S0-BIN-225

A CULTURAL INTRODUCTION TO PHILOSOPHY

FROM ANTIQUITY TO DESCARTES

	PEOPLE AND EVENTS	LITERATURE
2000–800 B.C.	Etruscans (ca.900)	Egyptian *Book of the Dead* (1000) *Psalms* (1000?–300?) *Vedas* (ca.2000) *Brahmanas* (ca.1000) *Gilgamesh* epic (ca.1200) Greek alphabet—Cnossus (ca.1250) 1st Chinese dictionary—40,000 characters (1500–1000) Hebrew Bible
800–700 B.C.	Rome founded (ca.753)	Homer: *Iliad, Odyssey* (ca.750) Hesiod: *Works and Days, Theogony* (fl.ca.735) Pre-Confucian *Classics* (ca.800)
700–600 B.C.		Sappho Archilochos
600–500 B.C.	Solon (638?–559)	Aeschylus: *Prometheus Bound, Oresteia* (525–456) Pindar (ca.518–438) Anacreon (580–495) Aesop's *Fables* Cratinus (520–421)
500–400 B.C.	Battle of Marathon (490) Battle of Thermopylae (480) Age of Pericles (461–431) Hippocrates (ca.460–377) Peloponnesian War (430–404)	Sophocles: *Oedipus, Electra* (496–406) Herodotus (ca.485–425) Euripides: *Medea, Hippolytus, Alcestis, Trojan Women* (484–406) Thucydides: *History of the Peloponnesian War* (ca.460–396) Aristophanes: *The Clouds, The Birds, Lysistrata, The Frogs* (ca.450–380) Xenophon: *The Anabasis* (434–355)
400–300 B.C.	Alexander the Great (356–323)	*Torah* (ca.400) *Bhagavad-Gita* (500 B.C.–A.D. 200) Theocritus (320–250) Menander (342–290) Ch'ü Yüan (343–277) Demosthenes (384–322)
300–200 B.C.	First Punic War (264–241) Second Punic War (218–201) Hannibal (246–182)	Apollonius of Rhodes (ca.293–215) Plautus (ca.250–184)
200–100 B.C.	Greek city-states under hegemony of Rome (200–168) Third Punic War (149–146) Roman civil wars (133–127)	Terence (ca.195–159)

RELIGION	ARTS	PHILOSOPHY
Moses (fl.1220–1200) David (1013–973) Solomon (ca.972–ca.932) Elijah (ca.850) Abraham (ca.1900)	Cretan-Mycenaean culture (1500–1200) Ziggurat, Ur (ca.2100) Stonehenge (ca.1500) Tutankhamen throne (ca.1400)	
Isaiah (ca.750)		
Deuteronomy (ca.625) Zoroaster (660–583)		Thales (ca.640–546) Anaximander (ca.610–545)
Ezekiel (ca.580) Daniel (ca.570)	Ishtar Gate (ca.570) Perseus and Medusa (ca.550) Parthenon (437–432) Temple of Apollo, Corinth Temple of Olympian Zeus, Athens	Pythagoras (ca.581–507) Xenophanes (ca.570–480) Anaximenes (fl.550) Heraclitus (ca.535–470) Lao-tzu (570–510) Confucius (551–479) Siddhartha Gautama (Buddha) (566–486)
Nehemiah (ca.440) Malachi (ca.420) Job (ca.400) Early Buddhism	Phidias (ca.500–435) Temple of Castor and Pollux, Rome (484) Classical period of Greek pottery Temple of Apollo, Delphi (ca.478) Temple of Zeus, Olympia (ca.460) Polyclitus (fl.420–415)	Parmenides (fl.500–450) Anaxagoras (ca.500–428) Empedocles (ca.490–445) Gorgias (483–375) Protagoras (490–420) Zeno of Elea (fl.475) Socrates (469–399) Democritus (460–370) Leucippus (fl.445) Antisthenes (445–365) Melissus (fl.440) Aristippus (435–356) Plato (427–347) Cratylus (ca.475) Antiphon
	Praxiteles (400–330) Scopas (420–340) Hellenistic period (320–100)	Aristotle (384–322) Euclid (335–275) Theophrastus (ca.372–287) Pyrrho (360–270) Epicurus (341–277) Zeno the Stoic (336–265) Timon (320–230) Isocrates (436–338) Diogenes (413–323) Cleanthes (331–232)
	Colossus of Rhodes (ca.275) Pharos lighthouse, Alexandria (ca.275)	Straton (fl.288) Chrysippus (279–206)
	Aphrodite of Melos (ca.150) Venus of Milo (ca.140)	

	PEOPLE AND EVENTS	LITERATURE
100–1 B.C.	Julius Caesar conquers Gaul (58–51) Julius Caesar assassinated (44) Augustus ruler of the Roman Empire (27 B.C.–A.D. 14) Strabo (63 B.C.–A.D. 21)	Cicero (106–43) Vergil: *Eclogues, Georgics, Aeneid* (70–19) Horace (65–8) Livy: *The Annals* (59 B.C.–A.D. 17) Julius Caesar: *Commentaries on the Gallic War* (ca.58–44) Ovid: *The Metamorphosis* (43 B.C.–A.D. 17) *Upanishads* (ca.900 B.C. ff.) Catullus (87–54)
1 B.C.–A.D. 100	Roman occupation of Britain (43–410)	Seneca (ca.3 B.C.–A.D. 65) Plutarch: *Parallel Lives* (ca.46–120) Tacitus: *Agricola, Histories* (ca.55–117) Petronius: *The Satyricon* (d.65) Juvenal (58–138) Christian Gospels
A.D. 100–200	Ptolemy (d.160)	Apuleius (b.114)
A.D. 200–300	Emperor Diocletian	
A.D. 300–400	Constantine's Christian Roman Empire (324–337) Council of Nicea (325)	
A.D. 400–500	Rome plundered by Visigoths (410) Anglo-Saxon invasions of Britain begin (449) Fall of Rome (476)	
A.D. 500–600	Justinian Laws, *Digest Code, Institutes* (527– 565)	
A.D. 600–700	Moslem conquest of N. Africa and Spain	
A.D. 700–800	Charlemagne (742–814)	Bede, *Ecclesiastical History of England* (ca.673–735) Alcuin (735–804)
A.D. 800–900	Alfred the Great reigns (871–900) Treaty of Verdun (843)	*Anglo-Saxon Chronicle* compiled (ca.892) *1001 Nights* Carolingian classical revival First printed book, China (868) Gospel Book of Ebbo
A.D. 900–1000	Capetian Dynasty founded in France (987)	Chinese encyclopedia, 1,000 vols. (978– 984)

RELIGION	ARTS	PHILOSOPHY
	Laocoön (ca.50) Vitruvius: "De architectura" (90)	Lucretius (94–55) Aenesidemus (fl.80–50) Philo Judaeus (30 B.C.–A.D. 50)
Jesus (d.30?) Paul (d.64) John (d.98)	Colosseum (75–82) Arch of Titus (ca.82)	Epictetus (50–125)
	Trajan Forum (112) Pantheon (124) Column of Marcus Aurelius (190)	Irenaeus (ca.130–200) Clement of Alexandria (ca.150–200) Justin Martyr (ca.153) Tertullian (ca.160–230) Origen (185–254) Galen (131–201) Marcus Aurelius (121–180)
	Caracalla Baths (211–217)	Plotinus (ca.205–269) Porphyry (ca.233–300) Jamblichus (ca.270–330) Sextus Empiricus (ca.200–250) Longinus (213?–273)
	Arch of Constantine (315) Old St. Peter's (ca.330–354)	St. Augustine (354–430)
Split between Eastern and Western churches (451)		Proclus (ca.410–485) Boethius (480–524)
Codex Bezae (500)		St. Benedict (480–543)
Mohammed leaves Mecca (622) Mohammed (570–632) Koran (652)		
St. Boniface (d.755)	Gregorian music Mosque at Cordova	
		John Scotus Erigena (ca.810–ca.877)
	St. Mark's Cathedral, Venice (976) Monastery at Cluny (980)	

	PEOPLE AND EVENTS	LITERATURE
A.D. 1000–1100	Norman conquest of England (1066) First crusades against the Moslems (1095–1099) Leif Erikson sails to America (1002)	*Beowulf* (ca.1000) *Song of Roland* (ca.1100)
A.D. 1100–1200	Paris University (1150) Oxford University (1167) Genghis Khan (1162–1227) Aztec, Inca, Maya civilizations rising Viking explorations	Omar Khayyam (1027–1123) Chrétien de Troyes (1144–1190) First vernacular literature
A.D. 1200–1300	Cambridge University (1200) Magna Carta (1215) Marco Polo (1254–1324) Mongol ascendancy Arabic numerals introduced in Europe Spectacles invented (1290) Honorius of Autun (ca.1200)	Dante Alighieri (1265–1321) *Carmina Burana* manuscript
A.D. 1300–1400	Black Death Plague (1347–1350) Ming Dynasty (1368–1644) Hundred Years War between England and France begins (1337)	Chaucer's *Canterbury Tales* (ca.1387) Boccaccio (1313–1375)
A.D. 1400–1500	Columbus in America (1492) Joan of Arc burned at the stake for heresy (1431) John Cabot in North America (1497) Amerigo Vespucci (1451–1512)	Gutenberg invents printing with movable type (1446–1450)
A.D. 1500–1550	Thomas More (1478–1535) Magellan circumnavigates the world (1519–1522) Copernicus (d.1543) Henry VIII (d.1547)	Machiavelli's *The Prince* (1532) Erasmus' *Praise of Folly* (1511) Calvin's *Institutes of the Christian Religion* (1536) Thomas More's *Utopia* (1516) Castiglione's *The Courtier* (1528)
A.D. 1550–1600	Gregorian calendar (1582) Council of Trent (1545–1563) Ivan the Terrible (r.1547–1584) Elizabeth I (r.1558–1603) Spanish Armada defeated by England (1588)	Montaigne (1533–1592) Cervantes (1547–1616) Vasari's *Lives* (1564) William Shakespeare (1564–1616) Sir Philip Sidney (1554–1586) John Donne (1572–1631)
A.D. 1600–1650	Richelieu in power (1624–1642) Jamestown, Virginia, founded (1607) Plymouth, Mass., founded (1620) Harvey describes circulation of the blood (1628)	
A.D. 1650–1700	Charles II restores monarchy in England (1660) Louis XIV (r.1661–1715) Great fire and plague of London (1665–1666) Peter the Great (r.1682–1725)	Racine (1639–1699) Milton's *Paradise Lost* (1667) Bunyan's *Pilgrim's Progress* (1678)

RELIGION	ARTS	PHILOSOPHY
College of Cardinals formed (1059) Gospel Book of Otto III	St. Paul's Cathedral (1016) Baptistry, Florence Bayeux Tapestry	St. Anselm (ca.1033–1109) Avicenna (980–1037)
Concordat of Worms (1122) Thomas Becket (1118–1170) St. Francis of Assisi (1182–1226)	French troubadour music Chartres Cathedral	Averroës (1126–1198) Peter Abailard (1079–1142) Moses Maimonides (1135–1204) John of Salisbury (1120–1180)
Spanish Inquisition (1203)	Cimabue (1240–ca.1300) Giotto (1266–1336) Reims Cathedral Florence Cathedral Palazzo Vecchio, Florence	Thomas Aquinas (1225–1274) Bonaventure (1221–1274) Albertus Magnus (1206–1280) John Duns Scotus (1265–1308) Sa'di (*Gulistan*) (ca.1200–1290) Roger Bacon (1214–1292) Siger of Brabant (ca.1235–1281) Meister Eckhart (1260–1327) Condemnation of 1277
John Wycliffe (1320–1384)		William of Ockham (1280?–1348) Petrarch (1304–1374) Nicolaus of Autrecourt (ca. 1300)
Savonarola (1452–1498)	Leonardo da Vinci (1452–1519) Hieronymus Bosch (d.1518) Botticelli (1444–1510) Dürer (1471–1528) Masaccio (1401–ca.1428) Titian (1477–1576)	Pico della Mirandola (1463–1494) Marsilios Ficino (1433–1499) Desiderius Erasmus (1467–1536) Nicholas of Cusa (1401–1464) Niccolo Machiavelli (1469–1527) Pietro Pomponazzi (1462–1525)
Peter Ramus (1515–1572) Luther's Reformation (1517) Calvin at Geneva (1541) Henry VIII founds Anglican Church (1534) Jesuit Order founded by Ignatius of Loyola (1534)	Correggio (1494–1534) Hans Holbein, the Younger (1497–1543) Michelangelo (1475–1564) Tintoretto (1518–1594)	Paracelsus (1493–1541) François Rabelais (1494–1553) Martin Luther (1483–1546) John Calvin (1509–1564) Nicholaus Copernicus (1473–1543)
Jakob Böhme (1575–1624) Edict of Nantes (1598) John Knox founds Presbyterian Church (1560)	Breughel (1564–1638) Caravaggio (1569–1609) Rubens (1577–1640)	Giordano Bruno (1548–1600) Francis Bacon (1561–1626) Johannes Kepler (1571–1630) Galileo Galilei (1564–1642)
King James Bible (1611) Society of Friends (Quakers) founded (1668)	Poussin (1594–1665) Velasquez (1599–1660) Rembrandt (1606–1669)	Descartes (1596–1650) Pascal (1623–1662) Spinoza (1632–1677) Hobbes (1588–1679) Robert Boyle (1627–1691) William Harvey (1578–1657)
Cotton Mather (1663–1728)		Locke (1632–1704) Pierre Bayle (1647–1706) Malebranche (1638–1715) Fénelon (1651–1715) Leibniz (1646–1716) Newton (1642–1727) Vico (1668–1744)

A CULTURAL INTRODUCTION TO PHILOSOPHY

FROM ANTIQUITY TO DESCARTES

edited by
John J. McDermott
TEXAS A&M UNIVERSITY

Alfred A. Knopf  New York

THIS IS A BORZOI BOOK PUBLISHED BY ALFRED A. KNOPF, INC.

First Edition
987654321

All inquiries should be addressed to Alfred A. Knopf, Inc., 201 East 50th Street, New York, N.Y. 10022. Published in the United States by Alfred A. Knopf, Inc., New York, and simultaneously in Canada by Random House of Canada Limited, Toronto. Distributed by Random House, Inc., New York.

Library of Congress Cataloging in Publication Data
Main entry under title:

A Cultural introduction to philosophy.

Includes bibliographies.
Contents: [1] From antiquity to Descartes.
1. Philosophy—Addresses, essays, lectures.
I. McDermott, John J. (John Joseph), 1932–
BD21.C85 1984 109 84-15454
ISBN 0-394-32781-0 (v. 1)

Manufactured in the United States of America

The School of Plato, a Roman mosaic showing Plato with his pupils. Photo by Alinari/Art Resource (see also p. 169).

The Greek epigraph facing the first page of the text is from *Philosophical Greek: An Introduction* by Francis H. Forbes (Chicago: University of Chicago Press, 1957), p. 1.

MAP ACKNOWLEDGMENTS

EARLY AND CLASSICAL GREECE, p. 52: from *A Short History of Western Civilization*, 5th ed., John B. Harrison and Richard E. Sullivan, ed. (New York: Alfred A. Knopf, 1980), p. 58. Reprinted with permission of Alfred A. Knopf.

ARISTOTLE'S AND PTOLEMY'S COSMOGRAPHY, p. 216: from A. C. Crombie, *Augustine to Galileo* (Cambridge: Harvard University Press, 1953), p. 57. Reprinted by permission of the publisher. Copyright 1952 by A. C. Crombie.

GREECE AND ITALY, p. 260: from *The Philosophers of Greece* by Robert S. Brumbaugh (New York: Thomas Y. Crowell, 1964), pp. 6 and 7. Reprinted from *The Philosophers of Greece* by Robert S. Brumbaugh by permission of the State University of New York Press. Copyright © 1964 by Robert S. Brumbaugh.

SOUTHERN ITALY AND SICILY, p. 272: from John Mansley Robinson: *An Introduction to Early Greek Philosophy*, p. 342. Copyright © 1968 by Houghton Mifflin Company. Used by permission.

PALESTINE AT THE TIME OF CHRIST, SHOWING THE PRINCIPAL TOWNS OF THE AREA, p. 345: from *The New Catholic Encyclopedia*, Vol. X (Washington, D.C.: The Catholic University of America Press, 1967), p. 899. Reprinted with permission of The Catholic University of America Press.

PLAN OF THE CITY OF JERUSALEM IN THE TIME OF CHRIST, p. 346: from ibid., Vol. VII, p. 883. Reprinted with permission of The Catholic University of America Press.

THE ROMAN EMPIRE, A.D. 362, p. 376: from *The Penguin Atlas of Medieval History* by Colin McEvedy (London: Penguin Books, 1961), p. 15. Copyright © Colin McEvedy, 1961. Reprinted by permission of Penguin Books Ltd.

EUROPE, A.D. 476, p. 402: from ibid., p. 23. Reprinted by permission of Penguin Books Ltd.

EUROPE, A.D. 1028, p. 422: from ibid., p. 59. Reprinted by permission of Penguin Books Ltd.

EUROPE, A.D. 1092, p. 423: from ibid., p. 63. Reprinted by permission of Penguin Books Ltd.

EUROPE, A.D. 1478, p. 638: from ibid., p. 85. Reprinted by permission of Penguin Books Ltd.

SIXTEENTH-CENTURY MAP OF THE WORLD BY ROBERT THORNE, A.D. 1527, pp. 724–725: from *Facsimile-Atlas to the Early History of Cartography* by A. E. Nordenskiold (New York: Dover, 1973), Map XLI.

EUROPEAN DISCOVERIES, A.D. 1450–1600, p. 728: reprinted from *A History of the Modern World*, 6th ed., revised, by R. R. Palmer and Joel Colton. Copyright 1950, © 1956, 1965, 1971, 1978, 1983 by Alfred A. Knopf, Inc. Copyright renewed 1978 by Robert Palmer and Alfred A. Knopf, Inc. Reprinted by permission of Alfred A. Knopf, Inc.

For
BRIAN McDERMOTT
1956–
Our Fourth Born
—Seeker of Novelty
Generous Teacher and Craftsman

PREFACE

This book has grown out of more than thirty years of teaching introductory philosophy and Western civilization courses to literally thousands of students in large public institutions, small private colleges, medical schools, and adult education programs. Those years and the many students have taught me that complete texts, where these are appropriate, and longer segments of textual material are necessary if students are to gain a real sense of the range of a philosopher's work. This book aims to fulfill that need.

I have found most of the material in this book to be easily accessible to most students, and frequently intellectually stimulating as well. There are, however, a few pieces—those by Aristotle and Duns Scotus, for example—that are more difficult. Their historical and philosophical importance demand that students concentrate on them, for with reflective effort, they too can be understood.

My convictions about teaching lead inevitably to a book as full as this one. There is a wealth of material here—more than many instructors will use—but the extensiveness of the material offers considerable latitude in organizing a course. It provides a variety of opportunities for teaching a dramatic and enriching historical introduction to Western philosophy and civilizations. I am convinced that all students are capable of gleaning some significant insights from these philosophical selections.

THE FOCUS

In order to be able to explore other cultures, we must be intimately acquainted with our own intellectual and cultural lineage, with its weaknesses as well as its strengths. This text provides the framework for such an understanding.

The origins and development of Western civilization are in fact wider in intellectual, cultural, religious, and geographical scope than is indicated by the material found in most philosophy texts. In addition to the sources rooted in Greece and Rome, I have included, therefore, material from the ancient Hebrew and Egyptian civilizations and have also represented the continual influence of the religion and philosophy of Islam. In effect, we reach far back into that area of the ancient world presently known as the Middle East and come forward through ancient Greece, the Roman Empire, the North Africa of Islam, and Christendom to the explosive sixteenth century of the Renaissance, the Reformation, and the Scientific Revolution.

The chronicling of this tradition is by no means exemplary of all of world history, but in twentieth-century terms, it represents the origins of a tradition essential to any understanding of world culture. Since the limitations of space make it impossible to present an integrated world history of philosophical texts, students are encouraged to make comparisons with other cultures, especially those of China, India, and Japan.

THE PLAN

The plan of this book is basically chronological rather than topical. The selections in this volume include works from antiquity through the seventeenth century. A second volume will cover material from the seventeenth century through the late twentieth century. In addition to representative selections from the major figures of this period—Plato, Aristotle, Augustine, Anselm, Aquinas, and Descartes—I also have included extensive selections from the Pre-Socratics, the Stoics, the Scriptures, and other leading thinkers of antiquity, the Middle Ages, the Renaissance, the Reformation, and the Scientific Revolution.

Pieces that are characteristic of the cultural ambience of their period are found throughout this volume. The maps and the illustrations provide a further dimension of the cultural settings in which the selections were written. I encourage the reader to make use of the time line at the beginning of the book, which places the philosophical activity in relation to the other, allied, cultural, historical, and scientific events of the same period. The headnotes serve to locate the period and the thinker in a proper historical context. I have been careful in them not to intrude my own interpretations on the texts. At their origin and ever since, these texts have been controversial, and the excitement of philosophy has been the often irresolvable arguments over matters of interpretation. With the exception of the Introduction and an occasional personal opinion here and there, I offer that these texts speak for themselves, as subject to the interpretive assistance of the instructor.

The chronological organization does not mean that this text cannot be used in a course devoted to the introduction to philosophy. An instructor may choose to concentrate on a few of the many themes extant in the book and select the works that best illustrate these themes in each historical period. There is, for example, ample material for a course concentrating on the development of Western ethics, epistemology, religion, or metaphysics, or better, some combination thereof. This book can also be used as a companion text in courses devoted to the history of Western civilization because much of the material, although of a philosophical cast, is interdisciplinary in style and intent.

I look forward to hearing of others' experiences with this book, whether they be complaints, suggestions, or a report of a rich and successful pedagogical result. I have every intention of responding to all correspondence in this regard, for I believe that if we are to succeed in educating others, we ourselves must live within the spirit of a community of inquiry as promulgated by the American philosopher Charles Sanders Peirce.

EDITORIAL NOTES ON THE TEXT

The texts included in this volume are generally a complete work, chapter, section, or some such division. In only a few instances have the texts been edited, and these instances are all clearly marked by ellipsis points. Translations have been chosen with the need of the student as the paramount criterion. The intent has been to combine the latest scholarship with the reading accessibility of the text.

The materials gathered under "Suggestions for Further Reading" are precisely as titled. These books have been helpful to students in understanding the period and thinkers under discussion. They are not meant to be exhaustive or exclusive. These works are intended as aids to further in-depth study, preparation of research papers, and, frequently, as models of scholarship in philosophy and the humanities. Although I have searched the recent secondary sources, a majority of the recommended readings have been prepared by previous generations of scholars. I have found the more general approach of these works to be the most helpful to students. I would appreciate suggestions concerning any serious omissions from these "Suggestions for Further Reading."

I have made every effort to ensure the internal integrity of the text, notations, and citations. Nonetheless, the massive character of this volume, prepared over many years, makes it probable that some aspects may have gone awry. I would welcome corrections, suggestions, and complaints. If the suggestion involves the introduction of new material for a second edition, it would then be helpful if the correspondent would accompany the request with a suggestion for deletion of some present material. Even in a book of this girth, space, after all, is finite.

ACKNOWLEDGMENTS

In a work of this topical and chronological scope, the scholarly debt incurred by the editor is extensive. In the list of scholarly advisers that follows, I have attempted to include all of those who assisted. Should I have forgotten some persons, I hereby apologize.

I have learned from the wise advice of Alexander P. D. Mourelatos, Manuel Davenport, Robert Burch, Larry Hickman, Michael Levy, Paul Parrish, Salvatore Saladino, Paul Colella, Eugene Fontinell, Peter Manicas, David Myers, Joseph Grassi, John Lachs, Anita Silvers, John Stuhr, Herman Saatkaamp, Jr., Beth Singer, Louis Mackey, Jonathan Moreno, James Gouinlock, Lee Miller, Marvin Henberg, Gerald Galgan, John Smith, Robert Cunningham, Joseph Kupfer, James Campbell, Patrick Hill, Charlene Seigfried, Charles White, Graham Horsley, John Bricke, Laurence McCullough, Henry Wolz, Marise McDermott, and especially Donald McQuade. These respondents to my requests represent every region of the nation and most of the major approaches to the teaching of philosophy. I am also indebted to my graduate school education at Fordham University, which concentrated on the history of philosophy. In that regard I offer gratitude for the pedagogical genius of Robert C. Pollock.

The initial preparation of the manuscript was aided by the work of Gwen Stacell, Laura Young, and Edith Schaffer. Early on, Michele McDermott combed all of the introductory texts extant in order to determine which selections had been most desired by previous anthologists and students. Robert McDermott was invaluable in his suggestions as to the selections from the Hebrew and Christian Scriptures. Melvin Dodd of the Texas A&M University library provided quick and efficient interlibrary loan service. Dean Robert S. Stone has been generous in providing me time for research.

This book owes its origin to the persuasive prodding of Ms. Jane Cullen, formerly of Random House publishers. Inasmuch as it was she who convinced me to undertake this project, every student who finds the book helpful and enlightening is in her debt. After the project began, it came under the acute editorial supervision of David Follmer and then Steven Pensinger, both editors at Random House/Knopf. I thank them for their generous support of this book and their protection of its editorial integrity. I am grateful to Randee Falk and Cynthia Ward for their excellent copyediting and management of the manuscript. The final stages of the manuscript were expertly handled by the project editor, Mary Shuford.

The preparation of the manuscript, with its seemingly infinite set of details, is due to three persons. First, Alden Turner, my graduate student, now a Ph.D. in literature, whose wisdom and loyalty to the project never wavered. He prepared much of the manuscript for publication, and it is he who was largely responsible for the work on the illustrations and the maps. His criticisms were always correct and his suggestions for improvement were always helpful. Second, Gregory Moses, a professional journalist and also my graduate student, who prepared other extensive sections of the manuscript. Moses was responsible for a final presubmission proofreading of the manuscript, which he performed with creative accuracy. Third, Patricia Bond, my indefatigable administrative assistant, who, in the midst of dozens of competing obligations, has shepherded this book to press. She is also responsible for obtaining the multiple permissions, and for a superb proofreading at the final stage of the manuscript. An unerring typist and an accomplished manager of academic interruptions, she enabled me to bring to closure a project that would otherwise be no more than a scholarly fantasy.

Finally, in this, as in all of my endeavors, the deepest gratitude is offered to the generous personal support of my wife of more than thirty years, Virginia Picarelli McDermott. She has an uncanny ability to help me distract myself from distractions so that I can complete the major task at hand. And it was Virginia who braced me when I became depressed at the amount of detail and who was unflagging in her commitment to the worthiness of this project as an introduction to the philosophical classics of the Western world.

CONTENTS

Ἀρχὴ δέ τοι ἥμισυ παντός

Well begun is half done.

Introduction

Philosophic study is the habit of always seeing an alternative.

—*William James*

The most succinct paragraph on the distinctive character of philosophical inquiry is to be found in the first book of the *Metaphysics*, by the Greek philosopher Aristotle:

> For it is owing to their wonder that men both now begin and at first began to philosophize; they wondered originally at the obvious difficulties, then advanced little by little and stated difficulties about the greater matters, e.g., about the phenomena of the moon and those of the sun and the stars, and about the genesis of the universe. And a man who is puzzled and wonders thinks himself ignorant (whence even the lover of myth is in a sense a lover of Wisdom, for the myth is composed of wonders); therefore since they philosophized in order to escape from ignorance, evidently they were pursuing science in order to know, and not for any utilitarian end. And this is confirmed by the facts; for it was when almost all the necessities of life and the things that make for comfort and recreation had been secured, that such knowledge began to be sought. Evidently then we do not seek it for the sake of any other advantage; but as the man is free, we say, who exists for his own sake and not for another's, so we pursue this as the only free science, for it alone exists for its own sake.*

The history of philosophy in western civilization has been characterized by periods of speculative explosions, followed by longer periods of absorption and redress. If we accept the common wisdom that western civilization began with the Greeks, then the paramount role of philosophy is obvious, for philosophical speculation was the formative dimension of Greek civilization. Philosophy is the mother of most of the intellectual and academic disciplines as we now know them. Western theology would be bare bones were it not for philosophical ideas. Rhetoric, logic, the social sciences, and the natural sciences all trace their lineage to philosophy. Indeed, as late as the eighteenth century, scientists were actually philosophers. Mathematics and physics were brought into being by philosophers, as witness the invention of the calculus, an attempted philosphical resolution of the problem of infinity. If, in the twentieth century, the sciences contend that they are independent of philosophical ideas, we can still point to the

---

*Aristotle, "Metaphysics," *The Basic Works of Aristotle*, ed. Richard McKeon (New York: Random House, 1941), p. 692 (982b).

work of Neils Bohr and Werner Heisenberg, who were profoundly influenced by philosophy and wrote philosophical treatises. Quantum mechanics, which points to the molecular structure of beings, is as much a philosophical hypothesis as it is a scientific one.

The influence of philosophers throughout the centuries is dazzling and greatly disproportionate to the number of philosophers recognized in the canon of important thinkers. We note, for example, Aristotle's organization of the intellectual disciplines and his pioneering work in biology and astronomy. Of significance also is Francis Bacon's stress on the inductive method and Descartes' invention of analytic geometry. The doctrine of toleration, so central to our democratic form of civilization, owes much to John Stuart Mill's defense of liberty. Educational theory is deeply indebted to the philosophical imagination of Plato, Rousseau, Herbart, Montessori and, above all, John Dewey. The major reason why contemporary educational theory is not at the forefront of our intellectual life is that it has been shorn of philosophical imagination. Finally, we should not forget that one of the most influential thinkers in human history is a philosopher—Karl Marx.

This pantheon of influential philosophers could be continued indefinitely, but suffice it to say that to be ignorant of the history of philosophy while pursuing a study of the meaning of human life is akin to studying the human body while remaining ignorant of the brain and the liver. Socrates once said that the unexamined life is not worth living, and for William James philosophy was the habit of always seeing an alternative. For me, the importance of philosophy proceeds from the fact that it is not afraid of anything. No idea is too daring to be pursued to its realization. Please notice that I did not say "afraid of nothing," for "nothing" is a serious problem in philosophy. In fact, the most important philosophical question is still with us and it reads, why is there something rather than nothing? To this question there is neither a perceivable nor a conceivable answer, yet having asked it some two thousand years ago we are burdened with reasking it and probing its significance. In effect, philosophy does not become tired and does not jettison its old questions; rather, it adds new ones. It is in this way that we can speak of philosophy as culturally immortal, for so long as life exists, questions as to its origin, meaning, and future are of paramount concern. On occasion, the response to these perennial questions takes on such a dramatic and novel formulation that it becomes a permanent deposit in our cultural history and our collective consciousness.

This volume is divided into six parts, each of which represents a historical period in philosophy. Within each part are sections devoted either to single thinkers, such as Plato and Aristotle, or to clusters of thinkers gathered under a chronological and thematic umbrella. Headnotes to the individual selections provide useful biographical details. Further, the cultural context for each philosopher's writings is conveyed by the inclusion of texts from companion thinkers, orators, historians, poets, scientists, and religious thinkers and scriptures. This material should enable the reader to obtain a richer sense of the world from which the philosophers took their cue and to which they responded.

In order to assist the reader, and especially the student, I shall now briefly recapitulate each part of this volume, and, along the way, offer a cameo version of four central thinkers—Plato, Aristotle, Augustine, and Descartes—in terms of their most dramatic intention. In this way, I hope to provide an overview of speculative philosophy, as well as examples of its powerful and influential character.

Part One is devoted to both prephilosophical literature and the earliest philosophical reasoning of Greek culture. The former includes what we can refer to as the literature of myth and the literature of the claims of revelation. *The Egyptian Book of the Dead* and the works of Homer are shrouded in mythic assumptions and beliefs to which human customs are a response. Myth is rooted in real human experience, but its articulation is mingled with fable, exaggeration, and above all, anthropomorphism, by which is meant that the gods act like human beings. The mystery of death and the human saga, with its tragedy, heroism, foibles, and weaknesses, are constant themes in ancient mythic literature. The origin of the world, and especially of human life, is also central to this literature, as will be found in the intriguing selection from the *Theogony* of the Greek poet Hesiod.

Running counter to the mythic version of origins is the Hebrew Bible, which introduces western civilization to the belief in one, creating God and which denies that human history is repetitive or cyclic. The Jews thus bequeath to us the doctrine of history as eschatological, in which all events are interpreted as being prophetic and are thought to take their meaning from their relationship to the future, to the end of time. Whereas Greek mythic thought is characterized by fate and resignation, ancient Hebrew thought features hope and a sense of possible liberation. In subsequent centuries, both Christianity and Islam were to become indebted to the Jewish doctrine of history. They also continued a version of the Jewish belief in revelation, that is, the belief that God speaks directly to human history and is witnessed as so doing by sacred scriptures.

Greek civilization, however, took a quite different tack, for the Greeks slowly abandoned their mythological assumptions and began a remarkable effort to understand the world by reliance on human reason. Beginning in the sixth century B.C., there emerged a number of thinkers who have come to be known by the term Pre-Socratics. Scattered among the Greek islands and from as far away as the coast of Italy, these thinkers sought to explain natural phenomena and the way of human knowing. Most important, they sought the basic causes, *archai,* that govern the activities of nature, *physis.* The fundamental question was whether nature was "one" and could be explained by an appeal to a single principle, or whether it was "many" and therefore required multiple principles of explanation. Ingenious strategies were devised to answer this question, with the four basic elements of air, earth, fire, and water subjected to a host of variant configurations.

As the texts included here will reveal, the Milesians, the Atomists, the Pythagoreans, Heraclitus, and Parmenides, among others, vied for the most trenchant and satisfactory version of the relationship between the one and the many. Although we are limited to fragments of their work, it is clear that the overall endeavor was sustained and profound. Perhaps the radical break of the Pre-Socratics with previous mythic thought is best caught by the following fragment from

Xenophanes, wherein he subjects Iris, the goddess of the rainbow, to some empirical scrutiny,

> She whom men call "Iris," too, is
> in reality a cloud, purple, red, and
> green to the sight.

Early in the fifth century B.C., Greek political and social life underwent a change in the direction of more active participation by citizens. The activity of questioning underwent a comparable change, with the focus of inquiry shifting from nature to human nature. A group of intrepid, ambitious, and itinerant teachers sought, for a fee, to educate the young in getting ahead, especially in political terms. Known as the Sophists, they introduced methods of argumentation that excelled in dialectical cleverness and often attempted to make the weaker appear the stronger in debate. Some commentators attribute to the Sophists the doctrine of cultural and ethical relativism—the position that truth is a function of human perception and social custom, hence not amenable to analysis by any objective criteria. A moderate and a more plausible view is that the Sophists believed that the truth is neither totally objective nor totally subjective, but rather results from a combination of the forces of nature, human perspective, and social and political circumstances.

Into this setting arrived one of the most fascinating figures in the history of thought, Socrates. Refusing to accept payment for his wisdom, Socrates would appear at gatherings of Sophists and their students, frequently to make a shamble of the sophistic position. Socrates himself taught no final doctrine and usually left his listeners bewildered as to where he stood on the issue under consideration, although it was clear that he had successfully dismantled their positions. Socrates was clearly not a relativist, but it is difficult to know just what he held to be the truth of key ethical and personal issues such as the nature of virtue. We do know, however, that Socrates believed that true knowledge began in an acknowledgment of ignorance and that dialectic was necessary to detect the presence of false statements.

Granted profound differences in their truth claims, Socrates resembles Jesus in at least two ways: he was put to death for his beliefs, and he left no published writings. Our knowledge of Socrates comes mainly from Plato's *Dialogues*, especially the early ones, which feature a brilliant rendition of Socrates' conversations with the Sophists and with groups of students. Yet Plato was incomparably more important as a thinker than as a recorder of the Socratic legacy. In fact, even in the *Dialogues* devoted to Socrates, it is difficult, if not impossible, to separate the teachings of Socrates from the overlay of Plato's original philosophical thought.

Unquestionably we find profound philosophical gleanings in earlier thinkers; yet Plato must be acknowledged as the first fully developed philosopher in western civilization. If the Pre-Socratics founded the western philosophical attitude, it was Plato who founded philosophy. It was only slightly excessive of the Anglo-American philosopher Alfred North Whitehead to write that "the safest general characterization of the European philosophical tradition is that it consists of a series of footnotes to Plato."* With rhetorical flourish and poetical style, Plato brought wisdom to bear on every conceivable aspect of human existence—the heavens, the interpersonal, the inner life, the emotions, the vices, the virtues, the numbers, the arts, and above all, the relationship among sense knowledge, imagination, and intuition.

In my judgment, the most telling way to present the philosophy of Plato is to analyze the meaning of the allegory of the cave.† In Book VII of the *Republic,* Plato introduces an allegory to detail what he takes to be our fundamental situation. We are imprisoned in a cave, fettered by the neck and the legs so that we can only look forward to a wall in front of us. On the wall are cast shadows of human figures, some bearing baskets of food on their heads and others carrying animals. The shadows are projected by the light of a fire behind the parapet on which pass the figures. A slight diffusion of daylight breaks in from the entrance to the cave, high above and to the side of the parapet. Because, as prisoners, we see only shadows, we take these images to be real. For reasons not given in the allegory, one of the prisoners is compelled to leave his chains and make his way to the upper world. After a period of adjustment to the emergence of light, the former prisoner stands in the glare of the sun. Returning to the cave, he attempts to instruct his fellow prisoners that they see only shadows and that he brings them the knowledge of the real sensible world. The prisoners threaten to kill him if he persists in this attempt to unmask their view of the world—a clear reference to the trial and death of Socrates for comparable activities.

In order to explicate this deceptively simple allegory, I have to introduce another theme, this time from Plato's *Dialogue* entitled "Meno." Socrates asks Meno to tell him the nature of virtue. Meno responds with a series of definitions, which Socrates rejects as instances of virtue but not explanatory of its nature, that is, its *eidos* or form. Meno becomes irritated at Socrates for constantly confusing him and strikes back with two devastating questions. First, if you do not know what you seek, how do you know that it exists? Second, should you find it, how would you know that it is what you have been seeking? To these questions, Socrates, representing Plato, introduces a myth, the upshot of which is that before our present embodiment, our souls had access to another world wherein we knew

---

*Alfred N. Whitehead, *Process and Reality* (New York: The Macmillan Co., 1979), p. 63.

†Plato, "Republic," *The Dialogues of Plato,* trans. Benjamin Jowett (New York: Random House, 1937), pp. 773–777. I interject here a personal note. In the allegory, Plato uses masculine pronouns in referring to human beings. This usage occurs throughout the selections in this book, just as it is in virtually all of our literature until very recently. I deplore this and made every effort to avoid it in my own writing, but obviously we cannot rewrite the past. Equally obvious is that the female pronoun should be present equivalently in all discussions of these texts. As for the allegory, female readers should read "she" instead of "he," for we now know that the cave, as well as opportunity for liberty, should be democratic as to gender. The prisoner in Plato's rendition is clearly Socrates, yet Joan of Arc could be a modern version.

the true forms of reality. Our task now is to recall these forms and to shed ourselves of the material world which blocks our vision. True pedagogy moves us from the world of shadows, through the world of material things, and then through the mathematical forms, until we have access to the forms themselves, especially those of truth, beauty, and the good.

The paradox of Plato's position can be stated as follows: we know more than we should but less than we can. As human beings, we sense the world one thing at a time—a chair, a book, a person. Yet we can use "book," "chair," and "person" to include endless individual instances. Our percepts are singular but our concepts are general. How is this possible? The history of philosophy has provided a variety of responses to this basic and puzzling question. It is not Plato's response so much as the question itself that is intriguing. More than two thousand years before Freud, Plato informs us that the world is not what it seems to be. Further, he tells us that we can be in touch with powers beyond our immediate ken. Physics is a local discipline, for our minds can penetrate the physical world and reach to the forms of things, independent of their singular, sensate characteristics.

Now, if we return to the cave, we find our situation deepened, considerably. The cave is a description of our life, our neighborhood, our region, our university, our state, our career, our family, our religion, and our politics. We are, at any given time, in one cave or another. The task is to know that—a task more subtle and more arduous than would appear at first glance. In our self-deception we think that where we are, what we do, and what we believe is where others are, what they do, and what they believe. Worse, we think that this is what others should do and believe. The crucial question pertaining to Plato's cave has to do with the person leaving. How did that happen? Was he helped to escape? If so, who had informed him of the self-deception in which he was mired? And why did not they respond positively when he returned? Or, is it that the escaped prisoner was in touch with powers that transcended the cave, powers given only to the few? Or, perhaps the fetters are self-inflicted and can be dropped by an act of the will, if we but had the will.

As I see our situation, there are three versions of the cave. The first is that of those who have broken out and are proceeding toward the light. I have not met any such persons and am dubious about reports that they exist, although my readings tell me of occasional examples. The second version is of those of us who are in the cave but are aware of its self-deception. We are restless and of good will, yet we lack either the energy, the courage, or the originality to escape. The third version is that of the opponent—those who are in the cave and refuse to admit to their situation. Such individuals become hostile to any effort directed toward enlightening them as to their actual plight. The more we insist on the existence of the cave, the more stubborn they become as to the righteousness of their way, their cause, and above all, their blindness. The Greeks had a word for this attitude. They called it *hybris,* roughly translated as stubborn pride in an unworthy, unworkable, inelegant, and self-deceiving cause. For Plato, the dissolving, unmasking, or disarming of this attitude was the key issue in pedagogy. And that is why for Plato philosophy is *therapeia,* an attempted healing of our wounded and encapsulated psyche. Thus, Shakespeare was a Platonist when he wrote, "There are more things in heaven and earth, Horatio, than are dreamt of in your philosophy." Plato's dreams may not be yours or mine, but his philosophy makes it clear that we should dream of things unseen and unknown.

As remarkable as was the appearance of Plato early in the development of western philosophy, equally remarkable was the fact that in Plato's lifetime there came to the fore a comparably great philosopher, namely, Aristotle. A student of Plato for twenty years, Aristotle forged an independent view of the task of philosophy and of the meaning of nature, knowing, and discourse. Many commentators hold that Aristotle's philosophy is less imaginative than that of Plato but also wiser and more accurately diagnostic of our actual human situation. Other commentators see Plato and Aristotle as comprising the two major alternatives in any attempt to understand the meaning of human existence. In that vein, altering the remark of Whitehead quoted earlier, western philosophy is a series of footnotes to Plato and Aristotle. For myself, I am too committed to the presence of real, historical novelty and to the profound changes in the nature of reality brought about by modern science to accept the contention that Plato and Aristotle exhaust the philosophically viable positions. This does not, however, alter the fact that Aristotle represents one of those major positions.

Although many of Aristotle's extant writings are highly complex, his basic philosophical message is crystal clear. Contrary to most of his predecessors, especially Parmenides and Plato, he believed that the world is just as it seems to be given to us in the primitives of our sense experience. For Aristotle, being *is,* that is, something *is.* Equivalently, being—something—can change to become something else, although the changing thing is being all the while. The movement from being to becoming, while remaining being, is an irreducible characteristic of reality. Put more simply, the world, nature, reality *is* just as we see, feel, and hear it. The senses are to be trusted, despite occasional circumstantial lapses, which occur, for example, when, in water, we "see" a straight stick as crooked. Aristotle, then, does not have us in a cave, subject to massive self-deception brought on by sense experience which yields only shadows.

In keeping with this thoroughgoing realist position in which the world is consonant with our everyday experience of it, Aristotle believes that language names and corresponds to a world of pre-existing givens. If used properly, it can accurately reflect the inherent order of reality. Given these two assertions—that the world is as we experience it and that language is capable of unearthing the principles that govern the world—Aristotle sees two resultant activities. The first, the task of the speculative intellect, is to grasp and articulate the basic principles of reality. For Aristotle, this is the province not only of first philosophy or metaphysics but of physics as well. The second, the task of the practical intellect, is to learn how "things" work and how "events" happen and how both may be used for human ends. This is the province of politics and ethics.

As an accompaniment to this dual activity of the intellect, Aristotle develops a logic or, in his terms, *analytics,* to provide a schematic latticework for all reasoning processes. Deeply influenced by his early researches into the organizational principles of the biological world, Aristotle carries this diligent concern for order and hierarchy into his logic. As a result, Aristotle's philosophy has an impressive coherence. The world comes ready-made, complete with governing principles and, moreover, it is accessible to human reason. This accessibility is given credence by the parallel accuracy of human language, which is able to articulate the fundamental principles. The entire transaction is governed by a logic, which separates out inductive reasoning from deductive reasoning, false premises and conclusions from true premises and conclusions, and which generates a series of categories to account for everything in its "natural" place. The world is intelligible in principle, in fact, and in deed. Being, becoming, structure, reasoning, and articulation are all of a continuous piece. There is a startling obviousness to the philosophy of Aristotle, and he may be right, for he describes the experience of most people, most of the time. His categories are still the basis for terms common to the languages of western civilization. The question is, of course, whether Aristotle's influence is attributable to the fact that he correctly described the world as it is or whether, because he was the first to describe our world so systematically, we simply concluded that the world must be that way.

After the death of Aristotle in 322 B.C., no philosophical thinker of similar stature appears until Augustine in the fourth and fifth century A.D. This is not to say that the intervening period was without important philosophical thought. After Aristotle, we witness the flowering of Stoicism, in both Greece and the new empire of Rome. Zeno of Citium, the acknowledged founder, as well as Cicero, Seneca, Epictetus, and Marcus Aurelius, each contributed to the development of the Stoic philosophy. Although in contemporary English language "stoicism" is identified with passivity and resignation, classical Stoicism was quite the reverse. The Stoics taught that we must positively enter into a harmonious relationship with the messagings of nature. In so doing, we ward off the bad and dissonant relationships, which cause pain and alienation.

A second significant philosophical approach to the quest for the good life is found in Epicureanism. As with Stoicism, shallow contemporary misunderstanding lurks here also, for Epicureanism is frequently identified with hedonism, or sheer pleasure seeking. In Epicurus' thought, pleasure was sought by practice of the virtues of prudence and justice, that is, by an integral ethical life. Lucretius' *On the Nature of Things* is a magnificent interpretation of the doctrines of Epicurus, especially on the problem of death.

Perhaps the most important figure in the attempts of this period to provide a regimen for living a profound life was Plotinus. Influenced by Plato and by eastern mysticism, Plotinus stressed the doctrine of ascent from the trap of matter, our bodies, up to union with the ineffable, the inexplicable, the One. As with the leaders of Stoicism and Epicureanism, Plotinus had a loyal following of students. Through their efforts, his work was passed on and became the central arch in the promulgation of neo-Platonism, itself a pervasive influence on later Christian theology, especially that of Augustine.

Not all the thinkers of this period between Aristotle and Augustine were impressed with these efforts to make life better; the period was also characterized by a resurgence of cynicism and skepticism. The biting critique of the often confusing character of competing philosophical claims is seldom better expressed than in our selection from the writings of Sextus Empiricus.

The great, even epochal, event during this time was not strictly philosophical, although it has had extraordinary influence on philosophical thought. This event was, of course, the birth and death of Jesus Christ. It is neither the province nor the task of philosophy to assess the transcendent claims of Christ or of his followers. Yet, some of them, especially those known as the Fathers of the Church, began to weave a liturgy and a theology out of pagan mysticism, the teachings of Jesus, Stoic philosophy, Neoplatonic philosophy, and Roman law. This effort, as history soon displayed, became inordinately successful, and Christianity took its place as one of the half-dozen major religions of the world. The three most radical claims of Jesus, as interpreted by his followers, are the Incarnation, the Redemption, and the Resurrection. Regarded by Christian theologians as mysteries and therefore unintelligible to reason, they nonetheless carry important philosophical implications, for each assumes that God cares, is accessible to human beings, and is responsible for the course of history.

Philosophers and even theologians who were Christians could not resist the temptation to probe these mysteries with the light of reason, in an attempt to understand them. Two phrases capture this effort, which stretched throughout the entire Christian period until the Renaissance of the fourteenth century, and by analogy, were operative also in medieval Judaism and medieval Islam. The phrases were, first; "I believe so that I may know" and, second, "faith seeking understanding." Canopied by the legitimacy of these justifications of inquiry and set against the more orthodox religious believers in all three revelation religions, philosophy prospered throughout the Middle Ages, although there existed many conflicts between the proponents of either faith or reason as the source of inquiry.

Unquestionably the most seminal evocation of the struggle to remain theologically orthodox and yet be philosophically inquisitive is found in the writings of Augustine. And nowhere is this attempt at faith seeking understanding more explicit than in Augustine's writing on the doctrine of the Trinity, the most baffling of all of the Christian theological mysteries. It is precisely the philosophical implication of Augustine's doctrine of the Trinity that interests philosophers, for it continues Plato's view of the world and casts a spell over the intellectual life of Europe for one thousand years, until it is replaced by the secular Platonism of René Descartes in the seventeenth century. I refer here to the Augustinian contention that human beings can be in direct touch with a higher power and as such can know a world which consequently becomes illuminated. In Plato's philosophy this is the pedagogy of using mathematics to approach knowledge of the world of forms. For Augustine, each person is an image of God and can know the world precisely to the extent that such imaging is acknowledged. Descartes traces this power to our "innate ideas" and to the capacity of our minds to know the ultimate principles of reality.

The doctrine of the Trinity is a brilliant intellectual construction of one of the most implausible contentions in the history of religion, namely, that one God is three persons, each exactly and equivalently God. Augustine states the quandary clearly in his treatise "On the Trinity":

> Some persons, however, find a difficulty in this faith; when they hear that the Father is God, and the Son God, and the Holy Spirit God, and yet that this Trinity is not three Gods, but one God; and they ask how they are to understand this: especially when it is said that the Trinity works indivisibly in everything that God works, and yet that a certain voice of the Father spoke, which is not the voice of the Son; and that none except the Son was born in the flesh, and suffered, and rose again, and ascended into heaven; and that none except the Holy Spirit came in the form of a dove. They wish to understand how the Trinity uttered that voice which was only of the Father; and how the same Trinity created that flesh in which the Son only was born of the Virgin; and how the very same Trinity itself wrought that form of a dove, in which the Holy Spirit only appeared. Yet, otherwise, the Trinity does not work indivisibly, but the Father does some things, the Son other things, and the Holy Spirit yet others: or else, if they do some things together, some severally, then the Trinity is not indivisible. It is a difficulty, too, to them, in what manner the Holy Spirit is in the Trinity, whom neither the Father nor the son, nor both, have begotten, although He is the Spirit of both the Father and of the Son. Since, then, men weary us with asking such questions, let us unfold to them, as we are able, whatever wisdom God's gift has bestowed upon our weakness on this subject; . . . *

The rudiments of the doctrine itself are quite simple. God is infinite and therefore has infinite knowledge. Further, in that God knows all, he knows himself. Infinite knowledge of himself is equivalent to an infinite person, the Son. Where there are two there is a relationship, in this case an infinite relationship, equivalent to the Spirit, the third person of the Trinity. The entire agreement hinges on the philosophical proposition that what is infinite must exist, for if it were only conceptual, then any existing thing would be superior, thereby denying the infinite.

There is no question that philosophical difficulties abound in this formulation. Aside from the obvious difficulty that we have no rational verification that the infinite God exists in the first place, we have to ask, why do these infinite relationships stop at three? Should it not follow that the Son and the Spirit have such a relationship and, likewise, the Spirit and the Father? Fortunately, these problems are not at the center of the present discussion. Rather, we focus on the nature of the Son and the remarkable contention that in the person of Christ, God became human. Our concern here is not with the religious claim but rather with its import for epistemology, that is, what and how we know.

---

*Augustine, "On the Trinity," *Basic Writings of St. Augustine,* ed. Whitney J. Oates (New York: Random House, 1948), vol. II, p. 673.

Et verbum caro factum est is the message of the Christian scriptures. The Word was made flesh. In the original Greek of St. John, the word for the Word, for the Christ, was *logos.* For five hundred years of Greek philosophy, beginning with Heraclitus, *logos* was the term used to describe the deepest manifestation of *physis,* of nature, of all that is or could be. John places the *logos* at the origin of nature by saying: In the beginning was the *logos.* This was not new to the Greeks. That God the Son is an idea, an *eidos,* would not have been new to Plato. But what was new, staggeringly new, was the notion that the *logos* chose flesh, matter, to appear to the world. In order to explicate the claim that God appeared to the world (a theophany), early Christian thought made use of Neoplatonic philosophy, yet made a radical break with its most cherished assumption. The Platonists believed that the material world is an obfuscation, which has to be transcended if one is to reach for the *eidai,* the ultimate forms. Augustine, however, was influenced not only by the Platonists, but also by the Greek and Roman Stoics. They taught him that the human world is penetrated by the *eidai,* known as, significantly, *logoi spermatikoi,* or in the Latin of Augustine, as *rationes seminales.* These seeded reasons or ideas are open to us if we practice the doctrine of *apatheia,* that is, allow nature to take an unhindered course within the very fabric of our being. The task, then, is for each of us as a microcosm to become continuous with nature as a macrocosm, and in so doing, we shall be consumed in the fire of an ultimate harmony. Despite the power of this position, we face a serious difficulty in accepting it. If Plato's world of forms is unreachable, the Stoic doctrine of consummation in nature obliviates our personal lives. Nowhere is this more graphically stated than in the *Meditations* of the Roman emperor and stoic philosopher, Marcus Aurelius:

> Of human life the time is a point, and the substance is in a flux, and the perception dull, and the composition of the whole body subject to putrefaction, and the soul a whirl, and fortune hard to divine, and fame a thing devoid of judgement. And, to say all in a word, everything which belongs to the body is a stream, and what belongs to the soul is a dream and a vapour, and life is a warfare and a stranger's sojourn, and after-fame is oblivion.*

Despite the problems with Plato's world of ideas and the Stoics' doctrine of *apatheia,* if we merge them, as Augustine does, they provide an excellent explanatory framework for the person of Christ in relation to the problems of knowledge. Christ is the supreme *eidos,* the idea that God has of himself. He is also the *logos,* the way in which God appears to the world. And it is extremely noteworthy that the "way" of the Christ is to be the true light that enlightens every one who comes into the world. Following Plato and the Jewish–Christian teaching of original sin, we are born prisoners in the cave of our own making. Following the doctrine in the Trinity, Christ, the *logos,* is the light that appears to us in the cave and summons us to liberation. Augustinean epistemology holds that to be a

*Marcus Aurelius, *Meditations* (Chicago: Henry Regnery Company, 1956), pp. 18–19.

Christian is to be in a world that is bathed with light, and to be able to behold the seeded reasons of the Stoics as alive and obvious. For Augustine, the world is laced with *vestigia Dei,* the traces and shadows of God. Yet, this scenario is definitely that of Plato, for both the world of ideas and the cave are central themes in early Christian teaching. The radical difference is that by virtue of the Incarnation, Christian thinkers, especially Augustine, find a way for the supreme idea, the *logos,* to penetrate the cave while remaining superior to it.

Plato is vague about how and why the one prisoner escapes. Augustine is not vague. We have it within our power, if called, to convert, to turn toward the light. In the Jewish sense of a *teshuvah,* we must 'turn' our whole body, have a change of heart and not just a change of mind if we are truly to seek and find the light. In the words of Baruch Spinoza, the great Jewish philosopher of the seventeenth century, we must be prepared for a *De Emendatione Intellectus,* a moral healing of the understanding, if we are to know at all. And still later, in the nineteenth century, William James can say that belief helps to create its own verification. It was Augustine who gave decisive impetus to a moral epistemology. His person and his thought dominated medieval culture. He is a key figure in the powerful doctrines of conversion as found in Luther and Calvin. And long after Christianity ceased to be at the center of European intellectual life, Augustine's stress on a change of heart, if we are to see and to know, remains with us, an abiding remembrance of the omnipresence of Plato's cave and of mine and of yours.

It soon becomes obvious that Augustine's thought, carrying with it the vestiges of Neoplatonism and Stoicism, was to be the dominant influence on speculative philosophy and theology in the Christian Middle Ages until the thirteenth century. Philosophers as original and creative as John Scotus Erigena and Anselm would attribute their most salient insights to Augustine. A dramatic change was brewing, however, for the writings of Aristotle, unknown to the Christian west, had filtered through the Middle East, where they were intensively analyzed by both Jewish and Moslem thinkers, for example, Maimonides and Averroes.

As a result of increased trade with the east and, unfortunately, the Crusades, the Christian west obtained access to the writings of Aristotle, which had been shepherded for many centuries by Arabic culture. A Dominican friar, Thomas Aquinas, found Aristotle to be a better philosopher than his scholastic heritage had led him to believe. In a series of detailed commentaries on Aristotle's works and in his own work, Aquinas brought Aristotle to the center of the medieval stage. Severe philosophical and theological controversy set in, and much of the work of Aquinas was condemned at Oxford in 1277, but the total hold of Augustinianism was broken. In the fourteenth century, the scholastic philosophy that grew out of Aquinas' work was subjected to severe and, some say, fatal criticism, by Ockham, among others. The writings of Aristotle, meanwhile, once again were put to the side, only to be re-resurrected for the nefarious purpose of aiding the Church in its battle against Galileo and the architects of the Scientific Revolution.

The dominance of the three revelation scriptures of Judaism, Christianity, and Islam notwithstanding, the medieval period generated a host of brilliant philosophers in each of those traditions. In reading Maimonides, Avicenna, Averroës, Aquinas, Duns Scotus, and Bonaventure, we should not let the frequent theological or religious stylistic garb detract from the originality of the philosophical thought and especially from the sophistication of reasoning.

The thought and assumptions of the medieval period did not simply come to an end. Rather they were slowly transformed by the Renaissance and abruptly challenged by the Reformation and the Scientific Revolution.

The Renaissance differs from the Reformation and the Scientific Revolution in that it was not inspired by an event nor even by a series of events. It is better described as a change in mood, attitude, and cultural style. Thus it began in Italy as early as the fifteenth century and remained vibrant in seventeenth-century Holland and England. Literally, the term Renaissance means rebirth, and the Renaissance is often referred to as a rebirth of learning after the alleged intellectual doldrums of the medieval period. This is patent and offensive nonsense, for medieval civilization was laced with learning, and surely the medieval world of Giotto, Dante, Chaucer, and the Gothic cathedral (of the fourteenth century) deserves fairer interpretive fate. Actually, the meaning of the Renaissance is twofold: first, it means a rebirth of classical or secular learning, especially that traceable to ancient Rome, and second, it means an intense and new concentration on the meaning of the individual. These developments are the source of much of the magnificent painting and sculpture of the Renaissance; they are expressed in the work of Michelangelo, Da Vinci, and later, Rembrandt. The Renaissance, known also as the age of humanism, remains a glittering cultural diamond, poised between the end of medieval civilization and the beginning of modern civilization, which features the rise of the nation-state and the Industrial Revolution.

Even a cursory survey of the fascinating figures and events of the fifteenth and especially the sixteenth century would prove to be virtually interminable. Hence, I will focus on the main intellectual concerns of these centuries, which were in essence an attack on the unitary principles undergirding medieval culture, promulgated and intensively protected by the Church. As late as the fifteenth century, European thought held to the existence of one continent, one true religion, and one finite, ordered universe with the earth as its stable center. These medieval cartographical, theological, and cosmological assumptions came apart at the seams in the tumultuous sixteenth century. In 1507, the Waldseemüller map presented the earth in two distinct hemispheres. Following the voyage reports of Amerigo Vespucci, a fourth part—America—was added to the map that had once contained only Europe, Asia, and Africa. The gravity of this event is revealed in the name awarded the new hemisphere, for it was called a *Mundus Novus*, a new world. And "world" it was, for previously the earth had been perceived as a single, unified continent surrounded by water. The implications of the "New World" for medieval consciousness were far-reaching. Who were the people of this new land? Were they descendents of Adam? Does the Bible account for them? If there is a "New World," does that not mean that European civilization is an old world? The ramifications of these and other questions were to be worked out in the experiences of the sixteenth- and seventeenth-century Dutch,

Spanish, English, and French colonists. During the Renaissance, however, it was clear that the medieval unitary version of geography had received a severe and lasting setback.

In the midst of the turmoil brought on by the discoveries of the explorers, an event took place which was to rent the ostensibly seamless garment of Christendom. In 1517, Martin Luther, critical of the Church, posted his theses on the castle door at Wittenberg and the Protestant Reformation began. The Church underestimated the theological power of Luther's position and grievously underestimated his political support. Soon a host of religious thinkers competed with Luther in opposing the Church, or better, the "Roman Catholic Church," soon to be its distinctive name. Among these reformers was the gifted theologian and dialectician John Calvin. The corruption characteristic of the Church in the Renaissance, coupled with northern European resentment of the excessive taxation levied by Rome, brought on a major and irreparable schism. The second unitary assumption of medieval consciousness was shattered. By the middle of the sixteenth century, Europe had to acknowledge two geographical "worlds" and two Christian religions, Roman Catholicism and Protestantism, the latter being further divided by the creation of multiple sects. Modern pluralism was born in the sixteenth century.

As if these two changes were not sufficiently staggering, the sixteenth century brought forward still another revolution in thought—this one of such a magnitude that it can rightly be called the intellectual watershed of modern history. Despite their bold, speculative character, Judaism, Christianity, and Islam each accepted the finite world bequeathed by the cosmology of the Greeks, especially as promulgated by Aristotle. The orthodox religious establishment of western Europe, including the Protestant Reformers, was ill prepared for the year 1643, when Nicholas Copernicus, a Polish astronomer, published *The Revolution of the Heavenly Spheres,* a work that was to spell the end of the Aristotelian–Ptolemaic geocentric cosmology. Although this treatise of Copernicus was not sufficient to prove heliocentrism, the subsequent researches of Tycho Brahe and Johannes Kepler soon provided verification. The third unitary assumption of medieval consciousness was now challenged. The earth moves, and with that movement, the great hierarchical system of metaphors and beliefs, so exquisitely portrayed by Dante, now found itself in mortal jeopardy.

The controversy surrounding the heliocentric theory of Copernicus was to become one of the most fascinating and complex in European intellectual history; in time it would involve the Roman Catholic Church, the Inquisition, and the persons of Galileo, Cusanus, Melancthon, Bruno, and finally Newton. In this ferment, the thinker who is the most intriguing is René Descartes, for it is he who most directly responds to the implications of the Copernican revolution.

One of the casualties of Copernicanism was the Aristotelian doctrine of natural place, whereby everything that exists, celestial or terrestrial, has its proper place in the rational scheme. The most important implication of this doctrine was that the earth was the center of the universe and concomitantly, human life, as the center of the earth, was central to cosmic life. Copernicanism rendered the earth as but a satellite, moving both around the sun and on its own axis. The crisis was clear. If stability and physical centrality were essential for metaphysical importance, the post-Copernican version of human life rendered us trite, trivial, dwarfed, and inconsequential. The English poet John Donne says it best in his "Anatomy of the World":

> . . . new Philosophy calls all in doubt,
> The Element of fire is quite put out;
> The Sun is lost, and the earth, and no man's wit
> Can well direct him where to look for it.
> And freely men confess that this world's spent,
> When in the Planets, and the Firmament
> They seek so many new; then see that this
> Is crumbled out again to his Atomies.
> 'Til all in pieces, all coherence gone;
> All just supply, and all Relation:
> Prince, Subject, Father, Son, are things forgot,
> For every man alone thinks he hath got
> To be a Phenix, and that then can be
> None of that kind, of which he is, but he.*

Or perhaps you prefer the plaintive remark of Pascal: "The eternal silence of these infinite spaces frightens me." Whether it be Donne or Pascal or whoever, a crisis in the meaning of the human self had erupted in the late sixteenth century. In my view, the crucial difference between Aristotelianism and Copernicanism traces to the doctrine of place. In the Aristotelian perspective, everything had a natural place, and the human organism was not an exception. Copernicanism dealt a devastating blow to this domestic version of the cosmos by casting deep doubt on the fixed character of the planets. For Aristotle, the importance of human life was inextricably tied to the importance of the planet earth as nothing less than the physical center of the cosmos. The eradication of that centrality by Copernicanism forebode a deep disquiet about the ontological status of human life. The period between Copernicanism and the twentieth century witnessed an effort at temporary repair by Newtonian physics. But the die was cast, and the full implications of Copernicanism finally arrived in our century, sustained by quantum mechanics, a new cosmology, and the socially derived collapse of religious, political, and ideological eschatologies. In a word, the deepest contemporary ontological problem is that of *Unheimlichkeit* or homelessness. The vast, limitless, perhaps infinite universe does not award us a place. The planet earth is a node in the midst of cosmic unintelligibility. According to Aristotle, who we are is where we are. But with the overturning of Aristotle's geocentric cosmology, the claim of a natural place and a fixed center is rejected. If that is so, we are now no one, for we are nowhere, in that we do not know the extent of the cosmos, or for that matter, whether it has any periphery at all, and consequently cannot know our place.

It is in the context of this dramatic situation that we consider one aspect of the philosophy of René Descartes, who is the founder of modern philosophy and the

---

*John Donne, *The Complete Poetry and Selected Prose of John Donne* (New York: The Modern Library, 1941), p. 191.

transitional figure between this book and the next volume. He was clearly sympathetic with Copernicanism, as we see in his early work *Le Monde*, which he had to suppress after the condemnation of Galileo. The implications of Copernicanism acted as a specter behind all of the works of Descartes. If heliocentrism is true, then the Aristotelian doctrine of natural place is wrecked. Further, if the earth is not the center of the universe, then human life cannot count on physical centrality for the source of its epistemic certitude. In a series of bold and ingenious methodological and philosophical moves, Descartes sets out to reanchor the possibility of human certitude. He proceeds in the following way: It is conceivable that God does not exist. In that God is the guarantor of our sense experience, it is also conceivable that I am deluded as to the existence of the physical world, including my body. What is not conceivable, however, is that I, as a thinking being, do not exist, for as Descartes states, in what is to become one of the most famous of all philosophical phrases, *cogito ergo sum*—in that I think, I exist. In the Fourth Part of the *Discourse Concerning Method*, Descartes writes:

> But immediately afterward I noticed that, while I thus wished to think that everything was false, it was necessary that I who was thinking be something. And noting that this truth, I think, therefore I am, was so firm and so assured that all the most extravagant suppositions of the skeptics were not capable of disturbing it, I judged that I could receive it, without scruple, as the first principle of the philosophy I was seeking.*

The philosophy Descartes sought was one in which the foundation was not subject to doubt, and especially not subject to the foibles and snares of sense experience. To that end, he opposes Aristotle and the Scholastics, such as Thomas Aquinas, by holding that the *res cogitans*, the thinking thing, the human mind, has no need of the physical world, the *res extensa*, for its existence. The *res cogitans* is a complete substance and, as such, is self-guaranteeing of its existence and its knowledge. The thinking self comes equipped with innate ideas of such power that they are able to reconstruct the existence of God and of the material world, with indubitability. In order to achieve this power, however, Descartes began a tradition known as psychophysical dualism, in which the mind and body were regarded as separate substances. This dualism shattered the experiential unity of the human self and caused serious disarray in the behavioral sciences until the middle of the nineteenth century and the birth of experimental psychology, which focused on the organic continuity of mind and body.

Nonetheless, Descartes bequeathed also an intriguing possibility, namely, that the human mind has innate powers which are independent of sense experience and of the physical place that the mind occupies at any given time. Further, with Plato, he holds that we can know infinitely more than we do, even to knowing the ultimate principles of reality, equivalent to the knowledge of perfect being.

---

*René Descartes, "Discourse Concerning Method," *The Essential Writings*, trans. John J. Blom (New York: Harper Torchbooks, 1977), p. 134.

This is a heady claim, but we should not forget that Descartes was the father of modern mathematics. As we of the twentieth century know, modern mathematics creates physics and physics creates versions of nature never imagined heretofore. Looked at from a traditional view, Pascal was right, inifinite space does terrify us. In the philosophy of Descartes, however, even infinite space is but a local box, potentially transcended by the power of the human mind.

I come now to the end of my attempt to highlight some of the paramount themes and some of the major thinkers, all to be found represented in the selections that follow. The cameo versions of the thought of Plato, Aristotle, Augustine, and Descartes should provide students with at least a hint of the interpretative possibilities present as they read the other philosophers' writings contained in this book. I trust that the reader will find these selections, as I do, philosophically rich, subtle, creative, imaginative, and worthy of inclusion in a volume dedicated to the cultural immortality of philosophy. Heed the warning of the German philosopher Friedrich Nietzsche, and "read slowly." Philosophy does not yield to the quick of wit nor to the impatient soul. To obtain philosophical wisdom, one must be both cautious and daring, critical and reverent. Following Heraclitus, if you arrive at the proper tension between those opposites, you will be on the edge of genuine insight.

SUGGESTIONS FOR FURTHER READING

Copleston, Frederick. *A History of Philosophy.* 8 vols. Westminster, Maryland: Newman Press, 1957.

Edwards, Paul, ed. *The Encyclopedia of Philosophy.* 8 vols. New York: Macmillan, 1967.

Randall, John Herman, Jr. *The Career of Philosophy.* 3 vols. New York: Columbia University Press, 1962–1977.

Runes, Dagobert D., ed. *Pictorial History of Philosophy.* New York: Bramhall House, 1959.

The reader is urged to seek out companion volumes in the history of western civilization. Among many possibilities, I suggest:

Chambers, Mortimer *et al. The Western Experience.* 2 vols. New York: Knopf, 1983.

Part 1

Wisdom Literature of Western Civilization

The Birth of Western Philosophy—The Pre-Socratics

Wisdom Literature of Western Civilization

Ancient wisdom is by no means confined to philosophy. It is to be found in a variety of writings representative of the cultures of Egypt, Israel, and Greece. Were this book able to be truly comprehensive, in the scale of world culture, writings from the ancient Chinese and Indian cultures would be presented as well. The religious and philosophical parallels between ancient eastern and western civilizations are remarkable, and students are urged to seek them out.

The following selections are characterized by a style that alternates among the epic narrative, the admonishing, and the poetic. Although philosophical style develops along significantly different lines, the philosophical implications of the wisdom literature are considerable, affecting western philosophy throughout its history.

THE BOOK OF THE DEAD

The Book of the Dead is a classic in the literature of death and dying. It is devoted to the funeral rituals of the Egyptians, and it presents many of the basic tenets of ancient Egyptian religion. Some of the Book's contents are more than 4,000 years old. It is apparent that the Egyptians long anticipated the Western tradition of a quest for immortality. As even this brief excerpt makes clear, the Egyptians believed in a form of eternal life.

Because of the comparative strangeness of the hieroglyphic form of writing, the commentary of E. A. Wallis Budge is included with the selection.

From The Doctrine of Eternal Life

The ideas and beliefs which the Egyptians held in reference to a future existence are not easily to be described in detail, owing to the many difficulties in translating religious texts and in harmonizing the statements made in different works of different periods. Some confusion of details also seems to have existed in the minds of the Egyptians themselves, which cannot be cleared up until the literature of the subject has been further studied and until more texts have been published. That the Egyptians believed in a future life is certain; and the doctrine of eternal existence is the leading feature of their religion, and is

Papyrus painting from The Book of the Dead by Ani, a scribe (19th Dynasty). The souls of the dead are weighed on a scale to determine their future—an afterlife or oblivion. (British Museum, London; Archives AME)

enunciated with the utmost clearness in all periods. And it is quite certain that the belief in immortality among the Egyptians is one of the oldest of their religious beliefs. The attainment of a renewal of life in the Other World was the aim and object of every Egyptian believer. To this end all the religious literature of Egypt was composed. Let us take the following extracts from texts of the VIth dynasty as illustrations:

1. Hail Unȧs, not hast thou gone, behold, [as] one dead, thou hast gone [as] one living to sit upon the throne of Osiris.

2. O Rā-Tum, cometh to thee thy son, cometh to thee Unȧs ..... thy son is this of thy body for ever.

3. O Tum, thy son is this Osiris; thou hast given his sustenance and he liveth; he liveth, and liveth Unȧs this; not dieth he, not dieth Unȧs this.

4. Setteth Unȧs in life in Ȧmenta.

5. He hath eaten the knowledge of god every, [his] existence eternity, his limit everlastingness in his *sāḥ* this; what he willeth he doeth, [what] he hateth not doth he do.

6. Live life, not shalt thou die.

In the Papyrus of Ani . . . the deceased is represented as having come to a place remote and far away, where there is neither air to breathe nor water to drink, but where he holds converse with Temu.

From *The Book of the Dead: The Hieroglyphic Transcript of the Papyrus of Ani,* trans. and ed. E. A. Wallis Budge (Secaucus, N.J.: University Books, 1977), pp. 66–82 (selected passages).

In answer to his question, "How long have I to live?" the great god of Anu answers:

Thou shalt exist for millions of millions of years, a period of millions of years.

In the LXXXIVth Chapter, as given in the same papyrus, the infinite duration of the past and future existence of the soul, as well as its divine nature, is proclaimed by Ani in the words:

I am Shu of divine company. My soul is God my soul is eternity.

When the deceased identifies himself with Shu, he makes the period of his existence coeval with that of Temu-Rā, *i.e.*, he existed before Osiris and the other gods of his company. These two passages prove the identity of the belief in eternal life in the XVIIIth dynasty with that of the Vth and VIth dynasties.

But while we have this evidence of the Egyptian belief in eternal life, we are nowhere told that man's corruptible body will rise again; indeed, the following extracts show that the idea prevailed that the body lay in the earth while the soul or spirit lived in heaven:

1. Soul to heaven body to earth. (Vth dynasty.)
2. Thy essence is in heaven, thy body to earth. (VIth dynasty.)
3. Heaven hath thy soul, earth hath thy body. (Ptolemaic Period.)

There is, however, no doubt that from first to last the Egyptians firmly believed that besides the soul there was some other element of the man that would rise again. The preservation of the corruptible body, too, was in some way connected with the life in the world to come, and its existence was necessary to ensure eternal life; otherwise the prayers recited to this end would have been futile, and the time-honoured custom of mummifying the dead would have had no meaning. The never-ending existence of the soul is asserted in a passage quoted above without reference to Osiris; but the frequent mention of the uniting of his bones, and of the gathering together of his members, and the doing away with all corruption from his body, seems to show that the pious Egyptian connected these things with the resurrection of his own body in some form, and he argued that what had been done for him who was proclaimed to be giver and source of life must be necessary for mortal man.

The physical body of man considered as a whole was called *khat*, a word which seems to be connected with the idea of something which is liable to decay. The word is also applied to the mummified body in the tomb, as we know from the words "My body *(khat)* is buried." Such a body was attributed to the god Osiris; in the CLXIInd Chapter of the Book of the Dead "his great divine body rested in Anu." In this respect the god and the deceased were on an equality. As we have seen above, the body neither leaves the tomb nor reappears on earth; yet its preservation was necessary. . . .

In close connection with the natural and spiritual bodies stood the heart, or rather that part of it which was the seat of the power of life and the fountain of good and evil thoughts. And in addition to the Natural-body and Spirit-body, man also had an abstract individuality or personality endowed with all his characteristic attributes. This abstract personality had an absolutely independent existence. It could move freely from place to place, separating itself from, or uniting itself to, the body at will, and also enjoying life with the gods in heaven. This was the KA.

To that part of man which beyond all doubt was believed to enjoy an eternal existence after the death of the body, the Egyptians gave the name BA, a word which has been thought to mean something like "sublime," "noble," and which has always hitherto been translated by "soul," or "heart-soul." It was closely associated with the KA and the AB, or heart, and it was one of the principles of life in man. In form it is depicted as a human-headed hawk, and in nature and substance it is stated to be exceedingly refined or ethereal. It revisited the body in the tomb and re-animated it, and conversed with it; it could take upon itself any shape that it pleased; and it had the power of passing into heaven and of dwelling with the perfected souls there. It was eternal. As the BA was closely associated with the KA, it partook of the funeral offerings, and in one aspect of its existence at least it was liable to decay if not properly and sufficiently nourished. In the Pyramid Texts the permanent dwellingplace of the BA or soul is heaven with the gods, whose life it shares:

1. Behold Unȧs cometh forth on day this in the form real of a soul living.

2. Their soul is in Unȧs.

3. Standeth thy soul among the gods.

4. Hail, Pepi this! cometh to thee the eye of Horus, it speaketh with thee. Cometh to thee thy soul which is among the gods.

5. Pure is thy soul among the gods.

6. As liveth Osiris, and as liveth the soul in Netat, so liveth Pepi this.

7. It placeth thy soul Pepi this among {the greater and lesser cycles of the gods} in the form of the uraei [which] are on thy brow.

8. Behold Pepi this, thy soul is the Souls of Ȧnu; behold thy soul is the Souls of Nekhen; behold thy soul is the Souls of Pe; behold thy soul is a star living, behold, among its brethren.

In connection with the KA and BA must be mentioned the KHAIBIT , or shadow of the man, which the Egyptians regarded as a part of the human economy. It may be compared with the σκιά and *umbra* of the Greeks and Romans. It was supposed to have an entirely independent existence and to be able to separate itself from the body; it was free to move wherever it pleased, and, like the KA and BA, it partook of the funeral offerings in the tomb, which it visited at will. The mention of the shade, whether of a god or man, in the Pyramid Texts is unfrequent, and it is not easy to ascertain what views were held concerning it; but from the passage in the text of Unȧs, where it is mentioned together with the souls and spirits and bones of the gods, it is evident that already at that early date its position in relation to man was well defined. From the collection of illustrations which Dr. Birch appended to his paper *On the Shade or Shadow of the Dead,* it is quite clear that in later times at least the shadow was always associated with the soul and was believed to be always near it; and this view is supported by a passage in the XCIInd Chapter of the Book of the Dead, where it is said:

Let not be shut in my soul, let not be fettered my shadow, let be opened the way for my soul and for my shadow, may it see the great god.

And again, in the LXXXIXth Chapter the deceased says:—

May I look upon my soul and my shadow.

Another important and apparently eternal part of man was the KHU, , which, judging from the meaning of the word, may be defined as a "shining" or translucent Spirit-soul. For want of a better word KHU has often been translated "shining one," "glorious," "intelligence," and the like, but its true meaning must be Spirit-soul. The Pyramid Texts show us that the KHU'S of the gods lived in heaven, and thither wended the KHU of a man as soon as ever the body died. Thus it is said, "Unȧs standeth with the KHU'S," and one of the gods is asked to "give him his sceptre among the KHU'S"; when the souls of the gods enter into Unȧs, their KHU's are with and round about him. To King Tetȧ it is said:

He hath plucked his eye from himself, he hath given it unto thee to strengthen thee therewith, that thou mayest prevail with it among the KHU's.

Thus, as we have seen, the whole man consisted of a natural body, a Spirit-body, a heart, a double, a Heart-soul, a shadow, a Spirit-soul, and a name. All these were, however, bound together inseparably, and the welfare of any single one of them concerned the welfare of all. For the well-being of the spiritual parts it was necessary to preserve from decay the natural body; and certain passages in the Pyramid Texts seem to show that a belief in the resurrection of the natural body existed in the earliest dynasties.

The texts are silent as to the time when the immortal part began its beatified existence; but it is probable that the Osiriș of a man only attained to the full enjoyment of spiritual happiness after the funeral ceremonies had been duly performed and the ritual recited. Comparatively few particulars are known of the manner of life of the soul in heaven, and though a number of interesting facts may be gleaned from the texts of all periods, it is very difficult to harmonize them. This result is due partly to the different views held by different schools of thought in ancient Egypt, and partly to the fact that on some points the Egyptians themselves seem to have had no decided opinions. We depend upon the Pyramid Texts for our knowledge of their earliest conceptions of a future life.

THE HEBREW BIBLE

The Hebrew Bible is one of the most influential and fascinating documents in the history of world culture. It is regarded as a sacred and prophetic book by Jews, Christians, and Moslems. Many Jews and Christians hold that the Hebrew Bible is divinely inspired. The Hebrew Bible is philosophically significant in that it introduces an explicit doctrine pertaining to the creation of the world and a deep commitment to the historical and developmental character of the human quest for liberation and salvation. Its religious and ethical teachings have become a cornerstone of Western civilization. And although the literal truth of the events recorded in the Hebrew Bible is subject to continuing controversy, Biblical themes and attitudes resonate in all our lives. Deliverance from bondage of one kind or another and the possibility of a providential resolution of the human debacle are themes of enduring concern.

The selections that follow are from Genesis, Exodus, Proverbs, and Ecclesiastes. Genesis and Exodus are the first two books of the Pentateuch, which is the first five books of the Bible and is known in Jewish tradition as the law or the Torah. Genesis tells us of the creation of the world and of the special relationship between God and the people of Israel, as mediated by Abraham, who is to be "the father of a multitude of nations." Exodus tells how God, through Moses, led the Israelites out of Egyptian bondage and gave them the Ten Commandments. Following a small selection from the Proverbs, which is a series of maxims devoted to moral practice, is a complete version of Ecclesiastes, the most philosophical and, perhaps, most secular book of the Hebrew Bible. Skeptical of salvation, the author of Ecclesiastes gives us a grim, if accurate, version of the human condition. The last entries, 12:9–14, seem to be intended as a correction to the pessimism of the text and as an orthodox warning.

From Genesis

1. In the beginning God created the heavens and the earth. [2]The earth was without form and void, and darkness was upon the face of the deep; and the Spirit of God was moving over the face of the waters.

3 And God said, "Let there be light"; and there was light. [4]And God saw that the light was good; and God separated the light from the darkness. [5]God called the light Day, and the darkness he called Night. And there was evening and there was morning, one day.

6 And God said, "Let there be a firmament in the midst of the waters, and let it separate the waters from the waters." [7]And God made the firmament and separated the waters which were under the firmament from the waters which were above the firmament. And it was so. [8]And God called the firmament Heaven. And there was evening and there was morning, a second day.

9 And God said, "Let the waters under the heavens be gathered together into one place, and let the dry land appear." And it was so. [10]God called the dry land Earth, and the waters that were gathered together he called Seas. And God saw that it was good. [11]And God said, "Let the earth put forth vegetation, plants yielding seed, and fruit trees bearing fruit in which is their seed, each according to its kind, upon the earth." And it was so. [12]The earth brought forth vegetation, plants yielding seed according to their own kinds, and trees bearing fruit in which is their seed, each according to its kind. And God saw that it was good. [12]And there was evening and there was morning, a third day.

14 And God said, "Let there be lights in the firmament of the heavens to separate the day from the night; and let them be for signs and for seasons and for days and years, [15]and let them be lights in the firmament of the heavens to give light upon the earth." And it was so. [16]And God made the two great lights, the greater light to rule the day, and the lesser light to rule the night; he made the stars also. [17]And God set them in the firmament of the heavens to give light upon the earth, [18]to rule over the day and over the night, and to separate the light from the darkness. And God saw that it was good. [19]And there was evening and there was morning, a fourth day.

20 And God said, "Let the waters bring forth swarms of living creatures, and let birds fly above the earth across the firmament of the heavens." [21]So God created the great sea monsters and every living creature that moves, with which the waters swarm, according to their kinds, and every winged bird according to its kind. And God saw that it was good. [22]And God blessed them, saying, "Be fruitful and multiply and fill the waters in the seas, and let birds multiply on the earth." [23]And there was evening and there was morning, a fifth day.

24 And God said, "Let the earth bring forth living creatures according to their kinds: cattle and creeping things and beasts of the earth according to their kinds." And it was so. [25]And God made the beasts of the earth according to their kinds and the cattle according to their kinds, and everything that creeps upon the ground according to its kind. And God saw that it was good.

26 Then God said, "Let us make man in our image, after our likeness; and let them have dominion over the fish of the sea, and over the birds of the air, and over the cattle, and over all the earth, and over every creeping thing that creeps upon the earth." [27]So God created man in his own image, in the image of God he created him; male and female he created them. [28]And God blessed them, and God said to them, "Be fruitful and multiply, and fill the earth and subdue it; and have dominion over the fish of the sea and over the birds of the air and over every living thing that moves upon the earth." [29]And God said, "Behold, I have given you every plant yielding seed which is upon the face of all the earth, and every tree with seed in its fruit; you shall have them for food. [30]And to every beast of the earth, and to every bird of the air, and to everything that creeps on the earth, everything that has the breath of life, I have given every green plant for food." And it was so. [31]And God saw everything that he had made, and behold, it was very good. And there was evening and there was morning, a sixth day.

2. Thus the heavens and the earth were finished, and all the host of them. [2]And on the seventh day God finished his work which he had done, and he rested on the seventh day from all his work which he had done. [3]So God blessed the seventh day and hallowed it, because on it God rested from all his work which he had done in creation.

3. Now the serpent was more subtle than any other wild creature that the LORD God had made. He said to the woman, "Did God say, 'You shall not eat of any tree of the garden'?" [2]And the woman said to the serpent, "We may eat of the fruit of the trees of the garden; [3]but God said, 'You shall not eat of the fruit of the tree which is in the midst of the garden, neither shall you touch it, lest you die.'" [4]But the serpent said to the woman, "You will not die. [5]For God knows that when you eat of it your eyes will be opened, and you will be like God, knowing good and evil." [6]So when the woman saw that the tree was good for food, and that it was a delight to the eyes, and that the tree was to be desired to make one wise, she took of its fruit and ate; and she also gave some to her husband, and he ate. [7]Then the eyes of both were opened, and they knew that they were naked; and they sewed fig leaves together and made themselves aprons.

8 And they heard the sound of the LORD God walking in the garden in the cool of the day, and the man and his wife hid themselves from the presence of the LORD God among the trees of the garden. [9]But the LORD God called to the man, and said to him, "Where are you?" [10]And he said, "I heard the sound of thee in the garden, and I was afraid, because I was naked; and I hid myself." [11]He said, "Who told you that you were naked? Have you eaten of the tree of which I commanded you not to eat?" [12]The man said, "The woman whom thou gavest to be with me, she gave me fruit of the tree, and I ate." [13]Then the LORD God said to the woman. "What is this that you have done?" The woman said, "The serpent beguiled me, and I ate." [14]The LORD God said to the serpent,

"Because you have done this,
    cursed are you above all cattle,
    and above all wild animals;
upon your belly you shall go,
    and dust you shall eat
    all the days of your life.
[15]I will put enmity between you and the woman,
    and between your seed and her seed;
he shall bruise your head,
    and you shall bruise his heel."

[16]To the woman he said,

"I will greatly multiply your pain in childbearing;
    in pain you shall bring forth children,
yet your desire shall be for your husband,
    and he shall rule over you."

[17]And to Adam he said,

"Because you have listened to the voice of your
    wife,
    and have eaten of the tree
of which I commanded you,
    'You shall not eat of it,'
cursed is the ground because of you;
    in toil you shall eat of it all the days of your
      life;
[18]thorns and thistles it shall bring forth to you;
    and you shall eat the plants of the field.
[19]In the sweat of your face
    you shall eat bread,
till you return to the ground,
    for out of it you were taken;
you are dust,
    and to dust you shall return."

20 The man called his wife's name Eve, because she was the mother of all living. [21]And the LORD God made for Adam and for his wife garments of skins, and clothed them.

22 Then the LORD God said, "Behold, the man has become like one of us, knowing good and evil; and now, lest he put forth his hand and take also of the tree of life, and eat, and live for ever"— [23]therefore the LORD God sent him forth from the garden of Eden, to till the ground from which he was taken. [24]He drove out the man; and at the east of the garden of Eden he placed the cherubim, and a flaming sword which turned every way, to guard the way to the tree of life. . . .

17. When Abram was ninety-nine years old the LORD appeared to Abram, and said to him, "I am God Almighty; walk before me, and be blameless. [2]And I will make my covenant between me and you, and will multiply you exceedingly." [3]Then Abram fell on his face; and God said to him, [4]"Behold, my covenant is with you, and you shall be the father of a multitude of nations. [5]No longer shall your name be Abram, but your name shall be Abraham; for I have made you the father of a multitude of nations. [6]I will make you exceedingly fruitful; and I will make na-

tions of you, and kings shall come forth from you.
[7]And I will establish my covenant between me and
you and your descendants after you throughout
their generations for an everlasting covenant, to be
God to you and to your descendants after you. [8]And
I will give to you, and to your descendants after you,
the land of your sojournings, all the land of Canaan,
for an everlasting possession; and I will be their
God."

From Exodus

12. 21 Then Moses called all the elders of Israel,
and said to them, "Select lambs for yourselves according to your families, and kill the passover lamb.
[22]Take a bunch of hyssop and dip it in the blood
which is in the basin, and touch the lintel and the
two doorposts with the blood which is in the basin;
and none of you shall go out of the door of his house
until the morning. [23]For the LORD will pass through
to slay the Egyptians; and when he sees the blood on
the lintel and on the two doorposts, the LORD will
pass over the door, and will not allow the destroyer
to enter your houses to slay you. [24]You shall observe
this rite as an ordinance for you and for your sons
for ever. [25]And when you come to the land which the
LORD will give you, as he has promised, you shall
keep this service. [26]And when your children say to
you, 'What do you mean by this service?' [27]you shall
say, 'It is the sacrifice of the LORD'S passover, for he
passed over the houses of the people of Israel in
Egypt, when he slew the Egyptians but spared our
houses.'" And the people bowed their heads and
worshiped.

28 Then the people of Israel went and did so; as
the LORD had commanded Moses and Aaron, so they
did.

29 At midnight the LORD smote all the first-born
in the land of Egypt, from the first-born of Pharaoh
who sat on his throne to the first-born of the captive
who was in the dungeon, and all the first-born of the
cattle. [30]And Pharaoh rose up in the night, he, and
all his servants, and all the Egyptians; and there was
a great cry in Egypt, for there was not a house where
one was not dead. [31]And he summoned Moses and
Aaron by night, and said, "Rise up, go forth from
among my people, both you and the people of Israel;
and go, serve the LORD, as you have said. [32]Take your
flocks and your herds, as you have said, and be gone;
and bless me also!" . . .

19. . . . [20]And the LORD came down upon Mount
Sinai, to the top of the mountain; and the LORD
called Moses to the top of the mountain, and Moses
went up. [21]And the LORD said to Moses, "Go down
and warn the people, lest they break through to the
LORD to gaze and many of them perish. [22]And also let
the priests who come near to the LORD consecrate
themselves, lest the LORD break out upon them."
[23]And Moses said to the LORD, "The people cannot
come up to Mount Sinai; for thou thyself didst
charge us, saying, 'Set bounds about the mountain,
and consecrate it.'" [24]And the LORD said to him, "Go
down, and come up bringing Aaron with you; but
do not let the priests and the people break through
to come up to the LORD, lest he break out against
them." [25]So Moses went down to the people and told
them.

20. And God spoke all these words, saying,

2 "I am the LORD your God, who brought you out
of the land of Egypt, out of the house of bondage.

3 "You shall have no other gods before me.

4 "You shall not make for yourself a graven image,
or any likeness of anything that is in heaven above,
or that is in the earth beneath, or that is in the water
under the earth; [5]you shall not bow down to them or
serve them; for I the LORD your God am a jealous
God, visiting the iniquity of the fathers upon the
children to the third and the fourth generation of
those who hate me, [6]but showing steadfast love to
thousands of those who love me and keep my
commandments.

7 "You shall not take the name of the LORD your
God in vain; for the LORD will not hold him guiltless
who takes his name in vain.

8 "Remember the sabbath day, to keep it holy. [9]Six
days you shall labor, and do all your work; [10]but the
seventh day is a sabbath to the LORD your God; in it
you shall not do any work, you, or your son, or your
daughter, your manservant, or your maidservant, or
your cattle, or the sojourner who is within your

gates; 11 for in six days the LORD made heaven and
earth, the sea, and all that is in them, and rested the
seventh day; therefore the LORD blessed the sabbath
day and hallowed it.
12 "Honor your father and your mother, that your
days may be long in the land which the LORD your
God gives you.
13 "You shall not kill.
14 "You shall not commit adultery.
15 "You shall not steal.
16 "You shall not bear false witness against your
neighbor.
17 "You shall not covet your neighbor's house;
you shall not covet your neighbor's wife, or his manservant, or his maidservant, or his ox, or his ass, or
anything that is your neighbor's."
18 Now when all the people perceived the thun-
derings and the lightnings and the sound of the
trumpet and the mountain smoking, the people were
afraid and trembled; and they stood afar off, 19 and
said to Moses, "You speak to us, and we will hear;
but let not God speak to us, lest we die." 20 And Moses
said to the people, "Do not fear; for God has come to
prove you, and that the fear of him may be before
your eyes, that you may not sin."

From Proverbs

6. 6 Go to the ant, O sluggard;
consider her ways, and be wise.
7 Without having any chief,
officer or ruler,
8 she prepares her food in summer,
and gathers her sustenance in harvest.
9 How long will you lie there, O sluggard?
When will you arise from your sleep?
10 A little sleep, a little slumber,
a little folding of the hands to rest,
11 and poverty will come upon you like a
vagabond,
and want like an armed man.

12 A worthless person, a wicked man,
goes about with crooked speech,
13 winks with his eyes, scrapes with his feet,
points with his finger,
14 with perverted heart devises evil,
continually sowing discord;
15 therefore calamity will come upon him
suddenly;
in a moment he will be broken beyond
healing.

16 There are six things which the LORD hates,
seven which are an abomination to him:
17 haughty eyes, a lying tongue,
and hands that shed innocent blood,
18 a heart that devises wicked plans,
feet that make haste to run to evil,
19 a false witness who breathes out lies,
and a man who sows discord among brothers.

Ecclesiastes

1. The words of the preacher, the son of David,
king in Jerusalem.
2 Vanity of vanities, says the Preacher,
vanity of vanities! All is vanity.
3 What does man gain by all the toil
at which he toils under the sun?
4 A generation goes, and a generation comes,
but the earth remains for ever.
5 The sun rises and the sun goes down,
and hastens to the place where it rises.
6 The wind blows to the south,
and goes round to the north;
round and round goes the wind,
and on its circuits the wind returns.
7 All streams run to the sea,
but the sea is not full;
to the place where the streams flow,
there they flow again.
8 All things are full of weariness;
a man cannot utter it;

the eye is not satisfied with seeing,
nor the ear filled with hearing.
[9]What has been is what will be,
and what has been done is what will be done;
and there is nothing new under the sun.
[10]Is there a thing of which it is said,
"See, this is new"?
It has been already,
in the ages before us.
[11]There is no remembrance of former things,
nor will there be any remembrance
of later things yet to happen
among those who come after.

12 I the Preacher have been king over Israel in Jerusalem. [13]And I applied my mind to seek and to
search out by wisdom all that is done under heaven;
it is an unhappy business that God has given to the
sons of men to be busy with. [14]I have seen everything that is done under the sun; and behold, all is
vanity and a striving after wind.

[15]What is crooked cannot be made straight,
and what is lacking cannot be numbered.

16 I said to myself, "I have acquired great wisdom,
surpassing all who were over Jerusalem before me;
and my mind has had great experience of wisdom
and knowledge." [17]And I applied my mind to know
wisdom and to know madness and folly. I perceived
that this also is but a striving after wind.

[18]For in much wisdom is much vexation,
and he who increases knowledge increases
sorrow.

2. I said to myself, "Come now, I will make a test
of pleasure; enjoy yourself." But behold, this also
was vanity. [2]I said of laughter, "It is mad," and of
pleasure, "What use is it?" [3]I searched with my mind
how to cheer my body with wine—my mind still
guiding me with wisdom—and how to lay hold on
folly, till I might see what was good for the sons of
men to do under heaven during the few days of their
life. [4]I made great works; I built houses and planted
vineyards for myself; [5]I made myself gardens and
parks, and planted in them all kinds of fruit trees. [6]I
made myself pools from which to water the forest of
growing trees. [7]I bought male and female slaves, and
had slaves who were born in my house; I had also
great possessions of herds and flocks, more than any
who had been before me in Jerusalem. [8]I also gathered for myself silver and gold and the treasure of
kings and provinces; I got singers, both men and
women, and many concubines, man's delight.

9 So I became great and surpassed all who were
before me in Jerusalem; also my wisdom remained
with me. [10]And whatever my eyes desired I did not
keep from them; I kept my heart from no pleasure,
for my heart found pleasure in all my toil, and this
was my reward for all my toil. [11]Then I considered
all that my hands had done and the toil I had spent
in doing it, and behold, all was vanity and a striving
after wind, and there was nothing to be gained
under the sun.

12 So I turned to consider wisdom and madness
and folly; for what can the man do who comes after
the king? Only what he has already done. [13]Then I
saw that wisdom excels folly as light excels darkness.
[14]The wise man has his eyes in his head, but the fool
walks in darkness; and yet I perceived that one fate
comes to all of them. [15]Then I said to myself, "What
befalls the fool will befall me also; why then have I
been so very wise?" And I said to myself that this
also is vanity. [16]For of the wise man as of the fool
there is no enduring remembrance, seeing that in
the days to come all will have been long forgotten.
How the wise man dies just like the fool! [17]So I hated
life, because what is done under the sun was grievous to me; for all is vanity and a striving after
wind.

18 I hated all my toil in which I had toiled under
the sun, seeing that I must leave it to the man who
will come after me; [19]and who knows whether he
will be a wise man or a fool? Yet he will be master
of all for which I toiled and used my wisdom under
the sun. This also is vanity. [20]So I turned about and
gave my heart up to despair over all the toil of my
labors under the sun, [21]because sometimes a man
who has toiled with wisdom and knowledge and
skill must leave all to be enjoyed by a man who did
not toil for it. This also is vanity and a great evil.
[22]What has a man from all the toil and strain with
which he toils beneath the sun? [23]For all his days are
full of pain, and his work is a vexation; even in the
night his mind does not rest. This also is vanity.

24 There is nothing better for a man than that he
should eat and drink, and find enjoyment in his toil.
This also, I saw, is from the hand of God; [25]for apart
from him who can eat or who can have enjoyment?
[26]For to the man who pleases him God gives wisdom
and knowledge and joy; but to the sinner he gives
the work of gathering and heaping, only to give to
one who pleases God. This also is vanity and a striving after wind.

3. For everything there is a season, and a time for every matter under heaven:

[2]a time to be born, and a time to die;
a time to plant, and a time to pluck up what is planted;
[3]a time to kill, and a time to heal;
a time to break down, and a time to build up;
[4]a time to weep, and a time to laugh;
a time to mourn, and a time to dance;
[5]a time to cast away stones, and a time to gather stones together;
a time to embrace, and a time to refrain from embracing;
[6]a time to seek, and a time to lose;
a time to keep, and a time to cast away;
[7]a time to rend, and a time to sew;
a time to keep silence, and a time to speak;
[8]a time to love, and a time to hate;
a time for war, and a time for peace.

[9]What gain has the worker from his toil?

10 I have seen the business that God has given to the sons of men to be busy with. [11]He has made everything beautiful in its time; also he has put eternity into man's mind, yet so that he cannot find out what God has done from the beginning to the end. [12]I know that there is nothing better for them than to be happy and enjoy themselves as long as they live; [13]also that it is God's gift to man that every one should eat and drink and take pleasure in all his toil. [14]I know that whatever God does endures for ever; nothing can be added to it, nor anything taken from it; God has made it so, in order that men should fear before him. [15]That which is, already has been; that which is to be, already has been; and God seeks what has been driven away.

16 Moreover I saw under the sun that in the place of justice, even there was wickedness, and in the place of righteousness, even there was wickedness. [17]I said in my heart, God will judge the righteous and the wicked, for he has appointed a time for every matter, and for every work. [18]I said in my heart with regard to the sons of men that God is testing them to show them that they are but beasts. [19]For the fate of the sons of men and the fate of beasts is the same; as one dies, so dies the other. They all have the same breath, and man has no advantage over the beasts; for all is vanity. [20]All go to one place; all are from the dust, and all turn to dust again. [21]Who knows whether the spirit of man goes upward and the spirit of the beast goes down to the earth? [22]So I saw that there is nothing better than that a man should enjoy his work, for that is his lot; who can bring him to see what will be after him?

4. Again I saw all the oppressions that are practiced under the sun. And behold, the tears of the oppressed, and they had no one to comfort them! On the side of their oppressors there was power, and there was no one to comfort them. [2]And I thought the dead who are already dead more fortunate than the living who are still alive; [3]but better than both is he who has not yet been, and has not seen the evil deeds that are done under the sun.

4 Then I saw that all toil and all skill in work come from a man's envy of his neighbor. This also is vanity and a striving after wind.

5 The fool folds his hands, and eats his own flesh.

6 Better is a handful of quietness than two hands full of toil and a striving after wind.

7 Again, I saw vanity under the sun: [8]a person who has no one, either son or brother, yet there is no end to all his toil, and his eyes are never satisfied with riches, so that he never asks, "For whom am I toiling and depriving myself of pleasure?" This also is vanity and an unhappy business.

9 Two are better than one, because they have a good reward for their toil. [10]For if they fall, one will lift up his fellow; but woe to him who is alone when he falls and has not another to lift him up. [11]Again, if two lie together, they are warm; but how can one be warm alone? [12]And though a man might prevail against one who is alone, two will withstand him. A threefold cord is not quickly broken.

13 Better is a poor and wise youth than an old and foolish king, who will no longer take advice, [14]even though he had gone from prison to the throne or in his own kingdom had been born poor. [15]I saw all the living who move about under the sun, as well as that youth, who was to stand in his place; [16]there was no end of all the people; he was over all of them. Yet those who come later will not rejoice in him. Surely this also is vanity and a striving after wind.

5. Guard your steps when you go to the house of God; to draw near to listen is better than to offer the sacrifice of fools; for they do not know that they are doing evil. [2]Be not rash with your mouth, nor let your heart be hasty to utter a word before God, for God is in heaven, and you upon earth; therefore let your words be few.

3 For a dream comes with much business, and a fool's voice with many words.

4 When you vow a vow to God, do not delay paying it; for he has no pleasure in fools. Pay what you vow. [5]It is better that you should not vow than that you should vow and not pay. [6]Let not your mouth lead you into sin, and do not say before the messenger that it was a mistake; why should God be angry at your voice, and destroy the work of your hands?

7 For when dreams increase, empty words grow many: but do you fear God.

8 If you see in a province the poor oppressed and justice and right violently taken away, do not be amazed at the matter; for the high official is watched by a higher, and there are yet higher ones over them. [9]But in all, a king is an advantage to a land with cultivated fields.

10 He who loves money will not be satisfied with money; nor he who loves wealth, with gain: this also is vanity.

11 When goods increase, they increase who eat them; and what gain has their owner but to see them with his eyes?

12 Sweet is the sleep of a laborer, whether he eats little or much; but the surfeit of the rich will not let him sleep.

13 There is a grievous evil which I have seen under the sun: riches were kept by their owner to his hurt, [14]and those riches were lost in a bad venture; and he is father of a son, but he has nothing in his hand. [15]As he came from his mother's womb he shall go again, naked as he came, and shall take nothing for his toil, which he may carry away in his hand. [16]This also is a grievous evil: just as he came, so shall he go; and what gain has he that he toiled for the wind, [17]and spent all his days in darkness and grief, in much vexation and sickness and resentment?

18 Behold, what I have seen to be good and to be fitting is to eat and drink and find enjoyment in all the toil with which one toils under the sun the few days of his life which God has given him, for this is his lot. [19]Every man also to whom God has given wealth and possessions and power to enjoy them, and to accept his lot and find enjoyment in his toil—this is the gift of God. [20]For he will not much remember the days of his life because God keeps him occupied with joy in his heart.

6. There is an evil which I have seen under the sun, and it lies heavy upon men: [2]a man to whom God gives wealth, possessions, and honor, so that he lacks nothing of all that he desires, yet God does not give him power to enjoy them, but a stranger enjoys them; this is vanity; it is a sore affliction. [3]If a man begets a hundred children, and lives many years, so that the day of his years are many, but he does not enjoy life's good things, and also has no burial, I say that an untimely birth is better off than he. [4]For it comes into vanity and goes into darkness, and in darkness its name is covered; [5]moreover it has not seen the sun or known anything; yet it finds rest rather than he. [6]Even though he should live a thousand years twice told, yet enjoy no good—do not all go to the one place?

7 All the toil of man is for his mouth, yet his appetite is not satisfied. [8]For what advantage has the wise man over the fool? And what does the poor man have who knows how to conduct himself before the living? [9]Better is the sight of the eyes than the wandering of desire; this also is vanity and a striving after wind.

10 Whatever has come to be has already been named, and it is known what man is, and that he is not able to dispute with one stronger than he. [11]The more words, the more vanity, and what is man the better? [12]For who knows what is good for man while he lives the few days of his vain life, which he passes like a shadow? For who can tell man what will be after him under the sun?

7. A good name is better than
precious ointment.
and the day of death, than the day of birth.
[2]It is better to go to the house of mourning
than to go to the house of feasting;
for this is the end of all men,
and the living will lay it to heart.
[3]Sorrow is better than laughter,
for by sadness of countenance the heart is made glad.
[4]The heart of the wise is in the house of mourning;
but the heart of fools is in the house of mirth.
[5]It is better for a man to hear the rebuke of the wise
than to hear the song of fools.
[6]For as the crackling of thorns under a pot,
so is the laughter of the fools;
this also is vanity.

[7]Surely oppression makes the wise man foolish,
and a bribe corrupts the mind.
[8]Better is the end of a thing than its beginning;
and the patient in spirit is better than the
proud in spirit.
[9]Be not quick to anger,
for anger lodges in the bosom of fools.
[10]Say not, "Why were the former days better than
these?".
For it is not from wisdom that you ask this.
[11]Wisdom is good with an inheritance,
an advantage to those who see the sun.
[12]For the protection of wisdom is like the
protection of money;
and the advantage of knowledge is that
wisdom preserves the life of him who has
it.
[13]Consider the work of God:
who can make straight what he has made
crooked?

14 In the day of prosperity be joyful, and in the
day of adversity consider; God has made the one as
well as the other, so that man may not find out anything that will be after him.

15 In my vain life I have seen everything; there is
a righteous man who perishes in his righteousness,
and there is a wicked man who prolongs his life in
his evil-doing. [16]Be not righteous overmuch, and do
not make yourself overwise; why should you destroy
yourself? [17]Be not wicked overmuch, neither be a
fool; why should you die before your time? [18]It is
good that you should take hold of this, and from that
withhold not your hand; for he who fears God shall
come forth from them all.

19 Wisdom gives strength to the wise man more
than ten rulers that are in a city.

20 Surely there is not a righteous man on earth
who does good and never sins.

21 Do not give heed to all the things that men say,
lest you hear your servant cursing you; [22]your heart
knows that many times you have yourself cursed
others.

23 All this I have tested by wisdom; I said, "I will
be wise"; but it was far from me. [24]That which is, is
far off, and deep, very deep; who can find it out? [25]I
turned my mind to know and to search out and to
seek wisdom and the sum of things, and to know the
wickedness of folly and the foolishness which is
madness. [26]And I found more bitter than death the
woman whose heart is snares and nets, and whose
hands are fetters; he who pleases God escapes her,
but the sinner is taken by her. [27]Behold, this is what
I found, says the Preacher, adding one thing to another to find the sum, [28]which my mind has sought
repeatedly, but I have not found. One man among a
thousand I found, but a woman among all these I
have not found. [29]Behold, this alone I found, that
God made man upright, but they have sought out
many devices.

8. Who is like the wise man?
And who knows the interpretation of a thing?
A man's wisdom makes his face shine,
and the hardness of his countenance is
changed.

2 Keep the king's command, and because of your
sacred oath be not dismayed; [3]go from his presence,
do not delay when the matter is unpleasant, for he
does whatever he pleases. [4]For the word of the king
is supreme, and who may say to him, "What are you
doing?" [5]He who obeys a command will meet no
harm, and the mind of a wise man will know the
time and way. [6]For every matter has its time and
way, although man's trouble lies heavy upon him.
[7]For he does not know what is to be, for who can tell
him how it will be? [8]No man has power to retain the
spirit, or authority over the day of death; there is no
discharge from war, nor will wickedness deliver
those who are given to it. [9]All this I observed while
applying my mind to all that is done under the sun,
while man lords it over man to his hurt.

10 Then I saw the wicked buried; they used to go
in and out of the holy place, and were praised in the
city where they had done such things. This also is
vanity. [11]Because sentence against an evil deed is not
executed speedily, the heart of the sons of men is
fully set to do evil. [12]Though a sinner does evil a
hundred times and prolongs his life, yet I know that
it will be well with those who fear God, because they
fear before him; [13]but it will not be well with the
wicked, neither will he prolong his days like a
shadow, because he does not fear before God.

14 There is a vanity which takes place on earth,
that there are righteous men to whom it happens according to the deeds of the wicked, and there are
wicked men to whom it happens according to the
deeds of the righteous. I said that this also is vanity.
[15]And I commend enjoyment, for man has no good
thing under the sun but to eat and drink, and enjoy
himself, for this will go with him in his toil through
the days of life which God gives him under the sun.

16 When I applied my mind to know wisdom, and to see the business that is done on earth, how neither day nor night one's eyes see sleep; [17]then I saw all the work of God, that man cannot find out the work that is done under the sun. However much man may toil in seeking, he will not find it out; even though a wise man claims to know, he cannot find it out.

9. But all this I laid to heart, examining it all, how the righteous and the wise and their deeds are in the hand of God; whether it is love or hate man does not know. Everything before them is vanity, [2]since one fate comes to all, to the righteous and the wicked, to the good and the evil, to the clean and the unclean, to him who sacrifices and him who does not sacrifice. As is the good man, so is the sinner; and he who swears is as he who shuns an oath. [3]This is an evil in all that is done under the sun, that one fate comes to all; also the hearts of men are full of evil, and madness is in their hearts while they live, and after that they go to the dead. [4]But he who is joined with all the living has hope, for a living dog is better than a dead lion. [5]For the living know that they will die, but the dead know nothing, and they have no more reward; but the memory of them is lost. [6]Their love and their hate and their envy have already perished, and they have no more for ever any share in all that is done under the sun.

7 Go, eat your bread with enjoyment, and drink your wine with a merry heart; for God has already approved what you do.

8 Let your garments be always white; let not oil be lacking on your head.

9 Enjoy life with the wife whom you love, all the days of your vain life which he has given you under the sun, because that is your portion in life and in your toil at which you toil under the sun. [10]Whatever your hand finds to do, do it with your might; for there is no work or thought or knowledge or wisdom in Sheol, to which you are going.

11 Again I saw that under the sun the race is not to the swift, nor the battle to the strong, nor bread to the wise, nor riches to the intelligent, nor favor to the men of skill; but time and chance happen to them all. [12]For man does not know his time. Like fish which are taken in an evil net, and like birds which are caught in a snare, so the sons of men are snared at an evil time, when it suddenly falls upon them.

13 I have also seen this example of wisdom under the sun, and it seemed great to me. [14]There was a little city with few men in it; and a great king came against it and besieged it, building great siegeworks against it. [15]But there was found in it a poor wise man, and he by his wisdom delivered the city. Yet no one remembered that poor man. [16]But I say that wisdom is better than might, though the poor man's wisdom is despised, and his words are not heeded.

17 The words of the wise heard in quiet are better than the shouting of a ruler among fools. [18]Wisdom is better than weapons of war, but one sinner destroys much good.

10. Dead flies make the perfumer's ointment give
off an evil odor;
so a little folly outweighs wisdom and honor.
[2]A wise man's heart inclines him toward the
right,
but a fool's heart toward the left.
[3]Even when the fool walks on the road, he lacks
sense,
and he says to every one that he is a fool.
[4]If the anger of the ruler rises against you, do not
leave your place,
for deference will make amends for great
offenses.

5 There is an evil which I have seen under the sun, as it were an error proceeding from the ruler: [6]folly is set in many high places, and the rich sit in a low place. [7]I have seen slaves on horses, and princes walking on foot like slaves.

[8]He who digs a pit will fall into it;
and a serpent will bite him who breaks
through a wall.
[9]He who quarries stones is hurt by them;
and he who splits logs is endangered by them.
[10]If the iron is blunt, and one does not whet the
edge,
he must put forth more strength;
but wisdom helps one to succeed.
[11]If the serpent bites before it is charmed,
there is no advantage in a charmer.

[12]The words of a wise man's mouth win him favor,
but the lips of a fool consume him.
[13]The beginning of the words of his mouth is
foolishness,
and the end of his talk is wicked madness.
[14]A fool multiplies words,
though no man knows what is to be,
and who can tell him what will be after him?
[15]The toil of a fool wearies him,
so that he does not know the way to the city.

16 Woe to you, O land, when your king is a child,
and your princes feast in the morning!
17 Happy are you, O land, when your king is the son of free men,
and your princes feast at the proper time,
for strength, and not for drunkenness!
18 Through sloth the roof sinks in,
and through indolence the house leaks.
19 Bread is made for laughter,
and wine gladdens life,
and money answers everything.
20 Even in your thought, do not curse the king,
nor in your bedchamber curse the rich;
for a bird of the air will carry your voice,
or some winged creature tell the matter.

11. Cast your bread upon the waters,
for you will find it after many days.
2 Give a portion to seven, or even to eight,
for you know not what evil may happen on earth.
3 If the clouds are full of rain,
they empty themselves on the earth;
and if a tree falls to the south or to the north,
in the place where the tree falls, there it will lie.
4 He who observes the wind will not sow;
and he who regards the clouds will not reap.

5 As you do not know how the spirit comes to the bones in the womb of a woman with child, so you do not know the work of God who makes everything.

6 In the morning sow your seed, and at evening withhold not your hand; for you do not know which will prosper, this or that, or whether both alike will be good.

7 Light is sweet, and it is pleasant for the eyes to behold the sun.

8 For if a man lives many years, let him rejoice in them all; but let him remember that the days of darkness will be many. All that comes is vanity.

9 Rejoice, O young man, in your youth, and let your heart cheer you in the days of your youth; walk in the ways of your heart and the sight of your eyes. But know that for all these things God will bring you into judgment.

10 Remove vexation from your mind, and put away pain from your body; for youth and the dawn of life are vanity.

12. Remember also your Creator in the days of
your youth, before the evil days come, and the years
draw nigh, when you will say, "I have no pleasure
in them"; 2 before the sun and the light and the moon
and the stars are darkened and the clouds return
after the rain; 3 in the day when the keepers of the
house tremble, and the strong men are bent, and the
grinders cease because they are few, and those that
look through the windows are dimmed, 4 and the
doors on the street are shut; when the sound of the
grinding is low, and one rises up at the voice of a
bird, and all the daughters of song are brought low;
5 they are afraid also of what is high, and terrors are
in the way; the almond tree blossoms, the grasshop-
per drags itself along and desire fails; because man
goes to his eternal home, and the mourners go about
the streets; 6 before the silver cord is snapped, or the
golden bowl is broken, or the pitcher is broken at the
fountain, or the wheel broken at the cistern, 7 and the
dust returns to the earth as it was, and the spirit returns to God who gave it. 8 Vanity of vanities, says
the Preacher; all is vanity.

9 Besides being wise, the Preacher also taught the
people knowledge, weighing and studying and arranging proverbs with great care. 10 The Preacher
sought to find pleasing words, and uprightly he
wrote words of truth.

11 The sayings of the wise are like goads, and like
nails firmly fixed are the collected sayings which are
given by one Shepherd. 12 My son, beware of anything beyond these. Of making many books there is
no end, and much study is a weariness of the flesh.

13 The end of the matter; all has been heard. Fear
God, and keep his commandments; for this is the
whole duty of man. 14 For God will bring every deed
into judgment, with every secret thing, whether
good or evil.

HOMER

Homer is now widely regarded, after considerable scholarly controversy, as the author of the two magnificent epics, The Iliad *and* The Odyssey, *composed in the eighth century* B.C. The Iliad *tells of the Trojan War, the battle between the Greeks and the Trojans that was precipitated by the kidnapping of Helen of Sparta by Paris of Troy.*

The Odyssey *is the story of the wanderings of Odysseus, whose journey home after the Trojan War took ten years. The philosophical significance of the Homeric epics is twofold: first, they present the gods as anthropomorphic, that is, as similar to human beings in their behavior; and, second, they mark the emergence of a distinctive Greek ethos, especially in their emphasis on the evil of* hubris, *stubborn pride. Moreover, as a source of the western moral tradition,* The Iliad *and* The Odyssey *rival the Hebrew Bible.*

The following selection from The Odyssey *occurs midway in the poem, when Odysseus visits Hades, the land of the dead. Students are encouraged to compare and contrast Homer's version with that of the* Egyptian Book of the Dead, *the* Tibetan Book of the Dead, *and with the "Inferno" of Dante's* Divine Comedy.

The Land of the Dead, *from* The Odyssey

'Now when we had gone down again to the sea and our vessel,
first of all we dragged the ship down into the bright water,
and in the black hull set the mast in place, and set sails,
and took the sheep and walked them aboard, and ourselves also
embarked, but sorrowful, and weeping big tears. Circe
of the lovely hair, the dread goddess who talks with mortals,
sent us an excellent companion, a following wind, filling
the sails, to carry from astern the ship with the dark prow.
We ourselves, over all the ship making fast the running gear,
sat still, and let the wind and the steersman hold her steady.
All day long her sails were filled as she went through the water,
and the sun set, and all the journeying-ways were darkened.
'She made the limit, which is of the deep-running Ocean.
There lie the community and city of Kimmerian people,
hidden in fog and cloud, nor does Helios, the radiant
sun, ever break through the dark, to illuminate them with his shining,
neither when he climbs up into the starry heaven,
nor when he wheels to return again from heaven to earth,
but always a glum night is spread over wretched mortals.
Making this point, we ran the ship ashore, and took out
the sheep, and ourselves walked along by the stream of the Ocean
until we came to that place of which Circe had spoken.
'There Perimedes and Eurylochos held the victims
fast, and I, drawing from beside my thigh my sharp sword,
dug a pit, of about a cubit in each direction,
and poured it full of drink offerings for all the dead, first
honey mixed with milk, and the second pouring was sweet wine,
and the third, water, and over it all I sprinkled white barley.
I promised many times to the strengthless heads of the perished

The Laokoön Group (2nd Century, B.C.*). Laokoön was a priest of Apollo who warned the Trojans against accepting the gift of the wooden horse from the Greeks at the end of the Trojan War. The Trojans doubted Laokoön's warning after he and his sons were crushed to death by serpents, and allowed the horse, which secretly contained Greek soldiers, to be brought within the walled city of Troy. (Museo Vaticano, Rome)*

dead that, returning to Ithaka, I would slaughter a barren
cow, my best, in my palace, and pile the pyre with treasures,
and to Teiresias apart would dedicate an all-black
ram, the one conspicuous in all our sheep flocks.
Now when, with sacrifices and prayers, I had so entreated
the hordes of the dead, I took the sheep and cut their throats
over the pit, and the dark-clouding blood ran in, and the souls
of the perished dead gathered to the place, up out of Erebos,

brides, and young unmarried men, and long-suffering elders,
virgins, tender and with the sorrows of young hearts upon them,
and many fighting men killed in battle, stabbed with brazen
spears, still carrying their bloody armor upon them.
These came swarming around my pit from every direction
with inhuman clamor, and green fear took hold of me.
Then I encouraged my companions and told them, taking
the sheep that were lying by, slaughtered with the pitiless
bronze, to skin these, and burn them, and pray to the divinities,
to Hades the powerful, and to revered Persephone,
while I myself, drawing from beside my thigh my sharp sword,
crouched there, and would not let the strengthless heads of the perished
dead draw nearer to the blood, until I had questioned Teiresias.
'But first there came the soul of my companion, Elpenor,
for he had not yet been buried under earth of the wide ways,
since we had left his body behind in Circe's palace,
unburied and unwept, with this other errand before us.
I broke into tears at the sight of him, and my heart pitied him,
and so I spoke aloud to him and addressed him in winged words:
"Elpenor, how did you come here beneath the fog and the darkness?
You have come faster on foot than I could in my black ship."
'So I spoke, and he groaned aloud and spoke and answered:
"Son of Laertes and seed of Zeus, resourceful Odysseus,
the evil will of the spirit and the wild wine bewildered me.
I lay down on the roof of Circe's palace, and never thought,
when I went down, to go by way of the long ladder,
but blundered straight off the edge of the roof, so that my neck bone
was broken out of its sockets, and my soul went down to Hades'.
But now I pray you, by those you have yet to see, who are not here,
by your wife, and by your father, who reared you when you were little,
and by Telemachos whom you left alone in your palace;
for I know that after you leave this place and the house of Hades
you will put back with your well-made ship to the island, Aiaia;
there at that time, my lord, I ask that you remember me,
and do not go and leave me behind unwept, unburied,
when you leave, for fear I might become the gods' curse upon you;
but burn me there with all my armor that belongs to me,
and heap up a grave mound beside the beach of the gray sea,
for an unhappy man, so that those to come will know of me.
Do this for me, and on top of the grave mound plant the oar
with which I rowed when I was alive and among my companions."
'So he spoke, and I in turn spoke to him in answer:
"All this, my unhappy friend, I will do for you as you ask me."
'So we two stayed there exchanging our sad words, I on
one side holding my sword over the blood, while opposite
me the phantom of my companion talked long with me.
'Next there came to me the soul of my dead mother,
Antikleia, daughter of great-hearted Autolykos,
whom I had left alive when I went to sacred Ilion.
I broke into tears at the sight of her and my heart pitied her,

but even so, for all my thronging sorrow, I would not
let her draw near the blood until I had questioned Teiresias.
'Now came the soul of Teiresias the Theban, holding
a staff of gold, and he knew who I was, and spoke to me:
"Son of Laertes and seed of Zeus, resourceful Odysseus,
how is it then, unhappy man, you have left the sunlight
and come here, to look on dead men, and this place without pleasure?
Now draw back from the pit, and hold your sharp sword away from me,
so that I can drink of the blood and speak the truth to you."
'So he spoke, and I, holding away the sword with the silver
nails, pushed it back in the sheath, and the flawless prophet,
after he had drunk the blood, began speaking to me.
"Glorious Odysseus, what you are after is sweet homecoming,
but the god will make it hard for you. I think you will not
escape the Shaker of the Earth, who holds a grudge against you
in his heart, and because you blinded his dear son, hates you.
But even so and still you might come back, after much suffering,
if you can contain your own desire, and contain your companions',
at that time when you first put in your well-made vessel
at the island Thrinakia, escaping the sea's blue water,
and there discover pasturing the cattle and fat sheep
of Helios, who sees all things, and listens to all things.
Then, if you keep your mind on homecoming, and leave these unharmed,
you might all make your way to Ithaka, after much suffering;
but if you do harm them, then I testify to the destruction
of your ship and your companions, but if you yourself get clear,
you will come home in bad case, with the loss of all your companions,
in someone else's ship, and find troubles in your household,
insolent men, who are eating away your livelihood
and courting your godlike wife and offering gifts to win her.
You may punish the violences of these men, when you come home.
But after you have killed these suitors in your own palace,
either by treachery, or openly with the sharp bronze,
then you must take up your well-shaped oar and go on a journey
until you come where there are men living who know nothing
of the sea, and who eat food that is not mixed with salt, who never
have known ships whose cheeks are painted purple, who never
have known well-shaped oars, which act for ships as wings do.
And I will tell you a very clear proof, and you cannot miss it.
When, as you walk, some other wayfarer happens to meet you,
and says you carry a winnow-fan on your bright shoulder,
then you must plant your well-shaped oar in the ground, and render
ceremonies sacrifice to the lord Poseidon,
one ram and one bull, and a mounter of sows, a boar pig,
and make your way home again and render holy hecatombs
to the immortal gods who hold the wide heaven, all
of them in order. Death will come to you from the sea, in
some altogether unwarlike way, and it will end you
in the ebbing time of a sleek old age. Your people
about you will be prosperous. All this is true that I tell you."

'So he spoke, but I in turn said to him in answer:
"All this, Teiresias, surely must be as the gods spun it..
But come now, tell me this and give me an accurate answer.
I see before me now the soul of my perished mother,
but she sits beside the blood in silence, and has not yet deigned
to look directly at her own son and speak a word to me.
Tell me, lord, what will make her know me, and know my presence?"
'So I spoke, and he at once said to me in answer:
"Easily I will tell you and put it in your understanding.
Any one of the perished dead you allow to come up
to the blood will give you a true answer, but if you begrudge this
to any one, he will return to the place where he came from."
'So speaking, the soul of the lord Teiresias went back into
the house of Hades, once he had uttered his prophecies, while I
waited steadily where I was standing, until my mother
came and drank the dark-clouding blood, and at once she knew me,
and full of lamentation she spoke to me in winged words:
"My child, how did you come here beneath the fog and the darkness
and still alive? All this is hard for the living to look on,
for in between lie the great rivers and terrible waters
that flow, Ocean first of all, which there is no means of crossing
on foot, not unless one has a well-made ship. Are you
come now to this place from Troy, with your ship and your companions,
after wandering a long time, and have you not yet come
to Ithaka, and there seen your wife in your palace?"
'So she spoke, and I in turn said to her in answer:
"Mother, a duty brought me here to the house of Hades.
I had to consult the soul of Teiresias the Theban.
For I have not yet been near Achaian country, nor ever
set foot on our land, but always suffering I have wandered
since the time I first went along with great Agamemnon
to Ilion, land of good horses, and the battle against the Trojans.
But come now, tell me this, and give me an accurate answer.
What doom of death that lays men low has been your undoing?
Was it a long sickness, or did Artemis of the arrows
come upon you with her painless shafts, and destroy you?
And tell me of my father and son whom I left behind. Is
my inheritance still with them, or does some other
man hold them now, and thinks I will come no more? Tell me
about the wife I married, what she wants, what she is thinking,
and whether she stays fast by my son, and guards everything,
or if she has married the best man among the Achaians."
'So I spoke, and my queenly mother answered me quickly:
"All too much with enduring heart she does wait for you
there in your own palace, and always with her the wretched
nights and the days also waste her away with weeping.
No one yet holds your fine inheritance, but in freedom
Telemachos adminsters your allotted lands, and apportions
the equal feasts, work that befits a man with authority
to judge, for all call him in. Your father remains, on the estate

where he is, and does not go to the city. There is no bed there
nor is there bed clothing nor blankets nor shining coverlets,
but in the winter time he sleeps in the house, where the thralls do,
in the dirt next to the fire, and with foul clothing upon him;
but when the summer comes and the blossoming time of harvest,
everywhere he has places to sleep on the ground, on fallen
leaves in piles along the rising ground of his orchard,
and there he lies, grieving, and the sorrow grows big within him
as he longs for your homecoming, and harsh old age is on him.
And so it was with me also and that was the reason I perished,
nor in my palace did the lady of arrows, well-aiming,
come upon me with her painless shafts, and destroy me,
nor was I visited by sickness, which beyond other
things takes the life out of the body with hateful weakness,
but, shining Odysseus, it was my longing for you, your cleverness
and your gentle ways, that took the sweet spirit of life from me."
'So she spoke, but I, pondering it in my heart, yet wished
to take the soul of my dead mother in my arms. Three times
I started toward her, and my heart was urgent to hold her,
and three times she fluttered out of my hands like a shadow
or a dream, and the sorrow sharpened at the heart within me,
and so I spoke to her and addressed her in winged words, saying:
"Mother, why will you not wait for me, when I am trying
to hold you, so that even in Hades' with our arms embracing
we can both take the satisfaction of dismal mourning?
Or are you nothing but an image that proud Persephone
sent my way, to make me grieve all the more for sorrow?
'So I spoke, and my queenly mother answered me quickly:
"Oh my child, ill-fated beyond all other mortals,
this is not Persephone, daughter of Zeus, beguiling you,
but it is only what happens, when they die, to all mortals.
The sinews no longer hold the flesh and the bones together.
and once the spirit has left the white bones, all the rest
of the body is made subject to the fire's strong fury,
but the soul flitters out like a dream and flies away. Therefore
you must strive back toward the light again with all speed; but remember
these things for your wife, so you may tell her hereafter."

HESIOD

Hesiod was a poet of the late eighth century B.C. His Works and Days *extols the virtues of peasant life and warns against laziness and carelessness. His* Theogony *catalogs the history and activities of the Greek divinities. Before the work of Hesiod, the gods were the source of all power but were idiosyncratic in their behavior and organization. It is Hesiod who introduces the human focus and prepares the way for the slow erosion of mythology as the explanation of nature and human activity.*

The selection from the Theogony *pertains to the origin of the earth and provides an informative contrast with Genesis in the Hebrew Bible. The selection from* Works and Days *tells of the creation of the first five races of human beings.*

From Theogony

First of all was Chaos born;
Then, after him, wide-bosomed Earth,
a sure, eternal dwelling-place
for all the deathless gods who rule
Olympus' snowy peaks.
Next, Tartarus of the dark mist was born
in a nook of the wide-wayed earth;
then Love, most beautiful by far
of all the immortals, the looser of limbs,
who overcomes, of all the gods
and all mankind, the mind within them
and their clever counsels.
From Chaos there sprang Erebos
and dark-robed Night.
From Night the Upper Air was born
and Day, borne in her womb,
the offspring of her love for Erebos.
The Earth's first offspring,
equal to herself, was Heaven
filled with stars, to cover her entire
and be a sure, eternal dwelling-place
for the blessed gods.
Then she bore the lofty hills
the happy haunts of goddess nymphs
who dwell in mountain glens.
Without sweet union of love
she bore the sea, Pontus,
unharvested, with raging swell of surge
and, having lain with Heaven, bore
the deeply whirling Ocean River stream.
The whole earth seethed with it,
and the streams of the Ocean river,
and the unharvested sea.
The blazing vapor engulfed
the earthborn Titans.
A flame unquenchable pierced through
the shining upper air.
A blazing beam of thunder flash
and lightning blast
blinded their eyes, despite their strength.
The wondrous blaze confounded Chaos.
To the eyes the sight was such
and the sound was such to the ears
as the collision of Earth

---

might seem with the mighty Heaven above.
Not from me but from my mother
comes the tale how earth and sky
were once one form, but being separated,
brought forth all things, sending into light
trees, birds, wild beasts,
those nourished by the salt sea
and the race of mortals.
The minute that each child was born
he would hide them all away
in a hidden place of Earth
and conceal them from the light.
Heaven exulted in his evil work,
but mighty Earth, within her heart,
groaned from pressure's pain,
and conceived a crafty plan
of wicked treachery.
Straightaway she made the spark
of hard grey flint, and made
a mighty sickle of it.
The she told her children
of the plan and spoke
encouraging words to them
born of her heart's distress:
"Children of mine, born of a wicked father,
obey me if you will, that we might punish
the vile and wicked outrage of your father
who was the first to plan such deeds of shame."
So she spoke; but fear laid hold of all
and not one said a word.
But mighty Cronus, crooked in his counsel,
took courage, and addressed his mother thus:
"Mother, I undertake to do this deed;
for I do not respect our ill-named father,
who was the first to plan such deeds of shame."
So he spoke; and mighty Earth rejoiced
within her heart, and in an ambush
made him lie, concealed.
She placed within his hand a sickle,
jagged sharp, and then revealed her plan.
Great Heaven then approached, and in his train
came Night; he longed for love and lay
spreading himself entirely over Earth.
Then from his ambush, his own son
stretched out his left hand; with his right
he seized the monstrous sickle,
long, and jagged sharp, and swiftly chopped
and cut his father's genitals,
and hurled them far behind him.
Nor did they fall in vain.

For every bloody drop that poured forth
Earth received; and as the seasons changed
she bore the powerful Furies
and the mightly Giants ablaze with armor,
holding in their hands long javelins.
Holy sky desires to penetrate the earth.
Love seizes earth with longing for this marriage.
And rain, falling from her bedfellow the sky,
impregnates earth; and she brings forth for men
pasture for their flocks, and grain for them.

From Works and Days

First of all, the immortals who dwell on Olympus
created the golden race of mortal men.
These lived in Cronus' time
when he held sway in heaven.
Like gods they lived their lives
with hearts released from care,
released from pain and sorrow.
They never felt the misery
of age; with never-failing limbs
they banqueted with pleasure,
remote from every ill.
Their death was like a sweet subduing sleep.
All good things were theirs.
The fruitful earth poured forth
her fruits unbidden in boundless plenty.
In peaceful ease they kept their lands
with good abundance,
rich in flocks, and dear to the immortals.
Now the earth has covered over
these men who are called
"pure spirits who dwell on earth,"
"good men," "defenders from evil,"
"warders of moral men" (who keep watch
over lawsuits and wicked deeds
and roam the earth enveloped in mist),
"givers of wealth."
Next after these the gods who dwell in Olympus
made a race of silver men
far baser than the first,
unlike the race of gods, in stature
and in spirit.

Poseidon, bronze statue from the island of Euboea. Poseidon was the Greek god of earthquakes and water. (Hirmer Fotoarchiv)

Kore. She was the idealization of feminine ("maiden") physical perfection for the Greeks. Sixth-century dedicatory statue from the Acropolis in Athens. (Alinari/Art Resource)

A child was nurtured at his mother's side
a hundred years, an utter simpleton,
playing a child's part in his house.
But when he was full grown
and reached the prime of life
he lived a meager span of years
in sorrow for his folly.
For they could not restrain themselves
from sin and wrong,
nor would they serve the gods
nor sacrifice upon the holy altars
of the blessed ones,
which is man's lawful duty.
Then Zeus the son of Cronus
engulfed them in his rage
because they paid no honors to the gods,
the blessed ones who dwell upon Olympus.
Then the earth engulfed these men
who are called by mortals
"blessed gods of the underworld,"
men of inferior rank, but still

honor attends them too.
Then Father Zeus devised another race,
a third, of mortal men,
a race of bronze, in no way like the silver,
dreadful and mighty, sprung from shafts of ash.
The all-lamented sinful works of Ares
were their chief care.
They ate no grain, but hearts of flint
were theirs, unyielding and unconquered.
Great was their strength,
invincible the arms
which grew from mighty shoulders
on strong limbs.
Bronze were their weapons,
their houses too were bronze,
with bronze they worked.
Black iron did not exist.
Subdued by their own hands
nameless they went to icy Hades'
dank and drear abode.
Black death laid hold upon them;
in spite of their great strength
they left the sun's bright light.
Then the earth engulfed this race,
and Zeus the son of Cronus made
another race, the fourth
he set upon the fruitful earth.
This was more just, and nobler
than the last—a godlike race
of heroes, who are called
"half-gods,"—the race before our own
upon the boundless earth.
Some of these men, grim war
and battle strife destroyed,
some fighting round the seven-gated city,
Thebes, the land of Cadmus,
for the flocks of Oedipus;
others, brought to Troy by ships
across the great surge of the mighty sea,
for fair-haired Helen's sake.
There death came as the end
to some of them, and with his pall
he shrouded them.
Father Zeus, the son of Cronus,
gave the rest to live their lives
apart from men, and made them dwell
at the far corners of the earth.
And there they live, beside the surge
of the deep Ocean in the blessed isles
with hearts released from care,

these heroes blest.
Three times each year the earth
in fruitfulness bestows on them
her fruits, as sweet as honey.
Far from the gods they live;
their king is Cronus, whom
the father of the gods and men
released from bondage.
Still, upon these last attend
honor and glory.
Then Zeus, farseeing, made another race
of men, the fifth, who live
upon the fruitful earth.
Would that I had no share
in this fifth race of men.
Would that I had died before
or afterwards been born.
This is the race of iron.
Not for a day do they cease
from toil and labor, not for a night
does their corruption cease.
The gods will give them
bitter sorrow to endure.
Yet still some good things
shall be mingled with the bad.
Zeus will destroy this race too
of mortal men, as soon as infants
at their birth have gray hair
on their temples;
when father and children can be
no longer like-minded,
nor guest agree with host,
nor friend with friend;
when love no longer exists
from brother to brother
as once it did.
Then they will swiftly dishonor
their aging parents, and chide them
with harsh rebukes, in bitterness,
with no respect for gods.
They will not repay their aged parents
for their childhood care,
but take the law in their own hands.
One man will sack another's city;
favor will not be shown to him
who keeps an oath, is just,
or good. The evil-doer's
arrogance will win men's praise.
Right shall depend on might
and piety will cease to be.

The wicked will slander the noble
and do him harm, and forswear himself.
Among all wretched men
envy will go her way
with shrill and evil tongue
delighting in disaster,
her face a face of hate.
And then the time will come
when, to Olympus from the wide-wayed earth,
enveloped in white robes
to hide their lovely flesh
Shame and Respect shall go,
leaving mankind, to join the blessed gods.
Bitter heartache they bequeath
to mortal men, nor leave
defense from evil.

SAPPHO

Sappho lived during the late seventh and early sixth centuries B.C. *Details of her life are few, although it is known that she was born on the island of Lesbos and spent some time as an exile in Sicily. Most of her poetry has been lost or survives only in fragments; what remains provides a tantalizing indication of her exquisite reflective and poetic gifts. Despite the loveliness of her verse, it clearly represents the deep sense of the tragic and the hold of fate on human life, themes which are constant in the thought and culture of ancient Greece.*

Poems

There are those who say
an array of horsemen,
and others of marching men,
and others of ships, is
the most beautiful thing on the dark earth.

But I say it is whatever one loves.

It is very easy
to show this to all:
for Helen,
by far the most beautiful of mortals,
left her husband
and sailed to Troy
giving no thought at all

---

to her child nor dear parents,
but was led . . .
[by her love alone.]

Now, far away, Anactoria
comes to my mind.
For I would rather watch her
moving in her lovely way,
and see her face, flashing radiant,
than all the force of Lydian chariots,
and their infantry in full display of arms.

When you have died, there will be nothing.
No memory of you will remain,
not a trace
to linger after:
you do not share
the rose of the Muses with us,
and will wander unseen
in the hall of the dead,
a fitful shade among the blinded ghosts.

I don't know
what
to do: I am
of two minds.

ARCHILOCHOS

A Greek poet who is regarded as second only to Homer, Archilochos lived during the seventh century B.C. *He was born on Parlos, in the Cyclades, a group of islands between the Greek coast and Asia Minor. His works were read and revered by no less than Horace and Catullus. We, however, are unfortunate in that his poetic remains are now mostly fragments. A soldier, indeed a mercenary, Archilochos has left us the satiric and skeptical poetry of a man of experience. Centuries before the advent of philosophy in Greece, Archilochos demonstrates an independence of thought and an ironic approach to the supremacy of the gods.*

Poems

These golden matters
Of Gyges and his treasuries
Are no concern of mine.

From Carmina Archilochos, *The Fragments of Archilochos,* trans. Guy Davenport (Berkeley: University of California Press, 1964), pp. 7, 10, 11, 42, and 64. Reprinted with the permission of the publisher.

Jealousy has no power over me,
Nor do I envy a god his work,
And I don't burn to rule.
Such things have no
Fascination for my eyes.

Attribute all to the gods.
They pick a man up,
Stretched on the black loam,
And set him on his two feet,
Firm, and then again
Shake solid men until
They fall backward
Into the worst of luck,
Wandering hungry,
Wild of mind.

The oxherd picks tarantulas from his oxen,
The cocksman keeps his prick dainty and clean:
The nature of man is surprising and diverse,
Each finding his pleasure where the heart wills,
And each can say, I alone among mankind
Have what's best, what's fine and good
From Zeus, God, Father of men and gods.
Yet Eurymas finds fault with everybody.

There's nothing now
We can't expect to happen!
Anything at all, you can bet,
Is ready to jump out at us.
No need to wonder over it.
Father Zeus has turned
Noon to night, blotting out
The sunshine utterly,
Putting cold terror
At the back of the throat.
Let's believe all we hear.
Even that dolphins and cows
Change place, porpoises and goats,
Rams booming along in the offing,
Mackerel nibbling in the hill pastures.
I wouldn't be surprised,
I wouldn't be surprised.

Fox knows many,
Hedgehog one
Solid trick.

Aliter,
Fox knows
Eleventythree
Tricks and still
Gets caught;
Hedgehog knows
One but it
Always works.

SUGGESTIONS FOR FURTHER READING

Epstein, Isadore. *Judaism: A Historical Presentation.* Baltimore: Penguin, 1959.

Kirk, G. S. *The Nature of Greek Myths.* Harmondsworth, Middlesex: Penguin, 1974.

Morford, Mark P. O., and Lenardon, Robert J. *Classical Mythology.* New York: David McKay, 1971.

Noss, John B. *Man's Religions.* New York: Macmillan, 1980.

Pritchard, James B. *The Ancient Near East.* 2 vols. Princeton: Princeton University Press, 1958, 1973.

Raju, P. T. *Introduction to Comparative Philosophy.* Lincoln: University of Nebraska Press, 1962.

Rose, H. J. *Religion in Greece and Rome.* New York: Harper & Row, 1959.

Smart, Ninian. *The Religious Experience of Mankind.* New York: Scribner, 1969.

The Birth of Western Philosophy— The Pre-Socratics

After the poetic utterances of Homer and Hesiod, Greek thought became more directly philosophical. Beginning in the sixth century B.C., with the work of the Milesian thinkers, Thales, Anaximander, and Anaximenes, philosophical speculation focused on the affairs of nature and the problems of being and knowing. This emphasis continued until the time of Socrates (470–399 B.C.), when human activities—social, political, and ethical—took the center of the philosophical stage. The writings of the Pre-Socratics have a haunting originality about them. No culture is totally unique but this period of Greek thought, with its profound and original inquiry into nature, reason, and the problems of being and becoming, has no equivalent parallel in other ancient cultures.

The selections that follow are of two kinds. One group is referred to as fragments, because, quite literally, they are the partial remains of ancient manuscripts. The second group comes from doxographical sources, that is, from quotations given by later thinkers, especially Theophrastus, a pupil of Aristotle. The scholarly assumption is that the doxographers, the collectors of extracts, had access to the original works. We have made no distinctions within the selections as to their origin, for there is extensive agreement on their authenticity. A bibliography of sources is presented at the end of this section.

THALES

Although traditionally Thales (fl. 580 B.C.) is said to be the first philosopher in western civilization, this assertion has been challenged by recent commentators, who accord the distinction to Anaximander. Born in Miletus, a port in Ionia on the coast of Asia Minor, Thales has become a legendary figure. Many of his alleged scientific achievements are now the subject of doubt, although we are confident that he correctly predicted a solar eclipse and was responsible for several important engineering accomplishments. No fragments of Thales' writings are extant. For the most part, our knowledge of his teachings derives from some cryptic remarks of Aristotle. According to Aristotle, Thales contended that the nature of reality would be comprehensible were we to analyze water as the element that provided life and motion. This contention was partially scientific, but it also reflected Thales' involvement with the ritualistic and mythic thought

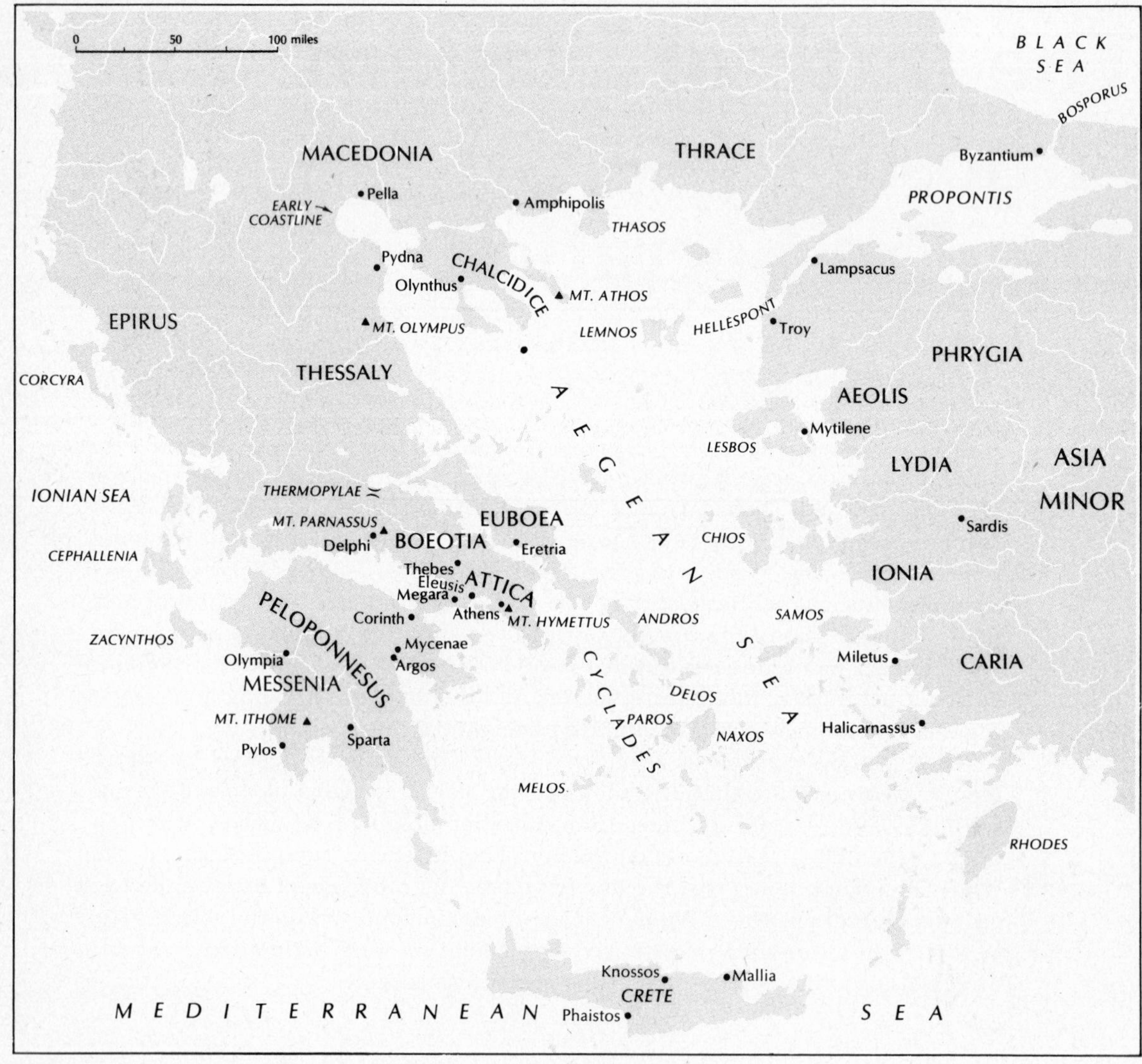

Early and Classical Greece

of sixth-century Greece. Nonetheless, if Thales did in fact hold that the fundamental explanatory principle of reality was water, then we have our first public philosophical statement in western civilization. That is, Thales held that, on the basis of a rational interpretation of observed facts, it is possible to denote a single and universal principle to account for the nature of reality. The question of whether "water" is a plausible candidate for this principle of accountability is not of paramount concern. Rather, the importance of Thales' alleged statement is contained in its claim of universality as based on rationality and observation. Put differently, the gods have not spoken; a human being has spoken.

Thales [1-6]

[1] Thales is traditionally the first to have revealed the investigation of nature to the Greeks; he had many predecessors, as also Theophrastus thinks, but so far surpassed them as to blot out all who came before him. He is said to have left nothing in the form of writings except the so-called *Nautical star-guide.*

[2] Others say the earth rests upon water. This, indeed, is the oldest theory that has been preserved, and is attributed to Thales of Miletus. It was supposed to stay still because it floated like wood and other similar substances, which are so constituted as to rest upon water but not upon air. As if the same account had not to be given of the water which carries the earth as of the earth itself!

[3] Of the first philosophers, then, most thought the principles which were of the nature of matter were the only principles of all things. That of which all things that are consist, the first from which they come to be, the last into which they are resolved (the substance remaining, but changing in its modifications), this they say is the element and this the principle of things, and therefore they think nothing is either generated or destroyed, since this sort of entity is always conserved, as we say Socrates neither comes to be absolutely when he comes to be beautiful or musical, nor ceases to be when he loses these characteristics, because the substratum, Socrates himself, remains. Just so they say nothing else comes to be or ceases to be; for there must be some entity—either one or more than one—from which all other things come to be, it being conserved.

Yet they do not all agree as to the number and the nature of these principles. Thales, the founder of this type of philosophy, says the principle is water (for which reason he declared that the earth rests on water), getting the notion perhaps from seeing that the nutriment of all things is moist, and that heat itself is generated from the moist and kept alive by it (and that from which they come to be is a principle of all things). He got his notion from this fact, and from the fact that the seeds of all things have a moist nature, and that water is the origin of the nature of moist things.

[4] For Thales says that the earth is supported by water and sails like a ship; and when it is said to quake it is pitching because of the movement of the water.

[5] Thales, too, to judge from what is recorded about him, seems to have held soul to be a motive force, since he said that the magnet has a soul in it because it moves the iron.

[6] Certain thinkers say that soul is intermingled in the whole universe, and it is perhaps for that reason that Thales came to the opinion that all things are full of gods.

ANAXIMANDER

Born in Miletus ca. 610 B.C., Anaximander lived until 546 B.C. He was a student of and a successor to Thales. His scientific achievements, especially with regard to mapping the heavens, are said to have been considerable. Anaximander wrote a very influential book, entitled On the Nature of Things. *There survives only a long quotation, which is treasured as the oldest philosophical fragment extant in western civilization, despite historical conflict as to its exact wording.*

This text of Anaximander, buttressed by doxographical sources, does provide us with an understanding of his fundamental philosophical contribution. He believed that the basic principle of reality was that of the apeiron. *Virtually untranslatable,* apeiron *has been rendered as the "boundless," the "limitless," and, more controversially, the "infinite." The* apeiron *of Anaximander is the source and regulator of the coming and going of all that was, is, or will be. Not identified with a single element, the* apeiron *functions as both cause and sustenance. Although subsequent Greek and medieval philosophy became far more sophisticated than that of the Pre-Socratics, the* apeiron *of Anaximander remains a tantalizing evocation of our deepest problem: How, after all, do things come to be? And where do they go when they no longer be? Deeper still, why do things come and go? The question is one of cosmic justice and necessity. Anaximander anticipates the struggles of two thousand years of philosophy in holding that there is a principle that neither comes nor goes but is the reason why all else must come and go.*

Anaximander [7-9]

[7] Of those who say that it is one, moving, and infinite, Anaximander, son of Praxiades, a Milesian, the successor and pupil of Thales, said that the principle and element of existing things was the *apeiron* [indefinite, or infinite], being the first to introduce this name of the material principle. He says that it is neither water nor any other of the so-called elements, but some other *apeiron* nature, from which come into being all the heavens and the worlds in them. And the source of coming-to-be for existing things is that into which destruction, too, happens 'according to necessity; for they pay penalty and retribution to each other for their injustice according to the assessment of Time', as he describes it in these rather poetical terms.

[8] Was there a time before motion began?—a time before which it had no existence? Does it cease again, so that nothing moves? Or is it the case that motion neither comes into existence nor passes away, but always was and always will be, and is a deathless and unfailing source of existing things—the life, as it were, of all things constituted by nature?

[9] Anaximander held that motion, through which it comes about that the heavens arise, is eternal.

ANAXIMENES

The third in a succession of philosophers from Miletus, Anaximenes (fl. 545 B.C.) is believed to have died between 528 and 526 B.C. He was a student of Anaximander and ancient writers refer to his "book," although nothing of it has survived.

From the doxographical tradition, we do know that Anaximenes continued the work of his predecessors by searching for the basic principle of explanation for the meaning and activity of nature. He chose air as the principle (arche) *that governs all existence, divine as well as human. The principle of condensation and rarefaction reveals the deepest activity of nature* (physis)*. The coming and going of the* apeiron *of Anaximander is hereby given a more explicit physical description. Just as our souls, being air, keep us together as human beings, so, too, does the cosmic air sustain the world.*

Anaximenes' doctrine had considerable influence, as witness the forceful statement of Diogenes of Apollonia, uttered almost a century later:

> *It seems to me that that which has intelligence is what men call air, and that all men are steered by this, and that it has power over all things. For this very thing seems to be a god and to reach everywhere and to dispose all things and to be in everything.*

The basic principle may not be the water of Thales, nor the apeiron *of Anaximander, nor the air of Anaximenes. Their question, however, is still with us after more than two millennia of thought and speculation. It is this quest for the principles that govern the nature and activity of reality which characterizes the centuries-long tradition of philosophy.*

Anaximenes [10-14]

[10] Anaximenes of Miletus, son of Eurystratus and associate of Anaximander, also says that the underlying nature of things is one and infinite. But he does not regard it as indeterminate, as Anaximander does, but as determinate, calling it air; and he says that it differs in respect of thinness and thickness in different things. When dilated it becomes fire; when compressed, wind and then cloud. When it is compressed further it becomes water, then earth, then stone. The rest are produced from these. He too makes motion eternal, through which for him also change comes about.

[11] The form of air is as follows. When it is most evenly distributed it is invisible to the eye; but it is made visible by cold or heat or moisture or motion. It is in constant motion; for things that change would not do so unless there were motion. When it is compressed or dilated it appears different. When it is dilated and becomes rarer, it becomes fire. Winds, on the other hand, are air that has been compressed. Cloud is produced from air by "felting"; when compressed further it becomes water; when compressed still further, earth; and when compressed as far as possible, stone.

[12] He says that what is contracted and compressed is cold, while what is dilated or "loosely-packed" (this is the word he himself uses) is hot. Thus it is quite proper to say of a man that he blows both hot and cold; for when the breath is compressed by the lips it is chilled, whereas when it issues from a relaxed mouth it is hot because of its dilation.

[13] Anaximenes says that air is a god.

[14] Just as our soul (being air) controls us, so breath and air encompass the whole world-order.

XENOPHANES

Born in Colophon, in Ionia, Xenophanes lived from ca. 570 B.C. until ca. 500 B.C., although some scholars contend that he lived far longer. He is alleged to be the first Greek philosopher to posit one god who was not anthropomorphic, that is, a god who did not imitate human qualities.

Xenophanes' writings often deal satirically with the immoral and humanlike characteristics of the traditional deities of Olympian theology. He was also skeptical about the ability of human beings to know the ultimate truth. His combination of irony, dubiety, and common sense makes him unusually refreshing in the pantheon of Pre-Socratic philosophers.

Xenophanes [15-28]

[15] She whom men call "Iris," too, is in reality a cloud, purple, red, and green to the sight.

[16] Mortals believe that the gods are begotten, and that they wear clothing like our own, and have a voice and a body.

[17] The Ethiopians make their gods snub-nosed and black; the Thracians make theirs gray-eyed and red-haired.

[18] And if oxen and horses and lions had hands, and could draw with their hands and do what man

can do, horses would draw the gods in the shape of horses, and oxen in the shape of oxen, each giving the gods bodies similar to their own.

[19] One god, greatest among gods and men, in no way similar to mortals either in body or mind.

[20] Fixing his gaze upon the heaven as a whole, Xenophanes declared that the one, *i.e.*, god, exists.

[21] The being of god is spherical, not like that of man. He sees all over and hears all over, but does not breathe. He is the totality of mind and thought, and is eternal.

[22] He says that there are innumerable world-orders, but that they do not overlap.

[23] Homer and Hesiod have attributed to the gods all those things which in men are a matter for reproach and censure: stealing, adultery, and mutual deception.

[24] It is proper for reasonable men to celebrate god with stories that are meet and with pure words. And when they have poured a libation and prayed for the power to do what is right (for it is of this that we stand most in need), then it is not unseemly for a man to drink as much as he can hold and still get home without help, unless he be very old. But among men he is to be praised who after drinking performs skillfully—telling not of the battles of the Titans or of Giants or of Centaurs (those fictions of the men of old) nor of violent civil war, in which there is no good, but to hold the gods in reverence: *that* is good always.

[25] The gods have not revealed all things from the beginning to mortals; but, by seeking, men find out, in time, what is better.

[26] If god had not created yellow honey, men would think figs sweeter than they do.

[27] No man knows the truth, nor will there be a man who has knowledge about the gods and what I say about everything. For even if he were to hit by chance upon the whole truth, he himself would not be aware of having done so, but each forms his own opinion.

[28] Let these things, then, be taken as *like* the truth. . . .

PYTHAGORAS AND PYTHAGOREANISM

Although we do not know for certain of any writings by Pythagoras (570 B.C.–ca. 490 B.C.), he is regarded as one of the most influential of ancient thinkers. He founded a religious and philosophical society at Croton in southern Italy, but severe community pressure against its existence forced him to flee. This pattern of grouping and then fleeing became a persistent one for the Pythagoreans. Such periodic travail, however, enabled them to spread their teachings and hence accounts in part for their extraordinary influence in western thought. In time, Pythagoreanism found its way into the thought of Parmenides, Plato, Philo of Alexandria, and Clement of Alexandria. It is even cited in the fifteenth century by Copernicus as an important factor in his heliocentric theory of the universe.

The key theme in Pythagoreanism is that of order, especially as derived from the study of numbers. The Pythagoreans believed that "things are numbers" and when combined with geometric figures, provide insight into harmony, both cosmic and personal. It follows that Pythagoreanism would contribute to mathematics, music theory, and cosmology. In addition, their doctrine of the transmigration of souls and series of taboos, such as ritual silence and abstention from animal flesh, gave the Pythagoreans a cultic character, which enhanced both the mystery and the attractiveness of their movement.

Pythagoras and the Pythagoreans [29–44]

[29] Down to the time of Philolaus it was impossible to obtain any knowledge of any Pythagorean doctrine.

[30] What he taught his disciples no one can say for certain, for they maintained a remarkable silence. All the same, the following became generally

known. First, he said that the soul is immortal; second, that it migrates into other kinds of animals; third, that the same events are repeated in cycles, nothing being new in the strict sense; and finally, that all things with souls should be regarded as akin. Pythagoras seems to have been the first to introduce these beliefs into Greece.

[31] For the sake of punishment the soul is yoked to the body and buried in it as in a tomb.

[32] The air about the earth is sluggish and unhealthy, and all things in it are mortal; but the uppermost air is always in motion and pure and wholesome, and all things in it are immortal and therefore divine. The sun, moon, and other heavenly bodies are gods; for in them the hot predominates, and this is the cause of life. . . . The rays of the sun penetrate the cold and the dense ether (they call air "cold ether" and sea and moisture "dense ether"), even to the depths, quickening all things. All things live which have a share of the hot; hence plants, too, are living things. But not all have soul. Soul is a detached portion of the ether—of the hot and the cold both, for it has a share of the cold ether, too. Soul is distinct from life and is immortal, since that from which it is detached is immortal.

[33] They say that once when a puppy was being whipped, Pythagoras, who was passing by, took pity on it, saying, "Stop! Do not beat it! It is the soul of a friend; I recognize his voice!"

[34] Pythagoras forbade even the killing, let alone the eating, of animals which share with us the privilege of having a soul.

[35] Some say that he was satisfied with honey alone, or a bit of honeycomb or bread (he did not touch wine during the day); or, for a treat, vegetables boiled or raw. Seafood he ate but rarely. His robe, which was white and spotless, and his bedclothes, which were also white, were of wool; for linen had not yet reached those parts. He was never observed to relieve himself, or to have intercourse, or to be drunk. He used to avoid laughter and all pandering to scurrilous jokes and vulgar stories.

[36] The first to use it, and to call himself a philosopher [*i.e.*, a "lover of wisdom"] was Pythagoras. For no one, he said, *is* wise except god.

[37] It was he who brought geometry to perfection, Moeris having been the first to find the beginnings of its elements, as Anticleides says in the second book of his *Alexander*. He goes on to say that Pythagoras worked very hard at the arithmetical side of geometry, and discovered the musical intervals on the monochord. Nor did he neglect even medicine. Apollodorus the calculator says that Pythagoras sacrificed a hecatomb when he discovered that the square on the hypotenuse of a right-angled triangle is equal to the sum of the squares on the sides enclosing the right angle.

[38] Eudemus the Peripatetic ascribes to the Pythagoreans the discovery of the theorem that any triangle has its interior angles equal to two right angles. He says that they proved the theorem in this way:

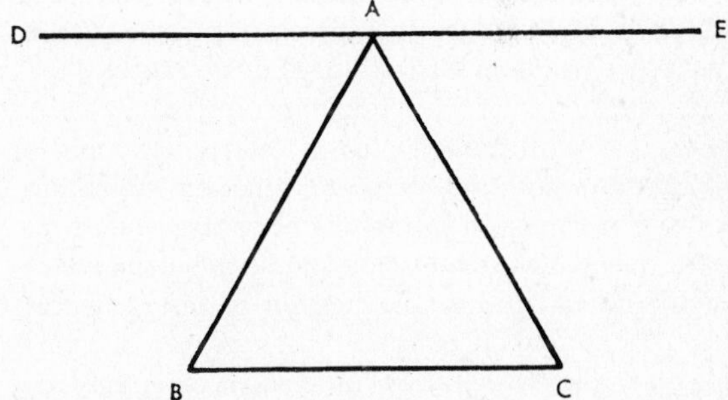

Let *ABC* be a triangle, and let the line *DE* be drawn through *A* parallel to *BC*. Now since *BC* and *DE* are parallel, and the alternate angles are equal, the angle *DAB* is equal to the angle *ABC* and the angle *EAC* is equal to the angle *ACB*.

Let the angle *BAC* be added to them both. Then the angles *DAB, BAC,* and *CAE* (that is to say, the angles *DAB* and *BAE, i.e.,* two right angles) are equal to the three angles of the triangle *ABC*.

Hence the three angles of the triangle are equal to two right angles.

[39] According to most accounts, geometry was discovered first among the Egyptians, and originated in the measurement of areas; for it was forced upon them by the flooding of the Nile, which obliterated everyone's boundaries. Nor is it astonishing that the discovery of this and of the other sciences should have arisen from practical needs, since everything that is in process of development proceeds from the imperfect to the perfect. . . . Pythagoras transformed this study into a form of liberal education, examining its principles from the beginning and tracking down the theorems immaterially and conceptually. It was he who discovered both the theory of proportionals and the construction of the cosmic figures

[*i.e.*, the pyramid, cube, octahedron, dodecahedron and icosahedron].

[40] Contemporaneously with these philosophers and before them, the so-called Pythagoreans, who were the first to take up mathematics, not only advanced this study, but also having been brought up in it they thought its principles were the principles of all things. Since of these principles numbers are by nature the first, and in numbers they seemed to see many resemblances to the things that exist and come into being—more than in fire and earth and water (such and such a modification of numbers being justice, another being soul and reason, another being opportunity—and similarly almost all other things being numerically expressible); since, again, they saw that the modifications and the ratios of the musical scales were expressible in numbers;—since, then, all other things seemed in their whole nature to be modelled on numbers, and numbers seemed to be the first things in the whole of nature, they supposed the elements of numbers to be the elements of all things, and the whole heaven to be a musical scale and a number. And all the properties of numbers and scales which they could show to agree with the attributes and parts and the whole arrangement of the heavens, they collected and fitted into their scheme; and if there was a gap anywhere, they readily made additions so as to make their whole theory coherent. E. g. as the number 10 is thought to be perfect and to comprise the whole nature of numbers, they say that the bodies which move through the heavens are ten, but as the visible bodies are only nine, to meet this they invent a tenth—the 'counter-earth'.

[41] The 'Pythagoreans' treat of principles and elements stranger than those of the physical philosophers (the reason is that they got the principles from non-sensible things, for the objects of mathematics, except those of astronomy, are of the class of things without movement); yet their discussions and investigations are all about nature; for they generate the heavens, and with regard to their parts and attributes and functions they observe the phenomena, and use up the principles and the causes in explaining these, which implies that they agree with the others, the physical philosophers, that the *real* is just all that which is perceptible and contained by the so-called 'heavens'. But the causes and the principles which they mention are, as we said, sufficient to act as steps even up to the higher realms of reality, and are more suited to these than to theories about nature. They do not tell us at all, however, how there can be movement if limit and unlimited and odd and even are the only things assumed, or how without movement and change there can be generation and destruction, or the bodies that move through the heavens can do what they do.

Further, if one either granted them that spatial magnitude consists of these elements, or this were proved, still how would some bodies be light and others have weight? To judge from what they assume and maintain they are speaking no more of mathematical bodies than of perceptible; hence they have said nothing whatever about fire or earth or the other bodies of this sort, I suppose because they have nothing to say which applies *peculiarly* to perceptible things.

[42] But the Pythagoreans have said in the same way that there are two principles, but added this much, which is peculiar to them, that they thought that finitude and infinity were not attributes of certain other things, e.g. of fire or earth or anything else of this kind, but that infinity itself and unity itself were the substance of the things of which they are predicated. This is why number was the substance of all things.

[43] But the Italian philosophers known as Pythagoreans take the contrary view. At the centre, they say, is fire, and the earth is one of the stars, creating night and day by its circular motion about the centre. They further construct another earth in opposition to ours to which they give the name counter-earth. In all this they are not seeking for theories and causes to account for observed facts, but rather forcing their observations and trying to accommodate them to certain theories and opinions of their own. But there are many others who would agree that it is wrong to give the earth the central position, looking for confirmation rather to theory than to the facts of observation. Their view is that the most precious place befits the most precious thing: but fire, they say, is more precious than earth, and the limit than the intermediate, and the circumference and the centre are limits. Reasoning on this basis they take the view that it is not earth that lies at the centre of the sphere, but rather fire.

[44] Pythagoras was the first to call what surrounds us a cosmos, because of the order in it.

HERACLITUS

Heraclitus (fl. 504–501 B.C.) is often referred to as the "obscure one," partly because the dates of his life and death are shrouded in mystery and partly because his extant writings are often aphoristic and frequently ambiguous. We do not know whether his writings are fragments of a book that was traditionally composed or whether the book itself was originally a series of oracular sayings. We do know that Heraclitus was born in Ephesus, an Ionian city of Asia Minor. Some commentators say that he was of noble birth, and his writings do reveal a condescension to the common citizens of his time.

Despite the scholarly controversy over his life and texts, it is safe to say that Heraclitus taught a doctrine which, in contemporary terms, we can call consciousness raising. Nature speaks to humankind through its "word," the logos. *But humankind is busy and deaf to the logos. The basic message of the logos is the paradoxical principle that all is one, the one being the irreducible presence of change or flux. It follows that for Heraclitus the basic element is fire, ever on the move, ever changing. His doctrine of the logos and his naming of fire as the central element in nature both became influential on the subsequent teaching of the Stoics and, through them, on early Christian thought. Heraclitus is also invoked as a forerunner of modern process philosophy, especially that of Henri Bergson.*

Heraclitus [45-82]

[45] Wisdom is one thing: to understand the thought which steers all things through all things.

[46] Heraclitus describes change as a way up and down, and the world-order as coming into being in accordance with it. For fire, when it is contracted, becomes moist; when it is contracted still further it becomes water; and water, when it is contracted, turns to earth. This is the downward way. And earth liquifies again; and from it water arises; and from water the rest. For he refers nearly everything to the evaporation of the sea. And this is the upward way.

[47] This world-order, the same for all, no god made or any man, but it always was and is and will be an ever-living fire, kindling by measure and going out by measure.

[48] Heraclitus, you know, says that everything moves on and that nothing is at rest; and, comparing existing things to the flow of a river, he says that you could not step into the same river twice.

[49] To god all things are beautiful and good and just; but men suppose some things to be just and others unjust.

[50] It is necessary to understand that war is universal and justice is strife, and that all things take place in accordance with strife and necessity.

[51] For fire lives the death of earth, and air lives the death of fire; water lives the death of air, and earth that of water.

[52] War is the father and king of all. . . .

[53] In a circle, beginning and end are common.

[54] The way up and the way down are the same.

[55] For the many do not understand such things when they meet with them; nor having learned do they comprehend, though they think they do.

[56] Though the *logos* is as I have said, men always fail to comprehend it, both before they hear it and when they hear it for the first time. For though all things come into being in accordance with this *logos,* they seem like men without experience, though in fact they do have experience both of words and deeds such as I have set forth, distinguishing each thing in accordance with its nature and declaring what it is. But other men are as unaware of what they do when awake as they are when they are asleep.

[57] Though they are in daily contact with the *logos* they are at variance with it, and what they meet with appears alien to them.

[58] Listening not to me but to the *logos,* it is wise to acknowledge that all things are one.

[59] We ought to follow what is common to all; but

though the *logos* is common to all, the many live as though their thought were private to themselves.

[60] If you do not expect the unexpected, you will not find it; for it is hard to find and difficult.

[61] Those who dig for gold dig up much dirt and find little.

[62] Nature loves to hide.

[63] They do not comprehend how, though it is at variance with itself, it agrees with itself. It is a harmony of opposed tensions, as in the bow and the lyre.

[64] In opposition there is agreement; between unlikes, the fairest harmony.

[65] Changing, it rests.

[66] It is not good for men to get all they wish.

[67] It is sickness that makes health pleasant and good; hunger, satiety; weariness, rest.

[68] Physicians who cut, burn, stab, and rack the sick demand a fee for it.

[69] According to Heraclitus we become intelligent by drawing in the divine *logos* when we breathe. We become forgetful during sleep, but on waking we regain our senses. For in sleep the channels of perception are shut, and the intelligence in us is severed from its kinship with the environment—our only connection with it being through breathing, by which we are, as it were, rooted in it. When it is separated in this way, the mind loses the power of remembering which it formerly had; but in the waking state it once more flows forth through the channels of perception as through so many openings, and making contact with the environment recovers the power of reasoning.

Just as coals, when they are brought close to the fire, begin to glow, and die down when they are removed from it, so it is with that portion of the environment which sojourns in our own bodies. When it is separated from its source, it loses nearly all power of thought; but when it makes contact with it through the many channels of sense, it becomes of like nature to the whole.

[70] Thinking is common to all.

[71] There is more need to stamp out insolence than a fire.

[72] I searched out myself.

[73] The soul has a *logos* which increases itself.

[74] You would not find out the boundaries of the soul though you travelled every road, so deep is its *logos*.

[75] A dry soul is wisest and best.

[76] Moderation is the greatest virtue, and wisdom is to speak the truth and to act according to nature, giving heed to it.

[77] Corpses are fitter to be cast out than dung.

[78] He says that the soul, passing out into the soul of the all, returns to its own kind.

[79] It is necessary for men who speak with common sense to place reliance on what is common to all, as a city relies upon law, and even more firmly. For all human laws are nourished by the one divine law. For it governs as far as it will, and is sufficient for all things, and outlasts them.

[80] Uncomprehending, even when they have heard, they are like the deaf. The old saying bears witness to them: "Though present they are absent."

[81] Dogs bark at those whom they do not recognize.

[82] The Ephesians ought to hang themselves—every grown man of them—and leave their city to adolescents, now that they have expelled Hermodorus, the best man among them, saying, "Let there be no best man among us; or if there is, let him be so elsewhere and among others!"

PARMENIDES

Plato tells us that Parmenides, at age 65, conversed with the young Socrates in Athens in 450 B.C., which places his birth at 515 B.C. Parmenides was the founder of a school known as the Eleatics, which also included Zeno and Melissus.

Parmenides was the author of a work which has been referred to as "On Nature" or "On Truth." It is thought that approximately one-third of this book survives. The major bequest of Parmenides is his strong affirmation of the irreducible character of being: namely, that which is, is, and that which is not, cannot be discussed. For Parmenides, being is, always was, and always will be. The parallel is clear. Either something which is, comes from being, which is, and therefore does not involve change, or one assumes that something comes from not-being, which is obviously impossible. The first way is that of truth, for it comes from the acknowledgment that being is. The second way, proceeding from non-being, is the way of opinion.

Throughout the centuries, philosophers have attempted to saddle Parmenides with a logical confusion between is, an existential predicate, and is, a copula, or a mere connector. Parmenides' thought, however, is much deeper than this accusation of a logical fallacy would suggest. In fact, it is Parmenides who introduces into western thought the most profound of all questions, namely, why is there something rather than nothing? The reader is well advised to ponder the seemingly obvious but subtle utterance that being is.

Parmenides [83-91]

[83] The mares that draw me as far as my heart would go escorted me, when the goddesses who were driving set me on the renowned road that leads through all cities the man who knows. Along this I was borne; for along it the wise horses drew at full stretch the chariot, and maidens led the way. The axle, urged round by the whirling wheels at either end, shrilled in its sockets and glowed, as the daughters of the sun, leaving the house of night and pushing the veils from their heads with their hands, hastened to escort me towards the light.

There are the gates of the ways of night and day, enclosed by a lintel and a threshold of stone; and these, high in the ether, are fitted with great doors, and avenging Justice holds the keys which control these ways. The maidens entreated her with gentle words, and wisely persuaded her to thrust back quickly the bolts of the gate. The leaves of the door, swinging back, made a yawning gap as the brazen pins on either side turned in their sockets. Straight through them, along the broad way, the maidens guided mares and chariot; and the goddess received me kindly, and taking my right hand in hers spoke these words to me:

"Welcome, youth, who come attended by immortal charioteers and mares which bear you on your journey to our dwelling. For it is no evil fate that has set you to travel on this road, far from the beaten paths of men, but right and justice. It is meet that you learn all things—both the unshakable heart of well-rounded truth and the opinions of mortals in which there is no true belief. But these, too, you must learn completely, seeing that appearances have to be acceptable, since they pervade everything."

[84] Come now, and I will tell you (and you, when

Athena Lemnia, by Phidias (450–448 B.C.). The goddess of both war and peace, Athena was also patron of the arts in classical Greece. (Albertinum, Dresden)

you have heard my speech shall bear it away with you) the ways of inquiry which alone exist for thought. The one is the way of how it is, and how it is not possible for it not to be; this is the way of persuasion, for it attends Truth. The other is the way of how it is not, and how it is necessary for it not to be; this, I tell you, is a way wholly unknowable. For you could not know what is not—that is impossible—nor could you express it.

[85] For thought and being are the same.

[86] Thinking and the thought that it is are the same; for you will not find thought apart from what is, in relation to which it is uttered.

[87] It is necessary to speak and to think what is; for being is, but nothing is not. These things I bid you consider. For I hold you back from this first way of inquiry; but also from that way on which mortals knowing nothing wander, of two minds. For helplessness guides the wandering thought in their breasts; they are carried along deaf and blind alike, dazed, beasts without judgment, convinced that to be and not to be are the same and not the same, and that the road of all things is a backward-turning one.

[88] For never shall this prevail: that things that are not, are. But hold back your thought from this way of inquiry, nor let habit born of long experience force you to ply an aimless eye and droning ear along this road; but judge by reasoning the much-contested argument that I have spoken.

[89] One way remains to be spoken of: the way how it is. Along this road there are very many indications that what is is unbegotten and imperishable; for it is whole and immovable and complete. Nor was it at any time, nor will it be, since it is now, all at once, one and continuous.

For what begetting of it would you search for? How and whence did it grow? I shall not let you say or think "from what is not"; for it is not possible either to say or to think how it is not. Again, what need would have driven it, if it began from nothing, to grow later rather than sooner? Thus it must exist fully or not at all. Nor will the force of conviction ever allow anything over and above itself to arise out of what is not; wherefore Justice does not loosen her fetters so as to allow it to come into being or pass away, but holds it fast.

Concerning these things the decision lies here: either it is, or it is not. But it has been decided, as was necessary, that the one way is unknowable and unnamable (for it is no true road) and that the other is real and true. How could what is perish? How could it have come to be? For if it came into being, it is not; nor is it if ever it is going to be. Thus coming into being is extinguished, and destruction unknown.

[90] Here I end my trustworthy account and thought concerning truth. Learn henceforth the beliefs of mortals, harkening to the deceitful ordering of my words. For they have made up their minds to name two forms, one of which it is not right to name—here is where they have gone astray—and have distinguished them as opposite in bodily form and have assigned to them marks distinguishing them from one another: to one ethereal flame of fire, which is gentle, very light, the same with itself in every direction but not the same with the other. That other too, in itself, is opposite: dark night, dense in bodily form and heavy. The whole arrangement of these I tell to you as it seems likely, so that no thought of mortals shall ever outstrip you.

[91] First of all the gods she devised Eros.

ZENO OF ELEA

Not to be confused with Zeno of Citium, the founder of Stoicism, ca. 300 B.C., Zeno of Elea was born ca. 490 B.C. He was a follower and defender of the thought of Parmenides and, as such, was an opponent of the Pythagoreans, who challenged the Parmenidean doctrine that being is one. Zeno subjected the pluralism of the Pythagoreans to a series of paradoxes, each of which was intended to show that reality is not made up of units and that motion is an illusion.

True to the doctrine of Parmenides, Zeno's paradoxes deny the validity of our sense experience. Yet, their logic has a compelling obviousness to them, and they have challenged philosophers throughout the centuries, including William James and Bertrand

Russell. The paradoxes are successfully refuted only in the work of contemporary mathematics and physics, which have developed radically new doctrines of time, space, and infinity.

Zeno of Elea [92–105]

[92] [Antiphon] told us that Pythodorus had described to him the appearance of Parmenides and Zeno; they came to Athens, as he said, at the great Panathenaea; the former was, at the time of his visit, about 65 years old, very white with age, but well favoured. Zeno was nearly 40 years of age, tall and fair to look upon; in the days of his youth he was reported to have been beloved by Parmenides. He said that they lodged with Pythodorus in the Ceramicus, outside the wall, whither Socrates, then a very young man, came to see them, and many others with him; they wanted to hear the writings of Zeno, which had been brought to Athens for the first time on the occasion of their visit. These Zeno himself read to them in the absence of Parmenides, and had very nearly finished when Pythodorous entered, and with him Parmenides and Aristoteles who was afterwards one of the Thirty, and heard the little that remained of the dialogue. Pythodorus had heard Zeno repeat them before.

When the recitation was completed, Socrates requested that the first thesis of the first argument might be read over again, and this having been done, he said: What is your meaning, Zeno? Do you maintain that if being is many, it must be both like and unlike, and that this is impossible, for neither can the like be unlike, nor the unlike like—is that your position?

Just so, said Zeno.

And if the unlike cannot be like, or the like unlike, then according to you, being could not be many; for this would involve an impossibility. In all that you say have you any other purpose except to disprove the being of the many? and is not each division of your treatise intended to furnish a separate proof of this, there being in all as many proofs of the not-being of the many as you have composed arguments? Is that your meaning, or have I misunderstood you?

No, said Zeno; you have correctly understood my general purpose.

I see, Parmenides, said Socrates, that Zeno would like to be not only one with you in friendship but your second self in his writings too; he puts what you say in another way, and would fain make believe that he is telling us something which is new. For you, in your poems, say The All is one, and of this you adduce excellent proofs; and he on the other hand says There is no many; and on behalf of this he offers overwhelming evidence. You affirm unity, he denies plurality. And so you deceive the world into believing that you are saying different things when really you are saying much the same. This is a strain of art beyond the reach of most of us.

Yes, Socrates, said Zeno. But although you are as keen as a Spartan hound in pursuing the track, you do not fully apprehend the true motive of the composition, which is not really such an artificial work as you imagine; for what you speak of was an accident; there was no pretence of a great purpose; nor any serious intention of deceiving the world. The truth is, that these writings of mine were meant to protect the arguments of Parmenides against those who make fun of him and seek to show the many ridiculous and contradictory results which they suppose to follow from the affirmation of the one. My answer is addressed to the partisans of the many, whose attack I return with interest by retorting upon them that their hypothesis of the being of many, if carried out, appears to be still more ridiculous than the hypothesis of the being of one. Zeal for my master led me to write the book in the days of my youth, but some one stole the copy; and therefore I had no choice whether it should be published or not; the motive, however, of writing, was not the ambition of an elder man, but the pugnacity of a young one. This you do not seem to see, Socrates; though in other respects, as I was saying, your notion is a very just one.

[93] Zeno showed . . . that nothing has size, because each of the many is identical with itself, and one.

[94] If it existed, it would have to be one. But if it were one, it could have no body. If it had thickness, it would have parts, and then it would no longer be one.

[95] For if it were added to another thing, it would not make it any larger. For, having no size, it could not contribute anything to the size of that to which it was added. And thus the thing added would be nothing. If, when it is taken away, the thing from which it is taken is no smaller; and if, when it is added to a thing, the thing to which it is added is not increased, then it is obvious that what is added or subtracted is nothing.

[96] Zeno has four arguments concerning motion which present difficulties to those who would solve them. The first says that there is no motion because the moving object must reach the halfway point before it reaches the end.

[97] The argument of Zeno . . . was as follows. If there is motion, there will be something which has traversed an infinite series of distances in a finite time. For since the process of dichotomy has no limit, in any continuum there will be an infinite number of halves, since every part of it has a half. A body, therefore, which has traversed a finite distance will have traversed an infinite number of halves in a finite time, *i.e.*, in the time which it actually took to traverse the finite distance in question. He assumes . . . that it is impossible to traverse an infinite distance in a finite time (because it is impossible to complete an infinite series), and thus does away with the existence of motion.

"THE ACHILLES"

[98] The second [argument] is the so-called Achilles. This is, that the slowest runner will never be overtaken by the swiftest. For the pursuer must first reach the point from which the pursued started, so that the slower must always be some distance ahead.

[99] This argument too is based on infinite divisibility, but is set up differently. It would run as follows. If there is motion, the slowest will never be overtaken by the swiftest. But this is impossible, therefore there is no motion. . . .

The argument is called the "Achilles" because of the introduction into it of Achilles who, the argument says, cannot overtake the tortoise he is chasing. For the pursuer, before he overtakes the pursued, must first arrive at the point from which the latter started. But during the time which it takes the pursuer to get to this point, the pursued has advanced some distance. Even though the pursued, being the slower of the two, covers less ground, he still advances, for he is not at rest. . . . Thus, assuming the distances to be successively less without limit, on the principle of the infinite divisibility of magnitudes, it turns out that Achilles will fail not only to overtake Hector but even the tortoise.

"THE ARROW"

[The third argument follows:]

[100] If, he says, everything is at rest when it is in a place equal to itself, and if the moving object is always in the present [and therefore in a place equal to itself], then the moving arrow is motionless.

[101] Zeno argues thus. Either the moving object moves in the place where it is, or in the place where it is not. And it does not move in the place where it is, nor in the place where it is not; therefore nothing moves.

"THE STADIUM"

[102] The fourth argument is the one about the equal bodies which move in a stadium past equal bodies in opposite directions at equal velocities—some moving from the end of the stadium, some from the midpoint. This, he thinks, involves the conclusion that half the time is equal to its double. . . .

For example, let the *A's* be stationary bodies of equal size; let the *B's*, starting from the midpoint, be bodies equal in number and size to the *A's*; and let the *C's*, starting from the end, be bodies equal in number and size to the *A's*, and move with a velocity equal to that of the *B's*. What happens, as the *B's* and *C's* move past each other, is that the first *B* reaches its goal at the same moment that the first *C* reaches its. But the first *C* has passed all the *B's*, whereas the first *B* has passed only half that number of bodies, so that it has taken only half the time. For each takes an equal time to pass each body. Further, at the same moment the first *B* has passed all the *C's*; for the first *C* and the first *B* arrive at opposite ends at the same time, since both take an equal time to pass the *A's*.

[103] If place is something that exists, where will it be? The difficulty raised by Zeno requires some answer.

For if *everything* that exists has a place, it is clear that place too will have a place, and so on without limit.

"THE MILLET SEED"

[104] "Tell me, Protagoras," he said, "does a single millet seed, or the ten-thousandth part of one, make a noise when it falls?"

Protagoras replied that it did not.

"What about a bushel of millet?" said Zeno. "Does that make a noise when it falls?"

Protagoras replied that it did.

"Well," said Zeno, "but is there no ratio between the bushel and a single seed, or the ten-thousandth part of it?"

Protagoras admitted that there was.

"Then," said Zeno, "will not the sounds made in the two cases stand in the same ratio? For if the things making the sounds stand in a certain ratio to one another, so must the sounds that they make. And if the bushel of millet makes a noise, then a single millet seed, or the ten-thousandth part of one, will also make a noise."

This was the way Zeno used to put his questions.

[105] According to Aristotle, Zeno was the founder of dialectic.

MELISSUS

Melissus was born in Samos sometime during the fifth century B.C. We know that he led the Samian fleet to victory over the Athenians in 441 B.C. Melissus was a follower of Parmenides and attempted to buttress the argument in favor of unity and against the reality of change. Simplicius, the commentator on Aristotle, who lived in the sixth century A.D. and who has provided us with so many writings of the Pre-Socratics, differentiates between Melissus and Parmenides as follows: "Melissus simply says that there is no becoming at all, whereas Parmenides says that there is in seeming though not in truth." Melissus was firmly committed to the view that "knowledge" by our senses is an illusion.

Melissus [106-110]

[106] What was always was and always will be. For if it had come into being it necessarily follows that before it came into being nothing was. But if nothing was, nothing could in any way come to be out of nothing.

[107] Since, therefore, it did not come into being, it is and always was and always will be, and has no beginning or end, but is infinite. For if it had come into being, it would have a beginning (for it would have begun to come into being at some time) and an end (for it would have ceased to come into being at some time). But since it neither began nor ceased, it is and was and always will be, and has neither beginning nor end. For it is impossible for anything to be forever, unless it exists entire.

[108] If it were not one, it would be limited by another.

[109] For if it were infinite, it would be one. For if it were two, they could not be inifinite, but would be limited by one another.

[110] This argument, then, is the greatest proof that it is one only; but the following also are proofs of it.

For if there were a many, they would have to be of the same sort as I say that the one is. For if there is earth and water and air and fire and iron and gold, and one thing lives and another dies; and if things are black and white, and all the other things that men say are true—if, I say, these are so, and if we see and hear rightly, then each must be such as we first decided, and may not change or come to be different, but each of them must always be what it is.

Now we say that we see and hear and perceive rightly. Yet it appears to us that what is hot becomes cold, and that what is cold becomes hot, that what is hard becomes soft, and the soft hard, and that what is alive dies and comes to be out of what is not living, and that all these change, and that what they were and what they are now is not the same. We suppose that iron, which is hard, is rubbed away by contact with our finger, along with gold and stone and everything else that appears to us to be strong, and that earth and stone come into being from water. So, as it turns out, we neither see nor perceive the things which are.

Now these things do not agree with one another. For we said that existing things were a many and eternal, having forms and strength. Yet all seem to change and alter from what we see them to be at one moment to what we see them to be at another. It is evident, therefore, that we do not see rightly after all, and that existing things do not rightly appear to be a many. For they would not change if they were real, but each would be just what it seemed to be. For nothing is stronger than true being. If it has changed, what is has passed away and what is not has come into being.

So, then, if there were a many, they would have to be such as the one is.

EMPEDOCLES

Born in Acragas, Sicily, in the early fifth century B.C., Empedocles lived until at least 444 B.C. Empedocles was a poet as well as a philosopher and also claimed to have healing powers. He wrote two poems, "On the Nature of Things" and "Purifications." Empedocles is the first Greek thinker known to have postulated a single, incorporeal deity. His theory of the four elements—earth, air, fire, and water—as the "roots of all things" became very influential in later Greek philosophy. These elements combined and separated on behalf of the powers of love and strife, which are cosmic in origin but which also penetrate to the nature of living things, plants, creatures, and human beings.

Empedocles [111-118]

[111] Hear first the four roots of all things: shining Zeus, life-bearing Hera, Aidoneus, and Nestis, who with her tears waters the mortal spring. [Earth, Air, Fire, and Water]

[112] When these [the elements] have been mingled in the form of a man, or some kind of wild animal or plant or bird, men call this "coming into being"; and when they separate men call it "evil destiny" [passing away]. This is established usage, and I myself assent to the custom.

[113] Fools! they have no far-reaching thoughts who imagine that what was not before can come into being, or that anything can perish and be utterly destroyed.

[114] . . . there is no real coming into being of any mortal creature, nor any end in wretched death, but only mingling and separation of what has been mingled, and "coming into being" is merely a name given to them by men.

[115] These alone exist; but running through one another they become men and the tribes of other animals—at one time coming together into a single order through Love, at another time each being borne apart again through the hostility of Strife until, grown together once more, they are wholly subdued.

Thus insofar as they have learned to grow into one from many and, when the one grows apart, to become many again, to this extent they come into being and have no lasting life; but insofar as they never cease changing places continually, they remain inviolate throughout the cycle.

[116] I shall tell a twofold tale. For at one time it grew to be one only from many, while at another it dispersed again to be many from one. And there is a twofold generation of mortal creatures, and a twofold passing away; for one [generation] is begotten and brought to ruin at the coming together of all things, and the other grows up and is dispersed as these are scattered again. And these never cease changing places continually—at one time all coming together into one through Love, at another each being borne apart again through the hostility of Strife.

[117] But come, harken to my words; for learning will increase your understanding. As I said before,

The Twelfth Labor of Hercules and the Capture of Cerberus, Greek vase painting. This painting depicts the last labor of Hercules—a Greek mythological hero, fabled to have extraordinary strength—in his quest for immortality: the capture of the creature that guarded the entrance to the underworld, Hades. (Giraudon/Art Resource)

in declaring the limits of my story, I shall tell a twofold tale.

At one time it grew to be one only from many; at another it dispersed again, to be many from one: fire and water and earth and the boundless height of air; dread Strife too, apart from these, evenly balanced in every direction, and Love in their midst, equal in length and breadth. Observe her with your mind; do not sit with dazed eyes. She it is who is known as inborn in mortal limbs, through whom they think friendly thoughts and do well-fitted deeds, calling her Joy and Aphrodite. No mortal man has perceived her as she circles among them; but do you attend to the undeceitful progress of my argument.

[118] Come now, look at the things which bear witness to what I said earlier, lest anything in my previous account be defective in form. Behold the sun, bright and warm everywhere, and the immortals bathed in its bright radiance; rain, everywhere dark and chill; and from the earth pour forth things compact and solid. In the presence of Strife all these are different in form and separated; but in the presence of Love they come together and long for one another. For from these spring all the things that were and are and will be: trees and men and women and beasts and birds and fishes who dwell in the sea—even the long-lived gods who are highest in honor. For there are these alone, but running through one another they assume different forms, so much do they change through mingling.

ANAXAGORAS

*Anaxagoras is believed to have lived from ca. 500 B.C. until ca. 428 B.C. He was born in Clazomenae in Asia Minor and most likely was a Persian citizen. Anaxagoras rejected Empedocles' doctrine of the four elements and his reliance on the powers of love and strife. For Anaxagoras, the moving and causing power is that of mind (*Nous*). This assertion seems to break with the sheerly physical explanations characteristic of the Pre-Socratic philosophers. Socrates, however, doubted that Anaxagoras understood the full implication of "mind" as a principle of explanation. We include the text of his famous repudiation of Anaxagoras, although the reader should be cautioned that Anaxagoras' doctrine is more profound than Socrates acknowledges.*

Anaxagoras [119-127]

[119] The Greeks are accustomed to speak of "coming into being" and "passing away"—but mistakenly; for nothing comes to be or passes away. There is only a mingling and separation of what is. It would be more correct, therefore, to call coming into being "mingling" and passing away "separation."

[120] Anaxagoras and Empedocles hold opposing views concerning the elements. For Empedocles says that fire and its fellow elements are the elements of bodies, and everything else is constituted from these. But Anaxagoras says just the opposite; he holds that the elements are the bodies which are made up of parts like themselves—such as flesh and bone and things of that sort.

[121] He says that nearly all the things that are made up of parts like themselves, such as water or fire, come into being and pass away through coming together and separation only, and do not in any other sense come to be or pass away, but remain eternal.

[122] When Anaxagoras speaks of the *homoiomeria* of things he means that bones are made up of tiny, miniature bones; flesh, of tiny, miniature bits of flesh; blood, through the coming together of many droplets of blood. Gold, he thinks, is made up of grains of gold, earth is a concretion of tiny earths, fire of fires, moisture of moistures. And he fashions and conceives of everything else in the same way.

[123] We take in nourishment that is simple and of one kind, such as bread and water, and by this hair, veins, arteries, flesh, sinews, bones, and the other parts of the body are nourished. This being so, we must agree that all existing things are in the nourishment that is taken in, and that by these everything is increased. There exist in the nourishment "portions," of which some are productive of blood, others of sinews, others of bones, and so on—these "portions" being perceptible to reason [alone].

[124] Things appear different from one another and receive different names depending upon which of the innumerable constituents of the mixture are present in the greatest numbers. For nothing is purely or simply black or white or sweet or flesh or bone, but the nature of each thing is taken to be that of which it contains the most.

[125] In everything there is a portion of everything except mind; and in some things there is mind too.

[126] Other things have a share of everything, but mind is infinite and self-ruled and not mixed with anything, but is alone by itself. For if it were not by itself, but were mixed with anything else, it would, by virtue of being mixed with this, have a share of all things; for there is a portion of everything in everything, as I said before. And the things that were mixed in it would hinder it, so that it could control nothing as it does now, being alone by itself. For it is the finest of all things and the purest, and it has all knowledge concerning all things and the greatest power; and over everything that has soul, large or small, mind rules.

And mind controlled the whole rotation, so that it rotated in the beginning. And at first it began to rotate from a small beginning, but now it rotates over a larger area, and it will rotate over a still larger area. And mind knows all the things that are mingled and separated out and distinguished. And what sort of things were to be, and what sort of things were (which now no longer are), and what now is, and what sort of things will be—all these mind arranged, and the rotation in which now rotate the stars and the sun and the moon and the air and the ether that are being separated off. The rotation caused them to separate off. And the dense was separated from the rare, and the hot from the cold, and the bright from the dark, and the dry from the moist.

There exist many portions of many things. Nothing is separated entirely, or distinguished one from another, except mind. Mind is all alike, both the greater and the smaller; but nothing else is like anything else, but each individual thing is and was most manifestly whatever that of which it has the most [portions].

[127] Then I heard some one reading, as he said, from a book of Anaxagoras, that mind was the disposer and cause of all, and I was delighted at this notion, which appeared quite admirable, and I said to myself: If mind is the disposer, mind will dispose all for the best, and put each particular in the best place; and I argued that if any one desired to find out the cause of the generation or destruction or existence of anything, he must find out what state of being or doing or suffering was best for that thing, and therefore a man had only to consider the best for himself and others, and then he would also know the worse, since the same science comprehended both. And I rejoiced to think that I had found in Anaxagoras a teacher of the causes of existence such as I desired, and I imagined that he would tell me first whether the earth is flat or round; and whichever was true, he would proceed to explain the cause and the necessity of this being so, and then he would teach me the nature of the best and show that this was best; and if he said that the earth was in the centre, he would further explain that this position was the best, and I should be satisfied with the ex-

planation given, and not want any other sort of cause. And I thought that I would then go on and ask him about the sun and moon and stars, and that he would explain to me their comparative swiftness, and their returnings and various states, active and passive, and how all of them were for the best. For I could not imagine that when he spoke of mind as the disposer of them, he would give any other account of their being as they are, except that this was best; and I thought that when he had explained to me in detail the cause of each and the cause of all, he would go on to explain to me what was best for each and what was good for all. These hopes I would not have sold for a large sum of money, and I seized the books and read them as fast as I could in my eagerness to know the better and the worse.

What expectations I had formed, and how grievously was I disappointed! As I proceeded, I found my philosopher altogether forsaking mind or any other principle of order, but having recourse to air, and ether, and water, and other eccentricities.

LEUCIPPUS AND DEMOCRITUS

Leucippus (fl. 436 B.C.) is a shadowy figure in the history of Greek philosophy. Some, such as Epicurus (341–270 B.C.), denied that Leucippus existed. Others, such as Aristotle, attributed to Leucippus the founding of a philosophy of nature called atomism. He is the author of a treatise "On Mind," from which there remains only the admonition that nothing happens randomly, for all takes place by necessity.

Of Democritus we know more. He was born at Abdêra in Thrace and lived from ca. 460 B.C. until ca. 370 B.C. Democritus wrote more than sixty works, and from them we have reports of several hundred fragments. In addition to his work on the theory of atoms, Democritus is also well known for his writings on ethics.

The atomistic theory of Leucippus and Democritus was the first cogent and defensible alternative to the Parmenidean dilemma that if being is one, change is illusory. To the contrary, the atomists held that reality is made up of a plurality of unchanging particles literally indivisible, which accounted for change by their multiple configurations or transformations of shape, relation, and sensible quality. This position allows for the "one" of Parmenides, but also grants that the changes accounted for by our sense experience are not illusory. It took into consideration the Pythagorean emphasis on the conjoining of numbers, an arrangement which created natural harmony. Atomism influenced Epicurus and, of course, anticipated the basic concerns of modern physics.

Leucippus and Democritus [128–142]

[128] For some of the older philosophers thought that 'what is' must of necessity be 'one' and immovable. The void, they argue, 'is not': but unless there is a void with a separate being of its own, 'what is' cannot be moved—nor again can it be 'many', since there is nothing to keep things apart. And in *this* respect, they insist, the view that the universe is not 'continuous' but 'discretes-in-contact' is no better than the view that there are 'many' (and not 'one') and a void. . . .

Reasoning in this way, therefore, they were led to transcend sense-perception, and to disregard it on the ground that 'one ought to follow the argument': and so they assert that the universe is 'one' and immovable. Some of them add that it is 'infinite', since the limit (if it had one) would be a limit against the void. . . .

Leucippus, however, thought he had a theory which harmonized with sense-perception and would not abolish either coming-to-be and passing-away or motion and the multiplicity of things. He made these concessions to the facts of perception: on the other hand, he conceded to the Monists that there could be no motion without a void. The result is a theory which he states as follows: 'The void is a "not-being", and no part of "what is" is a "not-being", for what "is" in the strict sense of the term is an absolute *plenum*. This *plenum*, however, is not "one": on the contrary, it is a "many" infinite in number and invisible owing to the minuteness of their bulk. The "many" move in the void (for there is a void): and by coming together they produce "coming-to-be", while by separating they produce "passing-away". Moreover, they act and suffer action wherever they chance to be in contact (for *there* they are not "one"), and they generate by being put together and becoming intertwined. From the genuinely-one, on the other hand, there never could have come-to-be a multiplicity, nor from the genuinely-many a "one": that is impossible. But (just as Empedocles and some of the other philosophers say that things suffer action through their pores, so) all "alteration" and all "passion" take place in the way that has been explained: breaking-up (i.e. passing-away) is effected by means of the void, and so too is growth—solids creeping in to fill the void places.'

[129] Leucippus and his associate Democritus say that the full and the empty are the elements, calling the one being and the other non-being—the full and solid being being, the empty non-being (whence they say being no more is than non-being, because the solid no more is than the empty); and they make these the material causes of things. And as those who make the underlying substance one generate all other things by its modifications, supposing the rare and the dense to be the sources of the modifications, in the same way these philosophers say the differences in the elements are the causes of all other qualities. These differences, they say, are three—shape and order and position. For they say the real is differentiated only by 'rhythm' and 'inter-contact' and 'turning'; and of these rhythm is shape, inter-contact is order, and turning is position; for A differs from N in shape, AN from NA in order, ⌶ from H in position.

[130] Democritus gives to space the names "void," "no-thing," and "the infinite." To each of his substances [*i.e.*, the atoms] he gives the name "thing," and "the compact," and "being." He supposes them to be so small that they elude our senses; but they have forms of all sorts and shapes of all sorts and differ in size. So that already he is able to create from these, as elements, by aggregation, the masses that are perceptible to sight and the other senses.

[131] They jostle and move in the void because of their unlikeness and the other differences mentioned above and as they move they collide and become entangled so as to touch and make contact with one another—though not so as to come to have a single nature, for it would be silly to suppose that two or more things could ever become one. Their coherence with one another for a time he explains by the interlocking and clinging of the [primary] bodies; for some of them are angular, some are hooked, some concave, some convex, and they differ in countless other ways. And so, he thinks, they cling to one another and remain together until such time as some stronger necessity from outside shakes them loose and scatters them abroad.

[132] Democritus does not give the same account of all the objects of sense, but distinguishes between some on the basis of size, some on the basis of shape, and others on the basis of arrangement and position. . . .

Heavy and light he distinguishes on the basis of size. For if each thing were divided up into units, even if these were to differ in shape their weight would depend on their size. Among compounds, however, the lighter is the one containing the most void, the heavier the one containing less. In some places he speaks thus; in others he says that the light is simply the fine.

He speaks of hard and soft in just the same way. The hard is the dense, the soft is the rare; and the differences in degree are accounted for accordingly. But because of differences in the amount of void enclosed in it, a hard body may be light or a heavy body soft. Thus, while iron is harder than lead, lead is heavier than iron. For iron is not uniformly put together; it has in it many void spaces of considerable extent, and though close-packed in some places it contains, generally speaking, much empty space. Lead, on the other hand, which contains less empty space, is uniformly put together throughout and therefore, though softer than iron, is heavier. This, then, is what he has determined concerning heavy and light and hard and soft.

Of the other objects of sense he says that they have no existence in nature, but that all are affects of our sense organs as they undergo the alteration which brings into being what appears to us. For neither hot nor cold has any reality, but the shape, "undergoing a change," works a change in us also. For whatever is present all at once prevails in each of us; but what is spread out over a long time is imperceptible.

An indication that the aforementioned qualities

do not exist in nature is that things do not appear the same to all living creatures, but what is sweet to us is bitter to others, and to still others sour or pungent or astringent; and so with the rest.

Moreover, he says that men "alter in makeup" according to age and condition—from which it is clear that a man's bodily state is a cause of what appears to him.

[133] In assigning shapes to each taste, Democritus made what is sweet to consist of atoms that are round and of a good size. What is sour consists of atoms that are bulky, jagged, and many-angled, without curves. Sharp-tasting things, as the name implies, consist of atoms that are themselves sharp, angular, crooked, fine, and without curves. Pungent things are made of atoms that are round, fine, angular, and crooked. Salty things, of atoms that are angular, of a good size, twisted, and with two sides equal. Bitter, of atoms that are curved and smooth but very crooked and small in size. Oily-tasting things consist of atoms that are fine, round, and small.

[134] In like manner he accounts for the other powers of each in terms of the shapes of the constituent atoms. Of all these shapes no one exists pure and unmixed with the others, but in each thing there are many shapes, and the same taste will have in it atoms that are smooth and rough, round and angular, and the rest. Whichever shape predominates in it will determine what sense-impression we receive and its strength, depending upon the sort of state it finds us in. For this matters not a little in explaining how it is that the same thing produces opposite effects and opposite things the same effect on us at different times.

[135] Democritus and Leucippus, postulating the "figures" [*i.e.*, the atoms], produce alteration and generation from these—generation and passing away by coming together and separation, alteration by configuration and position . . . so that, owing to changes in the compound, the same thing appears opposite at different times, and being altered by a small addition appears wholly different by virtue of this single alteration. For tragedy and comedy are made of the same letters.

[136] There are two forms of knowledge: one legitimate, one bastard. To the bastard sort belong all of the following: sight, hearing, smell, taste, touch. The legitimate is quite distinct from this. When the bastard form cannot see more minutely, nor hear nor smell nor taste nor perceive through touch, then another, finer form must be employed.

[137] The world-orders arise in this way. Many bodies of all sorts of shapes "split off" from the infinite into a great void where, being gathered together, they give rise to a single vortex, in which, colliding and circling in all sorts of ways, they begin to separate apart, like to like. Being unable to circle in equilibrium any longer because of their congestion, the light bodies go off into the outer void like chaff, while the rest "remain together" and, becoming entangled, unite their motions and produce first a spherical structure.

This stands apart like a "membrane," containing in itself all sorts of bodies; and, because of the resistance of the middle, as these revolve the surrounding membrane becomes thin as contiguous bodies continually flow together because of contact with the vortex. And in this way the earth arose, the bodies which were carried to the middle remaining together. Again, the surrounding membrane increases because of the acquisition of bodies from without; and as it moves with the vortex, whatever it touches it adds to itself. Certain of these, becoming entangled, form a structure at first very watery and muddy; but afterward they dry out, being carried about with the rotation of the whole, and ignite to form the substance of the heavenly bodies.

[138] For living things consort with their own kind: doves with doves, cranes with cranes, and similarly with other irrational creatures. So it is with inanimate things also, as one can observe in the sifting of seeds and in pebbles on the beach. For in the one case, by the rotation of the sieve beans are ranged separately with beans, barley with barley, and wheat with wheat; in the other, by the motion of the waves the oval pebbles are driven to the same place as the oval, and the round to the round—as if the similarity among them exercised some kind of attractive force.

[139] If the body were to bring suit against the soul for all the pain and suffering it had endured during life, and were judge of its own case, it would condemn the soul with pleasure for destroying some parts of the body through neglect and debauching them through drunkenness, and for corrupting others and dissipating them in the pursuit of pleasure—just as it would blame the man who used without due care some tool or implement which was in poor condition.

[140] What the body needs can be supplied generously without hardship or distress. The things which require hardship and distress and make life

disagreeable are desired not by the body but by an ill-constituted mind.

[141] That man seems more effective in promoting virtue who employs exhortation and verbal persuasion than he who relies on law and compulsion. For it is likely that a man who is prevented from injustice by law will do wrong secretly; but it is not likely that a man who is led by persuasion to do what he ought will do anything disastrous, either secretly or openly. Wherefore, one who acts rightly through intelligence and understanding becomes courageous and at the same time upright.

[142] The law wants to benefit the life of men; it achieves its end when men want to be benefited by it. When they obey it, it reveals its own virtue.

THE HIPPOCRATIC WRITINGS

Hippocrates (460–390 B.C.) was born on the island of Cos, southeast of Miletus. He is widely regarded as the founder of western scientific medicine, and in the field of medicine his name has historically represented both empirical wisdom and ethical integrity. The Hippocratic Writings are the result of many collaborators, so it is difficult to isolate the distinctive contribution of Hippocrates. The Writings, however, share a distaste for philosophical speculation that is not grounded in the actual experience of the human body and an insistence on the ethical dimension of medical practice.

The Hippocratic Writings [143-145]

[143] All who, on attempting to speak or to write on medicine, have assumed for themselves a postulate as a basis for their discussion—heat, cold, moisture, dryness, or anything else that they may fancy—who narrow down the causal principle of diseases and of death among men, and make it the same in all cases, postulating one thing or two, all these obviously blunder in many points even of their statements, but they are most open to censure because they blunder in what is an art, and one which all men use on the most important occasions, and give the greatest honours to the good craftsmen and practitioners in it. Some practitioners are poor, others very excellent; this would not be the case if an art of medicine did not exist at all, and had not been the subject of any research and discovery, but all would be equally inexperienced and unlearned therein, and the treatment of the sick would be in all respects haphazard. But it is not so; just as in all other arts the workers vary much in skill and in knowledge, so also is it in the case of medicine. Wherefore I have deemed that it has no need of an empty postulate, as do insoluble mysteries, about which any exponent must use a postulate, for example, things in the sky or below the earth. If a man were to learn and declare the state of these, neither to the speaker himself nor to his audience would it be clear whether his statements were true or not. For there is no test the application of which would give certainty.

But medicine has long had all its means to hand, and has discovered both a principle and a method, through which the discoveries made during a long period are many and excellent, while full discovery will be made, if the inquirer be competent, conduct his researches with knowledge of the discoveries already made, and make them his starting-point. But anyone who, casting aside and rejecting all these means, attempts to conduct research in any other way or after another fashion, and asserts that he has found out anything, is and has been the victim of deception. His assertion is impossible; the causes of its impossibility I will endeavour to expound by a statement and exposition of what the art is. In this way it will be manifest that by any other means discoveries are impossible. But it is particularly necessary, in my opinion, for one who discusses this art to discuss things familiar to ordinary folk. For the subject of inquiry and discussion is simply and solely the sufferings of these same ordinary folk when they are sick or in pain. Now to learn by themselves how their own sufferings come about and cease, and the reasons why they get worse or better, is not an easy task for ordinary folk; but when these things have been discovered and are set forth by another, it is simple. For merely an effort of memory is required of each man when he listens to a statement of his experiences. But if you miss being understood by laymen, and fail to put your hearers in this condition, you will miss reality. Therefore for this reason also medicine has no need of any postulate.

[144] Certain physicians and philosophers assert that nobody can know medicine who is ignorant what a man is; he who would treat patients properly must, they say, learn this. But the question they raise is one for philosophy; it is the province of those who, like Empedocles, have written on natural science, what man is from the beginning, how he came into being at the first, and from what elements he was originally constructed. But my view is, first, that all that philosophers or physicians have said or written on natural science no more pertains to medicine than to painting. I also hold that clear knowledge about natural science can be acquired from medicine and from no other source, and that one can attain this knowledge when medicine itself has been properly comprehended, but till then it is quite impossible—I mean to possess this information, what man is, by what causes he is made, and similar points accurately. Since this at least I think a physician must know, and be at great pains to know, about natural science, if he is going to perform aught of his duty, what man is in relation to foods and drinks, and to habits generally, and what will be the effects of each on each individual. It is not sufficient to learn simply that cheese is a bad food, as it gives a pain to one who eats a surfeit of it; we must know what the pain is, the reasons for it, and which constituent of man is harmfully affected. For there are many other bad foods and bad drinks, which affect a man in different ways. I would therefore have the point put thus:—"Undiluted wine, drunk in large quantity, produces a certain effect upon a man." All who know this would realise that this is a power of wine, and that wine itself is to blame, and we know through what parts of a man it chiefly exerts this power. Such nicety of truth I wish to be manifest in all other instances. To take my former example, cheese does not harm all men alike; some can eat their fill of it without the slightest hurt, nay, those it agrees with are wonderfully strengthened thereby. Others come off badly. So the constitutions of these men differ, and the difference lies in the constituent of the body which is hostile to cheese, and is roused and stirred to action under its influence. Those in whom a humour of such a kind is present in greater quantity, and with greater control over the body, naturally suffer more severely. But if cheese were bad for the human constitution without exception, it would have hurt all. He who knows the above truths will not fall into the following errors.

In convalescence from illness, and also in protracted illnesses, many disturbances occur, some spontaneously and some from things casually administered. I am aware that most physicians, like laymen, if the patient has done anything unusual near the day of the disturbance—taken a bath or a walk, or eaten strange food, these things being all beneficial—nevertheless assign the cause to one of them, and, while ignorant of the real cause, stop what may have been of the greatest value. Instead of so doing they ought to know what will be the result of a bath unseasonably taken or of fatigue. For the trouble caused by each of these things is also peculiar to each, and so with surfeit or such and such food. Whoever therefore fails to know how each of these particulars affects a man will be able neither to discover their consequences nor to use them properly.

[145] This lecture is not intended for those who are accustomed to hear discourses which inquire more deeply into the human constitution than is profitable for medical study. I am not going to assert that man is all air, or fire, or water, or earth, or in fact anything but what manifestly composes his body; let those who like discuss such matters. Nevertheless, when these things are discussed I perceive a certain discrepancy in the analyses for, although the same theory is employed, the conclusions do not agree. They all, theorizing, draw the same deduction, asserting that there is one basic substance which is unique and the basis of everything; but they call it by different names, one insisting that it is air, another that it is fire, another water, another earth. Each adds arguments and proofs to support his contention, all of which mean nothing. Now, whenever people arguing on the same theory do not reach the same conclusion, you may be sure that they do not know what they are talking about. A good illustration of this is provided by attending their disputations when the same disputants are present and the same audience; the same man never wins the argument three times running, it is first one and then the other and sometimes the one who happens to

have the glibbest tongue. Yet it would be expected that the man who asserts that he can provide the correct explanation of the subject, if, that is, he really knows what he is talking about and demonstrates it correctly, should always win the argument. I am of the opinion that these people wreck their own theories on the problem of terminology because they fail to understand the issue. Thus they serve, rather, to establish the theory of Melissus.

I need say no more about these theorists. But when we come to physicians, we find that some assert that man is composed of blood, others of bile and some of phlegm. But these, too, all make the same point asserting that there is a basic unity of substance, although they each give it a different name and so change its appearance and properties under stress of heat and cold, becoming sweet or bitter, white or black, and so forth. Now I do not agree with these people either, although the majority will declare that this, or something very similar, is the case. I hold that if man were basically of one substance, he would never feel pain, since, being one, there would be nothing to hurt. Moreover, if he should feel pain, the remedy likewise would have to be single. But in fact there are many remedies because there are many things in the body which when abnormally heated, cooled, dried or moistened by interaction, engender disease. As a result, disease has a plurality of forms and a plurality of cures.

I challenge the man who asserts that blood is the sole constituent of the human body, to show, not that it undergoes changes into all sorts of forms, but that there is a time of year or of human life when blood is obviously the sole constituent of the body. It is reasonable to suppose, were this theory true, that there is one period at which it appears in its proper form. The same applies to those who make the body of phlegm or bile.

I propose to show that the substances I believe compose the body are, both nominally and essentially, always the same and unchanging; in youth as well as in age, in cold weather as well as in warm. I shall produce proofs and demonstrate the causes both of the growth and decline of each of the constituents of the body.

In the first place, generation cannot arise from a single substance. For how could one thing generate another unless it copulated with some other? Secondly, unless the things which copulated were of the same species and had the same generative capabilities, we should not get these results. Again, generation would be impossible unless the hot stood in a fair and reasonable proportion to the cold, and likewise the dry to the wet; if, for instance, one preponderated over the other, one being much stronger and the other much weaker. It is likely, then, that anything should be generated from one thing, seeing that not even a number of things suffice unless they are combined in the right proportions? It follows, then, such being the nature of the human body and of everything else, that man is not a unity but each of the elements contributing to his formation preserves in the body the potentiality which it contributed. It also follows that each of the elements must return to its original nature when the body dies, the wet to the wet, the dry to the dry, the hot to the hot and the cold to the cold. The constitution of animals is similar and of everything else too. All things have a similar generation and a similar dissolution, for all are formed of the substances mentioned and are finally resolved in the same constituents as produced them; that too is how they disappear.

The human body contains blood, phlegm, yellow bile and black bile. These are the things that make up its constitution and cause its pains and health. Health is primarily that state in which these constituent substances are in the correct proportion to each other, both in strength and quantity, and are well mixed. Pain occurs when one of the substances presents either a deficiency or an excess, or is separated in the body and not mixed with the others. It is inevitable that when one of these is separated from the rest and stands by itself, not only the part from which it has come, but also that where it collects and is present in excess, should become diseased, and because it contains too much of the particular substance, cause pain and distress. Whenever there is more than slight discharge of one of these humours outside the body, then its loss is accompanied by pain. If, however, the loss, change or separation from the other humours is internal, then it inevitably causes twice as much pain, as I have said, for pain is produced both in the part whence it is derived and in the part where it accumulates.

Now I said that I would demonstrate that my proposed constituents of the human body were always constant, both nominally and essentially. I hold that these constituents are blood, phlegm and yellow and black bile. They have specific and different names because there are essential differences in their appearance. Phlegm is not like blood, nor is blood like bile, nor bile like phlegm. Indeed, how could they be alike when there is no similarity in appearance and when they are different to the sense of touch. They are dissimilar in their qualities of heat, cold, dryness and moisture. It follows then that substances so unlike in appearance and characteristics cannot basically be identical, at least if fire and water are not identical. As evidence of the fact that they are dissimilar, each possessing its own qualities and nature, consider the following case. If you give a man medicine which brings up phlegm, you will find his vomit is phlegm; if you give him one which brings up bile, he will vomit bile. Similarly, black bile can be eliminated by administering a medicine which brings it up, or, if you cut the body so as to form an open wound, it bleeds. These things will take place just the same every day and every night, winter and summer, so long as the subject can draw breath and expel it again, or until he is deprived of any of these congenital elements. For they must be congenital, firstly because it is obvious that they are present at every age so long as life is present and, secondly, because they were procreated by a human being who had them all and mothered in a human being similarly endowed with all the elements which I have indicated and demonstrated.

SOURCES OF THE FRAGMENTS

In addition to the modern edition of the Pre-Socratics, as translated by John Mansley Robinson, we refer the reader to the original sources of the fragments as reported in H. Diels, *Die Fragmente der Vorsokratiker,* ed., W. Kranz (Berlin, Weidmann, 1952). References to Diogenes Laertius are to *Lives of Eminent Philosophers,* 2 vols. (Cambridge: Harvard University Press, 1938). The authors and works given in parentheses refer to the ancient sources of the texts. Many of them are not translated and they are phrased in the Greek and Latin abbreviations and formulations by which they have come to be known. The reader will find these authors and most of their works discussed in *The Oxford Classical Dictionary,* ed. N. G. L. Hammond and H. H. Scullard (Oxford: At The Clarendon Press, 1970).

Thales

1. G. S. Kirk and J. E. Raven, *The Pre-Socratic Philosophers* (Cambridge: Cambridge University Press, 1957), p. 84 (Simplicius, *Physics,* 23, 29).
2. Aristotle, *On the Heavens,* ii. 13. 294a 13–35.
3. Aristotle, *Metaphysics,* i. 3. 983b 6–27.
4. from John Mansley Robinson, *An Introduction to Early Greek Philosophy* (Boston: Houghton Mifflin Company, 1968), p. 292 (Seneca, *Questions on Nature,* iii, 14). Hereafter cited as Robinson.
5. Aristotle, *On the Soul,* i. 2. 405a 20–22.
6. Aristotle, *On the Soul,* i. 5. 411a 7–8.

Anaximander

7. Kirk and Raven, pp. 105–107, col. A. (Simplicius, *Physics,* 24, 13).
8. Robinson, p. 40 (Aristotle, *Physics,* viii. 1. 250 b11).
9. Robinson, p. 40 (Hippolytus, *Refutation of All Heresies,* i. 6. 2).

Anaximenes

10. Robinson, p. 41 (Simplicius, *Physics,* 24, 26).
11. Robinson, p. 42 (Hippolytus, *Refutation,* i. 7. 2–3).
12. Robinson, p. 42 (Plutarch, *De prim. frig.* 7, p. 947 F).
13. Robinson, p. 47 (Aetius, i. 7. 13).
14. Robinson, p. 47 (Aetius, i. 3. 4).

Xenophanes

15. Robinson, p. 52 (*Schol. BLT Eust. ad Hom.* c. 44).
16. Robinson, p. 52 (Clement, *Stromateis,* v. 109).
17. Robinson, p. 52 (Clement, *Stromateis,* vii. 22).
18. Robinson, p. 52 (Clement, *Stromateis,* v. 110).
19. Robinson, p. 53 (Clement, *Stromateis,* v. 109).
20. Robinson, p. 54 (Aristotle, *Metaphysics,* i. 5. 986 b24).
21. Robinson, p. 54 (Diogenes Laertius, *Lives,* ix. 19).

22. Robinson, p. 54 (Diogenes Laertius, *Lives*, ix. 19).

23. Robinson, p. 55 (Sextus Empiricus, *Adversus Mathematicos*, ix. 193).

24. Robinson, p. 55 (Athenaeus, xi. 462 C).

25. Robinson, p. 56 (Stobaeus, *Ecl. phys.*, i. 8. 2).

26. Robinson, p. 56 (Sextus Empiricus, *Adversus Mathematicos*, vii. 110).

27. Robinson, p. 56 (Herodianus, *On Anomalous Words*, p. 41, 5).

28. Robinson, p. 56 (Plutarch, *Symposiaca*, ix. 7, p. 746 B).

Pythagoras and Pythagoreanism

29. Robinson, p. 57 (Diogenes Laertius, viii. 15).

30. Robinson, pp. 57–58 (Porphyrius, *Vita Pythagorae* 19).

31. Robinson, p. 58 (Clement, *Stromateis*, iii. 17).

32. Robinson, pp. 58–59 (Diogenes Laertius, viii. 26–28).

33. Robinson, p. 61 (Diogenes Laertius, viii. 36).

34. Robinson, p. 61 (Diogenes Laertius, viii. 13).

35. Robinson, p. 62 (Diogenes Laertius, viii. 19).

36. Robinson, p. 62 (Diogenes Laertius, i. 12).

37. Robinson, p. 63 (Diogenes Laertius, viii. 11–12).

38. Robinson, pp. 63–64 (Proclus *in Euclid* I, 32, p. 379, 2).

39. Robinson, p. 67 (Proclus *in Euclid* I, p. 64, 16).

40. Aristotle, *Metaphysics*, i. 5. 985b 23–986a 13.

41. Aristotle, *Metaphysics*, i. viii. 980b29–990a19.

42. Aristotle, *Metaphysics*, i. 5. 098a14–19.

43. Aristotle, *On the Heavens*, ii, 13. 293a20–293b1.

44. Robinson, p. 77 (Aetius, ii. 1. 1).

Heraclitus

45. Robinson, p. 88 (Diogenes Laertius, ix. 1).

46. Robinson, p. 89 (Diogenes Laertius, ix. 8–9).

47. Robinson, p. 90 (Clement, *Stromateis*, v. 105).

48. Robinson, pp. 90–91 (Plato, *Cratylus*, 402A).

49. Robinson, p. 92 (Porphyry, *in Iliadem* 4, 4).

50. Robinson, p. 93 (Origen, *Contra Celsum*, vi. 42).

51. Robinson, p. 93 (Maximus Tyrius, xii. 4, p. 489).

52. Robinson, p. 93 (Hippolytus, *Refutation*, ix. 9. 4).

53. Robinson, p. 93 (Porphyry, *in Iliadem* 7, 200).

54. Robinson, p. 94 (Hippolytus, *Refutation*, ix. 10).

55. Robinson, p. 94 (Clement, *Stromateis*, ii. 8).

56. Robinson, p. 94 (Sextus Empiricus, *Adversus Mathematicos*, vii. 132).

57. Robinson, p. 94 (Marcus Aurelius Antoninus, iv. 46).

58. Robinson, p. 95 (Hippolytus, *Refutation*, ix. 9).

59. Robinson, p. 95 (Sextus Empiricus, *Adversus Mathematicos*, vii. 133).

60. Robinson, p. 95 (Clement, *Stromateis*, ii. 17).

61. Robinson, p. 95 (Clement, *Stromateis*, iv. 4).

62. Robinson, p. 96 (Themistius, *Orations* 5, p. 69).

63. Robinson, p. 96 (Hippolytus, *Refutation*, ix. 9).

64. Robinson, p. 96 (Aristotle, *Nicomachean Ethics*, ix. 2. 1155 b4).

65. Robinson, p. 97 (Plotinus, *Enneads*, iv. 8. 1).

66. Robinson, p. 97 (Stobaeus, *Florilegium*, i. 176).

67. Robinson, p. 97 (Stobaeus, *Florilegium*, ii. 177).

68. Robinson, p. 97 (Hippolytus, *Refutation*, ix. 9).

69. Robinson, p. 98 (Sextus Empiricus, *Adversus Mathematicos*, vii. 129).

70. Robinson, p. 99 (Stobaeus, *Florilegium*, i. 179).

71. Robinson, p. 100 (Diogenes Laertius, ix. 2).

72. Robinson, p. 100 (Plutarch, *Adv. Coloten* 20, p. 1118 C).

73. Robinson, p. 100 (Stobaeus, *Florilegium,* i. 180a).

74. Robinson, p. 100 (Diogenes Laertius, ix. 7).

75. Robinson, p. 101 (Stobaeus, *Florilegium,* v. 8).

76. Robinson, p. 101 (Stobaeus, *Florilegium,* i. 178).

77. Robinson, p. 102 (Plutarch, *Symposiaca,* iv. 4. 3).

78. Robinson, p. 102 (Aetius iv. 7.2).

79. Robinson, p. 103 (Stobaeus, *Florilegium,* i. 179).

80. Robinson, p. 104 (Clement, *Stromateis,* v. 116).

81. Robinson, p. 104 (Plutarch, *An seni resp.* 7, p. 787 C).

82. Robinson, p. 104 (Strabo, xiv. 25, p. 642).

Parmenides

83. Robinson, p. 108 (Sextus Empiricus, *Adversus Mathematicos,* vii. 3 and Simplicius, *On the Heavens,* 557, 25).

84. Robinson, p. 110 (Proclus, *in Tim.,* i. 345. 18).

85. Robinson, p. 110 (Clement, *Stromateis,* vi. 23).

86. Robinson, p. 110 (Simplicius, *Physics,* 146, 7).

87. Robinson, p. 111 (Simplicius, *Physics,* 117, 4).

88. Robinson, p. 111 (Plato, *Sophist,* 237 A and Sextus Empiricus, *Adversus Mathematicos,* vii. 114).

89. Robinson, p. 113 (Simplicius, *Physics,* 145, 1).

90. Robinson, p. 118 (Simplicius, *Physics,* 30, 17 and 39, 8).

91. Robinson, p. 123 (Plato, *Symposium,* 178 B).

Zeno

92. Benjamin Jowett, trans., *The Dialogues of Plato,* 2 vols. (New York: Random House, 1937) (Plato, *Parmenides,* 127–128).

93. Robinson, p. 129 (Simplicius, *Physics,* 131, 9).

94. Robinson, p. 129 (Simplicius, *Physics,* 109, 34).

95. Robinson, p. 129 (Simplicius, *Physics,* 139, 5).

96. Robinson, p. 132 (Aristotle, *Physics,* vi. 9. 239 b 10–14).

97. Robinson, p. 132 (Simplicius, *Physics,* 1289, 5).

98. Robinson, p. 133 (Aristotle, *Physics,* vi. 9. 273 b 14–17).

99. Robinson, p. 133 (Simplicius, *Physics,* 1013, 31).

100. Robinson, p. 134 (Aristotle, *Physics,* vi. 9. 239 b 5–9).

101. Robinson, p. 134 (Epiphanius, *Adv. haer.,* iii. 11).

102. Robinson, p. 134 (Aristotle, *Physics,* vi. 9. 239 b 33–240 a 18).

103. Robinson, p. 136 (Aristotle, *Physics,* iv. 1. 209 a 23–25).

104. Robinson, p. 137 (Simplicius, *Physics,* 1108, 18).

105. Robinson, p. 137 (Diogenes Laertius, ix. 25).

Melissus

106. Robinson, p. 141 (Simplicius, *Physics,* 162, 24).

107. Robinson, pp. 141–142 (Simplicius, *Physics,* 29, 22 and 109, 20).

108. Robinson, p. 143 (Simplicius, *Physics,* 110, 5).

109. Robinson, p. 143 (Simplicius, *On the Heavens,* 557, 14).

110. Robinson, p. 148 (Simplicius, *On the Heavens,* 558, 19).

Empedocles

111. Robinson, p. 157 (Aetius, i. 3. 20).

112. Robinson, pp. 157–158 (Plutarch, *Adv. Coloten* 11, p. 1113 A).

113. Robinson, p. 158 (Plutarch, *Adv. Coloten* 12, p. 1113 C).

114. Robinson, p. 158 (Plutarch, *Adv. Coloten* 12, p. 1113 C).

115. Robinson, p. 158 (Simplicius, *Physics*, 33, 21).

116. Robinson, pp. 158–159 (Simplicius, *Physics*, 158, 1).

117. Robinson, p. 159 (Simplicius, *Physics*, 158, 1).

118. Robinson, p. 172 (Simplicius, *Physics*, 159, 13).

Anaxagoras

119. Robinson, p. 175 (Simplicius, *Physics*, 163, 18).

120. Robinson, p. 176 (Aristotle, *On the Heavens*, iv. 3. 302 a 28).

121. Robinson, p. 176 (Aristotle, *Metaphysics*, i. 3. 984 a 14).

122. Robinson, p. 176 (Lucretius, *On the Nature of Things*, i. 834–842).

123. Robinson, p. 177 (Aetius, i. 3. 5).

124. Robinson, p. 179 (Aristotle, *Physics*, i. 4. 187 b 2).

125. Robinson, p. 181 (Simplicius, *Physics*, 164, 22).

126. Robinson, p. 181 (Simplicius, *Physics*, 164, 22 and 156, 13).

127. Plato, *Phaedo*, 97–98.

Leucippus and Democritus

128. Aristotle, *On Generation and Corruption*, i. 8. 325a4–325b5.

129. Aristotle, *Metaphysics*, 985b4–b18.

130. Robinson, p. 197 (Simplicius, *On the Heavens*, 295, 1).

131. Robinson, pp. 198–199 (Simplicius, *On the Heavens*, 295, 9).

132. Robinson, pp. 199–200 (Theophrastus, *On Sensation*, 60–64).

133. Robinson, p. 200 (Theophrastus, *Etiology of Plants*, vi. 1. 6).

134. Robinson, pp. 200–201 (Theophrastus, *On Sensation*, 67).

135. Robinson, p. 201 (Aristotle, *On Generation and Corruption*, i. 2. 315 b 6).

136. Robinson, pp. 203–204 (Sextus Empiricus, *Adversus Mathematicos*, vii. 139).

137. Robinson, p. 206 (Diogenes Laertius, ix. 31) (This account by Laertius traces to Leucippus).

138. Robinson, p. 209 (Sextus Empiricus, *Adversus Mathematicos*, vii. 116).

139. Robinson, p. 222 (Plutarch, *De libid. et aegr.* 2).

140. Robinson, p. 223 (Stobaeus, *Florilegium*, iii. 10. 65).

141. Robinson, p. 234 (Stobaeus, *Ethical Fragments*, ii. 9. 3).

142. Robinson, p. 236 (Stobaeus, *Florilegium*, iv. i. 33).

Hippocrates

143. Hippocrates, "Ancient Medicine," trans. W. H. S. Jones (Cambridge: Harvard University Press, 1923), i, ii, pp. 13–15 (The Loeb Classical Library, Hippocrates, vol. I). (Reprinted by permission of the publishers and The Loeb Classical Library.)

144. Hippocrates, "Ancient Medicine," xx, xxi, pp. 53–57.

145. Hippocrates, "The Nature of Man," *The Medical Works of Hippocrates*, trans. John Chadwick and W. N. Mann (Oxford, Blackwell Scientific Publications, Ltd., 1950), 1–5, pp. 202–205. (Reprinted by permission of the publisher.)

SUGGESTIONS FOR FURTHER READING

Anton, John P., and Kustas, George L., eds. *Essays in Ancient Greek Philosophy*. Albany: State University of New York Press, 1971.

Burnet, John. *Early Greek Philosophy*. New York: Meridian, 1960.

Furley, David J., and Allen, R. E., eds. *Studies in Presocratic Philosophy.* 2 vols. New York: Humanities Press, 1970.

Guthrie, W. K. C. *A History of Greek Philosophy.* 6 vols. Cambridge: Cambridge University Press, 1962–1981.

Jaeger, Werner. *The Theology of the Early Greek Philosophers.* Oxford: Clarendon Press, 1947.

Kahn, Charles H. *The Art and Thought of Heraclitus.* Cambridge: Cambridge University Press, 1979.

Kirk, G. S., and Raven, J. E. *The Pre-Socratic Philosophers.* Cambridge: Cambridge University Press, 1957.

Mourelatos, Alexander P. D. *The Pre-Socratics.* New York: Doubleday, 1974.

Mourelatos, Alexander, P. D. *The Route of Parmenides.* New Haven: Yale University Press, 1970.

Robinson, John Mansley. *An Introduction to Early Greek Philosophy.* Boston: Houghton Mifflin, 1968.

West, M. L. *Early Greek Philosophy and the Orient.* Oxford: Clarendon Press, 1971.

Part 2

The Sophists and Socrates: From Nature to the Public

Protagoras
From Theaetetus
From Protagoras
From Theaetetus

Antiphon
From On Truth

Callicles
From Gorgias

Gorgias
Sextus Empiricus' Epitome of On Nature

Socrates
Euthyphro
Apology
Crito
From the Phaedo
From the Symposium

Sophocles
From Antigone

Aristophanes
From The Clouds

Plato: Philosophy as Imagination

Plato
Meno
From the Republic
From the Timaeus

Pericles
Pericles' Funeral Oration

Thucydides
The Athenian Destruction of Melos

Isocrates
The Primacy of Athens

The Sophists and Socrates: From Nature to the Public

The Sophists were a group of traveling teachers in Greece during the late fifth and early fourth centuries B.C. They shared a disdain and a skepticism towards the teachings of the earlier philosophers. After the Persian wars (500–499 B.C.), Greece gave its citizens more opportunity for political power. Consequently, the Sophists turned their attention to social and political matters, rather than to the study of the natural cosmos and the principles of being and becoming, or the problem of the one and the many. The Sophists charged money for their teaching, thus drawing the subsequent wrath and condescension of Plato and Aristotle. It is from Plato, especially, that the term "sophist" came to connote trickery, shallowness, and self-aggrandizement.

Plato was partially correct, for among the Sophists, many were hucksters and intellectually shallow. This critique, however, does not apply to the brilliant arguments of Protagoras and Gorgias, among several other Sophists whose wisdom rivaled that of Socrates. The paradox is that Plato is of two minds about the Sophists. In general terms, especially in his dialogue the *Sophist*, he finds them bankrupt of philosophical wisdom. Yet, in several other dialogues, especially the *Protagoras, Gorgias,* and *Theaetetus,* he represents their views as intellectually acute and demanding of a careful response.

Plato's ambivalence was embodied in his teacher, Socrates. In one sense, Socrates was a Sophist, for he taught the young to be skeptical of previous teachings, both religious and philosophical. Socrates, however, did not share the Sophists' emphasis on the relativism of moral values, nor their dubiety about the possibility of ultimate philosophical truth. Socrates' style was similar to that of the Sophists, although he charged no fee, but he claimed the potential access to a deeper wisdom. It is that possibility which Plato was to pursue, and in so doing he bequeathed us some of the most brilliant and provocative philosophical works in the history of civilization.

PROTAGORAS

Protagoras, the best known of the Sophists, lived from ca. 490 B.C. until ca. 420 B.C. He was born in Abdera, Thrace, but spent much of his life in Athens. Among his writings were pieces entitled "On Truth" and "On the Gods." Very little of his writings survive, and most of our insight into his teaching derives from Plato. He was a friend of the Athenian statesman Pericles and assisted him in an effort to develop democratic institutions.

A shortened version of one of Protagoras' surviving fragments has become a famous saying in western civilization, namely, "Man is the measure of all things." Controversy abounds over whether Protagoras meant man, the individual, or man, the human race. Plato interpreted Protagoras to mean the first and therefore chastised his relativism. A second conflict concerns whether Protagoras meant only that sense perception was relative or whether he viewed relativism as extending to ethical and political judgments as well. These conflicts are clearly represented in the following selections from Plato's version of the teachings of Protagoras.

From Theaetetus

> Of all things the measure is man: of existing things, that they exist; of nonexistent things, that they do not exist.*

Theaetetus. At any rate, Socrates, after such an exhortation I should be ashamed of not trying to do my best. Now he who knows perceives what he knows, and, as far as I can see at present, knowledge is perception.

Socrates. Bravely said, boy; that is the way in which you should express your opinion. And now, let us examine together this conception of yours, and see whether it is a true birth or a mere wind-egg:—You say that knowledge is perception?

Theaet. Yes

Soc. Well, you have delivered yourself of a very important doctrine about knowledge; it is indeed the opinion of Protagoras, who has another way of expressing it. Man, he says, is the measure of all things, of the existence of things that are, and of the non-existence of things that are not:—You have read him?

Theaet. O yes, again and again.

Soc. Does he not say that things are to you such as they appear to you, and to me such as they appear to me, and that you and I are men?

Theaet. Yes, he says so.

Soc. A wise man is not likely to talk nonsense. Let us try to understand him: the same wind is blowing, and yet one of us may be cold and the other not, or one may be slightly and the other very cold?

Theaet. Quite true.

Soc. Now is the wind, regarded not in relation to us but absolutely, cold or not; or are we to say, with Protagoras, that the wind is cold to him who is cold, and not to him who is not?

Theaet. I suppose the last.

Soc. Then it must appear so to each of them?

Theaet. Yes.

Soc. And 'appears to him' means the same as 'he perceives.'

Theaet. True.

Soc. Then appearing and perceiving coincide in the case of hot and cold, and in similar instances; for things appear, or may be supposed to be, to each one such as he perceives them?

Theaet. Yes.

Soc. Then perception is always of existence, and being the same as knowledge is unerring?

Theaet. Clearly.

Soc. In the name of the Graces, what an almighty wise man Protagoras must have been! He spoke

---

*John Mansley Robinson, *An Introduction to Early Greek Philosophy.* Copyright © 1968 by Houghton Mifflin Company. Used by permission. P. 245 (Sextus Empiricus, *Adversus Mathematicos,* vii, 60).

From Plato, *Theaetetus,* 151–152. Unless noted all Plato selections are from *The Dialogues of Plato,* trans. Benjamin Jowett, 2 vols. (New York: Random House, 1937). The citations given are to the paragraph numbers of Plato's *Dialogues* so that the reader can consult any edition.

these things in a parable to the common herd, like you and me, but told the truth, 'his Truth,' in secret to his own disciples.

Theaet. What do you mean, Socrates?

Soc. I am about to speak of a high argument, in which all things are said to be relative; you cannot rightly call anything by any name, such as great or small, heavy or light, for the great will be small and the heavy light—there is no single thing or quality, but out of motion and change and admixture all things are becoming relatively to one another, which 'becoming' is by us incorrectly called being, but is really becoming, for nothing ever is, but all things are becoming. Summon all philosophers—Protagoras, Heracleitus, Empedocles, and the rest of them, one after another, and with the exception of Parmenides they will agree with you in this.

From Protagoras

When we were all seated, Protagoras said: Now that the company are assembled, Socrates, tell me about the young man of whom you were just now speaking.

I replied: I will begin again at the same point, Protagoras, and tell you once more the purport of my visit: this is my friend Hippocrates, who is desirous of making your acquaintance; he would like to know what will happen to him if he associates with you. I have no more to say.

Protagoras answered: Young man, if you associate with me, on the very first day you will return home a better man than you came, and better on the second day than on the first, and better every day than you were on the day before.

When I heard this, I said: Protagoras, I do not at all wonder at hearing you say this; even at your age, and with all your wisdom, if any one were to teach you what you did not know before, you would become better no doubt: but please to answer in a different way—I will explain how by an example. Let me suppose that Hippocrates, instead of desiring your acquaintance, wished to become acquainted with the young man Zeuxippus of Heraclea, who has lately been in Athens, and he had come to him as he has come to you, and had heard him say, as he has heard you say, that every day he would grow and become better if he associated with him: and then suppose that he were to ask him, 'In what shall I become better, and in what shall I grow?'—Zeuxippus would answer, 'In painting.' And suppose that he went to Orthagoras the Theban, and heard him say the same thing, and asked him, 'In what shall I become better day by day?' he would reply, 'In flute-playing.' Now I want you to make the same sort of answer to this young man and to me, who am asking questions on his account. When you say that on the first day on which he associates with you he will return home a better man, and on every day will grow in like manner,—in what, Protagoras, will he be better? and about what?

When Protagoras heard me say this, he replied: You ask questions fairly, and I like to answer a question which is fairly put. If Hippocrates comes to me he will not experience the sort of drudgery with which other Sophists are in the habit of insulting their pupils; who, when they have just escaped from the arts, are taken and driven back into them by these teachers, and made to learn calculation, and astronomy, and geometry, and music (he gave a look at Hippias as he said this); but if he comes to me, he will learn that which he comes to learn. And this is prudence in affairs private as well as public; he will learn to order his own house in the best manner, and he will be able to speak and act for the best in the affairs of the state.

Do I understand you, I said; and is your meaning that you teach the art of politics, and that you promise to make men good citizens?

That, Socrates, is exactly the profession which I make.

Then, I said, you do indeed possess a noble art, if there is no mistake about this; for I will freely confess to you, Protagoras, that I have a doubt whether this art is capable of being taught, and yet I know not how to disbelieve your assertion. And I ought to

From Plato, *Protagoras*, 317–328.

tell you why I am of opinion that this art cannot be taught or communicated by man to man. I say that the Athenians are an understanding people, and indeed they are esteemed to be such by the other Hellenes. Now I observe that when we are met together in the assembly, and the matter in hand relates to building, the builders are summoned as advisers; when the question is one of ship-building, then the ship-wrights; and the like of other arts which they think capable of being taught and learned. And if some person offers to give them advice who is not supposed by them to have any skill in the art, even though he be good-looking, and rich, and noble, they will not listen to him, but laugh and hoot at him, until either he is clamoured down and retires of himself; or if he persist, he is dragged away or put out by the constables at the command of the prytanes. This is their way of behaving about professors of the arts. But when the question is an affair of state, then everybody is free to have a say—carpenter, tinker, cobbler, sailor, passenger; rich and poor, high and low—any one who likes gets up, and no one reproaches him, as in the former case, with not having learned, and having no teacher, and yet giving advice; evidently because they are under the impression that this sort of knowledge cannot be taught. And not only is this true of the state, but of individuals; the best and wisest of our citizens are unable to impart their political wisdom to others: as for example, Pericles, the father of these young men, who gave them excellent instruction in all that could be learned from masters, in his own department of politics neither taught them, nor gave them teachers: but they were allowed to wander at their own free will in a sort of hope that they would light upon virtue of their own accord. Or take another example: there was Cleinias the younger brother of our friend Alcibiades, of whom this very same Pericles was the guardian; and he being in fact under the apprehension that Cleinias would be corrupted by Alcibiades, took him away, and placed him in the house of Ariphron to be educated; but before six months had elapsed, Ariphron sent him back, not knowing what to do with him. And I could mention numberless other instances of persons who were good themselves, and never yet made any one else good, whether friend or stranger. Now I, Protagoras, having these examples before me, am inclined to think that virtue cannot be taught. But then again, when I listen to your words, I waver; and am disposed to think that there must be something in what you say, because I know that you have great experience, and learning, and invention. And I wish that you would, if possible, show me a little more clearly that virtue can be taught. Will you be so good?

That I will, Socrates, and gladly. But what would you like? Shall I, as an elder, speak to you as younger men in an apologue or myth, or shall I argue out the question?

To this several of the company answered that he should choose for himself.

Well, then, he said, I think that the myth will be more interesting.

Once upon a time there were gods only, and no mortal creatures. But when the time came that these also should be created, the gods fashioned them out of earth and fire and various mixtures of both elements in the interior of the earth; and when they were about to bring them into the light of day, they ordered Prometheus and Epimetheus to equip them, and to distribute to them severally their proper qualities. Epimetheus said to Prometheus: 'Let me distribute, and do you inspect.' This was agreed, and Epimetheus made the distribution. There were some to whom he gave strength without swiftness, while he equipped the weaker with swiftness; some he armed, and others he left unarmed; and devised for the latter some other means of preservation, making some large, and having their size as a protection, and others small, whose nature was to fly in the air or burrow in the ground; this was to be their way of escape. Thus did he compensate them with the view of preventing any race from becoming extinct. And when he had provided against their destruction by one another, he contrived also a means of protecting them against the seasons of heaven; clothing them with close hair and thick skins sufficient to defend them against the winter cold and able to resist the summer heat, so that they might have a natural bed of their own when they wanted to rest; also he furnished them with hoofs and hair and hard and callous skins under their feet. Then he gave them varieties of food,—herb of the soil to some, to others fruits of trees, and to others roots, and to some again he gave other animals as food. And some he made to have few young ones, while those who were their prey were very prolific; and in this manner the race was preserved. Thus did Epimetheus, who, not being very wise, forgot that he had distributed among the brute animals all the qualities which he had to give,—and when he came to man, who was still unprovided, he was terribly perplexed. Now while he was in this perplexity, Prometheus came to inspect the distribution, and he found that the other animals were suitably furnished, but that man alone was naked and shoeless, and had neither bed nor arms of defence. The appointed hour was approaching when man in his turn was to go forth into the light of day; and Prometheus, not knowing how he could devise his salvation, stole the mechanical arts of Hephaestus and Athene, and fire with them (they could neither have been acquired nor used without fire), and gave them to man. Thus man had the wisdom necessary to the support of life, but political wisdom he had not; for that was in the keeping of Zeus, and the power of Prometheus did not extend to entering into the citadel of heaven, where Zeus dwelt, who moreover had terrible sentinels; but he did enter by stealth into the common workshop of Athene and Hephaestus, in which they used to practise their favourite arts, and carried off Hephaestus' art of working by fire, and also the art of Athene, and gave them to man. And in this way man was supplied with the means of life. But Prometheus is said to have been afterwards prosecuted for theft, owing to the blunder of Epimetheus.

Now man, having a share of the divine attributes, was at first the only one of the animals who had any gods, because he alone was of their kindred; and he would raise altars and images of them. He was not long in inventing articulate speech and names; and he also constructed houses and clothes and shoes and beds, and drew sustenance from the earth. Thus provided, mankind at first lived dispersed, and there were no cities. But the consequence was that they were destroyed by the wild beasts, for they were utterly weak in comparison of them, and their art was only sufficient to provide them with the means of life, and did not enable them to carry on war against the animals: food they had, but not as yet the art of government, of which the art of war is a part. After a while the desire of self-preservation gathered them into cities; but when they were gathered together, having no art of government, they evil intreated one another, and were again in process of dispersion and destruction. Zeus feared that the entire race would be exterminated, and so he sent Hermes to them, bearing reverence and justice to be the ordering principles of cities and the bonds of friendship and conciliation. Hermes asked Zeus how he should impart justice and reverence among men:—Should he distribute them as the arts are distributed; that is to say, to a favoured few only, one skilled individual having enough of medicine or of any other art for many unskilled ones? 'Shall this be the manner in which I am to distribute justice and reverence among men, or shall I give them to all?' 'To all,' said Zeus; 'I should like them all to have a share; for cities cannot exist, if a few only share in the virtues, as in the arts. And further, make a law by my order, that he who has no part in reverence and justice shall be put to death, for he is a plague of the state.'

And this is the reason, Socrates, why the Athenians and mankind in general, when the question relates to carpentering or any other mechanical art, allow but a few to share in their deliberations; and when any one else interferes, then, as you say, they object, if he be not of the favoured few; which, as I reply, is very natural. But when they meet to deliberate about political virtue, which proceeds only by way of justice and wisdom, they are patient enough of any man who speaks of them, as is also natural, because they think that every man ought to share in this sort of virtue, and that states could not exist if this were otherwise. I have explained to you, Socrates, the reason of this phenomenon.

And that you may not suppose yourself to be deceived in thinking that all men regard every man as having a share of justice or honesty and of every other political virtue, let me give you a further proof, which is this. In other cases, as you are aware, if a man says that he is a good flute-player, or skillful in any other art in which he has no skill, people either laugh at him or are angry with him, and his relations think that he is mad and go and admonish him; but when honesty is in question, or some other political virtue, even if they know that he is dishonest, yet, if the man comes publicly forward and tells the truth about his dishonesty, then, what in the other case was held by them to be good sense, they now deem to be madness. They say that all men ought to profess honesty whether they are honest or not, and that a man is out of his mind who says anything else. Their notion is, that a man must have some degree of honesty; and that if he has none at all he ought not to be in the world.

I have been showing that they are right in admitting every man as a counsellor about this sort of virtue, as they are of opinion that every man is a partaker of it. And I will now endeavour to show further that they do not conceive this virtue to be given by nature, or to grow spontaneously, but to be a thing which may be taught; and which comes to a man by taking pains. No one would instruct, no one would rebuke, or be angry with those whose calamities they suppose to be due to nature or chance; they do not try to punish or to prevent them from being what they are; they do but pity them. Who is so foolish as to chastise or instruct the ugly, or the diminutive, or the feeble? And for this reason. Because he knows that good and evil of this kind is the work of nature and of chance; whereas if a man is wanting in those good qualities which are attained by study and exercise and teaching, and has only the contrary evil qualities, other men are angry with him, and punish and reprove him—of these evil qualities one is impiety, another injustice, and they may be described generally as the very opposite of political virtue. In such cases any man will be angry with another, and reprimand him,—clearly because he thinks that by study and learning, the virtue in which the other is deficient may be acquired. If you will think, Socrates, of the nature of punishment, you will see at once that in the opinion of mankind virtue may be acquired; no one punishes the evil-doer under the notion, or for the reason, that he has done wrong,—only the unreasonable fury of a beast acts in that manner. But he who desires to inflict rational punishment does not retaliate for a past wrong which cannot be undone; he has regard to the future, and is desirous that the man who is punished, and he who sees him punished, may be deterred from doing wrong again. He punishes for the sake of prevention, thereby clearly implying that virtue is capable of being taught. This is the notion of all who retaliate upon others either privately or publicly. And the Athenians, too, your own citizens, like other men, punish and take vengeance on all whom they regard as evil doers; and hence, we may infer them to be of the number of those who think that virtue may be acquired and taught. Thus far, Socrates, I have shown you clearly enough, if I am not mistaken, that your countrymen are right in admitting the tinker and the cobbler to advise about politics, and also that they deem virtue to be capable of being taught and acquired.

There yet remains one difficulty which has been raised by you about the sons of good men. What is the reason why good men teach their sons the knowledge which is gained from teachers, and make them wise in that, but do nothing towards improving them in the virtues which distinguish themselves? And here, Socrates, I will leave the apologue and resume the argument. Please to consider: Is there or is there not some one quality of which all the citizens must be partakers, if there is to be a city at all? In the answer to this question is contained the only solution of your difficulty; there is no other. For if there be any such quality, and this quality or unity is not the art of the carpenter, or the smith, or the potter, but justice and temperance and holiness and, in a word, manly virtue—if this is the quality of which all men must be partakers, and which is the very condition of their learning or doing anything else, and if he who is wanting in this, whether he be a child only or a grown-up man or woman, must be taught and punished, until by punishment he becomes better, and he who rebels against instruction and punishment is either exiled or condemned to death under the idea that he is incurable—if what I am saying be true, good men have their sons taught other things and not this, do consider how extraordinary their conduct would appear to be. For we have shown that they think virtue capable of being taught and cultivated both in private and public; and, notwithstanding, they have their sons taught lesser matters, ignorance of which does not involve the punishment of death: but greater things, of which the ignorance may cause death and exile to those who have no training or knowledge of them—aye, and confiscation as well as death, and, in a word, may be the ruin of families—those things, I say, they are supposed not to teach them,—not to take the utmost care that they should learn. How improbable is this, Socrates!

Education and admonition commence in the first years of childhood, and last to the very end of life. Mother and nurse and father and tutor are vying with one another about the improvement of the child as soon as ever he is able to understand what is being said to him: he cannot say or do anything without their setting forth to him that this is just and that is unjust; this is honourable, that is dishonourable; this is holy, that is unholy; do this and abstain from that. And if he obeys, well and good; if not, he is straightened by threats and blows, like a piece of bent or warped wood. At a later stage they send him to teachers, and enjoin them to see to his manners even more than to his reading and music; and the teachers do as they are desired. And when the boy has learned his letters and is beginning to understand what is written, as before he understood only what was spoken, they put into his hands the works of great poets, which he reads sitting on a bench at school; in these are contained many admonitions, and many tales, and praises, and encomia of ancient famous men, which he is required to learn by heart, in order that he may imitate or emulate them and desire to become like them. Then, again, the teachers of the lyre take similar care that their young disciple is temperate and gets into no mischief; and when they have taught him the use of the lyre, they introduce him to the poems of other excellent poets, who are the lyric poets; and these they set to music, and make their harmonies and rhythms quite familiar to the children's souls, in order that they may learn to be more gentle, and harmonious, and rhythmical, and so more fitted for speech and action; for the life of man in every part has need of harmony and rhythm. Then they send them to the master of gymnastic, in order that their bodies may better minister to the virtuous mind, and that they may not be compelled through bodily weakness to play the coward in war or on any other occasion. This is what is done by those who have the means, and those who have the means are the rich; their children begin to go to school soonest and leave off latest. When they have done with masters, the state again compels them to learn the laws, and live after the pattern which they furnish, and not after their own fancies; and just as in learning to write, the writing-master first draws lines with a style for the use of the young beginner, and gives him the tablet and makes him follow the lines, so the city draws the laws, which were the invention of good lawgivers living in the olden time; these are given to the young man, in order to guide him in his conduct whether he is commanding or obeying; and he who transgresses them is to be corrected, or, in other words, called to account, which is a term used not only in your country, but also in many others, seeing that justice calls men to account. Now when there is all this care about virtue private and public, why, Socrates, do you still wonder and doubt whether virtue can be taught? Cease to wonder, for the opposite would be far more surprising.

But why then do the sons of good fathers often turn out ill? There is nothing very wonderful in this; for, as I have been saying, the existence of a state implies that virtue is not any man's private possession. If so—and nothing can be truer—then I will further ask you to imagine, as an illustration, some other pursuit or branch of knowledge which may be assumed equally to be the condition of the existence of a state. Suppose that there could be no state unless we were all flute-players, as far as each had the capacity, and everybody was freely teaching everybody the art, both in private and public, and reproving the bad player as freely and openly as every man now teaches justice and the laws, not concealing them as he would conceal the other arts, but imparting them—for all of us have a mutual interest in the justice and virtue of one another, and this is the reason why every one is so ready to teach justice and the laws;—suppose, I say, that there were the same readiness and liberality among us in teaching one another flute-playing, do you imagine, Socrates, that the sons of good flute-players would be more likely to be good than the sons of bad ones? I think not. Would not their sons grow up to be distinguished or undistinguished according to their own natural capacities as flute-players, and the son of a good player would often turn out to be a bad one, and the son of a bad player to be a good one, and all flute-players would be good enough in comparison of those who were ignorant and unacquainted with the art of flute-playing? In like manner I would have you consider that he who appears to you to be the worst of those who have been brought up in laws and humanities, would appear to be a just man and a master of justice if he were to be compared with men who had no education, or courts of justice, or laws, or any restraints upon them which compelled them to practise virtue—with the savages, for example, whom the poet Pherecrates exhibited on the stage at the last year's Lenaean festival. If you were living among men such as the man-haters in his Chorus, you would be only too glad to meet with Eurybates and Phrynondas, and you would sorrowfully long to revisit the rascality of this part of the world. And you, Socrates, are discontented, and why? Because all men are teachers of virtue, each one according to his ability; and you say, Where are the teachers? You might as well ask, Who teaches Greek? For of that too there will not be any teachers found. Or you might ask, Who is to teach the sons of our artisans this same art which they have learned of their fathers? He and his fellow-workmen have taught them to the best of their ability,—but who will carry them further in their arts? And you would certainly have a difficulty, Socrates, in finding a teacher of them; but there would be no difficulty in finding a teacher of those who are wholly ignorant. And this is true of virtue or of anything else; if a man is better able than we are to promote virtue ever so little, we must be content with the result. A teacher of this sort I believe myself to be, and above all other men to have the knowledge which makes a man noble and good; and I give my pupils their money's-worth, and even more, as they themselves confess. And therefore I have introduced the following mode of payment:—When a man has been my pupil, if he likes he pays my price, but there is no compulsion; and if he does not like, he has only to go into a temple and take an oath of the value of the instructions, and he pays no more than he declares to be their value.

Such is my Apologue, Socrates, and such is the argument by which I endeavour to show that virtue may be taught, and that this is the opinion of the Athenians.

From Theaetetus

Socrates. Shall I tell you, Theodorus, what amazes me in your acquaintance Protagoras?

Theodorus. What is it?

Soc. I am charmed with his doctrine, that what appears is to each one, but I wonder that he did not begin his book on Truth with a declaration that a pig or a dog-faced baboon, or some other yet stranger monster which has sensation, is the measure of all things; then he might have shown a magnificent contempt for our opinion of him by informing us at the outset that while we were reverencing him like a God for his wisdom he was no better than a tadpole, not to speak of his fellow-men—would not this have produced an overpowering effect? For if truth is only sensation, and no man can discern another's feelings better than he, or has any superior right to determine whether his opinion is true or false, but each, as we have several times repeated, is to himself the sole judge, and everything that he judges is true and right, why, my friend, should Protagoras be preferred to the place of wisdom and instruction, and deserve to be well paid, and we poor ignoramuses have to go to him, if each one is the measure of his own wisdom? Must he not be talking 'ad captandum' in all this? I say nothing of the ridiculous predicament in which my own midwifery and the whole art of dialectic is placed; for the attempt to supervise or refute the notions or opinions of others would be a tedious and enormous piece of folly, if to each man his own are right; and this must be the case if Protagoras' Truth is the real truth, and the philosopher is not merely amusing himself by giving oracles out of the shrine of his book. . . .

Socrates. Yes, my marvel, and there might have been yet worse things in store for you, if an opponent had gone on to ask whether you can have a sharp and also a dull knowledge, and whether you can know near, but not at a distance, or know the same thing with more or less intensity, and so on without end. Such questions might have been put to you by a light-armed mercenary, who argued for pay. He would have lain in wait for you, and when you took up the position, that sense is knowledge, he would have made an assault upon hearing, smelling, and the other senses;—he would have shown you no mercy; and while you were lost in envy and admiration of his wisdom, he would have got you into his net, out of which you would not have escaped until you had come to an understanding about the sum to be paid for your release. Well, you ask, and how will Protagoras reinforce his position? Shall I answer for him?

Theaetetus. By all means.

Soc. He will repeat all those things which we have been urging on his behalf, and then he will close with us in disdain, and say:—The worthy Socrates asked a little boy, whether the same man could remember and not know the same thing, and the boy said No, because he was frightened, and could not

From Plato, *Theaetetus,* 161–162, 165–168.

see what was coming, and then Socrates made fun of poor me. The truth is, O slatternly Socrates, that when you ask questions about any assertion of mine, and the person asked is found tripping, if he has answered as I should have answered, then I am refuted, but if he answers something else, then he is refuted and not I. For do you really suppose that any one would admit the memory which a man has of an impression which has passed away to be the same with that which he experienced at the time? Assuredly not. Or would he hesitate to acknowledge that the same man may know and not know the same thing? Or, if he is afraid of making this admission, would he ever grant that one who has become unlike is the same as before he became unlike? Or would he admit that a man is one at all, and not rather many and infinite as the changes which take place in him? I speak by the card in order to avoid entanglements of words. But, O my good sir, he will say, come to the argument in a more generous spirit; and either show, if you can, that our sensations are not relative and individual, or, if you admit them to be so, prove that this does not involve the consequence that the appearance becomes, or, if you will have the word, is, to the individual only. As to your talk about pigs and baboons, you are yourself behaving like a pig, and you teach your hearers to make sport of my writings in the same ignorant manner; but this is not to your credit. For I declare that the truth is as I have written, and that each of us is a measure of existence and of non-existence. Yet one man may be a thousand times better than another in proportion as different things are and appear to him. And I am far from saying that wisdom and the wise man have no existence; but I say that the wise man is he who makes the evils which appear and are to a man, into goods which are and appear to him. And I would beg you not to press my words in the letter, but to take the meaning of them as I will explain them. Remember what has been already said,—that to the sick man his food appears to be and is bitter, and to the man in health the opposite of bitter. Now I cannot conceive that one of these men can be or ought to be made wiser than the other: nor can you assert that the sick man because he has one impression is foolish, and the healthy man because he has another is wise; but the one state requires to be changed into the other, the worse into the better. As in education, a change of state has to be effected, and the sophist accomplishes by words the change which the physician works by the aid of drugs. Not that any one ever made another think truly, who previously thought falsely. For no one can think what is not, or think anything different from that which he feels; and this is always true. But as the inferior habit of mind has thoughts of kindred nature, so I conceive that a good mind causes men to have good thoughts; and these which the inexperienced call true, I maintain to be only better, and not truer than others. And, O my dear Socrates, I do not call wise men tadpoles: far from it; I say that they are the physicians of the human body, and the husbandmen of plants—for the husbandmen also take away the evil and disordered sensations of plants, and infuse into them good and healthy sensations—aye and true ones; and the wise and good rhetoricians make the good instead of the evil to seem just to states; for whatever appears to a state to be just and fair, so long as it is regarded as such, is just and fair to it; but the teacher of wisdom causes the good to take the place of evil, both in appearance and in reality. And in like manner the Sophist who is able to train his pupils in this spirit is a wise man, and deserves to be well paid by them. And so one man is wiser than another; and no one thinks falsely, and you, whether you will or not, must endure to be a measure. On these foundations the argument stands firm, which you, Socrates, may, if you please, overthrow by an opposite argument, or if you like you may put questions to me—a method to which no intelligent person will object, quite the reverse. But I must beg you to put fair questions: for there is great inconsistency in saying that you have a zeal for virtue, and then always behaving unfairly in argument. The unfairness of which I complain is that you do not distinguish between mere disputation and dialectic: the disputer may trip up his opponent as often as he likes, and make fun; but the dialectician will be in earnest, and only correct his adversary when necessary, telling him the errors into which he has fallen through his own fault, or that of the company which he has previously kept. If you do so, your adversary will lay the blame of his own confusion and perplexity on himself, and not on you. He will follow and love you, and will hate himself, and escape from himself into philosophy, in order that he may become different from what he was. But the other mode of arguing, which is practised by the many, will have just the opposite effect upon him; and as he grows older, instead of turning philosopher, he will come to hate philosophy. I would recommend you, therefore, as I said before, not to encourage yourself in this polemical and controversial temper, but to find out, in a friendly and congenial spirit, what we really mean when we say that all things are in motion, and that to every individual and state what appears, is. In this manner you will consider whether knowledge and sensation are the same or different, but you will not argue, as you were just now doing, from the customary use of names and words, which the vulgar pervert in all sorts of ways, causing infinite perplexity to one another. Such, Theodorus, is the very slight help which I am able to offer to your old friend; had he been living, he would have helped himself in a far more gloriose style.

ANTIPHON

To this day, the identity and life span of Antiphon the Sophist are unknown. It is believed that he was an Athenian contemporary of Socrates in the fifth century B.C. *But because the name Antiphon was common at that time, it is possible that two or even three persons authored the works "On Truth" and "On Concord."*

Despite the vagueness as to the author, the remaining fragments from "On Truth" are extremely important, for they highlight one of the central conflicts in classical Greek thought, that between nature and convention. The abiding question was whether the laws of nature (physis) *or human law* (nomos) *should take precedence. The text of Antiphon is ancient, but the problem remains with us and is particularly clear in the environmental crisis, in which nature has begun to strike back at human technological interference.*

From On Truth

Justice [on the ordinary reckoning] consists in not breaking the rules of the city of which one is a citizen. A man will be just, then, in a way most advantageous to himself if, in the presence of witnesses, he holds the laws of the city in high esteem, and in the absence of witnesses, when he is alone, those of nature. For the laws of men are adventitious, but those of nature are necessary; and the laws of men are fixed by agreement, not by nature, whereas the laws of nature are natural and not fixed by agreement. He who breaks the rules, therefore, and escapes detection by those who have agreed to them, incurs no shame or penalty; if detected, he does. But if a man is forced to do something impossible according to the laws of nature, the evil that befalls him is no less if no one observes him, and no greater if everyone does. For he is not hurt because of opinion, but because of truth.

The point of the inquiry is this: that most of the things which are just by law are hostile to nature. For a law has even been passed stating what the eyes should and should not see, what the ears should and should not hear, what the tongue should and should not speak, what the hands should and should not do, where the feet should and should not go, and what the mind should and should not desire. And those acts which the laws prohibit are no more agreeable or more akin to nature than those which they enjoin. But life and death are the concern of nature, and living creatures live by what is advantageous to them and die from what is not advantageous; and the advantages which accrue from law are chains upon nature, whereas those which accrue from nature are free. . . .

If some benefit accrued to those who subscribed to the laws, while loss accrued to those who did not subscribe to them but opposed them, then obedience to the laws would not be without profit. But as things stand, it seems that legal justice is not strong enough to benefit those who subscribe to laws of this sort. For in the first place it permits the injured party to suffer injury and the man who inflicts it to inflict injury, and it does not prevent the injured party from suffering injury nor the man who does the injury from doing it. And if the case comes to trial, the injured party has no more of an advantage than the one who has done the injury; for he must convince his judges that he has been injured, and must be able, by his plea, to exact justice. And it is open to the one who has done the injury to deny it; for he can defend himself against the accusation, and he has the same opportunity to persuade his judges that his accuser has. For the victory goes to the best speaker.

CALLICLES

Callicles is a character in Plato's dialogue Gorgias. *The depiction may or may not be based on the life and thought of a real person. Whatever may be the true origin of Callicles, he represents the most aggressive and challenging critique leveled by the Sophists against philosophy in its Pre-Socratic formulation. The name may change, but throughout the centuries, wherever and whenever philosophy is thought or taught, the opponent will present a version of the argument of Callicles against Socrates.*

From Gorgias

Socrates. And from the opposite point of view, if indeed it be our duty to harm another, whether an enemy or not—I except the case of self-defence—then I have to be upon my guard—but if my enemy injures a third person, then in every sort of way, by word as well as deed, I should try to prevent his being punished, or appearing before the judge; and if he appears, I should contrive that he should escape, and not suffer punishment: if he has stolen a sum of money, let him keep what he has stolen and spend it on him and his, regardless of religion and justice; and if he have done things worthy of death, let him not die, but rather be immortal in his wickedness; or, if this is not possible, let him at any rate be allowed to live as long as he can. For such purposes, Polus, rhetoric may be useful, but is of small if of any use to him who is not intending to commit injustice; at least, there was no such use discovered by us in the previous discussion.

Callicles. Tell me, Chaerephon, is Socrates in earnest, or is he joking?

Chaerephon. I should say, Callicles, that he is in most profound earnest; but you may as well ask him.

Cal. By the gods, and I will. Tell me, Socrates, are you in earnest, or only in jest? For if you are in earnest, and what you say is true, is not the whole of human life turned upside down; and are we not doing, as would appear, in everything the opposite of what we ought to be doing?

Soc. O Callicles, if there were not some community of feelings among mankind, however varying in different persons—I mean to say, if every man's feelings were peculiar to himself and were not shared by the rest of his species—I do not see how we could ever communicate our impressions to one another. I make this remark because I perceive that you and I have a common feeling. For we are lovers both, and both of us have two loves apiece:—I am the lover of Alcibiades, the son of Cleinias, and of philosophy; and you of the Athenian Demus, and of Demus the son of Pyrilampes. Now, I observe that you, with all your cleverness, do not venture to contradict your favourite in any word or opinion of his; but as he changes you change, backwards and forwards. When the Athenian Demus denies anything that you are saying in the assembly, you go over to his opinion;

From Plato, *Gorgias,* 481–484.

and you do the same with Demus, the fair young son of Pyrilampes. For you have not the power to resist the words and ideas of your loves; and if a person were to express surprise at the strangeness of what you say from time to time when under their influence, you would probably reply to him, if you were honest, that you cannot help saying what your loves say unless they are prevented; and that you can only be silent when they are. Now you must understand that my words are an echo too, and therefore you need not wonder at me; but if you want to silence me, silence philosophy, who is my love, for she is always telling me what I am now telling you, my friend; neither is she capricious like my other love, for the son of Cleinias says one thing to-day and another thing to-morrow, but philosophy is always true. She is the teacher at whose words you are now wondering, and you have heard her yourself. Her you must refute, and either show, as I was saying, that to do injustice and to escape punishment is not the worst of all evils; or, if you leave her word unrefuted, by the dog the god of Egypt, I declare, O Callicles, that Callicles will never be at one with himself, but that his whole life will be a discord. And yet, my friend, I would rather that my lyre should be inharmonious, and that there should be no music in the chorus which I provided; aye, or that the whole world should be at odds with me, and oppose me, rather than that I myself should be at odds with myself, and contradict myself.

Cal. O Socrates, you are a regular declaimer, and seem to be running riot in the argument. And now you are declaiming in this way because Polus has fallen into the same error himself of which he accused Gorgias:—for he said that when Gorgias was asked by you whether, if some one came to him who wanted to learn rhetoric, and did not know justice, he would teach him justice, Gorgias in his modesty replied that he would, because he thought that mankind in general would be displeased if he answered 'No;' and then in consequence of this admission, Gorgias was compelled to contradict himself, that being just the sort of thing in which you delight. Whereupon Polus laughed at you deservedly, as I think; but now he has himself fallen into the same trap. I cannot say very much for his wit when he conceded to you that to do is more dishonourable than to suffer injustice, for this was the admission which led to his being entangled by you; and because he was too modest to say what he thought, he had his mouth stopped. For the truth is, Socrates, that you, who pretend to be engaged in the pursuit of truth, are appealing now to the popular and vulgar notions of right, which are not natural, but only conventional. Convention and nature are generally at variance with one another: and hence, if a person is too modest to say what he thinks, he is compelled to contradict himself; and you, in your ingenuity perceiving the advantage to be thereby gained, slyly ask of him who is arguing conventionally a question which is to be determined by the rule of nature; and if he is talking of the rule of nature, you slip away to custom: as, for instance, you did in this very discussion about doing and suffering injustice. When Polus was speaking of the conventionally dishonourable, you assailed him from the point of view of nature; for by the rule of nature, to suffer injustice is the greater disgrace because the greater evil; but conventionally, to do evil is the more disgraceful. For the suffering of injustice is not the part of a man, but of a slave, who indeed had better die than live; since when he is wronged and trampled upon, he is unable to help himself, or any other about whom he cares. The reason, as I conceive, is that the makers of laws are the majority who are weak; and they make laws and distribute praises and censures with a view to themselves and to their own interests; and they terrify the stronger sort of men, and those who are able to get the better of them, in order that they may not get the better of them; and they say, that dishonesty is shameful and unjust; meaning by the word injustice, the desire of a man to have more than his neighbours; for knowing their own inferiority, I suspect that they are too glad of equality. And therefore the endeavour to have more than the many, is conventionally said to be shameful and unjust, and is called injustice, whereas nature herself intimates that it is just for the better to have more than the worse, the more powerful than the weaker; and in many ways she shows, among men as well as among animals, and indeed among whole cities and races, that justice consists in the superior ruling over and having more than the inferior. For on what principle of justice did Xerxes invade Hellas, or his father the Scythians? (not to speak of numberless other examples). Nay, but these are the men who act according to nature; yes, by Heaven, and according to the law of nature: not, perhaps, according to that artificial law, which we invent and impose upon our fellows, of whom we take the best and strongest from their youth upwards, and tame them like young lions,—charming them with the sound of the voice, and saying to them, that with equality they must be content, and that the equal is the honourable and the just. But if there were a man who had sufficient force, he would shake off and break through, and escape from all this; he would trample under foot all our formulas and spells and charms, and all our laws which are against nature: the slave would rise in rebellion and be lord over us, and the light of natural justice would shine forth. And this I take to be the sentiment of Pindar, when he says in his poem, that

> 'Law is the king of all, of mortals as well as of immortals;'

this, as he says,

> 'Makes might to be right, doing violence with
> highest hand; as I infer from the deeds of
> Heracles, for without buying them—'

—I do not remember the exact words, but the meaning is, that without buying them, and without their being given to him, he carried off the oxen of Geryon, according to the law of natural right, and that the oxen and other possessions of the weaker and inferior properly belong to the stronger and superior. And this is true, as you may ascertain, if you will leave philosophy and go on to higher things: for philosophy, Socrates, if pursued in moderation and at the proper age, is an elegant accomplishment, but too much philosophy is the ruin of human life. Even if a man has good parts, still, if he carries philosophy into later life, he is necessarily ignorant of all those things which a gentleman and a person of honour ought to know; he is inexperienced in the laws of the State, and in the language which ought to be used in the dealings of man with man, whether private or public, and utterly ignorant of the pleasures and desires of mankind and of human character in general. And people of this sort, when they betake themselves to politics or business, are as ridiculous as I imagine the politicians to be, when they make their appearance in the arena of philosophy.

GORGIAS

Gorgias was born in Leontini, Sicily. He is believed to have lived from ca. 480 B.C. until ca. 375 B.C. Gorgias is the author of a treatise "On That Which Is Not, or On Nature." This work has been interpreted as an attack on two of the main Pre-Socratic traditions, the Pythagorean and the Parmenidean. A superb rhetorician, Gorgias was famous for his teaching of the art of persuasion, and he was the mentor of the great classical rhetorician Isocrates. He also influenced the literary style of the historian Thucydides and, allegedly, of many other important figures in classical Athens, including Pericles. The text that follows is a summary of Gorgias' treatise "On Nature" by Sextus Empiricus in the second century A.D. When combined with Callicles' attack on Pre-Socratic philosophy, the skepticism of Gorgias provides an important backdrop to the cautious but nonetheless optimistic attitude of Socrates. The question at stake is whether human beings can know anything for sure or whether all claims of knowledge are transient and of only local or individual significance.

Sextus Empiricus' Epitome of On Nature

In his book *On Not-Being* or *On Nature* Gorgias sets out to prove three successive points: first, that nothing exists; second, that even if it does it is incomprehensible by men; and third, that even if it is comprehensible it is certainly not expressible and cannot be communicated to another.

That nothing exists he proves in the following way. If anything exists, it must be either what is or what is not or what is *and* what is not. But, as he proceeds to show, what is does not exist, nor does what is not exist, nor does what is *and* what is not exist. Therefore nothing exists.

Now what is not does not exist. For if what is not exists it will at one and the same time be and not be. For insofar as it is conceived as what is not it will not exist; while on the other hand, insofar as it *is* what is not it *will* exist. But it is completely absurd that something should exist and not exist at one and the same time. Therefore what is not does not exist. (Moreover, if what is not *does* exist, what is will not exist; for these are contrary to one another. Thus, if existence were to characterize what is not, nonexistence will characterize what is. But it is not the case that what is does not exist; neither, therefore, will what is not exist.)

Furthermore, what is does not exist either. For if what is exists, either it is eternal or created or both eternal *and* created at the same time. But, as we shall prove, it is neither eternal nor created nor both eternal *and* created. Therefore what is does not exist.

For if what is is eternal (this is the first possibility to be considered), it has no beginning. For everything that is created has some beginning; but the eternal, being uncreated, had no beginning. And having no beginning it is infinite. But if it is infinite it is nowhere. For if it is somewhere, that in which it is is different from it, and thus what is, since it is encompassed by something, will no longer be infinite. For what encompasses is greater than that which is encompassed, but nothing is greater than the infinite. So, then, the infinite is not anywhere. (Nor is it encompassed by itself. For in that case that in which it is will be the same as that which is in it, and what is will become two different things: place and body. For that in which it is is place, while that which is in it is body. But this is absurd; therefore what is does not exist in itself.) Hence, if what is is eternal it is infinite; but if it is infinite it is nowhere; and if it does not exist anywhere it does not exist. Therefore, if what is is eternal it does not exist in respect to having a beginning.

Furthermore, it is impossible for what is to be created. For if it has been created, it has been created either out of what is or out of what is not. But it has not been created out of what is. For if it *is* it has not been created but exists already. Nor has it been created out of what is not; for what is not cannot create anything, since that which is creative of anything must of necessity have a share of existence. What is, then, is not created either.

For the same reasons it is not both together, *i.e.*, eternal *and* created; for these are destructive of one another. If what is is eternal it has not been created, and if it has been created it is not eternal. Therefore, if what is is neither eternal nor created, nor both together, it will not exist.

(Moreover, if it exists it is either one or many. But, as will be shown, it is neither one nor many; therefore, what is does not exist. For if it is one, either it is a quantity or it is continuous or it is a magnitude or it is a body; but whichever of these it is it is not one. For if it is a quantity it will be divided [*i.e.*, into the units which make up that quantity]; if it is continuous it will be cut up; similarly, if it be conceived as a magnitude it will not be indivisible; and if it is a body it will be threefold, for it will have length, breadth, and depth. But it is absurd to say that what is is none of these; therefore, what is is not one. Nor is it many. For if it is not one it is not many either; for the many is made up of ones, so that if the one is destroyed the many are destroyed too.)

From the foregoing it will be evident that neither what is nor what is not exists. That they do not both exist together—both what is and what is not—is easy to prove. For if both what is not *and* what is exist, what is not will be the same as what is so far as existence is concerned. And for this reason neither of them exists. For it is admitted that what is not does not exist; and it has been shown that what is is the same as what is not. Therefore it too will not exist. Not only that, but if what is is the same as what is not, both of them cannot exist. For if both exist they are *not* the same; and if they *are* the same, both cannot exist. For if what is does not exist and what is not does not exist, and both together do not exist, and if besides these possibilities no other is conceived, then nothing exists.

The next thing to be proved is that even if anything exists it is unknowable and inconceivable by man. For (says Gorgias) if the objects of thought are not things that exist, then what is is not thought. . . . But the objects of thought (to take them first) are not existing things, as we shall show, and therefore what is is not thought.

Now it is clear that the objects of thought are not existing things. For if the objects of thought are existing things, *all* objects of thought exist, and in whatever way anyone thinks them—which is ridiculous. For if someone thinks of a man flying, or of a chariot running along on the sea, it does not follow straightway that a man *is* flying or that a chariot *is* running along on the sea. So the objects of thought are not existing things.

Furthermore, if the objects of thought are existing things, nonexistent things will not be thought. For opposites characterize opposites, and what is not is opposite to what is. Hence if "being thought" characterizes what is, then "not being thought" characterizes what is not. But this is absurd; for Scylla and Chimera and many things that do not exist are thought. Therefore what is is not thought.

And just as things are called visible things because they are seen, and things heard audible because they are heard, and we do not reject visible things because they are not heard or dismiss audible things because they are not seen (for each ought to be judged by the sense peculiar to it and not by another), so also objects of thought will exist even though they are not visible to sight or audible to hearing, because they are apprehended by the test proper to them [merely by being thought]. So that if someone *thinks* that a chariot is running along on the sea, then he ought to believe that there *is* a chariot running along on the sea, even though he does not see it—which is absurd. Therefore what is is not thought or comprehended.

But even if it be comprehended it cannot be communicated to another person. For if existing things are *objects* seen and heard and, in general, perceived by the senses, and exist outside us; and if those that are visible are comprehended through vision while those that are audible are comprehended through hearing, and not the other way around; how, then, *can* they be conveyed to another person? For it is by means of *words* that we communicate, and words are not real, existent things. We do not, therefore, indicate existing things to our fellow men but words, which are different from real things. Thus, just as what is visible cannot become audible, and *vice versa*, so too, since what is is outside of us, it could not become our words. And not being words, it cannot be made apparent to another person.

(Indeed, words arise, he says, from the impression which external objects, *i.e.*, the objects of sensation, make on us. For when we meet with a taste the word which expresses that quality is produced in us, and when we meet with a color the word which expresses the color. But if so, words are not suited to the explanation of what lies outside us, but on the contrary what lies outside us is that which indicates our words. Moreover, it is not possible to object that words exist in the same sense that the objects of vision and hearing exist, and can therefore indicate real, existent things, being real and existent themselves. For even if words are real, he says, they differ from the rest of the things that are real, and visible bodies differ very greatly from words. For what is visible is apprehended by one sense organ, words by another. Words, therefore, do not manifest most real things, just as they do not make clear another's nature.)

SOCRATES

Socrates (490–399 B.C.) is one of the most enigmatic and elusive major figures in the history of philosophy. As with Jesus, there is controversy about his very existence. Two further parallels with Jesus are intriguing. Neither left any writings, although they are both the main figure in writings by others, and both went to their death willingly, although escape was possible. In the case of Socrates, as the court offered the options of either probation after a slight fine or exile, some commentators judge that his taking the third alternative, poisonous hemlock, was a form of suicide.

The major source of our information about Socrates is the Dialogues *of Plato. We have further information, some of it contradictory, from Aristophanes, Xenophon, and Aristotle. Present-day scholarship, despite occasional and fervid disagreement, generally takes the position that Plato's version of Socrates is an accurate representation of an actual historical figure of the fifth century B.C. in Athens. Following Plato, who as a young man met and listened to Socrates, we know that Socrates was a person of unusual gifts and temperament. He exhibited rare courage as a member of the infantry in the Peloponnesian War, and he had a reputation for having remarkable control of his body, being seemingly impervious to fatigue.*

Initially, Socrates taught like the Sophists, with the important exception that he charged no fee. Soon, however, it became apparent that Socrates was profoundly different from the Sophists. With a subtle mixture of humility and arrogance, Socrates announced that through a friend, he had learned that the Delphic oracle had named him the wisest man of all. Socrates accepted this praise, but in an early instance of what came to be known as "Socratic irony," he claimed that he was the wisest because he admitted to knowing nothing. True knowledge, then, begins in the acknowledgment of ignorance. Armed with this formidable dialectical and argumentative weapon, Socrates demolished the positions of the earlier philosophers and of his Sophistic contemporaries. Socrates, however, came to no definite conclusions in his discussions and thereby contributed to the erosion of confidence, especially among the young, in the political, religious, and ethical values of Athenian society. In time, the attitude and activity of Socrates generated severe opposition, and he was brought to trial. Falsely charged with corrupting the young and showing impiety to the gods, Socrates brilliantly defended himself. Yet, when he refused to accept a minor penalty, Socrates invoked the wrath of the jury and was condemned to death. Arrangements were made for his escape and exile, but Socrates rejected them on the grounds that to leave would be to admit his guilt and deny the integrity of his lifelong commitment to philosophy and to Athens.

The selections that follow represent the major themes in the life and thought of Socrates as given by Plato. The Euthyphro *is a classic rendition of the Socratic dialectic, directed to the question of the nature of piety. The* Apology, Crito, *and* Phaedo *tell of the trial and death of Socrates, his defense of the law, and his doctrine of immortality. The selection from the* Symposium *reports Socrates' speech on the meaning of love. Again, we caution the reader that it is inconclusive as to whether these views are those of Socrates or those of Plato, retrospectively attributed to Socrates. Fortunately, we do not have to resolve that scholarly dispute in order to enjoy these writings of Plato, for they are among the most rhetorically and intellectually exquisite pieces of literature in the history of humankind.*

Euthyphro

SCENE:—*The Porch of the King Archon*

Euthyphro. Why have you left the Lyceum, Socrates? and what are you doing in the Porch of the King Archon? Surely you cannot be concerned in a suit before the King, like myself?

Socrates. Not in a suit, Euthyphro; impeachment is the word which the Athenians use.

Euth. What! I suppose that some one has been prosecuting you, for I cannot believe that you are the prosecutor of another.

Soc. Certainly not.

Euth. Then some one else has been prosecuting you?

Soc. Yes.

Euth. And who is he?

Soc. A young man who is little known, Euthyphro; and I hardly know him: his name is Meletus, and he is of the deme of Pitthis. Perhaps you may remember his appearance; he has a beak, and long straight hair, and a beard which is ill grown.

Euth. No, I do not remember him, Socrates. But what is the charge which he brings against you?

Soc. What is the charge? Well, a very serious charge, which shows a good deal of character in the young man, and for which he is certainly not to be despised. He says he knows how the youth are

Plato, *Euthyphro*, complete.

corrupted and who are their corruptors. I fancy that he must be a wise man, and seeing that I am the reverse of a wise man, he has found me out, and is going to accuse me of corrupting his young friends. And of this our mother the state is to be the judge. Of all our political men he is the only one who seems to me to begin in the right way, with the cultivation of virtue in youth; like a good husbandman, he makes the young shoots his first care, and clears away us who are the destroyers of them. This is only the first step; he will afterwards attend to the elder branches; and if he goes on as he has begun, he will be a very great public benefactor.

Euth. I hope that he may; but I rather fear, Socrates, that the opposite will turn out to be the truth. My opinion is that in attacking you he is simply aiming a blow at the foundation of the state. But in what way does he say that you corrupt the young?

Soc. He brings a wonderful accusation against me, which at first hearing excites surprise: he says that I am a poet or maker of gods, and that I invent new gods and deny the existence of old ones; this is the ground of his indictment.

Euth. I understand, Socrates; he means to attack you about the familiar sign which occasionally, as you say, comes to you. He thinks that you are a neologian, and he is going to have you up before the court for this. He knows that such a charge is readily received by the world, as I myself know too well; for when I speak in the assembly about divine things, and foretell the future to them, they laugh at me and think me a madman. Yet every word that I say is true. But they are jealous of us all; and we must be brave and go at them.

Soc. Their laughter, friend Euthyphro, is not a matter of much consequence. For a man may be thought wise; but the Athenians, I suspect, do not much trouble themselves about him until he begins to impart his wisdom to others; and then for some reason or other, perhaps, as you say, from jealousy, they are angry.

Euth. I am never likely to try their temper in this way.

Soc. I dare say not, for you are reserved in your behaviour, and seldom impart your wisdom. But I have a benevolent habit of pouring out myself to everybody, and would even pay for a listener, and I am afraid that the Athenians may think me too talkative. Now if, as I was saying, they would only laugh at me, as you say that they laugh at you, the time might pass gaily enough in the court; but perhaps they may be in earnest, and then what the end will be you soothsayers only can predict.

Euth. I dare say that the affair will end in nothing, Socrates, and that you will win your cause; and I think that I shall win my own.

Soc. And what is your suit, Euthyphro? are you the pursuer or the defendant?

Euth. I am the pursuer.

Soc. Of whom?

Euth. You will think me mad when I tell you.

Soc. Why, has the fugitive wings?

Euth. Nay, he is not very volatile at his time of life.

Soc. Who is he?

Euth. My father.

Soc. Your father! my good man?

Euth. Yes.

Soc. And of what is he accused?

Euth. Of murder, Socrates.

Soc. By the powers, Euthyphro! how little does the common herd know of the nature of right and truth. A man must be an extraordinary man, and have made great strides in wisdom, before he could have seen his way to bring such an action.

Euth. Indeed, Socrates, he must.

Soc. I suppose that the man whom your father murdered was one of your relatives—clearly he was; for if he had been a stranger you would never have thought of prosecuting him.

Euth. I am amused, Socrates, at your making a distinction between one who is a relation and one who is not a relation; for surely the pollution is the same in either case, if you knowingly associate with the murderer when you ought to clear yourself and him by proceeding against him. The real question is whether the murdered man has been justly slain. If justly, then your duty is to let the matter alone; but if unjustly, then even if the murderer lives under the same roof with you and eats at the same table, proceed against him. Now the man who is dead was a poor dependant of mine who worked for us as a field labourer on our farm in Naxos, and one day in a fit of drunken passion he got into a quarrel with one of our domestic servants and slew him. My father bound him hand and foot and threw him into a ditch, and then sent to Athens to ask of a diviner what he should do with him. Meanwhile he never attended to him and took no care about him, for he regarded him as a murderer; and thought that no great harm would be done even if he did die. Now this was just what happened. For such was the effect of cold and hunger and chains upon him, that before the messenger returned from the diviner, he was dead. And my father and family are angry with me for taking the part of the murderer and prosecuting my father. They say that he did not kill him, and that if he did, the dead man was but a murderer, and I ought not to take any notice, for that a son is impious who prosecutes a father. Which shows, Socrates, how little they know what the gods think about piety and impiety.

Soc. Good heavens, Euthyphro! and is your knowledge of religion and of things pious and impious so very exact, that, supposing the circumstances to be as you state them, you are not afraid lest you too may be doing an impious thing in bringing an action against your father?

Euth. The best of Euthyphro, and that which distinguishes him, Socrates, from other men, is his exact knowledge of all such matters. What should I be good for without it?

Soc. Rare friend! I think that I cannot do better than be your disciple. Then before the trial with Meletus comes on I shall challenge him, and say that I have always had a great interest in religious questions, and now, as he charges me with rash imaginations and innovations in religion, I have become your disciple. You, Meletus, as I shall say to him, acknowledge Euthyphro to be a great theologian, and sound in his opinions; and if you approve of him you ought to approve of me, and not have me into court; but if you disapprove, you should begin by indicting him who is my teacher, and who will be the ruin, not of the young, but of the old; that is to say, of myself whom he instructs, and of his old father whom he admonishes and chastises. And if Meletus refuses to listen to me, but will go on, and will not shift the indictment from me to you, I cannot do better than repeat this challenge in the court.

Euth. Yes, indeed, Socrates; and if he attempts to indict me I am mistaken if I do not find a flaw in him; the court shall have a great deal more to say to him than to me.

Soc. And I, my dear friend, knowing this, am desirous of becoming your disciple. For I observe that no one appears to notice you—not even this Meletus; but his sharp eyes have found me out at once, and he has indicted me for impiety. And therefore, I adjure you to tell me the nature of piety and impiety, which you said that you knew so well, and of murder, and of other offences against the gods. What are they? Is not piety in every action always the same? and impiety, again—is it not always the opposite of piety, and also the same with itself, having, as impiety, one notion which includes whatever is impious?

Euth. To be sure, Socrates.

Soc. And what is piety, and what is impiety?

Euth. Piety is doing as I am doing; that is to say, prosecuting any one who is guilty of murder, sacrilege, or of any similar crime—whether he be your father or mother, or whoever he may be—that makes no difference; and not to prosecute them is impiety. And please to consider, Socrates, what a notable proof I will give you of the truth of my words, a proof which I have already given to others:—of the principle, I mean, that the impious, whoever he may be, ought not to go unpunished. For do not men regard Zeus as the best and most righteous of the gods?—and yet they admit that he bound his father (Cronos) because he wickedly devoured his sons, and that he too had punished his own father (Uranus) for a similar reason, in a nameless manner. And yet when I proceed against my father, they are angry with me. So inconsistent are they in their way of talking when the gods are concerned, and when I am concerned.

Soc. May not this be the reason, Euthyphro, why I am charged with impiety—that I cannot away with these stories about the gods? and therefore I suppose that people think me wrong. But, as you who are well informed about them approve of them, I cannot do better than assent to your superior wisdom. What else can I say, confessing as I do, that I know nothing about them? Tell me, for the love of Zeus, whether you really believe that they are true.

Euth. Yes, Socrates; and things more wonderful still, of which the world is in ignorance.

Soc. And do you really believe that the gods fought with one another, and had dire quarrels, battles, and the like, as the poets say, and as you may see represented in the works of great artists? The temples are full of them; and notably the robe of Athene, which is carried up to the Acropolis at the great Panathenaea, is embroidered with them. Are all these tales of the gods true, Euthyphro?

Euth. Yes, Socrates; and, as I was saying, I can tell you, if you would like to hear them, many other things about the gods which would quite amaze you.

Soc. I dare say; and you shall tell me them at some other time when I have leisure. But just at present I would rather hear from you a more precise answer, which you have not as yet given, my friend, to the question, What is 'piety'? When asked, you only replied, Doing as you do, charging your father with murder.

Euth. And what I said was true, Socrates.

Soc. No doubt, Euthyphro; but you would admit that there are many other pious acts?

Euth. There are.

Soc. Remember that I did not ask you to give me two or three examples of piety, but to explain the general idea which makes all pious things to be pious. Do you not recollect that there was one idea which made the impious impious, and the pious pious?

Euth. I remember.

Soc. Tell me what is the nature of this idea, and then I shall have a standard to which I may look, and by which I may measure actions, whether yours or those of any one else, and then I shall be able to say that such and such an action is pious, such another impious.

Euth. I will tell you, if you like.

Soc. I should very much like.

Euth. Piety, then, is that which is dear to the gods, and impiety is that which is not dear to them.

Soc. Very good, Euthyphro; you have now given me the sort of answer which I wanted. But whether what you say is true or not I cannot as yet tell, although I make no doubt that you will prove the truth of your words.

Euth. Of course.

Soc. Come, then, and let us examine what we are saying. That thing or person which is dear to the gods is pious, and that thing or person which is hateful to the gods is impious, these two being the extreme opposites of one another. Was not that said?

Euth. It was.

Musicians (ca. 480–470 B.C.). An example of Etruscan decorative tomb painting. (Alinari/Art Resource)

Soc. And well said?

Euth. Yes, Socrates, I thought so; it was certainly said.

Soc. And further, Euthyphro, the gods were admitted to have enmities and hatreds and differences?

Euth. Yes, that was also said.

Soc. And what sort of difference creates enmity and anger? Suppose for example that you and I, my good friend, differ about a number; do differences of this sort make us enemies and set us at variance with one another? Do we not go at once to arithmetic, and put an end to them by a sum?

Euth. True.

Soc. Or suppose that we differ about magnitudes, do we not quickly end the differences by measuring?

Euth. Very true.

Soc. And we end a controversy about heavy and light by resorting to a weighing machine?

Euth. To be sure.

Soc. But what differences are there which cannot be thus decided, and which therefore make us angry and set us at enmity with one another? I dare say the answer does not occur to you at the moment, and therefore I will suggest that these enmities arise when the matters of difference are the just and unjust, good and evil, honourable and dishonourable. Are not these the points about which men differ, and about which when we are unable satisfactorily to decide our differences, you and I and all of us quarrel, when we do quarrel?

Euth. Yes, Socrates, the nature of the differences about which we quarrel is such as you describe.

Soc. And the quarrels of the gods, noble Euthyphro, when they occur, are of a like nature?

Euth. Certainly they are.

Soc. They have differences of opinion, as you say, about good and evil, just and unjust, honourable and dishonourable: there would have been no quarrels among them, if there had been no such differences—would there now?

Euth. You are quite right.

Soc. Does not every man love that which he deems noble and just and good, and hate the opposite of them?

Euth. Very true.

Soc. But, as you say, people regard the same things, some as just and others as unjust,—about these they dispute; and so there arise wars and fightings among them.

Euth. Very true.

Soc. Then the same things are hated by the gods and loved by the gods, and are both hateful and dear to them?

Euth. True.

Soc. And upon this view the same things, Euthyphro, will be pious and also impious?

Euth. So I should suppose.

Soc. Then, my friend, I remark with surprise that you have not answered the question which I asked. For I certainly did not ask you to tell me what action is both pious and impious: but now it would seem that what is loved by the gods is also hated by them. And therefore, Euthyphro, in thus chastising your father you may very likely be doing what is agreeable to Zeus but disagreeable to Cronos or Uranus, and what is acceptable to Hephaestus but unacceptable to Herè, and there may be other gods who have similar differences of opinion.

Euth. But I believe, Socrates, that all the gods would be agreed as to the propriety of punishing a murderer: there would be no difference of opinion about that.

Soc. Well, but speaking of men, Euthyphro, did you ever hear any one arguing that a murderer or any sort of evil-doer ought to be let off?

Euth. I should rather say that these are the questions which they are always arguing, especially in courts of law: they commit all sorts of crimes, and there is nothing which they will not do or say in their own defence.

Soc. But do they admit their guilt, Euthyphro, and yet say that they ought not to be punished?

Euth. No; they do not.

Soc. Then there are some things which they do not venture to say and do: for they do not venture to argue that the guilty are to be unpunished, but they deny their guilt, do they not?

Euth. Yes.

Soc. Then they do not argue that the evil-doer should not be punished, but they argue about the fact of who the evil-doer is, and what he did and when?

Euth. True.

Soc. And the gods are in the same case, if as you assert they quarrel about just and unjust, and some of them say while others deny that injustice is done among them. For surely neither God nor man will ever venture to say that the doer of injustice is not to be punished?

Euth. That is true, Socrates, in the main.

Soc. But they join issue about the particulars—gods and men alike; and, if they dispute at all, they dispute about some act which is called in question, and which by some is affirmed to be just, by others to be unjust. Is not that true?

Euth. Quite true.

Soc. Well then, my dear friend Euthyphro, do tell me, for my better instruction and information, what proof have you that in the opinion of all the gods a servant who is guilty of murder, and is put in chains by the master of the dead man, and dies because he is put in chains before he who bound him can learn from the interpreters of the gods what he ought to do with him, dies unjustly; and that on behalf of such an one a son ought to proceed against his father and accuse him of murder. How would you show that all the gods absolutely agree in approving of his act? Prove to me that they do, and I will applaud your wisdom as long as I live.

Euth. It will be a difficult task; but I could make the matter very clear indeed to you.

Soc. I understand; you mean to say that I am not so quick of apprehension as the judges: for to them you will be sure to prove that the act is unjust, and hateful to the gods.

Euth. Yes indeed, Socrates; at least if they will listen to me.

Soc. But they will be sure to listen if they find that you are a good speaker. There was a notion that came into my mind while you were speaking; I said to myself: 'Well, and what if Euthyphro does prove to me that all the gods regarded the death of the serf as unjust, how do I know anything more of the nature of piety and impiety? for granting that this action may be hateful to the gods, still piety and impiety are not adequately defined by these distinctions, for that which is hateful to the gods has been shown to be also pleasing and dear to them.' And therefore, Euthyphro, I do not ask you to prove this; I will suppose, if you like, that all the gods condemn and abominate such an action. But I will amend the definition so far as to say that what all the gods hate is impious, and what they love pious or holy; and what some of them love and others hate is both or neither. Shall this be our definition of piety and impiety?

Euth. Why not, Socrates?

Soc. Why not! certainly, as far as I am concerned, Euthyphro, there is no reason why not. But whether this admission will greatly assist you in the task of instructing me as you promised, is a matter for you to consider.

Euth. Yes, I should say that what all the gods love is pious and holy, and the opposite which they all hate, impious.

Soc. Ought we to enquire into the truth of this, Euthyphro, or simply to accept the mere statement on our own authority and that of others? What do you say?

Euth. We should enquire; and I believe that the statement will stand the test of enquiry.

Soc. We shall know better, my good friend, in a little while. The point which I should first wish to understand is whether the pious or holy is beloved by the gods because it is holy, or holy because it is beloved of the gods.

Euth. I do not understand your meaning, Socrates.

Soc. I will endeavour to explain: we speak of carrying and we speak of being carried, of leading and being led, seeing and being seen. You know that in all such cases there is a difference, and you know also in what the difference lies?

Euth. I think that I understand.

Soc. And is not that which is beloved distinct from that which loves?

Euth. Certainly.

Soc. Well; and now tell me, is that which is carried in this state of carrying because it is carried, or for some other reason?

Euth. No; that is the reason.

Soc. And the same is true of what is led and of what is seen?

Euth. True.

Soc. And a thing is not seen because it is visible, but conversely, visible because it is seen; nor is a thing led because it is in the state of being led, or carried because it is in the state of being carried, but the converse of this. And now I think, Euthyphro, that my meaning will be intelligible; and my meaning is, that any state of action or passion implies previous action or passion. It does not become because it is becoming, but it is in a state of becoming because it becomes; neither does it suffer because it is in a state of suffering, but it is in a state of suffering because it suffers. Do you not agree?

Euth. Yes.

Soc. Is not that which is loved in some state either of becoming or suffering?

Euth. Yes.

Soc. And the same holds as in the previous instances; the state of being loved follows the act of being loved, and not the act the state.

Euth. Certainly.

Soc. And what do you say of piety, Euthyphro: is not piety, according to your definition, loved by all the gods?

Euth. Yes.

Soc. Because it is pious or holy, or for some other reason?

Euth. No, that is the reason.

Soc. It is loved because it is holy, not holy because it is loved?

Euth. Yes.

Soc. And that which is dear to the gods is loved by them, and is in a state to be loved of them because it is loved of them?

Euth. Certainly.

Soc. Then that which is dear to the gods, Euthyphro, is not holy, nor is that which is holy loved of God, as you affirm; but they are two different things.

Euth. How do you mean, Socrates?

Soc. I mean to say that the holy has been acknowledged by us to be loved of God because it is holy, not to be holy because it is loved.

Euth. Yes.

Soc. But that which is dear to the gods is dear to them because it is loved by them, not loved by them because it is dear to them.

Euth. True.

Soc. But, friend Euthyphro, if that which is holy is the same with that which is dear to God, and is loved because it is holy, then that which is dear to God would have been loved as being dear to God; but if that which is dear to God is dear to him because loved by him, then that which is holy would have been holy because loved by him. But now you see that the reverse is the case, and that they are quite different from one another. For one (*θεοφιλὲς*) is of a kind to be loved because it is loved, and the other (*ὅσιον*) is loved because it is of a kind to be loved. Thus you appear to me, Euthyphro, when I ask you what is the essence of holiness, to offer an attribute only, and not the essence—the attribute of being loved by all the gods. But you still refuse to explain to me the nature of holiness. And therefore, if you please, I will ask you not to hide your treasure, but to tell me once more what holiness or piety really is, whether dear to the gods or not (for that is a matter about which we will not quarrel); and what is impiety?

Euth. I really do not know, Socrates, how to express what I mean. For somehow or other our arguments, on whatever ground we rest them, seem to turn round and walk away from us.

Soc. Your words, Euthyphro, are like the handiwork of my ancestor Daedalus; and if I were the sayer or propounder of them, you might say that my arguments walk away and will not remain fixed where they are placed because I am a descendant of his. But now, since these notions are your own, you must find some other gibe, for they certainly, as you yourself allow, show an inclination to be on the move.

Euth. Nay, Socrates, I shall still say that you are the Daedalus who sets arguments in motion; not I, certainly, but you make them move or go round, for they would never have stirred, as far as I am concerned.

Soc. Then I must be a greater than Daedalus: for whereas he only made his own inventions to move, I move those of other people as well. And the beauty of it is, that I would rather not. For I would give the wisdom of Daedalus, and the wealth of Tantalus, to be able to detain them and keep them fixed. But enough of this. As I perceive that you are lazy, I will myself endeavor to show you how you might instruct me in the nature of piety; and I hope that you will not grudge your labour. Tell me, then,—Is not that which is pious necessarily just?

Euth. Yes.

Soc. And is, then, all which is just pious? or, is that which is pious all just, but that which is just, only in part and not all, pious?

Euth. I do not understand you, Socrates.

Soc. And yet I know that you are as much wiser than I am, as you are younger. But, as I was saying, revered friend, the abundance of your wisdom makes you lazy. Please to exert yourself, for there is no real difficulty in understanding me. What I mean I may explain by an illustration of what I do not mean. The poet (Stasinus) sings—

> 'Of Zeus, the author and creator of all these
> things,
> You will not tell: for where there is fear there
> is also reverence.'

Now I disagree with this poet. Shall I tell you in what respect?

Euth. By all means.

Soc. I should not say that where there is fear there is also reverence; for I am sure that many persons fear poverty and disease, and the like evils, but I do not perceive that they reverence the objects of their fear.

Euth. Very true.

Soc. But where reverence is, there is fear; for he who has a feeling of reverence and shame about the commission of any action, fears and is afraid of an ill reputation.

Euth. No doubt.

Soc. Then we are wrong in saying that where there is fear there is also reverence; and we should say, where there is reverence there is also fear. But there is not always reverence where there is fear; for fear is a more extended notion, and reverence is a part of fear, just as the odd is a part of number, and number is a more extended notion than the odd. I suppose that you follow me now?

Euth. Quite well.

Soc. That was the sort of question which I meant to raise when I asked whether the just is always the pious, or the pious always the just; and whether there may not be justice where there is not piety; for justice is the more extended notion of which piety is only a part. Do you dissent?

Euth. No, I think that you are quite right.

Soc. Then, if piety is a part of justice, I suppose that we should enquire what part? If you had pursued the enquiry in the previous cases; for instance, if you had asked me what is an even number, and what part of number the even is, I should have had no difficulty in replying, a number which represents a figure having two equal sides. Do you not agree?

Euth. Yes, I quite agree.

Soc. In like manner, I want you to tell me what part of justice is piety or holiness, that I may be able to tell Meletus not to do me injustice, or indict me for impiety, as I am now adequately instructed by you in the nature of piety or holiness, and their opposites.

Euth. Piety or holiness, Socrates, appears to me to be that part of justice which attends to the gods, as there is the other part of justice which attends to men.

Soc. That is good, Euthyphro; yet still there is a little point about which I should like to have further information, What is the meaning of 'attention'? For attention can hardly be used in the same sense when applied to the gods as when applied to other things. For instance, horses are said to require attention, and not every person is able to attend to them, but only a person skilled in horsemanship. Is it not so?

Euth. Certainly.

Soc. I should suppose that the art of horsemanship is the art of attending to horses?

Euth. Yes.

Soc. Nor is every one qualified to attend to dogs, but only the huntsman?

Euth. True.

Soc. And I should also conceive that the art of the huntsman is the art of attending to dogs?

Euth. Yes.

Soc. As the art of the oxherd is the art of attending to oxen?

Euth. Very true.

Soc. In like manner holiness or piety is the art of attending to the gods?—that would be your meaning, Euthyphro?

Euth. Yes.

Soc. And is not attention always designed for the good or benefit of that to which the attention is given? As in the case of horses, you may observe that when attended to by the horseman's art they are benefited and improved, are they not?

Euth. True.

Soc. As the dogs are benefited by the huntsman's art, and the oxen by the art of the oxherd, and all other things are tended or attended for their good and not for their hurt?

Euth. Certainly, not for their hurt.

Soc. But for their good?

Euth. Of course.

Soc. And does piety or holiness, which has been defined to be the art of attending to the gods, benefit or improve them? Would you say that when you do a holy act you make any of the gods better?

Euth. No, no; that was certainly not what I meant.

Soc. And I, Euthyphro, never supposed that you did. I asked you the question about the nature of the attention, because I thought that you did not.

Euth. You do me justice, Socrates; that is not the sort of attention which I mean.

Soc. Good: but I must still ask what is this attention to the gods which is called piety?

Euth. It is such, Socrates, as servants show to their masters.

Soc. I understand—a sort of ministration to the gods.

Euth. Exactly.

Soc. Medicine is also a sort of ministration or service, having in view the attainment of some object—would you not say of health?

Euth. I should.

Soc. Again, there is an art which ministers to the ship-builder with a view to the attainment of some result?

Euth. Yes, Socrates, with a view to the building of a ship.

Soc. As there is an art which ministers to the house-builder with a view to the building of a house?

Euth. Yes.

Soc. And now tell me, my good friend, about the art which ministers to the gods: what work does that help to accomplish? For you must surely know if, as you say, you are of all men living the one who is best instructed in religion.

Euth. And I speak the truth, Socrates.

Soc. Tell me then, oh tell me—what is that fair work which the gods do by the help of our ministrations?

Euth. Many and fair, Socrates, are the works which they do.

Soc. Why, my friend, and so are those of a general. But the chief of them is easily told. Would you not say that victory in war is the chief of them?

Euth. Certainly.

Soc. Many and fair, too, are the works of the husbandman, if I am not mistaken; but his chief work is the production of food from the earth?

Euth. Exactly.

Soc. And of the many and fair things done by the gods, which is the chief or principal one?

Euth. I have told you already, Socrates, that to learn all these things accurately will be very tiresome. Let me simply say that piety or holiness is learning how to please the gods in word and deed, by prayers and sacrifices. Such piety is the salvation of families and states, just as the impious, which is unpleasing to the gods, is their ruin and destruction.

Soc. I think that you could have answered in much fewer words the chief question which I asked, Euthyphro, if you had chosen. But I see plainly that you are not disposed to instruct me—clearly not: else why, when we reached the point, did you turn aside? Had you only answered me I should have truly learned of you by this time the nature of piety. Now, as the asker of a question is necessarily dependent on the answerer, whither he leads I must follow; and can only ask again, what is the pious, and what is piety? Do you mean that they are a sort of science of praying and sacrificing?

Euth. Yes, I do.

Soc. And sacrificing is giving to the gods, and prayer is asking of the gods?

Euth. Yes, Socrates.

Soc. Upon this view, then, piety is a science of asking and giving?

Euth. You understand me capitally, Socrates.

Soc. Yes, my friend; the reason is that I am a votary of your science, and give my mind to it, and therefore nothing which you say will be thrown away upon me. Please then to tell me, what is the nature of this service to the gods? Do you mean that we prefer requests and give gifts to them?

Euth. Yes, I do.

Soc. Is not the right way of asking to ask of them what we want?

Euth. Certainly.

Soc. And the right way of giving is to give to them in return what they want of us. There would be no meaning in an art which gives to any one that which he does not want.

Euth. Very true, Socrates.

Soc. Then piety, Euthyphro, is an art which gods and men have of doing business with one another?

Euth. That is an expression which you may use, if you like.

Soc. But I have no particular liking for anything but the truth. I wish, however, that you would tell me what benefit accrues to the gods from our gifts. There is no doubt about what they give to us; for there is no good thing which they do not give; but how we can give any good thing to them in return is far from being equally clear. If they give everything and we give nothing, that must be an affair of business in which we have very greatly the advantage of them.

Euth. And do you imagine, Socrates, that any benefit accrues to the gods from our gifts?

Soc. But if not, Euthyphro, what is the meaning of gifts which are conferred by us upon the gods?

Euth. What else, but tributes of honour; and, as I was just now saying, what pleases them?

Soc. Piety, then, is pleasing to the gods, but not beneficial or dear to them?

Euth. I should say that nothing could be dearer.

Soc. Then once more the assertion is repeated that piety is dear to the gods?

Euth. Certainly.

Soc. And when you say this, can you wonder at your words not standing firm, but walking away? Will you accuse me of being the Daedalus who makes them walk away, not perceiving that there is another and far greater artist than Daedalus who makes them go round in a circle, and he is yourself; for the argument, as you will perceive, comes round to the same point. Were we not saying that the holy or pious was not the same with that which is loved of the gods? Have you forgotten?

Euth. I quite remember.

Soc. And are you not saying that what is loved of the gods is holy; and is not this the same as what is dear to them—do you see?

Euth. True.

Soc. Then either we were wrong in our former assertion; or, if we were right then, we are wrong now.

Euth. One of the two must be true.

Soc. Then we must begin again and ask, What is piety? That is an enquiry which I shall never be weary of pursuing as far as in me lies; and I entreat you not to scorn me, but to apply your mind to the utmost, and tell me the truth. For, if any man knows, you are he; and therefore I must detain you, like Proteus, until you tell. If you had not certainly known the nature of piety and impiety, I am confident that you would never, on behalf of a serf, have charged your aged father with murder. You would not have run such a risk of doing wrong in the sight of the gods, and you would have had too much respect for the opinions of men. I am sure, therefore, that you know the nature of piety and impiety. Speak out then, my dear Euthyphro, and do not hide your knowledge.

Euth. Another time, Socrates; for I am in a hurry, and must go now.

Soc. Alas! my companion, and will you leave me in despair? I was hoping that you would instruct me in the nature of piety and impiety; and then I might have cleared myself of Meletus and his indictment. I would have told him that I had been enlightened by Euthyphro, and had given up rash innovations and speculations, in which I indulged only through ignorance, and that now I am about to lead a better life.

Apology

How you, O Athenians, have been affected by my accusers, I cannot tell; but I know that they almost made me forget who I was—so persuasively did they speak; and yet they have hardly uttered a word of truth. But of the many falsehoods told by them, there was one which quite amazed me;—I mean when they said that you should be upon your guard and not allow yourselves to be deceived by the force of my eloquence. To say this, when they were certain to be detected as soon as I opened my lips and proved myself to be anything but a great speaker, did indeed appear to me most shameless—unless by the force of eloquence they mean the force of truth; for if such is their meaning, I admit that I am eloquent. But in how different a way from theirs! Well, as I was saying, they have scarcely spoken the truth at all; but from me you shall hear the whole truth: not, however, delivered after their manner in a set oration duly ornamented with words and phrases. No, by heaven! but I shall use the words and arguments which occur to me at the moment; for I am confident in the justice of my cause: at my time of life I ought not to be appearing before you, O men of Athens, in the character of a juvenile orator—let no one expect it of me. And I must beg of you to grant me a favour:—If I defend myself in my accustomed manner, and you hear me using the words which I have been in the habit of using in the agora, at the tables of the money-changers, or anywhere else, I would ask you not to be surprised, and not to interrupt me on this account. For I am more than seventy years of age, and appearing now for the first time in a court of law, I am quite a stranger to the language of the place; and therefore I would have you regard me as if I were really a stranger, whom you would excuse if he spoke in his native tongue, and after the fashion of his country:—Am I making an unfair request of you? Never mind the manner, which may or may not be good; but think only of the truth of my words, and give heed to that: let the speaker speak truly and the judge decide justly.

And first, I have to reply to the older charges and

Plato, *Apology*, complete.

But far more dangerous are the others, who began when you were children, and took possession of your minds with their falsehoods, telling of one Socrates, a wise man, who speculated about the heaven above, and searched into the earth beneath, and to my first accusers, and then I will go on to the later ones. For of old I have had many accusers, who have accused me falsely to you during many years; and I am more afraid of them than of Anytus and his associates, who are dangerous, too, in their own way. made the worse appear the better cause. The disseminators of this tale are the accusers whom I dread; for their hearers are apt to fancy that such enquirers do not believe in the existence of the gods. And they are many, and their charges against me are of ancient date, and they were made by them in the days when you were more impressible than you are now—in childhood, or it may have been in youth—and the cause when heard went by default, for there was none to answer. And hardest of all, I do not know and cannot tell the names of my accusers; unless in the chance case of a Comic poet. All who from envy and malice have persuaded you—some of them having first convinced themselves—all this class of men are most difficult to deal with; for I cannot have them up here, and cross-examine them, and therefore I must simply fight with shadows in my own defence, and argue when there is no one who answers. I will ask you then to assume with me, as I was saying, that my opponents are of two kinds; one recent, the other ancient: and I hope that you will see the propriety of my answering the latter first, for these accusations you heard long before the others, and much oftener.

Well, then, I must make my defence, and endeavor to clear away in a short time, a slander which has lasted a long time. May I succeed, if to succeed be for my good and yours, or likely to avail me in my cause! The task is not an easy one; I quite understand the nature of it. And so leaving the event with God, in obedience to the law I will now make my defence.

I will begin at the beginning, and ask what is the accusation which has given rise to the slander of me, and in fact has encouraged Meletus to prefer this charge against me. Well, what do the slanderers say? They shall be my prosecutors, and I will sum up their words in an affidavit: 'Socrates is an evil-doer, and a curious person, who searches into things under the earth and in heaven, and he makes the worse appear the better cause; and he teaches the aforesaid doctrines to others.' Such is the nature of the accusation: it is just what you have yourselves seen in the comedy of Aristophanes, who has introduced a man whom he calls Socrates, going about and saying that he walks in air, and talking a deal of nonsense concerning matters of which I do not pretend to know either much or little—not that I mean to speak disparagingly of any one who is a student of natural philosophy. I should be very sorry if Meletus could bring so grave a charge against me. But the simple truth is, O Athenians, that I have nothing to do with physical speculations. Very many of those here present are witnesses to the truth of this, and to them I appeal. Speak then, you who have heard me, and tell your neighbours whether any of you have ever known me hold forth in few words or in many upon such matters. . . . You hear their answer. And from what they say of this part of the charge you will be able to judge of the truth of the rest.

As little foundation is there for the report that I am a teacher, and take money; this accusation has no more truth in it than the other. Although, if a man were really able to instruct mankind, to receive money for giving instruction would, in my opinion, be an honour to him. There is Gorgias of Leontium, and Prodicus of Ceos, and Hippias of Elis, who go the round of the cities, and are able to persuade the young men to leave their own citizens by whom they might be taught for nothing, and come to them whom they not only pay, but are thankful if they may be allowed to pay them. There is at this time a Parian philosopher residing in Athens, of whom I have heard; and I came to hear of him in this way:—I came across a man who has spent a world of money on the Sophists, Callias, the son of Hipponicus, and knowing that he had sons, I asked him: 'Callias,' I said, 'if your two sons were foals or calves, there would be no difficulty in finding some one to put over them; we should hire a trainer of horses, or a farmer probably, who would improve and perfect them in their own proper virtue and excellence; but as they are human beings, whom are you thinking of placing over them? Is there any one who understands human and political virtue? You must have thought about the matter, for you have sons; is there any one?' 'There is,' he said. 'Who is he?' said I; 'and of what country? and what does he charge?' 'Evenus the Parian,' he replied; 'he is the man, and his charge is five minae.' Happy is Evenus, I said to myself, if he really has this wisdom, and teaches at such a moderate charge. Had I the same, I should have been very proud and conceited; but the truth is that I have no knowledge of the kind.

I dare say, Athenians, that some one among you will reply, 'Yes, Socrates, but what is the origin of these accusations which are brought against you; there must have been something strange which you have been doing? All these rumours and this talk about you would never have arisen if you had been like other men: tell us, then, what is the cause of them, for we should be sorry to judge hastily of you.' Now I regard this as a fair challenge, and I will endeavour to explain to you the reason why I am called wise and have such an evil fame. Please to attend then. And although some of you may think that I am joking, I declare that I will tell you the entire truth. Men of Athens, this reputation of mine has come of a certain sort of wisdom which I possess. If you ask me what kind of wisdom, I reply, wisdom such as may perhaps be attained by man, for to that extent I am inclined to believe that I am wise; whereas the persons of whom I was speaking have a superhuman wisdom, which I may fail to describe, because I have it not myself; and he who says that I have, speaks falsely, and is taking away my character. And here, O men of Athens, I must beg you not to interrupt me, even if I seem to say something extravagant. For the word which I will speak is not mine. I will refer you to a witness who is worthy of credit; that witness shall be the God of Delphi—he will tell you about my wisdom, if I have any, and of what sort it is. You must have known Chaerephon; he was early a friend of mine, and also a friend of yours, for he shared in the recent exile of the people, and returned with you. Well, Chaerephon, as you know, was very impetuous in all his doings, and he went to Delphi and boldly asked the oracle to tell him whether—as I was saying, I must beg you not to interrupt—he asked the oracle to tell him whether any one was wiser than I was, and the Pythian prophetess answered, that there was no man wiser. Chaerephon is dead himself; but his brother, who is in court, will confirm the truth of what I am saying.

Why do I mention this? Because I am going to explain to you why I have such an evil name. When I heard the answer, I said to myself, What can the god mean? and what is the interpretation of his riddle? for I know that I have no wisdom, small or great. What then can he mean when he says that I am the wisest of men? And yet he is a god, and cannot lie; that would be against his nature. After long consideration, I thought of a method of trying the question. I reflected that if I could only find a man wiser than myself, then I might go to the god with a refutation in my hand. I should say to him, 'Here is a man who is wiser than I am; but you said that I was the wisest.' Accordingly I went to one who had the reputation of wisdom, and observed him—his name I need not mention; he was a politician whom I selected for examination—and the result was as follows: When I began to talk with him, I could not help thinking that he was not really wise, although he was thought wise by many, and still wiser by himself; and thereupon I tried to explain to him that he thought himself wise, but was not really wise; and the consequence was that he hated me, and his enmity was shared by several who were present and heard me. So I left him, saying to myself, as I went away: Well, although I do not suppose that either of us knows anything really beautiful and good, I am better off than he is,—for he knows nothing, and thinks that he knows; I neither know nor think that I know. In this latter particular, then, I seem to have slightly the advantage of him. Then I went to another who had still higher pretensions to wisdom, and my conclusion was exactly the same. Whereupon I made another enemy of him, and of many others besides him.

Then I went to one man after another, being not unconscious of the enmity which I provoked, and I lamented and feared this: But necessity was laid upon me,—the word of God, I thought, ought to be considered first. And I said to myself, Go I must to all who appear to know, and find out the meaning of the oracle. And I swear to you, Athenians, by the dog I swear!—for I must tell you the truth—the result of my mission was just this: I found that the men most in repute were all but the most foolish; and that others less esteemed were really wiser and better. I will tell you the tale of my wanderings and of the 'Herculean' labours, as I may call them, which I endured only to find at last the oracle irrefutable. After the politicians, I went to the poets; tragic, dithyrambic, and all sorts. And there, I said to myself, you will be instantly detected; now you will find out that you are more ignorant than they are. Accordingly, I took them some of the most elaborate passages in their own writings, and asked what was the meaning of them—thinking that they would teach me something. Will you believe me? I am almost ashamed to confess the truth, but I must say that there is hardly a person present who would not have talked better about their poetry than they did themselves. Then I knew that not by wisdom do poets write poetry, but by a sort of genius and inspiration; they are like diviners or soothsayers who also say many fine things, but do not understand the meaning of them. The poets appeared to me to be much in the same case; and I further observed that upon the strength of their poetry they believed themselves to be the wisest of men in other things in which they were not wise. So I departed, conceiving myself to be superior to them for the same reason that I was superior to the politicians.

At last I went to the artisans, for I was conscious that I knew nothing at all, as I may say, and I was sure that they knew many fine things; and here I was not mistaken, for they did know many things of which I was ignorant, and in this they certainly were wiser than I was. But I observed that even the good artisans fell into the same error as the poets;—because they were good workmen they thought that they also knew all sorts of high matters, and this defect in them overshadowed their wisdom; and therefore I asked myself on behalf of the oracle, whether I would like to be as I was, neither having their knowledge nor their ignorance, or like them in both; and I made answer to myself and to the oracle that I was better off as I was.

This inquisition has led to my having many enemies of the worst and most dangerous kind, and has given occasion also to many calumnies. And I am called wise, for my hearers always imagine that I myself possess the wisdom which I find wanting in others: but the truth is, O men of Athens, that God only is wise; and by his answer he intends to show that the wisdom of men is worth little or nothing; he is not speaking of Socrates, he is only using my name by way of illustration, as if he said, He, O men, is the wisest, who, like Socrates, knows that his wisdom is in truth worth nothing. And so I go about the world, obedient to the god, and search and make enquiry into the wisdom of any one, whether citizen or stranger, who appears to be wise; and if he is not wise, then in vindication of the oracle I show him that he is not wise; and my occupation quite absorbs me, and I have no time to give either to any public matter of interest or to any concern of my own, but I am in utter poverty by reason of my devotion to the god.

There is another thing:—young men of the richer classes, who have not much to do, come about me of their own accord; they like to hear the pretenders examined, and they often imitate me, and proceed to examine others; there are plenty of persons, as they quickly discover, who think that they know something, but really know little or nothing; and then those who are examined by them instead of being angry with themselves are angry with me: This confounded Socrates, they say; this villainous misleader of youth!—and then if somebody asks them, Why, what evil does he practise or teach? they do not know, and cannot tell; but in order that they may not appear to be at a loss, they repeat the ready-made charges which are used against all philosophers about teaching things up in the clouds and under the earth, and having no gods, and making the worse appear the better cause; for they do not like to confess that their pretence of knowledge has been detected—which is the truth; and as they are numerous and ambitious and energetic, and are drawn up in battle array and have persuasive tongues, they have filled your ears with their loud and inveterate calumnies. And this is the reason why my three accusers, Meletus and Anytus and Lycon, have set upon me; Meletus, who has a quarrel with me on behalf of the poets; Anytus, on behalf of the craftsmen and politicians; Lycon, on behalf of the rhetoricians: and as I said at the beginning, I cannot expect to get rid of such a mass of calumny all in a moment. And this, O men of Athens, is the truth and the whole truth; I have concealed nothing, I have dissembled nothing. And yet, I know that my plainness of speech makes them hate me, and what is their hatred but a proof that I am speaking the truth?—Hence has arisen the prejudice against me; and this is the reason of it, as you will find out either in this or in any future enquiry.

I have said enough in my defence against the first class of my accusers; I turn to the second class. They are headed by Meletus, that good man and true lover of his country, as he calls himself. Against these, too, I must try to make a defence:—Let their affidavit be read: it contains something of this kind: It says that Socrates is a doer of evil, who corrupts the youth; and who does not believe in the gods of the state, but has other new divinities of his own. Such is the charge; and now let us examine the particular counts. He says that I am a doer of evil, and corrupt the youth; but I say, O men of Athens, that Meletus is a doer of evil, in that he pretends to be in earnest when he is only in jest, and is so eager to bring men to trial from a pretended zeal and interest about matters in which he really never had the smallest interest. And the truth of this I will endeavour to prove to you.

Come hither, Meletus, and let me ask a question of you. You think a great deal about the improvement of youth?

Yes, I do.

Tell the judges, then, who is their improver; for you must know, as you have taken the pains to discover their corrupter, and are citing and accusing me before them. Speak, then, and tell the judges who their improver is.—Observe, Meletus, that you are silent, and have nothing to say. But is not this rather disgraceful, and a very considerable proof of what I was saying, that you have no interest in the matter? Speak up, friend, and tell us who their improver is.

The laws.

But that, my good sir, is not my meaning. I want to know who the person is, who, in the first place, knows the laws.

The judges, Socrates, who are present in court.

What, do you mean to say, Meletus, that they are able to instruct and improve youth?

Certainly they are.

What, all of them, or some only and not others?

All of them.

By the goddess Herè, that is good news! There are plenty of improvers, then. And what do you say of the audience,—do they improve them?

Yes, they do.

And the senators?

Yes, the senators improve them.

But perhaps the members of the assembly corrupt them?—or do they too improve them?

They improve them.

Then every Athenian improves and elevates them; all with the exception of myself; and I alone am their corrupter? Is that what you affirm?

That is what I stoutly affirm.

I am very unfortunate if you are right. But suppose I ask you a question: How about horses? Does one man do them harm and all the world good? Is not the exact opposite the truth? One man is able to do them good, or at least not many;—the trainer of horses, that is to say, does them good, and others who have to do with them rather injure them? Is not that true, Meletus, of horses, or of any other animals? Most assuredly it is; whether you and Anytus say yes or no. Happy indeed would be the condition of youth if they had one corrupter only, and all the rest of the world were their improvers. But you, Meletus, have sufficiently shown that you never had a thought about the young: your carelessness is seen in your not caring about the very things which you bring against me.

And now, Meletus, I will ask you another question—by Zeus I will: Which is better, to live among bad citizens, or among good ones? Answer, friend, I say; the question is one which may be easily answered. Do not the good do their neighbours good, and the bad do them evil?

Certainly.

And is there any one who would rather be injured than benefited by those who live with him? Answer, my good friend, the law requires you to answer—does any one like to be injured?

Certainly not.

And when you accuse me of corrupting and deteriorating the youth, do you allege that I corrupt them intentionally or unintentionally?

Intentionally, I say.

But you have just admitted that the good do their neighbours good, and evil do them evil. Now, is that a truth which your superior wisdom has recognized thus early in life, and am I, at my age, in such darkness and ignorance as not to know that if a man with whom I have to live is corrupted by me, I am very likely to be harmed by him; and yet I corrupt him, and intentionally, too—so you say, although neither I nor any other human being is ever likely to be convinced by you. But either I do not corrupt them, or I corrrupt them unintentionally; and on either view of the case you lie. If my offence is unintentional, the law has no cognizance of unintentional offences: you ought to have taken me privately, and warned and admonished me; for if I had been better advised, I should have left off doing what I only did unintentionally—no doubt I should; but you would have nothing to say to me and refused to teach me. And now you bring me up in this court, which is a place not of instruction, but of punishment.

It will be very clear to you, Athenians, as I was saying, that Meletus has no care at all, great or small, about the matter. But still I should like to know, Meletus, in what I am affirmed to corrupt the young. I suppose you mean, as I infer from your indictment, that I teach them not to acknowledge the gods which the state acknowledges, but some other new divinities or spiritual agencies in their stead. These are the lessons by which I corrupt the youth, as you say.

Yes, that I say emphatically.

Then, by the gods, Meletus, of whom we are speaking, tell me and the court, in somewhat plainer terms, what you mean! for I do not as yet understand whether you affirm that I teach other men to acknowledge some gods, and therefore that I do believe in gods, and am not an entire atheist—this you do not lay to my charge,—but only you say that they are not the same gods which the city recognizes—the charge is that they are different gods. Or, do you mean that I am an atheist simply, and a teacher of atheism?

I mean the latter—that you are a complete atheist.

What an extraordinary statement! Why do you think so, Meletus? Do you mean that I do not believe in the godhead of the sun or moon, like other men?

I assure you, judges, that he does not: for he says that the sun is stone, and the moon earth.

Friend Meletus, you think that you are accusing Anaxagoras: and you have but a bad opinion of the judges, if you fancy them illiterate to such a degree as not to know that these doctrines are found in the books of Anaxagoras the Clazomenian, which are full of them. And so, forsooth, the youth are said to be taught them by Socrates, when there are not unfrequently exhibitions of them at the theatre (price of admission one drachma at the most); and they might pay their money, and laugh at Socrates if he pretends to father these extraordinary views. And so, Meletus, you really think that I do not believe in any god?

I swear by Zeus that you believe absolutely in none at all.

Nobody will believe you, Meletus, and I am pretty sure that you do not believe yourself. I cannot help thinking, men of Athens, that Meletus is reckless and impudent, and that he has written this indictment in a spirit of mere wantonness and youthful bravado. Has he not compounded a riddle, thinking to try me? He said to himself:—I shall see whether the wise Socrates will discover my facetious contradiction, or whether I shall be able to deceive him and the rest of them. For he certainly does appear to me to contradict himself in the indictment as much as if he said that Socrates is guilty of not believing in the gods, and yet of believing in them—but this is not like a person who is in earnest.

I should like you, O men of Athens, to join me in examining what I conceive to be his inconsistency; and do you, Meletus, answer. And I must remind the audience of my request that they would not make a disturbance if I speak in my accustomed manner:

Did ever man, Meletus, believe in the existence of human things, and not of human beings? . . . I wish, men of Athens, that he would answer, and not be always trying to get up an interruption. Did ever any man believe in horsemanship, and not in horses? or in flute-playing, and not in flute-players? No, my friend; I will answer to you and to the court, as you refuse to answer for yourself. There is no man who ever did. But now please to answer the next question: Can a man believe in spiritual and divine agencies, and not in spirits or demigods?

He cannot.

How lucky I am to have extracted that answer, by the assistance of the court! But then you swear in the indictment that I teach and believe in divine or spiritual agencies (new or old, no matter for that); at any rate, I believe in spiritual agencies,—so you say and swear in the affidavit; and yet if I believe in divine beings, how can I help believing in spirits or demigods;—must I not? To be sure I must; and therefore I may assume that your silence gives consent. Now what are spirits or demigods? are they not either gods or the sons of gods?

Certainly they are.

But this is what I call the facetious riddle invented by you: the demigods or spirits are gods, and you say first that I do not believe in gods, and then again that I do believe in gods; that is, if I believe in demigods. For if the demigods are the illegitimate sons of gods, whether by the nymphs or by any other mothers, of whom they are said to be the sons—what human being will ever believe that there are no gods if they are the sons of gods? You might as well affirm the existence of mules, and deny that of horses and asses. Such nonsense, Meletus, could only have been intended by you to make trial of me. You have put this into the indictment because you had nothing real of which to accuse me. But no one who has a particle of understanding will ever be convinced by you that the same men can believe in divine and superhuman things, and yet not believe that there are gods and demigods and heroes.

I have said enough in answer to the charge of Meletus: any elaborate defence is unnecessary; but I know only too well how many are the enmities which I have incurred, and this is what will be my destruction if I am destroyed;—not Meletus, nor yet Anytus, but the envy and detraction of the world, which has been the death of many good men, and will probably be the death of many more; there is no danger of my being the last of them.

Some one will say: And are you not ashamed, Socrates, of a course of life which is likely to bring you to an untimely end? To him I may fairly answer: There you are mistaken: a man who is good for anything ought not to calculate the chance of living or dying; he ought only to consider whether in doing anything he is doing right or wrong—acting the part of a good man or of a bad. Whereas, upon your view, the heroes who fell at Troy were not good for much, and the son of Thetis above all, who altogether despised danger in comparison with disgrace; and when he was so eager to slay Hector, his goddess mother said to him, that if he avenged his companion Patroclus, and slew Hector, he would die himself—'Fate,' she said, in these or the like words, 'waits for you next after Hector;' he, receiving this warning, utterly despised danger and death, and instead of fearing them, feared rather to live in dishonour, and not to avenge his friend. 'Let me die forthwith,' he replies, 'and be avenged of my enemy, rather than abide here by the beaked ships, a laughing-stock and a burden of the earth.' Had Achilles any thought of death and danger? For wherever a man's place is, whether the place which he has chosen or that in which he has been placed by a commander, there he ought to remain in the hour of danger; he should not think of death or of anything but of disgrace. And this, O men of Athens, is a true saying.

Strange, indeed, would be my conduct, O men of Athens, if I who, when I was ordered by the generals whom you chose to command me at Potidaea and Amphipolis and Delium, remained where they placed me, like any other man, facing death—if now, when, as I conceive and imagine, God orders me to fulfil the philosopher's mission of searching into myself and other men, I were to desert my post through fear of death, or any other fear; that would indeed be strange, and I might justly be arraigned in court for denying the existence of the gods, if I disobeyed the oracle because I was afraid of death, fancying that I was wise when I was not wise. For the fear of death is indeed the pretence of wisdom, and not real wisdom, being a pretence of knowing the unknown; and no one knows whether death, which men in their fear apprehend to be the greatest evil, may not be the greatest good. Is not this ignorance of a disgraceful sort, the ignorance which is the conceit that man knows what he does not know? And in this respect only I believe myself to differ from men in general, and may perhaps claim to be wiser than they are:—that whereas I know but little of the world below, I do not suppose that I know: but I do know that injustice and disobedience to a better, whether God or man, is evil and dishonourable, and I will never fear or avoid a possible good rather than a certain evil. And therefore if you let me go now, and are not convinced by Anytus, who said that since I had been prosecuted I must be put to death (or if not that I ought never to have been prosecuted at all); and that if I escape now, your sons will all be utterly ruined by listening to my words—if you say to me, Socrates, this time we will not mind Anytus, and you shall be let off, but upon one condition, that you are not to enquire and speculate in this way any more, and that if you are caught doing so again you shall die;—if this was the condition on which you let me go, I should reply: Men of Athens, I honour and love you; but I shall obey God rather than you, and while I have life and strength I shall never cease from the practice and teaching of philosophy, exhorting any one whom I meet and saying to him after my manner: You, my friend,—a citizen of the great and mighty and wise city of Athens,—are you not ashamed of heaping up the greatest amount of money and honour and reputation, and caring so little about wisdom and truth and the greatest improvement of the soul, which you never regard or heed at all? And if the person with whom I am arguing, says: Yes, but I do care; then I do not leave him or let him go at once; but I proceed to interrogate and examine and cross-examine him, and if I think that he has no virtue in him, but only says that he has, I reproach him with undervaluing the greater, and overvaluing the less. And I shall repeat the same words to every one whom I meet, young and old, citizen and alien, but especially to the citizens, inasmuch as they are my brethren. For know that this is the command of God; and I believe that no greater good has ever happened in the state than my service to the God. For I do nothing but go about persuading you all, old and young alike, not to take thought for your persons or your properties, but first and chiefly to care about the greatest improvement of the soul. I tell you that virtue is not given by money, but that from virtue comes money and every other good of man, public as well as private. This is my teaching, and if this is the doctrine which corrupts the youth, I am a mischievous person. But if any one says that this is not my teaching, he is speaking an untruth. Wherefore, O men of Athens, I say to you, do as Anytus bids or not as Anytus bids, and either acquit me or not; but whichever you do, understand that I shall never alter my ways, not even if I have to die many times.

Men of Athens, do not interrupt, but hear me; there was an understanding between us that you should hear me to the end: I have something more to say, at which you may be inclined to cry out; but I believe that to hear me will be good for you, and therefore I beg that you will not cry out. I would have you know, that if you kill such an one as I am, you will injure yourselves more than you will injure me. Nothing will injure me, not Meletus nor yet Anytus—they cannot, for a bad man is not permitted to injure a better than himself. I do not deny that Anytus may, perhaps, kill him, or drive him into exile, or deprive him of civil rights; and he may imagine, and others may imagine, that he is inflicting a great injury upon him: but there I do not agree. For the evil of doing as he is doing—the evil of unjustly taking away the life of another—is greater far.

And now, Athenians, I am not going to argue for my own sake, as you may think, but for yours, that you may not sin against the God by condemning me, who am his gift to you. For if you kill me you will not easily find a successor to me, who, if I may use such a ludicrous figure of speech, am a sort of gadfly, given to the state by God; and the state is a great and noble steed who is tardy in his motions owing to his very size, and requires to be stirred into life. I am that gadfly which God has attached to the state, and all day long and in all places am always fastening upon you, arousing and persuading and reproaching you. You will not easily find another like me, and therefore I would advise you to spare me. I dare say that you may feel out of temper (like a person who is suddenly awakened from sleep), and you think that you might easily strike me dead as Anytus advises, and then you would sleep on for the remainder of your lives, unless God in his care of you sent you another gadfly. When I say that I am given to you by God, the proof of my mission is this:—if I had been like other men, I should not have neglected all my own concerns or patiently seen the neglect of them during all these years, and have been doing yours, coming to you individually like a father or elder brother, exhorting you to regard virtue; such conduct, I say, would be unlike human nature. If I had gained anything, or if my exhortations had been paid, there would have been some sense in my doing so; but now, as you will perceive, not even the impudence of my accusers dares to say that I have ever exacted or sought pay of any one; of that they have no witness. And I have a sufficient witness to the truth of what I say—my poverty.

Some one may wonder why I go about in private giving advice and busying myself with the concerns of others, but do not venture to come forward in public and advise the state. I will tell you why. You have heard me speak at sundry times and in divers places of an oracle or sign which comes to me, and is the divinity which Meletus ridicules in the indictment. This sign, which is a kind of voice, first began to come to me when I was a child; it always forbids but never commands me to do anything which I am going to do. This is what deters me from being a politician. And rightly, as I think. For I am certain, O men of Athens, that if I had engaged in politics, I should have perished long ago, and done no good either to you or to myself. And do not be offended at my telling you the truth: for the truth is, that no man who goes to war with you or any other multitude, honestly striving against the many lawless and unrighteous deeds which are done in a state, will save his life; he who will fight for the right, if he would live even for a brief space, must have a private station and not a public one.

I can give you convincing evidence of what I say, not words only, but what you value far more—actions. Let me relate to you a passage of my own life which will prove to you that I should never have yielded to injustice from any fear of death, and that 'as I should have refused to yield' I must have died at once. I will tell you a tale of the courts, not very interesting perhaps, but nevertheless true. The only office of state which I ever held, O men of Athens, was that of senator: the tribe Antiochis, which is my tribe, had the presidency at the trial of the generals who had not taken up the bodies of the slain after the battle of Arginusae; and you proposed to try them in a body, contrary to law, as you all thought afterwards; but at the time I was the only one of the Prytanes who was opposed to the illegality, and I gave my vote against you; and when the orators threatened to impeach and arrest me, and you called and shouted, I made up my mind that I would run the risk, having law and justice with me, rather than take part in your injustice because I feared imprisonment and death. This happened in the days of the democracy. But when the oligarchy of the Thirty was in power, they sent for me and four others into the rotunda, and bade us bring Leon the Salaminian from Salamis, as they wanted to put him to death. This was a specimen of the sort of commands which they were always giving with the view of implicating as many as possible in their crimes; and then I showed, not in word only but in deed, that, if I may be allowed to use such an expression, I cared not a straw for death, and that my great and only care was lest I should do an unrighteous or unholy thing. For the strong arm of that oppressive power did not frighten me into doing wrong; and when we came out of the rotunda the other four went to Salamis and fetched Leon, but I went quietly home. For which I might have lost my life, had not the power of the Thirty shortly afterwards come to an end. And many will witness to my words.

Now do you really imagine that I could have survived all these years, if I had led a public life, supposing that like a good man I had always maintained the right and had made justice, as I ought, the first thing? No indeed, men of Athens, neither I nor any other man. But I have been always the same in all my actions, public as well as private, and never have I yielded any base compliance to those who are slanderously termed my disciples, or to any other. Not that I have any regular disciples. But if any one likes to come and hear me while I am pursuing my mission, whether he be young or old, he is not excluded. Nor do I converse only with those who pay; but any one, whether he be rich or poor, may ask and answer me and listen to my words; and whether he turns out to be a bad man or a good one, neither result can be justly imputed to me; for I never taught or professed to teach him anything. And if any one says that he has ever learned or heard anything from me in private which all the world has not heard, let me tell you that he is lying.

But I shall be asked, Why do people delight in continually conversing with you? I have told you already, Athenians, the whole truth about this matter: they like to hear the cross-examination of the pretenders to wisdom; there is amusement in it. Now this duty of cross-examining other men has been imposed upon me by God; and has been signified to me by oracles, visions, and in every way in which the will of divine power was ever intimated to any one. This is true, O Athenians; or, if not true, would be soon refuted. If I am or have been corrupting the youth, those of them who are now grown up and become sensible that I gave them bad advice in the days of their youth should come forward as accusers, and take their revenge; or if they do not like to come themselves, some of their relatives, fathers, brothers, or other kinsmen, should say what evil their families have suffered at my hands. Now is their time. Many of them I see in the court. There is Crito, who is of the same age and of the same deme with myself, and there is Critobulus his son, whom I also see. Then again there is Lysanias of Sphettus, who is the father of Aeschines—he is present; and also there is Antiphon of Cephisus, who is the father of Epigenes; and there are the brothers of several who have associated with me. There is Nicostratus the son of Theosdotides, and the brother of Theodotus (now Theodotus himself is dead, and therefore he, at any rate, will not seek to stop him); and there is Paralus the son of Demodocus, who had a brother Theages; and Adeimantus the son of Ariston, whose brother Plato is present; and Aeantodorus, who is the brother of Apollodorus, whom I also see. I might mention a great many others, some of whom Meletus should have produced as witnesses in the course of his speech; and let him still produce them, if he has forgotten—I will make way for him. And let him say, if he has any testimony of the sort which he can produce. Nay, Athenians, the very opposite is the truth. For all these are ready to witness on behalf of the corrupter, of the injurer of their kindred, as Meletus and Anytus call me; not the corrupted youth only—there might have been a motive for that—but their uncorrupted elder relatives. Why should they too support me with their testimony? Why, indeed, except for the sake of truth and justice, and because they know that I am speaking the truth, and that Meletus is a liar.

Well, Athenians, this and the like of this is all the defence which I have to offer. Yet a word more. Perhaps there may be some one who is offended at me, when he calls to mind how he himself on a similar, or even a less serious occasion, prayed and entreated the judges with many tears, and how he produced his children in court, which was a moving spectacle, together with a host of relations and friends;

whereas I, who am probably in danger of my life, will do none of these things. The contrast may occur to his mind, and he may be set against me, and vote in anger because he is displeased at me on this account. Now if there be such a person among you,—mind, I do not say that there is,—to him I may fairly reply: My friend, I am a man, and like other men, a creature of flesh and blood, and not 'of wood or stone,' as Homer says; and I have a family, yes, and sons, O Athenians, three in number, one almost a man, and two others who are still young; and yet I will not bring any of them hither in order to petition you for an acquittal. And why not? Not from any self-assertion or want of respect for you. Whether I am or am not afraid of death is another question, of which I will not now speak. But, having regard to public opinion, I feel that such conduct would be discreditable to myself, and to you, and to the whole state. One who has reached my years, and who has a name for wisdom, ought not to demean himself. Whether this opinion of me be deserved or not, at any rate the world has decided that Socrates is in some way superior to other men. And if those among you who are said to be superior in wisdom and courage, and any other virtue, demean themselves in this way, how shameful is their conduct! I have seen men of reputation, when they have been condemned, behaving in the strangest manner: they seemed to fancy that they were going to suffer something dreadful if they died, and that they could be immortal if you only allowed them to live; and I think that such are a dishonour to the state, and that any stranger coming in would have said of them that the most eminent men of Athens, to whom the Athenians themselves give honour and command, are no better than women. And I say that these things ought not to be done by those of us who have a reputation; and if they are done, you ought not to permit them; you ought rather to show that you are far more disposed to condemn the man who gets up a doleful scene and makes the city ridiculous, than him who holds his peace.

But, setting aside the question of public opinion, there seems to be something wrong in asking a favour of a judge, and thus procuring an acquittal, instead of informing and convincing him. For his duty is, not to make a present of justice, but to give judgment; and he has sworn that he will judge according to the laws, and not according to his own good pleasure; and we ought not to encourage you, nor should you allow yourself to be encouraged, in this habit of perjury—there can be no piety in that. Do not then require me to do what I consider dishonourable and impious and wrong, especially now, when I am being tried for impiety on the indictment of Meletus. For if, O men of Athens, by force of persuasion and entreaty I could overpower your oaths, then I should be teaching you to believe that there are no gods, and in defending should simply convict myself of the charge of not believing in them. But that is not so—far otherwise. For I do believe that there are gods, and in a sense higher than that in which any of my accusers believe in them. And to you and to God I commit my cause, to be determined by you as is best for you and me.

There are many reasons why I am not grieved, O men of Athens, at the vote of condemnation. I expected it, and am only surprised that the votes are so nearly equal; for I had thought that the majority against me would have been far larger; but now, had thirty votes gone over to the other side, I should have been acquitted. And I may say, I think, that I have escaped Meletus. I may say more; for without the assistance of Anytus and Lycon, any one may see that he would not have had a fifth part of the votes, as the law requires, in which case he would have incurred a fine of a thousand drachmae.

And so he proposes death as the penalty. And what shall I propose on my part, O men of Athens? Clearly that which is my due. And what is my due? What return shall be made to the man who has never had the wit to be idle during his whole life; but has been careless of what the many care for—wealth, and family interests, and military offices, and speaking in the assembly, and magistracies, and plots, and parties. Reflecting that I was really too honest a man to be a politician and live, I did not go where I could do no good to you or to myself; but where I could do the greatest good privately to every one of you, thither I went, and sought to persuade every man among you that he must look to himself, and seek virtue and wisdom before he looks to his private interests, and look to the state before he looks to the interests of the state; and that this should be the order which he observes in all his actions. What shall be done to such an one? Doubtless some good thing, O men of Athens, if he has his reward; and the good should be of a kind suitable to him. What would be a reward suitable to a poor man who is your benefactor, and who desires leisure that he may instruct you? There can be no reward so fitting as maintenance in the Prytaneum, O men of Athens, a reward which he deserves far more than the citizen who has won the prize at Olympia in the horse or chariot race, whether the chariots were drawn by two horses or by many. For I am in want, and he has enough; and he only gives you the appearance of happiness, and I give you the reality. And if I am to estimate the penalty fairly, I should say that maintenance in the Prytaneum is the just return.

Perhaps you think that I am braving you in what I am saying now, as in what I said before about the tears and prayers. But this is not so. I speak rather because I am convinced that I never intentionally wronged any one, although I cannot convince you—the time has been too short; if there were a law at Athens, as there is in other cities, that a capital cause should not be decided in one day, then I believe that I should have convinced you. But I cannot in a moment refute great slanders; and, as I am convinced that I never wronged another, I will assuredly not wrong myself. I will not say of myself that I deserve any evil, or propose any penalty. Why should I? Because I am afraid of the penalty of death which Meletus proposes? When I do not know whether death is a good or an evil, why should I propose a penalty which would certainly be an evil? Shall I say imprisonment? And why should I live in prison, and be the slave of the magistrates of the year—of the Eleven? Or shall the penalty be a fine, and imprisonment until the fine is paid? There is the same objection. I should have to lie in prison, for money I have none, and cannot pay. And if I say exile (and this may possibly be the penalty which you will affix), I must indeed be blinded by the love of life, if I am so irrational as to expect that when you, who are my own citizens, cannot endure my discourses and words, and have found them so grievous and odious that you will have no more of them, others are likely to endure me. No indeed, men of Athens, that is not very likely. And what a life should I lead, at my age, wandering from city to city, ever changing my place of exile, and always being driven out! For I am quite sure that wherever I go, there, as here, the young men will flock to me; and if I drive them away, their elders will drive me out at their request; and if I let them come, their fathers and friends will drive me out for their sakes.

Some one will say: Yes, Socrates, but cannot you hold your tongue, and then you may go into a foreign city, and no one will interfere with you? Now I have great difficulty in making you understand my answer to this. For if I tell you that to do as you say would be a disobedience to the God, and therefore that I cannot hold my tongue, you will not believe that I am serious; and if I say again that daily to discourse about virtue, and of those other things about which you hear me examining myself and others, is the greatest good of man, and that the unexamined life is not worth living, you are still less likely to believe me. Yet I say what is true, although a thing of which it is hard for me to persuade you. Also, I have never been accustomed to think that I deserve to suffer any harm. Had I money I might have estimated the offence at what I was able to pay, and not have been much the worse. But I have none, and therefore I must ask you to proportion the fine to my means. Well, perhaps I could afford a mina, and therefore I propose that penalty: Plato, Crito, Critobulus, and Apollodorus, my friends here, bid me say thirty minae, and they will be the sureties. Let thirty minae be the penalty; for which sum they will be ample security to you.

Not much time will be gained, O Athenians, in return for the evil name which you will get from the detractors of the city, who will say that you killed Socrates, a wise man; for they will call me wise, even although I am not wise, when they want to reproach you. If you had waited a little while, your desire would have been fulfilled in the course of nature. For I am far advanced in years, as you may perceive, and not far from death. I am speaking now not to all of you, but only to those who have condemned me to death. And I have another thing to say to them: You think that I was convicted because I had no words of the sort which would have procured my acquittal—I mean, if I had thought fit to leave nothing undone or unsaid. Not so; the deficiency which led to my conviction was not of words—certainly not. But I had not the boldness or impudence or inclination to address you as you would have liked me to do, weeping and wailing and lamenting, and saying and doing many things which you have been accustomed to hear from others, and which, as I maintain, are unworthy of me. I thought at the time that I ought not to do anything common or mean when in danger: nor do I now repent of the style of my defence; I would rather die having spoken after my manner, than speak in your manner and live. For neither in war nor yet at law ought I or any man to use every way of escaping death. Often in battle there can be no doubt that if a man will throw away his arms, and fall on his knees before his pursuers, he may escape death; and in other dangers there are other ways of escaping death, if a man is willing to say and do anything. The difficulty, my friends, is not to avoid death, but to avoid unrighteousness; for that runs faster than death. I am old and move slowly, and the slower runner has overtaken me, and my accusers are keen and quick, and the faster runner, who is unrighteousness, has overtaken them. And now I depart hence condemned by you to suffer the penalty of death,—they too go their ways condemned by the truth to suffer the penalty of villainy and wrong; and I must abide by my award—let them abide by theirs. I suppose that these things may be regarded as fated,—and I think that they are well.

And now, O men who have condemned me, I would fain prophesy to you; for I am about to die, and in the hour of death men are gifted with prophetic power. And I prophesy to you who are my murderers, that immediately after my departure punishment far heavier than you have inflicted on me will surely await you. Me you have killed because you wanted to escape the accuser, and not to give an account of your lives. But that will not be as you suppose: far otherwise. For I say that there will be more accusers of you than there are now; accusers whom hitherto I have restrained: and as they are younger they will be more inconsiderate with you, and you will be more offended at them. If you think that by killing men you can prevent some one from censuring your evil lives, you are mistaken; that is not a way of escape which is either possible or honourable; the easiest and the noblest way is not to be disabling others, but to be improving yourselves. This is the prophecy which I utter before my departure to the judges who have condemned me.

Friends, who would have acquitted me, I would like also to talk with you about the thing which has come to pass, while the magistrates are busy, and before I go to the place at which I must die. Stay then a little, for we may as well talk with one another while there is time. You are my friends, and I should like to show you the meaning of this event which has happened to me. O my judges—for you I may truly call judges—I should like to tell you of a wonderful circumstance. Hitherto the divine faculty of which the internal oracle is the source has constantly been in the habit of opposing me even about trifles, if I was going to make a slip or error in any matter; and now as you see there has come upon me that which may be thought, and is generally believed to be, the last and worst evil. But the oracle made no sign of opposition, either when I was leaving my house in the morning, or when I was on my way to the court, or while I was speaking, at anything which I was going to say; and yet I have often been stopped in the middle of a speech, but now in nothing I either said or did touching the matter in hand has the oracle opposed me. What do I take to be the explanation of this silence? I will tell you. It is an intimation that what has happened to me is a good, and that those of us who think that death is an evil are in error. For the customary sign would surely have opposed me had I been going to evil and not to good.

Let us reflect in another way, and we shall see that there is great reason to hope that death is a good; for one of two things—either death is a state of nothingness and utter unconsciousness, or, as men say, there is a change and migration of the soul from this world to another. Now if you suppose that there is no consciousness, but a sleep like the sleep of him who is undisturbed even by dreams, death will be an unspeakable gain. For if a person were to select the night in which his sleep was undisturbed even by dreams, and were to compare with this the other days and nights of his life, and then were to tell us how many days and nights he had passed in the course of his life better and more pleasantly than this one, I think that any man, I will not say a private man, but even the great king will not find many such days or nights, when compared with the others. Now if death be of such a nature, I say that to die is gain; for eternity is then only a single night. But if death is the journey to another place, and there, as men say, all the dead abide, what good, O my friends and judges, can be greater than this? If indeed when the pilgrim arrives in the world below, he is delivered from the professors of justice in this world, and finds the true judges who are said to give judgment there, Minos and Rhadamanthus and Aeacus and Triptolemus, and other sons of God who were righteous in their own life, that pilgrimage will be worth making. What would not a man give if he might converse with Orpheus and Musaeus and Hesiod and

Homer? Nay, if this be true, let me die again and again. I myself, too, shall have a wonderful interest in there meeting and conversing with Palamedes, and Ajax the son of Telamon, and any other ancient hero who has suffered death through an unjust judgment; and there will be no small pleasure, as I think, in comparing my own sufferings with theirs. Above all, I shall then be able to continue my search into true and false knowledge; as in this world, so also in the next; and I shall find out who is wise, and who pretends to be wise, and is not. What would not a man give, O judges, to be able to examine the leader of the great Trojan expedition; or Odysseus or Sisyphus, or numberless others, men and women too! What infinite delight would there be in conversing with them and asking them questions! In another world they do not put a man to death for asking questions: assuredly not. For besides being happier than we are, they will be immortal, if what is said is true.

Wherefore, O judges, be of good cheer about death, and know of a certainty, that no evil can happen to a good man, either in life or after death. He and his are not neglected by the gods; nor has my own approaching end happened by mere chance. But I see clearly that the time had arrived when it was better for me to die and be released from trouble; wherefore the oracle gave no sign. For which reason, also, I am not angry with my condemners, or with my accusers; they have done me no harm, although they did not mean to do me any good; and for this I may gently blame them.

Still I have a favour to ask of them. When my sons are grown up, I would ask you, O my friends, to punish them; and I would have you trouble them, as I have troubled you, if they seem to care about riches, or anything, more than about virtue; or if they pretend to be something when they are really nothing,—then reprove them, as I have reproved you, for not caring about that for which they ought to care, and thinking that they are something when they are really nothing. And if you do this, both I and my sons will have received justice at your hands.

The hour of departure has arrived, and we go our ways—I to die, and you to live. Which is better God only knows.

Crito

SCENE:—*The Prison of Socrates*

Socrates. Why have you come at this hour, Crito? it must be quite early?

Crito. Yes, certainly.

Soc. What is the exact time?

Cr. The dawn is breaking.

Soc. I wonder that the keeper of the prison would let you in.

Cr. He knows me, because I often come, Socrates; moreover, I have done him a kindness.

Soc. And are you only just arrived?

Cr. No, I came some time ago.

Soc. Then why did you sit and say nothing, instead of at once awakening me?

Cr. I should not have liked myself, Socrates, to be in such great trouble and unrest as you are—indeed I should not: I have been watching with amazement your peaceful slumbers; and for that reason I did not awake you, because I wished to minimize the pain. I have always thought you to be of a happy disposition; but never did I see anything like the easy, tranquil manner in which you bear this calamity.

Soc. Why, Crito, when a man has reached my age he ought not to be repining at the approach of death.

Cr. And yet other old men find themselves in similar misfortunes, and age does not prevent them from repining.

Soc. That is true. But you have not told me why you come at this early hour.

Cr. I come to bring you a message which is sad and painful; not, as I believe, to yourself, but to all of us who are your friends, and saddest of all to me.

Soc. What? Has the ship come from Delos, on the arrival of which I am to die?

Cr. No, the ship has not actually arrived, but she

Plato, *Crito*, complete.

will probably be here to-day, as persons who have come from Sunium tell me that they left her there; and therefore to-morrow, Socrates, will be the last day of your life.

Soc. Very well, Crito; if such is the will of God, I am willing; but my belief is that there will be a delay of a day.

Cr. Why do you think so?

Soc. I will tell you. I am to die on the day after the arrival of the ship.

Cr. Yes; that is what the authorities say.

Soc. But I do not think that the ship will be here until to-morrow; this I infer from a vision which I had last night, or rather only just now, when you fortunately allowed me to sleep.

Cr. And what was the nature of the vision?

Soc. There appeared to me the likeness of a woman, fair and comely, clothed in bright raiment, who called to me and said: O Socrates,

> 'The third day hence to fertile Phthia shalt
> thou go.'

Cr. What a singular dream, Socrates!

Soc. There can be no doubt about the meaning, Crito, I think.

Cr. Yes; the meaning is only too clear. But, oh! my beloved Socrates, let me entreat you once more to take my advice and escape. For if you die I shall not only lose a friend who can never be replaced, but there is another evil: people who do not know you and me will believe that I might have saved you if I had been willing to give money, but that I did not care. Now, can there be a worse disgrace than this—that I should be thought to value money more than the life of a friend? For the many will not be persuaded that I wanted you to escape, and that you refused.

Soc. But why, my dear Crito, should we care about the opinion of the many? Good men, and they are the only persons who are worth considering, will think of these things truly as they occurred.

Cr. But you see, Socrates, that the opinion of the many must be regarded, for what is now happening shows that they can do the greatest evil to any one who has lost their good opinion.

Soc. I only wish it were so, Crito; and that the many could do the greatest evil; for then they would also be able to do the greatest good—and what a fine thing this would be! But in reality they can do neither; for they cannot make a man either wise or foolish; and whatever they do is the result of chance.

Cr. Well, I will not dispute with you; but please to tell me, Socrates, whether you are not acting out of regard to me and your other friends: are you not afraid that if you escape from prison we may get into trouble with the informers for having stolen you away, and lose either the whole or a great part of our property; or that even a worse evil may happen to us? Now, if you fear on our account, be at ease; for in order to save you, we ought surely to run this, or even a greater risk; be persuaded, then, and do as I say.

Soc. Yes, Crito, that is one fear which you mention, but by no means the only one.

Cr. Fear not—there are persons who are willing to get you out of prison at no great cost; and as for the informers, they are far from being exorbitant in their demands—a little money will satisfy them. My means, which are certainly ample, are at your service, and if you have a scruple about spending all mine, here are strangers who will give you the use of theirs; and one of them, Simmias the Theban, has brought a large sum of money for this very purpose; and Cebes and many others are prepared to spend their money in helping you to escape. I say, therefore, do not hesitate on our account, and do not say, as you did in the court, that you will have a difficulty in knowing what to do with yourself anywhere else. For men will love you in other places to which you may go, and not in Athens only; there are friends of mine in Thessaly, if you like to go to them, who will value and protect you, and no Thessalian will give you any trouble. Nor can I think that you are at all justified, Socrates, in betraying your own life when you might be saved; in acting thus you are playing into the hands of your enemies, who are hurrying on your destruction. And further I should say that you are deserting your own children; for you might bring them up and educate them; instead of which you go away and leave them, and they will have to take their chance; and if they do not meet with the usual fate of orphans, there will be small thanks to you. No man should bring children into the world who is unwilling to persevere to the end in their nurture and education. But you appear to be choosing the easier part, not the better and manlier, which would have been more becoming in one who professes to care for virtue in all his actions, like yourself. And indeed, I am ashamed not only of you, but of us who are your friends, when I reflect that the whole business will be attributed entirely to our want of courage. The trial need never have come on, or might have been managed differently; and this last act, or crowning folly, will seem to have occurred through our negligence and cowardice, who might have saved you, if we had been good for anything; and you might have saved yourself, for there was no difficulty at all. See now, Socrates, how sad and discreditable are the consequences, both to us and you. Make up your mind then, or rather have your mind already made up, for the time of deliberation is over, and there is only one thing to be done, which must be done this very night, and if we delay at all will be no longer practicable or possible; I beseech you therefore, Socrates, be persuaded by me, and do as I say.

Soc. Dear Crito, your zeal is invaluable, if a right one; but if wrong, the greater the zeal the greater the danger; and therefore we ought to consider whether I shall or shall not do as you say. For I am and always have been one of those natures who must be guided by reason, whatever the reason may be which upon reflection appears to me to be the best; and now that this chance has befallen me, I cannot repudiate my own words: the principles which I have hitherto honoured and revered I still honour, and unless we can at once find other and better principles, I am certain not to agree with you; no, not even if the power of the multitude could inflict many more imprisonments, confiscations, deaths, frightening us like children with hobgoblin terrors. What will be the fairest way of considering the question? Shall I return to your old argument about the opinions of men?—we were saying that some of them are to be regarded, and others not. Now were we right in maintaining this before I was condemned? And has the argument which was once good now proved to be talk for the sake of talking—mere childish nonsense? That is what I want to consider with your help, Crito:—whether, under my present circumstances, the argument appears to be in any way different or not; and is to be allowed by me or disallowed. That argument, which, as I believe, is maintained by many persons of authority, was to the effect, as I was saying, that the opinions of some men are to be regarded, and of other men not to be regarded. Now you, Crito, are not going to die to-morrow—at least, there is no human probability of this—and therefore you are disinterested and not liable to be deceived by the circumstances in which you are placed. Tell me then, whether I am right in saying that some opinions, and the opinions of some men only, are to be valued, and that other opinons, and the opinions of other men, are not to be valued. I ask you whether I was right in maintaining this?

Cr. Certainly.

Soc. The good are to be regarded, and not the bad?

Cr. Yes.

Soc. And the opinions of the wise are good, and the opinions of the unwise are evil?

Cr. Certainly.

Soc. And what was said about another matter? Is the pupil who devotes himself to the practice of gymnastics supposed to attend to the praise and blame and opinion of every man, or of one man only—his physician or trainer, whoever he may be?

Cr. Of one man only.

Soc. And he ought to fear the censure and welcome the praise of that one only, and not of the many?

Cr. Clearly so.

Soc. And he ought to act and train, and eat and drink in the way which seems good to his single master who has understanding, rather than according to the opinion of all other men put together?

Cr. True.

Soc. And if he disobeys and disregards the opinion and approval of the one, and regards the opinion of the many who have no understanding, will he not suffer evil?

Cr. Certainly he will.

Soc. And what will the evil be, whither tending and what affecting, in the disobedient person?

Cr. Clearly, affecting the body; that is what is destroyed by the evil.

Soc. Very good; and is not this true, Crito, of other things which we need not separately enumerate? In questions of just and unjust, fair and foul, good and evil, which are the subjects of our present consultation, ought we to follow the opinion of the many and to fear them; or the opinion of the one man who has understanding? ought we not to fear and reverence him more than all the rest of the world: and if we desert him shall we not destroy and injure that principle in us which may be assumed to be improved by justice and deteriorated by injustice;—there is such a principle?

Cr. Certainly there is, Socrates.

Soc. Take a parallel instance:—if, acting under the advice of those who have no understanding, we destroy that which is improved by health and is deteriorated by disease, would life be worth having? And that which has been destroyed is—the body?

Cr. Yes.

Soc. Could we live, having an evil and corrupted body?

Cr. Certainly not.

Soc. And will life be worth having, if that higher part of man be destroyed, which is improved by justice and depraved by injustice? Do we suppose that principle, whatever it may be in man, which has to do with justice and injustice, to be inferior to the body?

Cr. Certainly not.

Soc. More honourable than the body?

Cr. Far more.

Soc. Then, my friend, we must not regard what the many say of us: but what he, the one man who has understanding of just and unjust, will say, and what the truth will say. And therefore you begin in error when you advise that we should regard the opinion of the many about just and unjust, good and evil, honourable and dishonourable.—'Well,' some one will say, 'but the many can kill us.'

Cr. Yes, Socrates; that will clearly be the answer.

Soc. And it is true: but still I find with surprise that the old argument is unshaken as ever. And I should like to know whether I may say the same of another proposition—that not life, but a good life, is to be chiefly valued?

Cr. Yes, that also remains unshaken.

Soc. And a good life is equivalent to a just and honourable one—that holds also?

Cr. Yes, it does.

Soc. From these premisses I proceed to argue the qustion whether I ought or ought not to try and escape without the consent of the Athenians: and if I am clearly right in escaping, then I will make the attempt; but if not, I will abstain. The other considerations which you mention, of money and loss of character and the duty of educating one's children, are, I fear, only the doctrines of the multitude, who would be as ready to restore people to life, if they were able, as they are to put them to death—and with as little reason. But now, since the argument has thus far prevailed, the only question which remains to be considered is, whether we shall do rightly either in escaping or in suffering others to aid in our escape and paying them in money and thanks, or whether in reality we shall not do rightly; and if the latter, then death or any other calamity which may ensue on my remaining here must not be allowed to enter into the calculation.

Cr. I think you are right, Socrates; how then shall we proceed?

Soc. Let us consider the matter together, and do you either refute me if you can, and I will be convinced; or else cease, my dear friend, from repeating to me that I ought to escape against the wishes of the Athenians: for I highly value your attempts to persuade me to do so, but I may not be persuaded against my own better judgment. And now please to consider my first position, and try how you can best answer me.

Cr. I will.

Soc. Are we to say that we are never intentionally to do wrong, or that in one way we ought and in another we ought not to do wrong, or is doing wrong always evil and dishonourable, as I was just now saying, and as has been already acknowledged by us? Are all our former admissions which were made within a few days to be thrown away? And have we, at our age, been earnestly discoursing with one another all our life long only to discover that we are no better than children? Or, in spite of the opinion of the many, and in spite of consequences whether better or worse, shall we insist on the truth of what was then said, that injustice is always an evil and dishonour to him who acts unjustly? Shall we say so or not?

Cr. Yes.

Soc. Then we must do no wrong?

Cr. Certainly not.

Soc. Nor when injured injure in return, as the many imagine; for we must injure no one at all?

Cr. Clearly not.

Soc. Again, Crito, may we do evil?

Cr. Surely not, Socrates.

Soc. And what of doing evil in return for evil, which is the morality of the many—is that just or not?

Cr. Not just.

Woman Playing the Flute. For the Greeks and Romans, the aesthetic and the sensuous were continuous. (Alinari/Art Resource)

Soc. For doing evil to another is the same as injuring him?

Cr. Very true.

Soc. Then we ought not to retailiate or render evil for evil to any one, whatever evil we may have suffered from him. But I would have you consider, Crito, whether you really mean what you are saying. For this opinion has never been held, and never will be held, by any considerable number of persons; and those who are agreed and those who are not agreed upon this point have no common ground, and can only despise one another when they see how widely they differ. Tell me, then, whether you agree with and assent to my first principle, that neither injury nor retaliation nor warding off evil by evil is ever right. And shall that be the premiss of our argument? Or do you decline and dissent from this? For so I have ever thought, and continue to think; but, if you are of another opinion, let me hear what you have to say. If, however, you remain of the same mind as formerly, I will proceed to the next step.

Cr. You may proceed, for I have not changed my mind.

Soc. Then I will go on to the next point, which may be put in the form of a question:—Ought a man to do what he admits to be right, or ought he to betray the right?

Cr. He ought to do what he thinks right.

Soc. But if this is true, what is the application? In leaving the prison against the will of the Athenians, do I wrong any? or rather do I not wrong those whom I ought least to wrong? Do I not desert the principles which were acknowledged by us to be just—what do you say?

Cr. I cannot tell, Socrates; for I do not know.

Soc. Then consider the matter in this way:—Imagine that I am about to play truant (you may call the proceeding by any name which you like), and the laws and the government come and interrogate me: 'Tell us, Socrates,' they say; 'what are you about? are you not going by an act of yours to overturn us—the laws, and the whole state, as far as in you lies? Do you imagine that a state can subsist and not be overthrown, in which the decisions of law have no power, but are set aside and trampled upon by individuals?' What will be our answer, Crito, to these and the like words? Any one, and especially a rhetorician, will have a good deal to say on behalf of the law which requires a sentence to be carried out. He will argue that this law should not be set aside; and shall we reply, 'Yes; but the state has injured us and given an unjust sentence.' Suppose I say that?

Cr. Very good, Socrates.

Soc. 'And was that our agreement with you?' the law would answer; 'or were you to abide by the sentence of the state?' And if I were to express my astonishment at their words, the law would probably add: 'Answer, Socrates, instead of opening your eyes—you are in the habit of asking and answering questions, Tell us,—What complaint have you to make against us which justifies you in attempting to destroy us and the state? In the first place did we not bring you into existence? Your father married your mother by our aid and begat you. Say whether you have any objection to urge against those of us who regulate marriage?' None, I should reply. 'Or against those of us who after birth regulate the nurture and education of children, in which you also were trained? Were not the laws, which have the charge of education, right in commanding your father to train you in music and gymnastic?' Right, I should reply. 'Well then, since you were brought into the world and nurtured and educated by us, can you deny in the first place that you are our child and slave, as your fathers were before you? And if this is true you are not on equal terms with us; nor can you think that you have a right to do to us what we are doing to you. Would you have any right to strike or revile or do any other evil to your father or your master, if you had one, because you have been struck or reviled by him, or received some other evil at his hands?—you would not say this? And because we think right to destroy you, do you think that you have any right to destroy us in return, and your country as far as in you lies? Will you, O professor of true virtue, pretend that you are justified in this? Has a philosopher like you failed to discover that our country is more to be valued and higher and holier far than mother or father or any ancestor, and more to be regarded in the eyes of the gods and of men of understanding? also to be soothed, and gently and reverently entreated when angry, even more than a father, and either to be persuaded, or if not persuaded, to be obeyed? And when we are punished by her, whether with imprisonment or stripes, the punishment is to be endured in silence; and if she leads us to wounds or death in battle, thither we follow as is right; neither may any one yield or retreat or leave his rank, but whether in battle or in a court of law, or in any other place, he must do what his city and his country order him; or he must change their view of what is just: and if he may do no violence to his father or mother, much less may he do violence to his country.' What answer shall we make to this, Crito? Do the laws speak truly, or do they not?

Cr. I think that they do.

Soc. Then the laws will say, 'Consider, Socrates, if we are speaking truly that in your present attempt you are going to do us an injury. For, having brought you into the world, and nurtured and educated you, and given you and every other citizen a share in every good which we had to give, we further proclaim to any Athenian by the liberty which we allow him, that if he does not like us when he has become of age and has seen the ways of the city, and made our acquaintance, he may go where he pleases and take his goods with him. None of us laws will forbid him or interfere with him. Any one who does not like us and the city, and who wants to emigrate to a colony or to any other city, may go where he likes, retaining his property. But he who has experience of the manner in which we order justice and administer the state, and still remains, has entered into an implied contract that he will do as we command him. And he who disobeys us is, as we maintain, thrice wrong; first, because in disobeying us he is disobeying his parents; secondly, because we are the authors of his education; thirdly, because he has made an agreement with us that he will duly obey our commands; and he neither obeys them nor convinces us that our commands are unjust; and we do not rudely impose them, but give him the alternative of obeying or convincing us;—that is what we offer, and he does neither.

'These are the sort of accusations to which, as we were saying, you, Socrates, will be exposed if you accomplish your intentions; you, above all other Athenians.' Suppose now I ask, why I rather than anybody else? they will justly retort upon me that I above all other men have acknowledged the agreement. 'There is clear proof,' they will say, 'Socrates, that we and the city were not displeasing to you. Of all Athenians you have been the most constant resident in the city, which, as you never leave, you may be supposed to love. For you never went out of the city either to see the games, except once when you went to the Isthmus, or to any other place unless when you were on military service; nor did you travel as other men do. Nor had you any curiosity to know other states or their laws: your affections did not go beyond us and our state; we were your special favourites, and you acquiesced in our government of you; and here in this city you begat your children, which is a proof of your satisfaction. Moreover, you might in the course of the trial, if you had liked, have fixed the penalty at banishment; the state which refuses to let you go now would have let you go then. But you pretended that you preferred death to exile, and that you were not unwilling to die. And now you have forgotten these fine sentiments, and pay no respect to us the laws, of whom you are the destroyer; and are doing what only a miserable slave would do, running away and turning your back upon the compacts and agreements which you made as a citizen. And first of all answer this very question: Are we right in saying that you agreed to be governed according to us in deed, and not in word only? Is that true or not?' How shall we answer, Crito? Must we not assent?

Cr. We cannot help it, Socrates.

Soc. Then will they not say: 'You, Socrates, are breaking the covenants and agreements which you made with us at your leisure, not in any haste or under any compulsion or deception, but after you have had seventy years to think of them, during which time you were at liberty to leave the city, if we were not to your mind, or if our covenants appeared to you to be unfair. You had your choice, and might have gone either to Lacedaemon or Crete, both which states are often praised by you for their good government, or to some other Hellenic or foreign state. Whereas you, above all other Athenians, seemed to be so fond of the state, or, in other words, of us her laws (and who would care about a state which has no laws?), that you never stirred out of her; the halt, the blind, the maimed were not more stationary in her than you were. And now you run away and forsake your agreements. Not so, Socrates, if you will take our advice; do not make yourself ridiculous by escaping out of the city.

'For just consider, if you transgress and err in this sort of way, what good will you do either to yourself or to your friends? That your friends will be driven into exile and deprived of citizenship, or will lose their property, is tolerably certain; and you yourself, if you fly to one of the neighbouring cities, as, for example, Thebes or Megara, both of which are well governed, will come to them as an enemy, Socrates, and their government will be against you, and all patriotic citizens will cast an evil eye upon you as a subverter of the laws, and you will confirm in the minds of the judges the justice of their own condemnation of you. For he who is a corrupter of the laws is more than likely to be a corrupter of the young and foolish portion of mankind. Will you then flee from well-ordered cities and virtuous men? and is existence worth having on these terms? Or will you go to them without shame, and talk to them, Socrates? And what will you say to them? What you say here about virtue and justice and institutions and laws being the best things among men? Would that be decent of you? Surely not. But if you go away from well-governed states to Crito's friends in Thessaly, where there is great disorder and licence, they will be charmed to hear the tale of your escape from prison, set off with ludicrous particulars of the manner in which you were wrapped in a goatskin or some other disguise, and metamorphosed as the manner is of runaways; but will there be no one to remind you that in your old age you were not ashamed to violate the most sacred laws from a miserable desire of a little more life? Perhaps not, if you keep them in a good temper; but if they are out of temper you will hear many degrading things; you will live, but how?—as the flatterer of all men, and the servant of all men; and doing what?—eating and drinking in Thessaly, having gone abroad in order that you may get a dinner. And where will be your fine sentiments about justice and virtue? Say that you wish to live for the sake of your children—you want to bring them up and educate them—will you take them into Thessaly and deprive them of Athenian citizenship? Is this the benefit which you will confer upon them? Or are you under the impression that they will be better cared for and educated here if you are still alive, although absent from them; for your friends will take care of them? Do you fancy that if you are an inhabitant of Thessaly they will take care of them, and if you are an inhabitant of the other world that they will not take care of them? Nay; but if they who call themselves friends are good for anything, they will—to be sure they will.

'Listen, then, Socrates, to us who have brought you up. Think not of life and children first, and of justice afterwards, but of justice first, that you may be justified before the princes of the world below. For neither will you nor any that belong to you be happier or holier or juster in this life, or happier in another, if you do as Crito bids. Now you depart in innocence, a sufferer and not a doer of evil; a victim, not of the laws but of men. But if you go forth, returning evil for evil, and injury for injury, breaking the covenants and agreements which you have made with us, and wronging those whom you ought least of all to wrong, that is to say, yourself, your friends, your country, and us, we shall be angry with you while you live, and our brethren, the laws in the world below, will receive you as an enemy; for they will know that you have done your best to destroy us. Listen, then, to us and not to Crito.'

This, dear Crito, is the voice which I seem to hear murmuring in my ears, like the sound of the flute in the ears of the mystic; that voice, I say, is humming in my ears, and prevents me from hearing any other. And I know that anything more which you may say will be vain. Yet speak, if you have anything to say.

Cr. I have nothing to say, Socrates.

Soc. Leave me then, Crito, to fulfil the will of God, and to follow whither he leads.

From the Phaedo

And now, [Socrates] said, let us begin again; and do not you answer my question in the words in which I ask it: let me have not the old safe answer of which I spoke at first, but another equally safe, of which the truth will be inferred by you from what has been just said. I mean that if any one asks you 'what that is, of which the inherence makes the body hot,' you will reply not heat (this is what I call the safe and stupid answer), but fire, a far superior answer, which we are now in a condition to give. Or if any one asks you 'why a body is diseased,' you will not say from disease, but from fever; and instead of saying that oddness is the cause of odd numbers, you will say that the monad is the cause of them: and so of things in general, as I dare say that you will understand sufficiently without my adducing any further examples.

Yes, [Cebes] said, I quite understand you.

Tell me, then, what is that of which the inherence will render the body alive?

The soul, he replied.

And is this always the case?

Yes, he said, of course.

Then whatever the soul possesses, to that she comes bearing life?

Yes, certainly.

And is there any opposite to life?

There is, he said.

And what is that?

Death.

Then the soul, as has been acknowledged, will never receive the opposite of what she brings.

Impossible, replied Cebes.

And now, he said, what did we just now call that principle which repels the even?

The odd.

And that principle which repels the musical or the just?

The unmusical, he said, and the unjust.

And what do we call that principle which does not admit of death?

The immortal, he said.

And does the soul admit of death?

No.

Then the soul is immortal?

Yes, he said.

And may we say that this has been proven?

Yes, abundantly proven, Socrates, he replied.

Supposing that the odd were imperishable, must not three be imperishable?

Of course.

And if that which is cold were imperishable, when the warm principle came attacking the snow, must not the snow have retired whole and unmelted—for it could never have perished, nor could it have remained and admitted the heat?

True, he said.

Again, if the uncooling or warm principle were imperishable, the fire when assailed by cold would not have perished or have been extinguished, but would have gone away unaffected?

Certainly, he said.

And the same may be said of the immortal: if the immortal is also imperishable, the soul when attacked by death cannot perish; for the preceding argument shows that the soul will not admit of death, or ever be dead, any more than three or the odd number will admit of the even, or fire, or the heat in the fire, of the cold. Yet a person may say: 'But although the odd will not become even at the approach of the even, why may not the odd perish and the even take the place of the odd?' Now to him who makes this objection, we cannot answer that the odd principle is imperishable; for this has not been acknowledged, but if this had been acknowledged, there would have been no difficulty in contending that at the approach of the even the odd principle and the number three took their departure; and the same argument would have held good of fire and heat and any other thing.

Very true.

And the same may be said of the immortal: if the immortal is also imperishable, then the soul will be imperishable as well as immortal; but if not, some other proof of her imperishableness will have to be given.

No other proof is needed, he said; for if the immortal, being eternal, is liable to perish, then nothing is imperishable.

Yes, replied Socrates, and yet all men will agree

From Plato, *Phaedo,* 105–118.

that God, and the essential form of life, and the immortal in general, will never perish.

Yes, all men, he said—that is true; and what is more, gods, if I am not mistaken, as well as men.

Seeing then that the immortal is indestructible, must not the soul, if she is immortal, be also imperishable?

Most certainly.

Then when death attacks a man, the mortal portion of him may be supposed to die, but the immortal retires at the approach of death and is preserved safe and sound?

True.

Then, Cebes, beyond question, the soul is immortal and imperishable, and our souls will truly exist in another world!

I am convinced, Socrates, said Cebes, and have nothing more to object; but if my friend Simmias, or any one else, has any further objection to make, he had better speak out, and not keep silence, since I do not know to what other season he can defer the discussion, if there is anything which he wants to say or to have said.

But I have nothing more to say, replied Simmias; nor can I see any reason for doubt after what has been said. But I still feel and cannot help feeling uncertain in my own mind, when I think of the greatness of the subject and the feebleness of man.

Yes, Simmias, replied Socrates, that is well said: and I may add that first principles, even if they appear certain, should be carefully considered; and when they are satisfactorily ascertained, then, with a sort of hesitating confidence in human reason, you may, I think, follow the course of the argument; and if that be plain and clear, there will be no need for any further enquiry.

Very true.

But then, O my friends, he said, if the soul is really immortal, what care should be taken of her, not only in respect of the portion of time which is called life, but of eternity! And the danger of neglecting her from this point of view does indeed appear to be awful. If death had not been the end of all, the wicked would have had a good bargain in dying, for they would have been happily quit not only of their body, but of their own evil together with their souls. But now, inasmuch as the soul is manifestly immortal, there is no release or salvation from evil except the attainment of the highest virtue and wisdom. For the soul when on her progress to the world below takes nothing with her but nurture and education; and these are said greatly to benefit or greatly to injure the departed, at the very beginning of his journey thither.

For after death, as they say, the genius of each individual, to whom he belonged in life, leads him to a certain place in which the dead are gathered together, whence after judgment has been given they pass into the world below, following the guide, who is appointed to conduct them from this world to the other: and when they have there received their due and remained their time, another guide brings them back again after many revolutions of ages. Now this way to the other world is not, as Aeschylus says in the Telephus, a single and straight path—if that were so no guide would be needed, for no one could miss it; but there are many partings of the road, and windings, as I infer from the rites and sacrifices which are offered to the gods below in places where three ways meet on earth. The wise and orderly soul follows in the straight path and is conscious of her surroundings; but the soul which desires the body, and which, as I was relating before, has long been fluttering about the lifeless frame and the world of sight, is after many struggles and many sufferings hardly and with violence carried away by her attendant genius; and when she arrives at the place where the other souls are gathered, if she be impure and have done impure deeds, whether foul murders or other crimes which are the brothers of these, and the works of brothers in crime—from that soul every one flees and turns away; no one will be her companion, no one her guide, but alone she wanders in extremity of evil until certain times are fulfilled, and when they are fulfilled, she is borne irresistibly to her own fitting habitation; as every pure and just soul which has passed through life in the company and under the guidance of the gods has also her own proper home.

Now the earth has divers wonderful regions, and is indeed in nature and extent very unlike the notions of geographers, as I believe on the authority of one who shall be nameless.

What do you mean, Socrates? said Simmias. I have myself heard many descriptions of the earth, but I do not know, and I should very much like to know, in which of these you put faith.

And I, Simmias, replied Socrates, if I had the art of Glaucus would tell you; although I know not that the art of Glaucus could prove the truth of my tale, which I myself should never be able to prove, and even if I could, I fear, Simmias, that my life would come to an end before the argument was completed. I may describe to you, however, the form and regions of the earth according to my conception of them.

That, said Simmias, will be enough.

Well then, he said, my conviction is, that the earth is a round body in the centre of the heavens, and therefore has no need of air or of any similar force to be a support, but is kept there and hindered from falling or inclining any way by the equability of the surrounding heaven and by her own equipoise. For that which, being in equipoise, is in the centre of that which is equably diffused, will not incline any way in any degree, but will always remain in the same state and not deviate. And this is my first notion.

Which is surely a correct one, said Simmias.

Also I believe that the earth is very vast, and that we who dwell in the region extending from the river Phasis to the Pillars of Heracles inhabit a small portion only about the sea, like ants or frogs about a marsh, and that there are other inhabitants of many other like places; for everywhere on the face of the earth there are hollows of various forms and sizes, into which the water and the mist and the lower air collect. But the true earth is pure and situated in the pure heaven—there are the stars also; and it is the heaven which is commonly spoken of by us as the ether, and of which our own earth is the sediment gathering in the hollows beneath. But we who live in these hollows are deceived into the notion that we are dwelling above on the surface of the earth; which is just as if a creature who was at the bottom of the sea were to fancy that he was on the surface of the water, and that the sea was the heaven through which he saw the sun and the other stars, he having never come to the surface by reason of his feebleness and sluggishness, and having never lifted up his head and seen, nor ever heard from one who had seen, how much purer and fairer the world above is than his own. And such is exactly our case: for we are dwelling in a hollow of the earth, and fancy that we are on the surface; and the air we call heaven, in which we imagine that the stars move. But the fact is, that owing to our feebleness and sluggishness, we are prevented from reaching the surface of the air: for if any man could arrive at the exterior limit, or take the wings of a bird and come to the top, then like a fish who puts his head out of the water and sees this world, he would see a world beyond; and, if the nature of man could sustain the sight, he would acknowledge that this other world was the place of the true heaven and the true light and the true earth. For our earth, and the stones, and the entire region which surrounds us, are spoilt and corroded, as in the sea all things are corroded by the brine, neither is there any noble or perfect growth, but caverns only, and sand, and an endless slough of mud; and even the shore is not to be compared to the fairer sights of this world. And still less is this our world to be compared with the other. Of that upper earth which is under the heaven, I can tell you a charming tale, Simmias, which is well worth hearing.

And we, Socrates, replied Simmias, shall be charmed to listen to you.

The tale, my friend, he said, is as follows:—In the first place, the earth, when looked at from above, is in appearance streaked like one of those balls which have leather coverings in twelve pieces, and is decked with various colours, of which the colours used by painters on earth are in a manner samples. But there the whole earth is made up of them, and they are brighter far and clearer than ours; there is a purple of wonderful lustre, also the radiance of gold, and the white which is in the earth is whiter than any chalk or snow. Of these and other colours the earth is made up, and they are more in number and fairer than the eye of man has ever seen; the very hollows (of which I was speaking) filled with air and water have a colour of their own, and are seen like light gleaming amid the diversity of the other colours, so that the whole presents a single and continuous appearance of variety in unity. And in this fair region everything that grows—trees, and flowers, and fruits—are in a like degree fairer than any here; and there are hills, having stones in them in a like degree smoother, and more transparent, and fairer in colour than our highly-valued emeralds and sardonyxes and jaspers, and other gems, which are but minute fragments of them: for there all the stones are like our precious stones, and fairer still. The reason is, that they are pure, and not, like our precious stones, infected or corroded by the corrupt briny elements which coagulate among us, and which breed foulness and disease both in earth and stones, as well as in animals and plants. They are the jewels of the upper earth, which also shines with gold and silver and the like, and they are set in the light of day and are large and abundant and in all places, making the earth a sight to gladden the beholder's eye. And there are animals and men, some in a middle region, others dwelling about the air as we dwell about the sea; others in islands which the air flows round, near the continent; and in a word, the air is used by them as the water and the sea are by us, and the ether is to them what the air is to us. Moreover, the temperament of their seasons is such that they have no disease, and live much longer than we do, and have sight and hearing and smell, and all the other senses, in far greater perfection, in the same proportion that air is purer than water or the ether than air. Also they have temples and sacred places in which the gods really dwell, and they hear their voices and receive their answers, and are conscious of them and hold converse with them; and they see the sun, moon, and stars as they truly are, and their other blessedness is of a piece with this.

Such is the nature of the whole earth, and of the things which are around the earth; and there are divers regions in the hollows on the face of the globe everywhere, some of them deeper and more extended than that which we inhabit, others deeper but with a narrower opening than ours, and some are shallower and also wider. All have numerous perforations, and there are passages broad and narrow in the interior of the earth, connecting them with one another; and there flows out of and into them, as into basins, a vast tide of water, and huge subterranean streams of perennial rivers, and springs hot and cold, and a great fire, and great rivers of fire, and streams of liquid mud, thin or thick (like the rivers of mud in Sicily, and the lava streams which follow them), and the regions about which they happen to flow are filled up with them. And there is a swinging or see-saw in the interior of the earth which moves all this up and down, and is due to the following cause:—There is a chasm which is the vastest of them all, and pierces right through the whole earth; this is that chasm which Homer describes in the words.—

> 'Far off, where is the inmost depth beneath
> the earth;'

and which he in other places, and many other poets, have called Tartarus. And the see-saw is caused by the streams flowing into and out of this chasm, and they each have the nature of the soil through which they flow. And the reason why the streams are always flowing in and out, is that the watery element has no bed or bottom, but is swinging and surging up and down, and the surrounding wind and air do the same; they follow the water up and down, hither and thither, over the earth—just as in the act of respiration the air is always in process of inhalation and exhalation;—and the wind swinging with the water in and out produces fearful and irresistible blasts: when the waters retire with a rush into the lower parts of the earth, as they are called, they flow through the earth in those regions, and fill them up like water raised by a pump, and then when they leave those regions and rush back hither, they again fill the hollows here, and when these are filled, flow through subterranean channels and find their way to their several places, forming seas, and lakes, and rivers, and springs. Thence they again enter the earth, some of them making a long circuit into many lands, others going to a few places and not so distant; and again fall into Tartarus, some at a point a good deal lower than that at which they rose, and others not much lower, but all in some degree lower than the point from which they came. And some burst forth again on the opposite side, and some on the same side, and some wind round the earth with one or many folds like the coils of a serpent, and descend as far as they can, but always return and fall into the chasm. The rivers flowing in either direction can descend only to the centre and no further, for opposite to the rivers is a precipice.

Now these rivers are many, and mighty, and diverse, and there are four principal ones, of which the greatest and outermost is that called Oceanus, which flows round the earth in a circle; and in the opposite direction flows Acheron, which passes under the earth through desert places into the Acherusian lake: this is the lake to the shores of which the souls of the many go when they are dead, and after waiting an appointed time, which is to some a longer and to some a shorter time, they are sent back to be born again as animals. The third river passes out between the two, and near the place of outlet pours into a vast region of fire, and forms a lake larger than the Mediterranean Sea, boiling with water and mud; and proceeding muddy and turbid, and winding about the earth, comes, among other places, to the extremities of the Acherusian lake, but mingles not with the waters of the lake, and after making many coils about the earth plunges into Tartarus at a deeper level. This is that Pyriphlegethon, as the stream is called, which throws up jets of fire in different parts of the earth. The fourth river goes out on the opposite side, and falls first of all into a wild and savage region, which is all of a dark blue colour, like lapis lazuli; and this is that river which is called the Stygian river, and falls into and forms the Lake Styx, and after falling into the lake and receiving strange powers in the waters, passes under the earth, winding round in the opposite direction, and comes near the Acherusian lake from the opposite side of Pyriphlegethon. And the water of this river too mingles with no other, but flows round in a circle and falls into Tartarus over against Pyriphlegethon; and the name of the river, as the poets say, is Cocytus.

Such is the nature of the other world; and when the dead arrive at the place to which the genius of each severally guides them, first of all, they have sentence passed upon them, as they have lived well and piously or not. And those who appear to have lived neither well nor ill, go to the river Acheron, and embarking in any vessels which they may find, are carried in them to the lake, and there they dwell and are purified of their evil deeds, and having suffered the penalty of the wrongs which they have done to others, they are absolved, and receive the rewards of their good deeds, each of them according to his deserts. But those who appear to be incurable by reason of the greatness of their crimes—who have committed many and terrible deeds of sacrilege, murders foul and violent, or the like—such are hurled into Tartarus which is their suitable destiny, and they never come out. Those again who have committed crimes, which, although great, are not irremediable—who in a moment of anger, for example, have done some violence to a father or a mother, and have repented for the remainder of their lives, or who have taken the life of another under the like extenuating circumstances—these are plunged into Tartarus, the pains of which they are compelled to undergo for a year, but at the end of the year the wave casts them forth—mere homicides by way of Cocytus, parricides and matricides by Pyriphlegethon—and they are borne to the Acherusian lake, and there they lift up their voices and call upon the victims whom they have slain or wronged, to have pity on them, and to be kind to them, and let them come out into the lake. And if they prevail, then they come forth and cease from their troubles; but if not, they are carried back again into Tartarus and from thence into the rivers unceasingly, until they obtain mercy from those whom they have wronged: for that is the sentence inflicted upon them by their judges. Those too who have been pre-eminent for holiness of life are released from this earthly prison, and go to their pure home which is above, and dwell in the purer earth; and of these, such as have duly purified themselves with philosophy live henceforth altogether without the body, in mansions fairer still, which may not be described, and of which the time would fail me to tell.

Wherefore, Simmias, seeing all these things, what ought not we to do that we may obtain virtue and wisdom in this life? Fair is the prize, and the hope great!

A man of sense ought not to say, nor will I be very confident, that the description which I have given of the soul and her mansions is exactly true. But I do say that, inasmuch as the soul is shown to be immortal, he may venture to think, not improperly or unworthily, that something of the kind is true. The venture is a glorious one, and he ought to comfort himself with words like these, which is reason why I lengthen out the tale. Wherefore, I say, let a man be of good cheer about his soul, who having cast away the pleasures and ornaments of the body as alien to him and working harm rather than good, has sought after the pleasures of knowledge; and has arrayed the soul, not in some foreign attire, but in her own proper jewels, temperance, and justice, and courage, and nobility, and truth—in these adorned she is ready to go on her journey to the world below, when her hour comes. You, Simmias and Cebes, and all other men, will depart at some time or other. Me already, as a tragic poet would say, the voice of fate calls. Soon I must drink the poison; and I think that I had better repair to the bath first, in order that the women may not have the trouble of washing my body after I am dead.

When he had done speaking, Crito said: And have you any commands for us, Socrates—anything to say about your children, or any other matter in which we can serve you?

Nothing particular, Crito, he replied: only, as I have always told you, take care of yourselves; that is a service which you may be ever rendering to me and mine and to all of us, whether you promise to do so or not. But if you have no thought for yourselves, and care not to walk according to the rule which I have prescribed for you, not now for the first time, however much you may profess or promise at the moment, it will be of no avail.

We will do our best, said Crito: And in what way shall we bury you?

In any way that you like; but you must get hold of me, and take care that I do not run away from you. Then he turned to us, and added with a smile:—I cannot make Crito believe that I am the same Socrates who has been talking and conducting the argument; he fancies that I am the other Socrates whom he will soon see, a dead body—and he asks, How shall he bury me? And though I have spoken many words in the endeavour to show that when I have drunk the poison I shall leave you and go to the joys of the blessed,—these words of mine, with which I was comforting you and myself, have had, as I perceive, no effect upon Crito. And therefore I want you to be surety for me to him now, as at the trial he was surety to the judges for me: but let the promise be of another sort; for he was surety for me to the judges that I would remain, and you must be my surety to him that I shall not remain, but go away and depart; and then he will suffer less at my death, and not be grieved when he sees my body being burned or buried. I would not have him sorrow at my hard lot, or say at the burial, Thus we lay out Socrates, or, Thus we follow him to the grave or bury him; for false words are not only evil in themselves, but they infect the soul with evil. Be of good cheer then, my dear Crito, and say that you are burying my body only, and do with that whatever is usual, and what you think best.

When he had spoken these words, he arose and went into a chamber to bathe; Crito followed him and told us to wait. So we remained behind, talking and thinking of the subject of discourse, and also of the greatness of our sorrow; he was like a father of whom we were being bereaved, and we were about to pass the rest of our lives as orphans. When he had taken the bath his children were brought to him—(he had two young sons and an elder one); and the women of his family also came, and he talked to them and gave them a few directions in the presence of Crito; then he dismissed them and returned to us.

Now the hour of sunset was near, for a good deal of time had passed while he was within. When he came out, he sat down with us again after his bath, but not much was said. Soon the jailer, who was the servant of the Eleven, entered and stood by him, saying:—To you, Socrates, whom I know to be the noblest and gentlest and best of all who ever came to this place, I will not impute the angry feelings of other men, who rage and swear at me, when, in obedience to the authorities, I bid them drink the poison—indeed, I am sure that you will not be angry with me; for others, as you are aware, and not I, are to blame. And so fare you well, and try to bear lightly what must needs be—you know my errand. Then bursting into tears he turned away and went out.

Socrates looked at him and said: I return your good wishes, and will do as you bid. Then turning to us, he said, How charming the man is: since I have been in prison he has always been coming to see me, and at times he would talk to me, and was as good to me as could be, and now see how generously he sorrows on my account. We must do as he says, Crito; and therefore let the cup be brought, if the poison is prepared: if not, let the attendant prepare some.

Yet, said Crito, the sun is still upon the hill-tops, and I know that many a one has taken the draught late, and after the announcement has been made to him, he has eaten and drunk, and enjoyed the society of his beloved; do not hurry—there is time enough.

Socrates said: Yes, Crito, and they of whom you speak are right in so acting, for they think that they will be gainers by the delay; but I am right in not following their example, for I do not think that I should gain anything by drinking the poison a little later; I should only be ridiculous in my own eyes for sparing and saving a life which is already forfeit. Please then to do as I say, and not to refuse me.

Crito made a sign to the servant, who was standing by; and he went out, and having been absent for some time, returned with the jailer carrying the cup of poison. Socrates said: You, my good friend, who are experienced in these matters, shall give me directions how I am to proceed. The man answered: You have only to walk about until your legs are heavy, and then to lie down, and the poison will act. At the same time he handed the cup to Socrates, who in the easiest and gentlest manner, without the least fear or change of colour or feature, looking at the man with all his eyes, Echecrates, as his manner was, took the cup and said: What do you say about making a libation out of this cup to any god? May I, or not? The man answered: We only prepare, Socrates, just so much as we deem enough. I understand, he said: but I may and must ask the gods to prosper my journey from this to the other world—even so—and so be it according to my prayer. Then raising the cup to his lips, quite readily and cheerfully he drank off the poison. And hitherto most of us had been able to control our sorrow; but now when we saw him drinking, and saw too that he had finished the draught, we could no longer forbear, and in spite of myself my own tears were flowing fast; so that I covered my face and wept, not for him, but at the thought of my own calamity in having to part from such a friend. Nor was I the first; for Crito, when he found himself unable to restrain his tears, had got up, and I followed; and at that moment, Apollodorus, who had been weeping all the time, broke out in a loud and passionate cry which made cowards of us all. Socrates alone retained his calmness: What is this strange outcry? he said. I sent away the women mainly in order that they might not misbehave in this way, for I have been told that a man should die in peace. Be quiet then, and have patience. When we heard his words we were ashamed, and refrained our tears; and he walked about until, as he said, his legs began to fail, and then he lay on his back, according to the directions, and the man who gave him the poison now and then looked at his feet and legs; and after a while he pressed his foot hard, and asked him if he could feel; and he said, No; and then his leg, and so upwards and upwards, and showed us that he was cold and stiff. And he felt them himself, and said: When the poison reaches the heart, that will be the end. He was beginning to grow cold about the groin, when he uncovered his face, for he had covered himself up, and said—they were his last words—he said: Crito, I owe a cock to Asclepius; will you remember to pay the debt? The debt shall be paid, said Crito; is there anything else? There was no answer to this question; but in a minute or two a movement was heard, and the attendants uncovered him; his eyes were set, and Crito closed his eyes and mouth.

Such was the end, Echecrates, of our friend; concerning whom I may truly say, that of all the men of his time whom I have known, he was the wisest and justest and best.

From the Symposium

When Agathon had done speaking, Aristodemus said that there was a general cheer; the young man was thought to have spoken in a manner worthy of himself, and of the god. And Socrates, looking at Eryximachus, said: Tell me, son of Acumenus, was there not reason in my fears? and was I not a true prophet when I said that Agathon would make a wonderful oration, and that I should be in a strait?

The part of the prophecy which concerns Agathon, replied Eryximachus, appears to me to be true; but not the other part—that you will be in a strait.

Why, my dear friend, said Socrates, must not I or any one be in a strait who has to speak after he has heard such a rich and varied discourse? I am especially struck with the beauty of the concluding words—who could listen to them without amazement? When I reflected on the immeasurable inferiority of my own powers, I was ready to run away for shame, if there had been a possibility of escape. For I was reminded of Gorgias, and at the end of his speech I fancied that Agathon was shaking at me the Gorginian or Gorgonian head of the great master of rhetoric, which was simply to turn me and my speech into stone, as Homer says, and strike me dumb. And then I perceived how foolish I had been in consenting to take my turn with you in praising love, and saying that I too was a master of the art, when I really had no conception how anything ought to be praised. For in my simplicity I imagined that the topics of praise should be true, and that this being presupposed, out of the true the speaker was to choose the best and set them forth in the best manner. And I felt quite proud, thinking that I knew the nature of true praise, and should speak well. Whereas I now see that the intention was to attribute to Love every species of greatness and glory, whether really belonging to him or not, without regard to truth or falsehood—that was no matter; for the original proposal seems to have been not that each of you should really praise Love, but only that

From Plato, *Symposium*, 198–212.

you should appear to praise him. And so you attribute to Love every imaginable form of praise which can be gathered anywhere; and you say that 'he is all this,' and 'the cause of all that,' making him appear the fairest and best of all to those who know him not, for you cannot impose upon those who know him. And a noble and solemn hymn of praise have you rehearsed. But as I misunderstood the nature of the praise when I said that I would take my turn, I must beg to be absolved from the promise which I made in ignorance, and which (as Euripides would say) was a promise of the lips and not of the mind. Farewell then to such a strain: for I do not praise in that way; no, indeed, I cannot. But if you like to hear the truth above love, I am ready to speak in my own manner, though I will not make myself ridiculous by entering into any rivalry with you. Say then, Phaedrus, whether you would like to have the truth about love, spoken in any words and in any order which may happen to come into my mind at the time. Will that be agreeable to you?

Aristodemus said that Phaedrus and the company bid him speak in any manner which he thought best. Then, he added, let me have your permission first to ask Agathon a few more questions, in order that I may take his admissions as the premisses of my discourse.

I grant the permission, said Phaedrus: put your questions. Socrates then proceeded as follows:—

In the magnificent oration which you have just uttered, I think that you were right, my dear Agathon, in proposing to speak of the nature of Love first and afterwards of his works—that is a way of beginning which I very much approve. And as you have spoken so eloquently of his nature, may I ask you further, Whether love is the love of something or of nothing? And here I must explain myself: I do not want you to say that love is the love of a father or the love of a mother—that would be ridiculous; but to answer as you would, if I asked is a father a father of something? to which you would find no difficulty in replying, of a son or daughter: and the answer would be right.

Very true, said Agathon.

And you would say the same of a mother?

He assented.

Yet let me ask you one more question in order to illustrate my meaning: Is not a brother to be regarded essentially as a brother of something?

Certainly, he replied.

That is, of a brother or sister?

Yes, he said.

And now, said Socrates, I will ask about Love:—Is Love of something or of nothing?

Of something, surely, he replied.

Keep in mind what this is, and tell me what I want to know—whether Love desires that of which love is.

Yes, surely.

And does he possess, or does he not possess, that which he loves and desires?

Probably not, I should say.

Nay, replied Socrates, I would have you consider whether 'necessarily' is not rather the word. The inference that he who desires something is in want of something, and that he who desires nothing is in want of nothing, is in my judgment, Agathon, absolutely and necessarily true. What do you think?

I agree with you, said Agathon.

Very good. Would he who is great, desire to be great, or he who is strong, desire to be strong?

That would be inconsistent with our previous admissions.

True. For he who is anything cannot want to be that which he is?

Very true.

And yet, added Socrates, if a man being strong desired to be strong, or being swift desired to be swift, or being healthy desired to be healthy, in that case he might be thought to desire something which he already has or is. I give the example in order that we may avoid misconception. For the possessors of these qualities, Agathon, must be supposed to have their respective advantages at the time, whether they choose or not; and who can desire that which he has? Therefore, when a person says, I am well and wish to be well, or I am rich and wish to be rich, and I desire simply to have what I have—to him we shall reply: 'You, my friend, having wealth and health and strength, want to have the continuance of them; for at this moment, whether you choose or no, you have them. And when you say, I desire that which I have and nothing else, is not your meaning that you want to have what you now have in the future?' He must agree with us—must he not?

He must, replied Agathon.

Then, said Socrates, he desires that what he has at present may be preserved to him in the future, which is equivalent to saying that he desires something which is non-existent to him, and which as yet he has not got.

Very true, he said.

Then he and every one who desires, desires that which he has not already, and which is future and not present, and which he has not, and is not, and of which he is in want;—these are the sort of things which love and desire seek?

Very true, he said.

Then now, said Socrates, let us recapitulate the argument. First, is not love of something, and of something too which is wanting to a man?

Yes, he replied.

Remember further what you said in your speech, or if you do not remember I will remind you: you said that the love of the beautiful set in order the empire of the gods, for that of deformed things there is no love—did you not say something of that kind?

Yes, said Agathon.

Yes, my friend, and the remark was a just one. And if this is true, Love is the love of beauty and not of deformity?

He assented.

And the admission has been already made that Love is of something which a man wants and has not?

True, he said.

Then Love wants and has not beauty?

Certainly, he replied.

And would you call that beautiful which wants and does not possess beauty?

Certainly not.

Then would you still say that love is beautiful?

Agathon replied: I fear that I did not understand what I was saying.

You made a very good speech, Agathon, replied Socrates; but there is yet one small question which I would fain ask:—Is not the good also the beautiful?

Yes.

Then in wanting the beautiful, love wants also the good?

I cannot refute you, Socrates, said Agathon:—Let us assume that what you say is true.

Say rather, beloved Agathon, that you cannot refute the truth; for Socrates is easily refuted.

And now, taking my leave of you, I will rehearse a tale of love which I heard from Diotima of Mantineia, a woman wise in this and in many other kinds of knowledge, who in the days of old, when the Athenians offered sacrifice before the coming of the plague, delayed the disease ten years. She was my instructress in the art of love, and I shall repeat to you what she said to me, beginning with the admissions made by Agathon, which are nearly if not quite the same which I made to the wise woman when she questioned me: I think that this will be the easiest way, and I shall take both parts myself as well as I can. As you, Agathon, suggested, I must speak first of the being and nature of Love, and then of his works. First I said to her in nearly the same words which he used to me, that Love was a mighty god, and likewise fair; and she proved to me as I proved to him that, by my own showing, Love was neither fair nor good. 'What do you mean, Diotima,' I said, 'is love then evil and foul?' 'Hush,' she cried; 'must that be foul which is not fair?' 'Certainly,' I said. 'And is that which is not wise, ignorant? do you not see that there is a mean between wisdom and ignorance?' 'And what may that be?' I said. 'Right opinion,' she replied; 'which, as you know, being incapable of giving a reason, is not knowledge (for how can knowledge be devoid of reason? nor again, ignorance, for neither can ignorance attain the truth), but is clearly something which is a mean between ignorance and wisdom.' 'Quite true,' I replied. 'Do not then insist,' she said, 'that what is not fair is of necessity foul, or what is not good evil; or infer that because love is not fair and good he is therefore foul and evil; for he is in a mean between them.' 'Well,' I said, 'Love is surely admitted by all to be a great god.' 'By those who know or by those who do not know?' 'By all.' 'And how, Socrates,' she said with a smile, 'can Love be acknowledged to be a great god by those who say that he is not a god at all?' 'And who are they?' I said. 'You and I are two of them,' she replied. 'How can that be?' I said. 'It is quite intelligible,' she replied; 'for you yourself would acknowledge that the gods are happy and fair—of course you would—would you dare to say that any god was not?' 'Certainly not,' I replied. 'And you mean by the happy, those who are the possessors of things good or fair?' 'Yes.' 'And you admitted that Love, because he was in want, desires those good and fair things of which he is in want?' 'Yes, I did.' 'But how can he be a god who has no portion in what is either good or fair?' 'Impossible.' 'Then you see that you also deny the divinity of Love.'

'What then is Love?' I asked; 'Is he mortal?' 'No.' 'What then?' 'As in the former instance, he is neither mortal nor immortal, but in a mean between the two.' 'What is he, Diotima?' 'He is a great spirit (δχίμων), and like all spirits he is intermediate between the divine and the mortal.' 'And what,' I said, 'is his power?' 'He interprets,' she replied, 'between gods and men, conveying and taking across to the gods the prayers and sacrifices of men, and to men the commands and replies of the gods; he is the mediator who spans the chasm which divides them, and therefore in him all is bound together, and through him the arts of the prophet and the priest, their sacrifices and mysteries and charms, and all prophecy and incantation, find their way. For God mingles not with man; but through Love all the intercourse and converse of god with man, whether awake or asleep, is carried on. The wisdom which understands this is spiritual; all other wisdom, such as that of arts and handicrafts, is mean and vulgar. Now these spirits or intermediate powers are many and diverse, and one of them is Love.' 'And who,' I said, 'was his father, and who his mother?' 'The tale,' she said, 'will take time; nevertheless I will tell you. On the birthday of Aphrodite there was a feast of the gods, at which the god Poros or Plenty, who is the son of Metis or Discretion, was one of the guests. When the feast was over, Penia or Poverty, as the manner is on such occasions, came about the doors to beg. Now Plenty, who was the worse for nectar (there was no wine in those days), went into the garden of Zeus and fell into a heavy sleep; and Poverty considering her own straitened circumstances, plotted to have a child by him, and accordingly she lay down at his side and conceived Love, who partly because he is naturally a lover of the beautiful, and because Aphrodite is herself beautiful, and also because he was born on her birthday, is her follower and attendant. And as his parentage is, so also are his fortunes. In the first place he is always poor, and anything but tender and fair, as the many imagine him; and he is rough and squalid, and has no shoes, nor a house to dwell in; on the bare earth exposed he lies under the open heaven, in the streets, or at the doors of houses, taking his rest; and like his mother he is always in distress. Like his father too, whom he also partly resembles, he is always plotting against the fair and good; he is bold, enterprising, strong, a mighty hunter, always weaving some intrigue or other, keen in the pursuit of wisdom, fertile in resources: a philosopher at all times, terrible as an enchanter, sorcerer, sophist. He is by nature neither mortal nor immortal, but alive and flourishing at one moment when he is in plenty, and dead at another moment, and again alive by reason of his father's nature. But that which is always flowing in is always flowing out, and so he is never in want and never in wealth; and, further, he is in a mean between ignorance and knowledge. The truth of the matter is this: No god is a philosopher or seeker after wisdom, for he is wise already; nor does any man who is wise seek after wisdom. Neither do the ignorant seek after wisdom. For herein is the evil of ignorance, that he who is neither good nor wise is nevertheless satisfied with himself: he has no desire for that of which he feels no want.' 'But who then, Diotima,' I said, 'are the lovers of wisdom, if they are neither the wise nor the foolish?' 'A child may answer that question,' she replied; 'they are those who are in a mean between the two; Love is one of them. For wisdom is a most beautiful thing, and Love is of the beautiful; and therefore Love is also a philosopher or lover of wisdom, and being a lover of wisdom is in a mean between the wise and the ignorant. And of this too his birth is the cause; for his father is wealthy and wise, and his mother poor and foolish. Such, my dear Socrates, is the nature of the spirit Love. The error in your conception of him was very natural, and as I imagine from what you say, has arisen out of a confusion of love and the beloved, which made you think that love was all beautiful. For the beloved is the truly beautiful, and delicate, and perfect, and blessed; but the principle of love is another nature, and is such as I have described.'

I said: 'O thou stranger woman, thou sayest well; but, assuming Love to be such as you say, what is the use of him to men?' 'That, Socrates,' she replied, 'I will attempt to unfold: of his nature and birth I have already spoken; and you acknowledge that love is of the beautiful. But some one will say: Of the beautiful in what, Socrates and Diotima?—or rather let me put the question more clearly, and ask: When a man loves the beautiful, what does he desire?' I answered her 'That the beautiful may be his.' 'Still,' she said, 'the answer suggests a further question: What is given by the possession of beauty?' 'To what you have asked,' I replied, 'I have no answer ready.' 'Then,' she said, 'let me put the word "good" in the place of the beautiful, and repeat the question once more: If he who loves loves the good, what is it then that he loves?' 'The possession of the good,' I said. 'And what does he gain who possesses the good?' 'Happiness,' I replied; 'there is less difficulty in answering that question.' 'Yes,' she said, 'the happy are made happy by the aquisition of good things. Nor is there any need to ask why a man desires happiness; the answer is already final.' 'You are right,' I said. 'And is this wish and this desire common to all? and do all men always desire their own good, or only some men?—what say you?' 'All men,' I replied; 'the desire is common to all.' 'Why, then,' she rejoined, 'are not all men, Socrates, said to love, but only some of them? whereas you say that all men are always loving the same things.' 'I myself wonder,' I said, 'why this is.' 'There is nothing to wonder at,' she replied; 'the reason is that one part of love is separated off and receives the name of the whole, but the other parts have other names.' 'Give an illustration,' I said. She answered me as follows: 'There is poetry, which, as you know, is complex and manifold. All creation or passage of non-being into being is poetry or making, and the processes of all art are creative; and the masters of arts are all poets or makers.' 'Very true.' 'Still,' she said, 'you know that they are not called poets, but have other names; only that portion of the art which is separated off from the rest, and is concerned with music and metre, is termed poetry, and they who possess poetry in this sense of the word are called poets.' 'Very true,' I said. 'And the same holds of love. For you may say generally that all desire of good and happiness is only the great and subtle power of love; but they who are drawn towards him by any other path, whether the path of money-making or gymnastics or philosophy, are not called lovers—the name of the whole is appropriated to those whose affection takes one form only—they alone are said to love, or to be lovers.' 'I dare say,' I replied, 'that you are right.' 'Yes,' she added, 'and you hear people say that lovers are seeking for their other half; but I say that they are seeking neither for the half of themselves, nor for the whole, unless the half or the whole be also a good. And they will cut off their own hands and feet and cast them away, if they are evil: for they love not what is their own, unless perchance there be some one who calls what belongs to him the good, and what belongs to another the evil. For there is nothing which men love but the good. Is there anything?' 'Certainly, I should say, that there is nothing.' 'Then,' she said, 'the simple truth is, that men love the good.' 'Yes,' I said. 'To which must be added that they love the possession of the good?' 'Yes, that must be added.' 'And not only the possession, but the everlasting possession of the good?' 'That must be added too.' 'Then love,' she said, 'may be described generally as the love of the everlasting possession of the good?' 'That is most true.'

'Then if this be the nature of love, can you tell me further,' she said, 'what is the manner of the pursuit? what are they doing who show all this eagerness and heat which is called love? and what is the object which they have in view? Answer me.' 'Nay, Diotima,' I replied, 'if I had known, I should not have wondered at your wisdom, neither should I have come to learn from you about this very matter.' 'Well,' she said, 'I will teach you:—The object which they have in view is birth in beauty, whether of body or soul.' 'I do not understand you,' I said; 'the oracle requires an explanation.' 'I will make my meaning clearer,' she replied. 'I mean to say, that all men are bringing to the birth in their bodies and in their souls. There is a certain age at which human nature is desirous of procreation—procreation which must be in beauty and not in deformity; and this procreation is the union of man and woman, and is a divine thing; for conception and generation are an immortal principle in the mortal creature, and in the inharmonious they can never be. But the deformed is always inharmonious with the divine, and the beautiful harmonious. Beauty, then, is the destiny or goddess of parturition who presides at birth, and therefore, when approaching beauty, the conceiving power is propitious, and diffusive, and benign, and begets and bears fruit: at the sight of ugliness she frowns and contracts and has a sense of pain, and turns away, and shrivels up, and not without a pang refrains from conception. And this is the reason why, when the hour of conception arrives, and the teeming nature is full, there is such a flutter and ecstasy about beauty whose approach is the alleviation of the pain of travail. For love, Socrates, is not, as you imagine, the love of the beautiful only.' 'What then?' 'The love of generation and of birth in beauty.' 'Yes,' I said. 'Yes, indeed,' she replied. 'But why of generation?' 'Because to the mortal creature, generation is a sort of eternity and immortality,' she replied; 'and if, as has been already admitted, love is of the everlasting possession of the good, all men will necessarily desire immortality together with good: Wherefore love is of immortality.'

All this she taught me at various times when she spoke of love. And I remember her once saying to me, 'What is the cause, Socrates, of love, and the attendant desire? See you not how all animals, birds, as well as beasts, in their desire of procreation, are in agony when they take the infection of love, which begins with the desire of union; whereto is added the care of offspring, on whose behalf the weakest are ready to battle against the strongest even to the uttermost, and to die for them, and will let themselves be tormented with hunger or suffer anything in order to maintain their young. Man may be supposed to act thus from reason; but why should animals have these passionate feelings? Can you tell me why?' Again I replied that I did not know. She said to me: 'And do you expect ever to become a master in the art of love, if you do not know this?' 'But I have told you already, Diotima, that my ignorance is the reason why I come to you; for I am conscious that I want a teacher; tell me then the cause of this and of the other mysteries of love.' 'Marvel not,' she said, 'if you believe that love is of the immortal, as we have several times acknowledged; for here again, and on the same principle too, the mortal nature is seeking as far as is possible to be everlasting and immortal: and this is only to be attained by generation, because generation always leaves behind a new existence in the place of the old. Nay even in the life of the same individual there is succession and not absolute unity: a man is called the same, and yet in the short interval which elapses between youth and age, and in which every animal is said to have life and identity, he is undergoing a perpetual process of loss and reparation—hair, flesh, bones, blood, and the whole body are always changing. Which is true not only of the body, but also of the soul, whose habits, tempers, opinions, desires, pleasures, pains, fears, never remain the same in any one of us, but are always coming and going; and equally true of knowledge, and what is still more surprising to us mortals, not only do the sciences in general spring up and decay, so that in respect of them we are never the same; but each of them individually experiences a like change. For what is implied in the word "recollection," but the departure of knowledge, which is ever being forgotten, and is renewed and preserved by recollection, and appears to be the same although in reality new, according to that law of succession by which all mortal things are preserved, not absolutely the same, but by substitution, the old worn-out mortality leaving another new and similar existence behind—unlike the divine, which is always the same and not another? And in this way, Socrates, the mortal body, or mortal anything, partakes of immortality; but the immortal in another way. Marvel not then at the love which all men have of their offspring; for that universal love and interest is for the sake of immortality.'

I was astonished at her words, and said: 'Is this really true, O thou wise Diotima?' And she answered with all the authority of an accomplished sophist: 'Of that, Socrates, you may be assured;—think only of the ambition of men, and you will wonder at the senselessness of their ways, unless you consider how they are stirred by the love of an immortality of fame. They are ready to run all risks greater far than they would have run for their children, and to spend money and undergo any sort of toil, and even to die, for the sake of leaving behind them a name which shall be eternal. Do you imagine that Alcestis would have died to save Admetus, or Achilles to avenge Patroclus, or your own Codrus in order to preserve the kingdom for his sons, if they had not imagined that the memory of their virtues, which still survives among us, would be immortal? Nay,' she said, 'I am persuaded that all men do all things, and the better they are the more they do them, in hope of the glorious fame of immortal virtue; for they desire the immortal.

'Those who are pregnant in the body only, betake themselves to women and beget children—this is the character of their love; their offspring, as they hope, will preserve their memory and give them the blessedness and immortality which they desire in the future. But souls which are pregnant—for there certainly are men who are more creative in their souls than in their bodies—conceive that which is proper for the soul to conceive or contain. And what are these conceptions?—wisdom and virtue in general. And such creators are poets and all artists who are deserving of the name inventor. But the greatest and fairest sort of wisdom by far is that which is concerned with the ordering of states and families, and which is called temperance and justice. And he who in youth has the seed of these implanted in him and is himself inspired, when he comes to maturity desires to beget and generate. He wanders about seeking beauty that he may beget offspring—for in deformity he will beget nothing—and naturally embraces the beautiful rather than the deformed body; above all when he finds a fair and noble and well-nurtured soul, he embraces the two in one person, and to such an one he is full of speech about virtue and the nature and pursuits of a good man; and he tries to educate him; and at the touch of the beautiful which is ever present to his memory, even when absent, he brings forth that which he had conceived long before, and in company with him tends that which he brings forth; and they are married by a far nearer tie and have a closer friendship than those who beget mortal children, for the children who are their common offspring are fairer and more immortal. Who, when he thinks of Homer and Hesiod and other great poets, would not rather have their children than ordinary human ones? Who would not emulate them in the creation of children such as theirs, which have preserved their memory and given them everlasting glory? Or who would not have such children as Lycurgus left behind him to be the saviours, not only of Lacedaemon, but of Hellas, as one may say? There is Solon, too, who is the revered father of Athenian laws; and many others there are in many other places, both among Hellenes and barbarians, who have given to the world many noble works, and have been the parents of virtue of every kind; and many temples have been raised in their honour for the sake of children such as theirs; which were never raised in honour of any one, for the sake of his mortal children.

'These are the lesser mysteries of love, into which even you, Socrates, may enter; to the greater and more hidden ones which are the crown of these, and to which, if you pursue them in a right spirit, they will lead, I know not whether you will be able to attain. But I will do my utmost to inform you, and do you follow if you can. For he who would proceed aright in this matter should begin in youth to visit beautiful forms; and first, if he be guided by his instructor aright, to love one such form only—out of that he should create fair thoughts; and soon he will of himself perceive that the beauty of one form is akin to the beauty of another; and then if beauty of form in general is his pursuit, how foolish would he be not to recognize that the beauty in every form is one and the same! And when he perceives this he will abate his violent love of the one, which he will despise and deem a small thing, and will become a lover of all beautiful forms; in the next stage he will consider that the beauty of the mind is more honourable than the beauty of the outward form. So that if a virtuous soul have but a little comeliness, he will be content to love and tend him, and will search out and bring to the birth thoughts which may improve the young, until he is compelled to contemplate and see the beauty of institutions and laws, and to understand that the beauty of them all is of one family, and that personal beauty is a trifle; and after laws and institutions he will go on to the sciences, that he may see their beauty, being not like a servant in love with the beauty of one youth or man or institution, himself a slave mean and narrow-minded, but drawing towards and contemplating the vast sea of beauty, he will create many fair and noble thoughts and notions in boundless love of wisdom; until on that shore he grows and waxes strong, and at last the vision is revealed to him of a single science, which is the science of beauty everywhere. To this I will proceed; please to give me your very best attention:

'He who has been instructed thus far in the things of love, and who has learned to see the beautiful in due order and succession, when he comes toward the end will suddenly perceive a nature of wondrous beauty (and this, Socrates, is the final cause of all our former toils)—a nature which in the first place is everlasting, not growing and decaying, or waxing and waning; secondly, not fair in one point of view and foul in another, or at one time or in one relation or at one place fair, at another time or in another relation or at another place foul, as if fair to some and foul to others, or in the likeness of a face or hands or any other part of the bodily frame, or in any form of speech or knowledge, or existing in any other being, as for example, in an animal, or in heaven, or in earth, or in any other place; but beauty absolute, separate, simple, and everlasting, which without diminution and without increase, or any change, is imparted to the ever-growing and perishing beauties of all other things. He who from these ascending under the influence of true love, begins to perceive that beauty, is not far from the end. And the true order of going, or being led by another, to the things of love, is to begin from the beauties of earth and mount upwards for the sake of that other beauty, using these as steps only, and from one going on to two, and from two to all fair forms, and from fair forms to fair practices, and from fair practices to fair notions, until from fair notions he arrives at the notion of absolute beauty, and at last knows what the essence of beauty is. This, my dear Socrates,' said the stranger of Mantineia, 'is that life above all others which man should live, in the contemplation of beauty absolute; a beauty which if you once beheld, you would see not to be after the measure of gold, and garments, and fair boys and youths, whose presence now entrances you; and you and many a one would be content to live seeing them only and conversing with them without meat or drink, if that were possible—you only want to look at them and to be with them. But what if man had eyes to see the true beauty—the divine beauty, I mean, pure and clear and unalloyed, not clogged with the pollutions of mortality and all the colours and vanities of human life—thither looking, and holding converse with the true beauty simple and divine? Remember how in that communion only, beholding beauty with the eye of the mind, he will be enabled to bring forth, not images of beauty, but realities (for he has hold not of an image but of a reality), and bringing forth and nourishing true virtue to become the friend of God and be immortal, if mortal man may. Would that be an ignoble life?'

Such, Phaedrus—and I speak not only to you, but to all of you—were the words of Diotima; and I am persuaded of their truth. And being persuaded of them, I try to persuade others, that in the attainment of this end human nature will not easily find a helper better than love. And therefore, also, I say that every man ought to honour him as I myself honour him, and walk in his ways, and exhort others to do the same, and praise the power and spirit of love according to the measure of my ability now and ever.

The words which I have spoken, you, Phaedrus, may call an encomium of love, or anything else which you please.

SOPHOCLES

Sophocles, Aeschylus, and Euripides were the three great tragedians of the ancient Greek world. Born in 496 B.C., Sophocles lived for 90 years a fruitful, creative, and successful life, dying just two years before the fall of Athens to Sparta in 404 B.C., the end of the Peloponnesian War. Regarded by Aristotle as the master of theatrical tragedy, Sophocles is best known for his play Oedipus Rex, *which chronicles the fated downfall of a king who kills his father and marries his mother, unaware that he is their son. In the following selection from* Antigone, *Sophocles pits the defense of the civil law by Creon against that of an alleged higher law as invoked by Antigone, who wishes to bury her dead brother, fallen in battle against the state. The issue of the conflict between personal values and the law of the state is, of course, one that remains active to this very day.*

From Antigone

GUARD: O king, against nothing should men pledge their word; for the afterthought belies the first intent. I could have vowed that I should not soon be here again,—scared by thy threats, with which I had just been lashed: but,—since the joy that surprises and transcends our hopes is like in fulness to no other pleasure,—I have come, though 'tis in breach of my sworn oath, bringing this maid; who was taken showing grace to the dead. This time there was no casting of lots; no, this luck hath fallen to me, and to none else. And now, sire,

---

take her thyself, question her, examine her, as thou wilt; but I have a right to free and final quittance of this trouble.

CREON: And thy prisoner here—how and whence hast thou taken her?

GUARD: She was burying the man; thou knowest all.

CREON: Dost thou mean what thou sayest? Dost thou speak aright?

GUARD: I saw her burying the corpse that thou hadst forbidden to bury. Is that plain and clear?

CREON: And how was she seen? how taken in the act?

GUARD: It befell on this wise. When we had come to the place,—with those dread menaces of thine upon us,—we swept away all the dust that covered the corpse, and bared the dank body well; and then sat us down on the brow of the hill, to windward, heedful that the smell from him should not strike us; every man was wide awake, and kept his neighbour alert with torrents of threats, if anyone should be careless of this task.

So went it, until the sun's bright orb stood in mid heaven, and the heat began to burn: and then suddenly a whirlwind lifted from the earth a storm of dust, a trouble in the sky, and filled the plain, marring all the leafage of its woods; and the wide air was choked therewith: we closed our eyes, and bore the plague from the gods.

And when, after a long while, this storm had passed, the maid was seen; and she cried aloud with the sharp cry of a bird in its bitterness,—even as when, within the empty nest, it sees the bed stripped of its nestlings. So she also, when she saw the corpse bare, lifted up a voice of wailing, and called down curses on the doers of that deed. And straightway she brought thirsty dust in her hands; and from a shapely ewer of bronze, held high, with thrice-poured drink-offering she crowned the dead.

We rushed forward when we saw it, and at once closed upon our quarry, who was in no wise dismayed. Then we taxed her with her past and present doings; and she stood not on denial of aught,—at once to my joy and to my pain. To have escaped from ills one's self is a great joy; but 'tis painful to bring friends to ill. Howbeit, all such things are of less account to me than mine own safety.

CREON: Thou—thou whose face is bent to earth—dost thou avow, or disavow, this deed?

ANTIGONE: I avow it; I make no denial.

CREON (*to* GUARD): Thou canst betake thee whither thou wilt, free and clear of a grave charge.

(*Exit* GUARD)

(To ANTIGONE): Now, tell me thou—not in many words, but briefly—knewest thou that an edict had forbidden this?

ANTIGONE: I knew it: could I help it? It was public.

CREON: And thou didst indeed dare to transgress that law?

ANTIGONE: Yes; for it was not Zeus that had published me that edict; not such are the laws set among men by the Justice who dwells with the gods below; nor deemed I that thy decrees were of such force, that a mortal could override the unwritten and unfailing statutes of heaven. For their life is not of to-day or yesterday, but from all time, and no man knows when they were first put forth.

Not through dread of any human pride could I answer to the gods for breaking *these*. Die I must,—I knew that well (how should I not?)—even without thy edicts. But if I am to die before my time, I count that a gain: for when any one lives, as I do, compassed about with evils, can such an one find aught but gain in death?

So for me to meet this doom is trifling grief; but if I had suffered my mother's son to lie in death an unburied corpse, that would have grieved me; for this, I am not grieved. And if my present deeds are foolish in thy sight, it may be that a foolish judge arraigns my folly.

LEADER OF THE CHORUS: The maid shows herself passionate child of passionate sire, and knows not how to bend before troubles.

CREON: Yet I would have thee know that o'er-stubborn spirits are most often humbled; 'tis the stiffest iron, baked to hardness in the fire, that thou shalt oftenest see snapped and shivered; and I have known horses that show temper brought to order by a little curb; there is no room for pride when thou art thy neighbour's slave.—This girl was already versed in insolence when she transgressed the laws that had been set forth; and, that done, lo, a second insult,—to vaunt of this, and exult in her deed.

Now verily I am no man, she is the man, if this victory shall rest with her, and bring no penalty. No! be she sister's child, or nearer to me in blood than any that worships Zeus at the altar of our house,—she and her kinsfolk shall not avoid a doom most dire; for indeed I charge that other with a like share in the plotting of this burial.

And summon her—for I saw her e'en now within,—raving, and not mistress of her wits. So oft, before the deed, the mind stands self-convicted in its treason, when folks are plotting mischief in the dark. But verily this, too, is hateful,—when one who hath been caught in wickedness then seeks to make the crime a glory.

ANTIGONE: Wouldst thou do more than take and slay me?

CREON: No more, indeed; having that, I have all.

ANTIGONE: Why then dost thou delay? In thy discourse there is nought that pleases me,—never may there be!—and so my words must needs be unpleasing to thee. And yet, for glory—whence could I have won a nobler, than by giving burial to mine own brother? All here would own that they thought it well, were not their lips sealed by fear. But royalty, blest in so much besides, hath the power to do and say what it will.

CREON: Thou differest from all these Thebans in that view.

ANTIGONE: These also share it; but they curb their tongues for thee.

CREON: And art thou not ashamed to act apart from them?

ANTIGONE: No; there is nothing shameful in piety to a brother.

CREON: Was it not a brother, too, that died in the opposite cause?

ANTIGONE: Brother by the same mother and the same sire.

CREON: Why, then, dost thou render a grace that is impious in his sight?

ANTIGONE: The dead man will not say that he so deems it.

CREON: Yea, if thou makest him but equal in honour with the wicked.

ANTIGONE: It was his brother, not his slave, that perished.

CREON: Wasting this land; while *he* fell as its champion.

ANTIGONE: Nevertheless, Hades desires these rites.

CREON: But the good desires not a like portion with the evil.

ANTIGONE: Who knows but this seems blameless in the world below?

CREON: A foe is never a friend—not even in death.

ANTIGONE: 'Tis not my nature to join in hating, but in loving.

ARISTOPHANES

One of the great comic writers of the Greek classical world, Aristophanes lived from ca. 448 until some time after 388 B.C. No person or institution was too sacred for him to lampoon with ironic humor, slapstick, or profound mockery. One of his most famous comedies, The Clouds, *is an attack on the Sophists and on Socrates. Produced in 423 B.C.,* The Clouds *was poorly received by the Athenian audience, for its caricature of Socrates was too excessive, even for the work of Aristophanes. Yet the high seriousness in the activity of the Sophists, as well as that of Socrates, was appropriately lampooned. Some 25 years later, Socrates is quoted in Plato's* Apology *as saying that the satire by Aristophanes had seriously damaged his reputation. It may be, however, that Socrates was better served by this critique than the philosophers of our own time, who are rarely rewarded with either satire or praise.*

From The Clouds

SOCRATES *(coming out)*: By Respiration, the Breath of Life! By Chaos! By the Air! I have never seen a man so gross, so inept, so stupid, so forgetful. All the little quibbles, which I teach him, he forgets even before he has learnt them. Yet I will not give it up, I will make him come out here into the open air. Where are you, Strepsiades? Come, bring your couch out here.

STREPSIADES *(from within)*: But the bugs will not allow me to bring it.

SOCRATES: Have done with such nonsense! place it there and pay attention.

STREPSIADES *(coming out, with the bed)*: Well, here I am.

SOCRATES: Good! Which science of all those you have never been taught, do you wish to learn first? The measures, the rhythms or the verses?

STREPSIADES: Why, the measures; the flour dealer cheated me out of two *choenixes* the other day.

SOCRATES: It's not about that I ask you, but which, according to you, is the best measure, the trimeter or the tetrameter?

STREPSIADES: The one I prefer is the semisextarius .

SOCRATES: You talk nonsense, my good fellow.

STREPSIADES: I will wager your tetrameter is the semisextarius.

SOCRATES: Plague seize the dunce and the fool! Come, perchance you will learn the rhythms quicker.

STREPSIADES: Will the rhythms supply me with food?

SOCRATES: First they will help you to be pleasant in company, then to know what is meant by enhoplian rhythm and what by the dactylic.

STREPSIADES: Of the dactyl? I know that quite well.

SOCRATES: What is it then, other than this finger here?

STREPSIADES: Formerly, when a child, I used this one.

SOCRATES: You are as low-minded as you are stupid.

STREPSIADES: But, wretched man, I do not want to learn all this.

SOCRATES: Then what *do* you want to know?

STREPSIADES: Not that, not that, but the art of false reasoning.

SOCRATES: But you must first learn other things. Come, what are the male quadrupeds?

STREPSIADES: Oh! I know the males thoroughly. Do you take me for a fool then? The ram, the buck, the bull, the dog, the pigeon.

SOCRATES: Do you see what you are doing; is not the female pigeon called the same as the male?

STREPSIADES: How else? Come now!

SOCRATES: How else? With you then it's pigeon and pigeon!

STREPSIADES: That's right, by Posidon! but what names do you want me to give them?

SOCRATES: Term the female pigeonnette and the male pigeon.

STREPSIADES: Pigeonnette! hah! by the Air! That's splendid! for that lesson bring out your kneading-trough and I will fill him with flour to the brim.

SOCRATES: There you are wrong again; you make *trough* masculine and it should be feminine.

STREPSIADES: What? if I say, *him,* do I make the *trough* masculine?

SOCRATES: Assuredly! would you not say him for Cleonymus?

STREPSIADES: Well?

SOCRATES: Then trough is of the same gender as Cleonymus?

STREPSIADES: My good man! Cleonymus never had a kneading-trough; he used a round mortar for the purpose. But come, tell me what I *should* say!

SOCRATES: For trough you should say *her* as you would for Sostraté.

STREPSIADES: *Her?*

SOCRATES: In this manner you make it truly female.

STREPSIADES: That's it! *Her* for trough and *her* for Cleonymus.

SOCRATES: Now I must teach you to distinguish the masculine proper names from those that are feminine.

STREPSIADES: Ah! I know the female names well.

SOCRATES: Name some then.

STREPSIADES: Lysilla, Philinna, Clitagora, Demetria.

SOCRATES: And what are masculine names?

STREPSIADES: They are countless—Philoxenus, Melesias, Amynias.

SOCRATES: But, wretched man, the last two are not masculine.

STREPSIADES: You do not count them as masculine?

SOCRATES: Not at all. If you met Amynias, how would you hail him?

STREPSIADES: How? Why, I should shout, "Hi, there, Amynia!"

SOCRATES: Do you see? it's a female name that you give him.

STREPSIADES: And is it not rightly done, since he refuses military service? But what use is there in learning what we all know?

SOCRATES: You know nothing about it. Come, lie down there.

STREPSIADES: What for?

SOCRATES: Ponder awhile over matters that interest you.

STREPSIADES: Oh! I pray you, not there! but, if I must lie down and ponder, let me lie on the ground.

SOCRATES: That's out of the question. Come! on the couch!

STREPSIADES *(as he lies down)*: What cruel fate! What a torture the bugs will this day put me to!

(Socrates turns aside.)

CHORUS *(singing)*: Ponder and examine closely, gather your thoughts together, let your mind turn to every side of things; if you meet with a difficulty, spring quickly to some other idea; above all, keep your eyes away from all gentle sleep.

STREPSIADES *(singing)*: Ow, Wow, Wow, Wow is me!

Chorus *(singing)*: What ails you? why do you cry so?

Strepsiades: Oh! I am a dead man! Here are these cursed Corinthians advancing upon me from all corners of the couch; they are biting me, they are gnawing at my sides, they are drinking all my blood, they are yanking off my balls, they are digging into my arse, they are killing me!

Leader of the Chorus: Not so much wailing and clamour, if you please.

Strepsiades: How can I obey? I have lost my money and my complexion, my blood and my slippers, and to cap my misery, I must keep awake on this couch, when scarce a breath of life is left in me.

(A brief interval of silence ensues.)

Socrates: Well now! what are you doing? are you reflecting?

Strepsiades: Yes, by Posidon!

Socrates: What about?

Strepsiades: Whether the bugs will entirely devour me.

Socrates: May death seize you, accursed man!

(He turns aside again.)

Strepsiades: Ah! it has already.

Socrates: Come, no giving way! Cover up your head; the thing to do is to find an ingenious alternative.

Strepsiades: An alternative! ah! I only wish one would come to me from within these coverlets!

(Another interval of silence ensues.)

Socrates: Wait! let us see what our fellow is doing! Ho! you, are you asleep?

Strepsiades: No, by Apollo!

Socrates: Have you got hold of anything?

Strepsiades: No, nothing whatever.

Socrates: Nothing at all?

Strepsiades: No, nothing except my tool, which I've got in my hand.

Socrates: Aren't you going to cover your head immediately and ponder?

Strepsiades: On what? Come, Socrates, tell me.

Socrates: Think first what you want, and then tell me.

Strepsiades: But I have told you a thousand times what I want. Not to pay any of my creditors.

Socrates: Come, wrap yourself up; concentrate your mind, which wanders too lightly; study every detail, scheme and examine thoroughly.

Strepsiades: Alas! Alas!

Socrates: Keep still, and if any notion troubles you, put it quickly aside, then resume it and think over it again.

STREPSIADES: *My dear* little Socrates!

SOCRATES: What is it, old greybeard?

STREPSIADES: I have a scheme for not paying my debts.

SOCRATES: Let us hear it.

STREPSIADES: Tell me, if I purchased a Thessalian witch, I could make the moon descend during the night and shut it, like a mirror, into a round box and there keep it carefully. . . .

SOCRATES: How would you gain by that?

STREPSIADES: How? why, if the moon did not rise, I would have no interest to pay.

SOCRATES: Why so?

STREPSIADES: Because money is lent by the month.

SOCRATES: Good! but I am going to propose another trick to you. If you were condemned to pay five talents, how would you manage to quash that verdict? Tell me.

STREPSIADES: How? how? I don't know, I must think.

SOCRATES: Do you always shut your thoughts within yourself? Let your ideas fly in the air, like a may-bug, tied by the foot with a thread.

STREPSIADES: I have found a very clever way to annul that conviction; you will admit that much yourself.

SOCRATES: What is it?

STREPSIADES: Have you ever seen a beautiful, transparent stone at the druggists' with which you may kindle fire?

SOCRATES: You mean a crystal lens.

STREPSIADES: That's right. Well, now if I placed myself with this stone in the sun and a long way off from the clerk, while he was writing out the conviction, I could make all the wax, upon which the words were written, melt.

SOCRATES: Well thought out, by the Graces!

STREPSIADES: Ah! I am delighted to have annulled the decree that was to cost me five talents.

SOCRATES: Come, take up this next question quickly.

STREPSIADES: Which?

SOCRATES: If, when summoned to court, you were in danger of losing your case for want of witnesses, how would you make the conviction fall upon your opponent?

STREPSIADES: That's very simple and easy.

SOCRATES: Let me hear.

STREPSIADES: This way. If another case had to be pleaded before mine was called, I should run and hang myself.

SOCRATES: You talk rubbish!

STREPSIADES: Not so, by the gods! if I were dead, no action could lie against me.

SOCRATES: You are merely beating the air. Get out! I will give you no more lessons.

STREPSIADES *(imploringly)*: Why not? Oh! Socrates! in the name of the gods!

SOCRATES: But you forget as fast as you learn. Come, what was the thing I taught you first? Tell me.

STREPSIADES: Ah! let me see. What was the first thing? What was it then? Ah! that thing in which we knead the bread, oh! my god! what do you call it?

SOCRATES: Plague take the most forgetful and silliest of old addlepates!

STREPSIADES: Alas! what a calamity! what will become of me? I am undone if I do not learn how to ply my tongue. Oh! Clouds! give me good advice.

CHORUS-LEADER: Old man, we counsel you, if you have brought up a son, to send him to learn in your stead.

STREPSIADES: Undoubtedly I have a son, as well endowed as the best, but he is unwilling to learn. What will become of me?

CHORUS-LEADER: And you don't make him obey you?

STREPSIADES: You see, he is big and strong; moreover, through his mother he is a descendant of those fine birds, the race of Coesyra. Nevertheless, I will go and find him, and if he refuses, I will turn him out of the house. Go in, Socrates, and wait for me awhile.

(SOCRATES *goes into the Thoughtery,* STREPSIADES *into his own house.*)

CHORUS *(singing)*: Do you understand, Socrates, that thanks to us you will be loaded with benefits? Here is a man, ready to obey you in all things. You see how he is carried away with admiration and enthusiasm. Profit by it to clip him as short as possible; fine chances are all too quickly gone.

STREPSIADES *(coming out of his house and pushing his son in front of him)*: No, by the Clouds! you stay here no longer; go and devour the ruins of your uncle Megacles' fortune.

PHIDIPPIDES: Oh! my poor father! what has happened to you? By the Olympian Zeus! you are no longer in your senses!

STREPSIADES: Look! "the Olympian Zeus." Oh! you fool! to believe in Zeus at your age!

PHIDIPPIDES: What is there in that to make you laugh?

STREPSIADES: You are then a tiny little child, if you credit such antiquated rubbish! But come here, that I may teach you; I will tell you something very necessary to know to be a man; but do not repeat it to anybody.

PHIDIPPIDES: Tell me, what is it?

STREPSIADES: Just now you swore by Zeus.

PHIDIPPIDES: Sure I did.

STREPSIADES: Do you see how good it is to learn? Phidippides, there is no Zeus.

PHIDIPPIDES: What is there then?

STREPSIADES: The Whirlwind has driven out Zeus and is King now.

PHIDIPPIDES: What drivel!

STREPSIADES: You must realize that it is true.

PHIDIPPIDES: And who says so?

STREPSIADES: Socrates, the Melian, and Chaerephon, who knows how to measure the jump of a flea.

PHIDIPPIDES: Have you reached such a pitch of madness that you believe those bilious fellows?

STREPSIADES: Use better language, and do not insult men who are clever and full of wisdom, who, to economize, never shave, shun the gymnasia and never go to the baths, while you, you only await my death to eat up my wealth. But come, come as quickly as you can to learn in my stead.

PHIDIPPIDES: And what good can be learnt of them?

STREPSIADES: What good indeed? Why, all human knowledge. Firstly, you will know yourself grossly ignorant. But await me here awhile.

(He goes back into his house.)

PHIDIPPIDES: Alas! what is to be done? Father has lost his wits. Must I have him certificated for lunacy, or must I order his coffin?

STREPSIADES *(returning with a bird in each hand)*: Come! what kind of bird is this? Tell me.

PHIDIPPIDES: A pigeon.

STREPSIADES: Good! And this female?

PHIDIPPIDES: A pigeon.

STREPSIADES: The same for both? You make me laugh! In the future you must call this one a pigeonnette and the other a pigeon.

PHIDIPPIDES: A pigeonnette! These then are the fine things you have just learnt at the school of these sons of Earth!

STREPSIADES: And many others; but what I learnt I forgot at once, because I am too old.

PHIDIPPIDES: So this is why you have lost your cloak?

STREPSIADES: I have not lost it, I have consecrated it to Philosophy.

PHIDIPPIDES: And what have you done with your sandals, you poor fool?

STREPSIADES: If I have lost them, it is for what was necessary, just as Pericles did. But come, move yourself, let us go in; if necessary, do wrong to obey your father. When you were six years old and still lisped, I was the one who obeyed you. I remember at the feasts of Zeus you had a consuming wish for a little chariot and I bought it for you with the first obolus which I received as a juryman in the courts.

PHIDIPPIDES: You will soon repent of what you ask me to do.

STREPSIADES: Oh! now I am happy! He obeys. *(loudly)* Come, Socrates, come! Come out quick! Here I am bringing you my son; he refused, but I have persuaded him.

SOCRATES: Why, he is but a child yet. He is not used to these baskets, in which we suspend our minds.

PHIDIPPIDES: To make you better used to them, I would you were hung.

STREPSIADES: A curse upon you! you insult your master!

SOCRATES: "I would you were hung!" What a stupid speech! and so emphatically spoken! How can one ever get out of an accusation with such a tone, summon witnesses or touch or convince? And yet when we think Hyperbolus learnt all this for one talent!

STREPSIADES: Rest undisturbed and teach him. He has a most intelligent nature. Even when quite little he amused himself at home with making houses, carving boats, constructing little chariots of leather, and understood wonderfully how to make frogs out of pomegranate rinds. Teach him both methods of reasoning, the strong and also the weak, which by false arguments triumph over the strong; if not the two, at least the false, and that in every possible way.

SUGGESTIONS FOR FURTHER READING

Dover, Kenneth. *The Greeks.* Austin: University of Texas Press, 1980.

Guthrie, W. K. C. *A History of Greek Philosophy,* Vol. 3. Cambridge: Cambridge University Press, 1969.

Jaeger, Werner. *Paideia,* Vol. 1. New York: Oxford University Press, 1945.

Levin, Richard, ed. *The Question of Socrates.* New York: Harcourt, Brace and World, 1961.

Spiegelberg, Herbert, ed. *The Socratic Engima.* Indianapolis: Bobbs-Merrill, 1964.

Taylor, A. E. *Socrates.* Garden City, New York: Doubleday–Anchor, 1953.

Untersteiner, Mario. *The Sophists.* Oxford: Basil Blackwell, 1954.

Versényi, Laszlo. *Socratic Humanism.* New Haven: Yale University Press, 1963.

Vlastos, Gregory, ed. *The Philosophy of Socrates.* Garden City, New York: Doubleday–Anchor, 1971.

Plato: Philosophy as Imagination

Plato (ca. 429–347 B.C.) was born of distinguished Athenian parents. After the death of Socrates in 399 B.C., Plato went to Megara, and he subsequently traveled to many places, including Egypt, Italy, and Sicily. Sometime after 387 B.C., Plato founded his Academy, in which he taught for the rest of his life. The most famous student and "research associate" at the Academy was Aristotle, who was a member for 20 years.

During the decade between 367 and 357 B.C., Plato made two trips to Syracuse in Sicily, where he attempted to structure his ideal of the philosopher-king in the person of Dionysius II. Unfortunately, Plato's plans went awry, and he became caught up in considerable local political intrigue, leading, at one point, to brief imprisonment. Some commentators trace both the detailed pragmatic character and the religious rigidity of the *Laws*, Plato's late dialogue, to his disappointing experiences in Syracuse.

Although there exists doubt about some of Plato's writings, we are confident that at least two dozen dialogues are genuine. The term "dialogue" is somewhat misleading, for the *Apology* is more a report of Socrates' trial and the later "dialogues" have very little dramatic or interpersonal transaction. Scholars have divided Plato's writings into several different chronological arrangements. A division into three periods will suffice here. The first or early period includes the following dialogues: the *Apology, Lysis, Ion, Crito, Laches, Euthyphro, Charmides, Hippias Major* and *Hippias Minor, Protagoras, Euthydemus, Meno,* and *Gorgias.* The second or middle period includes the *Phaedo, Symposium, Phaedrus,* and the *Republic.* The third or late period features the *Sophist, Statesman, Philebus, Politicus, Timaeus, Theatetus,* and the *Laws.*

With Plato, the often brilliant but tentative gropings of the Pre-Socratic philosophers are brought to a mature form, in both literary and argumentative style. His dramatic style in the early dialogues enables us to discover philosophical inquiry in its richest form. In his later works, Plato bequeaths a powerful and imaginative philosophical vision, which has been the seedbed of speculation for all subsequent centuries in western civilization. The outline of Plato's philosophical doctrine is quite straightforward, yet the texture of its exposition is subtle and complex.

Plato believed that we know more than we should, yet less than we can. By this Plato means that we are embodied creatures who are trapped by the deceptions of our senses. Nonetheless, we know more than our single sense impressions tell us, such that we can speak of "chair" and "table," although our senses give us the experience of this chair and that table. Our access to concepts, universals, and classes convinces Plato that we are not limited to the knowledge of sense impressions. The task before us is, through philosophical education, to approximate so far as we can knowledge of the "forms" (*eidai*). Plato envisions us as being prisoners in a cave, wherein we see only the shadows of reality. So conditioned are we that attempts to teach us of another, real world are met with cynicism and even violence. Only philosophical education, especially in its dialectical form of argument, can break us from this mind-set and free us to seek the meaning of the "forms," which enable us to know in the deepest and most profound sense the meaning of good, beauty, and truth.

The selections that follow provide the major themes of Plato's doctrine. The *Meno* tells us his belief that true knowledge can be recollected (*anamnesis*). The material from the *Republic* presents his analysis of the hierarchy of knowledge as found in his allegory of the line, his theory of forms, and his description of our plight in the allegory of the cave. We find also his doctrine of the philosopher-king as one method of assuring a creative body politic. Finally, in the *Timaeus* we have Plato's description of the beginning of the world, a description reminiscent of the efforts of the Pre-Socratics.

PLATO

Meno

Meno. Can you tell me, Socrates, whether virtue is acquired by teaching or by practice; or if neither by teaching nor practice, then whether it comes to man by nature, or in what other way?

Socrates. O Meno, there was a time when the Thessalians were famous among the other Hellenes only for their riches and their riding; but now, if I am not mistaken, they are equally famous for their wisdom, especially at Larisa, which is the native city of your friend Aristippus. And this is Gorgias' doing; for when he came there, the flower of the Aleuadae, among them your admirer Aristippus, and the other chiefs of the Thessalians, fell in love with his wisdom. And he has taught you the habit of answering questions in a grand and bold style, which becomes those who know, and is the style in which he himself answers all comers; and any Hellene who likes may ask him anything. How different is our lot! my dear Meno. Here at Athens there is a dearth of the commodity, and all wisdom seems to have emigrated from us to you. I am certain that if you were to ask any Athenian whether virtue was natural or acquired, he would laugh in your face, and say: 'Stranger, you have far too good an opinion of me, if you think that I can answer your question. For I literally do not know what virtue is, and much less whether it is acquired by teaching or not.' And I myself, Meno, living as I do in this region of poverty, am as poor as the rest of the world; and I confess with shame that I know literally nothing about virtue; and when I do not know the 'quid' of anything how can I know the 'quale'? How, if I knew nothing at all of Meno, could I tell if he was fair, or the opposite of fair; rich and noble, or the reverse of rich and noble? Do you think that I could?

Men. No, indeed. But are you in earnest, Socrates,

Plato, *Meno,* complete.

in saying that you do not know what virtue is? And am I to carry back this report of you to Thessaly?

Soc. Not only that, my dear boy, but you may say further that I have never known of any one else who did, in my judgment.

Men. Then you have never met Gorgias when he was at Athens?

Soc. Yes, I have.

Men. And did you not think that he knew?

Soc. I have not a good memory, Meno, and therefore I cannot now tell what I thought of him at the time. And I dare say that he did know, and that you know what he said: please, therefore, to remind me of what he said; or, if you would rather, tell me your own view; for I suspect that you and he think much alike.

Men. Very true.

Soc. Then as he is not here, never mind him, and do you tell me: By the gods, Meno, be generous, and tell me what you say that virtue is; for I shall be truly delighted to find that I have been mistaken, and that you and Gorgias do really have this knowledge; although I have been just saying that I have never found anybody who had.

Men. There will be no difficulty, Socrates, in answering your question. Let us take first the virtue of a man—he should know how to administer the state, and in the administration of it to benefit his friends and harm his enemies; and he must also be careful not to suffer harm himself. A woman's virtue, if you wish to know about that, may also be easily described: her duty is to order her house, and keep what is indoors, and obey her husband. Every age, every condition of life, young or old, male or female, bond or free, has a different virtue: there are virtues numberless, and no lack of definitions of them; for virtue is relative to the actions and ages of each of us in all that we do. And the same may be said of vice, Socrates.

Soc. How fortunate I am, Meno! When I ask you for one virtue, you present me with a swarm of them, which are in your keeping. Suppose that I carry on the figure of the swarm, and ask of you, What is the nature of the bee? and you answer that there are many kinds of bees, and I reply: But do bees differ as bees, because there are many and different kinds of them; or are they not rather to be distinguished by some other quality, as for example beauty, size, or shape? How would you answer me?

Men. I should answer that bees do not differ from one another, as bees.

Soc. And if I went on to say: That is what I desire to know, Meno; tell me what is the quality in which they do not differ, but are all alike;—would you be able to answer?

Men. I should.

Soc. And so of the virtues, however many and different they may be, they have all a common nature which makes them virtues; and on this he who would answer the question, 'What is virtue?' would do well to have his eye fixed: Do you understand?

Men. I am beginning to understand; but I do not as yet take hold of the question as I could wish.

Soc. When you say, Meno, that there is one virtue of a man, another of a woman, another of a child, and so on, does this apply only to virtue, or would you say the same of health, and size, and strength? Or is the nature of health always the same, whether in man or woman?

Men. I should say that health is the same, both in man and woman.

Soc. And is not this true of size and strength? If a woman is strong, she will be strong by reason of the same form and of the same strength subsisting in her which there is in the man. I mean to say that strength, as strength, whether of man or woman, is the same. Is there any difference?

Men. I think not.

Soc. And will not virtue, as virtue, be the same, whether in a child or in a grown-up person, in a woman or in a man?

Men. I cannot help feeling, Socrates, that this case is different from the others.

Soc. But why? Were you not saying that the virtue of a man was to order a state, and the virtue of a woman was to order a house?

Men. I did say so.

Soc. And can either house or state or anything be well ordered without temperance and without justice?

Men. Certainly not.

Soc. Then they who order a state or a house temperately or justly order them with temperance and justice?

Men. Certainly.

Soc. Then both men and women, if they are to be good men and women, must have the same virtues of temperance and justice?

Men. True.

Soc. And can either a young man or an elder one be good, if they are intemperate and unjust?

Men. They cannot.

Soc. They must be temperate and just?

Men. Yes.

Soc. Then all men are good in the same way, and by participation in the same virtues?

Men. Such is the inference.

Soc. And they surely would not have been good in the same way, unless their virtue has been the same?

Men. They would not.

Soc. Then now that the sameness of all virtue has been proven, try and remember what you and Gorgias say that virtue is.

Men. Will you have one definition of them all?

Soc. That is what I am seeking.

Men. If you want to have one definition of them all, I know not what to say, but that virtue is the power of governing mankind.

Soc. And does this definition of virtue include all virtue? Is virtue the same in a child and in a slave, Meno? Can the child govern his father, or the slave his master; and would he who governed be any longer a slave?

Men. I think not, Socrates.

Soc. No, indeed; there would be small reason in that. Yet once more, fair friend; according to you, virtue is 'the power of governing;' but do you not add 'justly and not unjustly'?

Men. Yes, Socrates; I agree there; for justice is virtue.

Soc. Would you say 'virtue,' Meno, or 'a virtue'?

Men. What do you mean?

Soc. I mean as I might say about anything; that a round, for example, is 'a figure' and not simply 'figure,' and I should adopt this mode of speaking, because there are other figures.

Men. Quite right; and that is just what I am saying about virtue—that there are other virtues as well as justice.

Soc. What are they? tell me the names of them, as I would tell you the names of the other figures if you asked me.

Men. Courage and temperance and wisdom and magnanimity are virtues; and there are many others.

Soc. Yes, Meno; and again we are in the same case: in searching after one virtue we have found many, though not in the same way as before; but we have been unable to find the common virtue which runs through them all.

Men. Why, Socrates, even now I am not able to follow you in the attempt to get at one common notion of virtue as of other things.

Soc. No wonder; but I will try to get nearer if I can, for you know that all things have a common notion. Suppose now that some one asked you the question which I asked before: Meno, he would say, what is figure? And if you answered 'roundness,' he would reply to you, in my way of speaking, by asking whether you would say that roundness is 'figure' or 'a figure;' and you would answer 'a figure.'

Men. Certainly.

Soc. And for this reason—that there are other figures?

Men. Yes.

Soc. And if he proceeded to ask, What other figures are there? you would have told him.

Men. I should.

Soc. And if he similarly asked what colour is, and you answered whiteness, and the questioner rejoined, Would you say that whiteness is colour or a colour? you would reply, A colour, because there are other colours as well.

Men. I should.

Soc. And if he had said, Tell me what they are?—you would have told him of other colours which are colours just as much as whiteness.

Men. Yes.

Soc. And suppose that he were to pursue the matter in my way, he would say: Ever and anon we are landed in particulars, but this is not what I want; tell me then, since you call them by a common name, and say that they are all figures, even when opposed to one another, what is that common nature which you designate as figure—which contains straight as well as round, and is no more one than the other—that would be your mode of speaking?

Men. Yes.

Soc. And in speaking thus, you do not mean to say that the round is round any more than straight, or the straight any more straight than round?

Men. Certainly not.

Soc. You only assert that the round figure is not more a figure than the straight, or the straight than the round?

Men. Very true.

Soc. To what then do we give the name of figure? Try and answer. Suppose that when a person asked you this question either about figure or colour, you were to reply, Man, I do not understand what you want, or know what you are saying; he would look rather astonished and say: Do you not understand that I am looking for the 'simile in multis'? And then he might put the question in another form: Meno, he might say, what is that 'simile in multis' which you call figure, and which includes not only round and straight figures, but all? Could you not answer that question, Meno? I wish that you would try; the attempt will be good practice with a view to the answer about virtue.

Men. I would rather that you should answer, Socrates.

Soc. Shall I indulge you?

Men. By all means.

Soc. And then you will tell me about virtue?

Men. I will.

Soc. Then I must do my best, for there is a prize to be won.

Men. Certainly.

Soc. Well, I will try and explain to you what figure is. What do you say to this answer?—Figure is the only thing which always follows colour. Will you be satisfied with it, as I am sure that I should be, if you would let me have a similar definition of virtue?

Men. But, Socrates, it is such a simple answer.

Soc. Why simple?

Men. Because, according to you, figure is that which always follows colour.

(*Soc.* Granted.)

Men. But if a person were to say that he does not know what colour is, any more than what figure is—what sort of answer would you have given him?

Soc. I should have told him the truth. And if he were a philosopher of the eristic and antagonistic sort, I should say to him: You have my answer, and if I am wrong, your business is to take up the argument and refute me. But if we were friends, and were talking as you and I are now, I should reply in a milder strain and more in the dialectician's vein; that is to say, I should not only speak the truth, but I should make use of premisses which the person interrogated would be willing to admit. And this is the way in which I shall endeavour to approach you. You will acknowledge, will you not, that there is such a thing as an end, or termination, or extremity?—all which words I use in the same sense, although I am aware that Prodicus might draw distinctions about them: but still you, I am sure, would speak of a thing as ended or terminated—that is all which I am saying—not anything very difficult.

Men. Yes, I should; and I believe that I understand your meaning.

Soc. And you would speak of a surface and also of a solid, as for example in geometry.

Men. Yes.

Soc. Well then, you are now in a condition to understand my definition of figure. I define figure to be that in which the solid ends; or, more concisely, the limit of solid.

Men. And now, Socrates, what is colour?

Soc. You are outrageous, Meno, in thus plaguing a poor old man to give you an answer, when you will not take the trouble of remembering what is Gorgias' definition of virtue.

Men. When you have told me what I ask, I will tell you, Socrates.

Soc. A man who was blindfolded has only to hear you talking, and he would know that you are a fair creature and have still many lovers.

Men. Why do you think so?

Soc. Why, because you always speak in imperatives: like all beauties when they are in their prime, you are tyrannical; and also, as I suspect, you have found out that I have a weakness for the fair, and therefore to humour you I must answer.

Men. Please do.

Soc. Would you like me to answer you after the manner of Gorgias, which is familiar to you?

Men. I should like nothing better.

Soc. Do not he and you and Empedocles say that there are certain effluences of existence?

Men. Certainly.

Soc. And passages into which and through which the effluences pass?

Men. Exactly.

Soc. And some of the effluences fit into the passages, and some of them are too small or too large?

Men. True.

Soc. And there is such a thing as sight?

Men. Yes.

Soc. And now, as Pindar says, 'read my meaning:'—colour is an effluence of form, commensurate with sight, and palpable to sense.

Men. That, Socrates, appears to me to be an admirable answer.

Soc. Why, yes, because it happens to be one which you have been in the habit of hearing: and your wit will have discovered, I suspect, that you may explain in the same way the nature of sound and smell, and of many other similar phenomena.

Men. Quite true.

Soc. The answer, Meno, was in the orthodox

solemn vein, and therefore was more acceptable to you than the other answer about figure.

Men. Yes.

Soc. And yet, O son of Alexidemus, I cannot help thinking that the other was the better; and I am sure that you would be of the same opinion, if you would only stay and be initiated, and were not compelled, as you said yesterday, to go away before the mysteries.

Men. But I will stay, Socrates, if you will give me many such answers.

Soc. Well then, for my own sake as well as for yours, I will do my very best; but I am afraid that I shall not be able to give you very many as good: and now, in your turn, you are to fulfil your promise, and tell me what virtue is in the universal; and do not make a singular into a plural, as the facetious say of those who break a thing, but deliver virtue to me whole and sound, and not broken into a number of pieces: I have given you the pattern.

Men. Well, then, Socrates, virtue, as I take it, is when he, who desires the honourable, is able to provide it for himself; so the poet says, and I say too—

> 'Virtue is the desire of things honourable and
> the power of attaining them.'

Soc. And does he who desires the honourable also desire the good?

Men. Certainly.

Soc. Then are there some who desire the evil and others who desire the good? Do not all men, my dear sir, desire good?

Men. I think not.

Soc. There are some who desire evil?

Men. Yes.

Soc. Do you mean that they think the evils which they desire, to be good; or do they know that they are evil and yet desire them?

Men. Both, I think.

Soc. And do you really imagine, Meno, that a man knows evils to be evils and desires them notwithstanding?

Men. Certainly I do.

Soc. And desire is of possession?

Men. Yes, of possession.

Soc. And does he think that the evils will do good to him who possesses them, or does he know that they will do him harm?

Men. There are some who think that the evils will do them good, and others who know that they will do them harm.

Soc. And, in your opinion, do those who think that they will do them good know that they are evils?

Men. Certainly not.

Soc. Is it not obvious that those who are ignorant of their nature do not desire them; but they desire what they suppose to be goods although they are really evils; and if they are mistaken and suppose the evils to be goods they really desire goods?

Men. Yes, in that case.

Soc. Well, and do those who, as you say, desire evils, and think that evils are hurtful to the possessor of them, know that they will be hurt by them?

Men. They must know it.

Soc. And must they not suppose that those who are hurt are miserable in proportion to the hurt which is inflicted upon them?

Men. How can it be otherwise?

Soc. But are not the miserable ill-fated?

Men. Yes, indeed.

Soc. And does any one desire to be miserable and ill-fated?

Men. I should say not, Socrates.

Soc. But if there is no one who desires to be miserable, there is no one, Meno, who desires evil; for what is misery but the desire and possession of evil?

Men. That appears to be the truth, Socrates, and I admit that nobody desires evil.

Soc. And yet, were you not saying just now that virtue is the desire and power of attaining good?

Men. Yes, I did say so.

Soc. But if this be affirmed, then the desire of good is common to all, and one man is no better than another in that respect?

Men. True.

Soc. And if one man is not better than another in desiring good, he must be better in the power of attaining it?

Men. Exactly.

Soc. Then, according to your definition, virtue would appear to be the power of attaining good?

Men. I entirely approve, Socrates, of the manner in which you now view this matter.

Soc. Then let us see whether what you say is true from another point of view; for very likely you may be right:—You affirm virtue to be the power of attaining goods?

Men. Yes.

Soc. And the goods which you mean are such as health and wealth and the possession of gold and silver, and having office and honour in the state—those are what you would call goods?

Men. Yes, I should include all those.

Soc. Then, according to Meno, who is the hereditary friend of the great king, virtue is the power of getting silver and gold; and would you add that they must be gained piously, justly, or do you deem this to be of no consequence? And is any mode of acquisition, even if unjust and dishonest, equally to be deemed virtue?

Men. Not virtue, Socrates, but vice.

Soc. Then justice or temperance or holiness, or some other part of virtue, as would appear, must accompany the acquisition, and without them the mere acquisition of good will not be virtue.

Men. Why, how can there be virtue without these?

Soc. And the non-acquisition of gold and silver in a dishonest manner for oneself or another, or in other words the want of them, may be equally virtue?

Men. True.

Soc. Then the acquisition of such goods is no more virtue than the non-acquisition and want of them, but whatever is accompanied by justice or honesty is virtue, and whatever is devoid of justice is vice.

Men. It cannot be otherwise, in my judgment.

Soc. And were we not saying just now that justice, temperance, and the like, were each of them a part of virtue?

Men. Yes.

Soc. And so, Meno, this is the way in which you mock me.

Men. Why do you say that, Socrates?

Soc. Why, because I asked you to deliver virtue into my hands whole and unbroken, and I gave you a pattern according to which you were to frame your answer; and you have forgotten already, and tell me that virtue is the power of attaining good justly, or with justice; and justice you acknowledge to be a part of virtue.

Men. Yes.

Soc. Then it follows from your own admissions, that virtue is doing what you do with a part of virtue; for justice and the like are said by you to be parts of virtue.

Men. What of that?

Soc. What of that! Why, did not I ask you to tell me the nature of virtue as a whole? And you are very far from telling me this; but declare every action to be virtue which is done with a part of virtue; as though you had told me and I must already know the whole of virtue, and this too when frittered away into little pieces. And, therefore, my dear Meno, I fear that I must begin again and repeat the same question: What is virtue? for otherwise, I can only say, that every action done with a part of virtue is virtue; what else is the meaning of saying that every action done with justice is virtue? Ought I not to ask the question over again; for can any one who does not know virtue know a part of virtue?

Men. No: I do not say that he can.

Soc. Do you remember how, in the example of figure, we rejected any answer given in terms which were as yet unexplained or unadmitted?

Men. Yes, Socrates; and we were quite right in doing so.

Soc. But then, my friend, do not suppose that we can explain to any one the nature of virtue as a whole through some unexplained portion of virtue, or anything at all in that fashion; we should only have to ask over again the old question, What is virtue? Am I not right?

Men. I believe that you are.

Soc. Then begin again, and answer me, What, according to you and your friend Gorgias, is the definition of virtue?

Men. O Socrates, I used to be told, before I knew you, that you were always doubting yourself and making others doubt; and now you are casting your spells over me, and I am simply getting bewitched and enchanted, and am at my wits' end. And if I may venture to make a jest upon you, you seem to me both in your appearance and in your power over others to be very like the flat torpedo fish, who torpifies those who come near him and touch him, as you have now torpified me, I think. For my soul and my tongue are really torpid, and I do not know how to answer you; and though I have been delivered of an infinite variety of speeches about virtue before now, and to many persons—and very good ones they were, as I thought—at this moment I cannot even say what virtue is. And I think that you are very wise in not voyaging and going away from home, for if you did in other places as you do in Athens, you would be cast into prison as a magician.

Soc. You are a rogue, Meno, and had all but caught me.

Men. What do you mean, Socrates?

Soc. I can tell why you made a simile about me.

Men. Why?

Soc. In order that I might make another simile about you. For I know that all pretty young gentlemen like to have pretty similes made about them—as well they may—but I shall not return the compliment. As to my being a torpedo, if the torpedo is torpid as well as the cause of torpidity in others, then indeed I am a torpedo, but not otherwise; for I perplex others, not because I am clear, but because I am utterly perplexed myself. And now I know not what virtue is, and you seem to be in the same case, although you did once perhaps know before you touched me. However, I have no objection to join with you in the enquiry.

Men. And how will you enquire, Socrates, into that which you do not know? What will you put forth as the subject of enquiry? And if you find what you want, how will you ever know that this is the thing which you did not know?

Soc. I know, Meno, what you mean; but just see what a tiresome dispute you are introducing. You argue that a man cannot enquire either about that which he knows, or about that which he does not know; for if he knows, he has no need to enquire; and if not, he cannot; for he does not know the very subject about which he is to enquire.

Men. Well, Socrates, and is not the argument sound?

Soc. I think not.

Men. Why not?

Soc. I will tell you why: I have heard from certain wise men and women who spoke of things divine that—

Men. What did they say?

Soc. They spoke of a glorious truth, as I conceive.

Men. What was it? and who were they?

Soc. Some of them were priests and priestesses, who had studied how they might be able to give a reason of their profession: there have been poets also, who spoke of these things by inspiration, like Pindar, and many others who were inspired. And they say—mark, now, and see whether their words are true—they say that the soul of man is immortal, and at one time has an end, which is termed dying, and at another time is born again, but is never destroyed. And the moral is, that a man ought to live always in perfect holiness. '*For in the ninth year Persephone sends the souls of those from whom she has received the penalty of ancient crime back again from beneath into the light of the sun above, and these are they who become noble kings and mighty men and great in wisdom and are called saintly heroes in after ages.*' The soul, then, as being immortal, and having been born again many times, and having seen all things that exist, whether in this world or in the world below, has knowledge of them all; and it is no wonder that she should be able to call to remembrance all that she ever knew about virtue, and about everything; for as all nature is akin, and the soul has learned all things, there is no difficulty in her eliciting or as men say learning, out of a single recollection all the rest, if a man is strenuous and does not faint; for all enquiry and all learning is but recollection. And therefore we ought not to listen to this sophistical argument about the impossibility of enquiry: for it will make us idle, and is sweet only to the sluggard; but the other saying will make us active and inquisitive. In that confiding, I will gladly enquire with you into the nature of virtue.

Men. Yes, Socrates; but what do you mean by saying that we do not learn, and that what we call learning is only a process of recollection? Can you teach me how this is?

Soc. I told you, Meno, just now that you were a rogue, and now you ask whether I can teach you, when I am saying that there is no teaching, but only recollection; and thus you imagine that you will involve me in a contradiction.

Men. Indeed, Socrates, I protest that I had no such intention. I only asked the question from habit; but if you can prove to me that what you say is true, I wish that you would.

Soc. It will be no easy matter, but I will try to please you to the utmost of my power. Suppose that you call one of your numerous attendants, that I may demonstrate on him.

Men. Certainly. Come hither, boy.

Soc. He is Greek, and speaks Greek, does he not?

Men. Yes, indeed; he was born in the house.

Soc. Attend now to the questions which I ask him, and observe whether he learns of me or only remembers.

Men. I will.

Soc. Tell me, boy, do you know that a figure like this is a square?

Boy. I do.

Soc. And you know that a square figure has these four lines equal?

Boy. Certainly.

Soc. And these lines which I have drawn through the middle of the square are also equal?

Boy. Yes.

Soc. A square may be of any size?

Boy. Certainly.

Soc. And if one side of the figure be of two feet, and the other side be of two feet, how much will the whole be? Let me explain: if in one direction the space was of two feet, and in the other direction of one foot, the whole would be of two feet taken once?

Boy. Yes.

Soc. But since this side is also of two feet, there are twice two feet?

Boy. There are.

Soc. Then the square is of twice two feet?

Boy. Yes.

Soc. And how many are twice two feet? count and tell me.

Boy. Four, Socrates.

Soc. And might there not be another square twice as large as this, and having like this the lines equal?

Boy. Yes.

Soc. And of how many feet will that be?

Boy. Of eight feet.

Soc. And now try and tell me the length of the line which forms the side of that double square: this is two feet—what will that be?

Boy. Clearly, Socrates, it will be double.

Soc. Do you observe, Meno, that I am not teaching the boy anything, but only asking him questions; and now he fancies that he knows how long a line is necessary in order to produce a figure of eight square feet; does he not?

Men. Yes.

Soc. And does he really know?

Men. Certainly not.

Soc. He only guesses that because the square is double, the line is double.

Men. True.

Soc. Observe him while he recalls the steps in regular order. *(To the Boy.)* Tell me, boy, do you assert that a double space comes from a double line? Remember that I am not speaking of an oblong, but of a figure equal every way, and twice the size of this—that is to say of eight feet; and I want to know whether you still say that a double square comes from a double line?

Boy. Yes.

Soc. But does not this line become doubled if we add another such line here?

Boy. Certainly.

Soc. And four such lines will make a space containing eight feet?

Boy. Yes.

Soc. Let us describe such a figure: Would you not say that this is the figure of eight feet?

Boy. Yes.

Soc. And are there not these four divisions in the figure, each of which is equal to the figure of four feet?

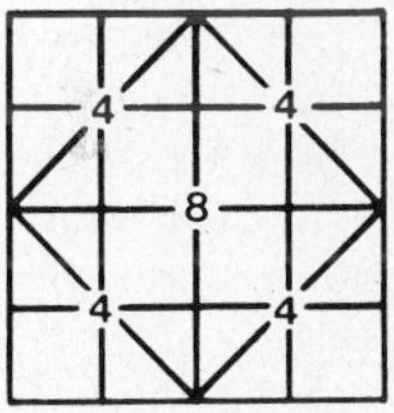

Boy. True.

Soc. And is not that four times four?

Boy. Certainly.

Soc. And four times is not double?

Boy. No, indeed.

Soc. But how much?

Boy. Four times as much.

Soc. Therefore the double line, boy, has given a space, not twice, but four times as much.

Boy. True.

Soc. Four times four are sixteen—are they not?

Boy. Yes.

Soc. What line would give you a space of eight feet, as this gives one of sixteen feet;—do you see?

Boy. Yes.

Soc. And the space of four feet is made from this half line?

Boy. Yes.

Soc. Good; and is not a space of eight feet twice the size of this, and half the size of the other?

Boy. Certainly.

Soc. Such a space, then, will be made out of a line greater than this one, and less than that one?

Boy. Yes; I think so.

Soc. Very good; I like to hear you say what you think. And now tell me, is not this a line of two feet and that of four?

Boy. Yes.

Soc. Then the line which forms the side of eight feet ought to be more than this line of two feet, and less than the other of four feet?

Boy. It ought.

Soc. Try and see if you can tell me how much it will be.

Boy. Three feet.

Soc. Then if we add a half to this line of two, that will be the line of three. Here are two and there is one; and on the other side, here are two also and there is one: and that makes the figure of which you speak?

Boy. Yes.

Soc. But if there are three feet this way and three feet that way, the whole space will be three times three feet?

Boy. That is evident.

Soc. And how much are three times three feet?

Boy. Nine.

Soc. And how much is the double of four?

Boy. Eight.

Soc. Then the figure of eight is not made out of a line of three?

Boy. No.

Soc. But from what line?—tell me exactly; and if you would rather not reckon, try and show me the line.

Boy. Indeed, Socrates, I do not know.

Soc. Do you see, Meno, what advances he has made in his power of recollection? He did not know at first, and he does not know now, what is the side of a figure of eight feet: but then he thought that he knew, and answered confidently as if he knew, and had no difficulty; now he has a difficulty, and neither knows nor fancies that he knows.

Men. True.

Soc. Is he not better off in knowing his ignorance?

Men. I think that he is.

Soc. If we have made him doubt, and given him the 'torpedo's shock,' have we done him any harm?

Men. I think not.

Soc. We have certainly, as would seem, assisted him in some degree to the discovery of the truth; and now he will wish to remedy his ignorance, but then he would have been ready to tell all the world again and again that the double space should have a double side.

Men. True.

Soc. But do you suppose that he would ever have enquired into or learned what he fancied that he knew, though he was really ignorant of it, until he had fallen into perplexity under the idea that he did not know, and had desired to know?

Men. I think not, Socrates.

Soc. Then he was the better for the torpedo's touch?

Men. I think so.

Soc. Mark now the farther development. I shall only ask him, and not teach him, and he shall share the enquiry with me: and do you watch and see if you find me telling or explaining anything to him, instead of eliciting his opinion. Tell me, boy, is not this a square of four feet which I have drawn?

Boy. Yes.

Soc. And now I add another square equal to the former one?

Boy. Yes.

Soc. And a third, which is equal to either of them?

Boy. Yes.

Soc. Suppose that we fill up the vacant corner?

Boy. Very good.

Soc. Here, then, there are four equal spaces?

Boy. Yes.

Soc. And how many times larger is this space than this other?

Boy. Four times.

Soc. But it ought to have been twice only, as you will remember.

Boy. True.

Soc. And does not this line, reaching from corner to corner, bisect each of these spaces?

Boy. Yes.

Soc. And are there not here four equal lines which contain this space?

Boy. There are.

Soc. Look and see how much this space is.

Boy. I do not understand.

Soc. Has not each interior line cut off half of the four spaces?

Boy. Yes.

Soc. And how many spaces are there in this section?

Boy. Four.

Soc. And how many in this?

Boy. Two.

Soc. And four is how many times two?

Boy. Twice.

Soc. And this space is of how many feet?

Boy. Of eight feet.

Soc. And from what line do you get this figure?

Boy. From this.

Soc. That is, from the line which extends from corner to corner of the figure of four feet?

Boy. Yes.

Soc. And that is the line which the learned call the diagonal. And if this is the proper name, then you, Meno's slave, are prepared to affirm that the double space is the square of the diagonal?

Boy. Certainly, Socrates.

Soc. What do you say of him, Meno? Were not all these answers given out of his own head?

Men. Yes, they were all his own.

Soc. And yet, as we were just now saying, he did not know?

Men. True.

Soc. But still he had in him those notions of his—had he not?

Men. Yes.

Soc. Then he who does not know may still have true notions of that which he does not know?

Men. He has.

Soc. And at present these notions have just been stirred up in him, as in a dream; but if he were frequently asked the same questions, in different forms, he would know as well as any one at last?

Men. I dare say.

Soc. Without any one teaching him he will recover his knowledge for himself, if he is only asked questions?

Men. Yes.

Soc. And this spontaneous recovery of knowledge in him is recollection?

Men. True.

Soc. And this knowledge which he now has must he not either have acquired or always possessed?

Men. Yes.

Soc. But if he always possessed this knowledge he would always have known; or if he has acquired the knowledge he could not have acquired it in this life, unless he has been taught geometry; for he may be made to do the same with all geometry and every other branch of knowledge. Now, has any one ever taught him all this? You must know about him, if, as you say, he was born and bred in your house.

Men. And I am certain that no one ever did teach him.

Soc. And yet he has the knowledge?

Men. The fact, Socrates, is undeniable.

Soc. But if he did not acquire the knowledge in this life, then he must have had and learned it at some other time?

Men. Clearly he must.

Soc. Which must have been the time when he was not a man?

Men. Yes.

Soc. And if there have been always true thoughts in him, both at the time when he was and was not a man, which only need to be awakened into knowledge by putting questions to him, his soul must have always possessed this knowledge, for he always either was or was not a man?

Men. Obviously.

Soc. And if the truth of all things always existed in the soul, then the soul is immortal. Wherefore be of good cheer, and try to recollect what you do not know, or rather what you do not remember.

Men. I feel, somehow, that I like what you are saying.

Soc. And I, Meno, like what I am saying. Some things I have said of which I am not altogether confident. But that we shall be better and braver and less helpless if we think that we ought to enquire, than we should have been if we indulged in the idle fancy that there was no knowing and no use in seeking to know what we do not know;—that is a theme upon which I am ready to fight, in word and deed, to the utmost of my power.

Men. There again, Socrates, your words seem to me excellent.

Soc. Then, as we are agreed that a man should enquire about that which he does not know, shall you and I make an effort to enquire together into the nature of virtue?

Men. By all means, Socrates. And yet I would much rather return to my original question. Whether in seeking to acquire virtue we should regard it as a thing to be taught, or as a gift of nature, or as coming to men in some other way?

Soc. Had I the command of you as well as of myself, Meno, I would not have enquired whether virtue is given by instruction or not, until we had first ascertained 'what it is.' But as you think only of controlling me who am your slave, and never of controlling yourself,—such being your notion of freedom, I must yield to you, for you are irresistible. And therefore I have now to enquire into the qualities of a thing of which I do not as yet know the nature. At any rate, will you condescend a little, and allow the question 'Whether virtue is given by instruction, or in any other way,' to be argued upon hypothesis? As the geometrician, when he is asked whether a certain triangle is capable of being inscribed in a certain circle, will reply: 'I cannot tell you as yet; but I will offer a hypothesis which may assist us in forming a conclusion: If the figure be such that when you have produced a given side of it, the given area of the triangle falls short by an area corresponding to the part produced, then one consequence follows, and if this is impossible then some other; and therefore I wish to assume a hypothesis before I tell you whether this triangle is capable of being inscribed in the circle:'—that is a geometrical hypothesis. And we too, as we know not the nature and qualities of virtue, must ask, whether virtue is or is not taught, under a hypothesis: as thus, if virtue is of such a class of mental goods, will it be taught or not? Let the first hypothesis be that virtue is or is not knowledge,—in that case will it be taught or not? or, as we were just now saying, 'remembered'? For there is no use in disputing about the name. But is virtue taught or not? or rather, does not every one see that knowledge alone is taught?

Men. I agree.

Soc. Then if virtue is knowledge, virtue will be taught?

Men. Certainly.

Soc. Then now we have made a quick end of this question: if virtue is of such a nature, it will be taught; and if not, not?

Men. Certainly.

Soc. The next question is, whether virtue is knowledge or of another species?

Men. Yes, that appears to be the question which comes next in order.

Soc. Do we not say that virtue is good?—This is a hypothesis which is not set aside.

Men. Certainly.

Soc. Now, if there be any sort of good which is distinct from knowledge, virtue may be that good; but if knowledge embraces all good, then we shall be right in thinking that virtue is knowledge?

Men. True.

Soc. And virtue makes us good?

Men. Yes.

Soc. And if we are good, then we are profitable; for all good things are profitable?

Men. Yes.

Soc. Then virtue is profitable?

Men. That is the only inference.

Soc. Then now let us see what are the things which severally profit us. Health and strength, and beauty and wealth—these, and the like of these, we call profitable?

Men. True.

Soc. And yet these things may also sometimes do us harm: would you not think so?

Men. Yes.

Soc. And what is the guiding principle which makes them profitable or the reverse? Are they not profitable when they are rightly used, and hurtful, when they are not rightly used?

Men. Certainly.

Soc. Next, let us consider the goods of the soul: they are temperance, justice, courage, quickness of apprehension, memory, magnanimity, and the like?

Men. Surely.

Soc. And such of these as are not knowledge, but of another sort, are sometimes profitable and sometimes hurtful; as, for example, courage wanting prudence, which is only a sort of confidence? When a man has no sense he is harmed by courage, but when he has sense he is profited?

Men. True.

Soc. And the same may be said of temperance and quickness of apprehension; whatever things are learned or done with sense are profitable, but when done without sense they are hurtful?

Men. Very true.

Soc. And in general, all that the soul attempts or endures, when under the guidance of wisdom, ends in happiness; but when she is under the guidance of folly, in the opposite?

Men. That appears to be true.

Soc. If then virtue is a quality of the soul, and is admitted to be profitable, it must be wisdom or prudence, since none of the things of the soul are either profitable or hurtful in themselves, but they are all made profitable or hurtful by the addition of wisdom or of folly; and therefore if virtue is profitable, virtue must be a sort of wisdom or prudence?

Men. I quite agree.

Soc. And the other goods, such as wealth and the like, of which we were just now saying that they are sometimes good and sometimes evil, do not they also become profitable or hurtful, accordingly as the soul guides and uses them rightly or wrongly; just as the things of the soul herself are benefited when under the guidance of wisdom and harmed by folly?

Men. True.

Soc. And the wise soul guides them rightly, and the foolish soul wrongly.

Men. Yes.

Soc. And is not this universally true of human nature? All other things hang upon the soul, and the things of the soul herself hang upon wisdom, if they are to be good; and so wisdom is inferred to be that which profits—and virtue, as we say, is profitable?

Men. Certainly.

Soc. And thus we arrive at the conclusion that virtue is either wholly or partly wisdom?

Men. I think that what you are saying, Socrates, is very true.

Soc. But if this is true, then the good are not by nature good?

Men. I think not.

Soc. If they had been, there would assuredly have been discerners of characters among us who would have known our future great men; and on their showing we should have adopted them, and when we had got them, we should have kept them in the citadel out of the way of harm, and set a stamp upon them far rather than upon a piece of gold, in order that no one might tamper with them; and when they grew up they would have been useful to the state?

Men. Yes, Socrates, that would have been the right way.

Soc. But if the good are not by nature good, are they made good by instruction?

Men. There appears to be no other alternative, Socrates. On the supposition that virtue is knowledge, there can be no doubt that virtue is taught.

Soc. Yes, indeed; but what if the supposition is erroneous?

Men. I certainly thought just now that we were right.

Soc. Yes, Meno; but a principle which has any soundness should stand firm not only just now, but always.

Men. Well; and why are you so slow of heart to believe that knowledge is virtue?

Soc. I will try and tell you why, Meno. I do not retract the assertion that if virtue is knowledge it may be taught; but I fear that I have some reason in doubting whether virtue is knowledge: for consider now and say whether virtue, and not only virtue but anything that is taught, must not have teachers and disciples?

Men. Surely.

Soc. And conversely, may not the art of which neither teachers nor disciples exist be assumed to be incapable of being taught?

Men. True; but do you think that there are no teachers of virtue?

Soc. I have certainly often enquired whether there were any, and taken great pains to find them, and have never succeeded; and many have assisted me in the search, and they were the persons whom I thought the most likely to know. Here at the moment when he is wanted we fortunately have sitting by us Anytus, the very person of whom we should make enquiry; to him then let us repair. In the first place, he is the son of a wealthy and wise father, Anthemion, who acquired his wealth, not by accident or gift, like Ismenias the Theban (who has recently made himself as rich as Polycrates), but by his own skill and industry, and who is a well-conditioned, modest man, not insolent, or over-bearing, or annoying; moreover, this son of his has received a good education, as the Athenian people certainly appear to think, for they choose him to fill the highest offices. And these are the sort of men from whom you are likely to learn whether there are any teachers of virtue, and who they are. Please, Anytus, to help me and your friend Meno in answering our question, Who are the teachers? Consider the matter thus: If we wanted Meno to be a good physician, to whom should we send him? Should we not send him to the physicians?

Anytus. Certainly.

Soc. Or if we wanted him to be a good cobbler, should we not send him to the cobblers?

Any. Yes.

Soc. And so forth?

Any. Yes.

Soc. Let me trouble you with one more question. When we say that we should be right in sending him to the physicians if we wanted him to be a physician, do we mean that we should be right in sending him to those who profess the art, rather than to those who do not, and to those who demand payment for teaching the art, and profess to teach it to any one who will come and learn? And if these were our reasons, should we not be right in sending him?

Any. Yes.

Soc. And might not the same be said of flute-playing, and of the other arts? Would a man who wanted to make another a flute-player refuse to send him to those who profess to teach the art for money, and be plaguing other persons to give him instruction, who are not professed teachers and who never had a single disciple in that branch of knowledge which he wishes him to acquire—would not such conduct be the height of folly?

Any. Yes, by Zeus, and of ignorance too.

Soc. Very good. And now you are in a position to

advise with me about my friend Meno. He has been telling me, Anytus, that he desires to attain that kind of wisdom and virtue by which men order the state or the house, and honour their parents, and know when to receive and when to send away citizens and strangers, as a good man should. Now, to whom should he go in order that he may learn this virtue? Does not the previous argument imply clearly that we should send him to those who profess and avouch that they are the common teachers of all Hellas, and are ready to impart instruction to any one who likes, at a fixed price?

Any. Whom do you mean, Socrates?

Soc. You surely know, do you not, Anytus, that these are the people whom mankind call Sophists?

Any. By Heracles, Socrates, forbear! I only hope that no friend or kinsman or acquaintance of mine, whether citizen or stranger, will ever be so mad as to allow himself to be corrupted by them; for they are a manifest pest and corrupting influences to those who have to do with them.

Soc. What, Anytus? Of all the people who profess that they know how to do men good, do you mean to say that these are the only ones who not only do them no good, but positively corrupt those who are entrusted to them, and in return for this disservice have the face to demand money? Indeed, I cannot believe you; for I know of a single man, Protagoras, who made more out of his craft than the illustrious Pheidias, who created such noble works, or any ten other statuaries. How could that be? A mender of old shoes, or patcher up of clothes, who made the shoes or clothes worse than he received them, could not have remained thirty days undetected, and would very soon have starved; whereas during more than forty years, Protagoras was corrupting all Hellas, and sending his disciples from him worse than he received them, and he was never found out. For, if I am not mistaken, he was about seventy years old at his death, forty of which were spent in the practice of his profession; and during all that time he had a good reputation, which to this day he retains: and not only Protagoras, but many others are well spoken of; some who lived before him, and others who are still living. Now, when you say that they deceived and corrupted the youth, are they to be supposed to have corrupted them consciously or unconsciously? Can those who were deemed by many to be the wisest men of Hellas have been out of their minds?

Any. Out of their minds! No, Socrates; the young men who gave their money to them were out of their minds, and their relations and guardians who entrusted their youth to the care of these men were still more out of their minds, and most of all, the cities who allowed them to come in, and did not drive them out, citizen and stranger alike.

Soc. Has any of the Sophists wronged you, Anytus? What makes you so angry with them?

Any. No, indeed, neither I nor any of my belongings has ever had, nor would I suffer them to have, anything to do with them.

Soc. Then you are entirely unacquainted with them?

Any. And I have no wish to be acquainted.

Soc. Then, my dear friend, how can you know whether a thing is good or bad of which you are wholly ignorant?

Any. Quite well; I am sure that I know what manner of men these are, whether I am acquainted with them or not.

Soc. You must be a diviner, Anytus, for I really cannot make out, judging from your own words, how, if you are not acquainted with them, you know about them. But I am not enquiring of you who are the teachers who will currupt Meno (let them be, if you please, the Sophists); I only ask you to tell him who there is in this great city who will teach him how to become eminent in the virtues which I was just now describing. He is the friend of your family, and you will oblige him.

Any. Why do you not tell him yourself?

Soc. I have told him whom I supposed to be the teachers of these things; but I learn from you that I am utterly at fault, and I dare say that you are right. And now I wish that you, on your part, would tell me to whom among the Athenians he should go. Whom would you name?

Any. Why single out individuals? Any Athenian gentleman, taken at random, if he will mind him, will do far more good to him than the Sophists.

Soc. And did those gentlemen grow of themselves; and without having been taught by any one, were they nevertheless able to teach others that which they had never learned themselves?

Any. I imagine that they learned of the previous generation of gentlemen. Have there not been many good men in this city?

Soc. Yes, certainly, Anytus; and many good statesmen also there always have been and there are still, in the city of Athens. But the question is whether they were also good teachers of their own virtue;—not whether there are, or have been, good men in this part of the world, but whether virtue can be taught, is the question which we have been discussing. Now, do we mean to say that the good men of our own and of other times knew how to impart to others that virtue which they had themselves; or is virtue a thing incapable of being communicated or imparted by one man to another? That is the question which I and Meno have been arguing. Look at the matter in your own way: Would you not admit that Themistocles was a good man?

Any. Certainly; no man better.

Soc. And must not he then have been a good teacher, if any man ever was a good teacher, of his own virtue?

Any. Yes, certainly,—if he wanted to be so.

Soc. But would he not have wanted? He would, at any rate, have desired to make his own son a good man and a gentlemen; he could not have been jealous of him, or have intentionally abstained from imparting to him his own virtue. Did you never hear that he made his son Cleophantus a famous horseman; and had him taught to stand upright on horseback and hurl a javelin, and to do many other marvellous things; and in anything which could be learned from a master he was well trained? Have you not heard from our elders of him?

Any. I have.

Soc. Then no one could say that his son showed any want of capacity?

Any. Very likely not.

Soc. But did any one, old or young, ever say in your hearing that Cleophatus, son of Themistocles, was a wise or good man, as his father was?

Any. I have certainly never heard any one say so.

Soc. And if virtue could have been taught, would his father Themistocles have sought to train him in these minor accomplishments, and allowed him who, as you must remember, was his own son, to be no better than his neighbours in those qualities in which he himself excelled?

Any. Indeed, indeed, I think not.

Soc. Here was a teacher of virtue whom you admit to be among the best men of the past. Let us take another,—Aristides, the son of Lysimachus: would you not acknowledge that he was a good man?

Any. To be sure I should.

Soc. And did not he train his son Lysimachus better than any other Athenian in all that could be done for him by the help of masters? But what has been the result? Is he a bit better than any other mortal? He is an acquaintance of yours, and you see what he is like. There is Pericles, again, magnificent in his wisdom; and he, as you are aware, had two sons, Paralus and Xanthippus.

Any. I know.

Soc. And you know, also, that he taught them to be unrivalled horsemen, and had them trained in music and gymnastics and all sorts of arts—in these respects they were on a level with the best—and had he no wish to make good men of them? Nay, he must have wished it. But virtue, as I suspect, could not be taught. And that you may not suppose the incompetent teachers to be only the meaner sort of Athenians and few in number, remember again that Thucydides had two sons, Melesias and Stephanus, whom, besides giving them a good education in other things, he trained in wrestling, and they were the best wrestlers in Athens: one of them he committed to the care of Xanthias, and the other of Eudorus, who had the reputation of being the most celebrated wrestlers of that day. Do you remember them?

Any. I have heard of them.

Soc. Now, can there be a doubt that Thucydides, whose children were taught things for which he had to spend money, would have taught them to be good men, which would have cost him nothing, if virtue could have been taught? Will you reply that he was a mean man, and had not many friends among the Athenians and allies? Nay, but he was of a great family, and a man of influence at Athens and in all Hellas, and, if virtue could have been taught, he would have found out some Athenian or foreigner who would have made good men of his sons, if he could not himself spare the time from cares of state. Once more, I suspect, friend Anytus, that virtue is not a thing which can be taught?

Any. Socrates, I think that you are too ready to speak evil of men: and, if you will take my advice, I would recommend you to be careful. Perhaps there is no city in which it is not easier to do men harm than to do them good, and this is certainly the case at Athens, as I believe that you know.

Soc. O Meno, I think that Anytus is in a rage. And he may well be in a rage, for he thinks, in the first place, that I am defaming these gentlemen; and in the second place, he is of opinion that he is one of them himself. But some day he will know what is the meaning of defamation, and if he ever does, he will forgive me. Meanwhile I will return to you, Meno; for I suppose that there are gentlemen in your region too?

Men. Certainly there are.

Soc. And are they willing to teach the young? and do they profess to be teachers? and do they agree that virtue is taught?

Men. No indeed, Socrates, they are anything but agreed; you may hear them saying at one time that virtue can be taught, and then again the reverse.

Soc. Can we call those teachers who do not acknowledge the possibility of their own vocation?

Men. I think not, Socrates.

Soc. And what do you think of these Sophists, who are the only professors? Do they seem to you to be teachers of virtue?

Men. I often wonder, Socrates, that Gorgias is never heard promising to teach virtue: and when he hears others promising he only laughs at them; but he thinks that men should be taught to speak.

Soc. Then do you not think that the Sophists are teachers?

Men. I cannot tell you, Socrates; like the rest of the world, I am in doubt, and sometimes I think that they are teachers and sometimes not.

Soc. And are you aware that not you only and other politicians have doubts whether virtue can be taught or not, but that Theognis the poet says the very same thing?

Men. Where does he say so?

Soc. In these elegiac verses:—

> 'Eat and drink and sit with the mighty, and make yourself agreeable to them; for from the good you will learn what is good, but if you mix with the bad you will lose the intelligence which you already have.'

Do you observe that here he seems to imply that virtue can be taught?

Men. Clearly.

Soc. But in some other verses he shifts about and says:—

> 'If understanding could be created and put into a man, then they' [who were able to perform this feat] 'would have obtained great rewards.'

And again:—

> 'Never would a bad son have sprung from a good sire, for he would have heard the voice of instruction; but not by teaching will you ever make a bad man into a good one.'

And this, as you may remark, is a contradiction of the other.

Men. Clearly.

Soc. And is there anything else of which the professors are affirmed not only not to be teachers of others, but to be ignorant themselves, and bad at the knowledge of that which they are professing to teach? or is there anything about which even the acknowledged 'gentlemen' are sometimes saying that 'this thing can be taught,' and sometimes the opposite? Can you say that they are teachers in any true sense whose ideas are in such confusion?

Men. I should say, certainly not.

Soc. But if neither the Sophists nor the gentlemen are teachers, clearly there can be no other teachers?

Men. No.

Soc. And if there are no teachers, neither are there disciples?

Men. Agreed.

Soc. And we have admitted that a thing cannot be taught of which there are neither teachers nor disciples?

Men. We have.

Soc. And there are no teachers of virtue to be found anywhere?

Men. There are not.

Soc. And if there are no teachers, neither are there scholars?

Men. That, I think, is true.

Soc. Then virtue cannot be taught?

Men. Not if we are right in our view. But I cannot believe, Socrates, that there are no good men: And if there are, how did they come into existence?

Soc. I am afraid, Meno, that you and I are not good for much, and that Gorgias has been as poor an educator of you as Prodicus has been of me. Certainly we shall have to look to ourselves, and try to find some one who will help in some way or other to improve us. This I say, because I observe that in the previous discussion none of us remarked that right and good action is possible to man under other guidance than that of knowledge (ἐπιστήμη);—and indeed if this be denied, there is no seeing how there can be any good men at all.

Men. How do you mean, Socrates?

Soc. I mean that good men are necessarily useful or profitable. Were we not right in admitting this? It must be so.

Men. Yes.

Soc. And in supposing that they will be useful only if they are true guides to us of action—there we were also right?

Men. Yes.

Soc. But when we said that a man cannot be a good guide unless he have knowledge (*φρόνησις*), in this we were wrong.

Men. What do you mean by the word 'right'?

Soc. I will explain. If a man knew the way to Larisa, or anywhere else, and went to the place and led others thither, would he not be a right and good guide?

Men. Certainly.

Soc. And a person who had a right opinion about the way, but had never been and did not know, might be a good guide also, might he not?

Men. Certainly.

Soc. And while he has true opinion about that which the other knows, he will be just as good a guide if he thinks the truth, as he who knows the truth?

Men. Exactly.

Soc. Then true opinion is as good a guide to correct action as knowledge; and that was the point which we omitted in our speculation about the nature of virtue, when we said that knowledge only is the guide of right action; whereas there is also right opinion.

Men. True.

Soc. Then right opinion is not less useful than knowledge?

Men. The difference, Socrates, is only that he who has knowledge will always be right; but he who has right opinion will sometimes be right, and sometimes not.

Soc. What do you mean? Can he be wrong who has right opinion, so long as he has right opinion?

Men. I admit the cogency of your argument, and therefore, Socrates, I wonder that knowledge should be preferred to right opinion—or why they should ever differ.

Soc. And shall I explain this wonder to you?

Men. Do tell me.

Soc. You would not wonder if you had ever observed the images of Daedalus; but perhaps you have not got them in your country?

Men. What have they to do with the question?

Soc. Because they require to be fastened in order to keep them, and if they are not fastened they will play truant and run away.

Men. Well, what of that?

Soc. I mean to say that they are not very valuable possessions if they are at liberty, for they will walk off like runaway slaves; but when fastened, they are of great value, for they are really beautiful works of art. Now this is an illustration of the nature of true opinions: while they abide with us they are beautiful and fruitful, but they run away out of the human soul, and do not remain long, and therefore they are not of much value until they are fastened by the tie of the cause; and this fastening of them, friend Meno, is recollection, as you and I have agreed to call it. But when they are bound, in the first place, they have the nature of knowledge; and, in the second place, they are abiding. And this is why knowledge is more honourable and excellent than true opinion, because fastened by a chain.

Men. What you are saying, Socrates, seems to be very like the truth.

Soc. I too speak rather in ignorance; I only conjecture. And yet that knowledge differs from true opinion is no matter of conjecture with me. There are not many things which I profess to know, but this is most certainly one of them.

Men. Yes, Socrates; and you are quite right in saying so.

Soc. And am I not also right in saying that true opinion leading the way perfects action quite as well as knowledge?

Men. There again, Socrates, I think you are right.

Soc. Then right opinion is not a whit inferior to knowledge, or less useful in action; nor is the man who has right opinion inferior to him who has knowledge?

Men. True.

Soc. And surely the good man has been acknowledged by us to be useful?

Men. Yes.

Soc. Seeing then that men become good and useful to states, not only because they have knowledge, but because they have right opinion, and that neither knowledge nor right opinion is given to man by nature or acquired by him—(do you imagine either of them to be given by nature?

Men. Not I.)

Soc. Then if they are not given by nature, neither are the good by nature good?

Men. Certainly not.

Soc. And nature being excluded, then came the question whether virtue is acquired by teaching?

Men. Yes.

Soc. If virtue was wisdom [or knowledge], then, as we thought, it was taught?

Men. Yes.

Soc. And if it was taught it was wisdom?

Men. Certainly.

Soc. And if there were teachers, it might be taught; and if there were no teachers, not?

Men. True.

Soc. But surely we acknowledged that there were no teachers of virtue?

Men. Yes.

Soc. Then we acknowledged that it was not taught, and was not wisdom?

Men. Certainly.

Soc. And yet we admitted that it was a good?

Men. Yes.

Soc. And the right guide is useful and good?

Men. Certainly.

Soc. And the only right guides are knowledge and true opinion—these are the guides of man; for things which happen by chance are not under the guidance of man: but the guides of man are true opinion and knowledge.

Men. I think so too.

Soc. But if virtue is not taught, neither is virtue knowledge.

Men. Clearly not.

Soc. Then of two good and useful things, one, which is knowledge, has been set aside, and cannot be supposed to be our guide in political life.

Men. I think not.

Soc. And therefore not by any wisdom, and not because they were wise, did Themistocles and those others of whom Anytus spoke govern states. This was the reason why they were unable to make others like themselves—because their virtue was not grounded on knowledge.

Men. That is probably true, Socrates.

Soc. But if not by knowledge, the only alternative which remains is that statesmen must have guided states by right opinion, which is in politics what divination is in religion; for diviners and also prophets say many things truly, but they know not what they say.

Men. So I believe.

Soc. And may we not, Meno, truly call those men 'divine' who, having no understanding, yet succeed in many a grand deed and word?

Men. Certainly.

Soc. Then we shall also be right in calling divine those whom we were just now speaking of as diviners and prophets, including the whole tribe of poets. Yes, and statemen above all may be said to be divine and illumined, being inspired and possessed of God, in which condition they say many grand things, not knowing what they say.

Men. Yes.

Soc. And the women too, Meno, call good men divine—do they not? and the Spartans, when they praise a good man, say 'that he is a divine man.'

Men. And I think, Socrates, that they are right; although very likely our friend Anytus may take offence at the word.

Soc. I do not care; as for Anytus, there will be another opportunity of talking with him. To sum up our enquiry—the result seems to be, if we are at all right in our view, that virtue is neither natural nor acquired, but an instinct given by God to the virtuous. Nor is the instinct accompanied by reason, unless there may be supposed to be among statesmen some one who is capable of educating statesmen. And if there be such an one, he may be said to be among the living what Homer says that Tiresias was among the dead, 'he alone has understanding; but the rest are flitting shades;' and he and his virtue in like manner will be a reality among shadows.

Men. That is excellent, Socrates.

Soc. Then, Meno, the conclusion is that virtue comes to the virtuous by the gift of God. But we shall never know the certain truth until, before asking how virtue is given, we enquire into the actual nature of virtue. I fear that I must go away, but do you, now that you are persuaded yourself, persuade our friend Anytus. And do not let him be so exasperated; if you can conciliate him, you will have done good service to the Athenian people.

From the Republic

Let me [Socrates] next endeavour to show what is that fault in States which is the cause of their present maladministration, and what is the least change which will enable a State to pass into the truer form; and let the change, if possible, be of one thing only, or, if not, of two; at any rate, let the changes be as few and slight as possible.

Certainly, he [Glaucon] replied.

I think, I said, that there might be a reform of the State if only one change were made, which is not a slight or easy though still a possible one.

What is it? he said.

Now then, I said, I go to meet that which I liken to the greatest of the waves; yet shall the word be spoken, even though the wave break and drown me in laughter and dishonour; and do you mark my words.

Proceed.

I said: *Until philosophers are kings, or the kings and princes of this world have the spirit and power of philosophy, and political greatness and wisdom meet in one, and those commoner natures who pursue either to the exclusion of the other are compelled to stand aside, cities will never have rest from their evils,—no, nor the human race, as I believe,—and then only will this our State have a possibility of life and behold the light of day.* Such was the thought, my dear Glaucon, which I would fain have uttered if it had not seemed too extravagant; for to be convinced that in no other State can there be happiness private or public is indeed a hard thing.

Socrates, what do you mean? I would have you consider that the word which you have uttered is one at which numerous persons, and very respectable persons too, in a figure pulling off their coats all in a moment, and seizing any weapon that comes to hand, will run at you might and main, before you know where you are, intending to do heaven knows what; and if you don't prepare an answer, and put yourself in motion, you will be 'pared by their fine wits,' and no mistake.

You got me into the scrape, I said.

And I was quite right; however, I will do all I can to get you out of it; but I can only give you good-will and good advice, and, perhaps, I may be able to fit answers to your questions better than another—that is all. And now, having such an auxiliary, you must do your best to show the unbelievers that you are right.

I ought to try, I said, since you offer me such invaluable assistance. And I think that, if there is to be a chance of our escaping, we must explain to them whom we mean when we say that philosophers are to rule in the State; then we shall be able to defend ourselves: There will be discovered to be some natures who ought to study philosophy and to be leaders in the State; and others who are not born to be philosophers, and are meant to be followers rather than leaders.

Then now for a definition, he said.

Follow me, I said, and I hope that I may in some way or other be able to give you a satisfactory explanation.

Proceed.

I dare say that you remember, and therefore I need not remind you, that a lover, if he is worthy of the name, ought to show his love, not to some one part of that which he loves, but to the whole.

I really do not understand, and therefore beg of you to assist my memory.

Another person, I said, might fairly reply as you do; but a man of pleasure like yourself ought to know that all who are in the flower of youth do somehow or other raise a pang or emotion in a lover's breast, and are thought by him to be worthy of his affectionate regards. Is not this a way which you have with the fair: one has a snub nose, and you praise his charming face; the hook-nose of another has, you say, a royal look; while he who is neither snub nor hooked has the grace of regularity: the dark visage is manly, the fair are children of the gods; and as to the sweet 'honey pale,' as they are called, what is the very name but the invention of a lover who talks in diminutives, and is not adverse to paleness if appearing on the cheek of youth? In a word, there is no excuse which you will not make, and nothing which you will not say, in order not to lose a single flower that blooms in the spring-time of youth.

From Plato, *Republic*, 473–480, 507–511, 514–521, 595–598.

If you make me an authority in matters of love, for the sake of the argument, I assent.

And what do you say of lovers of wine? Do you not see them doing the same? They are glad of any pretext of drinking any wine.

Very good.

And the same is true of ambitious men; if they cannot command an army, they are willing to command a file; and if they cannot be honoured by really great and important persons, they are glad to be honoured by lesser and meaner people,—but honour of some kind they must have.

Exactly.

Once more let me ask: Does he who desires any class of goods, desire the whole class or a part only?

The whole.

And may we not say of the philosopher that he is a lover, not of a part of wisdom only, but of the whole?

Yes, of the whole.

And he who dislikes learning, especially in youth, when he has no power of judging what is good and what is not, such an one we maintain not to be a philosopher or a lover of knowledge, just as he who refuses his food is not hungry, and may be said to have a bad appetite and not a good one?

Very true, he said.

Whereas he who has a taste for every sort of knowledge and who is curious to learn and is never satisfied, may be justly termed a philosopher? Am I not right?

Glaucon said: If curiosity makes a philosopher, you will find many a strange being will have a title to the name. All the lovers of sights have a delight in learning, and must therefore be included. Musical amateurs, too, are a folk strangely out of place among philosophers, for they are the last persons in the world who would come to anything like a philosophical discussion, if they could help, while they run about at the Dionysiac festivals as if they had let out their ears to hear every chorus; whether the performance is in town or country—that makes no difference—they are there. Now are we to maintain that all these and any who have similar tastes, as well as the professors of quite minor arts, are philosophers?

Certainly not, I replied; they are only an imitation.

He said: Who then are the true philosophers?

Those, I said, who are lovers of the vision of truth.

That is also good, he said; but I should like to know what you mean?

To another, I replied, I might have a difficulty in explaining; but I am sure that you will admit a proposition which I am about to make.

What is the proposition?

That since beauty is the opposite of ugliness, they are two?

Certainly.

And inasmuch as they are two, each of them is one?

True again.

And of just and unjust, good and evil, and of every other class, the same remark holds: taken singly, each of them is one; but from the various combinations of them with actions and things and with one another, they are seen in all sorts of lights and appear many?

Very true.

And this is the distinction which I draw between the sight-loving, art-loving, practical class and those of whom I am speaking, and who are alone worthy of the name of philosophers.

How do you distinguish them? he said.

The lovers of sounds and sights, I replied, are, as I conceive, fond of fine tones and colours and forms and all the artificial products that are made out of them, but their mind is incapable of seeing or loving absolute beauty.

True, he replied.

Few are they who are able to attain to the sight of this.

Very true.

And he who, having a sense of beautiful things has no sense of absolute beauty, or who, if another lead him to a knowledge of that beauty is unable to follow—of such an one I ask, Is he awake or in a dream only? Reflect: is not the dreamer, sleeping or waking, one who likens dissimilar things, who puts the copy in the place of the real object?

I should certainly say that such an one was dreaming.

But take the case of the other, who recognises the existence of absolute beauty and is able to distinguish the idea from the objects which participate in the idea, neither putting the objects in the place of the idea nor the idea in the place of the objects—is he a dreamer, or is he awake?

He is wide awake.

The School of Plato, Roman Mosaic. Philosophers are shown gathering for conversations in the agora, an Athenian public square hospitable for discourse. (Alinari/Art Resource)

And may we not say that the mind of the one who knows has knowledge, and that the mind of the other, who opines only, has opinion?

Certainly.

But suppose that the latter should quarrel with us and dispute our statement, can we administer any soothing cordial or advice to him, without revealing to him that there is sad disorder in his wits?

We must certainly offer him some good advice, he replied.

Come, then, and let us think of something to say to him. Shall we begin by assuring him that he is welcome to any knowledge which he may have, and that we are rejoiced at his having it? But we should like to ask him a question: Does he who has knowledge know something or nothing? (You must answer for him.)

I answer that he knows something.

Something that is or is not?

Something that is; for how can that which is not ever be known?

And are we assured, after looking at the matter from many points of view, that absolute being is or may be absolutely known, but that the utterly non-existent is utterly unknown?

Nothing can be more certain.

Good. But if there be anything which is of such a nature as to be and not to be, that will have a place intermediate between pure being and the absolute negation of being?

Yes, between them.

And, as knowledge corresponded to being and ignorance of necessity to not-being, for that intermediate between being and not being there has to be discovered a corresponding intermediate between ignorance and knowledge, if there be such?

Certainly.

Do we admit the existence of opinion?

Undoubtedly.

As being the same with knowledge, or another faculty?

Another faculty.

Then opinion and knowledge have to do with different kinds of matter corresponding to this difference of faculties?

Yes.

And knowledge is relative to being and knows being. But before I proceed further I will make a division.

What division?

I will begin by placing faculties in a class by themselves: they are powers in us, and in all other things, by which we do as we do. Sight and hearing, for example, I should call faculties. Have I clearly explained the class which I mean?

Yes, I quite understand.

Then let me tell you my view about them. I do not see them, and therefore the distinctions of figure, colour, and the like, which enable me to discern the differences of some things, do not apply to them. In speaking of a faculty I think only of its sphere and its result; and that which has the same sphere and the same result I call the same faculty, but that which has another sphere and another result I call different. Would that be your way of speaking?

Yes.

And will you be so very good as to answer one more question? Would you say that knowledge is a faculty, or in what class would you place it?

Certainly knowledge is a faculty, and the mightiest of all faculties.

And is opinion also a faculty?

Certainly, he said; for opinion is that with which we are able to form an opinion.

And yet you were acknowledging a little while ago that knowledge is not the same as opinion?

Why, yes, he said: how can any reasonable being ever identify that which is infallible with that which errs?

An excellent answer, proving, I said, that we are quite conscious of a distinction between them.

Yes.

Then knowledge and opinion having distinct powers have also distinct spheres or subject-matters?

That is certain.

Being is the sphere or subject-matter of knowledge, and knowledge is to know the nature of being?

Yes.

And opinion is to have an opinion?

Yes.

And do we know what we opine? or is the subject-matter of opinion the same as the subject-matter of knowledge?

Nay, he replied, that has been already disproven; if difference in faculty implies difference in the sphere or subject-matter, and if, as we were saying, opinion and knowledge are distinct faculties, then the sphere of knowledge and of opinion cannot be the same.

Then if being is the subject-matter of knowledge,

something else must be the subject-matter of opinion?

Yes, something else.

Well then, is not-being the subject-matter of opinion? or, rather, how can there be an opinion at all about not-being? Reflect: when a man has an opinion, has he not an opinion about something? Can he have an opinion which is an opinion about nothing?

Impossible.

He who has an opinion has an opinion about some one thing?

Yes.

And not-being is not one thing but, properly speaking, nothing?

True.

Of not-being, ignorance was assumed to be the necessary correlative; of being, knowledge?

True, he said.

Then opinion is not concerned either with being or with not-being?

Not with either.

And can therefore neither be ignorance nor knowledge?

That seems to be true.

But is opinion to be sought without and beyond either of them, in a greater clearness than knowledge, or in a greater darkness than ignorance?

In neither.

Then I suppose that opinion appears to you to be darker than knowledge, but lighter than ignorance?

Both; and in no small degree.

And also to be within and between them?

Yes.

Then you would infer that opinion is intermediate?

No question.

But were we not saying before, that if anything appeared to be of a sort which is and is not at the same time, that sort of thing would appear also to lie in the interval between pure being and absolute not-being; and that the corresponding faculty is neither knowledge nor ignorance, but will be found in the interval between them?

True.

And in that interval there has now been discovered something which we call opinion?

There has.

Then what remains to be discovered is the object which partakes equally of the nature of being and not-being, and cannot rightly be termed either, pure and simple; this unknown term, when discovered, we may truly call the subject of opinion, and assign each to their proper faculty,—the extremes to the faculties of the extremes and the mean to the faculty of the mean.

True.

This being premised, I would ask the gentleman who is of opinion that there is no absolute or unchangeable idea of beauty—in whose opinion the beautiful is the manifold—he, I say, your lover of beautiful sights, who cannot bear to be told that the beautiful is one, and the just is one, or that anything is one—to him I would appeal, saying, Will you be so very kind, sir, as to tell us whether, of all these beautiful things, there is one which will not be found ugly; or of the just which will not be found unjust; or of the holy, which will not also be unholy?

No, he replied; the beautiful will in some point of view be found ugly; and the same is true of the rest.

And may not the many which are doubles be also halves?—doubles, that is, of one thing, and halves of another?

Quite true.

And things great and small, heavy and light, as they are termed, will not be denoted by these any more than by the opposite names?

True; both these and the opposite names will always attach to all of them.

And can any one of those many things which are called by particular names be said to be this rather than not to be this?

He replied: They are like the punning riddles which are asked at feasts or the children's puzzle about the eunuch aiming at the bat, with what he hit him, as they say in the puzzle, and upon what the bat was sitting. The individual objects of which I am speaking are also a riddle, and have a double sense: nor can you fix them in your mind, either as being or not-being, or both, or neither.

Then what will you do with them? I said. Can they have a better place than between being and not-being? For they are clearly not in greater darkness or negation than not-being, or more full of light and existence than being.

That is quite true, he said.

Thus then we seem to have discovered that the many ideas which the multitude entertain about the beautiful and about all other things are tossing about in some region which is half-way between pure being and pure not-being?

We have.

Yes; and we had before agreed that anything of this kind which we might find was to be described as matter of opinion, and not as matter of knowledge; being the intermediate flux which is caught and detained by the intermediate faculty.

Quite true.

Then those who see the many beautiful, and who yet neither see absolute beauty, nor can follow any guide who points the way thither; who see the many just, and not absolute justice, and the like,—such persons may be said to have opinion but not knowledge?

That is certain.

But those who see the absolute and eternal and immutable may be said to know, and not to have opinion only?

Neither can that be denied.

The one love and embrace the subjects of knowledge, the other those of opinion? The latter are the same, as I dare say you will remember, who listened to sweet sounds and gazed upon fair colours, but would not tolerate the existence of absolute beauty.

Yes, I remember.

Shall we then be guilty of any impropriety in calling them lovers of opinion rather than lovers of wisdom, and will they be very angry with us for thus describing them?

I shall tell them not to be angy; no man should be angry at what is true.

But those who love the truth in each thing are to be called lovers of wisdom and not lovers of opinion

Assuredly. [473–480]

Yes, I [Socrates] said, but I must first come to an understanding with you, and remind you of what I have mentioned in the course of this discussion, and at many other times.

What?

The old story, that there is a many beautiful and a many good, and so of other things which we describe and define; to all of them 'many' is applied.

True, he [Glaucon] said.

And there is an absolute beauty and an absolute good, and of other things to which the term 'many' is applied there is an absolute; for they may be brought under a single idea, which is called the essence of each.

Very true.

The many, as we say, are seen but not known, and the ideas are known but not seen.

Exactly.

And what is the organ with which we see the visible things?

The sight, he said.

And with the hearing, I said, we hear, and with the other senses perceive the other objects of sense?

True.

But have you remarked that sight is by far the most costly and complex piece of workmanship which the artificer of the senses ever contrived?

No, I never have, he said.

Then reflect: has the ear or voice need of any third or additional nature in order that the one may be able to hear and the other to be heard?

Nothing of the sort.

No, indeed, I replied; and the same is true of most, if not all, the other senses—you would not say that any of them requires such an addition?

Certainly not.

But you see that without the addition of some other nature there is no seeing or being seen?

How do you mean?

Sight being, as I conceive, in the eyes, and he who has eyes wanting to see; colour being also present in them, still unless there be a third nature specially adapted to the purpose, the owner of the eyes will see nothing and the colours will be invisible.

Of what nature are you speaking?

Of that which you term light, I replied.

True, he said.

Noble, then, is the bond which links together sight and visibility, and great beyond other bonds by no small difference of nature; for light is their bond, and light is no ignoble thing?

Nay, he said, the reverse of ignoble.

And which, I said, of the gods in heaven would you say was the lord of this element? Whose is that light which makes the eye to see perfectly and the visible to appear?

You mean the sun, as you and all mankind say.

May not the relation of sight to this deity be described as follows?

How?

Neither sight nor the eye in which sight resides is the sun?

No.

Yet of all the organs of sense the eye is the most like the sun?

By far the most like.

And the power which the eye possesses is a sort of effluence which is dispensed from the sun?

Exactly.

Then the sun is not sight, but the author of sight who is recognised by sight.

True, he said.

And this is he whom I call the child of the good, whom the good begat in his own likeness, to be in the visible world, in relation to sight and the things of sight, what the good is in the intellectual world in relation to mind and the things of mind.

Will you be a little more explicit? he said.

Why, you know, I said, that the eyes, when a person directs them towards objects on which the light of day is no longer shining, but the moon and stars only, see dimly, and are nearly blind; they seem to have no clearness of vision in them?

Very true.

But when they are directed towards objects on which the sun shines, they see clearly and there is sight in them?

Certainly.

And the soul is like the eye: when resting upon that on which truth and being shine, the soul perceives and understands and is radiant with intelligence; but when turned towards the twilight of becoming and perishing, then she has opinion only, and goes blinking about, and is first of one opinion and then of another, and seems to have no intelligence?

Just so.

Now, that which imparts truth to the known and the power of knowing to the knower is what I would have you term the idea of good, and this you will deem to be the cause of science, and of truth in so far as the latter becomes the subject of knowledge, beautiful too, as are both truth and knowledge, you will be right in esteeming this other nature as more beautiful than either; and, as in the previous instance, light and sight may be truly said to be like the sun, and yet not to be the sun, so in this other sphere, science and truth may be deemed to be like the good, but not the good; the good has a place of honour yet higher.

What a wonder of beauty that must be, he said, which is the author of science and truth, and yet surpasses them in beauty; for you surely cannot mean to say that pleasure is the good?

God forbid, I replied; but may I ask you to consider the image in another point of view?

In what point of view?

You would say, would you not, that the sun is not only the author of visibility in all visible things, but of generation and nourishment and growth, though he himself is not generation?

Certainly.

In like manner the good may be said to be not only the author of knowledge to all things known, but of their being and essence, and yet the good is not essence, but far exceeds essence in dignity and power.

Glaucon said, with a ludicrous earnestness: By the light of heaven, how amazing!

Yes, I said, and the exaggeration may be set down to you; for you made me utter my fancies.

And pray continue to utter them; at any rate let us hear if there is anything more to be said about the similitude of the sun.

Yes, I said, there is a great deal more.

Then omit nothing, however slight.

I will do my best, I said; but I should think that a great deal will have to be omitted.

You have to imagine, then, that there are two ruling powers, and that one of them is set over the intellectual world, the other over the visible. I do not say heaven, lest you should fancy that I am playing upon the name (οὐρανός, ὁρατός). May I suppose that you have this distinction of the visible and intelligible fixed in your mind?

I have.

Now take a line which has been cut into two unequal parts, and divide each of them again in the same proportion, and suppose the two main divisions to answer, one to the visible and the other to the intelligible, and then compare the subdivisions in respect of their clearness and want of clearness, and you will find that the first section in the sphere of the visible consists of images. And by images I mean, in the first place, shadows, and in the second place, reflections in water and in solid, smooth and polished bodies and the like: Do you understand?

Yes, I understand.

Imagine, now, the other section, of which this is only the resemblance, to include the animals which we see, and everything that grows or is made.

Very good.

Would you not admit that both the sections of this division have different degrees of truth, and that the copy is to the original as the sphere of opinion is to the sphere of knowledge?

Most undoubtedly.

Next proceed to consider the manner in which the sphere of the intellectual is to be divided.

In what manner?

Thus:—There are two subdivisions, in the lower of which the soul uses the figures given by the former division as images; the enquiry can only be hypothetical, and instead of going upwards to a principle descends to the other end; in the higher of the two, the soul passes out of hypotheses, and goes up to a principle which is above hypotheses, making no use of images as in the former case, but proceeding only in and through the ideas themselves.

I do not quite understand your meaning, he said.

Then I will try again; you will understand me better when I have made some preliminary remarks. You are aware that students of geometry, arithmetic, and the kindred sciences assume the odd and the even and the figures and three kinds of angles and the like in their several branches of science; these are their hypotheses, which they and every body are supposed to know, and therefore they do not deign to give any account of them either to themselves or others; but they begin with them, and go on until they arrive at last, and in a consistent manner, at their conclusion?

Yes, he said, I know.

And do you not know also that although they make use of the visible forms and reason about them, they are thinking not of these but of the ideals which they resemble; not of the figures which they draw, but of the absolute square and the absolute diameter, and so on—the forms which they draw or make, and which have shadows and reflections in water of their own, are converted by them into images, but they are really seeking to behold the things themselves, which can only be seen with the eye of the mind?

That is true.

And of this kind I spoke as the intelligible, although in the search after it the soul is compelled to use hypotheses; not ascending to a first principle, because she is unable to rise above the region of hypothesis, but employing the objects of which the shadows below are resemblances in their turn as images, they having in relation to the shadows and reflections of them a greater distinctness, and therefore a higher value.

I understand, he said, that you are speaking of the province of geometry and the sister arts.

And when I speak of the other division of the intelligible, you will understand me to speak of that other sort of knowledge which reason herself attains by the power of dialectic, using the hypotheses not as first principles, but only as hypotheses—that is to say, as steps and points of departure into a world which is above hypotheses, in order that she may soar beyond them to the first principle of the whole; and clinging to this and then to that which depends on this, by successive steps she descends again without the aid of any sensible object, from ideas, through ideas, and in ideas she ends.

I understand you, he replied; not perfectly, for you seem to me to be describing a task which is really tremendous; but, at any rate, I understand you to say that knowledge and being, which the science of dialectic contemplates, are clearer than the notions of the arts, as they are termed, which proceed from hypotheses only: these are also contemplated by the understanding, and not by the senses: yet, because they start from hypotheses and do not ascend to a principle, those who contemplate them appear to you not to exercise the higher reason upon them, although when a first principle is added to them they are cognizable by the higher reason. And the habit which is concerned with geometry and the cognate sciences I suppose that you would term understanding and not reason, as being intermediate between opinion and reason.

You have quite conceived my meaning, I said; and now, corresponding to these four divisions, let there be four faculties in the soul—reason answering to the highest, understanding to the second, faith (or conviction) to the third, and perception of shadows to the last—and let there be a scale of them and let us suppose that the several faculties have clearness in the same degree that their objects have truth.

I understand, he replied, and give my assent, and accept your arrangement. [507–511]

And now, I [Socrates] said, let me show in a figure how far our nature is enlightened or unenlightened:—Behold! human beings living in an underground den, which has a mouth open towards the light and reaching all along the den; here they have been from their childhood, and have their legs and necks chained so that they cannot move, and can only see before them, being prevented by the chains from turning round their heads. Above and behind them a fire is blazing at a distance, and between the fire and the prisoners there is a raised way; and you will see, if you look, a low wall built along the way, like the screen which marionette players have in front of them, over which they show the puppets.

I [Glaucon] see.

And do you see, I said, men passing along the wall carrying all sorts of vessels, and statues and figures of animals made of wood and stone and various materials, which appear over the wall? Some of them are talking, others silent.

You have shown me a strange image, and they are strange prisoners.

Like ourselves, I replied; and they see only their own shadows, or the shadows of one another, which the fire throws on the opposite wall of the cave?

True, he said; how could they see anything but the shadows if they were never allowed to move their heads?

And of the objects which are being carried in like manner they would only see the shadows?

Yes, he said.

And if they were able to converse with one another, would they not suppose that they were naming what was actually before them?

Very true.

And suppose further that the prison had an echo which came from the other side, would they not be sure to fancy when one of the passers-by spoke that the voice which they heard came from the passing shadow?

No question, he replied.

To them, I said, the truth would be literally nothing but the shadows of the images.

That is certain.

And now look again, and see what will naturally follow if the prisoners are released and disabused of their error. At first, when any of them is liberated and compelled suddenly to stand up and turn his neck round and walk and look towards the light, he will suffer sharp pains; the glare will distress him, and he will be unable to see the realities of which in his former state he had seen the shadows; and then conceive some one saying to him, that what he saw before was an illusion, but that now, when he is approaching nearer to being and his eye is turned towards more real existence, he has a clearer vision,—what will be his reply? And you may further imagine that his instructor is pointing to the objects as they pass and requiring him to name them,—will he not be perplexed? Will he not fancy that the shadows which he formerly saw are truer than the objects which are now shown to him?

Far truer.

And if he is compelled to look straight at the light, will he not have a pain in his eyes which will make him turn away to take refuge in the objects of vision which he can see, and which he will conceive to be in reality clearer than the things which are now being shown to him?

True, he said.

And suppose once more, that he is reluctantly dragged up a steep and rugged ascent, and held fast until he is forced into the presence of the sun himself, is he not likely to be pained and irritated? When he approaches the light his eyes will be dazzled, and he will not be able to see anything at all of what are now called realities.

Not all in a moment, he said.

He will require to grow accustomed to the sight of the upper world. And first he will see the shadows best, next the reflections of men and other objects in the water, and then the objects themselves; then he will gaze upon the light of the moon and the stars and the spangled heaven; and he will see the sky and the stars by night better than the sun or the light of the sun by day?

Certainly.

Last of all he will be able to see the sun, and not mere reflections of him in the water, but he will see him in his own proper place, and not in another; and he will contemplate him as he is.

Certainly.

He will then proceed to argue that this is he who gives the season and the years, and is the guardian of all that is in the visible world, and in a certain way the cause of all things which he and his fellows have been accustomed to behold?

Clearly, he said, he would first see the sun and then reason about him.

And when he remembered his old habitation, and the wisdom of the den and his fellow-prisoners, do you not suppose that he would felicitate himself on the change, and pity them?

Certainly, he would.

And if they were in the habit of conferring

honours among themselves on those who were quickest to observe the passing shadows and to remark which of them went before, and which followed after, and which were together; and who were therefore best able to draw conclusions as to the future, do you think that he would care for such honours and glories, or envy the possessors of them? Would he not say with Homer,

> 'Better to be the poor servant of a poor master,'

and to endure anything, rather than think as they do and live after their manner?

Yes, he said, I think that he would rather suffer anything than entertain these false notions and live in this miserable manner.

Imagine once more, I said, such an one coming suddenly out of the sun to be replaced in his old situation; would he not be certain to have his eyes full of darkness?

To be sure, he said.

And if there were a contest, and he had to compete in measuring the shadows with the prisoners who had never moved out of the den, while his sight was still weak, and before his eyes had become steady (and the time which would be needed to acquire this new habit of sight might be very considerable), would he not be ridiculous? Men would say of him that up he went and down he came without his eyes; and that it was better not even to think of ascending; and if any one tried to loose another and lead him up to the light, let them only catch the offender, and they would put him to death.

No question, he said.

This entire allegory, I said, you may now append, dear Glaucon, to the previous argument; the prison-house is the world of sight, the light of the fire is the sun, and you will not misapprehend me if you interpret the journey upwards to be the ascent of the soul into the intellectual world according to my poor belief, which, at your desire, I have expressed—whether rightly or wrongly God knows. But, whether true or false, my opinion is that in the world of knowledge the idea of good appears last of all, and is seen only with an effort; and, when seen, is also inferred to be the universal author of all things beautiful and right, parent of light and of the lord of light in this visible world, and the immediate source of reason and truth in the intellectual; and that this is the power upon which he who would act rationally either in public or private life must have his eye fixed.

I agree, he said, as far as I am able to understand you.

Moreover, I said, you must not wonder that those who attain to this beatific vision are unwilling to descend to human affairs; for their souls are ever hastening into the upper world where they desire to dwell; which desire of theirs is very natural, if our allegory may be trusted.

Yes, very natural.

And is there anything surprising in one who passes from divine contemplations to the evil state of man, misbehaving himself in a ridiculous manner; if, while his eyes are blinking and before he has become accustomed to the surrounding darkness, he is compelled to fight in courts of law, or in other places, about the images or the shadows of images of justice, and is endeavouring to meet the conceptions of those who have never yet seen absolute justice?

Anything but surprising, he replied.

Any one who has common sense will remember that the bewilderments of the eyes are of two kinds, and arise from two causes, either from coming out of the light or from going into the light, which is true of the mind's eye, quite as much as of the bodily eye; and he who remembers this when he sees any one whose vision is perplexed and weak, will not be too ready to laugh; he will first ask whether that soul of man has come out of the brighter life, and is unable to see because unaccustomed to the dark, or having turned from darkness to the day is dazzled by excess of light. And he will count the one happy in his condition and state of being, and he will pity the other; or, if he have a mind to laugh at the soul which comes from below into the light, there will be more reason in this than in the laugh which greets him who returns from above out of the light into the den.

That, he said, is a very just distinction.

But then, if I am right, certain professors of education must be wrong when they say that they can put a knowledge into the soul which was not there before, like sight into blind eyes.

They undoubtedly say this, he replied.

Whereas, our argument shows that the power and capacity of learning exists in the soul already; and that just as the eye was unable to turn from darkness to light without the whole body, so too the instrument of knowledge can only by the movement of the whole soul be turned from the world of becoming into that of being, and learn by degrees to endure the sight of being, and of the brightest and best of being, or in other words, of the good.

Very true.

And must there not be some art which will effect conversion in the easiest and quickest manner; not implanting the faculty of sight, for that exists already, but has been turned in the wrong direction, and is looking away from the truth?

Yes, he said, such an art may be presumed.

And whereas the other so-called virtues of the soul seem to be akin to bodily qualities, for even when they are not originally innate they can be implanted later by habit and exercise, the virtue of wisdom more than anything else contains a divine element which always remains, and by this conversion is rendered useful and profitable; or, on the other hand, hurtful and useless. Did you never observe the narrow intelligence flashing from the keen eye of a clever rogue—how eager he is, how clearly his paltry soul sees the way to his end; he is the reverse of blind, but his keen eye-sight is forced into the service of evil, and he is mischievous in proportion to his cleverness?

Very true, he said.

But what if there had been a circumcision of such natures in the days of their youth; and they had been severed from those sensual pleasures, such as eating and drinking, which, like leaden weights, were attached to them at their birth, and which drag them down and turn the vision of their souls upon the things that are below—if, I say, they had been released from these impediments and turned in the opposite direction, the very same faculty in them would have seen the truth as keenly as they see what their eyes are turned to now.

Very likely.

Yes, I said; and there is another thing which is likely, or rather a necessary inference from what has preceded, that neither the uneducated and uninformed of the truth, nor yet those who never make an end of their education, will be able ministers of State; not the former, because they have no single aim of duty which is the rule of all their actions, private as well as public; nor the latter, because they will not act at all except upon compulsion, fancying that they are already dwelling apart in the islands of the blest.

Very true, he replied.

Then, I said, the business of us who are the founders of the State will be to compel the best minds to attain that knowledge which we have already shown to be the greatest of all—they must continue to ascend until they arrive at the good; but when they have ascended and seen enough we must not allow them to do as they do now.

What do you mean?

I mean that they remain in the upper world: but this must not be allowed; they must be made to descend again among the prisoners in the den, and partake of their labours and honours, whether they are worth having or not.

But is not this unjust? he said; ought we to give them a worse life, when they might have a better?

You have again forgotten, my friend, I said, the intention of the legislator, who did not aim at making any one class in the State happy above the rest; the happiness was to be in the whole State, and he held the citizens together by persuasion and necessity, making them benefactors of the State, and therefore benefactors of one another; to this end he created them, not to please themselves, but to be his instruments in binding up the State.

True, he said, I had forgotten.

Observe, Glaucon, that there will be no injustice in compelling our philosophers to have a care and providence of others; we shall explain to them that in other States, men of their class are not obliged to share in the toils of politics: and this is reasonable, for they grow up at their own sweet will, and the government would rather not have them. Being self-taught, they cannot be expected to show any gratitude for a culture which they have never received. But we have brought you into the world to be rulers of the hive, kings of yourselves and of the other citizens, and have educated you far better and more perfectly than they have been educated, and you are better able to share in the double duty. Wherefore each of you, when his turn comes, must go down to the general underground abode, and get the habit of seeing in the dark. When you have acquired the habit, you will see ten thousand times better than the inhabitants of the den, and you will know what the several images are, and what they represent, because you have seen the beautiful and just and good in their truth. And thus our State which is also yours will be a reality, and not a dream only, and will be administered in a spirit unlike that of other States, in which men fight with one another about shadows only and are distracted in the struggle for power, which in their eyes is a great good. Whereas the truth is that the State in which the rulers are most reluctant to govern is always the best and most quietly governed, and the State in which they are most eager, the worst.

Quite true, he replied.

And will our pupils, when they hear this, refuse to take their turn at the toils of State, when they are allowed to spend the greater part of their time with one another in the heavenly light?

Impossible, he answered; for they are just men, and the commands which we impose upon them are just; there can be no doubt that every one of them will take office as a stern necessity, and not after the fashion of our present rulers of State.

Yes, my friend, I said; and there lies the point. You must contrive for your future rulers another and a better life than that of a ruler, and then you may have a well-ordered State; for only in the State which offers this, will they rule who are truly rich, not in silver and gold, but in virtue and wisdom, which are the true blessings of life. Whereas if they go to the administration of public affairs, poor and hungering after their own private advantage, thinking that hence they are to snatch the chief good, order there can never be; for they will be fighting about office, and the civil and domestic broils which thus arise will be the ruin of the rulers themselves and of the whole State. [514–521]

Of the many excellences which I [Socrates] perceive in the order of our State, there is none which upon reflection pleases me better than the rule about poetry.

To what do you refer?

To the rejection of imitative poetry, which certainly ought not to be received; as I see far more clearly now that the parts of the soul have been distinguished.

What do you mean?

Speaking in confidence, for I should not like to have my words repeated to the tragedians and the rest of the imitative tribe—but I do not mind saying to you, that all poetical imitations are ruinous to the understanding of the hearers, and that the knowledge of their true nature is the only antidote to them.

Explain the purport of your remark.

Well, I will tell you, although I have always from my earliest youth had an awe and love of Homer, which even now makes the words falter on my lips, for he is the great captain and teacher of the whole of that charming tragic company; but a man is not to be reverenced more than the truth, and therefore I will speak out.

Very good, he said.

Listen to me then, or rather, answer me.

Put your question.

Can you tell me what imitation is? for I really do not know.

A likely thing, then, that I should know.

Why not? for the duller eye may often see a thing sooner than the keener.

Very true, he said; but in your presence, even if I had any faint notion, I could not muster courage to utter it. Will you enquire yourself?

Well then, shall we begin the enquiry in our usual manner: Whenever a number of individuals have a common name, we assume them to have also a corresponding idea or form:—do you understand me?

I do.

Let us take any common instance: there are beds and tables in the world—plenty of them, are there not?

Yes.

But there are only two ideas or forms of them—one the idea of a bed, the other of a table.

True.

And the maker of either of them makes a bed or he makes a table for our use, in accordance with the idea—that is our way of speaking in this and similar instances—but no artificer makes the ideas themselves: how could he?

Impossible.

And there is another artist,—I should like to know what you would say of him.

Who is he?

One who is the maker of all the works of all other workmen.

What an extraordinary man!

Wait a little, and there will be more reason for your saying so. For this is he who is able to make not only vessels of every kind, but plants and animals, himself and all other things—the earth and heaven, and the things which are in heaven or under the earth; he makes the gods also.

He must be a wizard and no mistake.

Oh! you are incredulous, are you? Do you mean that there is no such maker or creator, or that in one sense there might be a maker of all these things but in another not? Do you see that there is a way in which you could make them all yourself?

What way?

An easy way enough; or rather, there are many ways in which the feat might be quickly and easily accomplished, none quicker than that of turning a mirror round and round—you would soon enough make the sun and the heavens, and the earth and yourself, and other animals and plants, and all the other things of which we were just now speaking, in the mirror.

Yes, he said; but they would be appearances only.

Very good, I said, you are coming to the point now. And the painter too is, as I conceive, just such another—a creator of appearances, is he not?

Of course.

But then I suppose you will say that what he creates is untrue. And yet there is a sense in which the painter also creates a bed?

Yes, he said, but not a real bed.

And what of the maker of the bed? were you not saying that he too makes, not the idea which, according to our view, is the essence of the bed, but only a particular bed?

Yes, I did.

Then if he does not make that which exists he cannot make true existence, but only some semblance of existence; and if any one were to say that the work of the maker of the bed, or of any other workman, has real existence, he could hardly be supposed to be speaking the truth.

At any rate, he replied, philosophers would say that he was not speaking the truth.

No wonder, then, that his work too is an indistinct expression of truth.

No wonder.

Suppose now that by the light of the examples just offered we enquire who this imitator is?

If you please.

Well then, here are three beds: one existing in nature, which is made by God, as I think that we may say—for no one else can be the maker?

No.

There is another which is the work of the carpenter?

Yes.

And the work of the painter is a third?

Yes.

Beds, then, are of three kinds, and there are three artists who superintend them: God, the maker of the bed, and the painter?

Yes, there are three of them.

God, whether from choice or from necessity, made one bed in nature and one only; two or more such ideal beds neither ever have been nor ever will be made by God.

Why is that?

Because even if He had made but two, a third would still appear behind them which both of them would have for their idea, and that would be the ideal bed and not the two others.

Very true, he said.

God knew this, and He desired to be the real maker of a real bed, not a particular maker of a particular bed, and therefore He created a bed which is essentially and by nature one only.

So we believe.

Shall we, then, speak of Him as the natural author or maker of the bed?

Yes, he replied; inasmuch as by the natural process of creation He is the author of this and of all other things.

And what shall we say of the carpenter—is not he also the maker of the bed?

Yes.

But would you call the painter a creator and maker?

Certainly not.

Yet if he is not the maker, what is he in relation to the bed?

I think, he said, that we may fairly designate him as the imitator of that which the others make.

Good, I said; then you call him who is third in the descent from nature an imitator?

Certainly, he said.

And the tragic poet is an imitator, and therefore, like all other imitators, he is thrice removed from the king and from the truth?

That appears to be so.

Then about the imitator we are agreed. And what about the painter?—I would like to know whether he may be thought to imitate that which originally exists in nature, or only the creations of artists?

The latter.

As they are or as they appear? you have still to determine this.

What do you mean?

I mean, that you may look at a bed from different points of view, obliquely or directly or from any other point of view, and the bed will appear different, but there is no difference in reality. And the same of all things.

Yes, he said, the difference is only apparent.

Now let me ask you another question: Which is the art of painting designed to be—an imitation of things as they are, or as they appear—of appearance or of reality?

Of appearance.

Then the imitator, I said, is a long way off the truth, and can do all things because he lightly touches on a small part of them, and that part an image. For example: A painter will paint a cobbler, carpenter, or any other artist, though he knows nothing of their arts; and, if he is a good artist, he may deceive children or simple persons, when he shows them his picture of a carpenter from a distance, and they will fancy that they are looking at a real carpenter.

Certainly.

And whenever any one informs us that he has found a man who knows all the arts, and all things else that anybody knows, and every single thing with a higher degree of accuracy than any other man—whoever tells us this, I think that we can only imagine him to be a simple creature who is likely to have been deceived by some wizard or actor whom he met, and whom he thought all-knowing, because he himself was unable to analyse the nature of knowledge and ignorance and imitation.

Most true. [595–598]

From the Timaeus

Socrates. I see that I shall receive in my turn a perfect and splendid feast of reason. And now, Timaeus, you, I suppose, should speak next, after duly calling upon the Gods.

Timaeus. All men, Socrates, who have any degree of right feeling at the beginning of every enterprise, whether small or great, always call upon God. And we, too, who are going to discourse of the nature of the universe, how created or how existing without creation, if we be not altogether out of our wits, must invoke the aid of Gods and Goddesses and pray that our words may be acceptable to them and consistent with themselves. Let this, then, be our invocation of the Gods, to which I add an exhortation of myself to speak in such manner as will be most intelligible to you, and will most accord with my own intent.

First then, in my judgment, we must make a distinction and ask, What is that which always is and has no becoming; and what is that which is always becoming and never is? That which is apprehended by intelligence and reason is always in the same state; but that which is conceived by opinion with the help of sensation and without reason, is always in a process of becoming and perishing and never really is. Now everything that becomes or is created must of necessity be created by some cause, for without a cause nothing can be created. The work of the creator, whenever he looks to the unchangeable and fashions the form and nature of his work after an unchangeable pattern, must necessarily be made fair and perfect; but when he looks to the created only, and uses a created pattern, it is not fair or perfect. Was the heaven then or the world, whether called by this or by any other more appropriate name—assuming the name, I am asking a question which has to be asked at the beginning of any enquiry about anything—was the world, I say, always in existence and without beginning? or created, and had it a beginning? Created, I reply, being visible and tangible and having a body, and therefore sensible; and all sensible things are apprehended by opinion and sense and are in a process of creation and created. Now that which is created must, as we affirm, of necessity be created by a cause. But the father and maker of all this universe is past finding out; and even if we found him, to tell of him to all men would be impossible. And there is still a question to be asked about him: Which of the patterns had the artificer in view when he made the world,—the pattern of the unchangeable, or of that which is cre-

From Plato, *Timaeus,* 27–35.

ated? If the world be indeed fair and the artificer good, it is manifest that he must have looked to that which is eternal; but if what cannot be said without blasphemy is true, then to the created pattern. Every one will see that he must have looked to the eternal; for the world is the fairest of creations and he is the best of causes. And having been created in this way, the world has been framed in the likeness of that which is apprehended by reason and mind and is unchangeable, and must therefore of necessity, if this is admitted, be a copy of something. Now it is all-important that the beginning of everything should be according to nature. And in speaking of the copy and the original we may assume that words are akin to the matter which they describe; when they relate to the lasting and permanent and intelligible, they ought to be lasting and unalterable, and, as far as their nature allows, irrefutable and immovable—nothing less. But when they express only the copy or likeness and not the eternal things themselves, they need only be likely and analogous to the real words. As being is to becoming, so is truth to belief. If then, Socrates, amid the many opinions about the gods and the generation of the universe, we are not able to give notions which are altogether and in every respect exact and consistent with one another, do not be surprised. Enough, if we adduce probabilities as likely as any others; for we must remember that I who am the speaker, and you who are the judges, are only mortal men, and we ought to accept the tale which is probable and enquire no further.

Soc. Excellent, Timaeus; and we will do precisely as you bid us. The prelude is charming, and is already accepted by us—may we beg of you to proceed to the strain?

Tim. Let me tell you then why the creator made this world of generation. He was good, and the good can never have any jealousy of anything. And being free from jealousy, he desired that all things should be as like himself as they could be. This is in the truest sense the origin of creation and of the world, as we shall do well in believing on the testimony of wise men: God desired that all things should be good and nothing bad, so far as this was attainable. Wherefore also finding the whole visible sphere not at rest, but moving in an irregular and disorderly fashion, out of disorder he brought order, considering that this was in every way better than the other. Now the deeds of the best could never be or have been other than the fairest; and the creator, reflecting on the things which are by nature visible, found that no unintelligent creature taken as a whole was fairer than the intelligent taken as a whole; and that intelligence could not be present in anything which was devoid of soul. For which reason, when he was framing the universe, he put intelligence in soul, and soul in body, that he might be the creator of a work which was by nature fairest and best. Wherefore, using the language of probability, we may say that the world became a living creature truly endowed with soul and intelligence by the providence of God.

This being supposed, let us proceed to the next stage: In the likeness of what animal did the Creator make the world? It would be an unworthy thing to liken it to any nature which exists as a part only; for nothing can be beautiful which is like any imperfect thing; but let us suppose the world to be the very image of that whole of which all other animals both individually and in their tribes are portions. For the original of the universe contains in itself all intelligible beings, just as this world comprehends us and all other visible creatures. For the Deity, intending to make this world like the fairest and most perfect of intelligible beings, framed one visible animal comprehending within itself all other animals of a kindred nature. Are we right in saying that there is one world, or that they are many and infinite? There must be one only, if the created copy is to accord with the original. For that which includes all other intelligible creatures cannot have a second or companion; in that case there would be need of another living being which would include both, and of which they would be parts, and the likeness would be more truly said to resemble not them, but that other which included them. In order then that the world might be solitary, like the perfect animal, the creator made not two worlds or an infinite number of them; but there is and ever will be one only-begotten and created heaven.

Now that which is created is of necessity corporeal, and also visible and tangible. And nothing is visible where there is no fire, or tangible which has no solidity, and nothing is solid without earth. Wherefore also God in the beginning of creation made the body of the universe to consist of fire and earth. But two things cannot be rightly put together without a third; there must be some bond of union between them. And the fairest bond is that which makes the most complete fusion of itself and the things which it combines; and proportion is best adapted to effect such a union. For whenever in any three numbers, whether cube or square, there is a mean, which is to the last term what the first term is to it; and again, when the mean is to the first term as the last term is to the mean,—then the mean becoming first and last, and the first and last both becoming means, they will all of them of necessity come to be the same, and having become the same with one another will be all one. If the universal frame had been created a surface only and having no depth, a single mean would have sufficed to bind together itself and the other terms; but now, as the world must be solid, and solid bodies are always compacted not by one mean but by two, God placed water and air in the mean between fire and earth, and made them to have the same proportion so far as was possible (as fire is to air so is air to water, and as air is to water so is water to earth); and thus he bound and put together a visible and tangible heaven. And for these reasons, and out of such elements which are in number four, the body of the world was created, and it was harmonized by proportion, and therefore has the spirit of friendship; and having been reconciled to itself, it was indissoluble by the hand of any other than the framer.

Now the creation took up the whole of each of the four elements; for the Creator compounded the world out of all the fire and all the water and all the air and all the earth, leaving no part of any of them nor any power of them outside. His intention was, in the first place, that the animal should be as far as possible a perfect whole and of perfect parts: secondly, that it should be one, leaving no remnants out of which another such world might be created: and also that it should be free from old age and unaffected by disease. Considering that if heat and cold and other powerful forces which unite bodies surround and attack them from without when they are unprepared, they decompose them, and by bringing diseases and old age upon them, make them waste away—for this cause and on these grounds he made the world one whole, having every part entire, and being therefore perfect and not liable to old age and disease. And he gave to the world the figure which was suitable and also natural. Now to the animal which was to comprehend all animals, that figure was suitable which comprehends within itself all other figures. Wherefore he made the world in the form of a globe, round as from a lathe, having its extremes in every direction equidistant from the centre, the most perfect and the most like itself of all figures; for he considered that the like is infinitely fairer than the unlike. This he finished off, making the surface smooth all around for many reasons; in the first place, because the living being had no need of eyes when there was nothing remaining outside him to be seen; nor of ears when there was nothing to be heard; and there was no surrounding atmosphere to be breathed; nor would there have been any use of organs by the help of which he might receive his food or get rid of what he had already digested, since there was nothing which went from him or came into him: for there was nothing beside him. Of design he was created thus, his own waste providing his own food, and all that he did or suffered taking place in and by himself. For the Creator conceived that a being which was self-sufficient would be far more excellent than one which lacked anything; and, as he had no need to take anything or defend himself against any one, the Creator did not think it necessary to bestow upon him hands: nor had he any need of feet, nor of the whole apparatus of walking; but the movement suited to his spherical form was assigned to him, being of all the seven that which is most appropriate to mind and intelligence; and he was made to move in the same manner and on the same spot, within his own limits revolving in a circle. All the other six motions were taken away from him, and he was made not to partake of their deviations. And as this circular movement required no feet, the universe was created without legs and without feet.

Such was the whole plan of the eternal God about the god that was to be, to whom for this reason he gave a body, smooth and even, having a surface in every direction equidistant from the centre, a body entire and perfect, and formed out of perfect bodies. And in the centre he put the soul, which he diffused throughout the body, making it also to be the exterior environment of it; and he made the universe a circle moving in a circle, one and solitary, yet by reason of its excellence able to converse with itself, and needing no other friendship or acquaintance. Having these purposes in view he created the world a blessed god.

Now God did not make the soul after the body, although we are speaking of them in this order; for having brought them together he would never have allowed that the elder should be ruled by the younger; but this is a random manner of speaking which we have, because somehow we ourselves too are very much under the dominion of chance. Whereas he made the soul in origin and excellence prior to and older than the body, to be the ruler and mistress, of whom the body was to be the subject. And he made her out of the following elements and on this wise: Out of the indivisible and unchangeable, and also out of that which is divisible and has to do with material bodies, he compounded a third and intermediate kind of essence, partaking of the nature of the same and of the other, and this compound he placed accordingly in a mean between the indivisible, and the divisible and material. He took the three elements of the same, the other, and the essence, and mingled them into one form, compressing by force the reluctant and unsociable nature of the other into the same. When he had mingled them with the essence and out of three made one, he again divided this whole into as many portions as was fitting, each portion being a compound of the same, the other, and the essence.

PERICLES

Pericles, born ca. 495 B.C., had an illustrious and embattled career as an Athenian statesman. The activity of Pericles was contemporary with that of Socrates (469–399 B.C.). From 445 until 431 B.C., Pericles was a leader in the artistic and political development of Athens, and was influential in the construction of the Parthenon, the famous temple honoring the Greek goddess Athena. In 431 B.C., the Peloponnesian War with Sparta began, and Pericles became an important figure in rallying support for the Athenian army and navy. At the end of the first year of the war, he delivered a stirring oration on behalf of the war dead. But pestilence infected Athens, and Pericles died of its effects in 429 B.C. The war, bitter and complicated, lasted until 404 B.C., when Sparta conquered Athens and ended its hegemony as the premier city of the classical world. The following selection is as reported by Thucydides in his History.

The Parthenon, Athens (445–432 B.C.). Built on the Acropolis, the Parthenon is the finest monument of Greek architecture. (Alinari/Art Resource)

Pericles' Funeral Oration

'Most of my predecessors in this place have commended him who made this speech part of the law, telling us that it is well that it should be delivered at the burial of those who fall in battle. For myself, I should have thought that the worth which had displayed itself in deeds, would be sufficiently rewarded by honours also shown by deeds; such as you now see in this funeral prepared at the people's cost. And I could have wished that the reputations of many brave men were not to be imperilled in the mouth of a single individual, to stand or fall according as he spoke well or ill. For it is hard to speak properly upon a subject where it is even difficult to convince your hearers that you are speaking the truth. On the one hand, the friend who is familiar with every fact of the story, may think that some point has not been set forth with that fulness which he wishes and knows it to deserve; on the other, he who is a stranger to the matter may be led by envy to suspect exaggeration if he hears anything above his own nature. For men can endure to hear others praised only so long as they can severally persuade themselves of their own ability to equal the actions recounted: when this point is passed, envy comes in and with it incredulity. However, since our ancestors have stamped this custom with their approval, it becomes my duty to obey the law and to try to satisfy your several wishes and opinions as best I may.

'I shall begin with our ancestors: it is both just and proper that they should have the honour of the first mention on an occasion like the present. They dwelt in the country without break in the succession from generation to generation, and handed it down free to the present time by their valour. And if our more remote ancestors deserve praise, much more do our own fathers, who added to their inheritance the empire which we now possess, and spared no pains to be able to leave their acquisitions to us of the present generation. Lastly, there are few parts of our dominions that have not been augmented by those of us here, who are still more or less in the vigour of life; while the mother country has been furnished by us with everything that can enable her to depend on her own resources whether for war or for peace. That part of our history which tells of the military achievements which gave us our several possessions, or of the ready valour with which either we or our fathers stemmed the tide of Hellenic or foreign aggression, is a theme too familiar to my hearers for me to dilate on, and I shall therefore pass it by. But what was the road by which we reached our position, what the form of government under which our greatness grew, what the national habits out of which it sprang; these are questions which I may try to solve before I proceed to my panegyric upon these men; since I think this to be a subject upon which on the present occasion a speaker may properly dwell, and to which the whole assemblage, whether citizens or foreigners, may listen with advantage.

'Our constitution does not copy the laws of neighbouring states; we are rather a pattern to others than imitators ourselves. Its administration favours the many instead of the few; this is why it is called a democracy. If we look to the laws, they afford equal justice to all in their private differences; if to social standing, advancement in public life falls to reputation for capacity, class considerations not being allowed to interfere with merit; nor again does poverty bar the way, if a man is able to serve the state, he is not hindered by the obscurity of his condition. The freedom which we enjoy in our government extends also to our ordinary life. There, far from exercising a jealous surveillance over each other, we do not feel called upon to be angry with our neighbour for doing what he likes, or even to indulge in those injurious looks which cannot fail to be offensive, although they inflict no positive penalty. But all this ease in our private relations does not make us lawless as citizens. Against this fear is our chief safeguard, teaching us to obey the magistrates and the laws, particularly such as regard the protection of the injured, whether they are actually on the statute book, or belong to that code which, although unwritten, yet cannot be broken without acknowledged disgrace.

'Further, we provide plenty of means for the mind to refresh itself from business. We celebrate games and sacrifices all the year round, and the elegance of

From Thucydides, "The Peloponnesian War," *The Complete Writings of Thucydides*, trans. Joseph Gavorse (New York: The Modern Library, 1934), pp. 102–109.

our private establishments forms a daily source of pleasure and helps to banish the spleen; while the magnitude of our city draws the produce of the world into our harbour, so that to the Athenian the fruits of other countries are as familiar a luxury as those of his own.

'If we turn to our military policy, there also we differ from our antagonists. We throw open our city to the world, and never by alien acts exclude foreigners from any opportunity of learning or observing, although the eyes of an enemy may occasionally profit by our liberality; trusting less in system and policy than to the native spirit of our citizens; while in education, where our rivals from their very cradles by a painful discipline seek after manliness, at Athens we live exactly as we please, and yet are just as ready to encounter every legitimate danger. In proof of this it may be noticed that the Lacedæmonians do not invade our country alone, but bring with them all their confederates; while we Athenians advance unsupported into the territory of a neighbour, and fighting upon a foreign soil usually vanquish with ease men who are defending their homes. Our united force was never yet encountered by any enemy, because we have at once to attend to our marine and to despatch our citizens by land upon a hundred different services; so that, wherever they engage with some such fraction of our strength, a success against a detachment is magnified into a victory over the nation, and a defeat into a reverse suffered at the hands of our entire people. And yet if with habits not of labour but of ease, and courage not of art but of nature, we are still willing to encounter danger, we have the double advantage of escaping the experience of hardships in anticipation and of facing them in the hour of need as fearlessly as those who are never free from them.

'Nor are these the only points in which our city is worthy of admiration. We cultivate refinement without extravagance and knowledge without effeminacy; wealth we employ more for use than for show, and place the real disgrace of poverty not in owning to the fact but in declining the struggle against it. Our public men have, besides politics, their private affairs to attend to, and our ordinary citizens, though occupied with the pursuits of industry, are still fair judges of public matters; for, unlike any other nation, regarding him who takes no part in these duties not as unambitious but as useless, we Athenians are able to judge at all events if we cannot originate, and instead of looking on discussion as a stumbling-block in the way of action, we think it an indispensable preliminary to any wise action at all. Again, in our enterprises we present the singular spectacle of daring and deliberation, each carried to its highest point, and both united in the same persons; although usually decision is the fruit of ignorance, hesitation of reflexion. But the palm of courage will surely be adjudged most justly to those, who best know the difference between hardship and pleasure and yet are never tempted to shrink from danger. In generosity we are equally singular, acquiring our friends by conferring not by receiving favours. Yet, of course, the doer of the favour is the firmer friend of the two, in order by continued kindness to keep the recipient in his debt; while the debtor feels less keenly from the very consciousness that the return he makes will be a payment, not a free gift. And it is only the Athenians who, fearless of consequences, confer their benefits not from calculations of expediency, but in the confidence of liberality.

'In short, I say that as a city we are the school of Hellas; while I doubt if the world can produce a man, who where he has only himself to depend upon, is equal to so many emergencies, and graced by so happy a versatility as the Athenian. And that this is no mere boast thrown out for the occasion, but plain matter of fact, the power of the state acquired by these habits proves. For Athens alone of her contemporaries is found when tested to be greater than her reputation, and alone gives no occasion to her assailants to blush at the antagonist by whom they have been worsted, or to her subjects to question her title by merit to rule. Rather, the admiration of the present and succeeding ages will be ours, since we have not left our power without witness, but have shown it by mighty proofs; and far from needing a Homer for our panegyrist, or other of his craft whose verses might charm for the moment only for the impression which they gave to melt at the touch of fact, we have forced every sea and land to be the highway of our daring, and everywhere, whether for evil or for good, have left imperishable monuments behind us. Such is the Athens for which these men, in the assertion of their resolve not to lose her, nobly fought and died; and well may every one of their survivors be ready to suffer in her cause.

'Indeed if I have dwelt at some length upon the character of our country, it has been to show that our stake in the struggle is not the same as theirs who have no such blessings to lose, and also that the panegyric of the men over whom I am now speaking might be by definite proofs established. That panegyric is now in a great measure complete; for the Athens that I have celebrated is only what the heroism of these and their like have made her, men whose fame, unlike that of most Hellenes, will be found to be only commensurate with their deserts. And if a test of worth be wanted, it is to be found in their closing scene, and this not only in the cases in which it set the final seal upon their merit, but also in those in which it gave the first intimation of their having any. For there is justice in the claim that steadfastness in his country's battles should be as a cloak to cover a man's other imperfections; since the good action has blotted out the bad, and his merit as a citizen more than outweighed his demerits as an individual. But none of these allowed either wealth with its prospect of future enjoyment to unnerve his spirit, or poverty with its hope of a day of freedom and riches to tempt him to shrink from danger. No, holding that vengeance upon their enemies was more to be desired than any personal blessings, and reckoning this to be the most glorious of hazards, they joyfully determined to accept the risk, to make sure of their vengeance and to let their wishes wait; and while committing to hope the uncertainty of final success, in the business before them they thought fit to act boldly and trust in themselves. Thus choosing to die resisting, rather than to live submitting, they fled only from dishonour, but met danger face to face, and after one brief moment, while at the summit of their fortune, escaped, not from their fear, but from their glory.

'So died these men as became Athenians. You, their survivors, must determine to have as unaltering a resolution in the field, though you may pray that it may have a happier issue. And not contented with ideas derived only from words of the advantages which are bound up with the defence of your country, though these would furnish a valuable text to a speaker even before an audience so alive to them as the present, you must yourselves realise the power of Athens, and feed your eyes upon her from day to day, till love of her fills your hearts; and then when all her greatness shall break upon you, you must reflect that it was by courage, sense of duty, and a keen feeling of honour in action that men were enabled to win all this, and that no personal failure in an enterprise could make them consent to deprive their country of their valour, but they laid it at her feet as the most glorious contribution that they could offer. For this offering of their lives made in common by them all they each of them individually received that renown which never grows old, and for a sepulchre, not so much that in which their bones have been deposited, but that noblest of shrines wherein their glory is laid up to be eternally remembered upon every occasion on which deed or story shall fall for its commemoration. For heroes have the whole earth for their tomb; and in lands far from their own, where the column with its epitaph declares it, there is enshrined in every breast a record unwritten with no tablet to preserve it, except that of the heart. These take as your model, and judging happiness to be the fruit of freedom and freedom of valour, never decline the dangers of war. For it is not the miserable that would most justly be unsparing of their lives; these have nothing to hope for: it is rather they to whom continued life may bring reverses as yet unknown, and to whom a fall, if it came, would be most tremendous in its consequences. And surely, to a man of spirit, the degradation of cowardice must be immeasurably more grievous that the unfelt death which strikes him in the midst of his strength and patriotism!

'Comfort, therefore, not condolence, is what I have to offer to the parents of the dead who may be here. Numberless are the chances to which, as they know, the life of man is subject; but fortunate indeed are they who draw for their lot a death so glorious as that which has caused your mourning, and to whom life has been so exactly measured as to terminate in the happiness in which it has been passed. Still I know that this is a hard saying, especially when those are in question of whom you will constantly be reminded by seeing in the homes of others blessings of which once you also boasted: for grief is felt not so much for the want of what we have never known, as for the loss of that to which we have been long accustomed. Yet you who are still of an age to beget children must bear up in the hope of having others in their stead; not only will they help you to forget those whom you have lost, but will be to the state at once a reinforcement and a security; for never can a fair or just policy be expected of a citizen who does not, like his fellows, bring to the decision the interests and apprehensions of a father. While those of you who have passed your prime must congratulate yourselves with the thought that the best part of your life was fortunate, and that the brief span that remains will be cheered by the fame of the departed. For it is only the love of honour that never grows old; and honour it is, not gain, as some would have it, that rejoices the heart of age and helplessness.

'Turning to the sons or brothers of the dead, I see an arduous struggle before you. When a man is gone, all are wont to praise him, and should your merit be ever so transcendent, you will still find it difficult not merely to overtake, but even to approach their renown. The living have envy to contend with, while those who are no longer in our path are honoured with a goodwill into which rivalry does not enter. On the other hand, if I must say anything on the subject of female excellence to those of you who will now be in widowhood, it will be all comprised in this brief exhortation. Great will be your glory in not falling short of your natural character; and greatest will be hers who is least talked of among the men whether for good or for bad.

'My task is now finished. I have performed it to the best of my ability, and in words, at least, the requirements of the law are now satisfied. If deeds be in question, those who are here interred have received part of their honours already, and for the rest, their children will be brought up till manhood at the public expense: the state thus offers a valuable prize, as the garland of victory in this race of valour, for the reward both of those who have fallen and their survivors. And where the rewards for merit are greatest, there are found the best citizens.

'And now that you have brought to a close your lamentations for your relatives, you may depart.'

THUCYDIDES

As a commander for the Athenian forces against the skilled general Brasidas of Sparta, Thucydides (ca. 460–ca. 400 B.C.) learned firsthand of the fortunes and misfortunes of war. Because he lost the city of Amphipolis to Brasidas in 424 B.C., Thucydides was banished for 20 years. It was this period of exile that enabled him to study the military and political events of his time and to write his brilliant History of the Peloponnesian War. *After presenting Thucydides' version of Pericles' speech in praise of Athens, we now offer his devastating report of the Athenian destruction of Melos despite the Melians' offer of neutrality. It is of note that Thucydides takes the very objective position of an observer-participator in his* History, *thereby anticipating the modern philosophical debate about the scientific worth of historiography, that is, the writing of history.*

The Athenian Destruction of Melos

SIXTEENTH YEAR OF THE WAR—THE MELIAN CONFERENCE—FATE OF MELOS

B.C. 416: Athenian Expedition to Melos—Discussion of Envoys—Melians Refuse to Submit—Siege of Melos—Melians Massacred and Made Slaves.

The next summer Alcibiades sailed with twenty ships to Argos and seized the suspected persons still left of the Lacedæmonian [Spartan] faction to the number of three hundred, whom the Athenians forthwith lodged in the neighbouring islands of their empire. The Athenians also made an expedition against the isle of Melos with thirty ships of their own, six Chian, and two Lesbian vessels, sixteen hundred heavy infantry, three hundred archers, and twenty mounted archers from Athens, and about fifteen hundred heavy infantry from the allies

From Thucydides, "The Peloponnesian War," *The Complete Writings of Thucydides*, trans. Joseph Gavorse (New York: The Modern Library, 1934), pp. 330–337.

and the islanders. The Melians are a colony of Lacedæmon that would not submit to the Athenians like the other islanders, and at first remained neutral and took no part in the struggle, but afterwards upon the Athenians using violence and plundering their territory, assumed an attitude of open hostility. Cleomedes, son of Lycomedes, and Tisias, son of Tisimachus, the generals, encamping in their territory with the above armament, before doing any harm to their land, sent envoys to negotiate. These the Melians did not bring before the people, but bade them state the object of their mission to the magistrates and the few; upon which the Athenian envoys spoke as follows:—

Athenians. 'Since the negotiations are not to go on before the people, in order that we may not be able to speak straight on without interruption, and deceive the ears of the multitude by seductive arguments which would pass without refutation (for we know that this is the meaning of our being brought before the few), what if you who sit there were to pursue a method more cautious still! Make no set speech yourselves, but take us up at whatever you do not like, and settle that before going any farther. And first tell us if this proposition of ours suits you.'

The Melian commissioners answered:—

Melians. 'To the fairness of quietly instructing each other as you propose there is nothing to object; but your military preparations are too far advanced to agree with what you say, as we see you are come to be judges in your own cause, and that all we can reasonably expect from this negotiation is war, if we prove to have right on our side and refuse to submit, and in the contrary case, slavery.

Athen. 'If you have met to reason about presentiments of the future, or for anything else than to consult for the safety of your state upon the facts that you see before you, we will give over; otherwise we will go on.

Mel. 'It is natural and excusable for men in our position to turn more ways than one both in thought and utterance. However, the question in this conference is, as you say, the safety of our country; and the discussion, if you please, can proceed in the way which you propose.

Athen. 'For ourselves, we shall not trouble you with specious pretences—either of how we have a right to our empire because we overthrew the Mede, or are now attacking you because of wrong that you have done us—and make a long speech which would not be believed; and in return we hope that you, instead of thinking to influence us by saying that you did not join the Lacedæmonians, although their colonists, or that you have done us no wrong, will aim at what is feasible, holding in view the real sentiments of us both; since you know as well as we do that right, as the world goes, is only in question between equals in power, while the strong do what they can and the weak suffer what they must.

Mel. 'As we think, at any rate, it is expedient—we speak as we are obliged, since you enjoin us to let right alone and talk only of interest—that you should not destroy what is our common protection, the privilege of being allowed in danger to invoke what is fair and right, and even to profit by arguments not strictly valid if they can be got to pass current. And you are as much interested in this as any, as your fall would be a signal for the heaviest vengeance and an example for the world to meditate upon.

Athen. 'The end of our empire, if end it should, does not frighten us: a rival empire like Lacedæmon, even if Lacedæmon was our real antagonist, is not so terrible to the vanquished as subjects who by themselves attack and overpower their rulers. This, however, is a risk that we are content to take. We will now proceed to show you that we are come here in the interest of our empire, and that we shall say what we are now going to say, for the preservation of your country; as we would fain exercise that empire over you without trouble, and see you preserved for the good of us both.

Mel. 'And how, pray, could it turn out as good for us to serve as for you to rule?

Athen. 'Because you would have the advantage of submitting before suffering the worst, and we should gain by not destroying you.

Mel. 'So that you would not consent to our being neutral, friends instead of enemies, but allies of neither side.

Athen. 'No; for your hostility cannot so much hurt us as your friendship will be an argument to our subjects of our weakness, and your enmity of our power.

Mel. 'Is that your subjects' idea of equity, to put those who have nothing to do with you in the same category with peoples that are most of them your own colonists, and some conquered rebels?

Athen. 'As far as right goes they think one has as much of it as the other, and that if any maintain their independence it is because they are strong, and that if we do not molest them it is because we are afraid; so that besides extending our empire we should gain in security by your subjection; the fact that you are islanders and weaker than others rendering it all the more important that you should not succeed in baffling the masters of the sea.

Mel. 'But do you consider that there is no security in the policy which we indicate? For here again if you debar us from talking about justice and invite us to obey your interest, we also must explain ours, and try to persuade you, if the two happen to coincide. How can you avoid making enemies of all existing neutrals who shall look at our case and conclude from it that one day or another you will attack them? And what is this but to make greater the enemies that you have already, and to force others to become so who would otherwise have never thought of it?

Athen. 'Why, the fact is that continentals generally give us but little alarm; the liberty which they enjoy will long prevent their taking precautions against us; it is rather islanders like yourselves, outside our empire, and subjects smarting under the yoke, who would be the most likely to take a rash step and lead themselves and us into obvious danger.

Mel. 'Well then, if you risk so much to retain your empire, and your subjects to get rid of it, it were surely great baseness and cowardice in us who are still free not to try everything that can be tried, before submitting to your yoke.

Athen. 'Not if you are well advised, the contest not being an equal one, with honour as the prize and shame as the penalty, but a question of self-preservation and of not resisting those who are far stronger than you are.

Mel. 'But we know that the fortune of war is sometimes more impartial than the disproportion of numbers might lead one to suppose; to submit is to give ourselves over to despair, while action still preserves for us a hope that we may stand erect.

Athen. 'Hope, danger's comforter, may be indulged in by those who have abundant resources, if not without loss at all events without ruin; but its nature is to be extravagant, and those who go so far as to put their all upon the venture see it in its true colours only when they are ruined; but so long as the discovery would enable them to guard against it, it is never found wanting. Let not this be the case with you, who are weak and hang on a single turn of the scale; nor be like the vulgar, who, abandoning such security as human means may still afford, when visible hopes fail them in extremity, turn to invisible, to prophecies and oracles, and other such inventions that delude men with hopes to their destruction.

Mel. 'You may be sure that we are as well aware as you of the difficulty of contending against your power and fortune, unless the terms be equal. But we trust that the gods may grant us fortune as good as yours, since we are just men fighting against unjust, and that what we want in power will be made up by the alliance of the Lacedæmonians, who are bound, if only for very shame, to come to the aid of their kindred. Our confidence, therefore, after all is not so utterly irrational.

Athen. 'When you speak of the favour of the gods, we may as fairly hope for that as yourselves; neither our pretensions nor our conduct being in any way contrary to what men believe of the gods, or practise among themselves. Of the gods we believe, and of men we know, that by a necessary law of their nature they rule wherever they can. And it is not as if we were the first to make this law, or to act upon it when made: we found it existing before us, and shall leave it to exist for ever after us; all we do is to make use of it, knowing that you and everybody else, having the same power as we have, would do the same as we do. Thus, as far as the gods are concerned, we have no fear and no reason to fear that we shall be at a disadvantage. But when we come to your notion about the Lacedæmonians, which leads you to believe that shame will make them help you, here we bless your simplicity but do not envy your folly. The Lacedæmonians, when their own interests or their country's laws are in question, are the worthiest men alive; of their conduct towards others much might be said, but no clearer idea of it could be given than by shortly saying that of all the men we know they are most conspicuous in considering what is agreeable honourable, and what is expedient just. Such a way of thinking does not promise much for the safety which you now unreasonably count upon.

Mel. 'But it is for this very reason that we now trust to their respect for expediency to prevent them from betraying the Melians, their colonists, and thereby losing the confidence of their friends in Hellas and helping their enemies.

Athen. 'Then you do not adopt the view that expediency goes with security, while justice and honour cannot be followed without danger; and danger the Lacedæmonians generally court as little as possible.

Mel. 'But we believe that they would be more likely to face even danger for our sake, and with more confidence than for others, as our nearness to Peloponnese makes it easier for them to act, and our common blood insures our fidelity.

Athen. 'Yes, but what an intending ally trusts to, is not the goodwill of those who ask his aid, but a decided superiority of power for action; and the Lacedæmonians look to this even more than others. At least, such is their distrust of their home resources that it is only with numerous allies that they attack a neighbour; now is it likely that while we are masters of the sea they will cross over to an island?

Mel. 'But they would have others to send. The Cretan sea is a wide one, and it is more difficult for those who command it to intercept others, than for those who wish to elude them to do so safely. And should the Lacedæmonians miscarry in this, they would fall upon your land, and upon those left of your allies whom Brasidas did not reach; and instead of places which are not yours, you will have to fight for your own country and your own confederacy.

Athen. 'Some diversion of the kind you speak of you may one day experience, only to learn as others have done, that the Athenians never once yet withdrew from a siege for fear of any. But we are struck by the fact, that after saying you would consult for the safety of your country, in all this discussion you have mentioned nothing which men might trust in and think to be saved by. Your strongest arguments depend upon hope and the future, and your actual resources are too scanty, as compared with those arrayed against you, for you to come out victorious. You will therefore show great blindness of judgment, unless, after allowing us to retire, you can find some counsel more prudent than this. You will surely not be caught by that idea of disgrace, which in dangers that are disgraceful, and at the same time too plain to be mistaken, proves so fatal to mankind; since in too many cases the very men that have their eyes perfectly open to what they are rushing into, let the thing called disgrace, by the mere influence of a seductive name, lead them on to a point at which they become so enslaved by the phrase as in fact to fall wilfully into hopeless disaster, and incur disgrace more disgraceful as the companion of error, than when it comes as the result of misfortune. This, if you are well advised, you will guard against; and you will not think it dishonourable to submit to the greatest city in Hellas, when it makes you the moderate offer of becoming its tributary ally, without ceasing to enjoy the country that belongs to you; nor when you have the choice given you between war and security, will you be so blinded as to choose the worse. And it is certain that those who do not yield to their equals, who keep terms with their superiors, and are moderate towards their inferiors, on the whole succeed best. Think over the matter, therefore, after our withdrawal, and reflect once and again that it is for your country that you are consulting, that you have not more than one, and that upon this one deliberation depends its prosperity or ruin.'

The Athenians now withdrew from the conference; and the Melians, left to themselves, came to a decision corresponding with what they had maintained in the discussion, and answered, 'Our resolution, Athenians, is the same as it was at first. We will not in a moment deprive of freedom a city that has been inhabited these seven hundred years; but we put our trust in the fortune by which the gods have preserved it until now, and in the help of men, that is, of the Lacedæmonians; and so we will try and save ourselves. Meanwhile we invite you to allow us to be friends to you and foes to neither party, and to retire from our country after making such a treaty as shall seem fair to us both.'

Such was the answer of the Melians. The Athenians now departing from the conference said, 'Well, you alone, as it seems to us, judging from these resolutions, regard what is future as more certain than what is before your eyes, and what is out of sight, in your eagerness, as already coming to pass; and as you have staked most on, and trusted most in, the Lacedæmonians, your fortune, and your hopes, so will you be most completely deceived.'

The Athenian envoys now returned to the army; and the Melians showing no signs of yielding, the generals at once betook themselves to hostilities, and drew a line of circumvallation round the Melians, dividing the work among the different states. Subsequently the Athenians returned with most of their army, leaving behind them a certain number of their own citizens and of the allies to keep guard by land and sea. The force thus left stayed on and besieged the place.

About the same time the Argives invaded the territory of Phlius and lost eighty men cut off in an ambush by the Phliasians and Argive exiles. Meanwhile the Athenians at Pylos took so much plunder from the Lacedæmonians that the latter, although they still refrained from breaking off the treaty and going to war with Athens, yet proclaimed that any of their people that chose might plunder the Athenians. The Corinthians also commenced hostilities with the Athenians for private quarrels of their own; but the rest of the Peloponnesians stayed quiet. Meanwhile the Melians attacked by night and took the part of the Athenian lines over against the market, and killed some of the men, and brought in corn and all else that they could find useful to them, and so returned and kept quiet, while the Athenians took measures to keep better guard in future.

Summer was now over. The next winter the Lacedæmonians intended to invade the Argive territory, but arriving at the frontier found the sacrifices for crossing unfavourable, and went back again. This intention of theirs gave the Argives suspicions of certain of their fellow-citizens, some of whom they arrested; others, however, escaped them. About the same time the Melians again took another part of the Athenian lines which were but feebly garrisoned. Reinforcements afterwards arriving from Athens in consequence, under the command of Philocrates, son of Demeas, the siege was now pressed vigorously; and some treachery taking place inside, the Melians surrendered at discretion to the Athenians, who put to death all the grown men whom they took, and sold the women and children for slaves, and subsequently sent out five hundred colonists and inhabited the place themselves.

ISOCRATES

Although Isocrates was not an orator, he was the greatest teacher of oratory in the Greek world. He lived for 98 years, from 436 until 338 B.C., when he allegedly committed suicide by self-starvation in a protest against the insolence of Philip of Macedon. Isocrates was a follower of Socrates and he was educated also by the Sophists. In turn, he has been influential in the history of education, especially with regard to the use of dialectic and the significance of the art of ancient rhetoric. Among his many extant writings is the following panegyric, "The Primacy of Athens," in which that city is praised and favorably contrasted with its enemy, Sparta. The occasion for this contrast is the quest for leadership in the proposed war against the Persians.

The Primacy of Athens

In the first place, then, the first need of our nature was supplied by the agency of our state; for even though the story is a mythical one, yet it is fit to be told even at the present day. When Demeter came into the country in her wandering, after the rape of Persephone, and was kindly disposed to our forefathers on account of the services they rendered her, which can be told to none but the initiated, she bestowed two gifts which surpass all others: the fruits of the earth, which have saved us from the life of wild beasts, and the mystic rite, the partakers in which have brighter hopes concerning the end of life and the eternity beyond,—under these circumstances Athens showed such love for men, as well as for the gods, that, when she became mistress of these great blessings, she did not grudge them to the rest of the world, but shared her advantages with all. Now as to the festival, we to this day celebrate it every year; and as to the fruits of the earth, Athens has once for all taught the uses to which they can be put, the operations which they require, and the benefits which arise from them. Indeed no one will venture to disbelieve this statement, after I have made a few additional remarks. For in the first place, the

---

Isocrates, "The Primacy of Athens," trans. J. H. Freese, in *Greek Literature in Translation*, ed. George Howe, G. A. Harrer, and P. H. Epps (New York: Harper & Row, 1948), pp. 529–537. Reprinted by permission of Gustave A. Harrer, III.

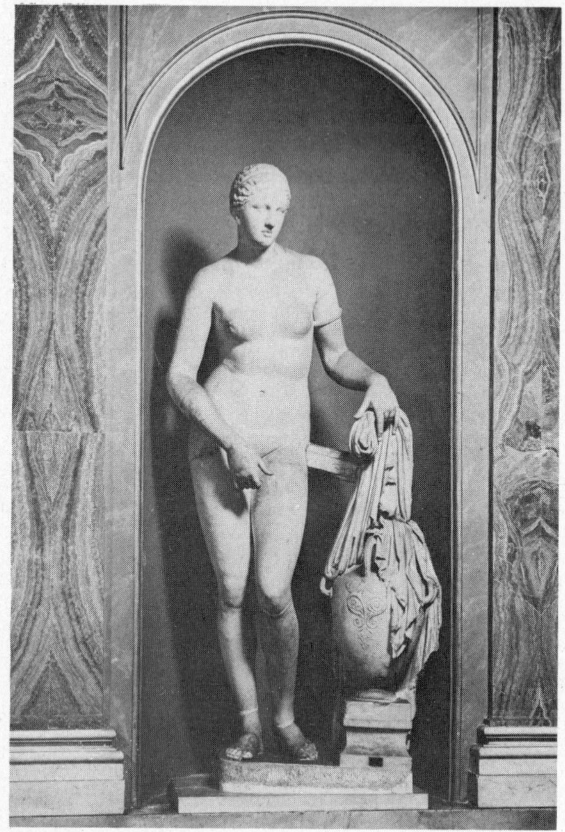

Cnidian Aphrodite, by Praxiteles (ca. 340 B.C.). This sculpture depicts the goddess of love and beauty, Aphrodite, in ancient Greek religion. (Scala/Art Resource)

very considerations which would lead a man to despise the story on account of its antiquity, would give him probable reason to suppose that the events had actually happened; for that many have told the story of these events, and all have heard it, should make us regard it, though not recent, yet as worthy of belief. In the second place, we can not only take refuge in the fact that we have received the tradition and rumour from a distant period, but we can also produce greater proofs than this of these things. For most of the cities of Hellas, as a memorial of our old services, send to us each years first-fruits of their corn, and those that omit to do so have often been commanded by the Pythia to pay the due proportion of their produce and perform their ancestral duties to our state. Yet can anything have stronger claims on our belief than that which is the subject of divine ordinance and of widespread approval in Hellas, where ancient story bears common witness to present deeds, and modern events agree with the legends of men of old? Besides this, if we leave all this out of consideration and take a survey from the beginning, we shall find that those who first appeared upon the earth did not at once find life in its present condition, but little by little procured for themselves its advantages. Whom then should we think most likely either to receive it as a gift from the gods or to win it by their own efforts? Surely those who are admitted to have been the first to exist, and are at once most highly gifted for the pursuits of life and most piously disposed towards the gods. Now what high honour ought to accrue to those who have produced such great blessings, it were a superfluous task to point out; for no one could find a reward commensurate with what has been achieved.

So much then concerning the greatest of our good works, first accomplished and most universal in its effects. But, in the same period, Athens, seeing the barbarians occupying the greater part of the country, and the Hellenes confined in a small space and driven by scarcity of land into intestine conspiracies and civil wars, and perishing, either from want of daily necessities or in war, was not content to leave things so, but sent forth leaders into the states who took those most in need of subsistence, made themselves their generals and conquered the barbarians in war, founded many states on both continents, colonized all the islands, and saved both those who followed them and those who stayed behind; for to the latter they left the home country sufficient for their needs, and the former they provided with more territory than they already possessed; for they acquired all the surrounding districts of which we are now in occupation. In this way too they afforded great facilities to those who in later times wished to send out colonists and to imitate our state; for it was not necessary for them to run risk in acquiring new territory, but they could go and live on land which we had marked out. Now who can show a leadership more ancestral than one which arose before most Hellenic cities were founded, or more beneficial than one which drove the barbarians from their homes, and led on the Hellenes to such prospertiy?

Yet, after aiding in the accomplishment of the most pressing duties, Athens did not neglect the rest, but deemed it the first step only in a career of beneficence to find food for those in want, a step which is incumbent upon a people who aim at good government generally, and thinking that life which was

men desire to live, she devoted such close attention limited to mere subsistence was not enough to make to the other interests of man, that of all the benefits which men enjoy, not derived from the gods but which we owe to our fellow-men, none have arisen without the aid of Athens, and most of them have been brought about by her agency. For finding the Hellenes living in lawlessness and dwelling in a scattered fashion, oppressed by tyrannies or being destroyed by anarchy, she also released them from these evils, either by becoming mistress of them or by making herself an example; for she was the first to lay down laws and establish a consititution. This is clear from the fact that, when men in the earliest times introduced indictments for homicide, and determined to settle their mutual disputes by argument and not by violence, they followed our laws in the mode of trial which they adopted.

Nay more, the arts also, whether useful for the necessities of life or contrived for pleasure, were by her either invented or put to proof and offered to the rest of the world for their use. In other respects, moreover, she ordered her administration in such a spirit of welcome to strangers and of friendliness to all, as to suit both those who were in want of money and those who desired to enjoy the wealth they possessed, and not to fail in serving either the prosperous, or those who were unfortunate in their own states, but so that each of these classes finds with us a delightful sojourn or a safe refuge. And further, since the territory possessed by the several states was not in every case self-sufficing, but was defective in some products and bore more than was sufficient of others, and much embarrassment arose where to dispose of the latter, and from whence to import the former, she provided a remedy for these troubles also; for she established the Piræus as a market in the centre of Hellas, of such superlative excellence that articles, which it is difficult for the several states to supply to each other one by one, can all be easily procured from Athens.

Now those who established the great festivals are justly praised for handing down to us a custom which leads us to make treaties with one another, to reconcile the enmities that exist among us, and to assemble in one place; besides that, in making common prayers and sacrifices we are reminded of the original bond of kinship between us, and are more kindly disposed towards each other for the future, we renew old friendships and make new ones, and neither for ordinary men nor for those of distinguished qualities is the time idly spent, but by the concourse of Hellenes opportunity arises for the latter to display their natural excellencies, and for the former to be spectators of their mutual contests, and neither spend their time dissatisfied, but each has whereof to be proud, the spectators when they see the competitors toiling on their behalf, and the competitors when they think that everyone has come to look at them. Great then as are the benefits we derive from the assemblies, in these respects, too, our state is not left behind. For indeed she can show many most beautiful spectacles, some passing all bounds in expenditure, others of high artistic repute, and some excelling in both these respects; then, the multitude of strangers who visit us is so great, that if there is any advantage in mutual intercourse, that also has been compassed by her. In addition to this, you can find with us the truest friendships and the most varied acquaintanceships; and, moreover, see contests not merely of speed and strength, but also of oratory and mind, and in all other productions of art, and for these the greatest prizes. For in addition to those which the state herself offers, she also helps to persuade others to bestow the like; for those recognized by us receive such credit as to be universally approved. Apart from this, whereas the other festivals are assembled at long intervals and soon dispersed, our state, on the contrary, is for those who visit her one long festival without ceasing.

Practical philosophy, moreover, which helped to discover and establish all these institutions, which at once educated us for action and softened our mutual intercourse, which distinguished calamities due to ignorance from those which spring from necessity, and taught us to avoid the former and nobly to endure the latter, was introduced by Athens; she also paid honour to eloquence, which all men desire, and begrudge to those who are skilled in it; for she was aware that this is the only distinguishing characteristic which we of all creatures possess, and that by this we have won our position of superiority to all the rest of them; she saw that in other spheres of action men's fortunes are so capricious that often in them the wise fail and the foolish succeed, and that the proper and skilful use of language is beyond the reach of men of poor capacity, but is the function of a soul of sound wisdom, and that those who are considered clever or stupid differ from each other mainly in this respect; she saw, besides, that men who have received a liberal education from the very first are not to be known by courage, or wealth, or such-like advantages, but are most clearly recognized by their speech, and that this is the surest token which is manifested of the education of each one of us, and that those who make good use of language are not only influential in their own states, but also held in honour among other people. So far has Athens left the rest of mankind behind in thought and expression that her pupils have become the teachers of the world, and she has made the name of Hellas distinctive no longer of race but of intellect, and the title of Hellene a badge of education rather than of common descent.

But that I may not seem to be lingering over details of my subject when I proposed to treat of the whole, nor to be eulogizing Athens on these grounds from inability to praise her for her achievements in war, I will say no more to those who take pride in what I have mentioned; but I think that our forefathers deserve to be honoured as much for the dangers they incurred as for the rest of their services. Neither small nor few nor obscure were the struggles they endured, but many and terrible and great, some for their own country, others for the general liberty; for during the whole time they did not cease to open their state to all, and were the champions of those among the Hellenes who from time to time were the victims of oppression. For that very reason some accuse us of a foolish policy, in that we have been accustomed to support the weaker, as if such arguments did not rather justify our admirers. For it was not in ignorance of the superiority of great alliances in regard to security that we took these counsels concerning them, but, while knowing much more accurately than other men the results of such a course, we nevertheless preferred to help the weak even against our interest rather than for profit's sake to join in the oppressions of the strong. . . .

Now I ought, I think, to speak also of the achievements of Athens against the barbarians, especially as the leadership of Hellas against them was the original subject of my speech. Now if I were to enumerate all the perils we went through I should be telling too long a tale; but in dealing with the greatest of them I will try to adopt the same method of narration that I followed just now. For the races best fitted for rule and the possessors of the widest imperial power are the Scythians, the Thracians, and the Persians, and it happens that all these have had hostile designs against us, and that our state has fought decisively against all of them. Now what argument will be left for my opponents, if I can prove that, if any of the Hellenes were unable to get justice, it was to Athens that they directed their petitions, and that, when barbarians wished to enslave Hellas, Athens was the first object of their attacks? . . .

Now honourable indeed are these deeds, and befitting those who dispute for the leadership; but akin to those which I have mentioned, and such as were to be expected from the descendants of men so great, were the achievements of those who made war against Darius and Xerxes. For although that was the greatest war ever set on foot, and never had so many perilous struggles taken place at one and the same time—against enemies who fancied themselves irresistible on account of their numbers, and allies who considered their valour unsurpassable—our ancestors conquered both, in the way that was suitable in each case, and proving superior in the face of every danger, earned as an immediate reward the meed of valour, and not long afterwards obtained the dominion of the sea, at the gift of the rest of the Hellenes, and without dispute from those who now seek to rob us of it.

Now let no one think me ignorant that the Lacedæmonians, too, in those critical times deserved credit for many good services to Hellas; but on this account I have even more reason to praise our state, in that, in conflict with such great competitors, she proved so far superior to them. But I wish to speak a little more at length about these two states, and not to skim over the subject too quickly, that it may be to us a memorial, both of the valour of our ancestors and of the hatred of the barbarians. And yet I am not unaware that it is difficult for one who comes latest to the task to speak of a subject long ago occupied by previous speakers, and on which those citizens best able to speak have often spoken on the occasion of public funerals; for it follows that the chief part must have been already used up, and only a few unimportant points omitted. Nevertheless, starting from what still remains to be said, since it is convenient for my purpose, I must not shrink from making mention concerning them.

Now I think that the greatest services have been rendered and the greatest praises deserved by those who exposed their persons in the forefront of danger for the sake of Hellas; yet it is not fair either to forget those who lived before this war and held power in these two states respectively. For they it was who trained beforehand those coming after them, inclined the multitude to virtue, and created formidable antagonists for the barbarians. For they did not despise the public interests, nor enjoy the resources of the state as their own, while neglecting her interests as no concern of theirs; but they were as solicitous for the common welfare as for their own domestic happiness, and at the same time properly stood aloof from matters which did not affect them. They did not estimate happiness by the standard of money, but they thought that the surest and best wealth was possessed by the man who pursued such conduct as would enable him to gain the best reputation for himself and leave behind the greatest fame for his children. They did not emulate one another's shameless audacity, nor cultivate effrontery in their own persons, but deemed it more terrible to be ill-spoken of by their fellow-citizens than to die nobly for the state, and were more ashamed of public errors than they are now of their own personal faults. The reason of this was that they took care that their laws should be exact and good, those concerned with the relations of every-day life even more than those that had to do with private contracts. For they knew that good men and true will have no need of many written documents, but, whether on public or private matters, will easily come to an agreement by the aid of a few recognised principles. Such was their public spirit, that the object of their political parties was to dispute, not which should destroy the other and rule over the rest, but which should be first in doing some service to the state; and they organized their clubs, not for their private interests, but for the benefit of the people. They pursued the same method in their dealings with other states, treating the Hellenes with deference and not with insolence, considering that their rule over them should be that of a general, not of a despot, and desiring to be addressed as leaders rather than masters, and to be entitled saviours and not reviled as destroyers; they won over states by kindness instead of overthrowing them by force; they made their word more trustworthy than their oath is now, and thought it their duty to abide by treaties as by the decrees of necessity; not proud of their power so much as ambitious to live in self-restraint, they thought it right to have the same feelings towards their inferiors as they expected their superiors to have towards them, and they considered their own cities as merely private towns, while they looked upon Hellas as their common fatherland. Possessed of such ideas, and educating the younger generation in such manners, they brought to light such valiant men in those who fought against the barbarians from Asia, that no one, either poet or sophist, has ever yet been able to speak in a manner worthy of their achievements. And I can readily excuse them; for it is just as hard to praise those who have surpassed the virtues of other men as those who have never done anything good; for whereas the latter have no deeds to support them, the former have no language befitting them. For what language could be commensurate with the deeds of men who were so far superior to those who made the expedition against Troy, that, while they spent ten years against one city, those men in a short time defeated the whole might of Asia, and not only saved their own countries but also liberated the whole of Hellas? And what deeds or toils or dangers would they have shrunk from attempting in order to win living reputations, when they were so readily willing to lose their lives for the sake of a posthumous fame? And I even think that the war must have been contrived by one of the gods in admiration of their valour, that men of such quality should not remain in obscurity nor end their lives ingloriously, but should be thought worthy of the same reward as those children of the gods who are called demi-gods; for even their bodies the gods rendered up to the inflexible laws of nature, but made immortal the memory of their valour.

Now, continuous as was the jealousy between our ancestors and the Lacedæmonians, yet in those times they exercised their rivalry for the highest objects, considering themselves to be not enemies but competitors, and not courting the barbarian with a view to the servitude of Hellas, but having one aim in the common safety, their only rivalry being which of them should achieve it. Now the first proof they gave of their high qualities was on the occasion of the expedition sent by Darius: for when the enemy landed in Attica our ancestors on their part did not wait for their allies; but, treating the public peril as if it were their own, they went with their own forces alone to meet a foe who had despised the whole of Hellas, prepared with their small numbers to encounter many myriads, as if other men's lives and not their own were at stake; and the Lacedæmonians no sooner heard of the war in Attica than, neglecting everything else, they came to help us, making as much haste as if their own country were being laid waste. A proof of their rapidity and emulation is that our ancestors are said on one and the same day to have heard of the landing of the barbarians, marched out to protect the borders of their territory, fought a victorious engagement and set up a trophy over their enemies, while the Lacedæmonians in three days and as many nights traversed twelve hundred stadia in marching order. So strenuously did they hasten, the one to share in the dangers, and the others to fight before reinforcements should arrive. The next occasion was that of the subsequent expedition, which Xerxes led in person, leaving his royal residence and making bold to become a general, and collecting all Asia together; in the description of whose fall the highest flights of eloquence have fallen short of the reality. He reached such a pitch of arrogance that, deeming it a small task to subdue Hellas, and wishing to leave such a memorial behind him as human nature cannot attain to, he did not cease till he had devised and forced to completion the feat which is in everyone's mouth, of sailing with his army across the mainland and marching on foot through the sea, by bridging the Hellespont, and cutting a canal through Athos.

It was one, then, of such lofty pride and such great achievements, master of so many men, that they went to encounter, dividing the risk between them,—the Lacedæmonians to Thermopylæ against his land forces, choosing a thousand of their number and taking a few of their allies with them, intending in the narrow pass to bar their further advance, and our ancestors to Artemisium, having manned sixty triremes against the whole fleet of the enemy. And they took heart to do these things, not so much from contempt of their enemies as in rivalry with each other, the Lacedæmonians envying our state the battle of Marathon and seeking to do the like, and fearing lest twice in succession Athens should bring deliverance to the Hellenes, while our people on their part wished above all to preserve their existing fame, and to make it clear to all that their former victory too was due to valour and not to luck, and in the next place also to encourage the Hellenes to undertake a sea-fight, by proving to them that in naval ventures just as in those by land it is the prowess of the common people that prevails. But though they displayed equal daring, their fortunes were not alike; the Lacedæmonians were destroyed—their spirits were victorious—their bodies only fainted and failed (for indeed it would be a sin to say that they were defeated; for no one of them deigned to flee); our ancestors on their part defeated the advanced squadron, but when they heard that the enemy were masters of the pass, they sailed back home, arranged affairs in the city, and directed the remainder of their efforts so well, that, many and glorious as were their previous achievements, they excelled yet more in the closing scenes of their perils. For . . . though they might have not merely escaped the dangers besetting them, but have received special distinctions, which the Great King offered them in the belief that, if he added the fleet of our state to his forces, he would immediately conquer Peloponnesus as well,—they would hear nothing of his gifts, nor did they in anger against the Hellenes for their betrayal gladly hasten to make terms with the barbarians, but for their own part they made ready to fight for freedom, and forgave the others for preferring slavery. For they considered that, though the humble states were right in seeking safety by every means, those which claimed to be at the head of Hellas could not possibly try to escape their peril. . . .

Now when an expedition against the barbarians is being proposed, who ought to have the leadership? Surely they who in the former war won the greatest fame, having often borne the brunt on their own shoulders, and in united contests having gained the prize of valour. Surely they who abandoned their own country for the general deliverance, and who not only in olden times founded most of the Hellenic states, but also in later days rescued them from the greatest disasters. Should we not be most hardly treated, if, after having endured the largest share of troubles, we should be thought worthy of a lesser share of honours, and, after having in those days occupied the foremost post, should now be compelled to follow the lead of others?

SUGGESTIONS FOR FURTHER READING

Crombie, I. M. *An Examination of Plato's Doctrines.* 2 vols. New York: Humanities Press, 1962.

Findlay, J. N. *Plato: The Written and Unwritten Doctrines.* New York: Humanities Press, 1974.

Gross, Barry, ed. *The Great Thinkers on Plato.* New York: Capricorn Books, 1968.

Guthrie, W. K. C. *A History of Greek Philosophy,* Vol. 4. Cambridge: Cambridge University Press, 1975.

Hamilton, Edith, and Cairns, Huntington, eds. *The Collected Dialogues of Plato.* New York: Pantheon, 1963.

Jaeger, Werner. *Paedeia,* Vols. 2 and 3. New York: Oxford University Press, 1943, 1944.

Randall, John Herman, Jr. *Plato: Dramatist of the Life of Reason.* New York: Columbia University Press, 1970.

Ryle, Gilbert. *Plato's Progress.* Cambridge: Cambridge University Press, 1966.

Taylor, A. E. *Plato: The Man and His Work.* New York: Humanities Press, 1950.

Vlastos, Gregory. *Plato's Universe.* Seattle: University of Washington Press, 1975.

Vlastos, Gregory, ed. *Plato, A Collection of Cultural Essays.* 2 vols. Garden City, New York: Doubleday–Anchor, 1971.

Wolz, Henry G. *Plato and Heidegger: In Search of Selfhood.* Lewisburg, Pennsylvania: Bucknell University Press, 1981.

Part 3

Aristotle: Philosophy as System

Aristotle: Philosophy as System

Aristotle (384–322 B.C.) was born in Stagira, in Chalcidice. He was the son of Nicomachus, court physician to Amnytas II, the Macedonian king. At the age of 17 he became a student in Plato's school, where he remained until the death of Plato in 347 B.C. Aristotle then lived in Assos, a city in Asia Minor, and in Mytilene on the island of Lesbos. It was during this period that he conducted many of his path-breaking zoological studies.

In 343 B.C., Philip of Macedon invited Aristotle to Pella, for the purpose of educating Philip's son, Alexander. In 335 B.C., Aristotle returned to Athens, where he founded a school known as the Lyceum. As it was held under a covered court *(peripatos)*, the students of Aristotle were known as *peripatetics*. The Lyceum was more of a community than a school, and Aristotle and his colleagues carried on teaching and research in virtually every field then known to human experience.

With the death of Alexander the Great in 323 B.C., Athens became a hostile environment for Macedonians such as Aristotle. Mindful of the death of Socrates, Aristotle left Athens "lest they sin twice against philosophy." He retired to Chalcis, where he died the following year.

Aristotle's writings are divided into the exoteric and the esoteric, that is, into those directed at an audience beyond the Lyceum and those directed at an audience within the Lyceum. Of the first group, only fragments remain. Many of the exoteric writings were in dialogue form, reminiscent of the Platonic dialogues. Ancient commentators praised Aristotle's prose style, especially in his work *On Philosophy*. The second group of writings, also referred to as treatises, were in the form of lecture notes for the Lyceum and, as such, they are ponderous and difficult to read. Considerable discussion has been devoted to the authenticity of the treatises; even more has been devoted to the question of how much the various editors and commentators throughout the centuries may have added and subtracted, thereby rendering the text of Aristotle a source of continuing controversy. Another item of dispute concerns the chronological order of the treatises and of the various books within each treatise, especially the *Metaphysics*.

Relative agreement exists on the authenticity of the following major works: *Categories, On Interpretation, Prior Analytics* and *Posterior Analytics, Physics, On the Heavens, On Coming-to-be and Passing Away, On the Soul, On the Parts of Animals, Metaphysics, Nicomachean Ethics, Politics,* and *Rhetoric and Poetics.* Most of these treatises have exercised an extraordinary influence on the development of western civilization, especially in logic, grammar, physics, biology, and astronomy. In fact, if it were not for the invention of the telescope and the microscope, the thought of Aristotle would still be at the center of the scientific stage.

The basic position of Aristotle in both science and philosophy was that of an observational empiricist, for whom human sense knowledge was trustworthy. Aristotle agreed with Plato that true knowledge should result in access to a universal form of which particular sense experiences are instances or examples. He disagreed with Plato on the separability of these universals from the objects experienced. Plato's position on this matter is ambiguous, but Aristotle's version of Plato is clear: he believed that, for Plato, sense experience is a block to intuiting the universal forms that exist apart from the physical world. Aristotle's belief in the trustworthy character of human sense experience spurred him to a series of brilliant explorations of human activity and consequently led to his establishing the fundamental principles that govern the cosmos, the animals, speech, and the physical world.

Aristotle saw human knowledge as being divided into the theoretical, the practical, and the productive. Although his treatises often cross over these lines, it can be said that the theoretical or speculative is best represented by the *Metaphysics,* the practical by the *Ethics* and the *Politics,* and the productive by the *Poetics.*

Aristotle is the philosopher's philosopher. His works are the acme of philosophical method. To him we owe the syllogism, the notion of substance, the classification of the disciplines, and eternal wisdom on ethics and politics. As the great medieval poet Dante wrote, Aristotle was *"il maestro di color che sanno,"* that is, the master of them that know.

From the Categories

Expressions which are in no way composite signify substance, quantity, quality, relation, place, time, position, state, action, or affection. To sketch my meaning roughly, examples of substance are 'man' or 'the horse', of quantity, such terms as 'two cubits long' or 'three cubits long', of quality, such attributes as 'white', 'grammatical'. 'Double', 'half', 'greater', fall under the category of relation; 'in the market place', 'in the Lyceum', under that of place; 'yesterday', 'last year', under that of time. 'Lying', 'sitting', are terms indicating position; 'shod', 'armed', state; 'to lance', 'to cauterize', action; 'to be lanced', 'to be cauterized', affection.

No one of these terms, in and by itself, involves

Aristotle, *Categories,* from Richard McKeon, ed., *The Basic Works of Aristotle* (New York: Random House, 1941) 4–5, 1b-25–4b-19. All of the selections from Aristotle are taken from this text, and are identified by the title of the work, the section numbers, and by the paragraph numbers that are universally used to code Aristotle's writings. Individual line numbers are only given when they are necessary to locate the passage. This translation was originally published in *The Oxford Translation of Aristotle,* edited by W. D. Ross.

an affirmation; it is by the combination of such terms that positive or negative statements arise. For every assertion must, as is admitted, be either true or false, whereas expressions which are not in any way composite, such as 'man', 'white', 'runs', 'wins', cannot be either true or false.

Substance, in the truest and primary and most definite sense of the word, is that which is neither predicable of a subject nor present in a subject; for instance, the individual man or horse. But in a secondary sense those things are called substances within which, as species, the primary substances are included; also those which, as genera, include the species. For instance, the individual man is included in the species 'man', and the genus to which the species belongs is 'animal'; these, therefore—that is to say, the species 'man' and the genus 'animal'—are termed secondary substances.

It is plain from what has been said that both the name and the definition of the predicate must be predicable of the subject. For instance, 'man' is predicated of the individual man. Now in this case the name of the species 'man' is applied to the individual, for we use the term 'man' in describing the individual; and the definition of 'man' will also be predicated of the individual man, for the individual man is both man and animal. Thus, both the name and the definition of the species are predicable of the individual.

With regard, on the other hand, to those things which are present in a subject, it is generally the case that neither their name nor their definition is predicable of that in which they are present. Though, however, the definition is never predicable, there is nothing in certain cases to prevent the name being used. For instance, 'white' being present in a body is predicated of that in which it is present, for a body is called white: the definition, however, of the color 'white' is never predicable of the body.

Everything except primary substances is either predicable of a primary substance or present in a primary substance. This becomes evident by reference to particular instances which occur. 'Animal' is predicated of the species 'man', therefore of the individual man, for if there were no individual man of whom it could be predicated, it could not be predicated of the species 'man' at all. Again, colour is present in body, therefore in individual bodies, for if there were no individual body in which it was present, it could not be present in body at all. Thus everything except primary substances is either predicated of primary substances, or is present in them, and if these last did not exist, it would be impossible for anything else to exist.

Of secondary substances, the species is more truly substance than the genus, being more nearly related to primary substance. For if any one should render an account of what a primary substance is, he would render a more instructive account, and one more proper to the subject, by stating the species than by stating the genus. Thus, he would give a more instructive account of an individual man by stating that he was man than by stating that he was animal, for the former description is peculiar to the individual in a greater degree, while the latter is too general. Again, the man who gives an account of the nature of an individual tree will give a more instructive account by mentioning the species 'tree' than by mentioning the genus 'plant'.

Moreover, primary substances are most properly called substances in virtue of the fact that they are the entities which underlie everything else, and that everything else is either predicated of them or present in them. Now the same relation which subsists between primary substance and everything else subsists also between the species and the genus: for the species is to the genus as subject is to predicate, since the genus is predicated of the species, whereas the species cannot be predicated of the genus. Thus we have a second ground for asserting that the species is more truly substance than the genus.

Of species themselves, except in the case of such as are genera, no one is more truly substance than another. We should not give a more appropriate account of the individual man by stating the species to which he belonged, than we should of an individual horse by adopting the same method of definition. In the same way, of primary substances, no one is more truly substance than another; an individual man is not more truly substance than an individual ox.

It is, then, with good reason that of all that remains, when we exclude primary substances, we concede to species and genera alone the name 'secondary substance', for these alone of all the predicates convey a knowledge of primary substance. For it is by stating the species or the genus that we appropriately define any individual man; and we shall make our definition more exact by stating the former than by stating the latter. All other things that we state, such as that he is white, that he runs, and so on, are irrelevant to the definition. Thus it is just that these alone, apart from primary substances, should be called substances.

Further, primary substances are most properly so called, because they underlie and are the subjects of everything else. Now the same relation that subsists between primary substance and everything else subsists also between the species and the genus to which the primary substance belongs, on the one hand, and every attribute which is not included within these, on the other. For these are the subjects of all such. If we call an individual man 'skilled in grammar', the predicate is applicable also to the species and to the genus to which he belongs. This law holds good in all cases.

It is a common characteristic of all substance that it is never present in a subject. For primary substance is neither present in a subject nor predicated of a subject; while, with regard to secondary substances, it is clear from the following arguments (apart from others) that they are not present in a subject. For 'man' is predicated of the individual man, but is not present in any subject: for manhood is not present in the individual man. In the same way, 'animal' is also predicated of the individual man, but is not present in him. Again, when a thing is present in a subject, though the name may quite well be applied to that in which it is present, the definition cannot be applied. Yet of secondary substances, not only the name, but also the definition, applies to the subject: we should use both the definition of the species and that of the genus with reference to the individual man. Thus substance cannot be present in a subject.

Yet this is not peculiar to substance, for it is also the case that differentiae cannot be present in subjects. The characteristics 'terrestrial' and 'two-footed' are predicated of the species 'man', but not present in it. For they are not *in* man. Moreover, the definition of the differentia may be predicated of that of which the differentia itself is predicated. For instance, if the characteristic 'terrestrial' is predicated of the species 'man', the definition also of that characteristic may be used to form the predicate of the species 'man': for 'man' is terrestrial.

The fact that the parts of substances appear to be present in the whole, as in a subject, should not make us apprehensive lest we should have to admit that such parts are not substances: for in explaining the phrase 'being present in a subject', we stated that we meant 'otherwise than as parts in a whole'.

It is the mark of substances and of differentiae that, in all propositions of which they form the predicate, they are predicated univocally. For all such propositions have for their subject either the individual or the species. It is true that, inasmuch as primary substance is not predicable of anything, it can never form the predicate of any proposition. But of secondary substances, the species is predicated of the individual, the genus both of the species and of the individual. Similarly the differentiae are predicated of the species and of the individuals. Moreover, the definition of the species and that of the genus are applicable to the primary substance, and that of the genus to the species. For all that is predicated of the predicate will be predicated also of the subject. Similarly, the definition of the differentiae will be applicable to the species and to the individuals. But it was stated above that the word 'univocal' was applied to those things which had both name and definition in common. It is, therefore, established that in every proposition, of which either substance or a differentia forms the predicate, these are predicated univocally.

All substance appears to signify that which is individual. In the case of primary substance this is indisputably true, for the thing is a unit. In the case of secondary substances, when we speak, for instance, of 'man' or 'animal', our form of speech gives the impression that we are here also indicating that which is individual, but the impression is not strictly true; for a secondary substance is not an individual, but a class with a certain qualification; for it is not one and single as a primary substance is; the words 'man', 'animal', are predicable of more than one subject.

Yet species and genus do not merely indicate quality, like the term 'white'; 'white' indicates quality and nothing further, but species and genus determine the quality with reference to a substance: they signify substance qualitatively differentiated. The determinate qualification covers a larger field in the case of the genus than in that of the species: he who uses the word 'animal' is herein using a word of wider extension than he who uses the word 'man'.

Another mark of substance is that it has no contrary. What could be the contrary of any primary substance, such as the individual man or animal? It has none. Nor can the species or the genus have a contrary. Yet this characteristic is not peculiar to substance, but is true of many other things, such as quantity. There is nothing that forms the contrary of 'two cubits long' or of 'three cubits long', or of 'ten', or of any such term. A man may contend that 'much' is the contrary of 'little', or 'great' of 'small', but of definite quantitative terms no contrary exists.

Substance, again, does not appear to admit of variation of degree. I do not mean by this that one substance cannot be more or less truly substance than another, for it has already been stated that this is the case; but that no single substance admits of varying degrees within itself. For instance, one particular substance, 'man', cannot be more or less man either than himself at some other time or than some other man. One man cannot be more man than another, as that which is white may be more or less white than some other white object, or as that which is beautiful may be more or less beautiful than some other beautiful object. The same quality, moreover, is said to subsist in a thing in varying degrees at different times. A body, being white, is said to be whiter at one time than it was before, or, being warm, is said to be warmer or less warm than at some other time. But substance is not said to be more or less that which it is: a man is not more truly a man at one time than he was before, nor is anything, if it is substance, more or less what it is. Substance, then, does not admit of variation of degree.

The most distinctive mark of substance appears to be that, while remaining numerically one and the same, it is capable of admitting contrary qualities. From among things other than substance, we should find ourselves unable to bring forward any which possessed this mark. Thus, one and the same colour cannot be white and black. Nor can the same one action be good and bad: this law holds good with everything that is not substance. But one and the self-same substance, while retaining its identity, is yet capable of admitting contrary qualities. The same individual person is at one time white, at another black, at one time warm, at another cold, at one time good, at another bad. This capacity is found nowhere else, though it might be maintained that a statement or opinion was an exception to the rule. The same statement, it is agreed, can be both true and false. For if the statement 'he is sitting' is true, yet, when the person in question has risen, the same statement will be false. The same applies to opinions. For if any one thinks truly that a person is sitting, yet, when that person has risen, this same opinion, if still held, will be false. Yet although this exception may be allowed, there is, nevertheless, a difference in the manner in which the thing takes place. It is by themselves changing that substances admit contrary qualities. It is thus that that which was hot becomes cold, for it has entered into a different state. Similarly that which was white becomes black, and that which was bad good, by a process of change; and in the same way in all other cases it is by changing that substances are capable of admitting contrary qualities. But statements and opinions themselves remain unaltered in all respects: it is by the alteration in the facts of the case that the contrary quality comes to be theirs. The statement 'he is sitting' remains unaltered, but it is at one time true, at another false, according to circumstances. What has been said of statements applies also to opinions. Thus, in respect of the manner in which the thing takes place, it is the peculiar mark of substance that it should be capable of admitting contrary qualities; for it is by itself changing that it does so.

If, then, a man should make this exception and contend that statements and opinions are capable of admitting contrary qualities, his contention is unsound. For statements and opinions are said to have this capacity, not because they themselves undergo modification, but because this modification occurs in the case of something else. The truth or falsity of a statement depends on facts, and not on any power on the part of the statement itself of admitting contrary qualities. In short, there is nothing which can alter the nature of statements and opinions. As, then, no change takes place in themselves, these cannot be said to be capable of admitting contrary qualities.

But it is by reason of the modification which takes place within the substance itself that a substance is said to be capable of admitting contrary qualities; for a substance admits within itself either disease or health, whiteness or blackness. It is in this sense that it is said to be capable of admitting contrary qualities.

To sum up, it is a distinctive mark of substance, that, while remaining numerically one and the same, it is capable of admitting contrary qualities, the modification taking place through a change in the substance itself.

Let these remarks suffice on the subject of substance.

From the Posterior Analytics

BOOK I

All instruction given or received by way of argument proceeds from pre-existent knowledge. This becomes evident upon a survey of all the species of such instruction. The mathematical sciences and all other speculative disciplines are acquired in this way, and so are the two forms of dialectical reasoning, syllogistic and inductive; for each of these latter makes use of old knowledge to impart new, the syllogism assuming an audience that accepts its premisses, induction exhibiting the universal as implicit in the clearly known particular. Again, the persuasion exerted by rhetorical arguments is in principle the same, since they use either example, a kind of induction, or enthymeme, a form of syllogism.

The pre-existent knowledge required is of two kinds. In some cases admission of the fact must be assumed, in others comprehension of the meaning of the term used, and sometimes both assumptions are essential. Thus, we assume that every predicate can be either truly affirmed or truly denied of any subject, and that 'triangle' means so and so; as regards 'unit' we have to make the double assumption of the meaning of the word and the existence of the thing. The reason is that these several objects are not equally obvious to us. Recognition of a truth may in some cases contain as factors both previous knowledge and also knowledge acquired simultaneously with that recognition—knowledge, this latter, of the particulars actually falling under the universal and therein already virtually known. For example, the student knew beforehand that the angles of every triangle are equal to two right angles; but it was only at the actual moment at which he was being led on to recognize this as true in the instance before him that he came to know 'this figure inscribed in the semicircle' to be a triangle. For some things (viz. the singulars finally reached which are not predicable of anything else as subject) are only learnt in this way, i.e. there is here no recognition through a middle of a minor term as subject to a major. Before he was led on to recognition or before he actually drew a conclusion, we should perhaps say that in a manner he knew, in a manner not.

If he did not in an unqualified sense of the term *know* the existence of this triangle, how could he know without qualification that its angles were equal to two right angles? No: clearly he *knows* not without qualification but only in the sense that he *knows* universally. If this distinction is not drawn, we are faced with the dilemma in the *Meno:* either a man will learn nothing or what he already knows; for we cannot accept the solution which some people offer. A man is asked, 'Do you, or do you not, know that every pair is even?' He says he does know it. The questioner then produces a particular pair, of the existence, and so *a fortiori* of the evenness, of which he was unaware. The solution which some people offer is to assert that they do not know that every pair is even, but only that everything which they know to be a pair is even: yet what they know to be even is that of which they have demonstrated evenness, i.e. what they made the subject of their premiss, viz. not merely every triangle or number which they know to be such, but any and every number or triangle without reservation. For no premiss is ever couched in the form 'every number which you know to be such', or 'every rectilinear figure which you know to be such': the predicate is always construed as applicable to any and every instance of the thing. On the other hand, I imagine there is nothing to prevent a man in one sense knowing what he is learning, in another not knowing it. The strange thing would be, not if in some sense he knew what he was learning, but if he were to know it in that precise sense and manner in which he was learning it.

We suppose ourselves to possess unqualified scientific knowledge of a thing, as opposed to knowing it in the accidental way in which the sophist knows, when we think that we know the cause on which the fact depends, as the cause of that fact and of no other, and, further, that the fact could not be other than it is. Now that scientific knowing is something of this

---

Posterior Analytics, I, 1–2, 71a–72b.

sort is evident—witness both those who falsely claim it and those who actually possess it, since the former merely imagine themselves to be, while the latter are also actually, in the condition described. Consequently the proper object of unqualified scientific knowledge is something which cannot be other than it is.

There may be another manner of knowing as well—that will be discussed later. What I now assert is that at all events we do know by demonstration. By demonstration I mean a syllogism productive of scientific knowledge, a syllogism, that is, the grasp of which is *eo ipso* such knowledge. Assuming then that my thesis as to the nature of scientific knowing is correct, the premisses of demonstrated knowledge must be true, primary, immediate, better known than and prior to the conclusion, which is further related to them as effect to cause. Unless these conditions are satisfied, the basic truths will not be 'appropriate' to the conclusion. Syllogism there may indeed be without these conditions, but such syllogism, not being productive of scientific knowledge, will not be demonstration. The premisses must be true: for that which is non-existent cannot be known—we cannot know, e.g., that the diagonal of a square is commensurate with its side. The premisses must be primary and indemonstrable; otherwise they will require demonstration in order to be known, since to have knowledge, if it be not accidental knowledge, of things which are demonstrable, means precisely to have a demonstration of them. The premisses must be the causes of the conclusion, better known than it, and prior to it; its causes, since we possess scientific knowledge of a thing only when we know its cause; prior, in order to be causes; antecedently known, this antecedent knowledge being not our mere understanding of the meaning, but knowledge of the fact as well. Now 'prior' and 'better known' are ambiguous terms, for there is a difference between what is prior and better known in the order of being and what is prior and better known to man. I mean that objects nearer to sense are prior and better known to man; objects without qualification prior and better known are those further from sense. Now the most universal causes are furthest from sense and particular causes are nearest to sense, and they are thus exactly opposed to one another. In saying that the premisses of demonstrated knowledge must be primary, I mean that they must be the 'appropriate' basic truths, for I identify primary premiss and basic truth. A 'basic truth' in a demonstration is an immediate proposition. An immediate proposition is one which has no other proposition prior to it. A proposition is either part of an enunciation, i.e. it predicates a single attribute of a single subject. If a proposition is dialectical, it assumes either part indifferently; if it is demonstrative, it lays down one part to the definite exclusion of the other because that part is true. The term 'enunciation' denotes either part of a contradiction indifferently. A contradiction is an opposition which of its own nature excludes a middle. The part of a contradiction which conjoins a predicate with a subject is an affirmation; the part disjoining them is a negation. I call an immediate basic truth of syllogism a 'thesis' when, though it is not susceptible of proof by the teacher, yet ignorance of it does not constitute a total bar to progress on the part of the pupil: one which the pupil must know if he is to learn anything whatever is an axiom. I call it an axiom because there are such truths and we give them the name of axioms *par excellence.* If a thesis assumes one part or the other of an enunciation, i.e. asserts either the existence or the non-existence of a subject, it is a hypothesis; if it does not so assert, it is a definition. Definition is a 'thesis' or a 'laying something down', since the arithmetician lays it down that to be a unit is to be quantitatively indivisible; but it is not a hypothesis, for to define what a unit is is not the same as to affirm its existence.

Now since the required ground of our knowledge—i.e. of our conviction—of a fact is the possession of such a syllogism as we call demonstration, and the ground of the syllogism is the facts constituting its premisses, we must not only know the primary premisses—some if not all of them—beforehand, but know them better than the conclusion: for the cause of an attribute's inherence in a subject always itself inheres in the subject more firmly than that attribute; e.g. the cause of our loving anything is dearer to us than the object of our love. So since the primary premisses are the cause of our knowledge—i.e. of our conviction—it follows that we know them better—that is, are more convinced of them—than their consequences, precisely because our knowledge of the latter is the effect of our knowledge of the premisses. Now a man cannot believe in anything more than in the things he knows, unless he has either actual knowledge of it or something better than actual knowledge. But we are faced with this paradox if a student whose belief rests on demonstration has not prior knowledge; a man must believe in some, if not in all, of the basic truths more than in the conclusion. Moreover, if a man sets out to acquire the scientific knowledge that comes through demonstration, he must not only have a better knowledge of the basic truths and a firmer conviction of them than of the connexion which is being demonstrated: more than this, nothing must be more certain or better known to him than these basic truths in their character as contradicting the fundamental premisses which lead to the opposed and erroneous conclusion. For indeed the conviction of pure science must be unshakable.

Some hold that, owing to the necessity of knowing the primary premisses, there is no scientific knowledge. Others think there is, but that all truths are demonstrable. Neither doctrine is either true or a necessary deduction from the premisses. The first school, assuming that there is no way of knowing other than by demonstration, maintain that an infinite regress is involved, on the ground that if behind the prior stands no primary, we could not know the posterior through the prior (wherein they are right, for one cannot traverse an infinite series): if on the other hand—they say—the series terminates and there are primary premisses, yet these are unknowable because incapable of demonstration, which according to them is the only form of knowledge. And since thus one cannot know the primary premisses, knowledge of the conclusions which follow from them is not pure scientific knowledge nor properly knowing at all, but rests on the mere supposition that the premisses are true. The other party agree with them as regards knowing, holding that it is only possible by demonstration, but they see no difficulty in holding that all truths are demonstrated, on the ground that demonstration may be circular and reciprocal.

Our own doctrine is that not all knowledge is demonstrative: on the contrary, knowledge of the immediate premisses is independent of demonstration. (The necessity of this is obvious; for since we must know the prior premisses from which the demonstration is drawn, and since the regress must end in immediate truths, those truths must be indemonstrable.) Such, then, is our doctrine, and in addition we maintain that besides scientific knowledge there is its originative source which enables us to recognize the definitions.

Now demonstration must be based on premisses prior to and better known than the conclusion; and the same things cannot simultaneously be both prior and posterior to one another: so circular demonstration is clearly not possible in the unqualified sense of 'demonstration', but only possible if 'demonstration' be extended to include that other method of argument which rests on a distinction between truths prior to us and truths without qualification prior, i.e. the method by which induction produces knowledge. But if we accept this extension of its meaning, our definition of unqualified knowledge will prove faulty; for there seem to be two kinds of it. Perhaps, however, the second form of demonstration, that which proceeds from truths better known to us, is not demonstration in the unqualified sense of the term.

The advocates of circular demonstration are not only faced with the difficulty we have just stated: in addition their theory reduces to the mere statement that if a thing exists, then it does exist—an easy way of proving anything. That this is so can be clearly shown by taking three terms, for to constitute the circle it makes no difference whether many terms or few or even only two are taken. Thus by direct proof, if *A* is, *B* must be; if *B* is, *C* must be; therefore if *A* is, *C* must be. Since then—by the circular proof—if *A* is, *B* must be, and if *B* is, *A* must be, *A* may be substituted for *C* above. Then 'if *B* is, *A* must be' = 'if *B* is, *C* must be', which above gave the conclusion 'if *A* is, *C* must be': but *C* and *A* have been identified. Consequently the upholders of circular demonstration are in the position of saying that if *A* is, *A* must be—a simple way of proving anything. Moreover, even such circular demonstration is impossible except in the case of attributes that imply one another, viz. 'peculiar' properties.

Now, it has been shown that the positing of one thing—be it one term or one premiss—never involves a necessary consequent: two premisses constitute the first and smallest foundation for drawing a conclusion at all and therefore *a fortiori* for the demonstrative syllogism of science. If, then, *A* is implied in *B* and *C*, and *B* and *C* are reciprocally implied in one another and in *A*, it is possible, as has been shown in my writings on the syllogism, to prove all the assumptions on which the original conclusion rested, by circular demonstration in the first figure. But it has also been shown that in the other figures either no conclusion is possible, or at least none which proves both the original premisses. Propositions the terms of which are not convertible cannot be circularly demonstrated at all, and since convertible terms occur rarely in actual demonstrations, it is clearly frivolous and impossible to say that demonstration is reciprocal and that therefore everything can be demonstrated.

From the Physics

BOOK II

Of things that exist, some exist by nature, some from other causes. 'By nature' the animals and their parts exist, and the plants and the simple bodies (earth, fire, air, water)—for we say that these and the like exist 'by nature'.

All the things mentioned present a feature in which they differ from things which are *not* constituted by nature. Each of them has within *itself* a principle of motion and of stationariness (in respect of place, or of growth and decrease, or by way of alteration). On the other hand, a bed and a coat and anything else of that sort, *qua* receiving these designations—i.e. in so far as they are products of art—have no innate impulse to change. But in so far as they happen to be composed of stone or of earth or of a mixture of the two, they do have such an impulse, and just to that extent—which seems to indicate that *nature is a source or cause of being moved and of being at rest in that to which it belongs primarily,* in virtue of itself and not in virtue of a concomitant attribute.

I say 'not in virtue of a concomitant attribute', because (for instance) a man who is a doctor might cure himself. Nevertheless it is not in so far as he is a patient that he possesses the art of medicine: it merely has happened that the same man is doctor and patient—and that is why these attributes are not always found together. So it is with all other artificial products. None of them has in itself the source of its own production. But while in some cases (for instance houses and the other products of manual labour) that principle is in something else external to the thing, in others—those which may cause a change in themselves in virtue of a concomitant attribute—it lies in the things themselves (but not in virtue of what they are).

'Nature' then is what has been stated. Things 'have a nature' which have a principle of this kind. Each of them is a substance; for it is a subject, and nature always implies a subject in which it inheres.

The term 'according to nature' is applied to all these things and also to the attributes which belong to them in virtue of what they are, for instance the property of fire to be carried upwards—which is not a 'nature' nor 'has a nature' but is 'by nature' or 'according to nature'.

What nature is, then, and the meaning of the terms 'by nature' and 'according to nature', has been stated. *That* nature exists, it would be absurd to try to prove; for it is obvious that there are many things of this kind, and to prove what is obvious by what is not is the mark of a man who is unable to distinguish what is self-evident from what is not. (This state of mind is clearly possible. A man blind from birth might reason about colours. Presumably therefore such persons must be talking about words without any thought to correspond.)

Some identify the nature or substance of a natural object with that immediate constituent of it which taken by itself is without arrangement, e.g. the wood is the 'nature' of the bed, and the bronze the 'nature' of the statue.

As an indication of this Antiphon points out that if you planted a bed and the rotting wood acquired the power of sending up a shoot, it would not be a bed that would come up, but *wood*—which shows that the arrangement in accordance with the rules of the art is merely an incidental attribute, whereas the real nature is the other, which, further, persists continuously through the process of making.

But if the material of each of these objects has itself the same relation to something else, say bronze (or gold) to water, bones (or wood) to earth and so on,

---

Physics, II, 1–7, 192b–198b.

that (they say) would be their nature and essence. Consequently some assert earth, others fire or air or water or some or all of these, to be the nature of the things that are. For whatever any one of them supposed to have this character—whether one thing or more than one thing—this or these he declared to be the whole of substance, all else being its affections, states, or dispositions. Every such thing they held to be eternal (for it could not pass into anything else), but other things to come into being and cease to be times without number.

This then is one account of 'nature', namely that it is the immediate material substratum of things which have in themselves a principle of motion or change.

Another account is that 'nature' is the shape or form which is specified in the definition of the thing.

For the word 'nature' is applied to what is according to nature and the natural in the same way as 'art' is applied to what is artistic or a work of art. We should not say in the latter case that there is anything artistic about a thing, if it is a bed only potentially, not yet having the form of a bed; nor should we call it a work of art. The same is true of natural compounds. What is potentially flesh or bone has not yet its own 'nature', and does not exist 'by nature', until it receives the form specified in the definition, which we name in defining what flesh or bone is. Thus in the second sense of 'nature' it would be the shape or form (not separable except in statement) of things which have in themselves a source of motion. (The combination of the two, e.g. man, is not 'nature' but 'by nature' or 'natural'.)

The form indeed is 'nature' rather than the matter; for a thing is more properly said to be what it is when it has attained to fulfilment than when it exists potentially. Again man is born from man, but not bed from bed. That is why people say that the figure is not the nature of a bed, but the wood is—if the bed sprouted not a bed but wood would come up. But even if the figure *is* art, then on the same principle the shape of man is his nature. For man is born from man.

We also speak of a thing's nature as being exhibited in the process of growth by which its nature is attained. The 'nature' in this sense is not like 'doctoring', which leads not to the art of doctoring but to health. Doctoring must start from the art, not lead to it. But it is not in this way that nature (in the one sense) is related to nature (in the other). What grows *qua* growing grows from something into something. Into what then does it grow? Not into that from which it arose but into that to which it tends. The shape then is nature.

'Shape' and 'nature', it should be added, are used in two senses. For the privation too is in a way form. But whether in unqualified coming to be there is privation, i.e. a contrary to what comes to be, we must consider later.

We have distinguished, then, the different ways in which the term 'nature' is used.

The next point to consider is how the mathematician differs from the physicist. Obviously physical bodies contain surfaces and volumes, lines and points, and these are the subject-matter of mathematics.

Further, is astronomy different from physics or a department of it? It seems absurd that the physicist should be supposed to know the nature of sun or moon, but not to know any of their essential attributes, particularly as the writers on physics obviously do discuss their shape also and whether the earth and the world are spherical or not.

Now the mathematician, though he too treats of these things, nevertheless does not treat of them as the limits of a physical body; nor does he consider the attributes indicated as the attributes of such bodies. That is why he separates them; for in thought they are separable from motion, and it makes no difference, nor does any falsity result, if they are separated. The holders of the theory of Forms do the same, though they are not aware of it; for they separate the objects of physics, which are less separable than those of mathematics. This becomes plain if one tries to state in each of the two cases the definitions of the things and of their attributes. 'Odd' and 'even', 'straight' and 'curved', and likewise 'number', 'line', and 'figure', do not involve motion; not so 'flesh' and 'bone' and 'man'—*these* are defined like 'snub nose', not like 'curved'.

Similar evidence is supplied by the more physical of the branches of mathematics, such as optics, harmonics, and astronomy. These are in a way the converse of geometry. While geometry investigates physical lines but not *qua* physical, optics investigates mathematical lines, but *qua* physical, not *qua* mathematical.

Since 'nature' has two senses, the form and the

matter, we must investigate its objects as we would the essence of snubness. That is, such things are neither independent of matter nor can be defined in terms of matter only. Here too indeed one might raise a difficulty. Since there are two natures, with which is the physicist concerned? Or should he investigate the combination of the two? But if the combination of the two, then also each severally. Does it belong then to the same or to different sciences to know each severally?

If we look at the ancients, physics would seem to be concerned with the *matter*. (It was only very slightly that Empedocles and Democritus touched on the forms and the essence.)

But if on the other hand art imitates nature, and it is the part of the same discipline to know the form and the matter up to a point (e.g. the doctor has a knowledge of health and also of bile and phlegm, in which health is realized and the builder both of the form of the house and of the matter, namely that it is bricks and beams, and so forth): if this is so, it would be the part of physics also to know nature in both its senses.

Again, 'that for the sake of which', or the end, belongs to the same department of knowledge as the means. But the nature is the end or 'that for the sake of which'. For if a thing undergoes a continuous change and there is a stage which is last, this stage is the end or 'that for the sake of which'. (That is why the poet was carried away into making an absurd statement when he said 'he has the end for the sake of which he was born'. For not every stage that is last claims to be an end, but only that which is best.)

For the arts make their material (some simply 'make' it, others make it serviceable), and we use everything as if it was there for our sake. (We also are in a sense an end. 'That for the sake of which' has two senses: the distinction is made in our work *On Philosophy*.) The arts, therefore, which govern the matter and have knowledge are two, namely the art which uses the product and the art which directs the production of it. That is why the using art also is in a sense directive; but it differs in that it knows the form, whereas the art which is directive as being concerned with production knows the matter. For the helmsman knows and prescribes what sort of form a helm should have, the other from what wood it should be made and by means of what operations. In the products of art, however, we make the material with a view to the function, whereas in the products of nature the matter is there all along.

Again, matter is a relative term: to each form there corresponds a special matter. How far then must the physicist know the form or essence? Up to a point, perhaps, as the doctor must know sinew or the smith bronze (i.e. until he understands the purpose of each): and the physicist is concerned only with things whose forms are separable indeed, but do not exist apart from matter. Man is begotten by man and by the sun as well. The mode of existence and essence of the separable it is the business of the primary type of philosophy to define.

Now that we have established these distinctions, we must proceed to consider causes, their character and number. Knowledge is the object of our inquiry, and men do not think they know a thing till they have grasped the 'why' of it (which is to grasp its primary cause). So clearly we too must do this as regards both coming to be and passing away and every kind of physical change, in order that, knowing their principles, we may try to refer to these principles each of our problems.

In one sense, then, (1) that out of which a thing comes to be and which persists, is called 'cause', e.g. the bronze of the statue, the silver of the bowl, and the genera of which the bronze and the silver are species.

In another sense (2) the form or the archetype, i.e. the statement of the essence, and its genera, are called 'causes' (e.g. of the octave the relation of 2:1, and generally number), and the parts in the definition.

Again (3) the primary source of the change or coming to rest; e.g. the man who gave advice is a cause, the father is cause of the child, and generally what makes of what is made and what causes change of what is changed.

Again (4) in the sense of end or 'that for the sake of which' a thing is done, e.g. health is the cause of walking about. ('Why is he walking about?' we say, 'To be healthy', and, having said that, we think we have assigned the cause.) The same is true also of all the intermediate steps which are brought about through the action of something else as means towards the end, e.g. reduction of flesh, purging, drugs, or surgical instruments are means towards health. All these things are 'for the sake of' the end, though they differ from one another in that some are activities, others instruments.

This then perhaps exhausts the number of ways in which the term 'cause' is used.

As the word has several senses, it follows that there are several causes of the same thing (not merely in virtue of a concomitant attribute), e.g. both the art of the sculptor and the bronze are causes of the statue. These are causes of the statue *qua* statue, not in virtue of anything else that it may be—only not in the same way; the one being the material cause, the other the cause whence the motion comes. Some things cause each other reciprocally, e.g. hard work causes fitness and *vice versa,* but again not in the same way, but the one as end, the other as the origin of change. Further the same thing is the cause of contrary results. For that which by its presence brings about one result is sometimes blamed for bringing about the contrary by its absence. Thus we ascribe the wreck of a ship to the absence of the pilot whose presence was the cause of its safety.

All the causes now mentioned fall into four familiar divisions. The letters are the causes of syllables, the material of artificial products, fire, &c., of bodies, the parts of the whole, and the premisses of the conclusion, in the sense of 'that from which'. Of these pairs the one set are causes in the sense of substratum, e.g. the parts, the other set in the sense of essence—the whole and the combination and the form. But the seed and the doctor and the adviser, and generally the maker, are all sources whence the change or stationariness originates, while the others are causes in the sense of the end or the good of the rest; for 'that for the sake of which' means what is best and the end of the things that lead up to it. (Whether we say the 'good itself' or the 'apparent good' makes no difference.)

Such then is the number and nature of the kinds of cause.

Now the modes of causation are many, though when brought under heads they too can be reduced in number. For 'cause' is used in many senses and even within the same kind one may be prior to another (e.g. the doctor and the expert are causes of health, the relation 2:1 and number of the octave), and always what is inclusive to what is particular. Another mode of causation is the incidental and its genera, e.g. in one way 'Polyclitus', in another 'sculptor' is the cause of a statue, because 'being Polyclitus' and 'sculptor' are incidentally conjoined. Also the classes in which the incidental attribute is included; thus 'a man' could be said to be the cause of a statue or, generally, 'a living creature'. An incidental attribute too may be more or less remote, e.g. suppose that 'a pale man' or 'a musical man' were said to be the cause of the statue.

All causes, both proper and incidental, may be spoken of either as potential or as actual; e.g. the cause of a house being built is either 'house-builder' or 'house-builder building'.

Similar distinctions can be made in the things of which the causes are causes, e.g. of 'this statue' or of 'statue' or of 'image' generally, of 'this bronze' or of 'bronze' or of 'material' generally. So too with the incidental attributes. Again we may use a complex expression for either and say, e.g., neither 'Polyclitus' nor 'sculptor' but 'Polyclitus, sculptor'.

All these various uses, however, come to six in number, under each of which again the usage is twofold. Cause means either what is particular or a genus, or an incidental attribute or a genus of that, and these either as a complex or each by itself; and all six either as actual or as potential. The difference is this much, that causes which are actually at work and particular exist and cease to exist simultaneously with their effect, e.g. this healing person with this being-healed person and that housebuilding man with that being-built house; but this is not always true of potential causes—the house and the housebuilder do not pass away simultaneously.

In investigating the cause of each thing it is always necessary to seek what is most precise (as also in other things): thus man builds because he is a builder, and a builder builds in virtue of his art of building. This last cause then is prior: and so generally.

Further, generic effects should be assigned to generic causes, particular effects to particular causes, e.g. statue to sculptor, this statue to this sculptor; and powers are relative to possible effects, actually operating causes to things which are actually being effected.

This must suffice for our account of the number of causes and the modes of causation.

But chance also and spontaneity are reckoned among causes: many things are said both to be and to come to be as a result of chance and spontaneity. We must inquire therefore in what manner chance and spontaneity are present among the causes enumerated, and whether they are the same or different, and generally what chance and spontaneity are.

Some people even question whether they are real or not. They say that nothing happens by chance, but that everything which we ascribe to chance or spontaneity has some definite cause, e.g. coming 'by chance' into the market and finding there a man whom one wanted but did not expect to meet is due to one's wish to go and buy in the market. Similarly in other cases of chance it is always possible, they maintain, to find something which is the cause; but not chance, for if chance were real, it would seem strange indeed, and the question might be raised, why on earth none of the wise men of old in speaking of the causes of generation and decay took account of chance; whence it would seem that they too did not believe that anything is by chance. But there is a further circumstance that is surprising. Many things both come to be and are by chance and spontaneity, and although all know that each of them can be ascribed to some cause (as the old argument said which denied chance), nevertheless they speak of some of these things as happening by chance and others not. For this reason also they ought to have at least referred to the matter in some way or other.

Certainly the early physicists found no place for chance among the causes which they recognized—love, strife, mind, fire, or the like. This is strange, whether they supposed that there is no such thing as chance or whether they thought there is but omitted to mention it—and that too when they sometimes used it, as Empedocles does when he says that the air is not always separated into the highest region, but 'as it may chance'. At any rate he says in his cosmogony that 'it happened to run that way at that time, but it often ran otherwise.' He tells us also that most of the parts of animals came to be by chance.

There are some too who ascribe this heavenly sphere and all the worlds to spontaneity. They say that the vortex arose spontaneously, i.e. the motion that separated and arranged in its present order all that exists. This statement might well cause surprise. For they are asserting that chance is not responsible for the existence or generation of animals and plants, nature or mind or something of the kind being the cause of them (for it is not any chance thing that comes from a given seed but an olive from one kind and a man from another); and yet at the same time they assert that the heavenly sphere and the divinest of visible things arose spontaneously, having no such cause as is assigned to animals and plants. Yet if this is so, it is a fact which deserves to be dwelt upon, and something might well have been said about it. For besides the other absurdities of the statement, it is the more absurd that people should make it when they see nothing coming to be spontaneously in the heavens, but much happening by chance among the things which as they say are not due to chance; whereas we should have expected exactly the opposite.

Others there are who, indeed, believe that chance is a cause, but that it is inscrutable to human intelligence, as being a divine thing and full of mystery.

Thus we must inquire what chance and spontaneity are, whether they are the same or different, and how they fit into our division of causes.

First then we observe that some things always come to pass in the same way, and others for the most part. It is clearly of neither of these that chance is said to be the cause, nor can the 'effect of chance' be identified with any of the things that come to pass by necessity and always, or for the most part. But as there is a third class of events besides these two—events which all say are 'by chance'—it is plain that there is such a thing as chance and spontaneity; for we know that things of this kind are due to chance and that things due to chance are of this kind.

But, secondly, some events are for the sake of something, others not. Again, some of the former class are in accordance with deliberate intention, others not, but both are in the class of things which are for the sake of something. Hence it is clear that even among the things which are outside the necessary and the normal, there are some in connexion with which the phrase 'for the sake of something' is applicable. (Events that are for the sake of something include whatever may be done as a result of thought or of nature.) Things of this kind, then, when they come to pass incidentally are said to be 'by chance'. For just as a thing is something either in virtue of itself or incidentally, so may it be a cause. For instance, the housebuilding faculty is in virtue of itself the cause of a house, whereas the pale or the musical is the incidental cause. That which is *per se* cause of the effect is determinate, but the incidental cause is indeterminable, for the possible attributes of an individual are innumerable. To resume then; when a thing of this kind comes to pass among events which are for the sake of something, it is said to be spontaneous or by chance. (The distinction between the two must be made later—for the present it is sufficient if it is plain that both are in the sphere of things done for the sake of something.)

Example: A man is engaged in collecting subscriptions for a feast. He would have gone to such and such a place for the purpose of getting the money, if he had known. He actually went there for another purpose, and it was only incidentally that he got his money by going there; and this was not due to the fact that he went there as a rule or necessarily, nor is the end effected (getting the money) a cause present in himself—it belongs to the class of things that are intentional and the result of intelligent deliberation. It is when these conditions are satisfied that the man is said to have gone 'by chance'. If he had gone of deliberate purpose and for the sake of this—if he always or normally went there when he was collecting payments—he would not be said to have gone 'by chance'.

It is clear then that chance is an incidental cause in the sphere of those actions for the sake of something which involve purpose. Intelligent reflection, then, and chance are in the same sphere, for purpose implies intelligent reflection.

It is necessary, no doubt, that the causes of what comes to pass by chance be indefinite; and that is why chance is supposed to belong to the class of the indefinite and to be inscrutable to man, and why it might be thought that, in a way, nothing occurs by chance. For all these statements are correct, because they are well grounded. Things *do,* in a way, occur by chance, for they occur incidentally and chance is an *incidental* cause. But strictly it is not the *cause*—without qualification—of anything, for instance, a housebuilder is the cause of a house; incidentally, a flute-player may be so.

And the causes of the man's coming and getting the money (when he did not come for the sake of that) are innumerable. He may have wished to see somebody or been following somebody or avoiding somebody, or may have gone to see a spectacle. Thus to say that chance is a thing contrary to rule is correct. For 'rule' applies to what is always true or true for the most part, whereas chance belongs to a third type of event. Hence, to conclude, since causes of this kind are indefinite, chance too is indefinite. (Yet in some cases one might raise the question whether *any* incidental fact might be the cause of the chance occurrence, e.g. of health the fresh air or the sun's heat may be the cause, but having had one's hair cut *cannot;* for some incidental causes are more relevant to the effect than others.)

Chance or fortune is called 'good' when the result is good, 'evil' when it is evil. The terms 'good fortune' and 'ill fortune' are used when either result is of considerable magnitude. Thus one who comes within an ace of some great evil or great good is said to be fortunate or unfortunate. The mind affirms the presence of the attribute, ignoring the hair's breadth of difference. Further, it is with reason that good fortune is regarded as unstable; for chance is unstable, as none of the things which result from it can be invariable or normal.

Both are then, as I have said, incidental causes—both chance and spontaneity—in the sphere of things which are capable of coming to pass not necessarily, nor normally, and with reference to such of these as might come to pass for the sake of something.

They differ in that 'spontaneity' is the wider term. Every result of chance is from what is spontaneous, but not everything that is from what is spontaneous is from chance.

Chance and what results from chance are appropriate to agents that are capable of good fortune and of moral action generally. Therefore necessarily chance is in the sphere of moral actions. This is indicated by the fact that good fortune is thought to be the same, or nearly the same, as happiness, and happiness to be a kind of moral action, since it is well-doing. Hence what is not capable of moral action cannot do anything by chance. Thus an inanimate thing or a lower animal or a child cannot do anything by chance, because it is incapable of deliberate intention; nor can 'good fortune' or 'ill fortune' be ascribed to them, except metaphorically, as Protarchus, for example, said that the stones of which altars are made are fortunate because they are held in honour, while their fellows are trodden under foot. Even these things, however, can in a way be affected by chance, when one who is dealing with them does something to them by chance, but not otherwise.

The spontaneous on the other hand is found both in the lower animals and in many inanimate objects. We say, for example, that the horse came 'spontaneously', because, though his coming saved him, he did not come for the sake of safety. Again, the tripod fell 'of itself', because, though when it fell it stood on its feet so as to serve for a seat, it did not fall for the sake of that.

Hence it is clear that events which (1) belong to the general class of things that may come to pass for the sake of something, (2) do not come to pass for the sake of what actually results, and (3) have an external cause, may be described by the phrase 'from spontaneity'. These 'spontaneous' events are said to be 'from chance' if they have the further characteristics of being the objects of deliberate intention and due to agents capable of that mode of action. This is indicated by the phrase 'in vain', which is used when *A*, which is for the sake of *B*, does not result in *B*. For instance, taking a walk is for the sake of evacuation of the bowels; if this does not follow after walking, we say that we have walked 'in vain' and that the walking was 'vain'. This implies that what is naturally the means to an end is 'in vain', when it does not effect the end towards which it was the natural means—for it would be absurd for a man to say that he had bathed in vain because the sun was not eclipsed, since the one was not done with a view to the other. Thus the spontaneous is even according to its derivation the case in which the thing itself happens in vain. The stone that struck the man did not fall for the purpose of striking him; therefore it fell spontaneously, because it might have fallen by the action of an agent and for the purpose of striking. The difference between spontaneity and what results by chance is greatest in things that come to be by nature; for when anything comes to be contrary to nature, we do not say that it came to be by chance, but by spontaneity. Yet strictly this too is different from the spontaneous proper; for the cause of the latter is external, that of the former internal.

We have now explained what chance is and what spontaneity is, and in what they differ from each other. Both belong to the mode of causation 'source of change', for either some natural or some intelligent agent is always the cause; but in this sort of causation the number of possible causes is infinite.

Spontaneity and chance are causes of effects which, though they might result from intelligence or nature, have in fact been caused by something *incidentally*. Now since nothing which is incidental is prior to what is *per se*, it is clear that no incidental cause can be prior to a cause *per se*. Spontaneity and chance, therefore, are posterior to intelligence and nature. Hence, however true it may be that the heavens are due to spontaneity, it will still be true that intelligence and nature will be prior causes of this All and of many things in it besides.

It is clear then that there are causes, and that the number of them is what we have stated. The number is the same as that of the things comprehended under the question 'why'. The 'why' is referred ultimately either (1), in things which do not involve motion, e.g. in mathematics, to the 'what' (to the definition of 'straight line' or 'commensurable', &c.), or (2) to what initiated a motion, e.g. 'why did they go to war?—because there had been a raid'; or (3) we are inquiring 'for the sake of what?'—'that they may rule'; or (4), in the case of things that come into being, we are looking for the matter. The causes, therefore, are these and so many in number.

Now, the causes being four, it is the business of the physicist to know about them all, and if he refers his problems back to all of them, he will assign the 'why' in the way proper to his science—the matter, the form, the mover, 'that for the sake of which'. The last three often coincide; for the 'what' and 'that for the sake of which' are one, while the primary source of motion is the same in species as these (for man generates man), and so too, in general, are all things which cause movement by being themselves moved; and such as are not of this kind are no longer inside the province of physics, for they cause motion not by possessing motion or a source of motion in themselves, but being themselves incapable of motion. Hence there are three branches of study, one of things which are incapable of motion, the second of things in motion, but indestructible, the third of destructible things.

The question 'why', then, is answered by reference to the matter, to the form, and to the primary moving cause. For in respect of coming to be it is mostly in this last way that causes are investigated—'what comes to be after what? what was the primary agent or patient?' and so at each step of the series.

Now the principles which cause motion in a physical way are two, of which one is not physical, as it has no principle of motion in itself. Of this kind is whatever causes movement, not being itself moved, such as (1) that which is completely unchangeable, the primary reality, and (2) the essence of that which is coming to be, i.e. the form; for this is the end or 'that for the sake of which'. Hence since nature is for the sake of something, we must know this cause also. We must explain the 'why' in all the senses of the term, namely, (1) that from this that will necessarily result ('from this' either without qualification or in most cases); (2) that 'this must be so if that is to be so' (as the conclusion presupposes the premisses); (3) that this was the essence of the thing; and (4) because it is better thus (not without qualification, but with reference to the essential nature in each case).

From On the Heavens

Let us first decide the question whether the earth moves or is at rest. For, as we said, there are some who make it one of the stars, and others who, setting it at the centre, suppose it to be 'rolled' and in motion about the pole as axis. That both views are untenable will be clear if we take as our starting-point the fact that the earth's motion, whether the earth be at the centre or away from it, must needs be a constrained motion. It cannot be the movement of the earth itself. If it were, any portion of it would have this movement; but in fact every part moves in a straight line to the centre. Being, then, constrained and unnatural, the movement could not be eternal. But the order of the universe is eternal. Again, everything that moves with the circular movement, except the first sphere, is observed to be passed, and to move with more than one motion. The earth, then, also, whether it move about the centre or as stationary at it, must necessarily move with two motions. But if this were so, there would have to be passings and turnings of the fixed stars. Yet no such thing is observed. The same stars always rise and set in the same parts of the earth.

Further, the natural movement of the earth, part and whole alike, is to the centre of the whole—whence the fact that it is now actually situated at the centre—but it might be questioned, since both centres are the same, which centre it is that portions of earth and other heavy things move to. Is this their goal because it is the centre of the earth or because it is the centre of the whole? The goal, surely, must be the centre of the whole. For fire and other light things move to the extremity of the area which contains the centre. It happens, however, that the centre of the earth and of the whole is the same. Thus they do move to the centre of the earth, but accidentally, in virtue of the fact that the earth's centre lies at the centre of the whole. That the centre of the earth is the goal of their movement is indicated by the fact that heavy bodies moving towards the earth do not move parallel but so as to make equal angles, and thus to a single centre, that of the earth. It is clear, then, that the earth must be at the centre and immovable, not only for the reasons already given, but also because heavy bodies forcibly thrown quite straight upward return to the point from which they started, even if they are thrown to an infinite distance. From these considerations then it is clear that the earth does not move and does not lie elsewhere than at the centre.

From what we have said the explanation of the earth's immobility is also apparent. If it is the nature of earth, as observation shows, to move from any point to the centre, as of fire contrariwise to move from the centre to the extremity, it is impossible that any portion of earth should move away from the centre except by constraint. For a single thing has a single movement, and a simple thing a simple: contrary movements cannot belong to the same thing, and movement away from the centre is the contrary of movement to it. If then no portion of earth can move away from the centre, obviously still less can the earth as a whole so move. For it is the nature of the whole to move to the point to which the part naturally moves. Since, then, it would require a force greater than itself to move it, it must needs stay at the centre. This view is further supported by the contributions of mathematicians to astronomy, since the observations made as the shapes change by which the order of the stars is determined, are fully accounted for on the hypothesis that the earth lies at the centre. Of the position of the earth and of the manner of its rest or movement, our discussion may here end.

Its shape must necessarily be spherical. For every portion of earth has weight until it reaches the

---

On the Heavens III, 1, 296a–298a.

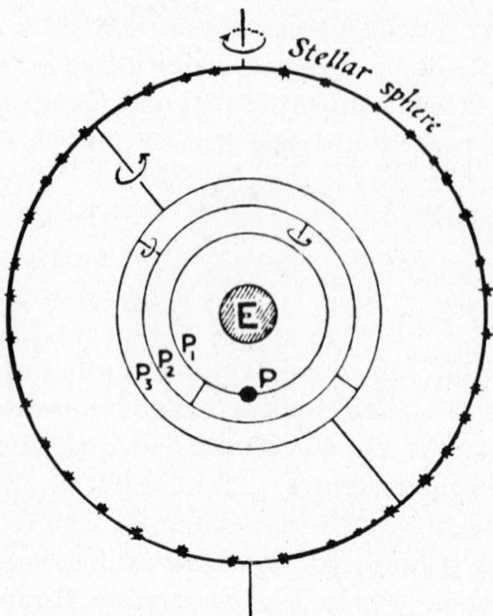

Fig. 1. The system of concentric spheres adopted by Aristotle, showing the system of spheres (p_1, p_2, p_3) for one planet P with the axes all placed in the plane of the paper. If P were Saturn the other planets' spheres would come inside this. The stellar sphere rotates about an axis passing through the centre of the stationary earth E.

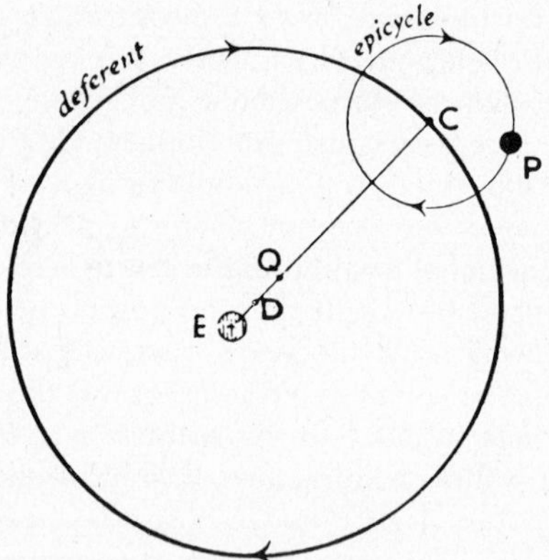

Fig. 2. The device of the epicycle in Ptolemy's system for the motion of a planet P. The centre of the deferent is D which does not coincide with E, the centre of the earth and of the universe. The centre of the epicycle, C, does not rotate uniformly about D but moves so that the line CQ, connecting C with the equant Q, moves through equal angles in equal times. If necessary for the better 'saving of appearances' the system could be complicated by adding further epicycles, as, for example, a second whose centre C_1 revolves round C, a third whose centre C_2 revolves round C_1, and so on, the planet itself always being on the outermost epicycle.

Aristotle's and Ptolemy's Cosmography

centre, and the jostling of parts greater and smaller would bring about not a waved surface, but rather compression and convergence of part and part until the centre is reached. The process should be conceived by supposing the earth to come into being in the way that some of the natural philosophers describe. Only they attribute the downward movement to constraint, and it is better to keep to the truth and say that the reason of this motion is that a thing which possesses weight is naturally endowed with a centripetal movement. When the mixture, then, was merely potential, the things that were separated off moved similarly from every side towards the centre. Whether the parts which come together at the centre were distributed at the extremities evenly, or in some other way, makes no difference. If, on the one hand, there were a similar movement from each quarter of the extremity to the single centre, it is obvious that the resulting mass would be similar on every side. For if an equal amount is added on every side the extremity of the mass will be everywhere equidistant from its centre, i.e. the figure will be spherical. But neither will it in any way affect the argument if there is not a similar accession of concurrent fragments from every side. For the greater quantity, finding a lesser in front of it, must necessarily drive it on, both having an impulse whose goal is the centre, and the greater weight driving the lesser forward till this goal is reached. In this we have also the solution of a possible difficulty. The earth, it might be argued, is at the centre and spherical in shape: if, then, a weight many times that of the earth were added to one hemisphere, the centre of the earth and of the whole will no longer be coincident. So that either the earth will not stay still at the centre, or if it does, it will be at rest without having its centre at the place to which it is still its nature to move. Such is the difficulty. A short consideration will give us an easy answer, if we first give precision to our postulate that any body endowed with weight, of whatever size moves towards the centre. Clearly it will not stop when its edge touches the centre. The greater quantity must prevail until the body's centre occupies the centre. For that is the goal of its impulse. Now it makes no difference whether we apply this to a clod or common fragment of earth or to the earth as a whole. The fact indicated does not depend upon degrees of size but applies universally to everything that has the centripetal impulse. Therefore earth in motion, whether in a mass or in fragments, necessarily continues to move until it occupies the centre equally every way, the less being forced to equalize itself by the greater owing to the forward drive of the impulse.

If the earth was generated, then, it must have been formed in this way, and so clearly its generation was spherical; and if it is ungenerated and has remained so always, its character must be that which the initial generation, if it had occurred, would have given it. But the spherical shape, necessitated by this argument, follows also from the fact that the motions of heavy bodies always make equal angles, and are not parallel. This would be the natural form of movement towards what is naturally spherical. Either then the earth is spherical or it is at least naturally spherical. And it is right to call anything that which nature intends it to be, and which belongs to it, rather than that which it is by constraint and contrary to nature. The evidence of the senses further corroborates this. How else would eclipses of the moon show segments shaped as we see them? As it is, the shapes which the moon itself each month shows are of every kind—straight, gibbous, and concave—but in eclipses the outline is always curved: and, since it is the interposition of the earth that makes the eclipse, the form of this line will be caused by the form of the earth's surface, which is therefore spherical. Again, our observations of the stars make it evident, not only that the earth is circular, but also that it is a circle of no great size. For quite a small change of position to south or north causes a manifest alteration of the horizon. There is much change, I mean, in the stars which are overhead, and the stars seen are different, as one moves northward or southward. Indeed there are some stars seen in Egypt and in the neighbourhood of Cyprus which are not seen in the northerly regions; and stars, which in the north are never beyond the range of observation, in those regions rise and set. All of which goes to show not only that the earth is circular in shape, but also that it is a sphere of no great size: for otherwise the effect of so slight a change of place would not be so quickly apparent. Hence one should not be too sure of the incredibility of the view of those who conceive that there is continuity between the parts about the pillars of Hercules and the parts about India, and that in this way the ocean is one. As further evidence in favour of this they quote the case of elephants, a species occurring in each of these extreme regions, suggesting that the common characteristic of these extremes is explained by their continuity. Also, those mathematicians who try to calculate the size of the earth's circumference arrive at the figure 400,000 stades. This indicates not only that the earth's mass is spherical in shape, but also that as compared with the stars it is not of great size.

From On the Soul

Let the foregoing suffice as our account of the views concerning the soul which have been handed on by our predecessors; let us now dismiss them and make as it were a completely fresh start, endeavouring to give a precise answer to the question, What is soul? i.e. to formulate the most general possible definition of it.

We are in the habit of recognizing, as one determinate kind of what is, substance, and that in several senses, (*a*) in the sense of matter or that which in itself is not 'a this', and (*b*) in the sense of form or essence, which is that precisely in virtue of which a thing is called 'a this', and thirdly (*c*) in the sense of that which is compounded of both (*a*) and (*b*). Now matter is potentiality, form actuality; of the latter there are two grades related to one another as e.g. knowledge to the exercise of knowledge.

Among substances are by general consent reckoned bodies and especially natural bodies; for they are the principles of all other bodies. Of natural bodies some have life in them, others not; by life we mean self-nutrition and growth (with its correlative decay). It follows that every natural body which has life in it is a substance in the sense of a composite.

But since it is also a *body* of such and such a kind, viz. having life, the *body* cannot be soul; the body is the subject or matter, not what is attributed to it. Hence the soul must be a substance in the sense of the form of a natural body having life potentially within it. But substance is actuality, and thus soul is

On the Soul, II, 1, 412a–413a.

the actuality of a body as above characterized. Now the word actuality has two senses corresponding respectively to the possession of knowledge and the actual exercise of knowledge. It is obvious that the soul is actuality in the first sense, viz. that of knowledge as possessed, for both sleeping and waking presuppose the existence of soul, and of these waking corresponds to actual knowing, sleeping to knowledge possessed but not employed, and, in the history of the individual, knowledge comes before its employment or exercise.

That is why the soul is the first grade of actuality of a natural body having life potentially in it. The body so described is a body which is organized. The parts of plants in spite of their extreme simplicity are 'organs'; e.g. the leaf serves to shelter the pericarp, the pericarp to shelter the fruit, while the roots of plants are analogous to the mouth of animals, both serving for the absorption of food. If, then, we have to give a general formula applicable to all kinds of soul, we must describe it as the first grade of actuality of a natural organized body. That is why we can wholly dismiss as unnecessary the question whether the soul and the body are one: it is as meaningless as to ask whether the wax and the shape given to it by the stamp are one, or generally the matter of a thing and that of which it is the matter. Unity has many senses (as many as 'is' has), but the most proper and fundamental sense of both is the relation of an actuality to that of which it is the actuality.

We have now given an answer to the question, What is soul?—an answer which applies to it in its full extent. It is substance in the sense which corresponds to the definitive formula of a thing's essence. That means that it is 'the essential whatness' of a body of the character just assigned. Suppose that what is literally an 'organ', like an axe, were a *natural* body, its 'essential whatness', would have been its essence, and so its soul; if this disappeared from it, it would have ceased to be an axe, except in name. As it is, it is just an axe; it wants the character which is required to make its whatness or formulable essence a soul; for that, it would have had to be a *natural* body of a particular kind, viz. one having in *itself* the power of setting itself in movement and arresting itself. Next, apply this doctrine in the case of the 'parts' of the living body. Suppose that the eye were an animal—sight would have been its soul, for sight is the substance or essence of the eye which corresponds to the formula, the eye being merely the matter of seeing; when seeing is removed the eye is no longer an eye, except in name—it is no more a real eye than the eye of a statue or of a painted figure. We must now extend our consideration from the 'parts' to the whole living body; for what the departmental sense is to the bodily part which is its organ, that the whole faculty of sense is to the whole sensitive body as such.

We must not understand by that which is 'potentially capable of living' what has lost the soul it had, but only what still retains it; but seeds and fruits are bodies which possess the qualification. Consequently, while waking is actuality in a sense corresponding to the cutting and the seeing, the soul is actuality in the sense corresponding to the power of sight and the power in the tool; the body corresponds to what exists in potentiality; as the pupil *plus* the power of sight constitutes the eye, so the soul *plus* the body constitutes the animal.

From this it indubitably follows that the soul is inseparable from its body, or at any rate that certain parts of it are (if it has parts)—for the actuality of some of them is nothing but the actualities of their bodily parts. Yet some may be separable because they are not the actualities of any body at all. Further, we have no light on the problem whether the soul may not be the actuality of its body in the sense in which the sailor is the actuality of the ship.

This must suffice as our sketch or outline determination of the nature of soul.

From the Metaphysics

All men by nature desire to know. An indication of this is the delight we take in our senses; for even apart from their usefulness they are loved for themselves; and above all others the sense of sight. For

---

Metaphysics, I, 1–2, 980a–983a; I, 10, 993a–12–27; III, 1, 995a–996a; IV, 1–2, 1003a–1005a; VII, 1–3, 1028a–1029b; VIII, 1–2, 1042a–1043a; IX, 1–2, 1045b–1046a; XII, 6, 1071b–1072a; XIV, 2, 1088b–1090a.

not only with a view to action, but even when we are not going to do anything, we prefer seeing (one might say) to everything else. The reason is that this, most of all the senses, makes us know and brings to light many differences between things.

By nature animals are born with the faculty of sensation, and from sensation memory is produced in some of them, though not in others. And therefore the former are more intelligent and apt at learning than those which cannot remember; those which are incapable of hearing sounds are intelligent though they cannot be taught, e.g. the bee, and any other race of animals that may be like it; and those which besides memory have this sense of hearing can be taught.

The animals other than man live by appearances and memories, and have but little of connected experience; but the human race lives also by art and reasonings. Now from memory experience is produced in men; for the several memories of the same thing produce finally the capacity for a single experience. And experience seems pretty much like science and art, but really science and art come to men *through* experience; for 'experience made art', as Polus says, 'but inexperience luck'. Now art arises when from many notions gained by experience one universal judgement about a class of objects is produced. For to have a judgement that when Callias was ill of this disease this did him good, and similarly in the case of Socrates and in many individual cases, is a matter of experience; but to judge that it has done good to all persons of a certain constitution, marked off in one class, when they were ill of this disease, e.g. to phlegmatic or bilious people when burning with fever—this is a matter of art.

With a view to action experience seems in no respect inferior to art, and men of experience succeed even better than those who have theory without experience. (The reason is that experience is knowledge of individuals, art of universals, and actions and productions are all concerned with the individual; for the physician does not cure *man,* except in an incidental way, but Callias or Socrates or some other called by some such individual name, who happens to be a man. If, then, a man has the theory without the experience, and recognizes the universal but does not know the individual included in this, he will often fail to cure; for it is the individual that is to be cured.) But yet we think that *knowledge* and *understanding* belong to art rather than to experience, and we suppose artists to be wiser than men of experience (which implies that Wisdom depends in all cases rather on knowledge); and this because the former know the cause, but the latter do not. For men of experience know that the thing is so, but do not know why, while the others know the 'why' and the cause. Hence we think also that the master-workers in each craft are more honourable and know in a truer sense and are wiser than the manual workers, because they know the causes of the things that are done (we think the manual workers are like certain lifeless things which act indeed, but act without knowing what they do, as fire burns—but while the lifeless things perform each of their functions by a natural tendency, the labourers perform them through habit); thus we view them as being wiser not in virtue of being able to act, but of having the theory for themselves and knowing the causes. And in general it is a sign of the man who knows and of the man who does not know, that the former can teach, and therefore we think art more truly knowledge than experience is; for artists can teach, and men of mere experience cannot.

Again, we do not regard any of the senses as Wisdom; yet surely these give the most authoriative knowledge of particulars. But they do not tell us the 'why' of anything—e.g. why fire is hot; they only say *that* it is hot.

At first he who invented any art whatever that went beyond the common perceptions of man was naturally admired by men, not only because there was something useful in the inventions, but because he was thought wise and superior to the rest. But as more arts were invented, and some were directed to the necessities of life, others to recreation, the inventors of the latter were naturally always regarded as wiser than the inventors of the former, because their branches of knowledge did not aim at utility. Hence when all such inventions were already established, the sciences which do not aim at giving pleasure or at the necessities of life were discovered, and first in the places where men first began to have leisure. This is why the mathematical arts were founded in Egypt; for there the priestly caste was allowed to be at leisure.

We have said in the *Ethics* what the difference is between art and science and the other kindred faculties; but the point of our present discussion is this, that all men suppose what is called Wisdom to deal with the first causes and the principles of things; so that, as has been said before, the man of experience is thought to be wiser than the possessors of any sense-perception whatever, the artist wiser than the men of experience, the master-worker than the mechanic, and the theoretical kinds of knowledge to be more of the nature of Wisdom than the productive. Clearly then Wisdom is knowledge about certain principles and causes.

Since we are seeking this knowledge, we must inquire of what kind are the causes and the principles, the knowledge of which is Wisdom. If one were to take the notions we have about the wise man, this might perhaps make the answer more evident. We suppose first, then, that the wise man knows all things, as far as possible, although he has not knowledge of each of them in detail; secondly, that he who can learn things that are difficult, and not easy for man to know, is wise (sense-perception is common to all, and therefore easy and no mark of Wisdom); again, that he who is more exact and more capable of teaching the causes is wiser, in every branch of knowledge; and that of the sciences, also, that which is desirable on its own account and for the sake of knowing it is more of the nature of Wisdom than that which is desirable on account of its results, and the superior science is more of the nature of Wisdom than the ancillary; for the wise man must not be ordered but must order, and he must not obey another, but the less wise must obey *him*.

Such and so many are the notions, then, which we have about Wisdom and the wise. Now of these characteristics that of knowing all things must belong to him who has in the highest degree universal knowledge; for he knows in a sense all the instances that fall under the universal. And these things, the most universal, are on the whole the hardest for men to know; for they are farthest from the senses. And the most exact of the sciences are those which deal most with first principles; for those which involve fewer principles are more exact than those which involve additional principles, e.g. arithmetic than geometry. But the science which investigates causes is also *instructive*, in a higher degree, for the people who instruct us are those who tell the causes of each thing. And understanding and knowledge pursued for their own sake are found most in the knowledge of that which is most knowable (for he who chooses to know for the sake of knowing will choose most readily that which is most truly knowledge, and such is the knowledge of that which is most knowable); and the first principles and the causes are most knowable; for by reason of these, and from these, all other things come to be known, and not these by means of the things subordinate to them. And the science which knows to what end each thing must be done is the most authoritative of the sciences, and more authoritative than any ancillary science; and this end is the good of that thing, and in general the supreme good in the whole of nature. Judged by all the tests we have mentioned, then, the name in question falls to the same science; this must be a science that investigates the first principles and causes; for the good, i.e. the end, is one of the causes.

That it is not a science of production is clear even from the history of the earliest philosophers. For it is owing to their wonder that men both now begin and at first began to philosophize; they wondered originally at the obvious difficulties, then advanced little by little and stated difficulties about the greater matters, e.g. about the phenomena of the moon and those of the sun and of the stars, and about the genesis of the universe. And a man who is puzzled and wonders thinks himself ignorant (whence even the lover of myth is in a sense a lover of Wisdom, for the myth is composed of wonders); therefore since they philosophized in order to escape from ignorance, evidently they were pursuing science in order to know, and not for any utilitarian end. And this is confirmed by the facts; for it was when almost all the necessities of life and the things that make for comfort and recreation had been secured, that such knowledge began to be sought. Evidently then we do not seek it for the sake of any other advantage; but as the man is free, we say, who exists for his own sake and not for another's, so we pursue this as the only free science, for it alone exists for its own sake.

Hence also the possession of it might be justly regarded as beyond human power; for in many ways human nature is in bondage, so that according to Simonides 'God alone can have this privilege', and it is unfitting that man should not be content to seek the knowledge that is suited to him. If, then, there is something in what the poets say, and jealousy is natural to the divine power, it would probably occur in this case above all, and all who excelled in this knowledge would be unfortunate. But the divine power cannot be jealous (nay, according to the proverb, 'bards tell many a lie'), nor should any other science be thought more honourable than one of this sort. For the most divine science is also most honourable; and this science alone must be, in two ways, most divine. For the science which it would be most meet for God to have is a divine science, and so is any science that deals with divine objects; and this science alone has both these qualities; for (1) God is thought to be among the causes of all things and to be a first principle, and (2) such a science either God alone can have, or God above all others. All the sciences, indeed, are more necessary than this, but none is better.

Yet the acquisition of it must in a sense end in something which is the opposite of our original inquiries. For all men begin, as we said, by wondering that things are as they are, as they do about self-moving marionettes, or about the solstices or the incommensurability of the diagonal of a square with the side; for it seems wonderful to all who have not yet seen the reason, that there is a thing which cannot be measured even by the smallest unit. But we must end in the contrary and, according to the proverb, the better state, as is the case in these instances too when men learn the cause; for there is nothing which would surprise a geometer so much as if the diagonal turned out to be commensurable.

We have stated, then, what is the nature of the science we are searching for, and what is the mark which our search and our whole investigation must reach. [I, 1–2, 980a–983a]

It is evident, then, even from what we have said before, that all men seem to seek the causes named in the *Physics,* and that we cannot name any beyond these; but they seek these vaguely; and though in a sense they have all been described before, in a sense they have not been described at all. For the earliest philosophy is, on all subjects, like one who lisps, since it is young and in its beginnings. For even Empedocles says bone exists by virtue of the ratio in it. Now this is the essence and the substance of the thing. But it is similarly necessary that flesh and each of the other tissues should be the ratio of its elements, or that not one of them should; for it is on account of this that both flesh and bone and everything else will exist, and not on account of the matter, which *he* names—fire and earth and water and air. But while he would necessarily have agreed if another had said this, he has not said it clearly.

On these questions our views have been expressed before; but let us return to enumerate the difficulties that might be raised on these same points; for perhaps we may get from them some help towards our later difficulties. [I, 10, 993a–12–27]

We must, with a view to the science which we are seeking, first recount the subjects that should be first discussed. These include both the other opinions that some have held on the first principles, and any point besides these that happens to have been overlooked. For those who wish to get clear of difficulties it is advantageous to discuss the difficulties well; for the subsequent free play of thought implies the solution of the previous difficulties, and it is not possible to untie a knot of which one does not know. But the difficulty of our thinking points to a 'knot' in the object; for in so far as our thought is in difficulties, it is in like case with those who are bound; for in either case it is impossible to go forward. Hence one should have surveyed all the difficulties beforehand, both for the purposes we have stated and because people who inquire without first stating the difficulties are like those who do not know where they have to go; besides, a man does not otherwise know even whether he has at any given time found what he is looking for or not; for the end is not clear to such a man, while to him who has first discussed the difficulties it is clear. Further, he who has heard all the contending arguments, as if they were the parties to a case, must be in a better position for judging.

The first problem concerns the subject which we discussed in our prefatory remarks. It is this—(1) whether the investigation of the causes belongs to one or to more sciences, and (2) whether such a science should survey only the first principles of substance, or also the principles on which all men base their proofs, e.g. whether it is possible at the same time to assert and deny one and the same thing or not, and all other such questions; and (3) if the science in question deals with substance, whether *one* science deals with all substances, or more than one, and if more, whether all are akin, or some of them must be called forms of Wisdom and the others something else. And (4) this itself is also one of the things that must be discussed—whether sensible substances alone should be said to exist or others also besides them, and whether these others are of one kind or there are several classes of substances, as is supposed by those who believe both in Form and in mathematical objects intermediate between these and sensible things. Into these questions, then, as we say, we must inquire, and also (5) whether our investigation is concerned only with substances or also with the essential attributes of substances. Further, with regard to the same and other and like and unlike and contrariety, and with regard to prior and posterior and all other such terms about which the dialecticians try to inquire, starting their investigation from probable premises only—whose business is it to inquire into all these? Further, we must discuss the essential attributes of these themselves; and we must ask not only what each of these is, but also whether one thing always has one contrary. Again (6), are the principles and elements of things the *genera,* or the parts *present* in each thing, into which it is divided; and (7) if they are the genera, are they the genera that are predicated proximately of the individuals, or the highest genera, e.g. is animal or man the first principle and the more independent of the individual instance? And (8) we must inquire and discuss especially whether there is, besides the matter, any thing that is a cause in itself or not, and whether this can exist apart or not, and whether it is one or more in number, and whether there is something apart from the concrete thing (by the concrete thing I mean the matter with something already predicated of it), or there is nothing apart, or there is something in some cases though not in others, and what sort of cases these are. Again (9) we ask whether the principles are limited in number or in kind, both those in the definitions and those in the substratum; and (10) whether the principles of perishable and of imperishable things are the same or different; and whether they are all imperishable or those of perishable things are perishable. Further (11) there is the question which is hardest of all and most perplexing, whether unity and being, as the Pythagoreans and Plato said, are not attributes of something else but the substance of existing things, or this is not the case, but the substratum is something else—as Empedocles says, love; as some one else says, fire; while another says water or air. Again (12) we ask whether the principles are universal or like individual things, and (13) whether they exist potentially or actually, and further, whether they are potential or actual in any other sense than in reference to movement; for these questions also would present much difficulty. Further (14), are numbers and lines and figures and points a kind of substance or not, and if they are substances are they separate from sensible things or present in them? With regard to all these matters not only is it hard to get possession of the truth, but it is not easy even to think out the difficulties well. [III, 1, 995a–996a]

There is a science which investigates being as being and the attributes which belong to this in virtue of its own nature. Now this is not the same as any of the so-called special sciences; for none of these other treats universally of being as being. They cut off a part of being and investigate the attribute of this part; this is what the mathematical sciences for instance do. Now since we are seeking the first principles and the highest causes, clearly there must be some thing to which these belong in virtue of its own nature. If then those who sought the elements of existing things were seeking these same principles, it is necessary that the elements must be elements of being not by accident but just because it *is* being. Therefore it is of being as being that we also must grasp the first causes.

There are many senses in which a thing may be said to 'be', but all that 'is' is related to one central point, one definite kind of thing, and is not said to 'be' by a mere ambiguity. Everything which is healthy is related to health, one thing in the sense that it preserves health, another in the sense that it produces it, another in the sense that it is a symptom of health, another because it is capable of it. And that which is medical is relative to the medical art, one thing being called medical because it possesses it, another because it is naturally adapted to it, another because it is a function of the medical art. And we shall find other words used similarly to these. So, too, there are many senses in which a thing is said to be, but all refer to one starting-point; some things are said to be because they are substances, others because they are affections of substance, others because they are a process towards substance, or destructions or privations or qualities of substance, or productive or generative of substance, or of things which are relative to substance, or negations of one of these things or of substance itself. It is for this reason that we say even of non-being that it *is* non-being. As, then, there is one science which deals with all healthy things, the same applies in the other cases also. For not only in the case of things which have one common notion does the investigation belong to one science, but also in the case of things which are related to one common nature; for even these in a sense have one common notion. It is clear then that it is the work of one science also to study the things that are, *qua* being.—But everywhere science deals chiefly with that which is primary, and on which the other things depend, and in virtue of which they get their names. If, then, this is substance, it will be of substances that the philosopher must grasp the principles and the causes.

Now for each one class of things, as there is one perception, so there is one science, as for instance grammar, being one science, investigates all articulate sounds. Hence to investigate all the species of being *qua* being is the work of a science which is generically one, and to investigate the several species is the work of the specific parts of the science.

If, now, being and unity are the same and are one thing in the sense that they are implied in one another as principle and cause are, not in the sense that they are explained by the same definition (though it makes no difference even if we suppose them to be like that—in fact this would even strengthen our case); for 'one man' and 'man' are the same thing, and so are 'existent man' and 'man', and the doubling of the words in 'one man and one *existent* man' does not express anything different (it is clear that the two things are not separated either in coming to be or in ceasing to be); and similarly '*one* existent man' adds nothing to 'existent man', so that it is obvious that the addition in these cases means the same thing, and unity is nothing apart from being; and if, further, the substance of each thing is one in no merely accidental way, and similarly is from its very nature something that *is:*—all this being so, there must be exactly as many species of being as of unity. And to investigate the essence of these is the work of a science which is generically one—I mean, for instance, the discussion of the same and the similar and the other concepts of this sort; and nearly all contraries may be referred to this origin; let us take them as having been investigated in the 'Selection of Contraries'.

And there are as many parts of philosophy as there are kinds of substance, so that there must necessarily be among them a first philosophy and one which follows this. For being falls immediately into genera; for which reason the sciences too will correspond to these genera. For the philosopher is like the mathematician, as that word is used; for mathematics also has parts, and there is a first and a second science and other successive ones within the sphere of mathematics.

Now since it is the work of one science to investigate opposites, and plurality is opposed to unity—and it belongs to one science to investigate the negation and the privation because in both cases we are really investigating the one thing of which the negation or the privation is a negation or privation (for we either say simply that that thing is not present, or that it is not present in some particular class; in the latter case difference is present over and above what is implied in negation; for negation means just the absence of the thing in question, while in privation there is also employed an underlying nature of which the privation is asserted):—in view of all these facts, the contraries of the concepts we named above, the other and the dissimilar and the unequal, and everything else which is derived either from these or from plurality and unity, must fall within the province of the science above named. And contrariety is one of these concepts; for contrariety is a kind of difference, and difference is a kind of otherness. Therefore, since there are many senses in which a thing is said to be one, these terms also will have many senses, but yet it belongs to one science to know them all; for a term belongs to different sciences not if it has different senses, but if it has not one meaning *and* its definitions cannot be referred to one central meaning. And since all things are referred to that which is primary, as for instance all things which are called one are referred to the primary one, we must say that this holds good also of the same and the other and of contraries in general; so that after distinguishing the various senses of each, we must then explain by reference to what is primary in the case of each of the predicates in question, saying how they are related to it; for some will be called what they are called because they possess it, others because they produce it, and others in other such ways.

It is evident, then, that it belongs to one science to be able to give an account of these concepts as well as of substance (this was one of the questions in our book of problems), and that it is the function of the philosopher to be able to investigate all things. For if it is not the function of the philosopher, who is it who will inquire whether Socrates and Socrates seated are the same thing, or whether one thing has one contrary, or what contrariety is, or how many meanings it has? And similarly with all other such questions. Since, then, these are essential modifications of unity *qua* unity and of being *qua* being, not *qua* numbers or lines or fire, it is clear that it belongs to this science to investigate both the essence of these concepts and their properties. And those who study these properties err not by leaving the sphere of philosophy, but by forgetting that substance, of which they have no correct idea, is prior to these other things. For number *qua* number has peculiar attributes, such as oddness and evenness, commensurability and equality, excess and defect, and these belong to numbers either in themselves or in relation to one another. And similarly the solid and the motionless and that which is in motion and the weightless and that which has weight have other peculiar properties. So too there are certain properties peculiar to being as such, and it is about these that the philosopher has to investigate the truth.—An indication of this may be mentioned:—dialecticians and sophists assume the same guise as the philosopher, for sophistic is Wisdom which exists only in semblance, and dialecticians embrace all things in their dialectic, and being is common to all things; but evidently their dialectic embraces these subjects because these are proper to philosophy.—For sophistic and dialectic turn on the same class of things as philosophy, but this differs from dialectic in the nature of the faculty required and from sophistic in respect of the purpose of the philosophic life. Dialectic is merely critical where philosophy claims to know, and sophistic is what appears to be philosophy but is not.

Again, in the list of contraries one of the two columns is privative, and all contraries are reducible to being and non-being, and to unity and plurality, as for instance rest belongs to unity and movement to plurality. And nearly all thinkers agree that being and substance are composed of contraries; at least all name contraries as their first principles—some name odd and even, some hot and cold, some limit and the unlimited, some love and strife. And all the others as well are evidently reducible to unity and plurality (this reduction we must take for granted), and the principles stated by other thinkers fall entirely under these as their genera. It is obvious then from these considerations too that it belongs to one science to examine being *qua* being. For all things are either contraries or composed of contraries, and unity and plurality are the starting-points of all contraries. And these belong to one science, whether they have or have not one single meaning. Probably the truth is that they have not; yet even if 'one' has several meanings, the other meanings will be related to the primary meaning (and similarly in the case of the contraries), even if being or unity is not a universal and the same in every instance or is not separable from the particular instances (as in fact it probably is not; the unity is in some cases that of common reference, in some cases that of serial succession). And for this reason it does not belong to the geometer to inquire what is contrariety or completeness or unity or being or the same or the other, but only to presuppose these concepts and reason from this starting-point.—Obviously then it is the work of one science to examine being *qua* being, and the attributes which belong to it *qua* being, and the same science will examine not only substances but also their attributes, both those above named and the concepts 'prior' and 'posterior', 'genus' and 'species', 'whole' and 'part', and the others of this sort. [IV, 1–2, 1003a–1005a]

There are several senses in which a thing may be said to 'be', as we pointed out previously in our book on the various senses of words; for in one sense the 'being' meant is 'what a thing is' or a 'this', and in another sense it means a quality or quantity or one of the other things that are predicated as these are. While 'being' has all these senses, obviously that which 'is' primarily is the 'what', which indicates the substance of the thing. For when we say of what quality a thing is, we say that it is good or bad, not that it is three cubits long or that it is a man; but when we say *what* it is, we do not say 'white' or 'hot' or 'three cubits long', but 'a man' or 'a god'. And all other things are said to be because they are, some of them, quantities of that which *is* in this primary sense, others qualities of it, others affections of it, and others some other determination of it. And so one might even raise the question whether the words 'to walk', 'to be healthy', 'to sit' imply that each of these things is existent, and similarly in any other case of this sort; for none of them is either self-subsistent or capable of being separated from substance, but rather, if anything, it is that which walks or sits or is healthy that is an existent thing. Now these are seen to be more real because there is something definite which underlies them (i.e. the substance or individual), which is implied in such a predicate; for we never use the word 'good' or 'sitting' without implying this. Clearly then it is in virtue of this category that each of the others also *is*. Therefore that which is primarily, i.e. not in a qualified sense but without qualification, must be substance.

Now there are several senses in which a thing is said to be first; yet substance is first in every sense—(1) in definition, (2) in order of knowledge, (3) in time. For (3) of the other categories none can exist independently, but only substance. And (1) in definition also this is first; for in the definition of each term the definition of its substance must be present. And (2) we think we know each thing most fully, when we know what it is, e.g. what man is or what fire is, rather than when we know its quality, its quantity, or its place; since we know each of these predicates also, only when we know *what* the quantity or the quality *is.*

And indeed the question which was raised of old and is raised now and always, and is always the subject of doubt, viz. what being is, is just the question, what is substance? For it is this that some assert to be one, others more than one, and that some assert to be limited in number, others unlimited. And so we also must consider chiefly and primarily and almost exclusively what that is which *is* in *this* sense.

Substance is thought to belong most obviously to bodies; and so we say that not only animals and plants and their parts are substances, but also natural bodies such as fire and water and earth and everything of the sort, and all things that are either parts of these or composed of these (either of parts or of the whole bodies), e.g. the physical universe and its parts, stars and moon and sun. But whether these alone are substances, or there are also others, or only some of these, or others as well, or none of these but only some other things, are substances, must be considered. Some think the limits of body, i.e. surface, line, point, and unit, are substances, and more so than body or the solid.

Further, some do not think there is anything substantial besides sensible things, but others think there are eternal substances which are more in number and more real; e.g. Plato posited two kinds of substance—the Forms and the objects of mathematics—as well as a third kind, viz. the substance of sensible bodies. And Speusippus made still more kinds of substance, beginning with the One, and assuming principles for each kind of substance, one for numbers, another for spatial magnitudes, and then another for the soul; and by going on in this way he multiplies the kinds of substance. And some say Forms and numbers have the same nature, and the other things come after them—lines and planes—until we come to the substance of the material universe and to sensible bodies.

Regarding these matters, then, we must inquire which of the common statements are right and which are not right, and what substances there are, and whether there are or are not any besides sensible substances, and how sensible substances exist, and whether there is a substance capable of separate existence (and if so why and how) or no such substance, apart from sensible substances; and we must first sketch the nature of substance.

The word 'substance' is applied, if not in more senses, still at least to four main objects; for both the essence and the universal and the genus are thought to be the substance of each thing, and fourthly the substratum. Now the substratum is that of which everything else is predicated, while it is itself not predicated of anything else. And so we must first determine the nature of this; for that which underlies a thing primarily is thought to be in the truest sense its substance. And in one sense matter is said to be of the nature of substratum, in another, shape, and in a third, the compound of these. (By the matter I mean, for instance, the bronze, by the shape the pattern of its form, and by the compound of these the statue, the concrete whole.) Therefore if the form is prior to the matter and more real, it will be prior also to the compound of both, for the same reason.

We have now outlined the nature of substance, showing that it is that which is not predicated of a stratum, but of which all else is predicated. But we must not merely state the matter thus; for this is not enough. The statement itself is obscure, and further, on this view, *matter* becomes substance. For if this is not substance, it baffles us to say what else is. When all else is stripped off evidently nothing but matter remains. For while the rest are affections, products, and potencies of bodies, length, breadth, and depth are quantities and not substances (for a quantity is not a substance), but the substance is rather that to which these belong primarily. But when length and breadth and depth are taken away we see nothing left unless there is something that is bounded by these; so that to those who consider the question thus matter alone must seem to be substance. By matter I mean that which in itself is neither a particular thing nor of a certain quantity nor assigned to any other of the categories by which being is determined. For there is something of which each of these is predicated, whose being is different from that of each of the predicates (for the predicates other than substance are predicated of substance, while substance is predicated of matter). Therefore the ultimate substratum is of itself neither a particular thing nor of a particular quantity nor otherwise positively characterized; nor yet is it the negations of these, for negations also will belong to it only by accident.

If we adopt this point of view, then, it follows that matter is substance. But this is impossible; for both separability and 'thisness' are thought to belong chiefly to substance. And so form and the compound of form and matter would be thought to be substance, rather than matter. The substance compounded of both, i.e. of matter and shape, may be dismissed; for it is posterior and its nature is obvious. And matter also is in a sense manifest. But we must inquire into the third kind of substance; for this is the most perplexing.

Some of the sensible substances are generally admitted to be substances, so that we must look first among these. For it is an advantage to advance to that which is more knowable. For learning proceeds for all in this way—through that which is less knowable by nature to that which is more knowable; and just as in conduct our task is to start from what is good for each and make what is without qualification good good for each, so it is our task to start from what is more knowable to oneself and make what is knowable by nature knowable to oneself. Now what is knowable and primary for particular sets of people is often knowable to a very small extent, and has little or nothing of reality. But yet one must start from that which is barely knowable but knowable to oneself, and try to know what is knowable without qualification, passing, as has been said, by way of those very things which one does know. [VII, 1–3, 1028a–1029b]

We must reckon up the results arising from what has been said, and compute the sum of them, and put the finishing touch to our inquiry. We have said that the causes, principles, and elements of substances are the object of our search. And some substances are recognized by every one, but some have been advocated by particular schools. Those generally recognized are the natural substances, i.e. fire, earth, water, air, &c., the simple bodies; secondly, plants and their parts, and animals and the parts of animals; and finally the physical universe and its parts; while some particular schools say that Forms and the objects of mathematics are substances. But there are arguments which lead to the conclusion that there are other substances, the essence and the substratum. Again, in another way the genus seems more substantial than the various species, and the universal than the particulars. And with the universal and the genus the Ideas are connected; it is in virtue of the same argument that they are thought to be substances. And since the essence is substance, and the definition is a formula of the essence, for this reason we have discussed definition and essential predication. Since the definition is a formula, and a formula has parts, we had to consider also with respect to the notion of 'part', what are parts of the substance and what are not, and whether the parts of the substance are also parts of the definition. Further, too, neither the universal nor the genus is a substance; we must inquire later into the Ideas and the objects of mathematics; for some say these are substances as well as the sensible substances.

But now let us resume the discussion of the generally recognized substances. These are the sensible substances, and sensible substances all have matter. The substratum is substance, and this is in one sense the matter (and by matter I mean that which, not being a 'this' actually, is potentially a 'this'), and in another sense the formula or shape (that which being a 'this' can be separately formulated), and thirdly the complex of these two, which alone is generated and destroyed, and is, without qualification, capable of separate existence; for of substances completely expressible in a formula some are separable and some are not.

But clearly matter also is substance; for in all the opposite changes that occur there is something which underlies the changes, e.g. in respect of place that which is now here and again elsewhere, and in respect of increase that which is now of one size and again less or greater, and in respect of alteration that which is now healthy and again diseased; and similarly in respect of substance there is something that is now being generated and again being destroyed, and now underlies the process as a 'this' and again underlies it in respect of a privation of positive character. And in *this* change the others are involved. But in either one or two of the others this is not involved; for it is not necessary if a thing has matter for change of place that it should also have matter for generation and destruction.

The difference between becoming in the full sense and becoming in a qualified sense has been stated in our physical works.

Since the substance which exists as underlying and as matter is generally recognized, and this is that which exists potentially, it remains for us to say what is the substance, in the sense of *actuality*, of sensible things. Democritus seems to think there are three kinds of difference between things; the underlying body, the matter, is one and the same, but they differ either in rhythm, i.e. shape, or in turning, i.e. position, or in inter-contact, i.e. order. But evidently there are many differences; for instance, some things are characterized by the mode of composition of their matter, e.g. the things formed by blending, such as honey-water; and others by being bound together, e.g. a bundle; and others by being glued together, e.g. a book; and others by being nailed together, e.g. a casket; and others in more than one of these ways; and others by position, e.g. threshold and lintel (for these differ by being placed in a certain way); and others by time, e.g. dinner and breakfast; and others by place, e.g. the winds; and others by the affections proper to sensible things, e.g. hardness and softness, density and rarity, dryness and wetness; and some things by some of these qualities, others by them all, and in general some by excess and some by defect. Clearly, then, the word 'is' has just as many meanings; a thing *is* a threshold because it lies in such and such a position, and its being means its lying in that position, while being ice means having been solidified in such and such a way. And the being of some things will be defined by *all* these qualities, because some parts of them are mixed, others are blended, others are bound together, others are solidified, and others use the other differentiae; e.g. the hand or the foot requires such complex definition. We must grasp, then, the kinds of differentiae (for these will be the principles of the being of things), e.g. the things characterized by the more and the less, or by the dense and the rare, and by other such qualities; for all these are forms of excess and defect. And anything that is characterized by shape or by smoothness and roughness is characterized by the straight and the curved. And for other things their being will mean their being mixed, and their not being will mean the opposite.

It is clear, then, from these facts that, since its substance is the cause of each thing's being, we must seek in these differentiae what is the cause of the being of each of these things. Now none of these differentiae is substance, even when coupled with matter, yet it is what is analogous to substance in each case; and as in substances that which is predicated of the matter is the actuality itself, in all other definitions also it is what most resembles full actuality. E.g. if we had to define a threshold, we should say 'wood or stone in such and such a position', and a house we should define as 'bricks and timbers in such and such a position' (or a purpose may exist as well in some cases), and if we had to define ice we should say 'water frozen or solidified in such and such a way', and harmony is 'such and such a blending of high and low'; and similarly in all other cases.

Obviously, then, the actuality or the formula is different when the matter is different; for in some cases it is the composition, in others the mixing, and in others some other of the attributes we have named. And so, of the people who go in for defining, those who define a house as stones, bricks, and timbers are speaking of the potential house, for these are the matter; but those who propose 'a receptacle to shelter chattels and living beings', or something of the sort, speak of the actuality. Those who combine both of these speak of the third kind of substance, which is composed of matter and form (for the formula that gives the differentiae seems to be an account of the form or actuality, while that which gives the components is rather an account of the matter); and the same is true of the kind of definitions which Archytas used to accept; they are accounts of the combined form and matter. E.g. what is still weather? Absence of motion in a large expanse of air; air is the matter, and absence of motion is the actuality and substance. What is a calm? Smoothness of sea; the material substratum is the sea, and the actuality or shape is smoothness. It is obvious then, from what has been said, what sensible substance is and how it exists—one kind of it as matter, another as form or actuality, while the third kind is that which is composed of these two. [VIII, 1–2, 1042a–1043a]

We have treated of that which *is* primarily and to which all the other categories of being are referred—i.e. of substance. For it is in virtue of the concept of substance that the others also are said to be—quantity and quality and the like; for all will be found to involve the concept of substance, as we said in the first part of our work. And since 'being' is in one way divided into individual thing, quality, and quantity, and is in another way distinguished in respect of potency and complete reality, and of function, let us now add a discussion of potency and complete reality. And first let us explain potency in the strictest sense, which is, however, not the most *useful* for our present purpose. For potency and actuality extend beyond the cases that involve a reference to motion. But when we have spoken of this first kind, we shall in our discussions of actuality explain the other kinds of potency as well.

We have pointed out elsewhere that 'potency' and the word 'can' have several senses. Of these we may neglect all the potencies that are so called by an equivocation. For some are called so by analogy, as in geometry we say one thing is or is not a 'power' of another by virtue of the presence or absence of some relation between them. But all potencies that conform to the same type are originative sources of some kind, and are called potencies in reference to one primary kind of potency, which is an originative source of change in another thing or in the thing itself *qua* other. For one kind is a potency of being acted on, i.e. the originative source, in the very thing acted on, of its being passively changed by another thing or by itself *qua* other; and another kind is a state of insusceptibility to change for the worse and to destruction by another thing or by the thing itself *qua* other by virtue of an originative source of change. In all these definitions is implied the formula of potency in the primary sense.—And again these so-called potencies are potencies either of merely acting or being acted on, or of acting or being acted on *well*, so that even in the formulae of the latter the formulae of the prior kinds of potency are somehow implied.

Obviously, then, in a sense the potency of acting and of being acted on is one (for a thing may be 'capable' either because it can itself be acted on or because something else can be acted on by it), but in a sense the potencies are different. For the one is in the thing acted on; it is because it contains a certain originative source, and because even the matter is an originative source, that the thing acted on is acted on, and one thing by one, another by another; for that which is oily can be burnt, and that which yields in a particular way can be crushed; and similarly in all other cases. But the other potency is in the agent, e.g. heat and the art of building are present, one in that which can produce heat and the other in the man who can build. And so, in so far as a thing is an organic unity, it cannot be acted on by itself; for it is one and not two different things. And 'impotence' and 'impotent' stand for the privation which is contrary to potency of this sort, so that every potency belongs to the same subject and refers to the same process as a corresponding impotence. Privation has several senses; for it means (1) that which has not a certain quality and (2) that which might naturally have it but has not it, either (*a*) in general or (*b*) when it might naturally have it, and either (α) in some particular way, e.g. when it has not it completely, or (β) when it has not it at all. And in certain cases if things which naturally have a quality lose it by violence, we say they have suffered privation. [IX, 1–2, 1045b–1046a]

Since there were three kinds of substance, two of them physical and one unmovable, regarding the latter we must assert that it is necessary that there should be an eternal unmovable substance. For substances are the first of existing things, and if they are all destructible, all things are destructible. But it is impossible that movement should either have come into being or cease to be (for it must always have existed), or that time should. For there could not be a before and an after if time did not exist. Movement also is continuous, then, in the sense in which time is; for time is either the same thing as movement or an attribute of movement. And there is no continuous movement except movement in place, and of this only that which is circular is continuous.

But if there is something which is capable of moving things or acting on them, but is not actually doing so, there will not necessarily be movement; for that which has a potency need not exercise it. Nothing, then, is gained even if we suppose eternal substances, as the believers in the Forms do, unless there is to be in them some principle which can cause change; nay, even this is not enough, nor is another substance besides the Forms enough; for if it is not to *act*, there will be no movement. Further, even if it acts, this will not be enough, if its essence is potency; for there will not be *eternal* movement, since that which is potentially may possibly not be. There must, then, be such a principle, whose very essence is actuality. Further, then, these substances must be without matter; for they must be eternal, if *anything* is eternal. Therefore they must be actuality.

Yet there is a difficulty; for it is thought that everything that acts is able to act, but that not everything that is able to act acts, so that the potency is prior. But if this is so, nothing that is need be; for it is possible for all things to be capable of existing but not yet to exist.

Yet if we follow the theologians who generate the world from night, or the natural philosophers who say that 'all things were together', the same impossible result ensues. For how will there be movement, if there is no actually existing cause? Wood will surely not move itself—the carpenter's art must act on it; nor will the menstrual blood nor the earth set themselves in motion, but the seeds must act on the earth and the *semen* on the menstrual blood.

This is why some suppose eternal actuality—e.g. Leucippus and Plato; for they say there is always movement. But why and what this movement is they do not say, nor, if the world moves in this way or that, do they tell us the cause of its doing so. Now nothing is moved at random, but there must always be something present to move it; e.g. as a matter of fact a thing moves in one way by nature, and in another by force or through the influence of reason or something else. (Further, what sort of movement is primary? This makes a vast difference.) But again for Plato, at least, it is not permissible to name here that which he sometimes supposes to be the source of movement—that which moves itself; for the soul is later, and coeval with the heavens, according to his account. To suppose potency prior to actuality, then, is in a sense right, and in a sense not; and we have specified these senses. That actuality is prior is testified by Anaxagoras (for his 'reason' is actuality) and by Empedocles in his doctrine of love and strife, and by those who say that there is always movement, e.g. Leucippus. Therefore chaos or night did not exist for an infinite time, but the same things have always existed (either passing through a cycle of changes or obeying some other law), since actuality is prior to potency. If, then, there is a constant cycle, something must always remain, acting in the same way. And if there is to be generation and destruction, there must be something else which is always acting in different ways. This must, then, act in one way in virtue of itself, and in another in virtue of something else—either of a third agent, therefore, or of the first. Now it must be in virtue of the first. For otherwise this again causes the motion both of the second agent and of the third. Therefore it is better to say 'the first'. For it was the cause of eternal uniformity; and something else is the cause of variety, and evidently both together are the cause of eternal variety. This, accordingly, is the character which the motions actually exhibit. What need then is there to seek for other principles? [XII, 6, 1071b–1072a]

We must inquire generally, whether eternal things can consist of elements. If they do, they will have matter; for everything that consists of elements is composite. Since, then, even if a thing exists for ever, out of that of which it consists it would necessarily also, if it *had* come into being, have come into being, and since everything comes to be what it comes to be out of that which is it potentially (for it could not have come to be out of that which had not this capacity, nor could it consist of such elements), and since the potential can be either actual or not—this being so, however everlasting number or anything else that has matter is, it must be capable of not existing, just as that which is any number of years old is as capable of not existing as that which is a day old; if this is capable of not existing, so is that which has lasted for a time so long that it has no limit. They cannot, then, be eternal, since that which is capable of not existing is not eternal, as we had occasion to show in another context. If that which we are now saying is true universally—that no substance is eternal unless it is actuality—and if the elements are matter that underlies substance, no eternal substance can have elements present in it, of which it consists.

There are some who describe the element which acts with the One as an indefinite dyad, and object to 'the unequal', reasonably enough, because of the ensuing difficulties; but they have got rid only of those objections which inevitably arise from the treatment of the unequal, i.e. the relative, as an element; those which arise apart from this opinion must confront even these thinkers, whether it is ideal number, or mathematical, that they construct out of those elements.

There are many causes which led them off into these explanations, and especially the fact that they framed the difficulty in an obsolete form. For they thought that all things that are would be one (viz.

Being itself), if one did not join issue with and refute the saying of Parmenides:

> 'For never will this be proved, that things
> that are not are.'

They thought it necessary to prove that that which is not is; for only thus—of that which is *and something else*—could the things that are be composed, if they are many.

But, first, if 'being' has many senses (for it means sometimes substance, sometimes that it is of certain quality, sometimes that it is of a certain quantity, and at other times the other categories), what sort of 'one', then, are all the things that are, if non-being is to be supposed not to be? Is it the substances that are one, or the affections and similarly the other categories as well, or all together—so that the 'this' and the 'such' and the 'so much' and the other categories that indicate each some one class of being will all be one? But it is strange, or rather impossible, that the coming into play of a single thing should bring it about that part of that which is is a 'this', part a 'such', part a 'so much', part a 'here'.

Secondly, of what sort of non-being and being do the things that are consist? For 'non-being' also has many senses, since 'being' has; and 'not being a man' means not being a certain substance, 'not being straight' not being of a certain quality, 'not being three cubits long' not being of a certain quantity. What sort of being and non-being, then, by their union pluralize the things that are? This thinker means by the non-being, the union of which with being pluralizes the things that are, the false and the character of falsity. This is also why it used to be said that we must assume something that is false, as geometers assume the line which is not a foot long to be a foot long. But this cannot be so. For neither do geometers assume anything false (for the enunciation is extraneous to the inference), nor is it non-being in this sense that the things that are are generated from or resolved into. But since 'non-being' taken in its various cases has as many senses as there are categories, and besides this the false is said not to be, and so is the potential, it is from this that generation proceeds, man from that which is not man but potentially man, and white from that which is not white but potentially white, and this whether it is some one thing that is generated or many.

The question evidently is, how being, in the sense of 'the *substances*', is many; for the things that are generated are numbers and lines and bodies. Now it is strange to inquire how being in the sense of the 'what' is many, and not how either qualities or quantities are many. For surely the indefinite dyad or 'the great and the small' is not a reason why there should be two kinds of white or many colours or flavours or shapes; for then these also would be numbers and units. But if they *had* attacked these other categories, they would have seen the cause of the plurality in substances also; for the same thing or something analogous is the cause. This aberration is the reason also why in seeking the opposite of being and the one, from which with being and the one the things that are proceed, they posited the relative term (i.e. the unequal), which is neither the contrary nor the contradictory of these, and is one kind of being as 'what' and quality also are.

They should have asked this question also, how relative terms are many and not one. But as it is, they inquire how there are many units besides the first 1, but do not go on to inquire how there are many unequals besides *the* unequal. Yet they use them and speak of great and small, many and few (from which proceed numbers), long and short (from which proceeds the line), broad and narrow (from which proceeds the plane), deep and shallow (from which proceed solids); and they speak of yet more kinds of relative term. What is the reason, then, why there is a plurality of these?

It is necessary, then, as we say, to presuppose for each thing that which is it potentially; and the holder of these views further declared what that is which is potentially a 'this' and a substance but is not in itself being —viz. that it is the relative (as if he had said 'the qualitative'), which is neither potentially the one or being, nor the negation of the one nor of being, but one among beings. And it was much *more* necessary, as we said, if he was inquiring how beings are many, not to inquire about those in the same category—how there are many substances or many qualities—but how beings as a whole are many; for some are substances, some modifications, some relations. In the categories other than substance there is yet another problem involved in the existence of plurality. Since they are not separable from substances, qualities and quantities are many just because their substratum becomes and is many; yet there *ought* to be a matter for each category; only it cannot be separable from substances. But in the case of 'thises', it is possible to explain how the 'this' is many things, unless a thing is to be treated as both a 'this' and a general character. The difficulty arising from the facts about substances is rather this, how there are actually many substances and not one.

But further, if the 'this' and the quantitative are not the same, we are not told how and why the things that are are many, but how quantities are many. For all 'number' means a quantity, and so does the 'unit', unless it means a measure or the quantitatively indivisible. If, then, the quantitative and the 'what' are different, we are not told whence or how the 'what' is many; but if any one says they are the same, he has to face many inconsistencies.

One might fix one's attention also on the question, regarding the numbers, what justifies the belief that they exist. To the believer in Ideas they provide some sort of cause for existing things, since each number is an Idea, and the Idea is to other things somehow or other the cause of their being; for let this supposition be granted them. But as for him who does not hold this view because he sees the inherent objections to the Ideas (so that it is not for *this* reason that he posits numbers), but who posits *mathematical* number, why must we believe his statement that such number exists, and of what use is such number to other things? Neither does he who says it exists maintain that it is the cause of anything (he rather says it is a thing existing by itself), nor is it observed to be the cause of anything; for the theorems of arithmeticians will all be found true even of sensible things, as was said before. [XIV, 2, 1088b–1090a]

From the Nicomachean Ethics

BOOK I

Every art and every inquiry, and similarly every action and pursuit, is thought to aim at some good; and for this reason the good has rightly been declared to be that at which all things aim. But a certain difference is found among ends; some are activities, others are products apart from the activities that produce them. Where there are ends apart from the actions, it is the nature of the products to be better than the activities. Now, as there are many actions, arts, and sciences, their ends also are many; the end of the medical art is health, that of shipbuilding a vessel, that of strategy victory, that of economics wealth. But where such arts fall under a single capacity—as bridle-making and the other arts concerned with the equipment of horses fall under the art of riding, and this and every military action under strategy, in the same way other arts fall under yet others—in all of these the ends of the master arts are to be preferred to all the subordinate ends; for it is for the sake of the former that the latter are pursued. It makes no difference whether the activities themselves are the ends of the actions, or something else apart from the activities, as in the case of the sciences just mentioned.

If, then, there is some end of the things we do, which we desire for its own sake (everything else being desired for the sake of this), and if we do not choose everything for the sake of something else (for at that rate the process would go on to infinity, so that our desire would be empty and vain), clearly this must be the good and the chief good. Will not the knowledge of it, then, have a great influence on life? Shall we not, like archers who have a mark to aim at, be more likely to hit upon what is right? If so, we must try, in outline at least to determine what it is, and of which of the sciences or capacities it is the object. It would seem to belong to the most authoritative art and that which is most truly the master art. And politics appears to be of this nature; for it is this that ordains which of the sciences should be studied in a state, and which each class of citizens should learn and up to what point they should learn them; and we see even the most highly esteemed of capacities to fall under this, e.g. strategy, economics, rhetoric; now, since politics uses the rest of the

---

Nicomachean Ethics, I, 1–4, 1094a–1095b; I, 7, 1096a–1098b; I, 9–10, 1099b–1101a; II, 1, 1103a–1103b; II, 5–6, 1105b–1106b; V, 1, 1129a–1130a; VIII, 1–14, 1155a–1163b; IX, 9–12, 1169b–1172a.

sciences, and since, again, it legislates as to what we are to do and what we are to abstain from, the end of this science must include those of the others, so that this end must be the good for man. For even if the end is the same for a single man and for a state, that of the state seems at all events something greater and more complete whether to attain or to preserve; though it is worth while to attain the end merely for one man, it is finer and more godlike to attain it for a nation or for city-states. These, then, are the ends at which our inquiry aims, since it is political science, in one sense of that term.

Our discussion will be adequate if it has as much clearness as the subject-matter admits of, for precision is not to be sought for alike in all discussions, any more than in all the products of the crafts. Now fine and just actions, which political science investigates, admit of much variety and fluctuation of opinion, so that they may be thought to exist only by convention, and not by nature. And goods also give rise to a similar fluctuation because they bring harm to many people; for before now men have been undone by reason of their wealth, and others by reason of their courage. We must be content, then, in speaking of such subjects and with such premisses to indicate the truth roughly and in outline, and in speaking about things which are only for the most part true and with premisses of the same kind to reach conclusions that are no better. In the same spirit, therefore, should each type of statement be received; for it is the mark of an educated man to look for precision in each class of things just so far as the nature of the subject admits; it is evidently equally foolish to accept probable reasoning from a mathematician and to demand from a rhetorician scientific proofs.

Now each man judges well the things he knows, and of these he is a good judge. And so the man who has been educated in a subject is a good judge of that subject, and the man who has received an all-round education is a good judge in general. Hence a young man is not a proper hearer of lectures on political science; for he is inexperienced in the actions that occur in life, but its discussions start from these and are about these; and, further, since he tends to follow his passions, his study will be vain and unprofitable, because the end aimed at is not knowledge but action. And it makes no difference whether he is young in years or youthful in character; the defect does not depend on time, but on his living, and pursuing each successive object, as passion directs. For to such persons, as to the incontinent, knowledge brings no profit; but to those who desire and act in accordance with a rational principle knowledge about such matters will be of great benefit.

These remarks about the student, the sort of treatment to be expected, and the purpose of the inquiry, may be taken as our preface.

Let us resume our inquiry and state, in view of the fact that all knowledge and every pursuit aims at some good, what it is that we say political science aims at and what is the highest of all goods achievable by action. Verbally there is very general agreement; for both the general run of men and people of superior refinement say that it is happiness, and identify living well and doing well with being happy; but with regard to what happiness is they differ, and the many do not give the same account as the wise. For the former think it is some plain and obvious thing, like pleasure, wealth, or honour; they differ, however, from one another—and often even the same man identifies it with different things, with health when he is ill, with wealth when he is poor; but, conscious of their ignorance, they admire those who proclaim some great ideal that is above their comprehension. Now some thought that apart from these many goods there is another which is self-subsistent and causes the goodness of all these as well. To examine all the opinions that have been held were perhaps somewhat fruitless; enough to examine those that are most prevalent or that seem to be arguable.

Let us not fail to notice, however, that there is a difference between arguments from and those to the first principles. For Plato, too, was right in raising this question and asking, as he used to do, 'are we on the way from or to the first principles?' There is a difference, as there is in a race-course between the course from the judges to the turning-point and the way back. For, while we must begin with what is known, things are objects of knowledge in two senses—some to us, some without qualification. Presumably, then, we must begin with things known to *us*. Hence any one who is to listen intelligently to lectures about what is noble and just and, generally, about the subjects of political science must have been brought up in good habits. For the fact is the starting-point, and if this is sufficiently plain to him, he will not at the start need the reason as well; and the man who has been well brought up has or can easily get starting-points. And as for him who neither has nor can get them, let him hear the words of Hesiod:

> Far best is he who knows all things himself;
> Good, he that hearkens when men counsel right;
> But he who neither knows, nor lays to heart
> Another's wisdom, is a useless wight.

[I, 1–4, 1094a–1095b]

Let us again return to the good we are seeking, and ask what it can be. It seems different in different actions and arts; it is different in medicine, in strategy, and in the other arts likewise. What then is the good of each? Surely that for whose sake everything else is done. In medicine this is health, in strategy victory, in architecture a house, in any other sphere something else, and in every action and pursuit the end; for it is for the sake of this that all men do whatever else they do. Therefore, if there is an end for all that we do, this will be the good achievable by action, and if there are more than one, these will be the goods achievable by action.

So the argument has by a different course reached the same point; but we must try to state this even more clearly. Since there are evidently more than one end, and we choose some of these (e.g. wealth, flutes, and in general instruments) for the sake of something else, clearly not all ends are final ends; but the chief good is evidently something final. Therefore, if there is only one final end, this will be what we are seeking, and if there are more than one, the most final of these will be what we are seeking. Now we call that which is in itself worthy of pursuit more final than that which is worthy of pursuit for the sake of something else, and that which is never desirable for the sake of something else more final than the things that are desirable both in themselves and for the sake of that other thing, and therefore we call final without qualification that which is always desirable in itself and never for the sake of something else.

Now such a thing happiness, above all else, is held to be; for this we choose always for itself and never for the sake of something else, but honour, pleasure, reason, and every virtue we choose indeed for themselves (for if nothing resulted from them we should still choose each of them), but we choose them also for the sake of happiness, judging that by means of them we shall be happy. Happiness, on the other hand, no one chooses for the sake of these, nor, in general, for anything other than itself.

From the point of view of self-sufficiency the same result seems to follow; for the final good is thought to be self-sufficient. Now by self-sufficient we do not mean that which is sufficient for a man by himself, for one who lives a solitary life, but also for parents, children, wife, and in general for his friends and fellow citizens, since man is born for citizenship. But some limit must be set to this; for if we extend our requirement to ancestors and descendants and friends' friends we are in for an infinite series. Let us examine this question, however, on another occasion; the self-sufficient we now define as that which when isolated makes life desirable and lacking in nothing; and such we think happiness to be; and further we think it most desirable of all things, without being counted as one good thing among others—if it were so counted it would clearly be made more desirable by the addition of even the least of goods; for that which is added becomes an excess of goods, and of goods the greater is always more desirable. Happiness, then, is something final and self-sufficient, and is the end of action.

Presumably, however, to say that happiness is the chief good seems a platitude, and a clearer account of what it is is still desired. This might perhaps be given, if we could first ascertain the function of man. For just as for a flute-player, a sculptor, or any artist, and, in general, for all things that have a function or activity, the good and the 'well' is thought to reside in the function, so would it seem to be for man, if he has a function. Have the carpenter, then, and the tanner certain functions or activities, and has man none? Is he born without a function? Or as eye, hand, foot, and in general each of the parts evidently has a function, may one lay it down that man similarly has a function apart from all these? What then can this be? Life seems to be common even to plants, but we are seeking what is peculiar to man. Let us exclude, therefore, the life of nutrition and growth. Next there would be a life of perception, but it also seems to be common even to the horse, the ox, and every animal. There remains, then, an active life of the element that has a rational principle; of this, one part has such a principle in the sense of being obedient to one, the other in the sense of possessing one and exercising thought. And, as 'life of the rational element' also has two meanings, we must state that life in the sense of activity is what we mean; for this seems to be the more proper sense of the term. Now if the function of man is an activity of soul which follows or implies a rational principle, and if we say 'a so-and-so' and 'a good so-and-so' have a function which is the same in kind, e.g. a lyre-player and a good lyre-player, and so without qualification in all cases, eminence in respect of goodness being added to the name of the function (for the function of a lyre-player is to play the lyre, and that of a good lyre-player is to do so well): if this is the case, [and we state the function of man to be a certain kind of life, and this to be an activity or actions of the soul implying a rational principle, and the function of a good man to be the good and noble performance of these, and if any action is well performed when it is performed in accordance with the appropriate excellence: if this is the case,] human good turns out to be activity of soul in accordance with virtue, and if there are more than one virtue, in accordance with the best and most complete.

But we must add 'in a complete life'. For one swallow does not make a summer, nor does one day; and so too one day, or a short time, does not make a man blessed and happy.

Let this serve as an outline of the good; for we must presumably first sketch it roughly, and then later fill in the details. But it would seem that any one is capable of carrying on and articulating what has once been well outlined, and that time is a good discoverer or partner in such a work; to which facts the advances of the arts are due; for any one can add what is lacking. And we must also remember what has been said before, and not look for precision in all things alike, but in each class of things such precision as accords with the subject-matter, and so much as is appropriate to the inquiry. For a carpenter and a geometer investigate the right angle in different ways; the former does so in so far as the right angle is useful for his work, while the latter inquires what it is or what sort of thing it is; for he is a spectator of the truth. We must act in the same way, then, in all other matters as well, that our main task may not be subordinated to minor questions. Nor must we demand the cause in all matters alike; it is enough in some cases that the *fact* be well established, as in the case of the first principles; the fact is the primary thing or first principle. Now of first principles we see some by induction, some by perception, some by a certain habituation, and others too in other ways. But each set of principles we must try to investigate in the natural way, and we must take pains to state them definitely, since they have a great influence on what follows. For the beginning is thought to be more than half of the whole, and many of the questions we ask are cleared up by it. [I, 7, 1096a–1098b]

For this reason also the question is asked, whether happiness is to be acquired by learning or by habituation or some other sort of training, or comes in virtue of some divine providence or again by chance. Now if there is any gift of the gods to men, it is reasonable that happiness should be god-given, and most surely god-given of all human things inasmuch as it is the best. But this question would perhaps be more appropriate to another inquiry; happiness seems, however, even if it is not god-sent but comes as a result of virtue and some process of learning or training, to be among the most god-like things; for that which is the prize and end of virtue seems to be the best thing in the world, and something godlike and blessed.

It will also on this view be very generally shared; for all who are not maimed as regards their potentiality for virtue may win it by a certain kind of study and care. But if it is better to be happy thus than by chance, it is reasonable that the facts should be so, since everything that depends on the action of nature is by nature as good as it can be, and similarly everything that depends on art or any rational cause, and especially if it depends on the best of all causes. To entrust to chance what is greatest and most noble would be a very defective arrangement.

The answer to the question we are asking is plain also from the definition of happiness; for it has been said to be a virtuous activity of soul, of a certain kind. Of the remaining goods, some must necessarily preexist as conditions of happiness, and others are naturally co-operative and useful as instruments. And this will be found to agree with what we said at the outset; for we stated the end of political science to the best end, and political science spends most of its pains on making the citizens to be of a certain character, viz. good and capable of noble acts.

It is natural, then, that we call neither ox nor horse nor any other of the animals happy; for none of them is capable of sharing in such activity. For this reason also a boy is not happy; for he is not yet capable of such acts, owing to his age; and boys who are called happy are being congratulated by reason of the hopes we have for them. For there is required, as we said, not only complete virtue but also a complete life, since many changes occur in life, and all manner of chances, and the most prosperous may fall into great misfortunes in old age, as is told of Priam in the Trojan Cycle; and one who has experienced such chances and has ended wretchedly no one calls happy.

Must no one at all, then, be called happy while he lives; must we, as Solon says, see the end? Even if we are to lay down this doctrine, is it also the case that a man is happy when he is *dead?* Or is not this quite absurd, especially for us who say that happiness is an activity? But if we do not call the dead man happy, and if Solon does not mean this, but that one can then safely call a man blessed as being at last beyond evils and misfortunes, this also affords matter for discussion; for both evil and good are thought to exist for a dead man, as much as for one who is alive but not aware of them; e.g. honours and dishonours and the good or bad fortunes of children and in general of descendants. And this also presents a problem; for though a man has lived happily up to old age and has had a death worthy of his life, many reverses may befall his descendants—some of them may be good and attain the life they deserve, while with others the opposite may be the case; and clearly too the degrees of relationship between them and their ancestors may vary indefinitely. It would be odd, then, if the dead man were to share in these changes and become at one time happy, at another wretched; while it would also be odd if the fortunes of the descendants did not for *some* time have *some* effect on the happiness of their ancestors.

But we must return to our first difficulty; for perhaps by a consideration of it our present problem might be solved. Now if we must see the end and only then call a man happy, not as being happy but as having been so before, surely this is a paradox, that when he is happy the attribute that belongs to him is not to be truly predicated of him because we do not wish to call living men happy, on account of the changes that may befall them, and because we have assumed happiness to be something permanent and by no means easily changed, while a single man may suffer many turns of fortune's wheel. For clearly if we were to keep pace with his fortunes, we should often call the same man happy and again wretched, making the happy man out to be a 'chameleon and insecurely based'. Or is this keeping pace with his fortunes quite wrong? Success or failure in life does not depend on these, but human life, as we said, needs these as mere additions, while virtuous activities or their opposites are what constitute happiness or the reverse.

The question we have now discussed confirms our definition. For no function of man has so much permanence as virtuous activities (these are thought to be more durable even than knowledge of the sciences), and of these themselves the most valuable are more durable because those who are happy spend their life most readily and most continuously in these; for this seems to be the reason why we do not forget them. The attribute in question, then, will belong to the happy man, and he will be happy throughout his life; for always, or by preference to everything else, he will be engaged in virtuous action and contemplation, and he will bear the chances of life most nobly and altogether decorously, if he is 'truly good' and 'foursquare beyond reproach'.

Now many events happen by chance, and events differing in importance; small pieces of good fortune or of its opposite clearly do not weigh down the scales of life one way or the other, but a multitude of great events if they turn out well will make life happier (for not only are they themselves such as to add beauty to life, but the way a man deals with them may be noble and good), while if they turn out ill they crush and maim happiness; for they both bring pain with them and hinder many activities. Yet even in these nobility shines through, when a man bears with resignation many great misfortunes, not through insensibility to pain but through nobility and greatness of soul.

If activities are, as we said, what gives life its character, no happy man can become miserable; for he will never do the acts that are hateful and mean. For the man who is truly good and wise, we think, bears all the chances of life becomingly and always makes the best of circumstances, as a good general makes the best military use of the army at his command and a good shoemaker makes the best shoes out of the hides that are given him; and so with all other craftsmen. And if this is the case, the happy man can never become miserable—though he will not reach *blessedness,* if he meet with fortunes like those of Priam.

Nor, again, is he many-coloured and changeable; for neither will he be moved from his happy state easily or by any ordinary misadventures, but only by many great ones, nor, if he has had many great misadventures, will he recover his happiness in a short time, but if at all, only in a long and complete one in which he has attained many splendid successes.

Why then should we not say that he is happy who is active in accordance with complete virtue and is sufficiently equipped with external goods, not for some chance period but throughout a complete life? Or must we add 'and who is destined to live thus and die as befits his life'? Certainly the future is obscure to us, while happiness, we claim, is an end and something in every way final. If so, we shall call happy those among living men in whom these conditions are, and are to be, fulfilled—but happy *men*. So much for these questions. [I, 9–10, 1099b–1101a]

BOOK II

Virtue, then, being of two kinds, intellectual and moral, intellectual virtue in the main owes both its birth and its growth to teaching (for which reason it requires experience and time), while moral virtue comes about as a result of habit, whence also its name *ethike* is one that is formed by a slight variation from the word *ethos* (habit). From this it is also plain that none of the moral virtues arises in us by nature; for nothing that exists by nature can form a habit contrary to its nature. For instance the stone which by nature moves downwards cannot be habituated to move upwards, not even if one tries to train it by throwing it up ten thousand times; nor can fire be habituated to move downwards, nor can anything else that by nature behaves in one way be trained to behave in another. Neither by nature, then, nor contrary to nature do the virtues arise in us; rather we are adapted by nature to receive them, and are made perfect by habit.

Again, of all the things that come to us by nature we first acquire the potentiality and later exhibit the activity (this is plain in the case of senses; for it was not by often seeing or often hearing that we got these senses, but on the contrary we had them before we used them, and did not come to have them by using them); but the virtues we get by first exercising them, as also happens in the case of the arts as well. For the things we have to learn before we can do them, we learn by doing them, e.g. men become builders by building and lyre-players by playing the lyre; so too we become just by doing just acts, temperate by doing temperate acts, brave by doing brave acts.

This is confirmed by what happens in states; for legislators make the citizens good by forming habits in them, and this is the wish of every legislator, and those who do not effect it miss their mark, and it is in this that a good constitution differs from a bad one.

Again, it is from the same causes and by the same means that every virtue is both produced and destroyed, and similarly every art; for it is from playing the lyre that both good and bad lyre-players are produced. And the corresponding statement is true of builders and of all the rest; men will be good or bad builders as a result of building well or badly. For if this were not so, there would have been no need of a teacher, but all men would have been born good or bad at their craft. This, then, is the case with the virtues also; by doing the acts that we do in our transactions with other men we become just or unjust, and by doing the acts that we do in the presence of danger, and being habituated to feel fear or confidence, we become brave or cowardly. The same is true of appetites and feelings of anger; some men become temperate and good-tempered, others self-indulgent and irascible, by behaving in one way or the other in the appropriate circumstances. Thus, in one word, states of character arise out of like activities. This is why the activities we exhibit must be of a certain kind; it is because the states of character correspond to the differences between these. It makes no small difference, then, whether we form habits of one kind or of another from our very youth; it makes a very great difference, or rather *all* the difference. [II, 1, 1103a–1103b]

Next we must consider what virtue is. Since things that are found in the soul are of three kinds—passions, faculties, states of character, virtue must be one of these. By passions I mean appetite, anger, fear, confidence, envy, joy, friendly feeling, hatred, longing, emulation, pity and in general the feelings that are accompanied by pleasure or pain; by faculties the things in virtue of which we are said to be capable of feeling these, e.g. of becoming angry or being pained or feeling pity; by states of character the

Diskobolos, by Myron. A masterpiece of classical Greek relief sculpture of the fifth century, B.C. *(Scala/Art Resource)*

things in virtue of which we stand well or badly with reference to the passions, e.g. with reference to anger we stand badly if we feel it violently or too weakly, and well if we feel it moderately; and similarly with reference to the other passions.

Now neither the virtues nor the vices are *passions,* because we are not called good or bad on the ground of our passions, but are so called on the ground of our virtues and our vices, and because we are neither praised nor blamed for our passions (for the man who feels fear or anger is not praised, nor is the man who simply feels anger blamed, but the man who feels it in a certain way), but for our virtues and our vices we *are* praised or blamed.

Again, we feel anger and fear without choice, but the virtues are modes of choice or involve choice. Further, in respect of the passions we are said to be moved, but in respect of the virtues and the vices we are said not to be moved but to be disposed in a particular way.

For these reasons also they are not *faculties;* for we are neither called good nor bad, nor praised nor blamed, for the simple capacity of feeling the passions; again, we have the faculties by nature, but we are not made good or bad by nature; we have spoken of this before.

If, then, the virtues are neither passions nor faculties, all that remains is that they should be *states of character.*

Thus we have stated what virtue is in respect of its genus.

We must, however, not only describe virtue as a state of character, but also say what sort of state it is. We may remark, then, that every virtue or excellence both brings into good condition the thing of which it is the excellence and makes the work of that thing be done well; e.g. the excellence of the eye makes both the eye and its work good; for it is by the excellence of the eye that we see well. Similarly the excellence of the horse makes a horse both good in itself and good at running and at carrying its rider and at awaiting the attack of the enemy. Therefore, if this is true in every case, the virtue of man also will be the state of character which makes a man good and which makes him do his own work well.

How this is to happen we have stated already, but it will be made plain also by the following consideration of the specific nature of virtue. In everything that is continuous and divisible it is possible to take more, less, or an equal amount, and that either in terms of the thing itself or relatively to us; and the equal is an intermediate between excess and defect. By the intermediate in the object I mean that which is equidistant from each of the extremes, which is one and the same for all men; by the intermediate relatively to us that which is neither too much nor too little—and this is not one, nor the same for all. For instance, if ten is many and two is few, six is the intermediate taken in terms of the object; for it exceeds and is exceeded by an equal amount; this is intermediate according to arithmetical proportion. But the intermediate relatively to us is not to be taken so; if ten pounds are too much for a particular person to eat and two too little, it does not follow that the trainer will order six pounds; for this also is perhaps too much for the person who is to take it, or too little—too little for Milo, too much for the beginner in athletic exercises. The same is true of running and wrestling. Thus a master of any art avoids excess and defect, but seeks the intermediate and chooses this—the intermediate not in the object but relatively to us.

If it is thus, then, that every art does its work well—by looking to the intermediate and judging its works by this standard (so that we often say of good works of art that it is not possible either to take away or to add anything, implying that excess and defect destroy the goodness of works of art, while the mean preserves it; and good artists, as we say, look to this in their work), and if, further, virtue is more exact and better than any art, as nature also is, then virtue must have the quality of aiming at the intermediate. I mean moral virtue; for it is this that is concerned with passions and actions, and in these there is excess, defect, and the intermediate. For instance, both fear and confidence and appetite and anger and pity and in general pleasure and pain may be felt both too much and too little, and in both cases not well; but to feel them at the right times, with reference to the right objects, towards the right people, with the right motive, and in the right way, is what is both intermediate and best, and this is characteristic of virtue. Similarly with regard to actions also there is excess, defect, and the intermediate. Now virtue is concerned with passions and actions, in which excess is a form of failure, and so is defect, while the intermediate is praised and is a form of success; and being praised and being successful are both characteristics of virtue. Therefore virtue is a kind of mean, since, as we have seen, it aims at what is intermediate.

Again, it is possible to fail in many ways (for evil belongs to the class of the unlimited, as the Pythagoreans conjectured, and good to that of the limited), while to succeed is possible only in one way (for which reason also one is easy and the other difficult—to miss the mark easy, to hit it difficult); for these reasons also, then, excess and defect are characteristic of vice, and the mean of virtue;

> For men are good in but one way, but bad in many.

Virtue, then is a state of character concerned with choice, lying in a mean, i.e. the mean relative to us, this being determined by a rational principle, and by that principle by which the man of practical wisdom would determine it. Now it is a mean between two vices, that which depends on excess and that which depends on defect; and again it is a mean because the vices respectively fall short of or exceed what is right in both passions and actions, while virtue both finds and chooses that which is intermediate. Hence in respect of its substance and the definition which states its essence virtue is a mean, with regard to what is best and right an extreme.

But not every action nor every passion admits of a mean; for some have names that already imply badness, e.g. spite, shamelessness, envy, and in the case of actions adultery, theft, murder; for all of these and suchlike things imply by their names that they are themselves bad, and not the excesses or deficiencies of them. It is not possible, then, ever to be right with regard to them; one must always be wrong. Nor does goodness or badness with regard to such things depend on committing adultery with the right woman, at the right time, and in the right way, but simply to do any of them is to go wrong. It would be equally absurd, then, to expect that in unjust, cowardly, and voluptuous action there should be a mean, an excess, and a deficiency; for at that rate there would be a mean of excess and of deficiency, an excess of excess, and a deficiency of deficiency. But as there is no excess and deficiency of temperance and courage because what is intermediate is in a sense an extreme, so too of the actions we have mentioned there is no mean nor any excess and deficiency, but however they are done they are wrong; for in general there is neither a mean of excess and deficiency, nor excess and deficiency of a mean. [II, 5–6, 1105b–1106b]

BOOK V

With regard to justice and injustice we must consider (1) what kind of actions they are concerned with, (2) what sort of mean justice is, and (3) between what extremes the just act is intermediate. Our investigation shall follow the same course as the preceding discussions.

We see that all men mean by justice that kind of state of character which makes people disposed to do what is just and makes them act justly and wish for what is just; and similarly by injustice that state which makes them act unjustly and wish for what is unjust. Let us too, then, lay this down as a general basis. For the same is not true of the sciences and the faculties as of states of character. A faculty or a science which is one and the same is held to relate to contrary objects, but a state of character which is one of two contraries does *not* produce the contrary results; e.g. as a result of health we do not do what is the opposite of healthy, but only what is healthy; for we say a man walks healthily, when he walks as a healthy man would.

Now often one contrary state is recognized from its contrary, and often states are recognized from the subjects that exhibit them; for (A) if good condition is known, bad condition also becomes known, and (B) good condition is known from the things that are in good condition, and they from it. If good condition is firmness of flesh, it is necessary both that bad condition should be flabbiness of flesh and that the wholesome should be that which causes firmness in flesh. And it follows for the most part that if one contrary is ambiguous the other also will be ambiguous; e.g. if 'just' is so, that 'unjust' will be so too.

Now 'justice' and 'injustice' seem to be ambiguous, but because their different meanings approach near to one another the ambiguity escapes notice and is not obvious as it is, comparatively, when the meanings are far apart, e.g. (for here the difference in outward form is great) as the ambiguity in the use of *kleis* for the collar-bone of an animal and for that with which we lock a door. Let us take as a starting-point, then, the various meanings of 'an unjust man'. Both the lawless man and the grasping and unfair man are thought to be unjust, so that evidently both the law-abiding and the fair man will be just. The just, then, is the lawful and the fair, the unjust the unlawful and the unfair.

Since the unjust man is grasping, he must be concerned with goods—not all goods, but those with which prosperity and adversity have to do, which taken absolutely are always good, but for a particular person are not always good. Now men pray for and pursue these things; but they should not, but should pray that the things that are good absolutely may also be good for them, and should choose the things that are good for them. The unjust man does not always choose the greater, but also the less—in the case of things bad absolutely; but because the lesser evil is itself thought to be in a sense good, and graspingness is directed at the good, therefore he is thought to be grasping. And he is unfair; for this contains and is common to both.

Since the lawless man was seen to be unjust and the law-abiding man just, evidently all lawful acts are in a sense just acts; for the acts laid down by the legislative art are lawful, and each of these, we say, is just. Now the laws in their enactments on all subjects aim at the common advantage either of all or of the best or those who hold power, or something of the sort; so that in one sense we call those acts just that tend to produce and preserve happiness and its components for the political society. And the law bids us do both the acts of a brave man (e.g. not to desert our post nor take to flight nor throw away our arms), and those of a temperate man (e.g. not to commit adultery nor to gratify one's lust), and those of a good-tempered man (e.g. not to strike another nor to speak evil), and similarly with regard to the other virtues and forms of wickedness, commanding some acts and forbidding others; and the rightly-framed law does this rightly, and the hastily conceived one less well.

This form of justice, then, is complete virtue, but not absolutely, but in relation to our neighbour. And therefore justice is often thought to be the greatest of virtues, and 'neither evening nor morning star' is so wonderful; and proverbially 'in justice is every virtue comprehended'. And it is complete virtue in its fullest sense, because it is the actual exercise of complete virtue. It is complete because he who possesses it can exercise his virtue not only in himself but towards his neighbour also; for many men can exercise virtue in their own affairs, but not in their relations to their neighbour. This is why the saying of Bias is thought to be true, that 'rule will show the man'; for a ruler is necessarily in relation to other men and a member of a society. For this same reason justice, alone of the virtues, is thought to be 'another's good', because it is related to our neighbour; for it does what is advantageous to another, either a ruler or a copartner. Now the worst man is he who exercises his wickedness both towards himself and towards his friends, and the best man is not he who exercises his virtue towards himself but he who exercises it towards another; for this is a difficult task. Justice in this sense, then, is not part of virtue but virtue entire, nor is the contrary injustice a part of vice but vice entire. What the difference is between virtue and justice in this sense is plain from what we have said; they are the same but their essence is not the same; what, as a relation to one's neighbour, is justice is, as a certain kind of state without qualification, virtue. [V, 1, 1129a–1130a]

BOOK VIII

After what we have said, a discussion of friendship would naturally follow, since it is a virtue or implies virtue, and is besides most necessary with a view to living. For without friends no one would choose to live, though he had all other goods; even rich men and those in possession of office and of dominating power are thought to need friends most of all; for what is the use of such prosperity without the opportunity of beneficence, which is exercised chiefly and in its most laudable form towards friends? Or how can prosperity be guarded and preserved without friends? The greater it is, the more exposed is it to risk. And in poverty and in other misfortunes men think friends are the only refuge. It helps the young, too, to keep from error; it aids older people by ministering to their needs and supplementing the activities that are failing from weakness; those in the prime of life it stimulates to noble actions—'two going together'—for with friends men are more able both to think and to act. Again, parent seems by nature to feel it for offspring and offspring for parent, not only among men but among birds and among most animals; it is felt mutually by members of the same race, and especially by men, whence we praise lovers of their fellowmen. We may see even in our travels how near and dear every man is to every other. Friendship seems too to hold states together, and lawgivers to care more for it than for justice; for unanimity seems to be something like friendship, and this they aim at most of all, and expel faction as their worst enemy; and when men are friends they have no need of justice, while when they are just they need friendship as well, and the truest form of justice is thought to be a friendly quality.

But it is not only necessary but also noble; for we praise those who love their friends, and it is thought to be a fine thing to have many friends; and again we think it is the same people that are good men and are friends.

Not a few things about friendship are matters of debate. Some define it as a kind of likeness and say like people are friends, whence come the sayings 'like to like', 'birds of a feather flock together', and so on; others on the contrary say 'two of a trade never agree'. On this very question they inquire for deeper and more physical causes, Euripides saying that 'parched earth loves the rain, and stately heaven when filled with rain loves to fall to earth', and Heraclitus that 'it is what opposes that helps' and 'from different tones comes the fairest tune' and 'all things are produced through strife'; while Empedocles, as well as others, expresses the opposite view that like aims at like. The physical problems we may leave alone (for they do not belong to the present inquiry); let us examine those which are human and involve character and feeling, e.g. whether friendship can arise between any two people or people cannot be friends if they are wicked, and whether there is one species of friendship or more than one. Those who think there is only one because it admits of degrees have relied on an inadequate indication; for even things different in species admit of degree. We have discussed this matter previously.

The kinds of friendship may perhaps be cleared up if we first come to know the object of love. For not everything seems to be loved but only the lovable, and this is good, pleasant, or useful; but it would seem to be that by which some good or pleasure is produced that is useful, so that it is the good and the useful that are lovable as ends. Do men love, then, *the* good, or what is good for *them?* These sometimes clash. So too with regard to the pleasant. Now it is thought that each loves what is good for himself, and that the good is without qualification lovable, and what is good for each man is lovable for him; but each man loves not what is good for him but what seems good. This however will make no difference; we shall just have to say that this is 'that which seems lovable'. Now there are three grounds on which people love; of the love of lifeless objects we do not use the word 'friendship'; for it is not mutual love, nor is there a wishing of good to the other (for it would surely be ridiculous to wish wine well; if one wishes anything for it, it is that it may keep, so that one may have it oneself); but to a friend we say we ought to wish what is good for his sake. But to those who thus wish good we ascribe only goodwill, if the wish is not reciprocated; goodwill when it is reciprocal being friendship. Or must we add 'when it is recognized'? For many people have goodwill to those whom they have not seen but judge to be good or useful; and one of these might return this feeling. These people seem to bear goodwill to each other; but how could one call them friends when they do not know their mutual feelings? To be friends, then, they must be mutually recognized as bearing goodwill and wishing well to each other for one of the aforesaid reasons.

Now these reasons differ from each other in kind; so, therefore, do the corresponding forms of love and friendship. There are therefore three kinds of friendship, equal in number to the things that are lovable; for with respect to each there is a mutual and recognized love, and those who love each other wish well to each other in that respect in which they love one another. Now those who love each other for their utility do not love each other for themselves but in virtue of some good which they get from each other. So too with those who love for the sake of pleasure; it is not for their character that men love ready-witted people, but because they find them pleasant. Therefore those who love for the sake of utility love for the sake of what is good for *themselves,* and those who love for the sake of pleasure do so for the sake of what is pleasant to *themselves,* and not in so far as the other is the person loved but in so far as he is useful or pleasant. And thus these friendships are only incidental; for it is not as being the man he is that the loved person is loved, but as providing some good or pleasure. Such friendships, then, are easily dissolved, if the parties do not remain like themselves; for if the one party is no longer pleasant or useful the other ceases to love him.

Now the useful is not permanent but is always changing. Thus when the motive of the friendship is done away, the friendship is dissolved, inasmuch as it existed only for the ends in question. This kind of friendship seems to exist chiefly between old people (for at that age people pursue not the pleasant but the useful) and, of those who are in their prime or young, between those who pursue utility. And such people do not live much with each other either; for sometimes they do not even find each other pleasant; therefore they do not need such companionship unless they are useful to each other; for they are pleasant to each other only in so far as they rouse in each other hopes of something good to come. Among such friendships people also class the friendship of host and guest. On the other hand the friendship of young people seems to aim at pleasure; for they live under the guidance of emotion, and pursue above all what is pleasant to themselves and what is immediately before them; but with increasing age their pleasures become different. This is why they quickly become friends and quickly cease to be so; their friendship changes with the object that is found pleasant, and such pleasure alters quickly. Young people are amorous too; for the greater part of the friendship of love depends on emotion and aims at pleasure; this is why they fall in love and quickly fall out of love, changing often within a single day. But these people do wish to spend their days and lives together; for it is thus that they attain the purpose of their friendship.

Perfect friendship is the friendship of men who are good and alike in virtue, for these wish well alike to each other *qua* good, and they are good in themselves. Now those who wish well to their friends for their sake are most truly friends; for they do this by reason of their own nature and not incidentally; therefore their friendship lasts as long as they are good—and goodness is an enduring thing. And each is good without qualification and to his friend, for the good are both good without qualification and useful to each other. So too they are pleasant; for the good are pleasant both without qualification and to each other, since to each his own activities and others like them are pleasurable, and the actions of the good *are* the same or like. And such a friendship is as might be expected permanent, since there meet in it all the qualities that friends should have. For all friendship is for the sake of good or of pleasure—good or pleasure either in the abstract or such as will be enjoyed by him who has the friendly feeling—and is based on a certain resemblance; and to a friendship of good men all the qualities we have named belong in virtue of the nature of the friends themselves; for in the case of this kind of friendship the other qualities also are alike in both friends, and that which is good without qualification is also without qualification pleasant, and these are the most lovable qualities. Love and friendship therefore are found most and in their best form between such men.

But it is natural that such friendships should be infrequent; for such men are rare. Further, such friendship requires time and familiarity; as the proverb says, men cannot know each other till they have 'eaten salt together'; nor can they admit each other to friendship or be friends till each has been found lovable and been trusted by each. Those who quickly show the marks of friendship to each other wish to be friends, but are not friends unless they both are lovable and know the fact; for a wish for friendship may arise quickly, but friendship does not.

This kind of friendship, then, is perfect both in respect of duration and in all other respects, and in it each gets from each in all respects the same as, or something like what, he gives; which is what ought to happen between friends. Friendship for the sake of pleasure bears a resemblance to this kind; for good people too are pleasant to each other. So too does friendship for the sake of utility; for the good are also useful to each other. Among men of these inferior sorts too, friendships are most permanent when friends get the same thing from each other (e.g. pleasure), and not only that but also from the same source, as happens between ready-witted people, not as happens between lover and beloved. For these do not take pleasure in the same things, but the one in seeing the beloved and the other in receiving attentions from his lover; and when the bloom of youth is passing the friendship sometimes passes too (for the one finds no pleasure in the sight of the other, and the other gets no attentions from the first); but many lovers on the other hand are constant, if familiarity has led them to love each other's characters, these being alike. But those who exchange not pleasure but utility in their amour are both less truly friends and less constant. Those who are friends for the sake of utility part when the advantage is at an end; for they were lovers not of each other but of profit.

For the sake of pleasure or utility, then, even bad men may be friends of each other, or good men of bad, or one who is neither good nor bad may be a friend to any sort of person, but for their own sake clearly only good men can be friends; for bad men do not delight in each other unless some advantage come of the relation.

The friendship of the good too and this alone is proof against slander; for it is not easy to trust any one's talk about a man who has long been tested by oneself; and it is among good men that trust and the feeling that 'he would never wrong me' and all the other things that are demanded in true friendship are found. In the other kinds of friendship, however, there is nothing to prevent these evils arising.

For men apply the name of friends even to those whose motive is utility, in which sense states are said to be friendly (for the alliances of states seem to aim at advantage), and to those who love each other for the sake of pleasure, in which sense children are called friends. Therefore we too ought perhaps to call such people friends, and say that there are several kinds of friendship—firstly and in the proper sense that of good men *qua* good, and by analogy the other kinds; for it is in virtue of something good and something akin to what is found in true friendship that they are friends, since even the pleasant is good for the lovers of pleasure. But these two kinds of friendship are not often united, nor do the same people become friends for the sake of utility and of pleasure; for things that are only incidentally connected are not often coupled together.

Friendship being divided into these kinds, bad men will be friends for the sake of pleasure or of utility, being in this respect like each other, but good men will be friends for their own sake, i.e. in virtue of their goodness. These, then, are friends without qualification; the others are friends incidentally and through a resemblance to these.

As in regard to the virtues some men are called good in respect of a state of character, others in respect of an activity, so too in the case of friendship; for those who live together delight in each other and confer benefits on each other, but those who are asleep or locally separated are not performing, but are disposed to perform, the activities of friendship; distance does not break off the friendship absolutely, but only the activity of it. But if the absence is lasting, it seems actually to make men forget their friendship; hence the saying 'out of sight, out of mind'. Neither old people nor sour people seem to make friends easily; for there is little that is pleasant in them, and no one can spend his days with one whose company is painful, or not pleasant, since nature seems above all to avoid the painful and to aim at the pleasant. Those, however, who approve of each other but do not live together seem to be well-disposed rather than actual friends. For there is nothing so characteristic of friends as living together (since while it is people who are in need that desire benefits, even those who are supremely happy desire to spend their days together; for solitude suits such people least of all); but people cannot live together if they are not pleasant and do not enjoy the same things, as friends who are companions seem to do.

The truest friendship, then, is that of the good, as we have frequently said; for that which is without qualification good or pleasant seems to be lovable and desirable, and for each person that which is good or pleasant to him; and the good man is lovable and desirable to the good man for both these reasons. Now it looks as if love were a feeling, friendship a state of character; for love may be felt just as much towards lifeless things, but mutual love involves choice and choice springs from a state of character; and men wish well to those whom they love, for their sake not as a result of feeling but as a result of a state of character. And in loving a friend men love what is good for themselves; for the good man in becoming a friend becomes a good to his friend. Each, then, both loves what is good for himself, and makes an equal return in goodwill and in pleasantness; for friendship is said to be equality, and both of these are found most in the friendship of the good.

Between sour and elderly people friendship arises less readily; inasmuch as they are less good-tempered and enjoy companionship less; for these are thought to be the greatest marks of friendship and most productive of it. This is why, while young men become friends quickly, old men do not; it is because men do not become friends with those in whom they do not delight; and similarly sour people do not quickly make friends either. But such men may bear goodwill to each other; for they wish one another well and aid one another in need; but they are hardly *friends* because they do not spend their days together nor delight in each other, and these are thought the greatest marks of friendship.

One cannot be a friend to many people in the sense of having friendship of the perfect type with them, just as one cannot be in love with many people at once (for love is a sort of excess of feeling, and it is the nature of such only to be felt towards one person); and it is not easy for many people at the same time to please the same person very greatly, or perhaps even to be good in his eyes. One must, too, acquire some experience of the other person and become familiar with him, and that is very hard. But with a view to utility or pleasure it is possible that many people should please one; for many people are useful or pleasant, and these services take little time.

Of these two kinds that which is for the sake of pleasure is the more like friendship, when both parties get the same things from each other and delight in each other or in the same things, as in the friendships of the young; for generosity is more found in such friendships. Friendship based on utility is for the commercially minded. People who are supremely happy, too, have no need of useful friends, but do need pleasant friends: for they wish to live with *some one* and, though they can endure for a short time what is painful, no one could put up with it continuously, nor even with the Good itself if it were painful to him; this is why they look out for friends who are pleasant. Perhaps they should look out for friends who, being pleasant, are also good, and good for them, too; for so they will have all the characteristics that friends should have.

People in positions of authority seem to have friends who fall into distinct classes; some people are useful to them and others are pleasant, but the same people are rarely both; for they seek neither those whose pleasantness is accompanied by virtue nor those whose utility is with a view to noble objects, but in their desire for pleasure they seek for ready-witted people, and their other friends they choose as being clever at doing what they are told, and these characteristics are rarely combined. Now we have said that the *good* man *is* at the same time pleasant and useful; but such a man does not become the friend of one who surpasses him in station, unless he is surpassed also in virtue; if this is not so, he does not establish equality by being proportionally exceeded in both respects. But people who surpass him in both respects are not so easy to find.

However that may be, the aforesaid friendships involve equality; for the friends get the same things from one another and wish the same things for one another, or exchange one thing for another, e.g. pleasure for utility; we have said, however, that they are both less truly friendships and less permanent. But it is from their likeness and their unlikeness to the same thing that they are thought both to be and not to be friendships. It is by their likeness to the friendship of virtue that they seem to be friendships (for one of them involves pleasure and the other utility, and these characteristics belong to the friendship of virtue as well); while it is because the friendship of virtue is proof against slander and permanent, while these quickly change (besides differing from the former in many other respects), that they appear *not* to be friendships; i.e. it is because of their unlikeness to the friendship of virtue..

But there is another kind of friendship, viz. that which involves an inequality between the parties, e.g. that of father to son and in general of elder to younger, that of man to wife and in general that of ruler to subject. And these friendships differ also from each other; for it is not the same that exists between parents and children and between rulers and subjects, nor is even that of father to son the same as that of son to father, nor that of husband to wife the same as that of wife to husband. For the virtue and the function of each of these is different, and so are the reasons for which they love; the love and the friendship are therefore different also. Each party, then, neither gets the same from the other, nor ought to seek it; but when children render to parents what they ought to render to those who brought them into the world, and parents render what they should to their children, the friendship of such persons will be abiding and excellent. In all friendships implying inequality the love also should be proportional, i.e. the better should be more loved than he loves, and so should the more useful, and similarly in each of the other cases; for when the love is in proportion to the merit of the parties, then in a sense arises equality, which is certainly held to be characteristic of friendship.

But equality does not seem to take the same form in acts of justice and in friendship; for in acts of justice what is equal in the primary sense is that which is in proportion to merit, while quantitative equality is secondary, but in friendship quantitative equality is primary and proportion to merit secondary. This becomes clear if there is a great interval in respect of virtue or vice or wealth or anything else between the parties; for then they are no longer friends, and do not even expect to be so. And this is most manifest in the case of the gods; for they surpass us most decisively in all good things. But it is clear also in the case of kings; for with them, too, men who are much their inferiors do not expect to be friends; nor do men of no account expect to be friends with the best or wisest men. In such cases it is not possible to define exactly up to what point friends can remain friends; for much can be taken away and friendship remain, but when one party is removed to a great distance, as God is, the possibility of friendship ceases. This is in fact the origin of the question whether friends really wish for their friends the greatest goods, e.g. that of being gods; since in that case their friends will no longer be friends to them, and therefore will not be good things for them (for friends are good things). The answer is that if we were right in saying that friend wishes good to friend for his sake, his friend must remain the sort of being he is, whatever that may be; therefore it is for him only so long as he remains a man that he will wish the greatest goods. But perhaps not *all* the greatest goods; for it is for himself most of all that each man wishes what is good.

Most people seem, owing to ambition, to wish to be loved rather than to love; which is why most men love flattery; for the flatterer is a friend in an inferior position, or pretends to be such and to love more than he is loved; and being loved seems to be akin to being honoured, and this is what most people aim at. But it seems to be not for its own sake that people choose honour, but incidentally. For most people enjoy being honoured by those in positions of authority because of their hopes (for they think that if they want anything they will get it from them; and therefore they delight in honour as a token of favour to come); while those who desire honour from good men, and men who know, are aiming at confirming their own opinion of themselves; they delight in honour, therefore, because they believe in their own goodness on the strength of the judgement of those who speak about them. In being loved, on the other hand, people delight for its own sake; whence it would seem to be better than being honoured, and friendship to be desirable in itself. But it seems to lie in loving rather than in being loved, as is indicated by the delight mothers take in loving; for some mothers hand over their children to be brought up, and so long as they know their fate they love them and do not seek to be loved in return (if they cannot have both), but seem to be satisfied if they see them prospering; and they themselves love their children even if these owing to their ignorance give them nothing of a mother's due. Now since friendship depends more on loving, and it is those who love their friends that are praised, loving seems to be the characteristic virtue of friends, so that it is only those in whom this is found in due measure that are lasting friends, and only their friendship that endures.

It is in this way more than any other that even unequals can be friends; they can be equalized. Now equality and likeness are friendship, and especially the likeness of those who are like in virtue; for being steadfast in themselves they hold fast to each other, and neither ask nor give base services, but (one may say) even prevent them; for it is characteristic of good men neither to go wrong themselves nor to let their friends do so. But wicked men have no steadfastness (for they do not remain even like to themselves), but become friends for a short time because they delight in each other's wickedness. Friends who are useful or pleasant last longer; i.e. as long as they provide each other with enjoyments or advantages. Friendship for utility's sake seems to be that which most easily exists between contraries, e.g. between poor and rich, between ignorant and learned; for what a man actually lacks he aims at, and one gives something else in return. But under this head, too, we might bring lover and beloved, beautiful and ugly. This is why lovers sometimes seem ridiculous, when they demand to be loved as they love; if they are equally lovable their claim can perhaps be justified, but when they have nothing lovable about them it is ridiculous. Perhaps, however, contrary does not even aim at contrary by its own nature, but only incidentally, the desire being for what is intermediate; for that is what is good, e.g. it is good for the dry not to become wet but to come to the intermediate state, and similarly with the hot and in all other cases. These subjects we may dismiss; for they are indeed somewhat foreign to our inquiry.

Friendship and justice seem, as we have said at the outset of our discussion, to be concerned with the same objects and exhibited between the same persons. For in every community, there is thought to be some form of justice, and friendship too; at least men address as friends their fellow-voyagers and fellow-soldiers, and so too those associated with them in any other kind of community. And the extent of their association is the extent of their friendship, as it is the extent to which justice exists between them. And the proverb 'what friends have is common property' expresses the truth; for friendship depends on community. Now brothers and comrades have all things in common, but the others to whom we have referred have definite things in common—some more things, others fewer; for of friendships, too, some are more and others less truly friendships. And the claims of justice differ too; the duties of parents to children and those of brothers to each other are not the same nor those of comrades and those of fellow-citizens, and so, too, with the other kinds of friendship. There is a difference, therefore, also between the acts that are unjust towards each of these classes of associates, and the injustice increases by being exhibited towards those who are friends in a fuller sense; e.g. it is a more terrible thing to defraud a comrade than a fellow-citizen, more terrible not to help a brother than a stranger, and more terrible to wound a father than any one else. And the demands of justice also seem to increase with the intensity of the friendship, which implies that friendship and justice exist between the same persons and have an equal extension.

Now all forms of community are like parts of the political community; for men journey together with a view to some particular advantage, and to provide something that they need for the purposes of life; and it is for the sake of advantage that the political community too seems both to have come together originally and to endure, for this is what legislators aim at, and they call just that which is to the common advantage. Now the other communities aim at advantage bit by bit, e.g. sailors at what is advantageous on a voyage with a view to making money or something of the kind, fellow-soldiers at what is advantageous in war, whether it is wealth or victory or the taking of a city that they seek, and members of tribes and demes act similarly [Some communities seem to arise for the sake of pleasure, viz. religious guilds and social clubs; for these exist respectively for the sake of offering sacrifice and of companionship. But all these seem to fall under the political community; for it aims not at present advantage but at what is advantageous for life as a whole], offering sacrifices and arranging gatherings for the purpose, and assigning honours to the gods, and providing pleasant relaxations for themselves. For the ancient sacrifices and gatherings seem to take place after the harvest as a sort of firstfruits, because it was at these seasons that people had most leisure. All the communities, then, seem to be parts of the political community; and particular kinds of friendship will correspond to the particular kinds of community.

There are three kinds of constitution, and an equal number of deviation-forms—perversions, as it were, of them. The constitutions are monarchy, aristocracy, and thirdly that which is based on a property qualification, which it seems appropriate to call timocratic, though most people are wont to call it polity. The best of these is monarchy, the worst timocracy. The deviation from monarchy is tyranny; for both are forms of one-man rule, but there is the greatest difference between them; the tyrant looks to his own advantage, the king to that of his subjects. For a man is not a king unless he is sufficient to himself and excels his subjects in all good things; and such a man needs nothing further; therefore he will not look to his own interests but to those of his subjects; for a king who is not like that would be a mere titular king. Now tyranny is the very contrary of this; the tyrant pursues his own good. And it is clearer in the case of tyranny that it is the worst deviation-form; but it is the contrary of the best that is worst. Monarchy passes over into tyranny; for tyranny is the evil form of one-man rule and the bad king becomes a tyrant. Aristocracy passes over into oligarchy by the badness of the rulers, who distribute contrary to equity what belongs to the city—all or most of the good things to themselves, and office always to the same people, paying most regard to wealth; thus the rulers are few and are bad men instead of the most worthy. Timocracy passes over into democracy; for these are coterminous, since it is the ideal even of timocracy to be the rule of the majority, and all who have the property qualification count as equal. Democracy is the least bad of the deviations; for in its case the form of constitution is but a slight deviation. These then are the changes to which constitutions are most subject; for these are the smallest and easiest transitions.

One may find resemblances to the constitutions and, as it were, patterns of them even in households. For the association of a father with his son bears the form of monarchy, since the father cares for his children; and this is why Homer calls Zeus 'father'; it is the ideal of monarchy to be paternal rule. But among the Persians the rule of the father is tyrannical; they use their sons as slaves. Tyrannical too is the rule of a master over slaves; for it is the advantage of the master that is brought about in it. Now this seems to be a correct form of government, but the Persian type is perverted; for the modes of rule appropriate to different relations are diverse. The association of man and wife seems to be aristocratic; for the man rules in accordance with his worth, and in those matters in which a man should rule, but the matters that befit a woman he hands over to her. If the man rules in everything the relation passes over into oligarchy; for in doing so he is not acting in accordance with their respective worth, and not ruling in virtue of his superiority. Sometimes, however, women rule, because they are heiresses; so their rule is not in virtue of excellence but due to wealth and power, as in oligarchies. The association of brothers is like timocracy; for they are equal, except in so far as they differ in age; hence if they differ *much* in age, the friendship is no longer of the fraternal type. Democracy is found chiefly in masterless dwellings (for here every one is on an equality), and in those in which the ruler is weak and every one has license to do as he pleases.

Each of the constitutions may be seen to involve friendship just in so far as it involves justice. The friendship between a king and his subjects depends on an excess of benefits conferred; for he confers benefits on his subjects if being a good man he cares for them with a view to their well-being, as a shepherd does for his sheep (whence Homer called Agamemnon 'shepherd of the peoples'). Such too is the friendship of a father, though this exceeds the other in the greatness of the benefits conferred; for he is responsible for the existence of his children, which is thought the greatest good, and for their nurture and upbringing. These things are ascribed to ancestors as well. Further, by nature a father tends to rule over his sons, ancestors over descendants, a king over his subjects. These friendships imply superiority of one party over the other, which is why ancestors are honoured. The justice therefore that exists between persons so related is not the same on both sides but is in every case proportioned to merit; for that is true of the friendship as well. The friendship of man and wife, again, is the same that is found in an aristocracy; for it is in accordance with virtue—the better gets more of what is good, and each gets what befits him; and so, too, with the justice in these relations. The friendship of brothers is like that of comrades; for they are equal and of like age, and such persons are for the most part like in their feelings and their character. Like this, too, is the friendship appropriate to timocratic government; for in such a constitution the ideal is for the citizens to be equal and fair; therefore rule is taken in turn, and on equal terms; and the friendship appropriate here will correspond.

But in the deviation-forms, as justice hardly exists, so too does friendship. It exists least in the worst form; in tyranny there is little or no friendship. For where there is nothing common to ruler and ruled, there is not friendship either, since there is not justice, e.g. between craftsman and tool, soul and body, master and slave; the latter in each case is benefited by that which uses it, but there is no friendship nor justice towards lifeless things. But neither is there friendship towards a horse or an ox, nor to a slave *qua* slave. For there is nothing common to the two parties; the slave is a living tool and the tool a lifeless slave. *Qua* slave then, one cannot be friends with him. But *qua* man one can; for there seems to be some justice between any man and any other who can share in a system of law or be a party to an agreement; therefore there can also be friendship with him in so far as he is a man. Therefore while in tyrannies friendship and justice hardly exist, in democracies they exist more fully; for where the citizens are equal they have much in common.

Every form of friendship, then, involves association, as has been said. One might, however, mark off from the rest both the friendship of kindred and that of comrades. Those of fellow-citizens, fellow-tribesmen, fellow-voyagers, and the like are more like mere friendships of association; for they seem to rest on a sort of compact. With them we might class the friendship of host and guest.

The friendship of kinsmen itself, while it seems to be of many kinds, appears to depend in every case on parental friendship; for parents love their children as being a part of themselves, and children their parents as being something originating from them. Now (1) parents know their offspring better than their children know that they are their children, and (2) the originator feels his offspring to be his own more than the offspring do their begetter; for the product belongs to the producer (e.g. a tooth or hair or anything else to him whose it is), but the producer does not belong to the product, or belongs in a less degree. And (3) the length of time produces the same result; parents love their children as soon as these are born, but children love their parents only after time has elapsed and they have acquired understanding or the power of discrimination by the senses. From these considerations it is also plain why mothers love more than fathers do. Parents, then, love their children as themselves (for their issue are by virtue of their separate existence a sort of other selves), while children love their parents as being born of them, and brothers love each other as being born of the same parents; for their identity with them makes them identical with each other (which is the reason why people talk of 'the same blood', 'the same stock', and so on). They are, therefore, in a sense the same thing, though in separate individuals. Two things that contribute greatly to friendship are a common upbringing and similarity of age; for 'two of an age take to each other', and people brought up together tend to be comrades; whence the friendship of brothers is akin to that of comrades. And cousins and other kinsmen are bound up together by derivation from brothers, viz. by being derived from the same parents. They come to be closer together or farther apart by virtue of the nearness or distance of the original ancestor.

The friendship of children to parents, and of men to gods, is a relation to them as to something good and superior; for they have conferred the greatest benefits, since they are the causes of their being and of their nourishment, and of their education from their birth; and this kind of friendship possesses pleasantness and utility also, more than that of strangers, inasmuch as their life is lived more in common. The friendship of brothers has the characteristics found in that of comrades (and especially when these are good), and in general between people who are like each other, inasmuch as they belong more to each other and start with a love for each other from their very birth, and inasmuch as those born of the same parents and brought up together and similarly educated are more akin in character; and the test of time has been applied most fully and convincingly in their case.

Between other kinsmen friendly relations are found in due proportion. Between man and wife friendship seems to exist by nature; for man is naturally inclined to form couples—even more than to form cities, inasmuch as the household is earlier and more necessary than the city, and reproduction is more common to man with the animals. With the other animals the union extends only to this point, but human beings live together not only for the sake of reproduction but also for the various purposes of life; for from the start the functions are divided, and those of man and woman are different; so they help each other by throwing their peculiar gifts into the common stock. It is for these reasons that both utility and pleasure seem to be found in this kind of friendship. But this friendship may be based also on virtue, if the parties are good; for each has its own virtue and they will delight in the fact. And children seem to be a bond of union (which is the reason why childless people part more easily); for children are a good common to both and what is common holds them together.

How man and wife and in general friend and friend ought mutually to behave seems to be the same question as how it is just for them to behave; for a man does not seem to have the same duties to a friend, a stranger, a comrade, and a schoolfellow.

There are three kinds of friendship, as we said at the outset of our inquiry, and in respect of each some are friends on an equality and others by virtue of a superiority (for not only can equally good men become friends but a better man can make friends with a worse, and similarly in friendships of pleasure or utility the friends may be equal or unequal in the benefits they confer). This being so, equals must effect the required equalization on a basis of equality in love and in all other respects, while unequals must render what is in proportion to their superiority or inferiority.

Complaints and reproaches arise either only or chiefly in the friendship of utility, and this is only to be expected. For those who are friends on the ground of virtue are anxious to do well by each other (since that is a mark of virtue and of friendship), and between men who are emulating each other in this there cannot be complaints or quarrels; no one is offended by a man who loves him and does well by him—if he is a person of nice feeling he takes his revenge by doing well by the other. And the man who excels the other in the services he renders will not complain of his friend, since he gets what he aims at; for each man desires what is good. Nor do complaints arise much even in friendships of pleasure; for both get at the same time what they desire, if they enjoy spending their time together; and even a man who complained of another for *not* affording him pleasure would seem ridiculous, since it is in his power not to spend his days with him.

But the friendship of utility is full of complaints; for as they use each other for their own interests they always want to get the better of the bargain, and think they have got less than they should, and blame their partners because they do not get all they 'want and deserve'; and those who do well by others cannot help them as much as those whom they benefit want.

Now it seems that, as justice is of two kinds, one unwritten and the other legal, one kind of friendship of utility is moral and the other legal. And so complaints arise most of all when men do not dissolve the relation in the spirit of the same type of friendship in which they contracted it. The *legal* type is that which is on fixed terms; its purely commercial variety is on the basis of immediate payment, while the more liberal variety allows time but stipulates for a definite *quid pro quo*. In this variety the debt is clear and not ambiguous, but in the postponement it contains an element of friendliness; and so some states do not allow suits arising out of such agreements, but think men who have bargained on a basis of credit ought to accept the consequences. The *moral* type is not on fixed terms; it makes a gift, or does whatever it does, as to a friend; but one expects to receive as much or more, as having not given but lent; and if a man is worse off when the relation is dissolved than he was when it was contracted he will complain. This happens because all or most men, while they wish for what is noble, choose what is advantageous; now it is noble to do well by another without a view to repayment, but it is the receiving of benefits that is advantageous.

Therefore if we can we should return the equivalent of what we have received (for we must not make a man our friend against his will; we must recognize that we were mistaken at the first and took a benefit from a person we should not have taken it from—since it was not from a friend, nor from one who did it just for the sake of acting so—and we must settle up just as if we had been benefited on fixed terms). Indeed, one would agree to repay if one could (if one could not, even the giver would not have expected one to do so); therefore if it is possible we must repay. But at the outset we must consider the man by whom we are being benefited and on what terms he is acting, in order that we may accept the benefit on these terms, or else decline it.

It is disputable whether we ought to measure a service by its utility to the receiver and make the return with a view to that, or by the benevolence of the giver. For those who have received say they have received from their benefactors what meant little to the latter and what they might have got from others—minimizing the service; while the givers, on the contrary, say it was the biggest thing they had, and what could not have been got from others, and that it was given in times of danger or similar need. Now if the friendship is one that aims at *utility*, surely the advantage to the receiver is the measure. For it is he that asks for the service, and the other man helps him on the assumption that he will receive the equivalent; so the assistance has been precisely as great as the advantage to the receiver, and therefore he must return as much as he has received, or even more (for that would be nobler). In friendships based on *virtue* on the other hand, complaints do not arise, but the purpose of the doer is a sort of measure; for in purpose lies the essential element of virtue and character.

Differences arise also in friendships based on superiority; for each expects to get more out of them, but when this happens the friendship is dissolved. Not only does the better man think he ought to get more, since more should be assigned to a good man, but the more useful similarly expects this; they say a useless man should not get as much as they should, since it becomes an act of public service and not a friendship if the proceeds of the friendship do not answer to the worth of the benefits conferred. For they think that, as in a commercial partnership those who put more in get more out, so it should be in friendship. But the man who is in a state of need and inferiority makes the opposite claim; they think it is the part of a good friend to help those who are in need; what, they say, is the use of being the friend of a good man or a powerful man, if one is to get nothing out of it?

At all events it seems that each party is justified in his claim, and that each should get more out of the friendship than the other—not more of the same thing, however, but the superior more honour and the inferior more gain; for honour is the prize of virtue and of beneficence, while gain is the assistance required by inferiority.

It seems to be so in constitutional arrangements also; the man who contributes nothing good to the common stock is not honoured; for what belongs to the public is given to the man who benefits the public, and honour does belong to the public. It is not possible to get wealth from the common stock and at the same time honour. For no one puts up with the smaller share in *all* things; therefore to the man who loses in wealth they assign honour and to the man who is willing to be paid, wealth, since the proportion to merit equalizes the parties and preserves the friendship, as we have said.

This then is also the way in which we should associate with unequals; the man who is benefited in respect of wealth or virtue must give honour in return, repaying what he can. For friendship asks a man to do what he can, not what is proportional to the merits of the case; since that cannot always be done, e.g. in honours paid to the gods or to parents; for no one could ever return to them the equivalent of what he gets, but the man who serves them to the utmost of his power is thought to be a good man.

This is why it would not seem open to a man to disown his father (though a father may disown his son); being in debt, he should repay, but there is nothing by doing which a son will have done the equivalent of what he has received, so that he is always in debt. But creditors can remit a debt; and a father can therefore do so too. At the same time it is thought that presumably no one would repudiate a son who was not far gone in wickedness; for apart from the natural friendship of father and son it is human nature not to reject a son's assistance. But the son, if he *is* wicked, will naturally avoid aiding his father, or not be zealous about it; for most people wish to get benefits, but avoid doing them, as a thing unprofitable.—So much for these questions. [VIII, 1–14, 1155a–1163b]

BOOK IX

It is also disputed whether the happy man will need friends or not. It is said that those who are supremely happy and self-sufficient have no need of friends; for they have the things that are good, and therefore being self-sufficient they need nothing further, while a friend, being another self, furnishes what a man cannot provide by his own effort; whence the saying 'when fortune is kind, what needs of friends?' But it seems strange, when one assigns all good things to the happy man, not to assign friends, who are thought the greatest of external goods. And if it is more characteristic of a friend to do well by another than to be well done by, and to confer benefits is characteristic of the good man and of virtue, and it is nobler to do well by friends than by strangers, the good man will need people to do well by. This is why the question is asked whether we need friends more in prosperity or in adversity, on the assumption that not only does a man in adversity need people to confer benefits on him, but also those who are prospering need people to do well by. Surely it is strange, too, to make the supremely happy man a solitary; for no one would choose the whole world on condition of being alone, since man is a political creature and one whose nature is to live with others. Therefore even the happy man lives with others; for he has the things that are by nature good. And plainly it is better to spend his days with friends and good men than with strangers or any chance persons. Therefore the happy man needs friends.

What then is it that the first school means, and in what respect is it right? Is it that most men identify friends with useful people? Of such friends indeed the supremely happy man will have no need, since he already has the things that are good; nor will he need those whom one makes one's friends because of their pleasantness, or he will need them only to a small extent (for his life, being pleasant, has no need of adventitious pleasure); and because he does not need *such* friends he is thought not to need friends.

But that is surely not true. For we have said at the outset that happiness is an activity; and activity plainly comes into being and is not present at the start like a piece of property. If (1) happiness lies in living and being active, and the good man's activity is virtuous and pleasant in itself, as we have said at the outset, and (2) a thing's being one's own is one of the attributes that make it pleasant, and (3) we can contemplate our neighbours better than ourselves and their actions better than our own, and if the actions of virtuous men who are their friends are pleasant to good men (since these have both the attributes that are naturally pleasant)—if this be so, the supremely happy man will need friends of this sort, since his purpose is to contemplate worthy actions and actions that are his own, and the actions of a good man who is his friend have both these qualities.

Further, men think that the happy man ought to live pleasantly. Now if he were a solitary, life would be hard for him; for by oneself it is not easy to be continuously active; but with others and towards others it is easier. With others therefore his activity will be more continuous, and it is in itself pleasant, as it ought to be for the man who is supremely happy; for a good man *qua* good delights in virtuous actions and is vexed at vicious ones, as a musical man enjoys beautiful tunes but is pained at bad ones. A certain training in virtue arises also from the company of the good, as Theognis has said before us.

If we look deeper into the nature of things, a virtuous friend seems to be naturally desirable for a virtuous man. For that which is good by nature, we have said, is for the virtuous man good and pleasant in itself. Now life is defined in the case of animals by the power of perception, in that of man by the power of perception or thought; and a power is defined by reference to the corresponding activity, which is the essential thing; therefore life seems to be essentially the act of perceiving or thinking. And life is among the things that are good and pleasant in themselves, since it is determinate and the determinate is of the nature of the good; and that which is good by nature is also good for the virtuous man (which is the reason why life seems pleasant to all men); but we must not apply this to a wicked and corrupt life nor to a life spent in pain; for such a life is indeterminate, as are its attributes. The nature of pain will become plainer in what follows. But if life itself is good and pleasant (which it seems to be, from the very fact that all men desire it, and particularly those who are good and supremely happy; for to such men life is most desirable, and their existence is the most supremely happy); and if he who sees perceives that he sees, and he who hears, that he hears, and he who walks, that he walks, and in the case of all other activities similarly there is something which perceives that we are active, so that if we perceive, we perceive that we perceive, and if we think, that we think; and if to perceive that we perceive or think is to perceive that we exist (for existence was defined as perceiving or thinking); and if perceiving that one lives is in itself one of the things that are pleasant (for life is by nature good, and to perceive what is good present in oneself is pleasant); and if life is desirable, and particularly so for good men, because to them existence is good and pleasant (for they are pleased at the consciousness of the presence in them of what is in itself good); and if as the virtuous man is to himself, he is to his friend also (for his friend is another self):—if all this be true, as his own being is desirable for each man, so, or almost so, is that of his friend. Now his being was seen to be desirable because he perceived his own goodness, and such perception is pleasant in itself. He needs, therefore, to be conscious of the existence of his friend as well, and this will be realized in their living together and sharing in discussion and thought; for this is what living together would seem to mean in the case of man, and not, as in the case of cattle, feeding in the same place.

If, then, being is in itself desirable for the supremely happy man (since it is by its nature good and pleasant), and that of his friend is very much the same, a friend will be one of the things that are desirable. Now that which is desirable for him he must have, or he will be deficient in this respect. The man who is to be happy will therefore need virtuous friends.

Should we, then, make as many friends as possible, or—as in the case of hospitality it is thought to be suitable advice, that one should be 'neither a man of many guests nor a man with none'—will that apply to friendship as well; should a man neither be friendless nor have an excessive number of friends?

To friends made with a view to *utility* this saying would seem thoroughly applicable; for to do services to many people in return is a laborious task and life is not long enough for its performance. Therefore friends in excess of those who are sufficient for our own life are superfluous, and hindrances to the noble life; so that we have no need of them. Of friends made with a view to *pleasure*, also, few are enough, as a little seasoning in food is enough.

But as regards *good* friends, should we have as many as possible, or is there a limit to the number of one's friends, as there is to the size of a city? You cannot make a city of ten men, and if there are a hundred thousand it is a city no longer. But the proper number is presumably not a single number, but anything that falls between certain fixed points. So for friends too there is a fixed number—perhaps the largest number with whom one can live together (for that, we found, is thought to be very characteristic of friendship); and that one cannot live with many people and divide oneself up among them is plain. Further, they too must be friends of one another, if they are all to spend their days together; and it is a hard business for this condition to be fulfilled with a large number. It is found difficult, too, to rejoice and to grieve in an intimate way with many people, for it may likely happen that one has at once to be happy with one friend and to mourn with another. Presumably, then, it is well not to seek to have as many friends as possible, but as many as are enough for the purpose of living together; for it would seem actually impossible to be a great friend to many people. This is why one cannot love several people; love is ideally a sort of excess of friendship, and that can only be felt towards one person; therefore great friendship too can only be felt towards a few people. This seems to be confirmed in practice; for we do not find many people who are friends in the comradely way of friendship, and the famous friendships of this sort are always between two people. Those who have many friends and mix intimately with them all are thought to be no one's friend, except in the way proper to fellow-citizens, and such people are also called obsequious. In the way proper to fellow-citizens, indeed, it is possible to be the friend of many and yet not be obsequious but a genuinely good man; but one cannot have with many people the friendship based on virtue and on the character of our friends themselves, and we must be content if we find even a few such.

Do we need friends more in good fortune or in bad? They are sought after in both; for while men in adversity need help, in prosperity they need people to live with and to make the objects of their beneficence; for they wish to do well by others. Friendship, then, is more necessary in bad fortune, and so it is useful friends that one wants in this case; but it is more noble in good fortune, and so we also seek for good men as our friends, since it is more desirable to confer benefits on these and to live with these. For the very presence of friends is pleasant both in good fortune and also in bad, since grief is lightened when friends sorrow with us. Hence one might ask whether they share as it were our burden, or—without that happening—their presence by its pleasantness, and the thought of their grieving with us, make our pain less. Whether it is for these reasons or for some other that our grief is lightened, is a question that may be dismissed; at all events what we have described appears to take place.

But their presence seems to contain a mixture of various factors. The very seeing of one's friends is pleasant, especially if one is in adversity, and becomes a safeguard against grief (for a friend tends to comfort us both by the sight of him and by his words, if he is tactful, since he knows our character and the things that please or pain us); but to see him pained at our misfortunes is painful; for every one shuns being a cause of pain to his friends. For this reason people of a manly nature guard against making their friends grieve with them, and, unless he be exceptionally insensible to pain, such a man cannot stand the pain that ensues for his friends, and in general does not admit fellow-mourners because he is not himself given to mourning; but women and womanly men enjoy sympathisers in their grief, and love them as friends and companions in sorrow. But in all things one obviously ought to imitate the better type of person.

On the other hand, the presence of friends in our *prosperity* implies both a pleasant passing of our time and the pleasant thought of their pleasure at our own good fortune. For this cause it would seem that we ought to summon our friends readily to share our good fortunes (for the beneficent character is a noble one), but summon them to our bad fortunes with hesitation; for we ought to give them as little a share as possible in our evils—whence the saying 'enough is *my* misfortune'. We should summon friends to us most of all when they are likely by suffering a few inconveniences to do us a great service.

Conversely, it is fitting to go unasked and readily to the aid of those in adversity (for it is characteristic of a friend to render services, and especially to those who are in need and have not demanded them; such action is nobler and pleasanter for both persons); but when our friends are prosperous we should join readily in their activities (for they need friends for these too), but be tardy in coming forward to be the objects of their kindness; for it is not noble to be keen to receive benefits. Still, we must no doubt avoid getting the reputation of kill-joys by repulsing them; for that sometimes happens.

The presence of friends, then, seems desirable in all circumstances.

Does it not follow, then, that, as for lovers the sight of the beloved is the thing they love most, and they prefer this sense to the others because on it love depends most for its being and for its origin, so for friends the most desirable thing is living together? For friendship is partnership, and as a man is to himself, so is he to his friend; now in his own case the consciousness of his being is desirable, and so therefore is the consciousness of his friend's being, and the activity of this consciousness is produced when they live together, so that it is natural that they aim at this. And whatever existence means for each class of men, whatever it is for whose sake they value life, in *that* they wish to occupy themselves with their friends; and so some drink together, others dice together, others join in athletic exercises and hunting, or in the study of philosophy, each class spending their days together in whatever they love most in life; for since they wish to live with their friends, they do and share in those things which give them the sense of living together. Thus the friendship of bad men turns out an evil thing (for because of their instability they unite in bad pursuits, and besides they become evil by becoming like each other), while the friendship of good men is good, being augmented by their companionship; and they are thought to become better too by their activities and by improving each other; for from each other they take the mould of the characteristics they approve—whence the saying 'noble deeds from noble men'.—So much, then, for friendship; our next task must be to discuss pleasure. [IX, 9–12, 1169b–1172a]

From the Politics

BOOK I

Every state is a community of some kind, and every community is established with a view to some good; for mankind always act in order to obtain that which they think good. But, if all communities aim at some good, the state or political community, which is the highest of all, and which embraces all the rest, aims at good in a greater degree than any other, and at the highest good.

Some people think that the qualifications of a statesman, king, householder, and master are the same, and that they differ, not in kind, but only in the number of their subjects. For example, the ruler over a few is called a master; over more the manager of a household; over a still larger number, a statesman or king, as if there were no difference between a great household and a small state. The distinction which is made between the king and the statesman is as follows: When the government is personal, the

Politics, I, 1, 1252a; III, 6–7, 1278b–1279b.

ruler is a king; when, according to the rules of the political science, the citizens rule and are ruled in turn, then he is called a statesman.

But all this is a mistake; for governments differ in kind, as will be evident to any one who considers the matter according to the method which has hitherto guided us. As in other departments of science, so in politics, the compound should always be resolved into the simple elements or least parts of the whole. We must therefore look at the elements of which the state is composed, in order that we may see in what the different kinds of rule differ from one another, and whether any scientific result can be attained about each one of them. [I, 1, 1252a]

BOOK III

Having determined these questions, we have next to consider whether there is only one form of government or many, and if many, what they are, and how many, and what are the differences between them.

A constitution is the arrangement of magistracies in a state, especially of the highest of all. The government is everywhere sovereign in the state, and the constitution is in fact the government. For example, in democracies the people are supreme, but in oligarchies, the few; and, therefore, we say that these two forms of government also are different: and so in other cases.

First, let us consider what is the purpose of a state, and how many forms of government there are by which human society is regulated. We have already said, in the first part of this treatise, when discussing household management and the rule of a master, that man is by nature a political animal. And therefore, men, even when they do not require one another's help, desire to live together; not but that they are also brought together by their common interests in proportion as they severally attain to any measure of well-being. This is certainly the chief end, both of individuals and of states. And also for the sake of mere life (in which there is possibly some noble element so long as the evils of existence do not greatly overbalance the good) mankind meet together and maintain the political community. And we all see that men cling to life even at the cost of enduring great misfortune, seeming to find in life a natural sweetness and happiness.

There is no difficulty in distinguishing the various kinds of authority; they have been often defined already in discussions outside the school. The rule of a master, although the slave by nature and the master by nature have in reality the same interests, is nevertheless exercised primarily with a view to the interest of the master, but accidentally considers the slave, since, if the slave perish, the rule of the master perishes with him. On the other hand, the government of a wife and children and of a household, which we have called household management, is exercised in the first instance for the good of the governed or for the common good of both parties, but essentially for the good of the governed, as we see to be the case in medicine, gymnastic, and the arts in general, which are only accidentally concerned with the good of the artists themselves. For there is no reason why the trainer may not sometimes practise gymnastics, and the helmsman is always one of the crew. The trainer or the helmsman considers the good of those committed to his care. But, when he is one of the persons taken care of, he accidentally participates in the advantage, for the helmsman is also a sailor, and the trainer becomes one of those in training. And so in politics: when the state is framed upon the principle of equality and likeness, the citizens think that they ought to hold office by turns. Formerly, as is natural, every one would take his turn of service; and then again, somebody else would look after his interest, just as he, while in office, had looked after theirs. But nowadays, for the sake of the advantage which is to be gained from the public revenues and from office, men want to be always in office. One might imagine that the rulers, being sickly, were only kept in health while they continued in office; in that case we may be sure that they would be hunting after places. The conclusion is evident: that governments which have a regard to the common interest are constituted in accordance with strict principles of justice, and are therefore true forms; but those which regard only the interest of the rulers are all defective and perverted forms, for they are despotic, whereas a state is a community of freemen.

Having determined these points, we have next to consider how many forms of government there are, and what they are; and in the first place what are the true forms, for when they are determined the perversions of them will at once be apparent. The words constitution and government have the same meaning, and the government, which is the supreme authority in states, must be in the hands of one, or of a few, or of the many. The true forms of government, therefore, are those in which the one, or the few, or the many, govern with a view to the common interest; but governments which rule with a view to the private interest, whether of the one, or of the few, or of the many, are perversions. For the members of a state, if they are truly citizens, ought to participate in its advantages. Of forms of government in which one rules, we call that which regards the common interests, kingship or royalty; that in which more than one, but not many, rule, aristocracy; and it is so called, either because the rulers are the best men, or because they have at heart the best interests of the state and of the citizens. But when the citizens at large administer the state for the common interest, the government is called by the generic name—a constitution. And there is a reason for this use of language. One man or a few may excel in virtue; but as the number increases it becomes more difficult for them to attain perfection in every kind of virtue, though they may in military virtue, for this is found in the masses. Hence in a constitutional government the fighting-men have the supreme power, and those who possess arms are the citizens.

Of the above-mentioned forms, the perversions are as follows:—of royalty, tyranny; of aristocracy, oligarchy; of constitutional government, democracy. For tyranny is a kind of monarchy which has in view the interest of the monarch only; oligarchy has in view the interest of the wealthy; democracy, of the needy: none of them the common good of all. [III, 6–7, 1278b–1279b]

From the Poetics

Our subject being Poetry, I propose to speak not only of the art in general but also of its species and their respective capacities; of the structure of plot required for a good poem; of the number and nature of the constituent parts of a poem; and likewise of any other matters in the same line of inquiry. Let us follow the natural order and begin with the primary facts.

Epic poetry and Tragedy, as also Comedy, Dithyrambic poetry, and most flute-playing and lyre-playing, are all, viewed as a whole, modes of imitation. But at the same time they differ from one another in three ways, either by a difference of kind in their means, or by differences in the objects, or in the manner of their imitations.

Just as colour and form are used as means by some, who (whether by art or constant practice) imitate and portray many things by their aid, and the voice is used by others; so also in the above-mentioned group of arts, the means with them as a whole are rhythm, language, and harmony—used, however, either singly or in certain combinations. A combination of harmony and rhythm alone is the means in flute-playing and lyre-playing, and any other arts there may be of the same description, e.g. imitative piping. Rhythm alone, without harmony, is the means in the dancer's imitations; for even he, by the rhythms of his attitudes, may represent men's characters, as well as what they do and suffer. There is further an art which imitates by language alone, without harmony, in prose or in verse, and if in verse, either in some one or in a plurality of metres. This form of imitation is to this day without a name. We have no common name for a mime of Sophron or Xenarchus and a Socratic Conversation; and we should still be without one even if the imitation in the two instances were in trimeters or elegiacs or some other kind of verse—though it is the way with people to tack on 'poet' to the name of a metre, and talk of elegiac-poets and epic-poets, thinking that they call them poets not by reason of the imitative nature of their work, but indiscriminately by reason of the metre they write in. Even if a theory of medicine or physical philosophy be put forth in a metrical form, it is usual to describe the writer in this way; Homer and Empedocles, however, have really nothing in common apart from their metre; so that, if the one is to be called a poet, the other should be termed a physicist rather than a poet. We should be in the same position also, if the imitation in these instances were in all the metres, like the *Centaur* (a

---

Poetics, I, 1447a–1448b.

rhapsody in a medley of all metres) of Chaeremon; and Chaeremon one has to recognize as a poet. So much, then, as to these arts. There are, lastly, certain other arts, which combine all the means enumerated, rhythm, melody, and verse, e.g. Dithyrambic and Nomic poetry, Tragedy and Comedy; with this difference, however, that the three kinds of means are in some of them all employed together, and in others brought in separately, one after the other. These elements of difference in the above arts I term the means of their imitation.

The objects the imitator represents are actions, with agents who are necessarily either good men or bad—the diversities of human character being nearly always derivative from this primary distinction, since the line between virtue and vice is one dividing the whole of mankind. It follows, therefore, that the agents represented must be either above our own level of goodness, or beneath it, or just such as we are; in the same way as, with the painters, the personages of Polygnotus are better than we are, those of Pauson worse, and those of Dionysius just like ourselves. It is clear that each of the above-mentioned arts will admit of these differences, and that it will become a separate art by representing objects with this point of difference. Even in dancing, flute-playing, and lyre-playing such diversities are possible; and they are also possible in the nameless art that uses language, prose or verse without harmony, as its means; Homer's personages, for instance, are better than we are; Cleophon's are on our own level; and those of Hegemon of Thasos, the first writer of parodies, and Nicochares, the author of the *Diliad*, are beneath it. The same is true of the Dithyramb and the Nome: the personages may be presented in them with the difference exemplified in the Cyclopses of Timotheus and Philoxenus. This difference it is that distinguishes Tragedy and Comedy also; the one would make its personages worse, and the other better, than the men of the present day.

A third difference in these arts is in the manner in which each kind of object is represented. Given both the same means and the same kind of object for imitation, one may either (1) speak at one moment in narrative and at another in an assumed character, as Homer does; or (2) one may remain the same throughout, without any such change; or (3) the imitators may represent the whole story dramatically, as though they were actually doing the things described.

As we said at the beginning, therefore, the differences in the imitation of these arts come under three heads, their means, their objects, and their manner.

So that as an imitator Sophocles will be on one side akin to Homer, both portraying good men; and on another to Aristophanes, since both present their personages as acting and doing. This in fact, according to some, is the reason for plays being termed dramas, because in a play the personages act the story. Hence too both Tragedy and Comedy are claimed by the Dorians as their discoveries; Comedy by the Megarians—by those in Greece as having arisen when Megara became a democracy, and by the Sicilian Megarians on the ground that the poet Epicharmus was of their country, and a good deal earlier than Chionides and Magnes; even Tragedy also is claimed by certain of the Peloponnesian Dorians. In support of this claim they point to the words 'comedy' and 'drama'. Their word for the outlying hamlets, they say, is *comae*, whereas Athenians call them *demes*—thus assuming that comedians got the name not from their *comoe* or revels, but from their strolling from hamlet to hamlet, lack of appreciation keeping them out of the city. Their word also for 'to act', they say, is *dran*, whereas Athenians use *prattein*.

So much, then, as to the number and nature of the points of difference in the imitation of these arts.

It is clear that the general origin of poetry was due to two causes, each of them part of human nature. Imitation is natural to man from childhood, one of his advantages over the lower animals being this, that he is the most imitative creature in the world, and learns at first by imitation. And it is also natural for all to delight in works of imitation. The truth of this second point is shown by experience: though the objects themselves may be painful to see, we delight to view the most realistic representations of them in art, the forms for example of the lowest animals and of dead bodies. The explanation is to be found in a further fact: to be learning something is the greatest of pleasures not only to the philosopher but also to the rest of mankind, however small their capacity for it; the reason of the delight in seeing the picture is that one is at the same time learning—gathering the meaning of things, e.g. that the man there is so-and-so; for if one has not seen the thing before, one's pleasure will not be in the picture as an imitation of it, but will be due to the execution or colouring or some similar cause. Imitation, then, being natural to us—as also the sense of harmony and rhythm, the metres being obviously species of rhythms—it was through their original aptitude, and by a series of improvements for the most part gradual on their first efforts, that they created poetry out of their improvisations.

SUGGESTIONS FOR FURTHER READING

Brentano, Franz. *The Psychology of Aristotle.* Edited and translated by Rolfe George. Berkeley: University of California Press, 1977.

Clark, Stephen R. L. *Aristotle's Man.* Oxford: Clarendon Press, 1975.

Edel, Abraham. *Aristotle.* New York: Dell, 1967.

Edel, Abraham. *Aristotle and His Philosophy.* Chapel Hill: University of North Carolina Press, 1982.

Farrington, Benjamin. *Aristotle.* New York: Praeger, 1965.

Grene, Marjorie. *A Portrait of Aristotle.* Chicago: University of Chicago Press, 1963.

Jaeger, Werner. *Aristotle.* Oxford: Clarendon Press, 1948.

Lear, Jonathan. *Aristotle and Logical Theory.* Cambridge: Cambridge University Press, 1980.

Moravcsik, J. M. E., ed. *Aristotle: A Collection of Critical Essays.* Garden City, New York: Doubleday–Anchor, 1967.

Randall, John Herman, Jr. *Aristotle.* New York: Columbia University Press, 1960.

Ross, W. D. *Aristotle.* New York: Meridian, 1959.

Taylor, A. E. *Aristotle.* New York: Dover, 1955.

Veatch, Henry B. *Aristotle.* Bloomington: Indiana University Press, 1974.

Woodbridge, J. E. *Aristotle's Vision of Nature.* New York: Columbia University Press, 1965.

Part 4

Post-Aristotelian Philosophy in Greece and Rome: The Quest for the Good Life

Zeno of Citium
From Diogenes Laertius' "Zeno"

Cleanthes of Assos
Hymn to Zeus

The Stoics
Fragments

Strabo
The Earth and Its Zones

Cicero
From On Old Age
From the Tusculan Disputations

Seneca
From On the Happy Life
From On Tranquillity of Mind

Epictetus
The Manual of Epictetus

Marcus Aurelius
From The Meditations

Epicurus
Epicurus to Menoeceus
Principal Doctrines

Lucretius
From On the Nature of Things

Sextus Empiricus and Scepticism
From Outlines of Pyrrhonism

Plotinus
The Knowing Hypostases and the Transcendent

The Christian Gospels: The Redemption of Nature

From the Acts of the Apostles
From the Gospel of Matthew
From the Gospel of John
From the Book of Revelation
From the Epistles of Paul

Post-Aristotelian Philosophy in Greece and Rome: The Quest for the Good Life

After the death of Alexander the Great in 323 B.C., the Greek city-states found themselves in a more amorphous political and social situation. Indeed, Greece itself was soon to become but a province of the Roman Empire. These circumstances led to an increased emphasis on individuality and the ethical, practical, or good life for each person. The major philosophical schools and doctrines that flourished during the period from approximately 300 B.C. until A.D. 300 were Stoicism, Epicureanism, Scepticism, and Neoplatonism, especially that of Plotinus.

The most influential of these schools was Stoicism. Founded by Zeno of Citium in 300 B.C., Stoicism listed Cleanthes and Chrysippus among its adherents in Greece, while in Rome, Epictetus, Seneca, and Marcus Aurelius embraced Stoic teachings. Stoicism concerned itself with logic, physics, and ethics. Its major contention was that human life had to be lived in harmony with the rhythms and cycles of nature. The highest state for the Stoic is that of *apatheia,* which is not accurately translated by the English word "apathy." To the contrary, *apatheia* is the activity of purposively living within the order and demands of the natural world and especially avoiding the excesses of feelings. The Stoics also believed that the world was periodically consumed by fire and that this cleansing was itself part of the order of nature.

A second important philosophical movement of this post-Aristotelian period is Epicureanism. Often confused with hedonism, a sheer ethic of pleasure, Epicureanism was a serious statement on behalf of living a moral and wise life. The pursuit of pleasure must be done with great care and moderation. Above all, fear of the gods and fear of death must be eliminated.

A third climate of philosophical opinion is found in the Sceptics, led by Pyrro of Elis (ca. 360–ca. 270 B.C.) and later by Carneades of Cyrene (214–129 B.C.). The historian and collator of the ancient Sceptical tradition is Sextus Empiricus, for whom the classical doctrines of causality, the infinite nature of God, and the worthiness of the syllogism were subject to criticism and doubt. Actually, ancient

Scepticism, as found, for example, in the thought of Carneades, was dubious about any claims which transcended immediate experience.

Finally, toward the end of this post-Aristotelian period, we have the dazzling reconstruction of Plato's thought by the mystic and philosopher Plotinus. Deeply influenced by the wisdom of Persia and India, Plotinus merged philosophical doctrines from Plato, Aristotle, and the Stoics into an original philosophical system, which was further characterized by his insistence on the practice of a deep personal spiritual life in the search for unity with ultimate reality.

The selections that follow give an indication of the major themes present in these four different interpretations of the ethical and philosophical life. Of course, midway through the six centuries of this period, we witness the birth of Christianity, a version of human life that is to utilize most of the ancient philosophy so far presented, but that nonetheless, will challenge philosophy in a deep and pervasive way. The material included here is from the Greek and Roman Stoics, Epicurus and the Epicurean tradition, inclusive of Lucretius, the Scepticism of Sextus Empiricus, and the Neoplatonism of Plotinus.

ZENO OF CITIUM

The founder of Stoicism, Zeno (336–265 B.C.) taught on a painted porch (Stoa Poikile), *from which came the name Stoic. His teaching stressed that only virtue was worthwhile and that evil was traceable to moral weakness. In his physics, he was influenced by Heraclitus, especially by his doctrine of the* logos *and his emphasis on the element of fire. Zeno sought to develop a community of persons who were loyal to the call of nature and the cautions of reason. He stressed the positive aspects of life and was convinced that harmony of human life and nature was an attainable goal, if we abandoned our tendency to always concentrate on mishap and evil. The following brief selection sums up the response to the endeavors of Stoicism.*

From Diogenes Laertius' "Zeno"

And Athenaeus the epigrammatist speaks of all the Stoics in common as follows:

O ye who've learnt the doctrines of the Porch
And have committed to your books divine
The best of human learning, teaching men
That the mind's virtue is the only good!
She only it is who keeps the lives of men
And cities,—safer than high gates and walls.
But those who place their happiness in
pleasure
Are led by the least worthy of the Muses.

Reprinted by permission of the publishers and The Loeb Classical Library from *Lives of the Eminent Philosophers,* Vol. II, Diogenes Laertius, trans. by R. D. Hicks, Cambridge, Mass.: Harvard University Press, 1925. (pp. 141–142)

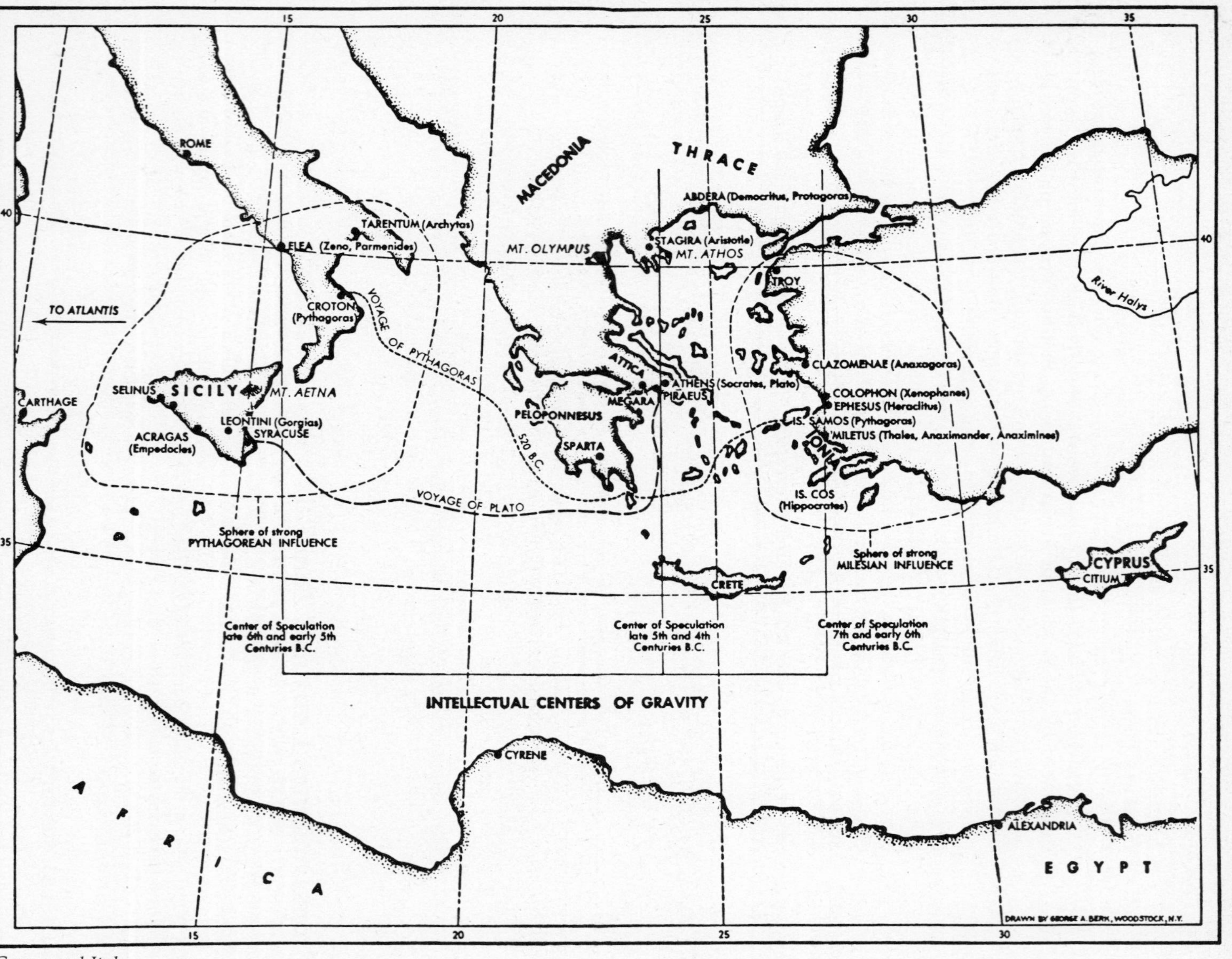

Greece and Italy

CLEANTHES OF ASSOS

Cleanthes (ca. 331–232 B.C.) succeeded Zeno as head of the Stoa. Like Zeno, Cleanthes was first influenced by the Cynics, especially by Crates of Thebes (365–285 B.C.). The Cynics were responsible for an intense critique of the sensual excesses of Greek and Roman society. They opposed traditional cultural inhibitions and stressed the radical freedom of the individual. The Cynics were more concerned with a critique of existing practice than they were with a developed positive philosophical alternative. The Stoics absorbed their critique but focused also on an original doctrine of how best to live within the possibilities and confines of nature.

More personable than Zeno, Cleanthes had a gentleness that attracted followers. His stress on the Stoic doctrine of dependence on nature and the order of the world is evident in the following selection, "Hymn to Zeus." After Cleanthes, the leadership of the Stoic school was held by Chrysippus of Soloi (279–206 B.C.).

Statue of Zeus, Cape Artemision (470 B.C.). The Greek god Zeus was believed to be the father of both gods and mortals. (Hirmer Fotoarchiv)

Hymn to Zeus

O God most glorious, called by many a name,
Nature's great King, through endless years the same;
Omnipotence, who by thy just decree
Controllest all, hail, Zeus, for unto thee
Behoves thy creatures in all lands to call.
We are thy children, we alone, of all
On earth's broad ways that wander to and fro,
Bearing thine image wheresoe'er we go.
Wherefore with songs of praise thy power I will forth show.
Lo! yonder Heaven, that round the earth is wheeled,
Follows thy guidance, still to thee doth yield
Glad homage; thine unconquerable hand
Such flaming minister, the levin brand,
Wieldeth, a sword two-edged, whose deathless might
Pulsates through all that Nature brings to light;
Vehicle of the universal Word, that flows
Through all, and in the light celestial glows
Of stars both great and small. A King of Kings
Through ceaseless ages, God, whose purpose brings
To birth, whate'er on land or in the sea
Is wrought, or in high heaven's immensity;
Save what the sinner works infatuate.
Nay, but thou knowest to make crooked straight:
Chaos to thee is order: in thine eyes
The unloved is lovely, who didst harmonize
Things evil with things good, that there should be
One Word through all things everlastingly.
One Word—whose voice alas! the wicked spurn;
Insatiate for the good their spirits yearn:
Yet seeing see not, neither hearing hear
God's universal law, which those revere,
By reason guided, happiness to win.
The rest, unreasoning, diverse shapes of sin
Self-prompted follow: for an idle name
Vainly they wrestle in the lists of fame:
Others inordinately riches woo,
Or dissolute, the joys of flesh pursue.
Now here, now there they wander, fruitless still,
For ever seeking good and finding ill.
Zeus the all-bountiful, whom darkness shrouds,
Whose lightning lightens in the thunder-clouds;
Thy children save from error's deadly sway:

Turn thou the darkness from their souls away:
Vouchsafe that unto knowledge they attain:
For thou by knowledge art made strong to reign
O'er all, and all things rulest righteously.
So by thee honoured, we will honour thee,
Praising thy works continually with songs,
As mortals should; nor higher meed belongs
E'en to the gods, than justly to adore
The universal law for evermore.

THE STOICS

The following selections are taken from writings by the Stoics or by commentators and even opponents, all of whom give versions of the basic Stoic philosophy. In these extracts, the dominating theme is the effort of the Stoics to go beyond the philosophical critique of society as found in the Cynics and the Sceptics. The material from Cicero is especially helpful in enabling us to understand the Stoic point of view.

Fragments

THE PARTS OF PHILOSOPHY

(SVF II, 38b)* Philosophy, they say, is like an animal, logic corresponding to the bones and sinews, ethics to the fleshy parts, physics to the soul. Another simile they use is that of an egg: the shell is logic, next comes the white, ethics, and the yolk in the center is physics. Or again, they liken philosophy to a fertile field: logic being the encircling fence, ethics the crop, physics the soil or the trees. . . .

Diogenes Laertius

(SVF II, 44) The Stoics teach that we should begin with logic, continue with ethics, and place physics last. For first it is necessary to make the mind sure so that it will be an invincible guardian of the teachings. And dialectic serves to make the reason secure. Second we must subscribe to ethics to improve our character, for the study of ethics is without danger to one who has previously mastered logic. And finally we must proceed to physics, for it is more divine and requires more profound attention.

Sextus Empiricus

LOGIC

(SVF I, 59b) Arcesilaus perhaps asked Zeno what would happen if the Wise Man could neither perceive anything nor have an opinion. I believe he replied that the Wise Man could never entertain an opinion because there was something which could be perceived. What is it then? Perceptions, no doubt. What sort of perception? Then he defined it as follows: It is an imitation, a seal, an impression from what exists just as it exists. Then it was asked further whether such a true perception was of the same type as a false perception. Here Zeno clearly saw that there was no perception which could be perceived if there could be one arising from that which exists,

**Stoicorum veterum fragmenta*

essentially similar to one arising from that which does not exist. . . .

Cicero

(SVF I, 59c) A comprehensive presentation is one which has been stamped and sealed by that which exists and just as it exists in such a way that it could not be produced by what does not exist.

Sextus Empiricus

(SVF II, 90) The Stoics, i.e., Zeno and Cleanthes say that three things are joined together: knowledge, opinion, and comprehension which stands between them. Knowledge is comprehension which is sure, certain and unchangeable by argument, whereas opinion is a weak and false assent. Comprehension which stands between them is assent to a comprehensive presentation. Now, a comprehensive presentation, according to them, is one that is true in such a way that it cannot become false. They say also that knowledge occurs only in wise men, opinion occurs only in foolish minds, but comprehension is common to both and is the criterion of truth.

Sextus Empiricus

(SVF II, 121) Suppose the Pyrrhonian suspension of judgment, the idea that nothing is certain: it is plain that, beginning with itself, it first invalidates itself. It either grants that something is true, that you are not to suspend your judgment on all things; or it objects in saying that there is nothing true. And it is evident that first it will not be true. For it either affirms what is true or it does not affirm what is true. But if the former, it concedes—though unwillingly—that something is true. If the latter, it leaves true what it wished to do away with. For, in so far as the skepticism which destroys is proved false, so the positions which are being destroyed are proved true (like the dream which says all dreams are false). For in confuting itself, it is confirmatory of the others. And, finally, if it is true, it will make a beginning with itself and not be skepticism of anything else but of itself first. Then if such a man comprehends that he is a man, or that he is skeptical, it is evident that he is not skeptical. . . . For how did he reply to the question? He is evidently no skeptic in respect to this. On the contrary, he affirms even that he does doubt.

And if we according to [the Stoics] suspend judgment in regard to everything, we shall first suspend our judgment in regard to our suspension of judgment itself, whether we are to trust it or not. And if this position is true—that we do not know what is true—then absolutely nothing is allowed to be true by it. But if he will say that even this is questionable—whether we know what is true—by this very statement he grants that truth is knowable, in the very act of appearing not to establish the doubt respecting it.

Then, if a philosophical sect is a leaning toward doctrines or, according to some, a leaning to a number of doctrines which are consistent with one another and with phenomena, tending to a well-lived life; and doctrine is logical comprehension, and comprehension is a state and assent of the mind, not merely skeptics, but every one who makes doctrine is accustomed in certain things to suspend his judgment, either through want of strength of mind, or want of clearness in the things, or equal force in the reasons.

Clement of Alexandria

(SVF II, 201a) A probable proposition is that which leads to assent, e.g., "If anything gave birth to something, the former is the mother of the latter." But it is false, because the bird is not the mother of an egg. Again, some propositions are possible, others impossible; and some are necessary, others not necessary. A possible proposition is one capable of being true, if nothing external prevents it from being true, as "Diocles is alive." A proposition is impossible if it is not capable of being true, as "the earth flies." The necessary proposition is that one which is both true and is not capable of being false, or, if capable, is prevented from being false by external circumstances, as, "Virtue is beneficial." Not necessary is that which is true although it can be false even when no external circumstance interferes, as, "Dion is walking about." A plausible proposition is one which has more occasions of being true than false as, "I shall be alive tomorrow." And there are other varieties of propositions. . . .

Diogenes Laertius

BASIC PHYSICAL THEORY

(SVF II, 346a) The Stoics believe in only one cause, i.e., the Maker. . . . This collection of causes, as defined by Aristotle and by Plato, comprehends either too much or too little. For if they regard as causes of any object that is to be made everything without

which the object cannot be made, they have named too few. Time must be included among the causes, for nothing can be made without time. Time must also include place, for if there be no place where a thing can be made, it will not be made. And motion too, for nothing is either made or destroyed without motion. There is also no art without motion, no change of any kind. Now, however, we are searching for the first, the general cause; this must be simple inasmuch as matter, too, is simple. Do we ask what cause is? It is surely Creative Reason, i.e., God.

Seneca

(SVF II, 421) The Stoics are accustomed to trace all things back to an elemental force of a fiery nature, herein following Heraclitus . . . ; their doctrine is that all force is of the nature of fire, and that, because of this, animate creatures perish when their heat fails; also in every domain of nature a thing is alive and vigorous if it is warm. . . . [They say that] there is no animate being contained within the whole universe of nature except fire. . . .

Cicero

(SVF II, 519) It is contrary to common sense that there should be a future time and a past time, but not present time; and that *recently* and *lately* subsist, but *now* is nothing at all. Yet this happens to the Stoics, who admit not the least time between, nor will they allow the present to be indivisible; but whatever anyone thinks to take and understand as present, one part of that, they say, is future, and the other part past.

Plutarch

THE WORLD

(SVF II, 524a) Now the philosophers of the Stoic school suppose that the whole differs from the universe; for they say that the whole is the world, whereas the universe is the external void together with the world; and on this account the whole is finite (for the world is finite), but the universe is infinite (as is also the void outside the world).

Sextus Empiricus

(SVF I, 98) Zeno said the fundamental substance of all existing things is fire, in this following Heraclitus, and the principles of fire were matter and God, here following Plato. But he asserted that they both were corporeal, an active and a passive, whereas Plato said that the primary, active cause was incorporeal. Next, the whole world, at certain fated periods, is dissolved by fire, and then formed again into a world. Now the primary fire is like a kind of seed, containing the reasons of all things and the causes of everything, past, present, and future. Now the union and sequence of these things is an inevitable and unavoidable fate, knowledge, truth, and law of existing things. And in this respect the events of the world are arranged very well, as in a well-governed city.

Eusebius

(SVF II, 620) Democritus and Epicurus and the greatest number of the Stoic philosophers affirm both the creation and the destructibility of the world, though not all in the same way; for some give a sketch of many worlds, etc. . . . But the Stoics speak of one world only, and assert that God is the cause of its creation, but that the cause of its destruction is no longer God, but [lies in] the power of the unceasingly raging fire which pervades all existing things, dissolving, in the long periods of time, everything into itself; while from it again a regeneration of the world takes place through the providence of the creator. And according to these men, there may be one world spoken of as eternal and another as destructible, the destructible in reference to the world's present arrangement, yet eternal is the world which in reference to the conflagration is rendered immortal by the regenerations and periodic revolutions which never cease.

Philo

(SVF II, 637) And why should you not believe that something of divinity exists in one who is a part of God? The whole universe which contains us is one, and is God; we are His associates and His members.

Seneca

THE NATURE OF THE SOUL

(SVF II, 845) The soul, in my opinion, is endowed with sense. Nothing, therefore, pertaining to the soul, is unconnected with sensation, nothing pertaining to sensation is unconnected with the soul. . . . Now, since it is the soul that imparts the faculty of perception to all things that have sensation, and since it is itself that perceives the senses, not to say properties of them all, how is it likely that it did not itself receive a sense of itself from the

beginning? Whence is it to know what is necessary for itself under given circumstances, from the very necessity of natural causes, if it does not know its own property, and what is necessary for it? This we can recognize, indeed, in every soul; I mean, it has a knowledge of itself, without which knowledge of itself no soul could possibly have exercised its own functions. I suppose, too, that it is especially suitable that man, the only rational animal, should have been furnished with such a soul as would make him the rational animal, itself being pre-eminently rational. Now, how can that soul which makes man a rational animal be itself rational if it be itself ignorant of its rationality, being ignorant of its own very self?

Tertullian

FATE, DESTINY, AND PROVIDENCE

(SVF II, 921) Now by fate I mean . . . an order and series of causes wherein cause is connected to cause and each cause of itself produces an effect. That is an immortal truth having its source in all eternity. Therefore, nothing has happened which was not going to happen, and, likewise, nothing is going to happen of which nature does not contain the efficient causes. Consequently, we know that fate is that which is called, not superstitiously, but scientifically [*physice*], "the eternal cause of things, the 'wherefore' of things past, of things present, and of things to come."

Cicero

(SVF II, 944) Since all things happen by fate, if there were a man whose mind could discern the inner connections of all causes, then surely he would never be mistaken in any prediction he might make. For he who knows the causes of future events necessarily knows what every future event will be. But since no one except God is capable of this, it is left to man to predict the future by means of certain signs which indicate what will follow them. Things which are to be do not suddenly spring into existence, but the evolution of time is like the unwinding of a cable; it creates nothing new but only unfolds each event in its order.

Cicero

(SVF II, 956) [Chrysippus is being criticized for "lazy reasoning."] If all things are determined, why go to a doctor for your health? If everything is determined by fate, then nothing is possible, and so on.

This argument is criticized by Chrysippus. For some things, he says, are simple, and some are complex. A simple event is: "Socrates will die on that day." Here, whether he does anything or not, the day of his death has been determined. But if it is fated that "Oedipus shall be born to Laius," it will not be possible to add "whether Laius has been with a woman or not"; for this is a complex fact and *confatal.* He calls it this because he thinks it is fated both that Laius will be with his wife and that thus Oedipus will be begotten. Likewise, if it should be said, "Milo will compete in the Olympic games," and someone adds, "Therefore, he will compete whether he has an opponent or not," he would be wrong; for the notion "will compete" is complex because there can be no competition without an opponent. All such captious arguments can be refuted in the same way. "Whether you call in a physician or not, you will be healed" is captious; for it is as much fated that you shall call in a physician as that you shall recover. These connected events, as I have said, are termed by Chrysippus *confatal.*

Cicero

(SVF II, 974) It seems to me that the ancient philosophers were of two opinions, one group holding that fate so controls everything that it exerts the force of necessity, . . . the other group holding that the voluntary motions of the soul occur without any influence of fate. Chrysippus, however, wished to hold a middle course like an honorary arbiter, but he rather attaches himself to those who believed that the motions of the soul are free from necessity. But by the expressions he uses, he falls back into the same difficulties so that unwillingly he affirms the necessity of fate. Let us see, therefore, how this affects assent. Those ancient philosophers, for whom everything occurs by fate, say that assent is produced by force and necessity. The others, however, who disagree, free assent from fate and assert that if fate rules assent, necessity cannot be avoided. . . . But Chrysippus, since he both rejects necessity and does not wish anything to happen without preceding causes, distinguishes two kinds of causes, so that he may escape necessity and retain fate. "For," he says, "perfect and principal causes are one thing, auxiliary and proximate causes are another. For which reason,

when we say everything happens by fate and antecedent causes, we do not mean perfect and principal causes, but auxiliary and proximate." And so, the position I argued above, he opposes as follows: "If everything happens by fate, of course it follows that everything happens by preceding causes, but they are not principal and perfect; they are auxiliary and proximate. And if these are not in our power, it does not follow that our appetites are not in our power. But this would follow if we should say everything happens by perfect and principal causes, so that when these causes are not in our power, our appetites are not in our power. For which reason those who so introduce fate as to join necessity with it, must accept that conclusion; but those who do not say that antecedent causes must be perfect and principal escape that conclusion." For as to saying that assent occurs by preceding causes, he thinks it easily explained. For although assent cannot occur without a sense stimulus, yet, since sensation has a proximate and not a principal cause, it has the explanation, as Chrysippus desired, which we gave above; not that something can happen without any external force—for assent requires sense stimulation—but it comes back to his illustration of the cylinder and the top, which cannot begin to move unless an impulse be given them. But when that happens, the top spins and the cylinder revolves according to their own natures. "As therefore," he says, "he who pushes the cylinder gives it a principle of motion, but does not give it a motion of revolution, so an object strikes our sense and as it were stamps its image in the soul, but the assent is in our power, which, as has been said in the case of the cylinder, while put in motion from without, moves for the rest by its own force and nature. But if anything happened without an antecedent cause, it would be false to say that everything happens by fate; but if it is likely that for everything which happens a cause precedes, what reason can be given why we should not admit that everything occurs by fate? Provided it is understood what is the distinction and dissimilarity between causes." . . . For Chrysippus, while admiting that the proximate and adjacent cause of assent is found in sensation, does not concede it to be the necessary cause of giving assent; with the result that if everything occurs by fate, everything occurs by antecedent and necessary causes.

Cicero

EARLY STOIC ETHICS

(SVF III, 4) Again, living virtuously is equivalent to living in accordance with experience of the actual course of nature, as Chrysippus says in the first book of his treatise *On Ends;* for our individual natures are parts of the nature of the whole universe. And this is why the end may be defined as life in accordance with nature, or, in other words, in accordance with our own human nature as well as that of the universe, a life in which we refrain from every action forbidden by the law common to all things, i.e., the right reason which pervades all things, and is identical with this Zeus, lord and ruler of all that is. And this very thing constitutes the virtue of the happy man and the smooth current of life, when all actions promote the harmony of the spirit dwelling in the individual man with the will of him who orders the universe.

Diogenes Laertius

(SVF III, 16) The end, they say, is to be happy, that for the sake of which everything is performed, but nothing is done for the sake of itself; to do this first, viz, to live according to virtue, to live consistently, which is further this, to live according to nature. Zeno spoke of happiness in this manner: happiness is the "smooth" life. And Cleanthes added to this limit in his treatises and Chrysippus and others of the Stoic school, saying that happiness was not different than the happiness of life, but was, they said, laid open to the public view, the end being that which chances to be happiness, so that the happy life is this. Therefore, it seems clear from these considerations, that 'to live according to nature' is of equal force with: 'to live in accordance with beauty' and 'to live well,' and again, 'the good and the beautiful' and 'the virtue and the participating virtue;' and that all good is beautiful, in the same way as all the disgraceful is bad; and on this account the Stoic conception of the End is equal to life according to virtue.

Stobaeus

(SVF III, 72) Since notions of things are produced in the mind when something has become known either by experience or combination of ideas or analogy or logical inference, the fourth and last method in this list is the one that has given us the conception of Good. For when the mind ascends by logical

inference from the things in accordance with nature, then finally it arrives at the notion of Good.

At the same time, Good is absolute, and is neither increased nor diminished; but Good is perceived and called good from its own inherent properties and not by comparison with other things. Just as honey, although extremely sweet, is yet perceived to be sweet by its own singular flavor and not by being compared with something else, so this Good which we are discussing is indeed of superlative value, yet its value depends on kind and not on quantity. Value is not counted as a Good nor yet as an Evil; so that however much you increase it in amount, it will still remain the same in kind. The value of Virtue is therefore singular and distinct; it depends on kind and not on degree.

Cicero

(SVF III, 135) Of things preferred some are preferred for their own sake, some for the sake of something else; and others again both for their own sake and for the sake of something else. To the first of these classes belong natural ability, moral improvement, and the like; to the second, wealth, noble birth, and the like; to the last, strength, perfect faculties, soundness of bodily organs. Things are preferred for their own sake because they accord with nature; not for their own sake, but for the sake of something else, because they secure not a few utilities. And similarly with the class of things rejected under the contrary heads.

Diogenes Laertius

(SVF III, 188) The initial principle being thus established that things in accordance with nature are "things to be taken" for their own sake, and their opposites similarly "things to be rejected," the first "appropriate act," [for so I render the Greek *(kathekon)*], is to preserve oneself in one's natural constitution; the next is to retain those things which are in accordance with nature and to repel those that are the contrary; then when this principle of choice and also of rejection has been discovered, there follows next in order choice conditioned by "appropriate action"; then, such choice becomes a fixed habit; and finally, choice fully rationalized and in harmony with nature.

Man's first attraction is towards the things in accordance with nature; but as soon as he has understanding, or rather become capable of "conception"—in Stoic phraseology *ennoia*—and has discerned the order and, so to speak, harmony that governs conduct, he therefore esteems this harmony far more highly than all the things for which he originally felt an affection, and by exercise of intelligence and reason infers the conclusion that herein resides the chief good of man, the thing that is praiseworthy and desirable for its own sake; and that inasmuch as this consists in what the Stoics term *homologia* and we "conformity"—inasmuch I say as in this resides that good which is the end to which all else is a means, moral conduct and moral worth itself, which alone is counted as a good, although of subsequent development, is nevertheless the sole thing that is for its own efficacy and value desirable, whereas none of the primary objects of nature is desirable for its own sake.

Cicero

(SVF II, 314) The law of all is the king of things, both human and divine; for it is necessary that law be as a superintendent and a principle and a ruling power both of the good and of the disgraceful, and, because of this, it is the measure both of justice and of injustice. And of those things which by nature are political animals, it commands what ought to be done and prohibits what ought not to be done.

Marcianus

(SVF III, 340) It is held by the Stoics to be important to understand that nature creates in parents an affection for their children; and parental affection is the source to which we trace the origin of the association of the human race in communities. This cannot but be clear in the first place from the conformation of the body and its members, which by themselves are enough to show that nature's scheme included the procreation of offspring. Yet it could not be consistent that nature should at once intend offspring to be born and make no provision for that offspring when born to be loved and cherished. Even in the lower animals nature's operation can be clearly discerned; when we observe the labor that they spend on bearing and rearing their young, we seem to be listening to the actual voice of nature. Hence, as it is manifest that it is natural for us to shrink from pain, so it is clear that we derive from nature herself the impulse to love those to whom we have given birth.

From this impulse is developed the sense of mutual attraction which unites human beings as such;

this also is bestowed by nature. The mere fact of their common humanity requires that one man should feel another man akin to him.

Cicero

(SVF III, 517) Conduct will not be right unless the will to act is right; for this is the source of conduct. Nor, again, can the will be right without a right attitude of mind; for this is the source of the will. Furthermore, such an attitude of mind will not be found even in the best of men unless he has learned the laws of life as a whole and has worked out a proper judgment about everything, and unless he has reduced facts to a standard of truth.

Seneca

(SVF I, 220) If poverty is an evil, no beggar can be happy, be he as wise as you like. But Zeno dared to say that a wise beggar was not only happy but also wealthy.

Cicero

(SVF III, 628) Nor yet will the Wise Man live in solitude; for he is naturally made for society and action.

Diogenes Laertius

STRABO

Strabo was a Greek geographer, historian, and philosopher, who became attached to Stoicism as both a way of life and an approach for understanding the makeup of the physical world. He found Stoicism satisfying, partially because it broke with what he regarded as the rigid system of Aristotle, especially Aristotle's doctrine of causality. During his lifetime (ca. 63 B.C.–ca. A.D. 21), Strabo published many historical sketches and a seventeen-volume study on geography. The following selection from his Geography *details the ancient knowledge of the five zones of the planet earth.*

The Earth and Its Zones

Since the taking in hand of my proposed task naturally follows the criticisms of my predecessors, let me make a second beginning by saying that the person who attempts to write an account of the countries of the earth must take many of the physical and mathematical principles as hypotheses and elaborate his whole treatise with reference to their intent and authority. For, as I have already said, no architect or engineer would be competent even to fix the site of a house or a city properly if he had no conception beforehand of "climata" and of the celestial phenomena, and of geometrical figures and magnitudes and heat and cold and other such things—much less a person who would fix positions for the whole of the inhabited world. For the mere drawing on one and the same plane surface of Iberia and India and the countries that lie between them and, in spite of its being a plane surface, the plotting of the sun's position at its settings, risings, and in meridian, as though these positions were fixed for all the people of the world—merely this exercise gives to the man who has previously conceived of the arrangement and movement of the celestial bodies and grasped the fact that the true surface of the earth is spherical but that it is depicted for the moment as a plane surface for the convenience of the eye—merely this exercise, I say, gives to that man instruction that is truly geographical but to the man not thus qualified it does not. Indeed, the case is not the same with us when we are dealing with geography as it is when we are travelling over great plains (those of Babylonia, for example) or over the sea: then all that is in

Reprinted by permission of the publishers and The Loeb Classical Library from *Geography*, Vol. I, Strabo, trans. by Horace L. Jones, Cambridge, Mass.: Harvard University Press, 1917. (pp. 417–433)

front of us and behind us and on either side of us is presented to our minds as a plane surface and offers no varying aspects with reference to the celestial bodies or the movements or the positions of the sun and the other stars relatively to us; but when we are dealing with geography the like parts must never present themselves to our minds in that way. The sailor on the open sea, or the man who travels through a level country, is guided by certain popular notions (and these notions impel not only the uneducated man but the man of affairs as well to act in the self-same way), because he is unfamiliar with the heavenly bodies and ignorant of the varying aspects of things with reference to them. For he sees the sun rise, pass the meridian, and set, but how it comes about he does not consider; for, indeed, such knowledge is not useful to him with reference to the task before him, any more than it is useful for him to know whether or not his body stands parallel to that of his neighbor. But perhaps he does consider these matters, and yet holds opinions opposed to the principles of mathematics—just as the natives of any given place do; for a man's place occasions such blunders. But the geographer does not write for the native of any particular place, nor yet does he write for the man of affairs of the kind who has paid no attention to the mathematical sciences properly so-called; nor, to be sure, does he write for the harvest-hand or the ditch-digger, but for the man who can be persuaded that the earth as a whole is such as the mathematicians represent it to be, and also all that relates to such an hypothesis. And the geographer urges upon his students that they first master those principles and then consider the subsequent problems; for, he declares, he will speak only of the results which follow from those principles; and hence his students will the more unerringly make the application of his teachings if they listen as mathematicians; but he refuses to teach geography to persons not thus qualified.

Now as for the matters which he regards as fundamental principles of his science, the geographer must rely upon the geometricians who have measured the earth as a whole; and in their turn the geometricians must rely upon the astronomers; and again the astronomers upon the physicists. Physics is a kind of Arete; and by Aretai they mean those sciences that postulate nothing but depend upon themselves, and contain within themselves their own principles as well as the proofs thereof. Now what we are taught by the physicists is as follows: The universe and the heavens are sphere-shaped. The tendency of the bodies that have weight is towards the centre. And, having taken its position about this centre, the earth is spherically concentric with the heavens, and it is motionless as is also the axis through it, which axis extends also through the centre of the heavens. The heavens revolve round both the earth and its axis from east to west; and along with the heavens revolve the fixed stars, with the same rapidity as the vault of the heavens. Now the fixed stars move along parallel circles, and the best known parallel circles are the equator, the two tropics, and the arctic circles; whereas the planets and the sun and the moon move along certain oblique circles whose positions lie in the zodiac. Now the astronomers first accept these principles, either in whole or in part, and then work out the subsequent problems, namely, the movements of the heavenly bodies, their revolutions, their eclipses, their sizes, their respective distances, and a host of other things. And, in the same way, the geometricians, in measuring the earth as a whole, adhere to the doctrines of the physicists and the astronomers, and, in their turn, the geographers adhere to those of the geometricians.

Thus we must take as an hypothesis that the heavens have five zones, and that the earth also has five zones, and that the terrestrial zones have the same names as the celestial zones (I have already stated the reasons for this division into zones). The limits of the zones can be defined by circles drawn on both sides of the equator and parallel to it, namely, by two circles which enclose the torrid zone, and by two others, following upon these, which form the two temperate zones next to the torrid zone and the two frigid zones next to the temperate zones. Beneath each of the celestial circles falls the corresponding terrestrial circle which bears the same name: and, in like manner, beneath the celestial zone, the terrestrial zone. Now they call "temperate" the zones that can be inhabited; the others they call uninhabitable, the one on account of the heat, and the other two on account of the cold. They proceed in the same manner with reference to the tropic and the arctic circles (that is, in countries that admit of arctic circles): they define their limits by giving the terrestrial circles the same names as the celestial—and thus they define all the terrestrial circles that fall beneath the several celestial circles. Since the celestial equator cuts the whole heavens in two, the earth also must of necessity be cut in two by the terrestrial equator. Of the two hemispheres—I refer to the two celestial as well as the two terrestrial hemispheres—one is called "the northern hemisphere" and the other "the southern hemisphere"; so also, since the torrid zone is cut in two by the same circle, the one part of it will be the northern and the other the southern. It is clear that, of the temperate zones also, the one will be northern and the other southern, each bearing the name of the hemisphere in which it lies. That hemisphere is called "northern hemisphere" which contains that temperate zone in which, as you look from the east to the west, the pole is on your right hand and the equator on your left, or in which, as you look towards the south, the west is on your right hand and the east on your left; and that hemisphere is called "southern hemisphere," in which the opposite is true; and hence it is clear that we are in one of the two hemispheres (that is, of course, in the northern), and that it is impossible for us to be in both. "Between them are great rivers; first, Oceanus," and then the torrid zone. But neither is there an Oceanus in the centre of our whole inhabited world, cleaving the whole of it, nor, to be sure, is there a torrid spot in it; not yet, indeed, is there a portion of it to be found whose "climata" are opposite to the "climata" which I have given for the northern temperate zone.

By accepting these principles, then, and also by making use of the sun-dial and the other helps given him by the astronomer—by means of which are found, for the several inhabited localities, both the circles that are parallel to the equator and the circles that cut the former at right angles, the latter being drawn through the poles—the geometrician can measure the inhabited portion of the earth by visiting it and the rest of the earth by his calculation of the intervals. In this way he can find the distance from the equator to the pole, which is a fourth part of the earth's largest circle; and then he has the circumference of the earth. Accordingly, just as the man who measures the earth gets his principles from the astronomer and the astronomer his from the physicist, so, too, the geographer must in the same way take his point of departure from the man who has measured the earth as a whole, having confidence in him and in those in whom he, in his turn, had confidence, and then explain, in the first instance, our inhabited world—its size, shape, and character, and its relations to the earth as a whole; for this is the peculiar task of the geographer. Then, secondly, he must discuss in a fitting manner the several parts of the inhabited world, both land and sea, noting in passing wherein the subject has been treated inadequately by those of our predecessors whom we have believed to be the best authorities on these matters.

Now let us take as hypothesis that the earth together with the sea is sphere-shaped and that the surface of the earth is one and the same with that of the high seas; for the elevations on the earth's surface would disappear from consideration, because they are small in comparison with the great size of the earth and admit of being overlooked; and so we use "sphere-shaped" for figures of this kind, not as though they were turned on a lathe, nor yet as the geometrician uses the sphere for demonstration, but as an aid to our conception of the earth—and that, too, a rather rough conception. Now let us conceive of a sphere with five zones, and let the equator be drawn as a circle upon that sphere, and let a second circle be drawn parallel thereto, bounding the frigid zone in the northern hemisphere, and let a third circle be drawn through the poles, cutting the other two circles at right angles. Then, since the northern hemisphere contains two-fourths of the earth, which are formed by the equator with the circle that passes through the poles, a quadrilateral area is cut off in each of the two fourths. The northern side of the quadrilateral is half of the parallel next to the pole; the southern side is half of the equator; and the two remaining sides are segments of the circle that runs through the poles, these segments lying opposite to each other and being equal in length. Now in one of these two quadrilaterals (it would seem to make no difference in which one) we say that our inhabited world lies, washed on all sides by the sea and like an island; for, as I have already said above, the evidence of our senses and of reason prove this. But if anyone disbelieve the evidence of reason, it would make no difference, from the point of view of the geographer, whether we make the inhabited world an island, or merely admit what experience has taught us, namely, that it is possible to sail round the inhabited world on both sides, from the east as well as from the west, with the exception of a few intermediate stretches. And, as to these stretches, it makes no difference whether they are bounded by sea or by uninhabited land; for the geographer undertakes to describe the known parts of the inhabited world, but he leaves out of consideration the unknown parts of it—just as he does what is outside of it. And it will suffice to fill out and complete the outline of what we term "the island" by joining with a straight line the extreme points reached on the coasting-voyages made on both sides of the inhabited world.

CICERO

Marcus Tullius Cicero (106–43 B.C.) was an eclectic thinker, drawing upon the wisdom of the Stoics, the Epicureans, the Platonists, the Aristotelians and the Sceptics, known also as the Academics. He lived a hectic political life, especially during the ascendancy of Julius Caesar (100–44 B.C.). Although he survived a conflict with Catiline, which resulted in Cicero's temporary exile in 58 B.C., he could not survive after the assassination of his protector, Julius Caesar. Betrayed by Octavian and condemned by Mark Antony, Cicero was murdered in 43 B.C.

In his writings, Cicero was also eclectic; he utilized many forms, including dialogues, disputations, and treatises. When his speeches, orations, and letters are taken into account, his stylistic diversity becomes even greater. In his philosophical work, Cicero is most indebted to the Stoics, particularly in his Theories of Ethics (De Finibus Bonorum et Malorum). *The following selection is from Cicero's treatise* On Old Age (De Senectute), *which reminds us of our own contemporary ideas on the meaning and inevitability of aging. Also included is a brief selection from the* Tusculan Disputations, *where Cicero stresses that only the virtuous person can be happy.*

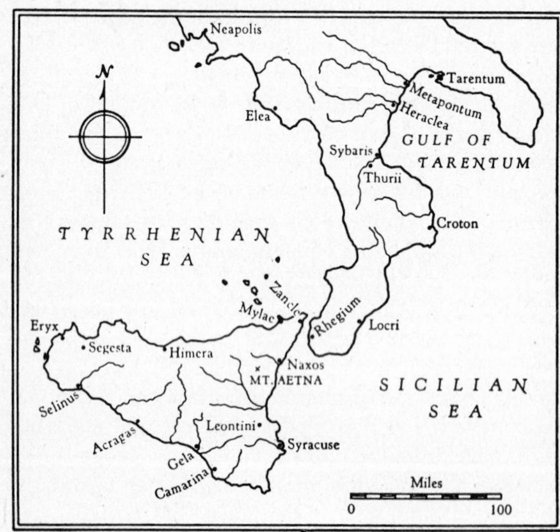

Southern Italy and Sicily

From On Old Age

It remains to consider now the fourth reason—one that seems especially calculated to render my time of life anxious and full of care—the nearness of death; for death, in truth, cannot be far away. O wretched indeed is that old man who has not learned in the course of his long life that death should be held of no account! For clearly death is negligible, if it utterly annihilates the soul, or even desirable, if it conducts the soul to some place where it is to live for ever. Surely no other alternative can be found. What, then, shall I fear, if after death I am destined to be either not unhappy or happy? And yet is there anyone so foolish, even though he is young, as to feel absolutely sure that he will be alive when evening comes? Nay, even youth, much more than old age, is subject to the accident of death; the young fall sick more easily, their sufferings are more intense, and

---

they are cured with greater difficulty. Therefore few arrive at old age, and, but for this, life would be lived in better and wiser fashion. For it is in old men that reason and good judgement are found, and had it not been for old men no state would have existed at all.

But I return to the question of impending death. What fault is this which you charge against old age, when, as you see, it is one chargeable likewise to youth? That death is common to every age has been brought home to me by the loss of my dearest son, and to you, Scipio, by the untimely end of your two brothers, when they were giving promise of attaining to the highest honours in the State. But, you may say, the young man hopes that he will live for a long time and this hope the old man cannot have. Such a hope is not wise, for what is more unwise than to mistake uncertainty for certainty, falsehood for truth? They say, also, that the old man has nothing even to hope for. Yet he is in better case than the young man, since what the latter merely hopes for, the former has already attained; the one wishes to live long, the other has lived long.

But, ye gods! what is there in human nature that is for long? For grant the utmost limit of life; let us hope to reach the age of the Tartessian king—for at Cadiz there was, as I have seen it recorded, a certain Arganthonius, who had reigned eighty and had lived one hundred and twenty years—,but to me nothing whatever seems "lengthy" if it has an end; for when that end arrives, then that which was is gone; naught remains but the fruit of good and virtuous deeds. Hours and days, and months and years, go by; the past returns no more, and what is to be we cannot know; but whatever the time given us in which to live, we should therewith be content.

The actor, for instance, to please his audience need not appear in every act to the very end; it is enough if he is approved in the parts in which he plays; and so it is not necessary for the wise man to stay on this mortal stage to the last fall of the curtain. For even if the allotted space of life be short, it is long enough in which to live honourably and well; but if a longer period of years should be granted, one has no more cause to grieve than the farmers have that the pleasant springtime has passed and that summer and autumn have come. For spring typifies youth and gives promise of future fruits; while the other seasons are designed for gathering in those fruits and storing them away.

Now the fruit of old age, as I have often said, is the memory of abundant blessings previously acquired. Moreover, whatever befalls in accordance with Nature should be accounted good; and indeed, what is more consonant with Nature than for the old to die? But the same fate befalls the young, though Nature in their case struggles and rebels. Therefore, when the young die I am reminded of a strong flame extinguished by a torrent; but when old men die it is as if a fire had gone out without the use of force and of its own accord, after the fuel had been consumed; and, just as apples when they are green are with difficulty plucked from the tree, but when ripe and mellow fall of themselves, so, with the young, death comes as a result of force, while with the old it is the result of ripeness. To me, indeed, the thought of this "ripeness" for death is so pleasant, that the nearer I approach death the more I feel like one who is in sight of land at last and is about to anchor in his home port after a long voyage.

But old age has no certain term, and there is good cause for an old man living so long as he can fulfil and support his proper duties and hold death of no account. By this means old age actually becomes more spirited and more courageous than youth. This explains the answer which Solon gave to the tyrant Pisistratus who asked, "Pray, what do you rely upon in opposing me so boldly?" and Solon replied, "Old age." But the most desirable end of life is that which comes while the mind is clear and the faculties are unimpaired, when Nature herself takes apart the work which she has put together. As the builder most readily destroys the ship or the house which he has built, so Nature is the agent best fitted to give dissolution to her creature, man. Now every structure when newly built is hard to pull apart, but the old and weather-beaten house comes easily down.

Hence, it follows that old men ought neither to cling too fondly to their little remnant of life, nor give it up without a cause. Pythagoras bids us stand like faithful sentries and not quit our post until God, our Captain, gives the word. Solon the Wise has a couplet in which he says that he does not want his death to be free from the grief and mourning of his friends. He wishes, no doubt to make out that he is dear to his friends, but I am inclined to think that Ennius has expressed it better when he says:

> I do not wish the honour of a tear,
> Or any wailing cries about my bier.

He does not think that death, which is followed by eternal life, should be a cause of grief.

Now, there may be some sensation in the process of dying, but it is a fleeting one, especially to the old; after death the sensation is either pleasant or there is none at all. But this should be thought on from our youth up, so that we may be indifferent to death, and without this thought no one can be in a tranquil state of mind. For it is certain that we must die, and, for aught we know, this very day. Therefore, since death threatens every hour, how can he who fears it have any steadfastness of soul? No very extended argument on this point seems necessary when I recall—not the conduct of Lucius Brutus, who was killed in liberating his country; nor that of the two Decii who rode full speed to a voluntary death; nor that of Marcus Atilius Regulus, who set out from home to undergo torture and keep the faith pledged to his foe; nor that of the two Scipios, who with their bodies sought to stay the Punic march; nor that, Scipio, of your grandfather Lucius Paulus who, in the shameful rout at Cannae, gave his life to atone for his colleague's folly; nor that of Marcus Marcellus, to whom not even his most pitiless foe denied the honours of a funeral—but rather when I recall, as I have noted in my *Antiquities,* how our legions have often marched with cheerful and unwavering courage into situations whence they thought they would never return. Then shall wise old men fear a thing which is despised by youths, and not only by those who are untaught, but by those also who are mere clowns?

Undoubtedly, as it seems to me at least, satiety of all pursuits causes satiety of life. Boyhood has certain pursuits: does youth yearn for them? Early youth has its pursuits: does the matured or so-called middle stage of life need them? Maturity, too, has such as are not even sought in old age, and finally, there are those suitable to old age. Therefore as the pleasures and pursuits of the earlier periods of life fall away, so also do those of old age; and when that happens man has his fill of life and the time is ripe for him to go.

Really I do not see why I should not venture to tell you what I, myself, think of death; for it seems to me that I apprehend it better as I draw nearer to it. It is my belief, Scipio, that your father, and yours, Laelius—both of them most illustrious men and very dear to me—are living yet, and living the only life deserving of the name. For while we are shut up within these frames of flesh we perform a sort of task imposed by necessity and endure grievous labour; for the soul is celestial, brought down from its most exalted home and buried, as it were, in earth, a place uncongenial to its divine and eternal nature. But I believe that the immortal gods implanted souls in human bodies so as to have beings who would care for the earth and who, while contemplating the celestial order, would imitate it in the moderation and consistency of their lives. Nor have I been driven to this belief solely by the force of reason and of argument, but also by the reputation and authority of philosophers of the highest rank.

I used to be told that Pythagoras and his disciples,—who were almost fellow-countrymen of ours, inasmuch as they were formerly called "Italian philosophers,"—never doubted that our souls were emanations of the Universal Divine Mind. Moreover, I had clearly set before me the arguments touching the immortality of the soul, delivered on the last day of his life by Socrates, whom the oracle of Apollo had pronounced the wisest of men. Why multiply words? That is my conviction, that is what I believe—since such is the lightning-like rapidity of the soul, such its wonderful memory of things that are past, such its ability to forecast the future, such its mastery of many arts, sciences, and inventions, that its nature, which encompasses all these things, cannot be mortal; and since the soul is always active and has no source of motion because it is self-moving, its motion will have no end, because it will never leave itself; and since in its nature the soul is of one substance and has nothing whatever mingled with it unlike or dissimilar to itself, it cannot be divided, and if it cannot be divided it cannot perish. And a strong argument that men's knowledge of numerous things antedates their birth is the fact that mere children, in studying difficult subjects, so quickly lay hold upon innumerable things that they seem not to be then learning them for the first time, but to be recalling and remembering them. This, in substance, is Plato's teaching.

Again, in Xenophon, Cyrus the Elder utters the following words as he is dying: "Think not, my dearest sons, that, when I have left you, I shall cease to be. For while I was with you you did not see my soul, but you knew that it was in this body from the deeds that I performed. Continue to believe, therefore, that it exists as before, even though you see it not. Nor, indeed, would the fame of illustrious men survive their death if the souls of those very men did not cause us to retain their memory longer. I, for my part, could never be persuaded that souls, which lived while they were in human bodies, perished when they left those bodies; nor, indeed, that the soul became incapable of thought when it had escaped from the unthinking corpse, but rather that, when it has been freed from every admixture of flesh and had begun to exist pure and undefiled, then only was it wise. And even when man is dissolved by death it is evident to the sight whither each bodily element departs; for the corporeal returns to the visible constituents from which it came, but the soul alone remains unseen, both when it is present and when it departs. Again, you really see nothing resembling death so much as sleep; and yet it is when the body sleeps that the soul most clearly manifests its divine nature; for when it is unfettered and free it sees many things that are to come. Hence we know what the soul's future state will be when it has been wholly released from the shackles of the flesh. Wherefore, if what I have said be true, cherish me as you would a god. But on the other hand, if my soul is going to perish along with my body, still you, who revere the gods as the guardians and rulers of this beautiful universe, will keep me in loving and sacred memory."

This was the view of the dying Cyrus. Let me, if you please, give my own.

No one, my dear Scipio, will ever convince me that your father Paulus, or your two grandfathers, Paulus and Africanus, or the latter's father and uncle, or many other illustrious men, unnecessary now to name, would have attempted such mighty deeds, to be remembered by posterity, if they had not known that posterity belonged to them. Or, to boast somewhat of myself after the manner of the old, do you think that I should have undertaken such heavy labours by day and by night, at home and abroad, if I had believed that the term of my earthly life would mark the limits of my fame? Would it not have been far better for me to spend a leisured and quiet life, free from toil and strife? But somehow, my soul was ever on the alert, looking forward to posterity, as if it realized that when it had departed from this life, then at last would it be alive. And, indeed, were it not true that the soul is immortal, it would not be the case that it is ever the souls of the best men that strive most for immortal glory. And what of the fact that the wisest men die with the greatest equanimity, the most foolish with the least? Is it not apparent to you that it is because the soul of the one, having a keener and wider vision, sees that it is setting out for a better country, while that of the other, being of duller sight, sees not its path?

Really, Scipio, I am carried away with the desire to see your father, and yours too, Laelius, both of whom I honoured and loved; and, indeed, I am eager to meet not only those whom I have known, but those also of whom I have heard and read and written. And when I shall have set out to join them, assuredly no one will easily draw me back, or boil me up again, as if I were a Pelias. Nay, if some god should give me leave to return to infancy from my old age, to weep once more in my cradle, I should vehemently protest; for, truly, after I have run my race I have no wish to be recalled, as it were, from the goal to the starting-place. For what advantage has life—or, rather, what trouble does it not have? But even grant that it has great advantage, yet undoubtedly it has either satiety or an end. I do not mean to complain of life as many men, and they learned ones, have often done; nor do I regret that I have lived, since I have so lived that I think I was not born in vain, and I quit life as if it were an inn, not a home. For Nature has given us an hostelry in which to sojourn, not to abide.

O glorious day, when I shall set out to join the assembled hosts of souls divine and leave this world of strife and sin! For I shall go to meet not only the men already mentioned, but my Cato, too, than whom no better man, none more distinguished for filial duty, was ever born. His body was burned by me, whereas, on the contrary it were more fitting that mine had been burned by him; but his soul, not deserting me, but ever looking back, has surely departed for that realm where it knew that I, myself, must come. People think that I have bravely borne my loss—not that I bore it with an untroubled heart, but I found constant solace in the thought that our separation would not be long.

For these reasons, Scipio, my old age sits light upon me (for you said that this has been a cause of wonder to you and Laelius), and not only is not burdensome, but is even happy. And if I err in my belief that the souls of men are immortal, I gladly err, nor do I wish this error which gives me pleasure to be wrested from me while I live. But if when dead I am going to be without sensation (as some petty philosophers think), then I have no fear that these seers, when they are dead, will have the laugh on me! Again, if we are not going to be immortal, nevertheless, it is desirable for a man to be blotted out at his proper time. For as Nature has marked the bounds of everything else, so she has marked the bounds of life. Moreover, old age is the final scene, as it were, in life's drama, from which we ought to escape when it grows wearisome and, certainly, when we have had our fill.

Such, my friends, are my views on old age. May you both attain it, and thus be able to prove by experience the truth of what you have heard from me.

From the Tusculan Disputations

A[uditor]. It does not appear to me that virtue can be sufficient for leading a happy life. M[arcus Cicero]. But, I can assure you, my friend Brutus thinks it sufficient and with your permission I put his judgment far above yours. A. No doubt you do and yet the question now before us is not the depth of your affection for him, but the view I have stated as it appears to me, and this I wish you to discuss. M. Do you really mean that virtue cannot be sufficient for leading a happy life? A. I do, absolutely. M. Tell me this, does virtue give sufficient aid for living rightly, honourably, praiseworthily, and in a word for leading a good life? A. Certainly it does. M. Can you then say either that the man who lives an evil life is not wretched, or that the man who, as you admit, leads a good life does not lead a happy one? A. Why should I not? for even in torture a man can live rightly, honourably, praiseworthily and for that reason lead a good life, provided only you understand the sense in which I now use the term good; for I mean living consistently, with dignity, wisdom, courage: these qualities too are thrown along with their possessor upon the rack, and for that happy life has no ambition. M. What then? is happy life, I ask, left in solitude outside the threshold and gate of the prison-house when consistency, dignity, courage, wisdom and the rest of the virtues are hurried along to the executioner and recoil from no torment or pain? A. If you are going to do any good, you must look out for some fresh arguments. Those you have given have no effect on me, not merely because they are hackneyed but much more because, as with certain light wines which lose their flavour in water, there is more delight in a sip than a draught of this Stoic vintage. For instance your troop of virtues, when laid upon the rack, bring before the eyes visions of majestic splendour, making it seem that happy life is on the point of hastening to them speedily and not suffering them to remain deserted by itself. When, however, one has led the soul away from the visions of that picture of the virtues to the truth of reality, there is left this bare question,—can anyone be happy as long as he is tormented? Let us therefore put this question now; as for the virtues, however, do not be afraid of their remonstrating and complaining that happy life has deserted them, for if there is no virtue without prudence, prudence by itself can see that not all good men are also happy, and recalls many memories of M. Atilius, Q. Caepio or Manius Aquilius, and when happy life (if resolved to resort to visions rather than actual facts) attempts to pass to the rack, prudence in person restrains it and says that it has no partnership with pain and agony.

M. I readily allow you to take such a line, although it is unfair of you to dictate the way in which you wish me to conduct the discussion. But I want to know whether we think any result was arrived at on the days previous to this or not. A. Certainly there was and a result of some moment. M. And yet, if that is so, this question has already been threshed out and brought well-nigh to its conclusion. A. How so, pray? M. Because troubled movements and agitations of the soul, roused and excited by ill-consid-

Reprinted by permission of the publishers and The Loeb Classical Library from *Tusculan Disputations,* Cicero, trans. by J. E. King, Cambridge, Mass.: Harvard University Press, 1927, revised 1945. (pp. 437–443, 507–509)

ered impulse, in scorn of all reason, leave no portion of happy life behind them. For who can fail to be wretched with the fear of death or pain upon him, one of which is always close at hand and the other always threatening? Further, if the same man (and this happens frequently) is afraid of poverty, disgrace, dishonour, if he is afraid of infirmity, blindness, if lastly he is afraid of slavery (the frequent fate, not of individual men but powerful communities): can anyone be happy with such fears before him? Again, the man who not merely fears such misfortunes in the future, but actually suffers and endures them in the present (add to the list exile, sorrow, childlessness), the man who is broken down by such blows and shipwrecked by distress, can he fail, pray, to be utterly wretched? Further, where we see a man passionately stirred with the madness of lust, desiring all things in a fury of unsatisfied longing, and the more copiously he drains the cup of pleasure wherever offered, the deeper and more consuming his thirst, would you not rightly pronounce him utterly wretched? Again, when a man is frivolously excited, and in a transport of empty delight and reckless extravagance, is he not all the more wretched, the happier his life appears in his own eyes? Therefore as such men are wretched, so on the contrary those are happy whom no fears alarm, no distresses corrode, no lusts inflame, no vain transports of delight dissolve in the melting lassitude of pleasure. Just therefore as the sea is understood to be calm when not even the lightest breath of air ruffles its waves; so a peaceful, still condition of the soul is discernible when there is no disturbance of strength enough to be able to ruffle it. Therefore if there is a man able to regard the power of fortune, to regard all human vicissitudes that can possibly befall, as so far endurable that neither fear nor worry touch him, and if the same man should covet nothing, feel no transport of empty pleasure in his soul, what reason is there why he should not be happy? And if virtue makes this possible, what reason is there why virtue of its own power alone should not make men happy?

A . . . But let us check our eloquence and return to the point at which we digressed. Happy life will give itself, I say, to torture, and following in the train of justice, temperance and above all of fortitude, of greatness of soul and patience will not halt at the sight of the face of the executioner, and, when all the virtues, while the soul remains undaunted, pass on to face torment, it will not stay behind outside the doors, as I have said, and threshold of the prison. For what could be more abominable, more hideous than to be left desolate, severed from its glorious companions? And yet this is by no means possible; for neither can the virtues subsist without happy life, nor happy life without the virtues. And so they will not suffer it to make evasions and will hurry it along with them to whatsoever pain and torment they shall themselves be led. For it is characteristic of the wise man to do nothing of which he can repent, nothing against his will, to do everything nobly, consistently, soberly, rightly, not to look forward to anything as if it were bound to come, to be astonished at no occurrence under the impression that its occurrence is unexpected and strange, to bring all things to the standard of his own judgment, to abide by his own decisions. And what can be happier than this I certainly cannot conceive.

For the Stoics indeed the conclusion is easy, since they hold it the sovereign good to live according to nature and in harmony with nature, seeing that not only is this the wise man's settled duty but also it lies in his power, and so for them it follows necessarily that where a man has the chief good in his power, he also has the power of happy life: thus the life of the wise is rendered happy always. Now you know the utterances I think the most courageous about happy life and, at the point we now are—unless you have something better to suggest—the truest as well.

SENECA

Seneca was born in Cordoba, Spain, ca. 4 B.C. He committed suicide in A.D. 65, following an alleged conspiracy to depose the Roman Emperor Nero. Educated in Rome, Seneca was an accomplished man of letters and rhetoric. Although a Stoic by persuasion, he was fond of the writings of Epicurus and of the Cynics. He was also influenced by the important Stoic philosopher Posidonius (ca. 135–ca. 51 B.C.), none of whose writings survive. Seneca's work On Physical Science *remains an important source for our knowledge of Posidonius' teachings. Seneca's published works were considerable. These include poetical works and tragedies, although his prose works are of most interest to philosophers, especially the* Moral Essays.

Seneca was a moralist in the tradition of the Stoics. For him, ethics was supreme among the Stoic disciplines of logic, ethics, and physics. He wrote that "there is no philosophy without goodness and no goodness without philosophy." His philosophical position includes the Stoic doctrine of apatheia, *that is, the acceptance of the law of nature and our obligation to abide by its demands.*

The two selections that follow, from "On the Happy Life" and "On Tranquillity of Mind," are taken from his Moral Essays. *They reflect the Stoic conviction that virtue, and only virtue, leads to happiness and tranquility.*

From On the Happy Life

To live happily, my brother Gallio, is the desire of all men, but their minds are blinded to a clear vision of just what it is that makes life happy; and so far from its being easy to attain the happy life, the more eagerly a man strives to reach it, the farther he recedes from it if he has made a mistake in the road; for when it leads in the opposite direction, his very speed will increase the distance that separates him.

First, therefore, we must seek what it is that we are aiming at; then we must look about for the road by which we can reach it most quickly, and on the journey itself, if only we are on the right path, we shall discover how much of the distance we overcome each day, and how much nearer we are to the goal toward which we are urged by a natural desire. But so long as we wander aimlessly, having no guide, and following only the noise and discordant cries of those who call us in different directions, life will be consumed in making mistakes—life that is brief even if we should strive day and night for sound wisdom. Let us, therefore, decide both upon the goal and upon the way, and not fail to find some experienced guide who has explored the region towards which we are advancing; for the conditions of this journey are different from those of most travel. On most journeys some well-recognized road and inquiries made of the inhabitants of the region prevent you from going astray; but on this one all the best beaten and the most frequented paths are the most deceptive. Nothing, therefore, needs to be more emphasized than the warning that we should not, like sheep, follow the lead of the throng in front of us, travelling, thus, the way that all go and not the way that we ought to go. Yet nothing involves us in greater trouble than the fact that we adapt ourselves to common report in the belief that the best things are those that have met with great approval,—the fact that, having so many to follow, we live after the rule, not of reason, but of imitation. The result of this is that people are piled high, one above another, as they rush to destruction. And just as it happens that in a great crush of humanity, when the people push against each other, no one can fall down without drawing along another, and those that are in front cause destruction to those behind—this same thing you may see happening everywhere in life. No man can go wrong to his own hurt only, but he will be both the cause and the sponsor of another's wrongdoing. For it is dangerous to attach one's self to the crowd in front, and so long as each one of us is more willing to trust another than to judge for himself, we never show any judgement in the matter of living, but always a blind trust, and a mistake that has been passed on from hand to hand finally involves us and works our destruction. It is the example of other people that is our undoing; let us merely separate our-

Reprinted by permission of the publishers and The Loeb Classical Library from *Moral Essays*, Vol. II, Seneca, trans. by John W. Basore, Cambridge, Mass: Harvard University Press, 1932. (pp. 99–121)

selves from the crowd, and we shall be made whole. But as it is, the populace, defending its own iniquity, pits itself against reason. And so we see the same thing happening that happens at the elections, where, when the fickle breeze of popular favour has shifted, the very same persons who chose the praetors wonder that those praetors were chosen. The same thing has one moment our favour, the next our disfavour; this is the outcome of every decision that follows the choice of the majority.

When the happy life is under debate, there will be no use for you to reply to me, as if it were a matter of votes: "This side seems to be in a majority." For that is just the reason it is the worse side. Human affairs are not so happily ordered that the majority prefer the better things; a proof of the worst choice is the crowd. Therefore let us find out what is best to do, not what is most commonly done—what will establish our claim to lasting happiness, not what finds favour with the rabble, who are the worst possible exponents of the truth. But by the rabble I mean no less the servants of the court than the servants of the kitchen; for I do not regard the colour of the garments that clothe the body. In rating a man I do not rely upon eyesight; I have a better and surer light, by which I may distinguish the false from the true. Let the soul discover the good of the soul. If the soul ever has leisure to draw breath and to retire within itself—ah! to what self-torture will it come, and how, if it confesses the truth to itself, it will say: "All that I have done hitherto, I would were undone; when I think of all that I have said, I envy the dumb; of all that I have prayed for, I rate my prayers as the curses of my enemies; of all that I have feared—ye gods! how much lighter it would have been than the load of what I have coveted! With many I have been at enmity, and, laying aside hatred, have been restored to friendship with them—if only there can be any friendship between the wicked; with myself I have not yet entered into friendship. I have made every effort to remove myself from the multitude and to make myself noteworthy by reason of some endowment. What have I accomplished save to expose myself to the darts of malice and show it where it can sting me? See you those who praise your eloquence, who trail upon your wealth, who court your favour, who exalt your power? All these are either now your enemies, or—it amounts to the same thing—can become such. To know how many are jealous of you, count your admirers. Why do I not rather seek some real good—one which I could feel, not one which I could display? These things that draw the eyes of men, before which they halt, which they show to one another in wonder, outwardly glitter, but are worthless within."

Let us seek something that is a good in more than appearance—something that is solid, constant, and more beautiful in its more hidden part; for this let us delve. And it is placed not far off; you will find it—you need only to know where to stretch out your hand. As it is, just as if we groped in darkness, we pass by things near at hand, stumbling over the very objects we desire.

Not to bore you, however, with tortuous details, I shall pass over in silence the opinions of other philosophers, for it would be tedious to enumerate and refute them all. Do you listen to ours. But when I say "ours," I do not bind myself to some particular one of the Stoic masters; I, too, have the right to form an opinion. Accordingly, I shall follow so-and-so, I shall request so-and-so to divide the question; perhaps, too, when called upon after all the rest, I shall impugn none of my predecessors' opinions, and shall say: "I simply have this much to add." Meantime, I follow the guidance of Nature—a doctrine upon which all Stoics are agreed. Not to stray from Nature and to mould ourselves according to her law and pattern—this is true wisdom.

The happy life, therefore, is a life that is in harmony with its own nature, and it can be attained in only one way. First of all, we must have a sound mind and one that is in constant possession of its sanity; second, it must be courageous and energetic, and, too, capable of the noblest fortitude, ready for every emergency, careful of the body and of all that concerns it, but without anxiety; lastly, it must be attentive to all the advantages that adorn life, but with over-much love for none—the user, but not the slave, of the gifts of Fortune. You understand, even if I do not say more, that, when once we have driven away all that excites or affrights us, there ensues unbroken tranquillity and enduring freedom; for when pleasures and fears have been banished, then, in place of all that is trivial and fragile and harmful just because of the evil it works, there comes upon us first a boundless joy that is firm and unalterable, then peace and harmony of the soul and true greatness coupled with kindliness; for all ferocity is born from weakness.

It is possible also to define this good of ours in

other terms—that is, the same idea may be expressed in different language. Just as an army remains the same, though at one time it deploys with a longer line, now is massed into a narrow space and either stands with hollowed centre and wings curved forward, or extends a straightened front, and, no matter what its formation may be, will keep the selfsame spirit and the same resolve to stand in defence of the selfsame cause,—so the definition of the highest good may at one time be given in prolix and lengthy form, and at another be restrained and concise. So it will come to the same thing if I say: "The highest good is a mind that scorns the happenings of chance, and rejoices only in virtue," or say: "It is the power of the mind to be unconquerable, wise from experience, calm in action, showing the while much courtesy and consideration in intercourse with others." It may also be defined in the statement that the happy man is he who recognizes no good and evil other than a good and an evil mind—one who cherishes honour, is content with virtue, who is neither puffed up, nor crushed, by the happenings of chance, who knows of no greater good than that which he alone is able to bestow upon himself, for whom true pleasure will be the scorn of pleasures. It is possible, too, if one chooses to be discursive, to transfer the same idea to various other forms of expression without injuring or weakening its meaning. For what prevents us from saying that the happy life is to have a mind that is free, lofty, fearless and steadfast—a mind that is placed beyond the reach of fear, beyond the reach of desire, that counts virtue the only good, baseness the only evil, and all else but a worthless mass of things, which come and go without increasing or diminishing the highest good, and neither subtract any part from the happy life nor add any part to it?

A man thus grounded must, whether he wills or not, necessarily be attended by constant cheerfulness and a joy that is deep and issues from deep within, since he finds delight in his own resources, and desires no joys greater than his inner joys. Should not such joys as these be rightly matched against the paltry and trivial and fleeting sensations of the wretched body? The day a man becomes superior to pleasure, he will also be superior to pain; but you see in what wretched and baneful bondage he must linger whom pleasures and pains, those most capricious and tyrannical of masters, shall in turn enslave. Therefore we must make our escape to freedom. But the only means of procuring this is through indifference to Fortune. Then will be born the one inestimable blessing, the peace and exaltation of a mind now safely anchored, and, when all error is banished, the great and stable joy that comes from the discovery of truth, along with kindliness and cheerfulness of mind; and the source of a man's pleasure in all of these will not be that they are good, but that they spring from a good that is his own.

Seeing that I am employing some freedom in treating my subject, I may say that the happy man is one who is freed from both fear and desire because of the gift of reason; since even rocks are free from fear and sorrow, and no less are the beasts of the field, yet for all that no one could say that these things are "blissful," when they have no comprehension of bliss. Put in the same class those people whose dullness of nature and ignorance of themselves have reduced them to the level of beasts of the field and of inanimate things. There is no difference between the one and the other, since in one case they are things without reason, and in the other their reason is warped, and works their own hurt, being active in the wrong direction; for no man can be said to be happy if he has been thrust outside the pale of truth. Therefore the life that is happy has been founded on correct and trustworthy judgement, and is unalterable. Then, truly, is the mind unclouded and freed from every ill, since it knows how to escape not only deep wounds, but even scratches, and, resolved to hold to the end whatever stand it has taken, it will defend its position even against the assaults of an angry Fortune. For so far as sensual pleasure is concerned, though it flows about us on every side, steals in through every opening, softens the mind with its blandishments, and employs one resource after another in order to seduce us in whole or in part, yet who of mortals, if he has left in him one trace of a human being, would choose to have his senses tickled night and day, and, forsaking the mind, devote his attention wholly to the body?

"But the mind also," it will be said, "has its own pleasures." Let it have them, in sooth, and let it pose as a judge of luxury and pleasures; let it gorge itself with all the things that are wont to delight the senses, then let it look back upon the past, and, recalling faded pleasures, let it intoxicate itself with former experiences and be eager now for those to come, and let it lay its plans, and, while the body lies helpless from present cramming, let it direct its thoughts to that to come—yet from all this, it seems to me, the mind will be more wretched than ever, since it is madness to choose evils instead of goods. But no man can be happy unless he is sane, and no man can be sane who searches for what will injure him in place of what is best. The happy man, therefore, is one who has right judgement; the happy man is content with his present lot, no matter what it is, and is reconciled to his circumstances; the happy man is he who allows reason to fix the value of every condition of existence.

Even those who declare that the highest good is in the belly see in what a dishonourable position they have placed it. And so they say that it is not possible to separate pleasure from virtue, and they aver that no one can live virtuously without also living pleasantly, nor pleasantly without also living virtuously. But I do not see how things so different can be cast in the same mould. What reason is there, I beg of you, why pleasure cannot be separated from virtue? Do you mean, since all goods have their origin in virtue, even the things that you love and desire must spring from its roots? But if the two were inseparable, we should not see certain things pleasant, but not honourable, and certain things truly most honourable, but painful and capable of being accomplished only through suffering. Then, too, we see that pleasure enters into even the basest life, but, on the other hand, virtue does not permit life to be evil, and there are people who are unhappy not without pleasure—nay, are so on account of pleasure itself—and this could not happen if pleasure were indissolubly joined to virtue; virtue often lacks pleasure, and never needs it. Why do you couple things that are unlike, nay, even opposites? Virtue is something lofty, exalted and regal, unconquerable, and unwearied; pleasure is something lowly, servile, weak, and perishable, whose haunt and abode are the brothel and the tavern. Virtue you will find in the temple, in the forum, in the senate-house—you will find her standing in front of the city walls, dusty and stained, and with calloused hands; pleasure you will more often find lurking out of sight, and in search of darkness, around the public baths and the sweatingrooms and the places that fear the police—soft, enervated, reeking with wine and perfume, and pallid, or else painted and made up with cosmetics like a corpse. The highest good is immortal, it knows no ending, it permits neither surfeit nor regret; for the right-thinking mind never alters, it neither is filled with self-loathing nor suffers any change in its life, that is ever the best. But pleasure is extinguished just when it is most enjoyed; it has but small space, and thus quickly fills it—it grows weary and is soon spent after its first assault. Nor is anything certain whose nature consists in movement. So it is not even possible that there should be any substance in that which comes and goes most swiftly and will perish in the very exercise of its power; for it struggles to reach a point at which it may cease, and it looks to the end while it is beginning.

What, further, is to be said of the fact that pleasure belongs alike to the good and the evil, and that the base delight no less in their disgrace than do the honourable in fair repute? And therefore the ancients have enjoined us to follow, not the most pleasant, but the best life, in order that pleasure should be, not the leader, but the companion of a right and proper desire. For we must use Nature as our guide; she it is that Reason heeds, it is of her that it takes counsel. Therefore to live happily is the same thing as to live according to Nature. What this is, I shall proceed to make clear. If we shall guard the endowments of the body and the needs of Nature with care and fearlessness, in the thought that they have been given but for a day and are fleeting, if we shall not be their slaves, nor allow these alien things to become our masters, if we shall count that the gratifications of the body, unessential as they are, have a place like to that of the auxiliaries and light-armed troops in camp—if we let them serve, not command—thus and thus only will these things be profitable to the mind. Let a man not be corrupted by external things, let him be unconquerable and admire only himself, courageous in spirit and ready for any fate, let him be the moulder of his own life; let not his confidence be without knowledge, nor his knowledge without firmness; let his decisions once made abide, and let not his decrees be altered by any erasure. It will be understood, even without my adding it, that such a man will be poised and well ordered, and will show majesty mingled with courtesy in all his actions. Let reason search into external things at the instigation of the senses, and, while it derives from them its first knowledge—for it has no other base from which it may operate, or begin its assault upon truth—yet let it fall back upon itself. For God also, the all-embracing world and the ruler of the universe, reaches forth into outward things, yet, withdrawing from all sides, returns into himself. And our mind should do the same; when, having followed the senses that serve it, it has through them reached to things without, let it be the master both of them and of itself. In this way will be born an energy that is united, a power that is at harmony with itself, and that dependable reason which is not divided against itself, nor uncertain either in its opinions, or its perceptions, or in its convictions; and this reason, when it has regulated itself, and established harmony between all its parts, and, so to speak, is in tune, has attained the highest good. For no crookedness, no slipperiness is left to it, nothing that will cause it to stumble or fall. It will do everything under its own authority and nothing unexpected will befall it, but whatever it does will turn out a good, and that, too, easily and readily and without subterfuge on the part of the doer; for reluctance and hesitation are an indication of conflict and instability. Wherefore you may boldly declare that the highest good is harmony of the soul; for where concord and unity are, there must the virtues be. Discord accompanies the vices.

From On Tranquillity of Mind

Let a man, however, hide himself away bearing in mind that, wherever he secretes his leisure, he should be willing to benefit the individual man and mankind by his intellect, his voice, and his counsel. For the man that does good service to the state is not merely he who brings forward candidates and defends the accused and votes for peace and war, but he also who admonishes young men, who instils virtue into their minds, supplying the great lack of good teachers, who lays hold upon those that are rushing wildly in pursuit of money and luxury, and draws them back, and, if he accomplishes nothing else, at least retards them—such a man performs a public service even in private life. Or does he accomplish more who in the office of praetor, whether in cases between citizens and foreigners or in cases between citizens, delivers to suitors the verdict his assistant has formulated, than he who teaches the meaning of justice, of pity, of endurance, of bravery, of contempt of death, of knowledge of the gods, and how secure and free is the blessing of a good conscience? If, then, the time that you have stolen from public duties is bestowed upon studies, you will neither have deserted, nor refused, your office. For a soldier is not merely one who stands in line and defends the right or the left wing, but he also who guards the gates and fills, not an idle, but a less dangerous, post, who keeps watch at night and has charge of the armoury; these offices, though they are bloodless, yet count as military service. If you devote yourself to studies, you will have escaped all your disgust at life, you will not long for night to come because you are weary of the light, nor will you be either burdensome to yourself or useless to others; you will attract many to friendship and those that gather about you will be the most excellent. For virtue, though obscured, is never concealed, but always gives signs of its presence; whoever is worthy will trace her out by her footsteps. But if we give up society altogether and, turning our backs upon the human race, live with our thoughts fixed only upon ourselves, this solitude deprived of every interest will be followed by a want of something to be accomplished. We shall begin to put up some buildings, to pull down others, to thrust back the sea, to cause waters to flow despite the obstacles of nature, and shall make ill disposition of the time which Nature has given us to be used. Some use it sparingly, others wastefully; some of us spend it in such a way that we are able to give an account of it, others in such a way—and nothing can be more shameful—that we have no balance left. Often a man who is very old in years has no evidence to prove that he has lived a long time other than his age.

To me, my dearest Serenus, Athenodorus seems to have surrendered too quickly to the times, to have retreated too quickly. I myself would not deny that sometimes one must retire, but it should be a gradual

Reprinted by permission of the publishers and The Loeb Classical Library from *Moral Essays*, Vol. II, Seneca, trans. by John W. Basore, Cambridge, Mass.: Harvard University Press, 1932. (pp. 223–235)

retreat without surrendering the standards, without surrendering the honour of a soldier; those are more respected by their enemies and safer who come to terms with their arms in their hands. This is what I think Virtue and Virtue's devotee should do. If Fortune shall get the upper hand and shall cut off the opportunity for action, let a man not straightway turn his back and flee, throwing away his arms and seeking some hiding-place, as if there were anywhere a place where Fortune could not reach him, but let him devote himself to his duties more sparingly, and, after making choice, let him find something in which he may be useful to the state. Is he not permitted to be a soldier? Let him seek public office. Must he live in a private station? Let him be a pleader. Is he condemned to silence? Let him help his countrymen by his silent support. Is it dangerous even to enter the forum? In private houses, at the public spectacles, at feasts, let him show himself a good comrade, a faithful friend, a temperate feaster. Has he lost the duties of a citizen? Let him exercise those of a man. The very reason for our magnanimity in not shutting ourselves up within the walls of one city, in going forth into intercourse with the whole earth, and in claiming the world as our country, was that we might have a wider field for our virtue. Is the tribunal closed to you, and are you barred from the rostrum and the hustings? Look how many broad stretching countries lie open behind you, how many peoples; never can you be blocked from any part so large that a still larger will not be left to you. But take care that this is not wholly your own fault; you are not willing to serve the state except as a consul or prytanis or herald or sufete. What if you should be unwilling to serve in the army except as a general or a tribune? Even if others shall hold the front line and your lot has placed you among those of the third line, from there where you are do service with your voice, encouragement, example, and spirit; even though a man's hands are cut off, he finds that he can do something for his side in battle if he stands his ground and helps with the shouting. Some such thing is what you should do. If Fortune has removed you from the foremost position in the state, you should, nevertheless, stand your ground and help with the shouting, and if someone stops your throat, you should, nevertheless, stand your ground and help in silence. The service of a good citizen is never useless; by being heard and seen, by his expression, by his gesture, by his silent stubbornness, and by his very walk he helps. As there are certain salutary things that without our tasting and touching them benefit us by their mere odour, so virtue sheds her advantage even from a distance, and in hiding. Whether she walks abroad and of her own right makes herself active, or has her appearances on sufferance and is forced to draw in her sails, or is inactive and mute and pent within narrow bounds, or is openly displayed, no matter what her condition is, she always does good. Why, then, do *you* think that the example of one who lives in honourable retirement is of little value? Accordingly, the best course by far is to combine leisure with business, whenever chance obstacles or the condition of the state shall prevent one's living a really active life; for a man is never so completely shut off from all pursuits that no opportunity is left for any honourable activity.

Can you find any city more wretched than was that of the Athenians when it was being torn to pieces by the Thirty Tyrants? They had slain thirteen hundred citizens, all the best men, and were not for that reason ready to stop, but their very cruelty fed its own flame. In the city in which there was the Areopagus, a most god-fearing court, in which there was a senate and a popular assembly that was like a senate, there gathered together every day a sorry college of hangmen, and the unhappy senate-house was made too narrow by tyrants! Could that city ever find peace in which there were as many tyrants as there might be satellites? No hope even of recovering liberty could offer itself, nor did there seem to be room for any sort of help against such mighty strength of wicked men. For where could the wretched state find enough Harmodiuses? Yet Socrates was in their midst and comforted the mourning city fathers, he encouraged those that were despairing of the state, reproached the rich men that were now dreading their wealth with a too late repentance of their perilous greed, while to those willing to imitate him he carried round with him a great example, as he moved a free man amid thirty masters. Yet this was the man that Athens herself murdered in prison, and Freedom herself could not endure the freedom of one who had mocked in security at a whole band of tyrants. And so you may learn both that the wise man has opportunity to display his power when the state is torn by trouble, and that effrontery, envy, and a thousand other cowardly vices hold sway when it is prosperous and happy. Therefore we shall either expand or contract our effort according as the state shall lend herself to us, according as Fortune shall permit us, but in any case we shall keep moving, and shall not be tied down and numbed by fear. Nay, he will be truly a man who, when perils are threatening from every side, when arms and chains are rattling around him, will neither endanger, nor conceal, his virtue; for saving oneself does not mean burying oneself. Curius Dentatus said, truly as I think, that he would rather be a dead man than a live one dead; for the worst of ills is to leave the number of the living before you die. But if you should happen upon a time when it is not at all easy to serve the state, your necessary course will be to claim more time for leisure and for letters, and, just as if you were making a perilous voyage, to put into harbour from time to time, and, without waiting for public affairs to release you, to separate yourself from them of your own accord.

EPICTETUS

Born in Hierapolis, in Asia Minor, Epictetus (ca. A.D. 50–ca. A.D. 130) was a slave until A.D. 68, when he was given his freedom by an official in the Roman government. He was sent to study with the Stoic teacher Rufus and became deeply committed to the thought and practice of the Stoics. He later founded a school while in exile at Epirus. His teachings were characterized by an extreme dependence on divine providence and by an absence of political and social involvement. He stressed the absolute responsibility of individuals for their own actions, and he pitied those who did wrong, believing that they suffered more than their victims. Epictetus was profoundly humble as a person and he lived a very abstemious life of self-sacrifice. The works of Epictetus were not published, so the versions we have were prepared from lecture notes taken by his student Flavius Arrianus. The following selection is from the Manual of Epictetus. *Known also as the* Enchiridion, *this work is a distillation by Arrianus of Epictetus'* Discourses.

The Manual of Epictetus

1

Of all existing things some are in our power, and others are not in our power. In our power are thought, impulse, will to get and will to avoid, and, in a word, everything which is our own doing. Things not in our power include the body, property, reputation, office, and, in a word, everything which is not our own doing. Things in our power are by nature free, unhindered, untrammelled; things not in our power are weak, servile, subject to hindrance, dependent on others. Remember then that if you imagine that what is naturally slavish is free, and what is naturally another's is your own, you will be hampered, you will mourn, you will be put to confusion, you will blame gods and men; but if you think that only your own belongs to you, and that what is another's is indeed another's, no one will ever put compulsion or hindrance on you, you will blame none, you will accuse none, you will do nothing against your will, no one will harm you, you will have no enemy, for no harm can touch you.

Aiming then at these high matters, you must remember that to attain them requires more than ordinary effort; you will have to give up some things entirely, and put off others for the moment. And if you would have these also—office and wealth—it may be that you will fail to get them, just because

From *The Stoic and Epicurean Philosophers,* edited by Whitney J. Oates (New York: Random House, Inc., 1940), pp. 468–484. Originally published in *Epictetus: The Discourses and Manual,* translated by P. E. Matheson (Oxford: Oxford University Press, 1917). Reprinted by permission of Oxford University Press.

your desire is set on the former, and you will certainly fail to attain those things which alone bring freedom and happiness.

Make it your study then to confront every harsh impression with the words, 'You are but an impression, and not at all what you seem to be'. Then test it by those rules that you possess; and first by this—the chief test of all—'Is it concerned with what is in our power or with what is not in our power?' And if it is concerned with what is not in our power, be ready with the answer that it is nothing to you.

2

Remember that the will to get promises attainment of what you will, and the will to avoid promises escape from what you avoid; and he who fails to get what he wills is unfortunate, and he who does not escape what he wills to avoid is miserable. If then you try to avoid only what is unnatural in the region within your control, you will escape from all that you avoid; but if you try to avoid disease or death or poverty you will be miserable.

Therefore let your will to avoid have no concern with what is not in man's power; direct it only to things in man's power that are contrary to nature. But for the moment you must utterly remove the will to get; for if you will to get something not in man's power you are bound to be unfortunate; while none of the things in man's power that you could honourably will to get is yet within your reach. Impulse to act and not to act, these are your concern; yet exercise them gently and without strain, and provisionally.

3

When anything, from the meanest thing upwards, is attractive or serviceable or an object of affection, remember always to say to yourself, 'What is its nature?' If you are fond of a jug, say you are fond of a jug; then you will not be disturbed if it be broken. If you kiss your child or your wife, say to yourself that you are kissing a human being, for then if death strikes it you will not be disturbed.

4

When you are about to take something in hand, remind yourself what manner of thing it is. If you are going to bathe put before your mind what happens in the bath—water pouring over some, others being jostled, some reviling, others stealing; and you will set to work more securely if you say to yourself at once: 'I want to bathe, and I want to keep my will in harmony with nature,' and so in each thing you do; for in this way, if anything turns up to hinder you in your bathing, you will be ready to say, 'I did not want only to bathe, but to keep my will in harmony with nature, and I shall not so keep it, if I lose my temper at what happens'.

5

What disturbs men's minds is not events but their judgements on events. For instance, death is nothing dreadful, or else Socrates would have thought it so. No, the only dreadful thing about it is men's judgement that it is dreadful. And so when we are hindered, or disturbed, or distressed, let us never lay the blame on others, but on ourselves, that is, on our own judgements. To accuse others for one's own misfortunes is a sign of want of education; to accuse oneself shows that one's education has begun; to accuse neither oneself nor others shows that one's education is complete.

6

Be not elated at an excellence which is not your own. If the horse in his pride were to say, 'I am handsome', we could bear with it. But when you say with pride, 'I have a handsome horse', know that the good horse is the ground of your pride. You ask then what you can call your own. The answer is—the way you deal with your impressions. Therefore when you deal with your impressions in accord with nature, then you may be proud indeed, for your pride will be in a good which is your own.

7

When you are on a voyage, and your ship is at anchorage, and you disembark to get fresh water, you may pick up a small shellfish or a truffle by the way, but you must keep your attention fixed on the ship, and keep looking towards it constantly, to see if the Helmsman calls you; and if he does, you have to leave everything, or be bundled on board with your legs tied like a sheep. So it is in life. If you have a dear wife or child given you, they are like the shell-fish or the truffle, they are very well in their way. Only, if the Helmsman call, run back to your ship, leave all else, and do not look behind you. And if you are old, never go far from the ship, so that when you are called you may not fail to appear.

8

Ask not that events should happen as you will, but let your will be that events should happen as they do, and you shall have peace.

9

Sickness is a hindrance to the body, but not to the will, unless the will consent. Lameness is a hindrance to the leg, but not to the will. Say this to yourself at each event that happens, for you shall find that though it hinders something else it will not hinder you.

10

When anything happens to you, always remember to turn to yourself and ask what faculty you have to deal with it. If you see a beautiful boy or a beautiful woman, you will find continence the faculty to exercise there; if trouble is laid on you, you will find endurance; if ribaldry, you will find patience. And if you train yourself in this habit your impressions will not carry you away.

11

Never say of anything, 'I lost it', but say, 'I gave it back'. Has your child died? It was given back. Has your wife died? She was given back. Has your estate been taken from you? Was not this also given back? But you say, 'He who took it from me is wicked'. What does it matter to you through whom the Giver asked it back? As long as He gives it you, take care of it, but not as your own; treat it as passers-by treat an inn.

12

If you wish to make progress, abandon reasonings of this sort: 'If I neglect my affairs I shall have nothing to live on'; 'If I do not punish my son, he will be wicked.' For it is better to die of hunger, so that you be free from pain and free from fear, than to live in plenty and be troubled in mind. It is better for your son to be wicked than for you to be miserable. Wherefore begin with little things. Is your drop of oil spilt? Is your sup of wine stolen? Say to yourself, 'This is the price paid for freedom from passion, this is the price of a quiet mind.' Nothing can be had without a price. When you call your slave-boy, reflect that he may not be able to hear you, and if he hears you, he may not be able to do anything you want. But he is not so well off that it rests with him to give you peace of mind.

13

If you wish to make progress, you must be content in external matters to seem a fool and a simpleton; do not wish men to think you know anything, and if any should think you to be somebody, distrust yourself. For know that it is not easy to keep your will in accord with nature and at the same time keep outward things; if you attend to one you must needs neglect the other.

14

It is silly to want your children and your wife and your friends to live for ever; for that means that you want what is not in your control to be in your control, and what is not your own to be yours. In the same way if you want your servant to make no mistakes, you are a fool, for you want vice not to be vice but something different. But if you want not to be disappointed in your will to get, you can attain to that.

Exercise yourself then in what lies in your power. Each man's master is the man who has authority over what he wishes or does not wish, to secure the one or to take away the other. Let him then who wishes to be free not wish for anything or avoid anything that depends on others; or else he is bound to be a slave.

15

Remember that you must behave in life as you would at a banquet. A dish is handed round and comes to you; put out your hand and take it politely. It passes you; do not stop it. It has not reached you;

do not be impatient to get it, but wait till your turn comes. Bear yourself thus towards children, wife, office, wealth, and one day you will be worthy to banquet with the gods. But if when they are set before you, you do not take them but despise them, then you shall not only share the gods' banquet, but shall share their rule. For by so doing Diogenes and Heraclitus and men like them were called divine and deserved the name.

16

When you see a man shedding tears in sorrow for a child abroad or dead, or for loss of property, beware that you are not carried away by the impression that it is outward ills that make him miserable. Keep this thought by you: 'What distresses him is not the event, for that does not distress another, but his judgement on the event.' Therefore do not hesitate to sympathize with him so far as words go, and if it so chance, even to groan with him; but take heed that you do not also groan in your inner being.

17

Remember that you are an actor in a play, and the Playwright chooses the manner of it: if he wants it short, it is short; if long, it is long. If he wants you to act a poor man you must act the part with all your powers; and so if your part be a cripple or a magistrate or a plain man. For your business is to act the character that is given you and act it well; the choice of the cast is Another's.

18

When a raven croaks with evil omen, let not the impression carry you away, but straightway distinguish in your own mind and say, 'These portents mean nothing to me; but only to my bit of a body or my bit of property or name, or my children or my wife. But for me all omens are favourable if I will, for, whatever the issue may be, it is in my power to get benefit therefrom.'

19

You can be invincible, if you never enter on a contest where victory is not in your power. Beware then that when you see a man raised to honour or great power or high repute you do not let your impression carry you away. For if the reality of good lies in what is in our power, there is no room for envy or jealousy. And you will not wish to be praetor, or prefect or consul, but to be free; and there is but one way to freedom—to despise what is not in our power.

20

Remember that foul words or blows in themselves are no outrage, but your judgement that they are so. So when any one makes you angry, know that it is your own thought that has angered you. Wherefore make it your first endeavour not to let your impressions carry you away. For if once you gain time and delay, you will find it easier to control yourself.

21

Keep before your eyes from day to day death and exile and all things that seem terrible, but death most of all, and then you will never set your thoughts on what is low and will never desire anything beyond measure.

22

If you set your desire on philosophy you must at once prepare to meet with ridicule and the jeers of many who will say, 'Here he is again, turned philosopher. Where has he got these proud looks?' Nay, put on no proud looks, but hold fast to what seems best to you, in confidence that God has set you at this post. And remember that if you abide where you are, those who first laugh at you will one day admire you, and that if you give way to them, you will get doubly laughed at.

23

If it ever happen to you to be diverted to things outside, so that you desire to please another, know that you have lost your life's plan. Be content then always to be a philosopher; if you wish to be regarded as one too, show yourself that you are one and you will be able to achieve it.

24

Let not reflections such as these afflict you: 'I shall live without honour, and never be of any account';

for if lack of honour is an evil, no one but yourself can involve you in evil any more than in shame. Is it your business to get office or to be invited to an entertainment?

Certainly not.

Where then is the dishonour you talk of? How can you be 'of no account anywhere', when you ought to count for something in those matters only which are in your power, where you may achieve the highest worth?

'But my friends,' you say, 'will lack assistance.'

What do you mean by 'lack assistance'? They will not have cash from you and you will not make them Roman citizens. Who told you that to do these things is in our power, and not dependent upon others? Who can give to another what is not his to give?

'Get them then,' says he, 'that we may have them.'

If I can get them and keep my self-respect, honour, magnanimity, show the way and I will get them. But if you call on me to lose the good things that are mine, in order that you may win things that are not good, look how unfair and thoughtless you are. And which do you really prefer? Money, or a faithful, modest friend? Therefore help me rather to keep these qualities, and do not expect from me actions which will make me lose them.

'But my country,' says he, 'will lack assistance, so far as lies in me.'

Once more I ask, What assistance do you mean? It will not owe colonnades or baths to you. What of that? It does not owe shoes to the blacksmith or arms to the shoemaker; it is sufficient if each man fulfils his own function. Would you do it no good if you secured to it another faithful and modest citizen?

'Yes.'

Well, then, you would not be useless to it.

'What place then shall I have in the city?'

Whatever place you can hold while you keep your character for honour and self-respect. But if you are going to lose these qualities in trying to benefit your city, what benefit, I ask, would you have done her when you attain to the perfection of being lost to shame and honour?

25

Has some one had precedence of you at an entertainment or a levée or been called in before you to give advice? If these things are good you ought to be glad that he got them; if they are evil, do not be angry that you did not get them yourself. Remember that if you want to get what is not in your power, you cannot earn the same reward as others unless you act as they do. How is it possible for one who does not haunt the great man's door to have equal shares with one who does, or one who does not go in his train equality with one who does; or one who does not praise him with one who does? You will be unjust then and insatiable if you wish to get these privileges for nothing, without paying their price. What is the price of a lettuce? An obol perhaps. If then a man pays his obol and get his lettuces, and you do not pay and do not get them, do not think you are defrauded. For as he has the lettuces so you have the obol you did not give. The same principle holds good too in conduct. You were not invited to some one's entertainment? Because you did not give the host the price for which he sells his dinner. He sells it for compliments, he sells it for attentions. Pay him the price then, if it is to your profit. But if you wish to get the one and yet not give up the other, nothing can satisfy you in your folly.

What! you say, you have nothing instead of the dinner?

Nay, you have this, you have not praised the man you did not want to praise, you have not had to bear with the insults of his doorstep.

26

It is in our power to discover the will of Nature from those matters on which we have no difference of opinion. For instance, when another man's slave has broken the wine-cup we are very ready to say at once, 'Such things must happen'. Know then that when your own cup is broken, you ought to behave in the same way as when your neighbour's was broken. Apply the same principle to higher matters. Is another's child or wife dead? Not one of us but would say, 'Such is the lot of man'; but when one's own dies, straightway one cries, 'Alas! miserable am I'. But we ought to remember what our feelings are when we hear it of another.

27

As a mark is not set up for men to miss it, so there is nothing intrinsically evil in the world.

28

If any one trusted your body to the first man he met, you would be indignant, but yet you trust your mind to the chance comer, and allow it to be disturbed and confounded if he revile you; are you not ashamed to do so?

29

In everything you do consider what comes first and what follows, and so approach it. Otherwise you will come to it with a good heart at first because you have not reflected on any of the consequences, and afterwards, when difficulties have appeared, you will desist to your shame. Do you wish to win at Olympia? So do I, by the gods, for it is a fine thing. But consider the first steps to it, and the consequences, and so lay your hand to the work. You must submit to discipline, eat to order, touch no sweets, train under compulsion, at a fixed hour, in heat and cold, drink no cold water, nor wine, except by order; you must hand yourself over completely to your trainer as you would to a physician, and then when the contest comes you must risk getting hacked, and sometimes dislocate your hand, twist your ankle, swallow plenty of sand, sometimes get a flogging, and with all this suffer defeat. When you have considered all this well, then enter on the athlete's course, if you still wish it. If you act without thought you will be behaving like children, who one day play at wrestlers, another day at gladiators, now sound the trumpet, and next strut the stage. Like them you will be now an athlete, now a gladiator, then orator, then philosopher, but nothing with all your soul. Like an ape, you imitate every sight you see, and one thing after another takes your fancy. When you undertake a thing you do it casually and halfheartedly, instead of considering it and looking at it all round. In the same way some people, when they see a philosopher and hear a man speaking like Euphrates (and indeed who can speak as he can?), wish to be philosophers themselves.

Man, consider first what it is you are undertaking; then look at your own powers and see if you can bear it. Do you want to compete in the pentathlon or in wrestling? Look to your arms, your thighs, see what your loins are like. For different men are born for different tasks. Do you suppose that if you do this you can live as you do now—eat and drink as you do now, indulge desire and discontent just as before? Nay, you must sit up late, work hard, abandon your own people, be looked down on by a mere slave, be ridiculed by those who meet you, get the worst of it in everything—in honour, in office, in justice, in every possible thing. This is what you have to consider: whether you are willing to pay this price for peace of mind, freedom, tranquillity. If not, do not come near; do not be, like the children, first a philosopher, then a tax-collector, then an orator, then one of Caesar's procurators. These callings do not agree. You must be one man, good or bad; you must develop either your Governing Principle, or your outward endowments; you must study either your inner man, or outward things—in a word, you must choose between the position of a philosopher and that of a mere outsider.

30

Appropriate acts are in general measured by the relations they are concerned with. 'He is your father.' This means you are called on to take care of him, give way to him in all things, bear with him if he reviles or strikes you.

'But he is a bad father.'

Well, have you any natural claim to a good father? No, only to a father.

'My brother wrongs me.'

Be careful then to maintain the relation you hold to him, and do not consider what he does, but what you must do if your purpose is to keep in accord with nature. For no one shall harm you, without your consent; you will only be harmed, when you think you are harmed. You will only discover what is proper to expect from neighbour, citizen, or praetor, if you get into the habit of looking at the relations implied by each.

31

For piety towards the gods know that the most important thing is this: to have right opinions about them—that they exist, and that they govern the universe well and justly—and to have set yourself to obey them, and to give way to all that happens, following events with a free will, in the belief that they are fulfilled by the highest mind. For thus you will never blame the gods, nor accuse them of neglecting you. But this you cannot achieve, unless you apply your conception of good and evil to those things only which are in our power, and not to those which are out of our power. For if you apply your notion of good or evil to the latter, then, as soon as you fail to get what you will to get or fail to avoid what you will to avoid, you will be bound to blame and hate those you hold responsible. For every living creature has a natural tendency to avoid and shun what seems harmful and all that causes it, and to pursue and admire what is helpful and all that causes it. It is not possible then for one who thinks he is harmed to take pleasure in what he thinks is the author of the harm, anymore than to take pleasure in the harm itself. That is why a father is reviled by his son, when he does not give his son a share of what the son regards as good things; thus Polynices and Eteocles were set at enmity with one another by thinking that a king's throne was a good thing. That is why the farmer, and the sailor, and the merchant, and those who lose wife or children revile the gods. For men's religion is bound up with their interest. Therefore he who makes it his concern rightly to direct his will to get and his will to avoid, is thereby making piety his concern. But it is proper on each occasion to make libation and sacrifice and to offer first-fruits according to the custom of our fathers, with purity and not in slovenly or careless fashion, without meanness and without extravagance.

32

When you make use of prophecy remember that while you know not what the issue will be, but are come to learn it from the prophet, you do know before you come what manner of thing it is, if you are really a philosopher. For if the event is not in our control, it cannot be either good or evil. Therefore do not bring with you to the prophet the will to get or the will to avoid, and do not approach him with trembling, but with your mind made up, that the whole issue is indifferent and does not affect you and that, whatever it be, it will be in your power to make good use of it, and no one shall hinder this. With confidence then approach the gods as counsellors, and further, when the counsel is given you, remember whose counsel it is, and whom you will be disregarding if you disobey. And consult the oracle, as Socrates thought men should, only when the whole question turns upon the issue of events, and neither reason nor any art of man provides opportunities for discovering what lies before you. Therefore, when it is your duty to risk your life with friend or country, do not ask the oracle whether you should risk your life. For if the prophet warns you that the sacrifice is unfavourable, though it is plain that this means death or exile or injury to some part of your body, yet reason requires that even at this cost you must stand by your friend and share your country's danger. Wherefore pay heed to the greater prophet, Pythian Apollo, who cast out of his temple the man who did not help his friend when he was being killed.

33

Lay down for yourself from the first a definite stamp and style of conduct, which you will maintain when you are alone and also in the society of men. Be silent for the most part, or, if you speak, say only what is necessary and in a few words. Talk, but rarely, if occasion calls you, but do not talk of ordinary things—of gladiators, or horse-races, or athletes, or of meats or drinks—these are topics that arise everywhere—but above all do not talk about men in blame or compliment or comparison. If you can, turn the conversation of your company by your talk to some fitting subject; but if you should chance to be isolated among strangers, be silent. Do not laugh much, nor at many things, nor without restraint.

Refuse to take oaths, altogether if that be possible, but if not, as far as circumstances allow.

Refuse the entertainments of strangers and the vulgar. But if occasion arise to accept them, then strain every nerve to avoid lapsing into the state of the vulgar. For know that, if your comrade have a stain on him, he that associates with him must needs share the stain, even though he be clean in himself.

For your body take just so much as your bare need requires, such as food, drink, clothing, house, servants, but cut down all that tends to luxury and outward show.

Avoid impurity to the utmost of your power before marriage, and if you indulge your passion, let it be done lawfully. But do not be offensive or censorious to those who indulge it, and do not be always bringing up your own chastity. If some one tells you that so and so speaks ill of you, do not defend yourself against what he says, but answer, 'He did not know my other faults, or he would not have mentioned these alone.'

It is not necessary for the most part to go to the games; but if you should have occasion to go, show that your first concern is for yourself; that is, wish that only to happen which does happen, and him only to win who does win, for so you will suffer no hindrance. But refrain entirely from applause, or ridicule, or prolonged excitement. And when you go away do not talk much of what happened there, except as far as it tends to your improvement. For to talk about it implies that the spectacle excited your wonder.

Do not go lightly or casually to hear lectures; but if you do go, maintain your gravity and dignity and do not make yourself offensive. When you are going to meet any one, and particularly some man of reputed eminence, set before your mind the thought, 'What would Socrates or Zeno have done?' and you will not fail to make proper use of the occasion.

When you go to visit some great man, prepare your mind by thinking that you will not find him in, that you will be shut out, that the doors will be slammed in your face, that he will pay no heed to you. And if in spite of all this you find it fitting for you to go, go and bear what happens and never say to yourself, 'It was not worth all this'; for that shows a vulgar mind and one at odds with outward things.

In your conversation avoid frequent and disproportionate mention of your own doings or adventures; for other people do not take the same pleasure in hearing what has happened to you as you take in recounting your adventures.

Avoid raising men's laughter; for it is a habit that easily slips into vulgarity, and it may well suffice to lessen your neighbour's respect.

It is dangerous too to lapse into foul language; when anything of the kind occurs, rebuke the offender, if the occasion allow, and if not, make it plain to him by your silence, or a blush or a frown, that you are angry at his words.

34

When you imagine some pleasure, beware that it does not carry you away, like other imaginations. Wait a while, and give yourself pause. Next remember two things: how long you will enjoy the pleasure, and also how long you will afterwards repent and revile yourself. And set on the other side the joy and self-satisfaction you will feel if you refrain. And if the moment seems come to realize it, take heed that you be not overcome by the winning sweetness and attraction of it; set in the other scale the thought how much better is the consciousness of having vanquished it.

35

When you do a thing because you have determined that it ought to be done, never avoid being seen doing it, even if the opinion of the multitude is going to condemn you. For if your action is wrong, then avoid doing it altogether, but if it is right, why do you fear those who will rebuke you wrongly?

36

The phrases, 'It is day' and 'It is night', mean a great deal if taken separately, but have no meaning if combined. In the same way, to choose the larger portion at a banquet may be worth while for your body, but if you want to maintain social decencies it is worthless. Therefore, when you are at meat with another, remember not only to consider the value of what is set before you for the body, but also to maintain your self-respect before your host.

37

If you try to act a part beyond your powers, you not only disgrace yourself in it, but you neglect the part which you could have filled with success.

38

As in walking you take care not to tread on a nail or to twist your foot, so take care that you do not harm your Governing Principle. And if we guard this in everything we do, we shall set to work more securely.

39

Every man's body is a measure of his property, as the foot is the measure for his shoe. If you stick to this limit, you will keep the right measure; if you go beyond it, you are bound to be carried away down a precipice in the end; just as with the shoe, if you once go beyond the foot, your shoe puts on gilding, and soon purple and embroidery. For when once you go beyond the measure there is no limit.

40

Women from fourteen years upwards are called 'madam' by men. Wherefore, when they see that the only advantage they have got is to be marriageable, they begin to make themselves smart and to set all their hopes on this. We must take pains then to make them understand that they are really honoured for nothing but a modest and decorous life.

41

It is a sign of a dull mind to dwell upon the cares of the body, to prolong exercise, eating, drinking, and other bodily functions. These things are to be done by the way; all your attention must be given to the mind.

42

When a man speaks evil or does evil to you, remember that he does or says it because he thinks it is fitting for him. It is not possible for him to follow what seems good to you, but only what seems good to him, so that, if his opinion is wrong, he suffers, in that he is the victim of deception. In the same way, if a composite judgement which is true is thought to be false, it is not the judgement that suffers, but the man who is deluded about it. If you act on this principle you will be gentle to him who reviles you, saying to yourself on each occasion, 'He thought it right.'

43

Everything has two handles, one by which you can carry it, the other by which you cannot. If your brother wrongs you, do not take it by that handle, the handle of his wrong, for you cannot carry it by that, but rather by the other handle—that he is a brother, brought up with you, and then you will take it by the handle that you can carry by.

44

It is illogical to reason thus, 'I am richer than you, therefore I am superior to you', 'I am more eloquent than you, therefore I am superior to you.' It is more logical to reason, 'I am richer than you, therefore my property is superior to yours', I am more eloquent than you, therefore my speech is superior to yours.' You are something more than property or speech.

45

If a man wash quickly, do not say that he washes badly, but that he washes quickly. If a man drink much wine, do not say that he drinks badly, but that he drinks much. For till you have decided what judgement prompts him, how do you know that he acts badly? If you do as I say, you will assent to your apprehensive impressions and to none other.

46

On no occasion call yourself a philosopher, nor talk at large of your principles among the multitude, but act on your principles. For instance, at a banquet do not say how one ought to eat, but eat as you ought. Remember that Socrates had so completely got rid of the thought of display that when men came and wanted an introduction to philosophers he took them to be introduced; so patient of neglect was he. And if a discussion arise among the multitude on some principle, keep silent for the most part; for you are in great danger of blurting out some undigested thought. And when some one says to you, 'You know nothing', and you do not let it provoke you, then know that you are really on the right road. For sheep do not bring grass to their shepherds and show them how much they have eaten, but they digest their fodder and then produce it in the form of wool and milk. Do the same yourself; instead of displaying your principles to the multitude, show them the results of the principles you have digested.

47

When you have adopted the simple life, do not pride yourself upon it, and if you are a water-drinker do not say on every occasion, 'I am a water-drinker.' And if you ever want to train laboriously, keep it to yourself and do not make a show of it. Do not embrace statues. If you are very thirsty take a good draught of cold water, and rinse your mouth and tell no one.

48

The ignorant man's position and character is this: he never looks to himself for benefit or harm, but to the world outside him. The philosopher's position and character is that he always look to himself for benefit and harm.

The signs of one who is making progress are: he blames none, praises none, complains of none, accuses none, never speaks of himself as if he were somebody, or as if he knew anything. And if any one compliments him he laughs in himself at his compliment; and if one blames him, he makes no defence. He goes about like a convalescent, careful not to disturb his constitution on its road to recovery, until it has got firm hold. He has got rid of the will to get, and his will to avoid is directed no longer to what is beyond our power but only to what is in our power and contrary to nature. In all things he exercises his will without strain. If men regard him as foolish or ignorant he pays no heed. In one word, he keeps watch and guard on himself as his own enemy, lying in wait for him.

49

When a man prides himself on being able to understand and interpret the books of Chrysippus, say to yourself, 'If Chrysippus had not written obscurely this man would have had nothing on which to pride himself.'

What is my object? To understand Nature and follow her. I look then for some one who interprets her, and having heard that Chrysippus does I come to him. But I do not understand his writings, so I seek an interpreter. So far there is nothing to be proud of. But when I have found the interpreter it remains for me to act on his precepts; that and that alone is a thing to be proud of. But if I admire the mere power of exposition, it comes to this—that I am turned into a grammarian instead of a philosopher, except that I interpret Chrysippus in place of Homer. Therefore, when some one says to me, 'Read me Chrysippus', when I cannot point to actions which are in harmony and correspondence with his teaching, I am rather inclined to blush.

50

Whatever principles you put before you, hold fast to them as laws which it will be impious to transgress. But pay no heed to what any one says of you; for this is something beyond your own control.

51

How long will you wait to think yourself worthy of the highest and transgress in nothing the clear pronouncement of reason? You have received the precepts which you ought to accept, and you have accepted them. Why then do you still wait for a master, that you may delay the amendment of yourself till he comes? You are a youth no longer, you are now a full-grown man. If now you are careless and indolent and are always putting off, fixing one day after another as the limit when you mean to begin attending to yourself, then, living or dying, you will make no progress but will continue unawares in ignorance. Therefore make up your mind before it is too late to live as one who is mature and proficient, and let all that seems best to you be a law that you cannot transgress. And if you encounter anything troublesome or pleasant or glorious or inglorious, remember that the hour of struggle is come, the Olympic contest is here and you may put off no longer, and that one day and one action determines whether the progress you have achieved is lost or maintained.

This was how Socrates attained perfection, paying heed to nothing but reason, in all that he encountered. And if you are not yet Socrates, yet ought you to live as one who would wish to be a Socrates.

52

The first and most necessary department of philosophy deals with the application of principles; for instance, 'not to lie.' The second deals with demonstrations; for instance, 'How comes it that one ought not to lie?' The third is concerned with establishing and analysing these processes; for instance, 'How comes it that this is a demonstration? What is demonstration, what is consequence, what is contradiction, what is true, what is false?' It follows then that the third department is necessary because of the second, and the second because of the first. The first is the most necessary part, and that in which we must rest. But we reverse the order: we occupy ourselves with the third, and make that our whole concern, and the first we completely neglect. Wherefore we lie, but are ready enough with the demonstration that lying is wrong.

53

On every occasion we must have these thoughts at hand,

'Lead me, O Zeus, and lead me, Destiny,
Whither ordainèd is by your decree.
I'll follow, doubting not, or if with will
Recreant I falter, I shall follow still.'
[Cleanthes]

'Who rightly with necessity complies
In things divine we count him skilled and wise.' [Euripides]

'Well, Crito, if this be the gods' will, so be it.' [Plato, *Crito*]

'Anytus and Meletus have power to put me to death,
but not to harm me.' [Plato, *Apology*]

MARCUS AURELIUS

Born in A.D. 121, Marcus Aurelius was both an emperor of Rome and a Stoic philosopher. He became emperor in A.D. 161, and for the next 19 years, until his death in A.D. 180, he waged many wars against threats to the Empire—both from without, as in the invasion of the Quadi and Marcomanni, and from within, as in the treason of Avidius Cassius. Throughout these perils, Aurelius distinguished himself by his administrative skill, and above all, by his compassion for the vanquished.

It was during his battles in the region of the river Danube that Aurelius composed his Meditations. *Written in Greek, they constitute one of the most profound moral self-explorations of classical literature. Aurelius bemoans the transient character of human life and concludes that only an acceptance of the eternal law of nature will provide life with sufficient meaning.*

The following selection is from The Meditations. *Seldom has a person of such high political importance reached an equivalently deep moral and philosophical point of view.*

From The Meditations

BOOK II

Begin the morning by saying to thyself, I shall meet with the busy-body, the ungrateful, arrogant, deceitful, envious, unsocial. All these things happen to them by reason of their ignorance of what is good and evil. But I who have seen the nature of the good that it is beautiful, and of the bad that it is ugly, and the nature of him who does wrong, that it is akin to me, not only of the same blood or seed, but that it participates in the same intelligence and the same portion of the divinity, I can neither be injured by any of them, for no one can fix on me what is ugly, nor can I be angry with my kinsman, nor hate him. For we are made for co-operation, like feet, like hands, like eyelids, like the rows of the upper and lower teeth. To act against one another then is contrary to nature; and it is acting against one another to be vexed and to turn away.

2. Whatever this is that I am, it is a little flesh and breath, and the ruling part. Throw away thy books; no longer distract thyself: it is not allowed; but as if thou wast now dying, despise the flesh; it is blood and bones and a network, a contexture of nerves, veins, and arteries. See the breath also, what kind of a thing it is, air, and not always the same, but every

moment sent out and again sucked in. The third then is the ruling part: consider thus: Thou art an old man; no longer let this be a slave, no longer be pulled by the strings like a puppet to unsocial movements, no longer be either dissatisfied with thy present lot, or shrink from the future.

3. All that is from the gods is full of Providence. That which is from fortune is not separated from nature or without an interweaving and involution with the things which are ordered by Providence. From thence all things flow; and there is besides necessity, and that which is for the advantage of the whole universe, of which thou art a part. But that is good for every part of nature which the nature of the whole brings, and what serves to maintain this nature. Now the universe is preserved, as by the changes of the elements so by the changes of things compounded of the elements. Let these principles be enough for thee, let them always be fixed opinions. But cast away the thirst after books, that thou mayest not die murmuring, but cheerfully, truly, and from thy heart thankful to the gods.

4. Remember how long thou hast been putting off these things, and how often thou hast received an opportunity from the gods, and yet dost not use it. Thou must now at last perceive of what universe thou art a part, and of what administrator of the universe thy existence is an efflux, and that a limit of time is fixed for thee, which if thou dost not use for clearing away the clouds from thy mind, it will go and thou wilt go, and it will never return.

5. Every moment think steadily as a Roman and a man to do what thou hast in hand with perfect and simple dignity, and feeling of affection, and freedom, and justice; and to give thyself relief from all other thoughts. And thou wilt give thyself relief, if thou doest every act of thy life as if it were the last, laying aside all carelessness and passionate aversion from the commands of reason, and all hypocrisy, and self-love, and discontent with the portion which has been given to thee. Thou seest how few the things are, the which if a man lays hold of, he is able to live a life which flows in quiet, and is like the existence of the gods; for the gods on their part will require nothing more from him who observes these things.

6. Do wrong to thyself, do wrong to thyself, my soul; but thou wilt no longer have the opportunity of honouring thyself. Every man's life is sufficient. But thine is nearly finished, though thy soul reverences not itself, but places thy felicity in the souls of others.

7. Do the things external which fall upon thee distract thee? Give thyself time to learn something new and good, and cease to be whirled around. But then thou must also avoid being carried about the other way. For those too are triflers who have wearied themselves in life by their activity, and yet have no object to which to direct every movement, and, in a word, all their thoughts.

8. Through not observing what is in the mind of another a man has seldom been seen to be unhappy; but those who do not observe the movements of their own minds must of necessity be unhappy.

9. This thou must always bear in mind, what is the nature of the whole, and what is my nature, and how this is related to that, and what kind of a part it is of what kind of a whole; and that there is no one who hinders thee from always doing and saying the things which are according to the nature of which thou art a part.

10. Theophrastus, in his comparison of bad acts—such a comparison as one would make in accordance with the common notions of mankind—says, like a true philosopher, that the offences which are committed through desire are more blameable than those which are committed through anger. For he who is excited by anger seems to turn away from reason with a certain pain and unconscious contraction; but he who offends through desire, being overpowered by pleasure, seems to be in a manner more intemperate and more womanish in his offences. Rightly then, and in a way worthy of philosophy, he said that the offence which is committed with pleasure is more blameable than that which is committed with pain; and on the whole the one is more like a person who has been first wronged and through pain is compelled to be angry; but the other is moved by his own impulse to do wrong, being carried towards doing something by desire.

11. Since it is possible that thou mayest depart from life this very moment, regulate every act and thought accordingly. But to go away from among men, if there are gods, is not a thing to be afraid of, for the gods will not involve thee in evil; but if indeed they do not exist, or if they have no concern about human affairs, what is it to me to live in a universe devoid of gods or devoid of Providence? But in truth they do exist, and they do care for human

things, and they have put all the means in man's power to enable him not to fall into real evils. And as to the rest, if there was anything evil, they would have provided for this also, that it should be altogether in a man's power not to fall into it. Now that which does not make a man worse, how can it make a man's life worse? But neither through ignorance, nor having the knowledge, but not the power to guard against or correct these things, is it possible that the nature of the universe has overlooked them: nor is it possible that it has made so great a mistake, either through want of power or want of skill, that good and evil should happen indiscriminately to the good and the bad. But death certainly, and life, honour and dishonour, pain and pleasure, all these things equally happen to good men and bad, being things which make us neither better nor worse. Therefore they are neither good nor evil.

12. How quickly all things disappear, in the universe the bodies themselves, but in time the remembrance of them; what is the nature of all sensible things, and particularly those which attract with the bait of pleasure or terrify by pain, or are noised abroad by vapoury fame; how worthless, and contemptible, and sordid, and perishable, and dead they are—all this it is the part of the intellectual faculty to observe. To observe too who these are whose opinions and voices give reputation; what death is, and the fact that, if a man looks at it in itself, and by the abstractive power of reflection resolves into their parts all the things which present themselves to the imagination in it, he will then consider it to be nothing else than an operation of nature; and if any one is afraid of an operation of nature, he is a child. This, however, is not only an operation of nature, but it is also a thing which conduces to the purposes of nature. To observe too how man comes near to the deity, and by what part of him, and when this part of man is so disposed.

13. Nothing is more wretched than a man who traverses everything in a round, and pries into the things beneath the earth, as the poet says, and seeks by conjecture what is in the minds of his neighbours, without perceiving that it is sufficient to attend to the daemon within him, and to reverence it sincerely. And reverence of the daemon consists in keeping it pure from passion and thoughtlessness, and dissatisfaction with what comes from gods and men. For the things from the gods merit veneration for their excellence; and the things from men should be dear to us by reason of kinship; and sometimes even, in a manner, they move our pity by reason of men's ignorance of good and bad; this defect being not less than that which deprives us of the power of distinguishing things that are white and black.

14. Though thou shouldst be going to live three thousand years, and as many times ten thousand years, still remember that no man loses any other life than this which he now lives, nor lives any other than this which he now loses. The longest and shortest are thus brought to the same. For the present is the same to all, though that which perishes is not the same; and so that which is lost appears to be a mere moment. For a man cannot lose either the past or the future: for what a man has not, how can any one take this from him? These two things then thou must bear in mind; the one, that all things from eternity are of like forms and come round in a circle, and that it makes no difference whether a man shall see the same things during a hundred years or two hundred, or an infinite time; and the second, that the longest liver and he who will die soonest lose just the same. For the present is the only thing of which a man can be deprived, if it is true that this is the only thing which he has, and that a man cannot lose a thing if he has it not.

15. Remember that all is opinion. For what was said by the Cynic Monimus is manifest: and manifest too is the use of what was said, if a man receives what may be got out of it as far as it is true.

16. The soul of man does violence to itself, first of all, when it becomes an abscess and, as it were, a tumour on the universe, so far as it can. For to be vexed at anything which happens is a separation of ourselves from nature, in some part of which the natures of all other things are contained. In the next place, the soul does violence to itself when it turns away from any man, or even moves towards him with the intention of injuring, such as are the souls of those who are angry. In the third place, the soul does violence to itself when it is overpowered by pleasure or by pain. Fourthly, when it plays a part, and does or says anything insincerely and untruly. Fifthly, when it allows any act of its own and any movement to be without an aim, and does anything thoughtlessly and without considering what it is, it being right that even the smallest things be done with reference to an end; and the end of rational animals is to follow the reason and the law of the most ancient city and polity.

17. Of human life the time is a point, and the substance is in a flux, and the perception dull, and the composition of the whole body subject to putrefaction, and the soul a whirl, and fortune hard to divine, and fame a thing devoid of judgement. And, to say all in a word, everything which belongs to the body is a stream, and what belongs to the soul is a dream and vapour, and life is a warfare and a stranger's sojourn, and after-fame is oblivion. What then is that which is able to conduct a man? One thing and only one, philosophy. But this consists in keeping the daemon within a man free from violence and unharmed, superior to pains and pleasures, doing nothing without a purpose, nor yet falsely and with hypocrisy, not feeling the need of another man's doing or not doing anything; and besides, accepting all that happens, and all that is allotted, as coming from thence, wherever it is, from whence he himself came; and, finally, waiting for death with a cheerful mind, as being nothing else than a dissolution of the elements of which every living being is compounded. But if there is no harm to the elements themselves in each continually changing into another, why should a man have any apprehension about the change and dissolution of all the elements? For it is according to nature, and nothing is evil which is according to nature.

This in Carnuntum. . . .

BOOK IV

That which rules within, when it is according to nature, is so affected with respect to the events which happen, that it always easily adapts itself to that which is possible and is presented to it. For it requires no definite material, but it moves towards its purpose, under certain conditions however; and it makes a material for itself out of that which opposes it, as fire lays hold of what falls into it, by which a small light would have been extinguished: but when the fire is strong, it soon appropriates to itself the matter which is heaped on it, and consumes it, and rises higher by means of this very material.

2. Let no act be done without a purpose, nor otherwise than according to the perfect principles of art.

3. Men seek retreats for themselves, houses in the country, sea-shores, and mountains; and thou too art wont to desire such things very much. But this is altogether a mark of the most common sort of men, for it is in thy power whenever thou shalt choose to retire into thyself. For nowhere either with more quiet or more freedom from trouble does a man retire than into his own soul, particularly when he has within him such thoughts that by looking into them he is immediately in perfect tranquillity; and I affirm that tranquillity is nothing else than the good ordering of the mind. Constantly then give to thyself this retreat, and renew thyself; and let thy principles be brief and fundamental, which, as soon as thou shalt recur to them, will be sufficient to cleanse the soul completely, and to send thee back free from all discontent with the things to which thou returnest. For with what art thou discontented? With the badness of men? Recall to thy mind this conclusion, that rational animals exist for one another, and that to endure is a part of justice, and that men do wrong involuntarily; and consider how many already, after mutual enmity, suspicion, hatred, and fighting, have been stretched dead, reduced to ashes; and be quiet at last.—But perhaps thou art dissatisfied with that which is assigned to thee out of the universe.—Recall to thy recollection this alternative; either there is providence or atoms, fortuitous concurrence of things; or remember the arguments by which it has been proved that the world is a kind of political community, and be quiet at last.—But perhaps corporeal things will still fasten upon thee.—Consider then further that the mind mingles not with the breath, whether moving gently or violently, when it has once drawn itself apart and discovered its own power, and think also of all that thou hast heard and assented to about pain and pleasure, and be quiet at last.—But perhaps the desire of the thing called fame will torment thee.—See how soon everything is forgotten, and look at the chaos of infinite time on each side of the present, and the emptiness of applause, and the changeableness and want of judgement in those who pretend to give praise, and the narrowness of the space within which it is circumscribed, and be quiet at last. For the whole earth is a point, and how small a nook in it is this thy dwelling, and how few are there in it, and what kind of people are they who will praise thee.

This then remains: Remember to retire into this little territory of thy own, and above all do not distract or strain thyself, but be free, and look at things as a man, as a human being, as a citizen, as a mortal. But among the things readiest to thy hand to which thou shalt turn, let there be these, which are two. One is that things do not touch the soul, for they are external and remain immovable; but our perturbations come only from the opinion which is within. The other is that all these things, which thou seest, change immediately and will no longer be; and constantly bear in mind how many of these changes thou hast already witnessed. The universe is transformation: life is opinion.

4. If our intellectual part is common, the reason also, in respect of which we are rational beings, is common: if this is so, common also is the reason which commands us what to do, and what not to do; if this is so, there is a common law also; if this is so, we are fellow-citizens; if this is so, we are members of some political community; if this is so, the world is in a manner a state. For of what other common political community will any one say that the whole human race are members? And from thence, from this common political community comes also our very intellectual faculty and reasoning faculty and our capacity for law; or whence do they come? For as my earthly part is a portion given to me from certain earth, and that which is watery from another element, and that which is hot and fiery from some peculiar source (for nothing comes out of that which is nothing, as nothing also returns to non-existence), so also the intellectual part comes from some source.

5. Death is such as generation is, a mystery of nature; a composition out of the same elements, and a decomposition into the same; and altogether not a thing of which any man should be ashamed, for it is not contrary to the nature of a reasonable animal, and not contrary to the reason of our constitution.

6. It is natural that these things should be done by such persons, it is a matter of necessity; and if a man will not have it so, he will not allow the fig-tree to have juice. But by all means bear this in mind, that within a very short time both thou and he will be dead; and soon not even your names will be left behind.

7. Take away thy opinion, and then there is taken away the complaint, 'I have been harmed.' Take away the complaint, 'I have been harmed,' and the harm is taken away.

8. That which does not make a man worse than he was, also does not make his life worse, nor does it harm him either from without or from within.

9. The nature of that which is universally useful has been compelled to do this.

10. Consider that everything which happens, happens justly, and if thou observest carefully, thou wilt find it to be so. I do not say only with respect to the continuity of the series of things, but with respect to what is just, and as if it were done by one who assigns to each thing its value. Observe then as thou hast begun; and whatever thou doest, do it in conjunction with this, the being good, and in the sense in which a man is properly understood to be good. Keep to this in every action.

11. Do not have such an opinion of things as he has who does thee wrong, or such as he wishes thee to have, but look at them as they are in truth.

12. A man should always have these two rules in readiness; the one, to do only whatever the reason of the ruling and legislating faculty may suggest for the use of men; the other, to change thy opinion, if there is any one at hand who sets thee right and moves thee from any opinion. But this change of opinion must proceed only from a certain persuasion, as of what is just or of common advantage, and the like, not because it appears pleasant or brings reputation.

13. Hast thou reason? I have.—Why then dost not thou use it? For if this does its own work, what else dost thou wish?

14. Thou hast existed as a part. Thou shalt disappear in that which produced thee; but rather thou shalt be received back into its seminal principle by transmutation.

15. Many grains of frankincense on the same altar: one falls before, another falls after; but it makes no difference.

16. Within ten days thou wilt seem a god to those to whom thou art now a beast and an ape, if thou wilt return to thy principles and the worship of reason.

17. Do not act as if thou wert going to live ten thousand years. Death hangs over thee. While thou livest, while it is in thy power, be good.

18. How much trouble he avoids who does not look to see what his neighbour says or does or thinks, but only to what he does himself, that it may be just and pure; or as Agathon says, look not round at the depraved morals of others, but run straight along the line without deviating from it.

19. He who has a vehement desire for posthumous fame does not consider that every one of those who remember him will himself also die very soon; then again also they who have succeeded them, until the whole remembrance shall have been extinguished as it is transmitted through men who foolishly admire and perish. But suppose that those who will remem-

ber are even immortal, and that the remembrance will be immortal, what then is this to thee? And I say not what is it to the dead, but what is it to the living? What is praise except indeed so far as it has a certain utility? For thou now rejectest unseasonably the gift of nature, clinging to something else. . . .

20. Everything which is in any way beautiful is beautiful in itself, and terminates in itself, not having praise as part of itself. Neither worse then nor better is a thing made by being praised. I affirm this also of the things which are called beautiful by the vulgar, for example, material things and works of art. That which is really beautiful has no need of anything; not more than law, nor more than truth, not more than benevolence or modesty. Which of these things is beautiful because it is praised, or spoiled by being blamed? Is such a thing as an emerald made worse than it was, if it is not praised? Or gold, ivory, purple, a lyre, a little knife, a flower, a shrub?

21. If souls continue to exist, how does the air contain them from eternity?—But how does the earth contain the bodies of those who have been buried from time so remote? For as here the mutation of these bodies after a certain continuance, whatever it may be, and their dissolution make room for other dead bodies; so the souls which are removed into the air after subsisting for some time are transmuted and diffused, and assume a fiery nature by being received into the seminal intelligence of the universe, and in this way make room for the fresh souls which come to dwell there. And this is the answer which a man might give on the hypothesis of souls continuing to exist. But we must not only think of the number of bodies which are thus buried, but also of the number of animals which are daily eaten by us and the other animals. For what a number is consumed, and thus in a manner buried in the bodies of those who feed on them! And nevertheless this earth receives them by reason of the changes of these bodies into blood, and the transformations into the aërial or the fiery element.

What is the investigation into the truth in this matter? The division into that which is material and that which is the cause of form, the formal.

22. Do not be whirled about, but in every movement have respect to justice, and on the occasion of every impression maintain the faculty of comprehension or understanding.

23. Everything harmonizes with me, which is harmonious to thee, O Universe. Nothing for me is too early nor too late, which is in due time for thee. Everything is fruit to me which thy seasons bring, O Nature: from thee are all things, in thee are all things, to thee all things return. The poet says, Dear city of Cecrops; and wilt not thou say, Dear city of Zeus?

24. Occupy thyself with few things, says the philosopher, if thou wouldst be tranquil.—But consider if it would not be better to say, Do what is necessary, and whatever the reason of the animal which is naturally social requires, and as it requires. For this brings not only the tranquillity which comes from doing well, but also that which comes from doing few things. For the greatest part of what we say and do being unnecessary, if a man takes this away, he will have more leisure and less uneasiness. Accordingly on every occasion a man should ask himself, Is this one of the unnecessary things? Now a man should take away not only unnecessary acts, but also, unnecessary thoughts, for thus superfluous acts will not follow after.

25. Try how the life of the good man suits thee, the life of him who is satisfied with his portion out of the whole, and satisfied with his own just acts and benevolent disposition.

26. Hast thou seen those things? Look also at these. Do not disturb thyself. Make thyself all simplicity. Does any one do wrong? It is to himself that he does the wrong. Has anything happened to thee? Well; out of the universe from the beginning everything which happens has been apportioned and spun out to thee. In a word, thy life is short. Thou must turn to profit the present by the aid of reason and justice. Be sober in thy relaxation.

27. Either it is a well-arranged universe or a chaos huddled together, but still a universe. But can a certain order subsist in thee, and disorder in the All? And this too when all things are so separated and diffused and sympathetic.

28. A black character, a womanish character, a stubborn character, bestial, childish, animal, stupid, counterfeit, scurrilous, fraudulent, tyrannical.

29. If he is a stranger to the universe who does not know what is in it, no less is he a stranger who does not know what is going on in it. He is a runaway, who flies from social reason; he is blind, who shuts the eyes of the understanding; he is poor, who has need of another, and has not from himself all things which are useful for life. He is an abscess on the

universe who withdraws and separates himself from the reason of our common nature through being displeased with the things which happen, for the same nature produces this, and has produced thee too: he is a piece rent asunder from the state, who tears his own soul from that of reasonable animals, which is one.

30. The one is a philosopher without a tunic, and the other without a book: here is another half naked: Bread I have not, he says, and I abide by reason.— And I do not get the means of living out of my learning, and I abide by my reason.

31. Love the art, poor as it may be, which thou hast learned, and be content with it; and pass through the rest of life like one who has intrusted to the gods with his whole soul all that he has, making thyself neither the tyrant nor the slave of any man.

32. Consider, for example, the times of Vespasian. Thou wilt see all these things, people marrying, bringing up children, sick, dying, warring, feasting, trafficking, cultivating the ground, flattering, obstinately arrogant, suspecting, plotting, wishing for some to die, grumbling about the present, loving, heaping up treasure, desiring consulship, kingly power. Well then, that life of these people no longer exists at all. Again, remove to the times of Trajan. Again, all is the same. Their life too is gone. In like manner view also the other epochs of time and of whole nations, and see how many after great efforts soon fell and were resolved into the elements. But chiefly thou shouldst think of those whom thou hast thyself known distracting themselves about idle things, neglecting to do what was in accordance with their proper constitution, and to hold firmly to this and to be content with it. And herein it is necessary to remember that the attention given to everything has its proper value and proportion. For thus thou wilt not be dissatisfied, if thou appliest thyself to smaller matters no further than is fit.

33. The words which were formerly familiar are now antiquated: so also the names of those who were famed of old, are now in a manner antiquated, Camillus, Caeso, Volesus, Leonnatus, and a little after also Scipio and Cato, then Augustus, then also Hadrian and Antoninus. For all things soon pass away and become a mere tale, and complete oblivion soon buries them. And I say this of those who have shone in a wondrous way. For the rest, as soon as they have breathed out their breath, they are gone, and no man speaks of them. And, to conclude the matter, what is even an eternal remembrance? A mere nothing. What then is that about which we ought to employ our serious pains? This one thing, thoughts just, and acts social, and words which never lie, and a disposition which gladly accepts all that happens, as necessary, as usual, as flowing from a principle and source of the same kind.

34. Willingly give thyself up to Clotho, one of the Fates, allowing her to spin thy thread into whatever things she pleases.

35. Everything is only for a day, both that which remembers and that which is remembered.

36. Observe constantly that all things take place by change, and accustom thyself to consider that the nature of the Universe loves nothing so much as to change the things which are and to make new things like them. For everything that exists is in a manner the seed of that which will be. But thou art thinking only of seeds which are cast into the earth or into a womb: but this is a very vulgar notion.

37. Thou wilt soon die, and thou art not yet simple, not free from perturbations, nor without suspicion of being hurt by external things, nor kindly disposed towards all; not dost thou yet place wisdom only in acting justly.

38. Examine men's ruling principles, even those of the wise, what kind of things they avoid, and what kind they pursue.

39. What is evil to thee does not subsist in the ruling principle of another; nor yet in any turning and mutation of thy corporeal covering. Where is it then? It is in that part of thee in which subsists the power of forming opinions about evils. Let this power then not form such opinions, and all is well. And if that which is nearest to it, the poor body, is cut, burnt, filled with matter and rottenness, nevertheless let the part which forms opinions about these things be quiet, that is, let it judge that nothing is either bad or good which can happen equally to the bad man and the good. For that which happens equally to him who lives contrary to nature and to him who lives according to nature, is neither according to nature nor contrary to nature.

40. Constantly regard the universe as one living being, having one substance and one soul; and observe how all things have reference to one perception, the perception of this one living being; and how all things act with one movement; and how all

things are the co-operating causes of all things which exist; observe too the continuous spinning of the thread and the contexture of the web.

41. Thou art a little soul bearing about a corpse, as Epictetus used to say.

42. It is no evil for things to undergo change, and no good for things to subsist in consequence of change.

43. Time is like a river made up of the events which happen, and a violent stream; for as soon as a thing has been seen, it is carried away, and another comes in its place, and this will be carried away too.

44. Everything which happens is as familiar and well known as the rose in spring and the fruit in summer; for such is disease, and death, and calumny, and treachery, and whatever else delights fools or vexes them.

45. In the series of things those which follow are always aptly fitted to those which have gone before; for this series is not like a mere enumeration of disjointed things, which has only a necessary sequence, but it is a rational connection: and as all existing things are arranged together harmoniously, so the things which come into existence exhibit no mere succession, but a certain wonderful relationship.

46. Always remember the saying of Heraclitus, that the death of earth is to become water, and the death of water is to become air, and the death of air is to become fire, and reversely. And think too of him who forgets whither the way leads, and that men quarrel with that with which they are most constantly in communion, the reason which governs the universe; and the things which they daily meet with seem to them strange: and consider that we ought not to act and speak as if we were asleep, for even in sleep we seem to act and speak; and that we ought not, like children who learn from their parents, simply to act and speak as we have been taught.

47. If any god told thee that thou shalt die to-morrow, or certainly on the day after to-morrow, thou wouldst not care much whether it was on the third day or on the morrow, unless thou wast in the highest degree mean-spirited—for how small is the difference?—so think it no great thing to die after as many years as thou canst name rather than to-morrow.

48. Think continually how many physicians are dead after often contracting their eyebrows over the sick; and how many astrologers after predicting with great pretensions the deaths of others; and how many philosophers after endless discourses on death or immortality; how many heroes after killing thousands; and how many tyrants who have used their power over men's lives with terrible insolence as if they were immortal; and how many cities are entirely dead, so to speak, Helice and Pompeii and Herculaneum, and others innumerable. Add to the reckoning all whom thou hast known, one after another. One man after burying another has been laid out dead, and another buries him: and all this in a short time. To conclude, always observe how ephemeral and worthless human things are, and what was yesterday a little mucus to-morrow will be a mummy or ashes. Pass then through this little space of time conformably to nature, and end thy journey in content, just as an olive falls off when it is ripe, blessing nature who produced it, and thanking the tree on which it grew.

49. Be like the promontory against which the waves continually break, but it stands firm and tames the fury of the water around it.

Unhappy am I, because this has happened to me.—Not so, but happy am I, though this has happened to me, because I continue free from pain, neither crushed by the present nor fearing the future. For such a thing as this might have happened to every man; but every man would not have continued free from pain on such an occasion. Why then is that rather a misfortune than this a good fortune? And dost thou in all cases call that a man's misfortune, which is not a deviation from man's nature? And does a thing seem to thee to be a deviation from man's nature, when it is not contrary to the will of man's nature? Well, thou knowest the will of nature. Will then this which has happened prevent thee from being just, magnanimous, temperate, prudent, secure against inconsiderate opinions and falsehood; will it prevent thee from having modesty, freedom, and everything else, by the presence of which man's nature obtains all that is its own? Remember too on every occasion which leads thee to vexation to apply this principle: not that this is a misfortune, but that to bear it nobly is good fortune.

50. It is a vulgar, but still a useful help towards contempt of death, to pass in review those who have tenaciously stuck to life. What more then have they gained than those who have died early? Certainly they lie in their tombs somewhere at last,

Cadicianus, Fabius, Julianus, Lepidus, or any one else like them, who have carried out many to be buried, and then were carried out themselves. Altogether the interval is small between birth and death; and consider with how much trouble, and in company with what sort of people and in what a feeble body this interval is laboriously passed. Do not then consider life a thing of any value. For look to the immensity of time behind thee, and to the time which is before thee, another boundless space. In this infinity then what is the difference between him who lives three days and him who lives three generations?

52. Always run to the short way; and the short way is the natural: accordingly say and do everything in conformity with the soundest reason. For such a purpose frees a man from trouble, and warfare, and all artifice and ostentatious display. . . .

BOOK VII

What is badness? It is that which thou hast often seen. And on the occasion of everything which happens keep this in mind, that it is that which thou hast often seen. Everywhere up and down thou wilt find the same things, with which the old histories are filled, those of the middle ages and those of our own day; with which cities and houses are filled now. There is nothing new: all things are both familiar and short-lived.

2. How can our principles become dead, unless the impressions (thoughts) which correspond to them are extinguished? But it is in thy power continuously to fan these thoughts into a flame. I can have that opinion about anything, which I ought to have. If I can, why am I disturbed? The things which are external to my mind have no relation at all to my mind.—Let this be the state of thy affects, and thou standest erect. To recover thy life is in thy power. Look at things again as thou didst use to look at them; for in this consists the recovery of thy life.

3. The idle business of show, plays on the stage, flocks of sheep, herds, exercises with spears, a bone cast to little dogs, a bit of bread into fish-ponds, labourings of ants and burden-carrying, runnings about of frightened little mice, puppets pulled by strings—all alike. It is thy duty then in the midst of such things to show good humour and not a proud air; to understand however that every man is worth just so much as the things are worth about which he busies himself.

4. In discourse thou must attend to what is said, and in every movement thou must observe what is doing. And in the one thou shouldst see immediately to what end it refers, but in the other watch carefully what is the thing signified.

5. Is my understanding sufficient for this or not? If it is sufficient, I use it for the work as an instrument given by the universal nature. But if it is not sufficient, then either I retire from the work and give way to him who is able to do it better; unless there be some reason why I ought not to do so; or I do it as well as I can, taking to help me the man who with the aid of my ruling principle can do what is now fit and useful for the general good. For whatsoever either by myself or with another I can do, ought to be directed to this only, to that which is useful and well suited to society.

6. How many after being celebrated by fame have been given up to oblivion; and how many who have celebrated the fame of others have long been dead.

7. Be not ashamed to be helped; for it is thy business to do thy duty like a soldier in the assault on a town. How then, if being lame thou canst not mount up on the battlements alone, but with the help of another it is possible?

8. Let not future things disturb thee, for thou wilt come to them, if it shall be necessary, having with thee the same reason which now thou usest for present things.

9. All things are implicated with one another, and the bond is holy; and there is hardly anything unconnected with any other thing. For things have been co-ordinated, and they combine to form the same universe (order). For there is one universe made up of all things, and one God who pervades all things, and one substance, and one law, one common reason in all intelligent animals, and one truth; if indeed there is also one perfection for all animals which are of the same stock and participate in the same reason.

10. Everything material soon disappears in the substance of the whole; and everything formal (causal) is very soon taken back into the universal reason; and the memory of everything is very soon overwhelmed in time.

11. To the rational animal the same act is according to nature and according to reason.

12. Be thou erect, or be made erect.

13. Just as it is with the members in those bodies which are united in one, so it is with rational beings

which exist separate, for they have been constituted for one co-operation. And the perception of this will be more apparent to thee, if thou often sayest to thyself that I am a member (μέλος) of the system of rational beings. But if (using the letter *r*) thou sayest that thou art a part (μέρος), thou dost not yet love men from thy heart; beneficence does not yet delight thee for its own sake; thou still doest it barely as a thing of propriety, and not yet as doing good to thyself.

14. Let there fall externally what will on the parts which can feel the effects of this fall. For those parts which have felt will complain, if they choose. But I, unless I think that what has happened is an evil, am not injured. And it is in my power not to think so.

15. Whatever any one does or says, I must be good, just as if the gold, or the emerald, or the purple were always saying this, Whatever any one does or says, I must be emerald and keep my colour.

16. The ruling faculty does not disturb itself; I mean, does not frighten itself or cause itself pain. But if any one else can frighten or pain it, let him do so. For the faculty itself will not by its own opinion turn itself into such ways. Let the body itself take care, if it can, that it suffer nothing, and let it speak, if it suffers. But the soul itself, that which is subject to fear, to pain, which has completely the power of forming an opinion about these things, will suffer nothing, for it will never deviate into such a judgement. The leading principle in itself wants nothing, unless it makes a want for itself; and therefore it is both free from perturbation and unimpeded, if it does not disturb and impede itself.

17. Eudaemonia (happiness) is a good daemon, or a good thing. What then art thou doing here, O imagination? Go away, I entreat thee by the gods, as thou didst come, for I want thee not. But thou art come according to thy old fashion. I am not angry with thee: only go away.

18. Is any man afraid of change? Why what can take place without change? What then is more pleasing or more suitable to the universal nature? And canst thou take a bath unless the wood undergoes a change? And canst thou be nourished, unless the food undergoes a change? And can anything else that is useful be accomplished without change? Dost thou not see then that for thyself also to change is just the same, and equally necessary for the universal nature?

19. Through the universal substance as through a furious torrent all bodies are carried, being by their nature united with and co-operating with the whole, as the parts of our body with one another. How many a Chrysippus, how many a Socrates, how many an Epictetus has time already swallowed up? And let the same thought occur to thee with reference to every man and thing.

20. One thing only troubles me, lest I should do something which the constitution of man does not allow, or in the way which it does not allow, or what it does not allow now.

21. Near is thy forgetfulness of all things; and near the forgetfulness of thee by all.

22. It is peculiar to man to love even those who do wrong. And this happens, if when they do wrong it occurs to thee that they are kinsmen, and that they do wrong through ignorance and unintentionally, and that soon both of you will die; and above all, that the wrong-doer has done thee no harm, for he has not made thy ruling faculty worse than it was before.

23. The universal nature out of the universal substance, as if it were wax, now moulds a horse, and when it has broken this up, it uses the material for a tree, then for a man, then for something else; and each of these things subsists for a very short time. But it is no hardship for the vessel to be broken up, just as there was none in its being fastened together.

24. A scowling look is altogether unnatural; when it is often assumed, the result is that all comeliness dies away, and at last is so completely extinguished that it cannot be again lighted up at all. Try to conclude from this very fact that it is contrary to reason. For if even the perception of doing wrong shall depart, what reason is there for living any longer?

25. Nature which governs the whole will soon change all things which thou seest, and out of their substance will make other things, and again other things from the substance of them, in order that the world may be ever new.

26. When a man has done thee any wrong, immediately consider with what opinion about good or evil he has done wrong. For when thou hast seen this, thou wilt pity him, and wilt neither wonder nor be angry. For either thou thyself thinkest the same thing to be good that he does or another thing of the same kind. It is thy duty then to pardon him. But if thou dost not think such things to be good or evil, thou wilt more readily be well disposed to him who is in error.

27. Think not so much of what thou hast not as of what thou hast: but of the things which thou hast select the best, and then reflect how eagerly they would have been sought, if thou hadst them not. At the same time however take care that thou dost not through being so pleased with them accustom thyself to overvalue them, so as to be disturbed if ever thou shouldst not have them.

28. Retire into thyself. The rational principle which rules has this nature, that it is content with itself when it does what is just, and so secures tranquillity.

29. Wipe out the imagination. Stop the pulling of the strings. Confine thyself to the present. Understand well what happens either to thee or to another. Divide and distribute every object into the causal (formal) and the material. Think of thy last hour. Let the wrong which is done by a man stay there where the wrong was done.

30. Direct thy attention to what is said. Let thy understanding enter into the things that are doing and the things which do them.

31. Adorn thyself with simplicity and modesty and with indifference towards the things which lie between virtue and vice. Love mankind. Follow God. The poet says that Law rules all.—And it is enough to remember that Law rules all.

32. About death: Whether it is a dispersion, or a resolution into atoms, or annihilation, it is either extinction or change.

33. About pain: The pain which is intolerable carries us off; but that which lasts a long time is tolerable; and the mind maintains its own tranquillity by retiring into itself, and the ruling faculty is not made worse. But the parts which are harmed by pain, let them, if they can, give their opinion about it.

34. About fame: Look at the minds of those who seek fame, observe what they are, and what kind of things they avoid, and what kind of things they pursue. And consider that as the heaps of sand piled on one another hide the former sands, so in life the events which go before are soon covered by those which come after.

35. From Plato: The man who has an elevated mind and takes a view of all time and of all substance, dost thou suppose it possible for him to think that human life is anything great? it is not possible, he said.—Such a man then will think that death also is no evil.—Certainly not.

36. From Antisthenes: It is royal to do good and to be abused.

37. It is a base thing for the countenance to be obedient and to regulate and compose itself as the mind commands, and for the mind not to be regulated and composed by itself.

38. It is not right to vex ourselves at things,
For they care nought about it.

39. To the immortal gods and us give joy.

40. Life must be reaped like the ripe ears of corn:
One man is born; another dies.

41. If gods care not for me and for my children,
There is a reason for it.

42. For the good is with me, and the just.

43. No joining others in their wailing, no violent emotion.

44. From Plato: But I would make this man a sufficient answer, which is this: Thou sayest not well, if thou thinkest that a man who is good for anything at all ought to compute the hazard of life or death, and should not rather look to this only in all that he does, whether he is doing what is just or unjust, and the works of a good or a bad man.

45. For thus it is, men of Athens, in truth: wherever a man has placed himself thinking it the best place for him, or has been placed by a commander, there in my opinion he ought to stay and to abide the hazard, taking nothing into the reckoning, either death or anything else, before the baseness of deserting his post.

46. But, my good friend, reflect whether that which is noble and good is not something different from saving and being saved; for as to a man living such or such a time, at least one who is really a man, consider if this is not a thing to be dismissed from the thoughts: and there must be no love of life: but as to these matters a man must intrust them to the deity and believe what the women say, that no man can escape his destiny, the next inquiry being how he may best live the time that he has to live.

47. Look round at the courses of the stars, as if thou wert going along with them; and constantly consider the changes of the elements into one another; for such thoughts purge away the filth of the terrene life.

48. This is a fine saying of Plato: That he who is discoursing about men should look also at earthly things as if he viewed them from some higher place; should look at them in their assemblies, armies, ag-

ricultural labours, marriages, treaties, births, deaths, noise of the courts of justice, desert places, various nations of barbarians, feasts, lamentations, markets, a mixture of all things and an orderly combination of contraries.

49. Consider the past; such great changes of political supremacies. Thou mayest foresee also the things which will be. For they will certainly be of like form, and it is not possible that they should deviate from the order of the things which take place now: accordingly to have contemplated human life for forty years is the same as to have contemplated it for ten thousand years. For what more wilt thou see?

50. That which has grown from the earth to the earth,
But that which has sprung from heavenly seed,
Back to the heavenly realms returns.

This is either a dissolution of the mutual involution of the atoms, or a similar dispersion of the unsentient elements.

51. With food and drinks and cunning magic arts
Turning the channel's course to 'scape from death.
The breeze which heaven has sent
We must endure, and toil without complaining.

52. Another may be more expert in casting his opponent; but he is not more social, nor more modest, nor better disciplined to meet all that happens, nor more considerate with respect to the faults of his neighbours.

53. Where any work can be done conformably to the reason which is common to gods and men, there we have nothing to fear: for where we are able to get profit by means of the activity which is successful and proceeds according to our constitution, there no harm is to be suspected.

54. Everywhere and at all times it is in thy power piously to acquiesce in thy present condition, and to behave justly to those who are about thee, and to exert thy skill upon thy present thoughts, that nothing shall steal into them without being well examined.

55. Do not look around thee to discover other men's ruling principles, but look straight to this, to what nature leads thee, both the universal nature through the things which happen to thee, and thy own nature through the acts which must be done by thee. But every being ought to do that which is according to its constitution; and all other things have been constituted for the sake of rational beings, just as among irrational things the inferior for the sake of the superior, but the rational for the sake of one another.

The prime principle then in man's constitution is the social. And the second is not to yield to the persuasions of the body, for it is the peculiar office of the rational and intelligent motion to circumscribe itself, and never to be overpowered either by the motion of the senses or of the appetites, for both are animal; but the intelligent motion claims superiority and does not permit itself to be overpowered by the others. And with good reason, for it is formed by nature to use all of them. The third thing in the rational constitution is freedom from error and from deception. Let then the ruling principle holding fast to these things go straight on, and it has what is its own.

56. Consider thyself to be dead, and to have completed thy life up to the present time; and live according to nature the remainder which is allowed thee.

57. Love that only which happens to thee and is spun with the thread of thy destiny. For what is more suitable?

58. In everything which happens keep before thy eyes those to whom the same things happened, and how they were vexed, and treated them as strange things, and found fault with them: and now where are they? Nowhere. Why then dost thou too choose to act in the same way? And why dost thou not leave these agitations which are foreign to nature, to those who cause them and those who are moved by them? And why art thou not altogether intent upon the right way of making use of the things which happen to thee? For then thou wilt use them well, and they will be a material for thee to work on. Only attend to thyself, and resolve to be a good man in every act which thou doest: and remember. . . .

59. Look within. Within is the fountain of good, and it will ever bubble up, if thou wilt ever dig.

60. The body ought to be compact, and to show no irregularity either in motion or attitude. For what the mind shows in the face by maintaining in it the expression of intelligence and propriety, that ought to be required also in the whole body. But all of these things should be observed without affectation.

61. The art of life is more like the wrestler's art

than the dancer's, in respect of this, that it should stand ready and firm to meet onsets which are sudden and unexpected.

62. Constantly observe who those are whose approbation thou wishest to have, and what ruling principles they possess. For then thou wilt neither blame those who offend involuntarily, nor wilt thou want their approbation, if thou lookest to the sources of their opinions and appetites.

63. Every soul, the philosopher says, is involuntarily deprived of truth; consequently in the same way it is deprived of justice and temperance and benevolence and everything of the kind. It is most necessary to bear this constantly in mind, for thus thou wilt be more gentle towards all.

64. In every pain let this thought be present, that there is no dishonour in it, nor does it make the governing intelligence worse, for it does not damage the intelligence either so far as the intelligence is rational or so far as it is social. Indeed in the case of most pains let this remark of Epicurus aid thee, that pain is neither intolerable nor everlasting, if thou bearest in mind that it has its limits, and if thou addest nothing to it in imagination: and remember this too, that we do not perceive that many things which are disagreeable to us are the same as pain, such as excessive drowsiness, and the being scorched by heat, and the having no appetite. When then thou art discontented about any of these things, say to thyself, that thou art yielding to pain.

65. Take care not to feel towards the inhuman, as they feel towards men.

66. How do we know if Telauges was not superior in character to Socrates? For it is not enough that Socrates died a more noble death, and disputed more skilfully with the sophists, and passed the night in the cold with more endurance, and that when he was bid to arrest Leon of Salamis, he considered it more noble to refuse, and that he walked in a swaggering way in the streets—though as to this fact one may have great doubts if it was true. But we ought to inquire, what kind of a soul it was that Socrates possessed, and if he was able to be content with being just towards men and pious towards the gods, neither idly vexed on account of men's villainy, nor yet making himself a slave to any man's ignorance, nor receiving as strange anything that fell to his share out of the universal, nor enduring it as intolerable, nor allowing his understanding to sympathise with the affects of the miserable flesh.

67. Nature has not so mingled the intelligence with the composition of the body, as not to have allowed thee the power of circumscribing thyself and of bringing under subjection to thyself all that is thy own; for it is very possible to be a divine man and to be recognised as such by no one. Always bear this in mind; and another thing too, that very little indeed is necessary for living a happy life. And because thou hast despaired of becoming a dialectician and skilled in the knowledge of nature, do not for this reason renounce the hope of being both free and modest and social and obedient to God.

68. It is in thy power to live free from all compulsion in the greatest tranquillity of mind, even if all the world cry out against thee as much as they choose, and even if wild beasts tear in pieces the members of this kneaded matter which has grown around thee. For what hinders the mind in the midst of all this from maintaining itself in tranquillity and in a just judgement of all surrounding things and in a ready use of the objects which are presented to it, so that the judgement may say to the thing which falls under its observation: This thou art in substance (reality), though in men's opinion thou mayest appear to be of a different kind; and the use shall say to that which falls under the hand: Thou art the thing that I was seeking; for to me that which presents itself is always a material for virtue both rational and political, and in a word, for the exercise of art, which belongs to man or God. For everything which happens has a relationship either to God or man, and is neither new nor difficult to handle, but usual and apt matter to work on.

69. The perfection of moral character consists in this, in passing every day as the last, and in being neither violently excited nor torpid nor playing the hypocrite.

70. The gods who are immortal are not vexed because during so long a time they must tolerate continually men such as they are and so many of them bad; and besides this, they also take care of them in all ways. But thou, who art destined to end so soon, art thou wearied of enduring the bad, and this too when thou art one of them?

71. It is a ridiculous thing for a man not to fly from his own badness, which is indeed possible, but to fly from other men's badness, which is impossible.

72. Whatever the rational and political (social) faculty finds to be neither intelligent nor social, it properly judges to be inferior to itself.

73. When thou hast done a good act and another has received it, why dost thou look for a third thing besides these, as fools do, either to have the reputation of having done a good act or to obtain a return?

74. No man is tired of receiving what is useful. But it is useful to act according to nature. Do not then be tired of receiving what is useful by doing it to others.

75. The nature of the All moved to make the universe. But now either everything that takes place comes by way of consequence or continuity; or even the chief things towards which the ruling power of the universe directs its own movement are governed by no rational principle. If this is remembered it will make thee more tranquil in many things.

EPICURUS

Epicurus was born in Samos, a Greek island, in 341 B.C. He died in Athens in 270 B.C. Introduced to philosophy by followers of Plato and Democritus, he established a school in Athens in 307 B.C. Known as the "Garden," this school was more of a commune, with strict moral and social bylaws. Despite the fact that the "Garden" stressed the necessity of a moral life, and although Epicurus constantly warned that the experience of pleasure should be devoid of self-indulgence, Epicureanism has been falsely mocked throughout history as devoted only to pleasure, that is, hedonistic.

In contemporary terms, Epicurus was a secular thinker. He stressed human mortality and the pervasiveness of chance in the design of the universe. Epicurus denied the possibility of divine providence, and he warned against living a life that was dictated by other than the wisdom and the needs of the individual person. The selections that follow tell of Epicurus' dedication to the doctrine of prudence and to the wisdom of leading a reasoned life, free of fears and artificial sanctions.

Epicurus to Menoeceus

Let no one when young delay to study philosophy, nor when he is old grow weary of his study. For no one can come too early or too late to secure the health of his soul. And the man who says that the age for philosophy has either not yet come or has gone by is like the man who says that the age for happiness is not yet come to him, or has passed away. Wherefore both when young and old a man must study philosophy, that as he grows old he may be young in blessings through the grateful recollection of what has been, and that in youth he may be old as well, since he will know no fear of what is to come. We must then meditate on the things that make our happiness, seeing that when that is with us we have all, but when it is absent we do all to win it.

The things which I used unceasingly to commend to you, these do and practise, considering them to be the first principles of the good life. First of all believe that god is a being immortal and blessed, even as the common idea of a god is engraved on men's minds, and do not assign to him anything alien to his immortality or ill-suited to his blessedness: but believe about him everything that can uphold his blessedness and immortality. For gods there are, since the knowledge of them is by clear vision. But they are not such as the many believe them to be: for indeed they do not consistently represent them as they believe them to be. And the impious man is not he who denies the gods of the many, but he who attaches to the gods the beliefs of the many. For the statements of the many about the gods are not conceptions

From *The Stoic and Epicurean Philosophers*, edited by Whitney J. Oates (New York: Random House, 1940), pp. 30–33. Originally published in *Epicurus: The Extant Remains*, translated by Cyril Bailey (Oxford: Oxford University Press, 1926). Reprinted by permission of Oxford University Press.

derived from sensation, but false suppositions, according to which the greatest misfortunes befall the wicked and the greatest blessings the good by the gift of the gods. For men being accustomed always to their own virtues welcome those like themselves, but regard all that is not of their nature as alien.

Become accustomed to the belief that death is nothing to us. For all good and evil consists in sensation, but death is deprivation of sensation. And therefore a right understanding that death is nothing to us makes the mortality of life enjoyable, not because it adds to it an infinite span of time, but because it takes away the craving for immortality. For there is nothing terrible in life for the man who has truly comprehended that there is nothing terrible in not living. So that the man speaks but idly who says that he fears death not because it will be painful when it comes, but because it is painful in anticipation. For that which gives no trouble when it comes, is but an empty pain in anticipation. So death, the most terrifying of ills, is nothing to us, since so long as we exist death is not with us; but when death comes, then we do not exist. It does not then concern either the living or the dead, since for the former it is not, and the latter are no more.

But the many at one moment shun death as the greatest of evils, at another yearn for it as a respite from the evils in life. But the wise man neither seeks to escape life nor fears the cessation of life, for neither does life offend him nor does the absence of life seem to be any evil. And just as with food he does not seek simply the larger share and nothing else, but rather the most pleasant, so he seeks to enjoy not the longest period of time, but the most pleasant.

And he who counsels the young man to live well, but the old man to make a good end, is foolish, not merely because of the desirability of life, but also because it is the same training which teaches to live well and to die well. Yet much worse still is the man who says it is good not to be born, but

> 'once born make haste to pass the gates of
> Death.' [*Theognis*]

For if he says this from conviction why does he not pass away out of life? For it is open to him to do so, if he had firmly made up his mind to this. But if he speaks in jest, his words are idle among men who cannot receive them.

We must then bear in mind that the future is neither ours, nor yet wholly not ours, so that we may not altogether expect it as sure to come, nor abandon hope of it, as if it will certainly not come.

We must consider that of desires some are natural, others vain, and of the natural some are necessary and others merely natural; and of the necessary some are necessary for happiness, others for the repose of the body, and others for very life. The right understanding of these facts enables us to refer all choice and avoidance to the health of the body and the soul's freedom from disturbance, since this is the aim of the life of blessedness. For it is to obtain this end that we always act, namely, to avoid pain and fear. And when this is once secured for us, all the tempest of the soul is dispersed, since the living creature has not to wander as though in search of something that is missing, and to look for some other thing by which he can fulfil the good of the soul and the good of the body. For it is then that we have need of pleasure, when we feel pain owing to the absence of pleasure; but when we do not feel pain, we no longer need pleasure. And for this cause we call pleasure the beginning and end of the blessed life. For we recognize pleasure as the first good innate in us, and from pleasure we begin every act of choice and avoidance, and to pleasure we return again, using the feeling as the standard by which we judge every good.

And since pleasure is the first good and natural to us, for this very reason we do not choose every pleasure, but sometimes we pass over many pleasures, when greater discomfort accrues to us as the result of them: and similarly we think many pains better than pleasures, since a greater pleasure comes to us when we have endured pains for a long time. Every pleasure then because of its natural kinship to us is good, yet not every pleasure is to be chosen: even as every pain also is an evil, yet not all are always of a nature to be avoided. Yet by a scale of comparison and by the consideration of advantages and disadvantages we must form our judgement on all these matters. For the good on certain occasions we treat as bad, and conversely the bad as good.

And again independence of desire we think a great good—not that we may at all times enjoy but a few things, but that, if we do not possess many, we may enjoy the few in the genuine persuasion that those have the sweetest pleasure in luxury who least need it, and that all that is natural is easy to be obtained, but that which is superfluous is hard. And so plain savours bring us a pleasure equal to a luxurious diet, when all the pain due to want is removed; and bread and water produce the highest pleasure, when one who needs them puts them to his lips. To grow accustomed therefore to simple and not luxurious diet gives us health to the full, and makes a man alert for the needful employments of life, and when after long intervals we approach luxuries, disposes us better towards them, and fits us to be fearless of fortune.

When, therefore, we maintain that pleasure is the end, we do not mean the pleasures of profligates and those that consist in sensuality, as is supposed by some who are either ignorant or disagree with us or do not understand, but freedom from pain in the body and from trouble in the mind. For it is not continuous drinkings and revellings, nor the satisfaction of lusts, nor the enjoyment of fish and other luxuries of the wealthy table, which produce a pleasant life, but sober reasoning, searching out the motives for all choice and avoidance, and banishing mere opinions, to which are due the greatest disturbance of the spirit.

Of all this the beginning and the greatest good is prudence. Wherefore prudence is a more precious thing even than philosophy: for from prudence are sprung all the other virtues, and it teaches us that it is not possible to live pleasantly without living prudently and honourably and justly, nor, again, to live a life of prudence, honour, and justice without living pleasantly. For the virtues are by nature bound up with the pleasant life, and the pleasant life is inseparable from them. For indeed who, think you, is a better man than he who holds reverent opinions concerning the gods, and is at all times free from fear of death, and has reasoned out the end ordained by nature? He understands that the limit of good things is easy to fulfil and easy to attain, whereas the course of ills is either short in time or slight in pain: he laughs at destiny, whom some have introduced as the mistress of all things. He thinks that with us lies the chief power in determining events, some of which happen by necessity and some by chance, and some are within our control; for while necessity cannot be called to account, he sees that chance is inconstant, but that which is in our control is subject to no master, and to it are naturally attached praise and blame. For, indeed, it were better to follow the myths about the gods than to become a slave to the destiny of the natural philosophers: for the former suggests a hope of placating the gods by worship, whereas the latter involves a necessity which knows no placation. As to chance, he does not regard it as a god as most men do (for in a god's acts there is no disorder), nor as an uncertain cause of all things: for he does not believe that good and evil are given by chance to man for the framing of a blessed life, but that opportunities for great good and great evil are afforded by it. He therefore thinks it better to be unfortunate in reasonable action than to prosper in unreason. For it is better in a man's actions that what is well chosen should fail, rather than that what is ill chosen should be successful owing to chance.

Meditate therefore on these things and things akin to them night and day by yourself, and with a companion like to yourself, and never shall you be disturbed waking or asleep, but you shall live like a god among men. For a man who lives among immortal blessings is not like to a mortal being.

Principal Doctrines

I. The blessed and immortal nature knows no trouble itself nor causes trouble to any other, so that it is never constrained by anger or favour. For all such things exist only in the weak.

II. Death is nothing to us: for that which is dissolved is without sensation; and that which lacks sensation is nothing to us.

III. The limit of quantity in pleasures is the

From *The Stoic and Epicurean Philosophers,* edited by Whitney J. Oates (New York: Random House, 1940), pp. 35–39. Originally published in *Epicurus: The Extant Remains,* translated by Cyril Bailey (Oxford: Oxford University Press, 1926). Reprinted by permission of Oxford University Press.

removal of all that is painful. Wherever pleasure is present, as long as it is there, there is neither pain of body nor of mind, nor of both at once.

IV. Pain does not last continuously in the flesh, but the acutest pain is there for a very short time, and even that which just exceeds the pleasure in the flesh does not continue for many days at once. But chronic illnesses permit a predominance of pleasure over pain in the flesh.

V. It is not possible to live pleasantly without living prudently and honourably and justly, nor again to live a life of prudence, honour, and justice without living pleasantly. And the man who does not possess the pleasant life, is not living prudently and honourably and justly, and the man who does not possess the virtuous life, cannot possibly live pleasantly.

VI. To secure protection from men anything is a natural good, by which you may be able to attain this end.

VII. Some men wished to become famous and conspicuous, thinking that they would thus win for themselves safety from other men. Wherefore if the life of such men is safe, they have obtained the good which nature craves; but if it is not safe, they do not possess that for which they strove at first by the instinct of nature.

VIII. No pleasure is a bad thing in itself: but the means which produce some pleasures bring with them disturbances many times greater than the pleasures.

IX. If every pleasure could be intensified so that it lasted and influenced the whole organism or the most essential parts of our nature, pleasures would never differ from one another.

X. If the things that produce the pleasures of profligates could dispel the fears of the mind about the phenomena of the sky and death and its pains, and also teach the limits of desires and of pains, we should never have cause to blame them: for they would be filling themselves full with pleasures from every source and never have pain of body or mind, which is the evil of life.

XI. If we were not troubled by our suspicions of the phenomena of the sky and about death, fearing that it concerns us, and also by our failure to grasp the limits of pains and desires, we should have no need of natural science.

XII. A man cannot dispel his fear about the most important matters if he does not know what is the nature of the universe but suspects the truth of some mythical story. So that without natural science it is not possible to attain our pleasures unalloyed.

XIII. There is no profit in securing protection in relation to men, if things above and things beneath the earth and indeed all in the boundless universe remain matters of suspicion.

XIV. The most unalloyed source of protection from men, which is secured to some extent by a certain force of expulsion, is in fact the immunity which results from a quiet life and the retirement from the world.

XV. The wealth demanded by nature is both limited and easily procured; that demanded by idle imaginings stretches on to infinity.

XVI. In but few things chance hinders a wise man, but the greatest and most important matters reason has ordained and throughout the whole period of life does and will ordain.

XVII. The just man is most free from trouble, the unjust most full of trouble.

XVIII. The pleasure in the flesh is not increased, when once the pain due to want is removed, but is only varied: and the limit as regards pleasure in the mind is begotten by the reasoned understanding of these very pleasures and of the emotions akin to them, which used to cause the greatest fear to the mind.

XIX. Infinite time contains no greater pleasure than limited time, if one measures by reason the limits of pleasure.

XX. The flesh perceives the limits of pleasure as unlimited and unlimited time is required to supply it. But the mind, having attained a reasoned understanding of the ultimate good of the flesh and its limits and having dissipated the fears concerning the time to come, supplies us with the complete life, and we have no further need of infinite time: but neither does the mind shun pleasure, nor, when circumstances begin to bring about the departure from life, does it approach its end as though it fell short in any way of the best life.

XXI. He who has learned the limits of life knows that that which removes the pain due to want and makes the whole of life complete is easy to obtain; so that there is no need of actions which involve competition.

XXII. We must consider both the real purpose and

all the evidence of direct perception, to which we always refer the conclusions of opinion; otherwise, all will be full of doubt and confusion.

XXIII. If you fight against all sensations, you will have no standard by which to judge even those of them which you say are false.

XXIV. If you reject any single sensation and fail to distinguish between the conclusion of opinion as to the appearance awaiting confirmation and that which is actually given by the sensation or feeling, or each intuitive apprehension of the mind, you will confound all other sensations as well with the same groundless opinion, so that you will reject every standard of judgement. And if among the mental images created by your opinion you affirm both that which awaits confirmation and that which does not, you will not escape error, since you will have preserved the whole cause of doubt in every judgement between what is right and what is wrong.

XXV. If on each occasion instead of referring your actions to the end of nature, you turn to some other nearer standard when you are making a choice or an avoidance, your actions will not be consistent with your principles.

XXVI. Of desires, all that do not lead to a sense of pain, if they are not satisfied, are not necessary, but involve a craving which is easily dispelled, when the object is hard to procure or they seem likely to produce harm.

XXVII. Of all the things which wisdom acquires to produce the blessedness of the complete life, far the greatest is the possession of friendship.

XXVIII. The same conviction which has given us confidence that there is nothing terrible that lasts for ever or even for long, has also seen the protection of friendship most fully completed in the limited evils of this life.

XXIX. Among desires some are natural and necessary, some natural but not necessary, and others neither natural nor necessary, but due to idle imagination.

XXX. Wherever in the case of desires which are physical, but do not lead to a sense of pain, if they are not fulfilled, the effort is intense, such pleasures are due to idle imagination, and it is not owing to their own nature that they fail to be dispelled, but owing to the empty imaginings of the man.

XXXI. The justice which arises from nature is a pledge of mutual advantage to restrain men from harming one another and save them from being harmed.

XXXII. For all living things which have not been able to make compacts not to harm one another or be harmed, nothing ever is either just or unjust; and likewise too for all tribes of men which have been unable or unwilling to make compacts not to harm or be harmed.

XXXIII. Justice never is anything in itself, but in the dealings of men with one another in any place whatever and at any time it is a kind of compact not to harm or be harmed.

XXXIV. Injustice is not an evil in itself, but only in consequence of the fear which attaches to the apprehension of being unable to escape those appointed to punish such actions.

XXXV. It is not possible for one who acts in secret contravention of the terms of the compact not to harm or be harmed, to be confident that he will escape detection, even if at present he escapes a thousand times. For up to the time of death it cannot be certain that he will indeed escape.

XXXVI. In its general aspect justice is the same for all, for it is a kind of mutual advantage in the dealings of men with one another: but with reference to the individual peculiarities of a country or any other circumstances the same thing does not turn out to be just for all.

XXXVII. Among actions which are sanctioned as just by law, that which is proved on examination to be of advantage in the requirements of men's dealings with one another, has the guarantee of justice, whether it is the same for all or not. But if a man makes a law and it does not turn out to lead to advantage in men's dealings with each other, then it no longer has the essential nature of justice. And even if the advantage in the matter of justice shifts from one side to the other, but for a while accords with the general concept, it is none the less just for that period in the eyes of those who do not confound themselves with empty sounds but look to the actual facts.

XXXVIII. Where, provided the circumstances have not been altered, actions which were considered just, have been shown not to accord with the general concept in actual practice, then they are not just. But where, when circumstances have changed, the same actions which were sanctioned as just no longer lead to advantage, there they were just at the time when they were of advantage for the dealings of fellow-citizens with one another; but subsequently they are no longer just, when no longer of advantage.

XXXIX. The man who has best ordered the element of disquiet arising from external circumstances has made those things that he could akin to himself and the rest at least not alien: but with all to which he could not do even this, he has refrained from mixing, and has expelled from his life all which it was of advantage to treat thus.

XL. As many as possess the power to procure complete immunity from their neighbours, these also live most pleasantly with one another, since they have the most certain pledge of security, and after they have enjoyed the fullest intimacy, they do not lament the previous departure of a dead friend, as though he were to be pitied.

LUCRETIUS

Biographical details about Lucretius are still contested. Most versions of his life trace to the report of Jerome (A.D. 348–420), who is known also as the translator and editor of the Latin Bible, the Vulgate edition. Jerome contends that Lucretius committed suicide at the age of 44, after being poisoned by a love potion and undergoing periods of insanity. He is believed to have lived from 99 B.C. until 55 B.C. and was most likely a member of an aristocratic Roman family.

Lucretius was profoundly influenced by Epicurus and to some extent by the Atomists. He has bequeathed one major philosophical work, On the Nature of Things (De Rerum Natura), *in which the major themes of Epicureanism are brilliantly orchestrated and developed. He was especially negative about the influence of Greek and Roman mythology, holding that the Gods held no power for we are in control of our own lives. Lucretius also followed Epicurus in his attempt to take the sting out of death by describing it as a perfectly natural and non-threatening human event. The following selection from* On the Nature of Things *praises human mortality and our relationship to nature.*

From On the Nature of Things

BOOK III

Thee, who first wast able amid such thick darkness to raise on high so bright a beacon and shed a light on the true interests of life, thee I follow, glory of the Greek race, and plant now my footsteps firmly fixed in thy imprinted marks, not so much from a desire to rival thee as that from the love I bear thee I yearn to imitate thee; for why need the swallow contend with swans, or what likeness is there between the feats of racing performed by kids with tottering limbs and by the powerful strength of the horse? Thou, father, art discoverer of things, thou furnishest us with fatherly precepts, and like as bees sip of all things in the flowery lawns, we, O glorious being, in like manner feed from out thy pages upon all the golden maxims, golden I say, most worthy ever of endless life. For soon as thy philosophy issuing from a godlike intellect has begun with loud voice to proclaim the nature of things, the terrors of the mind are dispelled, the walls of the world part asunder, I see things in operation throughout the whole void: the divinity of the gods is revealed and their tranquil abodes which neither winds do shake nor clouds drench with rains nor snow congealed by sharp frosts harms with hoary fall: an ever cloudless ether o'ercanopies them, and they laugh with light shed largely round. Nature too supplies all their wants and nothing ever impairs their peace of mind. But on the other hand the Acherusian quarters are nowhere to be seen, though earth is no bar to all things being descried, which are in operation underneath our feet throughout the void. At all this a kind of godlike delight mixed with shuddering awe comes over me to think that nature by thy power is laid thus visibly open, is thus unveiled on every side.

And now since I have shown what-like the beginnings of all things are and how diverse with varied shapes as they fly spontaneously driven on in everlasting motion, and how all things can be severally produced out of these, next after these questions the nature of the mind and soul should methinks be cleared up by my verses and that dread of Acheron be driven headlong forth, troubling as it does the life of man from its inmost depths and overspreading all things with the blackness of death, allowing no pleasure to be pure and unalloyed. For as to what men often give out that diseases and a life of shame are more to be feared than Tartarus, place of death, and that they know the soul to be of blood or it may be of wind, if haply their choice so direct, and that they have no need at all of our philosophy, you may perceive for the following reasons that all these boasts are thrown out more for glory's sake than because the thing is really believed. These very men, exiles from their country and banished far from the sight of men, live degraded by foul charge of guilt, sunk in a word in every kind of misery, and whithersoever the poor wretches are come, they yet do offer sacrifices to the dead and slaughter black sheep and make libations to the gods Manes and in times of distress turn their thoughts to religion much more earnestly. Wherefore you can better test the man in doubts and dangers and mid adversity learn who he is; for then and not till then the words of truth are forced out from the bottom of his heart: the mask is torn off, the reality is left. Avarice again and blind lust of honours which constrain unhappy men to overstep the bounds of right and sometimes as partners and agents of crimes to strive night and day with surpassing effort to struggle up the summit of power,—these sores of life are in no small measure fostered by the dread of death. For foul scorn and pinching want in every case are seen to be far removed from a life of pleasure and security and to be a loitering so to say before the gates of death. And while men driven on by an unreal dread wish to escape far away from these and keep them far from them, they amass wealth by civil bloodshed and greedily double their riches piling up murder on murder; cruelly triumph in the sad death of a brother and hate and fear the tables of kinsfolk. Often likewise from the same fear envy causes them to pine: they make moan that before their very eyes he is powerful, he attracts attention, who walks arrayed in gorgeous dignity, while they are wallowing in darkness and dirt. Some wear themselves to death for the sake of statues and a name. And often to such a degree through dread of death does hate of life and of the sight of daylight seize upon mortals, that they commit self-murder with a sorrowing heart, quite forgetting that this fear is the source of their cares, this fear which urges men to every sin, prompts this one to put all shame to rout, another to burst asunder the bonds of friendship, and in fine to overturn duty from its very base; since often ere now men have betrayed country and dear parents in seeking to shun the Acherusian quarters. For even as children are flurried and dread all things in the thick darkness, thus we in the daylight fear at times things not a whit more to be dreaded than what children shudder at in the dark and fancy sure to be. This terror therefore and darkness of mind must be dispelled not by the rays of the sun and glittering shafts of day, but by the aspect and law of nature.

First then I say that the mind which we often call the understanding, in which dwells the directing and governing principle of life, is no less part of the man, than hand and foot and eyes are parts of the whole living creature. Some however affirm that the sense of the mind does not dwell in a distinct part, but is a certain vital state of the body, which the Greeks call harmonia, because by it, they say, we live with sense, though the understanding is in no one part; just as when good health is said to belong to the body, though yet it is not any one part of the man in health. In this way they do not assign a distinct part to the sense of the mind; in all which they appear to me to be grievously at fault in more ways than one. Oftentimes the body which is visible to sight, is sick, while yet we have pleasure in another hidden part; and oftentimes the case is the very reverse, the man who is unhappy in mind feeling pleasure in his whole body; just as if, while a sick man's foot is pained, the head meanwhile should be in no pain at all. Moreover when the limbs are consigned to soft sleep and the burdened body lies diffused without sense, there is yet a something else in us which during that time is moved in many ways and admits into it all the motions of joy and unreal cares of the heart. Now that you may know that the soul as well is in the limbs and that the body is not wont to have sense by any harmony, this is a main proof: when much of the body has been taken away, still life often stays in the limbs; and yet the same life, when a few bodies of heat have been dispersed abroad and some air has been forced out through the mouth, abandons at once the veins and quits the bones: by this you may perceive that all bodies have not functions of like importance nor alike uphold existence, but rather that those seeds which constitute wind and heat, cause life to stay in the limbs. Therefore vital heat and wind are within the body and abandon our frame at death. Since then the nature of the mind and that of the soul have been proved to be a part as it were of the man, surrender the name of harmony, whether brought down to musicians from high Helicon, or whether rather they have themselves taken it from something else and transferred it to that thing which then was in need of a distinctive name; whatever it be, let them keep it: do you take in the rest of my precepts.

Now I assert that the mind and the soul are kept together in close union and make up a single nature, but that the directing principle which we call mind and understanding, is the head so to speak and reigns paramount in the whole body. It has a fixed seat in the middle region of the breast: here throb fear and apprehension, about these spots dwell soothing joys; therefore here is the understanding or mind. All the rest of the soul disseminated through the whole body obeys and moves at the will and inclination of the mind. It by itself alone knows for itself, rejoices for itself, at times when the impression does not move either soul or body together with it. And as when some part of us, the head or the eye, suffers from an attack of pain, we do not feel the anguish at the same time over the whole body, thus the mind sometimes suffers pain by itself or is inspirited with joy, when all the rest of the soul throughout the limbs and frame is stirred by no novel sensation. But when the mind is excited by some more vehement apprehension, we see the whole soul feel in unison through all the limbs, sweats and paleness spread over the whole body, the tongue falter, the voice die away, a mist cover the eyes, and ears ring, the limbs sink under one; in short we often see men drop down from terror of mind; so that anybody may easily perceive from this that the soul is closely united with the mind, and, when it has been smitten by the influence of the mind, forthwith pushes and strikes the body.

This same principle teaches that the nature of the mind and soul is bodily; for when it is seen to push the limbs, rouse the body from sleep, and alter the countenance and guide and turn about the whole man, and when we see that none of these effects can take place without touch nor touch without body, must we not admit that the mind and the soul are of a bodily nature? Again you perceive that our mind in our body suffers together with the body and feels in unison with it. When a weapon with a shudder-causing force has been driven in and has laid bare bones and sinews within the body, if it does not take life, yet there ensues a faintness and a lazy sinking to the ground and on the ground the turmoil of mind which arises, and sometimes a kind of undecided inclination to get up. Therefore the nature of the mind must be bodily, since it suffers from bodily weapons and blows.

I will now go on to explain in my verses of what kind of body the mind consists and out of what it is formed. First of all I say that it is extremely fine and formed of exceedingly minute bodies. That this is so you may, if you please to attend, clearly perceive from what follows: nothing that is seen takes place with a velocity equal to that of the mind when it starts some suggestion and actually sets it agoing; the mind therefore is stirred with greater rapidity than any of the things whose nature stands out visible to sight. But that which is so passing nimble, must consist of seeds exceedingly round and exceedingly minute, in order to be stirred and set in motion by a small moving power. Thus water is moved and heaves by ever so small a force, formed as it is of small particles apt to roll. But on the other hand the nature of honey is more sticky, its liquid more sluggish and its movement more dilatory; for the whole mass of matter coheres more closely, because sure enough it is made of bodies not so smooth, fine, and round. A breeze however gentle and light can force, as you may see, a high heap of poppy seed to be blown away from the top downwards; but on the other hand Eurus itself cannot move a heap of stones. Therefore bodies possess a power of moving in proportion to their smallness and smoothness; and on the other hand the greater weight and roughness bodies prove to have, the more stable they are. Since then the nature of the mind has been found to be eminently easy to move, it must consist of bodies exceedingly small, smooth, and round. The knowledge of which fact, my good friend, will on many accounts prove useful and be serviceable to you. The following fact too likewise demonstrates how fine the texture is of which its nature is composed, and how small the room is in which it can be contained, could it only be collected into one mass: soon as the untroubled sleep of death has gotten hold of a man and the nature of the mind and soul has withdrawn, you can perceive then no diminution of the entire body either in appearance or weight: death makes all good save the vital sense and heat. Therefore the whole soul must consist of very small seeds and be inwoven through veins and flesh and sinews; inasmuch as, after it has all withdrawn from the whole body, the exterior contour of the limbs preserves itself entire and not a tittle of the weight is lost. Just in the same way when the flavour of wine is gone or when the delicious aroma of a perfume has been dispersed into the air or when the savour has left some body, yet the thing itself does not therefore look smaller to the eye, nor does aught seem to have been taken from the weight, because sure enough many minute seeds make up the savours and the odour in the whole body of the several things. Therefore, again and again I say, you are to know that the nature of the mind and the soul has been formed of exceedingly minute seeds, since at its departure it takes away none of the weight.

We are not however to suppose that this nature is single. For a certain subtle spirit mixed with heat quits men at death, and then the heat draws air along with it; there being no heat which has not air too mixed with it: for since its nature is rare, many first-beginnings of air must move about through it. Thus the nature of the mind is proved to be threefold; and yet these things all together are not sufficient to produce sense; since the fact of the case does not admit that any of these can produce sense-giving motions and the thoughts which a man turns over in mind. Thus some fourth nature too must be added to these: it is altogether without name; than it nothing exists more nimble or more fine, or of smaller or smoother elements: it first transmits the sense-giving motions through the frame; for it is first stirred, made up as it is of small particles; next the heat and the unseen force of the spirit receive the motions, then the air; then all things are set in action, the blood is stirred, every part of the flesh is filled with sensation; last of all the feeling is transmitted to the bones and marrow, whether it be one of pleasure or an opposite excitement. No pain however can lightly pierce thus far nor any sharp malady make its way in, without all things being so thoroughly disordered that no room is left for life and the parts of the soul fly abroad through all the pores of the body. But commonly a stop is put to these motions on the surface as it were of the body: for this reason we are able to retain life.

Now though I would fain explain in what way these are mixed up together, by what means united, when they exert their powers, the poverty of my native speech deters me sorely against my will: yet will I touch upon them and in summary fashion to the best of my ability: the first-beginnings by their mutual motions are interlaced in such a way that none of them can be separated by itself, nor can the function of any go on divided from the rest by any interval; but they are so to say the several powers of one body. Even so in any flesh of living creature you please without exception there is smell and some colour and a savour, and yet out of all these is made up one single bulk of body. Thus the heat and the air and the unseen power of the spirit mixed together produce a single nature, together with that nimble force which transmits to them from itself the origin of motion; by which means sense-giving motion first takes its rise through the fleshly frame. For this nature lurks secreted in its inmost depths, and nothing in our body is farther beneath all ken than it, and more than this it is the very soul of the whole soul. Just in the same way as the power of the mind and the function of the soul are latent in our limbs and throughout our body, because they are each formed of small and few bodies: even so, you are to know, this nameless power made of minute bodies is concealed and is moreover the very soul so to say of the whole soul, and reigns supreme in the whole body. On a like principle the spirit and air and heat must, as they exert their powers, be mixed up together through the frame, and one must ever be more out of view or more prominent than another, that a single substance may be seen to be formed from the union of all, lest the heat and spirit apart by themselves and the power of the air apart by itself should destroy sense and dissipate it by their disunion. Thus the mind possesses that heat which it displays when it boils up in anger and fire flashes from the keen eyes; there is too much cold spirit comrade of fear, which spreads a shivering over the limbs and stirs the whole frame; yes and there is also that condition of still air which has place when the breast is calm and the looks cheerful. But they have more of the hot whose keen heart and passionate mind lightly boil up in anger. Foremost in this class comes the fierce violence of lions who often as they chafe break their hearts with their roaring and cannot contain within their breast the billows of their rage. Then the chilly mind of stags is fuller of the spirit and more quickly rouses through all the flesh its icy currents which cause a shivering motion to pass over the limbs. But the nature of oxen has its life rather from the still air, and never does the smoky torch of anger applied to it stimulate it too much, shedding over it the shadow of murky gloom, nor is it transfixed and stiffened by the icy shafts of fear: it lies between the other two, stags and cruel lions. And thus it is with mankind: however much teaching renders some equally refined, it yet leaves behind those earliest traces of the nature of each mind: and we are not to suppose that evil habits can be so thoroughly plucked up by the roots, that one man shall not be more prone than another to keen anger, a second shall not be somewhat more quickly assailed by fear, a third shall not take some things more meekly than is right. In many other points there must be differences between the varied natures of men and the tempers which follow upon these; though at present I am unable to set forth the hidden causes of these or to find names enough for the different shapes which belongs to the first-beginnings, from which shapes arises this diversity of things. What herein I think I may affirm is this: traces of the different natures left behind, which reason is unable to expel from us, are so exceedingly slight that there is nothing to hinder us from living a life worthy of gods.

Well this nature is contained by the whole body and is in turn the body's guardian and the cause of its existence; for the two adhere together with common roots and cannot it is plain be riven asunder without destruction. Even as it is not easy to pluck the perfume out of lumps of frankincense without quite destroying its nature as well; so it is not easy to withdraw from the whole body the nature of the mind and soul without dissolving all alike. With first-beginnings so interlaced from their earliest birth are they formed and gifted with a life of joint partnership, and it is plain that the faculty of the body and of the mind cannot feel separately, each alone without the other's power, but sense is kindled throughout our flesh and blown into flame between the two by the joint motions on the part of both. Moreover the body by itself is never either begotten or grows or, it is plain, continues to exist after death. For not in the way that the liquid of water often loses the heat which has been given to it, yet is not for that reason itself riven in pieces, but remains unimpaired,—not in this way, I say, can the abandoned frame endure the separation of the soul, but riven in pieces it utterly perishes and rots away. Thus the mutual connexions of body and soul from the first moment of their existence learn the vital motions even while hid in the body and womb of the mother, so that no separation can take place without mischief and ruin. Thus you may see that, since the cause of existence lies in their joint action, their nature too must be a joint nature.

Furthermore if any one tries to disprove that the body feels and believes that the soul mixed through the whole body takes upon it this motion which we name sense, he combats even manifest and undoubted facts. For who will ever bring forward any explanation of what the body's feeling is, except that which the plain fact of the case has itself given and taught to us? But when the soul it is said has departed, the body throughout is without sense; yes, for it loses what was not its own peculiar property in life; ay and much else it loses, before that soul is driven out of it.

Again to say that the eyes can see no object, but that the soul discerns through them as through an open door, is far from easy, since their sense contradicts this; for this sense e'en draws it and forces it out to the pupil: nay often we are unable to perceive shining things, because our eyes are embarrassed by the lights. But this is not the case with doors; for, because we ourselves see, the open doors do not therefore undergo any fatigue. Again if our eyes are in the place of doors, in that case when the eyes are removed the mind ought it would seem to have more power of seeing things, after doors, jambs and all, have been taken out of the way.

And herein you must by no means adopt the opinion which the revered judgment of the worthy man Democritus lays down, that the first-beginnings of body and mind placed together in successive layers come in alternate order and so weave the tissue of our limbs. For not only are the elements of the soul much smaller than those of which our body and flesh are formed, but they are also much fewer in number and are disseminated merely in scanty number through the frame, so that you can warrant no more than this: the first-beginnings of the soul keep spaces between them at least as great as are the smallest bodies which, if thrown upon it, are first able to excite in our body the sense-giving motions. Thus at times we do not feel the adhesion of dust when it settles on our body, nor the impact of chalk when it rests on our limbs, nor do we feel a mist at night nor a spider's slender threads as they come against us, when we are caught in its meshes in moving along, nor the same insect's flimsy web when it has fallen on our head, nor the feathers of birds and down of plants as it flies about, which commonly from exceeding lightness does not lightly fall, nor do we feel the tread of every creeping creature whatsoever nor each particular foot-print which gnats and the like stamp on our body. So very many first-beginnings must be stirred in us, before the seeds of the soul mixed up in our bodies feel that these have been disturbed, and by thumping with such spaces between can clash, unite, and in turn recoil.

The mind has more to do with holding the fastnesses of life and has more sovereign sway over it than the power of the soul. For without the understanding and the mind no part of the soul can maintain itself in the frame the smallest fraction of time, but follows at once in the other's train and passes away into the air and leaves the cold limbs in the chill of death. But he abides in life whose mind and understanding continue to stay with him: though the trunk is mangled with its limbs shorn all round about it, after the soul has been taken away on all sides and been severed from the limbs, the trunk yet lives and inhales the ethereal airs of life. When robbed, if not of the whole, yet of a large portion of the soul, it still lingers in and cleaves to life; just as, after the eye has been lacerated all round if the pupil has continued uninjured, the living power of sight remains, provided always you do not destroy the whole ball of the eye and pare close round the pupil and leave only it; for that will not be done even to the ball without the entire destruction of the eye. But if that middle portion of the eye, small as it is, is eaten into, the sight is gone at once and darkness ensues, though a man have the bright ball quite unimpaired. On such terms of union soul and mind are ever bound to each other.

Now mark me: that you may know that the minds and light souls of living creatures have birth and are mortal, I will go on to set forth verses worthy of your attention, got together by long study and invented with welcome effort. Do you mind to link to one name both of them alike, and when for instance I shall choose to speak of the soul, showing it to be mortal, believe that I speak of the mind as well, inasmuch as both make up one thing and are one united substance. First of all then since I have shown the soul to be fine and to be formed of minute bodies and made up of much smaller first-beginnings than is the liquid of water or mist or smoke:—for it far surpasses these in nimbleness and is moved, when struck by a far slenderer cause; inasmuch as it is moved by images of smoke and mist; as when for instance sunk in sleep we see altars steam forth their heat and send up their smoke on high; for beyond a doubt images are begotten for us from these things:—well then since you see on the vessels being shattered the water flow away on all sides, and since mist and smoke pass away into air, believe that the soul too is shed abroad and perishes much more quickly and dissolves sooner into its first bodies, when once it has been taken out of the limbs of a man and has withdrawn. For, when the body that serves for its vessel cannot hold it, if shattered from any cause and rarefied by the withdrawal of blood from the veins, how can you believe that this soul can be held by any air? How can that air which is rarer than our body hold it in?

Again we perceive that the mind is begotten along with the body and grows up together with it and becomes old along with it. For even as children go about with a tottering and weakly body, so slender sagacity of mind follows along with it; then when their life has reached the maturity of confirmed strength, the judgment too is greater and the power of the mind more developed. Afterwards when the body has been shattered by the mastering might of time and the frame has dropped with its forces dulled, then the intellect halts, the tongue dotes, the mind gives way, all faculties fail and are found wanting at the same time. It naturally follows then that the whole nature of the soul is dissolved, like smoke, into the high air; since we see it is begotten along with the body and grows up along with it and, as I have shown, breaks down at the same time worn out with age.

Moreover we see that even as the body is liable to violent diseases and severe pain, so is the mind to sharp cares and grief and fear; it naturally follows therefore that it is its partner in death as well. Again in diseases of the body the mind often wanders and goes astray; for it loses its reason and drivels in its speech and often in a profound lethargy is carried into deep and never-ending sleep with drooping eyes and head; out of which it neither hears the voices nor can recognise the faces of those who stand round calling it back to life and bedewing with tears, face and cheeks. Therefore you must admit that the mind too dissolves, since the infection of disease reaches to it; for pain and disease are both forgers of death: a truth we have fully learned ere now by the death of many. Again, when the pungent strength of wine has entered into a man and its spirit has been infused into and transmitted through his veins, why is it that a heaviness of the limbs follows along with this, his legs are hampered as he reels about, his tongue falters, his mind is besotted, his eyes swim, shouting, hiccuping, wranglings are rife, together with all the other usual concomitants, why is all this, if not because the overpowering violence of the wine is wont to disorder the soul within the body? But whenever things can be disordered and hampered, they give token that if a somewhat more potent cause gained an entrance, they would perish and be robbed of all further existence. Moreover it often happens that some one constrained by the violence of disease suddenly drops down before our eyes, as by a stroke of lightning, and foams at the mouth, moans and shivers through his frame, loses his reason, stiffens his muscles, is racked, gasps for breath fitfully, and wearies his limbs with tossing. Sure enough, because the violence of the disease spreads itself through his frame and disorders him, he foams as he tries to eject his soul, just as in the salt sea the waters boil with the mastering might of the winds. A moan too is forced out, because the limbs are seized with pain, and mainly because seeds of voice are driven forth and are carried in a close mass out by the mouth, the road which they are accustomed to take and where they have a well-paved way. Loss of reason follows, because the powers of the mind and soul are disordered and, as I have shown, are riven and forced asunder, torn to pieces by the same baneful malady. Then after the cause of the disease has bent its course back and the acrid humours of the distempered body return to their hiding-places, then he first gets up like one reeling, and by little and little comes back into full possession of his senses and regains his soul. Since therefore even within the body mind and soul are harassed by such violent distempers and so miserably racked by sufferings, why believe that they without the body in the open air can continue existence battling with fierce winds? And since we perceive that the mind is healed like the sick body, and we see that it can be altered by medicine, this too gives warning that the mind has a mortal existence. For it is natural that whosoever essays and attempts to change the mind or seeks to alter any other nature you like, should add new parts or change the arrangement of the present, or withdraw in short some tittle from the sum. But that which is immortal wills not to have its parts transposed nor any addition to be made nor one tittle to ebb away; for whenever a thing changes and quits its proper limits, this change is at once the death of that which was before. Therefore the mind, whether it is sick or whether it is altered by medicine, alike, as I have shown, gives forth mortal symptoms. So invariably is truth found to make head against false reason and to cut off all retreat from the assailant and by a two-fold refutation to put falsehood to rout.

Again we often see a man pass gradually away and limb by limb lose vital sense; first the toes of his feet and the nails turn livid, then the feet and shanks die, then next the steps of chilly death creep with slow pace over the other members. Therefore since the nature of the soul is rent and passes away and does not at one time stand forth in its entireness, it must be reckoned mortal. But if haply you suppose that it can draw itself in through the whole frame and mass its parts together and in this way withdraw sense from all the limbs, yet then that spot into which so great a store of soul is gathered, ought to show itself in possession of a greater amount of sense. But as this is nowhere found, sure enough as we said before, it is torn in pieces and scattered abroad, and therefore dies. Moreover if I were pleased for the moment to grant what is false and admit that the soul might be collected in one mass in the body of those who leave the light dying piecemeal, even then you must admit the soul to be mortal; and it makes no difference whether it perish dispersed in air, or gathered into one lump out of all its parts lose all feeling, since sense ever more and more fails the whole man throughout and less and less of life remains throughout.

And since the mind is one part of a man which remains fixed in a particular spot, just as are the ears and eyes and the other senses which guide and direct life; and just as the hand or eye or nose when separated from us cannot feel and exist apart, but in however short a time wastes away in putrefaction, thus the mind cannot exist by itself without the body and the man's self which as you see serves for the mind's vessel or any thing else you choose to imagine which implies a yet closer union with it, since the body is attached to it by the nearest ties.

Again the quickened powers of body and mind by their joint partnership enjoy health and life; for the nature of the mind cannot by itself alone without the body give forth vital motions nor can the body again bereft of the soul continue to exist and make use of its senses: just, you are to know, as the eye itself torn away from its roots cannot see anything when apart from the whole body, thus the soul and mind cannot it is plain do anything by themselves. Sure enough, because mixed up through veins and flesh, sinews and bones, their first-beginnings are confined by all the body and are not free to bound away leaving great spaces between, therefore thus shut in they make those sense-giving motions which they cannot make after death when forced out of the body into the air by reason that they are not then confined in a like manner; for the air will be a body and a living thing, if the soul shall be able to keep itself together and to enclose in it those motions which it used before to perform in the sinews and within the body. Moreover even while it yet moves within the confines of life, often the soul shaken from some cause or other is seen to wish to pass out and be loosed from the whole body, the features are seen to droop as at the last hour and all the limbs to sink flaccid over the bloodless trunk: just as happens, when the phrase is used, the mind is in a bad way, or the soul is quite gone; when all is hurry and every one is anxious to keep from parting the last tie of life; for then the mind and the power of the soul are shaken throughout and both are quite loosened together with the body; so that a cause somewhat more powerful can quite break them up. Why doubt I would ask that the soul when driven forth out of the body, when in the open air, feeble as it is, stript of its covering, not only cannot continue through eternity, but is unable to hold together the smallest fraction of time? Therefore, again and again I say, when the enveloping body has been all broken up and the vital airs have been forced out, you must admit that the senses of the mind and the soul are dissolved, since the cause of destruction is one and inseparable for both body and soul.

Again since the body is unable to bear the separation of the soul without rotting away in a noisome stench, why doubt that the power of the soul gathering itself up from the inmost depths of body has oozed out and dispersed like smoke, and that the crumbling body has changed and tumbled in with so total a ruin for this reason because its foundations throughout are stirred from their places, the soul oozing out abroad through the frame, through all the winding passages which are in the body, and all openings? So that in ways manifold you may learn that the nature of the soul has been divided piecemeal and gone forth throughout the frame, and that it has been torn to shreds within the body, ere it glided forth and swam out into the air. For no one when dying appears to feel the soul go forth entire from his whole body or first mount up to the throat and gullet, but all feel it fail in that part which lies in a particular quarter; just as they know that the senses as well suffer dissolution each in its own place. But if our mind were immortal, it would not when dying complain so much of its dissolution, as of passing abroad and quitting its vesture, like a snake.

Again why are the mind's understanding and judgement never begotten in the head or feet or hands, but cling in all alike to one spot and fixed quarter, if it be not that particular places are assigned for the birth of everything, and nature has determined where each is to continue to exist after it is born? Our body then must follow the same law and have such a manifold organisation of parts, that no perverted arrangement of its members shall ever show itself: so invariably effect follows cause, nor is flame wont to be born in rivers nor cold in fire.

Again if the nature of the soul is immortal and can feel when separated from our body, methinks we must suppose it to be provided with five senses; and in no other way can we picture to ourselves souls below flitting about Acheron. Painters therefore and former generations of writers have thus represented souls provided with senses. But neither eyes nor nose nor hand can exist for the soul apart from the body nor can tongue, nor can ears perceive by the sense of hearing or exist for the soul by themselves apart from the body.

And since we perceive that vital sense is in the whole body and we see that it is all endowed with life, if on a sudden any force with swift blow shall have cut it in twain so as quite to dissever the two halves, the power of the soul will without doubt at the same time be cleft and cut asunder and dashed in twain together with the body. But that which is cut and divides into any parts, you are to know disclaims for itself an everlasting nature. Stories are told how scythed chariots reeking with indiscriminate slaughter often lop off limbs so instantaneously that that which has fallen down lopped off from the frame is seen to quiver on the ground, while yet the mind and faculty of the man from the suddenness of the mischief cannot feel the pain; and because his mind once for all is wholly given to the business of fighting, with what remains of his body he mingles in the fray and carnage, and often perceives not that the wheels and devouring scythes have carried off among the horses' feet his left arm shield and all; another sees not that his right arm has dropped from him, while he mounts and presses forward. Another tries to get up after he has lost his leg, while the dying foot quivers with its toes on the ground close by. The head too when cut off from the warm and living trunk retains on the ground the expression of life and open eyes, until it has yielded up all the remnants of soul. To take another case, if, as a serpent's tongue is quivering, as its tail is darting out from its long body, you choose to chop with an axe into many pieces both tail and body, you will see all the separate portions thus cut off writhing under the fresh wound and bespattering the earth with gore, the fore part with the mouth making for its own hinder part, to allay with burning bite the pain of the wound with which it has been smitten. Shall we say than that there are entire souls in all those pieces? why from that argument it will follow that one living creature had many souls in its body; and this being absurd, therefore the soul which was one has been divided together with the body; therefore each alike must be reckoned mortal, since each is alike chopped up into many pieces.

Again if the nature of the soul is immortal and makes its way into our body at the time of birth, why are we unable to remember besides the time already gone, and why do we retain no traces of past actions? If the power of the mind has been so completely changed, that all remembrance of past things is lost, that methinks differs not widely from death; therefore you must admit that the soul which was before has perished and that which now is has now been formed.

Again if the quickened power of the mind is wont to be put into us after our body is fully formed, at the instant of our birth and our crossing the threshold of life, it ought agreeably to this to live not in such a way as to seem to have grown with the body and together with its members within the blood, but as in a den apart by and to itself: the very contrary to what undoubted fact teaches; for it is so closely united with the body throughout the veins, flesh, sinews, and bones, that the very teeth have a share of sense; as their aching proves and the sharp twinge of cold water and the crunching of a rough stone, when it has got into them out of bread. Wherefore, again and again I say, we must believe souls to be neither without a birth nor exempted from the law of death; for we must not believe that they could have been so completely united with our bodies, if they found their way into them from without, nor, since they are so closely inwoven with them, does it appear that they can get out unharmed and unloose themselves unscathed from all the sinews and bones and joints. But if haply you believe that the soul finds its way in from without and is wont to ooze through all our limbs, so much the more it will perish thus blended with the body; for what oozes through another is dissolved, and therefore dies. As food distributed through all the cavities of the body, while it is transmitted into the limbs and the whole frame, is destroyed and furnishes out of itself the matter of another nature, thus the soul and mind, though they pass entire into a fresh body, yet in oozing through it are dissolved, whilst there are transmitted so to say into the frame through all the cavities those particles of which this nature of mind is formed, which now is sovereign in our body, being born out of that soul which then perished when dispersed through the frame. Wherefore the nature of the soul is seen to be neither without a birthday nor exempt from death.

Again are seeds of the soul left in the dead body or not? If they are left and remain in it, the soul cannot fairly be deemed immortal, since it has withdrawn lessened by the loss of some parts; but if when taken away from the yet untainted limbs it has fled so entirely away as to leave in the body no parts of itself, whence do carcasses exude worms from the now rank flesh and whence does such a swarm of living things, boneless and bloodless, surge through the heaving frame? But if haply you believe that souls find their way into worms from without and can severally pass each into a body and you make no account of why many thousands of souls meet together in a place from which one has withdrawn, this question at least must, it seems, be raised and brought to a decisive test, whether souls hunt out the several seeds of worms and build for themselves a place to dwell in, or find their way into bodies fully formed so to say. But why they should on their part make a body or take such trouble, cannot be explained; since being without a body they are not plagued as they flit about with diseases and cold and hunger, the body being more akin to, more troubled by such infirmities, and by its contact with it the mind suffering many ills. Nevertheless be it ever so expedient for them to make a body, when they are going to enter, yet clearly there is no way by which they can do so. Therefore souls do not make for themselves bodies and limbs; no nor can they by any method find their way into bodies after they are fully formed; for they will neither be able to unite themselves with a nice precision nor will any connexion of mutual sensation be formed between them.

Again why does untamed fierceness go along with the sullen brood of lions, cunning with foxes and proneness to flight with stags? And to take any other instance of the kind, why are all qualities engendered in the limbs and temper from the very commencement of life, if not because a fixed power of mind derived from its proper seed and breed grows up together with the whole body? If it were immortal and wont to pass into different bodies, living creatures would be of interchangeable dispositions; a dog of Hyrcanian breed would often fly before the attack of an antlered stag, a hawk would cower in mid air as it fled at the approach of a dove, men would be without reason, the savage races of wild beasts would have reason. For the assertion that an immortal soul is altered by a change of body is advanced on a false principle. What is changed is dissolved, and therefore dies: the parts are transposed and quit their former order; therefore they must admit of being dissolved too throughout the frame, in order at last to die one and all together with the body. But if they shall say that souls of men always go into human bodies, I yet will ask how it is a soul can change from wise to foolish, and no child has discretion, and why the mare's foal is not so well trained as the powerful strength of the horse. You may be sure they will fly to the subterfuge that the mind grows weakly in a weakly body. But granting this is so, you must admit the soul to be mortal, since changed so completely throughout the frame it loses its former life and sense. Then too in what way will it be able to grow in strength uniformly with its allotted body and reach the coveted flower of age, unless it shall be its partner at its first beginning? Or what means it by passing out from the limbs when decayed with age? Does it fear to remain shut up in a crumbling body, fear that its tenement, worn out by protracted length of days, bury it in its ruins? Why an immortal being incurs no risks.

Again for souls to stand by at the unions of Venus and the birth-throes of beasts seems to be passing absurd, for them the immortals to wait for mortal limbs in number numberless and struggle with one another in forward rivalry, which shall first and by preference have entrance in; unless haply bargains are struck among the souls on these terms, that whichever in its flight shall first come up, shall first have right of entry, and that they shall make no trial at all of each other's strength.

Again a tree cannot exist in the ether, nor clouds in the deep sea nor can fishes live in the fields nor blood exist in woods nor sap in stones. Where each thing can grow and abide is fixed and ordained. Thus the nature of the mind cannot come into being alone without the body nor exist far away from the sinews and blood. But if (for this would be much more likely to happen than that) the force itself of the mind might be in the head or shoulders or heels or might be born in any other part of the body, it would after all be wont to abide in one and the same man or vessel. But since in our body even it is fixed and seen to be ordained where the soul and the mind can severally be and grow, it must still more strenuously be denied that it can abide and be born out of the body altogether. Therefore when the body has died, we must admit that the soul has perished, wrenched away throughout the body. To link forsooth a mortal thing with an everlasting and suppose that they can have sense in common and can be reciprocally acted upon, is sheer folly; for what can be conceived more incongruous, more discordant and inconsistent with itself, than a thing which is mortal, linked with an immortal and everlasting thing, trying in such union to weather furious storms? But if haply the soul is to be accounted immortal for this reason rather, because it is kept sheltered from death-bringing things, either because things hostile to its existence do not approach at all, or because those which do approach, in some way or other retreat discomfited before we can feel the harm they do, manifest experience proves that this cannot be true. For besides that it sickens in sympathy with the maladies of the body, it is often attacked by that which frets it on the score of the future and keeps it on the rack of suspense and wears it out with cares; and when ill deeds are in the past, remorse for sins yet gnaws: then there is madness peculiar to the mind and forgetfulness of all things; then too it often sinks into the black water of lethargy.

Death therefore to us is nothing, concerns us not a jot, since the nature of the mind is proved to be mortal; and as in time gone by we felt no distress, when the Poeni from all sides came together to do battle, and all things shaken by war's troublous uproar shuddered and quaked beneath high heaven, and mortal men were in doubt which of the two peoples it should be to whose empire all must fall by sea and land alike, thus when we shall be no more, when there shall have been a separation of body and soul, out of both of which we are each formed into a single being, to us, you may be sure, who then shall be no more, nothing whatever can happen to excite sensation, not if earth shall be mingled with sea and sea with heaven. And even supposing the nature of the mind and power of the soul do feel, after they have been severed from our body, yet that is nothing to us who by the binding tie of marriage between body and soul are formed each into one single being. And if time should gather up our matter after our death and put it once more into the position in which it now is, and the light of life be given to us again, this result even would concern us not at all, when the chain of our self-consciousness has once been snapped asunder. So now we give ourselves no concern about any self which we have been before, nor do we feel any distress on the score of that self. For when you look back on the whole past course of immeasurable time and think how manifold are the shapes which the motions of matter take, you may easily credit this too, that these very same seeds of which we now are formed, have often before been placed in the same order in which they now are; and yet we cannot recover this in memory: a break in our existence has been interposed, and all the motions have wandered to and fro far astray from the sensations they produced. For he whom evil is to befall, must in his own person exist at the very time it comes, if the misery and suffering are haply to have any place at all; but since death precludes this, and forbids him to be, upon whom the ills can be brought, you may be sure that we have nothing to fear after death, and that he who exists not, cannot become miserable, and that it matters not a whit whether he has been born into life at any other time, when immortal death has taken away his mortal life.

Therefore when you see a man bemoaning his hard case, that after death he shall either rot with his body laid in the grave or be devoured by flames or the jaws of wild beasts, you may be sure that his ring betrays a flaw and that there lurks in his heart a secret goad, though he himself declare that he does not believe that any sense will remain to him after death. He does not methinks really grant the conclusion which he professes to grant nor the principle on which he so professes, nor does he take and force himself root and branch out of life, but all unconsciously imagines something of self to survive. For when any one in life suggests to himself that birds and beasts will rend his body after death, he makes moan for himself: he does not separate himself from that self, nor withdraw himself fully from the body so thrown out, and fancies himself that other self and stands by and impregnates it with his own sense. Hence he makes much moan that he has been born mortal, and sees not that after real death there will be no other self to remain in life and lament to self that his own self has met death, and there to stand and grieve that his own self there lying is mangled or burnt. For if it is an evil after death to be pulled about by the devouring jaws of wild beasts, I cannot see why it should not be a cruel pain to be laid on fires and burn in hot flames, or to be placed in honey and stifled, or to stiffen with cold, stretched on the smooth surface of an icy slab of stone, or to be pressed down and crushed by a load of earth above.

'Now no more shall thy house admit thee with glad welcome, nor a most virtuous wife and sweet children run to be the first to snatch kisses and touch thy heart with a silent joy. No more mayst thou be prosperous in thy doings, a safeguard to thine own. One disastrous day has taken from thee luckless man in luckless wise all the many prizes of life.' This do men say; but add not thereto 'and now no longer does any craving for these things beset thee withal.' For if they could rightly perceive this in thought and follow up the thought in words, they would release themselves from great distress and apprehension of mind. 'Thou, even as now thou art, sunk in the sleep of death, shalt continue so to be all time to come, freed from all distressful pains; but we with a sorrow that would not be sated wept for thee, when close by thou didst turn to an ashen hue on thy appalling funeral pile, and no length of days shall pluck from our hearts our ever-during grief.' This question therefore should be asked of this speaker, what there is in it so passing bitter, if it come in the end to sleep and rest, that any one should pine in never-ending sorrow.

This too men often, when they have reclined at table cup in hand and shade their brows with crowns, love to say from the heart, 'short is this enjoyment for poor weak men; presently it will have been and never after may it be called back.' As if after their death it is to be one of their chiefest afflictions that thirst and parching drought is to burn them up hapless wretches, or a craving for anything else is to beset them. What folly! no one feels the want of himself and life at the time when mind and body are together sunk in sleep; for all we care this sleep might be everlasting, no craving whatever for ourselves then moves us. And yet by no means do those first-beginnings throughout our frame wander at that time far away from their sense-producing motions, at the moment when a man starts up from sleep and collects himself. Death therefore must be thought to concern us much less, if less there can be than what we see to be nothing; for a greater dispersion of the mass of matter follows after death, and no one wakes up, upon whom the chill cessation of life has once come.

Once more, if the nature of things could suddenly utter a voice and in person could rally any of us in such words as these, 'what hast thou, O mortal, so much at heart, that thou goest such lengths in sickly sorrows? Why bemoan and bewail death? For say thy life past and gone has been welcome to thee and thy blessings have not all, as if they were poured into a perforated vessel, run through and been lost without avail: why not then take thy departure like a guest filled with life, and with resignation, thou fool, enter upon untroubled rest? But if all that thou hast enjoyed, has been squandered and lost, and life is a grievance, why seek to make any addition, to be wasted perversely in its turn and lost utterly without avail? Why not rather make an end of life and travail? For there is nothing more which I can contrive and discover for thee to give pleasure: all things are ever the same. Though thy body is not yet decayed with years nor thy frame worn out and exhausted, yet all things remain the same, ay though in length of life thou shouldst outlast all races of things now living, nay even more if thou shouldst never die,' what answer have we to make save this, that nature sets up against us a well-founded claim and puts forth in her pleading a true indictment? If however one of greater age and more advanced in years should complain and lament poor wretch his death more than is right, would she not with greater cause raise her voice and rally him in sharp accents, 'Away from this time forth with thy tears, rascal; a truce to thy complainings: thou decayest after full enjoyment of all the prizes of life. But because thou ever yearnest for what is not present, and despisest what is, life has slipped from thy grasp unfinished and unsatisfying, and or ever thou thoughtest, death has taken his stand at thy pillow, before thou canst take thy departure sated and filled with good things. Now however resign all things unsuited to thy age, and with a good grace up and greatly go: thou must.' With good reason methinks she would bring her charge, with reason rally and reproach; for old things give way and are supplanted by new without fail, and one thing must ever be replenished out of other things; and no one is delivered over to the pit and black Tartarus: matter is needed for after generations to grow; all of which though will follow thee when they have finished their term of life; and thus it is that all these no less than thou have before this come to an end and hereafter will come to an end. Thus one thing will never cease to rise out of another, and life is granted to none in fee-simple, to all in usufruct. Think too how the bygone antiquity of everlasting time before our birth was nothing to us. Nature therefore holds this up to us as a mirror of the time yet to come after our death. Is there aught in this that looks appalling, aught that wears an aspect of gloom? Is it not more untroubled than any sleep?

And those things sure enough, which are fabled to be in the deep of Acheron, do all exist for us in this life. No Tantalus, numbed by groundless terror, as the story is, fears poor wretch a huge stone hanging in air; but in life rather a baseless dread of the god vexes mortals: the fall they fear is such fall of luck as chance brings to each. Nor do birds eat a way into Tityos laid in Acheron, nor can they sooth to say find during eternity food to peck under his large breast. However huge the bulk of body he extends, though such as to take up with outspread limbs not nine acres merely, but the whole earth, yet will he not be able to endure everlasting pain and supply food from his own body for ever. But he is for us a Tityos, whom, as he grovels in love, vultures rend and bitter bitter anguish eats up or troubled thoughts from any other passion do rive. In life too we have a Sisyphus before our eyes who is bent on asking from the people the rods and cruel axes, and always retires defeated and disappointed. For to ask for power, which empty as it is is never given, and always in the chase of it to undergo severe toil, this is forcing up-hill with much effort a stone which after all rolls back again from the summit and seeks in headlong haste the levels of the plain. Then to be ever feeding the thankless nature of the mind, and never to fill it full and sate it with good things, as the seasons of the year do for us, when they come round and bring their fruits and varied delights, though after all we are never filled with the enjoyments of life, this methinks is to do what is told of the maidens in the flower of their age, to keep pouring water into a perforated vessel which in spite of all can never be filled full. Moreover Cerberus and the furies and yon privation of light are idle tales, as well as all the rest, Ixion's wheel and black Tartarus belching forth hideous fires from his throat: things which nowhere are nor sooth to say can be. But there is in life a dread of punishment for evil deeds, signal as the deeds are signal, and for atonement of guilt, the prison and the frightful hurling down from the rock, scourgings, executioners, the dungeon of the doomed, the pitch, the metal plate, torches; and even though these are wanting, yet the conscience-stricken mind through boding fears applies to itself goads and frightens itself with whips, and sees not meanwhile what end there can be of ills or what limit at last is to be set to punishments, and fears lest these very evils be enhanced after death. The life of fools at length becomes a hell here on earth.

This too you may sometimes say to yourself, 'even worthy Ancus has quitted the light with his eyes, who was far far better than thou, unconscionable man. And since then many other kings and kesars have been laid low, who lorded it over mighty nations. He too, even he who erst paved a way over the great sea and made a path for his legions to march over the deep and taught them to pass on foot over the salt pools and set at naught the roarings of the sea, trampling on them with his horses, had the light taken from him and shed forth his soul from his dying body. The son of the Scipios, thunderbolt of war, terror of Carthage, yielded his bones to earth just as if he were the lowest menial. Think too of the inventors of all sciences and graceful arts, think of the companions of the Heliconian maids; among whom Homer bore the sceptre without a peer, and he now sleeps the same sleep as others. Then there is Democritus, who, when a ripe old age had warned him that the memory-waking motions of his mind were waning, by his own spontaneous act offered up his head to death. Even Epicurus passed away, when his light of life had run its course, he who surpassed in intellect the race of man and quenched the light of all, as the ethereal sun arisen quenches the stars.' Wilt thou then hesitate and think it a hardship to die? Thou for whom life is well nigh dead whilst yet thou livest and seest the light, who spendest the greater part of thy time in sleep and snorest wide awake and ceasest not to see visions and hast a mind troubled with groundless terror and canst not discover often what it is that ails thee, when besotted man thou art sore pressed on all sides with full many cares and goest astray tumbling about in the wayward wanderings of thy mind.

If, just as they are seen to feel that a load is on their mind which wears them out with its pressure, men might apprehend from what causes too it is produced and whence such a pile, if I may say so, of ill lies on their breast, they would not spend their life as we see them now for the most part do, not knowing any one of them what he means and wanting ever change of place as though he might lay his burden down. The man who is sick of home often issues forth from his large mansion, and as suddenly comes back to it, finding as he does that he is no better off abroad. He races to his country-house, driving his jennets in headlong haste, as if hurrying to bring help to a house on fire: he yawns the moment he has reached the door of his house, or sinks heavily into sleep and seeks forgetfulness, or even in haste goes back again to town. In this way each man flies from himself (but self from whom, as you may be sure is commonly the case, he cannot escape, clings to him in his own despite), hates too himself, because he is sick and knows not the cause of the malady; for if he could rightly see into this, relinquishing all else each man would study to learn the nature of things, since the point at stake is the condition for eternity, not for one hour, in which mortals have to pass all the time which remains for them to expect after death.

Once more what evil lust of life is this which constrains us with such force to be so mightily troubled in doubts and dangers? A sure term of life is fixed for mortals, and death cannot be shunned, but meet it we must. Moreover we are ever engaged, ever involved in the same pursuits, and no new pleasure is struck out by living on; but whilst what we crave is wanting, it seems to transcend all the rest; then, when it has been gotten, we crave something else, and ever does the same thirst of life possess us, as we gape for it open-mouthed. Quite doubtful it is what fortune the future will carry with it or what chance will bring us or what end is at hand. Nor by prolonging life do we take one tittle from the time past in death nor can we fret anything away, whereby we may haply be a less long time in the condition of the dead. Therefore you may complete as many generations as you please during your life; none the less however will that everlasting death await you; and for no less long a time will he be no more in being, who beginning with to-day has ended his life, than the man who has died many months and years ago.

SEXTUS EMPIRICUS AND SCEPTICISM

Very little is known about the life of Sextus Empiricus. He is thought to have lived sometime between A.D. *150 and* A.D. *225. Sextus was a medical doctor and an interpreter of philosophical scepticism. His attack on previous philosophers and other theoreticians is found in* Against the Dogmatists (Adversus Mathematicos). *As we saw in the material from the Pre-Socratics, this work by Sextus is a major source for "fragments" otherwise unavailable. The selection that follows presents a basic statement of the sceptical philosophical tradition. "Pyrrhonism" refers to the founder of ancient Scepticism, Pyrrho of Elis, who lived ca. 350–275* B.C. *Despite the contentious character of the writings of Sextus, especially with regard to the Stoics, he, too, sought a personal peace* (ataraxia) *through philosophical inquiry. The tradition of philosophical inquiry will always breed a parallel school of sceptics, who are dubious about the claims made by philosophers. The thought of Sextus Empiricus is a model of the sceptical approach to the claims of philosophy.*

From Outlines of Pyrrhonism

OF THE MAIN DIFFERENCE BETWEEN PHILOSOPHIC SYSTEMS

The natural result of any investigation is that the investigators either discover the object of search or deny that it is discoverable and confess it to be inapprehensible or persist in their search. So, too, with regard to the objects investigated by philosophy, this is probably why some have claimed to have discovered the truth, others have asserted that it cannot be apprehended, while others again go on inquiring. Those who believe they have discovered it are the "Dogmatists," specially so called—Aristotle, for example, and Epicurus and the Stoics and certain

---

Reprinted by permission of the publishers and The Loeb Classical Library from *Outlines of Pyrrhonism*, Sextus Empiricus, trans. R. G. Bury, Cambridge, Mass.: Harvard University Press, 1933. (I:3–21; II:203–213)

others; Cleitomachus and Carneades and other Academics treat it as inapprehensible: the Sceptics keep on searching. Hence it seems reasonable to hold that the main types of philosophy are three—the Dogmatic, the Academic, and the Sceptic. Of the other systems it will best become others to speak: our task at present is to describe in outline the Sceptic doctrine, first premising that of none of our future statements do we positively affirm that the fact is exactly as we state it, but we simply record each fact, like a chronicler, as it appears to us at the moment.

OF THE ARGUMENTS OF SCEPTICISM

Of the Sceptic philosophy one argument (or branch of exposition) is called "general," the other "special." In the general argument we set forth the distinctive features of Scepticism, stating its purport and principles, its logical methods, criterion, and end or aim; the "Tropes," also, or "Modes," which lead to suspension of judgment, and in what sense we adopt the Sceptic formulae, and the distinction between Scepticism and the philosophies which stand next to it. In the special argument we state our objections regarding the several divisions of so-called philosophy. Let us, then, deal first with the general argument, beginning our description with the names given to the Sceptic School.

OF THE NOMENCLATURE OF SCEPTICISM

The Sceptic School, then, is also called "Zetetic" from its activity in investigation and inquiry, and "Ephectic" or Suspensive from the state of mind produced in the inquirer after his search, and "Aporetic" or Dubitative either from its habit of doubting and seeking, as some say, or from its indecision as regards assent and denial, and "Pyrrhonean" from the fact that Pyrrho appears to us to have applied himself to Scepticism more thoroughly and more conspicuously than his predecessors.

WHAT SCEPTICISM IS

Scepticism is an ability, or mental attitude, which opposes appearances to judgments in any way whatsoever, with the result that, owing to the equipollence of the objects and reasons thus opposed, we are brought firstly to a state of mental suspense and next to a state of "unperturbedness" or quietude. Now we call it an "ability" not in any subtle sense, but simply in respect of its "being able." By "appearances" we now mean the objects of sense-perception, whence we contrast them with the objects of thought or "judgements." The phrase "in any way whatsoever" can be connected either with the word "ability," to make us take the word "ability," as we said, in its simple sense, or with the phrase "opposing appearances to judgements"; for inasmuch as we oppose these in a variety of ways—appearances to appearances, or judgements to judgements, or *alternando* appearances to judgements,—in order to ensure the inclusion of all these antitheses we employ the phrase "in any way whatsoever." Or, again, we join "in any way whatsoever" to "appearances and judgements" in order that we may not have to inquire how the appearances appear or how the thought-objects are judged, but may take these terms in the simple sense. The phrase "opposed judgements" we do not employ in the sense of negations and affirmations only but simply as equivalent to "conflicting judgements." "Equipollence" we use of equality in respect of probability and improbability, to indicate that no one of the conflicting judgements takes precedence of any other as being more probable. "Suspense" is a state of mental rest owing to which we neither deny nor affirm anything. "Quietude" is an untroubled and tranquil condition of soul. And how quietude enters the soul along with suspension of judgement we shall explain in our chapter (XII.) "Concerning the End."

OF THE SCEPTIC

In the definition of the Sceptic system there is also implicitly included that of the Pyrrhonean philosopher: he is the man who participates in this "ability."

OF THE PRINCIPLES OF SCEPTICISM

The originating cause of Scepticism is, we say, the hope of attaining quietude. Men of talent, who were perturbed by the contradictions of things and in doubt as to which of the alternatives they ought to accept, were led on to inquire what is true in things and what false, hoping by the settlement of this question to attain quietude. The main basic principle of the Sceptic system is that of opposing to every proposition an equal proposition; for we believe that as a consequence of this we end by ceasing to dogmatize.

DOES THE SCEPTIC DOGMATIZE?

When we say that the Sceptic refrains from dogmatizing we do not use the term "dogma," as some do, in the broader sense of "approval of a thing" (for the Sceptic gives assent to the feelings which are the necessary results of sense-impressions, and he would not, for example, say when feeling hot or cold "I believe that I am not hot or cold"); but we say that "he does not dogmatize" using "dogma" in the sense, which some give it, of "assent to one of the non-evident objects of scientific inquiry"; for the Pyrrhonean philosopher assents to nothing that is non-evident. Moreover, even in the act of enunciating the Sceptic formulae concerning things non-evident—such as the formula "No more (one thing than another)," or the formula "I determine nothing," or any of the others which we shall presently mention,—he does not dogmatize. For whereas the dogmatizer posits the things about which he is said to be dogmatizing as really existent, the Sceptic does not posit these formulae in any absolute sense; for he conceives that, just as the formula "All things are false" asserts the falsity of itself as well as of everything else, as does the formula "Nothing is true," so also the formula "No more" asserts that itself, like all the rest, is "No more (this than that)," and thus cancels itself along with the rest. And of the other formulae we say the same. If then, while the dogmatizer posits the matter of his dogma as substantial truth, the Sceptic enunciates his formulae so that they are virtually cancelled by themselves, he should not be said to dogmatize in his enunciation of them. And, most important of all, in his enunciation of these formulae he states what appears to himself and announces his own impression in an undogmatic way, without making any positive assertion regarding the external realities.

HAS THE SCEPTIC A DOCTRINAL RULE?

We follow the same lines in replying to the question "Has the Sceptic a doctrinal rule?" For if one defines a "doctrinal rule" as "adherence to a number of dogmas which are dependent both on one another and on appearances," and defines "dogma" as "assent to a non-evident proposition," then we shall say that he has not a doctrinal rule. But if one defines "doctrinal rule" as "procedure which, in accordance with appearance, follows a certain line of reasoning, that reasoning indicating how it is possible to seem to live rightly (the word 'rightly' being taken, not as referring to virtue only, but in a wider sense) and tending to enable one to suspend judgement, then we say that he has a doctrinal rule. For we follow a line of reasoning which, in accordance with appearances, points us to a life conformable to the customs of our country and its laws and institutions, and to our own instinctive feelings.

DOES THE SCEPTIC DEAL WITH PHYSICS?

We make a similar reply also to the question "Should the Sceptic deal with physical problems?" For while, on the one hand, so far as regards making firm and positive assertions about any of the matters dogmatically treated in physical theory, we do not deal with physics; yet, on the other hand, in respect of our mode of opposing to every proposition an equal proposition and of our theory of quietude we do treat of physics. This, too, is the way in which we approach the logical and ethical branches of so-called "philosophy."

DO THE SCEPTICS ABOLISH APPEARANCES?

Those who say that "the Sceptics abolish appearances," or phenomena, seem to me to be unacquainted with the statements of our School. For, as we said above, we do not overthrow the affective sense-impressions which induce our assent involuntarily; and these impressions are "the appearances." And when we question whether the underlying object is such as it appears, we grant the fact that it appears, and our doubt does not concern the appearance itself but the account given of the appearance,—and that is a different thing from questioning the appearance itself. For example, honey appears to us to be sweet (and this we grant, for we perceive sweetness through the senses), but whether it is also sweet in its essence is for us a matter of doubt, since this is not an appearance but a judgement regarding the appearance. And even if we do actually argue against the appearances, we do not propound such arguments with the intention of abolishing appearances, but by way of pointing out the rashness of the Dogmatists; for if reason is such a trickster as to all but snatch away the appearances from under our very eyes, surely we should view it with suspicion in the case of things non-evident so as not to display rashness by following it.

OF THE CRITERION OF SCEPTICISM

That we adhere to appearances is plain from what we say about the Criterion of the Sceptic School. The word "Criterion" is used in two senses: in the one it means "the standard regulating belief in reality or unreality," (and this we shall discuss in our refutation); in the other it denotes the standard of action by conforming to which in the conduct of life we perform some actions and abstain from others; and it is of the latter that we are now speaking. The criterion, then, of the Sceptic School is, we say, the appearance, giving this name to what is virtually the sense-presentation. For since this lies in feeling and involuntary affection, it is not open to question. Consequently, no one, I suppose, disputes that the underlying object has this or that appearance; the point in dispute is whether the object is in reality such as it appears to be.

Adhering, then, to appearances we live in accordance with the normal rules of life, undogmatically, seeing that we cannot remain wholly inactive. And it would seem that this regulation of life is fourfold, and that one part of it lies in the guidance of Nature, another in the constraint of the passions, another in the tradition of laws and customs, another in the instruction of the arts. Nature's guidance is that by which we are naturally capable of sensation and thought; constraint of the passions is that whereby hunger drives us to food and thirst to drink; tradition of customs and laws, that whereby we regard piety in the conduct of life as good, but impiety as evil; instruction of the arts, that whereby we are not inactive in such arts as we adopt. But we make all these statements undogmatically.

WHAT IS THE END OF SCEPTICISM?

Our next subject will be the End of the Sceptic system. Now an "End" is "that for which all actions or reasonings are undertaken, while it exists for the sake of none"; or, otherwise, "the ultimate object of appetency." We assert still that the Sceptic's End is quietude in respect of matters of opinion and moderate feeling in respect of things unavoidable. For the Sceptic, having set out to philosophize with the object of passing judgement on the sense-impressions and ascertaining which of them are true and which false, so as to attain quietude thereby, found himself involved in contradictions of equal weight, and being unable to decide between them suspended judgement; and as he was thus in suspense there followed, as it happened, the state of quietude in respect of matters of opinion. For the man who opines that anything is by nature good or bad is for ever being disquieted: when he is without the things which he deems good he believes himself to be tormented by things naturally bad and he pursues after the things which are, as he thinks, good; which when he has obtained he keeps falling into still more perturbations because of his irrational and immoderate elation, and in his dread of a change of fortune he uses every endeavour to avoid losing the things which he deems good. On the other hand, the man who determines nothing as to what is naturally good or bad neither shuns nor pursues anything eagerly; and, in consequence, he is unperturbed.

The Sceptic, in fact, had the same experience which is said to have befallen the painter Apelles. Once, they say, when he was painting a horse and wished to represent in the painting the horse's foam, he was so unsuccessful that he gave up the attempt and flung at the picture the sponge on which he used to wipe the paints off his brush, and the mark of the sponge produced the effect of a horse's foam. So, too, the Sceptics were in hopes of gaining quietude by means of a decision regarding the disparity of the objects of sense and of thought, and being unable to effect this they suspended judgement; and they found that quietude, as if by chance, followed upon their suspense, even as a shadow follows its substance. We do not, however, suppose that the Sceptic is wholly untroubled; but we say that he is troubled by things unavoidable; for we grant that he is cold at times and thirsty, and suffers various affections of that kind. But even in these cases, whereas ordinary people are afflicted by two circumstances,—namely, by the affections themselves and, in no less a degree, by the belief that these conditions are evil by nature,—the Sceptic, by his rejection of the added belief in the natural badness of all these conditions, escapes here too with less discomfort. Hence we say that, while in regard to matters of opinion the Sceptic's End is quietude, in regard to things unavoidable it is "moderate affection." But some notable Sceptics have added the further definition "suspension of judgement in investigations."

OF THE TRUE AND TRUTH

Even were we to grant, by way of hypothesis, that a criterion of truth exists, it is found to be useless and vain if we recall that, so far as the statements of the Dogmatists go, truth is unreal and the true non-substantial. The passage we recall is this: "The true is said to differ from truth in three ways—in essence, composition, potency. In essence, since the true is incorporeal (for it is judgement and "expression"), while truth is a body (for it is knowledge declaratory of all true things, and knowledge is a particular state of the regent part, just as the fist is a particular state of the hand, and the regent part is a body; for according to them it is breath). In composition, because the true is a simple thing, as for example 'I converse,' whereas truth is a compound of many true cognitions. In potency, since truth depends on knowledge but the true does not altogether so depend. Consequently, as they say, truth exists only in the good man, but the true in the bad man as well; for it is possible for the bad man to utter something true."

Such are the statements of the Dogmatists. But we,—having regard here again to the plan of our treatise,—shall confine our present discussion to the true, since its refutation entails that of truth as well, it being defined as the "system of the knowledge of things true." Again, since some of our arguments, whereby we dispute the very existence of the true, are more general, others of a specific kind, whereby we prove that the true does not exist in utterance or in expression or in the movement of the intellect, we deem it sufficient for the present to set forth only those of the more general kind. For just as, when the foundation of a wall collapses, all the superstructure collapses along with it, so also, when, the substantial existence of the true is refuted, all the particular inventions of the logic of the Dogmatists are included in the refutation.

DOES ANYTHING TRUE REALLY EXIST?

Seeing, then, that there is a controversy amongst the Dogmatists regarding "the true," since some assert that something true exists, others that nothing true exists, it is impossible to decide the controversy, because the man who says that something true exists will not be believed without proof, on account of the controversy; and if he wishes to offer proof, he will be disbelieved if he acknowledges that his proof is false, whereas if he declares that his proof is true he becomes involved in circular reasoning and will be required to show proof of the real truth of his proof, and another proof of that proof, and so on *ad infinitum.* But it is impossible to prove an infinite series; and so it is impossible also to get to know that something true exists.

Moreover, the "something," which is, they declare, the highest genus of all, is either true or false or neither false nor true or both false and true. If, then, they shall assert that it is false they will be confessing that all things are false. For just as it follows because "animal" is animate that all particular animals also are animate, so too if the highest genus of all ("something") is false all the particulars also will be false and nothing true. And this involves also the conclusion that nothing is false; for the very statements "all things are false," and "something false exists," being themselves included in the "all," will be false. And if the "something" is true, all things will be true; and from this again it follows that nothing is true, since this statement itself (I mean that "nothing is true") being "something" is true. And if the "something" is both false and true, each of its particulars will be both false and true. From which we conclude that nothing is really true; for that which has its real nature such that it is true will certainly not be false. And if the "something" is neither false nor true, it is acknowledged that all the particulars also, being declared to be neither false nor true, will not be true. So for these reasons it will be non-evident to us whether the true exists.

Furthermore, the true things are either apparent only, or non-evident only, or in part non-evident and in part apparent; but none of these alternatives is true, as we shall show; therefore nothing is true. If, however, the true things are apparent only, they will assert either that all or that some of the apparent are true. And if they say "all," the argument is overthrown; for it is apparent to some that nothing is true. If, again, they say "some," no one can assert without testing that these phenomena are true, those false, while if he employs a test or criterion he will say either that this criterion is apparent or that it is non-evident. But it is certainly not non-evident; for it is now being assumed that the apparent objects only are true. And if it is apparent, since the matter in question is what apparent things are true and what false, that apparent thing which is adopted for the purpose of judging the apparent objects will itself in turn require an apparent criterion, and this again another, and so on *ad infinitum.* But it is impossible to judge an infinite series; and hence it is impossible to apprehend whether the true things are apparent only.

Similarly also he who declares that the non-evident only are true will not imply that they are all true (for he will not say that it is true that the stars are even in number and that they are also odd); while if some are true, whereby shall we decide that these non-evident things are true and those false? Certainly not by an apparent criterion; and if by a non-evident one, then since our problem is which of the non-evident things are true and which false, this non-evident criterion will itself also need another to judge it, and this again a third, and so on *ad infinitum.* Neither, then, are the true things non-evident only.

The remaining alternative is to say that of the true some are apparent, some non-evident; but this too is absurd. For either all the apparent and all the non-evident are true, or some of the apparent and some of the non-evident. If, then, we say "all," the argument will again be overthrown, since the truth is granted of the statement "nothing is true," and the truth will be asserted of both the statements "the stars are even in number" and "they are odd." But if some of the apparent are true and some of the non-evident, how shall we judge that of the apparent these are true but those false? For if we do so by means of an apparent thing, the argument is thrown back *ad infinitum;* and if by means of a thing non-evident, then, since the non-evidents also require to be judged, by what means is this non-evident thing to be judged? If by an apparent thing, we fall into circular reasoning; and if by a thing non-evident, into the regress *ad infinitum.* And about the non-evident we must make a similar statement; for he who attempts to judge them by something non-evident is thrown back *ad infinitum,* while he who judges by a thing apparent or with the constant assistance of a thing apparent falls back *ad infinitum,* or, if he passes over to the apparent, is guilty of circular reasoning. It is false, therefore, to say that of the true some are apparent, some non-evident.

If, then, neither the apparent nor the non-evident alone are true, nor yet some apparent and some non-evident things, nothing is true. But if nothing is true, and the criterion seems to require the true for the purpose of judging, the criterion is useless and vain, even if we grant, by way of concession, that it possesses some substantial reality. And if we have to suspend judgement as to whether anything true exists, it follows that those who declare that "dialectic is the science of things true and false and neither" speak rashly.

And since the criterion of truth has appeared to be unattainable, it is no longer possible to make positive assertions either about those things which (if we may depend on the statements of the Dogmatists) seem to be evident or about those which are non-evident; for since the Dogmatists suppose they apprehend the latter from the things evident, if we are forced to suspend judgement about the evident, how shall we dare to make pronouncements about the non-evident? Yet, by way of super-addition, we shall also raise separate objections against the non-evident class of objects. And since they seem to be apprehended and confirmed by means of sign and proof, we shall show briefly that it is proper to suspend judgement also about sign and proof. We will begin with sign; for indeed proof seems to be a kind of sign.

PLOTINUS

Plotinus (A.D. 205–270) was born in Lykopolis, Upper Egypt. At the age of 28 he became a student of Ammonius Saccas, a very influential teacher of the time. Some 11 years later, Plotinus, searching for wisdom from the East, became involved with an expeditionary army in Persia. The venture proved a failure, and Plotinus returned to Rome to teach philosophy in A.D. 244. He subsequently attempted to form a community modeled after the thought of Plato but was unsuccessful.

The writings of Plotinus are known to us through his pupil Porphyry (A.D. 232–ca. A.D. 305), who edited and preserved them. The writings are arranged in six books and each book has nine treatises, hence the name the Enneads. *Plotinus, aided by Porphyry, is a major figure in the development of Neoplatonism, a doctrine that was to have profound influence on Christianity. It is important to note, however, that Plotinus was an original thinker. His philosophy differed from that of Plato in several ways, especially in his interpretation of the ideas* (eidai) *and in his doctrine of emanation. It is Plotinus' emphasis on the intimate relationship between the human soul and the One which becomes so influential in Christian thought, especially on that of St. Augustine (A.D. 354–430). The Augustinian doctrine of the person as an image of God* (imago Dei) *is rooted in the Neoplatonic treatment of the ideas, originally the platonic forms* (eidai).

For Plotinus, the highest principle is that of the One, which is beyond being and is ineffable, that is, without qualities and not subject to explanation. In descending order from the One are the Intelligence (Nous); *the Soul, sometimes disembodied and sometimes embodied; and, finally, Matter. Our spiritual life, under the guidance of philosophy, has as its goal to reverse this descendant pattern and make our way to union with the One.*

The Knowing Hypostases and the Transcendent

Are we to think that a being knowing itself must contain diversity, that self-knowledge can be affirmed only when some one phase of the self perceives other phases, and that therefore an absolutely simplex entity would be equally incapable of introversion and of self-awareness?

No: a being that has no parts or phases may have this consciousness; in fact there would be no real self-knowing in an entity presented as knowing itself in virtue of being a compound—some single element in it perceiving other elements—as we may know our own form and entire bodily organism by sense-perception: such knowing does not cover the whole field; the knowing element has not had the required cognizance at once of its associates and of itself; this is not the self-knower asked for; it is merely something that knows something else.

Either we must exhibit the self-knowing of an uncompounded being—and show how that is possible—or abandon the belief that any being can possess veritable self-cognition.

To abandon the belief is not possible in view of the many absurdities thus entailed.

It would be already absurd enough to deny this power to the Soul (or mind), but the very height of absurdity to deny it to the nature of the Intellectual-Principle, presented thus as knowing the rest of things but not attaining to knowledge, or even awareness, of itself.

It is the province of sense and in some degree of understanding and judgement, but not of the Intellectual-Principle, to handle the external, though whether the Intellectual-Principle holds the knowledge of these things is a question to be examined, but it is obvious that the Intellectual-Principle must have knowledge of the Intellectual objects. Now, can it know those objects alone or must it not simultaneously know itself, the being whose function it is to know just those things? Can it have self-knowledge in the sense (dismissed above as inadequate) of knowing its content while it ignores itself? Can it be aware of knowing its members and yet remain in ignorance of its own knowing self? Self and content must be simultaneously present: the method and degree of this knowledge we must now consider.

We begin with the Soul, asking whether it is to be allowed self-knowledge and what the knowing principle in it would be and how operating.

The sense-principle in it, we may at once decide, takes cognizance only of the external; even in any awareness of events within the body it occupies, this is still the perception of something external to a principle dealing with those bodily conditions not as within but as beneath itself.

The reasoning-principle in the Soul acts upon the representations standing before it as the result of sense-perception; these it judges, combining, distinguishing: or it may also observe the impressions, so to speak, rising from the Intellectual-Principle, and has the same power of handling these; and reasoning will develop to wisdom where it recognizes the new and late-coming impressions (those of sense) and adapts them, so to speak, to those it holds from long before—the act which may be described as the Soul's Reminiscence.

So far as this, the efficacy of the Intellectual-Principle in the Soul certainly reaches; but is there also introversion and self-cognition or is that power to be reserved strictly for the Divine Mind?

If we accord self-knowing to this phase of the Soul we make it an Intellectual-Principle and will have to show what distinguishes it from its prior; if we refuse it self-knowing, all our thought brings us step by step to some principle which has this power, and we must discover what such self-knowing consists in. If, again, we do allow self-knowledge in the lower we must examine the question of degree; for if there is no difference of degree, then the reasoning principle in Soul is the Intellectual-Principle unalloyed.

We ask, then, whether the understanding principle in the Soul has equally the power of turning inwards upon itself or whether it has no more than that of comprehending the impressions, superior and inferior, which it receives.

The first stage is to discover what this comprehension is.

Sense sees a man and transmits the impression to the understanding. What does the understanding say? It has nothing to say as yet; it accepts and waits; unless, rather, it questions within itself, 'Who is this?'—someone it has met before—and then, drawing on memory, says, 'Socrates.'

If it should go on to develop the impression received, it distinguishes various elements in what the representative faculty has set before it; supposing it to say 'Socrates, if the man is good', then, while it has spoken upon information from the senses, its total pronouncement is its own; it contains within itself a standard of good.

But how does it thus contain the good within itself?

It is, itself, of the nature of the good and it has been strengthened still towards the perception of all that is good by the irradiation of the Intellectual-Principle upon it; for this pure phase of the Soul welcomes to itself the images implanted from its prior.

But why may we not distinguish this understanding phase as Intellectual-Principle and take Soul to consist of the later phases from the sensitive downwards?

Because all the activities mentioned are within the scope of a reasoning faculty, and reasoning is characteristically the function of Soul.

Why not, however, absolve the question by assigning self-cognizance to this phase?

Because we have allotted to Soul the function of dealing—in thought and in multiform action—with the external, and we hold that observation of self and of the content of self must belong to Intellectual-Principle.

If any one says, 'Still; what precludes the reasoning Soul from observing its own content by some special faculty?' he is no longer positing a principle of understanding or of reasoning but, simply, bringing in the Intellectual-Principle unalloyed.

But what precludes the Intellectual-Principle from being present, unalloyed, within the Soul? Nothing, we admit; but are we entitled therefore to think of it as a phase of Soul?

We cannot describe it as belonging to the Soul though we do describe it as our Intellectual-Principle, something distinct from the understanding, advanced above it, and yet ours even though we cannot include it among soul-phases: it is ours and not ours; and therefore we use it sometimes and sometimes not, whereas we always have use of the understanding; the Intellectual-Principle is ours when we act by it, not ours when we neglect it.

But what is this acting by it? Does it mean that we become the Intellectual-Principle so that our utterance is the utterance of the Intellectual-Principle, or that (at best) we represent it?

We are not the Intellectual-Principle; we represent it in virtue of that highest reasoning faculty which draws upon it.

Again; we perceive by means of the perceptive faculty and are not, ourselves, the percipients: may we then say the same of the understanding (the principle of reasoning and discursive thought)?

No: our reasoning is our own; we ourselves think the thoughts that occupy the understanding—for this is actually the We—but the operation of the Intellectual-Principle enters from above us as that of the sensitive faculty from below; the We is the Soul at its highest, the mid-point between two powers, between the sensitive principle, inferior to us, and the intellectual principle superior. We think of the perceptive act as integral to ourselves because our sense-perception is uninterrupted; we hesitate as to the Intellectual-Principle both because we are not always occupied with it and because it exists apart, not a principle inclining to us but one to which we incline when we choose to look upwards.

The sensitive principle is our scout; the Intellectual-Principle our King.

But we, too, are king when we are moulded to the Intellectual-Principle.

That correspondence may be brought about in two ways: either through laws of conduct engraved upon our souls as tablets or else by our being, as it were, filled full of the Divine Mind, which again may have become to us a thing seen and felt as a presence.

Hence our self-knowing ensues because it is in virtue of this thing present that we know all other things; or because we know the faculty which discerns this principle of knowledge by means of the faculty itself; or because we become actually identical with the principle.

Thus the self-knower is a double person: there is the one that takes cognizance of the principle in virtue of which understanding occurs in the Soul or mind; and there is the higher, knowing himself by the Intellectual-Principle with which he becomes identical: this latter knows the self as no longer man but as a being that has become something other through and through: he has thrown himself as one thing over into the superior order, taking with him only that better part of the Soul which alone is winged for the Intellectual Act and gives the man, once established There, the power to appropriate what he has seen.

We can scarcely suppose this understanding faculty to be unaware that it has understanding; that it takes cognizance of things external; that in its judgements it decides by the rules and standards within itself held directly from the Intellectual-Principle; that there is something higher than itself, something which, moreover, it has no need to seek but fully possesses. What can we conceive to escape the self-knowledge of a principle which admittedly knows the place it holds and the work it has to do? It affirms that it springs from Intellectual-Principle whose second and image it is, that it holds all within itself, the universe of things, engraved, so to say, upon it as all is held There by the eternal engraver. Aware so far of itself, can it be supposed to halt at that? Are we to suppose that all we can do is to apply a distinct power of our nature and come thus to awareness of that Intellectual-Principle as aware of itself? Or may we not appropriate that principle—which belongs to us as we to it—and thus attain to awareness, at once, of it and of ourselves? Yes: this is the necessary way if we are to experience the self-knowledge vested in the Intellectual-Principle. And a man becomes Intellectual-Principle when, ignoring all other phases of his being, he sees through that only and sees only that and so knows himself by means of the self—in other words attains the self-knowledge which the Intellectual-Principle possesses.

Does it all come down, then, to one phase of the self knowing another phase?

That would be a case of knower distinguished from known, and would not be self-knowing.

What, then, if the total combination were supposed to be of one piece, knower quite undistinguished from known, so that, seeing any given part of itself as identical with itself, it sees itself by means of itself, knower and known thus being entirely without differentiation?

To begin with, the distinction in one self thus suggested is a strange phenomenon. How is the self to make the partition? The thing cannot happen of itself. And, again, which phase makes it? The phase that decides to be the knower or that which is to be the known? Then how can the knowing phase know itself in the known when it has chosen to be the knower and put itself apart from the known? In such self-knowledge by sundering it can be aware only of the object, not of the agent; it will not know its entire content, or itself as an integral whole; it knows the phase seen but not the seeing phase and thus has knowledge of something else, not self-knowledge.

In order to perfect self-knowing it must bring over

from itself the knowing phase as well: seeing subject and seen objects must be present as one thing. Now if in this coalescence of seeing subject with seen objects the objects were merely representations of the reality, the subject would not possess the realities: if it is to possess them it must do so not by seeing them as the result of any self-division but by knowing them, containing them, before any self-division occurs.

At that, the object known must be identical with the knowing act (or agent), the Intellectual-Principle, therefore, identical with the Intellectual Realm. And in fact, if this identity does not exist, neither does truth; the Principle that should contain realities is found to contain a transcript, something different from the realities; that constitutes non-Truth; Truth cannot apply to something conflicting with itself; what it affirms it must also be.

Thus we find that the Intellectual-Principle, the Intellectual Realm, and Real Being constitute one thing, which is the Primal Being; the primal Intellectual-Principle is that which contains the realities or, rather, which is identical with them.

But taking Primal Intellection and its intellectual object to be a unity, how does that give an Intellective Being knowing itself? An intellection enveloping its object or identical with it is far from exhibiting the Intellectual-Principle as self-knowing.

All turns on the identity. The intellectual object is itself an activity, not a mere potentiality; it is not lifeless; nor are the life and intellection brought into it as into something naturally devoid of them, some stone or other dead matter; no, the intellectual object is essentially existent, the primal reality. As an active force, the first activity, it must be, also itself, the noblest intellection, intellection possessing real being since it is entirely true; and such an intellection, primal and primally existent, can be no other than the primal principle of Intellection: for that primal principle is no potentiality and cannot be an agent distinct from its act and thus, once more, possessing its essential being as a mere potentiality. As an act—and one whose very being is an act—it must be undistinguishably identical with its act: but Being and the Intellectual object are also identical with that act; therefore the Intellectual-Principle, its exercise of intellection, and the object of intellection all are identical. Given its intellection identical with intellectual object and the object identical with the Principle itself, it cannot but have self-knowledge: its intellection operates by the intellectual act, which is itself, upon the intellectual object, which similarly is itself. It possesses self-knowing, thus, on every count; the act is itself; and the object, seen in that act-self, is itself.

Thus we have shown that there exists that which in the strictest sense possesses self-knowing.

This self-knowing agent, perfect in the Intellectual-Principle, is modified in the Soul.

The difference is that, while the Soul knows itself as within something else, the Intellectual-Principle knows itself as self-depending, knows all its nature and character, and knows by right of its own being and by simple introversion. When it looks upon the authentic existences it is looking upon itself; its vision is its effective existence, and this efficacy is itself since the Intellectual-Principle and the Intellectual Act are one: this is an integral seeing itself by its entire being, not a part seeing by a part.

But has our discussion issued in an Intellectual-Principle having a persuasive activity (furnishing us with probability)?

No: it brings compulsion, not persuasion; compulsion belongs to the Intellectual-Principle, persuasion to the Soul or mind, and we seem to desire to be persuaded rather than to see the truth in the pure intellect.

As long as we were Above, collected within the Intellectual nature, we were satisfied; we were held in the intellectual act; we had vision because we drew all into unity—for the thinker in us was the Intellectual Principle telling us of itself—and the Soul or mind was motionless, assenting to that act of its prior. But now that we are once more here—living in the secondary, the Soul—we seek for persuasive probabilities: it is through the image we desire to know the archetype.

Our way is to teach our Soul how the Intellectual-Principle exercises self-vision; the phase thus to be taught is that which already touches the intellective order, that which we call the understanding or intelligent Soul, indicating by the very name (*διά-νοια*) that it is already of itself in some degree an Intellectual-Principle or that it holds its peculiar power through and from that Principle. This phase must be brought to understand by what means it has knowledge of the thing it sees and warrant for what it affirms: if it became what it affirms, it would by that fact possess self-knowing. All its vision and affirmation being in the Supreme or deriving from it—There where itself also is—it will possess self-knowledge by its right as a Reason-Principle, claiming its kin and bringing all into accord with the divine imprint upon it.

The Soul therefore (to attain self-knowledge) has only to set this image (that is to say, its highest phase) alongside the veritable Intellectual-Principle which we have found to be identical with the truths constituting the objects of intellection, the world of Primals and Reality: for this Intellectual-Principle, by very definition, cannot be outside of itself, the Intellectual Reality: self-gathered and unalloyed, it is Intellectual-Principle through all the range of its being—for unintelligent intelligence is not possible—and thus it possesses of necessity self-knowing, as a being immanent to itself and one having for function and essence to be purely and solely Intellectual-Principle. This is no doer; the doer, not self-intent but looking outward, will have knowledge, in some kind, of the external, but, if wholly of this practical order, need have no self-knowledge; where, on the contrary, there is no action—and of course the pure Intellectual-Principle cannot be straining after any absent good—the intention can be only towards the self; at once self-knowing becomes not merely plausible but inevitable; what else could living signify in a being immune from action and existing in Intellect?

The contemplating of God, we might answer.

But to admit its knowing God is to be compelled to admit its self-knowing. It will know what it holds from God, what God has given forth or may; with this knowledge, it knows itself at the stroke, for it is itself one of those given things—in fact is all of them. Knowing God and His power, then, it knows itself, since it comes from Him and carries His power upon it; if, because here the act of vision is identical with the object, it is unable to see God clearly, then all the more, by equation of seeing and seen, we are driven back upon that self-seeing and self-knowing in which seeing and thing seen are undistinguishably one thing.

And what else is there to attribute to it?

Repose, no doubt; but to an Intellectual-Principle Repose is not an abdication from intellect; its Repose is an Act, the act of abstention from the alien: in all forms of existence repose from the alien leaves the characteristic activity intact, especially where the Being is not merely potential but fully realized.

In the Intellectual-Principle, the Being is an Act and in the absence of any other object it must be self-directed; by this self-intellection it holds its Act within itself and upon itself; all that can emanate from it is produced by this self-centering and self-intention; first self-gathered, it then gives itself or gives something in its likeness; fire must first be self-centered and be fire, true to fire's natural Act; then it may reproduce itself elsewhere.

Once more, then: the Intellectual-Principle is a self-intent activity, but Soul has the double phase, one inner, intent upon the Intellectual-Principle, the other outside it and facing to the external; by the one it holds the likeness to its source; by the other, even in its unlikeness, it still comes to likeness in this sphere, too, by virtue of action and production; in its action it still contemplates, and its production produces forms—detached intellections, so to speak—with the result that all its creations are representations of the divine Intellection and of the divine Intellect, moulded upon the archetype, of which all are emanations and images, the nearer more true, the very latest preserving some faint likeness of the source.

Now comes the question: what sort of thing does the Intellectual-Principle see in seeing the Intellectual Realm and what in seeing itself?

We are not to look for an Intellectual realm reminding us of the colour or shape to be seen on material objects: the intellectual antedates all such things; and even in our sphere the production is very different from the Reason-Principle in the seeds from which it is produced. The seed principles are invisible and the beings of the Intellectual still more characteristically so; the Intellectuals are of one same nature with the Intellectual Realm which contains them, just as the Reason-Principle in the seed is identical with the Soul, or life-principle, containing it.

But the Soul (considered as apart from the Intellectual-Principle) has no vision of what it thus contains, for it is not the producer but, like the Reason-Principles also, an image of its source: that source is the brilliant, the authentic, the primarily existent, the thing self-sprung and self-intent; but its image, Soul, is a thing which can have no permanence except by attachment, by living in that order; the very nature of an image is that as a secondary it shall have its being in something else, if at all it exist apart from its original. Hence this image (Soul) has not vision, for it has not the necessary light, and if it should see, then, as finding its completion elsewhere, it sees another, not itself.

In the pure Intellectual there is nothing of this: the vision and the envisioned are a unity; the seen is as the seeing and seeing as seen.

What, then, is there that can pronounce upon the nature of this all-unity?

That which sees: and to see is the function of the Intellectual-Principle. Even in our own sphere (we have a parallel to this self-vision of a unity), our vision is light or rather becomes one with the light, and it sees light for it sees colours. In the intellectual, the vision sees not through some medium but by and through itself alone, for its object is not external: by one light it sees another, not through any intermediate agency; a light sees a light, that is to say a thing sees itself. This light shining within the Soul enlightens it; that is, it makes the Soul intellective, working it into likeness with itself, the light above.

Think of the traces of this light upon the Soul, then say to yourself that such, and more beautiful and broader and more radiant, is the light itself; thus you will approach to the nature of the Intellectual-Principle and the Intellectual Realm, for it is this light, itself lit from above, which gives the Soul its brighter life.

It is not the source of the generative life of the Soul which, on the contrary, it draws inward, preserving it from such diffusion, holding it to the love of the splendour of its Prior.

Nor does it give the life of perception and sensation, for that looks to the external and to what acts most vigorously upon the senses, whereas one accepting that light of truth may be said no longer to see the visible, but the very contrary.

This means in sum that the life the Soul takes thence is an intellective life, a trace of the life in the (divine) Intellect, in which alone the authentic exists.

The life in the Divine Intellect is also an Act: it is the primal light outlamping to itself primarily, its own torch; lightgiver and lit at once; the authentic intellectual object, knowing at once and known, seen to itself and needing no other than itself to see by, self-sufficing to the vision, since what it sees it is; known to us by that very same light, our knowledge of it attained through itself, for from nowhere else could we find the means of telling of it. By its nature, its self-vision is the clearer but, using it as our medium, we too may come to see by it.

In the strength of such considerations we lead up our own Soul to the Divine, so that it poses itself as an image of that Being, its life becoming an imprint and a likeness of the Highest, its every act of thought making it over into the Divine and the Intellectual.

If the Soul is questioned as to the nature of that Intellectual-Principle—the perfect and all-embracing, the primal self-knower—it has but to enter into that Principle, or to sink all its activity into that, and at once it shows itself to be in effective possession of those priors whose memory it never lost: thus, as an image of the Intellectual-Principle, it can make itself the medium by which to attain some vision of it; it draws upon that within itself which is most closely resemblant, as far as resemblance is possible between divine Intellect and any phase of Soul.

In order, then, to know what the Divine Mind is we must observe Soul and especially its most Godlike phase.

One certain way to this knowledge is to separate first, the man from the body—yourself, that is, from your body; next to put aside that Soul which moulded the body, and, very earnestly, the system of sense with desires and impulses and every such futility, all setting definitely towards the mortal: what is left is the phase of the Soul which we have declared to be an image of the Divine Intellect, retaining some light from that source, like the light of the sun which goes beyond its spherical mass, issues from it and plays about it.

Of course we do not pretend that the sun's light (as the analogy might imply) remains a self-gathered and sun-centred thing: it is at once outrushing and indwelling; it strikes outward continuously, lap after lap, until it reaches us upon our earth: we must take it that all the light, including that which plays about the sun's orb, has travelled; otherwise we would have next to the orb a void expanse. The Soul, on the contrary—a light springing from the Divine Mind and shining about it—is in closest touch with that source; it is not in transit but remains centred there, and, in likeness to that principle, it has no place: the light of the sun is actually in the air, but the Soul is clean of all such contact so that its immunity is patent to itself and to any other of the same order.

And by its own characteristic act, though not without reasoning process, it knows the nature of the Intellectual-Principle which, on its side, knows itself without need of reasoning, for it is ever self-present whereas we become so by directing our Soul towards it; our life is broken and there are many lives, but that principle needs no changings of life or of things; the lives it brings to being are for others, not for itself: it cannot need the inferior; nor does it for itself produce the less when it possesses or is the all, nor the images when it possesses or is the prototype.

Anyone not of the strength to lay hold of the first Soul, that possessing pure intellection, must grasp that which has to do with our ordinary thinking and thence ascend: if even this prove too hard, let him turn to account the sensitive phase which carries the ideal forms of the less fine degree, that phase which, too, with its powers, is immaterial and lies just within the realm of Ideal-principles.

One may even, if it seem necessary, begin as low as the reproductive Soul and its very production and thence make the ascent, mounting from those ultimate ideal principles to the ultimates in the higher sense, that is to the primals.

This matter need not be elaborated at present: it suffices to say that if the created were all, it would not be ultimate: but the Supreme does include primals, the primals because the producers. In other words, there must be, with the made, the making source and these must be identical; otherwise there will be need of a Transcendent. But will not this Transcendent demand in turn a further transcendent? No: the demand comes from the Intellectual-Principle. If we are asked why this Transcendent also should not have self-vision (a duality to be transcended), our answer is that it has no need of vision; but this we will discuss later: for the moment we go back, since the question at issue is gravely important.

We repeat that the Intellectual-Principle must have, actually has, self-vision, firstly because it has multiplicity, next because it exists for the external and therefore must be a seeing power, one seeing that external; in fact its very essence is vision. Given some external, there must be vision; and if there be nothing external the Intellectual-Principle (Divine Mind) exists in vain. Unless there is something beyond bare unity, there can be no vision: vision must converge with a visible object. And this which the seer is to see can be only a multiple, no undistinguishable unity; nor could a universal unity find anything upon which to exercise any act; all, one and desolate, would be utter stagnation; in so far as there is action, there is diversity. If there be no distinctions, what is there to do, what direction in which to move? An agent must either act upon the extern or be a multiple and so able to act upon itself: making no advance towards anything other than itself, it is motionless, and where it could know only blank fixity it can know nothing.

The intellective power, therefore, when occupied with the intellectual act, must be in a state of duality, whether one of the two elements stand actually outside or both lie within: the intellectual act will always comport diversity as well as the necessary identity, and in the same way its characteristic objects (the Ideas) must stand to the Intellectual-Principle as at once distinct and identical. This applies equally to the single object; there can be no intellection except of something containing separable detail and, since the object is a Reason-Principle (a discriminated Idea), it has the necessary element of multiplicity. The Intellectual-Principle, thus, is formed of itself by the fact of being a multiple organ of vision, an eye receptive of many illuminated objects. If it had to direct itself to a memberless unity, it would be dereasoned: what could it say or know of such an object? The self-affirmation of (even) a memberless unity implies the repudiation of all that does not enter into the character: in other words, it must be multiple as a preliminary to being itself.

Then, again, in the assertion 'I am this particular thing', either the 'particular thing' is distinct from the assertor—and there is a false statement—or it is included within it, and, at once, multiplicity is asserted: otherwise the assertion is 'I am what I am', or 'I am I'.

If it be no more than a simple duality able to say 'I and that other phase', there is already multiplicity, for there is distinction and ground of distinction, there is number with all its train of separate things.

In sum, then, a knowing principle must handle distinct items: its object must, at the moment of cognition, contain diversity; otherwise the thing remains unknown; there is mere conjunction, such a contact, without affirmation or comprehension, as would precede knowledge, the intellect not yet in being, the impinging agent not percipient.

Similarly the knowing principle itself cannot remain simplex, especially in the act of self-knowing: all silent though its self-perception be, it is dual to itself.

Of course The One has no need of minute self-handling since it has nothing to learn by an intellective act; it is in full possession of its being before Intellect exists. Knowledge implies desire, for it is, so to speak, discovery crowning a search; the utterly undifferentiated remains self-centred and makes no inquiry about that self: anything capable of analysing its content must be a manifold.

Thus the Intellectual-Principle, in the act of knowing the Transcendent, is a manifold. It knows the Transcendent in very essence but, with all its effort to grasp that prior as a pure unity, it goes forth amassing successive impressions, so that, to it, the object becomes multiple: thus in its outgoing to its object it is not (fully realized) Intellectual-Principle; it is an eye that has not yet seen; in its return it is an eye possessed of the multiplicity which it has itself conferred: it sought something of which it found the vague presentment within itself; it returned with something else, the manifold quality with which it has of its own act invested the simplex.

If it had not possessed a previous impression of the Transcendent it could never have grasped it, but this impression, originally of unity, becomes an impression of multiplicity; and the Intellectual-Principle in taking cognizance of that multiplicity knows the Transcendent and so is realized as an eye possessed of its vision.

It is now Intellectual-Principle since it actually holds its object, and holds it by the act of intellection: before, it was no more than a tendance, an eye blank of impression: it was in motion towards the transcendental; now that it has attained, it has become Intellectual-Principle: always implicit (in the Transcendent), it now, in virtue of this intellection, holds the character of Intellectual-Principle, of Essential Existence, and of Intellectual Act where, previously, not possessing the Intellectual Object, it was not Intellectual Perception, and, not yet having exercised the Intellectual Act, it was not Intellectual-Principle.

The Principle before all these principles is no doubt the first principle of the universe, but not as immanent: immanence is not for primal sources but for engendering secondaries; that which stands as primal source of everything is not a thing but is distinct from all things: it is not, then, a member of the total but earlier than all, earlier, thus, than the Intellectual-Principle—which in fact envelops the entire train of things.

Thus we come, once more, to a Being above the Intellectual-Principle and, since the sequent amounts to no less than the All, we recognize, again, a Being above the All. This assuredly cannot be one of the things to which it is prior. We may not call it Intellect; therefore, too, we may not call it the Good, if the Good is to be taken in the sense of some one member of the universe; if we mean that which precedes the universe of things, the name may be allowed.

The Intellectual-Principle is established in multiplicity; its intellection, self-sprung though it be, is in the nature of something added to it (some accidental dualism) and makes it multiple: the utterly simplex, and therefore first of all beings, must, then, transcend the Intellectual-Principle; and, obviously, if this had intellection it would no longer transcend the Intellectual-Principle but be it, and at once be a multiple.

But why, after all, should it not be such a manifold as long as it remains one substantial existence, having the multiplicity not of a compound being but of a unity with a variety of activities?

Now, no doubt, if these various activities are not themselves substantial existences—but merely manifestations of latent potentiality—there is no compound; but, on the other hand, it remains incomplete until its substantial existence be expressed in act. If its substantial existence consists in its Act, and this Act constitutes multiplicity, then its substantial existence will be strictly proportioned to the extent of the multiplicity.

We allow this to be true for the Intellectual-Principle to which we have allotted (the multiplicity of) self-knowing; but for the first principle of all, never. Before the manifold, there must be The One, that from which the manifold rises: in all numerical series, the unit is the first.

But—we will be answered—for number, well and good, since the suite makes a compound; but in the real beings why must there be a unit from which the multiplicity of entities shall proceed?

Because (failing such a unity) the multiplicity would consist of disjointed items, each starting at its own distinct place and moving accidentally to serve to a total.

But, they will tell us, the Activities in question do proceed from a unity, from the Intellectual-Principle, a simplex.

By that they admit the existence of a simplex prior to the Activities; and they make the Activities perdurable and class them as substantial existences (hypostases); but as Hypostases they will be distinct from their source, which will remain simplex; while its product will in its own nature be manifold and dependent upon it.

Now if these activities arise from some unexplained first activity in that principle, then it too contains the manifold: if on the contrary they are the very earliest activities and the source and cause of any multiple product and the means by which that Principle is able, before any activity occurs, to remain self-centred, then they are allocated to the product of which they are the cause; for this principle is one thing, the activities going forth from it are another, since it is not, itself, in act. If this be not so, the first act cannot be the Intellectual-Principle: the One does not provide for the existence of an Intellectual-Principle which thereupon appears; that provision would be something (an Hypostasis) intervening between the One and the Intellectual-Principle its offspring. There could, in fact, be no such providing in The One, for it was never incomplete; and such provision could name nothing that ought to be provided. It cannot be thought to possess only some part of its content, and not the whole; nor did anything exist to which it could turn in desire. Clearly anything that comes into being after it arises without shaking to its permanence in its own habit. It is essential to the existence of any new entity that the First remain in self-gathered repose throughout: otherwise, it moved before there was motion and had intellectual act before any intellection—unless, indeed, that first act (as motionless and without intelligence) was incomplete, nothing more than a tendency. And what could be the object of such a tendency born of frustration?

The only reasonable explanation of act flowing from it lies in the analogy of light from a sun. The entire intellectual order may be figured as a kind of light with the One in repose at its summit as its King: but this manifestation is not cast out from it—that would cause us to postulate another light before the light—but the One shines eternally, resting upon the Intellectual Realm; this, not identical with its source, is yet not severed from it nor of so remote a nature as to be less than Real-Being; it is no blind thing, but is seeing, self-knowing, the primal knower.

The One, as transcending Intellect, transcends knowing: above all need, it is above the need of the knowing which pertains solely to the Secondary Nature. Knowing is a unitary thing, but defined: the first is One, but undefined: a defined One would not be the One-Absolute: the absolute is prior to the definite.

Thus The One is in truth beyond all statement: any affirmation is of a thing; but 'all-transcending, resting above even the most august divine Mind'—this is the only true description, since it does not make it a thing among things, nor name it where no name could identify it: we can but try to indicate, in our own feeble way, something concerning it. When in our perplexity we object, 'Then it is without self-perception, without self-consciousness, ignorant of itself', we must remember that we have been considering it only in its opposites.

If we assume within it the distinction of knowing and known, we make it a manifold; and if we allow intellection in it, we make it at that point indigent: supposing that in fact intellection accompanies it, intellection by it must be superfluous.

Self-intellection—which is the truest—implies the entire perception of a total self formed from a variety converging into an integral; every single unit in this variety is self-subsistent and has no need to look outside itself: if its intellectual act is, on the other hand, directed upon something outside, then the agent is deficient and the intellection faulty.

The wholly simplex and veritable self-sufficing can be lacking at no point: self-intellection begins in that principle which, secondarily self-sufficing, yet needs itself and therefore needs to know itself; this principle, by its self-presence, achieves its sufficiency in virtue of its entire content (it is the all): it becomes thus competent from the total of its being, in the act of living towards itself and looking upon itself.

Consciousness, as the very word indicates, is a conperception, an act exercised upon a manifold: and even intellection, earlier (nearer to the divine) though it is, implies that the agent turns back upon itself, upon a manifold, then. If that agent says no more than 'I am a being', it speaks (by the implied dualism) as a discoverer of the extern; and rightly so, for being is a manifold; when it faces towards the unmanifold and says, 'I am that being', it misses both itself and the being (since the simplex cannot be thus divided into knower and known): if it is to utter truth it cannot indicate by 'being' something (single) like a stone; in the one phrase multiplicity is asserted; for the being thus affirmed—the veritable, as distinguished from such a mere container of some trace of being as ought not to be called a being since it stands merely as image to archetype—this must possess multiplicity.

But will not each item in that multiplicity be an object of intellection to us?

Taken bare and single, no: but Being itself is manifold within itself, and whatever else you may name has Being.

This accepted, it follows that anything that is to be thought of as the most utterly simplex of all, cannot have self-intellection; to have that would mean being multiple. The Transcendent, thus, neither knows itself nor is known in itself.

How, then, do we ourselves come to be speaking of it?

No doubt we deal with it, but we do not state it; we have neither knowledge nor intellection of it.

But in what sense do we even deal with it when we have no hold upon it?

We do not, it is true, grasp it by knowledge, but that does not mean that we are utterly void of it; we hold it not so as to state it, but so as to be able to speak about it. And we can and do state what it is not, while we are silent as to what it is: we are, in fact, speaking of it in the light of its sequels; unable to state it, we may still possess it.

Those divinely possessed and inspired have at least the knowledge that they hold some greater thing within them though they cannot tell what it is; from the movements that stir them and the utterances that come from them they perceive the power, not themselves, that moves them: in the same way, it must be, we stand towards the Supreme when we hold the Intellectual-Principle pure; we know the divine Mind within, that which gives Being and all else of that order: but we know, too, that other, know that it is none of these, but a nobler principle than anything we know as Being; fuller and greater; above reason, mind, and feeling; conferring these powers, not to be confounded with them.

Conferring—but how? As itself possessing them or not? How can it convey what it does not possess, and yet if it does possess how is it simplex? And if, again, it does not, how is it the source of the manifold?

A single, unmanifold emanation we may very well allow—how even that can come from a pure unity may be a problem, but we may always explain it on the analogy of the irradiation from a luminary—but a multitudinous production raises question.

The explanation is, that what comes from the Supreme cannot be identical with it and assuredly cannot be better than it—what could be better than The One or could exceed it in any sense? The emanation, then, must be less good, that is to say, less self-sufficing: now what must that be which is less self-sufficing than The One? Obviously the Not-One, that is to say, multiplicity but a multiplicity striving towards unity; that is to say, a One-that-is-many.

All that is not One is conserved by virtue of the One, and from the One derives its characteristic nature: if it had not attained such unity as is consistent with being made up of multiplicty we could not affirm its existence: if we are able to affirm the nature of single things, this is in virtue of the unity, the identity even, which each of them possesses. But the all-transcendent, utterly void of multiplicity, has no mere unity of participation but is unity's self, independent of all else, as being that from which, by whatever means, all the rest take their degree of unity in their standing, near or far, towards it.

The second principle shows that it is next in order (after the all-transcendent One) by the fact that its multiplicity is at the same time an all-embracing unity: all the variety lies in the midst of a sameness, and identity cannot be separated from diversity since all stands as one; each item in that content, by the fact of participating in life, is a One-many: for the item could not make itself manifest as a One-and-all.

Only the Transcendent can be that; it is the great beginning, and the beginning must be a really existent One, wholly and truly One, while its sequent, poured down in some way from the One, is all, a total which has participation in unity and whose every member is similarly all and one.

What then is the All?

The total of which the Transcendent is the Source.

But in what way is it that source? In the sense, perhaps, of sustaining things as bestower of the unity of each single item?

That too; but also as having established them in being.

But how? As having, perhaps, contained them previously?

We have indicated that, thus, the First would be a manifold.

May we think, perhaps, that the First contained the universe as an indistinct total whose items are elaborated to distinct existence within the Second by the Reason-Principle there? That Second is certainly an Activity; the Transcendent would contain only the potentiality of the universe to come.

But the nature of this contained potentiality would have to be explained: it cannot be that of Matter, a receptivity, for thus the Source becomes passive, the very negation of production.

How then does it produce what it does not contain? Certainly not at haphazard and certainly not by selection. How then?

We have observed that anything that may spring from the One must be different from it. Differing, it is not One, since then it would be the Source. If unity has given place to duality, from that moment there is multiplicity; for there is variety side by side with identity, and this imports quality and all the rest.

We may take it as proved that the emanation of the Transcendent must be a Not-One, something other than pure unity: but that it is a multiplicity, and especially that it is such a multiplicity as is exhibited in the sequent universe, this is a statement worthy of deliberation: some further inquiry must be made, also, as to the necessity of any sequel to the First.

We have, of course, already seen that a secondary must follow upon the First, and that this is a power immeasurably fruitful; and we indicated that this truth is confirmed by the entire order of things since there is nothing, not even in the lowest ranks, void of the power of generating. We have now to add that, since things engendered tend downwards and not upwards and, especially, move towards multiplicity, the first principle of all must be less a manifold than any.

That which engenders the world of sense cannot itself be a sense-world; it must be the Intellect and the Intellectual world; similarly, the prior which engenders the Intellectual-Principle and the Intellectual world cannot be either, but must be something of less multiplicity. The manifold does not rise from the manifold: the intellectual multiplicity has its source in what is not manifold; by the mere fact of being manifold, the thing is not the first principle: we must look to something earlier.

All must be grouped under a unity which, as standing outside of all multiplicity and outside of any ordinary simplicity, is the veritably and essentially simplex.

But how does the offspring of unity become a Reason-Principle, characteristically a manifold, a total, when the source is obviously not a Reason-Principle? Yet if it is not, how can we explain the derivation of Reason-Principle from non-Reason-Principle?

And how does the secondarily good (the imaged Good) derive from The Good, the Absolute? What does it hold from the Absolute Good to entitle it to the name?

Similarity to the prior is not enough, it does not help towards goodness; we demand similarity only to an actually existent Good: the goodness must depend upon derivation from a Prior of such a nature that the similarity is desirable because that Prior is good, just as the similarity would be undesirable if the Prior were not good.

Does the similarity with the Prior consist, then, in a voluntary resting upon it?

It is rather that, finding its condition satisfying, it seeks nothing: the similarity depends upon the all-sufficiency of what it possesses; its existence is agreeable because all is present to it, and present in such a way as not to be even different from it (Intellectual-Principle is Being).

All life belongs to it, life brilliant and perfect; thus all in it is at once life-principle and Intellectual-Principle, nothing in it aloof from either life or intellect: it is therefore self-sufficing and seeks nothing: and if it seeks nothing this is because it has in itself what, lacking, it must seek. It has, therefore, its Good within itself, either by being of that order—in what we have called its life and intellect—or in some other quality or character going to produce these.

If this (secondary principle) were The Good (The Absolute) nothing could transcend these things, life and intellect: but, given the existence of something higher, this Intellectual-Principle must possess a life directed towards that Transcendent, dependent upon it, deriving its being from it, living towards it as towards its source. The First, then, must transcend this principle of life and intellect which directs thither both the life in itself, a copy of the Reality of the First, and the intellect in itself which is again a copy, though of what original there we cannot know.

But what can it be which is loftier than that existence—a life compact of wisdom, untouched by struggle and error, or than this Intellect which holds the Universe with all there is of life and intellect?

If we answer 'The Making Principle', there comes the question, 'making by what virtue'? and unless we can indicate something higher there than in the made, our reasoning has made no advance: we rest where we were.

We must go higher—if it were only for the reason that the self-sufficiency of the Intellectual-Principle is that of a totality of which each member is patently indigent, and that each has participated in The One and, as drawing on unity, is itself not unity.

What then is this in which each particular entity participates, the author of being to the universe and to each item of the total?

Since it is the author of all that exists, and since the multiplicity in each thing is converted into a self-sufficing existence by this presence of The One, so that even the particular itself becomes self-sufficing, then clearly this principle, author at once of Being and of self-sufficingness, is not itself a Being but is above Being and above even self-sufficing.

May we stop, content, with that? No: the Soul is yet, and even more, in pain. Is she ripe, perhaps, to bring forth, now that in her pangs she has come so close to what she seeks? No: we must call upon yet another spell if anywhere the assuagement is to be found. Perhaps in what has already been uttered, there lies the charm if only we tell it over often? No: we need a new, a further, incantation. All our effort may well skim over every truth, and through all the verities in which we have part, and yet the reality escapes us when we hope to affirm, to understand: for the understanding, in order to its affirmation, must possess itself of item after item; only so does it traverse all the field: but how can there be any such peregrination of that in which there is no variety?

All the need is met by a contact purely intellective. At the moment of touch there is no power whatever to make any affirmation; there is no leisure; reasoning upon the vision is for afterwards. We may know we have had the vision when the Soul has suddenly taken light. This light is from the Supreme and is the Supreme; we may believe in the Presence when, like that other God on the call of a certain man, He comes bringing light: the light is the proof of the advent. Thus, the Soul unlit remains without that vision; lit, it possesses what it sought. And this is the true end set before the Soul, to take that light, to see the Supreme by the Supreme and not by the light of any other principle—to see the Supreme which is also the means to the vision; for that which illumines the Soul is that which it is to see, just as it is by the sun's own light that we see the sun.

But how is this to be accomplished?

Cut away everything.

SUGGESTIONS FOR FURTHER READING

Armstrong, A. H. *Plotinus.* New York: Collier, 1962.

Caryl, M. J., and Haarhoff, T. J. *Life and Thought in the Greek and Roman World.* London: Methuen, 1961.

Davenport, Basil, ed. *The Portable Roman Reader.* New York: Viking, 1961.

Grant, Frederick C., ed. *Hellenistic Religions.* Indianapolis: Library of Liberal Arts, 1953.

Grant, Michael. *From Alexander to Cleopatra.* New York: Scribner, 1983.

Grant, Michael. *History of Rome.* New York: Scribner, 1978.

Hamilton, Edith. *The Roman Way.* New York: New American Library, 1957.

Haskell, H. J. *This Was Cicero.* New York: Knopf, 1942.

Hatch, Edwin. *The Influence of Greek Ideas on Christianity.* New York: Harper Torchbooks, 1957.

Nichols, James H., Jr. *Epicurean Political Philosophy.* Ithaca: Cornell University Press, 1976.

Oates, Whitney J., ed. *The Stoic and Epicurean Philosophers: The Complete Extant Writings of Epicurus, Epictetus, Lucretius, Marcus Aurelius.* New York: Random House, 1940.

O'Brien, Elmer, ed. *The Essential Plotinus.* New York: New American Library, 1964.

O'Meara, Dominic J., ed. *Neoplatonism and Christian Thought.* Norfolk, Virginia: International Society for Neoplatonic Studies, 1982.

Rist, John M., ed. *The Stoics.* Berkeley: University of California Press, 1978.

Saunders, Jason L., ed. *Greek and Roman Philosophy After Aristotle.* New York: Free Press, 1966.

Shapiro, Herman, and Curley, Edwin M. *Hellenistic Philosophy.* New York: Modern Library, 1965.

Tarn, W. W. *Hellenistic Civilization.* New York: Meridian, 1961.

The Christian Gospels: The Redemption of Nature

As with the Hebrew Bible, our commentary and selections from the Christian Bible do not indicate a belief or a sign of facticity relative to the claims put forth. Nonetheless, similar to the Hebrew Bible, the significance of the Christian scriptures for philosophy is enormous and pervasive. The imaginativeness, originality, and rhetorical power of religious beliefs have enabled them to penetrate the intellectual fabric of a culture and remain as touchstones for subsequent theory, influencing even those who do not accept them. So true is this that students will find western philosophy far into the modern period virtually unintelligible if they do not know the beliefs and assumptions of Christianity.

The founder of Christianity is Jesus Christ (ca. 5 B.C.–A.D. 30), who was a Jew. The Roman government condemned Jesus to death and crucified him. His disciples claim that he rose from the dead (the Resurrection), for Jesus, it is claimed, promised to come again (*parousia*) and in response to that promise, his followers, Christians, formed a community which followed his teaching in preparation for the "second coming." The central claim of Jesus was that he was the Son of God who had become man in order to atone for the sin of Adam (the Incarnation and the Redemption). The key phrase in the Gospels is that Jesus was the Word who became flesh *(et verbum caro factum est).* Given that the "Word" is "Logos" in Greek and, as it emerged in the previous sections on Heraclitus and the Stoics, the notion of *logos* is central to Greek thought, Christianity is, therefore, tied to Greek philosophy in an intimate and complicated way. For the Greeks, *logos* referred to the deepest and most profound message of *physis,* that is, of nature, of all that was, is, or could be. To hear and understand the *logos* was to live a life of profound continuity with the deepest recesses of reality. That the Christ, the Son of God, was called the Logos is a sign of the deep indebtedness of early Christian theology to the tradition of Greek philosophy.

The first centuries of Christian history were characterized by persecution from the Roman government and by conflicts over the nature of "true" Christian teaching. It was not until the promulgation of the Nicene Creed in A.D. 325 that there was some semblance of doctrinal order. The work of Augustine (A.D. 354–430) was also extremely important in clarifying the basic tenets of Christian theology and in opposing those views that became known as heresies.

The selections that follow provide the main events in the life of Jesus, the activities of his Apostles, and the development of the Church as found in the

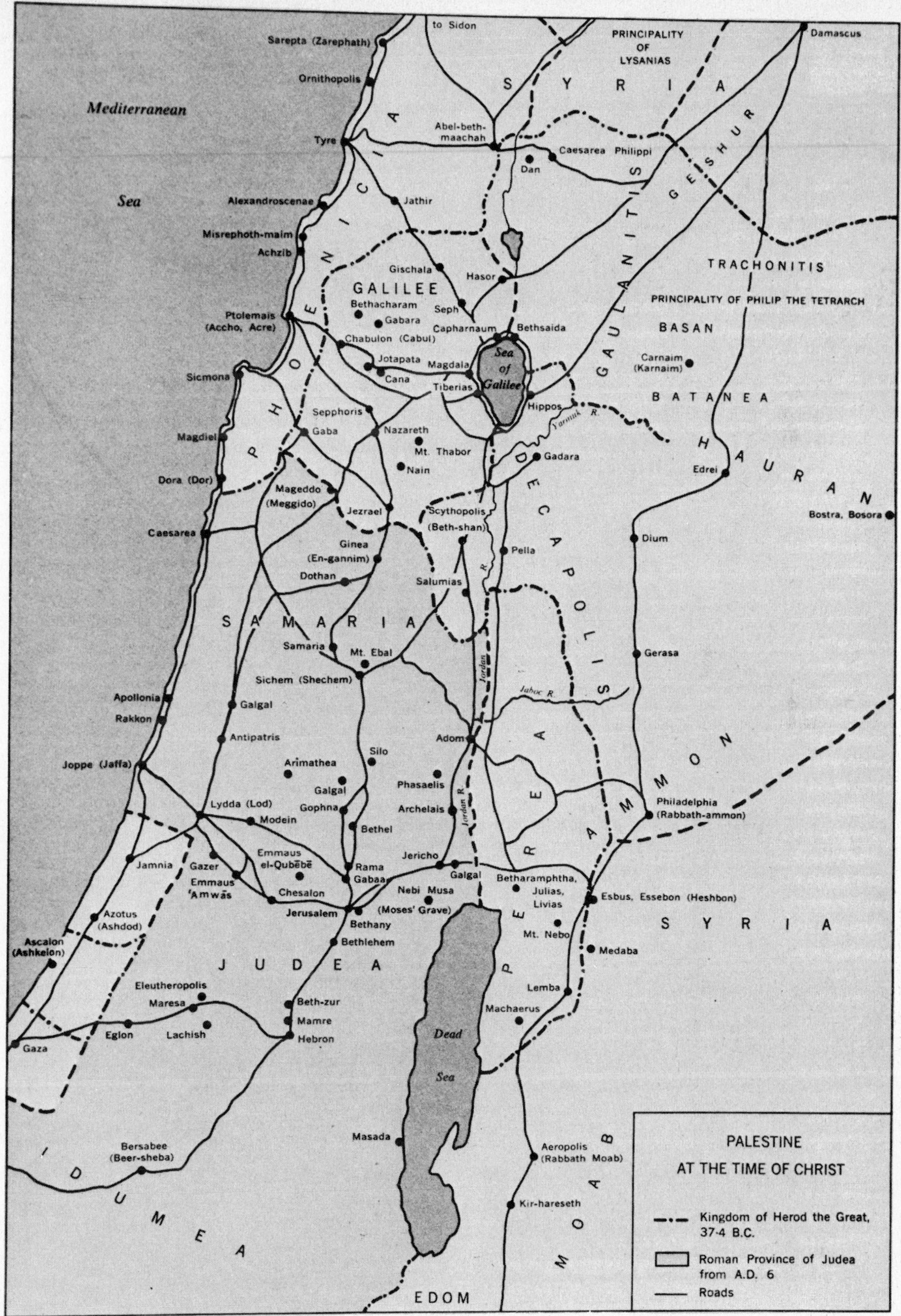

Palestine in the Time of Christ, Showing the Principal Towns of the Area

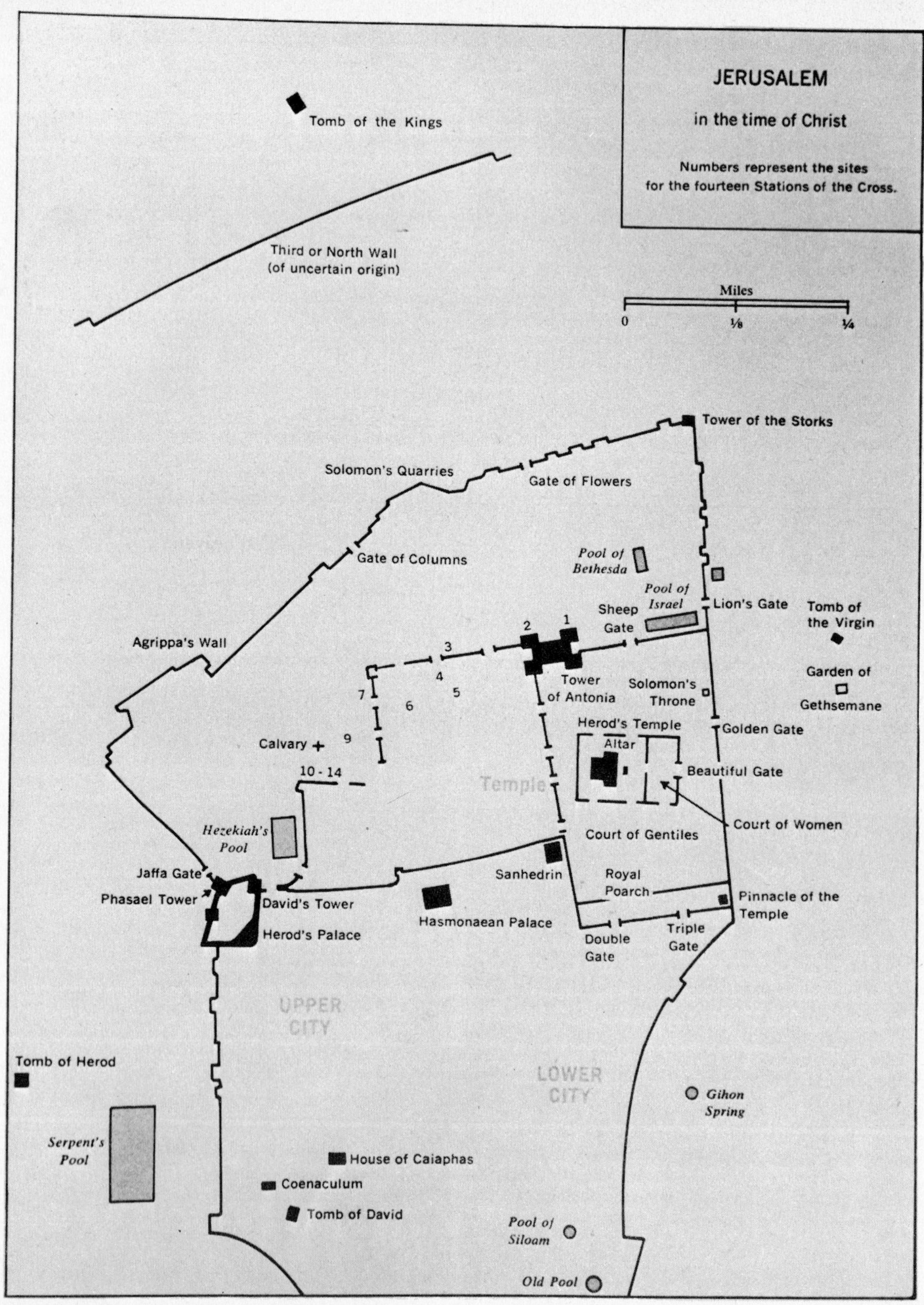

Plan of the City of Jerusalem in the Time of Christ

Epistles of Paul. Present also is the strong emphasis on the sacred character of the human community. Christianity, as distinct from most other cultures of western antiquity, awards to all human beings the inviolable and precious character of their personhood. In philosophical terms, Christian doctrine becomes a leading and seminal influence on the development of individual rights and in time, on the struggle to achieve a society in which each person is treated with dignity. Granted that Christian practice did not always honor this mandate, but it is an irreducible tenet of Christian doctrine. Of special importance in the selections that follow is the Prologue to the Gospel of John, for that is the heart of Christian theology, and is clearly indebted to Greek philosophy.

From the Acts of the Apostles

[THE COMING OF THE HOLY SPIRIT]

1. In the first book, O The-oph'i-lus, I have dealt with all that Jesus began to do and teach, [2]until the day when he was taken up, after he had given commandment through the Holy Spirit to the apostles whom he had chosen. [3]To them he presented himself alive after his passion by many proofs, appearing to them during forty days, and speaking of the kingdom of God. [4]And while staying with them he charged them not to depart from Jerusalem, but to wait for the promise of the Father, which, he said, "you heard from me, [5]for John baptized with water, but before many days you shall be bapized with the Holy Spirit."

6 So when they had come together, they asked him, "Lord, will you at this time restore the kingdom to Israel?" [7]He said to them, "It is not for you to know times or seasons which the Father has fixed by his own authority. [8]But you shall receive power when the Holy Spirit has come upon you; and you shall be my witnesses in Jerusalem and in all Judea and Sa-ma'ri-a and to the end of the earth." [9]And when he had said this, as they were looking on, he was lifted up, and a cloud took him out of their sight. [10]And while they were gazing into heaven as he went, behold, two men stood by them in white robes, [11]and said, "Men of Galilee, why do you stand looking into heaven? This Jesus, who was taken up from you into heaven, will come in the same way as you saw him go into heaven." . . .

2. When the day of Pentecost had come, they were all together in one place. [2]And suddenly a sound came from heaven like the rush of a mighty wind, and it filled all the house where they were sitting. [3]And there appeared to them tongues as of fire, distributed and resting on each one of them. [4]And they were all filled with the Holy Spirit and began to speak in other tongues, as the Spirit gave them utterance.

[THE CURING AND PREACHING OF THE APOSTLES]

3. Now Peter and John were going up to the temple at the hour of prayer, the ninth hour. [2]And a man lame from birth was being carried, whom they laid daily at that gate of the temple which is called Beautiful to ask alms of those who entered the temple. [3]Seeing Peter and John about to go into the temple, he asked for alms. [4]And Peter directed his gaze at him, with John, and said, "Look at us." [5]And he fixed his attention upon them, expecting to receive something from them. [6]But Peter said, "I have no silver and gold, but I give you what I have; in the name of Jesus Christ of Nazareth, walk." [7]And he took him by the right hand and raised him up; and immediately his feet and ankles were made strong. [8]And leaping up he stood and walked and entered the temple with them, walking and leaping and praising God. [9]And all the people saw him walking and praising God, [10]and recognized him as the one who sat for alms at the Beautiful Gate of the temple; and they were filled with wonder and amazement at what had happened to him.

11 While he clung to Peter and John, all the people ran together to them in the portico called Solomon's, astounded. [12]And when Peter saw it he addressed the people, "Men of Israel, why do you wonder at this, or why do you stare at us, as though by our own power or piety we had made him walk? [13]The God of Abraham and of Isaac and of Jacob, the God of our fathers, glorified his servant Jesus, whom you delivered up and denied in the presence of Pilate, when he had decided to release him. [14]But you denied the Holy and Righteous One, and asked for a murderer to be granted to you, [15]and killed the Author of life, whom God raised from the dead. To this we are witnesses. [16]And his name, by faith in his name, has made this man strong whom you see and know; and the faith which is through Jesus has given the man this perfect health in the presence of you all.

17 "And now, brethren, I know that you acted in ignorance, as did also your rulers. [18]But what God foretold by the mouth of all the prophets, that his Christ should suffer, he thus fulfilled. [19]Repent therefore, and turn again, that your sins may be blotted out, that times of refreshing may come from the presence of the Lord, [20]and that he may send the Christ appointed for you, Jesus, [21]whom heaven must receive until the time for establishing all that God spoke by the mouth of his holy prophets from of old. [22]Moses said, 'The Lord God will raise up for you a prophet from your brethren as he raised me up. You shall listen to him in whatever he tells you. [23]And it shall be that every soul that does not listen to that prophet shall be destroyed from the people.' [24]And all the prophets who have spoken, from Samuel and those who came afterwards, also proclaimed these days. [25]You are the sons of the prophets and of the covenant which God gave to your fathers, saying to Abraham, 'And in your posterity shall all the families of the earth be blessed.' [26]God, having raised up his servant, sent him to you first, to bless you in turning every one of you from your wickedness."

4. And as they were speaking to the people, the priests and the captain of the temple and the Sad'ducees came upon them, [2]annoyed because they were teaching the people and proclaiming in Jesus the resurrection from the dead. [3]And they arrested them and put them in custody until the morrow, for it was already evening. [4]But many of those who heard the word believed; and the number of the men came to about five thousand.

5 On the morrow their rulers and elders and scribes were gathered together in Jerusalem, [6]with Annas the high priest and Ca'ia-phas and John and Alexander, and all who were of the high-priestly family. [7]And when they had set them in the midst, they inquired, "By what power or by what name did you do this?" [8]Then Peter, filled with the Holy Spirit, said to them, "Rulers of the people and elders, [9]if we are being examined today concerning a good deed done to a cripple, by what means this man has been healed, [10]be it known to you all, and to all the people of Israel, that by the name of Jesus Christ of Nazareth, whom you crucified, whom God raised from the dead, by him this man is standing before you well. [11]This is the stone which was rejected by you builders, but which has become the head of the corner. [12]And there is salvation in no one else, for there is no other name under heaven given among men by which we must be saved."

[THE CONVERSION OF SAUL]

9. But Saul, still breathing threats and murder against the disciples of the Lord, went to the high priest [2]and asked him for letters to the synagogues at Damascus, so that if he found any belonging to the Way, men or women, he might bring them bound to Jerusalem. [3]Now as he journeyed he approached Damascus, and suddenly a light from heaven flashed about him. [4]And he fell to the ground and heard a voice saying to him, "Saul, Saul, why do you persecute me?" [5]And he said, "Who are you, Lord?" And he said, "I am Jesus, whom you are persecuting; [6]but rise and enter the city, and you will be told what you are to do." [7]The men who were traveling with him stood speechless, hearing the voice but seeing no one. [8]Saul arose from the ground; and when his eyes were opened, he could see nothing; so they led him by the hand and brought him into Damascus. [9]And for three days he was without sight, and neither ate nor drank.

10 Now there was a disciple at Damascus named An-a-ni'as. The Lord said to him in a vision. "An-a-ni'as." And he said, "Here I am, Lord." [11]And the Lord said to him, "Rise and go to the street called Straight, and inquire in the house of Judas for a man of Tarsus named Saul; for behold, he is praying, [13]and he has seen a man named An-a-ni'as come in and lay his hands on him so that he might regain his sight." [13]But An-a-ni'as answered, "Lord, I have heard from many about this man, how much evil he has done to thy saints at Jerusalem; [14]and here he has authority from the chief priests to bind all who call upon thy name." [15]But the Lord said to him, "Go, for he is a chosen instrument of mine to carry my name before the Gentiles and kings and the sons of Israel; [16]for I will show him how much he must suffer for the sake of my name." [17]So An-a-ni'as departed and entered the house. And laying his hands on him he said, "Brother Saul, the Lord Jesus who appeared to you on the road by which you came, has sent me that you may regain your sight and be filled with the Holy Spirit." [18]And immediately something like scales fell from his eyes and he regained his sight. Then he rose and was baptized, [19]and took food and was strengthened.

For several days he was with the disciples at Damascus. [20]And in the synagogues immediately he proclaimed Jesus, saying, "He is the Son of God." [21]And all who heard him were amazed, and said, "Is not this the man who made havoc in Jerusalem of those who called on this name? And he has come here for this purpose, to bring them bound before the chief priests." [22]But Saul increased all the more in strength, and confounded the Jews who lived in Damascus by proving that Jesus was the Christ.

[THE MOSAIC LAW]

15. But some men came down from Judea and were teaching the brethren, "Unless you are circumcised according to the custom of Moses, you cannot be saved." [2]And when Paul and Barnabas had no small dissension and debate with them, Paul and Barnabas and some of the others were appointed to go up to Jerusalem to the apostles and the elders about this question. [3]So, being sent on their way by the church, they passed through both Phoe-ni'ci-a and Sa-ma'ri-a, reporting the conversion of the Gentiles, and they gave great joy to all the brethren. [4]When they came to Jerusalem, they were welcomed by the church and the apostles and the elders, and they declared all that God had done with them. [5]But some believers who belonged to the party of the Pharisees rose up, and said, "It is necessary to circumcise them, and to change them to keep the law of Moses."

6 The Apostles and the elders were gathered together to consider this matter. [7]And after there had been much debate, Peter rose and said to them, "Brethren, you know that in the early days God made choice among you, that by my mouth the Gentiles should hear the word of the gospel and believe. [8]And God who knows the heart bore witness to them, giving them the Holy Spirit just as he did to us; [9]and he made no distinction between us and them, but cleansed their hearts by faith. [10]Now therefore why do you make trial of God by putting a yoke upon the neck of the disciples which neither our fathers nor we have been able to bear? [11]But we believe that we shall be saved through the grace of the Lord Jesus, just as they will."

12 And all the assembly kept silence; and they listened to Barnabas and Paul as they related what signs and wonders God had done through them among the Gentiles. [13]After they finished speaking, James replied, "Brethren, listen to me. [14]Symeon has related how God first visited the Gentiles, to take out of them a people for his name. [15]And with this the words of the prophets agree, as it is written,

[16]'After this I will return,
and I will rebuild the dwelling of David, which has fallen;
I will rebuild its ruins,
and I will set it up,
[17]that the rest of men may seek the Lord,
and all the Gentiles who are called by my name,
[18]says the Lord, who has made these things known from of old.'

[19]Therefore my judgement is that we should not trouble those of the Gentiles who turn to God, [20]but should write to them to abstain from the pollutions of idols and from unchastity and from what is strangled and from blood. [21]For from early generations Moses has had in every city those who preach him, for he is read every sabbath in the synagogues."

From the Gospel of Matthew

[THE BIRTH OF JESUS]

1. 18 Now the birth of Jesus Christ took place in this way. When his mother Mary had been betrothed to Joseph, before they came together she was found to be with child of the Holy Spirit; [19]and her husband Joseph, being a just man and unwilling to put her to shame, resolved to divorce her quietly. [20]But as he considered this, behold, an angel of the Lord appeared to him in a dream, saying, "Joseph, son of David, do not fear to take Mary your wife, for that which is conceived in her is of the Holy Spirit; [21]she will bear a son, and you shall call his name Jesus, for he will save his people from their sins." [22]All this took place to fulfil what the Lord had spoken by the prophet:

St. Matthew, from the Gospel Book of Ebbo (ca. A.D. *823). This manuscript illustration of Christ's apostle Matthew stylistically anticipates medieval painting. (Bibliothèque Municipals, Epernay)*

[23]"Behold, a virgin shall conceive and bear a son,
and his name shall be called Em·man'ū-ĕl"

(which means, God with us). [24]When Joseph woke from sleep, he did as the angel of the Lord commanded him; he took his wife, [25]but knew her not until she had borne a son; and he called his name Jesus.

2. Now when Jesus was born in Bethlehem of Judea in the days of Her'ȯd the king, behold, wise men from the East came to Jerusalem, saying, [2]"Where is he who has been born king of the Jews? For we have seen his star in the East, and have come to worship him." [3]When Her'ȯd the king heard this, he was troubled, and all Jerusalem with him; [4]and assembling all the chief priests and scribes of the people, he inquired of them where the Christ was to be born. [5]They told him, "In Bethlehem of Judea; for so it is written by the prophet:

[6]'And you, O Bethlehem, in the land of Judah,
are by no means least among the rulers of Judah;
for from you shall come a ruler
who will govern my people Israel.'"

7 Then Her'ȯd summoned the wise men secretly and ascertained from them what time the star appeared; [8]and he sent them to Bethlehem, saying, "Go and search diligently for the child, and when you have found him bring me word, that I too may come and worship him." [9]When they had heard the king they went their way; and lo, the star which they had seen in the East went before them, till it came to rest over the place where the child was. [10]When they saw the star, they rejoiced exceedingly with great joy; [11]and going into the house they saw the child with Mary his mother, and they fell down and worshiped him. Then, opening their treasures, they offered him gifts, gold and frankincense and myrrh. [12]And being warned in a dream not to return to Her'ȯd, they departed to their own country by another way.

13 Now when they had departed, behold, an angel of the Lord appeared to Joseph in a dream and said, "Rise, take the child and his mother, and flee to Egypt, and remain there till I tell you; for Her'ȯd is about to search for the child, to destroy him." [14]And he rose and took the child and his mother by night, and departed to Egypt, [15]and remained there until the death of Her'ȯd. This was to fulfil what the Lord had spoken by the prophet, "Out of Egypt have I called my son."

[THE BAPTISM OF JESUS]

3. In those days came John the Baptist, preaching in the wilderness of Judea, [2]"Repent, for the kingdom of heaven is at hand." [3]For this is he who was spoken of by the prophet I·sāi'āh when he said,

"The voice of one crying in the wilderness:
Prepare the way of the Lord,
make his paths straight."

[4]Now John wore a garment of camel's hair, and a leather girdle around his waist; and his food was locusts and wild honey. [5]Then went out to him Jerusalem and all Judea and all the region about the Jordan, [6]and they were baptized by him in the river Jordan, confessing their sins.

7 But when he saw many of the Pharisees and Sad'dū·cees coming for baptism, he said to them, "You brood of vipers! Who warned you to flee from the wrath to come: [8]Bear fruit that befits repentance, [9]and do not presume to say to yourselves, 'We have Abraham as our father'; for I tell you, God is able from these stones to raise up children to Abraham. [10]Even now the axe is laid to the root of the trees; every tree therefore that does not bear good fruit is cut down and thrown into the fire.

11 "I baptize you with water for repentance, but he who is coming after me is mightier than I, whose sandals I am not worthy to carry; he will baptize you with the Holy Spirit and with fire. [12]His winnowing fork is in his hand, and he will clear his threshing floor and gather his wheat into the granary, but the chaff he will burn with unquenchable fire."

13 Then Jesus came from Galilee to the Jordan to John, to be baptized by him. [14]John would have prevented him, saying, "I need to be baptized by you, and do you come to me?" [15]But Jesus answered him, "Let it be so now; for thus it is fitting for us to fulfil all righteousness." Then he consented. [16]And when Jesus was baptized, he went up immediately from the water, and behold, the heavens were opened and he saw the Spirit of God descending like a dove, and alighting on him; [17]and lo, a voice from heaven, saying, "This is my beloved Son, with whom I am well pleased."

The Baptism of Jesus by John. This mosaic, completed in the fifth century, is an early depiction of Christ, realistically rendered. (Scala/Art Resource)

[THE SERMON ON THE MOUNT]

5. Seeing the crowds, he went up to the mountain, and when he sat down his disciples came to him. [2]And he opened his mouth and taught them, saying:

3 "Blessed are the poor in spirit, for theirs is the kingdom of heaven.

4 "Blessed are those who mourn, for they shall be comforted.

5 "Blessed are the meek, for they shall inherit the earth.

6 "Blessed are those who hunger and thirst for righteousness, for they shall be satisfied.

7 "Blessed are the merciful, for they shall obtain mercy.

8 "Blessed are the pure in heart, for they shall see God.

9 "Blessed are the peacemakers, for they shall be called sons of God.

10 "Blessed are those who are persecuted for righteousness' sake, for theirs is the kingdom of heaven.

11 "Blessed are you when men revile you and persecute you and utter all kinds of evil against you

falsely on my account. [12]Rejoice and be glad, for your reward is great in heaven, for so men persecuted the prophets who were before you.

13 "You are the salt of the earth; but if salt has lost its taste, how can its saltness be restored? It is no longer good for anything except to be thrown out and trodden under foot by men.

14 "You are the light of the world. A city set on a hill cannot be hid. [15]Nor do men light a lamp and put it under a bushel, but on a stand, and it gives light to all in the house. [16]Let your light so shine before men, that they may see your good works and give glory to your Father who is in heaven.

17 "Think not that I have come to abolish the law and the prophets; I have come not to abolish them but to fulfil them. [18]For truly, I say to you, till heaven and earth pass away, not an iota, not a dot, will pass from the law until all is accomplished. [19]Whoever then relaxes one of the least of these commandments and teaches men so, shall be called least in the kingdom of heaven; but he who does them and teaches them shall be called great in the kingdom of heaven. [20]For I tell you, unless your righteousness exceeds that of the scribes and Pharisees, you will never enter the kingdom of heaven.

21 "You have heard that it was said to the men of old, 'You shall not kill; and whoever kills shall be liable to judgment.' [22]But I say to you that every one who is angry with his brother shall be liable to judgment; whoever insults his brother shall be liable to the council, and whoever says, 'You fool!' shall be liable to the hell of fire. [23]So if you are offering your gift at the altar, and there remember that your brother has something against you, [24]leave your gift there before the altar and go; first be reconciled to your brother, and then come and offer your gift. [25]Make friends quickly with your accuser, while you are going with him to court, lest your accuser hand you over to the judge, and the judge to the guard, and you be put in prison; [26]truly, I say to you, you will never get out till you have paid the last penny.

[THE LORD'S PRAYER]

6. "Beware of practicing your piety before men in order to be seen by them; for then you will have no reward from your Father who is in heaven.

2 "Thus, when you give alms, sound no trumpet before you, as the hypocrites do in the synagogues and in the streets, that they may be praised by men. Truly, I say to you, they have their reward. [3]But when you give alms, do not let your left hand know what your right hand is doing, [4]so that your alms may be in secret; and your Father who sees in secret will reward you.

5 "And when you pray, you must not be like the hypocrites; for they love to stand and pray in the synagogues and at the street corners, that they may be seen by men. Truly, I say to you, they have their reward. [6]But when you pray, go into your room and shut the door and pray to your Father who is in secret; and your Father who sees in secret will reward you.

7 "And in praying do not heap up empty phrases as the Gentiles do; for they think that they will be heard for their many words. [8]Do not be like them, for your Father knows what you need before you ask him. [9]Pray then like this:

Our Father who art in heaven.
Hallowed be thy name.
[10]Thy kingdom come,
Thy will be done,
On earth as it is in heaven.
[11]Give us this day our daily bread;
[12]And forgive us our debts,
As we also have forgiven our debtors;
[13]And lead us not into temptation,
But deliver us from evil.

[14]For if you forgive men their trepasses, your heavenly Father also will forgive you; [15]but if you do not forgive men their trespasses, neither will your Father forgive your trespasses.

[TRUST IN GOD]

6.16 "And when you fast, do not look dismal, like the hypocrites, for they disfigure their faces that their fasting may be seen by men. Truly, I say to you, they have their reward. [17]But when you fast, anoint your head and wash your face, [18]that your fasting may not be seen by men but by your Father who is in secret; and your Father who sees in secret will reward you.

19 "Do not lay up for yourselves treasures on earth, where moth and rust consume and where thieves break in and steal, [20]but lay up for yourselves treasures in heaven, where neither moth nor rust consumes and where thieves do not break in and

steal. [21]For where your treasure is, there will your heart be also.

22 "The eye is the lamp of the body. So, if your eye is sound, your whole body will be full of light; [23]but if your eye is not sound, your whole body will be full of darkness. If then the light in you is darkness, how great is the darkness!

24 "No one can serve two masters; for either he will hate the one and love the other, or he will be devoted to the one and despise the other. You cannot serve God and mammon.

25 "Therefore I tell you, do not be anxious about your life, what you shall eat or what you shall drink, nor about your body, what you shall put on. Is not life more than food, and the body more than clothing? [26]Look at the birds of the air: they neither sow nor reap nor gather into barns, and yet your heavenly Father feeds them. Are you not of more value than they? [27]And which of you by being anxious can add one cubit to his span of life? [28]And why be anxious about clothing? Consider the lilies of the field, how they grow; they neither toil nor spin; [29]yet I tell you, even Solomon in all his glory was not arrayed like one of these. [30]But if God so clothes the grass of the field, which today is alive and tomorrow is thrown into the oven, will he not much more clothe you, O men of little faith? [31]Therefore do not be anxious, saying, 'What shall we eat?' or 'What shall we drink?' or 'What shall we wear?' [32]For the Gentiles seek all these things; and your heavenly Father knows that you need them all. [33]But seek first his kingdom and his righteousness, and all these things shall be yours as well.

34 "Therefore do not be anxious about tomorrow, for tomorrow will be anxious for itself. Let the day's own trouble be sufficient for the day.

[HEARERS AND DOERS OF THE WORD]

7. "Judge not, that you be not judged. [2]For with the judgment you pronounce you will be judged, and the measure you give will be the measure you get. [3]Why do you see the speck that is in your brother's eye, but do not notice the log that is in your own eye? [4]Or how can you say to your brother, 'Let me take the speck out of your eye,' when there is the log in your own eye? [5]You hypocrite, first take the log out of your own eye, and then you will see clearly to take the speck out of your brother's eye.

6 "Do not give dogs what is holy; and do not throw your pearls before swine, lest they trample them underfoot and turn to attack you.

7 "Ask, and it will be given you; seek, and you will find; knock, and it will be opened to you. [8]For every one who asks receives, and he who seeks finds, and to him who knocks it will be opened. [9]Or what man of you, if his son asks him for a loaf, will give him a stone? [10]Or if he asks for a fish, will give him a serpent? [11]If you then, who are evil, know how to give good gifts to your children, how much more will your Father who is in heaven give good things to those who ask him? [12]So whatever you wish that men would do to you, do so to them; for this is the law and the prophets.

13 "Enter by the narrow gate; for the gate is wide and the way is easy, that leads to destruction, and those who enter by it are many. [14]For the gate is narrow and the way is hard, that leads to life, and those who find it are few.

15 "Beware of false prophets, who come to you in sheep's clothing but inwardly are ravenous wolves. [16]You will know them by their fruits. Are grapes gathered from thorns, or figs from thistles? [17]So, every sound tree bears good fruit, but the bad tree bears evil fruit. [18]A sound tree cannot bear evil fruit, nor can a bad tree bear good fruit. [19]Every tree that does not bear good fruit is cut down and thrown into the fire. [20]Thus you will know them by their fruits.

21 "Not every one who says to me, 'Lord, Lord,' shall enter the kingdom of heaven, but he who does the will of my Father who is in heaven. [22]On that day many will say to me, 'Lord, Lord, did we not prophesy in your name, and cast out demons in your name, and do many mighty works in your name?' [23]And then will I declare to them, 'I never knew you; depart from me, you evil-doers.'

24 "Every one then who hears these words of mine and does them will be like a wise man who built his house upon the rock; [25]and the rain fell, and the floods came, and the winds blew and beat upon that house, but it did not fall, because it had been founded on the rock. [26]And every one who hears these words of mine and does not do them will be like a foolish man who built his house upon the sand; [27]and the rain fell, and the floods came, and the winds blew and beat against that house, and it fell; and great was the fall of it."

28 And when Jesus finished these sayings, the

crowds were astonished at his teaching, [29]for he taught them as one who had authority, and not as their scribes.

[CHARGE TO THE TWELVE APOSTLES]

10. And he called to him his twelve disciples and gave them authority over unclean spirits, to cast them out, and to heal every disease and every infirmity. [2]The names of the twelve apostles are these: first, Simon, who is called Peter, and Andrew his brother; James the son of Zeb'e-dee, and John his brother; [3]Philip and Bartholomew; Thomas and Matthew the tax collector; James the son of Alphaeus, and Thaddaeus; [4]Simon the Cananaean, and Judas Iscariot, who betrayed him.

5 These twelve Jesus sent out, charging them, "Go nowhere among the Gentiles, and enter no town of the Samaritans, [6]but go rather to the lost sheep of the house of Israel. [7]And preach as you go, saying, 'The kingdom of heaven is at hand.' [8]Heal the sick, raise the dead, cleanse lepers, cast out demons. You received without pay, give without pay. [9]Take no gold, nor silver, nor copper in your belts, [10]no bag for your journey, nor two tunics, nor sandals, nor a staff; for the laborer deserves his food. [11]And whatever town or village you enter, find out who is worthy in it, and stay with him until you depart. [12]As you enter the house, salute it. [13]And if the house is worthy, let your peace come upon it; but if it is not worthy, let your peace return to you. [14]And if any one will not receive you or listen to your words, shake off the dust from your feet as you leave that house or town. [15]Truly, I say to you, it shall be more tolerable on the day of judgment for the land of Sodom and Gomor'rah than for that town.

16 "Lo, I send you out as sheep in the midst of wolves; so be wise as serpents and innocent as doves. [17]Beware of men; for they will deliver you up to councils, and flog you in their synagogues, [18]and you will be dragged before governors and kings for my sake, to bear testimony before them and the Gentiles. [19]When they deliver you up, do not be anxious how you are to speak or what you are to say; for what you are to say will be given to you in that hour; [20]for it is not you who speak, but the Spirit of your Father speaking through you. [21]Brother will deliver up brother to death, and the father his child, and children will rise against parents and have them put to death; [22]and you will be hated by all for my name's sake. But he who endures to the end will be saved. [23]When they persecute you in one town, flee to the next; for truly, I say to you, you will not have gone through all the towns of Israel, before the Son of man comes.

24 "A disciple is not above his teacher, nor a servant above his master; [25]it is enough for the disciple to be like his teacher, and the servant like his master. If they have called the master of the house Be-el'zebub, how much more will they malign those of his household.

26 "So have no fear of them; for nothing is covered that will not be revealed, or hidden that will not be known. [27]What I tell you in the dark, utter in the light; and what you hear whispered, proclaim upon the housetops. [28]And do not fear those who kill the body but cannot kill the soul; rather fear him who can destroy both soul and body in hell. [29]Are not two sparrows sold for a penny? And not one of them will fall to the ground without your Father's will. [30]But even the hairs of your head are all numbered. [31]Fear not, therefore; you are of more value than many sparrows. [32]So every one who acknowledges me before men, I also will acknowledge before my Father who is in heaven; [33]but whoever denies me before men, I also will deny before my Father who is in heaven.

34 "Do not think that I have come to bring peace on earth; I have not come to bring peace, but a sword. [35]For I have come to set a man against his father, and a daughter against her mother, and a daughter-in-law against her mother-in-law; [36]and a man's foes will be those of his own household. [37]He who loves father or mother more than me is not worthy of me; and he who loves son or daughter more than me is not worthy of me; [38]and he who does not take his cross and follow me is not worthy of me. [39]He who finds his life will lose it, and he who loses his life for my sake will find it.

40 "He who receives you receives me, and he who receives me receives him who sent me. [41]He who receives a prophet because he is a prophet shall receive a prophet's reward, and he who receives a righteous man because he is a righteous man shall receive a righteous man's reward. [42]And whoever gives to one of these little ones even a cup of cold water because he is a disciple, truly, I say to you, he shall not lose his reward."

[PARABLES]

13. That same day Jesus went out of the house and sat beside the sea. [2]And great crowds gathered about him, so that he got into a boat and sat there; and the whole crowd stood on the beach. [3]And he told them many things in parables, saying: "A sower went out to sow. [4]And as he sowed, some seeds fell along the path, and the birds came and devoured them. [5]Other seeds fell on rocky ground, where they had not much soil, and immediately they sprang up, since they had no depth of soil, [6]but when the sun rose they were scorched; and since they had no root they withered away. [7]Other seeds fell upon thorns, and the thorns grew up and choked them. [8]Other seeds fell on good soil and brought forth grain, some a hundredfold, some sixty, some thirty. [9]He who has ears, let him hear."

10 Then the disciples came and said to him, "Why do you speak to them in parables?" [11]And he answered them, "To you it has been given to know the secrets of the kingdom of heaven, but to them it has not been given. [12]For to him who has will more be given, and he will have abundance; but from him who has not, even what he has will be taken away. [13]This is why I speak to them in parables, because seeing they do not see, and hearing they do not hear, nor do they understand. [14]With them indeed is fulfilled the prophecy of I·ṡāi′ăh which says:

'You shall indeed hear but never understand,
and you shall indeed see but never perceive.
[15]For this people's heart has grown dull,
and their ears are heavy of hearing,
and their eyes they have closed,
lest they should perceive with their eyes,
and hear with their ears,
and understand with their heart,
and turn for me to heal them.'

[16]But blessed are your eyes, for they see, and your ears, for they hear. [17]Truly, I say to you, many prophets and righteous men longed to see what you see, and did not see it, and to hear what you hear, and did not hear it.

18 "Hear then the parable of the sower. [19]When any one hears the word of the kingdom and does not understand it, the evil one comes and snatches away what is sown in his heart; this is what was sown along the path. [20]As for what was sown on rocky ground, this is he who hears the word and immediately receives it with joy; [21]yet he has no root in himself, but endures for a while, and when tribulation or persecution arises on account of the word, immediately he falls away. [22]As for what was sown among thorns, this is he who hears the word, but the cares of the world and the delight in riches choke the word, and it proves unfruitful. [23]As for what was sown on good soil, this is he who hears the word and understands it; he indeed bears fruit, and yields, in one case a hundredfold, in another sixty, and in another thirty."

24 Another parable he put before them, saying, "The kingdom of heaven may be compared to a man who sowed good seed in his field; [25]but while men were sleeping, his enemy came and sowed weeds among the wheat, and went away. [26]So when the plants came up and bore grain, then the weeds appeared also. [27]And the servants of the householder came and said to him, 'Sir, did you not sow good seed in your field? How then has it weeds?' [28]He said to them, 'An enemy has done this.' The servants said to him, 'Then do you want us to go and gather them?' [29]But he said, 'No; lest in gathering the weeds you root up the wheat along with them. [30]Let both grow together until the harvest; and at harvest time I will tell the reapers, Gather the weeds first and bind them in bundles to be burned, but gather the wheat into my barn.'"

31 Another parable he put before them, saying, "The kingdom of heaven is like a grain of mustard seed which a man took and sowed in his field; [32]it is the smallest of all seeds, but when it has grown it is the greatest of shrubs and becomes a tree, so that the birds of the air come and make nests in its branches."

33 He told them another parable. "The kingdom of heaven is like leaven which a woman took and hid in three measures of meal, till it was all leavened."

34 All this Jesus said to the crowds in parables; indeed he said nothing to them without a parable. [35]This was to fulfill what was spoken by the prophet:

"I will open my mouth in parables,
I will utter what has been hidden since the
foundation of the world."

36 Then he left the crowds and went into the house. And his disciples came to him saying, "Explain to us the parable of the weeds of the field." [37]He answered, "He who sows the good seed is the Son of man; [38]the field is the world, and the good

seed means the sons of the kingdom; the weeds are the sons of the evil one, [39]and the enemy who sowed them is the devil; the harvest is the close of the age, and the reapers are angels. [40]Just as the weeds are gathered and burned with fire, so will it be at the close of the age. [41]The Son of man will send his angels, and they will gather out of his kingdom all causes of sin and all evil-doers, [42]and throw them into the furnace of fire; there men will weep and gnash their teeth. [43]Then the righteous will shine like the sun in the kingdom of their Father. He who has ears, let him hear.

44 "The kingdom of heaven is like treasure hidden in a field, which a man found and covered up; then in his joy he goes and sells all that he has and buys that field.

45 "Again, the kingdom of heaven is like a merchant in search of fine pearls, [46]who, on finding one pearl of great value, went and sold all that he had and bought it.

47 "Again, the kingdom of heaven is like a net which was thrown into the sea and gathered fish of every kind: [48]when it was full, men drew it ashore and sat down and sorted the good into vessels but threw away the bad. [49]So it will be at the close of the age. The angels will come out and separate the evil from the righteous, [50]and throw them into the furnace of fire; there men will weep and gnash their teeth. . . ."

[THE FOUNDING OF THE CHURCH]

16.13 Now when Jesus came into the district of Caes-a-re'a Philippi, he asked his disciples, "Who do men say that the Son of man is?" [14]And they said, "Some say John the Baptist, others say Elijah, and others Jeremiah or one of the prophets." [15]He said to them, "But who do you say that I am?" [16]Simon Peter replied, "You are the Christ, the Son of the living God." [17]And Jesus answered him, "Blessed are you, Simon Bar-Jona! For flesh and blood has not revealed this to you, but my Father who is in heaven. [18]And I tell you, you are Peter, and on this rock I will build my church, and the powers of death shall not prevail against it. [19]I will give you the keys of the kingdom of heaven, and whatever you bind on earth shall be bound in heaven, and whatever you loose on earth shall be loosed in heaven." [20]Then he strictly charged the disciples to tell no one that he was the Christ.

21 From that time Jesus began to show his disciples that he must go to Jerusalem and suffer many things from the elders and chief priests and scribes, and be killed, and on the third day be raised. [22]And Peter took him and began to rebuke him, saying, "God forbid, Lord! This shall never happen to you." [23]But he turned and said to Peter, "Get behind me, Satan! You are a hindrance to me; for you are not on the side of God, but of men."

24 Then Jesus told his disciples, "If any man would come after me, let him deny himself and take up his cross and follow me. [25]For whoever would save his life will lose it, and whoever loses his life for my sake will find it. [26]For what will it profit a man, if he gains the whole world and forfeits his life? Or what shall a man give in return for his life? [27]For the Son of man is to come with his angels in the glory of his Father, and then he will repay every man for what he has done. [28]Truly, I say to you, there are some standing here who will not taste death before they see the Son of man coming in his kingdom."

[MARRIAGE AND POSSESSIONS]

19. Now when Jesus had finished these sayings, he went away from Galilee and entered the region of Judea beyond the Jordan; [2]and large crowds followed him, and he healed them there.

3 And Pharisees came up to him and tested him by asking, "Is it lawful to divorce one's wife for any cause?" [4]He answered, "Have you not read that he who made them from the beginning made them male and female, [5]and said, 'For this reason a man shall leave his father and mother and be joined to his wife, and the two shall become one'? [6]So they are no longer two but one. What therefore God has joined together, let not man put asunder." [7]They said to him, "Why then did Moses command one to give a certificate of divorce, and to put her away?" [8]He said to them, "For your hardness of heart Moses allowed you to divorce your wives, but from the beginning it was not so. [9]And I say to you: whoever divorces his wife, except for unchastity, and marries another, commits adultery."

10 The disciples said to him, "If such is the case of

a man with his wife, it is not expedient to marry." [11]But he said to them, "Not all men can receive this precept, but only those to whom it is given. [12]For there are eunuchs who have been so from birth, and there are eunuchs who have been made eunuchs by men, and there are eunuchs who have made themselves eunuchs for the sake of the kingdom of heaven. He who is able to receive this, let him receive it."

13 Then children were brought to him that he might lay his hands on them and pray. The disciples rebuked the people; [14]but Jesus said, "Let the children come to me, and do not hinder them; for to such belongs the kingdom of heaven." [15] And he laid his hands on them and went away.

16 And behold, one came up to him saying, "Teacher, what good deed must I do, to have eternal life?" [17]And he said to him, "Why do you ask me about what is good? One there is who is good. If you would enter life, keep the commandments." [18]He said to him, "Which?" And Jesus said, "You shall not kill, You shall not commit adultery, You shall not steal, You shall not bear false witness, [19]Honor your father and mother, and, You shall love your neighbor as yourself." [20]The young man said to him, "All these I have observed; what do I still lack?" [21]Jesus said to him, "If you would be perfect, go, sell what you possess and give it to the poor, and you will have treasure in heaven; and come, follow me." [22]When the young man heard this he went away sorrowful; for he had great possessions.

23 And Jesus said to his disciples, "Truly, I say to you, it will be hard for a rich man to enter the kingdom of heaven. [24]Again I tell you, it is easier for a camel to go through the eye of a needle than for a rich man to enter the kingdom of God." [25]When the disciples heard this, they were greatly astonished, saying, "Who then can be saved?" [26]But Jesus looked at them and said to them, "With men this is impossible, but with God all things are possible." [27]Then Peter said in reply, "Lo, we have left everything and followed you. What then shall we have?" [28]Jesus said to them, "Truly, I say to you, in the new world, when the Son of man shall sit on his glorious throne, you who have followed me will also sit on twelve thrones, judging the twelve tribes of Israel. [29]And every one who has left houses or brothers or sisters or father or mother or children or lands, for my name's sake, will receive a hundredfold, and inherit eternal life. [30]But many that are first will be last, and the last first. . . ."

[THE TWO GREAT COMMANDMENTS]

22.15 Then the Pharisees went and took counsel how to entangle him in his talk. [16]And they sent their disciples to him, along with the He-ro'di-ans, saying, "Teacher, we know that you are true, and teach the way of God truthfully, and care for no man; for you do not regard the position of men. [17]Tell us, then, what you think. Is it lawful to pay taxes to Caesar, or not?" [18]But Jesus, aware of their malice, said, "Why put me to the test, you hypocrites? [19]Show me the money for the tax." And they brought him a coin. [20]And Jesus said to them, "Whose likeness and inscription is this?" [21]They said, "Caesar's." Then he said to them, "Render therefore to Caesar the things that are Caesar's, and to God the things that are God's." [22]When they heard it, they marveled; and they left him and went away.

23 The same day Sad'du-cees came to him, who say that there is no resurrection; and they asked him a question, [24]saying, "Teacher, Moses said, 'If a man dies, having no children, his brother must marry the widow, and raise up children for his brother.' [25]Now there were seven brothers among us; the first married, and died, and having no children left his wife to his brother. [26]So too the second and third, down to the seventh. [27]After them all, the woman died. [28]In the resurrection, therefore, to which of the seven will she be wife? For they all had her."

29 But Jesus answered them, "You are wrong, because you know neither the scriptures nor the power of God. [30]For in the resurrection they neither marry nor are given in marriage, but are like angels in heaven. [31]And as for the resurrection of the dead, have you not read what was said to you by God, [32]'I am the God of Abraham, and the God of Isaac, and the God of Jacob'? He is not God of the dead, but of the living." [33]And when the crowd heard it, they were astonished at his teaching.

34 But when the Pharisees heard that he had silenced the Sad'du-cees, they came together. [35]And one of them, a lawyer, asked him a question, to test him. [36]"Teacher, which is the great commandment in the law?" [37]And he said to him, "You shall love the Lord your God with all your heart, and with all your soul, and with all your mind. [38]This is the great and

first commandement. [39]And a second is like it, You shall love your neighbor as yourself. [40]On these two commandments depend all the law and the prophets."

[THE LAST JUDGMENT]

25.31 "When the Son of man comes in his glory, and all the angels with him, then he will sit on his glorious throne. [32]Before him will be gathered all the nations, and he will separate them one from another as a shepherd separates the sheep from the goats, [33]and he will place the sheep at his right hand, but the goats at the left. [34]Then the King will say to those at his right hand, 'Come, O blessed of my Father, inherit the kingdom prepared for you from the foundation of the world; [35]for I was hungry and you gave me food, I was thirsty and you gave me drink, I was a stranger and you welcomed me, [36]I was naked and you clothed me, I was sick and you visited me, I was in prison and you came to me.' [37]Then the righteous will answer him, 'Lord, when did we see thee hungry and feed thee, or thirsty and give thee drink? [38]And when did we see thee a stranger and welcome thee, or naked and clothe thee? [39]And when did we see thee sick or in prison and visit thee?' [40]And the King will answer them, 'Truly, I say to you, as you did it to one of the least of these my brethren, you did it to me.' [41]Then he will say to those at his left hand, 'Depart from me, you cursed, into the eternal fire prepared for the devil and his angels; [42]for I was hungry and you gave me no food, I was thirsty and you gave me no drink, [43]I was a stranger and you did not welcome me, naked and you did not clothe me, sick and in prison and you did not visit me.' [44]Then they also will answer, 'Lord, when did we see thee hungry or thirsty or a stranger or naked or sick or in prison, and did not minister to thee?' [45]Then he will answer them, 'Truly, I say to you, as you did it not to one of the least of these, you did it not to me.' [46]And they will go away into eternal punishment, but the righteous into eternal life."

[THE LAST SUPPER]

26.17 Now on the first day of Unleavened Bread the disciples came to Jesus, saying, "Where will you have us prepare for you to eat the passover?" [18]He said, "Go into the city to such a one, and say to him, 'The Teacher says, My time is at hand; I will keep the passover at your house with my disciples.'" [19]And the disciples did as Jesus had directed them, and they prepared the passover.

20 When it was evening, he sat at table with the twelve disciples; [21]and as they were eating, he said, "Truly, I say to you, one of you will betray me." [22]And they were very sorrowful, and began to say to him one after another, "Is it I, Lord?" [23]He answered, "He who has dipped his hand in the dish with me, will betray me. [24]The Son of man goes as it is written of him, but woe to that man by whom the Son of man is betrayed! It would have been better for that man if he had not been born." [25]Judas, who betrayed him, said, "Is it I, Master?" He said to him, "You have said so."

26 Now as they were eating, Jesus took bread, and blessed, and broke it, and gave it to the disciples and said, "Take, eat; this is my body." [27]And he took a cup, and when he had given thanks he gave it to them, saying, "Drink of it, all of you; [28]for this is my blood of the covenant, which is poured out for many for the forgiveness of sins. [29]I tell you I shall not drink again of this fruit of the vine until that day when I drink it new with you in my Father's kingdom."

30 And when they had sung a hymn, they went out to the Mount of Olives. [31]Then Jesus said to them, "You will all fall away because of me this night; for it is written, 'I will strike the shepherd, and the sheep of the flock will be scattered.' [32]But after I am raised up, I will go before you to Galilee." [33]Peter declared to him, "Though they all fall away because of you, I will never fall away." [34]Jesus said to him, "Truly, I say to you, this very night, before the cock crows, you will deny me three times." [35]Peter said to him, "Even if I must die with you, I will not deny you." And so said all the disciples.

36 Then Jesus went with them to a place called Geth-sem'a-ne, and he said to his disciples, "Sit here, while I go yonder and pray." [37]And taking with him Peter and the two sons of Zeb'e-dee, he began to be sorrowful and troubled. [38]Then he said to them, "My soul is very sorrowful, even to death; remain here, and watch with me." [39]And going a little farther he fell on his face and prayed, "My Father, if it be possible, let this cup pass from me; nevertheless, not as I will, but as thou wilt." [40]And he came to the disciples and found them sleeping; and he said to Peter, "So, could you not watch with me one hour? [41]Watch and pray that you may not enter into temptation; the

spirit indeed is willing, but the flesh is weak."
[42]Again, for the second time, he went away and
prayed, "My Father, if this cannot pass unless I drink
it, thy will be done." [43]And again he came and found
them sleeping, for their eyes were heavy. [44]So, leaving them again, he went away and prayed for the
third time, saying the same words. [45]Then he came
to the disciples and said to them, "Are you still sleeping and taking your rest? Behold, the hour is at
hand, and the Son of man is betrayed into the hands
of sinners. [46]Rise, let us be going; see, my betrayer is
at hand."

[THE PASSION AND DEATH]

27.11 Now Jesus stood before the governor; and
the governor asked him, "Are you the King of the
Jews?" Jesus said to him, "You have said so." [12]But
when he was accused by the chief priests and elders,
he made no answer. [13]Then Pilate said to him, "Do
you not hear how many things they testify against
you?" [14]But he gave him no answer, not even to a
single charge; so that the governor wondered
greatly.

15 Now at the feast the governor was accustomed
to release for the crowd any one prisoner whom they
wanted. [16]And they had then a notorious prisoner,
called Bar-ab'bas. [17]So when they had gathered, Pilate said to them, "Whom do you want me to release
for you, Bar-ab'bas or Jesus who is called Christ?
[18]For he knew that it was out of envy that they had
delivered him up. [19]Besides, while he was sitting on
the judgment seat, his wife sent word to him, "Have
nothing to do with that righteous man, for I have
suffered much over him today in a dream." [20]Now
the chief priests and the elders persuaded the people
to ask for Bar-ab'bas and destroy Jesus. [21]The governor again said to them, "Which of the two do you
want me to release for you?" And they said, "Bar-
ab'bas." [22]Pilate said to them, "Then what shall I do
with Jesus who is called Christ?" They all said, "Let
him be crucified." [23]And he said, "Why, what evil
has he done?" But they shouted all the more, "Let
him be crucified."

24 So when Pilate saw that he was gaining nothing, but rather that a riot was beginning, he took
water and washed his hands before the crowd, saying, "I am innocent of this man's blood; see to it
yourselves." [25]And all the people answered, "His
blood be on us and on our children!" [26]Then he released for them Bar-ab'bas, and having scourged
Jesus, delivered him to be crucified.

27 Then the soldiers of the governor took Jesus
into the praetorium, and they gathered the whole
battalion before him. [28]And they stripped him and
put a scarlet robe upon him, [29]and plaiting a crown
of thorns they put it on his head, and put a reed in
his right hand. And kneeling before him they
mocked him, saying, "Hail, King of the Jews!" [30]And
they spat upon him, and took the reed and struck
him on the head. [31]And when they had mocked him,
they stripped him of the robe, and put his own
clothes on him, and led him away to crucify him.

32 As they were marching out, they came upon a
man of Cy-re'ne, Simon by name; this man they
compelled to carry his cross. [33]And when they came
to a place called Gol'go-tha (which means the place
of the skull), [34]they offered him wine to drink, mingled with gall; but when he tasted it, he would not
drink it. [35]And when they had crucified him, they
divided his garments among them by casting lots;
[36]then they sat down and kept watch over him there.
[37]And over his head they put the charge against him,
which read; "This is Jesus the king of the Jews."
[38]Then two robbers were crucified with him, one on
the right and one on the left. [39]And those who passed
by derided him, wagging their heads [40]and saying,
"You who would destroy the temple and build it in
three days, save yourself! If you are the Son of God,
come down from the cross." [41]So also the chief
priests, with the scribes and elders, mocked him, saying, [42]"He saved others; he cannot save himself. He
is the King of Israel; let him come down now from
the cross, and we will believe in him. [43]He trusts in
God; let God deliver him now, if he desires him; for
he said, 'I am the Son of God.'" [44]And the robbers
who were crucified with him also reviled him in the
same way.

45 Now from the sixth hour there was darkness
over all the land until the ninth hour. [46]And about
the ninth hour Jesus cried with a loud voice, "Eli, Eli,
la'ma sa-bach-tha'ni?" that is, "My God, my God,
why hast thou forsaken me?" [47]And some of the by-
standers hearing it said, "This man is calling Elijah."
[48]And one of them at once ran and took a sponge,
filled it with vinegar, and put it on a reed, and gave
it to him to drink. [49]But the others said, "Wait, let us
see whether Elijah will come to save him." [50]And
Jesus cried again with a loud voice and yielded up
his spirit.

51 And behold, the curtain of the temple was torn in two, from top to bottom; and the earth shook, and the rocks were split; [52]the tombs also were opened, and many bodies of the saints who had fallen asleep were raised, [53]and coming out of the tombs after his resurrection they went into the holy city and appeared to many. [54]When the centurion and those who were with him, keeping watch over Jesus, saw the earthquake and what took place, they were filled with awe, and said, "Truly this was a son of God!"

55 There were also many women there, looking on from afar, who had followed Jesus from Galilee, ministering to him; [56]among whom were Mary Mag'da-lene, and Mary the mother of James and Joseph, and the mother of the sons of Zeb'e-dee.

57 When it was evening, there came a rich man from Ar-i-ma-the'a, named Joseph, who also was a disciple of Jesus. [58]He went to Pilate and asked for the body of Jesus. Then Pilate ordered it to be given to him. [59]And Joseph took the body, and wrapped it in a clean linen shroud, [60]and laid it in his own new tomb, which he had hewn in the rock; and he rolled a great stone to the entrance of the tomb, and departed. [61]Mary Mag'da-lene and the other Mary were there, sitting opposite the tomb.

62 Next day, that is, after the day of Preparation, the chief priests and the Pharisees gathered before Pilate [63]and said, "Sir, we remember how the impostor said, while he was still alive, 'After three days I will rise again.' [64]Therefore order the tomb to be made secure until the third day, lest his disciples go and steal him away, and tell the people, 'He has risen from the dead,' and the last fraud will be worse than the first." [65]Pilate said to them, "You have a guard of soldiers; go, make it as secure as you can." [66]So they went and made the tomb secure by sealing the stone and setting a guard.

[THE RESURRECTION]

28. Now after the sabbath, toward the dawn of the first day of the week, Mary Mag'da-lene and the other Mary went to see the tomb. [2]And behold, there was a great earthquake; for an angel of the Lord descended from heaven and came and rolled back the stone, and sat upon it. [3]His appearance was like lightning, and his raiment white as snow. [4]And for fear of him the guards trembled and became like dead men. [5]But the angel said to the women, "Do not be afraid; for I know that you seek Jesus who was crucified. [6]He is not here; for he has risen, as he said. Come, see the place where he lay. [7]Then go quickly and tell his disciples that he has risen from the dead, and behold, he is going before you to Galilee; there you will see him. Lo, I have told you." [8]So they departed quickly from the tomb with fear and great joy, and ran to tell his disciples. [9]And behold, Jesus met them and said, "Hail!" And they came up and took hold of his feet and worshiped him. [10]Then Jesus said to them, "Do not be afraid; go and tell my brethren to go to Galilee, and there they will see me."

11 While they were going, behold, some of the guard went into the city and told the chief priests all that had taken place. [12]And when they had assembled with the elders and taken counsel, they gave a sum of money to the soldiers [13]and said, "Tell people, 'His disciples came by night and stole him away while we were asleep.' [14]And if this comes to the governor's ears, we will satisfy him and keep you out of trouble." [15]So they took the money and did as they were directed; and this story has been spread among the Jews to this day.

16 Now the eleven disciples went to Galilee, to the mountain to which Jesus had directed them. [17]And when they saw him they worshiped him; but some doubted. [18]And Jesus came and said to him, "All authority in heaven and on earth has been given to me. [19]Go therefore and make disciples of all nations, baptizing them in the name of the Father and of the Son and of the Holy Spirit, [20]teaching them to observe all that I have commanded you; and lo, I am with you always, to the close of the age."

From the Gospel of John

[PROLOGUE]

1. In the beginning was the Word, and the Word was with God, and the Word was God. [2]He was in the beginning with God; [3]all things were made through him, and without him was not anything made that was made. [4]In him was life, and the life was the light of men. [5]The light shines in the darkness, and the darkness has not overcome it.

6 There was a man sent from God, whose name

St. John, from the Gospels of Godesalc. This eighth-century Carolingian manuscript illustration shows John transcribing the word of the dove, the Holy Spirit. (Bibliothèque Nationale, Paris.)

was John. [7]He came for testimony, to bear witness to the light, that all might believe through him. [8]He was not the light, but came to bear witness to the light.

9 The true light that enlightens every man was coming into the world; [10]he was in the world, and the world was made through him, yet the world knew him not; [11]he came to his own home, and his own people received him not. [12]But to all who received him, who believed in his name, he gave power to become children of God; [13]who were born, not of blood nor of the will of the flesh nor of the will of man, but of God.

14 And the Word became flesh and dwelt among us, full of grace and truth; we have beheld his glory, glory as of the only Son from the Father. ([15]John bore witness to him, and cried, "This was he of whom I said, 'He who comes after me ranks before me, for he was before me.'") [16]And from his fullness have we all received, grace upon grace. [17]For the law was given through Moses; grace and truth came through Jesus Christ. [18]No one has ever seen God; the only Son, who is in the bosom of the Father, he has made him known.

19 And this is the testimony of John, when the Jews sent priests and Levites from Jerusalem to ask him, "Who are you?" [20]He confessed, he did not deny, but confessed, "I am not the Christ." [21]And they asked him, "What then? Are you Elijah?" He said, "I am not." "Are you the prophet?" And he answered, "No." [22]They said to him then, "Who are you? Let us have an answer for those who sent us. What do you say about yourself?" [23]He said, "I am the voice of one crying in the wilderness, 'Make straight the way of the Lord,' as the prophet Isaiah said."

24 Now they had been sent from the Pharisees. [25]They asked him, "Then why are you baptizing, if you are neither the Christ, nor Elijah, nor the prophet?" [26]John answered them, "I baptize with water; but among you stands one whom you do not know, [27]even he who comes after me, the thong of whose sandal I am not worthy to untie." [28]This took place in Bethany beyond the Jordan, where John was baptizing.

29 The next day he saw Jesus coming toward him, and said, "Behold, the Lamb of God, who takes away the sin of the world! [30]This is he of whom I said, 'After me comes a man who ranks before me, for he was before me.' [31]I myself did not know him; but for this I came baptizing with water, that he might be revealed to Israel." [32]And John bore witness, "I saw the Spirit descend as a dove from heaven, and it remained on him. [33]I myself did not know him; but he who sent me to baptize with water said to me, 'He on whom you see the Spirit descend and remain, this is he who baptizes with the Holy Spirit.' [34]And I have seen and have borne witness that this is the Son of God."

[JESUS' RELATION TO THE FATHER]

5.19 Jesus said to them, "Truly, truly, I say to you, the Son can do nothing of his own accord, but only what he sees the Father doing; for whatever he does, that the Son does likewise. [20]For the Father loves the Son, and shows him all that he himself is doing; and greater works than these will he show him, that you may marvel. [21]For as the Father raises the dead and gives them life, so also the Son gives life to whom he will. 22 The Father judges no one, but has given all judgment to the Son, 23 that all may honor the Son, even as they honor the Father. He who does not honor the Son does not honor the Father who sent him. 24 Truly, truly, I say to you, he who hears my word and believes him who sent me, has eternal life; he does not come into judgment, but has passed from death to life.

25 "Truly, truly, I say to you, the hour is coming, and now is, when the dead will hear the voice of the Son of God, and those who hear will live. 26 For as the Father has life in himself, so he has granted the Son also to have life in himself, 27 and has given him authority to execute judgment, because he is the Son of man. 28 Do not marvel at this; for the hour is coming when all who are in the tombs will hear his voice 29 and come forth, those who have done good, to the resurrection of life, and those who have done evil, to the resurrection of judgment.

30 "I can do nothing on my own authority; as I hear, I judge; and my judgment is just, because I seek not my own will but the will of him who sent me. 31 If I bear witness to myself, my testimony is not true; 32 there is another who bears witness to me, and I know that the testimony which he bears to me is true. 33 You sent to John, and he has borne witness to the truth. 34 Not that the testimony which I receive is from man; but I say this that you may be saved. 35 He was a burning and shining lamp, and you were willing to rejoice for a while in his light. 36 But the testimony which I have is greater than that of John; for the works which the Father has granted me to accomplish, these very works which I am doing, bear me witness that the Father has sent me. 37 And the Father who sent me has himself borne witness to me. His voice you have never heard, his form you have never seen; 38 and you do not have his word abiding in you, for you do not believe him whom he has sent. 39 You search the scriptures, because you think that in them you have eternal life; and it is they that bear witness to me; 40 yet you refuse to come to me that you may have life. 41 I do not receive glory from men. 42 But I know that you have not the love of God within you. 43 I have come in my Father's name, and you do not receive me; if another comes in his own name, him you will receive. 44 How can you believe, who receive glory from one another and do not seek the glory that comes from the only God? 45 Do not think that I shall accuse you to the Father; it is Moses who accuses you, on whom you set your hope. 46 If you believed Moses, you would believe me, for he wrote of me. 47 But if you do not believe his writings, how will you believe my words?"

[JESUS THE CHRIST]

6.41 The Jews then murmured at him, because he said, "I am the bread which came down from heaven." 42 They said, "Is not this Jesus, the son of Joseph, whose father and mother we know? How does he now say, 'I have come down from heaven'?" 43 Jesus answered them, "Do not murmur among yourselves. 44 No one can come to me unless the Father who sent me draws him; and I will raise him up at the last day. 45 It is written in the prophets, 'And they shall all be taught by God.' Every one who has heard and learned from the Father comes to me. 46 Not that any one has seen the Father except him who is from God; he has seen the Father. 47 Truly, truly, I say to you, he who believes has eternal life. 48 I am the bread of life. 49 Your fathers ate the manna in the wilderness, and they died. 50 This is the bread which comes down from heaven, that a man may eat of it and not die. 51 I am the living bread which came down from heaven; if any one eats of this bread, he will live forever; and the bread which I shall give for the life of the world is my flesh."

52 The Jews then disputed among themselves, saying, "How can this man give us his flesh to eat?" 53 So Jesus said to them, "Truly, truly, I say to you, unless you eat the flesh of the Son of man and drink his blood, you have no life in you; 54 he who eats my flesh and drinks my blood has eternal life, and I will raise him up at the last day. 55 For my flesh is food indeed, and my blood is drink indeed. 56 He who eats my flesh and drinks my blood abides in me, and I in him. 57 As the living Father sent me, and I live because of the Father, so he who eats me will live because of me. 58 This is the bread which came down from heaven, not such as the fathers ate and died; he who eats this bread will live forever." 59 This he said in the synagogue, as he taught at Ca-per'na-um.

[BEFORE ABRAHAM WAS, I AM]

8. 51 Truly, truly, I say to you, if any one keeps my word, he will never see death." 52 The Jews said to him, "Now we know that you have a demon. Abraham died, as did the prophets; and you say, 'If any one keeps my word, he will never taste death.' [53]Are you greater than our father Abraham, who died? And the prophets died! Whom do you make yourself to be?" [54]Jesus answered, "If I glorify myself, my glory is nothing; it is my Father who glorifies me, of whom you say that he is your God. [55]But you have not known him; I know him. If I said, I do not know him, I should be a liar like you; but I do know him and I keep his word. [56]Your father Abraham rejoiced that he was to see my day; he saw it and was glad." [57]The Jews then said to him, "You are not yet fifty years old, and have you seen Abraham?" [58]Jesus said to them, "Truly, truly, I say to you, before Abraham was, I am." [59]So they took up stones to throw at him; but Jesus hid himself, and went out of the temple.

[ONE WITH THE FATHER]

14. "Let not your hearts be troubled; believe in God, believe also in me. [2]In my Father's house are many rooms; if it were not so, would I have told you that I go to prepare a place for you? [3]And when I go and prepare a place for you, I will come again and will take you to myself, that where I am you may be also. [4]And you know the way where I am going." [5]Thomas said to him, "Lord, we do not know where you are going; how can we know the way?" [6]Jesus said to him, "I am the way, and the truth, and the life; no one comes to the Father, but by me. [7]If you had known me, you would have known my Father also; henceforth you know him and have seen him."

8 Philip said to him, "Lord, show us the Father, and we will be satisfied." [9]Jesus said to him, "Have I been with you so long, and yet you do not know me, Philip? He who has seen me has seen the Father; how can you say, 'Show us the Father'? [10]Do you not believe that I am in the Father and the Father in me? The words that I say to you I do not speak on my own authority; but the Father who dwells in me does his works. [11]Believe me that I am in the Father and the Father in me; or else believe me for the sake of the works themselves.

12 "Truly, truly, I say to you, he who believes in me will also do the works that I do; and greater works than these will he do, because I go to the Father. [13]Whatever you ask in my name, I will do it, that the Father may be glorified in the Son; [14]if you ask anything in my name, I will do it.

15 "If you love me, you will keep my commandments. [16]And I will pray the Father, and he will give you another Counselor, to be with you forever, [17]even the Spirit of truth, whom the world cannot receive, because it neither sees him nor knows him; you know him, for he dwells with you, and will be in you.

18 "I will not leave you desolate; I will come to you. [19]Yet a little while, and the world will see me no more, but you will see me; because I live, you will live also. [20]In that day you will know that I am in my Father, and you in me, and I in you. [21]He who has my commandments and keeps them, he it is who loves me; and he who loves me will be loved by my Father, and I will love him and manifest myself to him." [22]Judas (not Iscariot) said to him, "Lord, how is it that you will manifest yourself to us, and not to the world?" [23]Jesus answered him, "If a man loves me, he will keep my word, and my Father will love him, and we will come to him and make our home with him. [24]He who does not love me does not keep my words; and the word which you hear is not mine but the Father's who sent me.

25 "These things I have spoken to you, while I am still with you. [26]But the Counselor, the Holy Spirit, whom the Father will send in my name, he will teach you all things, and bring to your remembrance all that I have said to you. [27]Peace I leave with you; my peace I give to you; not as the world gives do I give to you. Let not your hearts be troubled, neither let them be afraid. [28]You heard me say to you, 'I go away, and I will come to you.' If you loved me, you would have rejoiced, because I go to the Father; for the Father is greater than I. [29]And now I have told you before it takes place, so that when it does take place, you may believe.

[THE VINE AND THE BRANCHES]

15. "I am the true vine, and my Father is the vinedresser. [2]Every branch of mine that bears no fruit, he takes away, and every branch that does bear fruit he prunes, that it may bear more fruit. [3]You are already made clean by the word which I have spoken to you. [4]Abide in me, and I in you. As the branch cannot bear fruit by itself, unless it abides in the vine, neither can you, unless you abide in me. [5]I am the vine, you are the branches. He who abides in me, and I in him, he it is that bears much fruit, for apart from me you can do nothing. [6]If a man does not abide in me, he is cast forth as a branch and withers; and the branches are gathered, thrown into the fire and burned. [7]If you abide in me, and my words abide in you, ask whatever you will, and it shall be done for you. [8]By this my Father is glorified, that you bear much fruit, and so prove to be my disciples. [9]As the Father has loved me, so have I loved you; abide in my love. [10]If you keep my commandments, you will abide in my love, just as I have kept my Father's commandments and abide in his love. [11]These things I have spoken to you, that my joy may be in you, and that your joy may be full.

12 "This is my commandment, that you love one another as I have loved you. [13]Greater love has no man than this, that a man lay down his life for his friends. [14]You are my friends if you do what I command you. [15]No longer do I call you servants, for the servant does not know what his master is doing; but I have called you friends, for all that I have heard from my Father I have made known to you. [16]You did not choose me, but I chose you and appointed you that you should go and bear fruit and that your fruit should abide; so that whatever you ask the Father in my name, he may give it to you. [17]This I command you, to love one another.

18 "If the world hates you, know that it has hated me before it hated you. [19]If you were of the world, the world would love its own; but because you are not of the world, but I chose you out of the world, therefore the world hates you. [20]Remember the word that I said to you, 'A servant is not greater than his master.' If they persecuted me, they will persecute you; if they kept my word, they will keep yours also. [21]But all this they will do to you on my account, because they do not know him who sent me. [22]If I had not come and spoken to them, they would not have sin; but now they have no excuse for their sin. [23]He who hates me hates my Father also. [24]If I had not done among them the works which no one else did, they would not have sin; but now they have seen and hated both me and my Father. [25]It is to fulfill the word that is written in their law, 'They hated me without a cause.' [26]But when the Counselor comes, whom I shall send to you from the Father, even the Spirit of truth, who proceeds from the Father, he will bear witness to me; [27]and you also are witnesses, because you have been with me from the beginning.

[THE COMING OF THE HOLY SPIRIT]

16. "I have said all this to you to keep you from falling away. [2]They will put you out of the synagogues; indeed, the hour is coming when whoever kills you will think he is offering service to God. [3]And they will do this because they have not known the Father, nor me. [4]But I have said these things to you, that when their hour comes you may remember that I told you of them.

"I did not say these things to you from the beginning, because I was with you. [5]But now I am going to him who sent me; yet none of you asks me, 'Where are you going?' [6]But because I have said these things to you, sorrow has filled your hearts. [7]Nevertheless I tell you the truth: it is to your advantage that I go away, for if I do not go away, the Counselor will not come to you; but if I go, I will send him to you. [8]And when he comes, he will convince the world of sin and of righteousness and of judgment: [9]of sin, because they do not believe in me; [10]of righteousness, because I go to the Father, and you will see me no more; [11]of judgment, because the ruler of this world is judged.

12 "I have yet many things to say to you, but you cannot bear them now. [13]When the Spirit of truth comes, he will guide you into all the truth; for he will not speak on his own authority, but whatever he hears he will speak, and he will declare to you the things that are to come. [14]He will glorify me, for he will take what is mine and declare it to you. [15]All that the Father has is mine; therefore I said that he will take what is mine and declare it to you.

16 "A little while, and you will see me no more; again a little while, and you will see me." [17]Some of his disciples said to one another, "What is this that he says to us, 'A little while, and you will not see me, and again a little while, and you will see me'; and, 'because I go to the Father'?" [18]They said, "What does he mean by 'a little while'? We do not know what he means." [19]Jesus knew that they wanted to ask him; so he said to them, "Is this what you are asking yourselves, what I meant by saying, 'A little while, and you will not see me, and again a little while, and you will see me'? [20]Truly, truly, I say to you, you will weep and lament, but the world will rejoice; you will be sorrowful, but your sorrow will turn into joy. [21]When a woman is in travail she has sorrow, because her hour has come; but when she is delivered of the child, she no longer remembers the anguish, for joy that a child is born into the world. [22]So you have sorrow now, but I will see you again and your hearts will rejoice, and no one will take your joy from you. [23]On that day you will ask me no questions. Truly,

truly, I say to you, if you ask anything of the Father, he will give it to you in my name. [24]Hitherto you have asked nothing in my name; ask, and you will receive, that your joy may be full.

25 "I have said this to you in figures; the hour is coming when I shall no longer speak to you in figures but tell you plainly of the Father. [26]In that day you will ask in my name; and I do not say to you that I shall pray the Father for you; [27]for the Father himself loves you, because you have loved me and have believed that I came from the Father. [28]I came from the Father and have come into the world; again, I am leaving the world and going to the Father."

29 His disciples said, "Ah, now you are speaking plainly, not in any figure! [30]Now we know that you know all things, and need none to question you; by this we believe that you came from God." [31]Jesus answered them, "Do you now believe? [32]The hour is coming, indeed it has come, when you will be scattered, every man to his home, and will leave me alone; yet I am not alone, for the Father is with me. [33]I have said this to you, that in me you may have peace. In the world you have tribulation; but be of good cheer, I have overcome the world."

17. When Jesus had spoken these words, he lifted up his eyes to heaven and said, "Father, the hour has come; glorify thy Son that the Son may glorify thee, [2]since thou hast given him power over all flesh, so that he might give eternal life to all whom thou hast given him. [3]And this is eternal life, that they know thee the only true God, and Jesus Christ whom thou hast sent. [4]I glorified thee on earth, having accomplished the work which thou gavest me to do; [5]and now, Father, glorify thou me in thy own presence with the glory which I had with thee before the world was made.

6 "I have manifested thy name to the men whom thou gavest me out of the world; thine they were, and thou gavest them to me, and they have kept thy word. [7]Now they know that everything that thou hast given me is from thee; [8]for I have given them the words which thou gavest me, and they have received them and know in truth that I came from thee; and they have believed that thou didst send me. [9]I am praying for them; I am not praying for the world but for those whom thou hast given me, for they are thine; [10]all mine are thine, and thine are mine, and I am glorified in them. [11]And now I am no more in the world, but they are in the world, and I am coming to thee. Holy Father, keep them in thy name which thou hast given me, that they may be one, even as we are one. [12]While I was with them, I kept them in thy name which thou hast given me; I have guarded them, and none of them is lost but the son of perdition, that the scripture might be fulfilled. [13]But now I am coming to thee; and these things I speak in the world, that they may have my joy fulfilled in themselves. [14]I have given them thy word; and the world has hated them because they are not of the world, even as I am not of the world. [15]I do not pray that thou shouldst take them out of the world, but that thou shouldst keep them from the evil one. [16]They are not of the world, even as I am not of the world. [17]Sanctify them in the truth; thy word is truth. [18]As thou didst send me into the world, so I have sent them into the world. [19]And for their sake I consecrate myself, that they also may be consecrated in truth.

20 "I do not pray for these only, but also for those who are to believe in me through their word, [21]that they may all be one; even as thou, Father, art in me, and I in thee, that they also may be in us, so that the world may believe that thou hast sent me. [22]The glory which thou hast given me I have given to them, that they may be one even as we are one, [23]I in them and thou in me, that they may become perfectly one, so that the world may know that thou hast sent me and hast loved them even as thou hast loved me. [24]Father, I desire that they also, whom thou hast given me, may be with me where I am, to behold my glory which thou hast given me in thy love for me before the foundation of the world. [25]O righteous Father, the world has not known thee, but I have known thee; and these know that thou hast sent me. [26]I made known to them thy name, and I will make it known, that the love with which thou hast loved me may be in them, and I in them."

From the Book of Revelation

21. Then I saw a new heaven and a new earth; for the first heaven and the first earth had passed away, and the sea was no more. [2]And I saw the holy city, new Jerusalem, coming down out of heaven from

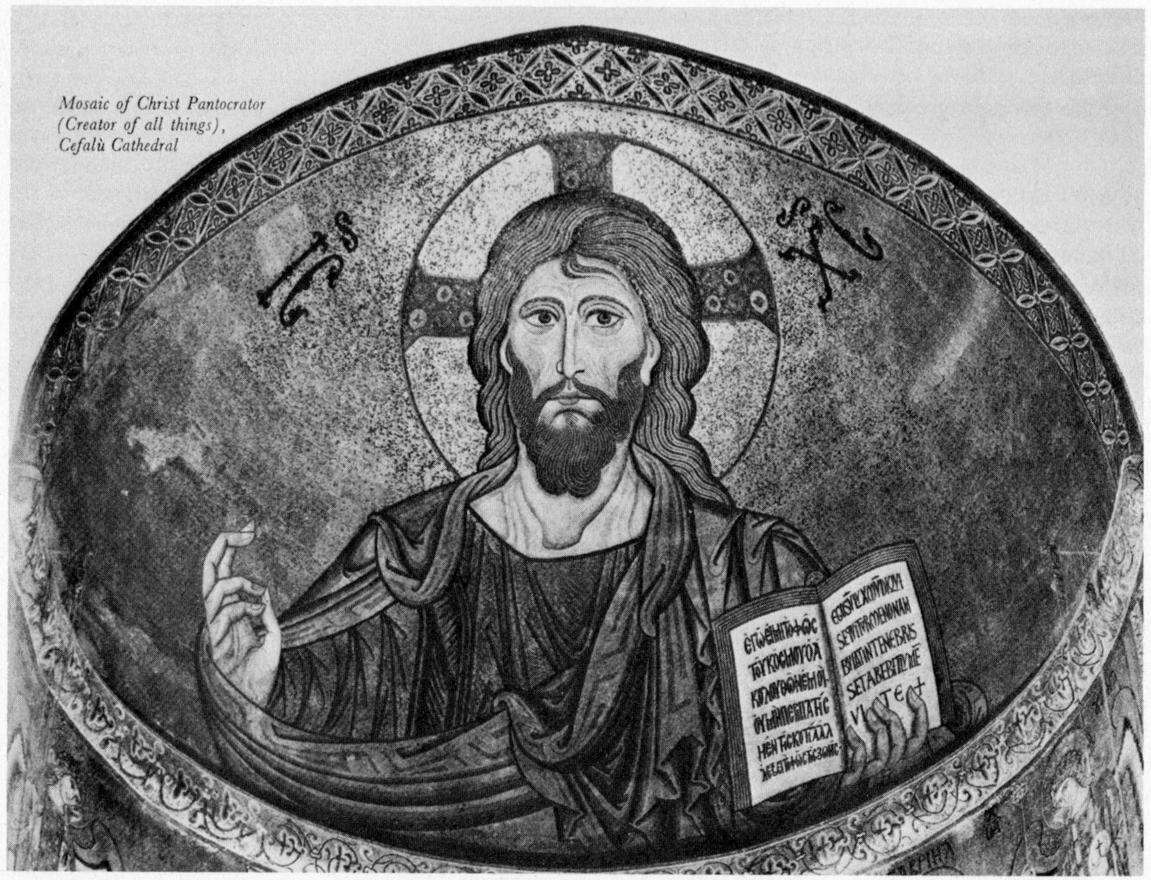

Mosaic of Christ Pantocrator (Creator of all things), Cefalù Cathedral

Christ as Supreme Emperor. The style of this picture demonstrates the iconographic influence of the East on Christian art. (From G. Pischel, A World History of Art *[New York: Simon & Schuster, 1975])*

God, prepared as a bride adorned for her husband; [3]and I heard a great voice from the throne saying, "Behold, the dwelling of God is with men. He will dwell with them, and they shall be his people, and God himself will be with them; [4]he will wipe away every tear from their eyes, and death shall be no more, neither shall there be mourning nor crying nor pain any more, for the former things have passed away."

5 And he who sat upon the throne said, "Behold, I make all things new." Also he said, "Write this, for these words are trustworthy and true." [6]And he said to me, "It is done! I am the Alpha and the Omega, the beginning and the end. To the thirsty I will give water without price from the fountain of the water of life. [7]He who conquers shall have this heritage, and I will be his God and he shall be my son. [8]But as for the cowardly, the faithless, the polluted, as for murderers, fornicators, sorcerers, idolaters, and all liars, their lot shall be in the lake that burns with fire and brimstone, which is the second death."

9 Then came one of the seven angels who had the seven bowls full of the seven last plagues, and spoke to me, saying, "Come, I will show you the Bride, the wife of the Lamb." [10]And in the Spirit he carried me away to a great, high mountain, and showed me the holy city Jerusalem coming down out of heaven from God, [11]having the glory of God, its radiance like a most rare jewel, like a jasper, clear as crystal. [12]It had a great, high wall, with twelve gates, and at the gates twelve angels, and on the gates the names of the twelve tribes of the sons of Israel were inscribed;

[13]on the east three gates, on the north three gates, on the south three gates, and on the west three gates. [14]And the wall of the city had twelve foundations, and on them the twelve names of the twelve apostles of the Lamb.

15 And he who talked to me had a measuring rod of gold to measure the city and its gates and walls. [16]The city lies foursquare; its length the same as its breadth; and he measured the city with his rod, twelve thousand stadia; its length and breadth and height are equal. [17]He also measured its wall, a hundred and forty-four cubits by a man's measure, that is, an angel's. [18]The wall was built of jasper, while the city was pure gold, clear as glass. [19]The foundations of the wall of the city were adorned with every jewel; the first was jasper, the second sapphire, the third agate, the fourth emerald,[20] the fifth onyx, the sixth carnelian, the seventh chrysolite, the eighth beryl, the ninth topaz, the tenth chrysoprase, the eleventh jacinth, the twelfth amethyst. [21]And the twelve gates were twelve pearls, each of the gates made of a single pearl, and the street of the city was pure gold, transparent as glass.

22 And I saw no temple in the city, for its temple is the Lord God the Almighty and the Lamb. [23]And the city has no need of sun or moon to shine upon it, for the glory of God is its light, and its lamp is the Lamb. [24]By its light shall the nations walk; and the kings of the earth shall bring their glory into it, [25]and its gates shall never be shut by day—and there shall be no night there; [26]they shall bring into it the glory and the honor of the nations. [27]But nothing unclean shall enter it, nor any one who practices abomination or falsehood, but only those who are written in the Lamb's book of life.

22. Then he showed me the river of the water of life, bright as crystal, flowing from the throne of God and of the Lamb [2]through the middle of the street of the city; also, on either side of the river, the tree of life with its twelve kinds of fruit, yielding its fruit each month; and the leaves of the tree were for the healing of the nations. [3]There shall no more be anything accursed, but the throne of God and of the Lamb shall be in it, and his servants shall worship him; [4]they shall see his face, and his name shall be on their foreheads. [5]And night shall be no more; they need no light of lamp or sun, for the Lord God will be their light, and they shall reign for ever and ever.

6 And he said to me, "These words are trustworthy and true. And the Lord, the God of the spirits of the prophets, has sent his angel to show his servants what must soon take place. [7]And behold, I am coming soon."

Blessed is he who keeps the words of the prophecy of this book.

8 I John am he who heard and saw these things. And when I heard and saw them, I fell down to worship at the feet of the angel who showed them to me; [9]but he said to me, "You must not do that! I am a fellow servant with you and your brethren the prophets, and with those who keep the words of this book. Worship God."

From the Epistles of Paul

[FREEDOM FROM THE LAW]

Romans

7.[14]We know that the law is spiritual; but I am carnal, sold under sin. [15]I do not understand my own actions. For I do not do what I want, but I do the very thing I hate. [16]Now if I do what I do not want, I agree that the law is good. [17]So then it is no longer I that do it, but sin which dwells within me. [18]For I know that nothing good dwells within me, that is, in my flesh. I can will what is right, but I cannot do it. [19]For I do not do the good I want, but the evil I do not want is what I do. [20]Now if I do what I do not want, it is no longer I that do it, but sin which dwells within me.

21 So I find it to be a law that when I want to do right, evil lies close at hand. [22]For I delight in the law of God, in my inmost self, [23]but I see in my members another law at war with the law of my mind and making me captive to the law of sin which dwells in my members. [24]Wretched man that I am! Who will deliver me from this body of death? [25]Thanks be to God through Jesus Christ our Lord! So then, I of myself serve the law of God with my mind, but with my flesh I serve the law of sin.

8. There is therefore now no condemnation for

those who are in Christ Jesus. [2]For the law of the
Spirit of life in Christ Jesus has set me free from the
law of sin and death. [3]For God has done what
the law, weakened by the flesh; could not do: sending his own Son in the likeness of sinful flesh and
for sin, he condemned sin in the flesh, [4]in order that
the just requirement of the law might be fulfilled in
us, who walk not according to the flesh but according to the Spirit. [5]For those who live according to the
flesh set their minds on the things of the flesh, but
those who live according to the Spirit set their minds
on the things of the Spirit. [6]To set the mind on the
flesh is death, but to set the mind on the Spirit is life
and peace. [7]For the mind that is set on the flesh is
hostile to God; it does not submit to God's law, indeed it cannot; [8]and those who are in the flesh cannot please God.

9 But you are not in the flesh, you are in the Spirit,
if the Spirit of God really dwells in you. Any one
who does not have the Spirit of Christ does not belong to him. [10]But if Christ is in you, although your
bodies are dead because of sin, your spirits are alive
because of righteousness. [11]If the Spirit of him who
raised Jesus from the dead dwells in you, he who
raised Christ Jesus from the dead will give life to
your mortal bodies also through his Spirit which
dwells in you.

12 So then, brethren, we are debtors, not to the
flesh, to live according to the flesh—[13]for if you live
according to the flesh you will die, but if by the
Spirit you put to death the deeds of the body you
will live. [14]For all who are led by the Spirit of God
are sons of God. [15]For you did not receive the spirit
of slavery to fall back into fear, but you have received the spirit of sonship. When we cry, "Abba!
Father!" [16]it is the Spirit himself bearing witness
with our spirit that we are children of God, [17]and if
children, then heirs, heirs of God and fellow heirs
with Christ, provided we suffer with him in order
that we may also be glorified with him.

[LOVE FULFILLS THE LAW]

1 Corinthians

13. Let every person be subject to the governing
authorities. For there is no authority except from
God, and those that exist have been instituted by
God. [2]Therefore he who resists the authorities resists
what God has appointed, and those who resist will
incur judgment. [3]For rulers are not a terror to good
conduct, but to bad. Would you have no fear of him
who is in authority? Then do what is good, and you
will receive his approval, [4]for he is God's servant for
your good. But if you do wrong, be afraid, for he
does not bear the sword in vain; he is the servant of
God to execute his wrath on the wrong-doer.
[5]Therefore one must be subject, not only to avoid
God's wrath but also for the sake of conscience. [6]For
the same reason you also pay taxes, for the authorities are ministers of God, attending to this very
thing. [7]Pay all of them their dues, taxes to whom
taxes are due, revenue to whom revenue is due, respect to whom respect is due, honor to whom honor
is due.

8 Owe no one anything, exept to love one another;
for he who loves his neighbor has fulfilled the law.
[9]The commandments, "You shall not commit adultery, You shall not kill, You shall not steal, You shall
not covet," and any other commandment, are
summed up in this sentence, "You shall love your
neighbor as yourself." [10]Love does no wrong to a
neighbor; therefore love is the fulfilling of the law.

11 Besides this you know what hour it is, how it is
full time now for you to wake from sleep. For salvation is nearer to us now than when we first believed; [12]the night is far gone, the day is at hand. Let
us then cast off the works of darkness and put on the
armor of light; [13]let us conduct ourselves becomingly
as in the day, not in reveling and drunkenness, not
in debauchery and licentiousness, not in quarreling
and jealousy. [14]But put on the Lord Jesus Christ, and
make no provision for the flesh, to gratify its desires.

[THE MYSTICAL BODY OF CHRIST]

Romans

12. I appeal to you therefore, brethren, by the mercies of God, to present your bodies as a living sacrifice, holy and acceptable to God, which is your spiritual worship. [2]Do not be conformed to this world
but be transformed by the renewal of your mind,
that you may prove what is the will of God, what is
good and acceptable and perfect.

3 For by the grace given to me I bid every one
among you not to think of himself more highly than
he ought to think, but to think with sober judgment,
each according to the measure of faith which God
has assigned him. [4]For as in one body we have many

members, and all the members do not have the same function, [5]so we, though many, are one body in Christ, and individually members one of another. [6]Having gifts that differ according to the grace given to us, let us use them: if prophecy, in proportion to our faith; [7]if service, in our serving; he who teaches, in his teaching; [8]he who exhorts, in his exhortation; he who contributes, in liberality; he who gives aid, with zeal; he who does acts of mercy, with cheerfulness.

9 Let love be genuine; hate what is evil, hold fast to what is good; [10]love one another with brotherly affection; outdo one another in showing honor. [11]Never flag in zeal, be aglow with the Spirit, serve the Lord. [12]Rejoice in your hope, be patient in tribulation, be constant in prayer. [13]Contribute to the needs of the saints, practice hospitality.

14 Bless those who persecute you; bless and do not curse them. [15]Rejoice with those who rejoice, weep with those who weep. [16]Live in harmony with one another; do not be haughty, but associate with the lowly; never be conceited. [17]Repay no one evil for evil, but take thought for what is noble in the sight of all. [18]If possible, so far as it depends upon you, live peaceably with all. [19]Beloved, never avenge yourselves, but leave it to the wrath of God; for it is written, "Vengeance is mine, I will repay, says the Lord." [20]No, "if your enemy is hungry, feed him; if he is thirsty, give him drink; for by so doing you will heap burning coals upon his head." [21]Do not be overcome by evil, but overcome evil with good.

[THE RESURRECTION OF THE BODY]

1 Corinthians

15.[16]For if the dead are not raised, then Christ has not been raised. [17]If Christ has not been raised, your faith is futile and you are still in your sins. [18]Then those also who have died in Christ have perished. [19]If in this life we who are in Christ have only hope, we are of all men most to be pitied.

20 But in fact Christ has been raised from the dead, the first fruits of those who have fallen asleep. [21]For as by a man came death, by a man has come also the resurrection of the dead. [22]For as in Adam all die, so also in Christ shall all be made alive. [23]But each in his own order: Christ the first fruits, then at his coming those who belong to Christ. [24]Then comes the end, when he delivers the kingdom to God the Father after destroying every rule and every authority and power. [25]For he must reign until he has put all his enemies under his feet. [26]The last enemy to be destroyed is death.

51 Lo! I tell you a mystery. We shall not all sleep, but we shall all be changed, [52]in a moment, in the twinkling of an eye, at the last trumpet. For the trumpet will sound, and the dead will be raised imperishable, and we shall be changed. [53]For this perishable nature must put on the imperishable, and this mortal nature must put on immortality. [54]When the perishable puts on the imperishable, and the mortal puts on immortality, then shall come to pass the saying that is written:

"Death is swallowed up in victory."
[55]"O death, where is thy victory?
O death, where is thy sting?"

[56]The sting of death is sin, and the power of sin is the law.[57]But thanks be to God who gives us the victory through our Lord Jesus Christ.

58 Therefore, my beloved brethren, be steadfast, immovable, always abounding in the work of the Lord, knowing that in the Lord your labor is not in vain.

SUGGESTIONS FOR FURTHER READING

Barrett, C. K., ed. *The New Testament Background: Selected Documents.* New York: Harper Torchbooks, 1961.

Bettenson, Henry. *Documents of the Christian Church.* New York: Oxford University Press, 1961.

Cochrane, Charles Norris. *Christianity and Classical Culture.* New York: Oxford University Press, 1944.

Fremantle, Anne, ed. *A Treasury of Early Christianity.* New York: New American Library, 1960.

Frye, Northrop. *The Great Code: The Bible and Literature.* New York: Harcourt Brace Jovanovich, 1982.

Grant, Robert M. *Early Christianity and Society.* New York: Harper & Row, 1977.

Jaeger, Werner. *Early Christianity and Greek Paideia.* Cambridge, Mass.: Harvard University Press, 1961.

Meeks, Wayne A. *The First Urban Christians: The Social World of the Apostle Paul.* New Haven: Yale University Press, 1983.

Musurillo, Herbert. *The Fathers of the Primitive Church.* New York: New American Library, 1966.

Perrin, Norman. *The New Testament.* New York: Harcourt Brace Jovanovich, 1974.

Randall, John Herman, Jr. *Hellenistic Ways of Deliverance and the Making of the Christian Synthesis.* New York: Columbia University Press, 1970.

West, James King. *Introduction to the Old Testament.* New York: Macmillan, 1981.

Part 5

Early Medieval Philosophy: Faith Seeking Understanding

Medieval Islamic and Jewish Philosophy: Revelation and the Use of Aristotle

Latin Scholasticism and the Recovery of Aristotle

The Fourteenth Century: Breakup of the Faith-Reason Synthesis

Early Medieval Philosophy: Faith Seeking Understanding

With the advent of Christianity, the various currents of thought were considerably intermingled. By the time of Augustine, in the late fourth century, the integration of Stoicism and Neoplatonism into the comprehensive thought of Christianity had become a fact. And from the time of Augustine on, most of the thinkers in the European world would be Christians.

The persistent refrain throughout the second until the twelfth century is that of "Faith Seeking Understanding" *(Credo ut Intelligam).* Although this motif is not dominant in the work of Boethius, who was more indebted to Aristotle than were other early medieval thinkers of this period, it is central to the thought of Augustine, John Scotus Erigena, and Anselm. By the time of Anselm's death in the early twelfth century, the stage was set for the great debates over the relationship between theology and philosophy, debates spiced by the appearance of philosophy from Islam. The key issue here was that of the "double truth," or whether a claim could be true in philosophy but not in theology. Logic, too, became more sophisticated, especially in the work of Abailard and in the refreshing, if somewhat cynical view of Abailard's student, John of Salisbury.

Commentators have sometimes referred to the early Middle Ages as the Dark Ages. Rome may have collapsed in the fifth century, but philosophy retained its brilliance and vitality, as attested by the selections that follow.

JUSTIN MARTYR

Justin Martyr (ca. A.D. *100–165) was born in Samaria of pagan parents. He died a Christian martyr in Rome. Justin wandered throughout the Middle East and Italy, searching for a true belief. He turned successively to Stoicism, Aristotelianism, Pythagoreanism, and Platonism. Finally, impressed by the constancy and courage of the Christian confessors, he embraced Christianity. The following selection from his "Dialogue" with the Jew, Trypho, tells something of his odyssey and decision.*

From Dialogue with Trypho

"I will tell you," said I, "what seems to me; for philosophy is, in fact, the greatest possession, and most honourable before God, to whom it leads us and alone commends us; and these are truly holy men who have bestowed attention on philosophy. What philosophy is, however, and the reason why it has been sent down to men, have escaped the observation of most; for there would be neither Platonists, nor Stoics, nor Peripatetics, nor Theoretics, nor Pythagoreans, this knowledge being *one*. I wish to tell you why it has become many-headed. It has happened that those who first handled it [i.e., philosophy], and who were therefore esteemed illustrious men, were succeeded by those who made no investigations concerning truth, but only admired the perseverance and self-discipline of the former, as well as the novelty of the doctrines; and each thought that to be true which he learned from his teacher: then, moreover, those latter persons handed down to *their* successors such things, and others similar to them; and this system was called by the name of him who was styled the father of the doctrine. Being at first desirous of personally conversing with one of these men, I surrendered myself to a certain Stoic; and having spent a considerable time with him, when I had not acquired any further knowledge of God (for he did not know himself, and said such instruction was unnecessary), I left him and betook myself to another, who was called a Peripatetic, and as *he* fancied, shrewd. And this man, after having entertained me for the first few days, requested me to settle the fee, in order that our intercourse might not be unprofitable. Him, too, for this reason I abandoned, believing him to be no philosopher at all. But when my soul was eagerly desirous to hear the peculiar and choice philosophy, I came to a Pythagorean, very celebrated—a man who thought much of his own wisdom. And then, when I had an interview with him, willing to become his hearer and disciple, he said, 'What then? Are you acquainted with music, astronomy, and geometry? Do you expect to perceive any of those things which conduce to a happy life, if you have not been first informed on those points which wean the soul from sensible objects, and render it fitted for objects which appertain to the mind, so that it can contemplate that which is honourable in its essence and that which is good in its essence?' Having commended many of these branches of learning, and telling me that they were necessary, he dismissed me when I confessed to him my ignorance. Accordingly I took it rather impatiently, as was to be expected when I failed in my hope, the more so because I deemed the man had some knowledge; but reflecting again on the space of time during which I would have to linger over those branches of learning, I was not able to endure longer procrastination. In my helpless condition it occurred to me to have a meeting with the Platonists, for their fame was great. I thereupon spent as much of my time as possible with one who had lately settled in our city,—a sagacious man, holding a high position among the Platonists,—and I progressed, and made the greatest improvements daily. And the perception of immaterial things quite overpowered me, and the contemplation of ideas furnished my mind with wings, so that in a little while I supposed that I had become wise; and such was my stupidity, I expected forthwith to look upon God, for this is the end of Plato's philosophy.

CLEMENT OF ALEXANDRIA

Born of pagan parents in A.D. 150, Clement was a student of Pantaenus, a former Stoic, who persuaded him to become a Christian. Clement, however, remained fascinated

---

Justin Martyr, "Dialogue with Trypho," in *Greek and Roman Philosophy After Aristotle* (New York: The Free Press, 1966), pp. 293–294, from Roberts and Donaldson, *Ante-Nicene Fathers*, Vol. I (Grand Rapids, Mich.: Wm. B. Eerdmans Publishing Company), Chapter 2. Reprinted by permission of the Wm. B. Eerdmans Publishing Company.

by the religious mysteries of his Greek heritage. He was especially attracted to a form of Christian gnosticism, which holds that true knowledge proceeds from faith in God. His Stromateis (Miscellanies) *is valuable for its presentation of the views of ancient writers whose published works no longer survive.*

The following selection presents Clement's advice to newly baptized Christians. The reader will find striking similarities to earlier texts from the Stoics and the Epicureans.

Exhortation to Endurance OR To the Newly Baptized

PRECEPTS OF CLEMENT

Cultivate quietness in word, quietness in deed, likewise in speech and gait; and avoid impetuous eagerness. For then the mind will remain steady, and will not be agitated by your eagerness and so become weak and of narrow discernment and see darkly; nor will it be worsted by gluttony, worsted by boiling rage, worsted by the other passions, lying a ready prey to them. For the mind, seated on high on a quiet throne looking intently towards God, must control the passions. By no means be swept away by temper in bursts of anger, nor be sluggish in speaking, nor all nervousness in movement; so that your quietness may be adorned by good proportion and your bearing may appear something divine and sacred. Guard also against the signs of arrogance, a haughty bearing, a lofty head, a dainty and high-treading footstep.

Let your speech be gentle towards those you meet, and your greetings kind; be modest towards women, and let your glance be turned to the ground. Be thoughtful in all your talk, and give back a useful answer, adapting the utterance to the hearers' need, just so loud that it may be distinctly audible, neither escaping the ears of the company by reason of feebleness nor going to excess with too much noise. Take care never to speak what you have not weighed and pondered beforehand; nor interject your own words on the spur of the moment and in the midst of another's; for you must listen and converse in turn, with set times for speech and for silence. Learn gladly, and teach ungrudgingly; never hide wisdom from others by reason of a grudging spirit, nor through false modesty stand aloof from instruction. Submit to elders just as to fathers. Honour God's servants. Be first to practise wisdom and virtue. Do not wrangle with your friends, nor mock at them and play the buffoon. Firmly renounce falsehood, guile and insolence. Endure in silence, as a gentle and high-minded man, the arrogant and insolent.

Let everything you do be done for God, both deeds and words; and refer all that is yours to Christ; and constantly turn your soul to God; and lean your thought on the power of Christ, as if in some harbour by the divine light of the Saviour it were resting from all talk and action. And often by day communicate your thoughts to men, but most of all to God at night as well as by day; for let not much sleep prevail to keep you from your prayers and hymns to God, since long sleep is a rival of death. Show yourself always a partner of Christ who makes the divine ray shine from heaven; let Christ be to you continual and unceasing joy.

Relax not the tension of your soul with feasting and indulgence in drink, but consider what is needful to be enough for the body. And do not hasten early to meals before the time for dinner comes; but let your dinner be bread, and let earth's grasses and the ripe fruits of trees be set before you; and go to your meal with composure, showing no sign of raging gluttony. Be not a flesh-eater nor a lover of wine,

---

Reprinted by permission of the publishers and The Loeb Classical Library from *Exhortation to the Newly Baptized*, Clement of Alexandria, trans. by G. W. Butterworth, Cambridge, Mass.: Harvard University Press, 1919. (pp. 370–377)

when no sickness leads you to this as a cure. But in place of the pleasures that are in these, choose the joys that are in divine words and hymns, joys supplied to you by wisdom from God; and let heavenly meditation ever lead you upward to heaven.

And give up the many anxious cares about the body by taking comfort in hopes towards God; because for you He will provide all necessary things in sufficiency, food to support life, covering for the body, and protection against winter cold. For to your King belongs the whole earth and all that is produced from it; and God treats the bodily parts of His servants with exceeding care, as if they were His, like His own shrines and temples. On this account do not dread severe diseases, nor the approach of old age, which must be expected in time: for even disease will come to an end, when with whole-hearted purpose we do His commandments.

Knowing this, make your soul strong even in face of diseases; be of good courage, like a man in the arena, bravest to submit to his toils with strength unmoved. Be not utterly crushed in soul by grief, whether disease lies heavily upon you, or any other hardship befalls, but nobly confront toils with your understanding, even in the midst of your struggles rendering thanks to God; since His thoughts are wiser than men's, and such as it is not easy nor possible for men to find out. Pity those who are in distress, and ask for men the help that comes from God; for God will grant grace to His friend when he asks, and will provide succour for those in distress, wishing to make His power known to men, in the hope that, when they have come to full knowledge, they may return to God, and may enjoy eternal blessedness when the Son of God shall appear and restore good things to His own.

AUGUSTINE

Augustine (A.D. 354–430) was born in Thagaste, in North Africa. His mother, Monica, was a devout Christian, and she exercised a profound influence on the restless soul of Augustine. After a life filled with controversy and changes of persuasion, Augustine died as Bishop of Hippo in North Africa, as the Vandals were at the gate of the city, bent on destruction.

The journey of Augustine illustrates the forces that were at work in the fourth century of the Christian era. He flirted with Manicheanism, which taught the irreducibility of the dualism between the principles of good and evil. He was attracted also by the Neoplatonists. Spurred on by his reading of Cicero's dialogue Hortensius, *which extolled the importance of philosophy, Augustine continued to search for a true belief. In 385, Augustine underwent a conversion experience, as reported in his* Confessions *(VIII, 12). He was baptized in 386, and subsequently ascended to the position of a Bishop and a defender of the Church against a slew of doctrinal enemies, especially the Pelagians and the Donatists. The former held that to be human was sufficient for the presence of salvific grace. Augustine opposed this view and asserted that an orthodox Christian commitment was necessary if grace were to be dispensed. The Donatists held the rigid view that only those priests in a state of grace could perform the sacraments. Augustine, rightly, opposed this position, for if held, the sacraments would be virtually unavailable.*

In girth, the works of Augustine rival those of Plato and Aristotle. He addressed virtually every subject and controversy known to his time. Augustine was deeply influenced by the style of the ancient rhetoricians, although he strove to free himself of their pagan influence. His Confessions, City of God, On the Trinity *and* On Free Will *are among the great classics of world literature. In spite of the majesty of his person and his work, he was a transitional figure—the last of the great ancients and the first of the great Christian thinkers. He was to be the inspiration for the whole of medieval Christian thought, as well as the main theological source for the Protestant reformers of the sixteenth century, Luther and Calvin.*

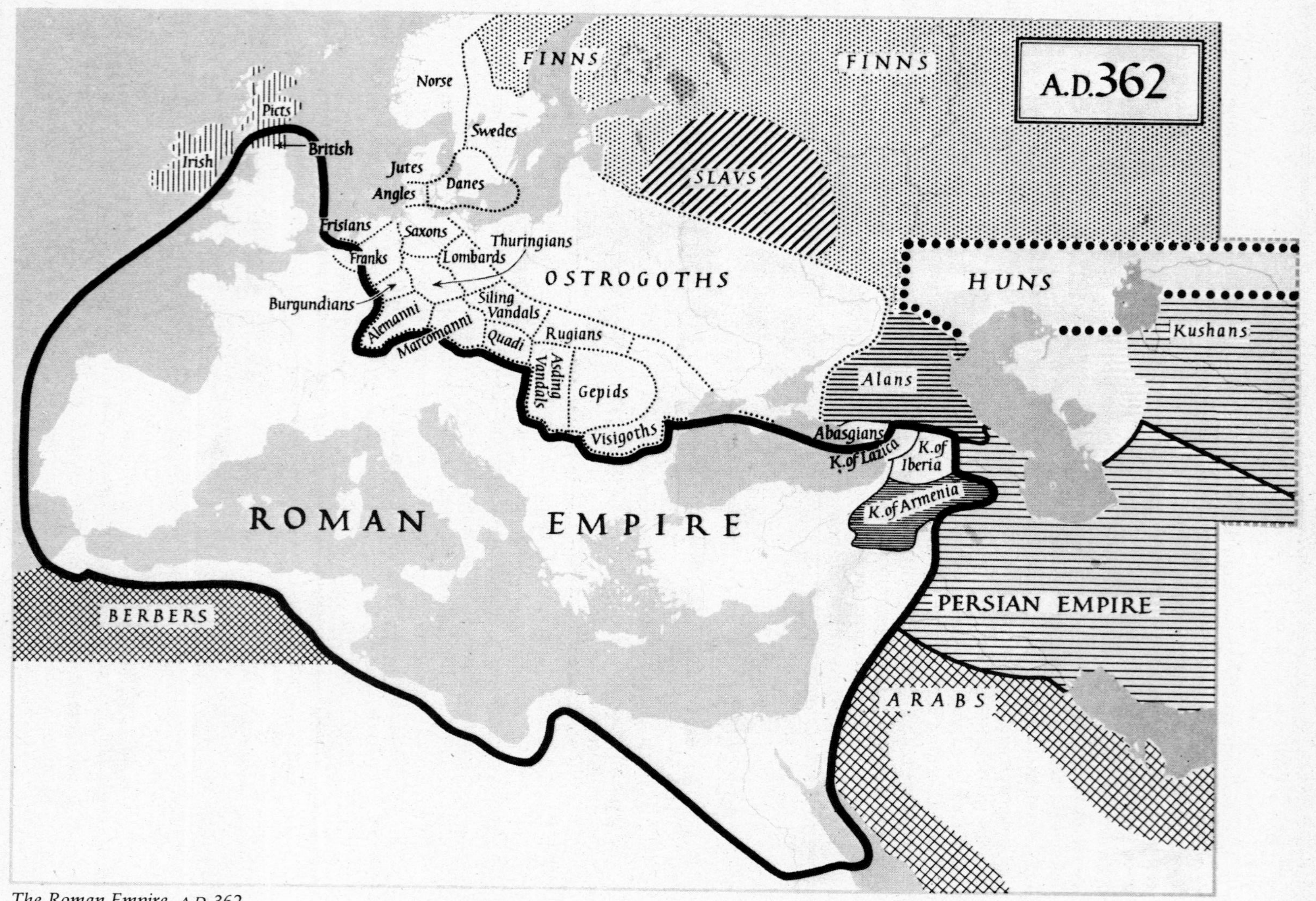

The Roman Empire, A.D. 362

The selections that follow are but a brief taste of the extraordinary range and quality of the writings of Augustine, Latin father of the Church, theologian, philosopher, and master of the interior life.

From On Free Will

Evodius—I should like you first to prove to me that free will is a good thing. Then I shall agree that God gave it, because I admit that all good things come from God. *Augustine*—Have I not proved this to your satisfaction after all the labour of our previous discussion? You admitted that every corporeal form derives its existence from the supreme form of all, that is, from the truth. And you agreed that every form was good. Truth himself, in the Gospel, tells us that even the hairs of our heads are numbered. Have you forgotten what we said about the supremacy of number, and its power which extends from one end to the other? What perversity it is to number our hairs among the good things though they are small and utterly contemptible, and to attribute their creation to God, the Creator of all good things because all good things, the greatest and the least, come from him from whom is all good; and yet to hesitate to ascribe free will to him, seeing that without it no one can live aright even on the testimony of those who live evil lives. Now tell me, pray, what in us seems to be superior, that without which we *can* live aright, or that without which we *cannot* live aright. *Ev.*—Now please spare me. I am ashamed of my blindness. Who can doubt that that is far superior without which there can be no right living? *Aug.*—Will you deny that a one-eyed man can live rightly? *Ev.*—Away with such shocking madness. *Aug.*—You agree that an eye is a good thing, and yet the loss of it does not prevent right living. Can you imagine that free will, without which no one can live aright, is no good thing?

Look at justice, of which no one can make a bad use. It is numbered among the best good things which a man can have. So are all the virtues of the soul which constitute the righteous and honourable life. No one makes a bad use of prudence or fortitude or temperance. In all of these, as in justice which you have chosen to mention, right reason prevails, without which there can be no virtues. And no one can make a bad use of right reason. These are therefore great good things. But you must remember that there can be no good things, great or small, save from him from whom all good things come, that is, God. So we were persuaded by our previous discussion, in the course of which you so often and so gladly expressed your assent. The virtues then, whereby life is rightly lived, are great goods. But the forms of bodies, without which life can be rightly lived, are the least of good things. And the powers of the soul, without which there can be no righteous life, are intermediate goods. No one makes a bad use of the virtues. But of the other goods, the intermediate and the small, anyone can make not only a good but also a bad use. No one makes a bad use of virtue, just because the function of virtue is the good use of the things of which we can also make a bad use. No one makes a bad use of anything when he uses it well. Wherefore God in his great and lavish goodness affords us not only great goods, but small ones too, and some intermediate between great and small. His goodness is more to be praised for the great goods than for the intermediate ones, and for the intermediate ones more than for the small ones. But for all, his goodness is to be praised more than if he had given only the great goods and not the lesser as well.

Ev.—I agree, but I have this difficulty. We see that free will makes use of other things either well or ill.

Reprinted from *Augustine: Earlier Writings*, edited by John H. S. Burleigh (Vol. VI: The Library of Christian Classics). Published simultaneously in Great Britain and the United States of America by the S.C.M. Press, Ltd., London, and the Westminster Press, Philadelphia, 1953. Reprinted and used by permission. (pp. 166–181)

How, then, is it to be numbered among the things we use? *Aug.*—Everything we know scientifically we know by means of reason, and yet reason itself is numbered among the things we know by reason. Have you forgotten that when we were inquiring as to the things we know by reason, you admitted that reason was known by reason? Do not marvel, therefore, if we use other things by free will, and can also use free will by itself. Will, which uses other things, somehow also uses itself, just as reason which knows other things knows itself also. Memory, too, contains not only all the other things which it remembers; but because we do not forget that we have memory, somehow memory remembers itself as well as other things. Or rather by memory we remember other things and memory too.

Will is therefore an intermediate good when it cleaves to the unchangeable good as something that is common property and not its own private preserve; of the same nature, that is to say, as truth of which we have spoken a great deal, but nothing worthy of so great a theme; when will cleaves to this good, man attains the happy life. And the happy life, that is, the disposition of soul cleaving to the unchangeable good, is the proper and first good of man. All the virtues are there which no one can use badly. However great and important the virtues may be, we know well enough that they are not common property, but are the property of each individual man. Truth and wisdom are common to all, and all wise men are also happy by cleaving to truth. But one man does not become happy by another's happiness. If one man seeks to attain happiness by imitating another, he seeks his happiness where he sees the other found his, that is to say in unchangeable and common truth. No one is made prudent by the prudence of another, or courageous by his courage, or temperate by his temperance, or just by his justice. A man is made virtuous by regulating his soul according to the rules and guiding lights of the virtues which dwell indestructibly in the truth and wisdom that are the common property of all. For so the virtuous man whom he set before him for imitation has regulated his soul, giving it a fixed objective.

The will, therefore, which cleaves to the unchangeable good that is common to all, obtains man's first and best good things though it is itself only an intermediate good. But the will which turns from the unchangeable and common good and turns to its own private good or to anything exterior or inferior, sins. It turns to its private good, when it wills to be governed by its own authority; to what is exterior, when it is eager to know what belongs to others and not to itself; to inferior things, when it loves bodily pleasure. In these ways a man becomes proud, inquisitive, licentious, and is taken captive by another kind of life which, when compared with the life we have just described, is really death. And yet it is still governed and disposed by divine providence, which appoints for all things their proper places, and distributes to each man his due according to his deserts. So it happens that the good things sought by sinners cannot in any way be bad, nor can free will be bad, for we found that it was to be numbered among the intermediate goods. What is bad is its turning away from the unchangeable good and its turning to changeable goods. That "aversion" and "conversion" is voluntary and is not coerced. Therefore it is followed by the deserved and just penalty of unhappiness.

But perhaps you are going to ask what is the cause of the movement of the will when it turns from the immutable to the mutable good. That movement is certainly evil, although free will must be numbered among good things since without it no one can live aright. We cannot doubt that that movement of the will, that turning away from the Lord God, is sin; but surely we cannot say that God is the author of sin? God, then, will not be the cause of that movement; but what will be its cause? If you ask this, and I answer that I do not know, probably you will be saddened. And yet that would be a true answer. That which is nothing cannot be known. Only hold fast to your pious opinion that no good thing can happen to you, to your senses or to your intelligence or to your thought, which does not come from God. Nothing of any kind can happen which is not of God. Do not hesitate to attribute to God as its maker every thing which you see has measure, number and order. When you take these things completely away nothing at all will remain. Wherever measure, number and order are found, there is perfect form. If there is some kind of inchoate form, wanting measure, number and order, you must remove it too, for inchoate form is a kind of material lying to the hand of the artificer to use for perfecting his work. For if the perfection of form is good, the beginning of form is not without some grain of good. Take away all good, and absolutely nothing will remain. All good is from God. Hence there is no natural existence which is not from God. Now that movement of "aversion," which we admit is sin, is a defective movement; and all defect comes from nothing. Observe where it belongs and you will have no doubt that it does not belong to God. Because that defective movement is voluntary, it is placed within our power. If you fear it, all you have to do is simply not to will it. If you do not will it, it will not exist. What can be more secure than to live a life where nothing can happen to you which you do not will. But since man cannot rise of his own free will as he fell by his own will spontaneously, let us hold with steadfast faith the right hand of God stretched out to us from above, even our Lord Jesus Christ. Let us wait for him with certain hope, and long for him with burning charity. If you think that we must still make diligent inquiry for the origin of sin—I myself think that there is no need at all for such inquiry—but if you think so, we must put it off till another discussion. *Ev.*—I bow to your will, but only so far as to postpone to another time the question you have raised. But I will not allow you to imagine that our inquiry has already gone far enough.

Ev.—It is sufficiently evident to me that free will is to be numbered among the good things, and, indeed, not among the least of our good things. We are, therefore, compelled to confess that it has been given us by God, and that he has rightly given it to us. But now, if you think a suitable time has come, I want to learn from you whence arises the movement by which the will itself turns from the unchangeable good, which is the common property of all, to its own interests or to the interests of others or to things beneath it, and so turns to mutable goods. *Aug.*—Why must you know this? *Ev.*—Because if free will is so given that it has that movement by nature, it turns of necessity to mutable goods; and no blame attaches where nature and necessity prevail. *Aug.*—Do you like or dislike that movement? *Ev.*—I dislike it. *Aug.*—So you find fault with it? *Ev.*—I do. *Aug.*—Then you find fault with a movement of the mind though it is faultless. *Ev.*—No, I do not. But I do not know whether there is any fault in abandoning the unchangeable good and turning towards the mutable goods. *Aug.*—Then you are finding fault with something which you do not know. *Ev.*—Don't insist on a verbal point. I said that I did not know whether there was any fault, but I meant to be understood really as having no doubt about it. Certainly I said I do not know, but obviously I was being ironical in suggesting that there could be any doubt about so clear a matter. *Aug.*—Just consider what is that truth you hold to be so certain that it has caused you so soon to forget what you said a moment ago. If that movement of the will exists by nature or necessity, it is in no way culpable. And yet you are so firmly convinced that it is culpable that you think fit to wax ironical about hesitation over a matter so certain. Why did you think it right to affirm, or at least to say with some hesitation, what you yourself show to be obviously false? You said: "If free will has been given in such fashion that it has that movement by nature, then it turns to mutable things of necessity, and no fault can be found where nature and necessity rule." But you ought to have had no doubt that it was not given in that fashion, since you do not doubt that that movement is culpable. *Ev.*—I said that the movement is culpable, and that therefore it displeases me, and that I cannot doubt that it is reprehensible. But I hold that a soul which is thereby drawn from the unchangeable good to mutable goods is not to be blamed if its nature is such that it is so moved by necessity.

Aug.—To whom belongs the movement which you admit is blameworthy? *Ev.*—I see that it is in the soul, but to whom it belongs I know not. *Aug.*—You do not deny that the soul is moved by that motion? *Ev.*—No. *Aug.*—Do you then deny that the motion by which a stone is moved is the motion of the stone? I don't mean the motion that we give to it, or that is given to it by some other force, when it is thrown upwards, but that by which of its own accord it falls back to earth. *Ev.*—I do not deny that the motion you refer to, by which it turns and falls downwards, is the motion of the stone, but it is its natural motion. If the motion of the soul is like that, it too is natural, and it cannot rightly be blamed for a motion that is natural. Even if it moves to its own destruction, it is compelled by the necessity of its own nature. Moreover because we have no doubt that the soul's motion is culpable we must absolutely deny that it is natural, and therefore not like the motion of the stone, which is natural motion. *Aug.*—Did we achieve anything in our two previous discussions? *Ev.*—I am sure we did. *Aug.*—No doubt you remember that in the first discussion we discovered that the mind can become the slave of lust only by its own will. No superior thing and no equal thing compels it to such dishonour, because that would be unjust.

And no inferior thing has the power. It remains that that must be the mind's own motion when it turns its will away from enjoyment of the Creator to enjoyment of the creature. If that motion is accounted blameworthy—and you thought anyone who doubted that deserved to be treated ironically—it is not natural but voluntary. It is like the motion of the falling stone, in so far as it is a motion of the soul as the former is the motion of the stone. But it is dissimilar in this, that it is not the power of a stone to arrest its downward motion, while if the soul is not willing it cannot be moved to abandon what is higher and to love what is lower. Thus the stone's motion is natural, the soul's voluntary. Hence anyone who says that a stone sins when it is carried downwards by its own weight is, I will not say more senseless than the stone but, completely mad. But we charge the soul with sin when we show that it has abandoned the higher things and prefers to enjoy lower things. What need is there, therefore, to seek the origin of the movement whereby the will turns from the unchangeable to the changeable good? We acknowledge that it is a movement of the soul, that it is voluntary and therefore culpable. And all useful learning in this matter has its object and value in teaching us to condemn and restrain that movement, and to convert our wills from falling into temporal delights to the enjoyment of the eternal good.

Ev.—I see, and in a sense grasp that what you say is true. There is nothing that I feel more certainly and more personally than that I have a will, and that it moves me to enjoy this or that. I know nothing I could call my own if the will by which I will "yea" or "nay" is not my own. If I use it to do evil, to whom is the evil to be attributed if not to myself? Since a good God has made me, and I can do nothing right except by willing, it is clearly evident that it was to this end that the will has been given to me by God who is good. Moreover, unless the movement of the will towards this or that object is voluntary and within our power, a man would not be praiseworthy when he turns to the higher objects nor blameworthy when he turns to lower objects, using his will like a hinge. There would be no use at all in warning him to pay no attention to temporal things and to will to obtain the eternal things, or to will to live aright and to be unwilling to live an evil life. But whoever thinks that man is not to be so warned ought to be cut off from membership in the human race.

That being so, I have a deep desire to know how it can be that God knows all things beforehand and that, nevertheless, we do not sin by necessity. Whoever says that anything can happen otherwise than as God has foreknown it, is attempting to destroy the divine foreknowledge with the most insensate impiety. If God foreknew that the first man would sin—and that anyone must concede who acknowledges with me that God has foreknowledge of all future events—I do not say that God did not make him, for he made him good, nor that the sin of the creature whom he made good could be prejudicial to God. On the contrary, God showed his goodness in making man, his justice in punishing his sin, and his mercy in delivering him. I do not say, therefore, that God did not make man. But this I say. Since God foreknew that man would sin, that which God foreknew must necessarily come to pass. How then is the will free when there is apparently this unavoidable necessity?

Aug.—You have knocked vigorously. May God in his mercy grant us his presence and open the door to those who knock. But I verily believe that the vast majority of men are troubled by that question for no other reason than that they do not ask it in a pious fashion. They are swifter to make excuses for their sins than to make confession of them. Some are glad to hold the opinion that there is no divine providence presiding over human affairs. They commit themselves, body and soul, to fortuitous circumstances, and deliver themselves to be carried about and tormented by lusts. They deny that there is any divine judgment, and deceive human judges when they are accused. They imagine that they are driven on by the favour of fortune. In sculpture or painting they are wont to represent Fortune as blind, either because they are better than the goddess by whom they think they are ruled, or because they confess that in their sentiments they are afflicted with that same blindness. In the case of such people it is not absurd to admit that they do everything by chance, seeing that they stumble in all that they do. But against this opinion, so full of foolish and senseless error, we have, I think, sufficiently spoken in our second disputation. Others do not venture to deny that the providence of God presides over human affairs, but they would rather indulge in the wicked error of believing that providence is weak or unjust or evil than confess their sins with suppliant piety. If all these would suffer themselves to be persuaded to believe that the goodness, justice and power of God are greater far, and far superior to any thought they can have of goodness, justice or might, if they would but take thought to themselves, they would know that they owe thanks to God, even if he had willed them to be somewhat lower in the scale of being than they actually are, and with all that is within them they would exclaim with the Psalmist: "I have spoken: Lord have mercy upon me; heal my soul for I have sinned against thee" (Ps. 41:5). So by stages the divine mercy would bring them to wisdom. They would be neither inflated by what they discover, nor rebellious when they fail to find the truth; by learning they would become better prepared to see the truth, and by recognizing their ignorance they would become more patient in seeking it. I am quite sure that these are your views too. Now first answer a few questions I am going to put to you, and you will see how easily I can find a solution to your tremendous problem.

Your trouble is this. You wonder how it can be that these two propositions are not contradictory and incompatible, namely that God has foreknowledge of all future events, and that we sin voluntarily and not by necessity. For if, you say, God foreknows that a man will sin, he must necessarily sin. But if there is necessity there is no voluntary choice in sinning, but rather fixed and unavoidable necessity. You are afraid that by that reasoning the conclusion may be reached either that God's foreknowledge of all future events must be impiously denied, or, if that cannot be denied, that sin is committed not voluntarily but by necessity. Isn't that your difficulty? *Ev.*—Exactly that. *Aug.*—You think, therefore, that all things of which God has foreknowledge happen by necessity and not voluntarily. *Ev.*—Yes. Absolutely. *Aug.*—Try an experiment, and examine yourself a little, and tell me what kind of will you are going to have to-morrow. Will you want to sin or to do right? *Ev.*—I do not know. *Aug.*—Do you think God also does not know? *Ev.*—I could in no wise think that. *Aug.*—If God knows what you are going to will to-morrow, and foresees what all men are going to will in the future, not only those who are at present alive but all who will ever be, much more will he foresee what he is going to do with the just and the impious? *Ev.*—Certainly if I say that God has foreknowledge of my deeds, I should say with even greater confidence that he has foreknowledge of his own acts, and foresees with complete certainty what he is going to do. *Aug.*—Don't you see that you will have to be careful lest someone say to you that, if all things of which God has foreknowledge are done by necessity and not voluntarily, his own future acts will be done not voluntarily but by necessity? *Ev.*—When I said that all future events of which God has foreknowledge happen by necessity, I was having regard only to things which happen within his creation, and not to things which happen in God himself. Indeed, in God nothing happens. Everything is eternal. *Aug.*—God, then, is not active within his creation? *Ev.*—He determined once for all how the order of the universe he created was to go on, and he never changes his mind. *Aug.*—Does he never make anyone happy? *Ev.*—Indeed he does. *Aug.*—He does it precisely at the time when the man in question actually becomes happy. *Ev.*—That is so. *Aug.*—If, then, for example, you yourself are happy one year from now, you will be made happy at that time. *Ev.*—Exactly. *Aug.*—God knows to-day what he is going to do a year hence? *Ev.*—He eternally had that foreknowledge, but I agree that he has it now, if indeed it is to happen so.

Aug.—Now tell me, are you not God's creature? And will not your becoming happy take place within your experience? *Ev.*—Certainly I am God's creature, and if I become happy it will be within my experience. *Aug.*—If God, then, makes you happy, your happiness will come by necessity and not by the exercise of your will? *Ev.*—God's will is my necessity. *Aug.*—Will you then be happy against your will? *Ev.*—If I had the power to be happy, I should be so at once. For I wish to be happy but am not, because not I but God makes me happy. *Aug.*—The truth simply cries out against you. You could not imagine that "having in our power" means anything else than "being able to do what we will." Therefore there is nothing so much in our power as is the will itself. For as soon as we will [*volumus*] immediately will [*voluntas*] is there. We can say rightly that we do not grow old voluntarily but necessarily, or that we do not die voluntarily but from necessity, and so with other similar things. But who but a raving fool would say that it is not voluntarily that we will? Therefore though God knows how we are going to will in the future, it is not proved that we do not voluntarily will anything. When you said that you did not make yourself happy, you said it as if I had denied it. What I say is that when you become happy in the future it will take place not against your will but in accordance with your willing. Therefore, though God has foreknowledge of your happiness in the future, and though nothing can happen otherwise than as he has foreknown it (for that would mean that there is no foreknowledge) we are not thereby compelled to think that you will not be happy voluntarily. That would be absurd and far from true. God's foreknowledge, which is even today quite certain that you are to be happy at a future date, does not rob you of your will to happiness when you actually attain happiness. Similarly if ever in the future you have a culpable will, it will be none the less your will because God had foreknowledge of it.

Observe, pray, how blind are those who say that if God has foreknowledge of what I am going to will, since nothing can happen otherwise than as he has foreknown it, therefore I must necessarily will what he has foreknown. If so, it must be admitted that I will, not voluntarily but from necessity. Strange folly! Is there, then, no difference between things that happen according to God's foreknowledge where there is no intervention of man's will at all, and things that happen because of a will of which he has foreknowledge? I omit the equally monstrous assertion of the man I mentioned a moment ago, who says I must necessarily so will. By assuming necessity he strives to do away with will altogether. If I must necessarily will, why need I speak of willing at all? But if he puts it in another way, and says that, because he must necessarily so will, his will is not in his own power, he can be countered by the answer you gave me when I asked whether you could become happy against your will. You replied that you would be happy now if the matter were in your power, for you willed to be happy but could not achieve it. And I added that the truth cries out against you; for we cannot say we do not have the power unless we do not have what we will. If we do not have the will, we may think we will but in fact we do not. If we cannot will without willing, those who will have will, and all that is in our power we have by willing. Our will would not be will unless it were in our power. Because it is in our power, it is free. We have nothing that is free which is not in our power, and if we have something it cannot be nothing. Hence it is not necessary to deny that God has foreknowledge of all things, while at the same time our wills are our own. God has foreknowledge of our will, so that of which he has foreknowledge must come to pass. In other words, we shall exercise our wills in the future because he has foreknowledge that we shall do so; and there can be no will or voluntary action unless it be in our power. Hence God has also foreknowledge of our power to will. My power is not taken from me by God's foreknowledge. Indeed I shall be more certainly in possession of my power because he whose foreknowledge is never mistaken, foreknows that I shall have the power. *Ev.*—Now I no longer deny that whatever God has foreknown must necessarily come to pass, nor that he has foreknowledge of our sins, but in such a way that our wills remain free and within our power.

Aug.—What further difficulty do you have? Perhaps you have forgotten what we established in our first disputation, and now wish to deny that we sin voluntarily and under no compulsion from anything superior, inferior or equal to us. *Ev.*—I do not venture to deny that at all. But I must confess I do not yet see how God's foreknowledge of our sins and our freedom of will in sinning can be other than mutually contradictory. We must confess that God is just and knows all things beforehand. But I should like to know with what justice he punishes sins which must necessarily be committed; or how they are not necessarily committed when he knows that they will be committed; or how the Creator is to escape having imputed to him anything that happens necessarily in his creature.

Aug.—Why do you think our free will is opposed to God's foreknowledge? Is it because it is foreknowledge simply, or because it is God's foreknowledge? *Ev.*—In the main because it is God's foreknowledge. *Aug.*—If you knew in advance that such and such a man would sin, there would be no necessity for him to sin. *Ev.*—Indeed there would, for I should have no real foreknowledge unless I knew for certain what was going to happen. *Aug.*—So it is foreknowledge generally and not God's foreknowledge specially that causes the events foreknown to happen by necessity? There would be no such thing as foreknowledge unless there was certain foreknowledge. *Ev.*—I agree. But why these questions? *Aug.*—Unless I am mistaken, you would not directly compel the man to sin, though you knew beforehand that he was going to sin. Nor does your prescience in itself compel him to sin even though he was certainly going to sin, as we must assume if you have real prescience. So there is no contradiction here. Simply you know beforehand what another is going to do with his own will. Similarly God compels no man to sin, though he sees beforehand those who are going to sin by their own will.

Why then should he not justly punish sins which, though he had foreknowledge of them, he did not compel the sinner to commit? Just as you apply no compulsion to past events by having them in your memory, so God by his foreknowledge does not use compulsion in the case of future events. Just as you remember your past actions, though all that you remember were not actions of your own, so God has foreknowledge of all his own actions, but is not the agent of all that he foreknows. Of evil actions he is not the agent but the just punisher. From this you may understand with what justice God punishes sins, for he has no responsibility for the future actions of men though he knows them beforehand. If he ought not to award punishment to sinners because he knew beforehand that they would sin, he ought not to reward the righteous, because he knew equally that they would be righteous. Let us confess that it belongs to his foreknowledge to allow no future event to escape his knowledge, and that it belongs to his justice to see that no sin goes unpunished by his judgment. For sin is committed voluntarily and not by any compulsion from his foreknowledge.

As to your third question how the Creator is to escape having imputed to him anything that happens necessarily in his creature, it is fitting for us to remember the rule of piety which says that we owe thanks to our Creator. That will provide us with the answer. His lavish goodness should be most justly praised even if he had made us with some lower rank in his creation. Though our soul be soiled with sins it is nevertheless loftier and better than if it were changed into visible light. And yet light is an eminent part of creation, as you can see by considering how much God is praised for it, even by souls wholly given over to bodily sense. Wherefore, though sinful souls are censured, do not let that provoke you to say in your heart that it would have been better if they did not exist. They are censured because they are compared with what they might have been if they had not willed to sin. God, their Maker, is to be gloriously praised for the human faculties with which he has endowed them, not only because he justly subjects them to his order when they sin, but also because he made them such that, even when soiled with sin, they are not surpassed in dignity by corporeal light, for which also God is rightly praised.

Possibly you would not go so far as to say that it would have been better if sinful souls did not exist, but take care also not to say that they should have been other than they are. Whatever better argument true reason may suggest to you, know at least that God made them, and that he is author of all good things. For it is not true reason but envious weakness that bids you think that anything ought to have been made better than it is, and that nothing inferior should have been made at all. That is as if you looked at the heavens and concluded that the earth ought not to have been made. That is all wrong. You would be quite right to find fault if you saw that the earth had been made, and no heavens, for then you might say the earth ought to have been made according to your ideal conception of the heavens. But now you see that your ideal earth has been made, only it is called not earth but heaven. I believe that since you have not been defrauded of the better creation you ought not to grudge that there is an inferior creation which we call the earth. In the earth again there is such a variety among its parts that you can think of nothing of an earthly nature which God has not made somewhere in the totality of his work. For the earth contains land of all kinds, passing by gradual stages from the most fruitful and pleasant to the most deceitful and infertile tracts, so that you can only find fault with one kind of land by comparing it with a better kind. So you ascend through all the grades of land with their varying praiseworthy qualities, and when you find the very best land you are glad that there are the other kinds as well. And yet what a difference there is between earth, in all its variety, and heaven! Water and air are interposed. Of these four elements various other forms and species of things are made, innumerable to us but all numbered by God. There may be things in the natural realm which you would never have thought of yourself, but the wholly and purely rational cannot but be. You can think of nothing better in the creation which the Creator did not think of. When the human soul says: "This is better than that," and if it says so truly, it will say so because of its relation to the divine reasons on which it depends. If it understands what it says, it does so likewise because of its relation to these reasons. Let it therefore believe that God has made what true reason knows he must have made, even if it is not evident in created things. If the heavens were invisible, but true reason led to the conclusion that such a thing must have been created, we ought to believe that it has been created though it do not appear to the eye. For thought would have no idea that it ought to have been created if it did not have some relation to the reasons through which all things were created. What does not exist can no more be thought than have true existence.

Many err because, beholding the better things with their minds, they look for them also with their eyes in the wrong places. That would be as if someone, who by reason understood perfect rotundity, should be annoyed that he did not observe it in a nut, assuming that he never saw any other round object besides that fruit. So when some people see with true reason that there are better creatures who, though they have free will, have ever adhered to God and have never sinned, they look at the sins of men and lament not that they may cease from sin but simply that men have been created at all. They say: "He did not create us such that we should will ever to enjoy his unchangeable truth and never to sin." Do not let them cry out or be annoyed. He did not compel them to sin by the mere fact that he created them and gave them power to choose good or evil as they would. He made them so far like those angels who never sinned and never will sin. If you delight in a creature which by voluntary perseverance never sins, there is no doubt you rightly prefer it to a sinful creature. Just as you give it the preference in your thought, so God gives it the preference in his universal order. You may believe that there are such creatures in the loftier regions of the heavens. For if God showed his goodness in creating creatures whom he knew beforehand would sin, he would show his goodness no less in creating creatures whom he knew beforehand would never sin.

Those sublime creatures have their happiness perpetually in the eternal enjoyment of their Creator; and their happiness they merit by their perpetual will to hold fast to righteousness. Below them sinful creatures have their proper order. By their sins they have lost happiness, but they have not lost the capacity to recover it. Herein they are superior to those creatures whose will is to remain perpetually in sin. Between these two extremes—those who continue in the will to righteousness and those who continue in the will to sin—there is this middle class who by the humility of repentance recover their exalted rank. But God did not withhold the lavishness of his bounty even from his creatures who he knew beforehand would not only sin but would continue in the will to sin; for he showed it in creating them. An errant horse is better than a stone that cannot err because it has neither motion nor feeling of its own. So a creature which sins by its own free will is more excellent than one which cannot sin because it has no free will. I would praise wine that was good of its kind, and would censure the man who drank it to excess. And yet I would hold the man whom I had censured, even while he was drunk, to be superior to the wine which made him drunk, even though I had praised it. So the corporeal creature is rightly to be praised in its own order, though those are to be censured who use it to excess and are thereby turned away from perception of the truth. And those perverse people, drunkards or the like, are to be preferred to the thing, laudable in its own order, greediness for which made them vain; not indeed because of their vices but because of the dignity of their nature which still remains.

Soul is universally superior to body. No soul can fall so far in sinfulness as to be changed into body. Its quality as soul cannot be taken from it, and it cannot in any way lose that which makes it superior to body. Now among corporeal objects light holds the first place. Consequently the worst soul is superior to the first of corporeal things. It is of course possible that some body may be preferable to the body in which a soul resides, but it cannot be preferred to the soul itself. Why, then, should not God be praised with all possible praise, who made souls that were to abide in the laws of righteousness, even if he also made other souls which he knew beforehand would sin or even persevere in sin? For even these are better than things that cannot sin because they have not reason or free choice of will. They are even better than the most splendid brilliance of bodies of any kind, though some people [the Manichees], greatly erring, venerate light as if it were the substance of God most high. In the order of corporeal creatures, from the sidereal choir down to the number of our hairs, the beauty of good things is so perfectly graded that it is a sign of lack of understanding to ask: "What is this?" or "To what purpose is that?" All things are created each in its own order. How much more does it show lack of understanding to ask such questions about any soul whatever? No matter how great a diminution of its glory it may suffer or what defects it may exhibit, nevertheless it will always and without any doubt surpass in dignity every kind of body.

Reason has a different standard of judgment from that of utility. Reason judges by the light of truth, and correctly subordinates lesser things to those that are greater. Utility, guided by experience of convenience, often attributes a higher value to things which reason convinces us are of lesser rank. Reason sets a vast difference in value between celestial and terrestrial bodies, but what carnal man would not prefer that several stars should be wanting in the heavens, than that one shrub should be lacking in his field or one cow from his herd? Older men pay no attention to, or at least are prepared patiently to correct, the judgments of children, who prefer the death of a man (except one of those bound to them by the ties of happy affection), to the death of a favourite sparrow, especially if the man was an object of terror to them, and the sparrow was tuneful and beautiful. So, if there are people, unskilled in judging the values of things, who praise God for his lesser creatures, finding them more easily appreciated by their carnal senses, and do not praise him for his better and superior creatures, or praise him less than they ought, or try to find fault with his creatures and to point out how they might have been better, or even do not believe that he created them, those who have advanced some way towards wisdom either entirely scorn such judgments or hear them with good-natured patience if they cannot correct them or until they are corrected.

Such being the case, it is far from the truth that the sins of the creature must be attributed to the Creator, even though those things must necessarily happen which he has foreknown. So much so that when you say you can find no reason why whatever necessarily happens in the creature should not be attributed to him, I on the contrary find no way, and I assert that none exists or can be found, of attributing to him what is done, necessarily no doubt, but also by the will of the sinner. If anyone says, I should prefer not to exist than to exist in unhappiness, I shall reply: That is a lie; for you are miserable now, and yet you do not wish to die, simply because you wish to exist. You don't want to be miserable but you want to continue in life all the same. Give thanks, therefore, because you exist, as you wish to do, so that the misery you do not wish may be taken from you. You exist as you wish to do, but you are unhappy against your will. If you are ungrateful for your existence you are rightly compelled to be unhappy, which you do not wish. I praise the goodness of the Creator because, even when you are ungrateful, you have what you wish. And I praise the justice of the Orderer of things because for your ingratitude you suffer what you do not wish.

From The Confessions

WHAT IS TIME?

At no time, therefore, did you do nothing, since you had made time itself. No times are coeternal with you, because you are permanent, whereas if they were permanent, they would not be times. What is time? Who can easily and briefly explain this? Who can comprehend this even in thought, so as to express it in a word? Yet what do we discuss more familiarly and knowingly in conversation than time? Surely we understand it when we talk about it, and also understand it when we hear others talk about it.

What, then, is time? If no one asks me, I know; if I want to explain it to someone who does ask me, I do not know. Yet I state confidently that I know this: if nothing were passing away, there would be no past time, and if nothing were coming, there would be no future time, and if nothing existed, there would be no present time. How, then, can these two kinds of time, the past and the future, be, when the past no longer is and the future as yet does not be?

But if the present were always present, and would not pass into the past, it would no longer be time, but eternity. Therefore, if the present, so as to be time, must be so constituted that it passes into the past, how can we say that it is, since the cause of its being is the fact that it will cease to be? Does it not follow that we can truly say that it is time, only because it tends toward non-being?

CAN TIME BE LONG OR SHORT?

Yet we say "a long time" and "a short time," and do not say this except of the past or the future. For example, we call a hundred years ago a long time in the past, and a hundred years from now we call a long time in the future. On the contrary, we term ten days ago, let us say, a short time past, and ten days to come, a brief future time. But in what sense is something non-existent either long or short? The past no longer exists, and the future is not yet in being. Therefore we should not say, "It is long," but we should say of the past, "It was long," and of the future, "It will be long." My lord, my light, shall not your truth here also jest at man? That past time which was so long, was it long when it was already past, or before that, when it was still present? It could be long at the time when that existed which could be long. Once past, it did not exist, hence it could not be long, since it in no wise existed. Therefore, let us not say, "Past time was long." We will not find anything which was long, since from the very fact that it is past, it is no more. Let us say, "That time once present was long," because it was long when it was present. It had not passed away, so as not to be, and therefore, there existed that which could be long. On the other hand, after it passed away, it instantly ceased to be long, because it ceased to be.

Let us see, then, O human soul, whether present time can be long, for it has been granted to you to perceive and to measure tracts of time. What answer do you make me? Are a hundred years, when present, a long time? See first whether a hundred years can be present. If the first of these years is going on, it is present, but the other ninety-nine are still in the future, and therefore as yet are not existent. If the second year is current, one is already past, another is present, and the rest are in the future. So it is if we posit any of the intervening years of the hundred as the present: before it will be past years, and after it, future years. For this reason, a hundred years cannot be present.

But see, at least, if the year now going on is itself present. If the first month is current, then all the rest are to come; if it is the second, then the first is already past and the others are not yet here. Therefore the current year is not wholly present, and if it is not wholly present, then the year is not present. A year is made up of twelve months, of which any one month, which is current, is the present, and the others are either past or future. However, not even the current month is present, but only a single day. If it is the first day, the others are to come; if the last day, the others are past; if any intervening day, it is between those past and those to come.

See how the present time, which alone we found worthy to be called long, is contracted to hardly the space of a single day. But let us examine it also, because not even a single day is present in its totality. It is completed in twenty-four hours of night and day, and of these the first has the others still to come, the last has them past it, and each of the intervening hours has those before it in the past and those after it in the future. That one hour itself goes on in fleeting moments; whatever part of it has flown away is past, whatever remains is future. If any point of time is conceived that can no longer be divided into even the most minute parts of a moment, that alone it is which may be called the present. It flies with such speed from the future into the past that it cannot be extended by even a trifling amount. For if it is extended, it is divided into past and future. The present has no space.

Where then is the time that we may call long? Is it to come? We do not say of it that it is long, because it does not yet exist, so as to be long. We say that it will be long. When, therefore, will it be? Even then, if it will still be to come, it will not be long, since that which will be long does not yet be. But suppose it will be long, at that time when out of the future, which does not yet be, it will first begin to be and will have become present, so that what may be long can actually exist. Then immediately present time cries out in the words above that it cannot be long.

TIME AND MEASUREMENT

Still, O Lord, we perceive intervals of time. We compare them to one another and say that some are longer and some shorter. Also, we measure how much longer or shorter this time may be than that, and answer that this is twice or three times as long as another, or that that one is identical with or just as much as this. But it is passing times that we measure, and we make these measurements in perceiving them. As to past times, which no longer exist, or future, which as yet do not exist, who can measure them, except perhaps a man rash enough to say that he can measure what does not exist? Therefore, as long as time is passing by, it can be perceived and measured, but when it has passed by, it cannot be measured since it does not exist.

PROPHECY AND HISTORY

Father, I ask questions; I do not make assertions. My God, govern me and guide me. Who is it that will tell me, not that there are three times, just as we learned as boys and as we have taught to boys, namely, past, present, and future, but that there is only present time, since the other two do not exist? Or do they too exist, but when the present comes into being from the future, does it proceed from some hidden source, and when past comes out of the present, does it recede into some hidden place? Where did they who foretold things to come see them, if they do not exist? A thing that does not exist cannot be seen. If those who narrate past events did not perceive them by their minds, they would not give true accounts. If such things were nothing at all, they could not be perceived in any way. Therefore, both future and past times have being.

St. Augustine in his Study. This fresco, by the Renaissance Neoplatonist Sandro Botticelli, details the doctrine of ascent from the world to unity with the divine. (The Granger Collection)

INDUCTION AND PREDICTION

Give me leave, "O Lord, my hope" to make further search: do not let my purpose be diverted. If future and past times exist, I wish to know where they are. But if I am not yet able to do this, I still know that wherever they are, they are there neither as future nor as past, but as present. For if they are in that place as future things, they are not yet there, and if they are in that place as past things, they are no longer there. Therefore, wherever they are, and whatever they are, they do not exist except as present things. However, when true accounts of the past are given, it is not the things themselves, which have passed away, that are drawn forth from memory, but words conceived from their images. These images they implanted in the mind like footsteps as they passed through the senses.

My boyhood, indeed, which no longer is, belongs to past time, which no longer is. However, when I recall it and talk about it, I perceive its image at the present time, because it still is in my memory. Whether there may be a like cause of predicting future events as well, namely, that actually existent images of things which as yet do not exist are perceived first, I confess, O my God, I do not know. But this I surely know, that we often premeditate our future actions and such premeditation is present to us, but the action that we premeditate does not yet exist, because it is to be. As soon as we have addressed ourselves to it and have begun to do what we were premeditating, then action will be existent. Then it will not be future, but present.

Howsoever this secret foresight of things to come takes place, nothing can be seen except what is present. But what now is is not future but present. Hence, when future things are said to be seen, it is not the things themselves, which are not yet existent, that is, the things that are to come, but their causes, or perhaps signs of them, which already exist, that are seen. Thus they are not future things, but things already present to the viewers, and from them future things are predicted as conceived in the mind. Again, these conceptions are already existent, and those who predict the future fix their gaze upon things present with them.

Let the vast multitude of such things offer me some example of this. I look at the dawn; I foretell the coming sunrise. What I look at is present; what I foretell is future. It is not the sun that is about to be, for it already exists, but its rising, which as yet is not. Yet if I did not picture within my mind this sunrise, just as when I now speak of it, I would be unable to predict it. Still that dawn, which I see in the sky, is not the sunrise, although it precedes the sunrise, nor is the picture in my mind the sunrise. Both these are perceived as present to me, so that the future sunrise may be foretold. Therefore, future things do not yet exist; if they do not yet exist, they are not; if they are not, they can in no wise be seen. However, they can be predicted from present things, which already exist and are seen.

A PRAYER FOR LIGHT

O you, the ruler of your creation, in what manner do you teach souls those things which are to come? You have taught your prophets. What is that way by which you teach things to come, you to whom nothing is future? Or is it rather that you teach things present concerning what is to come? What does not exist surely cannot be taught. Too distant is this way for my sight. It is too strong for me, and of myself I will not be able to attain it. But with your help I will be able to attain to it, when you will give it to me, you, the sweet light of my hidden eyes.

THREE KINDS OF TIME

It is now plain and clear that neither past nor future are existent, and that it is not properly stated that there are three times, past, present, and future. But perhaps it might properly be said that there are three times, the present of things past, the present of things present, and the present of things future. These three are in the soul, but elsewhere I do not see them: the present of things past is in memory; the present of things present is in intuition; the present of things future is in expectation. If we are permitted to say this, then I see three times, and I affirm that there are three times. It may also be said that there are three times, past, present, and future, as common usage correctly puts it. This may be stated. Note that I am not concerned over this, do not object to it, and do not criticize it, as long as we understand what we say, namely, that what is future is not now existent, nor is that which is past. There are few things that we state properly, and many that we speak improperly, but what we mean is understood.

MEASURES OF TIME

I said just a while ago that we measure passing times, so that we can say that this tract of time is double that single one, or that this one is just as long as the other, and whatever else as to periods of time we can describe by our measurements. Therefore, as I was saying, we measure passing times. If someone says to me, "How do you know this?" I may answer, "I know this because we make such measurements, and we cannot measure things that do not exist, and neither past nor future things exist." Yet how do we measure present time, since it has no extent? Therefore, it is measured as it passes by, but once it has passed by, it is not measured, for what would be measured will no longer exist. But from where, and on what path, and to what place does it pass, as it is measured? From where, except from the future? By what path, except by the present? To what place, except into the past? Therefore, it is from that which does not yet exist, by that which lacks space, and into that which no longer exists.

But what do we measure if time is not in a certain space? We do not say single, or double, or threefold, or equal, or anything else of this sort in the order of time, except with regard to tracts of time. In what space, then, do we measure passing time? In the future, out of which it passes? But we do not measure what does not yet exist. Or in the present, by which it passes? We do not measure what is without space. Or in the past, into which it passes? We do not measure what no longer exists.

A NEW TASK

My mind is on fire to understand this most intricate riddle. O Lord my God, good Father, I beseech you in the name of Christ, do not shut off, do not shut off these things, both familiar and yet hidden, from my desire, so that it may not penetrate into them, but let them grow bright, Lord, with your mercy bringing the light that lights them up. Of whom shall I inquire concerning them? To whom shall I more fruitfully confess my ignorance than to you, to whom my studies, strongly burning for your Scriptures, are not offensive.

Give me what I love, for in truth I love it, and this you have given to me. Give this to me, Father, for "truly you know how to give good gifts to your children." Give it to me, for "I studied that I might know this thing; it is a labor in your sight," until you open it up. I beseech you in the name of Christ, in the name of him, the saint of saints, let no man interrupt me. "I have believed, therefore do I speak." This is my hope, for this I live, "that I may contemplate the delight of the Lord." "Behold, you have made my days old," and they pass away, but how I do not know. We talk of time and time, of times and times: "How long ago did he say this?" "How long ago did he do this?" "How long a time since I saw that?" "This syllable takes twice the time of that short simple syllable." We say these things, and we hear them, and we are understood, and we understand. They are most clear and most familiar, but again they are very obscure, and their solution is a new task.

BODILY MOTION AS TIME

I have heard from a certain learned man that the movements of the sun, moon, and stars constitute time, but I did not agree with him. Why should not rather the movement of all bodies be times? In fact, if the lights of heaven should stop, while a potter's wheel was kept moving, would there be no time by which we might measure those rotations? Would we say either that it moved with equal speeds, or, if it sometimes moved more slowly and sometimes more swiftly, that some turns were longer and others shorter? Or while we were saying this, would we not also be speaking in time? Or would there be in our words some long syllables and others short, except for the fact that some were sounded for a longer and others for a shorter time? Grant to men, O God, that they may see in a little matter evidence common to things both small and great. The stars and the lights of heaven are "for signs, and for seasons, and for days, and for years." Truly they are such. Yet I should not say that the turning of that little wooden wheel constitutes a day, nor under those conditions should that learned man say that there is no time.

I desire to know the power and the nature of time, by which we measure bodily movements, and say, for instance, that this movement is twice as long as that. I put this question: "Since a day is defined not only as the sun's time over the earth—according to which usage, day is one thing and night another—but also as its entire circuit from east to east—and accordingly we say 'So many days have passed,' for they are termed 'so many days' with their nights included and are not reckoned as days apart from the night hours—since, then, a day is completed by the sun's movement and its circuit from east to east, I ask whether the movement itself constitutes a day, or the period in which the movement is performed, or both together?"

If the first were a day, then there would be a day even if the sun completed its course in a period of time such as an hour. If the second, then there would not be a day, if from one sunrise to another there were as brief a period as an hour, whereas the sun would have to go around twenty-four times to complete a day. If both, it could not be called a day if the sun ran its entire course in the space of an hour, nor if, while the sun stood still, just so much time passed by as the sun usually takes to complete its entire course from morning to morning.

Therefore, I will not now ask what is it that is called a day, but rather what is time, by which we would measure the sun's circuit and say that it was completed in half the time it usually takes, if it were finished in a period like twelve hours. Comparing both times, we should call the one a single period, the other a double period, even if the sun ran its course from east to east sometimes in the single period and sometimes in the double.

Let no man tell me, then, that movements of the heavenly bodies constitute periods of time. When at the prayer of a certain man, the sun stood still until he could achieve victory in battle, the sun indeed stood still, but time went on. That battle was waged and brought to an end during its own tract of time, which was sufficient for it. Therefore, I see that time is a kind of distention. Yet do I see this, or do I only seem to myself to see it? You, O light, will show this to me.

MEASURES OF MOVEMENT

Do you command me to agree with someone who says that time is the movement of a body? You do not command this. I hear that a body is never moved except in time: this you yourself affirm. But I do not hear that the movement of a body constitutes time: this you do not say. When a body is moved, I measure in time how long it is moved, from when it begins to be moved until it ceases. If I did not see when it began, and if it continues to be moved, so that I cannot see when it stops, I am unable to measure it, except perhaps from the time I begin to see it until I stop. If I look at it for long, I can merely report that it is a long time, but not how long. When we say how long, we say so by making a comparison, such as, "This is as long as that," or "Twice as long as that," or something of the sort.

But if we can mark off the distances of the places from which and to which the body that is moved goes—or its parts, if it is moved as on a lathe—then we can say in how much time the movement of that body, or its part, from this place to that, is completed. Since the movement of a body is one thing and that by which we measure how long it takes another, who does not perceive which of the two is better called time? For if a body is sometimes moved in different ways and sometimes stands still, then we measure in time not only its movement but also its standing still. We say, "It stood still just as long as it was moved," or "It stood still twice or three times as long as it was moved," and whatever else our measurements either determine or reckon, more or less, as the saying goes. Time, therefore, is not the movement of a body.

THE DEEPENING PROBLEM

I confess to you, O Lord, that I do not yet know what time is, and again I confess to you, O Lord, that I know that I say these things in time, and that I have now spoken at length of time, and that that very length of time is not long except by a period of time. How, then, do I know this, when I do not know what time is? Or perhaps I do not know how to express what I know? Woe is me, who do not even know what I do not know! Behold, O my God, before you I do not lie. As I speak, so is my heart. "You will light my lamp, O Lord, my God, you enlighten my darkness."

THE DEFINITION OF TIME

Does not my soul confess to you with a true confession that I measure tracts of time? Yes, O Lord my God, I measure them, and know not what I measure. I measure the motion of a body in time. But again, do I not measure time itself? In fact, could I measure a body's movement, as to how long it is and how long it takes from this place to that, unless I could measure the time in which it is moved? How, then, do I measure time itself? Do we measure a longer time by a shorter one, just as we measure the length of a rod by the length of a cubit? It is thus that we seem to measure the length of a long syllable by the length of a short syllable, and to say that it is twice as long. So also we measure the length of poems by the length of verses, the length of verses by the length of feet, the length of feet by the length of syllables, and the length of long syllables by the length of short ones. This is not as they are on the page—in that manner we measure spaces, not times—but as words pass by when we pronounce them. We say: "It is a long poem for it is composed of so many verses; the verses are long, for they consist of so many feet; the feet are long, for they extend over so many syllables; the syllable is long, for it is double a short one."

But a reliable measure of time is not comprehended in this manner, since it can be that a shorter verse, if pronounced more slowly, may sound for a longer stretch of time than a longer but more hurried verse. So it is for a poem, so for a foot, so for a syllable. For this reason it seemed to me that time is nothing more than distention: but of what thing I know not, and the marvel is, if it is not of the mind itself. For what do I measure, I beseech you, my God, when I say either indefinitely, "This time is longer than that," or even definitely, "This time is twice as long as that?" I measure time, I know. Yet I do not measure the future, because it does not yet exist; I do not measure the present, because it is not extended in space; I do not measure the past, because it no longer exists. What, then, do I measure? Times that pass, but are not yet past? So I have stated.

WHERE TIME IS MEASURED

Be steadfast, O my mind, and attend firmly. "God is our helper." "He made us, and not we ourselves." Look to where truth begins to dawn. See, as an example, a bodily voice begins to sound, and does sound, and still sounds, and then, see, it stops. There is silence now: that voice is past, and is no longer a voice. Before it sounded, the voice was to come, and could not be measured because it did not yet exist, and now it cannot be measured because it no longer is. Therefore, the time it was sounding, it could be measured, because at that time it existed. Even at that time it was not static, for it was going on and going away. Was it for that reason the more measurable? While passing away it was being extended over some tract of time, wherein it could be measured, for the present has no space. Therefore, if it could be measured at that time, let us suppose that another voice has begun to sound and still sounds on one continuous note without any break. Let us measure it while it is sounding, since when it has ceased to sound, it will be already past and there will be nothing that can be measured. Let us measure it exactly, and let us state how long it is. But it is still sounding, and it cannot be measured except from its beginning, when it begins to sound, up to its end, when it stops. We measure, in fact, the interval from some beginning up to some kind of end. Hence a voice that is never brought to a stop cannot be measured, so that one may say how long or short it is. Nor can it be said to be equal to another, or single or double or anything else with reference to something. But when it will be ended, it will no longer be. In what sense, then, can it be measured? Yet we do measure tracts of time, although not those which as yet are not, not those which no longer are, not those which are prolonged without a break, not those which have no limits. Neither future, nor past, nor present, nor passing times do we measure and still we measure tracts of time.

Deus creator omnium—"God, creator of all things"—this verse of eight syllables alternates between short and long syllables. Hence the four short syllables, the first, third, fifth and seventh, are simple with respect to the four long syllables the second, fourth, sixth, and eighth. Each long syllable has a double time with respect to each of the others. This I affirm, this I report, and so it is, in so far as it is plain to sense perception. In so far as sense perception is clear, I measure the long syllable by the short one, and I perceive that it is exactly twice as long. But when one syllable sounds after another, and if the first is short and the second long, how will I retain the short syllable and how will I apply it to the long syllable while measuring it, so as to find that the latter is twice as long? For the long syllable does not begin to sound until the short one has ceased to sound. Do I measure the long syllable itself while it is present, since I do not measure it until it is completed? Yet its completion is its passing away. Therefore, what is it that I measure? Where is the short syllable by which I measure? Where is the long syllable that I measure? Both of them have sounded, have flown off, have passed away, and now they are not. Yet I make measurements, and I answer confidently—in so far as sense activity is relied upon—that this syllable is single and that one double, namely, in length of time. Yet I cannot do this, unless because they have passed away and are ended. Therefore, I do not measure the syllables themselves, which no longer are, but something in my memory that remains fixed there.

It is in you, O my mind, that I measure my times. Do not interrupt me by crying that time is. Do not interrupt yourself with the noisy mobs of your prejudices. It is in you, I say, that I measure tracts of time. The impression that passing things make upon you remains, even after those things have passed. That present state is what I measure, not the things which pass away so that it be made. That is what I measure when I measure tracts of time. Therefore, either this is time, or I do not measure time.

How is it when we measure stretches of silence, and say that this silence has lasted for as much of time as that discourse lasted? Do we not apply our thought to measurement of the voice, just as though it were sounding, so that we may be able to report about the intervals of silence in a given tract of time? Even though both voice and mouth be silent, in our thought we run through poems and verses, and any discourse, and any other measurements of motion. We report about tracts of time: how great this one may be in relation to that, in the same manner as if we said them audibly.

If someone wished to utter a rather long sound and had determined by previous reflection how long it would be, he has in fact already silently gone through a tract of time. After committing it to memory, he has begun to utter that sound and he voices it until he has brought it to his proposed end. Yes, it has sounded and it will sound. For the part of it that is finished has surely sounded; what remains will sound. So it is carried out, as long as his present intention transfers the future into the past, with the past increasing by a diminution of future, until by the consumption of the future the whole is made past.

THE MENTAL SYNTHESIS

But how is the future, which as yet does not exist, diminished or consumed, or how does the past, which no longer exists, increase, unless there are three things in the mind, which does all this? It looks forward, it considers, it remembers, so that the reality to which it looks forward passes through what it considers into what it remembers. Who, then, denies that future things are not yet existent? Yet there is already in the mind an expectation of things to come. Who denies that past things no longer exist? Yet there is still in the soul the memory of past things. Who denies that present time lacks spatial extent, since it passes away in an instant? Yet attention abides, and through it what shall be present proceeds to become something absent. It is not, then, future time that is long, but a long future is a long expectation of the future. Nor is past time, which is not, long, but a long past is a long memory of the past.

I am about to recite a psalm that I know. Before I begin, my expectation extends over the entire psalm. Once I have begun, my memory extends over as much of it as I shall separate off and assign to the past. The life of this action of mine is distended into memory by reason of the part I have spoken and into forethought by reason of the part I am about to speak. But attention is actually present and that which was to be is borne along by it so as to become past. The more this is done and done again, so much the more is memory lengthened by a shortening of expectation, until the entire expectation is exhausted. When this is done the whole action is completed and passes into memory. What takes place in the whole psalm takes place also in each of its parts and in each of its syllables. The same thing holds for a longer action, of which perhaps the psalm is a small part. The same thing holds for a man's entire life, the parts of which are all the man's actions. The same thing holds throughout the whole age of the sons of men, the parts of which are the lives of all men.

From The City of God

About Social Life, Which, Though Very Greatly to Be Desired, Is Often Upset by Many Distresses.

But in that they believe that the life of the wise man must be social, we approve much more fully. For how could the City of God, about which we are already engaged in writing the nineteenth book, begin at the start or progress in its course or reach its appointed goal, if the life of the saints were not social? But who could reckon up the number and the magnitude of the woes with which human society overflows amid the worries of this our mortal state? Who could be equal to the task of assessing them? Let them give ear to a man in one of their own comedies, who says what every man concurs in: "I have taken a wife; what misery I have known therewith! Children were born; another responsibility." What of the ills that love breeds, as enumerated by that same Terence: "Slights, suspicions, enmities, war, then peace again"? Have they not everywhere made up the tale of human events? Do they not usually occur even when friends are united in a noble love? The history of man is in every cranny infested with them; in this list we count the slights, suspicions, enmities and war, as certainly evil; while peace is but a doubtful good, since we do not know the hearts of those with whom we choose to be at peace, and even if we could know them today, in any case we know not what they may be like tomorrow. Who, moreover, are wont to be more friendly, or at least ought to be, than those who dwell together in the same home? And yet who is free from doubt in such relations, seeing that from the hidden treachery of such persons great woes have often arisen,—woes the more bitter, as the peace was sweeter that was counted real when it was most cleverly feigned?

Reprinted by permission of the publishers and The Loeb Classical Library from *City of God*, Augustine, Book XIX, trans. by W. C. Greene, Cambridge, Mass.: Harvard University Press, 1960. (Chapters 5, 6, 8, 17, 24, 25, and 28; pp. 137–147, 151–155, 195–199, 231–235, 243–245)

That is why the words of Cicero so touch all men's hearts that we lament perforce: "No ambushed foes are harder to detect than those who mask their aim with a counterfeit loyalty or under the guise of some close tie. For against an open adversary you would be on your guard, and so easily escape him; but this hidden evil, being internal and domestic, not only arises but even crushes you before you have a chance to observe and investigate it." That is why the divine word has also been spoken: "A man's foes are even those of his own household," words that are heard with great sorrow of heart. For even if any man is strong enough to bear them with equanimity, or alert enough to guard with prudent foresight against the designs of a pretended friend, nevertheless, if he is himself a good man, he must needs feel grievous pain when he finds by experience that they are utterly base, whether they were always evil and feigned goodness or whether they underwent a change from goodwill to the evil mind that he finds in them. If, then, the home, our common refuge amid the ills of this human life, is not safe, what of the city? The larger it is, the more does its forum teem with lawsuits both civil and criminal, even though its calm be not disturbed by the turbulence, or more often the bloodshed, of sedition and civil wars. Cities are indeed free at times from such events, but never from the threat of them.

About the Error of Human Judgement, When the Truth Is Hidden.

What of those judgements pronounced by men on their fellow men, which are indispensable in cities however deep the peace that reigns in them? How sad, how lamentable we find them, since those who pronounce them cannot look into the consciences of those whom they judge. Therefore they are often compelled to seek the truth by torturing innocent witnesses though the case does not concern them. What shall I say of torture inflicted on the accused man himself? The question is whether he is guilty; yet he is tortured even if he is innocent, and for a doubtful crime he suffers a punishment that is not doubtful at all, not because it is discovered that he committed it but because it is not known that he did not commit it. Thus the ignorance of the judge generally results in the calamity of the innocent. And what is still more intolerable, and still more to be deplored and, were it possible, purged by floods of tears, is that the judge, in the act of torturing the accused for the express purpose of avoiding the unwitting execution of an innocent man, through pitiable ignorance puts to death, both tortured and innocent, the very man whom he has tortured in order not to execute him if innocent.

For if he has chosen, applying the wisdom of the philosophers mentioned above, to escape from this life rather than endure those torments any longer, he pleads guilty to a crime that he did not commit. And after he has been condemned and put to death, the judge still does not know whether it was a guilty or an innocent man whom he put to death and whom he tortured that he might not unwittingly execute an innocent man; so he has both tortured an innocent man in order to learn the truth and put him to death without learning it. Since there are such dark places in political life, will a wise judge sit on the bench, or will he not dare to do so? Clearly he will; for the claim of society constrains and draws him until he consents to serve; for to desert his duty to society he counts abominable.

For he does not think it abominable that innocent witnesses are tortured in other men's cases; or that the accused are often overcome by the pain of torture and so make false confessions and are punished, though innocent; or that, although not condemned to death, they often die under torture or as a consequence of torture; or that the accusers, perhaps moved by a desire to benefit society by seeing that crimes do not go unpunished, are themselves condemned by an ignorant judge, if both the evidence of witnesses is false and the defendant with fierce resistance to torture makes no admission of guilt, so that they have no way to prove the truth of their allegations, although those allegations are true. These many great evils he does not count as sins; for the wise judge does not commit them because of any will to do harm but because his action is determined by his ignorance, being also, however, determined by the binding claim of society that requires him to sit in judgement. Here, then, is a clear proof of man's miserable lot, of which I speak, even though we may not accuse the judge of evil intent. But if by ignorance and by office he is constrained to torture and punish the innocent, is it not enough that we acquit him of guilt? Must he be happy as well? How much more creditable is it for his powers of reflection and for his worth as a human being when he acknowledges our pitiable condition in that our acts are determined in spite of us, and loathes his own part in it, sending up, if he is wise as a religious man, a cry to God: "From my necessities deliver thou me!"

That the Friendship of Good Men Can Not Be Free From Anxiety, So Long as It Is Necessary to Worry About the Dangers of This Life.

If we escape from a kind of ignorance, akin to madness, that often befalls men in the wretched condition of this life, and that leads them to mistake a foe for a friend or a friend for a foe, what consolation have we in this human society, full of mistakes and distresses, save the unfeigned faith and mutual affection of true and good friends? But the more friends we have, and the more widely scattered they are, the further and more widely spread are our fears lest some evil may befall them among the accumulated evils of this age. For we are anxious not only for fear lest they may be afflicted by hunger, warfare, disease, captivity and the unimaginable sufferings of slavery, but also with far more bitter fear lest friendship be changed into perfidy, malice and villainy. And when these contingencies do occur, more frequently as our friends are the more numerous, and the tidings come to our knowledge, who, save the man who experiences them, can conceive of the pain that consumes our hearts? Indeed, we would rather hear that they were dead, although this, too, we could not hear without sorrow.

For if their lives delighted us with the comforts of friendship, how could it be that their death should bring us no sadness? He who would forbid such sadness must forbid, if he can, all friendly conversation, must interdict or intercept all friendly affection, must break with harsh brutality the bonds of all human relationships, or else lay down the law that they must be so indulged that no pleasure may be derived from them. But if this is utterly impossible, how can it be that a man's death shall not be bitter to us if his life be sweet to us? For hence it is that the sorrow of a heart not devoid of human feeling is like some wound or sore for whose healing we use as salve our kindly messages of comfort. Nor must it be supposed that there is nothing to be healed merely because healing is the easier and the more rapid the finer a man's spirit is. Since, then, the life of mortals is afflicted now more gently, again more harshly, by the death of those very dear to us, and especially of those whose performance of public duties is needful for human society, nevertheless we would rather hear of or behold the death of those whom we love than perceive that they have fallen from faith or virtue, that is, that the soul itself has suffered death. The earth is full of this vast store of evils; wherefore it is written: "Is man's life on earth anything but temptation?" And therefore the Lord himself says: "Woe to the world because of offences"; and again: "Because iniquity shall abound, the love of many shall wax cold." The result is that we feel thankful at the death of good men among our friends, and that, though their death brings sorrow, it is the more surely mitigated in that they have been spared those evils by which in this life even good men are crushed or contaminated or at least are in danger of either fate.

How Different the Uncertainty of the New Academy Is From the Certainty of the Christian Faith.

As to that peculiarity which Varro alleges to be a characteristic of the New Academy, the uncertainty of everything, the city of God utterly denounces such doubt, as madness. About matters that its mind and reason apprehend it has most certain knowledge, even though it is slight because of the corruptible body that weighs down the spirit; for, as the Apostle says: "We know in part." It also trusts in all matters the evidence of the senses, which the mind uses through the agency of the body; for wretchedly deceived indeed is he who supposes that they should never be trusted. It believes, too, in the holy Scriptures, old and new, that we call canonical, whence comes the very faith by which the just man lives; by this faith we walk without doubting, so long as we are exiled from the Lord on our pilgrimage. Provided that this faith is sound and certain, we may without just reproach feel doubt about some matters that neither sense nor reason have perceived, and that have not been revealed to us by the canonical Scriptures, and that have not come to our knowledge through witnesses whom it is absurd not to trust.

What Definition of a People and of a State Must Be Accepted If Not Only the Romans but Other Kingdoms Are to Claim These Titles.

But if a people be defined not in this but in some other manner, for example, in this way: "A people is a large gathering of rational beings united in fellowship by their agreement about the objects of their love," then surely, in order to perceive the character of each people, we must inspect the objects of its love. Yet whatever it loves, if it is a large gathering, not of cattle but of rational beings, and is united in fellowship by common agreement about the objects of its love, then there is no absurdity in using the term "people" of it; and surely the better the objects of its united love, the better the people, and the worse the objects of its love, the worse the people. According to this definition of ours, the Roman people is a people, and its estate is without doubt a state. But what this people loved in its early and in subsequent times, and by what moral decline it passed into bloody sedition and then into social and civil warfare, and disrupted and corrupted that very unity of heart, which is, so to speak, the health of a people, history bears witness, and I have dealt with it at length in the preceding books. And yet I shall not on this account say either that there is no people or that the people's estate is not a state, so long as there remains, however slight, a gathering of rational beings united in fellowship by a common agreement about the objects of its love. But what I have said about this people and about this state let me be understood to have said and meant about those of the Athenians, those of any other Greeks, of the Egyptians, of the earlier Babylon of the Assyrians and of any other nation whatsoever, when they maintained in their states an imperial sway, whether small or great. For in general a city of the impious, not governed by God, since it is disobedient to the command of God that sacrifice be not offered save to himself only, whereby in that city the soul should exercise righteous and faithful rule over the body and reason over the vices, has no true justice.

That There Can Be No True Virtues Where There Is No True Religion.

For however praiseworthy may seem to be the rule of the soul over the body and of the reason over the vices, if the soul and the reason do not serve God as God has commanded that he should be served, then in no wise do they rightly rule the body and the vices. For what kind of mistress over the body and the vices can a mind be that knows not the true God, and that instead of being subject to his command is prostituted to the corrupting power of the most vicious demons? Accordingly, the very virtues that it thinks it possesses, and by means of which it rules the body and the vices in order to obtain or keep any object whatsoever, if it does not subordinate them to God, are themselves vices rather than virtues. For although some suppose that virtues are true and honourable when they are made subject to themselves and are sought for no further end, even then they are puffed up and proud, and so must be reckoned as vices rather than as virtues. For as it is not something that comes from the flesh that makes the flesh live, but something above it, so it is not something that comes from man but something above man that makes him live a blessed life; and this is true not only of man but of every heavenly domination and power.

What End Awaits the Wicked.

But, on the other hand, those who do not belong to that city of God will receive everlasting wretchedness, which is called also the second death, because neither the soul that is alienated from God's life can be said to live there, nor the body, which will be subjected to everlasting torments; and this second death will be all the harder to bear in that it cannot find an end in death. But since, just as wretchedness is the opposite of blessedness, and death of life, so war is the opposite of peace, the question is properly raised what or what sort of war can be understood as present in the final state of the wicked, to correspond to the peace that is heralded and lauded in the final state of the righteous. But let the questioner note what is harmful or destructive in warfare, and he will see that it is nothing but the mutual opposition and conflict of things. Now what war can he imagine more grievous and bitter than one in which the will is so opposed to passion and passion to the will that their enmities can be ended by the victory of neither, and in which the power of pain so contends with the very nature of the body that neither yields to the other? For in this life, when such a conflict arises, either pain conquers, and death takes away feeling, or nature conquers, and health removes the pain. But in the life beyond, pain remains, on the one hand, to torment, and nature lasts, on the other, to feel it; neither ceases to be, lest the punishment also should cease.

But since these are the ultimate limits of good and evil, of which we should seek to win the former and escape the latter, and since there is a judgement through which good men will pass to the former and bad men to the latter, I will, so far as God may grant, deal with this judgement in the following book.

From On the Trinity

Of Difficulties Concerning the Trinity: In What Manner Three Are One God, and How, Working Indivisibly, They Yet Perform Some Things Severally

Some persons, however, find a difficulty in this faith; when they hear that the Father is God, and the Son God, and the Holy Spirit God, and yet that this Trinity is not three Gods, but one God; and they ask how they are to understand this: especially when it is said that the Trinity works indivisibly in everything that God works, and yet that a certain voice of the Father spoke, which is not the voice of the Son; and that none except the Son was born in the flesh, and suffered, and rose again, and ascended into heaven; and that none except the Holy Spirit came in the form of a dove. They wish to understand how the Trinity uttered that voice which was only of the Father; and how the same Trinity created that flesh in which the Son only was born of the Virgin; and how the very same Trinity itself wrought that form of a dove, in which the Holy Spirit only appeared. Yet, otherwise, the Trinity does not work indivisibly, but the Father does some things, the Son other things, and the Holy Spirit yet others: or else, if they do some things together, some severally, then the Trinity is not indivisible. It is a difficulty, too, to them, in what manner the Holy Spirit is in the Trinity, whom neither the Father nor the Son, nor both, have begotten, although He is the Spirit both of the Father and of the Son. Since, then, men weary us with asking such questions, let us unfold to them, as we are able, whatever wisdom God's gift has bestowed upon our weakness on this subject; neither "let us go on our way with consuming envy." Should we say that we are not accustomed to think about such things, it would not be true; yet if we acknowledge that such subjects commonly dwell in our thoughts, carried away as we are by the love of investigating the truth, then they require of us, by the law of charity, to make known to them what we have herein been able to find out. "Not as though I had already attained, either were already perfect" (for, if the Apostle Paul, how much more must I, who lie far beneath his feet, count myself not to have apprehended!); but, according to my measure, "if I forget those things that are behind, and reach forth unto those things which are before, and press towards the mark for the prize of the high calling," I am requested to disclose so much of the road as I have already passed, and the point to which I have reached, whence the course yet remains to bring me to the end. And those make the request, whom a generous charity compels me to serve. Needs must compel me too, and God will grant that, in supplying them with matter to read, I shall profit myself also; and that, in seeking to reply to their inquiries, I shall myself likewise find that for which I was inquiring. Accordingly, I have undertaken the task, by the bidding and help of the Lord my God, not so much of discoursing with authority respecting things I know already, as of learning those things by piously discoursing of them.

That The Son Is Very God, of the Same Substance With the Father. Not Only the Father, but the Trinity, Is Affirmed to Be Immortal. All Things Are Not From the Father Alone, but Also From the Son. That the Holy Spirit Is Very God, Equal With the Father and the Son

They who have said that our Lord Jesus Christ is not God, or not very God, or not with the Father the One and only God, or not truly immortal because changeable, are proved wrong by the most plain and unanimous voice of divine testimonies; as, for instance, "In the beginning was the Word, and the Word was with God, and the Word was God." For it is plain that we are to take the Word of God to be the only Son of God, of whom it is afterwards said, "And the Word was made flesh, and dwelt among us," on account of that birth of His incarnation, which was wrought in time of the Virgin. But herein is declared, not only that He is God, but also that He is of the same substance with the Father; because, after saying, "And the Word was God," it is said also, "The same was in the beginning with God: all things were made by Him, and without Him was not anything made." Not simply "all things;" but only all things that were *made*, that is, the whole creature. From which it appears clearly, that He Himself was not made, by whom all things were made. And if He was not made, then He is not a creature; but if He is not a creature, then He is of the same substance with the Father. For all substance that is not God is creature; and all that is not creature is God. And if the Son is not of the same substance with the Father, then He is a substance that was made: and if He is a substance that was made, then all things were not made by Him; but "all things were made by Him," therefore He is of one and the same substance with the Father. And so He is not only God, but also very God. And the same John most expressly affirms this in his epistle: "For we know that the Son of God is come, and hath given us an understanding, that we may know the true God, and that we may be in His true Son Jesus Christ. This is the true God, and eternal life."

Hence also it follows by consequence, that the Apostle Paul did not say, "Who alone has immortality," of the Father merely; but of the One and only God, which is the Trinity itself. For that which is itself eternal life is not mortal according to any changeableness; and hence the Son of God, because "He is Eternal Life," is also Himself understood with the Father, where it is said, "Who only hath immortality." For we, too, are made partakers of this eternal life, and become, in our own measure, immortal. But the eternal life itself, of which we are made partakers, is one thing; we ourselves, who, by partaking of it, shall live eternally, are another. For if He had said, "Whom in His own time the Father will show, who is the blessed and only Potentate, the King of kings, and Lord of lords; who only hath immortality;" not even so would it be necessarily understood that the Son is excluded. For neither has the Son separated the Father from Himself, because He Himself, speaking elsewhere with the voice of wisdom (for He Himself is the Wisdom of God), says, "I alone compassed the circuit of heaven." And therefore so much the more is it not necessary that the words, "Who hath immortality," should be understood of the Father alone, omitting the Son; when they are said thus: "That thou keep this commandment without spot, unrebukeable, until the appearing of our Lord Jesus Christ: whom in His own time He will show, who is the blessed and only Potentate, the King of kings, and Lord of lords; who only hath immortality, dwelling in the light which no man can approach unto; whom no man hath seen, nor can see: to whom be honor and power everlasting. Amen." In these words neither is the Father specially named, nor the Son, nor the Holy Spirit; but the blessed and only Potentate, the King of kings, and Lord of lords; that is, the One and only and true God, the Trinity itself.

But perhaps what follows may interfere with this meaning; because it is said, "Whom no man hath seen, nor can see:" although this may also be taken as belonging to Christ according to His divinity, which the Jews did not see, who yet saw and crucified Him in the flesh; whereas His divinity can in no wise be seen by human sight, but is seen with that sight with which they who see are no longer men, but beyond men. Rightly, therefore, is God Himself, the Trinity, understood to be the "blessed and only Potentate," who "shows the coming of our Lord Jesus Christ in His own time." For the words, "Who only hath immortality," are said in the same way as it is said, "Who only doeth wondrous things." And I should be glad to know of whom they take these words to be said. If only of the Father, how then is that true which the Son Himself says, "For what things soever the Father doeth, these also doeth the Son likewise?" Is there any, among wonderful works, more wonderful than to raise up and quicken the dead? Yet the same Son saith, "As the Father raiseth up the dead, and quickeneth them, even so the Son quickeneth whom He will." How, then, does the Father alone "do wondrous things," when these words allow us to understand neither the Father only, nor the Son only, but assuredly the one only true God, that is, the Father, and the Son, and the Holy Spirit?

Also, when the same apostle says, "But to us there is but one God, the Father, of whom are all things, and we in Him: and one Lord Jesus Christ, by whom are all things, and we by Him," who can doubt that he speaks of all things which are created; as does John, when he says, "All things were made by Him"? I ask, therefore, of whom he speaks in another place: "For of Him, and through Him, and in Him, are all things: to whom be glory for ever. Amen." For if of the Father, and the Son, and the Holy Spirit, so as to assign each clause severally to each person: of Him, that is to say, of the Father; through Him, that is to say, through the Son; in Him, that is to say, in the Holy Spirit—it is manifest that the Father, and the Son, and the Holy Spirit is one God, inasmuch as the words continue in the singular number, "To whom be glory for ever." For at the beginning of the passage he does not say, "O the depth of the riches both of the wisdom and knowledge" of the Father, or of the Son, or of the Holy Spirit, but "of the wisdom and knowledge of God!" "How unsearchable are His judgments, and His ways past finding out! For who hath known the mind of the Lord? or who hath been His counsellor? Or who hath first given to Him and it shall be recompensed unto him again? For of Him, and through Him, and in Him, are all things: to whom be glory for ever. Amen." But if they will have this to be understood only of the Father, then in what way are all things by the Father, as is said here; and all things by the son, as where it is said to the Corinthians, "And one Lord Jesus Christ, by whom are all things," and as in the Gospel of John, "All things were made by Him?" For if some things were made by the Father, and some by the Son, then all things were not made by the Father, nor all things by the Son; but if all things were made by the Father, and all things by the Son, then the same things were made by the Father and by the Son. The Son, therefore, is equal with the Father, and the working of the Father and the Son is indivisible. Because if the Father made even the Son, whom certainly the Son Himself did not make, then all things were not made by the Son; but all things *were* made by the Son: therefore He Himself was not made, that with the Father he might make all things that were made. And the apostle has not refrained from using the very word itself, but has said most expressly, "Who, being in the form of God, thought it not robbery to be equal with God;" using here the name of God specially of the Father; as elsewhere, "But the head of Christ is God."

Similar evidence has been collected also concerning the Holy Spirit, of which those who have discussed the subject before ouselves have most fully availed themselves, that He too is God, and not a creature. But if not a creature, then not only God (for men likewise are called gods), but also very God; and therefore absolutely equal with the Father and the Son, and in the unity of the Trinity consubstantial and co-eternal. But that the Holy Spirit is not a creature is made quite plain by that passage above all others, where we are commanded not to serve the creature, but the Creator; not in the sense in which we are commanded to "serve" one another by love, which is in Greek δουλεύειν, but in that in which God alone is served, which is in Greek λατρεύειν. From whence they are called idolaters who tender that service to images which is due to God. For it is this service concerning which it is said, "Thou shalt worship the Lord thy God, and Him only shalt thou serve." For this is found also more distinctly in the Greek Scriptures, which have λατρεύσεις. Now if we are forbidden to serve the creature with such a service, seeing that it is written, "Thou shalt worship the Lord thy God, and Him only shalt thou serve" (and hence, too, the apostle repudiates those who worship and serve the creature more than the Creator), then assuredly the Holy Spirit is not a creature, to whom such a service is paid by all the saints; as says the apostle, "For we are the circumcision, which serve the Spirit of God," which is in the Greek λατρεύοντες. For even most Latin copies also have it thus, "We who serve the Spirit of God;" but all Greek ones, or almost all, have it so. Although in some Latin copies we find, not "We worship the Spirit of God," but, "We worship God in the Spirit." But let those who err in this case, and refuse to give up to the more weighty authority, tell us whether they find this text also varied in the MSS.: "Know ye not that your body is the temple of the Holy Ghost, which is in you, which ye have of God?" Yet what can be more senseless or more profane, than that any one should dare to say that the members of Christ are the temple of one who, in their opinion, is a creature inferior to Christ? For the apostle says in another place, "Your bodies are members of Christ." But if the members of Christ are also the temple of the Holy Spirit, then the Holy Spirit is not a creature; because we must owe to Him, of whom our body is the temple, that service wherewith God only is to be served, which in Greek is called λατρεια. And accordingly the apostle says, "Therefore glorify God in your body."

All Are Sometimes Understood in One Person

But this is said, not on account of any inequality of the Word of God and of the Holy Spirit, but as though the presence of the Son of man with them would be a hindrance to the coming of Him, who was not less, because He did not "empty Himself, taking upon Him the form of a servant," as the Son did. It was necessary, then, that the form of a servant should be taken away from their eyes, because, through gazing upon it, they thought that alone which they saw to be Christ. Hence also is that which is said, "If ye loved me, ye would rejoice because I said, "I go unto the Father; for my Father is greater than I:" that is, on that account it is necessary for me to go to the Father, because, while you see me thus, you hold me to be less than the Father through that which you see; and so, being taken up with the creature and the "fashion" which I have taken upon me, you do not perceive the equality which I have with the Father. Hence, too, is this: "Touch me not; for I am not yet ascended to my Father." For touch, as it were, puts a limit to their conception, and He therefore would not have the thought of the heart, directed towards Himself, to be so limited as that He should be held to be only that which He seemed to be. But the "ascension to the Father" meant, so to appear as He is equal to the Father, that the limit of the sight which sufficeth us might be attained there. Sometimes also it is said of the Son alone, that He himself sufficeth, and the whole reward of our love and longing is held forth as in the sight of Him. For so it is said, "He that hath my commandments, and keepeth them, he it is that loveth me; and he that loveth me shall be loved of my Father; and I will love him, and will manifest myself to him." Pray, because He has not here said, And I will show the Father also to him, has He therefore excluded the Father? On the contrary, because it is true, "I and my Father are one," when the Father is manifested, the Son also, who is in Him, is manifested; and when the Son is manifested, the Father also, who is in Him, is manifested. As, therefore, when it is said, "And I will manifest myself to him," it is understood that He manifests also the Father; so likewise in that which is said, "When He shall have delivered up the kingdom to God, even the Father," it is understood that He does not take it away from Himself; since, when He shall bring believers to the contemplation of God, even the Father, doubtless He will bring them to the contemplation of Himself, who has said, "And I will manifest myself to him." And so, consequently, when Judas had said to Him, "Lord, how is it that Thou wilt manifest Thyself unto us, and not unto the world?" Jesus answered and said to him, "If a man love me, he will keep my words: and my Father will love him, and we will come unto him, and make our abode with him." Behold, that He manifests not only Himself to him by whom He is loved, because He comes to him together with the Father, and abides with him.

Will it perhaps be thought, that when the Father and the Son make their abode with him who loves them, the Holy Spirit is excluded from that abode? What, then, is that which is said above of the Holy Spirit: "Whom the world cannot receive, because it seeth Him not: but ye know Him; for He abideth with you, and is in you"? He, therefore, is not excluded from that abode, of whom it is said, "He abideth with you, and is in you;" unless, perhaps, any one be so senseless as to think, that when the Father and the Son have come that they may make their abode with him who loves them, the Holy Spirit will depart thence, and (as it were) give place to those who are greater. But the Scripture itself meets this carnal idea; for it says a little above: "I will pray the Father, and He shall give you another Comforter, that He may abide with you for ever." He will not therefore depart when the Father and the Son come, but will be in the same abode with them eternally; because neither will He come without them, nor they without Him. But in order to intimate the Trinity, some things are separately affirmed, the Persons being also each severally named; and yet are not to be understood as though the other Persons were excluded, on account of the unity of the same Trinity and the One substance and Godhead of the Father and of the Son and of the Holy Spirit.

BOETHIUS

The son of a Roman consul, Boethius (ca. A.D. *480–524) also became a consul. Unfortunately, he fell out of favor with King Theodoric and was condemned to death. While in prison awaiting his execution, Boethius wrote a dialogue between himself and philosophy. Entitled* The Consolation of Philosophy, *this work drew on Stoic and Neoplatonic wisdom for strength and insight, causing later Christian commentators to question Boethius's theological orthodoxy, despite the fact that many Christian thinkers kept their loyalty to Greek philosophy throughout the entire medieval period. Nonethe-*

less, it remained a powerful source of spiritual succor throughout the Christian Middle Ages.

Boethius did not finish his plan of translating all of Plato and Aristotle into Latin, although he did finish most of Aristotle's logic and the important commentary on Aristotle, the Isagoge of Porphyry. *His definitions of important philosophical terms, such as substance, person, and the problem of universals, made a distinctive and essential contribution to medieval philosophy.*

From The Consolation of Philosophy

IX

"Let it suffice that we have hitherto discovered the form of false felicity, which if thou hast plainly seen, order now requireth that we show thee in what true happiness consisteth." "I see," quoth I, "that neither sufficiency by riches, nor power by kingdoms, nor respect by dignities, nor renown by glory, nor joy can be gotten by pleasures." "Hast thou also understood the causes why it is so?" "Methink I have a little glimpse of them, but I had rather thou wouldst declare them more plainly."

"The reason is manifest, for that which is simple and undivided of itself, is divided by men's error, and is translated from true and perfect to false and unperfect. Thinkest thou that which needeth nothing, to stand in need of power?" "No," quoth I. "Thou sayest well, for if any power in any respect be weak, in this it must necessarily stand in need of help of others." "It is true," quoth I. "Wherefore sufficiency and power have one and the same nature." "So it seemeth." "Now thinkest thou, that which is of this sort ought to be despised, or rather that it is worthy to be respected above all other things?" "There can be no doubt of this," quoth I. "Let us add respect then to sufficiency and power, so that we judge these three to be one." "We must add it if we confess the truth."

"What now," quoth she, "thinkest thou this to be obscure and base, or rather most excellent and famous? Consider whether that which thou has granted to want nothing, to be most potent, and most worthy of honour, may seem to want fame, which it cannot yield itself, and for that cause be in some respect more abject." "I must needs confess," quoth I, "that, being what it is, this is also most famous." "Consequently then we must acknowledge that fame differeth nothing from the former three." We must so," quoth I. "Wherefore that which wanteth nothing, which can perform all things by its own power, which is famous and respected, is it not manifest that it is also most pleasant?" To which I answered: "How such a man should fall into any grief, I can by no means imagine. Wherefore if that which we have said hitherto be true, we must needs confess that he is most joyful and content." And by the same reason it followeth that sufficiency, power, fame, respect, pleasure have indeed divers names, but differ not in substance." "It followeth indeed," quoth I. "This then, which is one and simple by nature, man's wickedness divideth, and while he endeavoureth to obtain part of that which hath no parts, he neither getteth a part, which is none, nor the whole, which he seeketh not after." "How is this?" quoth I. "He who seeketh after riches," quoth she, "to avoid want, taketh no thought for power, he had rather be base and obscure, he depriveth himself even of many natural pleasures that he may not lose the money which he hath gotten. But by this means he attaineth not to sufficiency, whom power forsaketh, whom trouble molesteth, whom baseness maketh abject, whom obscurity overwhelmeth. Again, he that only desireth power, consumeth wealth, despiseth pleasures, and setteth light by honour or glory,

Reprinted by permission of the publishers and The Loeb Classical Library from *The Consolation of Philosophy,* Boethius, trans. by S. J. Tester, Cambridge, Mass.: Harvard University Press, 1973. (Book III, 9–12; pp. 257–263; 267–276; 277–285; 287–293)

which is not potent. But thou seest how many things are wanting to this man also. For sometimes he wanteth necessaries, and is perplexed with anxieties, and being not able to rid himself, ceaseth to be powerful, which was the only thing he aimed at. The like discourse may be made of honours, glory, pleasures. For since every one of these things is the same with the rest, whosoever seeketh for any of them without the rest obtaineth not that which he desireth." "What then?" quoth I. "If one should desire to have them all together, he should wish for the sum of happiness, but shall he find it in these things which we have showed cannot perform what they promise?" "No," quoth I. "Wherefore we must by no means seek for happiness in these things which are thought to afford the several portions of that which is to be desired." "I confess it," quoth I, "and nothing can be more true than this." "Now then," quoth she, "thou hast both the form and causes of false felicity; cast but the eyes of thy mind on the contrary, and thou shalt presently espy true happiness, which we promised to show thee." "This," quoth I, "is evident, even to him that is blind, and thou showedst it a little before, while thou endeavouredst to lay open the causes of the false. For, if I be not deceived, that is true and perfect happiness which maketh a man sufficient, potent, respected, famous, joyful. And that thou mayest know that I understood thee aright, that which can truly perform any one of these because they are all one, I acknowledge to be full and perfect happiness." "O my scholar, I think thee happy by having this opinion, if thou addest this also." "What?" quoth I. "Dost thou imagine that there is any mortal or frail thing which can cause this happy estate?" "I do not," quoth I, "and that hath been so proved by thee, that more cannot be desired." "Wherefore these things seem to afford men the images of the true good, or certain unperfect goods, but they cannot give them the true and perfect good itself." "I am of the same mind," quoth I. "Now then, since thou knowest wherein true happiness consisteth, and what have only a false show of it, it remaineth that thou shouldst learn where thou mayest seek for this which is true." "This is that," quoth I, "which I have long earnestly expected." "But since, as Plato teacheth (in Timaeus), we must implore God's assistance even in our least affairs, what, thinkest thou, must we do now, that we may deserve to find the seat of that sovereign good?" "We must," quoth I, "invocate the Father of all things, without whose remembrance no beginning hath a good foundation." "Thou sayest rightly," quoth she, and withal sung in this sort. . . .

X

Wherefore since thou hast seen what is the form of perfect and imperfect good, now I think we must show in what this perfection of happiness is placed. And inquire first whether there can be any such good extant in the world, as thou has defined; lest, contrary to truth, we be deceived with an empty show of thought. But it cannot be denied that there is some such thing extant which is as it were the fountain of all goodness. For all that is said to be imperfect is so termed for the want it hath of perfection. Whence it followeth that if in any kind we find something imperfect, there must needs be something perfect also in the same kind. For if we take away perfection we cannot so much as devise how there should be any imperfection. For the nature of things began not from that which is defective and not complete, but, proceeding from entire and absolute, falleth into that which is extreme and enfeebled. But *if*, as we showed before, there be a certain imperfect felicity of frail goods, it cannot be doubted but that there is some solid and perfect happiness also." "Thou hast," quoth I, "concluded most firmly and most truly." "Now where this good dwelleth," quoth she, "consider this. The common conceit of men's minds proveth that God the Prince of all things is good. For, since nothing can be imagined better than God, who doubteth but that is good than which is nothing better? And reason doth in such sort demonstrate God to be good that it convinceth Him to be perfectly good. For unless He were so, He could not be the chief of all things. For there would be something better than He, having perfect goodness, which could seem to be of greater antiquity and eminence than He. For it is already manifest that perfect things were before the imperfect. Wherefore, lest our reasoning should have no end, we must confess that the Sovereign God is most full of sovereign and perfect goodness. But we have concluded that perfect goodness is true happiness, wherefore true blessedness must necessarily be placed in the most high God." "I agree," quoth I, "neither can this be any way contradicted." "But I pray thee," quoth she, "see how boldly and inviolably thou approvest that which we said, that the Sovereign God is most full

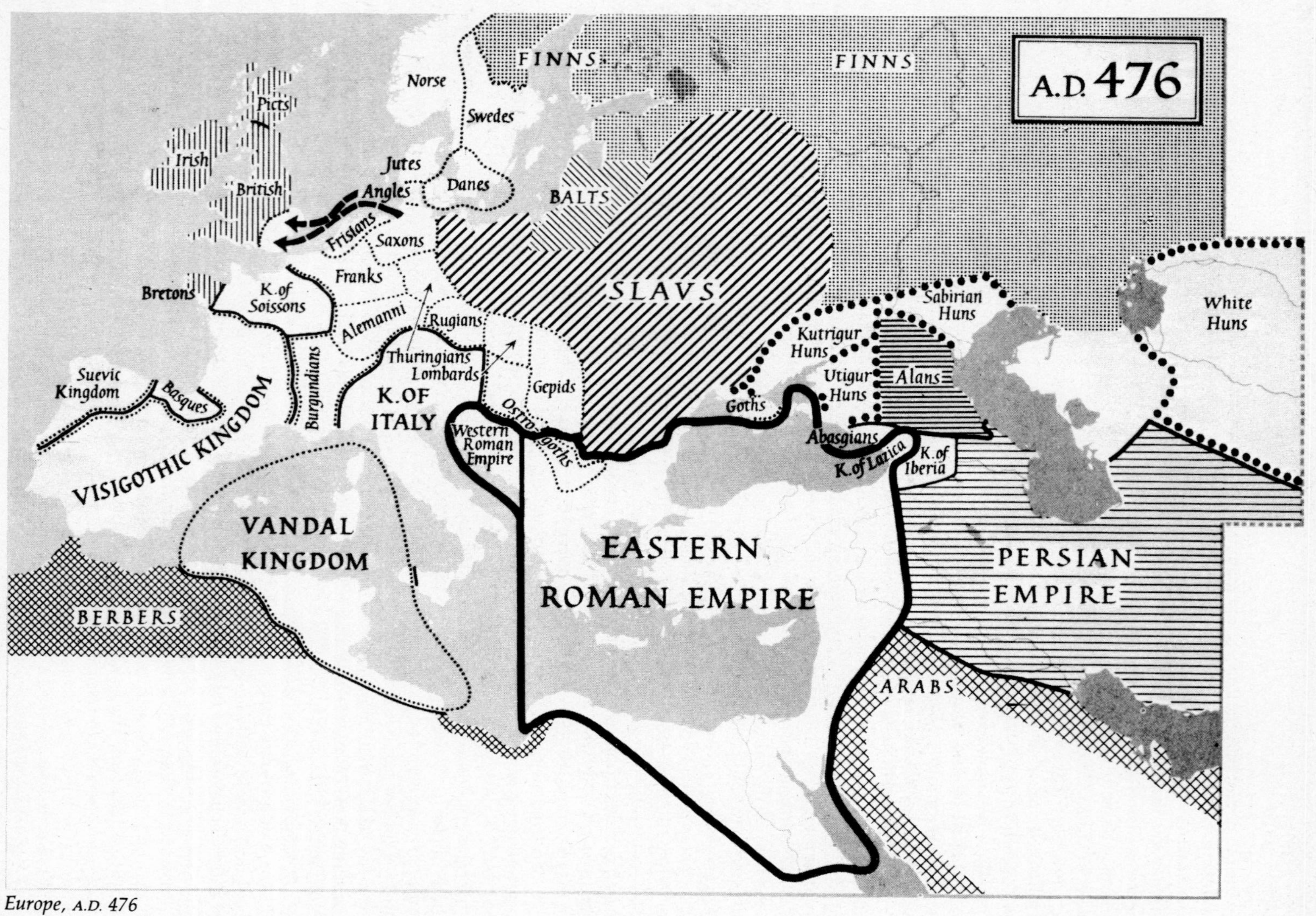
A.D. 476
FINNS
FINNS
Norse
Swedes
Picts
Irish
British
Jutes
Angles
Danes
BALTS
Frisians
Saxons
Franks
SLAVS
Bretons
K. of Soissons
Alemanni
Rugians
Thuringians
Lombards
Burgundians
K. OF ITALY
Gepids
Ostrogoths
Western Roman Empire
Suevic Kingdom
Basques
VISIGOTHIC KINGDOM
VANDAL KINGDOM
BERBERS
EASTERN ROMAN EMPIRE
Goths
Kutrigur Huns
Utigur Huns
Sabirian Huns
Alans
Abasgians
K. of Lazica
K. of Iberia
White Huns
PERSIAN EMPIRE
ARABS

Europe, A.D. 476

of sovereign goodness." "How?" quoth I. "That thou presumest not that this Father of all things hath either received from others that sovereign good with which He is said to be replenished, or hath it naturally in such sort that thou shouldst think that the substance of the blessedness which is had, and of God who hath it, were diverse. For if thou thinkest that He had it from others, thou mayest also infer that he who gave it was better than the receiver. But we most worthily confess that He is the most excellent of all things. And if He hath it by nature, but as a diverse thing, since we speak of God the Prince of all things, let him that can, invent who united these diverse things. Finally, that which is different from anything, is not that from which it is understood to differ. Wherefore that which is naturally different from the sovereign good, is not the sovereign good itself. Which it were impious to think of God, than whom, we know certainly, nothing is better. For doubtless the nature of nothing can be better than the beginning of it. Wherefore I may most truly conclude that which is the beginning of all things to be also in His own substance the chiefest good." "Most rightly," quoth I. "But it is granted that the chiefest good is blessedness?" "It is," quoth I. "Wherefore," quoth she, "we must needs confess that blessedness itself is God." "I can neither contradict," quoth I, "thy former propositions, and I see this illation followeth from them."

"Consider," saith she, "if the same be not more firmly proved hence, because there cannot be two chief goods, the one different from the other. For it is manifest that of those goods which differ, the one is not the other, wherefore neither of them can be perfect, wanting the other. But manifestly that which is not perfect, is not the chiefest, wherefore the chief goods cannot be diverse. Now we have proved that both blessedness and God are the chiefest good, wherefore that must needs be the highest blessedness which is the highest divinity." "There can be nothing," quoth I, "concluded more truly than this, nor more firmly in arguing, nor more worthy God himself." "Upon this then," quoth she, "as the geometricians are wont, out of their propositions which they have demonstrated, to infer something which they call *porismata* (deductions) so will I give thee as it were a *corollarium*. For since that men are made blessed by the obtaining of blessedness, and blessedness is nothing else but divinity, it is manifest that men are made blessed by the obtaining of divinity. And as men are made just by the obtaining of justice, and wise by the obtaining of wisdom, so they who obtain divinity must needs in like manner become gods. Wherefore everyone that is blessed is a god, but by nature there is only one God; but there may be many by participation." "This is," quoth I, "an excellent and precious *porisma* or *corollarium*." But there is nothing more excellent than that which reason persuades us to add." "What?" quoth I.

"Since," quoth she, "blessedness seemeth to contain many things, whether do they all concur as divers parts to the composition of one entire body of blessedness, or doth some one of them form the substance of blessedness to which the rest are to be referred?" "I desire," quoth I, "that thou wouldst declare this point, by the enumeration of the particulars." "Do we not think," quoth she, "that blessedness is good?" "Yea, the chiefest good," quoth I. "Thou mayest," quoth she, "add this to them all. For blessedness is accounted the chiefest sufficiency, the chiefest power, respect, fame, and pleasure. What then? Are all these—sufficiency, power, and the rest—the good, in the sense that they are members of it, or rather are they referred to good as to the head?" I understand," quoth I, "what thou proposest, but I desire to hear what thou concludest." "This is the decision of this matter. If all these were members of blessedness, they should differ one from another. For this is the nature of parts, that being divers they compose one body. But we have proved that all these are one and the same thing. Wherefore they are no members, otherwise blessedness should be compacted of one member, which cannot be." "There is no doubt of this," quoth I, "but I expect that which is behind." "It is manifest that the rest are to be referred to goodness; for sufficiency is desired, because it is esteemed good, and likewise power, because that likewise is thought to be good. And we may conjecture the same of respect, fame, and pleasure. Wherefore goodness is the sum and cause of all that is desired. For that which is neither good indeed, nor beareth any show of goodness, can by no means be sought after. And contrariwise those things which are not good of their own nature, yet, if they seem such, are desired as if they were truly good. So that the sum, origin, and cause of all that is sought after is rightly thought to be goodness. And that on account of which a thing is sought, seemeth to be the chief object of desire. As if one would ride for his health, he doth not so much desire the motion of riding, as the effect of health. Wherefore, since all things are desired in respect of goodness, they are not so much wished for as goodness itself. But we granted that to be blessedness for which other things are desired, wherefore in like manner only blessedness is sought after; by which it plainly appeareth, that goodness and blessedness have one and the self-same substance." "I see not how any man can dissent." "But we have showed that God and true blessedness are one and the self-same thing." "It is so," quoth I. "We may then securely conclude that the substance of God consisteth in nothing else but in goodness."

XI

"I consent," quoth I, "for all is grounded upon most firm reasons." "But what account wilt thou make," quoth she, "to know what goodness itself is?" "I will esteem it infinitely," quoth I, "because by this means I shall come to know God also, who is nothing else but goodness." "I will conclude this," quoth she, "most certainly, if those things be not denied which I have already proved." "They shall not," quoth I. "Have we not proved," quoth she, "that those things which are desired of many, are not true and perfect goods, because they differ one from another and, being separated, cannot cause complete and absolute goodness, which is only found when they are united as it were into one form and causality, that the same may be sufficiency, power, respect, fame, and pleasure? And except they be all one and the same thing, that they have nothing worth the desiring?" "It hath been proved," quoth I, "neither can it be any way doubted of." "Those things, then, which, when they differ, are not good and when they are one, become good, are they not made good by obtaining unity?" "So methink," quoth I. "But dost thou grant that all that is good is good by partaking goodness?" "It is so." "Thou must grant then likewise that unity and goodness are the same. For those things have the same substance, which naturally have not diverse effects." "I cannot deny it," quoth I. "Knowest thou then," quoth she, "that everything that is doth so long remain and subsist as it is one, and perisheth and is dissolved so soon as it ceaseth to be one?" "How?" "As in living creatures," quoth she, "so long as the body and soul remain united, the living creature remaineth. But when this unity is dissolved by their separation, it is manifest that it perisheth, and is no longer a living creature. The body also itself, so long as it remaineth in one form by the conjunction of the parts, appeareth the likeness of a man. But if the members of the body, being separated and sundered, have lost their unity, it is no longer the same. And in like manner it will be manifest to him that will descend to other particulars, that everything continueth so long as it is one, and perisheth when it loseth unity." "Considering more particulars, I find it to be no otherwise." "Is there anything," quoth she, "that in the course of nature, leaving the desire of being, seeketh to come to destruction and corruption?" "If," quoth I, "I consider living creatures which have any nature to will and nill, I find nothing that without extern compulsion forsake the intention to remain, and of their own accord hasten to destruction. For every living creature laboureth to preserve his health and escheweth death and detriment. But what I should think of herbs, and trees, and of all things without life, I am altogether doubtful."

"But there is no cause why thou shouldst doubt of this, if thou considerest first that herbs and trees grow in places agreeable to their nature, where, so much as their constitution permitteth, they cannot soon wither and perish. For some grow in fields, other upon hills, some in fenny, other in stony places, and the barren sands are fertile for some, which if thou wouldst transplant into other places they die. But nature giveth every one that which is fitting, and striveth to keep them from decaying so long as they can remain. What should I tell thee, if all of them, as it were thrusting their head into the ground, draw nourishment by their roots, and convey substance and bark by the inward pith? What, that always the softest, as the pith, is placed within, and is covered without by the strength of the wood, and last of all the bark is exposed to the weather, as being best able to bear it off? And how great is the diligence of nature that all things may continue by the multiplication of seed; all which who knoweth not to be, as it were, certain engines, not only to remain for a time, but successively in a manner to endure for ever? Those things also which are thought to be without all life, doth not every one in like manner desire that which appertaineth to their own good? For why doth levity lift up flames, or heaviness weigh down the earth, but because these places and motions are convenient for them? And that which is agreeable to everything conserveth it, as that which is opposite causeth corruption. Likewise those things which are hard, as stones, stick most firmly to their parts, and make great resistance to any dissolution. And liquid things, as air and water, are indeed easily divided, but do easily also join again. And fire flieth all division. Neither do we now treat of the voluntary motions of the understanding soul, but only of natural operations. Of which sort is, to digest that which we have eaten, without thinking of it, to breathe in our sleep not thinking what we do. For even in living creatures the love of life proceedeth not from the will of the soul, but from the principles of nature. For the will many times embraceth death upon urgent occasions, which nature abhorreth; and contrariwise the act of generation, by which alone the continuance of mortal things is maintained, is sometimes bridled by the will, though nature doth always desire it. So true it is that this self-love proceedeth not from any voluntary motion, but from natural intention. For providence gave to her creatures this as the greatest cause of continuance, that they naturally desire to continue so long as they may, wherefore there is no cause why thou shouldst any way doubt that all things which are desire naturally stability of remaining, and eschew corruption."

"I confess," quoth I, "that I now see undoubtedly that which before seemed very doubtful." "Now that," quoth she, "which desireth to continue and remain seeketh to have unity. For if this be taken away, being itself cannot remain." "It is true," quoth I. "All things then," quoth she, "desire unity." I granted it to be so. "But we have showed that unity is the same as goodness." "You have indeed." "All things then desire goodness, which thou mayest define thus: Goodness is that which is desired of all things." "There can be nothing imagined more true. For either all things have reference to no one principle and, being destitute as it were of one head, shall be in confusion without any ruler: or if there be anything to which all things hasten, that must be the chiefest of all goods." "I rejoice greatly O scholar," quoth she, "for thou hast fixed in thy mind the very mark of verity. But in this thou hast discovered that which a little before thou saidest thou wert ignorant of." "What is that?" quoth I. "What the end of all things is," quoth she. "For certainly it is that which is desired of all things, which since we have concluded to be goodness, we must also confess that goodness is the end of all things."

XII

Then I said that I did very well like of Plato's doctrine, for she had brought these things to my remembrance now the second time, first, because I lost their memory by the contagion of my body, and after when I was oppressed with the burden of grief. "If," quoth she, "thou reflectest upon that which heretofore hath been granted, thou wilt not be far from remembering that which in the beginning thou confessedst thyself to be ignorant of." "What?" quoth I. "By what government," quoth she, "the world is ruled." "I remember," quoth I, "that I did confess my ignorance, but though I foresee what thou wilt say, yet I desire to hear it more plainly from thyself." "Thou thoughtest a little before that it was not to be doubted that this world is governed by God." "Neither do I think now," quoth I, "neither will I ever think, that it is to be doubted of, and I will briefly explicate the reasons which move me to think so. This world could never have been compacted of so many divers and contrary parts, unless there were One that doth unite these so different things; and this disagreeing diversity of natures being united would separate and divide this concord, unless there were One that holdeth together that which He united. Neither would the course of nature continue so certain, nor would the different parts hold so well-ordered motions in due places, times, causality, spaces and qualities, unless there were One who, Himself remaining quiet, disposeth and ordereth this variety of motions. This, whatsoever it be, by which things created continue and are moved, I call God a name which all men use."

"Since," quoth she, "thou art of this mind, I think with little labour thou mayest be capable of felicity, and return to thy country in safety. But let us consider what we proposed. Have we not placed sufficiency in happiness, and granted that God is blessedness itself?" "Yes truly." "Wherefore," quoth she, "He will need no outward helps to govern the world, otherwise, if He needed anything, He had not full sufficiency." "That," quoth I, "must necessarily be so." "Wherefore He disposeth all things by Himself." "No doubt He doth," quoth I. "But it hath been proved that God is goodness itself." "I remember it very well," quoth I. "Then He disposeth all things by goodness: since He governeth all things by Himself, whom we have granted to be goodness. And this is as it were the helm and rudder by which the frame of the world is kept steadfast and uncorrupted." "I most willingly agree," quoth I, "and I foresaw a little before, though only with a slender guess, that thou wouldst conclude this." "I believe thee," quoth she, "for now I suppose thou lookest more watchfully about thee to discern the truth. But that which I shall say is no less manifest." "What?" quoth I. "Since that God is deservedly thought to govern all things with the helm of goodness, and all these things likewise, as I have showed, hasten to goodness with their natural contention, can there be any doubt made but that they are governed willingly, and that they frame themselves of their own accord to their disposer's beck, as agreeable and conformable to their ruler?" "It must needs be so," quoth I, "neither would it seem an happy government, if it were an imposed yoke, not a desired health." "There is nothing then which, following nature, endeavoureth to resist God." "Nothing," quoth I. "What if anything doth endeavour," quoth she, "can anything prevail against Him, whom we have granted to be most powerful by reason of His blessedness?" "No doubt," quoth I, "nothing could prevail." "Wherefore there is nothing which either will or can resist this sovereign goodness." "I think not," quoth I. "It is then the sovereign goodness which governeth all things strongly, and disposeth them sweetly." "How much," quoth I, "doth not only the reason which thou allegest, but much more the very words which thou usest, delight me, that folly which so much vexed me may at length be ashamed of herself."

"Thou hast heard in the poets' fables," quoth she, "how the giants provoked heaven, but this benign fortitude put them also down, as they deserved. But wilt thou have our arguments contend together? Perhaps by this clash there will fly out some beautiful spark of truth." "As it pleaseth thee," quoth I. "No man can doubt," quoth she, "but that God is almighty." "No man," quoth I, "that is well in his wits." "But," quoth she, "there is nothing that He who is almighty cannot do." "Nothing," quoth I, "Can God do evil?" "No," quoth I. "Wherefore," quoth she, "evil is nothing, since He cannot do it who can do anything." "Dost thou mock me," quoth I, "making with thy reasons an inextricable labyrinth, because thou dost now go in where thou meanest to go out again, and after go out, where thou camest in, or dost thou frame a wonderful circle of the simplicity of God? For a little before taking thy beginning from blessedness, thou affirmedst that to be the chiefest good which thou saidst was placed in God, and likewise thou provedst, that God Himself is the chiefest good and full happiness, out of which thou madest me a present of that inference, that no man shall be happy unless he be also a God. Again thou toldest me that the form of goodness is the substance of God and of blessedness, and that unity is the same with goodness, because it is desired by the nature of all things; thou didst also dispute that God governeth the whole world with the helm of goodness, and that all things obey willingly, and that there is no nature of evil, and thou didst explicate all these things with no foreign or far-fetched proofs, but with those which were proper and drawn from inward principles, the one confirming the other."

"We neither play nor mock," quoth she, "and we have finished the greatest matter that can be by the assistance of God, whose aid we implored in the beginning. For such is the form of the Divine substance that it is neither divided into outward things, nor receiveth any such into itself, but as Parmenides saith of it:

> In a body like a sphere well-rounded on all
> sides.

it doth roll about the moving orb of things, while it keepeth itself unmovable. And if we have used no far-fetched reasons, but such as were placed within the compass of the matter we handled, thou hast no cause to marvel, since thou hast learned in Plato's school that our speeches must be like and as it were akin to the things we speak of."

BENEDICT

Benedict (ca. A.D. *480–ca. 547) was born in Norcia, Italy. After a period of study in Rome, he went to Subiaco to live as a hermit. Subsequently, he founded an order of monks known as the Benedictines. He later founded a monastery at Monte Cassino in Italy and wrote "The Rule of St. Benedict," which was to become the source of order and purpose in monastic life until modern times. Its importance must not be underestimated, as monastic life was itself to be a major organizing principle in the development of medieval culture after the collapse of the Roman Empire. The daily life of the monastic orders was a prime factor in the acculturation of the nomadic people who made their way into the crumbling frontiers of the European region of the Roman Empire. The monks bequeathed order, a religious liturgy, and a theological and philosophical ethic to the development of medieval culture. The fundamental motto of the Benedictines, evident in the following selection from "The Rule," was to pray and to work* (ora et labora).

From The Rule of St. Benedict

Prologue. . . . We are about to found, therefore, a school for the Lord's service; in the organization of which we trust that we shall ordain nothing severe and nothing burdensome. But even if, the demands of justice dictating it, something a little irksome shall be the result, for the purpose of amending vices or preserving charity—thou shalt not therefore, struck by fear, flee the way of salvation, which can not be entered upon except through a narrow entrance. But as one's way of life and one's faith progresses, the heart becomes broadened, and, with the unutterable sweetness of love, the way of the mandates of the Lord is traversed. Thus, never departing from His guidance, continuing in the monastery in His teaching until death, through patience we are made partakers in Christ's passion, in order that we may merit to be companions in His kingdom.

Concerning the kinds of monks and their manner of living. It is manifest that there are four kinds of monks. The cenobites are the first kind; that is, those living in a monastery, serving under a rule or an abbot. Then the second kind is that of the anchorites; that is, the hermits—those who, not by the new fervour of a conversion but by the long probation of life in a monastery, have learned to fight against the devil, having already been taught by the solace of many. They, having been well prepared in the army of brothers for the solitary fight of the hermit, being secure now without the consolation of another, are able, God helping them, to fight with their own

Upper Cover of the Lindau Gospels (A.D. 870). The earliest form of a book (as distinct from a papyrus or tablet) was known as a codex, which was often brilliantly illustrated in an art form now mostly ignored. (The Pierpont Morgan Library)

From "The Rule of St. Benedict," trans. E. F. Henderson, *Select Historical Documents of the Middle Ages* (London: George Bell and Sons, 1896); pp. 274–314. (Selected passages)

hand or arm against the vices of the flesh or of their thoughts.

But a third very bad kind of monks are the sarabites, approved by no rule, experience being their teacher, as with the gold which is tried in the furnace. But, softened after the manner of lead, keeping faith with the world by their works, they are known through their tonsure to lie to God. These being shut up by twos or threes, or, indeed, alone, without a shepherd, not in the Lord's but in their own sheepfolds—their law is the satisfaction of their desires. For whatever they think good or choice, this they call holy; and what they do not wish, this they consider unlawful. But the fourth kind of monks is the kind which is called gyratory. During their whole life they are guests, for three or four days at a time, in the cells of the different monasteries, throughout the various provinces; always wandering and never stationary, given over to the service of their own pleasures and the joys of the palate, and in every way worse than the sarabites. Concerning the most wretched way of living of all such monks it is better to be silent than to speak. These things therefore being omitted, let us proceed, with the aid of God, to treat of the best kind, the cenobites.

What the Abbot should be like. An abbot who is worthy to preside over a monastery ought always to remember what he is called, and carry out with his deeds the name of a Superior. For he is believed to be Christ's representative, since he is called by His name, the apostle saying: "Ye have received the spirit of adoption of sons, whereby we call Abba, Father." And so the abbot should not—grant that he may not—teach, or decree, or order, any thing apart from the precept of the Lord; but his order or teaching should be sprinkled with the ferment of divine justice in the minds of his disciples. Let the abbot always be mindful that, at the tremendous judgment of God, both things will be weighed in the balance: his teaching and the obedience of his disciples. And let the abbot know that whatever the father of the family finds of less utility among the sheep is laid to the fault of the shepherd. Only in a case where the whole diligence of their pastor shall have been bestowed on an unruly and disobedient flock, and his whole care given to their morbid actions, shall that pastor, absolved in the judgment of the Lord, be free to say to the Lord with the prophet: "I have not hid Thy righteousness within my heart, I have declared Thy faithfulness and Thy salvation, but they despising have scorned me." And then at length let the punishment for the disobedient sheep under his care be death itself prevailing against them. Therefore, when anyone receives the name of abbot, he ought to rule over his disciples with a double teaching; that is, let him show forth all good and holy things by deeds more than by words. So that to ready disciples he may propound the mandates of God in words; but, to the hard-hearted and the more simple-minded, he may show forth the divine precepts by his deeds. But as to all the things that he has taught to his disciples to be wrong, he shall show by his deeds that they are not to be done; lest, preaching to others, he himself shall be found worthy of blame, and lest God may say at some time to him a sinner: "What hast thou to do to declare my statutes or that thou should'st take my covenant in thy mouth. Seeing that thou hatest instruction and casteth my words behind thee; and why beholdest thou the mote that is in thy brother's eye, but considerest not the beam that is in thine own eye?" He shall make no distinction of persons in the monastery. One shall not be more cherished than another, unless it be the one whom he finds excelling in good works or in obedience. A free-born man shall not be preferred to one coming from servitude, unless there be some other reasonable cause. But if, justice demanding that it should be thus, it seems good to the abbot, he shall do this no matter what the rank shall be. But otherwise they shall keep their own places; for whether we be bond or free we are all one in Christ; and, under one God, we perform an equal service of subjection; for God is no respecter of persons. Only in this way is a distinction made by Him concerning us: if we are found humble and surpassing others in good works. Therefore let him (the abbot) have equal charity for all: let the same discipline be administered in all cases according to merit. In his teaching indeed the abbot ought always to observe that form laid down by the apostle when he says: "reprove, rebuke, exhort." That is, mixing seasons with seasons, blandishments with terrors, let him display the feeling of a severe yet devoted master. He should, namely, rebuke more severely the unruly and the turbulent. The obedient, moreover, and the gentle and the patient, he should exhort, that they may progress to higher things. But the negligent and scorners, we warn him to admonish and reprove. Nor let him conceal the sins of the erring: but, in order that he may prevail, let him pluck them out by the roots as soon as they begin to spring up; being mindful of the danger of Eli the priest of Shiloh. And the more honest and intelligent minds, indeed, let him rebuke with words, with a first or second admonition; but the wicked and the hard-hearted and the proud, or the disobedient, let him restrain at the very beginning of their sin by castigation of the body, as it were, with whips: knowing that it is written: "A fool is not bettered by words." And again: "Strike thy son with the rod and thou shalt deliver his soul from death." The abbot ought always to remember what he is, to remember what he is called, and to know that from him to whom more is committed, the more is demanded. And let him know what a difficult and arduous thing he has undertaken—to rule the soul and aid the morals of many. And in one case indeed with blandishments, in another with rebukes, in another with persuasion—according to the quality or intelligence of each one—he shall so conform and adapt himself to all, that not only shall he not suffer detriment to come to the flock committed to him, but shall rejoice in the increase of a good flock. Above all things, let him not, dissimulating or undervaluing the safety of the souls committed to him, give more heed to transitory and earthly and passing things: but let him always reflect that he has undertaken to rule souls for which he is to render account. And, lest perchance he enter into strife for a lesser matter, let him remember that it is written: "Seek ye first the kingdom of God and His righteousness; and all these things shall be added unto you." And again: "They that fear Him shall lack nothing." And let him know that he who undertakes to rule souls must prepare to render account. And, whatever number of brothers he knows that he has under his care, let him know for certain that at the day of judgment he shall render account to God for all their souls; his own soul without doubt being included. And thus, always fearing the future interrogation of the shepherd concerning the flocks entrusted to him, while keeping free from foreign interests he is rendered careful for his own. And when, by his admonitions, he administers correction to others, he is himself cleansed from his vices.

About calling in the brethren to take council. As often as anything especial is to be done in the monastery, the abbot shall call together the whole congregation, and shall himself explain the question at issue. And, having heard the advice of the brethren, he shall think it over by himself, and shall do what he considers most advantageous. And for this reason, moreover, we have said that all ought to be called to take counsel: because often it is to a younger person that God reveals what is best. The brethren, moreover, with all subjection of humility, ought so to give their advice, that they do not presume boldly to defend what seems good to them; but it should rather depend on the judgment of the abbot; so that whatever he decided to be the more salutary, they should all agree to it. But even as it behooves the disciples to obey the master, so it is fitting that he should providently and justly arrange all matters. In all things, indeed, let all follow the Rule as their guide; and let no one rashly deviate from it. Let no one in the monastery follow the inclination of his own heart; and let no one boldly presume to dispute with his abbot, within or without the monastery. But, if he should so presume, let him be subject to the discipline of the Rule. The abbot, on the other hand, shall do all things fearing the Lord and observing the Rule; knowing that he, without a doubt, shall have to render account to God as to a most impartial judge, for all his decisions. But if any lesser matters for the good of the monastery are to be decided upon, he shall employ the counsel of the elder members alone, since it is written: "Do all things with counsel, and after it is done thou wilt not repent." . . .

Concerning obedience. The first grade of humility is obedience without delay. This becomes those who, on account of the holy service which they have professed, or on account of the fear of hell or the glory of eternal life consider nothing dearer to them than Christ: so that, so soon as anything is commanded by their superior, they may not know how to suffer delay in doing it, even as if it were a divine command. Concerning whom the Lord said: "As soon as he heard of me he obeyed me." And again he said to the learned men: "He who heareth you heareth me." Therefore let all such, straightway leaving their own affairs and giving up their own will, with unoccupied hands and leaving incomplete what they were doing—the foot of obedience being foremost—follow with their deeds the voice of him who orders. And, as it were, in the same moment, let the aforesaid command of the master and the perfected work of the disciple—both together in the swiftness of the fear of God—be called into being by those who are possessed with a desire of advancing to eternal life. And therefore let them seize the narrow way of which the Lord says: "Narrow is the way which leadeth unto life." Thus, not living according to their own judgment nor obeying their own desires and pleasures, but walking under another's judgment and command, passing their time in monasteries, let them desire an abbot to rule over them. Without doubt all such live up to that precept of the Lord in which he says: "I am not come to do My own will but the will of Him that sent Me." . . .

Concerning humility. . . . The sixth grade of humility is, that a monk be contented with all lowliness or extremity, and consider himself, with regard to everything which is enjoined on him, as a poor and unworthy workman; saying to himself with the prophet: "I was reduced to nothing and was ignorant; I was made as the cattle before thee, and I am always with thee." The seventh grade of humility is, not only that he, with his tongue, pronounce himself viler and more worthless than all; but that he also believe it in the innermost workings of his heart; humbling himself. . . . The eighth degree of humility is that a monk do nothing except what the common rule of the monastery, or the example of his elders, urges him to do. The ninth degree of humility is that a monk restrain his tongue from speaking; and, keeping silence, do not speak until he is spoken to. The tenth grade of humility is that he be not ready, and easily inclined, to laugh. . . . The eleventh grade of humility is that a monk, when he speaks, speak slowly and without laughter, humbly with gravity, using few and reasonable words; and that he be not loud of voice. . . . The twelfth grade of humility is that a monk shall, not only with his heart but also with his body, always show humility to all who see him: that is when at work, in the oratory, in the monastery, in the garden, on the road, in the fields. And everywhere, sitting or walking or standing, let him always be with head inclined, his looks fixed upon the ground; remembering every hour that he is guilty of his sins. Let him think that he is already being presented before the tremendous judgment of God, saying always to himself in his heart what that publican of the gospel, fixing his eyes on the earth, said: "Lord I am not worthy, I a sinner, so much as to lift up mine eyes unto Heaven.". . .

How the monks shall sleep. They shall sleep separately in separate beds. They shall receive positions for their beds, after the manner of their characters, according to the dispensation of their abbot. If it can be done, they shall all sleep in one place. If, however, their number do not permit it, they shall rest by tens or twenties, with elders who will concern themselves about them. A candle shall always be burning in that same cell until early in the morning. They shall sleep clothed, and girt with belts or with ropes; and they shall not have their knives at their sides while they sleep, lest perchance in a dream they should wound the sleepers. And let the monks be always on the alert; and, when the signal is given, rising without delay, let them hasten to mutually prepare themselves for the service of God—with all gravity and modesty, however. The younger brothers shall not have beds by themselves, but interpersed among those of the elder ones. And when they rise for the service of God, they shall exhort each other mutually with moderation, on account of the excuses that those who are sleepy are inclined to make. . . .

What care the abbot should exercise with regard to the excommunicated. With all solicitude the abbot shall exercise care with regard to delinquent brothers: "They that be whole need not a physician, but they that are sick." And therefore he ought to use every means, as a wise physician, to send in as it were secret consolers—that is, wise elder brothers who, as it were secretly, shall console the wavering brother and lead him to the atonement of humility. And they shall comfort him lest he be swallowed up by overmuch sorrow. On the contrary, as the same apostle says, charity shall be confirmed in him, and he shall be prayed for by all. For the abbot should greatly exert his solicitude, and take care with all sagacity and industry, lest he lose any of the sheep entrusted to him. For he should know that he has undertaken the care of weak souls, not the tyranny over sound ones. And he shall fear the threat of the prophet through whom the Lord says: "Ye did take that which ye saw to be strong, and that which was weak ye did cast out." And let him imitate the pious example of the good Shepherd, who, leaving the ninety and nine sheep upon the mountains, went out to seek the one sheep that had gone astray: and He had such compassion upon its infirmity, that He deigned to place it upon His sacred shoulders, and thus to carry it back to the flock. . . .

Whether the monks should have anything of their own. More than anything else is this special vice to be cut off root and branch from the monastery, that one should presume to give or receive anything without the order of the abbot, or should have anything of his own. He should have absolutely not anything:

neither a book, nor tablets, nor a pen—nothing at all. For indeed it is not allowed to the monks to have their own bodies or wills in their own power. But all things necessary they must expect from the Father of the monastery; nor is it allowable to have anything which the abbot did not give or permit. All things shall be common to all, as it is written: "Let not any man presume or call anything his own." But if any one shall have been discovered delighting in this most evil vice: being warned once again, if he do not amend, let him be subjected to punishment.

Whether all ought to receive necessaries equally. As it is written: "It was divided among them singly, according as each had need": whereby we do not say—far from it—that there should be an excepting of persons, but a consideration for infirmities. Wherefore he who needs less, let him thank God and not be dismayed; but he who needs more, let him be humiliated on account of his infirmity, and not exalted on account of the mercy that is shown him. And thus all members will be in peace. Above all, let not the evil of murmuring appear, for any cause, through any word or sign whatever. But, if such a murmurer is discovered, he shall be subjected to stricter discipline. . . .

Although human nature itself is prone to have pity for these ages—that is, old age and infancy—nevertheless the authority of the Rule also has regard for them. Their weakness shall always be considered, and in the matter of food, the strict tenor of the Rule shall by no means be observed, as far as they are concerned; but they shall be treated with pious consideration, and may anticipate the canonical hours. . . .

We believe, moreover, that, for the daily refection of the sixth as well as of the ninth hour, two cooked dishes, on account of the infirmities of the different ones, are enough for all tables: so that whoever, perchance, can not eat of one may partake of the other. Therefore let two cooked dishes suffice for all the brothers: and, if it is possible to obtain apples or growing vegetables, a third may be added. One full pound of bread shall suffice for a day, whether there be one refection, or a breakfast and a supper. But if they are going to have supper, the third part of that same pound shall be reserved by the cellarer, to be given back to those who are about to sup. But if, perchance, some greater labour shall have been performed, it shall be in the will and the power of the abbot, if it is expedient, to increase anything; surfeiting above all things being guarded against, so that indigestion may never seize a monk: for nothing is so contrary to every Christian as surfeiting. . . . But the eating of the flesh of quadrupeds shall be abstained from altogether by every one, excepting alone the weak and the sick. . . .

Concerning the daily manual labour. Idleness is the enemy of the soul. And therefore, at fixed times, the brothers ought to be occupied in manual labours; and again, at fixed times, in sacred reading. Therefore we believe that, according to this disposition, both seasons ought to be arranged: so that, from Easter until the Calends of October, going out early, from the first until the fourth hour they shall do what labour may be necessary. Moreover, from the fourth hour until about the sixth, they shall be free for reading. After the meal of the sixth hour, moreover, rising from table, they shall rest in their beds with all silence; or, perchance, he that wishes to read may so read to himself that he do not disturb another. And the nona (the second meal) shall be gone through with more moderately about the middle of the eighth hour; and again they shall work at what is to be done until Vespers. But, if the exigency or poverty of the place demands that they be occupied by themselves in picking fruits, they shall not be dismayed: for then they are truly monks if they live by the labours of their hands; as did also our fathers and the apostles. Let all things be done with moderation, however, on account of the faint-hearted. From the Calends of October, moreover, until the beginning of Lent they shall be free for reading until the second full hour. At the second hour the tertia (morning service) shall be held, and all shall labour at the task which is enjoined upon them until the ninth. The first signal, moreover, of the ninth hour having been given, they shall each one leave off his work: and be ready when the second signal strikes. Moreover after the refection they shall be free for their readings or for psalms. But in the days of Lent, from dawn until the third full hour, they shall be free for their readings; and, until the tenth full hour, they shall do the labour that is enjoined on them. In which days of Lent they shall all receive separate books from the library: which they shall read entirely through in order. These books are to be given out on the first day of Lent. Above all there shall certainly be appointed one or two elders, who shall go round the monastery at the hours in which the brothers are engaged in reading, and see to it that no troublesome brother chance to be found who is open to idleness and trifling, and is not intent on his reading; being not only of no use to himself, but also stirring up others. If such a one—may it not happen—be found, he shall be admonished once and a second time. If he do not amend, he shall be subject under the Rule to such punishment that the others may have fear. Nor shall brother join brother at unsuitable hours. Moreover on Sunday all shall engage in reading: excepting those who are deputed to various duties. But if anyone be so negligent and lazy that he will not or can not read, some task shall be imposed upon him which he can do; so that he be not idle. On feeble or delicate brothers such a labour or art is to be imposed, that they shall neither be idle, nor shall they be so oppressed by the violence of labour as to be driven to take flight. Their weakness is to be taken into consideration by the abbot.

Although at all times the life of the monk should be such as though Lent were being observed: nevertheless, since few have that virtue, we urge that, on those said days of Lent, he shall keep his life in all purity; and likewise wipe out, in those holy days, the negligencies of other times. This is then worthily done if we refrain from all vices, if we devote ourselves to prayer with weeping, to reading and compunction of heart, and to abstinence. Therefore, on these days, let us add of ourselves something to the ordinary amount of our service: special prayers, abstinence from food and drink; so that each one, over and above the amount allotted to him, shall offer of his own will something to God with rejoicing of the Holy Spirit. That is, he shall restrict his body in food, drink, sleep, talkativeness, and merry-making; and, with the joy of a spiritual desire, shall await the holy Easter. The offering, moreover, that each one makes, he shall announce to his abbot; that it may be done with his prayers and by his will. For what is done without the permission of the spiritual Father, shall be put down to presumption and vain-glory, and not to a monk's credit. Therefore all things are to be done according to the will of the abbot. . . .

Whether a monk should be allowed to receive letters or anything. By no means shall it be allowed to a monk—either from his relatives, or from any man, or from one of his fellows—to receive or to give, without order of the abbot, letters, presents, or any gift, however small. But even if, by his relatives, anything has been sent to him: he shall not presume to receive it, unless it have first been shown to the abbot. But if he order it to be received, it shall be in the power of the abbot to give it to whomever he may will. And the brother to whom it happened to have been sent shall not be chagrined; that an opportunity be not given to the devil. Whoever, moreover, presumes otherwise, shall be subject to the discipline of the Rule. . . .

Concerning the manner of receiving brothers. When any new comer applies for conversion, an easy entrance shall not be granted him: but, as the apostle says, "Try the spirits if they be of God." Therefore, if he who comes perseveres in knocking, and is seen after four or five days to patiently endure the insults inflicted upon him, and the difficulty of ingress, and to persist in his demand: entrance shall be allowed him, and he shall remain for a few days in the cell of the guests. After this, moreover, he shall be in the cell of the novices, where he shall meditate and eat and sleep. And an elder shall be detailed off for him who shall be capable of saving souls, who shall altogether intently watch over him, and make it a care to see if he reverently seek God, if he be zealous in the service of God, in obedience, in suffering shame. And all the harshness and roughness of the means through which God is approached shall be told him in advance. If he promise perseverance in his steadfastness, after the lapse of two months this Rule shall be read to him in order, and it shall be said to him: "Behold the law under which thou dost wish to serve; if thou canst observe it, enter; but if thou canst not, depart freely." If he have stood firm thus far, then he shall be led into the aforesaid cell of the novices; and again he shall be proven with all patience. And, after the lapse of six months, the Rule shall be read to him; that he may know upon what he is entering. And, if he stand firm thus far, after four months the same Rule shall again be re-read to him. And if, having deliberated with himself, he shall promise to keep everything, and to obey all the commands that are laid upon him: then he shall be received in the congregation; knowing that it is decreed, by the law of the Rule, that from that day he shall not be allowed to depart from the monastery, nor to shake free his neck from the yoke of the Rule, which, after such tardy deliberation, he was at liberty either to refuse or receive. He who is to be received, moreover, shall, in the oratory, in the presence of all, make promise concerning his steadfastness and the change in his manner of life and his obedience to God and to His saints; so that if, at any time, he act contrary, he shall know that he shall be condemned by Him whom he mocks. Concerning which promise he shall make a petition in the name of the saints whose relics are there, and of the abbot who is present. Which petition he shall write with his own hand. Or, if he really be not learned in letters, another, being asked by him, shall write it. And that novice shall make his sign; and with his own hand shall place it (the petition) above the altar. And when he has placed it there, the novice shall straightway commence this verse: "Receive me oh Lord according to thy promise and I shall live, and do not cast me down from my hope." Which verse the whole congregation shall repeat three times, adding: "Glory be to the Father." Then that brother novice shall prostrate himself at the feet of each one, that they may pray for him. And, already, from that day, he shall be considered as in the congregation. If he have any property, he shall either first present it to the poor, or, making a solemn donation, shall confer it on the monastery, keeping nothing at all for himself: as one, forsooth, who from that day, shall know that he shall not have power even over his own body. Straightway, therefore in the oratory, he shall take off his own garments in which he was clad, and shall put on the garments of the monastery. Moreover those garments which he has taken off shall be placed in the vestiary to be preserved; so that if, at any time, the devil persuading him, he shall consent to go forth from the monastery—may it not happen—then, taking off the garments of the monastery, he may be cast out. That petition of his, nevertheless, which the abbot took from above the altar, he shall not receive again; but it shall be preserved in the monastery.

Concerning the sons of nobles or of poor men who are presented. If by chance any one of the nobles offers his son to God in the monastery: if the boy himself is a minor in age, his parents shall make the petition which we spoke of above. And, with an oblation, they shall enwrap that petition and the hand of the boy in the linen cloth of the altar; and thus they shall offer him. Concerning their property, moreover, either they shall promise in the present petition, under an oath, that they never, either through some chosen person, or in any way whatever, will give him anything at any time, or furnish him with the means of possessing it. Or, indeed, if they be not willing to do this, and wish to offer something as alms to the monastery for their salvation, they shall make a donation of the things which they wish to give to the monastery; retaining for themselves, if they wish, the usufruct. And let all things be so observed that no suspicion may remain with the boy; by which being deceived he might perish—which God forbid—as we have learned by experience. The poorer ones shall also do likewise. Those, however, who have nothing at all shall simply make their petition; and, with an oblation, shall offer their son before witnesses. . . .

If any abbot seek to ordain for himself a priest or deacon, he shall elect from among his fold one who is worthy to perform the office of a priest. He who is ordained, moreover, shall beware of elation or pride. Nor shall he presume to do anything at all unless what he is ordered to by the abbot; knowing that he is all the more subject to the Rule. Nor, by reason of the priesthood, shall he forget obedience and discipline; but he shall advance more and more towards God. But he shall always expect to hold that position which he had when he entered the monastery: except when performing the service of the altar, and if, perchance, the election of the congregation and the will of the abbot inclines to promote him on account of his merit of life. He shall, nevertheless, know that he is to observe the Rule constituted for him by the deans or provosts: and that, if he presume otherwise, he shall be considered not a priest but a rebel. And if, having often been admonished, he do not amend: even the bishop shall be called in in testimony. But if, even then, he do not amend, his faults being glaring, he shall be thrust forth from the monastery. That is, if his contumaciousness shall have been of such a kind, that he was not willing to be subject to or to obey the Rule.

Concerning rank in the congregation. They shall preserve their rank in the monastery according as the time of their conversion and the merit of their life decrees; and as the abbot ordains. And the abbot shall not perturb the flock committed to him; nor, using as it were an arbitrary power, shall he unjustly dispose anything. But he shall always reflect that he is to render account to God for all his judgments and works. Therefore, according to the order which he has decreed, or which the brothers themselves have held: thus they shall go to the absolution, to the communion, to the singing of the psalm, to their place in the choir. And in all places, altogether, age does not decide the rank or affect it; for Samuel and Daniel, as boys, judged the priests. Therefore excepting those who, as we have said, the abbot has, for a higher reason, preferred, or, for certain causes, degraded: all the rest, as they are converted, so they remain. Thus, for example, he who comes to the monastery at the second hour of the day, may know that he is younger than he who came at the first hour of the day, of whatever age or dignity he be. And, in the case of boys, discipline shall be observed in all things by all. The juniors, therefore, shall honour their seniors; the seniors shall love their juniors. In the very calling of names, it shall be allowed to no one to call another simply by his name: but the seniors shall call their juniors by the name of brothers. The juniors, moreover, shall call their seniors "nonni," which indicates paternal reverence. The abbot, moreover, because he is believed to be Christ's representative, shall be called Master and Abbot; not by his assumption, but through honour and love for Christ. His thoughts moreover shall be such, and he shall show himself such,that he may be worthy of such honour. Moreover, wherever the brothers meet each other, the junior shall seek a blessing from the senior. When the greater one passes, the lesser one shall rise and give him a place to sit down. Nor shall the junior presume to sit unless his senior bid him; so that it shall be done as is written: "Vying with each other in honour." Boys, little ones or youths, shall obtain their places in the oratory or at table with discipline as the end in view. Out of doors, moreover, or wherever they are, they shall be guarded and disciplined; until they come to an intelligent age.

Concerning the ordination of an abbot. In ordaining an abbot this consideration shall always be observed: that such a one shall be put into office as the whole congregation, according to the fear of God, with one heart—or even a part, however small, of the congregation with more prudent counsel—shall have chosen. He who is to be ordained, moreover, shall be elected for merit of life and learnedness in wisdom; even though he be the lowest in rank in the congregation. But even if the whole congregation with one consent shall have elected a person consenting to their vices—which God forbid—and those vices shall in any way come clearly to the knowledge of the bishop to whose diocese that place pertains, or to the neighbouring abbots or Christians: the latter shall not allow the consent of the wicked to prevail, but shall set up a dispenser worthy of the house of God; knowing that they will receive a good reward for this, if they do it chastely and with zeal for God. Just so they shall know, on the contrary, that they have sinned if they neglect. The abbot who is ordained, moreover, shall reflect always what a burden he is undertaking, and to whom he is to render account of his stewardship. He shall know that he ought rather to be of help than to command. He ought, therefore, to be learned in the divine law, that he may know how to give forth both the new and the old; chaste, sober, merciful. He shall always exalt mercy over judgment, that he may obtain the same. He shall hate vice, he shall love the brethren. In his blame itself he shall act prudently and do nothing excessive; lest, while he is too desirous of removing the rust, the vessel be broken. And he shall always suspect his own frailty; and shall remember that a bruised reed is not to be crushed. By which we do not say that he shall permit vice to be nourished; but prudently, and with charity, he shall remove it, according as he finds it to be expedient in the case of each one, as we have already said. And he shall strive rather to be loved than feared. He shall not be troubled and anxious; he also shall not be too obstinate; he shall not be jealous and too suspicious; for then he will have no rest. In his commands he shall be provident, and shall consider whether they be of God or of the world. He shall use discernment and moderation with regard to the labours which he enjoins, thinking of the discretion of St. James who said: "if I overdrive my flocks they will die all in one day." Accepting therefore this and other testimony of discretion the mother of the virtues, he shall so temper all things that there may be both what the strong desire, and the weak do not flee. And, especially, he shall keep the present Rule in all things; so that, when he hath ministered well, he shall hear from the Lord what that good servant did who obtained meat for his fellow servants in his day: "Verily I say unto you," he said, "that he shall make him ruler over all his goods. . . ."

That they shall be mutually obedient. The virtue of obedience is not only to be exhibited by all to the abbot, but also the brothers shall be thus mutually obedient to each other; knowing that they shall approach God through this way of obedience. The command therefore of the abbot, or of the provosts who are constituted by him, being given the preference—since we do not allow private commands to have more weight than his—for the rest, all juniors shall obey their superiors with all charity and solicitude. But if any one is found contentious, he shall be punished. If, moreover, any brother, for any slight cause, be in any way rebuked by the abbot or by any one who is his superior; or if he feel, even lightly, that the mind of some superior is angered or moved against him, however little: straightway, without delay, he shall so long lie prostrate at his feet, atoning, until, with the benediction, that anger shall be appeased. But if any one scorn to do this, he shall either be subjected to corporal punishment; or, if he be contumacious, he shall be expelled from the monastery. . . .

Concerning the fact that not every just observance is decreed in this Rule. We have written out this Rule, indeed, that we may show those observing it in the monasteries how to have some honesty of character, or beginning of conversion. But for those who hasten to the perfection of living, there are the teachings of the holy Fathers: the observance of which leads a man to the heights of perfection. For what page, or what discourse, of Divine authority of the Old or the New Testament is not a most perfect rule for human life? Or what book of the holy Catholic Fathers does not trumpet forth how by the right path we shall come to our Creator? Also the reading aloud of the Fathers, and their decrees, and their lives; also the Rule of our holy Father Basil—what else are they except instruments of virtue for well-living and obedient monks? We, moreover, blush with confusion for the idle, and the evilly living and the negligent. Thou, therefore, whoever doth hasten to the celestial fatherland, perform with Christ's aid this Rule written out as the least of beginnings; and then at length, under God's protection, thou wilt come to the greater things that we have mentioned; to the summits of learning and virtue.

JOHN SCOTUS ERIGENA

Erigena was an Irish monk born ca. A.D. *810. The place, circumstances, and date of his death are unknown. We do know that in the year 850 he was teaching at the court of Charles the Bold in the Kingdom of the Franks. Erigena's thought was influenced by Augustine, although he also had access to the Neoplatonist interpretation of Christianity, especially the works of Gregory of Nyssa and the Pseudo-Dionysius (so-called because he was originally thought to be a disciple of Paul—*Acts, 17:34*). The central problem is as follows: Augustine, following Plato, the Neoplatonists, and Plotinus, developed a position in which the Platonic "ideas" became "ideas" in the mind of God. Given the Augustinian doctrine of the Trinity, the person became, literally, an "idea" in the mind of God, analogous to the logos, the Christ, who was the second person of the Trinity and yet fully God in every way. Erigena drew from this Augustinian source and concluded that the relationship between God and the person was one of phasing rather than one of a rigid cause-and-effect distinction. The doctrine of emanation, held by Plotinus and perhaps by Scotus Erigena, viewed the creation in more processive and temporal terms rather than in the traditional doctrine of an absolute God creating a world in one act of his will.*

Erigena's first work, On Predestination, *generated criticism because of its liberal views. But it was his major work,* De Divisione Naturae, *which caused Erigena's posthumous condemnation in the year 1225. Translated as* On the Division of Nature, *the title is somewhat misleading, for the fourfold structures of nature are not so much divisions as they are phases of a process of Neoplatonic emanation. Brilliantly conceived and argued, this work of Erigena does, despite its condemnation by Church authorities, represent a plausible and perhaps "orthodox" form of Trinitarian Christianity. After all, if God is infinite, as Christians contend, how can anything be totally other than God? Erigena is often accused of pantheism, which, theologically, may be what Christianity implies.*

From On the Division of Nature

Master. While thinking about and inquiring as diligently as my faculties permit into the first and highest division of all things capable of being perceived by the soul, or into those which transcend its reach—into those things which are, and those which are not—a general term embracing all of these occurred to me: in Greek the term is *physis,* in Latin, *natura.* Does the case seem otherwise to you?

Disciple. No; I quite agree. Indeed, even I, although just a novice when it comes to reasoning, can see this is the case.

Master. Consequently, *nature* is the general name for all things which are and which are not?

Disciple. Yes. For nothing that can be thought of as obtaining in the universe would remain outside this designation.

Master. As we are thus agreed with respect to the utter generality of this designation, I should enjoy hearing you discourse on the principle of its division, through *differentiae,* into species. Or would you prefer that I attempt this dividing while you evaluate my divisions?

Disciple. You go ahead, please. I am quite anxious to learn the true principle of these things from you.

Master. Now as I see it the division of nature consists in four species derived by means of four *differentia.* The first of these divisions being *that which creates and is not created;* the second, *that which is created and creates;* the third, *that which is created and does not create;* and the fourth, *that which neither creates nor is created.* In these four there are two pairs of opposites: the third division, that is, is opposed to the first, while the fourth is opposed to the second. Note, however, that the fourth is classed with the impossibles—*i.e.,* those things whose *differentia* is not-being-able-to-be. Does it seem to you that such a division obtains?

Disciple. Yes it does. But will you expand a bit, so that I may more clearly grasp the oppositions of which you spoke?

Master. Now, unless I'm mistaken, you do see the opposition between the first and third species. The first, that is, creates and is not created so that, *ex contrario,* that which is created and does not create is in opposition to it. Again, the second is opposed to the fourth inasmuch as the second—which is both created and creates—is universally contradicted by the fourth—which neither creates nor is created.

Disciple. I see. Yet the fourth species puzzles me. I feel no hesitation with respect to the other three, since the first is understood (if I see it correctly) in the cause of all that which is and which is not; while the second is understood in the primordial causes; and the third is understood in that of which we become aware in temporally and spatially located generations. Still, as I see it, it would help if we discuss each of these a bit more in detail.

Master. You are quite right. But which species of nature should be discussed first?

Disciple. It seems proper to me to speak of the first before discussing the others.

Master. So be it. But first of all I think that we should speak briefly of the highest and principal division of all things—that is, the division into those things which are and those which are not.

Disciple. All right. As a matter of fact, I can see that reasoning should proceed from this starting point; not only because this is the first *differentia* of all things, but because it appears that this is more obscure than the others.

Master. All right. Now, this basic class-producing *differentia* of all things is to be approached in various ways. The first of these ways leads us to observe that all things capable of being perceived by the senses or grasped by the intellect can reasonably be said to-be; while it seems just as reasonable that those things—owing to the excellence of their natures—which elude both the sensitive faculties and the intellect, be said not-to-be. This last group of things is not correctly understood save in God alone, and in matter, and in the principles and essences of all things constituted by Him. There is a good reason for this: only He who alone truly is, is the essence of all things. To quote Dionysius the Areopagite, "the being of all things is superbeing Divinity." Gregory the Theologian, too, adduces many reasons to prove that no intellect can grasp the *what* of any substance or essence, whether of a visible or invisible creature. For just as God Himself, in Himself, and beyond every creature can be understood by no intellect, just so the essence obtaining in the most secret recesses of his creations remains incomprehensible. For whatever is perceived by the corporeal senses, or grasped by the intellect, as being in any creature, is but a certain accident of each essence which remains, in itself, incomprehensible. The essence, that is, approached through the quality, quantity, form, matter, *differentia,* place or time, is not the *what* but the *that.*

Hence, this is the first and highest mode of the division of things which are said to-be and not-to-be. As I see it, that mode which appears to be reasonable—*i.e.,* the mode which consists in privations of relations with respect to substances (such as sight and blindness with respect to the eyes)—should not be admitted at all. For it seems to me to be wholly inadmissible to hold that that which entirely is-not, or is not-able-to-be, or which transcends the intellect owing to the excellence of its nature, can ever be received into the divisions of things unless one were to hold that the absences and privations of things which are, are not entirely nothing, but are rather supported in some unbelievable manner by the natural power of the things of which they are the privations, absences or oppositions, so that in this sense, they could be held to-be.

Now let the second way of approaching being and not-being be that which is accomplished by considering the orders and *differentiae* of the natures of creatures. This, which begins with the most pre-eminent intellectual power obtaining closest to God, descends to the lowest point of the rational and irrational creature—*i.e.,* from the most elevated angel to the lowest portion of the rational and irrational soul. Now in this way each order, including the very lowest one—the order of bodies in which the entire division is terminated—can in a certain extraordinary sense be said to-be and not-to-be. Affirmation, that is, of the inferior is a negation of the superior; while negation of the inferior is an affirmation of the superior. Similarly, affirmation of the superior is a negation of the inferior; while negation of the superior is an affirmation of the inferior. Clearly, the affirmation of man, insofar as he is mortal, is the negation of the angel. Again, negation of man is an affirmation of the angel, and so on. For if it is the case that man is a rational animal, mortal and visible, then clearly an angel is neither a rational animal, nor mortal, nor visible. Again, if an angel is an essential intellectual motion contemplating God and the causes of things, then man is not an essential intellectual motion contemplating God and the causes of things. And this same law obtains with respect to all celestial essences until the highest order of all things is attained. But this highest order terminates in a supreme upward negation. For its negation affirms no creature superior to itself.

Now upwards, there obtains three orders, the first of which are Cherubim, Seraphim and Thrones; the second, Virtues, Powers and Dominations; the third, Principles, Archangels and Angels. Downward, however, the lowest order of bodies only negates or affirms that which is superior to itself. Nothing, that is, obtains below this order to either affirm or negate, since it is preceded by all superiors but itself precedes no inferior. For this reason, every order of the rational and intellectual creature is said to-be and not-to-be. *It is,* that is to say, to the degree that it is known by superiors or by itself; while *it is not,* to the degree that it is incapable of comprehension by an inferior.

The third way is fittingly approached by observing those things by which the plenitude of this visible world is perfected, and by their prior causes obtaining in the most hidden of nature's recesses. Now, whichever of these causes obtain, formed-matter—that which is known through generation in space and time—is said by a peculiar human speech-pattern, to-be. Nevertheless, whatever does obtain within the recesses of nature and does not appear as formed-matter either in place, time or other accidents, is said by the same curious speech-pattern, not-to-be.

There are numerous examples of this approach, especially when it comes to regarding human nature. For as God made all men simultaneously in that first, single man created in His image; and as He did not constitute all of them at once, but rather in particular times and places; and that He thus brought the singly created nature of man into visible being in accordance with a certain order known to Himself; so it is the case that those who have already appeared and do now appear in the visible world are said to-be; while those who are yet latent, but nonetheless going-to-be, are said not-to-be.

Thus, this difference obtains between the first and

third modes: the first appears generally in all things which have been made simultaneously and singly in causes and effects. The third obtains particularly with respect to those things which are as yet partly latent in respect of their causes, and partly apparent in their effects. To this mode belongs that principle which refers to seeds—be they of animal, tree or herb. For the power of seed—at the time when it is quietly in repose within the recesses of nature—is said not-to-be, because it is not yet become manifest; but directly it has manifested itself by the generation of animals, or flowers or fruit, it is said to-be.

Now the fourth approach is that adopted by the philosophers who hold—not without reason—that only those things truly are, which are grasped by the intellect; while those things subject to generation and which are varied, united and separated by the additions and subtractions of matter, or intervals, or motions of time and place as are all bodies subject to generation and corruption, are held truly not-to-be.

A fifth approach derives from that which obtains in human nature alone. For when the human nature, through sin, has violated the dignity of the Divine image in which it subsists, and has thus deservedly lost its being, it is said, as a consequence, not-to-be. When human nature, however, restored by the grace of God's only-begotten Son, is led back to the original condition of its substance, in which it has been made according to the image of God, it then begins to-be, and begins to live in him who was made in God's image. The Apostle seems to be speaking in this mode when he says: "and He calls those things that are not, as those that are"—*i.e.,* God the Father calls through faith in his Son those who have been lost in the first man, so that they may be just as those who have been reborn in Christ. Again, this could also be understood as referring to those whom God calls daily out of the secret recesses of nature (where they are held not-to-be) into visible form and matter, and in all other ways in which hidden things can appear. But as I see it, enough has been said of these things for now. Does it seem so to you?

Disciple. Enough, indeed. . . .

Master. Then let us return to those things which we have already mentioned; that is, to the division of nature. . . . Now of these, the first *differentia,* as we saw, was into that which creates and is not created. Such a species of nature is correctly predicated of God alone: for He alone is understood as without beginning and creator of all things. And in virtue of the fact that He is thus principal cause of all things which have been made from Him and through Him, He is also the end of all that which is from Him. All things desire Him. He is, consequently, beginning, middle and end. Beginning, because all things participating in essence are from Him; middle, because they subsist and are moved in and through Him; and end, because they are moved to Him seeking the termination of their motion and the permanence of their perfection.

Disciple. This I do believe most devoutly; and to the degree that it is capable of being understood, I understand that this is predicated correctly only of the Divine cause of all things, since this cause alone causes all things which are from it, while it is itself created by nothing superior or precedent. For it is itself the highest and only cause of all things which subsist from it and in it.

Yet, I am puzzled, and should like to hear your opinion on this. Quite often—and it is this which puzzles me—I find that in the books of the holy fathers, when they are attempting to argue about the Divine Nature, they maintain that it not only creates all things which are, but is itself, as well, created. Hence, if this is the case, I don't see how our view can obtain: for we say that the Divine Nature alone creates, but is created by nothing.

Master. You have good reason to be disturbed. I, too, wonder about this, and I should have wished to know from you how these views, which appear to be contrary, could fail to be opposed to each other and what true reason could say about it.

Disciple. Please begin. I am anxious to hear what your opinion is on this, not mine.

Master. I suggest that we first consider the name itself—God—which is employed in sacred scripture. For although Divine Nature is called by many names, as Goodness, Being, Truth, and others of a like kind, nonetheless scripture most frequently employs this Divine name.

Disciple. That is clearly the case.

Master. Now, the etymology of this name is Greek. It derives either from the verb *theoreo* [I see], or from the verb *theo* [I run]. Or, as is more probable, it can be said to derive from both, because one and the same meaning is present. For when *theos* [God], is deduced from the verb *theoreo* [I see], He is interpreted as seeing. For He Himself sees in Himself all things which are, while He looks upon nothing outside Himself because there is nothing outside Himself. But when *theos* [God], is deduced from the verb *theo* [I run], *theos* [God], is correctly understood as running. For He Himself runs in all things, and is in no way quiescent, but fills all things by running. As the saying is: "His speech runs swiftly." Despite this, He is in no way moved; as restful-motion, and mobile-rest, are most truly predicated of God. God, that is, rests absolutely within Himself, never relapsing from His natural immobility. Still, He moves Himself through all things which subsist essentially from Him, so that they may *be* those things; for all things are made by His motion. Consequently, one and the same meaning obtains in the two interpretations of His name—God. To run through all things, that is, is nothing other to God than to see all things; and just as by seeing, so also by running are all things made.

Disciple. So much for the name. Still, I do not fully see how He moves Himself. For He who is everywhere; He without which nothing else can be; He, outside of whom nothing is extended; He is the place and limit of all things.

Master. Now, I have not said that God is moved outside Himself; but by Himself, in Himself, and to Himself. For no motion aside from the appetite of His will should be believed to be in Him; and it is by this appetite that He wills that all things be made. Similarly, His rest is not to be understood as following on motion; but rather as the incommutably commanded object of this same will by means of which He defines the permanence of all things in the incommutable stability of their principles. Neither rest nor motion are properly said to be in Him. These two, indeed, appear to be opposed to one another, and true reason forbids the attribution of opposites to Him. Rest is properly the end of motion, but God does not begin to be moved in order that He attain a certain state. Consequently, these names—as many such similar ones—are predicated by the creature to the creator as a kind of Divine metaphor. Now this is not unreasonable, since He is the cause of all things which are at rest and in motion. It is, indeed, by Him that they begin to run so that they may be, as He is the principle of all things; further, it is through Him that they are brought to Him by natural motion, so that they may rest in Him eternally and incommutably. For He is the end and the rest of all things, and they desire nothing beyond Him. It is in Him that they find the beginning and the end of their motion. Hence, God is said to be running; not because He, who stands immutably in Himself and fills all things, runs outside Himself, but because He makes everything run from non-existence to existence.

Disciple. This seems reasonable; let us now return to what was proposed.

Master. What proposal are you referring to? Often when we digress we forget the principal question.

Disciple. Haven't we proposed that we inquire—so far as we are able—into the reason that those who discuss the Divine Nature say that it both creates and is created? That it does create all things, surely no intelligent being can doubt; but in what manner it is said to be created has, so it seemed to us, not been sufficiently clarified.

Master. You are right. But as I see it, from what has been said before, a key to the solution of this problem has been provided. For we have deduced that by the motion of the Divine Nature we are to understand a proposal of the Divine Will as to the establishment of those things which are to be made. Divine Nature, which *is* Divine Will, is therefore said to be made in all things. For being and willing obtain in respect of the establishment of all things which are made. That is, for example, that one can hold that the motion of the Divine Will occurs so that those things which are, might be; and that therefore it creates all things out of nothing so that they may be in being from non-being; but that it is nonetheless created, since besides itself nothing else essentially is, for it is the essence of all things. Just, that is, as there is no natural good beside itself, but all which is said to be good is good by participation in the one highest good, so everything which is said to exist, does not exist in itself, but exists by participating in the Divine Nature. Thus, not only, as we have seen, is the Divine Nature said to be made in existing things, but as well in those who are reformed by faith, hope, charity and the other virtues. The word of God is thus born in a marvelous and ineffable way, as the Apostle says when saying of Christ: "Who has been made in wisdom from God, and justification and redemption." Again, it is not improper to say that it has been made, because it—which is invisible *per se*—appears in all things which are. Our intellect, too, in this way, is not improperly said to-be, even before it arrived at thought and memory; for it, too, is invisible *per se* and unknowable to all save God and ourselves. However, as soon as it has arrived at thought, and takes a form from certain phantasms, it is said, not without reason, to be made. For the intellect which was unformed prior to its attainment of memory, is made in memory by receiving certain forms of things, or words, or colors, or other sensibles. Then it receives, so to speak, a second formation: when by certain signs of forms, or of words—*i.e.*, letters, which are signs of words; and figures, which are signs of forms—it is formed by the mathematical or other sensible signs by which means it is suggested to the sense of those who experience these signs. This similarity, then (although far removed from the Divine Nature), I judge nonetheless as significant in showing how the Divine Nature—while it creates everything and cannot be created by anything—is yet created in a marvelous way in all the things that are from it. Hence, just as the mind's intelligence, or plan, or advice—or whatever manner this our innermost motion can be spoken of when it has arrived at thought and has received certain forms of phantasms, and has then proceeded by the sign of words, or the signs of sensible motions—is said, not without rectitude, to be made, just so the Divine Essence—which subsisting *per se* transcends every intellect—is correctly said to be created in those things which have been made from it, and through it, and in it, and for it, so that it can be known in them whether by the intellect (if they are intellectual), or by sense (if they are sensible), by those who investigate the Divine Essence by correct study.

Disciple. As I see it, enough has now been said of this. . . . Still, I find that I cannot grant motion to God who alone is immutable. There is nothing in respect of which He could move Himself, inasmuch as all things are in Him: or, and this is even stronger, since He himself *is* all things. Nonetheless, I cannot deny Him making, since He is the maker of all things.

Master. Therefore you see motion as separate from making?

Disciple. No; not that; for I see that they are inseparable from each other.

Master. Well then, what are you going to do?

Disciple. I don't know. I therefore fervently request that you clear some path for me and rid me of this difficulty.

Master. Very well. Now does it seem to you that God was before He made all things?

Disciple. Yes; it seems to me that He was.

Master. Consequently, making was an accident in respect of Him. For what is not co-eternal and co-essential with Him is either something outside of Him or something befalling Him.

Disciple. I find it hard to believe that there is something outside Him; for all things are in Him and there is nothing outside Him. Indeed, I should rather have said that He is not subject to accident; for if He were, He would not be simple but rather a certain composite of essence and accidents. Clearly, if something other than He is understood together with Him, or if in any manner something befalls Him, then He is neither infinite nor simple. This, however, is repugnant to the Catholic faith and true reason. For these hold God to be infinite: more than infinite, as He is the infinity of infinities; and simple: more than simple, as He is the simplicity of simples. Further, it believes or understands that there is nothing with Him, since He is Himself the limit of all things which are and are not, and which can and cannot be, and which appear to be either contrary and opposed, or similar and dissimilar, to Him. For He is the similitude of similars; the dissimilitude of dissimilars; the opposition of opposites and the contrariety of contraries. Indeed. He gathers and compounds all these things into one concord by means of a beautiful and ineffable harmony. For everything in the parts of the universe that appear to be opposed, contrary and dissonant with respect to one another, are harmonious and in consonance when considered in the most general harmony of the universe itself.

Master. You are correct in your understanding. But take care or you may leave yourself open to the charge of having granted to other things what you have just granted of these.

Disciple. What I have conceded, I shall not retract. Proceed now in any order that you wish and I shall follow.

Master. God, then, as you say, was not before He made all things?

Disciple. True. For if He was, He would have been subject to the accident of making all things; and were He thus subject, motion and time could be predicated of Him. For He would then have moved Himself in order to make those things which He had not yet made; and He would have thus preceded His action in time which was then neither co-essential nor co-eternal with Him.

Master. Therefore His making is co-eternal and co-essential with Him.

Disciple. I believe and understand this to be the case.

Master. Is it the case that God and His making—*i.e.,* his action—are two distinct things? Or are they one thing, simple and individual?

Disciple. They are one, as I see it. For God is innumerable and does not receive number in Himself. He is number without number, beyond all numbers, and the cause of all numbers.

Master. Hence, in God there is not one thing which is being and another which is making, but for Him being is also making?

Disciple. I cannot deny this conclusion.

Master. Therefore, when we are told that God made anything, what we should take this to mean is that God is in all things—*i.e.,* subsists as the essence of all things. For He alone truly is *per se;* and only He is that which is said to be in those things which are. For none of the things which are, truly are *per se,* except insofar as they receive their true being by a participation in Him—the one who alone truly is *per se.*

Disciple. I do not deny this.

Master. Do you not, therefore, see how it is that true reason completely separates the category of making from the Divine Nature, and from changes and places, and assigns the category of making to those mutable, temporal things which cannot lack a beginning and end?

Disciple. I now see this clearly; and I quite understand that no category is attributable to God.

ANSELM

Anselm (1033–1109) was born in Aosta, Italy. He was a Benedictine monk who became the Abbot of Bec and then, in 1093, the Archbishop of Canterbury, in which position he defended the Church against the King of England. Although Anselm published writings dealing with a range of subjects, including On Free Will *and* On Truth, *he is best known for his works on the existence of God, the* Monologion *and the* Proslogion. *The eighteenth-century philosopher Kant called Anselm's argument the ontological argument. It has been debated down to the present, with major thinkers such as Descartes, Spinoza, Leibniz, Locke, Kant, Hegel, and Royce each offering their interpretations.*

There are two major assumptions in Anselm's argument: the first is that one and only one necessary being can exist; the second is that human beings can have an "idea" of a perfect being. Although the first has a logical urgency about it, the second is subject to severe doubt. Anselm's assumption that something must exist, necessarily, is plausible; it is at least more plausible than the opposite assumption, namely, that at one time nothing existed. Following Parmenides, this opposite position leads us into a dead end—from nothing follows nothing, yet it is clear that something does exist. Anselm's second assumption is more questionable. In fact, commentators have judged the claim of the existence of a perfect being to be circular: that is, we claim that a perfect being exists and use the perfect being to verify our claim. Anselm's argument should be read with extreme care for it is a model of medieval philosophy in that it uses theological doctrine to spur philosophical inquiry. The contrary argument of Gaunilo, disappointingly repeated by Thomas Aquinas, misses the point entirely, for the question is not one of any other example than the singular, unique instance of a perfect being.

It can be said, paradoxically, that if God exists, then Anselm's argument could be valid. If God does not exist, then the argument is brilliant, seductive, but in the end, wrongheaded.

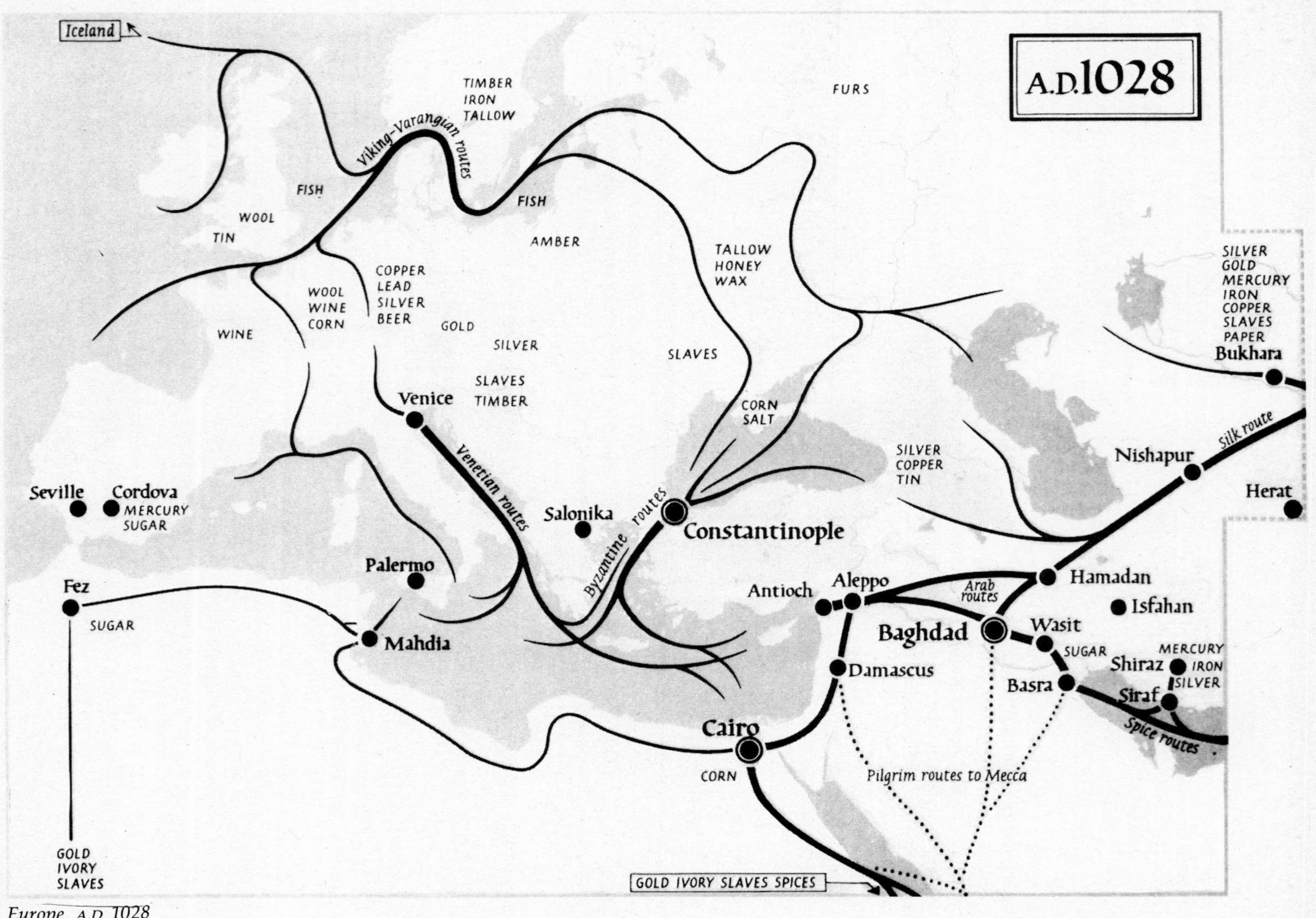

A.D. 1028
Iceland
TIMBER
IRON
TALLOW
FURS
Viking-Varangian routes
FISH
WOOL
TIN
FISH
AMBER
TALLOW
HONEY
WAX
COPPER
LEAD
SILVER
BEER
WOOL
WINE
CORN
WINE
GOLD
SILVER
SLAVES
SLAVES
TIMBER
Venice
CORN
SALT
SILVER
GOLD
MERCURY
IRON
COPPER
SLAVES
PAPER
Bukhara
Silk route
Nishapur
Herat
SILVER
COPPER
TIN
Venetian routes
Seville
Cordova
MERCURY
SUGAR
Salonika
Byzantine routes
Constantinople
Palermo
Fez
SUGAR
Mahdia
Antioch
Aleppo
Arab routes
Hamadan
Isfahan
Baghdad
Wasit
SUGAR
MERCURY
Shiraz
IRON
SILVER
Damascus
Basra
Siraf
Spice routes
Cairo
CORN
Pilgrim routes to Mecca
GOLD
IVORY
SLAVES
GOLD IVORY SLAVES SPICES

Europe, A.D. 1028

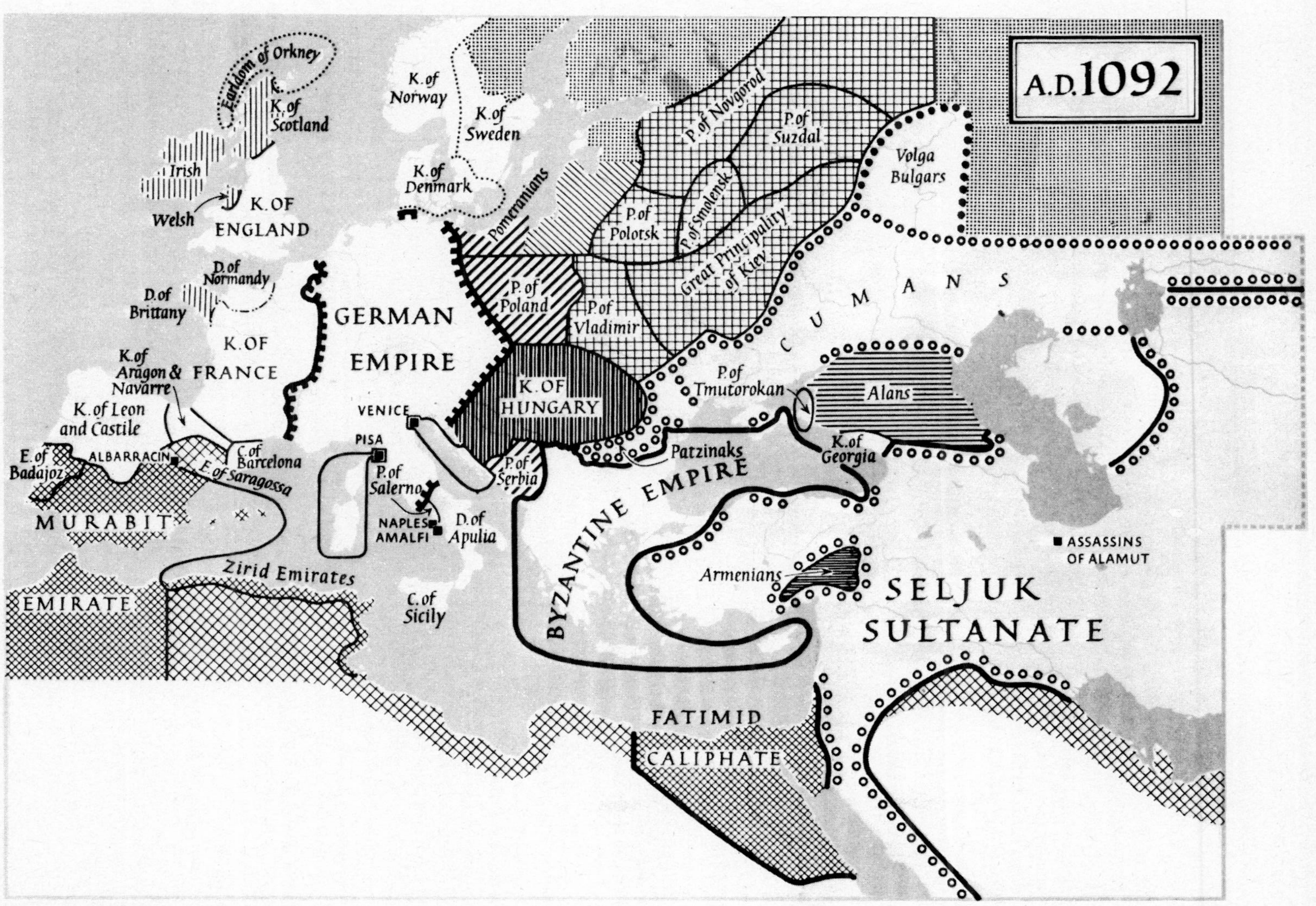

A.D. 1092
Earldom of Orkney
K. of Scotland
Irish
Welsh
K. OF ENGLAND
D. of Normandy
D. of Brittany
K. OF FRANCE
K. of Aragon & Navarre
K. of Leon and Castile
E. of Badajoz
ALBARRACIN
C. of Barcelona
E. of Saragossa
MURABIT
EMIRATE
Zirid Emirates
K. of Norway
K. of Sweden
K. of Denmark
Pomeranians
GERMAN EMPIRE
VENICE
PISA
P. of Salerno
NAPLES
AMALFI
D. of Apulia
C. of Sicily
P. of Poland
K. OF HUNGARY
P. of Serbia
P. of Vladimir
P. of Polotsk
P. of Smolensk
P. of Novgorod
P. of Suzdal
Great Principality of Kiev
Volga Bulgars
CUMANS
P. of Tmutorokan
Alans
Patzinaks
K. of Georgia
BYZANTINE EMPIRE
Armenians
SELJUK SULTANATE
ASSASSINS OF ALAMUT
FATIMID CALIPHATE

Europe, A.D. *1092*

From the Proslogion

A Rousing of the Mind to the Contemplation of God

Come now, insignificant man, fly for a moment from your affairs, escape for a little while from the tumult of your thoughts. Put aside now your weighty cares and leave your wearisome toils. Abandon yourself for a little to God and rest for a little in Him. Enter into the inner chamber of your soul, shut out everything save God and what can be of help in your quest for Him and having locked the door seek Him out [Matt. vi. 6]. Speak now, my whole heart, speak now to God: 'I seek Your countenance, O Lord, Your countenance I seek' [Ps. xxvi. 8].

Come, then, Lord my God, teach my heart where and how to seek You, where and how to find You. Lord, if You are not present here, where, since You are absent, shall I look for You? On the other hand, if You are everywhere why then, since You are present, do I not see You? But surely You dwell in 'light inaccessible' [1 Tim. vi. 16]. And where is this inaccessible light, or how can I approach the inaccessible light? Or who shall lead me and take me into it that I may see You in it? Again, by what signs, under what aspect, shall I seek You? Never have I seen You, Lord my God. I do not know Your face. What shall he do, most high Lord, what shall this exile do, far away from You as he is? What shall Your servant do, tormented by love of You and yet cast off 'far from your face' [Ps. i. 13]? He yearns to see You and Your countenance is too far away from him. He desires to come close to You, and Your dwelling place is inaccessible; he longs to find You and does not know where You are; he is eager to seek You out and he does not know Your countenance. Lord, You are my God and my Lord, and never have I seen You. You have created me and re-created me and You have given me all the good things I possess, and still I do not know You. In fine, I was made in order to see You, and I have not yet accomplished what I was made for.

I acknowledge, Lord, and I give thanks that You have created Your image in me, so that I may remember You, think of You, love You. But this image is so effaced and worn away by vice, so darkened by the smoke of sin, that it cannot do what it was made to do unless You renew it and reform it. I do not try, Lord, to attain Your lofty heights, because my understanding is in no way equal to it. But I do desire to understand Your truth a little, that truth that my heart believes and loves. For I do not seek to understand so that I may believe; but I believe so that I may understand. For I believe this also, that 'unless I believe, I shall not understand' [Is. vii. 9].

THAT GOD TRULY EXISTS

Well then, Lord, You who give understanding to faith, grant me that I may understand, as much as You see fit, that You exist as we believe You to exist, and that You are what we believe You to be. Now we believe that You are something than which nothing greater can be thought. Or can it be that a thing of such a nature does not exist, since 'the Fool has said in his heart, there is no God' [Ps. xiii. 1, lii. 1]? But surely, when this same Fool hears what I am speaking about, namely, 'something-than-which-nothing-greater-can-be-thought,' he understands what he hears, and what he understands is in his mind, even if he does not understand that it actually exists. For it is one thing for an object to exist in the mind, and another thing to understand that an object actually exists. Thus, when a painter plans beforehand what he is going to execute, he has [the picture] in his mind, but he does not yet think that it actually exists because he has not yet executed it. However, when he has actually painted it, then he both has it in his mind and understands that it exists because he has now made it. Even the Fool, then, is forced to agree that something-than-which-nothing-greater-can-be-thought exists in the mind, since he understands this when he hears it, and whatever is understood is in the mind. And surely that-than-which-a-greater-cannot-be-thought cannot exist in the mind alone. For if it exists solely in the mind even, it can be thought to exist in reality also, which is greater. If then that-than-which-a-greater-cannot-be-thought exists in the mind alone, this same that-than-which-a-greater-*cannot*-be-thought is that-than-which-a-greater-*can*-be-thought. But this is obviously impossible. Therefore there is absolutely no doubt that something-than-which-a-greater-cannot-be-thought exists both in the mind and in reality.

THAT GOD CANNOT BE THOUGHT NOT TO EXIST

And certainly this being so truly exists that it cannot be even thought not to exist. For something can be thought to exist that cannot be thought not to exist, and this is greater than that which can be thought not to exist. Hence, if that-than-which-a-greater-cannot-be-thought can be thought not to exist, then that-than-which-a-greater-cannot-be-thought is not the same as that-than-which-a-greater-cannot-be-thought, which is absurd. Something-than-which-a-greater-cannot-be-thought exists so truly then, that it cannot be even thought not to exist.

And You, Lord our God, are this being. You exist so truly, Lord my God, that You cannot even be thought not to exist. And this is as it should be, for if some intelligence could think of something better than You, the creature would be above its creator and would judge its creator—and that is completely absurd. In fact, everything else there is, except You alone, can be thought of as not existing. You alone, then, of all things most truly exist and therefore of all things possess existence to the highest degree; for anything else does not exist as truly, and so possesses existence to a lesser degree. Why then did 'the Fool say in his heart, there is no God' [Ps. xiii. 1, lii, 1] when it is so evident to any rational mind that You of all things exist to the highest degree? Why indeed, unless because he was stupid and a fool?

How 'the Fool Said in his Heart' What Cannot Be Thought

How indeed has he 'said in his heart' what he could not think; or how could he not think what he 'said in his heart', since to 'say in one's heart' and to 'think' are the same? But if he really (indeed, since he really) both thought because he 'said in his heart' and did not 'say in his heart' because he could not think, there is not only one sense in which something is 'said in one's heart' or thought. For in one sense a thing is thought when the word signifying it is thought; in another sense when the very object which the thing is is understood. In the first sense, then, God can be thought not to exist, but not at all in the second sense. No one, indeed, understanding what God is can think that God does not exist, even though he may say these words in his heart either without any [objective] signification or with some peculiar signification. For God is that-than-which-nothing-greater-can-be-thought. Whoever really understands this understands clearly that this same being so exists that not even in thought can it not exist. Thus whoever understands that God exists in such a way cannot think of Him as not existing.

I give thanks, good Lord, I give thanks to You, since what I believed before through Your free gift I now so understand through Your illumination, that if I did not want to *believe* that You existed, I should nevertheless be unable not to *understand* it. . . .

A Reply to the Foregoing by a Certain Writer on Behalf of the Fool [By Gaunilo]

To one doubting whether there is, or denying that there is, something of such a nature than which nothing greater can be thought, it is said here [in the *Proslogion*] that its existence is proved, first because the very one who denies or doubts it already has it in his mind, since when he hears it spoken of he understands what is said; and further, because what he understands is necessarily such that it exists not only in the mind but also in reality. And this is proved by the fact that it is greater to exist both in the mind and in reality than in the mind alone. For if this same being exists in the mind alone, anything that existed also in reality would be greater than this being, and thus that which is greater than everything would be less than some thing and would not be greater than everything, which is obviously contradictory. Therefore, it is necessarily the case that that which is greater than everything, being already proved to exist in the mind, should exist not only in the mind but also in reality, since otherwise it would not be greater than everything.

But he [the Fool] can perhaps reply that this thing is said already to exist in the mind only in the sense that I understand what is said. For could I not say that all kinds of unreal things, not existing in themselves in any way at all, are equally in the mind since if anyone speaks about them I understand whatever he says? Unless perhaps it is manifest that this being is such that it can be entertained in the mind in a different way from unreal or doubtfully real things, so that I am not said to think of or have in thought what is heard, but to understand and have it in mind, in that I cannot really think of this being in any other way save by understanding it, that is to say, by grasping by certain knowledge that the thing itself actually exists. But if this is the case, first, there will be no difference between having an object in mind (taken as preceding in time), and understanding that the object actually exists (taken as following in time), as in the case of the picture which exists first in the mind of the painter and then in the completed work. And thus it would be scarcely conceivable that, when this object had been spoken of and heard, it could not be thought not to exist in the same way in which God can [be thought] not to exist. For if He cannot, why put forward this whole argument against anyone denying or doubting that there is something of this kind? Finally, that it is such a thing that, as soon as it is thought of, it cannot but be certainly perceived by the mind as indubitably existing, must be proved to me by some indisputable argument and not by that proposed, namely, that it must already be in my mind when I understand what I hear. For this is in my view like [arguing that] any things doubtfully real or even unreal are capable of existing if these things are mentioned by someone whose spoken words I might understand, and, even more, that [they exist] if, though deceived about them as often happens, I should believe them [to exist]—which argument I still do not believe!

Hence, the example of the painter having the picture he is about to make already in his mind cannot support this argument. For this picture, before it is actually made, is contained in the very art of the painter and such a thing in the art of any artist is nothing but a certain part of his very understanding, since as St. Augustine says [*In Iohannem*, tract. 1. n. 16], 'when the artisan is about actually to make a box he has it beforehand in his art. The box which is actually made is not a living thing, but the box which is in his art is a living thing since the soul of the artist, in which these things exist before their actual realization, is a living thing'. Now how are these things living in the living soul of the artist unless they are identical with the knowledge or understanding of the soul itself? But, apart from those things which are known to belong to the very nature of the mind itself, in the case of any truth perceived by the mind by being either heard or understood, then it cannot be doubted that this truth is one thing and that the understanding which grasps it is another. Therefore even if it were true that there was something than which nothing greater could be thought, this thing, heard and understood, would not, however, be the same as the not-yet-made picture is in the mind of the painter.

To this we may add something that has already been mentioned, namely, that upon hearing it spoken of I can so little think of or entertain in my mind this being (that which is greater than all those others that are able to be thought of, and which it is said can be none other than God Himself) in terms of an object known to me either by species or genus, as I can think of God Himself, whom indeed for this very reason I can even think does not exist. For neither do I know the reality itself, nor can I form an idea from some other things like it since, as you say yourself, it is such that nothing could be like it. For if I heard something said about a man who was completely unknown to me so that I did not even know whether he existed, I could nevertheless think about him in his very reality as a man by means of that specific or generic notion by which I know what a man is or men are. However, it could happen that, because of a falsehood on the part of the speaker, the man I thought of did not actually exist, although I thought of him nevertheless as a truly existing object—not this particular man but any man in general. It is not, then, in the way that I have this unreal thing in thought or in mind that I can have that object in my mind when I hear 'God' or 'something greater than everything' spoken of. For while I was able to think of the former in terms of a truly existing thing which was known to me, I know nothing at all of the latter save for the verbal formula, and on the basis of this alone one can scarcely or never think of any truth. For when one thinks in this way, one thinks not so much of the word itself, which is indeed a real thing (that is to say, the sound of the letters or syllables), as of the meaning of the word which is heard. However, it [that which is greater than everything] is not thought of in the way of one who knows what is meant by that expression—thought of, that is, in terms of the thing [signified] or as true in thought alone. It is rather in the way of one who does not really know this object but thinks of it in terms of an affection of his mind produced by hearing the spoken words, and who tries to imagine what the words he has heard might mean. However, it would be astonishing if he could ever [attain to] the truth of the thing. Therefore, when I hear and understand someone saying that there is something greater than everything that can be thought of, it is agreed that it is in this latter sense that it is in my mind and not in any other sense. So much for the claim that that supreme nature exists already in my mind.

That, however, [this nature] necessarily exists in reality is demonstrated to me from the fact that, unless it existed, whatever exists in reality would be greater than it and consequently it would not be that which is greater than everything that undoubtedly had already been proved to exist in the mind. To this I reply as follows: if something that cannot even be thought in the true and real sense must be said to exist in the mind, then I do not deny that this also exists in my mind in the same way. But since from this one cannot in any way conclude that it exists also in reality, I certainly do not yet concede that it actually exists, until this is proved to me by an indubitable argument. For he who claims that it actually exists because otherwise it would not be that which is greater than everything does not consider carefully enough whom he is addressing. For I certainly do not yet admit this greater [than everything] to be any truly existing thing; indeed I doubt or even deny it. And I do not concede that it exists in a different way from that—if one ought to speak of 'existence' here—when the mind tries to imagine a completely unknown thing on the basis of the spoken words alone. How then can it be proved to me on that basis that that which is greater than everything truly exists in reality (because it is evident that it is greater than all others) if I keep on denying and also doubting that this is evident and do not admit that this greater [than everything] is either in my mind or thought, not even in the sense in which many doubtfully real and unreal things are? It must first of all be proved to me then that this same greater than everything truly exists in reality somewhere, and then only will the fact that it is greater than everything make it clear that it also subsists in itself.

For example: they say that there is in the ocean somewhere an island which, because of the difficulty (or rather the impossibility) of finding that which does not exist, some have called the 'Lost Island'. And the story goes that it is blessed with all manner of priceless riches and delights in abundance, much more even than the Happy Isles, and, having no owner or inhabitant, it is superior everywhere in abundance of riches to all those other lands that men inhabit. Now, if anyone tell me that it is like this, I shall easily understand what is said, since nothing is difficult about it. But if he should then go on to say, as though it were a logical consequence of this: You cannot any more doubt that this island that is more excellent than all other lands truly exists somewhere in reality than you can doubt that it is in your mind; and since it is more excellent to exist not only in the mind alone but also in reality, therefore it must needs be that it exists. For if it did not exist, any other land existing in reality would be more excellent than it, and so this island, already conceived by you to be more excellent than others, will not be more excellent. If, I say, someone wishes thus to persuade me that this island really exists beyond all doubt, I should either think that he was joking, or I should find it hard to decide which of us I ought to judge the bigger fool—I, if I agreed with him, or he, if he thought that he had proved the existence of this island with any certainty, unless he had first convinced me that its very excellence exists in my mind precisely as a thing existing truly and indubitably and not just as something unreal or doubtfully real.

Thus first of all might the Fool reply to objections. And if then someone should assert that this greater [than everything] is such that it cannot be thought not to exist (again without any other proof than that otherwise it would not be greater than everything), then he could make this same reply and say: When have I said that there truly existed some being that is 'greater than everything', such that from this it could be proved to me that this same being really existed to such a degree that it could not be thought not to exist? That is why it must first be conclusively proved by argument that there is some higher nature, namely that which is greater and better than all the things that are, so that from this we can also infer everything else which necessarily cannot be wanting to what is greater and better than everything. When, however, it is said that this supreme being cannot be *thought* not to exist, it would perhaps be better to say that it cannot be *understood* not to exist nor even to be able not to exist. For, strictly speaking, unreal things cannot be *understood*, though certainly they can be *thought* of in the same way as the Fool *thought* that God does not exist. I know with complete certainty that I exist, but I also know at the same time nevertheless that I can not-exist. And I *understand* without any doubt that that which exists to the highest degree, namely God, both exists and cannot not exist. I do not know, however, whether I can *think* of myself as not existing while I know with absolute certainty that I do exist; but if I can, why cannot [I do the same] with regard to anything else I know with the same certainty? If however I cannot, this will not be the distinguishing characteristic of God [namely, to be such that He cannot be thought not to exist].

The other parts of this tract are argued so truly, so brilliantly and so splendidly, and are also of so much worth and instinct with so fragrant a perfume of devout and holy feeling, that in no way should they be rejected because of those things at the beginning (rightly intuited, but less surely argued out). Rather the latter should be demonstrated more firmly and so everything received with very great respect and praise.

A Reply to the Foregoing by the Author of the Book in Question

Since it is not the Fool, against whom I spoke in my tract, who takes me up, but one who, though speaking on the Fool's behalf, is an orthodox Christian and no fool, it will suffice if I reply to the Christian.

You say then—you, whoever you are, who claim that the Fool can say these things—that the being than-which-a-greater-cannot-be-thought is not in the mind except as what cannot be thought of, in the true sense, at all. And [you claim], moreover, that what I say does not follow, namely, that 'that-than-which-a-greater-cannot-be-thought' exists in reality from the fact that it exists in the mind, any more than that the Lost Island most certainly exists from the fact that, when it is described in words, he who hears it described has no doubt that it exists in his mind. I reply as follows: If 'that-than-which-a-greater-cannot-be-thought' is neither understood nor thought of, and is neither in the mind nor in thought, then it is evident that *either* God is not that-than-which-a-greater-cannot-be-thought *or* is not understood nor thought of, and is not in the mind nor in thought. Now my strongest argument that this is false is to appeal to your faith and to your conscience. Therefore 'that-than-which-a-greater-cannot-be-thought' is truly understood and thought and is in the mind and in thought. For this reason, [the arguments] by which you attempt to prove the contrary are either not true, or what you believe follows from them does not in fact follow.

Moreover, you maintain that, from the fact that that-than-which-a-greater-cannot-be-thought is understood, it does not follow that it is in the mind, nor that, if it is in the mind, it therefore exists in reality. I insist, however, that simply if it can be thought it is necessary that it exists. For 'that-than-which-a-greater-cannot-be-thought' cannot be thought save as being without a beginning. But whatever can be thought as existing and does not actually exist can be thought as having a beginning of its existence. Consequently, 'that-than-which-a-greater-cannot-be-thought' cannot be thought as existing and yet not actually exist. If, therefore, it can be thought as existing, it exists of necessity.

Further: even if it can be thought of, then certainly it necessarily exists. For no one who denies or doubts that there is something-than-which-a-greater-cannot-be-thought, denies or doubts that, if this being were to exist, it would not be capable of not-existing either actually or in the mind—otherwise it would not be that-than-which-a-greater-cannot-be-thought. But, whatever can be thought as existing and does not actually exist, could, if it were to exist, possibly not exist either actually or in the mind. For this reason, if it can merely be thought, 'that-than-which-a-greater-cannot-be-thought' cannot not exist. However, let us suppose that it does not exist even though it can be thought. Now, whatever can be thought and does not actually exist would not be, if it should exist, 'that-than-which-a-greater-cannot-be-thought'. If, therefore, it were 'that-than-which-a-greater-cannot-be-thought' it would not be that-than-which-a-greater-cannot-be-thought, which is completely absurd. It is, then, false that something-than-which-a-greater-cannot-be-thought does not exist if it can merely be thought; and it is all the more false if it can be understood and be in the mind.

I will go further: It cannot be doubted that whatever does not exist in any one place or at any one time, even though it does exist in some place or at some time, can however be thought to exist at no place at no time, just as it does not exist in some place or at some time. For what did not exist yesterday and today exists can thus, as it is understood not to have existed yesterday, be supposed not to exist at any time. And that which does not exist here in this place, and does exist elsewhere can, in the same way as it does not exist here, be thought not to exist anywhere. Similarly with a thing some of whose particular parts do not exist in the place and at the time its other parts exist—all of its parts, and therefore the whole thing itself, can be thought to exist at no time and in no place. For even if it be said that time always exists and that the world is everywhere, the former does not, however, always exist as a whole, nor is the other as a whole everywhere; and as certain particular parts of time do not exist when other parts do exist, therefore they can be even thought not to exist at any time. Again, as certain particular parts of the world do not exist in the same place where other parts do exist, they can thus be supposed not to exist anywhere. Moreover, what is made up of parts can be broken up in thought and can possibly not exist. Thus it is that whatever does not exist as a whole at a certain place and time can be thought not to exist, even if it does actually exist. But 'that-than-which-a-greater-cannot-be-thought' cannot be thought not to exist if it does actually exist; otherwise, if it exists it is not that-than-which-a-greater-cannot-be-thought, which is absurd. In no way, then, does this being not exist as a whole in any particular place or at any particular time; but it exists as a whole at every time and in every place.

Do you not consider then that that about which we understand these things can to some extent be thought or understood, or can exist in thought or in the mind? For if it cannot, we could not understand these things about it. And if you say that, because it is not completely understood, it cannot be understood at all and cannot be in the mind, then you must say [equally] that one who cannot see the purest light of the sun directly does not see daylight, which is the same thing as the light of the sun. Surely then 'that-than-which-a-greater-cannot-be-thought' is understood and is in the mind to the extent that we understand these things about it.

I said, then, in the argument that you criticize, that when the Fool hears 'that-than-which-a-greater-cannot-be-thought' spoken of he understands what he hears. Obviously if it is spoken of in a known language and he does not understand it, then either he has no intelligence at all, or a completely obtuse one.

Next I said that, if it is understood it is in the mind; or does what has been proved to exist necessarily in actual reality not exist in any mind? But you will say that, even if it is in the mind, yet it does not follow that it is understood. Observe then that, from the fact that it is understood, it does follow that it is in the mind. For, just as what is thought is thought by means of a thought, and what is thought by a thought is thus, as thought, *in* thought, so also, what is understood is understood by the mind, and what is understood by the mind is thus, as understood, *in* the mind. What could be more obvious than this?

I said further that if a thing exists even in the mind alone, it can be thought to exist also in reality, which is greater. If, then, it (namely, 'that-than-which-a-greater-cannot-be-thought') exists in the mind alone, it is something than which a greater *can* be thought. What, I ask you, could be more logical? For if it exists even in the mind alone, cannot it be thought to exist also in reality? And if it can [be so thought], is it not the case that he who thinks this thinks of something greater than it, if it exists in the mind alone? What, then, could follow more logically than that, if 'that-than-which-a-greater-*cannot*-be thought' exists in the mind alone, it is the same as that-than-which-a-greater-*can*-be-thought? But surely 'that-than-which-a-greater-*can*-be-thought' is not for any mind [the same as] 'that-than-which-a-greater-*cannot*-be thought'. Does it not follow, then, that 'that-than-which-a-greater-*cannot*-be-thought', if it exists in anyone's mind, does not exist in the mind alone? For if it exists in the mind alone, it is that-than-which-a-greater-*can*-be-thought, which is absurd.

You claim, however, that this is as though someone asserted that it cannot be doubted that a certain island in the ocean (which is more fertile than all other lands and which, because of the difficulty or even the impossibility of discovering what does not exist, is called the 'Lost Island') truly exists in reality since anyone easily understands it when it is described in words. Now, I truly promise that if anyone should discover for me something existing either in reality or in the mind alone—except 'that-than-which-a-greater-cannot-be-thought'—to which the logic of my argument would apply, then I shall find that Lost Island and give it, never more to be lost, to that person. It has already been clearly seen, however, that 'that-than-which-a-greater-cannot-be-thought' cannot be thought not to exist, because it exists as a matter of such certain truth. Otherwise it would not exist at all. In short, if anyone says that he thinks that this being does not exist, I reply that, when he thinks of this, either he thinks of something than which a greater cannot be thought, or he does not think of it. If he does not think of it, then he does not think that what he does not think of does not exist. If, however, he does think of it, then indeed he thinks of something which cannot be even thought not to exist. For if it could be thought not to exist, it could be thought to have a beginning and an end—but this cannot be. Thus, he who thinks of it thinks of something that cannot be thought not to exist; indeed, he who thinks of this does not think of it as not existing, otherwise he would think what cannot be thought. Therefore 'that-than-which-a-greater-cannot-be-thought' cannot be thought not to exist.

You say, moreover, that when it is said that this supreme reality cannot be *thought* not to exist, it would perhaps be better to say that it cannot be *understood* not to exist or even to be able not to exist. However, it must rather be said that it cannot be *thought*. For if I had said that the thing in question could not be *understood* not to exist, perhaps you yourself (who claim that we cannot understand—if this word is to be taken strictly—things that are unreal) would object that nothing that exists can be understood not to exist. For it is false [to say that] what exists does not exist, so that it is not the distinguishing characteristic of God not to be able to be understood not to exist. But, if any of those things which exist with absolute certainty can be understood not to exist, in the same way other things that certainly exist can be understood not to exist. But, if the matter is carefully considered, this objection cannot be made apropos [the term] 'thought'. For even if none of those things that exist can be *understood* not to exist, all however can be *thought* as not existing, save that which exists to a supreme degree. For in fact all those things (and they alone) that have a beginning or end or are made up of parts and, as I have already said, all those things that do not exist as a whole in a particular place or at a particular time can be thought as not existing. Only that being in which there is neither beginning nor end nor conjunction of parts, and that thought does not discern save as a whole in every place and at every time, cannot be thought as not existing.

Know then that you can think of yourself as not existing while yet you are absolutely sure that you exist. I am astonished that you have said that you do not know this. For we think of many things that we know to exist, as not existing; and [we think of] many things that we know not to exist, as existing—not judging that it is really as we think but imagining it to be so. We *can*, in fact, think of something as not existing while knowing that it does exist, since we can [think of] the one and know the other at the same time. And we *cannot* think of something as not existing if yet we know that it does exist, since we cannot think of it as existing and not existing at the same time. He, therefore, who distinguishes these two senses of this assertion will understand that [in one sense] nothing can be thought as not existing while yet it is known to exist, and that [in another sense] whatever exists, save that-than-which-a-greater-cannot-be-thought, can be thought of as not existing even when we know that it does exist. Thus it is that, on the one hand, it is the distinguishing characteristic of God that He cannot be thought of as not existing, and that, on the other hand, many things, the while they do exist, cannot be thought of as not existing. In what sense, however, one can say that God can be thought of as not existing I think I have adequately explained in my tract.

As for the other objections you make against me on behalf of the Fool, it is quite easy to meet them, even for one weak in the head, and so I considered it a waste of time to show this. But since I hear that they appear to certain readers to have some force against me, I will deal briefly with them.

First, you often reiterate that I say that that which is greater than everything exists in the mind, and that if it is in the mind, it exists also in reality, for otherwise that which is greater than everything would not be that which is greater than everything. However, nowhere in all that I have said will you find such an argument. For 'that which is greater than everything' and 'that-than-which-a-greater-cannot-be-thought' are not equivalent for the purpose of proving the real existence of the thing spoken of. Thus, if anyone should say that 'that-than-which-a-greater-cannot-be-thought' is not something that actually exists, or that it can possibly not exist, or even can be thought of as not existing, he can easily be refuted. For what does not exist can possibly not exist, and what can not exist can be thought of as not existing. However, whatever can be thought of as not existing, if it actually exists, is not that-than-which-a-greater-cannot-be-thought. But if it does not exist, indeed even if it should exist, it would not be that-than-which-a-greater-cannot-be-thought. But it cannot be asserted that 'that-than-which-a-greater-cannot-be-thought' is not, if it exists, that-than-which-a-greater-cannot-be-thought, or that, if it should exist, it would not be that-than-which-a-greater-cannot-be-thought. It is evident, then, that it neither does not exist nor can not exist or be thought of as not existing. For if it does exist in another way it is not what it is said to be, and if it should exist [in another way] it would not be [what it was said to be].

However it seems that it is not as easy to prove this in respect of what is said to be greater than everything. For it is not as evident that that which can be thought of as not existing is not that which is greater than everything, as that it is not that-than-which-a-greater-cannot-be-thought. And, in the same way, neither is it indubitable that, if there is something which is 'greater than everything', it is identical with 'that-than-which-a-greater-cannot-be-thought'; nor, if there were [such a being], that no other like it might exist—as this is certain in respect of what is said to be 'that-than-which-a-greater-cannot-be-thought'. For what if someone should say that something that is greater than everything actually exists, and yet that this same being can be thought of as not existing, and that something greater than it can be thought, even if this does not exist? In this case can it be inferred as evidently that [this being] is therefore not that which is greater than everything, as it would quite evidently be said in the other case that it is therefore not that-than-which-a-greater-cannot-be-thought? The former [inference] needs, in fact, a premiss in addition to this which is said to be 'greater than everything'; but the latter needs nothing save this utterance itself, namely, 'that-than-which-a-greater-cannot-be-thought'. Therefore, if what 'that-than-which-a-greater-cannot-be-thought' of itself proves concerning itself cannot be proved in the same way in respect of what is said to be 'greater than everything', you criticize me unjustly for having said what I did not say, since it differs so much from what I did say.

If, however, it can [be proved] by means of another argument, you should not have criticized me for having asserted what can be proved. Whether it can [be proved], however, is easily appreciated by one who understands that it can [in respect of] 'that-than-which-a-greater-cannot-be-thought'. For one cannot in any way understand 'that-than-which-a-greater-cannot-be-thought' without [understanding that it is] that which alone is greater than everything. As, therefore, 'that-than-which-a-greater-cannot-be-thought' is understood and is in the mind, and is consequently judged to exist in true reality, so also that which is greater than everything is said to be understood and to exist in the mind, and so is necessarily inferred to exist in reality itself. You see, then, how right you were to compare me with that stupid person who wished to maintain that the Lost Island existed from the sole fact that being described it was understood.

You object, moreover, that any unreal or doubtfully real things at all can equally be understood and exist in the mind in the same way as the being I was speaking of. I am astonished that you urge this [objection] against me, for I was concerned to prove something which was in doubt, and for me it was sufficient that I should first show that it was understood and existed in the mind *in some way or other*, leaving it to be determined subsequently whether it was in the mind alone as unreal things are, or in reality also as true things are. For, if unreal or doubtfully real things are understood and exist in the mind in the sense that, when they are spoken of, he who hears them understands what the speaker means, nothing prevents what I have spoken of being understood and existing in the mind. But how are these [assertions] consistent, that is, when you assert that if someone speaks of unreal things you would understand whatever he says, and that, in the case of a thing which is not entertained in thought in the same way as even unreal things are, you do not say that you think of it or have it in thought upon hearing it spoken of, but rather that you understand it and have it in mind since, precisely, you cannot think of it save by understanding it, that is, knowing certainly that the thing exists in reality itself? How, I say, are both [assertions] consistent, namely that unreal things are understood, and that 'to understand' means knowing with certainty that something actually exists? You should have seen that nothing [of this applies] to me. But if unreal things are, in a sense, understood (this definition applying not to every kind of understanding but to a certain kind) then I ought not to be criticized for having said that 'that-than-which-a-greater-cannot-be-thought' is understood and is in the mind, even before it was certain that it existed in reality itself.

Next, you say that it can hardly be believed that when this [that-than-which-a-greater-cannot-be-thought] has been spoken of and heard, it cannot be thought not to exist, as even it can be thought that God does not exist. Now those who have attained even a little expertise in disputation and argument could reply to that on my behalf. For is it reasonable that someone should therefore deny what he understands because it is said to be [the same as] that which he denies since he does not understand it? Or if that is denied [to exist] which is understood only to some extent and is the same as what is not understood at all, is not what is in doubt more easily proved from the fact that it is in some mind than from the fact that it is in no mind at all? For this reason it cannot be believed that anyone should deny 'that-than-which-a-greater-cannot-be-thought' (which, being heard, he understands to some extent), on the ground that he denies God whose meaning he does not think of in any way at all. On the other hand, if it is denied on the ground that it is not understood completely, even so is not that which is understood in some way easier to prove than that which is not understood in any way? It was therefore not wholly without reason that, to prove against the Fool that God exists, I proposed 'that-than-which-a-greater-cannot-be-thought', since he would understand this in some way, [whereas] he would understand the former [God] in no way at all.

In fact, your painstaking argument that 'that-than-which-a-greater-cannot-be-thought' is not like the not-yet realized painting in the mind of the painter is beside the point. For I did not propose [the example] of the foreknown picture because I wanted to assert that what was at issue was in the same case, but rather that so I could show that something not understood as existing exists in the mind.

Again, you say that upon hearing of 'that-than-which-a-greater-cannot-be-thought' you cannot think of it as a real object known either generically or specifically or have it in your mind, on the grounds that you neither know the thing itself nor can you form an idea of it from other things similar to it. But obviously this is not so. For since everything that is less good is similar in so far as it is good to that which is more good, it is evident to every rational mind that, mounting from the less good to the more good we can from those things than which something greater can be thought conjecture a great deal about that-than-which-a-greater-cannot-be-thought. Who, for example, cannot think of this (even if he does not believe that what he thinks of actually exists) namely, that if something that has a beginning and end is good, that which, although it has had a beginning, does not, however, have an end, is much better? And just as this latter is better than the former, so also that which has neither beginning nor end is better again than this, even if it passes always from the past through the present to the future. Again, whether something of this kind actually exists or not, that which does not lack anything at all, nor is forced to change or move, is very much better still. Cannot this be thought? Or can we think of something greater than this? Or is not this precisely to form an idea of that-than-which-a-greater-cannot-be-thought from those things than which a greater can be thought? There is, then, a way by which one can form an idea of 'that-than-which-a-greater-cannot-be-thought'. In this way, therefore, the Fool who does not accept the sacred authority [of Revelation] can easily be refuted if he denies that he can form an idea from other things of 'that-than-which-a-greater-cannot-be-thought'. But if any orthodox Christian should deny this let him remember that 'the invisible things of God from the creation of the world are clearly seen through the things that have been made, even his eternal power and Godhead' [Rom. i. 20].

But even if it were true that [the object] that-than-which-a-greater-cannot-be-thought cannot be thought of nor understood, it would not, however, be false that [the formula] 'that-than-which-a-greater-cannot-be-thought' could be thought of and understood. For just as nothing prevents one from saying 'ineffable' although one cannot specify what is said to be ineffable; and just as one can think of the inconceivable—although one cannot think of what 'inconceivable' applies to—so also, when 'that-than-which-a-greater-cannot-be-thought' is spoken of, there is no doubt at all that what is heard can be thought of and understood even if the thing itself cannot be thought of and understood. For if someone is so witless as to say that there is not something than-which-a-greater-cannot-be-thought, yet he will not be so shameless as to say that he is not able to understand and think of what he was speaking about. Or if such a one is to be found, not only should his assertion be condemned, but he himself contemned. Whoever, then, denies that there is something than-which-a-greater-cannot-be-thought, at any rate understands and thinks of the denial he makes, and this denial cannot be understood and thought about apart from its elements. Now, one element [of the denial] is 'that-than-which-a-greater-cannot-be-thought'. Whoever, therefore, denies this understands and thinks of 'that-than-which-a-greater-cannot-be-thought'. It is evident, moreover, that in the same way one can think of and understand that which cannot not exist. And one who thinks of this thinks of something greater than one who thinks of what can not exist. When, therefore, one thinks of that-than-which-a-greater-cannot-be-thought, if one thinks of what can not exist, one does not think of that-than-which-a-greater-cannot-be-thought. Now the same thing cannot at the same time be thought of and not thought of. For this reason he who thinks of that-than-which-a-greater-cannot-be-thought does not think of something that can not exist but something that cannot not exist. Therefore what he thinks of exists necessarily, since whatever can not exist is not what he thinks of.

I think now that I have shown that I have proved in the above tract, not by a weak argumentation but by a sufficiently necessary one, that something-than-which-a-greater-cannot-be-thought exists in reality itself, and that this proof has not been weakened by the force of any objection. For the import of this proof is in itself of such force that what is spoken of is proved (as a necessary consequence of the fact that it is understood or thought of) both to exist in actual reality and to be itself whatever must be believed about the Divine Being. For we believe of the Divine Being whatever it can, absolutely speaking, be thought better to be than not to be. For example, it is better to be eternal than not eternal, good than not good, indeed goodness-itself than not goodness-itself. However, nothing of this kind cannot but be that-than-which-a-greater-cannot-be-thought. It is, then, necessary that 'that-than-which-a-greater-cannot-be-thought' should be whatever must be believed about the Divine Nature.

I thank you for your kindness both in criticizing and praising my tract. For since you praised so fulsomely those parts that appeared to you to be worthy of acceptance, it is quite clear that you have criticized those parts that seemed to you to be weak, not from any malice but from good will.

PETER ABAILARD

Peter Abailard was born in Brittany in 1079 and died in a monastery in 1142. The life of Abailard gives lie to the stereotype of philosophers as living an ivory-tower existence. He carried on a romance with the beautiful Heloise and secretly married her after she bore a child. Conflict with her uncle led Abailard to sequester Heloise, only to result in Abailard's being castrated by hired thugs. Subsequently, Heloise went to a convent and Abailard to the famous Abbey of Saint Denis, where he became a monk.

A student of William of Champeaux, Abailard was a brilliant and contentious itinerant teacher. He was notorious for showing up and taking students away from the resident faculty. Acerbic in style and master of medieval dialectic, Abailard was more than a match for his Scholastic opponents. His major philosophical concern was the problem of universals, that is, whether our ideas or concepts are themselves real or are only names for individual things. Abailard opposed both the nominalism of Roscelin and the extreme realism of William of Champeaux; he held that we experience only particulars but can, through the method of comparison, develop general ideas. He also bequeathed an interesting work in ethics, Know Thyself, *in which he stressed the importance of intention in moral culpability.*

From On Universals

Porphyry, as Boethius points out [in his Commentary on the *Isagoge*], raises three profitable questions whose answers are shrouded in mystery and though not a few philosophers have attempted to solve them, few have succeeded in doing so. The first is: Do genera and species really exist or are they simply something in the mind? It is as if [Porphyry] were asking whether their existence is a fact or merely a matter of opinion. The second is: Granting they do exist, are they corporeal or incorporeal? The third is: Do they exist apart from sensible things or only in them? For there are two types of incorporeal things. Some, like God or the soul, can subsist in their incorporeality apart from anything sensible. Others are unable to exist apart from the sensible objects in which they are found. A line, for example, is unable to exist apart from some bodily subject.

Porphyry sidesteps answering them with the remark: "For the present I refuse to be drawn into a discussion as to whether genus and species exist in reality or solely and simply in thought; or if they do exist whether they are corporeal or incorporeal, or whether, on the admission they are incorporeal, they are separated from sensibles or exist only in and dependent upon sensible things, and other things of this sort."

"Other things of this sort" can be interpreted in various ways. We could take him to mean: "I refuse to discuss these three questions and other related matters." For other relevant questions could be raised that pose similar problems. For instance, what is the common basis or reason for applying universal names to things, which boils down to explaining to what extent different things agree; or how should one understand those universal names wherein one seems to conceive of nothing, where the universal term in a word seems to have no referent? And there are many other difficult points. By understanding "other things of this sort" in this way, we can add a fourth question: Do genera and species, as long as they remain such, require that the subject they name have some reality or, if all the things they designate were destroyed, could the universal consist simply in its significance for the mind, as would be the case with the name "rose" when no roses are in bloom which it could designate in general? . . .

Since genera and species are obviously instances of universals and in mentioning them Porphyry touches on the nature of universals in general, we may distinguish the properties common to universals by studying them in these samples. Let us inquire then whether they apply only to *words* or to *things* as well.

Aristotle defines the universal as "that which is of such a nature as to be predicated of many." Porphyry, on the other hand, goes on to define the singular or individual as "that which is predicated of a single individual."

Authorities then seem to apply "universal" to things as much as they do to words. Aristotle himself does this, declaring by way of preface to his definition of the universal, that "some things are universal, others individual. Now by 'universal' I mean that which is of such a nature as to be predicated of many, whereas 'individual' is not something of this kind." Porphyry too, having stated that the species

---

is composed of a genus and difference, proceeds to locate it in the nature of things. From this it is clear that things themselves fall under a universal noun.

Nouns too are called universals. That is why Aristotle says: "The genus specifies the quality with reference to substance, for it signifies what sort of thing it is."

"It seems then that things as well as words are called universals." . . .

However, things taken either singly or collectively cannot be called universals, because they are not predicable of many. Consequently it remains to ascribe this form of universality to words alone. Just as grammarians call certain nouns proper and others appellative, so dialecticians call certain simple words particulars, that is, individuals, and others universals. A universal word is one which is able to be predicated of many by reason of its intention, such as the noun "man," which can be joined with the names of particular men by reason of the nature of the subject on which they are imposed. A particular word, however, is one which is predicable only of a single subject, as *Socrates* when it is taken as the name of but one individual. For if you take it equivocally, you give it the signification not of one word but of many. For according to Priscian, many nouns can obviously be brought together in a single word. When a universal then is described as "that which is predicable of many," *that which* indicates not only the simplicity of the word as a discrete expression, but also the unity of signification lacking in an equivocal term. . . .

Now that we have defined "universal" and "particular" in regard to words, let us investigate in particular the properties of those which are universal. For questions have been raised about universals, since serious doubts existed as to their meaning because there seemed to be no subject to which they referred. Neither did they express the sense of any one thing. These universal terms then appeared to be imposed on nothing, since it is clear that all things subsisting in themselves are individuals and, as has been shown, they do not share in some one thing by virtue of which a universal name could be given to them. Since it is certain then that (a) universals are not imposed on things by reason of their individual differences, for then they would not be common but singular, (b) nor can they designate things which share in some identical entity, for it is not a thing in which they agree, there seems to be nothing from which universals might derive their meaning, particularly since their sense is not restricted to any one thing. . . . Since "man" is imposed on individuals for an identical reason, viz. because each is a rational, mortal animal, the very generality of the designation prevents one from understanding the term of just one man in the way, for example, that one understands by Socrates just one unique person, which is why it is called a particular. But the common term "man" does not mean just Socrates, or any other man. Neither does it designate a collection, nor does it, as some think, mean just Socrates insofar as he is man. For even if Socrates alone were sitting in this house and because of that the proposition "A man sits in this house" is true, still by the name "man," there is no way of getting to Socrates except insofar as he too is a man. Otherwise, from the proposition itself, "sitting" would be understood to inhere in Socrates, so that from "A man sits in this house," one could infer "Socrates sits in this house." And the same applies to any other individual man. Neither can "A man sits in this house" be understood of a collection, since the proposition can be true if only one man is there. Consequently, there is not a single thing that "man" or any other universal term seems to signify, since there is not a single thing whose sense the term seems to express. Neither does it seem there could be any sense if no subject is thought of. Universals then appear to be totally devoid of meaning.

And yet this is not the case. For universals do signify distinct individuals to the extent of giving names to them, but this significative function does not require that one grasps a sense which arises out of them and which belongs to each of them. "Man," for example, does name individual things, but for the common reason that they are all men. That is why it is called a universal. Also there is a certain sense—common, not proper—that is applicable to those individuals which one conceives to be alike.

But let us look carefully now into some matters we have touched on only briefly, viz. (a) what is the common reason for imposing a universal name on things, (b) what is this intellectual conception of a common likeness, and (c) is a word said to be common because of some common cause by virtue of which all the things it designates are alike, or is it merely because we have a common concept for all of them, or is it for both of these reasons?

Let us consider first the question of the common

cause. As we noted earlier, each individual man is a discrete subject since he has as proper to himself not only an essence but also whatever forms [or qualifications] that essence may have. Nevertheless, they agree in this that they are all men. Since there is no man who is not a discrete or distinct individual thing, I do not say they agree "in man," but "in being a man." Now if you consider the matter carefully, man or any other thing is not the same as "to be a man," even as "not to be in a subject" is not a thing, nor is there anything which is "not to undergo contrariety" or "not to be subject to greater or lesser degrees," and still Aristotle says these are points in which all substances agree. Since there is no *thing* in which things could possibly agree, if there is any agreement among certain things, this must not be taken to be some *thing*. Just as Socrates and Plato are alike in being men, so a horse and donkey are alike in not being men. It is for this reason that they are called "nonmen." Different individuals then agree either in being the same or in not being the same, e.g. in being men or white, or in not being men or being white.

Still this agreement among things (which itself is not a thing) must not be regarded as a case of bringing together things which are real on the basis of nothing. In point of fact we do speak of this agreeing with that to the extent of their having the same status, that of man, i.e. the two agree in that they are men. But what we perceive is merely that they are men, and there is not the slightest difference between them, I say, in their being men, even though we may not call this an essence. But "being a man" (which is not a thing) we do call "the status of man" and we have also called it "the common cause for imposing on individuals a universal name." For we frequently give the name "cause" to some characteristic that is not itself a thing as when one says "He was beaten because he did not wish to appear in court." His not wishing to appear in court, cited here as a cause is not a [constitutive] essence [of his being beaten].

We can also designate as "the status of man" those things themselves in a man's nature which the one who imposed the word conceives according to a common likeness.

Having shown how universals signify, namely by functioning as names of things, and having presented what the reason for imposing such general names is, let us indicate just what these universal meanings consist of.

To begin with, let us point out the distinguishing features of all intellectual conception or understanding. Though sense perception as well as intellectual conception are both functions of the soul, there is a difference between the two. Bodies and what inhere in them are objects of sensory knowledge, e.g. a tower or its sensory qualities. In the exercise of this function, however, the soul makes use of corporeal instruments. In understanding or conceiving something intellectually, the soul needs no corporeal organ and consequently no bodily subject in which the thought object inheres is required. It is enough that the mind constructs for itself a likeness of these things and the action called intellection is concerned with this [cognitive content]. Hence, if the tower is removed or destroyed, the sense perception that dealt with it perishes, but the intellectual conception of the tower remains in the likeness preserved in the mind. As the act of sense perception is not the sensed thing itself, so the act of the intellect is not itself the form understood or conceived intellectually. Understanding is an activity of the soul by virtue of which it is said to understand, but the form toward which understanding is directed is a kind of image or construct *(res ficta)* which the mind fashions for itself at will, like those imaginary cities seen in dreams or the form of a projected building which the architect conceives after the manner of a blueprint. This construct is not something one can call either substance or accident.

Nevertheless, there are those who simply identify it with the act itself through which it is understood or conceived. Thus they speak of the tower building itself, which I think of when the tower is not there and which I conceive to be lofty, square, and situated in a spacious plain, as being the same as thinking of a tower. But we prefer to call the [conceptual] image as such the likeness of the thing.

There is of course nothing to prevent the act of understanding itself from being called in some sense a "likeness" because it obviously conceives what is, properly speaking, a likeness of the thing. Still, as we have said—and rightly so—the two are not the same. For, I ask: "Does the squareness or loftiness represent the actual form or quality possessed by the act of understanding itself when one thinks of the height and the way the tower is put together?"

Surely the actual squareness and height are present only in bodies and from an imagined quality no act of understanding or any other real essence can be constructed. What remains then but that the substance, like the quality of which it is the subject, is also fictive? Perhaps one could also say that a mirror or reflected image is not itself a true "thing," since there often appears on the whitish surface of the mirror a color of contrary quality. . . .

Having treated in general the nature of understanding, let us consider how a universal and a particular conception differ. The conception associated with a universal name is an image that is general and indiscriminate [*imago communis et confusa*], whereas the image associated with a singular word represents the proper and characteristic form, as it were, of a single thing, i.e. it applies to one and only one person. When I hear the word "man," for instance, a certain likeness arises in my mind which is so related to individual men that it is proper to none but common to all. But when I hear "Socrates," a certain form arises in my mind which is the likeness of a particular person. . . . Hence it is correct to say "man" does not rightly signify Socrates or any other man, since by virtue of this name no one in particular is identified; yet it is a name of particular things. "Socrates," on the other hand, must not only name a particular thing, but it must also determine just what thing is its subject. . . . To show what pertains to the nature of all lions, a picture can be constructed which represents nothing that is the peculiar property of only one of them. On the other hand, a picture suited to distinguish any one of them can be drawn by depicting something proper to the one in question, for example, by painting it as limping, maimed, or wounded by the spear of Hercules. Just as one can paint one figure that is general and another that is particular, so too can one form one conception of things that is common and another conception that is proper.

There is some question, however, and not without reason, whether or not this [universal] name also signifies this conceptual form to which the understanding is directed. Both authority and reason, however, seem to be unanimous in affirming that it does.

For Priscian, after first showing how universals were applied commonly to individuals, seemed to introduce another meaning they had, namely the common form. He states that "the general and special forms of things which were given intelligibility in the divine mind before being produced in bodies could be used to reveal what the natural genera and species of things are." In this passage he views God after the fashion of an artist who first conceives in his mind a [model or] exemplar form of what he is to fashion and who works according to the likeness of this form, which form is said to be embodied when a real thing is constructed in its likeness.

It may be all right to ascribe such a common conception to God, but not to man. For those works of God like a man, a soul, or a stone represent general or special states of nature, whereas those of a human artisan like a house or a sword do not. For "house" and "sword" do not pertain to nature as the other terms do. They are the names not of a substance but of something accidental and therefore they are neither genera not ultimate species. Conceptions by abstraction [of the true nature of things] may well be ascribed to the divine mind but may not be ascribed to that of man, because men, who know things only through the medium of their senses, scarcely ever arrive at such an ideal understanding and never conceive the [underlying] natures of things in their purity. But God knew all things he created for what they were and this even before they actually existed. He can discriminate between these individual states as they are in themselves; senses are no hindrance to him who alone has true understanding of things. Of those things which men have not experienced through the senses, they happen to have opinions rather than understanding, as we learn from experience. For having thought of some city before seeing it, we find on arriving there that it is quite different than we had thought.

And so I believe we have only an opinion about those forms like rationality, mortality, paternity, or what is within. Names for what we experience, however, produce understanding to the extent they can do so, for the one who coined the terms intended that they be imposed in accord with the [true] nature or properties of things, even though he himself was unable to do justice in thought to the nature or property of the thing. It is these common concepts, however, which Priscian calls general and special [i.e. generic and specific], that these general names or the names of species bring to the mind. He says that the universals function as proper names with regard to such conceptions, and although these names refer to the essences named only in an indiscriminate fashion, they direct the mind of the hearer immediately to that common conception in the same way that proper names direct attention to the one thing that they signify.

Porphyry too, in distinguishing between things constituted only in the likeness of matter and form and those actually composed of matter and form, seems to understand this common conception by the former. Boethius also, when he calls the conception gathered from a likeness of many things a genus or a species, seems to have in mind this same common conception. Some think that Plato subscribed to this view, i.e. to these common ideas—which he located in the *nous*—he gave the names of genus and species. On this point, perhaps, Boethius indicates some disagreement between Plato and Aristotle, where he speaks of Plato claiming not only that genera, species, and the rest should be understood to be universals, but also that they also have true existence and subsistence apart from bodies, as if to say that Plato understood these common concepts, which he assumed to exist in a bodiless form in the *nous*, to be universals. He means here by universal "a common likeness of many things" perhaps, rather than "predicable of many" as Aristotle understood the term. For this conception [itself] does not seem to be predicated of many in the way that a name is able to be applied to each of many things.

But his [i.e. Boethius'] statement that Plato thinks universals subsist apart from sensibles can be interpreted in another way, so that there is no disagreement between the philosophers. For Aristotle's statements about universals always subsisting in sensibles is to be understood of the way they actually do exist, because the animal nature (which the universal name "animal" designates and which is called a kind of universal in a transferred sense of the term) is never found to exist in anything which is not sensible. Plato, however, thinks this nature has such a natural subsistence in itself that it would retain its existence if it were not subject to sense [i.e. if it were not clothed with sensible accidents]. Hence what Aristotle denies to be actually the case, Plato, the investigator of the nature, ascribes to a natural capacity. Consequently there is no real disagreement between them.

Reason too seems to agree with these authorities in their apparent claim that the universal names designate these common concepts or forms. For what else does to conceive of them by name mean but that names signify them? But since we hold that these forms conceived are not simply the same as the acts of knowing them, there is in addition to the real thing and the act of understanding a third factor, viz. the signification or meaning of the name. Now while there is no authority for holding this, still it is not contrary to reason.

At this point, let us give an answer to the question we promised earlier to settle, namely whether the ability of universal words to refer to things in general is due to the fact that there is in them a common cause for imposing the words on them, or whether it is due to the fact that a common concept of them exists, or whether it is for both of these reasons. Now there seems to be no ground why it should not be for both of these reasons, but if we understand "common cause" as involving something of the nature of the things, then this seems to be the stronger of the two reasons.

Another point we must clarify is the one noted earlier, namely that these universal conceptions are formed by abstraction, and we must show how one can speak of them as isolated, naked, and pure without their being empty. But first about abstraction. Here we must remember that while matter and form are always fused together, the rational power of the mind is such that it can consider matter alone or form alone or both together. The first two are considerations by way of abstraction, since in order to study its precise nature, they abstract one thing from what does not exist alone. The third type of consideration is by way of synthesis. The substance of man, for instance, is a body, an animal, a man; it is invested with no end of forms. But when I turn my attention exclusively to the material essence of a substance, disregarding all its additional forms or qualifications, my understanding takes the form of a concept by abstraction. If I direct my attention, however, to nothing more than the corporeity of this substance, the resulting concept, though it represents a synthesis when compared with the previous concept (that of substance alone), is still formed by abstraction from the forms other than corporeity, such as animation, sensitivity, rationality, or whiteness, none of which I consider.

Such conceptions by abstraction might appear to be false or empty, perhaps, since they look to the thing in a way other than that in which it exists. For since they consider matter or form exclusively, and neither of these subsists separately, they clearly represent a conception of the thing otherwise than the way it is. Consequently, they seem to be vacuous, yet this is not really the case. For it is only when a thing is considered to have some property or nature which it does not actually possess that the conception which represents the thing otherwise than it is, is indeed empty. But this is not what happens in abstraction. For when I consider this man only in his nature as a substance or a body, but not as an animal, a man, or a grammarian, certainly I do not think of anything that is not in that nature, and still I do not attend to all that it has. And when I say that I attend only to what is in it, "only" refers to my attention and not to the way this characteristic exists, for otherwise my conception would be empty. For the thing does not only have this, but I only consider it as having this. And while I do consider it in some sense to be otherwise than it actually is, I do not consider it to be in a state or condition other than that in which it is, as was pointed out earlier. "Otherwise" means merely that the mode of thought is other than the mode of existing. For the thing in question is thought of not as separated, but separately from the other, even though it does not exist separately. Matter is perceived purely, form simply, even though the former does not exist purely nor the latter simply. Purity and simplicity, in a word, are features of our understanding, not of existence; they are characteristic of the way we think, not of the way things exist. Even the senses often function discriminatively where composite objects are concerned. If a statue is half gold, half silver, I can look separately at the gold and silver combined there, studying first the gold, then the silver exclusively, thus viewing piecemeal what is actually joined together, and yet I do not perceive to be divided what is not divided. In much the same way "understanding by way of abstraction" means "considering separately" but not "considering [it] as separated." Otherwise such understanding would be vacuous. . . .

But let us return to our *universal* conceptions, which must always be produced by way of abstraction. For when I hear "man" or "whiteness" or "white," I do not recall in virtue of the name all the natures or properties in those subjects to which the name refers. "Man" gives rise to the conception, indiscriminate, not discrete, of animal, rational and mortal only, but not of the additional accidents as well. Conceptions of individuals also can be formed by abstraction, as happens for example when one speaks of "this substance," "this body," "this animal," "this white," or "this whiteness." For by "this man," though I consider just man's nature, I do so as related to a certain subject, whereas by "man" I regard this nature simply in itself and not in relation to some one man. That is why a universal concept is correctly described as being *isolated, bare,* and *pure:* i.e. "isolated from sense," because it is not a perception of the thing as sensory; "bare," because it is abstracted from some or from all forms; "pure," because it is unadulterated by any reference to any single individual, since there is not just one thing, be it the matter or the form, to which it points, as we explained earlier when we described such a conception as indiscriminate.

Now that we have considered these matters, let us proceed to answer the questions posed by Porphyry about genera and species. This we can easily do now that we have clarified the nature of universals in general. The point of the first question was whether genera and species exist. More precisely, are they signs of something which really exists or of something that merely exists in thought, i.e. are they simply vacuous, devoid of any real reference, as is the case with words like "chimera" or "goat-stag," which fail to produce any coherent meaning? To this one has to reply that as a matter of fact they do serve to name things that actually exist and therefore are not the subjects of purely empty thoughts. But what they name are the selfsame things named by singular names. And still, there is a sense in which they exist as isolated, bare, and pure only in the mind, as we have just explained. . . .

The second question, viz. "Are they corporeal or incorporeal?" can be taken in the same way, that is, "Granting that they are signs of existing things, are these things corporeal or incorporeal?" For surely everything that exists, as Boethius puts it, is either corporeal or incorporeal, regardless of whether these words mean respectively: (1) a bodily or a bodiless substance, (2) something perceptible to the senses like man, wood, and whiteness, or something imperceptible in this way like justice or the soul. (3) "Corporeal" can also have the meaning of something discrete or individual, so that the question boils down to asking whether genera and species signify discrete individuals or not. A thoroughgoing investigator of truth considers not only what can be factually stated but also such possible opinions as might be proposed. Consequently, even though one is quite certain that only individuals are real, in view of the fact that someone might be of the opinion that there are other things that exist, it is justifiable to inquire about them. Now this third meaning of "corporeal" makes better sense of our question, reducing it to an inquiry as to whether it is discrete individuals or not that are signified. On the other hand, since nothing existing is incorporeal, i.e. nonindividual, "incorporeal" would seem to be superfluous in Boethius' statement that everything existing is either corporeal or incorporeal. Here the order of the questions, it seems, suggests nothing that would be of help except perhaps that corporeal and incorporeal, taken in another sense, do represent divisions of whatever exists and that this might also be the case here. The inquirer in this case would seem to be asking, in effect: "Since I see that some existing things are called corporeal and others incorporeal, I would like to know which of these names we should use for what universals signify?" The answer to this would be: "To some extent, 'corporeal' would be appropriate, since the *significata* are in essence discrete individuals. 'Incorporeal' would be a better description, however, of the way a universal term names things, for it does not point to them in an individual and specific fashion but points only in an indiscriminate way, as we have adequately explained above." Hence universal names are described both as corporeal (because of the nature of the things they point to) and as incorporeal (because of the way these things are signified, for although they name discrete individuals, universals do not name them individually or properly).

The third question ("Do they exist apart from or only in sensible things?") arises from the admission that they are incorporeal, since, as we noted [in the opening paragraph], there is a certain sense in which "existing in the sensible" and "not existing in the sensible" represent a division of the incorporeal. Now universals are said to exist in sensible things to the extent that they signify the inner substance of something which is sensible by reason of its external forms. While they signify this same substance actually existing in sensible garb, they point to what is by its nature something distinct from the sensible thing [i.e. as substance it is other than its accidental garb], as we said above in our reinterpretation of Plato. That is why Boethius does not claim that genera and species exist apart from sensible things, but only that they are understood apart from them, to the extent namely that the things conceived generically or specifically are viewed with reference to their nature in a rational fashion rather than in a sensory way, and they could indeed subsist in themselves [i.e. as individual substances] even if stripped of the exterior or [accidental] forms by which they come to the attention of the senses. For we admit that all genera and species exist in things perceptible to the senses. Since our understanding of them has always been described as something apart from the senses, however, they appeared not to be in sensible things in any way. There was every reason, then, to ask whether they could be in sensibles. And to this question, the answer is that some of them are, but only to the extent, as was explained, that they represent the enduring substrate that lies beneath the sensible.

We can take corporeal and incorporeal in this second question as equivalent to sensible and insensible, so that the sequence of questions becomes more orderly. And since our understanding of universals is derived solely from sense perceptions, as has been said, one could appropriately ask whether universals were sensible or insensible. Now the answer is that some of them are sensible (we refer here to the nature of those things classed as sensible) and the same time not sensible (we refer here to the way they are signified). For while it is sensible things that these universals name, they do not designate these things in the way they are perceived by the senses, i.e. as distinct individuals, and when things are designated only in universal terms the senses cannot pick them out. Hence the question arose: "Do universals designate only sensible things, or is there something else they signify?" And the answer to this is that they signify both the sensible things themselves and also that common concept which Priscian ascribes above all to the divine mind.

As for the fourth question we added to the others, our solution is this. We do not want to speak of there being universal *names* when the things they name have perished and they can no longer be predicated of many and are not common names of anything, as would be the case when all the roses were gone. Nevertheless, "rose" would still have meaning for the mind even though it names nothing. Otherwise, "There is no rose" would not be a proposition.

From Ethics *or* Know Thyself

PROLOGUE

In the study of morals we deal with the defects or qualities of the mind which dispose us to bad or good actions. Defects and qualities are not only mental, but also physical. There is bodily weakness; there is also the endurance which we call strength. There is sluggishness or speed; blindness or sight. When we now speak of defects, therefore, we pre-suppose defects of the mind, so as to distinguish them from the physical ones. The defects of the mind are opposed to the qualities; injustice to justice; cowardice to constancy; intemperance to temperance.

CHAPTER I

The Defect of Mind Bearing Upon Conduct

Certain defects or merits of mind have no connection with morals. They do not make human life a matter of praise or blame. Such are dull wits or quick insight; a good or a bad memory; ignorance or knowledge. Each of these features is found in good and bad alike. They have nothing to do with the system of morals, nor with making life base or honourable. To exclude these we safeguarded above the phrase 'defects of mind' by adding 'which dispose to bad actions,' that is, those defects which incline the will to what least of all either should be done or should be left undone.

CHAPTER II

How Does Sin Differ From a Disposition to Evil?

Defect of this mental kind is not the same thing as sin. Sin, too, is not the same as a bad action. For example, to be irascible, that is, prone or easily roused to the agitation of anger is a defect and moves the mind to unpleasantly impetuous and irrational action. This defect, however, is in the mind so that the mind is liable to wrath, even when it is not actually roused to it. Similarly, lameness, by reason of which a man is said to be lame, is in the man himself even when he does not walk and reveal his lameness. For the defect is there though action be lacking. So, also, nature or constitution renders many liable to luxury. Yet they do not sin because they are like this, but from this very fact they have the material of a struggle whereby they may, in the virtue of temperance, triumph over themselves and win the crown. As Solomon says: 'Better a patient than a strong man; and the Lord of his soul than he that taketh a city.' (Prov. xvi, 32.) For religion does not think it degrading to be beaten by man; but it is degrading to be beaten by one's lower self. The former defeat has been the fate of good men. But, in the latter, we fall below ourselves. The Apostle commends victory of this sort; 'No one shall be crowned who has not truly striven.' (2 Tim. ii, 5.) This striving, I repeat, means standing less against men than against myself, so that defects may not lure me into base consent. Though men cease to oppose us, our defects do not cease. The fight with them is the more dangerous because of its repetition. And as it is the more difficult, so victory is the more glorious. Men, however much they prevail over us, do not force baseness upon us, unless by their practice of vice they turn us also to it and overcome us through our own wretched consent. They may dominate our body; but while our mind is free, there is no danger to true freedom. We run no risk of base servitude. Subservience to vice, not to man, is degradation. It is the overlordship of defects and not physical serfdom which debases the soul.

CHAPTER III

Definition of 'Defect' and of Sin

Defect, then, is that whereby we are disposed to sin. We are, that is, inclined to consent to what we ought not to do, or to leave undone what we ought to do. Consent of this kind we rightly call sin. Here is the reproach of the soul meriting damnation or being declared guilty by God. What is that consent but to despise God and to violate his laws? God cannot be set at enmity by injury, but by contempt. He

From Peter Abailard, *Abailard's Ethics,* trans. J. Ramsay McCallum (New York: Richmond Publishing Co., 1976), pp. 15–37. Reprinted by permission of the publisher.

is the highest power, and is not diminished by any injury, but He avenges contempt of Himself. Our sin, therefore, is contempt of the Creator. To sin is to despise the Creator; that is, not to do for Him what we believe we should do for Him, or, not to renounce what we think should be renounced on His behalf. We have defined sin negatively by saying that it means not doing or not renouncing what we ought to do or renounce. Clearly, then, we have shown that sin has no reality. It exists rather in *not being* than in *being*. Similarly we could define shadows by saying: The absence of light where light usually is.

Perhaps you object that sin is the desire or will to do an evil deed, and that this will or desire condemns us before God in the same way as the will to do a good deed justifies us. There is as much quality, you suggest, in the good will as there is sin in the evil will; and it is no less 'in being' in the latter than in the former. By willing to do what we believe to be pleasing to God we please Him. Equally, by willing to do what we believe to be displeasing to God, we displease Him and seem either to violate or despise His nature.

But diligent attention will show that we must think far otherwise of this point. We frequently err; and from no evil will at all. Indeed, the evil will itself, when restrained, though it may not be quenched, procures the palm-wreath for those who resist it. It provides, not merely the materials for combat, but also the crown of glory. It should be spoken of rather as a certain inevitable weakness than as sin. Take, for example, the case of an innocent servant whose harsh master is moved with fury against him. He pursues the servant, drawing his sword with intent to kill him. For a while the servant flies and avoids death as best he can. At last, forced all unwillingly to it, he kills his master so as not to be killed by him. Let anyone say what sort of evil will there was in this deed. His will was only to flee from death and preserve his own life. Was this an evil will? You reply: 'I do not think this was an evil will. But the will that he had to kill the master who was pursuing him was evil.' Your answer would be admirable and acute if you could show that the servant really willed what you say that he did. But, as I insisted, he was unwillingly forced to his deed. He protracted his master's life as long as he could, knowing that danger also threatened his own life from such a crime. How, then was a deed done voluntarily by which he incurred danger to his own life?

Your reply may be that the action was voluntary because the man's will was to escape death even though it may not have been to kill his master. This charge might easily be preferred against him. I do not rebut it. Nevertheless, as has been said, that will be which he sought to evade death, as you urge, and not to kill his master, cannot at all be condemned as bad. He did, however, fail by consenting, though driven to it through fear of death, to an unjust murder which he ought rather to have endured than committed. Of his own will, I mean, he took the sword. It was not handed to him by authority. The Truth saith: 'Everyone that taketh the sword shall perish by the sword.' (Matt. xxvi, 52.) By his rashness he risked the death and damnation of his soul. The servant's wish, then, was not to kill has master, but to avoid death. Because he *consented,* however, as he should not have done, to murder, this wrongful consent preceding the crime was sin.

Someone may interpose: 'But you cannot conclude that he wished to kill his master because, in order to escape death, he was willing to kill his master. I might say to a man; I am willing for you to have my cape so that you may give me five shillings. Or, I am glad for you to have it at this price. But I do not hand it over because I desire you to have possession of it.' No, and if a man in prison desired under duresse, to put his son there in his place that he might secure his own ransom, should we therefore admit that he wished to send his son to prison?

It was only with many a tear and groan that he consented to such a course.

The fact is that this kind of will, existing with much internal regret, is not, if I may so say, *will,* but a passive submission of mind. It is so because the man wills one thing on account of another. He puts up with *this* because he really desires *that.* A patient is said to submit to cautery or lancet that he may obtain health. Martyrs endured that they might come to Christ; and Christ, too, that we may be saved by his passion.

Yet we are not bound to admit simply that these people therefore wish for this mental unease. Such unease can only be where something occurs contrary to wish. No man suffers so long as he fulfils his wish and does what he likes to experience. The Apostle says: 'I desire to depart and to be with Christ' (Phil. i, 23), that is, to die so that I may attain to him. Elsewhere this apostle says: 'We desire not to be despoiled of our garments, but to be clothed from above, that our mortal part may be swallowed up in life.' This notion, Blessed Augustine reminds us, was contained in the Lord's address to Peter: 'Thou shalt extend thy hands and another shall gird thee, and lead thee whither thou willest not.' (John xxi, 18.) The Lord also spoke to the Father out of the weakness of the human nature which he had taken upon himself: 'If it be possible, let this cup pass from me; nevertheless not as I will, but as thou willest.' (Matt. xxvi, 39.) His spirit naturally trembled before the great terror of death: and he could not speak of what he knew to be punishment as a matter of his own will. When elsewhere it is written of Him: 'He was offered because He himself willed it' (Isaiah liii, 7), it must be understood either of His divine nature, in whose will it was that he should suffer as a man, or 'He himself willed it' must be taken according to the Psalmist's phrase: 'Whatsoever he willed, that he did.' (Ps. cxiii, 3.)

Sin, therefore, is sometimes committed without an evil will. Thus sin cannot be defined as 'will.' True, you will say, when we sin under constraint, but not when we sin willingly, for instance, when we will to do something which we know ought not to be done by us. There the evil will and sin seem to be the same thing. For example a man sees a woman; his concupiscence is aroused; his mind is enticed by fleshly lust and stirred to base desire. This wish, this lascivious longing, what else can it be, you say, than sin?

I reply: What if that wish may be bridled by the power of temperance? What if its nature is never to be entirely extinguished but to persist in struggle and not fully fail even in defeat? For where is the battle if the antagonist is away? Whence the great reward without grave endurance? When the fight is over nothing remains but to reap the reward. Here we strive in contest in order elsewhere to obtain as victors a crown. Now, for a contest, an opponent is needed who will resist, not one who simply submits. This opponent is our evil will over which we triumph when we subjugate it to the divine will. But we do not entirely destroy it. For we needs must ever expect to encounter our enemy. What achievement before God is it if we undergo nothing contrary to our own will, but merely practice what we please? Who will be grateful to us if in what we say we do for him we merely satisfy our own fancy?

You will say, what merit have we with God in acting willingly or unwillingly? Certainly none: I reply. He weighs the intention rather than the deed in his recompense. Nor does the deed, whether it proceed from a good or an evil will, add anything to the merit, as we shall show shortly. But when we set His will before our own so as to follow His and not ours, our merit with God is magnified, in accordance with that perfect word of Truth: 'I came not to do mine own will, but the will of Him that sent me.' (John vi, 38.) To this end He exhorts us: 'If anyone comes to me, and does not hate father, and mother . . . yea his own soul also, he is not worthy of me.' (Luke xiv, 26.) That is to say, 'unless a man renounces his parents' influence and his own will and submits himself to my teaching, he is not worthy of me.' Thus we are bidden to hate our father, not to destroy him. Similarly with our own will. We must not be led by it; at the same time, we are not asked to root it out altogether.

When the Scripture says: 'Go not after your own desires' (Eccles. xviii, 30) and: 'Turn from your own will' (ibid.), it instructs us not to fulfil our desires. Yet it does not say that we are to be wholly without them. It is vicious to give in to our desires; but not to have any desires at all is impossible for our weak nature.

The sin, then, consists not in desiring a woman, but in consent to the desire, and not the wish for whoredom, but the consent to the wish is damnation.

Let us see how our conclusions about sexual intemperance apply to theft. A man crosses another's garden. At the sign of the delectable fruit his desire is aroused. He does not, however, give way to desire so as to take anything by theft or rapine, although his mind was moved to strong inclination by the thought of the delight of eating. Where there is desire, there, without doubt, will exists. The man desires the eating of that fruit wherein he doubts not that there will be delight. The weakness of nature in this man is compelled to desire the fruit which, without the master's permission, he has no right to take. He conquers the desire, but does not extinguish it. Since, however, he is not enticed into consent, he does not descend to sin.

What, then, of your objection? It should be clear from such instances, that the wish or desire itself of doing what is not seemly is never to be called sin, but rather, as we said, the consent is sin. We consent to what is not seemly when we do not draw ourselves back from such a deed, and are prepared, should opportunity offer, to perform it completely. Whoever is discovered in this intention, though his guilt has yet to be completed in deed, is already guily before God in so far as he strives with all his might to sin, and accomplishes within himself, as the blessed Augustine reminds us, as much as if he were actually taken in the act.

But while wish is not sin, and, as we have said, we sometimes commit sin unwillingly, there are nevertheless those who assert that every sin is voluntary. In this respect they discover a certain difference between sin and will. Will is one thing, they say, but a voluntary act is another. They mean that there is a distinction between will and what is done willingly. If, however, we call sin what we have already decided that it essentially is, namely, contempt of God or consent to that which we believe should not, for God's sake, be done how can we say that sin is voluntary? I mean, how can we say that we wish to despise God? What is sin but sinking below a standard, or becoming liable to damnation? For although we desire to do what we know deserves punishment, yet we do not desire to be punished. Thus plainly we are reprobate. We are willing to do wrong; but we are unwilling to bear the just punishment of wrongdoing. The punishment which is just displeases: the deed which is unjust pleases. Often we woo a married woman because of her charm. Our wish is not so much to commit adultery as a longing that she were unmarried. On the other hand, many covet the wives of influential men for the sake of their own fame, and not for the natural attractiveness of these ladies. Their wish is for adultery rather than sexual relationship, the major in preference to the minor excess. Some, too, are ashamed altogether of being betrayed into any consent to concupiscence or evil will; and thus from the weakness of the flesh are compelled to wish what they least of all wish to wish.

How, then, a wish which we do not wish to have can be called voluntary, as it is according to those thinkers I have mentioned, so that all sin becomes a matter of voluntary action, I assuredly do not understand, unless by voluntary is meant that no action is determined, since a sin is never a predestined event. Or perhaps we are to take 'voluntary' to be that which proceeds from some kind of will. For although the man who slew his master had no will to perform the actual murder, nevertheless he did it from some sort of will, because he certainly wished to escape or defer death.

Some are intensely indignant when they hear us assert that the act of sinning adds nothing to guilt or damnation before God. Their contention is that in this act of sinning a certain delight supervenes, which increases the sin, as in sexual intercourse or indulgence in food which we referred to above. Their statement is absurd unless they can prove that physical delight of this kind is itself sin, and that such pleasure cannot be taken without a sin being thereby committed. If it be as they suppose, then no one is permitted to enjoy physical pleasure. The married do not escape sin when they employ their physical privilege; nor yet the man who eats with relish his own fruits.

Invalids, too, who are treated to more delicate dishes to aid their recovery of strength would likewise be guilty, since they are not able to eat without a sense of delight and should this be lacking, the food does them no good. Finally, God, the Creator of nourishment and of the bodies which receive it, would not be without guilt for having instilled savours which necessarily involve in sin those who ignorantly use them. Yet how should He supply such things for our consumption, or permit them to be consumed, if it were impossible for us to eat them without sin? How, again, can it be said that there is sin in doing what is allowed? In regard to those matters which once were unlawful and forbidden, if they are later allowed and made lawful, they can be done entirely without sin. For instance, the eating of pork and many other things once out of bounds to the Jew are now free to us Christians. When, therefore, we see Jews turned Christian gladly eating food of this sort which the law had prohibited, how can we defend their rectitude except by affirming that this latitude has now been conceded to them by God?

Well, in what was formerly a food restriction and is now food freedom, the concession of freedom excludes sin and eliminates contempt of God. Who then shall say that a man sins in respect of a matter which the divine permission has made lawful for him? If the marriage-bed or the eating of even delicate food was permitted from the first day of our creation, when we lived in Paradise without sin, who can prove that we transgress in these enjoyments, so long as we do not pass the limits of the permission?

Another objection is that matrimonial intercourse and the eating of tasty food are only allowed on condition of being taken without pleasure. But, if this is so, then they are allowed to be done in a way in which they never can be done. That concession is not reasonable which concedes that a thing shall be so done as it is certain that it cannot be done. By what reasoning did the law aforetime enforce matrimony so that each might leave his seed to Israel? Or, how did the Apostle oblige wives to fulfil the mutual debt if these acts could not be done without sinning? How can he refer to this debt when already it is of necessity sin? Or how should a man be compelled to do what he will grieve God by doing? Hence, I think that it is plain that no natural physical delight can be set down as sin, nor can it be called guilt for men to delight in what, when it is done, must involve the feeling of delight.

For example, if anyone obliged a monk, bound in chains, to lie among women, and the monk by the softness of the couch and by contact with his fair flatterers is allured into delight, though not into consent, who shall presume to designate guilt the delight which is naturally awakened?

You may urge, with some thinkers, that the carnal pleasure, even in lawful intercourse, involves sin. Thus David says: 'Behold in sin was I conceived.' (Ps. l, 7.) And the Apostle, when he had said: 'Ye return to it again' (1 Cor. vii, 5), adds, nevertheless, 'This I say by way of concession, not of command.' (ibid., v, 6.) Yet authority rather than reason, seems to dictate the view that we should allow simple physical delight to be sin. For, assuredly, David was conceived not in fornication, but in matrimony: and concession, that is forgiveness, does not, as this standpoint avers, condone when there is no guilt to forgive. As for what David meant when he says that he had been conceived 'in iniquity' or 'in sin' and does not say 'whose' sin, he referred to the general curse of original sin, wherein from the guilt of our first parents each is subject to damnation, as it is elsewhere stated: 'None are pure of stain, not the infant a day old, if he has life on this earth.' As the blessed Jerome reminds us and as manifest reason teaches, the soul of a young child is without sin. If, then, it is pure of sin, how is it also impure by sinful corruption? We must understand the infant's purity from sin in reference to its personal guilt. But its contact with sinful corruption, its 'stain,' is in reference to penalty owed by mankind because of Adam's sin. He who has not yet perceived by reason what he ought to do cannot be guilty of contempt of God. Yet he is not free from the contamination of the sin of his first parents, from which he contracts the penalty, though not the guilt, and bears in penalty what they committed in guilt. When, therefore, David says that he was conceived in iniquity or sin, he sees himself subject to the general sentence of damnation from the guilt of his racial parents, and he assigns these sins, not to his father and mother but to his first parents.

When the Apostle speaks of indulgence, he must not be understood as some would wish to understand him, to mean permission to be equivalent to pardon for sin. His statement is: 'By way of indulgence not of command.' He might equally have said: 'By permission, not by force.' If husband and wife wish and decide upon mutual agreement they can abstain altogether from intercourse, and may not be compelled to it by command. But should they not so decide they have indulgence, that is, permission to substitute a less perfect for a more perfect rule of life. The Apostle, in this passage, did not therefore refer to pardon for sin, but to the permission of a less strict life for the avoidance of fornication. He meant that this lower level might elude the peaks of sin, and by its inferior standing escape the greater guilt.

We come, then, to this conclusion, that no one who sets out to assert that all fleshly desire is sin may say that the sin itself is increased by the doing of it. For this would mean extending the consent of the soul into the exercise of the action. In short, one would be stained not only by consent to baseness, but also by the mire of the deed, as if what happens externally in the body could possibly soil the soul. Sin is not, therefore, increased by the doing of an action: and nothing mars the soul except what is of its own nature, namely consent. This we affirmed was alone sin, preceding action in will, or subsequent to the performance of action. Although we wish for, or do, what is unseemly, we do not therefore sin. For such deeds not uncommonly occur without there being any sin. On the other hand, there may be consent without the external effects, as we have indicated. There was wish without consent in the case of the man who was attracted by a woman whom he caught sight of, or who was tempted by his neighbour's fruit, but who was not enticed into consent. There was evil consent without evil desire in the servant who unwillingly killed his master.

Certain acts which ought not to be done often are done, and without any sin, when, for instance, they are committed under force or ignorance. No one, I think, ignores this fact. A woman under constraint of violence, lies with another's husband. A man, taken by some trick, sleeps with one whom he supposed to be his wife, or kills a man, in the belief that he himself has the right to be both judge and executioner. Thus to desire the wife of another or actually to lie with her is not sin. But to consent to that desire or to that action is sin. This consent to covetousness the law calls covetousness in saying: 'Thou shalt not covet.' (Deut. v, 21.) Yet that which we cannot avoid ought not to be forbidden, nor that wherein, as we said, we do not sin. But we should be cautioned about the consent to covetousness. So, too, the saying of the Lord must be understood: 'Whosoever shall look upon a woman to desire her.' (Matt. v, 28.) That is, whosoever shall so look upon her as to slip into consent to covetousness, 'has already committed adultery with her in his heart' (Matt. v, 28), even though he may not have committed adultery in deed. He is guilty of sin, though there be no sequel to his intention.

Careful account will reveal that wherever actions are restricted by some precept or prohibition, these refer rather to will and consent than to the deeds themselves. Otherwise nothing relative to a person's moral merit could be included under a precept. Indeed, actions are so much the less worth prescribing as they are less in our power to do. At the same time, many things we are forbidden to do for which there exists in our will both the inclination and the consent.

The Lord God says: 'Thou shalt not kill. Thou shalt not bear false witness.' (Deut. v, 17, 20.) If we accept these cautions as being only about actions, as the words suggest, then guilt is not forbidden, but simply the activity of guilt. For we have seen that actions may be carried out without sin, as that it is not sin to kill a man or to lie with another's wife. And even the man who desires to bear false testimony, and is willing to utter it, so long as he is silent for some reason and does not speak, is innocent before the law, that is, if the prohibition in this matter be accepted literally of the action. It is not said that we should not *wish* to give false witness, or that we should not *consent* in bearing it, but simply that we should not bear false witness.

Similarly, when the law forbids us to marry or have intercourse with our sisters, if this prohibition relates to deed rather than to intention, no one can keep the commandment, for a sister unless we recognize her, is just a woman. If a man, then, marries his sister in error, is he a transgressor for doing what the law forbade? He is not, you will reply, because, in acting ignorantly in what he did, he did not consent to a transgression. Thus a transgressor is not one who *does* what is prohibited. He is one who *consents* to what is prohibited. The prohibition is, therefore, not about action, but about consent. It is as though in saying: 'Do not do this or that,' we meant: 'Do not consent to do this or that,' or 'Do not wittingly do this.'

Blessed Augustine, in his careful view of this question, reduces every sin or command to terms of charity and covetousness, and not to works. 'The law,' he says, 'inculcates nothing but charity, and forbids nothing but covetousness.' The Apostle, also, asserts: 'All the law is contained in one word: thou shalt love thy neighbour as thyself,' (Rom. xiii, 8, 10), and again, 'Love is the fulfilling of the law.' (ibid.)

Whether you actually give alms to a needy person, or charity makes you ready to give, makes no difference to the merit of the deed. The will may be there when the opportunity is not. Nor does it rest entirely with you to deal with every case of need which you encounter. Actions which are right and actions which are far from right are done by good and bad men alike. The intention alone separates the two classes of men.

Augustine reminds us that in the self-same action we find God the Father, the Lord Jesus Christ, and also Judas the betrayer. The betrayal of the Son was accomplished by God the Father, and by the Son, and by the betrayer. For 'the Father delivered up the Son, and the Son Himself' (Rom. viii, 32; Gal. ii, 22), as the Apostle says, and Judas delivered up his Master. The traitor, therefore, did the same thing as God Himself. But did Judas do anything well? No. Good certainly came of his act; but his act was not well done, nor was it destined to benefit him.

God considers not the action, but the spirit of the action. It is the intention, not the deed wherein the merit or praise of the doer consists. Often, indeed, the same action is done from different motives: for justice sake by one man, for an evil reason by another. Two men, for instance, hang a guilty person. The one does it out of zeal for justice; the other in resentment for an earlier enmity. The action of hanging is the same. Both men do what is good and what justice demands. Yet the diversity of their intentions causes the same deed to be done from different motives, in the one case good, in the other bad.

Everyone knows that the devil himself does nothing without God's permission, when he either punishes a wicked man according to his deserts, or is allowed to afflict a just man for moral cleansing or for an example of endurance. Since, however, in doing what God permits the devil moves at the spur of his own malice, the power which he has may be called good, or even just, while his will is for ever unjust. He receives, that is, the power from God, but his will is of himself.

Who, among the elect, can ever emulate the deeds of hypocrites? Who, for the love of God, ever endures or undertakes so much as they do from thirst for human praise? Who does not agree that sometimes what God forbids may rightly be done, while, contrarily, He may counsel certain things which of all things are least convenient? We note how He forbade certain miracles, whereby He had healed infirmities, to be made public. He set an example of humility lest any man should claim glory for the grace bestowed on him. Nevertheless, the recipients of those benefits did not cease to broadcast them, to the praise of Him who had done such things, and yet had forbidden them to be revealed. Thus we read: 'As much as He bade them not to speak, so much the more did they publish abroad, etc.' Will you judge these men guilty of a fault who acted contrary to the command which they had received, and did so wittingly? Who can acquit them of wrong-doing, unless by finding that they did not act out of contempt for the One who commanded, but decided to do what was to His honour? How, then, did the matter stand? Did Christ command what ought not to have been commanded? Or, did the newly-healed men disobey when they should have obeyed? The command was a good thing; yet it was not good for it to be obeyed.

In the case of Abraham, also, you will accuse God for first enjoining the sacrifice of Abraham's son, and then revoking the command. Has, then, God never *wisely commanded* anything which, if *it had come about*, would not have been good? If good, you will object, why was it afterwards forbidden? But conceive that it was good for the same thing to be prescribed and also to be prohibited. God, we know, permits nothing, and does not himself consent to achieve anything apart from rational cause. Thus it is the pure intention of the command, not the execution of the action which justifies God in wisely commanding what would not in actual fact be good. God did not intend Abraham to sacrifice his son, or command this sacrifice to be put into effect. His aim was to test Abraham's obedience, constancy of faith, and love towards Him, so that these qualities should be left to us as an example. This intention the Lord God plainly asserts afterwards in saying: 'Now know I that thou fearest the Lord.' (Gen. xxii, 12.) It is as if he frankly said: 'I commanded you: you showed yourself ready to obey Me. Both these things were done so that others might know what I had Myself known of you from the beginning.' There was a right intention on God's part; but it was not right for it to be put in practice. The prohibition, too, in the case of the miracles of healing was right. The object of this prohibition was not for it to be obeyed, but for an example to be given to our weak spirit in avoiding empty applause. God, in the one case enjoined an action which, if obeyed, would not have been good. In the other case, He forbade what was worth putting into fact, namely, a knowledge of Christ's miracles. The intention excuses Him in the first matter, just as the intention excuses the men who, in the second instance, were healed and did not carry out his injunction. They knew that the precept was not given to be practised, but in order that the aforenamed example of moderation in a successful miracle might be set. In keeping, then, the spirit of the command they showed, by actually disobeying no contempt for Him with whose intention they knew that they were acting.

A scrutiny of the deed rather than of the intention will reveal, then, cases where men frequently not only wish to go against God's bidding, but carry their wish knowingly into effect, and do so without any guilt of sin. An action or a wish must not be called bad because it does not in actual fact fall in with God's command. It may well be that the doer's intention does not at all differ from the will of his divine superior. The intention exonerates Him who gave a practically unseemly command: the intention excuses the man who, out of kindness, disobeyed the command to conceal the miracle.

Briefly to summarize the above argument: Four things were postulated which must be carefully distinguished from one another.

1. Imperfection of soul, making us liable to sin.
2. Sin itself, which we decided is consent to evil or contempt of God.

3. The will or desire of evil.

4. The evil deed.

To wish is not the same thing as to fulfil a wish. Equally, to sin is not the same as to carry out a sin. In the first case, we sin by consent of the soul: the second is a matter of the external effect of an action, namely, when we fulfil in deed that whereunto we have previously consented. When, therefore, temptation is said to proceed through three stages, suggestion, delight, consent, it must be understood that, like our first parents, we are frequently led along these three paths to the commission of sin. The devil's persuasion comes *first* promising from the taste of the forbidden fruit immortality. Delight follows. When the woman sees the beautiful tree, and perceives that the fruit is good, her appetite is whetted by the anticipated pleasure of tasting. This desire she ought to have repressed, so as to obey God's command. But in consenting to it, she was drawn *secondly* into sin. By penitence she should have put right this fault, and obtained pardon. Instead, she *thirdly* consummated the sin by the deed. Eve thus passed through the three stages to the commission of sin.

By the same avenues we also arrive not at sin, but at the action of sin, namely, the doing of an unseemly deed through the suggestion or prompting of something within us. If we already know that such a deed will be pleasant, our imagination is held by anticipatory delight and we are tempted thereby in thought. So long as we give consent to such delight, we sin. Lastly, we pass to the third stage, and actually commit the sin.

It is agreed by some thinkers that carnal suggestion, even though the person causing the suggestion be not present, should be included under sinful suggestion. For example, a man having seen a woman falls into a sensual desire of her. But it seems that this kind of suggestion should simply be called delight. This delight, and other delights of the like kind, arise naturally and, as we said above, they are not sinful. The Apostle calls them 'human temptations.' No temptation has taken you yet which was not common to men. God is faithful, and will not suffer you to be tempted above what you are able; but will, with the temptation make a way of escape, that you may be able to bear it.' By temptation is meant, in general, any movement of the soul to do something unseemly, whether in wish or consent. We speak of human temptation without which it is hardly or never possible for human weakness to exist. Such are sexual desire, or the pleasures of the table. From these the Psalmist asks to be delivered when he says: 'Deliver me from my wants, O Lord' (Ps. xxiv, 17); that is, from the temptations of natural and necessary appetites that they may not influence him into sinful consent. Or, he may mean: 'When this life is over, grant me to be without those temptations of which life has been full.'

When the Apostle says: 'No temptation has taken you but what is human,' his statement amounts to this: Even if the soul be stirred by that delight which is, as we said, human temptation, yet God would not lead the soul into that consent wherein sin consists. Someone may object: But by what power of our own are we able to resist those desires? We may reply: 'God is faithful, who will not allow you to be tempted,' as the Scripture says. In other words: We should rather trust him than rely upon ourselves. He promises help, and is true to his promises. He is faithful, so that we should have complete faith in him. Out of pity God diminishes the degree of human temptation, 'does not suffer us to be tempted above what we are able,' in order that it may not drive us to sin at a pace we cannot endure, when, that is, we strive to resist it. Then, too, God turns the temptation to our advantage: for He trains us thereby so that the recurrence of temptation causes us less care, and we fear less the onset of a foe over whom we have already triumphed, and whom we know how to meet.

Every encounter, not as yet undertaken, is for that reason, to us, a matter of more anxiety and dismay. But when such an encounter comes to those accustomed to victory, its force and terror alike vanish.

JOHN OF SALISBURY

John of Salisbury was born in England ca. 1125. As a secretary to Thomas Beckett, the Archbishop of Canterbury, John was exposed to the extreme intrigue characteristic of the politics of church and state in the twelfth century. His Policraticus *details some of these issues, especially the duties and problems of a medieval prince. For our purposes, a more interesting work is* The Metalogicon, *which praises a true philosophical education and satirizes the emptiness of the Scholastic logic then in vogue. A student of Abailard, John is witty and often sarcastic, but his message is telling and relevant to our own times. His attack on the formalism and rigidity of philosophical discourse anticipates the effort of many contemporary philosophers to widen both the scope and the applicability of philosophy to problems of direct and immediate concern to human life. This effort is to be construed as an addition to the philosophical enterprise, rather than as an anti-intellectual replacement of technical philosophy. In his later years, at the invitation of King Louis VII of France, John became Bishop of Chartres. He died in 1180 and was buried in Chartres.*

From The Metalogicon

CHAPTER 12

Why Some Arts Are Called "Liberal"

While there are many sorts of arts, the first to proffer their services to the natural abilities of those who philosophize are the liberal arts. All of the latter are included in the courses of the Trivium and Quadrivium. The liberal arts are said to have become so efficacious among our ancestors, who studied them diligently, that they enabled them to comprehend everything they read, elevated their understanding to all things, and empowered them to cut through the knots of all problems possible of solution. Those to whom the system of the Trivium has disclosed the significance of all words, or the rules of the Quadrivium have unveiled the secrets of all nature, do not need the help of a teacher in order to understand the meaning of books and to find the solutions of questions. They [the branches of learning included in the Trivium and Quadrivium] are called "arts" [either] because they delimit [*artant*] by rules and precepts; or from virtue, in Greek known as *ares,* which strengthens minds to apprehend the ways of wisdom; or from reason, called *arso* by the Greeks, which the arts nourish and cause to grow. They are called "liberal," either because the ancients took care to have their children instructed in them; or because their object is to effect man's liberation, so that, freed from cares, he may devote himself to wisdom. More often than not, they liberate us from cares incompatible with wisdom. They often even free us from worry about [material] necessities, so that the mind may have still greater liberty to apply itself to philosophy.

CHAPTER 13

Whence Grammar Gets Its Name

Among all the liberal arts, the first is logic, and specifically that part of logic which gives initial instruction about words. As has already been explained, the word "logic" has a broad meaning, and is not restricted exclusively to the science of argumentative reasoning. [It includes] Grammar [which] is "the science of speaking and writing correctly—the starting point of all liberal studies." Grammar is the cradle of all philosophy, and in a manner of speaking, the first nurse of the whole study of letters. It takes all of us as tender babes, newly born from nature's bosom. It nurses us in our infancy, and guides our every forward step in philosophy. With motherly care, it fosters and protects the philosopher from the start to the finish [of his pursuits]. It is called "grammar" from the basic elements of writing and speaking. *Grama* means a letter or line, and

From John of Salisbury, *The Metalogicon of John Salisbury: A Twelfth-Century Defense of the Verbal and Logical Arts of the Trivium,* trans. Daniel D. McGarry (Berkeley: University of California Press, 1955), pp. 36–38, 111–117. Reprinted by permission of Daniel McGarry.

grammar is "literal," since it teaches letters, that is, both the symbols which stand for simple sounds, and the elementary sounds represented by the symbols. It is also [in a way] linear. For in augmenting size, the length of lines is fundamental, and, as it were, the basic dimension of plane surfaces and solids. So also this branch, which teaches language, is the first of the arts to assist those who are aspiring to increase in wisdom. For it introduces wisdom both through ears and eyes by its facilitation of verbal intercourse. Words admitted into our ears knock on and arouse our understanding. The latter (according to Augustine) is a sort of hand of the soul, able to grasp and to perceive. Letters, that is written symbols, in the first place represent sounds. And secondly they stand for things, which they conduct into the mind through the windows of the eyes. Frequently they even communicate, without emitting a sound, the utterances of those who are absent. This art [grammar] accordingly imparts the fundamental elements of language, and also trains our faculties of sight and hearing. One who is ignorant of it [grammar] cannot philosophize any easier than one who lacks sight and hearing from birth can become an eminent philosopher.

CHAPTER 17

In What a Pernicious Manner Logic Is Sometimes Taught; and the Ideas of Moderns About [the Nature of] Genera and Species

To show off their knowledge, our contemporaries dispense their instruction in such a way that their listeners are at a loss to understand them. They seem to have the impression that every letter of the alphabet is pregnant with the secrets of Minerva. They analyze and press upon tender ears everything that anyone has ever said or done. Falling into the error condemned by Cicero, they frequently come to be unintelligible to their hearers more because of the multiplicity than the profundity of their statements. "It is indeed useful and advantageous for disputants," as Aristotle observes, "to take cognizance of several opinions on a topic." From the mutual disagreement thus brought into relief, what is seen to be poorly stated may be disproved or modified. Instruction in elementary logic does not, however, constitute the proper occasion for such procedure. Simplicity, brevity, and easy subject matter are, so far as is possible, appropriate in introductory studies. This is so true that it is permissible to expound many difficult points in a simpler way than their nature strictly requires. Thus, much that we have learned in our youth must later be amended in more advanced philosophical studies. Nevertheless, at present, all are here [in introductory logical studies] declaiming on the nature of universals, and attempting to explain, contrary to the intention of the author, what is really a most profound question, and a matter [that should be reserved] for more advanced studies. One holds that universals are merely word sounds, although this opinion, along with its author Roscelin, has already almost completely passed into oblivion. Another maintains that universals are word concepts, and twists to support his thesis everything that he can remember to have ever been written on the subject. Our Peripatetic of Pallet, Abelard, was ensnared in this opinion. He left many, and still has, to this day, some followers and proponents of his doctrine. They are friends of mine, although they often so torture the helpless letter that even the hardest heart is filled with compassion for the latter. They hold that it is preposterous to predicate a thing concerning a thing, although Aristotle is author of this monstrosity. For Aristotle frequently asserts that a thing is predicated concerning a thing, as is evident to anyone who is really familiar with his teaching. Another is wrapped up in a consideration of acts of the [intuitive] understanding, and says that genera and species are nothing more than the latter. Proponents of this view take their cue from Cicero and Boethius, who cite Aristotle as saying that universals should be regarded as and called "notions." "A notion," they tell us, "is the cognition of something, derived from its previously perceived form, and in need of unravelment." Or again [they say]: "A notion is an act of the [intuitive] understanding, a simple mental comprehension." They accordingly distort everything written, with an eye to making acts of [intuitive] understanding or "notions" include the universality of universals. Those who adhere to the view that universals are things, have various and sundry opinions. One, reasoning from the fact that everything which exists is singular in number, concludes that either the universal is numerically one, or it is non-existent. But since it is impossible for things that are substantial to be non-existent, if those things for which they are substantial exist, they further conclude that universals must be essentially one with particular things. Accordingly, following Walter of Mortagne, they distinguish [various] states [of existence], and say that Plato is an individual in so far as he is Plato; a species in so far as he is a man; a genus of a subaltern [subordinate] kind in so far as he is an animal; and a most general genus in so far as he is a substance. Although this opinion formerly had some proponents, it has been a long time since anyone has asserted it. Walter now upholds [the doctrine of] ideas, emulating Plato and imitating Bernard of Chartres, and maintains that genus and species are nothing more nor less than these, namely, ideas. "An idea," according to Seneca's definition, "is an eternal exemplar of those things which come to be as a result of nature." And since universals are not subject to corruption, and are not altered by the changes that transform particular things and cause them to come and go, succeeding one another almost momentarily, ideas are properly and correctly called "universals." Indeed, particular things are deemed incapable of supporting the substantive verb, [i.e., of being said "to be"], since they are not at all stable, and disappear without even waiting to receive names. For they vary so much in their qualities, time, location, and numerous different properties, that their whole existence seems to be more a mutual transition than a stable status. In contrast, Boethius declares: "We say that things 'are' when they may neither be increased nor diminished, but always continue as they are, firmly sustained by the foundations of their own nature." These [foundations] include their quantities, qualities, relations, places, times, conditions, and whatever is found in a way united with bodies. Although these adjuncts of bodies may seem to be changed, they remain immutable in their own nature. In like manner, although individuals [of species] may change, species remain the same. The waves of a stream wash on, yet the same flow of water continues, and we refer to the stream as the same river. Whence the statement of Seneca, which, in fact, he has borrowed from another: "In one sense it is true that we may descend twice into the same river, although in another sense this is not so." These "ideas," or "exemplary forms," are the original plans of all things. They may neither be decreased nor augmented; and they are so permanent and perpetual, that even if the whole world were to come to an end, they could not perish. They include all things, and, as Augustine seems to maintain in his book *On Free Will*, their number neither increases nor diminishes, because the ideas always continue on, even when it happens that [particular] temporal things cease to exist. What these men promise is wonderful, and familiar to philosophers who rise to the contemplation of higher things. But, as Boethius and numerous other authors testify, it is utterly foreign to the mind of Aristotle. For Aristotle very frequently opposes this view, as is clear from his books. Bernard of Chartres and his followers labored strenuously to compose the differences between Aristotle and Plato. But I opine that they arrived on the scene too late, so that their efforts to reconcile two dead men, who disagree as long as they were alive and could do so, were in vain. Still another, in his endeavor to explain Aristotle, places universality in "native forms," as does Gilbert, Bishop of Poitiers, who labors to prove that "native forms" and universals are identical. A "native form" is an example of an original [exemplar]. It [the native form, unlike the original] inheres in created things, instead of subsisting in the divine mind. In Greek it is called the *idos,* since it stands in relation to the idea as the example does to its exemplar. The native form is sensible in things that are perceptible by the senses; but insensible as conceived in the mind. It is singular in individuals, but universal in all [of a kind]. Another, with Joscelin, Bishop of Soissons, attributes universality to collections of things, while denying it to things as individuals. When Joscelin tries to explain the authorities, he has his troubles and is hard put, for in many places he cannot bear the gaping astonishment of the indignant letter. Still another takes refuge in a new tongue, since he does not have sufficient command of Latin. When he hears the words "genus" and "species," at one time he says they should be understood as universals, and at another that they refer to the *maneries* of things. I know not in which of the authors he has found this term or this distinction, unless perhaps he has dug it out of lists of abstruse and obsolete words, or it is an item of jargon [in the baggage] of present-day doctors. I am further at a loss to see what it can mean here, unless it refers to collections of things, which would be the same as Joscelin's view, or to a universal thing, which, however, could hardly be called a *maneries.* For a *maneries* may be interpreted as referring to both [collections and universals], since a number of things, or the status in which a thing of such and such a type continues to exist may be called a *maneries.* Finally, there are some who fix their attention on the status of things, and say that genera and species consist in the latter.

CHAPTER 18

That Men Always Alter the Opinions of Their Predecessors

It would take too long, and [also] be entirely foreign to my purpose, to propound the opinions and errors of everyone. The saying of the comic poet that "There are as many opinions as heads," has almost come to hold true. Rarely, if ever, do we find a teacher who is content to follow in the footsteps of his master. Each, to make a name for himself, coins his own special error. Wherewith, while promising to correct his master, he sets himself up as a target for correction and condemnation by his own disciples as well as by posterity. I recognize that the same rule threatens to apply in my own case. By disagreeing with others and committing my dissent to writing, I am, in fact, laying myself open to be criticized by many. He who speaks is judged merely by one or a few persons; whereas he who writes thereby exposes himself to criticism by all, and appears before the tribunal of the whole world and every age. However, not to be overly harsh with the doctors, I must observe that, very often, many of them seem to be wrangling over words, rather than disputing about facts. Nonetheless there is nothing that is less appropriate for a professor of this art [of logic], since such procedure ill befits a serious man. As Aristotle declares, "To dispute in this wise over a word is utterly abhorrent in dialectic, unless it be the sole possible way in which a proposition may be discussed." Of a truth, on points where they seem to be in profound disagreement, such [professors of logic] admit one another's interpretations, even though they may maintain that the latter are inadequate. They are mutually condemning, not the meaning, but the words of one another's statements.

SUGGESTIONS FOR FURTHER READING

Armstrong, A. H., ed. *The Cambridge History of Later Greek and Early Medieval Philosophy.* Cambridge: Cambridge University Press, 1967.

Bark, William Carroll. *Origins of the Medieval World.* New York: Doubleday-Anchor, 1960.

D'Arcy, M. C. et al. *Saint Augustine.* New York: Meridian, 1957.

Goodrich, Norma Lorre. *The Medieval Myths.* New York: New American Library, 1961.

Markus, R. A., ed. *Augustine.* New York: Doubleday-Anchor, 1972.

Marrou, Henri. *Saint Augustine.* New York: Harper Torchbooks, 1958.

Plantinga, Alvin, ed. *The Ontological Argument: From St. Anselm to Contemporary Philosophers.* New York: Doubleday-Anchor, 1965.

Previté-Orton, C. W. *The Shorter Cambridge Medieval History,* Vol. I. Cambridge: Cambridge University Press, 1952.

Pryzwara, Erich. *An Augustine Synthesis.* New York: Harper Torchbooks, 1958.

Stephenson, Carl. *Medieval Feudalism.* Ithaca: Cornell University Press, 1942.

Medieval Islamic and Jewish Philosophy: Revelation and the Use of Aristotle

The development of Islamic philosophy from the sixth to the twelfth centuries is a dazzling achievement. After Emperor Justinian closed the philosophical schools in Athens, philosophical activity moved east, especially to Syria. The works of Aristotle and some Neoplatonic sources were translated into Syriac. Meanwhile, beginning in the seventh century, Islam, the religion founded by Mohammed (571–632), became the dominant force in Western Asia, Northern Africa, and finally in much of Spain.

Just as Christianity had to adjudicate between the claims of the Bible and Greek philosophy, so Islam faced a similar problem with the Koran, the scriptural basis of Islam. This process of adjudication was carried on by a school of thinkers known as the "Mutazilites," who were inclined to philosophical reasoning as an aid to understanding the scriptures. They were opposed by the "Mutakallimoun," who held to a more rigorous orthodox theology. One can find a parallel development in the Christian West of the thirteenth century in the thought of Thomas Aquinas and Bonaventure—Aquinas being hospitable to secular philosophy and Bonaventure supporting a more strictly theological position.

In the development of Islamic philosophy, Aristotle was the dominant factor, although through false ascription his works were mixed with Neoplatonic texts. It is important to note that the full text of Aristotle's writings was not available to the Christian West until the thirteenth century. The significance of the philosophy of Aristotle for the revelation religions of Judaism, Christianity, and Islam was clear; without a scriptural source, Aristotle anticipated every major contention of these religions except, obviously, those having to do with divine intervention or divine messages. Philosophical and theological discussions centered around the themes of the freedom of the will, the nature of God and God's activity, and the relationship between ethical and religious responsibility. The major figures in the development of Islamic philosophy were Alkindi, Alfarabi, Avicenna, and Averroës.

Although the scriptural basis was profoundly different, medieval Jewish philosophy faced problems similar to those faced by Islamic philosophy. From the ninth to the thirteenth centuries, Jewish philosophers flourished in the Islamic world, and, in fact, often made the Islamic philosophical commentaries central to their own thought. Once again, Neoplatonism and Aristotelianism provided the sources for further philosophical development. Important medieval Jewish philosophers included Saadia, Ibn Gabirol, Judah Halevi, and Moses Maimonides, whose *Guide of the Perplexed* is one of the most significant philosophical and religious documents of the Middle Ages.

Medieval Islamic and Jewish philosophies are included here not only because of their considerable intellectual worth but also as a corrective to that naive provincialism which assumes that the wealth of western philosophy in the Middle Ages was circumscribed by the borders of Europe.

THE KORAN

The Prophet Mohammed was born in Mecca in the year 570. Mohammed was religiously sensitive and often meditated in a mountain cave. In 610, according to Muslim tradition, the Angel Gabriel appeared to Mohammed and began a series of revelations, the remainder of which came from God. Mohammed and others committed these revelations to memory and in time began to write them on palm leaves or stone. Divided into 114 suras, *or chapters, the authorized version of the Koran was established in 651–652, 20 years after the death of Mohammed. The exact chronology of the* suras *is not known, although it is believed that the larger ones are from a later period in the life of Mohammed. The central theme of the Koran is the absolute dependence of human beings on the will of God, who, although merciful, is irritated at humanity's previous failure to follow his teachings, as in Judaism and Christianity, for example. The God of the Koran is more demanding than the God of the Bible.*

The Prophet Mohammed saw himself as the Messenger of the one, true God, Allah. He made no claim to miraculous powers, holding rather that God had appointed him to set straight the meaning of the revelation as both the Jews and the Christians had failed in their divine mission. We reprint sura *II,* Al-Baqarah *("The Cow"), for although it is not as poetic as other selections, it provides a mini-version of the teaching of the Koran, still the sacred book of hundreds of millions of persons throughout the world.*

The Cow

In the Name of Allah, the Compassionate, the Merciful

Alif lam mim. This Book is not to be doubted. It is a guide to the righteous, who have faith in the unseen and are steadfast in prayer; who bestow in charity a part of what We have given them; who trust what has been revealed to you and to others before you, and firmly believe in the life to come. These are rightly guided by their Lord; these shall surely triumph.

As for the unbelievers, whether you forewarn them or not, they will not have faith. Allah has set a seal upon their hearts and ears; their sight is dimmed and a grievous punishment awaits them.

There are some who declare: 'We believe in Allah and the Last Day,' yet they are no true believers. They seek to deceive Allah and those who believe in Him: but they deceive none save themselves, though they may not perceive it. There is a sickness in their hearts which Allah has increased: they shall be sternly punished for their hypocrisy.

When it is said to them: 'Do not commit evil in the land,' they reply: 'We do nothing but good.' But it is they who are the evil-doers, though they may not perceive it.

And when it is said to them: 'Believe as others believe,' they reply: 'Are we to believe as fools believe?' It is they who are the fools, if they but knew it!

When they meet the faithful, they declare: 'We, too, are believers.' But when they are alone with their devils they say to them: 'We follow none but you: we were only mocking.' Allah will mock at them and keep them long in sin, blundering blindly along.

Such are those that barter away guidance for error: they profit nothing, nor are they on the right path. They are like one who kindled a fire, but as soon as it lit up all around him Allah put it out and he was left darkling: they do not see. Deaf, dumb, and blind, they shall never return to the right path.

Or like those who, beneath a dark storm-cloud charged with thunder and lightning, thrust their fingers in their ears at the sound of every thunder-clap for fear of death (Allah thus encompasses the unbelievers). The lightning almost takes away their sight: whenever it flashes upon them they walk on, but as soon as it darkens they stand still. Indeed, if Allah pleased, He could take away their sight and hearing: He has power over all things.

Men, serve your Lord, who has created you and those who have gone before you, so that you may guard yourselves against evil; who has made the earth a bed for you and the sky a dome, and has sent down water from the sky to bring forth fruits for your sustenance. Do not knowingly set up other gods besides Him.

If you doubt what We have revealed to Our servant, produce one chapter comparable to this Book. Call upon your idols to assist you, if what you say be true. But if you fail (as you are sure to fail) then guard yourselves against the fire whose fuel is men and stones, prepared for the unbelievers.

Proclaim good tidings to those who have faith and do good works. They shall dwell in gardens watered by running streams: whenever they are given fruit to eat they will say: 'This is what we used to eat before,' for they shall be given the like. Wedded to chaste virgins, they shall abide there for ever.

Allah does not disdain to give a parable about a gnat or a larger creature. The faithful know that it is the truth from their Lord, but the unbelievers ask: 'What could Allah mean by this parable?'

By such parables Allah enlightens some and misleads others. But He misleads none except the evil-doers, who break His covenant after accepting it and divide what He has bidden to be united and commit evil in the land. Truly, these shall have much to lose.

How can you deny Allah? Did He not give you life when you were dead, and will He not cause you to die and then restore you to life? Will you not return to Him at last? He created for you all that the earth contains; then, ascending to the sky, fashioned it into seven heavens. He has knowledge of all things.

When your Lord said to the angels: 'I am placing on the earth one that shall rule as My deputy,' they replied: 'Will You put there one that will do evil and shed blood, when we have for so long sung Your praises and sanctified Your name?'

He said: 'I know what you do not know.'

He taught Adam the names of all things and then set them before the angels, saying: 'Tell Me the names of these, if what you say be true.'

'Glory to You,' they replied, 'we have no knowledge except that which You have given us. You alone are wise and all-knowing.'

Then said He to Adam: 'Tell them their names.' And when Adam had named them, He said: 'Did I not tell you that I know the secrets of heaven and earth, and all that you hide and all that you reveal?'

And when We said to the angels: 'Prostrate yourselves before Adam,' they all prostrated themselves except Satan, who in his pride refused and became an unbeliever.

To Adam We said: 'Dwell with your wife in Paradise and eat of its fruits to your hearts' content wherever you will. But never approach this tree or you shall both become transgressors.'

But Satan made them fall from Paradise and brought about their banishment. 'Go hence,' We said, 'and may your offspring be enemies to each other. The earth will for a while provide your sustenance and dwelling-place.'

Then Adam learnt prayer from his Lord, and his Lord relented towards him. He is the Forgiving One, the Merciful.

'Go hence, all,' We said. 'When Our guidance is revealed those that accept it shall have nothing to fear or to regret; but those that deny and reject Our revelations shall be the heirs of Hell, and there they shall abide for ever.'

Children of Israel, remember the favours I have bestowed upon you. Keep your covenant and I will be true to Mine. Revere Me. Have faith in My revelations, which confirm your Scriptures, and do not be the first to deny them. Fear Me, and do not sell My revelations for a paltry price. Do not confound truth with falsehood, nor knowingly hide the truth. Attend to your prayers, pay the alms-tax, and worship with the worshippers. Would you enjoin righteousness on others and forget it yourselves? Yet you read the Scriptures. Have you no sense?

Fortify yourselves with patience and prayer. This may indeed be an exacting discipline, but not to the devout, who know that they will meet their Lord and that to Him they will return.

Children of Israel, remember that I have bestowed favours on you and exalted you above the nations. Guard yourselves against the day when every soul will stand alone: when neither intercession nor ransom shall be accepted from it, nor any help be given it.

Remember how We delivered you from Pharaoh's people, who had oppressed you cruelly, slaying your sons and sparing your daughters. Surely that was a great trial from your Lord. We parted the sea for you and, taking you to safety, drowned Pharaoh's men before your very eyes. We communed with Moses for forty nights, but in his absence you took up the calf and worshipped it, thus committing evil. Yet after that We pardoned you, so that you might give thanks.

We gave Moses the Scriptures and knowledge of right and wrong, so that you might be rightly guided. He said to his people: 'You have wronged yourselves, my people, in worshipping the calf. Turn in repentance to your Creator and slay the culprits. That will be best for you in His sight." And He relented towards you. He is the Forgiving One, the Merciful.

When you said to Moses: 'We will not believe in you until we see Allah with our own eyes,' a thunderbolt struck you whilst you were looking on. Then We revived you from your stupor, so that you might give thanks.

We caused the clouds to draw their shadow over you and sent down for you manna and quails, saying: 'Eat of the good things We have given you.' Indeed, they did not wrong Us, but they wronged themselves.

'Enter this city,' We said, 'and eat where you will to your hearts' content. Make your way reverently through the gates, saying: "We repent." We shall forgive you your sins and bestow abundance on the righteous among you.' But the wrongdoers perverted Our words and We let loose on them a scourge from heaven as a punishment for their misdeeds.

When Moses demanded water for his people We said to him: 'Strike the Rock with your staff.' Thereupon twelve springs gushed from the Rock, and each tribe knew their drinking-place. We said: 'Eat and drink of that which Allah has provided and do not corrupt the land with evil.'

'Moses,' you said, 'we are weary of this monotonous diet. Call on your Lord to give us some of the varied produce of the earth, green herbs and cucumbers, corn and lentils and onions.'

'What!' he answered. 'Would you exchange that which is good for what is worse? Go back to Egypt. There you shall find all that you have asked for.'

Shame and misery were stamped upon them and they incurred the wrath of Allah; because they disbelieved His signs and slew His prophets unjustly; because they were rebels and transgressors.

Believers, Jews, Christians, and Sabaeans—whoever believes in Allah and the Last Day and does what is right—shall be rewarded by their Lord; they have nothing to fear or to regret.

We made a covenant with you and raised the Mount above you, saying: 'Receive what We have given you with earnestness and bear in mind its precepts, that you may guard yourselves against evil.' Yet after that you turned away, and but for Allah's grace and mercy you would have surely been among the lost.

You have heard of those of you that broke the Sabbath. We said to them: 'You shall be changed into detested apes.' We made their fate an example to their own generation and to those who followed them, and a lesson to the righteous.

When Moses said to his people: 'Allah commands

you to sacrifice a cow,' they replied: 'Are you making game of us?'

'Allah forbid that I should be so foolish!' he rejoined.

'Call on your Lord,' they said, 'to make known to us what kind of cow she shall be.'

Moses replied: 'Your Lord says: "Let her be neither an old cow nor a young heifer, but in between." Do, therefore, as you are bidden.'

'Call on your Lord,' they said, 'to make known to us what her colour shall be.'

Moses replied: 'Your Lord says: "Let the cow be yellow, a rich yellow pleasing to the eye."'

'Call on your Lord,' they said, 'to make known to us the exact type of cow she shall be; for to us cows look all alike. If Allah wills we shall be rightly guided.'

Moses replied: 'Your Lord says: "Let her be a healthy cow, not worn out with ploughing the earth or watering the field; a cow free from any blemish."'

'Now you have told us all,' they answered. And they slaughtered a cow, after they had almost succeeded in evading the sacrifice.

And when you slew a man and then fell out with one another concerning him, Allah made known what you concealed. We said: 'Strike the corpse with a piece of it.' Thus Allah restores the dead to life and shows you His signs, that you may grow in understanding.

Yet after that your hearts became as hard as rock or even harder; for from some rocks rivers take their course: some break asunder and water gushes from them: and others tumble down through fear of Allah. Allah is watching over all your actions.

Do you then hope that they will believe in you, when some of them have already heard the Word of Allah and knowingly perverted it, although they understood its meaning?

When they meet the faithful they declare: 'We, too, are believers.' But when alone they say to each other: 'Must you preach to them what Allah has revealed to you? They will only dispute with you about it in your Lord's presence. Have you no sense?

Do they not know that Allah has knowledge of all they hide and all that they reveal?

There are illiterate men among them who, ignorant of the Scriptures, know of nothing except lies and vague fancies. Woe to those that write the Scriptures with their own hands and then declare: 'This is from Allah,' in order to gain some paltry end. Woeful shall be their fate, because of what their hands have written, because of that which they have gained!

They declare: 'We shall be punished in Hell only for a few days.' Say: 'Did Allah make you such a promise—Allah will not break His promise—or do you assert about Him what you have no means of knowing?

Truly, those that commit evil and become engrossed in sin are the heirs of Hell; in it they shall remain for ever. But those that have faith and do good works are the heirs of Paradise; for ever they shall abide in it.

When We made a covenant with the Israelites We said: 'Serve none but Allah. Show kindness to your parents, to your kinsfolk, to the orphans, and to the destitute. Exhort men to righteousness. Attend to your prayers and pay the alms-tax.' But you all broke your covenant except a few, and gave no heed.

And when We made a covenant with you We said: 'You shall not shed your kinsmen's blood or turn them out of their dwellings.' To this you consented and bore witness. Yet it was you that slew your kinsfolk and turned many of them out of their dwellings, helping others against them with sin and enmity in your hearts. Yet had they come to you as captives, you would have ransomed them. Surely their expulsion was unlawful. Can you believe in one part of the Scriptures and deny another?

Those of you that act thus shall be rewarded with disgrace in this world and with a grievous punishment on the Day of Resurrection. Allah is watching over all your actions.

Such are they who buy the life of this world at the price of the life to come. Their punishment shall not be lightened, nor shall they be helped.

To Moses We gave the Scriptures and after him We sent other apostles. We gave Jesus the son of Mary veritable signs and strengthened him with the Holy Spirit. Will you then scorn each apostle whose message does not suit your fancies, charging some with imposture and slaying others?

They say: 'Our hearts are sealed.' But Allah has cursed them for their unbelief. They have but little faith.

And now that a Book confirming their Scriptures has been revealed to them by Allah, they deny it, although they know it to be the truth and have long prayed for help against the unbelievers. May Allah's curse be upon the infidels! Evil is that for which they have bartered away their souls. To deny Allah's own revelation, grudging that He should reveal his bounty to whom He chooses from His servants! They have incurred Allah's most inexorable wrath. An ignominious punishment awaits the unbelievers.

When it is said to them: 'Believe in what Allah has revealed,' they reply: 'We believe in what was revealed to *us.*' But they deny what has since been revealed, although it is the truth, corroborating their own scriptures.

Say: 'Why did you kill the prophets of Allah, if you are true believers? Moses came to you with veritable signs, but in his absence you worshipped the calf and committed evil.'

When We made a covenant with you and raised the Mount above you, saying: 'Take what We have given you with willing hearts and hear Our commandments,' you replied: 'We hear but disobey.'

For their unbelief they were made to drink the calf into their very hearts. Say: 'Evil is that to which your faith prompts you, if you are indeed believers.'

Say: 'If your claim be true that Allah's paradise is for you alone and not for other men, then you must long for death!'

But they will never long for death, because of what they did; for Allah knows the evil-doers. Indeed, you will find that they love this life more than other men: more than the pagans do. Each one of them would willingly live a thousand years.

But even if their lives were indeed prolonged, that will surely not save them from Our scourge. Allah is watching over all their actions.

Say: 'Whoever is an enemy of Gabriel' (who has by Allah's grace revealed to you the Koran as a guide and joyful tidings for the faithful, confirming previous scriptures) 'whoever is an enemy of Allah, His angels, or His apostles, or of Gabriel or Michael, shall make Allah himself his enemy: Allah is the enemy of the unbelievers.'

We have sent down to you clear revelations: none will deny them except the evil-doers. What! Whenever they make a covenant, must some of them cast it aside? Most of them are unbelievers.

And now that an apostle has come to them from Allah confirming their own scriptures, some of those to whom the Scriptures were given cast off the Book of Allah behind their backs as though they know nothing and accept what the devils tell of Solomon's kingdom. Not that Solomon was an unbeliever: it is the devils who are unbelievers. They teach men witchcraft and that which was revealed to the angels Harut and Marut in Babylon. Yet they never instruct any man without saying to Him beforehand: 'We have been sent to tempt you; do not renounce your faith.' From these two, men learn a charm by which they can create discord between husband and wife, although they can harm none with what they learn except by Allah's leave. They learn, indeed, what harms them and does not profit them; yet they know full well that anyone who engaged in that traffic would have no share in the life to come. Vile is that for which they have sold their souls, if they but knew it! Had they believed in Allah and kept from evil, far better for them would His reward have been, if they but knew it.

Believers, do not say to Our apostle *Ra'ina,* but say *Undhurna.* Take heed; the unbelievers shall be sternly punished.

The unbelievers among the People of the Book, and the pagans, resent that any blessings should have been sent down to you from your Lord. But Allah chooses whom He will for his mercy. His grace is infinite.

If We abrogate any verse or cause it to be forgotten We will replace it by a better one or one similar. Do you not know that Allah has power over all things? Do you not know that it is to Allah that the kingdom of the heavens and the earth belongs, and that there is none besides Him to protect or help you?

Would you demand of your apostle that which was once demanded of Moses? He that barters faith for unbelief has surely strayed from the right path.

Many of those to whom the Scriptures were given wish, through envy, to lead you back to unbelief, now that you have embraced the faith and the truth has been made plain to them. Forgive them and bear with them until Allah makes known His will. He has power over all things.

Attend to your prayers and pay the alms-tax. Your good works shall be rewarded by Allah. He is watching over all your actions.

They declare: 'None but Jews and Christians shall be admitted to Paradise.' Such are their wishful fancies. Say: 'Let us have your proof, if what you say be true.' Indeed, those that surrender themselves to Allah and do good works shall be rewarded by their Lord: they shall have nothing to fear or to regret.

The Jews say the Christians are astray, and the Christians say it is the Jews who are astray. Yet they both read the Scriptures. And the pagans say the same of both. Allah will judge their disputes on the Day of Resurrection.

Who is more wicked than the men who seek to destroy the mosques of Allah and forbid His name

Capella Del Mihrab, Umayyad Mosque (965 A.D.). The Islamic-Moorish influence penetrated Western Europe, especially Spain, and remains as a telling and brilliant aesthetic presence until our own time. (Cordoba Mas, Barcelona)

to be mentioned in them, when it behooves these men to enter them with fear in their hearts? They shall be held to shame in this world and sternly punished in the next.

To Allah belongs the east and the west. Whichever way you turn there is the face of Allah. He is omnipresent and all-knowing.

They say: 'Allah has begotten a son.' Allah forbid! His is what the heavens and the earth contain; all things are obedient to Him. Creator of the heavens and the earth! When He decrees a thing, He need only say 'Be,' and it is.

The ignorant ask: 'Why does Allah not speak to us or give us a sign?' The same demand was made by those before them: their hearts are all alike. But to those whose faith is firm We have already revealed Our signs.

We have sent you forth to proclaim the truth and to give warning. You shall not be questioned about the heirs of hell.

You will please neither the Christians nor the Jews unless you follow their faith. Say: 'The guidance of Allah is the only guidance.' And if after all the knowledge you have been given you yield to their desires, there shall be none to help or protect you from the wrath of Allah. Those to whom We have given the Book, and who read it as it ought to be read, truly believe in it; those that deny it shall assuredly be lost.

Children of Israel, remember that I have bestowed favours upon you and exalted you above the nations. Fear the day when every soul shall stand alone: when neither intercession nor ransom shall be accepted from it, nor any help be given it.

When his Lord put Abraham to the proof by enjoining on him certain commandments and Abraham fulfilled them, He said: 'I have appointed you a leader of mankind.'

'And what of my descendants?' asked Abraham.

'My covenant,' said He, 'does not apply to the evildoers.'

We made the House a resort and a sanctuary for mankind, saying: 'Make the place where Abraham stood a house of worship.' We enjoined Abraham and Ishmael to cleanse Our house for those who walk round it, who meditate in it, and who kneel and prostrate themselves.

'Lord,' said Abraham, 'make this a land of peace and bestow plenty upon its people, those of them that believe in Allah and the Last Day.'

'As for those that do not,' He answered, 'I shall let them live awhile and then drag them to the scourge of Hell. Evil shall be their fate.'

Abraham and Ishmael built the House and dedicated it, saying: 'Accept this from us, Lord. You hear all and You know all. Make us submissive to You; make of our descendants a nation that will submit to You. Teach us our rites of worship and turn to us mercifully; You are forgiving and merciful. Send forth to them an apostle of their own who shall declare to them Your revelations and instruct them in the Scriptures and in wisdom and purify them of sin. You are the Mighty, the Wise One.'

Who but a foolish man would renounce the faith of Abraham? We chose him in this world, and in the world to come he shall dwell among the righteous. When his Lord said to him: 'Submit,' he answered: 'I have submitted to the Lord of the Creation.'

Abraham enjoined the faith on his children, and so did Jacob, saying: 'My children, Allah has chosen for you the true faith. Do not depart this life except as men who have submitted to Him.'

Were you present when death came to Jacob? He said to his children: 'What will you worship when I am gone?' They replied: 'We will worship your God and the God of your forefathers Abraham and Ishmael and Isaac: the One God. To Him we will surrender ourselves.'

That nation have passed away. Theirs is what they did, and yours what you have done. You shall not be questioned about their actions.

They say: 'Accept the Jewish or the Christian faith and you shall be rightly guided.'

Say: 'By no means! We believe in the faith of Abraham, the upright one. He was no idolater.'

Say: 'We believe in Allah and that which is revealed to us; we believe in what was revealed to Abraham, Ishmael, Isaac, Jacob, and the tribes; to Moses and Jesus and the other prophets. We make no distinction between any of them, and to Allah we have surrendered ourselves.'

If they accept your faith they shall be rightly guided; if they reject it, they shall surely be in schism. Against them Allah is your all-sufficient defender. He hears all and knows all.

We take on Allah's own dye. And who has a better dye than Allah's?

Say: 'Would you dispute with us about Him, who is our Lord and your Lord? We shall both be judged by our works. To Him alone we are devoted.'

Do you claim that Abraham, Ishmael, Isaac, Jacob, and the tribes, were all Jews or Christians? Do you know better than Allah Himself? Who is more wicked than the man who hides a testimony which he has received from Allah? He is watching over all your actions.

That nation have passed away. Theirs is what they did and yours what you have done. You shall not be questioned about their actions.

The foolish will ask: 'What has made them change their *qiblah?*'

Say: 'The east and the west are Allah's. He guides whom He will to the right path.'

We have made you a just nation, so that you may testify against mankind and that your own apostle may testify against you. We decreed your former *qiblah* only in order that We might know the Apostle's true adherents and those who were to disown him. It was indeed a hard test, but not to those whom Allah guided. He was not to make your faith fruitless. He is compassionate and merciful to men.

Many a time We have seen you turn your eyes towards heaven. We will make you turn towards a *qiblah* that will please you. Turn towards the Holy Mosque; wherever you be face towards it.

Those to whom the Scriptures were given know this to be the truth from their Lord. Allah is watching over all their actions. But even if you gave them every proof they would not accept your *qiblah*, nor would you accept theirs; nor would any of their sects accept the *qiblah* of the other. If after all the knowledge you have been given you yield to their desires, then you will surely become an evil-doer.

Those to whom We gave the Scriptures know Our apostle as they know their own sons. But some of them deliberately conceal the truth. This is the truth from your Lord: therefore never doubt it.

Each one has a goal towards which he turns. But wherever you be, emulate one another in good works. Allah will bring you all before Him. He has power over all things.

Whichever way you depart, face towards the Holy Mosque: and wherever you are, face towards it, so that men will have no cause to reproach you, except the evil-doers among them. Have no fear of them; fear Me, so that I may perfect My favour to you and that you may be rightly guided.

Thus We have sent forth to you an apostle of your own who will recite to you Our revelations and purify you of sin, who will instruct you in the Book and in wisdom and teach you that of which you have no knowledge. Remember Me, then, and I will remember you. Give thanks to Me and never deny Me.

Believers, fortify yourselves with patience and prayer. Allah is with those that are patient. Do not say that those who were slain in the cause of Allah are dead; they are alive, although you are not aware of them.

We shall test your steadfastness with fear and famine, with loss of life and property and crops. Give good news to those who endure with fortitude; who in adversity say: 'We belong to Allah, and to Him we shall return.' On such men will be Allah's blessing and mercy; such men are rightly guided.

Safa and Marwa are beacons of Allah. It shall be no offence for the pilgrim or the visitor to the Sacred House to walk round them. He that does good of his own accord shall be rewarded by Allah. Allah has knowledge of all things.

Those that hide the clear proofs and the guidance We have revealed after We have proclaimed them in the Scriptures, shall be cursed by Allah and man; except those that repent and mend their ways and make known the truth. Towards them I shall relent. I am the Relenting One, the Merciful. But the infidels who die unbelievers shall incur the curse of Allah, the angels, and those who invoke damnation.

Under it they shall remain for ever; their punishment shall not be lightened, nor shall they be reprieved.

Your God is one God. There is no god but Him. He is the Compassionate, the Merciful.

In the creation of the heavens and the earth; in the alternation of night and day; in the ships that sail the ocean with cargoes beneficial to man; in the water which Allah sends down from the sky and with which He revives the dead earth, dispersing over it all manner of beasts; in the movements of the winds, and in the clouds that are driven between earth and sky; surely in these there are signs for rational men.

Yet there are some who worship idols, bestowing on them the adoration due to Allah (though the love of Allah is stronger in the faithful). But when they face their punishment the wrongdoers will know that might is His alone and that Allah is stern in retribution. When they face their punishment the leaders will disown their followers, and the bonds which now unite them will break asunder. Those who followed them will say: 'Could we but live again, we would disown them as they have now disowned us.'

Thus Allah will show them their own works. They shall sigh with remorse, but shall never come out of Hell.

Men, eat of what is lawful and wholesome on the earth and do not walk in Satan's footsteps, for he is your sworn enemy. He enjoins you to commit evil and indecency and to assert about Allah what you do not know.

When it is said to them: 'Follow what Allah has revealed,' they reply: 'We will follow that which our fathers practised,' even though their fathers were senseless men lacking in guidance.

In preaching to the unbelievers the Apostle may be compared to one who calls on beasts that can hear nothing except a shout and a cry. Deaf, dumb, and blind, they understand nothing.

Believers, eat of the wholesome things with which We have provided you and give thanks to Allah, if it is He whom you worship

He has forbidden you the flesh of animals that die a natural death, blood, and pig's meat; also any flesh that is consecrated in the name of any other than Allah. But whoever is constrained to eat any of these, through neither appetite nor wilful sin, incurs no guilt. Allah is forgiving and merciful.

Those that suppress any part of the Scriptures which Allah has revealed in order to gain some paltry end shall swallow nothing but fire into their bellies. On the Day of Resurrection Allah will neither speak to them nor purify them. Theirs shall be a woeful punishment.

Such are those that barter guidance for error and forgiveness for punishment. How steadfastly they seek the fire of Hell! That is because Allah has revealed the Book with the truth; those that disagree about it are in schism.

Righteousness does not consist in whether you face towards the east or the west. The righteous man is he who believes in Allah and the Last Day, in the angels and the Scriptures and the prophets; who for the love of Allah gives his wealth to his kinsfolk, to the orphans, to the needy, to the wayfarers and to the beggars, and for the redemption of captives; who attends to his prayers and pays the alms-tax; who is true to his promises and steadfast in trial and adversity and in times of war. Such are the true believers; such are the God-fearing.

Believers, retaliation is decreed for you in bloodshed: a free man for a free man, a slave for a slave, and a female for a female. He who is pardoned by his aggrieved brother shall be prosecuted according to usage and shall pay him a liberal fine. This is a merciful dispensation from your Lord. He that transgresses thereafter shall be sternly punished.

Men of understanding! In retaliation you have a safeguard for your lives; perchance you will guard yourselves against evil.

It is decreed that when death approaches, those of you that leave property shall bequeath it equitably to parents and kindred. This is a duty incumbent on the righteous. He that alters a will after hearing it shall be accountable for his crime. Allah hears all and knows all.

He that suspects an error or an injustice on the part of a testator and brings about a settlement among the parties incurs no guilt. Allah is forgiving and merciful.

Believers, fasting is decreed for you as it was decreed for those before you; perchance you will guard yourselves against evil. Fast a certain number of days, but if any one of you is ill or on a journey let him fast a similar number of days later on; and for those that can afford it there is a ransom: the feeding of a poor man. He that does good of his own accord shall be well rewarded; but to fast is better for you, if you but knew it.

In the month of Ramadhan the Koran was revealed, a book of guidance with proofs of guidance distinguishing right from wrong. Therefore whoever of you is present in that month let him fast. But he who is ill or on a journey shall fast a similar number of days later on.

Allah desires your well-being, not your discomfort. He desires you to fast the whole month so that you may magnify Him and render thanks to Him for giving you His guidance.

When My servants question you about Me, tell them that I am near. I answer the prayer of the suppliant when he calls to Me; therefore let them answer My call and put their trust in Me, that they may be rightly guided.

It is now lawful for you to lie with your wives on the night of the fast; they are a comfort to you as you are to them. Allah knew that you were deceiving yourselves. He has relented towards you and pardoned you. Therefore you may now lie with them and seek what Allah has ordained for you. Eat and drink until you can tell a white thread from a black one in the light of the coming dawn. Then resume the fast till nightfall and do not approach them, but stay at your prayers in the mosques.

These are the bounds set by Allah: do not come near them. Thus He makes known His revelations to mankind that they may guard themselves against evil.

Do not usurp one another's property by unjust means, nor bribe with it the judges in order that you may knowingly and wrongfully deprive others of their possessions.

They question you about the phases of the moon. Say: 'They are seasons fixed for mankind and for the pilgrimage.'

Righteousness does not consist in entering your dwellings from the back. The righteous man is he that fears Allah. Enter your dwellings by their doors and fear Allah, so that you may prosper.

Fight for the sake of Allah those that fight against you, but do not attack them first. Allah does not love the aggressors.

Kill them wherever you find them. Drive them out of the places from which they drove you. Idolatry is worse than carnage. But do not fight them within the precincts of the Holy Mosque unless they attack you there; if they attack you put them to the sword. Thus shall the unbelievers be rewarded: but if they mend their ways, know that Allah is forgiving and merciful.

Fight against them until idolatry is no more and Allah's religion reigns supreme. But if they mend their ways, fight none except the evil-doers.

A sacred month for a sacred month: sacred things too are subject to retaliation. If any one attacks you, attack him as he attacked you. Have fear of Allah, and know that Allah is with the righteous.

Give generously for the cause of Allah and do not with your own hands cast yourselves into destruction. Be charitable; Allah loves the charitable.

Make the pilgrimage and visit the Sacred House for His sake. If you cannot, send such offerings as you can afford and do not shave your heads until the offerings have reached their destination. But if any of you is ill or suffers from an ailment of the head, he must pay a ransom either by fasting or by almsgiving or by offering a sacrifice.

If in peacetime anyone of you combines the visit with the pilgrimage, he must offer such gifts as he can afford; but if he lacks the means let him fast three days during the pilgrimage and seven when he has returned; that is, ten days in all. That is incumbent on him whose family are not present at the Holy Mosque. Have fear of Allah: know that He is stern in retribution.

Make the pilgrimage in the appointed months. He that intends to perform it in those months must abstain from sexual intercourse, obscene language, and acrimonious disputes while on pilgrimage. Allah is aware of whatever good you do. Provide yourselves well: the best provision is piety. Fear Me, then, you that are endowed with understanding.

It shall be no offence for you to seek the bounty of your Lord by trading. When you come running from Arafat remember Allah as you approach the sacred monument. Remember Him that gave you guidance when you were in error. Then go out from the place whence the pilgrims will go out and implore the forgiveness of Allah. He is forgiving and merciful. And when you have fulfilled your sacred duties, remember Allah as you remember your forefathers or with deeper reverence.

There are some who say: 'Lord, give us abundance in this world.' These shall have no share in the world to come. But there are others who say: 'Lord, give us what is good both in this world and in the next, and keep us from the fire of Hell.' These shall be rewarded for their deeds. Swift is the reckoning of Allah.

Give glory to Allah on the appointed days. He that departs on the second day incurs no sin, nor does he who stays longer, if he truly fears Allah. Have fear of Allah, then, and know that you shall all be gathered before Him.

There are some men whose views on this life please you: they even call on Allah to vouch for that which is in their hearts; whereas in fact they are the deadliest of your opponents. No sooner do they leave you than they hasten to commit evil in the land, destroying crops and cattle. Allah does not love evil.

When it is said to them: 'Have fear of Allah,' vanity carries them off to sin. Hell shall be enough for them, a dismal resting-place.

But there are others who would give away their lives in order to find favour with Allah. Allah is compassionate to His servants.

Believers, submit all of you to Allah and do not walk in Satan's footsteps; he is your sworn enemy. If you lapse back after the veritable signs that have been shown to you, know that Allah is mighty and wise.

Are they waiting for Allah to come down to them in the shadow of a cloud, with all the angels? Their fate will have been settled then. To Allah shall all things return.

Ask the Israelites how many veritable signs We have given them. He that tampers with the boon of Allah after it has been bestowed on him shall be severely punished. Allah is stern in retribution.

For the unbelievers the life of this world is decked with all manner of temptations. They scoff at the faithful, but those that fear Allah shall be above them on the Day of Resurrection. Allah gives without measure to whom He will.

Mankind were once one nation. Then Allah sent forth prophets to give them good news and to warn them, and with these He sent down the Book with the truth, that it might judge the disputes of men. (None disputed it save those to whom it was given, and that was through envy of one another, after veritable signs had been vouchsafed them.) So Allah guided by His will those who believed in the truth which had been disputed. Allah guides whom He will to the right path.

Did you think that you would go to Paradise untouched by the suffering which was endured by those before you? Affliction and adversity befell them; and so battered were they that each apostle, and those who shared his faith, cried out: 'When will the help of Allah come?' His help is ever near.

They will ask you about alms-giving. Say: 'Whatever you bestow in charity must go to your parents and to your kinsfolk, to the orphan and to the poor man and to the stranger. Allah is aware of whatever good you do.'

Fighting is obligatory for you, much as you dislike it. But you may hate a thing although it is good for you, and love it although it is bad for you. Allah knows, but you do not.

They ask you about fighting in the sacred month. Say: 'To fight in this month is a grave offence; but to debar others from the path of Allah, to deny Him, and to expel His worshippers from the Holy Mosque, is far more grave in His sight. Idolatry is worse than carnage.'

They will not cease to fight against you until they force you to renounce your faith—if they are able. But whoever of you recants and dies an unbeliever, his works shall come to nothing in this world and in the world to come. Such men shall be the tenants of Hell, and there they shall abide for ever.

Those that have embraced the faith and those that have fled their land and fought for the cause of Allah, may hope for Allah's mercy. Allah is forgiving and merciful.

They ask you about drinking and gambling. Say: 'There is great harm in both, although they have some benefit for men; but their harm is far greater than their benefit.'

They ask you what they should give in alms. Say: 'What you can spare.' Thus Allah makes plain to you His revelations, so that you may reflect upon this world and the hereafter.

They question you concerning orphans. Say: 'To deal justly with them is best. If you mix their affairs with yours, remember they are your brothers. Allah knows the just from the unjust. If Allah pleased, He could afflict you. He is mighty and wise.'

You shall not wed pagan women, unless they embrace the faith. A believing slave-girl is better than an idolatress, although she may please you. Nor shall you wed idolaters, unless they embrace the faith. A believing slave is better than an idolater, although he may please you. These call you to Hell-fire; but Allah calls you, by His will, to Paradise and to forgiveness. He makes plain His revelations to mankind, so that they may take heed.

They ask you about menstruation. Say: 'It is an indisposition. Keep aloof from women during their menstrual periods and do not touch them until they are clean again. Then have intercourse with them as Allah enjoined you. Allah loves those that turn to Him in repentance and strive to keep themselves clean.'

Women are your fields: go, then, into your fields as you please. Do good works and fear Allah. Bear in mind that you shall meet Him. Give good news to the believers.

Do not make Allah the subject of your oaths when you swear that you will deal justly and keep from evil and make peace among men. Allah knows all and hears all. He will not call you to account for that which is inadvertent in your oaths. But He will take you to task for that which is intended in your hearts. Allah is forgiving and lenient.

Those that renounce their wives on oath must wait four months. If they change their mind, Allah is forgiving and merciful; but if they decide to divorce them, know that He hears all and knows all.

Divorced women must wait, keeping themselves from men, three menstrual courses. It is unlawful for them, if they believe in Allah and the Last Day, to hide what He has created in their wombs: in which case their husbands would do well to take them back, should they desire reconciliation.

Women shall with justice have rights similar to those exercised against them, although men have a status above women. Allah is mighty and wise.

Divorce may be pronounced twice, and then a woman must be retained in honour or allowed to go with kindness. It is unlawful for husbands to take from them anything they have given them, unless both fear that they may not be able to keep within the bounds set by Allah; in which case it shall be no offence for either of them if the wife ransom herself.

These are the bounds set by Allah; do not transgress them. Those that transgress the bounds of Allah are wrongdoers.

If a man divorce his wife, he cannot remarry her until she has wedded another man and been divorced by him; in which case it shall be no offence for either of them to return to the other, if they think that they can keep within the limits set by Allah.

Such are the bounds of Allah. He makes them plain to men of understanding.

When you have renounced your wives and they have reached the end of their waiting period, either retain them in honour or let them go with kindness. but you shall not retain them in order to harm them or to wrong them. Whoever does this wrongs his own soul.

Do not make game of Allah's revelations. Remember the favours He has bestowed upon you, and the Book and the wisdom which He has revealed for your instruction. Fear Allah and know that He has knowledge of all things.

If a man has renounced his wife and she has reached the end of her waiting period, do not prevent her from remarrying her husband if they have come to an honourable agreement. This is enjoined on every one of you who believes in Allah and the Last Day; it is more honourable for you and more chaste. Allah knows, but you do not.

Mothers shall give suck to their children for two whole years if the father wishes the suckling to be completed. They must be maintained and clothed in a reasonable manner by the father of the child. None should be charged with more than one can bear. A mother should not be allowed to suffer on account of her child, nor should a father on account of his child. The same duties devolve upon the father's heir. But if, after consultation, they choose by mutual consent to wean the child, they shall incur no guilt. Nor shall it be any offence for you if you prefer to have a nurse for your children, provided that you pay her what you promise, according to usage. Have fear of Allah and know that He is cognizant of all your actions.

Widows shall wait, keeping themselves apart from men, for four months and ten days after their husbands' death. When they have reached the end of their waiting period, it shall be no offence for you to let them do whatever they choose for themselves, provided that it is decent. Allah is cognizant of all your actions.

It shall be no offence for you openly to propose marriage to such women or to cherish them in your hearts. Allah knows that you will remember them. Do not arrange to meet them in secret, and if you do, speak to them honourably. But you shall not consummate the marriage before the end of their waiting period. Know that Allah has knowledge of all your thoughts. Therefore take heed and bear in mind that Allah is forgiving and lenient.

It shall be no offence for you to divorce your wives before the marriage is consummated or the dowry settled. Provide for them with fairness; the rich man according to his means and the poor man according to his. This is binding on righteous men. If you divorce them before the marriage is consummated, but after their dowry has been settled, give them the half of their dowry, unless they or the husband agree to forgo it. But it is more proper that the husband should forgo it. Do not forget to show kindness to each other. Allah observes your actions.

Attend regularly to your prayers, including the middle prayer, and stand up with all devotion before Allah. When you are exposed to danger pray while riding or on foot; and when you are restored to safety remember Allah, as He has taught you what you did not know.

You shall bequeath your widows a year's maintenance without causing them to leave their homes; but if they leave of their own accord, no blame shall be attached to you for any course they may deem fit to pursue. Allah is mighty and wise. Reasonable provision should also be made for divorced women. That is incumbent on righteous men.

Thus Allah makes known to you His revelations that you may grow in understanding.

Consider those that fled their country in their thousands for fear of death. Allah said to them: 'You shall perish,' and then He brought them back to life. Surely Allah is bountiful to mankind, but most men do not give thanks.

Fight for the cause of Allah and bear in mind that He hears all and knows all.

Who will grant Allah a generous loan? He will repay him many times over. It is Allah who enriches and makes poor. To Him you shall all return.

Have you not heard of what the leaders of the Israelites demanded of one of their prophets after the death of Moses? 'Anoint for us a king,' they said, 'and we will fight for the cause of Allah.'

He replied: 'What if you refuse to fight, when ordered so to do?'

'Why should we refuse to fight for the cause of Allah,' they said, 'when we and all our children have been driven from our dwellings?'

But when at last they were ordered to fight, they all refused, except a few of them. Allah knows the evil-doers.

Their prophet said to them: 'Allah has appointed Saul to be your king.' But they replied: 'Should he be given the kingship, when we are more deserving of it than he? Besides, he is not rich at all.'

He said: 'Allah has chosen him to rule over you and made him grow in wisdom and in stature. Allah gives His sovereignty to whom He will. He is munificent and all-knowing.'

Their prophet also said to them: 'The advent of the Ark shall be the portent of his reign. Therein shall be a pledge of security from your Lord, and the relics which the House of Moses and the House of Aaron left behind. It will be borne by the angels. That will be a sign for you, if you are true believers.'

And when Saul marched out with his army, he said: 'Allah will put you to the proof at a certain river. He that drinks from it shall cease to be my soldier; but he that does not drink from it, or contents himself with a taste of it in the hollow of his hand, shall fight by my side.'

But they all drank from it, except a few of them. And when Saul had crossed the river with those who shared his faith, they said: 'We have no power this day against Goliath and his warriors.'

But those of them who believed that they would meet Allah on Judgement-day replied: 'Many a small band has, by Allah's grace, vanquished a mighty army. Allah is with those who endure with fortitude.'

When they met Goliath and his warriors they cried: 'Lord, fill our hearts with steadfastness. Make us firm of foot and help us against the unbelievers.'

By Allah's will they routed them. David slew Goliath, and Allah bestowed on him sovereignty and wisdom and taught him what He pleased. Had Allah not defeated some by the might of others, the earth would have been utterly corrupted. But Allah is bountiful to His creatures.

Such are the revelations of Allah. We recite them to you in all truth, for you are one of Our messengers. Of these messengers We have exalted some above others. To some Allah spoke directly; others He raised to a lofty status. We gave Jesus the son of Mary veritable signs and strengthened him with the Holy Spirit. Had Allah pleased, those who succeeded them would not have fought against one another after the veritable signs had been given them. But they disagreed among themselves; some had faith and others had none. Yet had Allah pleased they would not have fought against one another. Allah does what He will.

Believers, bestow in alms a part of what We have given you before that day arrives when there shall be neither trading nor friendship nor intercession.

Truly, it is the unbelievers who are the wrong-doers.

Allah: there is no god but Him, the Living, the Eternal One. Neither slumber nor sleep overtakes Him. His is what the heavens and the earth contain. Who can intercede with Him except by His permission? He knows what is before and behind men. They can grasp only that part of His knowledge which He wills. His throne is as vast as the heavens and the earth, and the preservation of both does not weary Him. He is the Exalted, the Immense One.

There shall be no compulsion in religion. True guidance is now distinct from error. He that renounces idol-worship and puts his faith in Allah shall grasp a firm handle that will never break. Allah hears all and knows all.

Allah is the Patron of the faithful. He leads them from darkness to the light. As for the unbelievers, their patrons are false gods, who lead them from light to darkness. They are the heirs of Hell and shall abide in it for ever.

Have you not heard of him who argued with Abraham about his Lord because He had bestowed on him the Kingdom? Abraham said: 'My Lord is He who has power to give life and to cause death.'

'I, too,' replied the other, 'have power to give life and to cause death.'

'Allah brings up the sun from the east,' said Abraham. 'Bring it up yourself from the west.'

The unbeliever was confounded. Allah does not guide the evil-doers.

Or of him, who, when passing by a ruined and desolate city, remarked: 'How can Allah give life to this city, now that it is dead?' Thereupon Allah caused him to die, and after a hundred years brought him back to life.

'How long have you stayed away?' asked Allah.

'A day,' he replied, 'or a few hours.'

'Know, then,' said Allah, 'that you have stayed away a hundred years. Yet look at your food and drink: they have not rotted. And look at the bones of your ass. We will make you a sign to mankind: see how We will raise them and clothe them with flesh.'

And when it had all become manifest to him, he said: 'I know now that Allah has power over all things.'

When Abraham said: 'Show me, Lord, how You raise the dead,' He replied: 'Have you no faith?'

'Yes,' said Abraham, 'but I wish to reassure my heart.'

'Take four birds,' said He, 'draw them to you, and cut their bodies to pieces. Scatter them over the mountain-tops, then call them. They will come swiftly to you. Know that Allah is mighty and wise.'

He that gives his wealth for the cause of Allah is like a grain of corn which brings forth seven ears, each bearing a hundred grains. Allah gives abundance to whom He will; He is munificent and all-knowing.

Those that give their wealth for the cause of Allah and do not follow their almsgiving with taunts and insults shall be rewarded by their Lord; they shall have nothing to fear or to regret.

A kind word with forgiveness is better than charity followed by insult. Allah is self-sufficient and indulgent.

Believers, do not mar your almsgiving with taunts and mischief-making, like those who spend their wealth for the sake of ostentation and believe neither in Allah nor in the Last Day. Such men are like a rock covered with earth: a shower falls upon it and leaves it hard and bare. They shall gain nothing from their works. Allah does not guide the unbelievers.

But those that give away their wealth from a desire to please Allah and to reassure their own souls are like a garden on a hill-side: if a shower falls upon it, it yields up twice its normal crop; and if no rain falls upon it, it is watered by the dew. Allah takes cognizance of all your actions.

Would any one of you, being a man well-advanced in age with helpless children to support, wish to have his garden—a garden planted with palm-trees, vines and all manner of fruits, and watered by running streams—blasted and consumed by a fiery whirlwind?

Thus Allah makes plain to you His revelations, so that you may give thought.

Believers, give in alms of the wealth you have lawfully earned and of that which We have brought out of the earth for you; not worthless things which you yourselves would only reluctantly accept. Know that Allah is self-sufficient and glorious.

Satan threatens you with poverty and orders you to commit what is indecent. But Allah promises you His forgiveness and His bounty. Allah is munificent and all-knowing.

He gives wisdom to whom He will; and he that receives the gift of wisdom is rich indeed. Yet none except men of sense bear this in mind.

Whatever alms you give and whatever vows you make are known to Allah. The evil-doers shall have none to help them.

To be charitable in public is good, but to give alms to the poor in private is better and will atone for some of your sins. Allah has knowledge of all your actions.

It is not for you to guide them. Allah gives guidance to whom He will.

Whatever alms you give shall redound to your own advantage, provided that you give them for the love of Allah. And whatever alms you give shall be paid back to you in full: you shall not be wronged.

As for those needy men who, being wholly preoccupied with fighting for the cause of Allah, cannot travel in the land in quest of trading ventures: the ignorant take them for men of wealth on account of their modest behaviour. But you can recognize them by their look—they never importune men for alms. Whatever alms you give are known to Allah.

Those that give alms by day and by night, in private and in public, shall be rewarded by their Lord. They have nothing to fear or to regret.

Those that live on usury shall rise up before Allah like men whom Satan has demented by his touch; for they claim that usury is like trading. But Allah has permitted trading and forbidden usury. He that receives an admonition from his Lord and mends his ways may keep what he has already earned; his fate is in the hands of Allah. But he that pays no heed shall be consigned to Hell-fire and shall remain in it for ever.

Allah has laid His curse on usury and blessed almsgiving with increase. He bears no love for the impious and the sinful.

Those that have faith and do good works, attend to their prayers and pay the alms-tax, will be rewarded by their Lord and will have nothing to fear or to regret.

Believers, have fear of Allah and waive what is still due to you from usury, if your faith be true; or war shall be declared against you by Allah and His apostle. If you repent, you may retain your principal, suffering no loss and causing loss to none.

If your debtor be in straits, grant him a delay until he can discharge his debt; but if you waive the sum as alms it will be better for you, if you but knew it.

Fear the day when you shall all return to Allah; when every soul shall be requited according to its deserts. None shall be wronged.

Believers, when you contract a debt for a fixed period, put it in writing. Let a scribe write it down for you with fairness; no scribe should refuse to write as Allah has taught him. Therefore let him write; and let the debtor dictate, fearing Allah his Lord and not diminishing the sum he owes. If the debtor be a feeble-minded or ignorant person, or one who cannot dictate, let his guardian dictate for him in fairness. Call in two male witnesses from among you, but if two men cannot be found, then one man and two women whom you judge fit to act as witnesses; so that if either of them commit an error, the other will remember. Witnesses must not refuse to give evidence if called upon to do so. So do not fail to put your debts in writing, be they small or big, together with the date of payment. This is more just in the sight of Allah; it ensures accuracy in testifying and is the best way to remove all doubt. But if the transaction in hand be a bargain concluded on the spot, it is no offence for you if you do not commit it to writing.

See that witnesses are present when you barter with one another, and let no harm be done to either scribe or witness. If you harm them you shall commit a transgression. Have fear of Allah, who teaches you; he has knowledge of all things.

If you are travelling the road and a scribe cannot be found, then let pledges be taken. If anyone of you entrusts another with a pledge, let the trustee restore the pledge to its owner; and let him fear Allah, his Lord.

You shall not withhold testimony. He that withholds it is a transgressor. Allah has knowledge of all your actions.

To Allah belongs all that the heavens and the earth contain. Whether you reveal your thoughts or hide them, Allah will bring you to account for them. He will forgive whom He will and punish whom He pleases; He has power over all things.

The Apostle believes in what has been revealed to him by his Lord, and so do the faithful. They all believe in Allah and His angels, His scriptures, and His apostles: We discriminate against none of His apostles. They say: 'We hear and obey. Grant us your forgiveness, Lord; to You we shall all return. Allah does not charge a soul with more than it can bear. It shall be requited for whatever good and whatever evil it has done. Lord, do not be angry with us if we forget or lapse into error. Lord, do not lay on us the burden You laid on those before us. Lord, do not charge us with more than we can bear. Pardon us, forgive us our sins, and have mercy upon us. You alone are our Protector. Give us victory over the unbelievers.

AVICENNA

Avicenna was a Persian, born near Bukhara in 980. Something of a child prodigy, he mastered the logic, mathematics, science, and medicine of his time. He was a physician, and his Canon of Medicine *provided a synthesis of Greek and Arabic medicine. He died in Hermadan, Persia, in 1037, while participating in a political and military conflict.*

Avicenna attempted to merge Aristotle's doctrine of motion, as found in the principles of matter and form, with that of emanation as taught by the Neoplatonists. The effort enabled him, to his own satisfaction, to hold both the Islamic doctrine of the supremacy of God and the ancient philosophical position that the world was eternal. The doctrine of emanation of the world from the Godhead also provided him with a rationale for the immortality of the human soul, for if the world and its creatures emanated from God rather than being created as separate entities, then the creation had the characteristics of God, namely, eternal life. Avicenna was the greatest of the eastern Islamic philosophers; his classification of the sciences and his work in medicine profoundly influenced subsequent Islamic thought, as well as being significant for Thomas Aquinas and the intellectual traditions of the Christian west.

From Essay on the Secret of Destiny

In the name of God, the Merciful, the Compassionate.

Someone asked the eminent *shaykh* Abū 'Alī b. Sīnā (may God the Exalted have mercy on him) the meaning of the Ṣūfī saying, 'He who knows the secret of destiny is an atheist'. In reply he stated that this matter contains the utmost obscurity, and is one of those matters which may be set down only in enigmatic form and taught only in a hidden manner, on account of the corrupting effects its open declaration would have on the general public. The basic principle concerning it is found in a Tradition of the Prophet (God bless and safeguard him): 'Destiny is the secret of God; do not declare the secret of God'. In another Tradition, when a man questioned the Prince of the Believers, 'Alī (may God be pleased with him), he replied, 'Destiny is a deep sea; do not sail out on it'. Being asked again he replied, 'It is a stony path; do not walk on it'. Being asked once more he said, 'It is a hard ascent; do not undertake it'.

The *shaykh* said: Know that the secret of destiny is based upon certain premisses, such as [1] the world order, [2] the report that there is Reward and Punishment, and [3] the affirmation of the resurrection of souls.

From Avicenna, "Essay on the Secret of Destiny," trans. George F. Hourani, in John F. Wippel and Allan B. Wolter, eds., *Medieval Philosophy: From St. Augustine to Nicholas of Cusa* (New York: Free Press, 1969), pp. 229–232. Originally published in the *Bulletin of the School of Oriental and African Studies* (University of London), vol. XXIX, Part I, 1966, pp. 31–33. Reprinted by permission of George F. Hourani.

[1] The first premiss is that you should know that in the world as a whole and in its parts, both upper and earthly, there is nothing which forms an exception to the facts that God is the cause of its being and origination and that God has knowledge of it, controls it, and wills its existence; it is all subject to His control, determination, knowledge, and will. This is a general and superficial account, although in these assertions we intend to describe it truly, not as the theologians understand it; and it is possible to produce proofs and demonstrations of that. Thus, if it were not that this world is composed of elements which give rise to good and evil things in it and produce both righteousness and wickedness in its inhabitants, there would have been no completion of an order for the world. For if the world had contained nothing but pure righteousness, it would not have been this world but another one, and it would necessarily have had a composition different from the present composition; and likewise if it had contained nothing but sheer wickedness, it would not have been this world but another one. But whatever is composed in the present fashion and order contains both righteousness and wickedness.

[2] The second premiss is that according to the ancients Reward is the occurrence of pleasure in the soul corresponding to the extent of its perfection, while Punishment is the occurrence of pain in the soul corresponding to the extent of its deficiency. So the soul's abiding in deficiency is its 'alienation from God the Exalted', and this is 'the curse', 'the Penalty', [God's] 'wrath' and 'anger', and pain comes to it from that deficiency; while its perfection is what is meant by [God's] 'satisfaction' with it, its 'closeness' and 'nearness' and 'attachment'. This, then, and nothing else is the meaning of 'Reward' and 'Punishment' according to them.

[3] The third premiss is that the resurrection is just the return of human souls to their own world: this is why God the Exalted has said, 'O tranquil soul, return to your Lord satisfied and satisfactory'.

These are summary statements, which need to be supported by their proper demonstrations.

[*a*] Now, if these premisses are established, we say that the apparent evils which befall this world are, on the principles of the Sage, not purposed for the world—the good things alone are what is purposed, the evil ones are a privation, while according to Plato both are purposed as well as willed; [*b*] and that the commanding and forbidding of acts to responsible beings, by revelation in the world, are just a stimulant to him of whom it was foreknown [by God] that there would occur in him [performance of] the commandments, or (in the case of a prohibition) a deterrent to him of whom it was foreknown that he would refrain from what is forbidden. Thus the commandment is a cause of the act's proceeding from him of whom it is foreknown that it will proceed, and the prohibition is a cause of intimidation to him who refrains from something bad because of it. Without the commandment the former would not have come to desire the act; without the prohibition the latter would not have been scared. It is as if one were to imagine that it would have been possible for 100 per cent of wickedness to befall in the absence of any prohibition, and that with the presence of the prohibitions 50 per cent of wickedness has befallen, whereas without prohibitions 100 percent would have befallen. Commandments must be judged in the same way: had there been no commandments nothing of righteousness would have befallen, but with the advent of the commandments 50 per cent of righteousness has occurred.

[*c*] As for praise and blame, these have just two objects. One is to incite a doer of good to repeat the like act which is willed to proceed from him; the second is to scare the one from whom the act has occurred from repeating the like of it, and [ensure] that the one from whom that act has [not] occurred will abstain from doing what is not willed to proceed from him, though it is in his capacity to do it.

[*d*] It is not admissible that Reward and Punishment should be such as the theologians suppose: chastisement of the fornicator, for example, by putting him in chains and shackles, burning him in the fire over and over again, and setting snakes and scorpions upon him. For this is the behaviour of one who wills to slake his wrath against his enemy, through injury or pain which he inflicts on him out of hostility against him; and that is impossible in the character of God the Exalted, for it is the act of one who wills that the very being who models himself on him should refrain from acts like his or be restrained from repeating such acts. And it is not to be imagined that after the resurrection there are obligations, commandments, and prohibitions for anyone, so that by witnessing Reward and Punishment they should be scared or refrain from what is

proscribed to them and desire what is commanded to them. So it is false that Reward and Punishment are as they have imagined them.

[*e*] As for the [system of] penalties ordained by the divine Law for those who commit transgressions, it has the same effect as the prohibitions in serving as a restraint upon him who abstains from transgression, whereas without it it is imaginable that the act might proceed from him. There may also be a gain to the one who is subject to penalty, in preventing him from further wickedness, because men must be bound by one of two bonds, either the bond of the divine Law or the bond of reason, that the order of the world may be completed. Do you not see that if anyone were let loose from both bonds the load of wickedness he would commit would be unbearable, and the order of the world's affairs would be upset by the dominance of him who is released from both bonds? But God is more knowing and wiser.

From Concerning the Soul

CHAPTER I

The Vegetative Soul

When the elements are mixed together in a more harmonious way, i.e. in a more balanced proportion than in the cases previously mentioned, other beings also come into existence out of them due to the powers of the heavenly bodies. The first of these are plants. Now some plants are grown from seed and set aside a part of the body bearing the reproductive faculty, while others grow from spontaneous generation without seeds.

Since plants nourish themselves they have the faculty of nutrition. And because it is of the nature of plants to grow, it follows that they have the faculty of growth. Again, since it is the nature of certain plants to reproduce their like and to be reproduced by their like, they have a reproductive faculty. The reproductive faculty is different from the faculty of nutrition, for unripe fruits possess the nutritive but not the reproductive faculty; just as they possess the faculty of growth, but not that of reproduction. Similarly, the faculty of nutrition differs from that of growth. Do you not see that decrepit animals have the nutritive faculty but lack that of growth?

The nutritive faculty transmits food and replaces what has been dissolved with it; the faculty of growth increases the substance of the main structural organs in length, breadth, and depth, not haphazard but in such a way that they can reach the utmost perfection of growth. The reproductive faculty gives the matter the form of the thing; it separates from the parent body a part in which a faculty derived from its origin inheres and which, when the matter and the place which are prepared to receive its activity are present, performs its functions.

It will be evident from the foregoing that all vegetable, animal, and human functions are due to faculties over and above bodily functions, and even over and above the nature of the mixture itself.

After the plant comes the animal, which emerges from a compound of elements whose organic nature is much nearer to the mean than the previous two and is therefore prepared to receive the animal soul, having passed through the stage of the vegetable soul. And so the nearer it approaches the mean the greater is its capacity for receiving yet another psychical faculty more refined than the previous one.

The soul is like a single genus divisible in some way into three parts. The first is the vegetable soul, which is the first entelechy of a natural body possessing organs in so far as it is reproduced, grows, and assimilates nourishment. Food is a body whose function it is to become similar to the nature of the body whose food it is said to be, and adds to that body either in exact proportion or more or less what is dissolved.

The second is the animal soul, which is the first entelechy of a natural body possessing organs in so far as it perceives individuals and moves by volition.

Avicenna, *The Book of Salvation*, Vol. 2, Sec. 6, trans. Fazlur Rahman, *Avicenna's Psychology* (Westport, Conn.: Hyperion Press, 1952), pp. 24–29, 32–33, 56–63.

The third is the human soul, which is the first entelechy of a natural body possessing organs in so far as it acts by rational choice and rational deduction, and in so far as it perceives universals.

The vegetable soul has three faculties. First, the nutritive faculty which transforms another body into a body similar to that in which it is itself present, and replaces what has been dissolved. Secondly, the faculty of growth which increases every aspect of the body in which it resides, by length, breadth, and depth in proportion to the quantity necessary to make it attain its perfection in growth. Thirdly, the reproductive faculty which takes from the body in which it resides a part which is potentially similar to it and acts upon it with the help of other similar bodies, generating and mixing them so as to render that part actually similar to the body (to which it had been only potentially similar).

CHAPTER II

The Animal Soul

The animal soul, according to the primary division, has two faculties—the motive and the perceptive. The motive faculty again is of two kinds: either it is motive in so far as it gives an impulse, or in so far as it is active. Now the motive faculty, in so far as it provides the impulse, is the faculty of appetence. When a desirable or repugnant image is imprinted on the imagination of which we shall speak before long, it rouses this faculty to movement. It has two subdivisions: one is called the faculty of desire which provokes a movement (of the organs) that brings one near to things imagined to be necessary or useful in the search for pleasure. The second is called the faculty of anger, which impels the subject to a movement of the limbs in order to repulse things imagined to be harmful or destructive, and thus to overcome them. As for the motive faculty in its active capacity, it is a power which is distributed through the nerves and muscles, and its function is to contract the muscles and to pull the tendons and ligaments towards the starting-point of the movement, or to relax them or stretch them so that they move away from the starting-point.

The perceptive faculty can be divided into two parts, the external sense and the internal sense. The external senses are the five or eight senses. One of them is sight, which is a faculty located in the concave nerve; it perceives the image of the forms of coloured bodies imprinted on the vitreous humour. These forms are transmitted through actually transparent media to polished surfaces. The second is the sense of hearing, which is a faculty located in the nerves distributed over the surface of the ear-hole; it perceives the form of what is transmitted to it by the vibration of the air which is compressed between two objects, one striking and the other being struck, the latter offering it resistance so as to set up vibrations in the air which produce the sound. This vibration of the air outside reaches the air which lies motionless and compressed in the cavity of the ear, moving it in a way similar to that in which it is itself moved. Its waves touch that nerve, and so it is heard.

The third sense is that of smell, a faculty located in the two protuberances of the front part of the brain which resemble the two nipples of the breasts. It perceives the odour conveyed to it by inhaled air, which is either mixed with the vapour in the air or is imprinted on it through qualitative change in the air produced by an odorous body.

The fourth sense is that of taste, a faculty located in the nerves distributed over the tongue, which perceives the taste dissolved from bodies touching it and mingling with the saliva it contains, thus producing a qualitative change in the tongue itself.

The fifth sense is that of touch, which is a faculty distributed over the entire skin and flesh of the body. The nerves perceive what touches them and are affected when it is opposed to them in quality, and changes are then wrought in their constitution or structure.

Probably this faculty is not one species but a genus including four faculties which are all distributed throughout the skin. The first of them judges the opposition between hot and cold; the second that between dry and moist; the third that between hard and soft; and the fourth that between rough and smooth. But their coexistence in the same organ gives the false impression that they are essentially one.

The forms of all the sensibles reach the organs of sense and are imprinted on them, and then the faculty of sensation perceives them. This is almost evident in touch, taste, smell, and hearing. But concerning sight, a different view has been maintained, for some people have thought that something issues from the eye, meets the object of sight, takes its form from without—and that this constitutes the act of seeing. They often call the thing which according to them issues from the eye, light.

But true philosophers hold the view that when an actually transparent body, i.e. a body which has no colour, intervenes between the eye and the object of sight, the exterior form of the coloured body on which light is falling is transmitted to the pupil of the eye and so the eye perceives it.

This transmission is similar to the transmission of colours by means of light being refracted from a coloured thing and giving its colour to another body. The resemblance is not complete, however, for the former is more like an image in a mirror.

The absurdity of the view that light issues from the eye is shown by the following consideration. What emanates is either a body or a non-body. If it is not a body it is absurd to attribute motion and change of place to it, except figuratively in that there may be a power in the eye which transforms the air and other things it encounters into some sort of quality, so that it may be said that this quality 'came out of the eye'. Likewise, it is absurd to hold the view that it is a body, because if so then either—

(1) it will remain intact, issuing from the eye and reaching to the sphere of the fixed stars. In this case there will have emerged from the eye, despite its smallness, a conical body of immense size, which will have compressed the air and repulsed all the heavenly bodies, or it will have traversed an empty space. Both these views are manifestly absurd. Or—

(2) it will be dispersed, diffused and split up. In that case the percipient animal will of necessity feel something being detached from him and then dispersed and diffused; also, he will perceive the spots where that ray falls to the exclusion of the spots where it does not fall, so that he will only partially perceive the body, sensing some points here and there but missing the major part. Or—

(3) this emanating body is united with the air and the heavens and becomes one with them, so that the uniform whole is like one organ of the animal. In this case the uniform whole in its entirety will possess sensation. This is a most peculiar change indeed! It follows necessarily that if many eyes co-operate, it will be more powerful. Thus a man when in the company of others would have keener sight than when alone, for many people can effect a more powerful change than a single person. Again, this emanating body will necessarily be either simple or composite, and its composite nature will also be of a particular kind. Its motion then must be either voluntary or natural. But we know that this movement is not voluntary and by choice, although the opening and closing of the eyelids are voluntary. The only remaining alternative is that the movement is natural. But the simple natural movement will be only in one direction, not in many; and so the composite movement will also be, according to the dominant element, only in one direction, not in many. But it is not so with this movement according to those who support the theory of the 'issuing body'.

Again, if the sensed object is seen through the base of the conical emanating body which touches it, and not through the angle, it will necessarily follow that the shape and magnitude of the object perceived at a distance will also be perceptible as well as its colour. This is because the percipient subject comes in contact with it and encompasses it. But if it is perceived through the angle, I mean the section between the vitrium and the hypothetical cone, then the remoter the object the smaller will be the angle and also the common section, and consequently the form imprinted on it will also be smaller and will be so perceived. Sometimes the angle will be so small that the object will fail to be perceived and so the form will not be seen at all.

As for the second part, namely that the emanating something is not a body but an accident or a quality, this 'changing' or 'being changed' will inevitably be more powerful with the increase of the percipient subjects. In that case the same absurdity which we mentioned before will arise. Again, the air will either be merely a medium of transmission or percipient in itself. If it is only a medium of transmission and not percipient, then, as we maintain, perception takes place *in* the pupil of the eye and not outside it. But if the percipient is the air, then the same absurdity which we have already mentioned will be repeated; and it will necessarily follow that whenever there is commotion or disturbance in the air, sight will be distorted with the renewal of 'change' and the renewed action of the percipient in perceiving one thing after another, just as when a man runs in calm air his perception of minute things is confused. All this shows that sight is not due to something issuing from us towards the sensed object. It must therefore be due to something coming towards us from the sensed object; since this is not the body of the object, it must be its form. If this view were not correct, the creation of the eye with all its strata and humours and their respective shape and structure would be useless.

CHAPTER IV

The Rational Soul

The human rational soul is also divisible into a practical and a theoretical faculty, both of which are equivocally called intelligence. The practical faculty is the principle of movement of the human body, which urges it to individual actions characterized by deliberation and in accordance with purposive considerations. This faculty has a certain correspondence with the animal faculties of appetence, imagination, and estimation, and a certain dual character in itself. Its relationship to the animal faculty of appetence is that certain states arise in it peculiar to man by which it is disposed to quick actions and passions such as shame, laughter, weeping, &c. Its relationship to the animal faculty of imagination and estimation is that it uses that faculty to deduce plans concerning transitory things and to deduce human arts. Finally, it own dual character is that with the help of the theoretical intelligence it forms the ordinary and commonly accepted opinions concerning actions, as, for instance, that lies and tyranny are evil and other similar premisses which, in books of logic, have been clearly distinguished from the purely rational ones. This faculty must govern all the other faculties of the body in accordance with the laws of another faculty which we shall mention, so that it should not submit to them but that they should be subordinated to it, lest passive dispositions arising from the body and derived from material things should develop in it. These passive dispositions are called bad morals. But far from being passive and submissive this faculty must govern the other bodily faculties so that it may have excellent morals.

It is also possible to attribute morals to the bodily faculties. But if the latter predominate they are in an active state, while the practical intelligence is in a passive one. Thus the same thing produces morals in both. But if the practical intelligence predominates, it is in an active state while the bodily faculties are in a passive one, and this is morals in the strict sense (even so there would be two dispositions or moral characters); or character is only one with two different relationships. If we examine them more closely the reason why morals are attributed to this faculty is that the human soul, as will be shown later, is a single substance which is related to two planes—the one higher and the other lower than itself. It has special faculties which establish the relationship between itself and each plane: the practical faculty which the human soul possesses in relation to the lower plane, which is the body, and its control and management; and the theoretical faculty in relation to the higher plane, from which it passively receives and acquires intelligibles. It is as if our soul has two faces: one turned towards the body, and it must not be influenced by any requirements of the bodily nature; and the other turned towards the higher principles, and it must always be ready to receive from what is There in the Higher Plane and to be influenced by it. So much for the practical faculty.

CHAPTER XII

Concerning the Temporal Origin of the Soul

We say that human souls are of the same species and concept. If they existed before the body, they would either be multiple entities or one single entity. But it is impossible for them to be either the one or the other, as will be shown later, therefore it is impossible for them to exist before the body. We now begin with the explanation of the impossibility of its numerical multiplicity and say that the mutual difference of the souls before [their attachment to] bodies is either due to their quiddity and form; or to the element and matter which is multiple in space, a particular part of which each matter occupies; or to the various times peculiar to every soul when it becomes existent in its matter; or to the causes which divide their matter. But their difference is not due to their quiddity or form, since their form is one, therefore their difference is due to the recipient of the quiddity or to the body to which the quiddity is specifically related. Before its attachment to the body the soul is quiddity pure and simple; thus it is impossible for one soul to be numerically different from another, or for the quiddity to admit of essential differentiation. This holds absolutely true in all cases; for the multiplicity of the species of those things whose essences are pure concepts is only due to the substrata which receive them and to what is affected by them, or due only to their times. But when they are absolutely separate, i.e. when the categories we have enumerated are not applicable to them, they cannot be diverse. It is therefore impossible for them to have any kind of diversity or multiplicity among them. Thus it is untrue that before they enter bodies souls have numerically different essences.

I say that it is also impossible for souls to have numerically one essence, for when two bodies come into existence two souls also come into existence in them. Then either—

(1) these two souls are two parts of the same single soul, in which case one single thing which does not possess any magnitude and bulk would be potentially divisible. This is manifestly absurd according to the principles established in physics. Or—

(2) a soul which is numerically one would be in two bodies. This also does not require much effort to refute.

It is thus proved that the soul comes into existence whenever a body does so fit to be used by it. The body which thus comes into being is the kingdom and instrument of the soul. In the very disposition of the substance of the soul which comes into existence together with a certain body—a body, that is to say, with the appropriate qualities to make it suitable to receive the soul which takes its origin from the first principles—there is a natural yearning to occupy itself with that body, to use it, control it, and be attracted by it. This yearning binds the soul specially to this body, and turns it away from other bodies different from it in nature so that the soul does not contact them except through it. Thus when the principle of its individualization, namely, its peculiar dispositions, occurs to it, it becomes an individual. These dispositions determine its attachment to that particular body and form the relationship of their mutual suitability, although this relationship and its condition may be obscure to us. The soul achieves its first entelechy through the body; its subsequent development, however, does not depend on the body but on its own nature.

But after their separation from their bodies the souls remain individual owing to the different matters in which they had been, and owing to the times of their birth and their different dispositions due to the bodies which necessarily differ because of their peculiar conditions.

CHAPTER XIII

The Soul Does Not Die With the Death of the Body; It Is Incorruptible

We say that the soul does not die with the death of the body and is absolutely incorruptible. As for the former proposition, this is because everything which is corrupted with the corruption of something else is in some way attached to it. And anything which in some way is attached to something else is either coexistent with it or posterior to it in existence or prior to it, this priority being essential and not temporal. If, then, the soul is so attached to the body that it is coexistent with it, and this is not accidental but pertains to its essence, then they are essentially interdependent. Then neither the soul nor the body would be a substance; but in fact they are substances. And if this is an accidental and not an essential attachment, then, with the corruption of the one term only the accidental relationship of the other term will be annulled, but its being will not be corrupted with its corruption. If the soul is so attached to the body that it is posterior to it in existence, then, in that case, the body will be the cause of the soul's existence. Now the causes are four; so either the body is the efficient cause of the soul and gives it existence, or it is its receptive and material cause—maybe by way of composition as the elements are for the body or by way of simplicity as bronze is for the statue—or the body is the soul's formal or final cause. But the body cannot be the soul's efficient cause, for body, as such, does not act; it acts only through its faculties. If it were to act through its essence, not through its faculites, every body would act in the same way. Again, the bodily faculties are all of them either accidents or material forms, and it is impossible that either accidents or forms subsisting in matter should produce the being of a self-subsisting entity independent of matter or that of an absolute substance. Nor is it possible that the body should be the receptive and material cause of the soul, for we have clearly shown and proved that the soul is in no way imprinted in the body. The body, then, is not 'informed' with the form of the soul, either by way of simplicity or composition so that certain parts of the body are composed and mixed together in a certain way and then the soul is imprinted in them. It is also impossible that the body should be the formal or the final cause of the soul, for the reverse is the more plausible case.

Thus the attachment of the soul to the body is not the attachment of an effect to a necessary cause. The truth is that the body and the temperament are an accidental cause of the soul, for when the matter of a body suitable to become the instrument of the soul and its proper subject comes into existence, the separate causes bring into being the individual soul, and that is how the soul originates from them. This is because it is impossible to bring arbitrarily into being different souls without any specific cause. Besides, the soul does not admit of numerical multiplicity, as we have shown. Again, whenever a new thing comes into being, it must be preceded by a matter which is prepared to receive it or to have a relationship with it, as has been shown in the other sciences. Again, if an individual soul were to come into being without an instrument through which it acts and attains perfection, its being would be purposeless; but there is nothing purposeless in nature. In truth, when the suitability and preparation for such a relationship exist in the instrument, it becomes necessary that such a thing as a soul should originate from the separate causes.

But if the existence of one thing necessitates the existence of another, the corruption of the former does not necessarily entail that of the latter. This happens only where its very being subsists through or in that thing. Many things originating from other things survive the latter's corruption; when their being does not subsist in them, and especially when they owe their existence to something other than what was merely preparatory for the emanation of their being. And the being of the soul does in fact emanate from something different from the body and bodily functions, as we have shown; its source of emanation must be something different from the body. Thus when the soul owes its being to that other thing and only the time of its realization to the body, its being would be independent of the body which is only its accidental cause; it cannot then be said that they have a mutual relationship which would necessitate the body preceding the soul as its necessary cause.

Let us turn to the third division which we mentioned in the beginning, namely, that the attachment of the soul to the body might be in the sense that the soul is prior to the body in existence. Now in that case the priority will be either temporal as well as essential, and so the soul's being could not possibly be attached to the body since it precedes the body in time, or the priority will be only essential and not temporal, for in time the soul will not be separate from the body. This sort of priority means that when the prior entity comes into existence, the being of the posterior entity must follow from it. Then the prior entity cannot exist, if the posterior is supposed to be non-existent. I do not say that the supposition of the non-existence of the posterior necessitates the non-existence of the prior, but that the posterior cannot be non-existent except when first something has naturally happened to the prior which has made it non-existent, too. Thus it is not the supposition of the non-existence of the posterior entity which necessitates the non-existence of the prior, but the supposition of the non-existence of the prior itself, for the posterior can be supposed to be non-existent only after the prior itself has ceased to exist. This being so, it follows that the cause of non-existence must occur in the substance of the soul necessitating the body's corruption along with it, and that the body cannot be corrupted through a cause special to itself. But in fact the corruption of the body does take place through a cause special to itself, namely, through changes in its composition and its temperament. Thus it is false to hold that the soul is attached to the body as essentially prior to it, and that at the same time the body is indeed corrupted through a cause in itself; so no such relationship subsists between the two.

This being so, all the forms of attachment between the body and the soul have proved to be false and it only remains that the soul, in its being, has no relationship with the body but is related with other principles which are not subject to change or corruption.

As for the proposition that the soul does not admit of corruption at all, I say that there is another conclusive reason for the immortality of the soul. Everything which might be corrupted through some cause has in itself the potentiality of corruption and, before corruption, has the actuality of persistence. But it is absurd that a single thing in the same sense should possess both, the potentiality of corruption and the actuality of persistence; its potentiality of corruption cannot be due to its actual persistence, for the concept of potentiality is contrary to that of actuality. Also, the relation of this potentiality is opposed to the relation of this actuality, for the one is related with corruption, the other with persistence. These two concepts, then, are attributable to two different factors in the concrete thing. Hence we say that the actuality of persistence and the potentiality of corruption may be combined in composite things and in such simple things as subsist in composite ones. But these two concepts cannot come together in simple things whose essence is separate. I say in another absolute sense that these two concepts cannot exist together in a simple thing whose essence is unitary. This is because everything which persists and has the potentiality of corruption also has the potentiality of persistence, since its persistence is not necessary. When it is not necessary, it is possible; and possibility is of the nature of potentiality. Thus the potentiality of persistence is in its very substance. But, of course, it is clear that the actuality of persistence of a thing is not the same as its potentiality of persistence. Thus its actuality of persistence is a fact which happens to the body which has the potentiality of persistence. Therefore that potentiality does not belong to something actual but to something of which actual existence is only an accident and does not constitute its real essence. From this it necessarily follows that its being is composed of a factor the possession of which gives actual existence to it (this factor is the form in every concrete existent), and another factor which attains this actual existence but which in itself has only the potentiality of existence (and this factor is the matter in the concrete existent).

So if the soul is absolutely simple and is not divisible into matter and form, it will not admit of corruption. But if it is composite, let us leave the composite and consider only the substance which is its matter. We say: either that matter will continue to be divisible and so the same analysis will go on being applied to it and we shall then have a regress *ad infinitum*, which is absurd; or this substance and base will never cease to exist. But if so, then our present discourse is devoted to this factor which is the base and origin (i.e. the substance) and not to the composite thing which is composed of this factor and some other. So it is clear that everything which is simple and not composite, or which is the origin and base (i.e. the substance) of the composite thing, cannot in itself possess both the actuality of persistence and the potentiality of corruption. If it has the potentiality of corruption, it cannot possibly have the actuality of persistence, and if it has the actuality of persistence and existence, it cannot have the potentiality of corruption. Obviously, then, the substance of the soul does not have the potentiality of corruption. Of those things which come to be and are corrupted, the corruptible is only the concrete composite. The potentiality of corruption and of persistence at the same time does not belong to something which gives unity to the composite, but to the matter which potentially admits of both contraries. So the corruptible composite as such possesses neither the potentiality of persistence nor that of corruption, let alone both. As to the matter itself, it either has persistence not due to any potentiality, which gives it the capacity for persistence—as some people think—or it has persistence through a potentiality which gives it persistence, but does not have the potentiality of corruption; this latter being something which it acquires. The potentiality of corruption of simple entities which subsist in matter is due to matter and is not in their own substance. The argument which proves that everything which comes to exist passes away on account of the finitude of the potentialities of persistence and corruption is relevant only to those things whose being is composed of matter and form. Matter has the potentiality that this form may persist in it, and at the same time the potentiality that this form may cease to exist in it. It is then obvious that the soul is absolutely incorruptible. This is the point which we wanted to make, and this is what we wanted to prove.

AVERROËS

Born in Cordoba, Spain, in 1126, Averroës rivals Avicenna as the greatest philosopher of Islam, although he was far more influential on medieval Jewish and Christian thought than on Islamic philosophy. Averroës lived alternately in Cordoba and Morocco, working both as a physician and as a qādi, *that is, a judge and lawyer. He opposed Avicenna's interpretation of Greek philosophy and believed that the doctrine of Aristotle had been presented in a confused manner throughout the history of Islamic philosophy.*

In order to rectify this confusion, Averroës wrote many commentaries on Aristotle.

Nevertheless, the Neoplatonic presence in Islam found its way into the thought of Averroës, particularly in his doctrine of the soul. This amalgam led to a controversial contention that the individual soul was not immortal although the universal intellect of all humankind was immortal. As might be expected, Christian philosophers, led by Thomas Aquinas, attacked this view of the immortality of the soul. A further complication in the thought of Averroës traced to the accusation that he taught a "double-truth," namely, a proposition that could be true in philosophy and false in theology or vice versa. Commentators on Averroës correctly deny that he held that position, yet "Latin Averroism," which is the Christian adoption of the "double-truth," had a brief but notorious history until it was condemned by the medieval church in 1277. In fact, Averroës held, as did Thomas Aquinas, that philosophy could use the light of reason to expose the truth of the laws of nature and the existence of God. Neither held the doctrine of the double-truth, but the writings of both Averroës and Aquinas were censored in 1277, for they trusted a source, reason, other than faith.

The writing of Averroës fared no better in Islamic circles, and with his death in 1198 Islamic philosophy went into a steep decline.

From Long Commentary on De Anima

BOOK III

Text 4. It is necessary, therefore, that, if [the intellect] understands all things, it be not mixed, as Anaxagoras has said, in order that it may dominate, that is in order that it may understand. For if [something] were to appear in it, that which appears would prevent something foreign [from appearing in it], since it is something other.

Commentary. After [Aristotle] has set down that the material, receiving intellect must belong to the genus of passive powers, and, that in spite of this, it is not altered by the reception [of that which it receives], for it is neither a body nor a power within a body, he provides a demonstration for this [opinion]. And he says: *It is necessary, therefore, that, if the intellect understands,* etc. That is, it is necessary, therefore, that, if [the intellect] understands all those things which exist outside the soul, it be described—prior to its understanding—as belonging to the genus of passive, not active, powers, and [it is necessary] that it be not mixed with bodies, that is, that it be neither a body nor a power within a body, be it a natural or animate [power], as Anaxagoras has said. Thereafter [Aristole] says: *in order that it may understand* etc. That is, it is necessary that it be not mixed, in order that it may understand all things and receive them. For if it were mixed, then it would be either a body or a power within a body, and if it were one of these, it would have a form proper to itself, which form would prevent it from receiving some foreign form.

This is what he has in mind when he says: *For if something were to appear in it* etc. That is, if [the passive intellect] were to have a form proper to itself, then that form would prevent it from receiving the various external forms, which are different from it. Thus, one must inquire into those propositions by means of which Aristotle shows these two things about the intellect, namely [1] that it belongs to the genus of passive powers, and [2] that it is not alterable, since it is neither a body nor a power within a body. For these two [propositions] are the starting point of all those things which are said about the intellect. As Plato said, the most extensive discussion must take place in the beginning; for the slightest

From Averroës, "Long Commentary on *De Anima*," trans. Arthur Hyman, in Arthur Hyman and James J. Walsh, eds., *Philosophy in the Middle Ages: The Christian, Islamic and Jewish Traditions* (Indianapolis: Hackett Publishing Co., Inc., 2d ed., 1983), pp. 324–334. Permission granted by the publisher.

error in the beginning is the cause of the greatest error in the end, as Aristotle says.

We say: That conception by the intellect belongs in some way to a passive power, just as in the case of a sensory power [perception by a sense belongs to a passive power], becomes clear through the following [considerations]. Now, the passive powers are moveable by that to which they are related *(attribuuntur)*, while active powers move that to which they are related *(attribuuntur)*. And since it is the case that something moves something else only insofar as it exists in actuality and [something] is moved insofar as it exists in potentiality, it follows necessarily, that since the forms of things exist in actuality outside the soul, they move the rational soul insofar as it understands them, just as in the case of sensible things it is necessary that they move the senses insofar as they are things existing in actuality and that the senses are moved by them. Therefore, the rational soul must consider the forms *(intentiones)* which are in the imaginative faculty, just as the senses must inspect sensible things. And since it appears that the forms of external things move this power in such a way that the mind abstracts these forms from material things and thereby makes them the first intelligibles in actuality, after they had been intelligibles in potentiality—it appears from this that this soul [the intellect] is [also] active, not [only] passive. For insofar as the intelligibles move [the intellect], it is passive, but insofar as they are moved by it, it is active. For this reason Aristotle states subsequently that it is necessary to posit in the rational soul the following two distinct [powers], namely, an active power and a passive power. And he states clearly that each one of [the rational soul's] parts is neither generable nor corruptible. In the present discussion, however, he begins to describe the nature *(substantiam)* of this passive power, to the extent to which it is necessary in this exposition. Therefore he states that this distinct [power], namely, that which is passive and receptive, exists in the rational faculty.

That the substance which receives these forms can not be a body or a power in a body, becomes clear from the propositions of which Aristotle makes use in this discussion. One of these is that this substance [the material intellect] receives all material forms, and this is [something well] known about this intellect. The other is that everything which receives something else must necessarily be devoid of the nature of that which it receives and that its essence *(substantiam)* is not the same in species as the essence *(substantiam)* of that which it receives. For, if that which receives is of the same nature as that which is received, then something would receive itself and that which moves would be the same as that which is moved. Wherefore it is necessary that the sense which receives color lacks color and the sense which receives sound lacks sound. And this proposition is necessarily [true] and there is no doubt about it. From these two propositions it follows that the substance which is called the material intellect does not have any of the material forms in its nature. And since the material forms are either a body or forms in a body, it is evident that the substance which is called the material intellect is not a body or a form in a body. For this reason it is not mixed with matter in any way at all. And you should know that what he states is necessarily [so], [namely] that, since it [the material intellect] is a substance, and since it receives the forms of material things or material [forms], it does not have in itself a material form, that is [it is not] composed of matter and form. Nor is it some one of the material forms, for the material forms are not separable [from bodies]. Nor, again, is it one of the first simple forms since these are separable [from bodies], but it [the material intellect] does not . . . receive forms except as differentiated and insofar as they are intelligible in potentiality, not in actuality [that is, it must be related to the body in some way]. Therefore it is something different from form and from matter and from that which is composed of these. But whether this substance [the material intellect] has a proper form which is different in its being from the material forms has not yet been explained in this discussion. For the proposition which states that that which receives must be devoid of the nature of that which it receives is understood as referring to the nature of the species, not to the nature of its genus, and even less to [the nature of] something remote, and still less to [the nature of] something which is predicated according to equivocation. Thus we say that in the sense of touch there exists something intermediate between the two contraries which it perceives, for contraries differ in species from intermediate things. Since this is the disposition of the material intellect, namely, that it is some existing thing, and that it is a power separate from body, and that it has no material form, it is clear that it is not passive [in the sense of being alterable] (for passive things, that is things which are alterable, are like material forms), and that it is simple, and separable from body, as Aristotle says. The nature of the material intellect is understood by Aristotle in this manner. We shall speak subsequently about the questions which he raised.

Text 5. And thus [the material intellect] has no other nature but that which is possible. Therefore that [part] of the soul which is called intellect (and I call intellect that [part] by means of which we distinguish and think) is not something existing in actuality before it thinks.

Commentary. After [Aristotle] has shown that the material intellect does not possess any of the forms of material things, he begins to define it in the following manner. And he says that it has no nature but the nature of the possibility for receiving the material intelligible forms. And he states: *And thus [the material intellect] has no other nature,* etc. That is, that [part] of the soul which is called the material intellect has no nature and essence through which it exists *(constituatur)* insofar as it is material but the nature of possibility, for it is devoid of all material and intelligible forms.

Thereafter he says: *and I call intellect,* etc. That is, and I intend by *intellect* that faculty of the soul which is truly called intellect, not that faculty which is called intellect in a general sense, that is, the imaginative faculty (in the Greek language), but [I intend] that faculty by means of which we distinguish speculative things and by means of which we think about things to be done in the future. Thereafter he says: *it is not something existing in actuality before it thinks.* That is, it is the definition of the material intellect that it is that which is in potentiality all the concepts *(intentiones)* of the universal material forms and it is not something in actuality before it understands them.

Since this is the definition of the material intellect, it is clear that it differs in respect to itself from prime matter in that it is in potentiality all the concepts *(intentiones)* of the universal material forms, while prime matter is in potentiality all these sensible forms, not [as] knowing and comprehending. And the reason why this nature, that is, the material intellect, distinguishes and knows, while prime matter does not distinguish or know, is that prime matter receives differentiated, that is, individual and particular forms, while [the material intellect] receives universal forms. And from this it is clear that this nature, [that is, the material intellect] is not some individual thing, either a body or a power in a body, for if it were, it would receive the forms insofar as they are differentiated and particular, and if this were the case, then the forms existing in [the material intellect] would be intelligible in potentiality and thus [this intellect] would not distinguish the nature of the forms insofar as they are forms, and the case would be the same as that of a disposition for individual forms, whether they are spiritual or corporeal. Therefore, if this nature, which is called intellect, receives forms, it is necessary that it receives [these] forms in a manner of reception different from that according to which these matters receive the forms whose determination in prime matter is the determination of prime matter in respect to them. Therefore it is not necessary that there belong to the genus of those matters by which the form is determined as particular anything but prime matter. For if there were other matters in this genus, then the reception of forms in these [matters] would be of the same genus, for diversity in the nature of the receptacle produces a diversity in the nature of that which is received. This consideration moved Aristotle to affirm that this nature, that is, the material intellect, differs from the nature of matter and from the nature of form and from the nature of the composite. . . .

All these things being as they are, it seems to me proper to write down what appears to me [to be correct] concerning this subject. And if that which appears to me [to be correct] will not be complete, let it be the starting point for something which can be completed. Now, I beg those brethren who see what has been written, that they write down their questions and perhaps in this way that which is true about this subject will be discovered, if I should not have discovered it. But should I have discovered [what is true], as I think I have, then [this truth] will become clear through these questions. For truth, as Aristotle says, agrees with itself and bears witness to itself in every way.

As for the question stating: in what way are the speculative intelligibles generable and corruptible, while [the intellect] producing them and that receiving them are eternal (and what need would there be to posit an agent intellect and a receiving [intellect] were there not something that is generated)—this question would not arise would there not exist something which is the cause of the generation of the speculative intelligibles. But what has been said concerning the fact that these [speculative] intelligibles consists of two [principles], one of which is generated, the other of which is not generated is according to the course of nature. For, since conception by the intellect, as Aristotle says, is like perception by the senses—but perception by a sense is accomplished through two principles, one of which is the object through which sense perception becomes true (and this is the sensible outside the soul), and the other is that subject through which sense perception is an existing form (and this is the first actuality of the sense organ), it is likewise necessary that the intelligibles in actuality have two principles, one of which is the object *(subiectum)* through which they are true, namely, the forms which are the true images, the other one of which is that subject *(subiectum)* through which the intelligibles are one of the things existing in the world, and this is the material intellect. But there is no difference between sense and intellect except that the object through which sense-perception is true exists outside the soul, while the object through which conception by the intellect is true exists within the soul. As will be seen subsequently, this is what was said by Aristotle about this intellect. . . .

This similarity exists in an even more perfect manner between the visible object which moves the sense of sight and the intelligible object which moves the intellect. For just as the visible object, which is color, moves the sense of sight only when through the presence of light it was made color in actuality after it had been [color] in potentiality, so also the imaginative forms *(intentiones)* move the material intellect only when they are made intelligibles in actuality after they had been [intelligibles] in potentiality. And for this reason (as will be seen later) it was necessary for Aristotle to posit an agent intellect, and this is the intellect which brings the imaginative forms from potentiality into actuality. Thus, just as the color which exists in potentiality is not the first actuality of that color which is the perceived form *(intentio),* while the subject which is actualized by this color is the sense of sight, so also the subject which is actualized by the intelligible object is not the imaginative forms *(intentiones)* which are intelligible in potentiality, but the material intellect is that subject which is actualized by the intelligibles. And the relation of the intelligible forms to the material intellect is as the relation of the form *(intentio)* of color to the faculty of sight.

All these matters being as we have related, it is only necessary that the intelligibles in actuality, that is the speculative intelligibles, are generable according to the object through which they are true, that is according to the imaginative forms, but not according to that subject through which they are one of the existing things, that is, according to the material intellect.

But the second question which states: in what way is the material intellect numerically one in all individual human beings, not generable nor corruptible, while the intelligibles existing in it in actuality (and this is the speculative intellect) are numbered according to the numeration of individual human beings, and generable and corruptible through the generation and corruption of individual [human beings]—this question is extremely difficult and one that has the greatest ambiguity.

If we posit that this material intellect is numbered according to the numeration of individual human beings, it follows that it is some individual thing, either a body or a power in a body. And if it were some individual thing, it would be the intelligible form *(intentio)* in potentiality. But the intelligible form in potentiality is an object which moves the receiving intellect, not a subject which is moved. For, if the receiving subject were assumed to be some individual thing, it would follow, as we have said, that something receives itself, and this is impossible.

[Even] if we were to admit that it receives itself, it would necessarily follow that it receives itself insofar as it is diverse. And thus the intellectual faculty would be the same as the sensory faculty, and there would be no distinction between the existence of the form outside the soul and in the soul. For this individual matter receives the forms only as particulars and individuals. And this is one of the arguments which provide evidence that Aristotle was of the opinion that the [material] intellect is not an individual form *(intentio).*

[On the other hand], were we to assert that [the material intellect] is not numbered according to the numeration of individual [human beings], it would follow that its relation to all individual human beings who possess its ultimate perfection through generation would be the same. Whence it would be necessary that if one of these individual [human beings] acquires some knowledge, this knowledge would be acquired by all of them. For, if the conjunction *(continuatio)* of these individual human beings [with what is known] occurs because of the conjunction *(propter continuationem)* of the material intellect with them, just as the conjunction of a human being with the sensory form *(intentione)* occurs because of the conjunction of the first perfection of the sense organ with him who receives the sensory form (but the conjunction of the material intellect with all human beings who exist in actuality in their ultimate perfection at some given time must be one and the same conjunction, for there is nothing which would produce any difference in the relation of conjunction between the two who are conjoined)—if, I say, this is the case, it is necessary that if you acquire some knowledge, I will acquire the same knowledge, which is absurd.

And regardless whether you assert that the ultimate perfection which is generated in some individual [human being]—that is, that perfection through which the material intellect is joined [to human beings] and through which it is as a form separable from the subject to which it is joined—inheres in the intellect, if something like that should be the case, or whether you assert that this perfection belongs to one of the faculties of the soul or to one of the faculties of the body, each of these assumptions leads to an absurd conclusion.

Therefore one must be of the opinion that if there exist some beings having a soul whose first perfection is a substance existing in separation from their subjects, as it is thought about the celestial bodies, it is impossible that there exist in each of their species more than one individual. For if there would exist in these, that is, in each of their species more than one individual, for example, in the body moved by the same mover, then the existence of these individuals would be unnecessary and superfluous, since their motion would result from the form *(intentio)* which is one in number. For example, it is unnecessary that one sailor (captain) should have more than one ship at the same time, and it is likewise unnecessary that one artisan should have more than one instrument of the same kind.

This is the meaning of what was said in the first book of *De Caelo*, namely that, if there existed another world, there would have to exist another celestial body [corresponding to a celestial body in this world]. And if there existed another celestial body, it would have to have a motive force numerically different from the motive force of this celestial body [that is, the one existing in this world]. If this were the case, then the motive force of the celestial body would be material and numbered through the numeration of the celestial bodies, since it is impossible that a motive force which is one in number should belong to two bodies which are different in number. Therefore, a craftsman does not use more than one instrument when only one action proceeds from him. And it is generally thought that necessarily absurd conclusions will follow from the assertion we have made, namely, that the intellect *in habitu* is one in number. Avempace enumerated most of these absurd conclusions in his Letter which he called *The Conjunction of the Intellect with Man.* Since this is so, of what sort is the road toward the solution of this difficult question?

We say that it is evident that a man is thinking in actuality only because of the conjunction of the intelligible in actuality with him. It is also evident that matter and form are joined to one another in such a way that something which is composed of them is a unitary thing and this is especially evident in the case of the conjunction of the material intellect and the intelligible form *(intentio)* in actuality. For that which is composed of these [the material intellect and the intelligible form] is not some third thing different from them as is the case in respect to other beings composed of matter and form. Hence the conjunction of the intelligible with man is only possible through the conjunction of one of these two parts with him, namely that part which belongs to it [the intelligible] as matter or that part which belongs to it (namely, the intelligible) as form.

Since it is clear from the previously mentioned difficulties that it is impossible that the intelligible be joined to each individual human being and that it be numbered according their numeration through that part which is to it as matter, that is, through the material intellect, it remains that the conjunction of the intelligibles with us human beings takes place through the conjunction of the intelligible forms (and they are the imaginative forms) with us, that is, through that part which is in us in respect to them in some way like a form. And therefore the statement that a boy is potentially thinking can be understood in two ways. One of these is insofar as the imaginative forms which exist in him are intelligible in potentiality; the other is insofar as the material intellect, to whose nature it belongs to receive the concept of this imaginative form, is receptive in potentiality and joined to us in potentiality.

It is clear, therefore, that the first perfection of the intellect differs from the first perfection of the other faculties of the soul and that the term *perfection* is predicated of them in an equivocal fashion, and this is the opposite of what Alexander [of Aphrodisias] thought. For this reason Aristotle said in his definition of the soul that the soul is the first perfection of a natural organic body, for it is not yet clear whether a body is perfected by all faculties in the same way, or whether there is among them some faculty by which a body is not perfected, or, if it is perfected by it, it will be perfected in some other way.

Now the predisposition of the intelligibles which exists in the imaginative faculty is similar to the predispositions which exist in the other faculties of the soul, namely, the predisposition for the first perfections of the other faculties of the soul, insofar as each of these predispositions is generated through the generation of the individual [in which it exists] and destroyed through the destruction of this individual and, generally, this predisposition is numbered according to the numeration of that individual.

But the two kinds of predisposition differ in that the first kind, namely, the predisposition which exists in the imaginative forms, is a predisposition in a moving principle, while the second kind, namely that predisposition which exists for the first perfections of the other parts of the soul, is a predisposition in a recipient.

Because of the similarity between these two kinds of predispositions Avempace thought that the only predisposition for the production of the intelligible concept is the predisposition existing in the imaginative forms. But these two predispositions differ as earth and heaven. For one of them is a predisposition in a moving principle insofar as it is a moving principle, while the other is a predisposition in something moved insofar as it is moved and is a recipient.

Thus one should hold the opinion which has already become clear to us from Aristotle's discussion, [namely] that there are two kinds of intellect in the soul. One of these is the receiving intellect whose existence has been shown here, the other is the agent intellect and this is the one which causes the forms which are in the imaginative faculty to move the material intellect in actuality, after they had only moved [it] potentially, as will be clear further on from Aristotle's discussion. And these two kinds [of intellect] are not generable or corruptible. And the agent intellect is to the receiving intellect as form to matter, as will be shown later on.

Now Themistius was of the opinion that we are the agent intellect, and that the speculative intellect is nothing but the conjunction of the agent intellect with the material intellect. And it is not as he thought, but one must be of the opinion that there are three kinds of intellect in the soul. One of these is the receiving intellect, the second is the producing [agent] intellect, and the third is the produced [speculative] intellect. Two of these intellects are eternal, namely the agent and receiving intellects, the third, however, is generable and corruptible in one way, eternal in another way.

Since as a result of this discussion we are of the opinion that the material intellect is a single one for all human beings and since we are also of the opinion that the human species is eternal, as has been shown in other places, it follows that the material intellect is never devoid of the natural principles which are common to the whole human species, namely, the first propositions and individual concepts which are common to all. For these intelligibles are one according to the recipient [the material intellect], and many according to the received form [the imaginative form].

Hence according to the manner in which they are one, they are necessarily eternal, for existence does not depart from the received object, namely the moving principle which is the form *(intentio)* of the imaginative forms, and there is nothing on part of the recipient which prevents [its reception]. For generation and corruption belongs to them only according to the multitude which befalls them, not according to the manner according to which they are one. Therefore, when in respect to some individual human being, some knowledge of the things first known is destroyed through the destruction of the object through which it is joined to us and through which it is true, that is the imaginative form, it does not follow that this knowledge is destroyed absolutely, but it is [only] destroyed in respect to some individual human being. Because of this we can say that the speculative intellect is one in all [human beings].

If one considers these intelligibles insofar as they exist absolutely, not in respect to some individual [human being], they are truly said to be eternal, and [it is not the case] that they are known at one time and not known at another time, but they are known always. And that existence belongs to them as intermediate between absence of existence and permanent existence. For in accordance with the quantitative difference [literally: according to the increase and decrease] which comes to the intelligibles from the ultimate perfection [of human beings] they are generable and corruptible, while insofar as they are one in number they are eternal.

This will be the case if it is not set down that the disposition in respect to the ultimate perfection in man is as the disposition in respect to the intelligibles which are common to all [men], that is, that the world [literally: worldly existence] is not devoid of such an individual existence. That this should be impossible is not obvious, but someone who affirms this must have an adequate reason and one that puts the mind at rest. For if knowledge belongs in some proper fashion to human beings, just as the various kinds of crafts belong in some proper fashions to human beings, one should think that it is impossible that philosophy should be without any abode, just as one must be of the opinion that it is impossible that all the natural crafts should be without any abode. For if some part [of the earth] lacks them, that is, these crafts, for example, the northern quarter of the earth, the other quarters will not lack them, since it is clear that they can have an abode in the southern part, just as in the northern.

Thus, perhaps, philosophy comes to be in the major portion of the subject at all times, just as man comes to be from man and horse from horse. According to this mode of existence the speculative intellect is neither generable nor corruptible.

In general, the case of the agent intellect which produces the intelligibles is the same as the case of the intellect which distinguishes and receives [the intelligibles]. For just as the agent intellect never ceases from generating and producing [intelligibles] in an absolute manner, even though some particular subject may be removed from this generation, so is it with the intellect that distinguishes.

Aristotle indicated this in the first treatise of this book [*De Anima*] when he said: *Conception and consideration by the intellect are differentiated, so that within the intellect something other is destroyed, while the intellect itself is not subject to destruction.* Aristotle intends by *something other* the human imaginative [forms]. And he intends by *conception by the intellect* the reception which exists always in the material intellect, about which he intends to raise questions in the present treatise as well as in the former when he says: [*And when it (the intellect) is set free*] . . . *we do not remember, since this intellect is not passive, but the passive intellect is corruptible, and without it nothing thinks.*

And by the *passive intellect* he intends the imaginative faculty, as will be shown later. Generally, this meaning seems to be remote, namely, that the soul, that is the speculative intellect, should be immortal.

For this reason Plato said that the universals are neither generable nor corruptible and that they exist outside the mind. This statement is true in the sense that the intelligibles inhering in the speculative intellect are immortal, but false according to the sound of his words (and this is the sense which Aristotle labored to destroy in the *Metaphysics*). In general, in regard of the nature *(intentio)* of the soul, there is something true in the probable propositions which attribute to the soul both kinds of existence, namely mortal and immortal, since it is impossible that probable propositions should be completely false. The Ancients give an account of this and all the religious laws agree in this account.

The third question (namely, in what way is the material intellect some existing thing, while it is not one of the material forms nor prime matter) is answered as follows. One should be of the opinion that there are four kinds of existence. For just as sensible being is divided into form and matter, so also must intelligible being be divided into principles similar to these, that is into something similar to form and something similar to matter. This distinction is necessary for every incorporeal intellect which understands another, for if this distinction did not apply there would be no multiplicity in regard to the incorporeal forms. It has been shown in *First Philosophy* [that is in the *Metaphysics*] that there exists no form absolutely free from potentiality except the first form which does not think anything outside itself, but its existence *(essentia)* is its quiddity, but other forms are differentiated in respect to quiddity and existence *(essentia)* in some way. Were there not this genus of beings which we know in the science of the soul, we could not think of multiplicity in the case of incorporeal beings, just as we would not know that incorporeal motive forces must be intellects, if we would not know the nature of the intellect.

This escaped many modern philosophers, so that

they deny what Aristotle said in the eleventh treatise of the *First Philosophy*, namely, that it is necessary, that the incorporeal forms which move the celestial bodies are [numbered] according to the number of the celestial bodies. Therefore, knowledge about the soul is necessary for the knowledge of First Philosophy. It is necessary that the receiving intellect knows the intellect which exists in actuality. For if [this intellect] understands the material forms, it is more fitting that it understands immaterial forms, and that which it knows of the incorporeal forms, for example, of the agent intellect, does not hinder it from knowing the material forms.

But the proposition which states that a recipient must not have anything in actuality insofar as it receives is not said in an absolute fashion, but with the provision, that it is not necessary that the receiving intellect be not anything whatsoever in actuality, but [only] that it is not something in actuality in respect to that which it receives, as we have stated previously. Indeed, you should know that the relation of the agent intellect to the receiving intellect is as the relation of light to the transparent medium, and that the relation of the material forms to the receiving intellect is as the relation of color to the transparent medium. For just as light is the perfection of the transparent medium, so is the agent intellect the perfection of the material [intellect]. And just as the transparent medium is only moved by color and receives it when it is illuminated, so also the [material] intellect only receives the intelligibles which exist in it when the material intellect is perfected by the agent intellect and illuminated by it. And just as light makes color in potentiality exist in actuality, as a result of which it [color] can move the transparent medium, so also the agent intellect makes the intelligible forms in potentiality exist in actuality, as a result of which the material intellect receives them. In this manner one must understand about the material and agent intellect.

When the material intellect becomes joined insofar as it is perfected through the agent intellect, then we are joined with the agent intellect. And this disposition is called *acquisition (adeptio)* and *acquired intellect (intellectus adeptus)*, as will be seen later. The manner in which we have described the essence of the material intellect answers all the questions arising about our statement that this intellect is one and many. For if something which is known by me and by you were one in all respects, it would follow that, if I know something, you would also know it, and many other absurdities [would also follow]. And if we were to assert that the material intellect is many, it would follow that something known by me and by you is one in respect to species and two in respect to individual, and thus something known would possess something else known and this would go on to infinity. Thus it will be impossible that a student learns from a teacher if the knowledge which exists in the teacher is not a force generating and producing the knowledge which is in the student, in the same manner as one fire produces another fire alike to it in species, which is absurd. The fact that something known by the teacher and the student is the same in this manner made Plato believe that learning is remembering. But if we assert that something known by me and by you is many in respect to that object *(in subiecto)* according to which it is true, that is in respect to the imaginative forms, and one in respect to the subject through which it is an existing intellect (and this is the material intellect), these questions are resolved completely.

MOSES MAIMONIDES

Born in Spain in 1135, Moses Maimonides is uncontestably the most important of the medieval Jewish thinkers. Fleeing an oppressive Muslim sect, the Almohads, Maimonides arrived in Egypt, where he became a physician. He died in Cairo in 1204.

Maimonides is celebrated in Jewish thought for his attempt to organize and systemize the Mishna, that is, Jewish oral law. Still more significant is his The Guide of the Perplexed, *which counts centuries of Christian as well as Jewish readers. Written in Arabic, the* Guide *was intended for literate and informed Jews who were puzzled over the complex relationship between philosophy and the Hebrew scriptures. Clearly influenced by Islamic thought, Maimonides, like many Muslims, took Aristotle as his philosopher.*

The themes of the Guide *are familiar to medieval thought: the existence and nature of God, his attributes, the creation of the world in time, and the moral questions that proceed from a people who live by a scriptural tradition. The* Guide *was soon translated into Hebrew, and Maimonides became the major, although often controversial, figure in medieval and early modern Jewish thought. More traditional Jewish thinkers viewed the work of Maimonides as anti-religious, although his philosophy clearly allows for both religious insight and religious experience. He was later read in the Christian west and despite the virulent anti-Semitism of Christianity, he was influential there as well, especially in his philosophical claim that the creation of the world was accessible to philosophical reason. The* Guide *is a complex and subtle book, worthy of thousands of years of Jewish history. It remains a challenging and classic interpretation of the relationship between philosophy and scriptural theology.*

From The Guide of the Perplexed

PART I

Chapter 51

There are many things in existence that are clear and manifest: primary intelligibles and things perceived by the senses and, in addition, the things that come near to these in respect to their clarity. If man had been left as he [naturally] is, he would not have needed a proof of them—for instance, for the existence of motion, the existence of man's ability to act, the manifestations of generation and corruption, the natures of the things that are apparent to the senses, like the hotness of fire, the coldness of water, and many other things of this kind. Yet since strange opinions have arisen due either to people who committed errors or to people who acted with some end in view, so that professing such opinion they ran counter to the nature of existence and denied a sensibly perceived thing or wished to suggest to the estimative faculty the existence of a nonexistent thing, the men of science have had to resort to proving those manifest things and to disproving the existence of things that are only thought to exist. Thus we find that Aristotle establishes the fact of motion, as it had been denied, and demonstrates the nonexistence of atoms, as their existence had been asserted. To this category belongs the denial of essential attributes to God, may He be exalted. For that denial is a primary intelligible, inasmuch as an attribute is not the essence of the thing of which it is predicated, but is a certain mode of the essence and hence an accident. If, however, the attribute were the essence of the thing of which it is predicated, the attribute would be either a tautology—as if you were saying that man is man—or the attribute would be a mere explanation of a term—as if you said that man is a rational living being. For being a rational animal is the essence and true reality of man, and there does not exist in this case a third notion, apart from those of animal and of rational, that constitutes man. For man is the being of which life and rationality are predicated. Thus those attributes merely signify an explanation of a term and nothing else. It is as if you said that the thing denoted by the term "man" is the thing composed of life and rationality. It is then clear that an attribute may be only one of two things. It is either the essence of the thing of which it is predicated, in which case it is an explanation of a term. We, in this respect, do not consider it impossible to predicate such an attribute of God, but do consider it impossible in another respect, as shall be

From Moses Maimonides, *The Guide of the Perplexed*, trans. Shlomo Pines (Chicago: University of Chicago Press, 1964), Part I, Chapters 51, 52, and 68; Part II, Introduction and Chapters 13 and 17; Part III, Chapter 12.

made clear. Or the attribute is different from the thing of which it is predicated, being a notion superadded to that thing. This would lead to the conclusion that that attribute is an accident belonging to that essence.

Now by denying the assertion that terms denoting accidents are attributes of the Creator, one does not deny the notion of accident. For every notion superadded to an essence is an adjunct to it and does not perfect its essence, and this is the meaning of accident. This should be considered in addition to the circumstances that there would be many eternal things if there were many attributes. For there is no oneness at all except in believing that there is one simple essence in which there is no complexity or multiplication of notions, but one notion only; so that from whatever angle you regard it and from whatever point of view you consider it, you will find that it is one, not divided in any way and by any cause into two notions; and you will not find therein any multiplicity either in the thing as it is outside of the mind or as it is in the mind, as shall be demonstrated in this Treatise.

In discussing this subject, some people engaged in speculation have ended by saying that His attributes, may He be exalted, are neither His essence nor a thing external to His essence. This is similar to what others say, namely, that the modes—by which term they mean the universals—are neither existent nor nonexistent, and, again similar to what others say, that the atom is not in a place, but occupies a locality, and that there is no act of a man but that there may be an acquisition of an act by him. These are things that are merely said; and accordingly they subsist only in words, not in the mind; all the more, they have no existence outside of the mind. But as you know and as everyone knows who does not deceive himself, these assertions are defended by means of many words and falsifying parables and are proved correct by shouting defamatory polemics and various complicated kinds of dialectic arguments and sophistries. Should, however, the man who proclaims these things and attempts to establish them in the ways indicated, reflect upon his belief, he would find nothing but confusion and incapacity. For he wants to make exist something that does not exist and to create a mean between two contraries that have no mean. Or is there a mean between that which exists and that which does not exist, or in the case of two things is there a mean between one of them being identical with the other or being something else? What forces him to this is, as we have said, the wish to preserve the conceptions of the imagination and the fact that all existent bodies are always represented to oneself as certain essences. Now every such essence is of necessity endowed with attributes, for we do not ever find an essence of a body that while existing is divested of everything and is without an attribute. This imagination being pursued, it was thought that He, may He be exalted, is similarly composed of various notions, namely, His essence and the notions that are superadded to His essence. Several groups of people pursued the likening of God to other beings and believed Him to be a body endowed with attributes. Another group raised themselves above this consequence and denied His being a body, but preserved the attributes. All this was rendered necessary by their keeping to the external sense of the revealed books as I shall make clear in later chapters that will deal with these notions.

Chapter 52

An attribute predicated of any thing, of which thing it is accordingly said that it is such and such, must necessarily belong to one of the following five groups:

The first group is characterized by the thing having its definition predicated of it—as when it is predicated of man that he is a rational living being. This attribute, which indicates the essence and true reality of a thing, is, as we have already made clear, merely the explanation of a term and nothing else. This kind of attribute should be denied to God according to everybody. For He, may He be exalted, has no causes anterior to Him that are the cause of His existence and by which, in consequence, He is defined. For this reason it is well known among all people engaged in speculation, who understand what they say, that God cannot be defined.

The second group is characterized by the thing having part of its definition predicated of it—as when it is predicated of man that he is a living being or a rational being. This attribute signifies an inseparable connection. For our saying, every man is rational, signifies that reason must be found in every being in whom humanity is found. This kind of attribute should be denied to God, may He be exalted, according to everybody. For if He has a part of an essence, His essence must be composite. The absurdity of divine attributes belonging to this group is like the absurdity recognized with regard to the first group.

The third group consists of attributes predicated of a thing that go beyond its true reality and its essence so that the attribute in question is not a thing through which the essence is perfected and constituted. Consequently that attribute is a certain quality with respect to the thing of which it is predicated. Now quality, considered one of the supreme genera, is regarded as one of the accidents. Thus if an attribute belonging to this group would subsist in Him, may He be exalted, He would be a substratum of accidents. This is sufficient to show how far from His true reality and essence this is, I mean the supposition that He is endowed with quality. It is, however, strange that those who proclaim the existence of attributes, deny with reference to Him, may He be exalted, the possibility of likening Him to something else and of qualifying Him. For what is the meaning of their saying that He may not be qualified unless it be that He is not endowed with quality? Now every attribute that is affirmed of a certain essence as pertaining to it essentially either constitutes the essence, in which case it is identical with the latter, or is a quality of that essence.

Now there are, as you know, four genera of qualities. I will accordingly give you examples in the way of attributes of every one of these genera, in order that the impossibility of the subsistence of attributes of this kind in God, may He be exalted, be made clear to you. The first example is as follows. You predicate of a man one of his speculative or moral habits or one of the dispositions subsisting in him qua an animate being, as when you say someone is a carpenter or chaste or ill. There is no difference between your saying a carpenter or your saying a learned man or a sage, all of these being dispositions subsisting in the soul. There is also no difference between your saying a chaste man and your saying a merciful man. For all arts, sciences, and settled moral characters are dispositions subsisting in the soul. All this is clear to whoever has occupied himself even to the slightest extent with the art of logic. The second example is as follows. You predicate of a thing a natural faculty that is in it or the absence of a natural faculty, as when you say soft or hard. And there is no difference between your saying soft and hard and your saying strong and weak, all these being natural dispositions. The third example is as follows. You predicate of a man a passive quality or an affection, as when you say someone is irascible, irritable, timid, or merciful, in cases in which this character is not firmly established. Your predicating a color, a taste, a smell, warmth, coldness, dryness, and humidity of a certain thing also belongs to this kind. The fourth example is as follows. You predicate of a thing that which pertains to it in respect of quantity considered as such, as when you say long, short, crooked, and straight and other similar things. Now when you consider all these attributes and what is akin to them, you will find that it is impossible to ascribe them to God. For He does not possess quantity so that there might pertain to Him a quality pertaining to quantity as such. Nor does He receive impressions and affections so that there might pertain to Him a quality belonging to the affections. Nor does He have dispositions so that there might be faculties and similar things pertaining to Him. Nor is He, may He be exalted, endowed with a soul, so that He might have a habitus pertaining to Him—such as clemency, modesty, and similar things—or have pertain to Him that which pertains to animate beings as such—for instance, health and illness. It is accordingly clear to you that no attribute that may be brought under the supreme genus of quality can subsist in Him, may He be exalted.

With regard to those three groups of attributes—which are the attributes indicative of the essence or of a part of the essence or of a certain quality subsisting in the essence—it has already been made clear that they are impossible with reference to Him, may He be exalted, for all of them are indicative of composition, and the impossibility of composition in respect to the deity we shall make clear by demonstration.

The fourth group of attributes is as follows. It is predicated of a thing that it has a relation to something other than itself. For instance, it is related to a time or to a place or to another individual, as for instance when you predicate of Zayd that he is the father of a certain individual or the partner of a certain individual or an inhabitant of a certain place or one who was at a certain time. Now this kind of attribute does not necessarily entail either multiplicity or change in the essence of the thing of which it is predicated. For the Zayd who is referred to may be the partner of Umar, the father of Bakr, the master of Khālid, a friend of Zayd, an inhabitant of such and such dwelling place, and one who was born in such and such a year. Those notions of relation are not the essence of the thing or something subsisting in its essence, as do the qualities. At first thought it seems that it is permissible to predicate of God, may He be exalted, attributes of this kind. However, when one knows true reality and achieves greater exactness in speculation, the fact that this is impossible becomes clear. There is no relation between God, may He be exalted, and time and place; and this is quite clear. For time is an accident attached to motion, when the notion of priority and posteriority is considered in the latter and when motion becomes numbered, as is made clear in the passages especially dealing with this subject. Motion, on the other hand, is one of the things attached to bodies, whereas God, may He be exalted, is not a body. Accordingly there is no relation between Him and time, and in the same way there is no relation between Him and place. The subject of investigation and speculation is therefore the question whether there is between Him, may He be exalted, and any of the substances created by Him a true relation of some kind so that this relation might be predicated of Him. It is clear at the first glance that there is no correlation between Him and the things created by Him. For one of the properties of two correlated things is the possibility of inverting the statement concerning them while preserving their respective relations. Now He, may He be exalted, has a necessary existence while that which is other than He has a possible existence, as we shall make clear. There accordingly can be no correlation between them. As for the view that there is some relation between them, it is deemed correct, but this is not correct. For it is impossible to represent oneself that a relation subsists between the intellect and color although, according to our school, both of them are comprised by the same "existence." How then can a relation be represented between Him and what is other than He when there is no notion comprising in any respect both of the two, inasmuch as existence is, in our opinion, affirmed of Him, may He be exalted, and of what is other than He merely by way of absolute equivocation. There is, in truth, no relation in any respect between Him and any of His creatures. For relation is always found between two things falling under the same—necessarily proximate—species, whereas there is no relation between the two things if they merely fall under the same genus. On this account one does not say that this red is more intense than this green or less or equally so, though both fall under the same genus, namely, color. If, however, two things fall under two different genera, there is no relation between them in any respect whatever, not even according to the inchoate notions of common opinion; this holds even for cases in which the two things fall in the last resort under one higher genus. For instance, there is no relation between a hundred cubits and the heat that is in pepper inasmuch as the latter belongs to the genus quality and the former to the genus quantity. There is no relation either between knowledge and sweetness or between clemency and bitterness, though all of them fall under the supreme genus quality. How then could there subsist a relation between Him, may He be exalted, and any of the things created by Him, given the immense difference between them with regard to the true reality of their existence, than which there is no greater difference? If a relation subsisted between them, it would necessarily follow that the accident of relation must be attached to God. Even if it is not an accident with regard to His essence, may He be exalted, nevertheless it is, generally speaking, some sort of accident. There is accordingly no way of escape offering the possibility of affirming that He has an attribute, not even with regard to relation, if one has knowledge of true reality. However, relation is an attribute with regard to which it is more appropriate than with regard to the others that indulgence should be exercised if it is predicated of God. For it does not entail the positing of a multiplicity of eternal things or the positing of alteration taking place in His essence, may He be exalted, as a consequence of an alteration of the things related to Him.

The fifth group of the affirmative attributes is as follows. A thing has its action predicated of it. I do not intend to signify by the words, his action, the habitus of an art that belongs to him who is described—as when you say a carpenter or a smith—inasmuch as this belongs to the species of quality, as we have mentioned. But I intend to signify by the words, his action, the action that he who is described has performed—as when you say Zayd is the one who carpentered this door, built that particular wall, or wove this garment. Now this kind of attribute is remote from the essence of the thing of which it is predicated. For this reason it is permitted that this kind should be predicated of God, may He be exalted, after you have—as shall be made clear—come to know that the acts in question need not be carried out by means of differing notions subsisting within the essence of the agent, but that all His different acts, may He be exalted, are all of them carried out by means of His essence, and not, as we have made clear, by means of a superadded notion.

A summary of the contents of the present chapter would be as follows: He, may He be exalted, is one in all respects; no multiplicity should be posited in Him; there is no notion that is superadded to His essence; the numerous attributes possessing diverse notions that figure in the Scriptures and that are indicative of Him, may He be exalted, are mentioned in reference to the multiplicity of His actions and not because of a multiplicity subsisting in His essence, and some of them, as we have made clear, also with a view to indicating His perfection according to what we consider as perfection. As for the question whether it is possible that one simple essence in which no multiplicity is posited should perform diverse actions, the answer shall be made clear by means of examples.

Chapter 68

You already know that the following dictum of the philosophers with reference to God, may He be exalted, is generally admitted: the dictum being that He is the intellect as well as the intellectually cognizing subject and the intellectually cognized object, and that those three notions form in Him, may He be exalted, one single notion in which there is no multiplicity. We have mentioned this likewise in our great compilation, since this, as we have made clear there, is one of the foundations of our Law; I mean the fact that He is one only and that no other thing can be added to Him, I mean to say that there is no external thing other than He. For this reason it is said, *by the Lord the living*, and not, *by the life of the Lord*. For His life is not something other than His essence, as we have made clear when speaking of the negation of attributes. However, there is no doubt that anyone who has not studied the books that have been composed concerning the intellect has not grasped the essence of the intellect, has not acquired knowledge of its quiddity, and has no understanding of it other than one that resembles his understanding of the notions of blackness and whiteness, has great difficulty in understanding this notion. In fact our saying that He is the intellectual cognition as well as the intellectually cognizing subject and the intellectually cognized object will appear to him as if we had said that whiteness, that which has become white, and that which whitens, are one and the same thing. How many ignoramuses there are who hasten to refute us by means of this and similar examples, and how many pretending to knowledge there are who have great difficulties with regard to this and who hold that the minds cannot attain the knowledge that it is correct that this matter should be necessarily true. Yet this notion is a matter of demonstration and is quite clear, as the theologizing philosophers have explained. Here I shall make clear to you that which they have demonstrated.

Know that before a man intellectually cognizes a thing, he is potentially the intellectually cognizing subject. Now if he has intellectually cognized a thing (it is as if you said that if a man has intellectually cognized this piece of wood to which one can point, has stripped its form from its matter, and has represented to himself the pure form—this being the action of the intellect), at that time the man would become one who has intellectual cognition in actu. Intellect realized in actu is the pure abstract form, which is in his mind, of the piece of wood. For intellect is nothing but the thing that is intellectually cognized. Accordingly it has become clear to you that the thing that is intellectually cognized is the abstract form of the piece of wood, that this form is identical with the intellect realized in actu, and that these are not two things—intellect and the intellectually cognized form of the piece of wood. For the intellect in actu is nothing but that which has been intellectually cognized; and the thing by means of which the form of wood was intellectually cognized and made abstract, that thing being the intellectually cognizing subject, is also indubitably identical with the intellect realized in actu. For in the case of every intellect, its act is identical in essence; for intellect in actu is not one thing and its act another thing; for the true reality and the quiddity of the intellect is apprehension. You should not then think that the intellect in actu is a certain thing existing by itself apart from apprehension and that apprehension is something else subsisting in that intellect. For the very being and true reality of the intellect is apprehension. Whenever, therefore, you assume that an intellect exists in actu, that intellect is identical with the apprehension of what has been intellectually cognized. This is most clear to whoever has attempted this kind of speculation. Accordingly it is clear that the act of the intellect, which is its apprehension, is the true reality and the essence of the intellect. Consequently the thing by means of which the form of that piece of wood was abstracted and apprehended, which thing is the intellect, is also the intellectually cognizing subject. For it is that very intellect that abstracted the form and apprehended it, this being its act because of which it is said to be an intellectually cognizing subject. Now its act is identical with its essence. Accordingly that which has been assumed to be an intellect in actu has nothing belonging to it except the form of the piece of wood. Accordingly it is clear that whenever intellect exists in actu, it is identical with the intellectually cognized thing. And it has become clear that the act of every intellect, which act consists in its being intellectually cognizing, is identical with the essence of that intellect. Consequently the intellect, the intellectually cognizing subject, and the intellectually cognized object are always one and the same thing in the case of everything that is cognized in actu.

If, however, potential cognition is assumed, they—that is, the intellect in potentia and the potentially cognizable object—are necessarily two things. It is as if you said the hylic intellect subsisting in Zayd is a potential intellect, and similarly this piece of wood is in potentia an intellectually cognized object. Indubitably these are two things. When thereupon the intellect becomes actual and the form of the piece of wood is realized as intellectually cognized, then the intellectually cognized form is identical with the intellect—that very intellect, which is an intellect in actu, being the one by means of which the form was abstracted and intellectually cognized. For everything that has an existing act exists in actu. Thus every intellect in potentia and potentially cognizable objects are two things. Moreover, everything that is in potentia must undoubtedly have a substratum supporting this potentiality, such a substratum as, for instance, man. Thus there are three things: the man who supports that potentiality and who is the intellectually cognizing subject in potentia; the potentiality that is the intellect in potentia; and the thing apt to be intellectually cognized, which is the potentially cognizable object. In the example in question, this would be as if you said: man, hylic intellect, and the form of the piece of wood—these being three separate notions. When, however, the intellect is realized in actu, the three notions become one. Accordingly you will never find in that case that intellect is one thing and the intellectually cognized object another thing, unless they are regarded as being in potentia.

Now when it is demonstrated that God, may He be held precious and magnified, is an intellect in actu and that there is absolutely no potentiality in Him—as is clear and shall be demonstrated—so that He is not by way of sometimes apprehending and sometimes not apprehending but is always an intellect in actu, it follows necessarily that He and the thing apprehended are one thing, which is His essence. Moreover, the act of apprehension owing to which He is said to be an intellectually cognizing subject is in itself the intellect, which is His essence. Accordingly He is always the intellect as well as the intellectually cognizing subject and the intellectually cognized object. It is accordingly also clear that the numerical unity of the intellect, the intellectually cognizing subject, and the intellectually cognized object, does not hold good with reference to the Creator only, but also with reference to every intellect. Thus in us too, the intellectually cognizing subject, the intellect, and the intellectually cognized object, are one and the same thing wherever we have an intellect in actu. We, however, pass intellectually from potentiality to actuality only from time to time. And the separate intellect too, I mean the active intellect, sometimes gets an impediment that hinders its act—even if this impediment does not proceed from this intellect's essence, but is extraneous to it—being a certain motion happening to it by accident.

We do not intend at present to explain this, our intention being to affirm that that which pertains solely to Him, may He be exalted, and which is specific to Him is His being constantly an intellect in actu and that there is no impediment either proceeding from His essence or from another that might hinder His apprehending. Accordingly it follows necessarily because of this that He is always and constantly an intellectually cognizing subject, an intellect, and an intellectually cognized object. Thus His essence is the intellectually cognizing subject, the intellectually cognized object, and the intellect, as is also necessarily the case with regard to every intellect in actu. We have repeated this notion several times in this chapter because the minds of men are very much strangers to this way of representing the thing to oneself. I do not consider that you might confuse intellectual representation with imagination and with the reception of an image of a sense object by the imaginative faculty, as this Treatise has been composed only for the benefit of those who have philosophized and have acquired knowledge of what has become clear with reference to the soul and all its faculties.

PART II

[Introduction]

The premises needed for establishing the existence of the deity, may He be exalted, and for the demonstration that He is neither a body nor a force in a body and that He, may His name be sublime, is one, are twenty-five—all of which are demonstrated without there being a doubt as to any point concerning them. For Aristotle and the Peripatetics after him have come forward with a demonstration for every one of them. There is one premise that we will grant them, for through it the objects of our quest will be demonstrated, as I shall make clear; this premise is the eternity of the world.

1. The first premise: The existence of any infinite magnitude is impossible.

2. The second premise: The existence of magnitudes of which the number is infinite is impossible—that is, if they exist together.

3. The third premise: The existence of causes and effects of which the number is infinite is impossible, even if they are not endowed with magnitude. For instance, the assumption that one particular intellect, for example, has as its cause a second intellect, and that the cause of this second intellect is a third one, and that of the third a fourth, and so on to infinity, is likewise clearly impossible.

4. The fourth premise: Change exists in four categories: it exists in the category of substance, the changes occurring in a substance being generation and corruption. It exists in the category of quantity, namely, as growth and decrease. It exists in the category of quality, namely, as alteration. It exists in the category of place, namely, as the motion of translation. It is this change in the category of place that is more especially called motion.

5. The fifth premise: Every motion is a change and transition from potentiality to actuality.

6. The sixth premise: Of motions, some are essential and some accidental, some are violent and some are motions of a part—this being a species of accidental motion. Now essential motion is, for example, the translation of a body from one place to another. Accidental motion is, for example, when a blackness existing in this particular body is said to be translated from one place to another. Violent motion is, for example, the motion of a stone upwards through the action of something constraining it to that. Motion of a part is, for example, the motion of a nail in a ship; for when the ship is in motion, we say that the nail is likewise in motion. Similarly when any compound is in motion as a whole, its parts are likewise said to be in motion.

7. The seventh premise: Everything changeable is divisible. Hence everything movable is divisible and is necessarily a body. But everything that is indivisible is not movable; hence it will not be a body at all.

8. The eighth premise: Everything that is moved owing to accident must of necessity come to rest, inasmuch as its motion is not in virtue of its essence. Hence it cannot be moved forever in that accidental motion.

9. The ninth premise: Every body that moves another body moves the latter only through being itself in motion when moving the other body.

10. The tenth premise: Everything that is said to be in a body is divided into two classes: either it subsists through the body, as do the accidents, or the body subsists through it, as in the case of the natural form. Both classes are to be considered as a force in the body.

11. The eleventh premise: Some of the things that subsist through body are sometimes divided through the division of the body and hence are divisible according to accident, as for instance the colors and the other forces that are distributed through the whole of the body. In a like manner some of the things that

constitute a body are not divisible in any way, as for instance the soul and the intellect.

12. The twelfth premise: Every force that is found distributed through a body is finite because the body is finite.

13. The thirteenth premise: It is impossible that one of the species of motion be continuous, except local motion, and of this only that which is circular.

14. The fourteenth premise: Local motion is the primary and the first by nature among all motions; for generation and corruption are preceded by alteration, and alteration is preceded by the approach of that which alters to that which is to be altered; and there is no growth and diminution except when they are preceded by generation and corruption.

15. The fifteenth premise: Time is an accident consequent upon motion and is necessarily attached to it. Neither of them exists without the other. Motion does not exist except in time, and time cannot be conceived by the intellect except together with motion. And all that with regard to which no motion can be found, does not fall under time.

16. The sixteenth premise: In whatsoever is not a body, multiplicity cannot be cognized by the intellect, unless the thing in question is a force in a body, for then the multiplicity of the individual forces would subsist in virtue of the multiplicity of the matters or substances in which these forces are to be found. Hence no multiplicity at all can be cognized by the intellect in the separate things, which are neither a body nor a force in a body, except when they are causes and effects.

17. The seventeenth premise: Everything that is in motion has of necessity a mover; and the mover either may be outside the moved object, as in the case of a stone moved by a hand, or the mover may be in the body in motion, as in the case of the body of a living being, for the latter is composed of a mover and of that which is moved. It is for this reason that when a living being dies and the mover—namely, the soul—is lacking from it, that which is moved—namely, the organic body—remains at the moment in its former state, except that it is not moved with that motion. However, inasmuch as the mover that exists in that which is moved is hidden and does not appear to the senses, it is thought of living beings that they are in motion without having a mover. Everything moved that has a mover within itself is said to be moved by itself—the meaning being that the force moving that which, in the object moved, is moving according to essence, exists in the whole of that object.

18. The eighteenth premise: Everything that passes from potentiality to actuality has something other than itself that causes it to pass, and this cause is of necessity outside that thing. For if that cause were that thing and there were no obstacle to prevent this passage, the thing would not have been for a certain time in potentia but would have always been in actu. If, however, the cause of the passage from potentiality to actuality subsisted in the thing, and if there was at the same time an obstacle to it, which was subsequently removed, there is no doubt that the factor that put an end to the obstacle is the one that caused that potentially to pass into actuality. Understand this.

19. The nineteenth premise: Everything that has a cause for its existence is only possible with regard to existence in respect to its own essence. For it exists if its causes are present. If, however, they are not present, or if they become nonexistent, or if their relation that entails the existence of the thing in question has changed, that thing does not exist.

20. The twentieth premise: Everything that is necessarily existent in respect to its own essence has no cause for its existence in any way whatever or under any condition.

21. The twenty-first premise: Everything that is composed of two notions has necessarily that composition as the cause of its existence as it really is, and consequently is not necessarily existent in respect to its own essence, for it exists in virtue of the existence of its two parts and of their composition.

22. The twenty-second premise: Every body is necessarily composed of two things and is necessarily accompanied by accidents. The two things constituting it are its matter and its form; and the accidents accompanying it are quantity, shape, and position.

23. The twenty-third premise: It is possible for whatsoever is in potentia and in whose essence there is a certain possibility, not to exist in actu at a certain time.

24. The twenty-fourth premise: Whatsoever is something in potentia is necessarily endowed with matter, for possibility is always in matter.

25. The twenty-fifth premise: The principles of an individual compound substance are matter and form. And there is no doubt about the necessity of there being an agent, I mean to say a mover that moves the substratum so as to predispose it to receive the form. That is the proximate mover, which predisposes the matter of a certain individual. At this point it is necessary to engage in speculation with regard to motion, the mover, and the moved. However, with regard to all this, everything that it was necessary to explain has already been explained. The text of the words of Aristotle is: Matter does not move itself. This therefore is the capital premise calling for an inquiry concerning the existence of the Prime Mover.

Of the twenty-five premises that I have put before you in the form of a preface, some become manifest with very little reflection and are demonstrative premises and first intelligibles or notions approaching the latter, as may be seen in the epitome we have made of their orderly exposition. Others require a number of demonstrations and premises leading up to them. However, all of them have been given demonstrations as to which no doubt is possible. With regard to some of them, this has been done in the Book of "Akroasis" and its commentaries; with regard to others, in the Book of "Metaphysics" and its commentary. I have already made it known to you that the purpose of this Treatise is not to transcribe the books of the philosophers and to explain the most remote of the premises, but to mention the proximate premises that are required for our purpose.

I shall add to the premises mentioned before, one further premise that affirms as necessary the eternity of the world. Aristotle deemed it to be correct and the most fitting to be believed. We shall grant him this premise by way of a hypothesis in order that the clarification of that which we intended to make clear should be achieved. This premise, which among them is the twenty-sixth, [consists in Aristotle's statement] that time and movement are eternal, perpetual, existing in actu. Hence it follows of necessity, in his opinion, that there is a body, moving with an eternal movement, existing in actu; and this is the fifth body. For this reason, he says that the heaven is not subject to generation and corruption. For according to him, movement is not subject to generation and corruption; for he says that every movement is necessarily preceded by another movement either of the same species as itself or of other species, and that what is thought with regard to living beings—namely, that their local movement is not preceded at all by another movement—is not correct. For the cause of their movement after rest goes back finally to things calling for this local movement; these things being either an alteration of temperament necessitating a desire to seek what agrees with the living being or to flee from what disagrees with it, or an imagination, or an opinion occurring to it. Accordingly, any one of these three factors sets the living being in motion, and every one of them is necessitated by other movements. Similarly he says that in the case of everything that comes about in time, the possibility of its coming-about precedes in time its coming-about. From this there follow necessarily several points liable to validate his premise. According to this premise, a finite moving object moves upon a finite distance an infinite number of times, going back over the same distance in a circle. Now this is impossible except in circular movement, as is demonstrated in the thirteenth of these premises. According to this premise, that which is infinite must necessarily exist as a succession and not simultaneously.

This is the premise that Aristotle constantly wishes to establish as true. Now to me it seems that he does not affirm categorically that the arguments he puts forward in its favor constitute a demonstration. The premise in question is rather, in his opinion, the most fitting and the most probable. However, his followers and the commentators of his books claim that the premise is necessary and not merely possible and that it has already been demonstrated. On the other hand, every Mutakallim desires to establish that it is impossible. They say that there can be no mental representation of the coming-about in succession of an infinite number of things occurring in time. The strength of their argument is that it constitutes, in their opinion, a first intelligible. But to me it seems that the premise in question is possible—that is, neither necessary, as is affirmed by the commentators of the writings of Aristotle, nor impossible, as is claimed by the Mutakallimūn. It is not the purpose now to explain the arguments of Aristotle, or to raise our doubts concerning him, or to explain my opinion concerning the creation of the world in time. But the purpose at this point is to circumscribe the premises that we need for our three problems; after first having set forth these premises and having agreed to take them as granted, I shall set out explaining what necessarily follows from them.

Chapter 13

There are three opinions of human beings, namely, of all those who believe that there is an existent deity, with regard to the eternity of the world or its production in time.

The first opinion, which is the opinion of all who believe in the Law of *Moses our Master, peace be on him,* is that the world as a whole—I mean to say, every existent other than God, may He be exalted—was brought into existence by God after having been purely and absolutely nonexistent, and that God, may He be exalted, had existed alone, and nothing else—neither an angel nor a sphere nor what subsists within the sphere. Afterwards, through His will and His volition, He brought into existence out of nothing all the beings as they are, time itself being one of the created things. For time is consequent upon motion, and motion is an accident in what is moved. Furthermore, what is moved—that is, that upon the motion of which time is consequent—is itself created in time and came to be after not having been. Accordingly one's saying: God "was" before He created the world—where the word "was" is indicative of time—and similarly all the thoughts that are carried along in the mind regarding the infinite duration of His existence before the creation of the world, are all of them due to a supposition regarding time or to an imagining of time and not due to the true reality of time. For time is indubitably an accident. According to us it is one of the created accidents, as are blackness and whiteness. And though it does not belong to the species of quality, it is nevertheless, generally stated, an accident necessarily following upon motion, as is made clear to whoever has understood the discourse of Aristotle on the elucidation of time and on the true reality of its existence.

We shall expound here a notion that, though it does not belong to the purpose that we pursue, is useful with regard to it. This notion is as follows. What caused the nature of time to be hidden from the majority of the men of knowledge so that that notion perplexed them—like Galen and others—and made them wonder whether or not time had a true reality in that which exists, is the fact that time is an accident subsisting in an accident. For the accidents that have a primary existence in bodies, as for instance colors and tastes, can be understood at the outset and a mental representation can be had of their notions. But the nature of the accidents whose substrata are other accidents, as for instance the glint of a color and the curve and circularity of a line, is most hidden—more particularly if, in addition, the accident that serves as a substratum has no permanent state, but passes from one state to another. For in consequence the matter becomes even more hidden. In time both characteristics are conjoined. For it is an accident concomitant with motion, the latter being an accident in that which is moved. Moreover, motion has not the status of blackness and whiteness, which constitute a permanent state. For the true reality and substance of motion consist in its not remaining in the same state even for the duration of the twinkling of an eye. This accordingly is what has rendered it necessary for the nature of time to be hidden. The purpose however is that, according to us, time is a created and generated thing as are the other accidents and the substances serving as substrata to these accidents. Hence God's bringing the world into existence does not have a temporal beginning, for time is one of the created things. Consider this matter thoroughly. For thus you will not be necessarily attached to objections from which there is no escape for him who does not know it. For if you affirm as true the existence of time prior to the world, you are necessarily bound to believe in the eternity [of the world]. For time is an accident which necessarily must have a substratum. Accordingly it follows necessarily that there existed some thing prior to the existence of this world existing now. But this notion must be avoided.

This is one of the opinions. And it is undoubtedly a basis of the Law of *Moses our Master*, peace be on him. And it is second to the basis that is the belief in the unity [of God]. Nothing other than this should come to your mind. It was *Abraham our Father, peace be on him,* who began to proclaim in public this opinion to which speculation had led him. For this reason, he made his proclamation *in the Name of the Lord, God of the world;* he had also explicitly stated this opinion in saying: *Maker of heaven and earth.*

The second opinion is that of all the philosophers of whom we have heard reports and whose discourses we have seen. They say that it is absurd that God would bring a thing into existence out of nothing. Furthermore, according to them, it is likewise not possible that a thing should pass away into nothing; I mean to say that it is not possible that a certain being, endowed with matter and form, should be generated out of the absolute nonexistence of that matter, or that it should pass away into the absolute nonexistence of that matter. To predicate of God that He is able to do this is, according to them, like predicating of Him that He is able to bring together two contraries in one instant of time, or that he is able to create something that is like Himself, may He be exalted, or to make Himself corporeal, or to create a square whose diagonal is equal to its side, and similar impossibilities. What may be understood from their discourse is that they say that just as His not bringing impossible things into existence does not argue a lack of power on His part—since what is impossible has a firmly established nature that is not produced by an agent and that consequently cannot be changed—it likewise is not due to lack of power on His part that He is not able to bring into existence a thing out of nothing, for this belongs to the class of all the impossible things. Hence they believe that there exists a certain matter that is eternal as the deity is eternal; and that He does not exist without it, nor does it exist without Him. They do not believe that it has the same rank in what exists as He, may He be exalted, but that He is the cause of its existence; and that it has the same relation toward Him as, for instance, clay has toward a potter or iron toward a smith; and that He creates in it whatever He wishes. Thus He sometimes forms out of it a heaven and an earth, and sometimes He forms out of it something else. The people holding this opinion believe that the heaven too is subject to generation and passing-away, but that it is not generated out of nothing and does not pass away into nothing. For it is generated and passes away just as the individuals that are animals are generated from existent matter and pass away into existent matter. The generation and passing-away of the heaven is thus similar to that of all the other existents that are below it.

The people belonging to this sect are in their turn divided into several sects. But it is useless to mention their various sects and opinions in this Treatise. However, the universal principle held by this sect is identical with what I have told you. This is also the belief of Plato. For you will find that Aristotle in the "Akroasis" relates of him that he, I mean Plato, believed that the heaven is subject to generation and passing-away. And you likewise will find his doctrine plainly set forth in his book to Timaeus. But he does not believe what we believe, as is thought by him who does not examine opinions and is not precise in speculation; he [the interpreter] imagines that our opinion and his [Plato's] opinion are identical. But this is not so. For as for us, we believe that the heaven was generated out of nothing after a state of absolute nonexistence, whereas he believes that it has come into existence and has been generated from some other thing. This then is the second opinion.

The third opinion is that of Aristotle, his followers, and the commentators of his books. He asserts what also is asserted by the people belonging to the sect that has just been mentioned, namely, that something endowed with matter can by no means be brought into existence out of that which has no matter. He goes beyond this by saying that the heaven is in no way subject to generation and passing-away. His opinion on this point may be summed up as follows. He thinks that this being as a whole, such as it is, has never ceased to be and will never do so; that the permanent thing not subject to generation and passing-away, namely, the heaven, likewise does not cease to be; that time and motion are perpetual and everlasting and not subject to generation and passing-away; and also that the thing subject to generation and passing-away, namely, that which is beneath the sphere of the moon, does not cease to be. I mean to say that its first matter is not subject in its essence to generation and passing-away, but that various forms succeed each other in it in such a way that it divests itself of one form and assumes another. He thinks furthermore that this whole higher and lower order cannot be corrupted and abolished, that no innovation can take place in it that is not according to its nature, and that no occurrence that deviates from what is analogous to it can happen in it in any way. He asserts—though he does not do so textually, but this is what his opinion comes to—that in his opinion it would be an impossibility that will should change in God or a new volition arise in Him; and that all that exists has been brought into existence, in the state in which it is at present, by God through His volition; but that it was not produced after having been in a state of nonexistence. He thinks that just as it is impossible that the deity should become nonexistent or that His essence should undergo a change, it is impossible that a volition should undergo a change in Him or a new will arise in Him. Accordingly it follows necessarily that this being as a whole has never ceased to be as it is at present and will be as it is in the future eternity.

This is a summary and the truth of these opinions. They are the opinions of those according to whom the existence of the deity for this world has been demonstrated. Those who have no knowledge of the existence of the deity, may He be held sublime and honored, but think that things are subject to generation and passing-away through conjunction and separation due to chance and that there is no one who governs and orders being, are Epicurus, his following, and those like him, as is related by Alexander. It is useless for us to mention these sects. For the existence of the deity has already been demonstrated, and there can be no utility in our mentioning the opinions of groups of people who built their doctrine upon a foundation the reverse of which has been demonstrated as true. Similarly it is useless for us to wish to prove as true the assertion of the people holding the second opinion, I mean that according to which the heaven is subject to generation and passing-away. For they believe in eternity; and there is, in our opinion, no difference between those who believe that heaven must of necessity be generated from a thing and pass away into a thing or the belief of Aristotle who believed that it is not subject to generation and corruption. For the purpose of every follower of the Law of *Moses and Abraham our Father* or of those who go the way of these two is to believe that there is nothing eternal in any way at all existing simultaneously with God; to believe also that the bringing into existence of a being out of nonexistence is for the deity not an impossibility, but rather an obligation, as is deemed likewise by some of the men of speculation.

After we have expounded those opinions, I shall begin to explain and summarize the proofs of Aristotle in favor of his opinion and the motive that incited him to adopt it.

Chapter 17

In the case of everything produced in time, which is generated after not having existed—even in those cases in which the matter of the thing was already existent and in the course of the production of the thing had merely put off one and put on another form—the nature of that particular thing after it has been produced in time, has attained its final state, and achieved stability, is different from its nature when it is being generated and is beginning to pass from potentiality to actuality. It is also different from the nature the thing had before it had moved so as to pass from potentiality to actuality. For example, the nature of the feminine seed, which is the blood in the blood vessels, is different from the nature of this seed as it exists in the state of pregnancy after it has encountered the masculine sperm and has begun to move toward the transition from potentiality to actuality. And even at the latter period, its nature is different from the nature of an animal that, after having been born, achieves perfection. No inference can be drawn in any respect from the nature of a thing after it has been generated, has attained its final state, and has achieved stability in its most perfect state, to the state of that thing while it moved toward being generated. Nor can an inference be drawn from the state of the thing when it moves toward being generated to its state before it begins to move thus. Whenever you err in this and draw an inference from the nature of a thing that has achieved actuality to its nature when it was only in potentia, grave doubts are aroused in you. Moreover, things that must exist become impossible in your opinion, and on the other hand things that are impossible become necessary in your opinion. Assume, according to an example we have made, that a man of a most perfect natural disposition was born and that his mother died after she had suckled him for several months. And the man, alone in an isolated island, took upon himself the entire upbringing of him who was born, until he grew up, became intelligent, and acquired knowledge. Now this child had never seen a woman or a female of one of the species of the other animals. Accordingly he puts a question, saying to a man who is with him: How did we come to exist, and in what way were we generated? Thereupon the man to whom the question was put replied: Every individual among us was generated in the belly of an individual belonging like us to our species, an individual who is female and has such and such a form. Every individual among us was—being small in body—within the belly, was moved and fed there, and grew up little by little—being alive—until it reached such and such limit in size. Thereupon an opening was opened up for him in the lower part of the body, from which he issued and came forth. Thereupon he does not cease growing until he becomes such as you see that we are. Now the orphaned child must of necessity put the question: Did every individual among us—when he was little, contained within a belly, but alive and moving and growing—did he eat, drink, breathe through the mouth and nose, produce excrements? He is answered: No. Thereupon he indubitably will hasten to set this down as a lie and will produce a demonstration that all these true statements are impossible, drawing inferences from perfect beings that have achieved stability. He will say: If any individual among us were deprived of breath for the fraction of an hour, he would die and his movements would cease. How then can one conceive that an individual among us could be for months within a thick vessel surrounding him, which is within a body, and yet be alive and in motion? If one of us were to swallow a sparrow, that sparrow would die immediately upon entering the stomach, and all the more the underbelly. Every individual among us would undoubtedly perish within a few days if he did not eat food with his mouth and drink water; how then can an individual remain alive for months without eating and drinking? Every individual among us, if he had taken food and had not given off excrements, would die in very great pain within a few days; how then could the individual in question remain for months without giving off excrements? If the belly of one of us were perforated, he would die after some days; how then can it be supposed that the navel of the fetus in question was open? How is it that he does not open his eyes, put out his palms, stretch his feet, while all the parts of his body are whole and have no defect as you thought? Similarly all the analogies will be carried on in order to show that it is in no respect possible that man should be generated in that manner.

Consider this example and reflect upon it, you who are engaged in speculation, and you shall find that this is exactly our position with regard to Aristotle. For we, the community of the followers of *Moses our Master and Abraham our Father,* may peace be on them, believe that the world was generated in such and such manner and came to be in a certain state from another state and was created in a certain state, which came after another state. Aristotle, on the other hand, begins to contradict us and to bring forward against us proofs based on the nature of what exists, a nature that has attained stability, is perfect, and has achieved actuality. As for us, we declare against him that this nature, after it has achieved stability and perfection, does not resemble in anything the state it was in while in the state of being generated, and that it was brought into existence from absolute nonexistence. Now what argument from among all that he advances holds good against us? For these arguments necessarily concern only those who claim that the stable nature of that which exists, gives an indication of its having been created in time. I have already made it known to you that I do not claim this.

Now I shall go back and set forth for your benefit the principles of his methods and shall show you that nothing in them of necessity concerns us in any respect, since we contend that God brought the world as a whole into existence after nonexistence and formed it until it has achieved perfection as you see it. He said that the first matter is subject to neither generation nor passing-away and began to draw inferences in favor of this thesis from the things subject to generation and passing-away and to make clear that it was impossible that the first matter was generated. And this is correct. For we do not maintain that the first matter is generated as man is generated from the seed or that it passes away as man passes away into dust. But we maintain that God has brought it into existence from nothing and that after being brought into existence, it was as it is now—I mean everything is generated from it, and everything generated from it passes away into it; it does not exist devoid of form; generation and corruption terminate in it; it is not subject to generation as are the things generated from it, nor to passing-away as are the things that pass away into it, but is created from nothing. And its Creator may, if He wishes to do so, render it entirely and absolutely nonexistent. We likewise say the same thing of motion. For he has inferred from the nature of motion that motion is not subject to generation and passing-away. And this is correct. For we maintain that after motion has come into existence with the nature characteristic of it when it has become stable, one cannot imagine that it should come into being as a whole and perish as a whole, as partial motions come into being and perish. This analogy holds good with regard to everything that is attached to the nature of motion. Similarly the assertion that circular motion has no beginning is correct. For after the spherical body endowed with circular motion has been brought into being, one cannot conceive that its motion should have a beginning. We shall make a similar assertion with regard to the possibility that must of necessity precede everything that is generated. For this is only necessary in regard to this being that is stabilized—in this being everything that is generated, is generated from some being. But in the case of a thing created from nothing, neither the senses nor the intellect point to something that must be preceded by its possibility. We make a similar assertion with regard to the thesis that there are no contraries in heaven. That thesis is correct. However, we have not claimed that the heavens have been generated as the horse and palm tree are. Nor have we claimed that their being composite renders necessary their passing-away as is the case with plants and animals because of the contraries that subsist in them.

The essential point is, as we have mentioned, that a being's state of perfection and completion furnishes no indication of the state of that being preceding its perfection. It involves no disgracefulness for us if someone says that the heavens were generated before the earth or the earth before the heavens or that the heavens have existed without stars or that a particular species of animals has existed without another species being in existence. For all this applies to the state of this universe when it was being generated. Similarly in the case of animals when they are being generated, the heart exists before the testicles—a circumstance that may be ocularly perceived—and the veins before the bones; and this is so in spite of the fact that after the animal has achieved perfection, no part of its body can exist in it if any part of all the others, without which the individual cannot possibly endure, does not exist.

All these assertions are needed if the text of Scripture is taken in its external sense, even though it must not be so taken, as shall be explained when we shall speak of it at length. You ought to memorize this notion. For it is a great wall that I have built around the Law, a wall that surrounds it warding off the stones of all those who project these missiles against it.

However, should Aristotle, I mean to say he who adopts his opinion, argue against us by saying: If this existent provides no indication for us, how do you know that it is generated and that there has existed another nature that has generated it—we should say: This is not obligatory for us in view of what we wish to maintain. For at present we do not wish to establish as true that the world is created in time. But what we wish to establish is the possibility of its being created in time. Now this contention cannot be proved to be impossible by inferences drawn from the nature of what exists, which we do not set at nought. When the possibility of this contention has been established, as we have made clear, we shall go back and we shall make prevail the opinion asserting creation in time.

In this question no way remains open to him except to show the impossibility for the world having been created in time, not by starting from the nature of being, but by starting from the judgments of the intellect with regard to the deity: these being the three methods that I have mentioned to you before. By means of these methods they wish to prove the eternity of the world, taking the deity as their starting point. I shall accordingly show you, in a following chapter, how doubts can be cast on these methods so that no proof whatever can be established as correct by means of them.

PART III

Chapter 12

Often it occurs to the imagination of the multitude that there are more evils in the world than there are good things. As a consequence, this thought is contained in many sermons and poems of all the religious communities, which say that it is surprising if good exists in the temporal, whereas the evils of the temporal are numerous and constant. This error is not found only among the multitude, but also among those who deem that they know something.

Rāzī has written a famous book, which he has entitled "Divine Things." He filled it with the enormity of his ravings and his ignorant notions. Among them there is a notion that he has thought up, namely, that there is more evil than good in what exists; if you compare man's well-being and his pleasures in the time span of his well-being with the pains, the heavy sufferings, the infirmities, the paralytic afflictions, the wretchedness, the sorrows, and the calamities that befall him, you find that his existence—he means the existence of man—is a punishment and a great evil inflicted upon him. He began to establish this opinion by inductively examining these misfortunes, so as to oppose all that is thought by the adherents of the truth regarding the beneficence and manifest munificence of the deity and regarding His being, may He be exalted, the absolute good and regarding all that proceeds from Him being indubitably an absolute good. The reason for this whole mistake lies in the fact that this ignoramus and those like him among the multitude consider that which exists only with reference to a human individual. Every ignoramus imagines that all that exists exists with a view to his individual sake; it is as if there were nothing that exists except him. And if something happens to him that is contrary to what he wishes, he makes the trenchant judgment that all that exists is an evil. However, if man considered and represented to himself that which exists and knew the smallness of his part in it, the truth would become clear and manifest to him. For this extensive raving entertained by men with regard to the multitude of evils in the world is not said by them to hold good with regard to the angels or with regard to the spheres and the stars or with regard to the elements and the minerals and the plants composed of them or with regard to the various species of animals, but their whole thought only goes out to some individuals belonging to the human species. If someone has eaten bad food and consequently was stricken with leprosy, they are astonished how this great ill has befallen him and how this great evil exists. They are also astonished when one who frequently copulates is stricken blind, and they think it a marvelous thing the calamity of blindness that has befallen such a man and other such calamities.

Now the true way of considering this is that all the existent individuals of the human species and, all the more, those of the other species of the animals are things of no value at all in comparison with the whole that exists and endures. It has made this clear, saying: *Man is like unto vanity, and so on. Man, that is a worm; and the son of man, that is a maggot. How much less in them that dwell in houses of clay, and so on. Behold, the nations are as a drop of a bucket, and so on.* There are also all the other passages figuring in the texts of the books of the prophets concerning this sublime and grave subject, which is most useful in giving man knowledge of his true value, so that he should not make the mistake of thinking that what exists is in existence only for the sake of him as an individual. According to us, on the other hand, what exists is in existence because of the will of its Creator; and among the things that are in existence, the species of man is the least in comparison to the superior existents—I refer to the spheres and the stars. As far as comparison with the angels is concerned, there is in true reality no relation between man and them. Man is merely the most noble among the things that are subject to generation, namely, in this our nether world; I mean to say that he is the noblest thing that is composed of the elements. Withal his existence is for him a great good and a benefit on the part of God because of the properties with which He has singled him out and perfected him. The greater part of the evils that befall its individuals are due to the latter, I mean the deficient individuals of the human species. It is because of our own deficiencies that we lament and we call for aid. We suffer because of evils that we have produced ourselves of our free will; but we attribute them to God, may He be exalted above this; just as He explains in His book, saying: *Is corruption His? No; His children's is the blemish, and so on. Solomon* too has explained this, saying: *The foolishness of man perverteth his way; and his heart fretteth against the Lord.* The explanation of this lies in the fact that all the evils that befall man fall under one of three species.

The first species of evil is that which befalls man because of the nature of coming-to-be and passing-away, I mean to say because of his being endowed with matter. Because of this, infirmities and paralytic afflictions befall some individuals either in consequence of their original natural disposition, or they supervene because of changes occurring in the elements, such as corruption of the air or a fire from heaven and a landslide. We have already explained that divine wisdom has made it obligatory that there should be no coming-to-be except through passing-away. Were it not for the passing-away of the individuals, the coming-to-be relating to the species would not continue. Thus that pure beneficence, that munificence, that activity causing good to overflow, are made clear. He who wishes to be endowed with flesh and bones and at the same time not be subject to impressions and not to be attained by any of the concomitants of matter merely wishes, without being aware of it, to combine two contraries, namely, to be subject to impressions and not to be subject to them. For if he were not liable to receive impressions, he would not have been generated, and what exists of him would have been one single individual and not a multitude of individuals belonging to one species. Galen has put it well in the third of the book of "Utilities," saying: Do not set your mind on the vain thought that it is possible that out of menstrual blood and sperm there should be generated a living being that does not die, is not subject to pain, is in perpetual motion, or is as brilliant as the sun. This dictum of Galen draws attention to one particular case falling under a general proposition. That proposition is as follows: Everything that is capable of being generated from any matter whatever, is generated in the most perfect way in which it is possible to be generated out of that specific matter; the deficiency attaining the individuals of the species corresponds to the deficiency of the particular matter of the individual. Now the ultimate term and the most perfect thing that may be generated out of blood and sperm is the human species with its well-known nature consisting in man's being a living, rational, and mortal being. Thus this species of evils must necessarily exist. Withal you will find that the evils of this kind that befall men are very few and occur only seldom. For you will find cities, existing for thousands of years, that have never been flooded or burned. Also thousands of people are born in perfect health whereas the birth of an infirm human being is an anomaly, or at least—if someone objects to the word anomaly and does not use it—such an individual is very rare; for they do not form a hundredth or even a thousandth part of those born in good health.

The evils of the second kind are those that men inflict upon one another, such as tyrannical domination of some of them over others. These evils are more numerous than those belonging to the first kind, and the reasons for that are numerous and well known. The evils in question also come from us. However, the wronged man has no device against them. At the same time, there is no city existing anywhere in the whole world in which evil of this kind is in any way widespread and predominant among the inhabitants of that city; but its existence is also rare—in the cases, for instance, when one individual surprises another individual and kills him or robs him by night. This kind of evil becomes common, reaching many people, only in the course of great wars; and such events too do not form the majority of occurrences upon the earth taken as a whole.

The evils of the third kind are those that are inflicted upon any individual among us by his own action; this is what happens in the majority of cases, and these evils are much more numerous than those of the second kind. All men lament over evils of this kind; and it is only seldom that you find one who is not guilty of having brought them upon himself. He who is reached by them deserves truly to be blamed. To him one may say what has been said: *This hath been to you of your own doing*. It has also been said: *He doeth it that would destroy his own soul. Solomon* has said about evils of this kind: *The foolishness of man perverteth his way, and so on.* He also has explained with reference to evils of this kind that they are done by man to himself; his dictum being: *Behold, this only have I found, that God made man upright; but they have sought out many thoughts;* these thoughts are those that have been vanquished by these evils. About this kind it has also been said: *For affliction cometh not forth from the dust, neither doth trouble spring out of the ground.* Immediately afterwards it is explained that this sort of evil is brought into existence by man, for it is said: *For man is born unto trouble, and so on.* This kind is consequent upon all vices, I mean concupiscence for eating, drinking, and copulation, and doing these things with excess in regard to quantity or irregularly or when the quality of the foodstuffs is bad. For this is the cause of all corporeal and psychical diseases and ailments. With regard to the diseases of the body, this is manifest. With regard to the diseases of the soul due to this evil regimen, they arise in two ways: In the first place, through the alteration necessarily affecting the soul in consequence of the alteration of the body, the soul being a corporeal faculty—it having already been said that the moral qualities of the soul are consequent upon the temperament of the body. And in the second place, because of the fact that the soul becomes familiarized with, and accustomed to, unnecessary things and consequently acquires the habit of desiring things that are unnecessary either for the preservation of the individual or for the preservation of the species; and this desire is something infinite. For whereas all necessary things are restricted and limited, that which is superfluous is unlimited. If, for instance, your desire is directed to having silver plate, it would be better if it were of gold; some have crystal plate; and perhaps plate is procured that is made out of emeralds and rubies, whenever these stones are to be found. Thus every ignoramus who thinks worthless thoughts is always sad and despondent because he is not able to achieve the luxury attained by someone else. In most cases such a man exposes himself to great dangers, such as arise in sea voyages and the service of kings; his aim therein being to obtain these unnecessary luxuries. When, however, he is stricken by misfortunes in these courses he has pursued, he complains about God's decree and predestination and begins to put the blame on the temporal and to be astonished at the latter's injustice in not helping him to obtain great wealth, which would permit him to procure a great deal of wine so as always to be drunk and a number of concubines adorned with gold and precious stones of various kinds so as to move him to copulate more than he is able so as to experience pleasure—as if the end of existence consisted merely in the pleasure of such an ignoble man. The error of the multitude has arrived at the point where they impute to the Creator deficiency of power because of His having produced that which exists and endowed it with a nature entailing, according to their imagination, these great evils; inasmuch as this nature does not help every vicious man to achieve the satisfaction of his vice so that his corrupt soul should reach the term of its demand, which, according to what we have explained, has no limit. On the other hand, men of excellence and knowledge have grasped and understood the wisdom manifested in that which exists, as *David* has set forth, saying: *All the paths of the Lord are mercy and truth unto such as keep His covenant and His testimonies.* By this he says that those who keep to the nature of that which exists, keep the commandments of the Law, and know the ends of both, apprehend clearly the excellency and the true reality of the whole. For this reason they take as their end that for which they were intended as men, namely, apprehension. And because of the necessity of the body, they seek what is necessary for it, *bread to eat, and raiment to put on,* without any luxury. If one restricts oneself to what is necessary, this is the easiest of things and may be obtained with a very small effort. Whatever in it that is seen as difficult and hard for us is due to the following reason: when one endeavors to seek what is unnecessary, it becomes difficult to find even what is necessary. For the more frequently hopes cling to the superfluous, the more onerous does the matter become; forces and revenues are spent for what is unnecessary and that which is necessary is not found. You ought to consider the circumstances in which we are placed with regard to its being found. For the more a thing is necessary for a living being, the more often it may be found and the cheaper it is. On the other hand, the less necessary it is, the less often it is found and it is very expensive. Thus, for instance, the necessary for man is air, water, and food. But air is the most necessary, for nobody can be without it for a moment without perishing. As for water, one can remain without it for a day or two. Accordingly air is indubitably easier to find and cheaper than water. Water is more necessary than food, for certain people may remain, if they drink and do not eat, for four or five days without food. Accordingly in every city you find water more frequently and at a cheaper price than food. Things are similar with regard to foodstuffs; those that are most necessary are easier to find at a given place and cheaper than the unnecessary. Regarding musk, amber, rubies, and emeralds, I do not think that anyone of sound intellect can believe that man has strong need for them unless it be for medical treatment; and even in such cases, they and other similar things can be replaced by numerous herbs and earths.

This is a manifestation of the beneficence and munificence of God, may He be exalted, shown even with regard to this weak living creature. Regarding manifestations of His justice, may He be exalted, and of the equality established by Him between them, they are very evident. For within the domain of natural generation and corruption, there is no case in which an individual animal belonging to any species whatever of animals is distinguished from another individual of the same species by having a special faculty possessed only by him or by having an additional part of the body. For all natural, psychic, and animal faculties and all the parts that are found in one particular individual are also found, as far as essence is concerned, in another—even though there be accidentally a deficiency because of something that has supervened and that is not according to nature. But this is rare, as we have made clear. There in no way exists a relation of superiority and inferiority between individuals conforming to the course of nature except that which follows necessarily from the differences in the disposition of the various kinds of matter; this being necessary on account of the nature of the matter of the particular species and not specially intended for one individual rather than another. As for the fact that one individual possesses many sachets and clothes adorned with gold whereas another lacks these superfluities of life, there is no injustice and no inequity in this. He who has obtained these luxuries has not gained thereby an increment in his substance. He has only obtained a false imagining or a plaything. And he who lacks the superfluities of life is not necessarily deficient. *And he that gathered much had nothing over, and he that gathered little had no lack; they gathered every man according to his eating.* This is what happens for the most part at every time and at every place. And, as we have made clear, no attention should be paid to anomalies.

Through the two considerations that have been set forth, His beneficence, may He be exalted, with regard to His creatures will become clear to you, in that He brings into existence what is necessary according to its order of importance and in that He makes individuals of the same species equal at their creation. With a view to this true consideration, the Master of those who know says: *For all His ways are judgment.* And *David* says: *All the paths of the Lord are mercy and truth, and so on,* as we have made clear. *David* also says explicitly: *The Lord is good to all; and His tender mercies are over all His works.* For His bringing us into existence is absolutely the great good, as we have made clear, and the creation of the governing faculty in the living beings is an indication of His mercifulness with regard to them, as we have made clear.

SUGGESTIONS FOR FURTHER READING

Corbin, Henry. *Avicenna and the Visionary Recital.* Willard R. Trask, trans. New York: Pantheon, 1960.

Fakhry, Majid. *A History of Islamic Philosophy.* New York: Columbia University Press, 1970.

Husik, Isaac. *A History of Medieval Jewish Philosophy.* New York: Meridian, 1958.

Lewis, Bernard, ed. *Islam.* 2 vols. New York: Harper & Row, 1974.

Marcus, Jacob R. *The Jew in the Medieval World.* New York: Harper Torchbooks, 1965.

Morewedge, Parviz. *The "Metaphysica" of Avicenna.* New York: Columbia University Press, 1973.

Peters, Francis E. *Aristotle and the Arabs: The Aristotelian Tradition in Islam.* New York: New York University Press, 1968.

Latin Scholasticism and the Recovery of Aristotle

By the twelfth century, the major writings of Aristotle had begun to filter into the Christian west. At the time, the west was dominated by Latin Scholasticism, a philosophical approach developed by the European universities that stressed logic, intellectual debate, and the supremacy of theological doctrine. Contacts with Muslim civilization in Spain and renewed transactions with Byzantine civilization and eastern Christendom made available increasingly accurate translations of Aristotle.

The thirteenth century witnessed the emergence of the great universities of European civilization, a development that was characterized by profound conflicts both between and within the disciplines of philosophy and theology. The recovery of Aristotle was auspicious for several reasons: first, it gave to Christian philosophy an enormous fund of technical philosophical terminology; second, it cast new and contentious light on the questions of the world as eternal or created, the immortality of the soul, and the relation between perception and conception; third, it reinforced the medieval commitment to a geocentric cosmology. But because the study of Aristotle was associated with Muslim thought, especially Averroës, it met with deep and intense opposition in much of the Christian west. Aristotle, due to his contention that nature can be understood by reason alone, was regarded by the theologians as a threat to the longstanding role of Neoplatonism and Augustinianism as the bedrock of Christian theology. Despite the brilliant defense of Aristotle by Thomas Aquinas, propositions reflecting the Averroistic-Aristotelian point of view were condemned in 1277 by Etienne Tempier, the Bishop of Paris. The following selections reveal some of the intellectual ferment of the thirteenth century, most of it swirling about the thought of Aristotle. The cultural version of this intellectual quest is provided by excerpts from one of the masterpieces of world literature, Dante's *Divine Comedy*.

BONAVENTURE

Bonaventure was born in 1217, in Bagnoregio, Italy. He early came under the influence of Francis of Assisi, the founder of the Franciscans, a monastic order which rivaled the Dominicans as the major teaching order of the thirteenth century. Bonaventure himself was active as a scholar and teacher at the University of Paris and in 1257 became minister general of the Franciscans. This appointment intensified his personal tension between the humble and even anti-intellectual bequest of Francis and his own ongoing participation in the contemporary philosophical and theological debates. A second conflict in the life of Bonaventure developed because of his loyalty to the Augustinian tradition. He had great doubt about the worth of Aristotle's philosophy, especially on questions concerning the nature of the soul and the creation of the world. Augustine, following the Neoplatonists, held that we could achieve an intimate relationship with ultimate reality if we were to undergo a spiritual transformation of our personal lives. Aristotle, to the contrary, trusted our reasoning powers to understand the ultimate fabric and organization of nature. Although skilled in philosophical debate, Bonaventure tended also toward a mystical version of human life, as attested in his moving work The Journey of the Mind to God.

Bonaventure's death, in 1274, came as he was organizing the Second Ecumenical Council of Lyons. Just a year before, he had written the Collations of the Six Days, *from which we take our first selection. This selection makes manifest both Bonaventure's Christian Platonism and his opposition to Aristotle, whose thought he regarded as a block to a true understanding of the power of the soul.*

From Collations of the Six Days

First Treatise on the First Vision; Which Is by Means of Understanding Naturally Given

God saw that the light was good. God separated the light from the darkness, etc. After every one of the works of the six days, with the exception of the second, it is said: *God saw that it was good.* And at the end: *God saw that all He had made was very good.* God is said to see, because He makes us see. The first vision of the soul is by means of understanding naturally given. Hence in the Psalm: *The light of Thy countenance, O Lord, is signed upon us.* And here all the difficulties of philosophy could be explained. The philosophers have offered nine sciences and promised a tenth: contemplation. But many philosophers, while attempting to avoid the darkness of error, have themselves become involved in major errors. *While professing to be wise, they have become fools.* Because they boasted of their knowledge, these philosophers have become the likes of Lucifer. With the Egyptians was the densest darkness, but with Your saints was the greatest light. All those who properly followed the Law of Nature, the patriarchs, the prophets, and the philosophers, were the sons of light.

Truth is the light of the soul. This light never fails. Indeed, it shines so powerfully upon the soul that this soul cannot possibly believe it to be non-existing, or abstain from expressing it, without an inner contradiction. For if truth does not exist, it is true that truth does not exist: and so something is true. And if something is true, it is true that truth exists. Hence if truth does not exist, truth exists! As Esdras says, *truth overcomes everything.*

2. Now, this light sends out three primary radiations, hence in Ecclesiasticus: *The sun, three times as much, burneth the mountains.* There is, indeed, a truth of things, a truth of signs or words and a truth of behavior. The truth of things is indivision between existence and essence, the truth of words is equality between expression and understanding, the truth of behavior is the rectitude of a morally good life. And these three are the three parts of philosophy which the philosophers did not invent, since they are: but because they already existed in the order of truth,

Reprinted with permission of the Franciscan Herald Press, Chicago, IL 60609 from *Collations of the Six Days: The Works of St. Bonaventure*, Vol. V, trans. José de Vinck. (pp. 69–72)

they became the concern of the soul, as Augustine explains.

3. This threefold radiation may be considered from the viewpoint of the originating principle, from that of the receiving subject, and from that of the object in which it terminates. For it concerns the originating principles in terms of the three causes: the primary (efficient), the exemplar (formal), and the final: *For from Him and through Him and unto Him are all things.* Hence truth indicates that our mind is carried by a natural inclination to the supreme Truth in that it is the cause of being, the reason of understanding and the norm of life. From the cause of being comes forth the truth of things; from the reason of understanding, the truth of words; from the norm of life, the truth of moral behavior.

4. On the part of the soul [the receiving subject], every radiation of truth over our power of understanding comes about in one of three ways: it shines upon it absolutely, and then refers to things to be seen; or in relation to the interpretative faculty, and then consists in the truth of words; or in relation to the affective or motive faculty, and then it is the truth of things to be done.

5. It is the same as regards the object. Everything that exists depends upon essence, reason, or will. The first leads to the knowledge of things, the second to the knowledge of words, and the third to the knowledge of behavior.

Hence, in relation to the principle, to the subject, and to the object, there is in the soul a threefold radiation of truth through which the soul may be lifted up to eternal matters and also to the cause of all. But if the spice of faith is added, things become easier: the cause of being is then attributed to the Father, the reason of understanding to the Son, and the norm of life to the Holy Spirit.

6. In so far as the vision of understanding naturally given is turned toward things, it is truth. But the soul wants the whole world to be described within itself. Now the world may be considered in three ways: in terms of essence, quantity, and nature. And so this radiation leads to the study of hidden differences between quiddities, to the manifest proportions of numbers, and to the properties containing a mixture of both which are found in natures. The consideration of natures is mixed, for at times it concerns causes, which are hidden, for instance, why is fire warm, why is this herb spicy, for they have such qualities from their species which is hidden. At other times, it concerns quality, or again quantity and the influence of other bodies which are sometimes visible and at other times hidden.

7. There are at present six ways of dividing according to hidden differences in the quiddities: that is, into substance and accident, universal and particular, potency and act, one and many, simple and composite, cause and caused. These are six lights that prepare the soul for knowledge and valid perception.

8. The division into SUBSTANCE AND ACCIDENT is obvious. But what are the things that may be included in it? Here there is the greatest error. For one man says that creation does not exist. Why? Because it is impossible that accident precede substance. Now creation is an accident. Hence, etc. I say that creation, in so far as it is the receiving of an effect is not an accident, because the relation of the creature to the Creator is not accidental, but essential. Likewise, the potency of matter is not an accident of matter, but is essential to it, for "by the very fact that it exists, it does so with a disposition toward something else." Likewise, differences may be reduced to the genus, as mere privations to their fulfillment.

9. The second division is into UNIVERSAL AND PARTICULAR; and here again there is a major error. For some philosophers say that the universal is nothing, except in the spirit. Plato stated that it existed only in God; others, that it existed only in the soul. I say that there is a universal oneness related to multiplicity, another existing in multiplicity, and yet another exceeding multiplicity. The universal oneness *related* to multiplicity is found in the potency of matter, which is not fulfilled; the universal oneness *existing* in multiplicity is the common nature found in particular individuals; and the universal oneness that *exceeds* multiplicity exists in the soul. And so, the one related to the many, the one in the many, and the one exceeding the many exist in Eternal Art; and by means of this Art and for this reason oneness exists in reality. For it is clear that two men are similar, but not a man and a donkey; hence it is necessary that this likeness be founded and stabilized in some stable form: and not in some form existing in another individual, since it is particular; hence it must exist in something universal. Now the universal principle is not contained exclusively within the soul, but exists in the object according to the process

of passing from genus into species, so that we communicate first with the substance as with the most general principle, then with the other principles, until we come in contact with the final (individual) form of a man.

10. The third division is into POTENCY AND ACT, and here there are many errors. For some philosophers say that act adds nothing to potency except a manner of being, that it stands in the same relationship to it as complete stands to incomplete. We are not speaking here of purely passive potency, but of that which proceeds to act. For since in every creature there is both active and passive potency, these two potencies must be founded on different principles within the object. Now this is the power of that potency which is the seminal reason: sometimes it adds a part of being or essence, as for instance over and above the principle "body" it adds "living" in relation to a given object, but in such a way that, while the attribute "living" is something in itself, it is ordained to sensitivity. And so, over and above "living," the seminal reason or potency adds "sensible," and so forth until the level of individual man is attained. It is the same with the potencies of the soul: for as the quadrangle has one more angle than the triangle, and the pentagon one more than the quadrangle, so "sensitive" is added to "vegetative" and "rational" to "sensitive."

But sometimes the seminal reason adds nothing more than a manner of being, if for instance it turns oneness in potency into oneness in act; it adds only a manner of being, for the "one" is not joined to matter unqualifiedly, but to matter having life rooted in itself as a potency.

Hence it is unsound to propose that the final form is added to prime matter without something that is a disposition or potency towards it, or without any other intermediate form.

11. The fourth division is into THE ONE AND THE MANY, and there are here a number of errors. Some philosophers claim that everything is one: as there is one matter, there is also one radical form, which is then multiplied and varied only through different manners of being. And this is nothing more than to say that the proposition: man is a donkey is true in itself but false by accident. Hence you should understand that rational and irrational differ not only accidentally, but also essentially.

12. The fifth division is into SIMPLE AND COMPOSITE, and here also there are many errors, as for instance to claim that a certain creature is simple, for then it would be pure act, which is an attribute of God alone, and it is most dangerous to attribute to a creature what belongs to God. Hence, it is less dangerous to say that an angel is composite, even if it is not true, than to say that it is simple: for I attribute composition to the angel because I refuse to attribute to it what belongs to God, and this out of respect for the reverence I have toward God. But, in truth, it does seem to be composite, for Boethius says: "Form cannot be a subject." So if the angel be pure form, nothing can happen to it in the accidental order, neither joy nor sadness.

13. The sixth division is into CAUSE AND CAUSED, and here once more there are a multiplicity of errors. For some philosophers say that the world has existed from all eternity. Wise men agree that a thing cannot be made out of nothing, and exist from all eternity. Indeed, it is necessary that, as when a being falls into nothingness, it ceases to be, so also when it comes forth from nothingness, it begins to be. But some thinkers are seen to suppose uncreated matter: and from this it would follow that God made nothing: He did not make matter since it was uncreated, and He did not make form, for it is made either out of something or out of nothing. It is not made out of matter, for the essence of the form cannot be made out of the essence of matter; nor out of nothing, since they suppose God cannot make anything out of nothing. But perish the thought that God's power depends upon a foundation of matter!

These then are the foundations of faith which every man should examine.

14. The second radiation of understanding naturally given consists in the consideration of the manifest proportions of quantities, and these are very clear because they offer themselves to the senses, and man willingly acts upon them, for they fall under the imagination, and imagination is strong within us while reason is obscured. Therefore man is very much involved in these things. This knowledge is most certain, because it is obvious to the eye, whereas all other sciences are, so to speak, occult.

15. Mathematical consideration covers six branches: mathematics, concerned with numbers in themselves, music concerned with numbers as sounds, geometry concerned with continuous quantity and general measurable proportions, perspective, which

adds the line of sight, astrology which concerns both and also numeral and substantial distinctions, or continous and discrete quantity. The latter is twofold, comprising astronomy which studies bodies in regular motion, and astrology properly so-called which is concerned with influences: and this science is partly safe and partly dangerous. It is dangerous because of the judgments that follow upon it, and because it gives birth to geomancy and necromancy and other kinds of divination.

16. Now these sciences prepare for the understanding of Scripture, as is clear in the case of perfect numbers, and of the decreased and increasing number, as it appears with the perfection of the number six, which is perfect of itself. Augustine explains: "The number six is not perfect because God created the world in this number of days; but God created the world in this number of days because it is perfect." Likewise, concerning the two first cubic numbers, 8 and 27: twice two times two equal 8, and three times three times three equal 27, and they can be related through no other numbers than 12 and 18, for 12 is to 18 as 18 is to 27, in the proportion of one and a half, which contains the whole and its intermediate.

The same is clear of the triangle, how it leads to the knowledge of the Trinity, for it is certain that as great as the Son is, so great is the Father, and as great as the Father is, so great are the Holy Spirit and the Son. Hence, consider the triangle each angle of which encloses the total area. Likewise, in perspective, in the case of the *direct* radiation of sight which is stronger and compares with the throwing of a stone: if you throw it straight down, the sound is louder; if you throw it obliquely, it is less. The *reflected* radiation comes from a clean and polished body, by virtue of its polish, and there it receives the species. The *diffracted* radiation is penetration into a transparent body.

17. The third radiation of understanding naturally given consists in searching the mixed properties of natures, that is, those that are partly hidden and partly manifest. For the Philosopher considers all things through motion: he studies motion as such, the principles and causes of motion, as for instance place and time. He studies the natures of heavenly bodies, that is, the ethereal and the meteorical; he studies bodies as elementary, vegetative, sensitive, and rational.

The heavenly bodies he considers in the book "On Heaven and the World," where he reduces all motion to perfect motion, that is, to local motion. Now this local motion is of three kinds: either *around* the center, in which case there is no opposition, and this is circular motion; or *away* from the center, and this is the motion of light bodies; or again *toward* the center, and this is the motion of heavy bodies, or straight motion. The meteoric bodies he considers in the book "On Meteors," where he speaks of impressions and minerals.

Concerning now the elementary bodies, he studies them in the book "On Generation and Corruption"; and the vegetative beings, he studies in the book "On Plants" where there are some marvelous considerations.

Finally, he considers sensitive beings in the book "On Animals," which we do not have in full, and rational beings in the book "On the Soul" and its appendices, "On Sense and the Sensible," "On Memory and Reminiscence," "On the Spirit and the Soul," "On Sleep and Wakefulness," "On Life and Death."

18. The second radiation of truth provides information for the consideration of speech, arguments and methods of rational persuasion, so that by this means a man may enjoy the art of speech that properly represents the concepts of the mind, of arguments that draw the assent of every mind, and of persuasive methods that incline the dispositions of the mind. For reason thinks of making whatever is in itself to exist in another, and whatever is in another to exist within itself: and this cannot be done except by means of speech. Whatever is contained in the soul, then, is there either as a concept, as an assent, or as an affective disposition. And so, to indicate concepts, there is grammar, to induce assent, there is logic, and to move affective dispositions, there is rhetoric.

19. According to the grammarian, every part of speech signifies a concept of the mind. For it has a part that signifies substance or quality, and that is the noun [and adjective]; it has a part that signifies the mood, and that is the verb, which tells of dispositions as in the indicative mood related to the rational power, the imperative mood related to the irascible power, the optative mood related to the concupiscible power, the subjunctive mood signifying both parts, and the infinitive mood which is

almost material. And according to Priscian, it is to these differences that all moods are reduced.

Likewise, the grammarian establishes the rules of the letter and syllable, of discourse and speech. For as in different languages there are different manners of signifying and terminating—as, for instance [in Latin] the terminal *a* generally indicating the feminine and *us* the masculine, and so forth—the grammarian is concerned with the rules of letters; but he cannot go down to this level except by means of the syllable. Finally, he is concerned with the interrelationship of expressions, likewise with the rules of prosody and syntax. For he expresses all things through the eight parts of speech. And so he studies the letter through the syllable, then prosody and rhythm, and these are then referred to the first. He also considers number and case, as for instance that a [singular] nominative is used with a singular verb, so that we cannot say: a man run, for from a single substance there can come but a single action. Again, he sees to it that after a transitive verb there be placed, not a noun in the nominative, but one in the accusative, which indicates something toward which the action is directed, not a principle of action as would the nominative.

Hence a grammarian draws the nature from things, nor can he be a good grammarian unless he knows things.

20. Another aspect is that which explains arguments leading to the assent of the mind. This is accomplished by a solid argumentation such as: things which are equal to one and the same thing are equal to each other. This type of argument has both a general and a special form and treat of things which are necessary and well established. Therefore we have the First Analysis and the Second Analysis which are concerned with the syllogism simply considered. They treat of the necessary syllogism which results in conclusions because of correct inference as in the First Analysis (or Solution), and in the Second Analysis (Solution) because of a correct inference based on the order of being. Since there cannot always be an induction based on necessary arguments, we have manners and forms of proof based on things which are probable, such as the topical proof. And then because there is room for error in such matters, there are added the sophistic manners of proving so that a man might know how to refute them. Thus one who refutes such arguments is not himself a sophist but is truly giving a response. Because these modes of argument take their origin from the nature of things (for instance, "There is smoke, therefore there was a fire"—which is a proof from effect) there are added the ten predicaments and also a treatment of statements.

21. The third direction is that by which the mind is enlightened for the sake of persuading or inclining the spirit: and this is achieved by means of rhetoric. Hence it is fitting that the orator provide for social good, since there may be danger in this area on account of the disagreement of minds. He proceeds by means of three attributes, of a threefold method: demonstrative, deliberative, and judicial.

22. The demonstrative is concerned with the person; it may praise or blame. Praise may be addressed to the goods of the soul which are three in number, virtue, understanding, and truth; or to the goods of the body, beauty, strength, etc.; or again, to the goods of status, for instance wealth, parenthood and citizenship.

23. The deliberative is concerned with something that needs to be done: a man is persuaded to act if there is security, usefulness, honesty; he is dissuaded if there is damage, danger, or dishonesty.

24. The judicial corresponds to a thing that is done, as seen from the viewpoint of the legitimacy of its foundation, conjecture, or reasonable doubt. A legitimate juridical foundation consists in this: "Did you do it?"—"I did not do it." It is what some people call a lawsuit. A legitimate juridical conjecture supposes the calling of a witness for the sake of proof. A legitimate juridical doubt consists in this: when the fact of a case is admitted, but the indictee claims he is not guilty, or was permitted to act because of a mandate from his superior, or was obliged to act.

25. For a man to be a powerful orator, he must first capture the audience's good will with an opening that is neither too long, nor obscure, nor excessively refined. He must then tell the story to expose the facts and to make his point—and he must avoid an excessive number of subdivisions. Then he must strengthen his point with arguments, then refute his adversary and show that the arguments of the opposition are worthless. Finally he must draw the conclusion. It is necessary for him to have inventiveness, organization, a good elocution, a reliable memory and clear diction.

From Conferences on the Hexaemeron

VISION I, DISCUSSION III

On God, the Causal Exemplar of Everything, and on the Four Cardinal Virtues Exemplified There and Their Three Degrees

"And God saw the light that it was good" (Genesis. I, 4). This text was chosen because of the first vision of understanding given through nature. "God saw the light," that is, he made the light to be seen. This was mentioned above in the two Discussions of scientific consideration and how the light radiates as the truth of things, of words, and of manners, concerning which there are nine partial instructions and three principal rays.

Again, "God saw the light," that is, he made [it] be seen through wisdom's contemplation by illuminating the soul in itself, in reflection, and in understanding. And this last illumination in understanding is distinguished by six conditions which that light impresses in the mind; for it is the first simple cause, etc., and in creatures there are opposed conditions. The soul raises itself to that understanding by reason, experience, and understanding of the simple. From all of which, every perfection is given in the soul in those six conditions, since it has substance, power, operation, etc.

To all these the understanding given through nature reaches, and hence the philosophers have come to them; and so in them just as in the angels, "Light is divided from darkness" (Genesis. I, 4). Thus they knew that light as it is great in the quiddity of things, clear in the pronunciation of words, best in the ordering of manners.

But there was a difference as to whether in that light there is the characteristic of being the exemplar of everything, some saying that it knows itself alone, as in Book XI of the *Metaphysics,* the last chapter: "And it moves through being loved and desired." These do not posit any exemplar at all. The first of these is Aristotle, who attacked eternal reasons and Ideas, as well as their defender, Plato. The commentator on Book I of the *Ethics,* where Aristotle proves that the highest good is not an Idea, replies to his arguments.

From this there follows a second error, namely, that the truth of divine providence and foreknowledge is put aside, if everything is not distinct in it. Whence they say that God knows nothing as a particular and that there is no truth of the future except by necessity, and so foreknowledge is removed and one must maintain that everything happens by chance. Hence fate is necessarily brought in, as the Arabs maintain, that is, the error that the substances moving the world are the causes of everything. And from this there follows the unsuitable position that the disposition of the world is beyond punishment and glory. For if those substances do not err in moving, neither hell nor demon is posited; whence Aristotle did not posit demons nor more angels than celestial spheres.

Most of all, then, the truth of divine providence and the disposition of the world is put aside in this way. And thus in the putting aside of the truth there is given the error of the eternity of the world, as even Aristotle himself seems to sense, according to the doctors who impute this to him, namely, Gregory of Nazianzus and Gregory of Nyssa. From this there follows the unity of the intellect or its transmigration into another body or what is corporeal; and since it is not proper to posit an infinite number of intellects, he thought to posit one for all. All these follow if it is held that the world is eternal. And further, it follows that after this life there is neither punishment nor glory.

Those holding such views, therefore, fall into these errors, the understanding of which is closed by the key to the bottomless pit from which a great fog arises. It is more circumspect, then, to say that Aristotle did not feel that the world is eternal, whether he felt so or not, since he was so great that everyone followed him and was devoted to saying the same things; thus all the light determined in his predeces-

From Bonaventure, "Conferences on the Hexaemeron," Vision I, Discussion III, trans. James J. Walsh, in *Philosophy in the Middle Ages,* Arthur Hyman and James J. Walsh, eds. (Indianapolis: Hackett Publishing Co., Inc., 2d ed. 1983), pp. 459–461.

sors was extinguished. But we follow him where he spoke well, not where he was in the dark, not on those matters of which he was ignorant or which he concealed. From doing that, men in this life are on the infinite precipice.

Thomas Aquinas

Born in Roccasecca, Italy, in 1225, Thomas Aquinas is unquestionably the greatest and the most influential of the medieval philosophers. Despite family objections, Aquinas became a Dominican friar. He studied with Albert the Great at the University of Paris, where he became interested in the philosophy of Aristotle. Despite his young age, Aquinas was soon the central figure in the conflict between traditional theology and the Averroist version of Aristotle, especially as promulgated by Siger of Brabant.

In general terms, Aquinas was loyal to the thought of Augustine and he opposed Latin Averroism. Nonetheless, in philosophical matters, he regarded Aristotle as the master, and he wrote a series of brilliant commentaries on Aristotle's works. Aquinas attempted to show that within the limits of human reason, Aristotle's philosophical treatment of the soul, the existence of God, ethics, logic, and physics constitutes an utterly appropriate and rich basis for a Christian philosophy. Only matters of faith as revealed by the Scriptures were considered by Aquinas to be out of the reach of Aristotle.

This interpretation and defense of Aristotle was very radical for the thirteenth century, and some of Aquinas' positions were included with those of the Latin Averroists in the Condemnation of 1277. But the recovery and defense of Aristotle does not exhaust the philosophical contribution of Aquinas. His metaphysics goes beyond Aristotle, particularly on the thorny question of existence. For this reason, Aquinas' classic treatise Concerning Being and Essence *has been included here in its entirety. Philosophical gleanings from his monumental* Summa Theologica *are most often wise and informed. The* Summa *is the most comprehensive philosophical treatment of the major philosophical questions ever published by a single author. The natural, the human, and speculation about the supernatural are all treated in detail by Aquinas. Moreover, Aquinas' habit of citing objections to his position has given us access to a rich deposit of ancient and medieval thought.*

In 1273, Aquinas reportedly had a mystical experience of such intensity that he stopped his theological and philosophical writing. Less than a year later, in March 1274, he died in a monastery. Aquinas' writings fell into virtual eclipse during the centuries dominated by the modern secular philosophies of Descartes, Kant, and Hegel. In 1879, Pope Leo XIII issued an encyclical, Aeterni Patris, *in which the teaching of Aquinas was made the official doctrine of the Roman Catholic Church. This doctrine, known as Thomism, soon was taught in an insulated and defensive manner. Such a development was most unfortunate, for of all the medieval philosophers, Thomas Aquinas was the most hospitable to different points of view. In recent decades, the irony has been compounded, for now that Thomism is no longer the exclusive pedagogical resource of Roman Catholic thought, Aquinas has been largely ignored. Contemporary Roman Catholic philosophers are more interested in twentieth-century existentialism and phenomenology as well as in nineteenth-century classical American philosophy. Aquinas, however, should be restored to his rightful place as one of the masters of the western philosophical tradition.*

From The Division and Methods of the Sciences

QUESTION FIVE

The Division of Speculative Science

There are two questions here. The first concerns the division of speculative science which the text proposes, the second concerns the methods it attributes to the parts of speculative science.

With regard to the first question there are four points of inquiry:

1. Is speculative science appropriately divided into these three parts: natural, mathematical, and divine?
2. Does natural philosophy treat of what exists in motion and matter?
3. Does mathematics treat, without motion and matter, of what exists in matter?
4. Does divine science treat of what exists without matter and motion?

Article One

Is Speculative Science Appropriately Divided into These Three Parts: Natural, Mathematical, and Divine?

We proceed thus with regard to the first article:

It seems that speculative science is not appropriately divided into these three parts, for

1. The parts of speculative science are the habits that perfect the contemplative part of the soul. But the Philosopher says in the *Ethics* that the scientific part of the soul, which is its contemplative part, is perfected by three habits, namely, wisdom, science, and understanding. Therefore these are the three divisions of speculative science, not those proposed in the text.

2. Again, Augustine says that rational philosophy, or logic, is included under contemplative or speculative philosophy. Consequently, since no mention is made of it, it seems the division is inadequate.

3. Again, philosophy is commonly divided into seven liberal arts, which include neither natural nor divine science, but only rational and mathematical science. Hence natural and divine should not be called parts of speculative science.

4. Again, medicine seems to be the most operative science, and yet it is said to contain a speculative part and a practical part. By the same token, therefore, all the other operative sciences have a speculative part. Consequently, even though it is a practical science, ethics or moral science should be mentioned in this division because of its speculative part.

5. Again, the science of medicine is a branch of physics, and similarly certain other arts called "mechanical," like the science of agriculture, alchemy, and others of the same sort. Therefore, since these sciences are operative, it seems that natural science should not be included without qualification under speculative science.

6. Again, a whole should not be contradistinguished from its part. But divine science seems to be a whole in relation to physics and mathematics, since their subjects are parts of its subject. For the subject of divine science or first philosophy is being; and changeable substance, which the natural scientist considers, and also quantity, which the mathematician considers, are parts of being. This is clear in the *Metaphysics*. Therefore, divine science should not be contradistinguished from natural science and mathematics.

7. Again, as it is said in the *De Anima*, sciences are divided in the same manner as things. But philosophy concerns being, for it is knowledge of being, as Dionysius says. Now being is primarily divided into potency and act, one and many, substance and accident. So it seems that the parts of philosophy ought to be distinguished by such divisions of being.

8. Again, there are many other divisions of beings studied by sciences more essential than the divisions into mobile and immobile and into abstract and non-abstract; for example, the divisions into corporeal and incorporeal and into living and non-living, and

---

the like. Therefore differences of this sort should be the basis for the division of the parts of philosophy rather than those mentioned here.

9. Again, that science on which others depend must be prior to them. Now all the other sciences depend on divine science because it is its business to prove their principles. Therefore Boethius should have placed divine science before the others.

10. Again, mathematics should be studied before natural science, for the young can easily learn mathematics, but only the more advanced natural science, as is said in the *Ethics.* This is why the ancients are said to have observed the following order in learning the sciences: first logic, then mathematics, then natural science, after that moral science, and finally men studied divine science. Therefore, Boethius should have placed mathematics before natural science. And so it seems that this division is unsuitable.

On the contrary, the Philosopher proves the appropriateness of this division in the *Metaphysics,* where he says, "There will be three philosophical and theoretical sciences: mathematics, physics, and theology."

Moreover, in the *Physics* three methods of the sciences are proposed which indeed seem to belong to these three.

Moreover, Ptolemy also uses this division in the beginning of his *Almagest.*

Reply: The theoretical or speculative intellect is properly distinguished from the operative or practical intellect by the fact that the speculative intellect has for its end the truth that it contemplates, while the practical intellect directs the truth under consideration to activity as to an end. So the Philosopher says in the *De Anima* that they differ from each other by their ends; and in the *Metaphysics* he states that "the end of speculative knowledge is truth, but the end of practical knowledge is action."

Now, since matter must be proportionate to the end, the subject-matter of the practical sciences must be things that can be made or done by us, so that we can direct the knowledge of them to activity as to an end. On the other hand, the subject-matter of the speculative sciences must be things that cannot be made or done by us, so that our knowledge of them cannot be directed to activity as to an end. And the speculative sciences must differ according to the distinctions among these things.

Now we must realize that when habits or powers are differentiated by their objects they do not differ according to just any distinction among these objects, but according to the distinctions that are essential to the objects as objects. For example, it is incidental to a sense object whether it be an animal or a plant. Accordingly, the distinction between the sense powers is not based upon this difference but rather upon the difference between color and sound. So the speculative sciences must be divided according to differences between objects of speculation, considered precisely as such. Now an object of this kind—namely, an object of a speculative power—derives one characteristic from the side of the power of intellect and another from the side of the habit of science that perfects the intellect. From the side of the intellect it has the fact that it is immaterial, because the intellect itself is immaterial. From the side of the habit of science it has the fact that it is necessary, for science treats of necessary matters, as is shown in the *Posterior Analytics.* Now everything that is necessary is, as such, immobile, because everything changeable is, as such, able to be or not to be, either absolutely or in a certain respect, as is said in the *Metaphysics.* Consequently, separation from matter and motion, or connection with them, essentially belongs to an object of speculation, which is the object of speculative science. As a result, the speculative sciences are differentiated according to their degree of separation from matter and motion.

Now there are some objects of speculation that depend on matter for their being, for they can exist only in matter. And these are subdivided. Some depend on matter both for their being and for their being understood, as do those things whose definition contains sensible matter and which, as a consequence, cannot be understood without sensible matter. For example, it is necessary to include flesh and bones in the definition of man. It is things of this sort that physics or natural science studies. On the other hand, there are some things that, although dependent upon matter for their being, do not depend upon it for their being understood, because sensible matter is not included in their definition. This is the case with lines and numbers—the kind of objects with which mathematics deals. There are still other objects of speculative knowledge that do not depend upon matter for their being, because they can exist without matter; either they never exist in matter, as in the case of God and the angels, or they exist in matter in some instances and not in others, as in the case of substance, quality, being, potency, act, one and many, and the like. The science that treats of all these is theology or divine science, which is so called because its principal object is God. By another name it is called metaphysics; that is to say, *beyond physics,* because it comes to us after physics among subjects to be learned; for we have to proceed from sensible things to those that are non-sensible. It is also called first philosophy, inasmuch as all the other sciences, receiving their principles from it, come after it. Now there can be nothing that depends upon matter for its being understood but not for its being, because by its very nature the intellect is immaterial. So there is no fourth kind of philosophy besides the ones mentioned.

Replies to the Opposing Arguments:

Reply to 1. In the *Ethics,* the Philosopher considers the intellectual habits insofar as they are intellectual virtues. Now they are called virtues because they perfect the intellect in its operation; for "virtue makes its possessor good and renders his work good." So he distinguishes between virtues of this sort inasmuch as speculative habits perfect the intellect in different ways. In one way the speculative part of the soul is perfected by understanding, which is the habit of principles, through which some things become known of themselves. In another way it is perfected by a habit through which conclusions demonstrated from these principles are known, whether the demonstration proceeds from inferior causes, as in science, or from the highest causes, as in wisdom. But when sciences are differentiated insofar as they are habits, they must be distinguished according to their objects, that is, according to the things of which the sciences treat. And it is in this way that both here and in the *Metaphysics* speculative philosophy is distinguished into three parts.

Reply to 2. As is evident in the beginning of the *Metaphysics,* the speculative sciences concern things the knowledge of which is sought for their own sake. However, we do not seek to know the things studied by logic for themselves, but as a help to the other sciences. So logic is not included under speculative philosophy as a principal part but as something brought under speculative philosophy as furnishing speculative thought with its instruments, namely, syllogisms, definitions, and the like, which we need in the speculative sciences. Thus, according to Boethius, logic is not so much a science as the instrument of science.

Reply to 3. The seven liberal arts do not adequately divide theoretical philosophy; but, as Hugh of St. Victor says, seven arts are grouped together (leaving out certain other ones), because those who wanted to learn philosophy were first instructed in them. And the reason why they are divided into the trivium and quadrivium is that "they are as it were paths *(viae)* introducing the quick mind to the secrets of philosophy." This is also in harmony with the Philosopher's statement in the *Metaphysics,* that we must investigate the method of scientific thinking before the sciences themselves. And the Commentator says in the same place that before all the other sciences a person should learn logic, which teaches the method of all the sciences; and the trivium concerns logic. The Philosopher also says in the *Ethics* that the young can know mathematics but not physics, because it requires experience. So we are given to understand that after physics we should learn mathematics, which the quadrivium concerns. These, then, are like paths leading the mind to the other philosophical disciplines.

We may add that among the other sciences these are called arts because they involve not only knowledge but also a work that is directly a product of reason itself; for example, producing a composition, syllogism or discourse, numbering, measuring, composing melodies, and reckoning the course of the stars. Other sciences (such as divine and natural science) either do not involve a work produced but only knowledge, and so we cannot call them arts, because, as the *Metaphysics* says, art is "productive reason"; or they involve some bodily activity, as in the case of medicine, alchemy, and other sciences of this kind. These latter, then, cannot be called liberal arts because such activity belongs to man on the side of his nature in which he is not free, namely, on the side of his body. And although moral science is directed to action, still that action is not the act of the science but rather of virtue, as is clear in the *Ethics.* So we cannot call moral science an art; but rather in these actions virtue takes the place of art. Thus, as

Augustine says, the ancients defined virtue as the art of noble and well-ordered living.

Reply to 4. As Avicenna says, the distinction between theoretical and practical is not the same when philosophy is divided into theoretical and practical, when the arts are divided into theoretical and practical, and when medicine is so divided. For when we distinguish philosophy or the arts into theoretical and practical we must do so on the basis of their end, calling that theoretical which is directed solely to knowledge of the truth, and that practical which is directed to operation. However, there is this difference when we distinguish the whole of philosophy and the arts on this basis: We divide philosophy with respect to the final end or happiness, to which the whole of human life is directed. For, as Augustine says, following Varro, "There is no other reason for a man philosophizing except to be happy." And since the philosophers teach that there is a twofold happiness, one contemplative and the other active, as is clear in the *Ethics,* they have accordingly also distinguished between two parts of philosophy, calling moral philosophy practical and natural and rational philosophy theoretical. But when they call some arts speculative and some practical, this is on the basis of some *special* ends of those arts; as when we say that agriculture is a practical art but dialectic is theoretical.

However, when we divide medicine into theoretical and practical, the division is not on the basis of the end. For on that basis the whole of medicine is practical, since it is directed to practice. But the above division is made on the basis of whether what is studied in medicine is proximate to, or remote from practice. Thus we call that part of medicine practical which teaches the method of healing; for instance, that these particular medicines should be given for these abscesses. On the other hand, we call that part theoretical which teaches the principles directing a man in his practice, although not immediately; for instance, that there are three virtues, and that there are so many kinds of fever. Consequently, if we call some part of a practical science theoretical, we should not on that account place that part under speculative philosophy.

Reply to 5. One science is contained under another in two ways: In one way, as its part, because its subject is part of the subject of that other science, as plant is a part of natural body. So the science of plants is also contained under natural science as one of its parts. In another way, one science is contained under another as subalternated to it. This occurs when in a higher science there is given the reason for what a lower science knows only as a fact. This is how music is contained under arithmetic.

Medicine, therefore, is not contained under physics as a part, for the subject of medicine is not part of the subject of natural science from the point of view from which it is the subject of medicine. For although the curable body is a natural body, it is not the subject of medicine insofar as it is curable by nature, but insofar as it is curable by art. But because art is nature's handmaid in healing (in which art too plays a part, for health is brought about through the power of nature with the assistance of art), it follows that the reason for the practices used in the art must be based on the properties of natural things. So medicine is subalternated to physics, and for the same reason so too are alchemy, the science of agriculture, and all sciences of this sort. We conclude, then, that physics in itself and in all its parts is speculative, although some practical sciences are subalternated to it.

Reply to 6. Although the subjects of the other sciences are parts of being, which is the subject of metaphysics, the other sciences are not necessarily parts of metaphysics. For each science treats of one part of being in a special way distinct from that in which metaphysics treats of being. So its subject is not properly speaking a part of the subject of metaphysics, for it is not a part of being from the point of view from which being is the subject of metaphysics; from this viewpoint it is a special science distinct from the others. However, the science treating of potency, or that treating of act or unity or anything of this sort, could be called a part of metaphysics, because these are considered in the same manner as being, which is the subject of metaphysics.

Reply to 7. These parts of being require the same manner of consideration as being-in-general *(ens commune)* because they too are independent of matter. For this reason the science dealing with them is not distinct from the science of being-in-general.

Reply to 8. The other diversities of things mentioned in the objection do not differentiate those things essentially as objects of knowledge. So the sciences are not distinguished according to them.

Reply to 9. Although divine science is by nature the first of all the sciences, with respect to us the other sciences come before it. For, as Avicenna says, the position of this science is that it be learned after the natural sciences, which explain many things used by metaphysics, such as generation, corruption, motion, and the like. It should also be learned after mathematics, because to know the separate substances metaphysics has to know the number and dispositions of the heavenly spheres, and this is impossible without astronomy, which presupposes the whole of mathematics. Other sciences, such as music, ethics, and the like, contribute to its fullness of perfection.

Nor is there necessarily a vicious circle because metaphysics presupposes conclusions proved in the other sciences while it itself proves their principles. For the principles that another science (such as natural philosophy) takes from first philosophy do not prove what the same first philosopher takes from the natural philosopher, but they are proved through other self-evident principles. Similarly the first philosopher does not prove the principles he gives the natural philosopher by principles he receives from him, but by other self-evident principles. So there is no vicious circle in their definitions.

Moreover, the sensible effects on which the demonstrations of natural science are based are more evident to us in the beginning. But when we come to know the first causes through them, these causes will reveal to us the reason for the effects, from which they were proved by a demonstration *quia*. In this way natural science also contributes something to divine science, and nevertheless it is divine science that explains its principles. That is why Boethius places divine science last, because it is the last relative to us.

Reply to 10. Although we should learn natural science after mathematics because the general proofs of natural science require experience and time, still, since natural things fall under the senses, they are by nature better known than the mathematical entities abstracted from sensible matter.

Concerning Being and Essence

INTRODUCTION

Because a small error in the beginning is a great one in the end, according to the Philosopher [Aristotle] in the first book of the *De Caelo et Mundo*, and since being and essence are what are first conceived by the intellect, as Avicenna says in the first book of his *Metaphysics*, therefore, lest error befall from ignorance of them (being and essence), in order to reveal their difficulty it should be said what is signified by the names being and essence, and how they are found in diverse things and how they are disposed with respect to *(se habeant ad)* logical intentions, namely, genus, species, and difference.

CHAPTER ONE

Because indeed we must receive knowledge of the simple from the composite and arrive at what is prior from what is posterior, in order that beginning with the less difficult instruction may be made more suitably, we should proceed from the meaning of being to the meaning of essence.

Therefore one should know, as the Philosopher [Aristotle] says in the fifth of the *Metaphysics*, that being by itself *(ens per se)* is said to be taken in two modes: in the one mode, that it is divided into ten genera; in the other, that it signifies the truth of propositions. Moreoever the difference between these is that in the second mode everything can be called being concerning which an affirmative proposition can be formed, even if it posits nothing in the thing *(in re)*; by virtue of this mode privations and negations are likewise called beings, for we say that affirmation is the opposite of negation, and that blindness is in the eye. But in the first mode only what posits something in the thing can be called being; consequently, according to the first mode blindness and such are not beings. The name essence, therefore, is not taken from being in the sec-

George G. Leckie, trans., *Concerning Being and Essence*, by St. Thomas Aquinas, © 1937, renewed 1965, pp. 3–38. Reprinted by permission of Prentice-Hall, Inc., Englewood Cliffs, N.J. (complete)

ond mode, for in this mode some things are said to have essence which have not being, as is evident in privations. But essence is taken from being only in the first mode; whence the Commentator [Averroës] says in the same place that "being in the first mode is said to be what signifies the essence of the thing." And because, as has been said, being in this mode is divided into ten genera, it follows that essence signifies something common to all natures by which diverse beings are disposed in different genera and species, as for instance humanity is the essence of man and so for others. And because that by means of which the thing is constituted in its proper genus or species is that which is signified by the definition indicating what the thing is, hence it is that the name essence has been changed by philosophers into the name quiddity. And this is what the Philosopher frequently calls *"quod quid erat esse,"* that is, that by virtue of which a thing (anything) has to be what it is (something), (τὸ τί ἦν εἶναι). And indeed it is called form according as by means of form the certitude of any single thing is signified, as Avicenna remarks in the second part of his *Metaphysics.* This is called by another name, nature, accepting nature according to the first of the four modes assigned by Boethius in his book *De Duabus Naturis,* namely, according as nature is said to be all that which can be comprehended by the intellect in any mode whatsoever; for a thing is not intelligible except by virtue of its definition and essence. And thus also the Philosopher in the Fourth book of his *Metaphysics* says that every substance is a nature. But the name nature taken in this sense is seen to signify the essence of a thing inasmuch as it has a disposition *(ordinem)* towards an operation proper to the thing, since no thing is lacking in its proper operation. Indeed the name quiddity is taken from that which signifies the definition; but it is called essence according as by virtue of it and in it being has existence *(esse).*

But because being is asserted absolutely and primarily of substances and secondarily and as if in a certain respect *(secundum quid)* of accidents, hence it is that essence also exists truly and properly in substances, but exists in accidents in a certain mode and in a certain respect. Some substances indeed are simple and others are composite, and in both there is an essence. But essence is possessed by simple substances in a truer and more noble mode according as simple substances have a more exalted existence, for they are the cause of those which are composite,—at least the primary substance, which is God, is. But since the essences of these substances are more concealed from us, therefore we must begin from the essences of composite substances in order that instruction may be made more suitably from what is easier.

CHAPTER TWO

In composite substances, therefore, matter and form are noted, as for instance in man soul and body are noted. Moreover it cannot be said that either of these alone is called essence. For it is evident that matter alone is not the essence of the thing, because it is by means of its essence that the thing is both known and ordered in its species and genus. But matter is not the principle of cognition, nor is anything determined as regards genus and species according to it (matter), but according to that by means of which something is in act. And furthermore neither can form alone be called the essence of composite substance, however much some attempt to assert this. From what has been said it is clear that essence is what is signified by the definition of the thing. But the definition of natural substances contains not only form but also matter; for otherwise natural definitions and mathematical definitions would not differ. Nor can it be said that matter is posited in the definition of a natural substance as an addition to its essence or as a being outside of its essence *(extra essentiam),* since this mode of definition is more proper to accidents which do not have a perfect essence; whence it follows that they must admit the subject into their definition, which (subject) is outside of their genus. It is clear, therefore, that essence comprehends matter and form. But it cannot be said that essence signifies a relation which is between matter and form, or that it is something superadded to them, since something superadded would of necessity be accidental or extraneous to the thing, nor could the thing be conceived by means of it, for everything is appropriate to its essence. For by the form, which is the actuality of matter, matter is made being in act and a this somewhat. Whence that which is superadded does not give existence *(esse)* in act simply to matter, but existence in act of such sort as likewise accidents make, as for instance whiteness makes something white in act. Wherefore whenever such form is acquired it is not said to be generated simply but in a certain respect *(secundum quid).* Hence it follows that in composite substances the name of essence signifies that which is composed of matter and form. And this agrees also with the opinion of Boethius in his commentary *Predicamentorum,* where he says that *ousia* signifies a composite. For *ousia* according to the Greeks is the same as essence according to us, as Boethius himself remarks in his book *De Duabus Naturis.* Avicenna also says that the quiddity of composite substances is itself a composition of matter and form. The Commentator also says concerning the seventh book of the *Metaphysics:* "The nature which species have in things capable of generation is something intermediate that is composed of matter and form." Reason also accords with this, because the existence of a composite substance is not the existence of form only, nor the existence of matter only, but of the composite itself; and indeed essence is that according to which a thing is said to exist. Whence it follows that the essence by virtue of which a thing is called being is not form alone, nor matter alone, but both; although in its mode the form is the cause of its existence. We discover it indeed thus in other things which are constituted from more than one principle, since a thing is not named from one of those principles alone, but from that which unites both. It appears thus in the case of tastes, because sweetness is caused from the action of warmth dissolving moisture, and although in this mode the warmth is the cause of the sweetness, yet a body is not called sweet from its warmth but from the taste which unites both the warmth and the moisture.

But because the principle of individuation is matter, it perhaps seems to follow from this that essence which unites in itself both matter and form would be only particular and not universal. From this it would follow that universals do not have definition, if essence is what is signified by means of the definition. One should therefore understand that matter in any mode whatsoever is not taken to be the principle of individuation, but only signated matter *(materia signata).* And I call signated matter that which is considered as under determinate dimensions. But now this matter is not posited in the definition of man inasmuch as he is man, but it would be posited in the definiton of Socrates if Socrates were to have a definition. But in the definition of man non-signated matter is posited; for in the definition of man this certain flesh and this certain bone are not posited, but bone and flesh absolutely, which are the non-signated matter of man. Accordingly, it is clear that the essence of Socrates and the essence of man do not differ except according to signate and non-signate. Whence the Commentator remarks upon the seventh of the *Metaphysics:* "Socrates is nothing other than animality and rationality which are his quiddity." Thus also the essence of genus and of species differ according to signate and non-signate, although there is a different mode of designation for each of them, because the designation of the individual with respect to species is by means of matter determined by dimensions, whereas the designation of species in respect to genus is by means of the constitutive difference which is taken from the form of the thing.

This determination or designation, however, which is in the species in respect to genus is not by means of something existing in the essence of species, which is in no mode in the essence of genus; nay, whatever is in species is in genus as something undetermined. For if animal is not the whole of man, but part of him, it is not predicated of him, since no integral part is predicated of its whole.

But how this is related can be seen if one observes how body differs according as animal is posited as part or as genus; for it cannot be genus in the same mode in which it is an integral part. This name body, therefore, is taken in several senses. For body according as it is in the genus of substance is asserted of that which has a nature such that three dimensions can be designated in it; in truth the three designated dimensions themselves are body which is in the genus of quantity. But it happens in things that what has one perfection may also aim at further perfection; as for instance is clear in the case of man, since he has both a sensitive nature and further, intellectual nature. Likewise indeed beyond this perfection which is to have such a form that three dimensions can be designated in it, another perfection can be added, as life or something of this sort. This name body, therefore, can signify a certain thing which has a form such that from it follows the possibility of designating three dimensions in it, with this limitation, namely, that from that form no further perfection may follow, but if anything else is added it is beyond the significance of body thus spoken of. And in this mode body is an integral and material part of animal, because thus soul will be beyond what is signified by the name body and will be something added to (excelling) body itself in such wise that from these two, that is, from soul and body, the animal is constituted as from its parts. This name body can also be taken so as to signify a certain thing which has a form such that from the form three dimensions can be designated in it, whatsoever that form may be, and whether any further perfection can issue from it or not. And in this mode body is the genus of animal, because in animal nothing is taken which is not contained implicitly in body; for soul is not a form different from that by means of which three dimensions can be designated in that thing. And therefore when it was said that body is what has a form such that from the form three dimensions can be designated in the body, it was to be understood of whatever the form might be, whether animality or lapidity or any other. And so the form of animal is contained implicitly in the form of body, according as body is its genus. And such too is the habitude (relation) of animal to man. For if animal denoted only a certain thing which has a perfection such that it can feel and be moved by virtue of a principle existing in itself, to the exclusion of any further perfections, then whatever further perfection supervened to the thing, would be disposed in respect to *(haberet se ad)* animal by means of the partitive mode *(modum partis)* and not as if implicitly beneath (included in) the principle of animal, and thus animal would not be a genus. But animal is a genus according as it signifies a certain thing from the form of which can issue feeling and motion, whatsoever this form may be, whether it be the sensible soul alone or the sensible and rational together. Thus, therefore, genus signifies indeterminately all that which is in species, for it does not signify matter alone. Similarly, difference signifies the whole, but it does not signify form alone. And definition likewise signifies a whole, and also species does. But yet in diverse ways: because genus signifies a whole as a certain determination determining what is material in a thing, without the determination of the proper form. Whence genus is taken from matter, although it is not matter, as is evident in the instance of what is called body because it has a perfection such that three dimensions can be designated in it, which certain perfection is materially disposed towards further perfection. In truth, on the contrary, difference is taken determinately as a certain determination by form, for the reason that determined matter is involved in the primary conception of it, as appears when it is called animate or that which has soul; for what it is, whether body or something else, is not determined. Whence Avicenna says that genus is not intellected in difference as a part of essence, but only as a being beyond its essence *(extra essentiam)*, just as a subject is in regard to the intellection of the passions. And therefore, likewise, speaking *per se*, genus is not predicated concerning difference, as the Philosopher remarks in the third of the *Metaphysics* and the fourth of the *Topics*, unless perchance as a subject is predicated of passion. But definition or species comprehends both, namely, determinate matter which the name of genus designates, and determinate form which the name of difference designates.

And from this the reason is clear why genus and species and difference are proportionally disposed towards *(se habeant ad)* matter and form and the composite in nature, although they are not the same as nature, since genus is not matter but taken from matter as signifying the whole, nor is difference form but taken from form as signifying the whole. Wherefore we call man a rational animal, not from the composite of animal and rational, as we say that he is composed of body and soul; for man is said to be composed of soul and body, just as from two things a third thing is truly constituted, which is neither of the two; for man is neither soul nor body. But if man can be said to be composed in some manner of animal and rational, it is not as a third thing from two things but as a third concept from two concepts; for the concept of animal is one expressing, without the determination of a special form, the nature of a thing, by that which is material in respect to its ultimate perfection. The concept, however, of the difference rational consists in the determination of a special form. And from the two concepts (animal and rational) is constituted the concept of the species or definition. And therefore just as a thing constituted from other things does not take the predication of those things, thus neither does the concept take the predication of those concepts from which it is constituted, for we do not say that the definition is genus or difference.

But, although genus signifies the whole essence of species, yet it does not follow that there is one essence of different species which have the same genus, because the unity of the genus proceeds from its very indetermination and indifference; not, however, because that which is signified by genus is one nature by number in different species to which supervenes something else which is the difference determining it, as for instance form determines matter which is numerically one; but because genus signifies some form, though not determinately this or that (form) which difference expresses determinately, which is none other than that (form) which is signified indeterminately through genus. And therefore the Commentator says in the twelfth book of the *Metaphysics* that prime matter is called one through the remotion of all forms (*scil.* pure potentiality in the order of substance), but genus is called one through the community of its signified form. Whence it is clear that by means of the addition of difference, which removes the indetermination which was the cause of the unity of genus, species remain different by virtue of essence.

And because, as has been said, the nature of species is indeterminate in respect to the individual, just as the nature of genus is indeterminate with respect to species, hence it is that, just as that which is genus according as it is predicated concerning species implies in its signification, although indistinctly, all that is determinate in species, thus likewise it follows that what is species, according as it is predicated of the individual, signifies all that which is in the individual essentially although indistinctly. And in this mode the essence of Socrates is signified by the name of man, and as a consequence man is predicated of Socrates. But if the nature of the species be signified with the exclusion of designated matter, which is the principle of individuation, it will thus be disposed *(se habebit)* as a part (by means of the partitive mode). And in this mode it is signified by the name humanity, for humanity signifies that in virtue of which man is man. But designated matter is not that in virtue of which man is man; and, therefore, in no mode is it contained among those things from which man possesses manness. Since therefore humanity includes in its concept only those things from which man possesses manness, it is clear that designated matter is excluded from or cut off from its signification. And since the part is not predicated of the whole, hence it is that humanity is not predicated either of man or of Socrates. Wherefore Avicenna says that the quiddity of a composite is not the composite itself of which it is the quiddity, although the quiddity itself is composite; as for instance humanity, although it is composite, still is not man. Nay rather, it must be received in something which is designated matter. But since, as has been said, the designation of species in respect to genus is by virtue of form, whereas the designation of the individual in respect to species is by virtue of matter, it follows therefore that the name signifying that whence the nature of genus is taken, with the exclusion of the determinate form perfecting the species, should signify the material part of the whole itself, as the body is the material part of man. But the name signifying that whence the nature of species is taken, with the exclusion of designated matter, signifies the formal part. And therefore humanity is signified as a certain form, and is spoken of as that which is the form of the whole; not indeed as if it were superadded to the essential parts, namely, to form and matter, as for instance the form of a house is superadded to its integral parts; but rather it is form that is the whole, that is, embracing form and matter, yet with the exclusion of those things by means of which matter is found to be designated. So, therefore, it is clear that the name man and the name humanity signify the essence of man, but in different modes, as has been said, since the name man signifies it as a whole, inasmuch as it does not exclude the designation of matter but contains it implicitly and indistinctly, as for instance it has been said that the genus contains the difference. And therefore the name man is predicated of individuals. But the name humanity signifies the essence as a part, since it does not contain in its signification anything except what is of man inasmuch as he is man, and because it excludes all designation of matter; whence it is not predicated of individual man. And for this reason likewise the name essence sometimes is found predicated of a thing, for Socrates is said to be an essence, and sometimes it is denied, as for instance it is said that the essence of Socrates is not Socrates.

CHAPTER THREE

Having seen, therefore, what is signified by the name of essence in composite substances, we should see in what mode it is disposed towards *(se habeat ad)* the ratio of genus, species, and difference. Since, however, that to which the ratio of genus or species or difference applies is predicated concerning this signate singular, it is impossible that the ratio of the universal, namely, that of genus and of species, should apply to essence according as it is signified by means of the partitive mode, as for instance by the name humanity or animality. And therefore Avicenna says that rationality is not the difference, but the principle of difference. And for the same reason humanity is not species nor is animality genus. Similarly, also, it cannot be said that the ratio of genus or of species applies to essence according as essence is a certain thing existing apart from singulars, as the Platonists were accustomed to assert, since thus genus and species would not be predicated of this individual. For it cannot be said that Socrates is what is separated from him, nor again that the separated conduces to the cognition of a singular. And therefore it follows that the ratio of genus or species applies to essence according as it is signified in the mode of a whole, as for instance by the name of man or animal, according as it contains implicitly and indistinctly all that is in the individual.

But nature or essence taken thus can be considered in two ways. In one mode according to its proper ratio, and this is the absolute consideration of it, and in this mode nothing is true concerning it except what applies to it according to this mode, whence whatever else is attributed to it is a false attribution. For example, to man inasmuch as he is man rational and animal applies and the other things which fall within his definition. White or black, however, and whatsoever of this mode, which is not of the ratio of humanity, does not apply to man inasmuch as he is man. Accordingly, if it were asked whether this nature thus considered can be said to be one or more than one, neither ought to be conceded, because each is outside the concept of humanity, and either one can happen to it *(accidere)*. For if plurality were to belong to the concept of humanity, it could never be one although nevertheless it is one according as it is in Socrates. Similarly, if unity were to belong to its ratio, then would it be one and the same of Socrates and of Plato, nor could it be multiplied *(plurificari)* in many. It is considered in another mode according to the existence *(esse)* which it has in this or that, and in this mode something is predicated concerning it by means of accident *(per accidens)*, by reason of that in which it is, as for instance it is said that man is white because Socrates is white, although this does not apply to man inasmuch as he is man.

But this nature has a twofold existence: having one existence in singulars and another in the soul, and according to both of the two, accident follows upon the nature spoken of, and in singulars also it has a manifold existence according to the diversity of the singulars. And nevertheless to this very nature according to its primary consideration, that is to say, its absolute one, none of these (existences) ought to belong. For it is false to say that the essence of man, inasmuch as he is man, has existence in this singular, because if existence in this singular applied to man as man, then (man) would never exist outside of this singular. Similarly, also, if it applied to man as man not to exist in this singular, (man) would never exist in it. But it is true to say that man as man does not have to be in this singular or in that or in the soul. Therefore it is clear that the nature of man absolutely considered abstracts from any sort of existence, yet in such wise that it does not exclude any of them. And this nature so considered is what is predicated of all individuals. Still it cannot be said that the ratio of universal applies to nature thus considered, because unity and community belong to the principle of the universal, whereas to human nature neither of these (two) applies according to its absolute consideration. For if community belonged to the concept of man, then in whatsoever humanity were found community would be found. And this is false because in Socrates there is not found any community, but whatever is in him is individuated. Similarly, also, it cannot be said that the ratio of genus or of species belongs to human nature according to the existence which it has in individuals, because human nature is not found in individuals according to its unity so that it is a one appropriate to all, which the ratio of the universal demands. It follows, therefore, that the ratio of species applies to human nature according to that existence *(esse)* which it has in the intellect. For human nature itself has an existence in the intellect abstracted from all individuations, and therefore it has a uniform ratio to all individuals which are outside the soul, according as it is equally the likeness *(similitudo)* of all and leads to the understanding of all inasmuch as they are men. And because it has such a relation to all individuals, the intellect discovers the ratio of species and attributes it to it (human nature). Whence the Commentator observes in the first book of the *De Anima* that intellect is what actuates *(agit)* universality in things. Avicenna also says this in his *Metaphysics*. Whence, although this intellectual nature has the ratio of universal according as it is compared to things which are outside of the soul because it is a single likeness of all, nevertheless according as it has existence in this intellect or that it is a certain particular intellected species. And therefore the error of the Commentator in book three on the *De Anima* is clear, seeing that he wished to conclude from the universality of the intellected form to the unity of the intellect in all men; because there is no universality of that form according to the existence which it has in the intellect, but according as it is referred to things as a likeness of things. Thus, too, if there were a single corporeal statue representing many men, it is clear that the image or species of the statue would have an existence singular and proper according as it existed in this matter, but it would have a ratio of community according as it were a common thing representing many. And because to human nature according to its absolute consideration belongs what is predicated of Socrates, and since the ratio of species does not belong to it according to its absolute consideration, but follows from accidents which issue from it according to the existence which it has in the intellect, therefore the name of species is not predicated of Socrates so that it is said that Socrates is a species, which would necessarily happen if the ratio of species belonged to man according to the existence which he has in Socrates, or according to man's absolute consideration, namely, inasmuch as he is man; for whatever applies to man inasmuch as he is man is predicated of Socrates. Yet to be predicated applies to genus by virtue of itself *(per se)*, since it is posited in its definition. For predication is a certain thing which is perfected by means of the action of the intellect composing and dividing, having in the very thing as its foundation the unity of those things of which one is asserted of the other. Whence the ratio of predicability can be included in the ratio of this mode of intention which is genus, which, similarly, is perfected by means of an act of the intellect. Yet, nevertheless, that to which the intellect attributes the intention of predication, composing the one with the other, is not the very intention of genus but rather that to which the intellect attributes the intention of genus, as for instance what is signified by the name animal. Thus, therefore, it is clear how essence or nature is disposed towards *(se habet ad)* the ratio of species, because the ratio of species does not belong to those things which are appropriate to it according to its absolute consideration, nor likewise does it belong to the accidents which issue from it according to the existence which it has outside the soul, as whiteness or blackness. But it does belong to the accidents which issue from it according to the existence which it has in the intellect. And it is according to this mode that the ratio of genus and of difference also applies to it.

CHAPTER FOUR

Now it remains to see through what mode essence exists in separate substances, namely, in the soul, in intelligences and in the first cause. But although all grant the simplicity of the first cause, yet certain ones strive to introduce a composition of form and matter in intelligences and in the soul. The author of this position appears to have been Avicebron, the writer of the book *Fons Vitae*. But this is opposed to what is commonly said by philosophers, seeing that they call them substances separated from matter and prove them to be devoid of all matter. The most powerful reason for the assertion is (taken) from the power *(virtute)* of understanding which is in them (separate substances). For we see that forms are not intelligible in act except according as they are separated from matter and its conditions, nor are they made intelligible in act except by the power *(per virtutem)* of intelligent substance, inasmuch as they are received in it and inasmuch as they are actuated by virtue of it. Whence it is necessary that in any intelligent substance there be entire immunity from matter in such wise that they neither have a material part to them nor yet exist as a form impressed in matter, as is the case respecting material forms. Nor can anyone say that intelligibility is not impeded by any sort of matter, but only by corporeal matter. For if this impediment were by reason of corporeal matter alone, since matter is not spoken of as corporeal except inasmuch as it stands under corporeal form, then it would follow necessarily that matter would impede intelligibility by means of its corporeal form. And this cannot be, because the very corporeal form also is intelligible in act, just as other forms are, inasmuch as it is abstracted from matter. Wherefore in the soul or in an intelligence there is in no way a composition of matter and form so that essence might be taken in them in the mode in which it is taken in corporeal substances. But there is there (in them) a composition of form and existence; whence it is said in the comment on the ninth proposition of the book *De Causis* that intelligence is having form and existence; and form is taken there for the very quiddity or simple nature.

But it is easy to see how this is. For whatever things are disposed towards *(se habent ad)* one another in such wise that one is the cause of the existence of the other, that which has the ratio of cause can possess existence without the other, but not conversely. But such is found to be the habitude of matter and form, because form gives existence to matter, and therefore it is impossible for matter to be without some form, yet it is not impossible for any form to exist without matter, for form inasmuch as it is form does not depend on matter. But if any forms should be discovered which cannot exist save in matter, this happens to them inasmuch as they are distant from the first principle which is the first and pure act. Whence those forms which have the greatest propinquity to the first principle are forms subsisting by virtue of themselves *(per se)* without matter. For form does not require matter according to its entire genus, as has been said, and forms of this sort are intelligences. And therefore it is not necessary that the essences or quiddities of these substances be anything save the very form. Therefore the essence of a composite substance and the essence of a simple substance differ in that the essence of a composite substance is not form alone but embraces form and matter, whereas the essence of a simple substance is form alone. And from this two other differences are derived. One is that the essence of a composite substance can be signified as a whole or as a part, which happens according to the designation of the matter, as has been stated. And therefore the essence of a composite thing is not predicated in any mode whatsoever of the composite thing itself; for it cannot be said that man is his quiddity. But the essence of a simple thing, which is its form, cannot be signified except as a whole, since there is nothing there except the form as form receiving, and, therefore, in whatever mode the essence of a simple substance is taken it is predicated of the substance. Whence Avicenna says that the quiddity of a simple (substance) is itself simple, because there is not anything else receptive of the quiddity. The second difference is that the essences of composite things, seeing that they are received in designated matter, are multiplied according to its division, whence it results that some things are the same in species and diverse numerically. But since the essence of simple substance is not received in matter, there cannot be there any such multiplication. And therefore it follows necessarily that in these substances more than one individual of the same species are not found, but however many individuals there are, just so many are the species, as Avicenna expressly says. (*scil.* "A species of this mode is one in number.")

And indeed substances of this sort, although they are forms alone without matter, still do not have an entire simplicity of nature so that they are pure act; on the contrary, they have a mixture of potency, which is evident thus: for whatsoever does not belong to the concept of essence or quiddity is something accruing from without and effecting a composition with the essence, since no essence can be conceived without those things which are parts of essence. But every essence or quiddity can be conceived aside from the condition that something be known concerning its existence, for I can conceive what a man or phoenix is and still not know whether it has existence in the nature of things. Therefore it is clear that existence is something other than essence or quiddity, unless perhaps there be something the quiddity of which is its very existence. And this thing can only be one and primary, because it is impossible that a multiplication of anything should be effected except by virtue of the addition of some difference, as the nature of genus is multiplied into species either by virtue of this, that the form is received in diverse matters, just as the nature of species is multiplied in diverse individuals, or by virtue of this, that it is one thing absolutely but another as received in something, as for instance if there were a certain separated heat it would be other than a non-separated heat from its very separation. But if some thing is posited which is existence alone such that the existence itself is subsisting, this existence does not receive an addition of difference, since then it would not be existence only but existence and beyond that some form; and much less does it receive an addition of matter because then it would be not a subsisting existence but a material existence. Wherefore it is clear that a thing such that it is its own existence cannot be except as one (unique). Whence it follows necessarily that in anything whatsoever except this (the unique) its existence must be one thing and its quiddity or nature or form another. Accordingly, in intelligences there is an existence over and beyond form, and therefore it has been said that an intelligence is form and existence.

But all that belongs to anything is either caused

from principles of its nature, as for instance risibility in man, or accrues to it through some extrinsic principle, as for instance light in air from the influence of the sun. But it cannot be that existence itself should be caused by the form or quiddity of the thing, caused, I say, as by means of an efficient cause, because thus something would be the cause of itself and would bring its very self into existence, which is impossible. Therefore it follows that everything such that its existence is other than its nature has existence from another *(ab alio).* And because everything which exists by virtue of another is reduced to that which exists in virtue of itself *(per se),* as to its first cause, it follows that there must be something which is the cause of the existence *(causa essendi)* of all things, because it is very existence alone; otherwise the causes would proceed to infinity, since everything which is not existence alone would have a cause of its existence, as has been said. It is clear, therefore, that an intelligence is form and existence, and that it has its existence from the first being which is existence alone, and this is the first cause which is God. But everything which receives something from something *(aliquid ab aliquo)* is in potency in respect to that, and what is received in it is its act. Therefore it follows that the very quiddity or form which is the intelligence is in potency in respect to the existence which it receives from God, and that existence is received according to the mode of act. And thus potency and act are found in intelligences, yet not form and matter, except equivocally. Whence, too, to suffer, to receive, to be a subject and all things of this kind which are seen to belong to things by reason of matter, belong equivocally to intellectual substances and to corporeal substances, as the Commentator says in the third book of the *De Anima.* And because, as has been said, the quiddity of an intelligence is the intelligence itself, therefore its quiddity or essence is the same thing as itself, and its existence, received from God, is that by means of which it subsists in the nature of things. And for this reason substances of this sort are said by some to be composed of that by virtue of which it is *(quo est)* and that which it is *(quod est),* or of that which it is and existence, as Boethius says.

And since potency and act are posited in intelligences it will not be difficult to find a multitude of intelligences, which would be impossible if there were no potency in them. Whence the Commentator says in the third book of the *De Anima,* that if the nature of the possible intellect were unknown we should not be able to discover multiplicity in separate substances. Therefore the distinction of these in regard to one another is according to their grade (measure) of potency and act, so that a superior intelligence which is more proximate to the first (being) has more of act and less of potency, and so for others. And this is fulfilled in the human soul which holds the lowest grade among intellectual substances. Whence its possible intellect is disposed towards *(se habet ad)* intelligible forms just as first matter, which holds the lowest grade in sensible existence, is disposed towards sensible forms, as the Commentator remarks in book three on the *De Anima.* And therefore the Philosopher compares it to a tablet upon which nothing is written, and for this reason among other intelligible substances it has more potency. Accordingly, it is made to be so close to material things that the material thing is drawn to participate in its existence, so that from soul and body results one existence in one composite, although that existence according as it pertains to soul is not dependent upon the body. And therefore after that form which is in the soul are discovered other forms having more potency and more propinquity to matter. In these, too, is found order *(ordo)* and grade (measure: *gradus*) all the way through to the first forms of elements which are in the greatest propinquity to matter. Accordingly, they do not have any operation except according to the exigency of active and passive qualities, and of the others by which matter is disposed to form.

CHAPTER FIVE

Having understood the above, one knows clearly how essence is found in different things. For there is a threefold way of having an essence in substances. One way is like God, whose essence is His very existence; and therefore some philosophers are found who say that God does not have a quiddity or essence, since His essence is none other than His existence. And from this it follows that God is not in a genus, since everything which is in a genus must have a quiddity in addition to its existence, seeing that the quiddity or nature of genus or species is not distinguished according to a principle of nature in those things of which it is genus and species, but existence is different in different things. And indeed if we say that God is existence alone it is not necessary that we fall into the error of those who said that God is that universal existence in which everything exists formally. For the existence which is God is of a condition such that no addition can be made to it. Whence by virtue of its very purity it is existence distinct from every other existence, as for instance a certain separated color would by its very separation be different from non-separated color. For this reason it is observed in the comment on the ninth proposition of the book *De Causis* that the individuation of the first cause which is existence alone is by means of its pure goodness. But common existence, just as it does not include an addition to its concept, so, too, does not include in its concept any exclusion of addition, because if this were so nothing could be conceived to exist in which something over and above were added to existence. Similarly, too, although a being be existence alone, it does not follow that it should be wanting in the rest of the perfections and nobilities. Indeed God has the perfections which are in all genera, and for this reason He is called perfect simply, as the Philosopher and Commentator say in the fifth book of the *Metaphysics*, but He has these (perfections) in a more excellent mode than other things, because in Him they are one, but in other things they have diversity. And this is because all of these perfections belong to Him according to his simple existence; just as, if someone were able by means of one quality to effect the operations of all qualities, in that one quality he would have all qualities, so God in His very existence has all perfections.

According to the second mode essence is found in created intellectual substances in which the essence is other than their existence, although their essence is without matter. Whence their existence is not absolute but received and therefore according to the capacity of the receiving nature, but their nature or quiddity is absolute and not received in any matter. And therefore it is said in the book *De Causis* that intelligences are infinite from beneath and finite from above. For they are finite in respect to their existence which they receive from above, but they are not finite from below, since their forms are not limited to the capacity of any matter receiving them. And therefore in such substances there is not found a multitude of individuals in one species, as has been said, except in the instance of the human soul because of the body which is united to it. And although its individuation depends on the body as its occasion inasmuch as its (that of the individuation) beginning is concerned, seeing that the soul does not acquire individuated existence except in a body of which it is the act, still it does not follow that, the body being removed, the individuation would perish; because, since it (the soul) has absolute existence from the time individuated existence is acquired, in that it is made the form of this body, that existence always remains individuated. And therefore Avicenna says that the individuation of souls and their multitude depends upon the body in respect to their beginning but not in respect to their end. And because in those substances quiddity is not the same as existence therefore they are capable of being ordered in a predicament (category) and for this reason genus, species, and difference are found in them, although their proper differences are hidden from us. For in sensible things likewise the essential differences themselves are unknown; hence they are signified by means of the accidental differences which arise from their essential differences, as a cause is signified by means of its effect, as for instance biped is posited as the difference of man. But the proper accidents of immaterial substances are not known to us, and accordingly their differences cannot be signified by us either by virtue of themselves or by virtue of their accidental differences.

Still one ought to know that genus and difference are not taken in the same mode in those substances and in sensible substances, because in sensible substances genus is taken from that which is material in the thing, but difference is taken from that which is formal in it. Whence Avicenna says in the beginning of his book *De Anima* that form in things composed of matter and form "is the simple difference of that which is constituted from it," not, however, so that the form itself is the difference, but because it is the principle of the difference, as he says in his *Metaphysics.* And such difference is called simple difference, because it is taken from what is a part of the quiddity of the thing, namely, from the form. But since immaterial substances are simple quiddities, difference in them cannot be taken from that which is a part of the quiddity but from the whole quiddity. And therefore in the beginning of the *De Anima* Avicenna says that "simple difference . . . is not possessed except in those species the essences of which are composed of matter and form." Similarly also in these substances genus is taken from the whole essence, yet in a different mode. For one separate substance agrees with others in immateriality, and these substances differ from one another in their grade of perfection according to their recession from potentiality and their accession to pure act. And therefore in them genus is appropriated from that which ensues from them inasmuch as they are immaterial, as intellectuality or something of this sort. Difference, however, is appropriated from that which ensues from the grade of perfection in them and this is unknown to us. And yet it is not necessary that these differences be accidental, because they are according to greater and less perfection which does not diversify species; for the grade of perfection in receiving the same form does not diversify species, just as more white and less white in participating in the same principle of whiteness (does not), but a different grade of perfection in the very forms or natures participated does diversify species, as for instance nature proceeds by grades from plants to animals through certain (levels) which are mediate between animals and plants, according to the Philosopher in the eighth book of the *De Animalibus.* Nor again is it necessary that the division of intellectual substances be always through two true differences, because it is impossible for this to happen in all things, as the Philosopher says in the eleventh book of the *De Animalibus.*

In the third mode essence is found in substances composed of matter and form, in which also existence is received and finite because they have existence from another, and again their nature or quiddity is received in signated matter. And therefore they are finite from above and below, and in them furthermore a multiplication of individuals in one species is possible, because of the division of signated matter. And how their essence is disposed towards *(se habeat ad)* logical intentions has been discussed above.

CHAPTER SIX

It now remains to see how essence exists in accidents, for how it exists in all substances has been discussed. And because, as has been said, essence is what is signified by means of definition it is necessary that they (accidents) possess essence in the mode in which they have definition. But they have an incomplete definition because they cannot be defined unless a subject is posited in their definition; and this is because they do not have existence by virtue of themselves *(per se)* freed from *(absolutum)* the subject. But just as a substantial existence ensues from form and matter when composited, so, too, an accidental existence ensues from accident and subject when the accident advenes to the subject. And therefore neither has the substantial form itself complete essence, nor has matter; because likewise in the definition of substantial form it is necessary to posit that of which it is the form, and so its definition is by virtue of the addition of something which is outside its genus, as is also the definition of the accidental form. Whence in the definition of soul body is posited by the naturalist who considers the soul only inasmuch as it is the form of a physical body. But nevertheless there is a difference between substantial form and accidental form because, just as substantial form does not have an absolute existence by virtue of itself without that to which it advenes, so neither does that to which it advenes, namely, matter. And therefore from the conjunction of both ensues that existence in which the thing subsists by virtue of itself *(per se),* and from them is effected a unity by virtue of itself (*unum per se:* a substantial unity) for the reason that a certain essence ensues from their conjunction. Whence the form, although considered in itself *(in se)* it does not possess the complete ratio of essence, is nevertheless part of a complete essence. But that to which the accident advenes is a being complete in itself *(in se),* subsisting in its own existence; which certain existence naturally precedes the accident which supervenes to it. And therefore the supervening accident, from its conjunction with that to which it advenes, does not cause that existence in which the thing subsists, through which the thing is a being by virtue of itself *(ens per se),* but it causes a certain secondary existence, without which the subsisting thing can be conceived, as the first can be conceived without the second. Whence from an accident and a subject is not effected a unity by virtue of itself (*unum per se:* substantial unity), but a unity by virtue of accident (*unum per accidens:* accidental unity). And therefore from their conjunction a certain essence does not result, as from the conjunction of form with matter. For which reason an accident has neither the ratio of complete essence, nor is it a part of complete essence; but just as it is being in a certain respect *(secundum quid),* so also it has essence in a certain respect.

But because that which is in the greatest degree and most truly asserted in any genus whatsoever is the cause of those things which are posterior in that genus, as for instance fire which is the extreme of hotness is the cause of heat in hot things, as is also said in the second book of the *Metaphysics,* therefore substance, which is first in the genus of being, having essence most truly and in the greatest degree, is necessarily the cause of accidents which participate in the principle of being only secondarily and, as it were, in a certain respect *(secundum quid).* This however happens in diverse ways. For since the parts of a substance are matter and form, therefore certain accidents principally follow upon form, and others upon matter. Moreover, some form is found the existence of which does not depend on matter, as the intellective soul does not; but matter does not exist except by means of form. Whence in accidents which ensue from form there is something which has no communication with matter, as for instance to intellect, which is not by means of any corporeal organ, as the Philosopher proves in the third book of *De Anima.* But some of the things ensuing from the form have communication with matter, as for instance to sense, and things of this sort; but no accident ensues from matter without communication with form. Yet in these accidents which ensue from matter there is found a certain diversity. For certain accidents ensue from matter according to an order which they have to a special form, as for instance masculine and feminine in animals, the diversity of which is reduced to matter, as is said in the tenth book of the *Metaphysics.* Whence the form of animal being removed, the accidents do not remain except equivocally. Certain (accidents) ensue from matter according to an order which it has to a general form, and therefore, the special form being removed, they still remain (in the matter), as for instance blackness of skin is in the Ethiopian from a mixture of elements and not by reason of his soul, and therefore remains in him after death. And because each and every thing is individuated from its matter and disposed in a genus or a species by virtue of its form, therefore accidents which ensue from matter are accidents of the individual, according to which individuals of the same species differ from one another. But the accidents which ensue from form are proper passions of the genus or of the species, whence they are found in all things participating in the nature of the genus or of the species, as for instance risibility in man ensues from the form, since a laugh arises from some apprehension in the soul of a man.

One should know, too, that accidents are sometimes caused by the essential principles according to perfect act, as for instance heat in fire which is always hot in act; but at times (they are caused) only according to an aptitude, with completion accruing to them from an exterior agent, as for instance transparency in the air which is completed by means of a lucid external body. And in such instances the aptitude is an inseparable accident, but the complement, which ensues to it from some principle which is outside the essence of the thing or which does not enter into its constitution, will be separable, as for instance to be moved and things of this sort.

One should know therefore that in accidents genus, species and difference are taken in a mode other than that in which they are taken in substances. For since in substances there is effected from the substantial form and the matter a unity by virtue of itself (*per se unum:* a substantial unity), a certain nature resulting from their conjunction which is properly placed in the predicament (category) of substance, therefore in substances the concrete names which signify the composite are properly said to be in a genus, whether species or genus, as man or animal. However, neither form nor matter is in a predicament (category) in this mode except through reduction, as the former is said to be in a genus. But a substantial unity *(unum per se)* is not effected from an accident and its subject, and therefore no nature results from their conjunction to which the intention of genus or species can be attributed. Accordingly, the accidental names expressing a concretion, as for instance white man or musician, are not placed in a predicament (category), either as species or as genus, except by reduction, for they can be placed in a predicament only according to what is signified in the abstract, as for instance white or musical. And because accidents are not composed of matter and form, therefore in them it is not possible to take the genus from the matter and the difference from the form as in composite substances. But the genus must be taken primarily from its very mode of being inasmuch as being is asserted in diverse modes of the ten predicamental genera (categories) in accordance with the (order of) prior and posterior. So likewise it is called quantity according as it is the measure of substance and quality inasmuch as it is said to be a disposition of substance, and likewise for the others (predicamental genera), as the Philosopher states in the fourth of the *Metaphysics.* Indeed, difference in accidents is taken from the diversity of the principles from which they are caused. And because proper passions are caused from proper principles of the subject, therefore a subject is posited in their definition in place of difference, if they are defined abstractly *(in absoluto),* according to which manner of definition they are properly in a genus, as for instance it is said that snub-nosedness is a curvature of the nose. But the converse would hold if their definition were taken concretely. For thus the subject would be posited in their definition as their genus, seeing that they would then be defined as composite substances are, in which the ratio of the genus is taken from matter, as we say that a snub-nose is a curved nose. If one accident be the principle of another accident, the case is similar to the above, as for instance the principle of relation is action and passion and quantity; and therefore according to this the Philosopher divides relation in the *Metaphysics.* But since the proper principles of accidents are not always manifest, therefore sometimes we take the difference of accidents from their effects, as condensing and dispersing are called differences of color, which are caused from the abundance or paucity of light from which the different species of color result.

Thus, therefore, it is clear in what mode essence is in substances and in accidents, and in what mode it is in composite substances and in simple substances, and after what manner universal logical intentions are found in all these; with the exception of the First which is the extreme of simplicity, and to which because of its simplicity neither the ratio of genus, nor of species, nor, consequently, definition applies.

In which may the end and consummation of this discourse be. Amen.

From the Summa Theologica (Part One)

SECTION I

Question I

The Nature and Domain of Sacred Doctrine (in Ten Articles)

To place our purpose within definite limits, we must first investigate the nature and domain of sacred doctrine. Concerning this there are ten points of inquiry:—

(1) Whether sacred doctrine is necessary? (2) Whether it is a science? (3) Whether it is one or many? (4) Whether it is speculative or practical? (5) How it is compared with other sciences? (6) Whether it is a wisdom? (7) Whether God is its subject-matter? (8) Whether it is argumentative? (9) Whether it rightly employs metaphors and similes? (10) Whether the Sacred Scripture of this doctrine may be expounded in different senses?

FIRST ARTICLE

Whether, Besides the Philosophical Sciences, Any Further Doctrine Is Required?

We proceed thus to the First Article:—

Objection 1. It seems that, besides the philosophical sciences, we have no need of any further knowledge. For man should not seek to know what is above reason: *Seek not the things that are too high for thee (Ecclus.* iii. 22*).* But whatever is not above reason is sufficiently considered in the philosophical sciences. Therefore any other knowledge besides the philosophical sciences is superfluous.

Obj. 2. Further, knowledge can be concerned only with being, for nothing can be known, save the true, which is convertible with being. But everything that is, is considered in the philosophical sciences—even God Himself; so that there is a part of philosophy

---

From St. Thomas Aquinas, *Summa Theologica,* Part One, Section I, Questions 1, 2, Part One, Section VI, Questions 75 and 76, *Basic Writings of St. Thomas Aquinas,* trans. Anton C. Pegis (New York: Random House, 1945), pp. 5–6, 18–24, and 682–718. Reprinted by permission of the A.C. Pegis Estate.

called theology, or the divine science, as is clear from Aristotle. Therefore, besides the philosophical sciences, there is no need of any further knowledge.

On the contrary, It is written (*2 Tim.* iii. 16): *All Scripture inspired of God is profitable to teach, to reprove, to correct, to instruct in justice.* Now Scripture, inspired of God, is not a part of the philosophical sciences discovered by human reason. Therefore it is useful that besides the philosophical sciences there should be another science—*i.e.,* inspired of God.

I answer that, It was necessary for man's salvation that there should be a knowledge revealed by God, besides the philosophical sciences investigated by human reason. First, because man is directed to God as to an end that surpasses the grasp of his reason: *The eye hath not seen, O God, besides Thee, what things Thou hast prepared for them that wait for Thee* (*Isa.* lxiv. 4). But the end must first be known by men who are to direct their thoughts and actions to the end. Hence it was necessary for the salvation of man that certain truths which exceed human reason should be made known to him by divine revelation. Even as regards those truths about God which human reason can investigate, it was necessary that man be taught by a divine revelation. For the truth about God, such as reason can know it, would only be known by a few, and that after a long time, and with the admixture of many errors; whereas man's whole salvation, which is in God, depends upon the knowledge of this truth. Therefore, in order that the salvation of men might be brought about more fitly and more surely, it was necessary that they be taught divine truths by divine revelation. It was therefore necessary that, besides the philosophical sciences investigated by reason, there should be a sacred science by way of revelation.

Reply Obj. 1. Although those things which are beyond man's knowledge may not be sought for by man through his reason, nevertheless, what is revealed by God must be accepted through faith. Hence the sacred text continues, *For many things are shown to thee above the understanding of man* (*Ecclus.* iii. 25). And in such things sacred science consists.

Reply Obj. 2. Sciences are diversified according to the diverse nature of their knowable objects. For the astronomer and the physicist both prove the same conclusion—that the earth, for instance, is round: the astronomer by means of mathematics (*i.e.,* abstracting from matter), but the physicist by means of matter itself. Hence there is no reason why those things which are treated by the philosophical sciences, so far as they can be known by the light of natural reason, may not also be treated by another science so far as they are known by the light of the divine revelation. Hence the theology included in sacred doctrine differs in genus from that theology which is part of philosophy.

Question II

The Existence of God (in Three Articles)

Because the chief aim of sacred doctrine is to teach the knowledge of God not only as He is in Himself, but also as He is the beginning of things and their last end, and especially of rational creatures, as is clear from what has been already said, therefore, in our endeavor to expound this science, we shall treat: (1) of God; (2) of the rational creature's movement towards God; (3) of Christ Who as man is our way to God.

In treating of God there will be a threefold division:—

For we shall consider (1) whatever concerns the divine essence. (2) Whatever concerns the distinctions of Persons. (3) Whatever concerns the procession of creatures from Him.

Concerning the divine essence, we must consider:—

(1) Whether God exists? (2) The manner of His existence, or, rather, what is *not* the manner of His existence. (3) Whatever concerns His operations—namely, His knowledge, will, power.

Concerning the first, there are three points of inquiry:—

(1) Whether the proposition *God exists* is self-evident? (2) Whether it is demonstrable? (3) Whether God exists?

FIRST ARTICLE

Whether the Existence of God Is Self-Evident?

We proceed thus to the First Article:—

Objection 1. It seems that the existence of God is self-evident. For those things are said to be self-evident to us the knowledge of which exists naturally in us, as we can see in regard to first principles. But as Damascene says, *the knowledge of God is naturally implanted in all.* Therefore the existence of God is self-evident.

Obj. 2. Further, those things are said to be self-evident which are known as soon as the terms are known, which the Philosopher says is true of the first principles of demonstration. Thus, when the nature of a whole and of a part is known, it is at once recognized that every whole is greater than its part. But as soon as the signification of the name *God* is understood, it is at once seen that God exists. For by this name is signified that thing than which nothing greater can be conceived. But that which exists actually and mentally is greater than that which exists only mentally. Therefore, since as soon as the name *God* is understood it exists mentally, it also follows that it exists actually. Therefore the proposition *God exists* is self-evident.

Obj. 3. Further, the existence of truth is self-evident. For whoever denies the existence of truth grants that truth does not exist: and, if truth does not exist, then the proposition *Truth does not exist* is true: and if there is anything true, there must be truth. But God is truth itself: *I am the way, the truth, and the life* (*Jo.* xiv. 60). Therefore *God exists* is self-evident.

On the contrary, No one can mentally admit the opposite of what is self-evident, as the Philosopher states concerning the first principles of demonstration. But the opposite of the proposition *God is* can be mentally admitted: *The fool said in his heart, There is no God* (*Ps.* lii. 1). Therefore, that God exists is not self-evident.

I answer that, A thing can be self-evident in either of two ways: on the one hand, self-evident in itself, though not to us; on the other, self-evident in itself, and to us. A proposition is self-evident because the predicate is included in the essence of the subject: *e.g., Man is an animal,* for animal is contained in the essence of man. If, therefore, the essence of the predicate and subject be known to all, the proposition will be self-evident to all; as is clear with regard to the first principles of demonstration, the terms of which are certain common notions that no one is ignorant of, such as being and non-being, whole and part, and the like. If, however, there are some to whom the essence of the predicate and subject is unknown, the proposition will be self-evident in itself, but not to those who do not know the meaning of the predicate and subject of the proposition. Therefore, it happens, as Boethius says, that there are some notions of the mind which are common and self-evident only to the learned, as that incorporeal substances are not in space. Therefore I say that this proposition, *God exists,* of itself is self-evident, for the predicate is the same as the subject, because God is His own existence as will be hereafter shown. Now because we do not know the essence of God, the proposition is not self-evident to us, but needs to be demonstrated by things that are more known to us, though less known in their nature—namely, by His effects.

Reply Obj. 1. To know that God exists in a general and confused way is implanted in us by nature, inasmuch as God is man's beatitude. For man naturally desires happiness, and what is naturally desired by man is naturally known by him. This, however, is not to know absolutely that God exists; just as to know that someone is approaching is not the same as to know that Peter is approaching, even though it is Peter who is approaching; for there are many who imagine that man's perfect good, which is happiness, consists in riches, and others in pleasures, and others in something else.

Reply Obj. 2. Perhaps not everyone who hears this name *God* understands it to signify something than which nothing greater can be thought, seeing that some have believed God to be a body. Yet, granted that everyone understands that by this name *God* is signified something than which nothing greater can be thought, nevertheless, it does not therefore follow that he understands that what the name signifies exists actually, but only that it exists mentally. Nor can it be argued that it actually exists, unless it be admitted that there actually exists something than which nothing greater can be thought; and this precisely is not admitted by those who hold that God does not exist.

Reply Obj. 3. The existence of truth in general is self-evident, but the existence of a Primal Truth is not self-evident to us.

SECOND ARTICLE

Whether It Can Be Demonstrated That God Exists?

We proceed thus to the Second Article:—

Objection 1. It seems that the existence of God cannot be demonstrated. For it is an article of faith that

God exists. But what is of faith cannot be demonstrated, because a demonstration produces scientific knowledge, whereas faith is of the unseen, as is clear from the Apostle (*Heb.* xi. 1). Therefore it cannot be demonstrated that God exists.

Obj. 2. Further, essence is the middle term of demonstration. But we cannot know in what God's essence consists, but solely in what it does not consist, as Damascene says. Therefore we cannot demonstrate that God exists.

Obj. 3. Further, if the existence of God were demonstrated, this could only be from His effects. But His effects are not proportioned to Him, since He is infinite and His effects are finite, and between the finite and infinite there is no proportion. Therefore, since a cause cannot be demonstrated by an effect not proportioned to it, it seems that the existence of God cannot be demonstrated.

On the contrary, The Apostle says: *The invisible things of Him are clearly seen, being understood by the things that are made* (*Rom.* i. 20). But this would not be unless the existence of God could be demonstrated through the things that are made; for the first thing we must know of anything is, whether it exists.

I answer that, Demonstration can be made in two ways: One is through the cause, and is called *propter quid,* and this is to argue from what is prior absolutely. The other is through the effect, and is called a demonstration *quia;* this is to argue from what is prior relatively only to us. When an effect is better known to us than its cause, from the effect we proceed to the knowledge of the cause. And from every effect the existence of its proper cause can be demonstrated, so long as its effects are better known to us; because, since every effect depends upon its cause, if the effect exists, the cause must pre-exist. Hence the existence of God, in so far as it is not self-evident to us, can be demonstrated from those of His effects which are known to us.

Reply Obj. 1. The existence of God and other like truths about God, which can be known by natural reason, are not articles of faith, but are preambles to the articles; for faith presupposes natural knowledge, even as grace presupposes nature and perfection the perfectible. Nevertheless, there is nothing to prevent a man, who cannot grasp a proof, from accepting, as a matter of faith, something which in itself is capable of being scientifically known and demonstrated.

Reply Obj. 2. When the existence of a cause is demonstrated from an effect, this effect takes the place of the definition of the cause in proving the cause's existence. This is especially the case in regard to God, because, in order to prove the existence of anything, it is necessary to accept as a middle term the meaning of the name, and not its essence, for the question of its essence follows on the question of its existence. Now the names given to God are derived from His effects, as will be later shown. Consequently, in demonstrating the existence of God from His effects, we may take for the middle term the meaning of the name *God.*

Reply Obj. 3. From effects not proportioned to the cause no perfect knowledge of that cause can be obtained. Yet from every effect the existence of the cause can be clearly demonstrated, and so we can demonstrate the existence of God from His effects; though from them we cannot know God perfectly as He is in His essence.

THIRD ARTICLE

Whether God Exists?

We proceed thus to the Third Article:—

Objection 1. It seems that God does not exist; because if one of two contraries be infinite, the other would be altogether destroyed. But the name *God* means that He is infinite goodness. If, therefore, God existed, there would be no evil discoverable; but there is evil in the world. Therefore God does not exist.

Obj. 2. Further, it is superfluous to suppose that what can be accounted for by a few principles has been produced by many. But it seems that everything we see in the world can be accounted for by other principles, supposing God did not exist. For all natural things can be reduced to one principle, which is nature; and all voluntary things can be reduced to one principle, which is human reason, or will. Therefore there is no need to suppose God's existence.

On the contrary, It is said in the person of God: *I am Who am* (*Exod.* iii. 14).

I answer that, The existence of God can be proved in five ways.

The first and more manifest way is the argument

from motion. It is certain, and evident to our senses, that in the world some things are in motion. Now whatever is moved is moved by another, for nothing can be moved except it is in potentiality to that towards which it is moved; whereas a thing moves inasmuch as it is in act. For motion is nothing else than the reduction of something from potentiality to actuality. But nothing can be reduced from potentiality to actuality, except by something in a state of actuality. Thus that which is actually hot, as fire, makes wood, which is potentially hot, to be actually hot, and thereby moves and changes it. Now it is not possible that the same thing should be at once in actuality and potentiality in the same respect, but only in different respects. For what is actually hot cannot simultaneously be potentially hot; but it is simultaneously potentially cold. It is therefore impossible that in the same respect and in the same way a thing should be both mover and moved, *i.e.*, that it should move itself. Therefore, whatever is moved must be moved by another. If that by which it is moved be itself moved, then this also must needs be moved by another, and that by another again. But this cannot go on to infinity, because then there would be no first mover, and, consequently, no other mover, seeing that subsequent movers move only inasmuch as they are moved by the first mover; as the staff moves only because it is moved by the hand. Therefore it is necessary to arrive at a first mover, moved by no other; and this everyone understands to be God.

The second way is from the nature of efficient cause. In the world of sensible things we find there is an order of efficient causes. There is no case known (neither is it, indeed, possible) in which a thing is found to be the efficient cause of itself; for so it would be prior to itself, which is impossible. Now in efficient causes it is not possible to go on to infinity, because in all efficient causes following in order, the first is the cause of the intermediate cause, and the intermediate is the cause of the ultimate cause, whether the intermediate cause be several, or one only. Now to take away the cause is to take away the effect. Therefore, if there be no first cause among efficient causes, there will be no ultimate, nor any intermediate, cause. But if in efficient causes it is possible to go on to infinity, there will be no first efficient cause, neither will there be an ultimate effect, nor any intermediate efficient causes; all of which is plainly false. Therefore it is necessary to admit a first efficient cause, to which everyone gives the name of God.

The third way is taken from possibility and necessity, and runs thus. We find in nature things that are possible to be and not to be, since they are found to be generated, and to be corrupted, and consequently, it is possible for them to be and not to be. But it is impossible for these always to exist, for that which can not-be at some time is not. Therefore, if everything can not-be, then at one time there was nothing in existence. Now if this were true, even now there would be nothing in existence, because that which does not exist begins to exist only through something already existing. Therefore, if at one time nothing was in existence, it would have been impossible for anything to have begun to exist; and thus even now nothing would be in existence—which is absurd. Therefore, not all beings are merely possible, but there must exist something the existence of which is necessary. But every necessary thing either has its necessity caused by another, or not. Now it is impossible to go on to infinity in necessary things which have their necessity caused by another, as has been already proved in regard to efficient causes. Therefore we cannot but admit the existence of some being having of itself its own necessity, and not receiving it from another, but rather causing in others their necessity. This all men speak of as God.

The fourth way is taken from the gradation to be found in things. Among beings there are some more and some less good, true, noble, and the like. But *more* and *less* are predicated of different things according as they resemble in their different ways something which is the maximum, as a thing is said to be hotter according as it more nearly resembles that which is hottest; so that there is something which is truest, something best, something noblest, and, consequently, something which is most being, for those things that are greatest in truth are greatest in being, as it is written in *Metaph.* ii. Now the maximum in any genus is the cause of all in that genus, as fire, which is the maximum of heat, is the cause of all hot things, as is said in the same book. Therefore there must also be something which is to all beings the cause of their being, goodness, and every other perfection; and this we call God.

The fifth way is taken from the governance of the world. We see that things which lack knowledge, such as natural bodies, act for an end, and this is evident from their acting always, or nearly always, in the same way, so as to obtain the best result. Hence it is plain that they achieve their end, not fortuitously, but designedly. Now whatever lacks knowledge cannot move towards an end, unless it be directed by some being endowed with knowledge and intelligence; as the arrow is directed by the archer. Therefore some intelligent being exists by whom all natural things are directed to their end; and this being we call God.

Reply Obj. 1. As Augustine says: *Since God is the highest good, He would not allow any evil to exist in His works, unless His omnipotence and goodness were such as to bring good even out of evil.* This is part of the infinite goodness of God, that He should allow evil to exist, and out of it produce good.

Reply Obj. 2. Since nature works for a determinate end under the direction of a higher agent, whatever is done by nature must be traced back to God as to its first cause. So likewise whatever is done voluntarily must be traced back to some higher cause other than human reason and will, since these can change and fail; for all things that are changeable and capable of defect must be traced back to an immovable and self-necessary first principle, as has been shown.

SECTION VI: TREATISE ON MAN

Question LXXV

On Man Who Is Composed of a Spiritual and a Corporeal Substance: And First, Concerning What Belongs to the Essence of the Soul (in Seven Articles)

Having treated of the spiritual and of the corporeal creature, we now proceed to treat of man, who is composed of a spiritual and of a corporeal substance. We shall treat first of the nature of man, and secondly of his origin. Now the theologian considers the nature of man in relation to the soul, but not in relation to the body, except in so far as the body has relation to the soul. Hence the first object of our consideration will be the soul. And since Dionysius says that three things are to be found in spiritual substances—essence, power and operation—we shall treat first of what belongs to the essence of the soul; secondly, of what belongs to its power; thirdly, of what belongs to its operation.

Concerning the first, two points have to be considered; the first is the nature of the soul considered in itself; the second is the union of the soul with the body. Under the first head there are seven points of inquiry.

(1) Whether the soul is a body? (2) Whether the human soul is something subsistent? (3) Whether the souls of brute animals are subsistent? (4) Whether the soul is man, or is man composed of soul and body? (5) Whether the soul is composed of matter and form? (6) Whether the soul is incorruptible? (7) Whether the soul is of the same species as an angel?

FIRST ARTICLE

Whether the Soul Is a Body?

We proceed thus to the First Article:—

Objection 1. It would seem that the soul is a body. For the soul is the mover of the body. Nor does it move unless moved. First, because apparently nothing can move unless it is itself moved, since nothing gives what it has not. For instance, what is not hot does not give heat. Secondly, because if there be anything that moves and is itself not moved, it must be the cause of eternal and uniform movement, as we find proved *Physics* viii. Now this does not appear to be the case in the movement of an animal, which is caused by the soul. Therefore the soul is a moved mover. But every moved mover is a body. Therefore the soul is a body.

Obj. 2. Further, all knowledge is caused by means of a likeness. But there can be no likeness of a body to an incorporeal thing. If, therefore, the soul were not a body, it could not have knowledge of corporeal things.

Obj. 3. Further, between the mover and the moved there must be contact. But contact is only between bodies. Since, therefore, the soul moves the body, it seems that the soul must be a body.

On the contrary, Augustine says that the soul *is simple in comparison with the body, inasmuch as it does not occupy space by any bulk.*

I answer that, To seek the nature of the soul, we must premise that the soul is defined as the first principle of life in those things in our world which live; for we call living things *animate,* and those things which have no life, *inanimate.* Now life is shown principally by two activities, knowledge and movement. The philosophers of old, not being able to rise above their imagination, supposed that the principle of these actions was something corporeal; for they asserted that only bodies were real things, and that what is not corporeal is nothing. Hence they maintained that the soul is some sort of body. This opinion can be proved in many ways to be false; but we shall make use of only one proof, which shows quite universally and certainly that the soul is not a body.

It is manifest that not every principle of vital action is a soul, for then the eye would be a soul, as it is a principle of vision; and the same might be applied to the other instruments of the soul. But it is the *first* principle of life which we call the soul. Now, though a body may be a principle of life, as the heart is a principle of life in an animal, yet no body can be the first principle of life. For it is clear that to be a principle of life, or to be a living thing, does not belong to a body as a body, since, if that were the case, every body would be a living thing, or a principle of life. Therefore a body is competent to be a living thing or even a principle of life, as *such* a body. Now that it is actually such a body it owes to some principle which is called its act. Therefore the soul, which is the first principle of life, is not a body, but the act of a body; just as heat, which is the principle of calefaction, is not a body, but an act of a body.

Reply Obj. 1. Since everything which is moved must be moved by something else, a process which cannot be prolonged indefinitely, we must allow that not every mover is moved. For, since to be moved is to pass from potentiality to actuality, the mover gives what it has to the thing moved, inasmuch as it causes it to be in act. But, as is shown in *Physics* viii., there is a mover which is altogether immovable, and which is not moved either essentially or accidentally; and such a mover can cause an eternally uniform movement. There is, however, another kind of mover, which, though not moved essentially, is moved accidentally; and for this reason it does not cause a uniform movement. Such a mover is the soul. There is, again, another mover, which is moved essentially—namely, the body. And because the philosophers of old believed that nothing existed but bodies, they maintained that every mover is moved, and that the soul is moved essentially, and is a body.

St. Francis Renouncing his Inheritance, by Giotto (ca. 1300). In his sophisticated use of space, the medieval Italian painter Giotto anticipated Renaissance art. (Alinari/Art Resource)

Reply Obj. 2. It is not necessary that the likeness of the thing known be actually in the nature of the knower. But given a being which knows potentially, and afterwards knows actually, the likeness of the thing known must be in the nature of the knower, not actually, but only potentially; and thus color is not actually in the pupil of the eye, but only potentially. Hence it is necessary, not that the likeness of corporeal things be actually in the nature of the soul, but that there be a potentiality in the soul for such a likeness. But the ancient naturalists did not know how to distinguish between actuality and potentiality; and so they held that the soul must be a body in order to have knowledge of a body, and that it must be composed of the principles of which all bodies are formed.

Reply Obj. 3. There are two kinds of contact, that of *quantity*, and that of *power*. By the former a body can be touched only by a body; by the latter a body can be touched by an incorporeal reality, which moves that body.

SECOND ARTICLE

Whether the Human Soul Is Something Subsistent?

We proceed thus to the Second Article:—

Objection 1. It would seem that the human soul is not something subsistent. For that which subsists is said to be *this particular thing.* Now *this particular thing* is said not of the soul, but of that which is composed of soul and body. Therefore the soul is not something subsistent.

Obj. 2. Further, everything subsistent operates. But the soul does not operate, for, as the Philosopher says, *to say that the soul feels or understands is like saying that the soul weaves or builds.* Therefore the soul is not subsistent.

Obj. 3. Further, if the soul were something subsistent, it would have some operation apart from the body. But it has no operation apart from the body, not even that of understanding; for the act of understanding does not take place without a phantasm, which cannot exist apart from the body. Therefore the human soul is not something subsistent.

On the contrary, Augustine says: *Whoever understands that the nature of the mind is that of substance and not that of a body, will see that those who maintain the corporeal nature of the mind are led astray because they associate with the mind those things without which they are unable to think of any nature—i.e.,* imaginary pictures of corporeal things. Therefore the nature of the human mind is not only incorporeal, but it is also a substance, that is, something subsistent.

I answer that, It must necessarily be allowed that the principle of intellectual operation, which we call the soul of man, is a principle both incorporeal and subsistent. For it is clear that by means of the intellect man can know all corporeal things. Now whatever knows certain things cannot have any of them in its own nature, because that which is in it naturally would impede the knowledge of anything else. Thus we observe that a sick man's tongue, being unbalanced by a feverish and bitter humor, is insensible to anything sweet, and everything seems bitter to it. Therefore, if the intellectual principle contained within itself the nature of any body, it would be unable to know all bodies. Now every body has its own determinate nature. Therefore it is impossible for the intellectual principle to be a body. It is also impossible for it to understand by means of a bodily organ, since the determinate nature of that organ would likewise impede knowledge of all bodies; as when a certain determinate color is not only in the pupil of the eye, but also in a glass vase, the liquid in the vase seems to be of that same color.

Therefore the intellectual principle, which we call the mind or the intellect, has essentially an operation in which the body does not share. Now only that which subsists in itself can have an operation in itself. For nothing can operate but what is actual, and so a thing operates according as it is; for which reason we do not say that heat imparts heat, but that what is hot gives heat. We must conclude, therefore, that the human soul, which is called intellect or mind, is something incorporeal and subsistent.

Reply Obj. 1. This particular thing can be taken in two senses. Firstly, for anything subsistent; secondly, for that which subsists and is complete in a specific nature. The former sense excludes the inherence of an accident or of a material form; the latter excludes also the imperfection of the part, so that a hand can be called *this particular thing* in the first sense, but not in the second. Therefore, since the human soul is a part of human nature, it can be called *this particular thing* in the first sense, as being something subsistent; but not in the second, for in this sense the composite of body and soul is said to be *this particiar thing.*

Reply Obj. 2. Aristotle wrote those words as expressing, not his own opinion, but the opinion of those who said that to understand is to be moved, as is clear from the context. Or we may reply that to operate through itself belongs to what exists through itself. But for a thing to exist through itself, it suffices sometimes that it be not inherent, as an accident or a material form; even though it be part of something. Nevertheless, that is rightly said to subsist through itself which is neither inherent in the above sense, nor part of anything else. In this sense, the eye or the hand cannot be said to subsist through itself; nor can it for that reason be said to operate through itself. Hence the operation of the parts is through each part attributed to the whole. For we say that man sees with the eye, and feels with the hand, and not in the same sense as when we say that what is hot gives heat by its heat; for heat, strictly speaking, does not give heat. We may therefore say that the soul understands just as the eye sees; but it is more correct to say that man understands through the soul.

Reply Obj. 3. The body is necessary for the action of the intellect, not as its organ of action, but on the part of the object; for the phantasm is to the intellect what color is to the sight. Neither does such a dependence on the body prove the intellect to be non-subsistent, or otherwise it would follow that an animal is non-subsistent simply because it requires external sensibles for sensation.

THIRD ARTICLE

Whether the Souls of Brute Animals Are Subsistent?

We proceed thus to the Third Article:—

Objection 1. It would seem that the souls of brute animals are subsistent. For man is of the same genus as other animals, and, as we have shown, the soul of man is subsistent. Therefore the souls of other animals are subsistent.

Obj. 2. Further, the relation of the sensitive power to sensible objects is like the relation of the intellectual power to intelligible objects. But the intellect, without the body, apprehends intelligible objects. Therefore the sensitive power, without the body, perceives sensible objects. Therefore, since the souls of brute animals are sensitive, they are subsistent, for the same reason that the human soul, which is intellectual, is subsistent.

Obj. 3. Further, the soul of brute animals moves the body. But the body is not a mover, but is moved. Therefore the soul of brute animals has an operation apart from the body.

On the contrary, Is what is written in the book *De Ecclesiasticis Dogmatibus: Man alone we believe to have a subsistent soul; whereas the souls of animals are not subsistent.*

I answer that, The early philosophers made no distinction between sense and intellect, and referred both to a corporeal principle, as has been said. Plato, however, drew a distinction between intellect and sense, but he referred both to an incorporeal principle, maintaining that sensing, like understanding, belongs to the soul as such. From this it follows that even the souls of brute animals are subsistent. But Aristotle held that, of the operations of the soul, understanding alone is performed without a corporeal organ. On the other hand, sensation and the attendant operations of the sensitive soul are evidently accompanied with change in the body; and thus, in the act of vision, the pupil of the eye is affected by the likeness of color. So with the other senses. Hence it is clear that the sensitive soul has no *per se* operation of its own, and that every operation of the sensitive soul belongs to the composite. Therefore we conclude that as the souls of brute animals have no *per se* operations they are not subsistent. For the operation of anything follows the mode of its being.

Reply Obj. 1. Although man is of the same *genus* as other animals, he is of a different *species.* Now, specific difference is derived form the difference of form; nor does every difference of form necessarily imply a diversity of *genus.*

Reply Obj. 2. The relation of the sensitive power to the sensible object is in one way the same as that of the intellectual power to the intelligible object, in so far as each is in potentiality to its object. But in another way their relations differ, inasmuch as the impression of the sensible on the sense is accompanied with change in the body; so that when the intensity of the sensible is excessive, the sense is corrupted. This is a thing that never occurs in the case of the intellect. For an intellect that understands the highest of intelligible objects is more able afterwards to understand those that are lower.—If, however, in the process of intellectual operation the body is weary, this result is accidental, inasmuch as the intellect requires the operation of the sensitive powers in the production of the phantasms.

Reply Obj. 3. A motive power is of two kinds. One, the appetitive power, which commands motion. The operation of this power in the sensitive soul is not without the body; for anger, joy and passions of a like nature are accompanied by some change in the body. The other motive power is that which executes motion in adapting the members for obeying the appetite; and the act of this power does not consist in moving, but in being moved. Whence it is clear that to move is not an act of the sensitive soul without the body.

FOURTH ARTICLE

Whether the Soul Is Man?

We proceed thus to the Fourth Article:—

Objection 1. It would seem that the soul is man. For it is written (*2 Cor.* iv. 16): *Though our outward man is corrupted, yet the inward man is renewed day by day.* But that which is within man is the soul. Therefore the soul is the inward man.

Obj. 2. Further, the human soul is a substance. But it is not a universal substance. Therefore it is a particular substance. Therefore it is a *hypostasis* or a person; and it can be only a human person. Therefore the soul is a man, for a human person is a man.

On the contrary, Augustine commends Varro as holding *that man is not the soul alone, nor the body alone, but both soul and body.*

I answer that, The assertion, *the soul is a man,* can be taken in two senses. First, that man is a soul, though this particular man (Socrates, for instance) is not a soul, but composed of soul and body. I say this, because some held that the form alone belongs to the species, while matter is part of the individual, and not of the species. This cannot be true, for to the nature of the species belongs what the definition signifies, and in natural things the definition does not signify the form only, but the form and the matter. Hence, in natural things the matter is part of the species; not, indeed, signate matter, which is the principle of individuation, but common matter. For just as it belongs to the nature of this particular man to be composed of this soul, of this flesh, and of these bones, so it belongs to the nature of man to be composed of soul, flesh, and bones; for whatever belongs in common to the substance of all the individuals contained under a given species must belong also to the substance of the species.

That *the soul is a man* may also be understood in this sense, namely, that this soul is this man. Now this could be held if it were supposed that the operation of the sensitive soul were proper to it without the body; because in that case all the operations which are attributed to man would belong only to the soul. But each thing is that which performs its own operations, and consequently that is man which performs the operations of a man. But it has been shown above that sensation is not the operation of the soul alone. Since, then, sensation is an operation of man, but not proper to the soul, it is clear that man is not only a soul, but something composed of soul and body.—Plato, through supposing that sensation was proper to the soul, could maintain man to be *a soul making use of a body.*

Reply Obj. 2. According to the Philosopher, each thing seems to be chiefly what is most important in it. Thus, what the governor of a state does, the state is said to do. In this way sometimes what is most important in man is said to be man: sometimes it is the intellectual part which, in accordance with truth, is called the *inward* man; and sometimes the sensitive part with the body is called man in the opinion of those who remain the slaves of sensible things. And this is called the *outward* man.

Reply Obj. 2. Not every particular substance is a hypostasis or a person, but that which has the complete nature of its species. Hence a hand, or a foot, is not called a hypostasis, or a person; nor, likewise, is the soul alone so called, since it is a part of the human species.

FIFTH ARTICLE

Whether the Soul Is Composed of Matter and Form?

We proceed thus to the Fifth Article:—

Objection 1. It would seem that the soul is composed of matter and form. For potentiality is opposed to actuality. Now, whatsoever things are in actuality participate in the First Act, which is God. It is by participation in God that all things are good, beings, and living things, as is clear from the teachings of Dionysius. Therefore, whatsoever things are in potentiality participate in the first potentiality. But the first potentiality is primary matter. Therefore, since the human soul is, after a manner, in potentiality (which appears from the fact that sometimes a man is potentially understanding), it seems that the human soul must participate in primary matter, as a part of itself.

Obj. 2. Further, wherever the properties of matter are found, there matter is. But the properties of matter are found in the soul—namely, to be a subject, and to be changed. For the soul is subject to science, and virtue; and it changes from ignorance to knowledge and from vice to virtue. Therefore there is matter in the soul.

Obj. 3. Further, things which have no matter have no cause of their being, as the Philosopher says in *Metaph.* viii. But the soul has a cause of its being, since it is created by God. Therefore the soul has matter.

Obj. 4. Further, what has no matter, and is only a form, is a pure act, and is infinite. But this belongs to God alone. Therefore the soul has matter.

On the contrary, Augustine proves that the soul was made neither of corporeal matter, nor of spiritual matter.

I answer that, The soul has no matter. We may consider this question in two ways. First, from the notion of a soul in general, for it belongs to the notion of a soul to be the form of a body. Now, either it is a form in its entirety, or by virtue of some part of itself. If in its entirety, then it is impossible that any part of it should be matter, if by matter we understand something purely potential; for a form, as such, is an act, and that which is purely potential cannot be part of an act, since potentiality is repugnant to actuality as being its opposite. If, however, it be a form by virtue of a part of itself, then we shall call that part the soul, and that matter, which it actualizes first, we shall call the *primary animate.*

Secondly, we may proceed from the specific notion of the human soul, inasmuch as it is intellectual. For it is clear that whatever is received into something is received according to the condition of the recipient. Now a thing is known in as far as its form is in the knower. But the intellectual soul knows a thing in its nature absolutely: for instance, it knows a stone absolutely as a stone; and therefore the form of a stone absolutely, as to its proper formal notion, is in the intellectual soul. Therefore the intellectual soul itself is an absolute form, and not something composed of matter and form. For if the intellectual soul were composed of matter and form, the forms of things would be received into it as individuals, and so it would only know the individual; just as it happens with the sensitive powers which receive forms in a corporeal organ. For matter is the principle by which forms are individuated. It follows, therefore, that the intellectual soul, and every intellectual substance which has knowledge of forms absolutely, is exempt from composition of matter and form.

Reply Obj. 1. The First Act is the universal principle of all acts, because It is infinite, *precontaining all things* in its power, as Dionysius says. Therefore It is participated in by things, not as a part of themselves, but by diffusion of Its processions. Now as potentiality is receptive of act, it must be proportionate to act. But the acts received which proceed from the First Infinite Act, and are participations thereof, are diverse, so that there cannot be one potentiality which receives all acts, in the same way that there is one act from which all participated acts are derived; for then the receptive potentiality would equal the active potentiality of the First Act. Now the receptive potentiality in the intellectual soul is other than the receptive potentiality of primary matter, as appears from the diversity of the things received by each. For primary matter receives individual forms; whereas the intellect receives absolute forms. Hence the existence of such a potentiality in the intellectual soul does not prove that the soul is composed of matter and form.

Reply Obj. 2. To be a subject and to be changed belong to matter by reason of its being in potentiality. Just as, therefore, the potentiality of the intellect is one thing and the potentiality of primary matter another, so in each is there a different manner of subjection and change. For the intellect is subject to knowledge, and is changed from ignorance to knowledge, by reason of its being in potentiality with regard to the intelligible species.

Reply Obj. 3. The form causes matter to be, and so does the agent; and so, the agent causes matter to be in so far as it changes it to the actuality of the form. A subsistent form, however, does not owe its being to some formal principle, nor has it a cause changing it from potentiality to act. So after the words quoted above, the Philosopher concludes that in things composed of matter and form *there is no other cause but that which moves from potentiality to act; while whatsoever things have no matter are truly beings in themselves.*

Reply Obj. 4. Everything participated is compared to the participator as its act. But whatever created form be supposed to subsist *per se,* must have being by participation, for *even life,* or anything of that sort, *is a participator of being,* as Dionysius says. Now participated being is limited by the capacity of the participator; so that God alone, Who is His own being, is pure act and infinite. But in intellectual substances, there is composition of actuality and potentiality, not, indeed, of matter and form, but of form and participated being. Therefore some say that they are composed of that *whereby they are* and that *which they are;* for being itself is that by which a thing is.

SIXTH ARTICLE

Whether the Human Soul Is Corruptible?

We proceed thus to the Sixth Article:—

Objection 1. It would seem that the human soul is corruptible. For those things that have a like beginning and process seemingly have a like end. But the beginning, by generation, of men is like that of animals, for they are made from the earth. And the process of life is alike in both; because *all things breathe alike, and man hath nothing more than the beast,* as it is written (*Eccles.* iii. 19). Therefore, as the same text concludes, *the death of man and beast is one, and the condition of both is equal.* But the souls of brute animals are corruptible. Therefore the human soul too is corruptible.

Obj. 2. Further, whatever is out of nothing can return to nothingness, because the end should correspond to the beginning. But as it is written (*Wis.* ii. 2), *We are born of nothing;* and this is true, not only of the body, but also of the soul. Therefore, as is concluded in the same passage, *After this we shall be as if we had not been,* even as to our soul.

Obj. 3. Further, nothing is without its own proper operation. But the operation proper to the soul, which is to understand through a phantasm, cannot be without the body. For the soul understands nothing without a phantasm, and *there is no phantasm without the body,* as the Philosopher says. Therefore the soul cannot survive the dissolution of the body.

On the contrary, Dionysius says that human souls owe to divine goodness that they are *intellectual,* and that they have *an incorruptible substantial life.*

I answer that, We must assert that the intellectual principle which we call the human soul is incorruptible. For a thing may be corrupted in two ways—in itself and accidentally. Now it is impossible for any subsistent being to be generated or corrupted accidentally, that is, by the generation or corruption of something else. For generation and corruption belong to a thing in the same way that being belongs to it, which is acquired by generation and lost by corruption. Therefore, whatever has being in itself cannot be generated or corrupted except in itself; while things which do not subsist, such as accidents and material forms, acquire being or lose it through the generation or corruption of composites. Now it was shown above that the souls of brutes are not self-subsistent, whereas the human soul is, so that the souls of brutes are corrupted, when their bodies are corrupted, while the human soul could not be corrupted unless it were corrupted in itself. This is impossible, not only as regards the human soul, but also as regards anything subsistent that is a form alone. For it is clear that what belongs to a thing by virtue of the thing itself is inseparable from it. But being belongs to a form, which is an act, by virtue of itself. And thus, matter acquires actual being according as it acquires form; while it is corrupted so far as the form is separated from it. But it is impossible for a form to be separated from itself; and therefore it is impossible for a subsistent form to cease to exist.

Granted even that the soul were composed of matter and form, as some pretend, we should nevertheless have to maintain that it is incorruptible. For corruption is found only where there is contrariety, since generation and corruption are from contraries and into contraries. Therefore the heavenly bodies, since they have no matter subject to contrariety, are incorruptible. Now there can be no contrariety in the intellectual soul; for it is a receiving subject according to the manner of its being, and those things which it receives are without contrariety. Thus, the notions even of contraries are not themselves contrary, since contraries belong to the same science. Therefore it is impossible for the intellectual soul to be corruptible.

Moreover we may take a sign of this from the fact that everything naturally aspires to being after its own manner. Now, in things that have knowledge, desire ensues upon knowledge. The senses indeed do not know being, except under the conditions of *here* and *now,* whereas the intellect apprehends being absolutely, and for all time; so that everything that has an intellect naturally desires always to exist. But a natural desire cannot be in vain. Therefore every intellectual substance is incorruptible.

Reply Obj. 1. Solomon reasons thus in the person of the foolish, as expressed in the words of *Wis.* ii. Therefore the saying that man and animals have a like beginning in generation is true of the body; for all animals alike are made of earth. But it is not true of the soul. For while the souls of brutes are produced by some power of the body, the human soul is produced by God. To signify this, it is written of other animals: *Let the earth bring forth the living soul* (*Gen.* i. 24); while of man it is written (*Gen.* ii. 7) that *He breathed into his face the breath of life.* And so in the last chapter of *Ecclesiastes* (xii. 7) it is concluded: *The dust returns into its earth from whence it was; and the spirit returns to God Who gave it.* Again, the process of life is alike as to the body, concerning which it is written (*Eccles.* iii. 19): *All things breathe alike,* and (*Wis.* ii. 2), *The breath in our nostrils is smoke.* But the process is not alike in the case of the soul, for man has understanding whereas animals do not. Hence it is false to say: *Man has nothing more than beasts.* Thus death comes to both alike as to the body, but not as to the soul.

Reply Obj. 2. As a thing can be created, not by reason of a passive potentiality, but only by reason of the active potentiality of the Creator, Who can produce something out of nothing, so when we say that a thing can be reduced to nothing, we do not imply in the creature a potentiality to non-being, but in the Creator the power of ceasing to sustain being. But a thing is said to be corruptible because there is in it a potentiality to non-being.

Reply Obj. 3. To understand through a phantasm is the proper operation of the soul by virtue of its union with the body. After separation from the body, it will have another mode of understanding, similar to other substances separated from bodies, as will appear later on.

SEVENTH ARTICLE

Whether the Soul Is of the Same Species as an Angel?

We proceed thus to the Seventh Article:—

Objection 1. It would seem that the soul is of the same species as an angel. For each thing is ordained to its proper end by the nature of its species, whence is derived its inclination for that end. But the end of the soul is the same as that of an angel—namely, eternal happiness. Therefore they are of the same species.

Obj. 2. Further, the ultimate specific difference is the noblest, because it completes the nature of the species. But there is nothing nobler either in an angel or in the soul than their intellectual being. Therefore the soul and the angel agree in the ultimate specific difference. Therefore they belong to the same species.

Obj. 3. Further, it seems that the soul does not differ from an angel except in its union with the body. But as the body is outside the essence of the soul, it does not seem to belong to its species. Therefore the soul and an angel are of the same species.

On the contrary, Things which have different natural operations are of different species. But the natural operations of the soul and of an angel are different, since, as Dionysius says, *Angelic minds have simple and blessed intellects, not gathering their knowledge of divine things from visible things.* Subsequently he says the contrary of this about the soul. Therefore the soul and an angel are not of the same species.

I answer that, Origen held that human souls and angels are all of the same species, and this because he supposed that in these substances the difference of degree was accidental, resulting from their free choice, as we have seen above. But this cannot be, for in incorporeal substances there cannot be diversity of number without diversity of species and inequality of nature; because, as they are not composed of matter and form, but are subsistent forms, it is clear that there is necessarily among them a diversity in species. For a separate form cannot be understood otherwise than as one of a single species. Thus, supposing a separate whiteness to exist, it could only be one, for one whiteness does not differ from another except as in this or that subject. But diversity of species is always accompanied by diversity of nature. Thus, in the species of colors, one is more perfect than another; and the same applies to other species, because differences which divide a *genus* are contrary to one another. Contraries, however, are compared to one another as the perfect to the imperfect, since the *principle of contrariety is habit and privation,* as is written, *Metaph.* x.

The same would follow if the aforesaid substances were composed of matter and form. For if the matter of one be distinct from the matter of another, it is required either that the form be the principle of the distinction of matter—that is to say, that the matter is distinct because of its relation to diverse forms, in which case there would still result a difference of species and an inequality of nature; or else that the matter is the principle of the distinction of forms.

But one matter cannot be distinct from another, except by a distinction of quantity, which has no place in these incorporeal substances, such as an angel and the soul. Hence, it is not possible for the angel and the soul to be of the same species. How it is that there can be many souls of one species will be explained later.

Reply Obj. 1. This argument is concerned with the proximate and natural end. Eternal happiness, however, is the ultimate and supernatural end.

Reply Obj. 2. The ultimate specific difference is the noblest because it is the most determinate, in the same way as actuality is nobler than potentiality. Thus, however, that which is intellectual is not the noblest, because it is indeterminate and common to many degrees of intellectuality; just as the sensible is common to many degrees of sensible being. Hence, just as all sensible things are not of one species, so neither are all intellectual beings of one species.

Reply Obj. 3. The body is not of the essence of the soul, but the soul, by nature of its essence, can be united to the body; so that, properly speaking, it is not even the soul, but rather the *composite*, which is in the species. And the very fact that the soul in a certain way requires the body for its operation proves that the soul is endowed with a grade of intellectuality inferior to that of an angel, who is not united to a body.

Question LXXVI

The Union of Body and Soul (in Eight Articles)

We now consider the union of the soul with the body, on which there are eight points for inquiry: (1) Whether the intellectual principle is united to the body as its form? (2) Whether the intellectual principle is multiplied numerically according to the number of bodies, or is there one intellect for all men? (3) Whether in a body, the form of which is an intellectual principle, there is some other soul? (4) Whether in that body there is any other substantial form? (5) Of the qualities required in the body of which the intellectual principle is the form? (6) Whether the intellectual soul is joined to the body by means of accidental dispositions? (7) Whether the intellectual soul is united to such a body by means of another body? (8) Whether the soul is wholly in each part of the body?

FIRST ARTICLE

Whether the Intellectual Principle Is United to the Body as Its Form?

We proceed thus to the First Article:—

Objection 1. It seems that the intellectual principle is not united to the body as its form. For the Philosopher says that *the intellect is separate,* and that it is not the act of any body. Therefore it is not united to the body as its form.

Obj. 2. Further, every form is determined according to the nature of the matter of which it is the form; otherwise no proportion would be required between matter and form. Therefore if the intellect were united to the body as its form, since every body has a determinate nature, it would follow that the intellect has a determinate nature; and thus, it would not be capable of knowing all things, as is clear from what has been said. This is contrary to the nature of the intellect. Therefore the intellect is not united to the body as its form.

Obj. 3. Further, whatever receptive power is an act of a body, receives a form materially and individually; for what is received must be received according to the condition of the receiver. But the form of the thing understood is not received into the intellect materially and individually, but rather immaterially and universally. Otherwise, the intellect would not be capable of knowing immaterial and universal objects, but only individuals, like the senses. Therefore the intellect is not united to the body as its form.

Obj. 4. Further, power and action have the same subject, for the same subject is what can, and does, act. But intellectual action is not the action of a body, as appears from the above. Therefore neither is the intellectual power a power of the body. But a virtue or a power cannot be more abstract or more simple than the essence from which the virtue or power is derived. Therefore, neither is the substance of the intellect the form of a body.

Obj. 5. Further, whatever has being in itself is not united to the body as its form, because a form is that *by which* a thing exists; which means that the very being of a form does not belong to the form by itself. But the intellectual principle has being in itself and is subsistent, as was said above. Therefore it is not united to the body as its form.

Obj. 6. Further, whatever exists in a thing by reason of its nature exists in it always. But to be united to matter belongs to the form by reason of its nature, because form is the act of matter, not by any accidental quality, but by its own essence; or otherwise matter and form would not make a thing substantially one, but only accidentally one. Therefore, a form cannot be without its own proper matter. But the intellectual principle, since it is incorruptible, as was shown above, remains separate from the body, after the dissolution of the body. Therefore the intellectual principle is not united to the body as its form.

On the contrary, According to the Philosopher in *Metaph.* viii., difference is derived from the form. But the difference which constitutes man is *rational,* which is said of man because of his intellectual principle. Therefore the intellectual principle is the form of man.

I answer that, We must assert that the intellect which is the principle of intellectual operation is the form of the human body. For that whereby primarily anything acts is a form of the thing to which the act is attributed. For instance, that whereby a body is primarily healed is health, and that whereby the soul knows primarily is knowledge; hence health is a form of the body, and knowledge is a form of the soul. The reason for this is that nothing acts except so far as it is in act; and so, a thing acts by that whereby it is in act. Now it is clear that the first thing by which the body lives is the soul. And as life appears through various operations in different degrees of living things, that whereby we primarily perform each of all these vital actions is the soul. For the soul is the primary principle of our nourishment, sensation, and local movement; and likewise of our understanding. Therefore this principle by which primarily we understand, whether it be called the intellect or the intellectual soul, is the form of the body. This is the demonstration used by Aristotle.

But if anyone say that the intellectual soul is not the form of the body, he must explain how it is that this action of understanding is the action of this particular man; for each one is conscious that it is he himself who understands. Now an action may be attributed to anyone in three ways, as is clear from the Philosopher. For a thing is said to move or act, either by virtue of its whole self, for instance, as a physician heals; or by virtue of a part, as a man sees by his eye; or through an accidental quality, as when we say that something that is white builds, because it is accidental to the builder to be white. So when we say that Socrates or Plato understands, it is clear that this is not attributed to him accidentally, since it is ascribed to him as man, which is predicated of him essentially. We must therefore say either that Socrates understands by virtue of his whole self, as Plato maintained, holding that man is an intellectual soul; or that the intellect is a part of Socrates. The first cannot stand, as was shown above, because it is one and the same man who is conscious both that he understands and that he senses. But one cannot sense without a body, and therefore the body must be some part of man. It follows therefore that the intellect by which Socrates understands is a part of Socrates, so that it is in some way united to the body of Socrates.

As to this union, the Commentator held that it is through the intelligible species, as having a double subject, namely, the possible intellect and the phantasms which are in the corporeal organs. Thus, through the intelligible species, the possible intellect *is linked* to the body of this or that particular man. But this link or union does not sufficiently explain the fact that the act of the intellect is the act of Socrates. This can be clearly seen from comparison with the sensitive power, from which Aristotle proceeds to consider things relating to the intellect. For the relation of phantasms to the intellect is like the relation of colors to the sense of sight, as he says *De Anima* iii. Therefore, just as the species of colors are in the sight, so the species of phantasms are in the possible intellect. Now it is clear that because the colors, the likenesses of which are in the sight, are on a wall, the action of seeing is not attributed to the wall; for we do not say that the wall sees, but rather that it is seen. Therefore, from the fact that the species of phantasms are in the possible intellect, it does not follow that Socrates, in whom are the phantasms, understands, but that he or his phantasms are understood.

Some, however, have tried to maintain that the intellect is united to the body as its mover, and hence that the intellect and body form one thing in such a way that the act of the intellect could be attributed to the whole. This is, however, absurd for many reasons. First, because the intellect does not move the body except through the appetite, whose movement presupposes the operation of the intellect. The reason therefore why Socrates understands is not because he is moved by his intellect, but rather, contrariwise, he is moved by his intellect because he understands.—Secondly, because, since Socrates is an individual in a nature of one essence composed of matter and form, if the intellect be not the form, it follows that it must be outside the essence, and then the intellect is to the whole Socrates as a motor to the thing moved. But to understand is an action that remains in the agent, and does not pass into something else, as does the action of heating. Therefore the action of understanding cannot be attributed to Socrates for the reason that he is moved by his intellect.—Thirdly, because the action of a mover is never attributed to the thing moved, except as to an instrument, just as the action of a carpenter is attributed to a saw. Therefore, if understanding is attributed to Socrates as the action of his mover, it follows that it is attributed to him as to an instrument. This is contrary to the teaching of the Philosopher, who holds that understanding is not possible through a corporeal instrument.—Fourthly, because, although the action of a part be attributed to the whole, as the action of the eye is attributed to a man, yet it is never attributed to another part, except perhaps accidentally; for we do not say that the hand sees because the eye sees. Therefore, if the intellect and Socrates are united in the above manner, the action of the intellect cannot be attributed to Socrates. If, however, Socrates be a whole composed of a union of the intellect with whatever else belongs to Socrates, but with the supposition that the intellect is united to the other parts of Socrates only as a mover, it follows that Socrates is not one absolutely, and consequently neither a being absolutely, for a thing is a being according as it is one.

There remains, therefore, no other explanation than that given by Aristotle—namely, that this particular man understands because the intellectual principle is his form. Thus from the very operation of the intellect it is made clear that the intellectual principle is united to the body as its form.

The same can be clearly shown from the nature of the human species. For the nature of each thing is shown by its operation. Now the proper operation of man as man is to understand, for it is in this that he surpasses all animals. Whence Aristotle concludes that the ultimate happiness of man must consist in this operation as properly belonging to him. Man must therefore derive his species from that which is the principle of this operation. But the species of each thing is derived from its form. It follows therefore that the intellectual principle is the proper form of man.

But we must observe that the nobler a form is, the more it rises above corporeal matter, the less it is subject to matter, and the more it excels matter by its power and its operation. Hence we find that the form of a mixed body has an operation not caused by its elemental qualities. And the higher we advance in the nobility of forms, the more we find that the power of the form excels the elementary matter; as the vegetative soul excels the form of the metal, and the sensitive soul excels the vegetative soul. Now the human soul is the highest and noblest of forms. Therefore, in its power it excels corporeal matter by the fact that it has an operation and a power in which corporeal matter has no share whatever. This power is called the intellect.

It is well to remark, furthermore, that if anyone held that the soul is composed of matter and form, it would follow that in no way could the soul be the form of the body. For since form is an act, and matter is being only in potentiality, that which is composed of matter and form cannot in its entirety be the form of another. But if it is a form by virtue of some part of itself, then that part which is the form we call the soul, and that of which it is the form we call the *primary animate,* as was said above.

Reply Obj. 1. As the Philosopher says, the highest natural form (namely, the human soul) to which the consideration of the natural philospher is directed is indeed separate, but it exists in matter. He proves this from the fact that *man and the sun generate man from matter.* It is separate according to its intellectual power, because an intellectual power is not the power of a corporeal organ, as the power of seeing is the act of the eye; for understanding is an act which cannot be performed by a corporeal organ, as can the act of seeing. But it exists in matter in so far as the soul itself, to which this power belongs, is the form of the body, and the term of human generation. And so the Philosopher says that *the intellect is separate,* because it is not the power of a corporeal organ.

From this it is clear how to answer the Second and Third objections. For in order that man may be able to understand all things by means of his intellect, and that his intellect may understand all things immaterial and universal, it is sufficient that the intellectual power be not the act of the body.

Reply Obj. 4. The human soul, by reason of its perfection, is not a form immersed in matter, or entirely embraced by matter. Therefore there is nothing to prevent some power of the soul from not being the act of the body, although the soul is essentially the form of the body.

Reply Obj. 5. The soul communicates that being in which it subsists to the corporeal matter, out of which and the intellectual soul there results one being; so that the being of the whole composite is also the being of the soul. This is not the case with other non-subsistent forms. For this reason the human soul retains its own being after the dissolution of the body; whereas it is not so with other forms.

Reply Obj. 6. To be united to the body belongs to the soul by reason of itself, just as it belongs to a light body by reason of itself to be raised up. And just as a light body remains light, when removed from its proper place, retaining meanwhile an aptitude and an inclination for its proper place, so the human soul retains its proper being when separated from the body, having an aptitude and a natural inclination to be united to the body.

SECOND ARTICLE

Whether the Intellectual Principle Is Multiplied According to the Number of Bodies?

We proceed thus to the Second Article:—

Objection 1. It would seem that the intellectual principle is not multiplied according to the number of bodies, but that there is one intellect in all men. For an immaterial substance is not multiplied numerically within one species. But the human soul is an immaterial substance, since it is not composed of matter and form, as was shown above. Therefore there are not many human souls in one species. But all men are of one species. Therefore there is but one intellect in all men.

Obj. 2. Further, when the cause is removed, the effect is also removed. Therefore, if human souls were multiplied according to the number of bodies, it would follow that if the bodies were removed, the number of souls would not remain, but from all the souls there would be but a single remainder. This is heretical, for it would do away with the distinction of rewards and punishments.

Obj. 3. Further, if my intellect is distinct from your intellect, my intellect is an individual, and so is yours; for individuals are things which differ in number but agree in one species. Now whatever is received into anything must be received according to the condition of the receiver. Therefore the species of things would be received individually into my intellect, and also into yours; which is contrary to the nature of the intellect, which knows universals.

Obj. 4. Further, the thing understood is in the intellect which understands. If, therefore, my intellect is distinct from yours, what is understood by me must be distinct from what is understood by you; and consequently it will be reckoned *as something individual,* and be only *potentially something understood.* Hence, the common intention will have to be abstracted from both, since from things which are diverse something intelligible and common to them may be abstracted. But this is contrary to the nature of the intellect, for then the intellect would not seem to be distinct from the imagination. It seems to follow, therefore, that there is one intellect in all men.

Obj. 5. Further, when the disciple receives knowledge from the teacher, it cannot be said that the teacher's knowledge begets knowledge in the disciple, because then knowledge too would be an active form, such as heat is; which is clearly false. It seems, therefore, that the same individual knowledge which is in the teacher is communicated to the disciple. This cannot be, unless there is one intellect in both. Seemingly, therefore, the intellect of the disciple and teacher is but one; and, consequently, the same applies to all men.

Obj. 6. Further, Augustine says: *If I were to say that there are many human souls, I should laugh at myself.* But the soul seems to be one chiefly because of the intellect. Therefore there is one intellect of all men.

On the contrary, The Philosopher says that the relation of universal causes to what is universal is like the relation of particular causes to individuals. But it is impossible that a soul, one in species, should belong to animals of different species. Therefore it is impossible that one individual intellectual soul should belong to several individuals.

I answer that, It is absolutely impossible for one intellect to belong to all men. This is clear if, as Plato maintained, man is the intellect itself. For if Socrates and Plato have one intellect, it would follow that Socrates and Plato are one man, and that they are not distinct from each other, except by something outside the essence of each. The distinction between Socrates and Plato would then not be other than that of one man with a tunic and another with a cloak; which is quite absurd.

It is likewise clear that this is impossible if, according to the opinion of Aristotle, it is supposed that the intellect is a part or a power of the soul which is the form of man. For it is impossible for many distinct individuals to have one form, just as it is impossible for them to have one being. For the form is the principle of being.

Again, this is clearly impossible, whatever one may hold as to the manner of the union of the intellect to this or that man. For it is manifest that, if there is one principal agent, and two instruments, we can say without qualification that there is one agent but several actions; as when one man touches several things with his two hands, there will be one who touches, but two contacts. If, on the contrary, we suppose one instrument and several principal agents, we can say that there are several agents, but one act; for example, if there be many pulling a ship by means of a rope, those who pull will be many, but the pulling will be one. If, however, there is one principal agent, and one instrument, we say that there is one agent and one action; as when the smith strikes with one hammer, there is one striker and one stroke. Now it is clear that no matter how the intellect is united or joined to this or that man, the intellect has the primacy among all the other things which pertain to man, for the sensitive powers obey the intellect, and are at its service. So if we suppose two men to have two intellects and one sense,—for instance, if two men had one eye,—there would be two seers, but one seeing. But if the intellect is held to be one, no matter how diverse may be all those things which the intellect uses as instruments, it is in no way possible to say that Socrates and Plato are more than one understanding man. And if to this we add that to understand, which is the act of the intellect, is not produced by any organ other than the intellect itself, it will further follow that there is but one agent and one action; in other words, all men are but one "understander," and have but one act of understanding,—I mean, of course, in relation to one and the same intelligible object.

Now, it would be possible to distinguish my intellectual action from yours by the distinction of the phantasms—because there is one phantasm of a stone in me, and another in you—if the phantasm itself, according as it is one thing in me and another in you, were a form of the possible intellect. For the same agent produces diverse actions through diverse forms. Thus, through the diverse forms in things in relation to the same eye, there are diverse "seeings." But the phantasm itself is not the form of the possible intellect; the intelligible species abstracted from phantasms is such a form. Now in one intellect, from different phantasms of the same species, only one intelligible species is abstracted; as appears in one man, in whom there may be different phantasms of a stone, and yet from all of them only one intelligible species of a stone is abstracted, by which the intellect of that one man, by one operation, understands the nature of a stone, notwithstanding the diversity of phantasms. Therefore, if there were one intellect for all men, the diversity of phantasms in this man and in that would not cause a diversity of intellectual operation in this man and that man, as the Commentator imagines. It follows, therefore, that it is altogether impossible and inappropriate to posit one intellect for all men.

Reply Obj. 1. Although the intellectual soul, like the angel, has no matter from which it is produced, yet it is the form of a certain matter; in which it is unlike an angel. Therefore, according to the division of matter, there are many souls of one species; while it is quite impossible for many angels to be of one species.

Reply Obj. 2. Everything has unity in the same way that it has being, and consequently we must judge of the multiplicity of a thing as we judge of its being. Now it is clear that the intellectual soul is according to its very being united to the body as its form. And yet, after the dissolution of the body, the intellectual soul retains its own being. In like manner, the multiplicity of souls is in proportion to the multiplicity of bodies; and yet, after the dissolution of the bodies, the souls remain multiplied in their being.

Reply Obj. 3. The individuality of the understanding being, or of the species whereby it understands, does not exclude the understanding of universals; or otherwise, since separate intellects are subsistent substances, and consequently individual, they could not understand universals. But it is the materiality of the knower, and of the species whereby he knows, that impedes the knowledge of the universal. For as every action is according to the mode of the form by which the agent acts, as heating is according to the mode of the heat, so knowledge is according to the mode of the species by which the knower knows. Now it is clear that the common nature becomes distinct and multiplied by reason of the individuating principles which come from the matter. Therefore if the form, which is the means of knowledge, is material—that is, not abstracted from material conditions—its likeness to the nature of a species or genus will be according to the distinction and multiplication of that nature by means of individuating principles; so that the knowledge of the nature in its community will be impossible. But if the species be abstracted from the conditions of individual matter, there will be a likeness of the nature without those things which make it distinct and multiplied. And thus there will be knowledge of the universal. Nor does it matter, as to this particular point, whether there be one intellect or many; because, even if there were but one, it would necessarily be an individual intellect, and the species whereby it understands, an individual species.

Reply Obj. 4. Whether the intellect be one or many, what is understood is one. For what is understood is in the intellect, not in itself, but according to its likeness; for *the stone is not in the soul, but its likeness is,* as is said *De Anima* iii. Yet it is the stone which is understood, not the likeness of the stone, except by a reflection of the intellect on itself. Otherwise, the objects of sciences would not be things, but only intelligible species. Now it is possible for different things, according to different forms, to be likened to the same thing. And since knowledge is begotten according to the assimilation of the knower to the thing known, it follows that the same thing can be known by several knowers; as is apparent in regard to the senses, for several see the same color by means of diverse likenesses. In the same way several intellects understand one thing. But there is this difference, according to the opinion of Aristotle, between the sense and the intellect—that a thing is perceived by the sense according to that disposition which it has outside the soul—that is, in its individuality; whereas, though the nature of the thing understood is outside the soul, yet its mode of being outside the soul is not the mode of being according to which it is known. For the common nature is understood as apart from the individuating principles; whereas such is not its mode of being outside the soul. (But according to the opinion of Plato, the thing understood exists outside the soul in the same way as it is understood. For Plato supposed that the natures of things exist separate from matter.)

Reply Obj. 5. One knowledge exists in the disciple and another in the teacher. How it is caused will be shown later on.

Reply Obj. 6. Augustine denies such a plurality of souls as would involve a denial of their communication in the one nature of the species.

THIRD ARTICLE

Whether Besides the Intellectual Soul There Are in Man Other Souls Essentially Different from One Another?

We proceed thus to the Third Article:—

Objection 1. It would seem that besides the intellectual soul there are in man other souls essentially different from one another, namely, the sensitive soul and the nutritive soul. For corruptible and incorruptible are not of the same substance. But the intellectual soul is incorruptible, whereas the other souls, namely, the sensitive and the nutritive, are corruptible, as was shown above. Therefore in man the essence of the intellectual soul, the sensitive soul and the nutritive soul, cannot be the same.

Obj. 2. Further, if it be said that the sensitive soul in man is incorruptible, against this is the dictum that the *corruptible and the incorruptible differ generically,* according to the Philosopher in *Metaph.* x. But the sensitive soul in the horse, the lion, and other brute animals, is corruptible. If, therefore, in man it be incorruptible, the sensitive soul in man and brute animals will not be of the same *genus.* Now, an animal is so called because it has a sensitive soul; and, therefore, *animal* will not be one genus common to man and other animals, which is absurd.

Obj. 3. Further, the Philosopher says that the embryo is an animal before it is a man. But this would be impossible if the essence of the sensitive soul were the same as that of the intellectual soul; for an animal is such by its sensitive soul, while a man is a man by the intellectual soul. Therefore in man the essence of the sensitive soul is not the same as the essence of the intellectual soul.

Obj. 4. Further, the Philosopher says in *Metaph.* viii., that the genus is taken from the matter, and difference from the form. But *rational,* which is the difference constituting man, is taken from the intellectual soul; while he is called *animal* by reason of his having a body animated by a sensitive soul. Therefore the intellectual soul is compared to the body animated by a sensitive soul as form to matter. Therefore in man the intellectual soul is not essentially the same as the sensitive soul, but presupposes it as a material subject.

On the contrary, It is said in the book *De Ecclesiasticis Dogmatibus: Nor do we say that there are two souls in one man, as James and other Syrians write,—one, animal, by which the body is animated, and which is mingled with the blood; the other, spiritual, which obeys the reason; but we say that it is one and the same soul in man which both gives life to the body by being united to it, and orders itself by its own reason.*

I answer that, Plato held that there were several souls in one body, distinct even according to organs. To these souls he referred the different vital actions, saying that the nutritive power is in the liver, the concupiscible in the heart, and the knowing power in the brain. Which opinion is rejected by Aristotle with reference to those parts of the soul which use corporeal organs. His reason is that in those animals which continue to live when they have been divided, in each part are observed the operations of the soul, such as those of sense and appetite. Now this would not be the case if the various principles of the soul's operations were essentially diverse in their distribution through the various parts of the body. But with regard to the intellectual part, Aristotle seems to leave it in doubt whether it be *only logically* distinct from the other parts of the soul, *or also locally.*

The opinion of Plato could be maintained if, as he held, the soul were united to the body, not as its form, but as its mover. For nothing incongruous is involved if the same movable thing be moved by several movers; and still less if it be moved according to its various parts. If we suppose, however, that the soul is united to the body as its form, it is quite impossible for several essentially different souls to be in one body. This can be made clear by three reasons.

In the first place, an animal in which there were several souls would not be absolutely one. For nothing is absolutely one except by one form, by which a thing has being; because a thing has both being and unity from the same source, and therefore things which are denominated by various forms are not absolutely one; as, for instance, *a white man.* If, therefore, man were *living* by one form, the vegetative soul, and *animal* by another form, the sensitive soul, and *man* by another form, the intellectual soul, it would follow that man is not absolutely one. Thus Aristotle argues in *Metaph.* viii., against Plato, that if the Idea of an animal is distinct from the Idea of a biped, then a biped animal is not absolutely one. For this reason, against those who hold that there are several souls in the body, he asks, *what contains them?*—that is, what makes them one? It cannot be said that they are united by the unity of the body; because it is rather the soul that contains the body and makes it one, than the reverse.

Secondly, this is proved to be impossible by the mode in which one thing is predicated of another. Those things which are derived from various forms are predicated of one another either accidentally (if the forms are not ordered one to another, as when we say that something white is sweet), or essentially, in the second mode of essential predication (if the forms are ordered one to another, as when the subject enters into the definition of the predicate; and thus a surface is presupposed for color, so that if we say that a body with a surface is colored, we have the second mode of essential predication). Therefore, if we have one form by which a thing is an animal, and another form by which it is a man, it follows either that one of these two things could not be predicated of the other, except accidentally (supposing these two forms not to be ordered to one another), or that one would be predicated of the other according to the second mode of essential predication, if one soul be presupposed to the other. But both of these consequences are clearly false. For *animal* is predicated of man essentially and not accidentally, and man is not part of the definition of an animal, but the other way about. Therefore it is of necessity by the same form that a thing is animal and man. Otherwise man would not really be the being which is an animal, so that animal could be essentially predicated of man.

Thirdly, this is shown to be impossible by the fact that when one operation of the soul is intense it impedes another; which could never be the case unless the principle of such actions were essentially one.

We must therefore conclude that the sensitive soul, the intellectual soul and the nutritive soul are in man numerically one and the same soul. This can easily be explained, if we consider the differences of species and forms. For we observe that the species and forms of things differ from one another as the perfect and the less perfect; just as in the order of things, the animate are more perfect than the inanimate, animals more perfect than plants, and man more perfect than brute animals. Furthermore, in each of these genera there are various degrees. For this reason Aristotle compares the species of things to numbers, which differ in species by the addition or subtraction of unity. He also compares the various souls to the species of figures, one of which contains another, as a pentagon contains and exceeds a tetragon. Thus the intellectual soul contains virtually whatever belongs to the sensitive soul of brute animals, and to the nutritive soul of plants. Therefore, just as a surface which is of a pentagonal shape is not tetragonal by one shape, and pentagonal by another—since a tetragonal shape would be superfluous, as being contained in the pentagonal—so neither is Socrates a man by one soul, and an animal by another; but by one and the same soul he is both animal and man.

Reply Obj. 1. The sensitive soul is incorruptible, not by reason of its being sensitive, but by reason of its being intellectual. When, therefore, a soul is sensitive only, it is corruptible; but when the intellectual is joined to the sensitive, then the sensitive soul is incorruptible. For although the sensitive does not give incorruptibility, yet it cannot deprive the intellectual of its incorruptibility.

Reply Obj. 2. Not forms, but composites, are classified either generically or specifically. Now man is corruptible like other animals. And so the difference of corruptible and incorruptible which is on the part of the forms does not involve a generic difference between man and the other animals.

Reply Obj. 3. The embryo has first of all a soul which is merely sensitive, and when this is removed, it is supplanted by a more perfect soul, which is both sensitive and intellectual, as will be shown farther on.

Reply Obj. 4. We must not base the diversity of natural things on the various logical notions or intentions which follow from our manner of understanding; for reason can apprehend one and the same thing in various ways. Therefore since, as we have said, the intellectual soul contains virtually what belongs to the sensitive soul, and something more, reason can consider separately what belongs to the power of the sensitive soul, as something imperfect and material. And because it observes that this is something common to man and to other animals, it forms thence the notion of the *genus.* On the other hand, that wherein the intellectual soul exceeds the sensitive soul, the reason takes as formal and perfecting; and thence it gathers the *difference* of man.

FOURTH ARTICLE

Whether in Man There Is Another Form Besides the Intellectual Soul?

We proceed thus to the Fourth Article:—

Objection 1. It would seem that in man there is another form besides the intellectual soul. For the Philosopher says that *the soul is the act of a physical body which has life potentially.* Therefore the soul is to the body as a form to matter. But the body has a substantial form by which it is a body. Therefore some other substantial form in the body precedes the soul.

Obj. 2. Further, man moves himself as every animal does. *Now everything that moves itself is divided into two parts, of which one moves, and the other is moved,* as the Philosopher proves. But the part which moves is the soul. Therefore the other part must be such that it can be moved. But primary matter cannot be moved since it is a being only potentially, while everything that is moved is a body. Therefore in man and in every animal there must be another substantial form, by which the body is constituted.

Obj. 3. Further, the order of forms depends on their relation to primary matter; for *before* and *after* apply by comparison to some beginning. Therefore, if there were not in man some other substantial form besides the rational soul, and if the rational soul inhered immediately to primary matter, it would follow that it ranks among the most imperfect forms which inhere to matter immediately.

Obj. 4. Further, the human body is a mixed body. Now mixture does not result from matter alone; for then we should have mere corruption. Therefore the forms of the elements must remain in a mixed body; and these are substantial forms. Therefore in the human body there are other substantial forms besides the intellectual soul.

On the contrary, Of one thing there is but one substantial being. But the substantial form gives substantial being. Therefore of one thing there is but one substantial form. But the soul is the substantial form of man. Therefore it is impossible that there be in man another substantial form besides the intellectual soul.

I answer that, If we supposed that the intellectual soul is not united to the body as its form, but only as its mover, as the Platonists maintain, it would necessarily follow that in man there is another substantial form by which the body is established in its being as movable by the soul. If, however, the intellectual soul is united to the body as its substantial form, as we have said above, it is impossible for another substantial form besides the intellectual soul to be found in man.

In order to make this evident, we must consider that the substantial form differs from the accidental form in this, that the accidental form does not make a thing *to be absolutely,* but *to be such,* as heat does not make a thing to be absolutely, but only to be hot. Therefore by the coming of the accidental form a thing is not said to be made or generated absolutely, but to be made such, or to be in some particular disposition; and in like manner, when an accidental form is removed, a thing is said to be corrupted, not absolutely, but relatively. But the substantial form gives being absolutely, and hence by its coming a thing is said to be generated absolutely, and by its removal to be corrupted absolutely. For this reason, the old natural philosophers, who held that primary matter was some actual being—for instance, fire or air, or something of that sort—maintained that nothing is generated absolutely, or corrupted absolutely, but that *every becoming is nothing but an alteration,* as we read *Physics* i. Therefore, if besides the intellectual soul there pre-existed in matter another substantial form by which the subject of the soul were made an actual being, it would follow that the soul does not give being absolutely, and consequently that it is not the substantial form; and so at the advent of the soul there would not be absolute generation, nor at its removal absolute corruption. All of which is clearly false.

Whence we must conclude that there is no other substantial form in man besides the intellectual soul; and that just as the soul contains virtually the sensitive and nutritive souls, so does it contain virtually all inferior forms, and does alone whatever the imperfect forms do in other things. The same is to be said of the sensitive soul in brute animals, and of the nutritive soul in plants, and universally of all more perfect forms in relation to the imperfect.

Reply Obj. 1. Aristotle does not say that the soul is the act of a body only, but *the act of a physical organic body which has life potentially;* and that this potentiality *does not exclude the soul.* Whence it is clear that in the being of which the soul is called the act, the soul itself is included; as when we say that heat is the act of what is hot, and light of what is lucid. And this means, not that the lucid is lucid in separation from light, but that it is lucid through light. In like manner, the soul is said to be the *act of a body,* etc., because it is by the soul that the body is a body, and is organic, and has life potentially. When the first act is said to be *in potentiality,* this is to be understood in relation to the second act, which is operation. Now such a potentiality *does not remove*—that is, does not exclude—the soul.

Reply Obj. 2. The soul does not move the body by its essence, as the form of the body, but by the motive power, whose act presupposes that the body is already actualized by the soul: so that the soul by its motive power is the part which moves; and the animate body is the part moved.

Reply Obj. 3. There are in matter various degrees of perfection, as *to be, to live, to sense, to understand.* Now what is added is always more perfect. Therefore that form which gives matter only the first degree of perfection is the most imperfect, while that form which gives the first, second, and third degree, and so on, is the most perfect: and yet it is present to matter immediately.

Reply Obj. 4. Avicenna held that the substantial forms of the elements remain entire in the mixed body, and that the mixture is made by the contrary qualities of the elements being reduced to an equilibrium. But this is impossible. For the various forms of the elements must necessarily be in various parts of matter, and for the distinction of the parts we must suppose dimensions, without which matter cannot be divisible. Now matter subject to dimension is not to be found except in a body. But several distinct bodies cannot be in the same place. Whence it follows that the elements in the mixed body would be distinct as to position. Hence, there would not be a real mixture which affects the whole, but only a mixture that seems so to the sense because of the juxtaposition of very small particles.

Averroës maintained that the forms of elements, by reason of their imperfection, are between accidental and substantial forms, and so can be *more* or *less;* and therefore in the mixture they are modified and reduced to an equilibrium, so that one form emerges among them. But this is even more impossible. For the substantial being of each thing consists in something indivisible, and every addition and subtraction varies the species, as in numbers, according to *Metaph.* viii. Consequently, it is impossible for any substantial form to receive *more* or *less*. Nor is it less impossible for anything to be between substance and accident.

Therefore we must say, in accordance with the Philosopher, that the forms of the elements remain in the mixed body, not actually, but virtually. For the proper qualities of the elements remain, though modified; and in these qualities is the power of the elementary forms. This quality of the mixture is the proper disposition for the substantial form of the mixed body; for instance, the form of a stone, or of any sort of soul.

FIFTH ARTICLE

Whether the Intellectual Soul Is Fittingly United to Such a Body?

We proceed thus to the Fifth Article:—

Objection 1. It would seem that the intellectual soul is not fittingly united to such a body. For matter must be proportionate to the form. But the intellectual soul is an incorruptible form. Therefore it is not fittingly united to a corruptible body.

Obj. 2. Further, the intellectual soul is a perfectly immaterial form. A proof of this is its operation in which corporeal matter does not share. But the more subtle is the body, the less has it of matter. Therefore the soul should be united to a most subtle body, to fire, for instance, and not to a mixed body, still less to a terrestrial body.

Obj. 3. Further, since the form is the principle of the species, one form cannot produce a variety of species. But the intellectual soul is one form. Therefore, it should not be united to a body which is composed of parts belonging to various species.

Obj. 4. Further, a more perfect form should have a more perfect subject. But the intellectual soul is the most perfect of souls. Therefore since the bodies of other animals are naturally provided with a covering, for instance, with hair instead of clothes, and hoofs instead of shoes, and are, moreover, naturally provided with arms, as claws, teeth, and horns:—it seems that the intellectual soul should not have been united to a body which is imperfect, in being deprived of the above means of protection.

On the contrary, The Philosopher says that *the soul is the act of a physical organic body having life potentially.*

I answer that, Since the form is not for the matter, but rather the matter for the form, we must gather from the form the reason why the matter is such as it is; and not conversely. Now the intellectual soul, as we have seen above, holds in the order of nature the lowest place among intellectual substances. So much so, that it is not naturally endowed with the knowledge of truth, as the angels are, but has to gather knowledge from individual things by way of the senses, as Dionysius says. But nature never fails anyone in what is necessary, and therefore the intellectual soul had to be endowed not only with the power of understanding, but also with the power of sensing. Now the action of the senses is not performed without a corporeal instrument. Therefore the intellectual soul had to be united to a body which could be the fitting organ of sense.

Now all the other senses are based on the sense of touch. But the organ of touch requires to be a medium between contraries, such as hot and cold, wet and dry, and the like, of which the sense of touch has the perception; and in this way it is in potentiality with regard to contraries, and is able to perceive them. Therefore the more the organ of touch is reduced to an equable complexion, the more sensitive will be the touch. But the intellectual soul has the power of sense in all its completeness, because what belongs to the inferior nature pre-exists more perfectly in the superior, as Dionysius says. Therefore the body to which the intellectual soul is united had to be a mixed body, above others reduced to the most equable complexion. For this reason, among animals man has the better sense of touch. And among men, those who have the better sense of touch have the better intellect. A sign of which is that we observe *those who are refined in body are well endowed in mind,* as is stated in *De Anima* ii.

Reply Obj. 1. Perhaps someone might try to avoid this objection by saying that before sin the human body was incorruptible. But such an answer does not seem sufficient, because before sin the human body was immortal, not by nature, but by a gift of divine grace; or otherwise its immortality would not be forfeited through sin, as neither was the immortality of the devil.

Therefore we answer in another way. Now in matter two conditions are to be found: one which is chosen in order that the matter be suitable to the form; the other which follows necessarily as a result of a previous disposition. The artisan, for instance, chooses iron for the making of a saw, because it is suitable for cutting through hard material; but that the teeth of the saw may become blunt and rusted, follows from a necessity imposed by the matter itself. So the intellectual soul requires a body of equable complexion, which, however, is corruptible by necessity of its matter. If, however, it be said that God could avoid this necessity, we answer that in the establishment of natural things, the question is not what God can do, but what befits the natures of things, as Augustine says. God, however, provided in this case by applying a remedy against death in the gift of grace.

Reply Obj. 2. A body is not necessary to the intellectual soul by reason of its intellectual operation considered as such, but because of the sensitive power, which requires an organ of equable temperament. Therefore the intellectual soul had to be united to such a body, and not to a simple element, or to a mixed body, in which fire was in excess; because otherwise there could not be an equability of temperament. And this body of an equable temperament has a dignity of its own in being remote from contraries. In this it resembles in a way a heavenly body.

Reply Obj. 3. The parts of an animal, for instance, the eye, hand, flesh, and bones, and so forth, do not make the species, but the whole does; and therefore, properly speaking, we cannot say that these have diverse species, but diverse dispositions. This is suitable to the intellectual soul, which, although it be one in its essence, yet because of its perfection, is manifold in its power. And so, for its various operations the soul requires various dispositions in the parts of the body to which it is united. For this reason we observe that there is a greater variety of parts in perfect than in imperfect animals; and in these a greater variety than in plants.

Reply Obj. 4. The intellectual soul, as comprehending universals, has a power that is open to infinite things. Therefore it cannot be limited by nature to certain fixed natural judgments or even to certain fixed means whether of defense or of clothing, as is the case with other animals, whose souls are endowed with a knowledge and a power for fixed particular things. Instead of all these, man has by nature his reason and his hands, which are *the organs of organs,* since by their means man can make for himself instruments of an infinite variety, and for any number of purposes.

SIXTH ARTICLE

Whether the Intellectual Soul Is United to the Body Through the Medium of Accidental Dispositions?

We proceed thus to the Sixth Article:—

Objection 1. It would seem that the intellectual soul is united to the body through the medium of accidental dispositions. For every form resides in its own disposed matter. But dispositions to a form are accidents. Therefore we must presuppose accidents to be in matter before the substantial form; and therefore before the soul, since the soul is a substantial form.

Obj. 2. Further, diverse forms of one species require diverse parts of matter. But diverse parts of matter are unintelligible without division in measurable quantity. Therefore we must suppose dimensions in matter before the substantial forms, which are many belonging to one species.

Obj. 3. Further, what is spiritual is connected with what is corporeal by virtual contact. But the virtue of the soul is its power. Therefore it seems that the soul is united to the body by means of a power, which is an accident.

On the contrary, Accident is posterior to substance, both in the order of time and in the order of reason, as the Philosopher says in *Metaph.* vii. Therefore it is unintelligible that any accidental form exist in matter before the soul, which is the substantial form.

I answer that, If the soul were united to the body merely as a mover, there would be nothing to prevent the existence of certain dispositions mediating between the soul and the body; on the contrary, they would be necessary, for on the part of the soul there would be required the power to move the body, and on the part of the body, a certain aptitude to be moved by the soul.

If, however, the intellectual soul is united to the body as the substantial form, as we have already said above, it is impossible for any accidental disposition to come between the body and the soul, or between any substantial form whatever and its matter. The reason is this. Since matter is in potentiality to all acts in a certain order, what is absolutely first among the acts must be understood as being first in matter.

Now the first among all acts is being. Therefore, it is impossible for matter to be apprehended as being hot, or quantified, before actually being. But matter has actual being by the substantial form, which makes it to be absolutely, as we have said above. Therefore it is impossible for any accidental dispositions to pre-exist in matter before the substantial form, and consequently before the soul.

Reply Obj. 1. As appears from what has been already said, the more perfect form virtually contains whatever belongs to the inferior forms; and therefore while remaining one and the same, it perfects matter according to the various degrees of perfection. For the same essential form makes man an *actual being,* a *body,* a *living being,* an *animal,* and a *man.* Now it is clear that to every *genus* follow its own proper accidents. Therefore as mattter is apprehended as perfected in its being, before it is understood as corporeal, and so on, so those accidents which belong to being are understood to exist before corporeity. And thus, dispositions are understood in matter before the form, not as regards all its effects, but as regards the subsequent effect.

Reply Obj. 2. Dimensions of quantity are accidents consequent upon the corporeity which belongs to the whole matter. Hence, once matter is understood as corporeal and measurable, it can be understood as distinct in its various parts, and as receptive of different forms according to further degrees of perfection. For although it is essentially the same form which gives to matter the various degrees of perfection, as we have said, yet it is considered as different according to the way that the reason thinks of it.

Reply Obj. 3. A spiritual substance, which is united to a body as its mover only, is united to it by power or virtue. But the intellectual soul is united to the body as a form by its very being; but it guides and moves the body by its power and virtue.

SEVENTH ARTICLE

Whether the Soul Is United to the Animal Body by Means of a Body?

We proceed thus to the Seventh Article:—

Objection 1. It seems that the soul is united to the animal body by means of a body. For Augustine says that *the soul administers the body by light* (that is, by fire) *and by air, which are most akin to a spirit.* But fire and air are bodies. Therefore the soul is united to the human body by means of a body.

Obj. 2. Further, a link between two things seems to be that thing the removal of which involves the cessation of their union. But when breathing ceases, the soul is separated from the body. Therefore the breath, which is a subtle body, is the means of union between soul and body.

Obj. 3. Further, things which are very distant from one another are not united except by something between them. But the intellectual soul is very distant from the body, both because it is incorporeal and because it is incorruptible. Therefore it seems to be united to the body by means of an incorruptible body: and such would be some heavenly light, which would harmonize the elements, and unite them together.

On the contrary, The Philosopher says: *We need not ask if the soul and body are one, just as neither do we ask if wax and its shape are one.* But the shape is united to the wax without a body intervening. Therefore also the soul is thus united to the body.

I answer that, If the soul, following the opinion of the Platonists, were united to the body merely as a mover, it would be right to say that some other bodies must intervene between the soul and body of man, or of any animal whatever; for a mover naturally moves what is distant from it by means of something nearer.

If, however, the soul is united to the body as its form, as we have said above, it is impossible for it to be united by means of another body. The reason for this is that a thing is one according as it is a being. Now the form, through itself, makes a thing to be actual, since it is itself essentially an act; nor does it give being by means of something else. Hence, the unity of a thing composed of matter and form is by virtue of the form itself, which by reason of its very nature is united to matter as its act. Nor is there any other cause of union except the agent, which causes matter to be in act, as the Philosopher says in *Metaph.* viii.

From this it is clear how false are the opinions of those who maintained the existence of some mediate bodies between the soul and body of man. Of these, certain Platonists said that the intellectual soul has an incorruptible body naturally united to it, from which it is never separated, and by means of which it is united to the corruptible body of man. Others said that the soul is united to the body by means of a corporeal spirit. Others, again, said it is united to the body by means of light, which, they say, is a body and of the nature of the fifth essence; so that the vegetative soul would be united to the body by means of the light of the sidereal heaven, the sensible soul, by means of the light of the crystal heaven, and the intellectual soul by means of the light of the empyrean heaven. Now all this is fictitious and ridiculous. For light is not a body, and the fifth essence does not enter materially into the composition of a mixed body (since it is unchangeable), but only virtually; and lastly, because the soul is immediately united to the body as the form to matter.

Reply Obj. 1. Augustine speaks there of the soul as it moves the body; whence he uses the word *administration.* It is true that it moves the grosser parts of the body by the more subtle parts. And the first instrument of the motive power is a kind of spirit, as the Philosopher says in *De causa motus animalium.*

Reply Obj. 2. The union of soul and body ceases at the cessation of breath, not because this is the means of union, but because of the removal of that disposition by which the body is disposed for such a union. Nevertheless the breath is a means of moving, as the first instrument of motion.

Reply Obj. 3. The soul is indeed very distant from the body, if we consider the condition of each separately; so that if each had a separate being, many means of connection would have to intervene. But inasmuch as the soul is the form of the body, it does not have being apart from the being of the body, but by its own being it is united to the body immediately. This is the case with every form which, if considered as an act, is very distant from matter, which is a being only in potentiality.

EIGHTH ARTICLE

Whether the Whole Soul Is in Each Part of the Body?

We proceed thus to the Eighth Article:—

Objection 1. It would seem that the whole soul is not in each part of the body. For the Philosopher says: *It is not necessary for the soul to be in each part of the body; it suffices that it be in some principle of the body causing the other parts to live, for each part has a natural movement of its own.*

Obj. 2. Further, the soul is in the body of which it is the act. But it is the act of an organic body. Therefore it exists only in an organic body. But each part of the human body is not an organic body. Therefore the whole soul is not in each part.

Obj. 3. Further, the Philosopher says that the relation of a part of the soul to a part of the body, such as the sight to the pupil of the eye, is the same as the relation of the whole soul to the whole body of an animal. If, therefore, the whole soul is in each part of the body, it follows that each part of the body is an animal.

Obj. 4. Further, all the powers of the soul are rooted in the essence of the soul. If, therefore, the whole soul be in each part of the body, it follows that all the powers of the soul are in each part of the body; and thus, the sight will be in the ear, and hearing in the eye, and this is absurd.

Obj. 5. Further, if the whole soul is in each part of the body, each part of the body is immediately dependent on the soul. Thus one part would not depend on another, nor would one part be nobler than another; which is clearly untrue. Therefore the soul is not in each part of the body.

On the contrary, Augustine says that *in each body the whole soul is in the whole body and wholly in each part.*

I answer that, As we have said, if the soul were united to the body merely as its mover, we might say that it is not in each part of the body, but only in one part, through which it would move the others. But since the soul is united to the body as its form, it must necessarily be in the whole body, and in each part thereof. For it is not an accidental form, but the substantial form of the body. Now the substantial form perfects not only the whole, but each part of the whole. For since a whole consists of parts, a form of the whole which does not give being to each of the parts of the body is a form consisting in composition and order, such as the form of a house; and such a form is accidental. But the soul is a substantial form, and therefore it must be the form and the act, not only of the whole, but also of each part. Therefore, on the withdrawal of the soul, just as we do not speak of an animal or a man unless equivocally (as we speak of a painted animal or a stone animal), so it is with the hand, the eye, the flesh and bones, as the Philosopher says. A proof of which is that, on the withdrawal of the soul, no part of the body retains its proper work; although that which retains its species or form retains the action of the species. But act is in that of which it is the act, and therefore the soul might be in the whole body, and in each part thereof.

That it is entire in each part of the body may be concluded from this, that since a whole is that which is divided into parts, there are three kinds of totality, corresponding to three kinds of division. There is a whole which is divided into parts of quantity, as a whole line, or a whole body. There is also a whole which is divided into logical and essential parts: as a thing defined is divided into the parts of a definition, and a composite into matter and form. There is, further, a third kind of whole which is potential, divided into virtual parts.

The first kind of totality does not apply to forms, except perhaps accidentally; and then only to those forms which have an indifferent relationship to a quantitative whole and its parts. Thus, whiteness, as far as its essence is concerned, is equally disposed to be in the whole surface, and in each part of the surface; and, therefore, when the surface is divided, the whiteness is accidentally divided. But a form which requires variety in the parts, such as a soul, and especially the soul of perfect animals, is not equally related to the whole and the parts. Hence it is not divided accidentally, namely, through the division of quantity. Quantitative totality, therefore, cannot be attributed to the soul, either essentially or accidentally. But the second kind of totality, which depends on logical and essential perfection, properly and essentially belongs to forms; and likewise virtual totality, because a form is the principle of operation. Therefore if it be asked whether the whole whiteness is in the whole surface and in each part thereof, it is necessary to distinguish. If we mean the quantitative totality which whiteness has accidentally, then the whole whiteness is not in each part of the surface. The same is to be said of totality of power, since the whiteness which is in the whole surface moves the sight more than the whiteness which is in a small part thereof. But if we mean totality of species and essence, then the whole whiteness is in each part of a surface.

Since, however, the soul has no quantitative totality, neither essentially, nor accidentally, as we have seen, it is enough to say that the whole soul is in each part of the body by totality of perfection and of essence, but not by totality of power. For it is not in each part of the body with regard to each of its powers; but with regard to sight, it is in the eye, and with regard to hearing, it is in the ear, and so forth. We must observe, however, that since the soul requires a variety of parts, its relation to the whole is not the same as its relation to the parts; for to the whole it is compared primarily and essentially as to its proper and proportionate perfectible; but to the parts, secondarily, inasmuch as they are ordained to the whole.

Reply Obj. 1. The Philosopher is speaking there of the motive power of the soul.

Reply Obj. 2. The soul is the act of an organic body, as of its primary and proportionate perfectible.

Reply Obj. 3. An animal is that which is composed of a soul and a whole body, which is the soul's primary and proportionate perfectible. *Thus* the soul is not in a part. Whence it does not follow that a part of an animal is an animal.

Reply Obj. 4. Some of the powers of the soul are in it according as it exceeds the entire capacity of the body, namely, the intellect and the will; and hence these powers are not said to be in any part of the body. Other powers are common to the soul and body; wherefore each of these powers need not be wherever the soul is, but only in that part of the body which is adapted to the operation of such a power.

Reply Obj. 5. One part of the body is said to be nobler than another because of the various powers, of which the parts of the body are the organs. For that part which is the organ of a nobler power is a nobler part of the body; as is also that part which serves the same power in a nobler manner.

SIGER OF BRABANT

Comparatively little is known of the life of Siger. His life span is given as ca. 1240 to ca. 1284, when, it is alleged, he was murdered by his secretary. We do know that he was a master in the faculty of arts at the University of Paris in 1266. Siger was the major target of the Condemnation of 1277, for he was associated with several doctrines that were anathema to the teaching of the medieval Church—namely, that the individual soul is not immortal, that the human will is determined, and that the world is eternal rather than created in time.

Further, Siger was accused of the sophistic embrace of the double-truth by which a proposition could be true in philosophy and false in theology or false in philosophy and true in theology. Commentators are divided as to whether Siger held these various positions in full, in part, or at all. Suffice to say that Siger was an able dialectician and controversial enough to be a lightning rod for opposition to the growing influence of Aristotle and his Muslim interpreter, Averroës. The selection that follows, "On the Necessity and Contingency of Causes," amply demonstrates both his dialectical ability and potential controversiality. It is also a quintessential medieval response to a philosophical question.

On the Necessity and Contingency of Causes

[Here] begins a difficult question resolved by Master Siger of Brabant.

Your question is justly debatable: whether it is necessary that all future things be going to be before they are, and with regard to present and past things also: whether it was necessary for them to be going to be before they came to be.

And it seems that this is the cause. 1. Every effect which comes to pass, results from a cause in relation to which its existence is necessary, as Avicenna says and as can be proved also. For if some effect results from a cause which when posited, the effect is able to be posited and not to be posited, then that cause is being-in-potency-to-producing-an-effect, and it will require something educing it from potency to act, which would make it a cause in act; wherefore it is necessary that every cause causing an effect be such that when posited, the effect is necessarily posited; and if that cause is [itself] the effect of another, the same is argued for it. For this [caused-cause] would come to be from such a cause as when posited, the former of necessity is posited, and so on up even to the first cause of all. Wherefore all effects seem to proceed from their causes in such a way that it is necessary for them to be going to be before they should come to be.

2. Moreover. In the things of the present there is the cause of all things which afterwards will come to be, so that all future things will come to be from present things, either without a medium or with a medium: one or more than one, many or few. But if in present things there exists the necessary cause of those which will come to be, what was proposed is a consequence; but if not, [if] rather from things of the present, future things are able to be and not to be, then the cause of future things is not in present things, except as matter. Whence no element of those future things which do not have a necessary cause in present things will come to be; or if it comes to be, matter proceeds [from potency] to act by itself without any agent. It is necessary, therefore, that in present things there exist the necessary cause of all future things; and the argument would be the same should someone appeal to what happened in times past.

3. Moreover. Everything which comes to be, comes to be either from an essential cause necessary to an effect, one which cannot be impeded, or from an essential cause which works frequently and in most cases, which nevertheless can be impeded, or from an accidental cause. And with regard to future things arising from a cause in the first way, it is clear

that their coming-to-be is necessary. The effect of a cause which works in most cases and exists in that disposition in which it is not impeded, is necessary, so that whenever that cause is posited in such disposition, it is also necessary that the effect be posited. The same is true also for an effect which results from an accidental cause. For an accidental cause, taken according to that disposition wherein it is a necessary cause of its effect, necessarily brings about its effect. But if someone should say that that accident through which it causes necessarily, cannot happen to that cause—because an accident is not necessary—it can be argued as before: because that accidental being or that accidental cause, since it is a certain effect, proceeds from a cause existing in some one of the three aforesaid ways, and thus the occurrence of that accident will be necessary as before.

4. Moreover. In the Sixth Book of the *Metaphysics* Aristotle maintains—and his commentator does also—that if there were no accidental being, all things would be necessary; and this is certainly clear for a cause-which-works-in-most-cases would be necessary unless something were to happen to it. Now the fact is, however, that nothing is accidental being absolutely; for although some effect, referred to some particular cause of it, results from this cause accidentally, as through the concurrence of another agent, either through the impediment of a contrary or from the indisposition of matter concurring with that agent, nevertheless those concurrences referred to a higher cause which extends itself to many, are brought together by it as by an essential cause with which neither of these concurs. But if all things were necessary, if there were no accidental being, as Aristotle says, as has been seen, and nothing is accidental being absolutely, as has been said and will be evident in solving the question, then, it would seem that all effects have some essential cause from which they necessarily follow, although in relation to some definite cause, some of them proceed from an accidental cause and some from a cause which works in most cases. But, as it seems, each of these is referred to some necessary cause.

5. Moreover. Every effect having a cause in the present or past from which it necessarily follows, necessarily comes to be, as Aristotle maintains in the Sixth Book of the *Metaphysics.* But every future effect has a cause in the present from which it necessarily follows; the proof of which is Divine providence. For if *a* will come to be, it has been foreseen by God that *a* will come to be, and this by an infallible providence; for Divine providence cannot err. Wherefore *a* necessarily follows from such a cause of it.

6. Moreover. From the same thing it can be argued even more efficaciously: whenever some conditional is true, the consequence is necessary from the supposition of the antecedent. But this consequence is true: if *a* is foreseen to come to be, *a* will come to be absolutely, no addition having been made in the consequent that it will come to be necessarily or contingently. But if the antecedent is already true, the consequent is necessarily going to be.

7. Moreover. Let it be said: how can there be an infallible providence about a fallible thing, since these do not seem to be compatible? For if the order of a thing or of a cause to some effect is fallible, then the knowledge *(ratio)* of the order of that cause to its effect, or providence, will be fallible. For if this situation: *b* to come to be from *a* or that *b* will come to be from *a,* is fallible, although it will not fail, then reason or intellect preconceiving that *b* will come to be from *a,* is fallible. And the same kind of deficiency exists and the argument is the same for divine foreknowledge of future things which precedes those future things. For in those three ways in which one argues for providence, one can argue for foreknowledge, as is clearly evident to anyone who tries. Divine foreknowledge of future things and providence are different, however; for divine foreknowledge of future things, under the aspect of foreknowledge, pertains to the divine intellect according as it contemplates them absolutely; however, since providence is the part of prudence being about future things—prudence however pertains to the practical intellect—providence about future things pertains to the divine intellect not only according as it contemplates them, but also according as it directs them; hence it belongs to providence to follow foresight. However, providence and foreknowledge agree in this, that each is infallible.

To the contrary. Aristotle maintains in the Sixth Book of the *Metaphysics* that not all things come to pass of necessity, and, *in the same place,* he maintains that some causes are such that when posited sometimes they cause their effects, sometimes they do not. Thus it is clearly his intention that not all things come to pass of necessity, since *in the same place* he says that not all future things come to pass, for example, that the living be going to die. For something is already a fact, as that contraries are found in a body, from which necessarily death will come about. But although someone ought to die from sickness or violence, yet it is not yet necessary that it be the fact nor that it be in the present that he ought necessarily to die in such a fashion, as is said *above.*

Moreover. This is clearly Aristotle's intention in the *Perihermeneias,* where he maintains that not all things come to pass of necessity, because then it would not be necessary to take counsel or to negotiate. Therefore, etc.

We have divided the solution of this question into four parts. For in the first place some things concerning the order of causes to effects must be considered. Secondly, how some people have erred because of that order, believing that all things come to pass necessarily on account of the connection of causes and the condition of the universe. Thirdly, in what those who err in this way were mistaken and how the question is answered. Fourthly and finally, from the determined truth the reasonings of the adversaries of the truth must be gotten rid of.

I

With respect to the first it must be known that five orders of causes-in-relation-to-the-caused are found in the universe, and this is according to the intention of the *Philosophers.* The first is that the First Cause, cause of the whole of being *(totius esse),* is the essential, immediate, necessary cause of the first intelligence, and is such that when posited, its first caused is also simultaneously posited; and this I affirm in accordance with the intention of the *Philosophers.* I say that it is the essential cause of [the first intelligence]; for the First Cause causes nothing accidentally, since nothing is able to concur with it, for then it would not be the cause of the whole of being *(totius entis);* for there is no causal order among accidents in relation to each other. I say that it is the immediate cause of [the first intelligence], because that is its first caused. It is also necessary cause of [the first intelligence] by reason of the fact that an essential cause, to which an impediment cannot happen and which does not cause through an intermediate impedible cause, is a necessary cause of its effect. But this is the way the First Cause is related to the first caused, and I also say, that it is necessary that it always exist simultaneous with its caused effect. For nothing prevents some present causes from being necessary in relation to future effects, by virtue of the fact that they are the cause of those effects through an intermediate motion and through an order to that which is moved, which causes posteriority in duration. But since the First Cause does not cause the first caused through an order to that which is moved nor through an intermediate motion, and since it is a necessary cause in relation to that which is its caused, they will be simultaneous as regards duration.

The second order is that the First Cause is the cause of the separated intelligences, of the spheres and of their motions, and universally of the ingenerables. The essential and necessary cause, I say, which also has being *(esse)* simultaneously with caused things of this kind; and this will be made clear in the same way in which it was made clear about the First Cause in relation to the first caused. But this order falls short of the previous order in this, that the First Cause is not the cause of the aforementioned except according to a certain order, and it is not the immediate cause of all of them, since from something one and simple only one proceeds immediately and not many except in a certain order; however as regards the order according to which the aforesaid proceed, nothing [is clear] to reason. Moreover the First Cause is not only the essential cause of any one of the aforesaid taking causality in the way indicated but also of the conjunction which occurs among them, as that this should have being with that.

The third order is that the First Cause is the cause that the moon at one time be in such a place, the sun in such a place, and so on for the other stars. And the First Cause is the essential and necessary cause of these, but not the immediate [cause], nor one which when posited these effects are posited, for the First Cause does not cause the said positions except through an order to the moved, which causes posteriority. Nevertheless, from the existence of the First Cause it will necessarily come about that at one time the sun is in such a place, the moon in such a place, and similarly for the other stars. And that it is a necessary cause is proved as before. For it is the essential cause of this, since it is first, to which nothing can happen, because it is not its nature to be impeded nor does it cause the aforesaid effects through intermediate impedible causes. The proper mover of any one star, however, is the essential, immediate and necessary cause of the aforesaid, but not such that when posited, the effect is posited. The

First Cause certainly is an essential, necessary but not immediate cause, nor one which when posited, the effect of any conjunction and of a division occurring among the celestial stars is posited, so that all these are going to come about in a time determined by the First Cause. And therefore Aristotle well says that, although from the celestial bodies something can come to be by chance and accidentally, nevertheless among them nothing happens by chance, since whatever comes to pass among them comes to pass from essential and necessary causes, as has been seen; such however does come to pass by chance. Moreover, no proper mover is the cause of the conjunctions or divisions among the celestial bodies, but rather a higher cause is what unites; for what does not fall under the order of an inferior cause, falls under the order of a higher cause, and under its causality as well. For the order of any cause extends just as far as its causality. Whence the First Cause, and not the proper movers, orders the conjunctions and divisions among the stars.

The fourth order of causes is that the celestial bodies cause something in these inferiors, but in different ways. For something of the revolutions of the celestial bodies causes something here below as an essential, necessary, immediate cause and one which when posited, the effect is posited; also [it causes] something as an essential and necessary cause, but not one which when posited, the effect is posited, since it causes through a mediating motion; and it causes something but not as an immediate cause; and a revolution certainly causes something here below as an essential cause which works in most cases, since the celestial revolutions are naturally constituted to be impeded by an incapacity of matter; and it also causes something accidentally. But that which a celestial body causes here below accidentally, and what is accidental to them offering an impediment according to that which is taken absolutely, since it is a certain disposition of matter, or something here below acting contrary, is reduced to something of the celestial bodies as to a cause, but the very concurrence of the accident with the celestial body is not; yet nevertheless this concurrence is reduced to a superior cause, for whatever happens among the celestial bodies, in whatever way they are connected, has a unifying cause, as has been seen. And since every disposition of matter is referred to something of the celestial bodies, then, indeed, so uniting the celestial bodies unites the disposition of matter, caused by one revolution, to that [caused] by another revolution, whether that disposition is simultaneous with its cause, or is caused later, or remains later than its cause. Therefore the celestial bodies have this defect with respect to inferiors in relation to the divine causes which cause something in celestial bodies, that celestial bodies cause something accidentally and are able to be impeded, while this is not true of those other causes.

The fifth and last order of causes however is that particular lower causes, whose causality extends to few, have to cause some effects essentially and necessarily, other [effects] essentially though working only in most cases, and [still] others accidentally; nevertheless of the essential causality which is in these, a greater quantity is non-necessary causing, but causing which is effective in most cases, since these causes are especially subject to change. Nevertheless accidents here below, whether they are two causes concurring, or an impeding contrary agent or some disposition of matter, are found to be ordered and to have an essential cause of their conjunction in higher causes. For these inferiors are caused by superiors; therefore these two concurrences are caused either by one among the celestial bodies, or by many. In the first way they have an essential ordering cause among celestial bodies; in the second way, among divine things, as is clear from what was said before. But these particular causes fall short of celestial bodies in this, that celestial causes, even if they are impeded from their effect on account of an indisposition of matter, nevertheless are not capable of suffering and are not movable in themselves as are inferiors; and accidents still lower, which do not have their conjoining cause in particular causes, are found sometimes to be joined by something in the celestial bodies, by reason of the fact that a celestial cause extends to more than a particular inferior cause.

II

From the aforesaid, the second member of what was proposed above is clear, namely, what led *some* into the error that it is necessary that all future things which will come to pass be going to be before they are; likewise for all present and past things, before they should come to be. For every effect, related to the First Cause, comes from it as from its essential cause, since to that cause nothing happens. Therefore it also comes from it as from a non-impedible cause. For no cause is impedible unless an impediment can happen to it. From which it is argued as follows: every effect which results from an essential, non-impedible cause, results necessarily; but everything which results, in relation to the first cause of its coming-to-be, results from it as from an essential, non-impedible cause, as has already been shown. Therefore it is necessary that everything which comes to be, before it is, be going to be from the existence of the First Cause, which is the essential and non-impedible cause of the futurity of every effect which comes to be in its own time. And this reasoning is manifested because *Aristotle* maintains that there are two situations which prevent it being the case that all things happen necessarily. One is that some things come from an essential cause, but an impedible one, and those are not necessary; for example, if someone drinking a warm beverage dies, still it is not necessary that a warm beverage drinker dies. The other is that certain [things] are accidents which certainly according to Aristotle are not necessary, as that someone digging out a grave find a treasure. But if effects which, in relation to some particular cause, result from it as from an impedible cause, yet in relation to the First Cause, result from it as from an essential cause to which no impediment of its effect in a determinate time happens, then effects of this kind, which come to be from a particular cause in most cases, nevertheless in relation to the First Cause will come to be necessarily. But if, in addition, those things which are accidents in themselves and in relation to some particular causes, are always found to have a unifying and ordering cause, as has been seen previously, so that accidents of this kind also come from an essential, non-impedible cause, then accidents notwithstanding, all things would result from their causes necessarily. And this was what moved certain *Parisian Doctors* speaking out against the doctrine of their master, Aristotle, others maintaining other opinions for other reasons: although, they say, certain future things, which we call contingent in comparison to some of their causes, do not come from these necessarily, nor is it necessary for them to be going to be, before they are, from these causes, nevertheless when future things of this kind are related to the First Cause, from which all intermediate causes up to the effect are and act, or to the whole connection of causes or the whole relationship of existing things, all things which will come to be, before they are, necessarily will be from the existence of the First Cause, the connection of causes, or the relationship of existents, so that it is absolutely true to say that all things which will come to be, before they are, have something in the relationship of existents so that it is necessary for them to be going to be.

III

Now we must consider the third item proposed above, namely, in what those who think in the aforementioned way err. And it is this: that although the First Cause is not an impedible cause or one with which an accidental impediment concurs, nevertheless it does not produce inferior effects immediately but through intermediate causes; and although these intermediate causes owe it to the order of the First Cause that they produce an effect, and at that time that they are not impeded, nevertheless they are still in their very nature impedible; therefore, although the First Cause is not impedible, nevertheless it produces an effect through an impedible cause. For which reason that effect, even in relation to the First Cause, was not necessarily going to be beforehand. And although all concurrences have an ordaining and unifying cause, yet not such a cause (as is apparent and the reason for which will be seen) as makes all accidents be necessary, so that some among them would not be rare, but rather all of them would be frequent, indeed necessary. However, if all things were to come to be necessarily, it would be necessary, not so much that the first cause of future things be not impedible, but that future things which come to be not come to be from the First Cause through intermediate impedible causes. It would also be necessary that in beings there would be no accident but that would have an essential cause unifying and ordaining it, not just any sort but one which would prevent it from being rare, so that, when Aristotle maintains that, if there were no accident, all things would be necessary, we must understand that the removal of accident in relation to the First Cause does not make all things necessary, rather it would be necessary to remove an accidental impediment in relation to particular causes, through which intermediate causes the First Cause acts. And therefore, if anyone should especially prize the truth, he would find Aristotle, in the Sixth Book of the *Metaphysics*, maintaining two things: one is that, if all future things were to come to be necessarily, then all things would come to be from essential, non-impedible causes; the other is that there would be no rare accident; in fact the two aforesaid accompany each other.

From these, summarily with Aristotle, we say, finishing the question, that only those future things will come to be necessarily which will come to be from an essential, non-impedible cause, and not only the first but also a proximate cause; and because not all future things are such, but some of them are accidents, some of them moreover will come to be from causes that are impedible, although not impeded, for that reason not all things will come to be necessarily. And this is clear in this way. If anyone directs his attention, something is said to be necessarily going to be not only because it will come to pass and will not be otherwise, but because it is not able to be otherwise than that it should come to pass. Moreover, a future thing is not said to be impossible to be otherwise than that it should come to be, unless because its already present cause is such, not only that it will not be otherwise than that this kind of effect result from it, but because in its very nature [it is] such that it is not possible [for it] to be otherwise than that the effect come from it. And because not all things which will come to be, will come to be in this way from their cause, therefore not all things will come to be necessarily. For it is necessary, if all things which will come to be are necessarily going to be, that each and every thing would have in present things some cause which cannot be impeded, from which this kind of future effect would come to be immediately, or through intermediate future causes likewise not impedible; as in a living thing there is a present cause of future death, not impedible from that effect. And therefore we call many effects contingently future, and not necessarily [future], even referring them to the whole connection of causes or interrelationship of present things, or even to the First Cause. For although in the interrelationship of present things or the whole connection of causes there is contained a cause which is not impeded or which is deprived of any future contingent impediment, nevertheless there is not contained in them a necessary, immobile, non-impedible cause, which cannot be otherwise; it is not the case for, if in the interrelationship of present things and the connection of causes there does not exist what moves, or impedes, or makes to be otherwise the present cause of a future contingent, not for that reason is there contained in the interrelationship of present things and the connection of causes the immobile cause of that future thing. And the First Cause, even if it is a non-impedible cause, nevertheless causes through the medium of an impedible cause, as has been said; neither is it necessary for contingent future things to come to pass with respect to Divine Providence, because it has been seen from the order and connection of causes and the interrelationship of present things that it is not necessary that many things come to be which will come to be; wherefore neither [will they come to be necessarily] from the reason and understanding of this order and of the connection of causes to caused. But divine providence is nothing other than the reason of the said order and the making of the said connection.

But now three doubts arise concerning what has been said. The first is this. How can these simultaneously be the case: The First Cause is a non-impedible cause with respect to any future thing which will come to be, and yet that effect proceeds from it through impedible causes; for if the intermediaries and the instruments are impedible from the effect, then the First Cause will be impedible from its effect, through those intermediaries.

The second doubt exists because, although a cause, which is called "a cause which works in most cases," taken essentially and absolutely, is able to be otherwise than that it produce an effect, nevertheless the same cause taken as not impeded is not able to be otherwise than that it produce the effect. In this way however it is a cause producing an effect, insofar, namely, as [it is] not impeded. Therefore it seems that the effect of necessity proceeds from that [cause].

The third doubt is this, how is it that not all accidents have necessary concomitance, although all have an essential and ordering cause, as has been said before. For the flowering of this tree and of that, which, considered in themselves, are accidents, have necessary, or at least frequent, concomitance on account of the fact that they have an essential cause unifying and conjoining them. But if all accidents, which, considered in themselves and related to some particular causes, have the nature of accidents reduced to a higher cause, are found to be ordered, why will the concomitance of all not be necessary, as [it is] of the aforesaid? And we ask this, for let it be the case that there should be some impedible causes from which something would also come to be accidentally: if the impediment happening were some one of the things necessary from a unifying and ordering cause, the necessity of futurity in those things which result, inasmuch as they result, is not taken away, although some [of them] would also come to be from causes sometimes impeded, since the concurrence of impediments would come to be necessarily.

The first of these is solved: for these are not the case simultaneously—the First Cause is the necessary cause to some effect which will come to be, and, that effect is produced through intermediate impedible causes. But for the First Cause to be a non-impedible cause is not for it to be necessary to some effect which will come to be, but is for it to be a cause to which no impediment is able to happen outside its order, so that from the fact that the First Cause is not impedible, it follows that the coming-to-be of something future cannot happen outside Its order. And therefore if under the order of the First Cause only one part of the contradiction of a contingent future would fall, so that the other is not able to fall under its order, as happens in the case of particular causes, that future would necessarily result from the First Cause. Now however, since such is not the particular order of the First Cause to the caused, what has been said does not occur. Whence from a particular and proximate cause a contingent future does not result necessarily, because it is possible for the coming-to-be of that future to occur otherwise and outside the order of that cause. Nor does that future thing result necessarily from the First Cause, for although it is not possible for the coming-to-be of that future thing to occur otherwise than according to the order of the First Cause by reason of the fact that it is not an impedible cause, nevertheless since not only does that future thing fall under its order but also the possible opposite of that future thing, therefore the coming-to-be of that future thing is not necessary even with respect to the First Cause.

With regard to the second one must know that, as Aristotle says in the First Book of the *De Caelo et Mundo,* he who is sitting, while he is sitting, has a potency to standing. But he who is sitting, while he is sitting does not have a potency-to-standing-while-he-is-sitting. And therefore it is said in the *Perihermeneias* that being which is, when it is, necessarily is; not however: what is, necessarily is. So also a non-impeded cause-which-works-in-most-cases, even when it is not impeded, is able to be such that the effect not result from it, although it is not possible that from a non-impeded cause, when not impeded, the effect not result; and since necessity is a certain impossibility-to-being-otherwise, it appears that there is a certain necessity in the coming-to-be of an effect from an impedible cause, and clearly, because a cause-which-works-in-most-cases, existing in that disposition in which it has to cause the effect, and not impeded, is not, when it is this way, in potency to not-causing the effect. And unless there were such necessity, nothing would result from such causes; and Avicenna had this necessity in mind when he said that every effect is necessary with respect to its cause. However this is not necessity absolutely, no more than is the necessity of any present thing. For a cause-which-works-in-most-cases, at the very time when it is not impeded, is impedible and has a potency to be such that the effect not come to be from it, although it does not have a potency-to-be-impeded-while-not-impeded. Not seeing these aforesaid necessities, however, *some* have fallen into diverse errors. For *some,* paying attention to the fact that a cause not impeded and universally existing in that disposition in which it has to cause the effect, is not, when it is this way, in potency to not causing that very effect, have said that all things come to pass necessarily; and it is already apparent in what they have erred. *Others,* however, in order that they might avoid this error, have fallen into a different one saying that a cause, existing in that disposition in which it has to cause the effect, would in no way be a cause necessary to the effect, because then counsel and free choice would be destroyed. However the aforesaid distinction of the necessary solves their ignorance. If all things were to result necessarily, viz., from non-impedible causes, counsel to prevent certain future effects would be idle, as if the drinking of poison were a non-impedible cause of death, it would be idle to seek advice about medicine. This case: that the very cause producing the effect, be a non-impedible and necessary cause, would take away freedom of choice, because then all our willing would be caused by a cause which the will could not resist. But this case: that the drinking of poison, when not impeded, is not in-potency-not-to-cause-death-while-not-impeded, does not remove counsel about medicine. But one should not consult in order that the drinking of poison, which is not impeded, might not induce death; rather one should consult because the drinking of poison, which is not impeded, was impedible, so that at other times the aforesaid drinking may be impeded by the aid of medicine and may not induce death. However this case: that the will is always moved to willing under a cause existing in that disposition in which it is naturally constituted to move the will, and with the will itself existing in that disposition in which it is naturally constituted to be moved by such, does not take away freedom of choice, by reason of the fact that nothing moves the will that is not impedible from the motion, even if it is not impeded when it does move the will. Whence one must consider that the freedom of the will in its works must not be understood in this way, that the will is the first cause of its act-of-willing and its operating, being able to move itself to opposites, not moved by anything prior. For the will is not moved to willing except by some apprehension. Nor is this freedom of the will, that, the will itself existing in that disposition in which it is naturally constituted to be moved to willing something, and the mover also existing in that disposition in which it is naturally constituted to move, the will sometimes may not have to be moved, or it may have the potency-not-to-be-moved-when-it-is-so-disposed, the agent likewise being so disposed; for this is impossible. Rather freedom of the will consists in this, that even if the will be sometimes found moved by certain things, when these kinds of movers of the will are not impeded, such is the nature of the will that any one of those which can move the will, can be impeded from its motion; which happens to the will as opposed to the sensitive appetite, because the will wills from the judgment of reason, the sensitive appetite however desires from the judgment of sense. Now the fact is that we are born with a determinate judgment of sense with respect to the pleasurable and the painful, perceiving this determinately [as] pleasurable, that with sorrow. And because of this the sensitive appetite does not freely desire or flee from anything. However we are not so born with a determinate judgment about good and evil, rather either is possible; on which account also [either is possible] in the case of the will.

To the third it must be said that accidents, which have one cause and which are such that one of them is not able to result except from a cause from which the other results, are necessary; indeed these are not properly accidents, as in the example posited before, that when this tree flowers, the other does also. But for those things which concur from a unifying cause, while it is still possible for them to result from diverse causes, and for one of them to result [but] not from the cause of the other, the concomitance of such things is not necessary. As for example with the creditor willing to go to the market-place, the debtor is also willing from a common cause, as the sterility of the oats and the failure of the cereal plant; because it is still possible for these to result from different causes, and one of them not from the cause of the other, so it is that it accidentally happens that they are from one cause: for this reason, it is not necessary that with the creditor willing to go to the forum the debtor also be willing. And because the accidental does not have a unifying proximate cause except accidentally, and the remote cause moreover, which is God, does not induce necessity into the concomitance of accidents, therefore Aristotle has well said that the accidental is not truly being but as it were only in name, nor truly one, and that there is no cause of its generation. Thus when any two are accidentally concurrent in being, it is true that they have a unifying cause, but just as it accidentally happens that these are united, so it happens that these are from one cause, since it is possible for one of them to come to be from its proper cause without the other coming to be. Therefore the fact that being-which-exists-only-in-most-cases will not result of necessity, for example, that someone drinking a warm beverage die, and the fact that those things which are accidental are certainly not necessary, for example, that someone digging find a treasure, these make it true that not all things are necessarily going to be but only those things which result from non-impedible causes and which have in present things such a cause as future death has in the body of an animal now living.

IV

To the first objection maintaining the opposite it must be said that a cause of an effect, which works in most cases, taken in itself, is not necessary to the effect; the same cause even taken as not impeded, while it remains impedible, is still not necessary to the effect. But it is true that a cause-which-works-in-most-cases, taken as not impeded and as in the disposition in which it is a cause, is not, while not impeded and being so disposed, in potency to not causing the effect; and thus Avicenna thought that every effect is necessary with respect to its cause, which necessity, as has been seen before, is no other kind than this: everything which is, is necessary-when-it-is. And since a cause-which-works-in-most-cases, posited as not-impeded, although at that time it also be in potency to be impeded and to the effect not being produced, nevertheless that cause not impeded is not in potency such that the effect is able not to be posited, the cause not being impeded, therefore for a cause-which-works-in-most-cases to be a cause actually causing an effect, nothing is required but the removal of the impediment nor does it need something essentially educing it from potency to act, since the cause impeded is not a cause in potency except accidentally.

To the second it must be said similarly, that a future contingent effect, which will come to pass, does not have in the interrelationship of present things only a cause which is as matter, but also a cause in act, not however a cause from which necessarily that effect will be going to be; and this is clear in this way. For it is able to have in the interrelationship of present things a non-impeded cause without an intermediate, or with one or more intermediates. And, as has been seen, such a cause is not necessary to the effect, nor is it a cause only as matter, requiring something which makes it a cause actually. Thus the reasoning is defective in supposing that, if a future effect does not have in the interrelationship of present things a cause which is a cause only as matter, that therefore there already exists presently some non-impeded and necessary cause of that effect.

The third objection is answered the same way as is apparent to anyone examining it.

To the fourth objection it must be said that in order for everything to come to pass necessarily even with respect to the First Cause and the whole connection of causes and the interrelationship of present things, it would be required that nothing would be accidental being, not only with respect to the First Cause, and that not only the First Cause would be a non-impedible cause, but also that no impediment would be able to happen with respect to intermediate causes, through which the First Cause produces its effects, as has been said before.

With regard to the other objection based on providence, it must be known that *some* have stated: everything that will come to be, is necessarily going to be on account of what is touched upon in the three reasonings about divine providence mentioned above. But they are mistaken. For divine providence does not impose necessity on things; which is apparent in this way. Divine providence is nothing other than the reason or intellect directing the connection and order of causes to the things which they cause. But if the said order and connection does not impose necessity on all future things, but only on some, [namely], whose which come to be from non-impedible causes, then neither does the reason [directing] the said connection impose necessity, because if the causes which the master of the house pre-ordains to some end, do not induce that [end] necessarily, then neither does the reason or intellect or providence of the master of the house.

On account of this *others* have said that through divine providence not only is it provided for some future thing that it will come to be, but also how it will come to be, as, according to the condition of the proximate cause, contingently or necessarily; and therefore with regard to the coming-to-be of future contingents they say that it is necessary that such come to be, contingently however. But this statement can be understood in three ways. In one way so that it might mean not that future things of this kind come to be necessarily, but that in the coming-to-be of future things of this kind, contingency is necessary, such that if they come to be, it is necessary for them to come to be contingently; and this is true; but this is not what they intend, who say that it is necessary that future things of this kind come to be, contingently however, since their intention is to posit necessity and infallibility in the coming-to-be of future things of this kind, by reason of the fact that it has been forseen that these come to be, by infallible providence. And therefore one can understand in a second way the statement which says that it is necessary that future things of this kind come to be, contingently however; namely, that future things of this kind come to be contingently in relation to some impedible cause of them, and that nevertheless it is necessary that they come to be, in relation to providence and the whole connection of causes. And this is to say that, simply they come to pass necessarily, although in relation to something they are contingent; but, as has been seen before, that all things are necessarily going to be, even in relation to the whole connection of causes, is false. In a third way one can understand that they wish to say that contingency is the case absolutely, even in relation to divine providence and the connection of causes, and not only in relation to some cause. But then opposites are implied in the said statement, opposites which cannot be the case simultaneously. For these cannot be the case simultaneously, that it is necessary that *a* come to be, and yet it come to be contingently. But they do not affirm such except as, on account of the infallibility of divine providence, they posit infallibility and necessity in the coming-to-be of all future things. But, as has been said before, if the connection, order, and interrelationship of present things does not impose necessity on all future things, then neither does the knowledge of that order and the directing of the interrelationship.

But it must be diligently noted that if it were foreknown with regard to any future thing which we call contingent, that it will come to be, and it was foreknown by that knowledge which was of that thing in itself and not in another, and through that thing's proper concept, and by an infallible knowledge, whether the knowledge was divine or some other kind, then that future thing would necessarily be going to be. Thus, because *some* liken the divine knowledge by which He knows of any future thing that it will come to be, to their own knowledge, also positing that divine knowledge to be infallible, it is necessary for them to say that all things are necessarily going to be, as *Averroës* also says in the Sixth Book of the *Metaphysics*, that according to that which is said in the *Legal Examples*, because all things are written in the tablet and because that which is written ought necessarily to pass into act, all things are necessarily going to be. For the *Legal Examples* accept that in the divine intellect is a knowledge about all things which will come to be, that they will be, and a knowledge by which these are known in themselves and not in another, and through their proper concept. For thus does the *Legal Examples* take it that all things are written in the tablet: Averroës intending through "written in the tablet" that which *some* call divine foreknowledge, providence, or predestination which is part of providence, or the book of life.

But it must be noticed that neither present things nor future things or the coming-to-be of future things are known through the divine intellect by a knowledge which is of them in themselves, but by that kind of knowledge by which something is known in another. For the aforesaid enjoy no knowledge in God except a knowledge which is of God's own self and is his substance. However it is not necessary that such an infallible and always true knowledge of future things impose necessity on future things, so that it must be said of any future contingent thing that it has not been foreseen and foreknown by God that this will be, because nothing is foreseen and foreknown by God unless it is true. Now however, as Aristotle maintains in the *Perihermeneias*, although it is true that a naval battle will be or will not be, nevertheless divisively to assert either truly does not happen. For if it were true that a naval battle will be, then it would be necessary that a naval battle will be, as is treated *in the same book*. Or if it sounds serious to the ears of some, that this is not foreknown by God, then it must be said, as has been said before, that, although the fact that *a* will be, does not enjoy knowledge in God, except such a knowledge which is of the divine substance itself and is the divine substance itself, even such a knowledge of the very fact that *a* will be, which is of *a* but in some other immutable thing, although that *a* will come to be is mutable, does not impose necessity on that *a* relative to coming to be.

From which one must answer to the first objection by conceding the major: that "a future effect which has a present cause from which it necessarily follows, will of necessity come to be"; and by denying the minor which takes it that "all things which will come to be have a present cause from which they follow necessarily"; and when it is proved: "because it has been foreseen that these will come to be," it can be denied, as has been said; and that it is not foreseen that *a* will come to be, since this is not true: or one must say that, although it has been foreseen that *a* will come to be, and by an infallible providence, nevertheless that *a* will come to be is fallible, by reason of the fact that that providence and knowledge of *a* itself is not infallible about *a* in itself, but in something else which is immutable. For in the divine intellect mutable things have immutable science and fallible future things also have an infallible foreknowledge and providence.

To the second objection about providence one must speak similarly, either by denying the antecedent, namely that it has been foreseen that *a* will come to be, for the aforesaid reason; or by destroying the consequent by which it is said that if it has been foreseen that *a* will come to be, therefore *a* will come to be. For if from the interrelationship of present things and the connection of causes it does not follow that *a* will come to pass—for then it would be necessarily going to be from these—then neither from the existence of the First Cause [does it follow], since the First Cause does not cause that except through intermediate causes; and, if from the aforesaid it does not follow that *a* will come to pass, then neither [does it follow] from the providence which God has, since the providence which God has, is God; and also for this reason, since from ordered causes it is not necessary for any effect to follow, then neither [is it necessary] from the reason directing that order. Moreover, this consequence lies hidden: that *a* be going to be, if it has been foreseen that *a* will come to be: this happens because providence in relation to that coming-to-be is understood by a similitude to our knowledge and our providence regarding any future thing, that it will come to be.

To the third objection about providence one must say that just as there can be in God an immutable science of any mutable thing, by reason of the fact that science is not understood as the kind which is of that thing in itself, but in something immutable, so also there can be an infallible providence about a fallible future thing. It must be noted, however, that, although it is fallible that *a* be going to be, nevertheless the coming-to-pass of that *a* cannot occur outside the order of the First Cause, but neither is *a*'s being able not to be going to be not outside its order.

And what has been said about divine providence would similarly be said if one argued from divine foreknowledge of future things or predestination.

And with this are terminated six problems and one question, and it has been determined by master Siger of Brabant.

THE CONDEMNATION OF 1277

In 1277, Etienne Tempier, the Bishop of Paris, issued a statement condemning 219 philosophical and theological propositions that supposedly were taught by those sympathetic to the thought of Aristotle. Many of these propositions were alleged to be held by Siger of Brabant, although he was subsequently absolved of heresy. More telling and more unsettling is the fact that at least fifteen of the condemned propositions were traceable to Albert the Great (ca. 1200–1266) and his pupil, Thomas Aquinas, both of whom were committed to integrating the thought of Aristotle and his Arabic commentators into the teaching of medieval Scholasticism. Included in the selection here are those propositions most revealing of the philosophical controversies of the thirteenth century. Although the condemnation was short-lived, especially in the case of Aquinas, it remains a dreadful warning of the danger that political and religious oppression represent to the human quest for the truth.

From The Condemnation of 219 Propositions

Stephen, by divine permission unworthy servant of the church of Paris, sends greetings in the Son of the glorious Virgin to all those who will read this letter.

We have received frequent reports, inspired by zeal for the faith, on the part of important and serious persons to the effect that some students of the arts in Paris are exceeding the boundaries of their

---

own faculty and are presuming to treat and discuss, as if they were debatable in the schools, certain obvious and loathsome errors, or rather *vanities and lying follies* [Ps. 39:5], which are contained in the roll joined to this letter. These students are not hearkening to the admonition of Gregory, "Let him who would speak wisely exercise great care, lest by his speech he disrupt the unity of his listeners," particularly when in support of the aforesaid errors they adduce pagan writings that—shame on their ignorance—they assert to be so convincing that they do not know how to answer them. So as not to appear to be asserting what they thus insinuate, however, they conceal their answers in such a way that, while wishing to avoid Scylla, they fall into Charybdis. For they say that these things are true according to philosophy but not according to the Catholic faith, as if there were two contrary truths and as if the truth of Sacred Scripture were contradicted by the truth in the sayings of the accursed pagans, of whom it is written, *I will destroy the wisdom of the wise* [I Cor. 1:19; cf. Isa. 29:14], inasmuch as true wisdom destroys false wisdom. Would that such students listen to the advice of the wise man when he says: *If you have understanding, answer your neighbor; but if not, let your hand be upon your mouth, lest you be suprised in an unskillful word and be confounded* [Ecclus. 5:14].

Lest, therefore, this unguarded speech lead simple people into error, we, having taken counsel with the doctors of Sacred Scripture and other prudent men, strictly forbid these and like things and totally condemn them. We excommunicate all those who shall have taught the said errors or any one of them, or shall have dared in any way to defend or uphold them, or even to listen to them, unless they choose to reveal themselves to us or to the chancery of Paris within seven days; in addition to which we shall proceed against them by inflicting such other penalties as the law requires according to the nature of the offense.

By this same sentence of ours we also condemn the book *De Amore*, or *De Deo Amoris*, which begins with the words, *Cogit me multum*, and so on, and ends with the words, *Cave, igitur, Galtere, amoris exercere mandata*, and so on, as well as the book of geomancy that begins with the words, *Existimaverunt Indi*, and so on, and ends with the words, *Ratiocinare ergo super eum invenies*, and so on. We likewise condemn the books, scrolls, and leaflets dealing with necromancy, or containing experiments in fortunetelling, invocations of devils or incantations endangering lives, or in which these and similar things evidently contrary to the orthodox faith and good morals are treated. We pronounce the sentence of excommunication against those who shall have taught the said scrolls, books, and leaflets, or listened to them, unless they reveal themselves to us or to the chancery of Paris within seven days in the manner described earlier in this letter; in addition to which we shall proceed to inflict such other penalties as the gravity of the offense demands.

Given in the year of the Lord 1277, on the Sunday on which *Laetare Jerusalem* is sung at the court of Paris.

ERRORS IN PHILOSOPHY

On the Nature of Philosophy

1. That there is no more excellent state than to study philosophy. (40)

2. That the only wise men in the world are the philosophers. (154)

3. That in order to have some certitude about any conclusion, man must base himself on self-evident principles.—The statement is erroneous because it refers in a general way both to the certitude of apprehension and to that of adherence. (151) [177]

4. That one should not hold anything unless it is self-evident or can be manifested from self-evident principles. (37)

5. That man should not be content with authority to have certitude about any question. (150)

6. That there is no rationally disputable question that the philosopher ought not to dispute and determine, because reasons are derived from things. It belongs to philosophy under one or another of its parts to consider all things. (145)

7. That, besides the philosophic disciplines, all the sciences are necessary but that they are necessary only on account of human custom. (24)

On the Knowability of God

8. That our intellect by its own natural power can attain to a knowledge of the first cause.—This does not sound well and is erroneous if what is meant is immediate knowledge. (211)

9. That we can know God by His essence in this mortal life. (36)

10. That nothing can be known about God except that He is, or His existence. (215)

On the Nature of God

11. That the proposition, "God is being per se positively," is not intelligible; rather God is being per se privatively. (216)

12. That the intellect by which God understands Himself is by definition different from that by which He understands other things.—This is erroneous because, although the proper reason of His understanding is different in each case, the intellect is not other by definition. (149)

On the Causation of the World

27. That the first cause cannot make more than one world. (34)

28. That from one first agent there cannot proceed a multiplicity of effects. (44)

29. That the first cause would be able to produce an effect equal to itself if it did not limit its power. (26)

30. That the first cause cannot produce something other than itself, because every difference between maker and made is through matter. (55) [179]

31. That in heavenly things there are three principles: the subject of eternal motion, the soul of the heavenly body, and the first mover as desired.—The error is in regard to the first two. (95)

32. That there are two eternal principles, namely, the body of the heaven and its soul. (94)

On the Eternity of the World

83. That the world, although it was made from nothing, was not newly-made, and, although it passed from nonbeing to being, the nonbeing did not precede being in duration but only in nature. (99)

84. That the world is eternal because that which has a nature by which it is able to exist for the whole future has a nature by which it was able to exist in the whole past. (98)

85. That the world is eternal as regards all the species contained in it, and that time, motion, matter, agent, and receiver are eternal, because the world comes from the infinite power of God and it is impossible that there be something new in the effect without there being something new in the cause. (87)

86. That eternity and time have no existence in reality but only in the mind. (200)

87. That nothing is eternal from the standpoint of its end that is not eternal from the standpoint of its beginning. (4)

88. That time is infinite as regards both extremes, for although it is impossible for an infinity to be passed through when one of its parts had to be passed through, it is not impossible for an infinity to be passed through when none of its parts had to be passed through. (205)

89. That it is impossible to refute the arguments of the Philosopher concerning the eternity of the world unless we say that the will of the first being embraces incompatibles. (89)

90. That the universe cannot cease to exist because the first agent is able to cause transmutations one after another eternally, now into this form, now into that, and similarly it is of the nature of matter to undergo change. (203)

91. That there has already been an infinite number of revolutions of the heaven, which it is impossible for the created intellect but not for the first cause to comprehend. (101) [183]

92. That with all the heavenly bodies coming back to the same point after a period of thirty-six thousand years, the same effects as now exist will reappear. (6)

On the Necessity and Contingency of Things

93. That some things can take place by chance with respect to the first cause, and that it is false that all things are preordained by the first cause, because then they would come about by necessity. (197)

94. That fate, which is the disposition of the universe, proceeds from divine providence, not immediately, but mediately through the motion of the higher bodies, and that this fate does not impose necessity upon the lower beings, since they have contrariety, but upon the higher. (195)

95. That for all effects to be necessary with respect to the first cause, it does not suffice that the first cause itself be not impedible, but it is also necessary that the intermediary causes be not impedible.—This is erroneous because then God could not produce a necessary effect without posterior causes. (60)

96. That beings depart from the order of the first cause considered in itself, although not in relation to the other causes operating in the universe.—This is erroneous because the order of beings to the first cause is more essential and more inseparable than their order to the lower causes. (47)

97. That it pertains to the dignity of the higher causes to be able to commit errors and produce monsters unintentionally, since nature is able to do this. (196)

98. That, among the efficient causes, the secondary cause has an action that it did not receive from the first cause. (198)

99. That there is more than one prime mover. (66)

100. That, among the efficient causes, if the first cause were to cease to act, the secondary cause would not, as long as the secondary cause operates according to its own nature. (199)

101. That no agent is in potency to one or the other of two things; on the contrary, it is determined. (160)

102. That nothing happens by chance, but everything comes about by necessity, and that all the things that will exist in the future will exist by necessity, and those that will not exist are impossible, and that nothing occurs contingently if all causes are considered.—This is erroneous because the concurrence of causes is included in the definition of chance, as Boethius says in his book *On Consolation.* (21)

103. That the necessity of events comes from the diversity of places. (142)

104. That the differences of condition among men, both as regards spiritual gifts and temporal assets, are traced back to the diverse signs of the heaven. (143) [184]

105. That at the time of the generation of a man in body, and hence in soul, which follows upon the body, there is in him a disposition produced by the order of the higher and lower causes by which he is inclined to certain actions or events.—This is erroneous unless it is understood of natural events and by way of disposition. (207)

106. That one attributes health, sickness, life, and death to the position of the stars and the glance of fortune by saying that if fortune looks down on him he will live, if it does not, he will die. (206)

107. That God was not able to make prime matter save through the mediation of a heavenly body. (38)

On the Human Will

150. That that which by its nature is not determined to being or nonbeing is not determined except by something that is necessary with respect to itself. (128)

151. That the soul wills nothing unless it is moved by another. Hence the following proposition is false: the soul wills by itself.—This is erroneous if what is meant is that the soul is moved by another, namely, by something desirable or an object in such a way that the desirable thing or object is the whole reason for the movement of the will itself. (194)

152. That all voluntary movements are reduced to the first mover.—This is erroneous unless one is speaking of the simply first, uncreated mover and of movement according to its substance, not according to its deformity. (209)

153. That the will and the intellect are not moved in act by themselves but by an eternal cause, namely, the heavenly bodies. (133)

154. That our will is subject to the power of the heavenly bodies. (162)

155. That a sphere is the cause of a doctor's willing to cure. (132)

156. That the effects of the stars upon free choice are hidden. (161)

157. That when two goods are proposed, the stronger moves more strongly.—This is erroneous unless one is speaking from the standpoint of the good that moves. (208)

158. That in all his actions man follows his appetite and always the greater appetite.—This is erroneous if what is meant is the greater in moving power. (164)

159. That the appetite is necessarily moved by a desirable object if all obstacles are removed. This is erroneous in the case of the intellectual appetite. (134)

160. That it is impossible for the will not to will when it is in the disposition in which it is natural

for it to be moved and when that which by nature moves remains so disposed. (131)

161. That in itself the will is undetermined to opposites, like matter, but it is determined by a desirable object as matter is determined by an agent. (135)

162. That the science of contraries alone is the cause for which the rational soul is in potency to opposites, and that a power that is simply one is not in potency to opposites except accidentally and by reason of something else. (173)

163. That the will necessarily pursues what is firmly held by reason, and that it cannot abstain from that which reason dictates. This necessitation, however, is not compulsion but the nature of the will. (163) [188]

164. That man's will is necessitated by his knowledge, like the appetite of a brute. (159)

165. That after a conclusion has been reached about something to be done, the will does not remain free, and that punishments are provided by law only for the correction of ignorance and in order that the correction may be a source of knowledge for others. (158)

166. That if reason is rectified, the will is also rectified.—This is erroneous because contrary to Augustine's gloss on this verse from the Psalms: *My soul hath coveted to long,* and so on [Ps. 118:20], and because according to this, grace would not be necessary for the rectitude of the will but only science, which is the error of Pelagius. (130)

167. That there can be no sin in the higher powers of the soul. And thus sin comes from passion and not from the will. (165)

168. That a man acting from passion acts by compulsion. (136)

169. That as long as passion and particular science are present in act, the will cannot go against them. (129)

On Ethics or Moral Matters

170. That all the good that is possible to man consists in the intellectual virtues. (144)

171. That a man who is ordered as to his intellect and his affections, in the manner in which this can be sufficiently accomplished by means of the intellectual and moral virtues of which the Philosopher speaks in the *Ethics,* is sufficiently disposed for eternal happiness. (157)

172. That happiness is had in this life and not in another. (176)

173. That happiness cannot be infused by God immediately. (22)

174. That after death man loses every good. (15)

175. That since Socrates was made incapable of eternity, if he is to be eternal it is necessary that he be changed in nature and species. (12)

176. That God or the intelligence does not infuse science into the human soul during sleep except through the mediation of a heavenly body. (65)

177. That raptures and visions are caused only by nature. (33)

178. That by certain signs one knows men's intentions and changes of intention, and whether these intentions are to be carried out, and that by means of these prefigurations one knows the arrival of strangers, the enslavement of men, the release of captives, and whether those who are coming are acquaintances or thieves. (167)

179. That natural law forbids the killing of irrational animals, although not only these. (20) [189]

HONORIUS OF AUTUN

In direct contrast to the extraordinary sophistication of theological and philosophical speculation, medieval cosmology limped behind, more a creature of fantasy than of scientific imagination. The following selection, by Honorius of Autun, a Benedictine monk of the twelfth century, presents a popular and readily accepted version of the nature of the cosmos. Copernicus and Galileo are more than 300 years in the future, and one can see that the confidence and the richness of descriptions such as Honorius' would engender an intense scepticism with regard to any subsequent attempt to replace this "picture" with one more scientific. The cosmology of Honorius is in complete harmony with the assumptions of theology and natural philosophy that the world is finite, intelligible, and governed by an all-knowing, beneficent God. The combination of scriptural sources and the wisdom of philosophy enables Honorius and his culture to feel comfortable in their knowledge of what they take to be the "world." Parenthetically, they did not have access to a telescope.

From A Picture of the World

1. The world [*mundus*] gets its name from *undique motus,* as it were, for it is in perpetual motion. It is round like a ball, yet it has distinct parts like an egg. A shell completely covers the outside of the egg. Inside the shell is the clear albumen; within the latter lies the yolk; within the yolk, the fatty germ. In similar fashion heaven covers the whole of the world like a shell, next comes the sphere of pure aether like the clear albumen, then the sphere of turbulent air like the yolk, and finally, like the fatty germ, comes the earth.

2. There are five ways of writing about the creation of the world. One has to do with the way the immensity of the universe is conceived before all ages in the divine mind. This conception is called the archetypal world, of which it is written: "Whatever has been made found life in him [the Logos]" (John 1). The second refers to the moment when this world, perceptible to the senses, was embodied in matter according to the archetype. Of this it is written: "He that liveth forever created all things together" [Eccles. 18:1]. The third refers to the six days during which this world was given form by fashioning the various kinds of things, as it is written: "For six days God made his wonderfully good things" (Genesis 1). The fourth has to do with one thing being born of another as man from man, beast from beast, tree from tree, and each from seed of its own kind, as it is said: "My father works even until now" [John 5:17]. The fifth refers to the future renovation of the universe, as it is written: "Behold I make all things new" (Apoc. 21).

3. The elements composing all things are called *elementa,* which comes from *hyle* and *ligamenta* (i.e., the bands in which matter is wrapped), *hyle* being Greek for *matter.* They are fire, air, water, and earth. In themselves they revolve in cyclic fashion, until fire turns into air, air into water, water into earth and back again, earth into water, water into air, and air into fire. Each has its own qualities that are like arms, so to speak, which clasp each other and merge their discordant natures into a peaceful alliance. For the dry, cold earth is linked with cold water, while water, being cold and wet, is in turn connected with humid air. Air, being damp and warm, is joined to fire with its heat. Fire, being hot and dry, is tied in again with the dry earth. Of these elements, earth is the heaviest and occupies the lowest place, whereas fire as the lightest rises to the highest. The two remaining elements occupy an intermediate position, supplying a kind of stable bond. Of these, water is the heavier and nearest to the earth; air is the lighter and has the place next to fire. Walking things like men or beasts are destined for the earth; things that swim like fish, for the water; things that fly like birds, for the air; radiant things like the sun and stars, for the sphere of fire.

4. The lowest element is known by seven names: *terra, tellus, humus, arida, sicca, solum,* and *ops. Terra,* derived from *terendo,* "treading upon," refers to the element earth as a whole. *Tellus* [land], derived from *tollens fructus* [bearing fruits], refers to what is suitable for farming or is planted with vineyards or fruit-bearing trees. *Humus,* from *humor* [fluid], refers to swampy, nonarable areas. *Arida,* "without water," are desert lands like Lybia, which are always kept dry by the heat of the sun. *Sicca* are places like Judea, which, though watered by rain at times, are quickly desiccated. *Solum* [ground] from "solidity," applies to mountainous regions. *Ops* [property, wealth] applies to lands like India, where treasures like gold and precious stones abound.

5. The form of the earth is round, hence it is called an orb. If someone were situated high in the air, looking down upon it, its mighty mountains and concave valleys would appear to be smaller than the finger of one who held a huge ball in his hand. The circumference of the earth, however, is measured at 180,000 *stadia,* which is estimated to be 12,502 miles. The earth is located in the center of the world, like a point in the exact center of a circle. Since the position it occupies as its own represents an end point, it rests on no other element for support, but is held where it is by the power of God, as written: "Do you not fear me, says the Lord, who hangeth the earth on nothingness, founding it on its own bases" (Ps. 103). The ocean encompasses it like a girdle, as is written: "The deep like a garment is its clothing" *(ibid).* Its dryness is irrigated throughout by channels of water within it like the veins of blood in the body. That is why wherever one digs into the earth, water is to be found.

6. The earth is divided into five zones or circles. Of these the two extremes where the sun never approaches are uninhabitable because of the cold. The central zone from which the sun never recedes is uninhabitable because of the heat. The two intermediary zones are habitable being tempered on the one hand by the heat and on the other by the cold. If a fire, for instance, is kindled outside in the winter it sets up five areas of which the two extremes are icy, the center hot, and the two in between temperate. If it moved in a circle like the sun, these would become five circular zones. Of the earth's zones, the first is called the arctic, the second gets its name from the summer solstice, the third from the equinox, the fourth from the winter solstice, and the fifth is called antarctic. Only the second we know to be inhabited.

7. The habitable zone in which we dwell is divided into three parts by the Mediterranean Sea. One of these is Asia, the other Europe, and the third Africa. Asia extends from the north by way of the east to the south; Europe, from the west to the north; Africa, from the south to the west.

8. Asia gets its name from a queen by the same name. The first region of this in the east is paradise, a place renowned for its pleasantness, but inaccessible to men because it is surrounded by a fiery wall extending up to heaven.

9. In it is the tree of life, namely the tree of the fruit of which is such that whoever eats of it will remain in a state of immortality. Here also is the fountain that splits up into four rivers. Within paradise they flow together over the earth but outside they spread out over great distances.

[Chapters 13–36 contain descriptions, some mythical, some factual, of the various regions of the earth, concluding with a brief mention of various known and legendary islands.]

. . . Among these is that great island of which Plato writes which sank into the sea with its inhabitants. It exceeded Africa and Europe in size and was located where the present Mare Concretum is. And there is a certain ocean island, known as the "Lost Island," which surpasses all others on earth in pleasantness and productivity, but its whereabouts is unknown to man. It was once discovered by chance and when men tried to find it afterwards without success, it came to be called the "Lost Island."

37. Hell [*infernus*] is so called because it lies below [*inferius*]. For just as the earth is in the center of the sphere of air, so hell is in the center of the earth. That is why it is also called the end of the earth. But it is actually a place, broader below and narrower at the top—a horrible place of fire and brimstone. It is also called the "Lake of the Dead" or "Land of the Dead" because the souls that descend into it are truly dead. It is also called the "Pool of Fire" because souls sink into it like stones into the sea. It is also referred to as the "Dark and Gloomy Land" because it is clouded by smoke and a murky stench. It is also known as the "Land of the Forgotten" because those who dwell there have forgotten God and are forgotten by his mercy. It is also called *Tartarus,* which is etymologically linked with "horror" and "tremor," for here there is "weeping and gnashing of teeth" (Matt. 8). Another name for it is *Gehenna,* i.e., "land of fire," for *ge* means a land, whose fire puts ours into the shade. Its deepest recesses, filled with dragons and fiery snakes, is called *Erebus.* This is also called an "open mouth" and a *Barathrum* [deep pit] because it is a kind of *atra vorago* or "black pit." The places emitting fetid vapors are called "Acheron" which means air-holes that breathe forth a filthy smell. Here is located the river Styx, which in Greek means "sadness." It is also called "Phlegeton," which means "infernal river" because of the proximity of fire and brimstone. It is horrible by reason of the heat and stench. There are many other dreadful places and islands of punishment, some by reason of the cold or raging winds, others by reason of the ever-burning fire and brimstone. Having reviewed

the fiery places of hell, let us now turn to the cooling sphere of the waters.

38. Water, the second element, gets its name from *aequalitas* [equality]. Hence the surface of the sea is level. Water collects in the sea, is scattered in rivers, is divided in springs, and is connected by flowing streams. It girds the entire earth, dividing all regions and provinces. Its deepest part is called *abyssus* [abyss] from *abest fundus* (i.e., having no bottom). Actually it does have a bottom, but it is exceedingly deep.

39. The ocean [*oceanus*] gets its name from *ocior annis* [swifter than years] or *limbus* [hem or border] of the zones, because it surrounds them like a hem.

40. The tides of the ocean, i.e., its ebbing and flowing, are caused by the moon, whose inhalation causes high tide and exhalation low tide. . . .

53. Air is the name given to everything resembling the void, extending from the earth to the moon, from which vital breath is drawn. Because [this element] is moist, birds fly in it as fish swim in water. Air is the place where demons dwell awaiting with horror the day of judgment; from it they fashion bodies when they appear to men.

54. From air the wind is created, which is nothing else but air that has been agitated and stirred up. . . .

67. The fourth element is fire or *ignis* which gets its name from *quasi non gignis* [not begotten as it were]. It extends from the moon to the firmament. It is more subtle than air, even as air is more tenuous than water or water less dense than earth. This is also called *aether* which is *purus aer*, as it were, i.e., pure or refined air. From this the angels take their bodies when they are sent on missions to men.

68. In this fire sphere, seven stars go their own way against [the general movement of] the world and because of their wandering course are called planets, i.e., erratic things. The immense velocity of the firmament carries them from east to west, though their natural course is in the opposite direction. They are like the fly carried about on the mill wheel. Nevertheless their proper motion seems to be counter to the direction of the revolution of the firmament. Because of the obliquity of the zodiac they do not wander above or below it. Being impeded by the rays of the sun, however, they become eccentric and move backwards or remain stationary.

69. The moon is the first of the planets and the smallest star. But to us it appears to be bigger because it is carried along the first sphere next to the earth. It is a globe-shaped body, of a fiery nature, but mixed with water. Hence it does not glow with a light of its own but, like a mirror, it is illumined by the light of the sun. That is why it is called *luna*, because it is, as it were, *lucina*, i.e., *a luce nata* [born from light]. The little clouds seen on it are believed to come from the water in its substance. For it is said that if water were not intermixed with it, it would shed its rays on earth like the sun. But in such a case, because of its proximity it would devastate the earth with its heat, for this globe is much larger than the earth. Still, because of the distance of its orbit, it appears to be hardly a half-measure larger. The moon shines by that portion of its surface which faces the sun, whereas the portion turned away from the sun is in darkness. At full moon it is most remote from the sun, neither waxing nor waning. But when it is in opposition to the earth its light is obscured. Although it is carried violently through the firmament every day from east to west, it strains against this motion and passes through all the signs of the zodiac in twenty-seven days. Its path is said to oscillate over a period of nine or ten years. On the fourth day after the new moon, if the moon has the hue of ruddy gold, it portends windy weather; if the upper horn is darkened with spots, it is the beginning of a month of rain; if it is the central portion that is clouded, come full moon, it will be serene.

70. The second planet is Mercury. It is also known as Stilbon. It has a spherical form and is formed of fire. Its size is in the neighborhood of the moon and it receives light from the sun. It moves around the zodiac in 339 days.

71. The third planet is Venus (also known as Hesperus, the son of Aurora and Cephalus). It is both the Morning Star and Evening Star. It too is formed of fire, is round, and moves like Mercury through the zodiac, but in 348 days.

72. The fourth planet is the sun [*sol*] or Phoebus. It is called *sol* from *solus* [sole], because when all the other stars are obscured, it is the sole thing that shines. It too is of spherical form and of the nature of fire. Over eight times the size of the earth, its light exceeds that of all the other stars. Borne from east to west by the impetus of the firmament, it has a gradual counter movement that takes it through the zodiac in a period of 365 days. The periodic variation of its path is believed to take twenty-one years. Its presence brings about day; its absence, night. Just as it shines above the earth during the whole day, so it

shines below the earth during the entire night. When it travels in the northern part of the heavens it produces long days and the summer; when it moves in the southern part of the heavens it brings winter and shorter days.

73. At daybreak, if the sun is hazy or hidden by clouds, it augurs a rainy day; if it looks pallid, stormy weather is in the offing; if the sun appears concave, emitting bright rays towards the north and south, it forebodes damp and windy weather; if it is pale at sunset or covered with black clouds, the wind will be from the north.

74. Mars, also called Pyrois, is the fifth planet. It is globular, fiery hot, and takes two years to move through the zodiac.

75. The sixth planet is Jupiter. Round and temperate, it moves around the zodiac in twelve years.

76. The seventh planet is Saturn. It is also called Phaeton, the son of Helios. . . . It is spherical, icy, and moves through the zodiac in thirty years.

All of these orbits change periodically. After a span of 532 years the cycle begins again.

77. With respect to the center of the earth, the higher apsis of each orbit occurs when Saturn is in Scorpio, Jupiter in Virgo, Mars in Leo, the sun in Gemini, Venus in Sagittarius, Mercury in Capricorn, the moon in Aries. Halfway around each orbit is the lower apsis, the point closest to the center of the earth.

78. Each planet has its peculiar shade. Saturn is white; Jupiter, clear and bright; Mars, fiery; the Morning Star, whitish; the Evening Star, refulgent; Mercury, radiant; the moon, serene; the sun, burning.

79. The zodiac, or circle of the twelve signs, through which the planets move is divided laterally into twelve bands. The sun moves only through the two middle bands; the moon through them all; Venus wanders two degrees beyond; Mercury moves through eight of them, four above, two in the middle, and two below. Saturn, like the sun, stays in the middle two.

80. Delightful music is produced by these seven spheres revolving in sweet harmony, but tremendous though it be, we hear it not, for our ears are not attuned to it and it originates beyond the atmosphere. The only sounds that we can hear, however, are such as occur in the atmosphere. Celestial music is measured on a scale that extends from earth to firmament, but our scale is said to be modeled upon it.

81. If, on earth, one puts *A* in the moon, *B* in Mercury, *C* in Venus, *D* in the sun, *E* in Mars, *F* in Jupiter and *G* in Saturn, the musical scale becomes immediately apparent, for from earth to the firmament seven tones are to be found. From earth to moon is one tone; from moon to Mercury, a halftone; from Mercury to Venus, a halftone; from Venus to the sun, three halftones; from the sun to Mars, a whole tone; then to Jupiter, a halftone; from there to Saturn, a halftone, and from Saturn to the zodiac, three halftones. A tone consists of 15,625 miles; a halftone of 7,812½ miles. Altogether the tones add up to seven. The reason the philosophers have distinguished nine Muses is because they discovered nine consonances between earth and heaven, consonances which are implanted by nature in man.

82. For as the tones in our world add up to seven, and we have seven notes in our music, so the human composite represents a sevenfold blend. The body is a harmony of the four elements; the soul, of three powers; and nature has brought them together through the art of music. That is why man is called a microcosm, or smaller world, when he is thus recognized to be numerically in tune with the music of the spheres.

83. The distance from earth to moon is 12,600 *stadia,* which equals 15,625 miles; from moon to Mercury, 7,812½ miles; from there to Venus, the same; from it to the sun, 23,437½ miles; from the sun to Mars, 15,625 miles; to Jupiter, 7,812½ miles; to Saturn, the same; from there to the firmament, 23,437½ miles. From earth to heaven therefore it is 109,375 miles.

With the planetary spheres we pass beyond fire; let us push on to the heavenly spheres.

84. Heaven is called *coelum,* since it is like a *casa ilios* [i.e., a home of the sun] or like a *vas coelatum* [i.e., an embossed vase], since it is set with stars. It is of a subtle, fiery nature. Being everywhere equally distant from the center of the earth, it has a round shape. Consequently, from all quarters, it appears as a hemisphere and it rotates daily with an indescribable rapidity. If the heavens are red in the evening, it portends a fine day; if they are so at dawn, it betokens stormy weather. There are two "Gates of Heaven," the east from which the sun comes forth, the west into which it enters.

85. The climes or regions of heaven are four: eastern, southern, western, and northern. . . .

86. The orient is named after *ortus solis* [where the sun rises]; the occident from *occasus solis* [where the

sun sets]; the meridian from *medidies* [midday] and the north [*septentrio*] from the seven stars known as the seven [*septem*] ploughing oxen [*triones*.] The first letter of the Greek names for these celestial zones can be arranged to spell the name of Adam, who is a microcosm.

87. The superior heaven is called the firmament, for it is like firm land in the midst of waters. It has a spherical form, is of an aqueous nature, and is everywhere adorned with stars. But the water, like ice, is solidified in crystal form. Hence it is called "firmament."

88. There are two poles, so called from *polire* [to smooth or polish]. One is the north pole, always visible to us; the other, the south pole, which we never see because the swelling of the earth prevents us from viewing the point on the sphere directly opposite to us. The heavens turn on these like a wheel on its axle.

89. The heavens are studded everywhere with stars but they do not appear to us during the day because they are blotted out by the brightness of the sun, even as the sun does not shine when clouds cover the sky. A star [*stella*] gets its name as it were from *stans luna* [i.e., a "standing moon"], for they stand fixed in the firmament and do not fall despite the amazing speed at which they are whirled about. While one star is called *stella*, many together are called *astra* or *sidera*.

90. *Sidera* comes from con*sider*ing, since those who are sailing or are traveling study the stars. All the stars are round and fiery. Only God knows how they are arranged or ordered. He who numbers the stars alone knows their names, their distinctive traits, their capacities, the course they run, their time and place. But the wise of this world give to them the names of animals or men so that we might tell them apart.

91. In the midst of the firmament are twelve signs which divide equally the circular path [through which the planets seem to move]. In Greek, it is called *zodiacus;* in Latin, *signifer,* because it contains the signs [*signa*] which bear the names of animals, *zoön* meaning "animal."

[Chapters 92–135 list the signs of the zodiac and explain how they and the principal other constellations got their names.]

136. The Milky Way is so white because all the stars pour their light into it.

137. Comets are stars with tails of flame, which appear towards the northern part of the Milky Way. They portend political revolutions, plague, war, tornadoes, scorching heat, or drought. They appear for seven days, or if longer, for eighty days.

Many untrue and vicious things we have seen ascribed to the stars, however. Let us look higher then to the Morning Star and the Sun of Suns.

138. Suspended above the firmament are waterlike clouds which are said to move through the heavens in a circular path and are referred to as the *aqueous heaven*.

139. Above this is a spiritual heaven unknown to men. It is the habitation of the nine orders or choirs of angels. Here is the paradise of paradises where the souls of the saints are received. It is this heaven that was created in the beginning with the earth, according to what we read [in the Scriptures].

140. Far surpassing even this is the heaven of heavens in which the King of Angels dwells.

DANTE ALIGHIERI

Widely regarded as one of the world's great poets, Dante was born in Florence, Italy, in 1265. In 1289, he fought with the Florentine cavalry in a victory at Campoldino. After the death of his spiritual inspiration, Beatrice, in 1290, Dante devoted his life to scholarship and writing, while remaining active in Florentine and Italian politics. He died in Ravenna in 1321.

Although Dante was the author of a range of works, including The New Life *and* On World Government, The Divine Comedy *is his masterpiece. A magnificent mirror image of medieval society and beliefs,* The Divine Comedy *tells of Dante's journey upward from Hell through Purgatory and finally to Paradise. Thus Dante charts, in an often wry and irreverent fashion, the life of the human soul in its journey to the light.* The Divine Comedy *is a poetic version of the medieval cathedral as well as of the* Summa Theologica *of Thomas Aquinas, in that Dante accepts the hierarchical theology, cosmology, architecture, and social structure of the medieval age. As the architectural movement is an upward progression from the dungeon to the steeple, from the dark nave to the luminescent glory of the stained glass windows of the medieval cathedral, so too is the journey of Dante from the Inferno to Purgatory and to Paradise characterized by ascension. The following excerpts have been chosen as particularly relevant for students of philosophy. It is hoped that this taste of* The Divine Comedy *will lead the student to a complete reading of this superb poetic rendition of human life.*

From The Divine Comedy

In *The Divine Comedy* Dante describes his imaginary journey through Hell, Purgatory, and Paradise. No other poem in any language has had such a wide appeal: the conception is so lofty, the music so beautiful, and the interest of the narrative so sustained, that its importance has steadily increased. For the last six hundred years learned commentaries have been accumulating; and so, inevitably, have the translations.

The luckless translator can never recapture the beauty of Dante's music. He must try to convey the meaning, often obscure, as musically as he can in another tongue. In this version the aim has been to tell Dante's story as simply and accurately as possible. Any archaic and unfamiliar constructions that would impede the swift pace of the narrative have been avoided, although the second person singular has been used in the Paradiso—for such is the language of heaven.

As the "terza rima" form of the original is alien to English, blank verse has been chosen, the form used by Milton in *Paradise Lost.* In his foreward to that poem, he says: "The measure is English heroic verse without rime, as that of Homer in Greek, and of Virgil in Latin—rime being no necessary adjunct or true ornament of poem or good verse, in longer works especially, but the invention of a barbarous age, to set off wretched matter and lame meter; graced indeed since by the use of some famous modern poets, carried away by custom, but much to their own vexation, hindrance, and constraint to express many things otherwise, and for the most part worse, than else they would have expressed them."

It is natural that the scenes so vividly described by Dante should have inspired many artists—such as Botticelli, Flaxman and Blake—to depict them. Most famous of all the illustrations are those of Gustave Doré (1833–1883) whose dramatic portrayals, particularly of the horrors of the Inferno, are unsurpassed.

INFERNO

Canto 1

MIDWAY upon the journey of our life
I found that I was in a dusky wood;
For the right path, whence I had strayed, was lost.
Ah me! How hard a thing it is to tell

 Specified excerpts from Translator's Note; Inferno, Canto I, ll. 1–27 and 61–136 (White, pp. 1–2); Canto III, ll. 1–59 (White, pp. 4–5); Canto IV, ll. 13–45 and 130–150 (White, pp. 6–8); Canto V, ll. 73–142 (White, pp. 9–10); Canto XI, ll. 70–112 (White, p. 19); Purgatorio, Canto XVII, ll. 82–139 (White, p. 95); Canto XVIII, ll. 1–75 (White, p. 96); Paradiso, Canto V, ll. 19–87 (White, pp. 136–137); Canto XI, ll. 43–108 (White, pp. 147–148); Canto XIX, ll. 67–108 (White, p. 162); Canto XX, ll. 88–138 (White, pp. 164–165); Canto XXXIII, ll. 1–57 (White, p. 187).

The wildness of that rough and savage place,
The very thought of which brings back my fear!
So bitter was it, death is little more so:
But that the good I found there may be told,
I will describe the other things I saw.
   How I arrived there, it were hard to tell:
So weary was my mind, so filled with sleep,
I reeled, and wandered from the path of truth.
When I had come before a mountain's base—
The ending of that steep and rugged valley
That lately had so struck my heart with fear—
I raised my eyes, and saw the mountain's shoulder
Already covered by the planet's rays
That safely guide the steps of other men.
Then was my terror somewhat quieted
That through the last night's anguish I had borne
Within the very wellsprings of my heart.
Like one who having battled with the waves,
In safety on the shore, with panting breath
Looks back upon the perils of the deep:
So did my soul, which still in terror fled,
Turn back to contemplate with awe and fear
That pass which man had never left alive.
   While I was stumbling down to lower ground,
Before my startled eyes appeared a man
Whose voice seemed weak from long-continued silence;
And when I saw him in that desert place,
"Help, pity me," I cried, "whate'er you are,
A living man, or spectre from the shades!"
   He answered me: "No man am I, though once
A man I was—from Lombard parents sprung
Who both were citizens of Mantua.
Late in the time of Julius I was born,
And lived in Rome while great Augustus reigned,
When false and lying gods still held their sway.
I was a poet, and sang the worthy son
Born to Anchises, who escaped from Troy
After proud Ilion was burned to ashes.
But why do you return to so much woe?
Why not climb upward to that happy mountain,
The origin and cause of every joy?"
   "Are you then Virgil—that great fountainhead
Whence such a flood of eloquence has flowed?"
I answered him abashed, with forehead bowed.
"O light and honor of all other poets,
May my long faithful study of your book,
And my great love for it, avail me now!
You are my master, and my very author:
It is from you alone that I have taken
The lofty style for which men honor me.

See yonder beast, from which I turned away:
Protect me from her, O illustrious sage—
My blood is trembling in my veins from fear!"
"Another passage you must seek," he said,
Perceiving that my eyes were filled with tears,
"If you would safely leave this savage place.
For that wild beast which makes you cry aloud
Suffers no man to pass along her way,
But blocks his passage till he has been slain.
Her nature is so evil and malign
That never is her greedy will appeased:
Food only makes her hungrier than before.
With many another animal she has bred,
And will with many more, until such time
The Hound shall come, to make her die of grief—
That Hound who shall not feed upon the land
Or riches, but on wisdom, love, and valor.
His fatherland shall lie between the Feltres:
The savior, he, of fallen Italy
For whom the maid Camilla died, and Turnus,
Euryalus, and Nixus shed their blood.
Through every city he shall drive her on
Until again she takes her place in hell,
Whence envy sent her forth to plague mankind.
Wherefore I think that it were best for you
To follow me: and I shall be your guide
To lead you hence through that eternal place
Where you shall hear despairing cries of woe,
And see the ancient spirits in their grief
Proclaiming they have died a second death.
Then you shall look on those who are content
To burn in flames, because they hope to join,
Whenever it may be, the blessed throng.
But should you wish to reach the realms of bliss,
For that there'll be a worthier soul than I:
I'll leave you in her care when I depart.
For the great Emperor who rules above
Forbids that I, rebellious to His law,
Approach unto His glorious citadel.
The Lord who ruleth all there sits on high:
There is His city, there His lofty throne.
How happy there is he whom God hath chosen!"
And I to him: "O poet, I beseech you,
By that same God whom you have never known,
That I may flee this wickedness, and worse!
O lead me where you said but now awhile,
So that I may behold St. Peter's gate,
And those you say are so oppressed by grief."
Then he moved on: I followed in his steps.

The Last Judgment: The Damned Falling into the Abyss of Hell, School of Roger van der Weyden (first half of the fifteenth century). This depiction of sufferers in Hell conveys the seriousness with which medieval culture held the possibility of eternal damnation. (The Bettmann Archive)

Canto 3

THROUGH ME LIES THE ROAD TO THE CITY OF GRIEF.
THROUGH ME LIES THE PATHWAY TO WOE EVERLASTING.
THROUGH ME LIES THE ROAD TO THE SOULS THAT ARE LOST.
JUSTICE IMPELLED MY MIGHTY ARCHITECT:
THE POWER DIVINE, AND PRIMAL LOVE AND WISDOM
SURPASSING ALL, HAVE HERE CONSTRUCTED ME.

BEFORE I WAS CREATED, NOTHING WAS
SAVE THINGS ETERNAL. I SHALL LAST FOREVER.
ABANDON HOPE, ALL YE WHO ENTER HERE!
   In characters obscure, above a gate
I saw these words inscribed upon the rock.
"Master," I said, "their meaning bodes me ill!"
   He answered me like one of understanding:
"Here must all misgiving be cast off;
All cowardice must here be overcome.
For now we have approached unto that place
Of which I spoke, where you shall see those souls
Who mourn the lack of intellect's true light."
   Then, after he had placed his hand in mine,
With radiant countenance that gave me heart,
He led me onward to the things unknown.
   Here sighs and wails and shrieks of every sort
Reverberated in the starless air,
So that at first it made me weep to hear.
In divers tongues, in accents horrible,
With groans of agony and screams of rage,
In voices weak and shrill, with sounds of blows,
A ceaseless tumult's everlasting roar
Seethed round about that timeless blackened air,
As sand is tossed before the whirlwind's blast.
I asked him, with my head in horror bound:
"O master, tell me what is this I hear,
And who are these so overcome by grief?"
   He answered me: "This miserable lot
Befalls the woe-begotten souls of those
Who lived their lives with neither praise nor blame.
Commingled with them here, that wretched choir
Of angels stand, who selfishly refused
To keep their faith with God, or to rebel.
Heaven expelled them, not to be less fair;
And yet deep hell refuses to receive them."
   And I: "O master, what can be the grief,
That makes them thus lament so bitterly?"
   He answered: "I will tell you very briefly.
These have no hope of death; existence here
Is so degraded and obscure, that they
Are envious of any other lot.
The world above has put them out of mind:
Mercy and justice scorn them, both alike.
We won't discuss them. Look, and pass them by."
   And as I looked, I saw a standard borne
So swiftly round about that it appeared
As if it were disdainful of repose.
Behind it surged so vast a multitude
Of souls, that I should never have believed

That death had overthrown so great a throng.
When I beheld there some that I had known,
I saw, and knew at once, the shade of him
Who basely made the great renunciation.

Canto 4

. . . "Into that sightless world let us descend,"
The poet said, his face as pale as death.
"I shall go first, and you shall come behind."
Perceiving his pale hue, I questioned him:
"How shall I go, when you, my only hope
Of comfort for my fears, do fear as well?"
He answered me: "The anguish of these people
Who suffer here, has painted on my face
Compassion—which you misread as fear.
Let us be on: our road is long and hard."
Then he stepped forth, and ushered me within
The topmost ring that girdles the abyss.
But in this ring—as far as one could judge—
There were no cries of woe, but only sighs
That quivered in the everlasting air.
This murmur came from multitudes of men,
Of women, and of children, who bewailed,
But suffered not. My goodly master said:
"You do not ask me who these spirits are
We see about us. Ere we pass beyond,
I wish to tell you that they have not sinned.
Though they are worthy, this does not suffice,
Because they never have received the joy
Of holy baptism, essence of your faith.
But those who lived before the time of Christ,
Could never worthily adore their God:
And I myself am of this company.
For this defect, and for no other wrong,
Our souls are lost: for this we must endure
A hopeless life of unfulfilled desire."
My heart was stricken when I understood;
For I knew there were many worthy souls
Eternally suspended there in limbo. . . .

. . . Then, as I slightly lifted up my brow,
I saw that overlord of all wise men
Among a philosophic family.
Plato was there, and Socrates as well,
Standing above the others, near his side;
Democritus, who thought all due to chance;
Diogenes and Anaxagoras,

Zeno, Empedocles, and Heraclitus.
I saw that pleasant gatherer of herbs,
Dioscorides; and Orpheus, and Linus;
Tullius, and Seneca the moralist;
Euclid the measurer, and Ptolemy,
Hippocrates, and Galen; Avicenna,
Averroës, who wrote the Commentary.
All that I saw I cannot well relate:
So lengthy is my theme, that oftentimes
My words are insufficient for the fact.
  Our group of six was now reduced to two.
My leader took me by another road,
Forth from that quiet air to gusty storms:
And I had come to where all light was gone.

Canto 5

. . . I said to him: "O poet, I would speak
To that sequestered pair that cling together
And seem to float so lightly on the wind."
  He answered me: "Take heed when they approach
More nearly to us: ask them by that love
Which bears them on, and they will come to you."
  Now when the wind had wafted them to us,
I raised my voice: "O wearied souls, unless
Forbidden by Another, come, and speak!"
Like doves that with their wings upraised and still
Are borne upon the air by their desire
When longing calls them back to their soft nest:
Just so these two left Dido's company
To come toward us through the fetid air,
So strongly were they drawn by my appeal.
  "O living creature, gracious and benign,
Who through this air as dark as pitch has come
To seek us who have stained the earth with blood—
Were He who rules the universe our friend,
We would beseech Him for your soul's repose
Because you have compassion for our lot.
Of what it pleases you to hear and speak
We will converse with both of you, so long
The bitter blast is lulled as it is now.
  The land where I was born lies on the shore
Where Po, with all his riot retinue
Pours toward the ocean stream in search of peace.
Love, which lies smouldering in each gentle heart,
Inflamed him for the beauty that was mine;
And how 'twas taken from me, shames me still.
Love, that will take for answer only love,
Caught me so fiercely up in his delight
That, as you see, he still is by my side.

Love led us to one death: Caina waits
For him who quenched the flame of both our lives."
These were the words that came to us from them.
When I had understood those injured souls,
I bowed my head, nor ever lifted it
Until the poet said: "What are your thoughts?"
I answered him, beginning in this manner:
"Alas, what loving thoughts, what fond desires
Have brought them to this lamentable pass!"
Once more I turned to them and raised my voice:
"Francesca, I am moved to bitter tears
By pity for the torments you have suffered.
But tell me, in that hour when sighs were sweet,
How did love let you know, or chance discover
The drift of all your fond imaginings?"
And she replied: "There is no greater grief
Than to recall a bygone happiness
In present misery: that your teacher knows.
But if you have so great a wish to learn
The very root whence sprang our sinful love,
I'll tell our tale, like one who speaks and weeps.
"One day, to pass the time, we read the book
Of Launcelot, and how love conquered him.
We were all unsuspecting and alone:
From time to time our eyes would leave the page
And meet to kindle blushes in our cheeks.
But at one point alone we were o'ercome:
When we were reading how those smiling lips
Were kissed by such a lover—Paolo here,
Who nevermore from me shall be divided,
All trembling, held and kissed me on the mouth.
Our Galeot was the book; and he that wrote it,
A Galeot! On that day we read no more."
While the first spirit told her tale, the other
Wept with a passionate grief that mastered me;
I felt a faintness, as it were of death,
And like a corpse fell headlong to the ground.

Canto 11

. . . But tell me why those in the reeking swamp,
Those others in the wind and in the rain,
And those who always meet with bitter speech,
Are not within the flaming citadel
For punishment—since God holds them in wrath?
If not, why are they in such sorry plight?"
He said to me: "Why goes your mind astray
So far beyond its usual boundaries,
Or has your memory forsaken you?
Do you not recollect those words in which

Your *Ethics* treats of those three dispositions—
Those dispositions never willed by heaven—
Incontinence, bestiality, and vice?
And how incontinence the least of all
Offends our God, incurring lesser blame?
If you can rightly understand my words,
And well remember who those spirits are
Who suffer punishment outside these walls
Above us there, then you will comprehend
Their separation from these guilty souls,
And why the heavenly vengeance strikes them less."
"O sun, that clarifies all faulty vision,
You so content me when you solve my doubts
That I like doubts themselves as much as knowledge.
Turn back again," I asked, "to where you said
That usury offends the Power Divine,
And pray explain to me this knotty point."
"Philosophy," my master answered me,
"To him who understands it, demonstrates
How nature takes her course, not only from
Wisdom divine, but from its art as well.
And if you read with care your book of physics,
After the first few pages, you will find
That art, as best it can, doth follow nature,
As pupil follows master; industry
Or art is, so to speak, grandchild to God.
From these two sources (if you call to mind
That passage in the Book of Genesis)
Mankind must take its sustenance and progress.
The moneylender takes another course,
Despising nature and her follower,
Because he sets his hope for gain elsewhere.
But follow me, for now we must proceed. . . .

PURGATORIO

Canto 17

. . . "My gracious father, tell me what offence
Is purged in this new cornice where we stand?
Even though our feet are resting, you can speak."
And he to me: "The love of what is good,
Defective in its duty, is here restored:
'Tis here the slackened oar is plied again.
But that you may more clearly understand,
Pray give me your attention: you will see
What good fruit you will gather by delay.
"Nor creature nor Creator," he began,
"Was ever without love—or spiritual
Or elective. This, my son, you know.
Elective love is always free of error;
That other love can err in its objective,

Or from too little or too much intensity.
While it is turned upon the heavenly blessings,
And, for the lesser, keeps within its bounds,
It cannot be the source of wicked joys;
But when it turns to evil, or pursues
The good with too much or too little zeal,
'Tis then the creature thwarts its own Creator.
Hence you will see that love must be the seed
Within yourselves, whence every virtue springs
And also every punishable action.
Now since the face of love can never turn
Away from what promotes its object's good,
All things are thus immune from their own hatred.
And since no being e'er can be imagined
As independent of its own Creator,
It is impossible to hate one's God.
It follows then, unless I am in error,
That lust of evil is toward your neighbor,
And rises in three ways within your clay.
"First there are those who through their neighbor's fall
Themselves hope to excel, and therefore crave
To see him cast down from his high position;
Then, those who fear to lose, should others rise,
Their power or fortune, honor and renown,
With fear so great, they wish the opposite;
Then, those with such resentment for a wrong
That they become insatiate for revenge,
And these must needs work injury on others.
This threefold love is wept for down below.
"Now I would tell you of that other kind
Pursuing good, but not with proper judgment.
Each person, in a way that is confused,
Conceives a good wherein his mind may rest,
And longs for it: so all strive to attain it.
If dilatory love should lead you on
To see or to obtain that good, this cornice,
After due penitence, torments you.
There is another good, which doth not yield
True happiness: for 'tis not the good essence
That is the root and fruit of every good.
The love that yields itself too much to this
Is wept for in three circles here above us.
But wherefore it is spoken of as threefold,
I tell you not: that you must learn yourself."

Canto 18

My teacher, who had ended his discourse
Now looked attentively upon my face
To see if I appeared content. But I,
Already goaded by another thirst,

Was silent, and was thinking: "Now perchance
He is annoyed by too much questioning."
But that true father, who had understood
My timid wish that still remained concealed,
By speaking first, emboldened me to say:
"I see so much more keenly in your light,
My master, that I clearly can discern
All that your reasoning described or means.
Therefore I pray that you expound to me
That love to which you, father, have ascribed
Every good action, and its opposite."
"Direct on me," he answered, "the keen eye
Of understanding: then will you perceive
The error of the blind who try to lead.
The mind, created well-disposed to love,
Is quickly moved toward everything that pleaseth,
So soon as pleasure rouses it to action.
Your apprehensive faculty will draw
An image from some object that exists,
And so display it, that your mind turns toward it.
And if, thus turned, the mind incline thereto,
That inclination is both love and nature,
Bound to you the more by pleasure's tie.
Then as a flame will move forever upward
By reason of its form, which is conceived
For rising to its proper element:
Just so the captivated mind aspires.
This yearning is a spiritual motion,
And rests not till it gains the thing it loves.
From this, it must be evident to you
How far the truth is hid from those who hold
That each love, in itself, is laudable
Because it may have matter that is good,
Yet every seal's impression is not good,
However good the wax itself may be."
"Your words," I answered him, "and my own mind,
Eager to follow them, have shown me love:
And yet my doubt is greater than before.
For if all love be sent us from without,
And if the soul proceeds not otherwise—
If it go right or wrong, 'tis not at fault."
And he: "As far as reason can explain,
I'll tell you here. Beyond that, you must look
To Beatrice: for this now deals with faith.
Every substantial form that is distinct
From matter, or is united with it,
Doth hold a power specific in itself,
That is not felt as long as it is dormant,
But demonstrates itself in its effect,
Even as in plants green leaves betoken life.

Man does not know whence comes his understanding
Of the existence of first principles,
Or of the trend of primal appetites
Innate in you, like instinct in the bee
For making honey; and this primal will
Can never in itself be praised or censured.
But so that all may harmonize with it,
The faculty of reason is inborn,
And should defend the threshold of assent.
This is the source of all mankind's deserts,
According as it gathers in the good
Or winnows out the bad loves in its path.
Those who have sought this out in argument
Perceived this innate freedom, and bequeathed
Moral philosophy unto the world.
If, therefore, we assume that every love
Rises within you of necessity,
In you exists the power to restrain it.
To Beatrice, this noble faculty
Denotes free will; so bear this well in mind
If she proceeds to speak of it to you." . . .

PARADISO

Canto 5

. . . "The greatest gift God's bounty has created,
The gift that most conforms to His own good,
That He himself of all most precious holds,
Is freedom of the will, wherewith are blest
All creatures that possess intelligence;
But they, and only they, are so endowed.
From this, to thee will now be evident
The exceeding value of a vow, if made
So God accept it when thou offerest it.
To close this compact between God and man,
That precious treasure must be sacrificed,
Though this is brought about by its own act.
What can be rendered, then, in recompense?
To use for other good what thou hast offered,
Would do good work, but with ill-gotten gain.
"Upon the greater point, thou art assured;
But since our Holy Church gives dispensation
In this regard—which seems to void my truth—
Thou yet shalt sit at table for a while,
Because partaking of such heavy food
Requires some further aid for its digestion.
Open thy mind to what I now reveal,
And treasure it therein: for ill he learns
Who hearing, yet retains not what he hears.
"This sacrifice is of two things combined:

The first, the very substance it is made of;
The other is the covenant itself.
The latter is ne'er cancelled if not kept—
Thou wilt remember that it was of this
I spoke a while ago with such precision.
And that is why the Hebrews were obliged
To make an offering only; 'twas allowed,
As thou shouldst know, to change the sacrifice.
The other—which is known to thee as substance—
May well be of such nature as permits
Exchange for other substance, without fault.
But let no person venture to exchange
His shoulder's burden at his own discretion,
Save that he turn both white and yellow key.
For every permutation is as naught,
If that which is put down, be not contained
In that assumed—even as four in six.
Hence anything of such intrinsic weight
That by itself it bears down every scale,
Is not redeemed by any other effort.
"A vow must never be considered lightly.
Be faithful—not unreasonably so,
Like Jepthah when he made his offering.
Better that he had said: 'I have done wrong,'
Than keeping faith to do a greater ill.
Insensate, too, that Grecian king, who made
Iphigenia mourn her beauty's loss,
Making both wise and foolish mourn for her,
When they were told of that strange sacrifice.
"O Christians, be more careful as ye move!
And be not like a feather to the wind,
Nor think that every water will absolve you!
Ye have the Testament, both New and Old,
The Shepherd of the Church to guide your steps:
Let these suffice to lead you to salvation!
If lust for evil cry to you aught else,
Be men, not silly sheep, so that the Jew
Who dwells among you, may not laugh in scorn;
And be not like the lamb that leaves its mother,
Foolish and wanton, fighting with itself
In useless frolics, for its own delight."
Thus Beatrice to me, even as I write it;
Then, burning with desire, she turned again
Unto that region which is most alive. . . .

Canto 11

. . . "Betwixt Topino and that stream which runs
Down from the hill that blessed Ubald chose,
There hangs a lofty mountain's fertile slope

From which Perugia feels the cold and heat
Through Porta Sole; and beneath her yoke
Gualdo and Nocera weep behind her.
From this slope, where breaks its steep ascent,
A sun arose to shine upon the world,
Even as the other dawns from out the Ganges.
Let him who speaks about that place not say
"Ascesi"—which is too inadequate—
But "Orient," if he would say aright.
"Ere he had travelled far from where he rose,
He soon began to influence the earth
And make it feel some comfort from his virtue.
While still a youth, he roused his father's wrath
By following a certain dame—to whom,
As unto death, none willingly pays suit—
And in the presence of the bishop's court,
And *coram patre,* joined himself to her,
Loving her more and more forever after.
A widow for eleven hundred years,
She had remained unwooed until his time;
It was of no avail for her to hear
That he who fear imposed on all the world
Found her with Amyclas, undisturbed—
Nor yet to be so constant and undaunted,
She mounted on the very Cross with Christ,
While even Mary stood beneath its foot.
"But that my language should not be obscure,
Henceforth assume that Poverty and Francis
Are the two lovers in my narrative.
Their concord, and their aspects luminous,
Made their sweet love, their joyful contemplation
Their wonder, to be cause of holy thoughts—
So much so, that the venerable Bernard
First bared his feet, then ran in quest of peace;
Yet as he ran, he seemed but slow of foot.
O rich, unknown rewards, O fertile good!
Egidius bares his feet, Sylvester also,
To follow the example of the bridegroom,
So pleasing now the bride appears to them.
"That father, that great master, went his way
Together with his bride and family
Who now had girded on the humble cord;
No cowardice of heart oppressed his brow,
That he was son to Pietro Bernardone,
Nor yet that he was wondrously despised;
But with a carriage worthy of a king,
He told his stern resolve to Innocent,
And gained from him approval for his order.
"Now after these poor folk had multiplied,
In following him, whose admirable life

Were best proclaimed amid the heavenly hosts,
The saintly purpose of this archimandrite
Was crowned with yet a second diadem,
Through Honorius, by the Holy Ghost.
And after that, through thirst for martyrdom,
And in the presence of the haughty sultan,
He preached the Christ, and those who followed Him.
And then, because he found the Saracens
Unripe for faith, he fled from idleness,
And sought to harvest the Italian crop.
Upon that rock 'twixt Tiber and the Arno,
He now received from Christ that final seal
Which two years long, appeared upon his limbs. . . .

Canto 19

. . . "Now is revealed to thee the hiding place
Where living justice was concealed from thee,
About which thou didst ask so frequently.
Thou saidst: 'A man is born on Indus' banks
Where no men live to speak to him of Christ,
Nor even any who can write or read;
His wishes and his actions all are good,
So far as human reason can discern;
Devoid of sin in action or in speech,
He dies without the faith, and unbaptized:
Where, then, is the justice that condemns him,
And where his fault, if he does not believe?'
"Who art thou, that wouldst pretend to judge
With thy short vision of a single span,
Of things that are a thousand miles away?
For one debating subtleties with me,
Indeed there would be wondrous cause for doubt,
If there were not the Scripture to direct you.
O earthly animals! O stupid minds!
The primal will—which of itself is good—
Has ne'er moved from itself, the good supreme.
Only so much is just, as matches it;
Created good cannot encompass it;
Radiant primal good remains the cause."
As when the stork will wheel above her nest
After she has given her young their food,
The nourished brood look back again at her:
In much this way I lifted up my brow,
And so, as well, became that blessed image
Which moved its wings impelled by many wills.
And while it wheeled about, it sang these words:
"As are my notes to thee, who know'st them not,
Such, to you mortals, is the eternal judgment."

When the Holy Spirit's shining flames
Were quieted, the voice within that sign
Which caused the world to venerate the Romans,
Began again: "No one has e'er attained
This kingdom, who did not believe in Christ,
Before or after He was crucified.
But mark you, there are many crying 'Christ!'
Who at the Judgment Day will be less near Him
Than one may be who ne'er has known the Christ. . . .

Canto 20

. . . "I see that thou believest in these things
Because I say them, seeing not the *how:*
Although believed in, still they lie concealed.
Thou art like one who knows a thing by name,
But is unable to conceive its essence,
If some one else reveal it not to him.
Regnum cœlorum suffers violence
From burning love, as well as living hope,
Which overcomes the will divine itself:
Not in the way that man prevails o'er man,
It lets itself be conquered willingly,
And being conquered, conquers by its goodness.
"The first and fifth who flame upon my brow
Cause thee to wonder, when thou dost perceive
That they adorn the region of the angels.
They did not leave their bodies—as thou thinkest—
As gentiles, but as Christians firm of faith
In Christ that died, or Christ that was to die.
For one of them returned to flesh from hell—
Whence none comes back through thirst for righteousness—
And this was recompense for living hope
That placed its strength in orisons to God
For his resuscitation, that his will
Might be employed for good upon the earth.
That glorious spirit—his of whom I speak—
Returning for a while into the flesh,
Had faith in Him who has the power to help;
And in believing, burned with such true love
Than when the spirit died a second time,
'Twas worthy of this joyful state of bliss.
"The other spirit—through the grace that springs
From well so deep that never mortal creature
Has gazed within the sources whence it flows,
Set all his love on justice in the world;
Wherefore, from grace to grace, Almighty God
Opened his eye to see salvation's way.
Thus he believed in it, and from that time

No longer could endure the pagan stench,
But e'er reproved the heathen for their folly.
And those three ladies by the right-hand wheel
For him were sanction of baptismal rite
A thousand years before its institution.
"Predestination! O how far removed
Thy root lies from the cognizance of those
Who do not see the first cause as a whole!
Ye mortals, have a care in how ye judge;
For even we ourselves, who look on God,
Do not as yet know all of the elect.
This lack of knowledge is the sweeter for us,
Because our good is fashioned in this good:
Thus what God wills, we also will ourselves." . . .

Canto 33

O Virgin Mother, daughter of thy Son,
Humbler and more exalted than all others,
Predestined object of the eternal will!
Thou gavest such nobility to man
That He who made mankind did not disdain
To make Himself a creature of His making.
Within thy womb, that love was re-enkindled
Whose heat has germinated this fair flower,
To blossom thus in everlasting peace.
Thou art our noonday torch of charity;
And down below thou art for mortal men
The living fount of hope. Thou art so great,
O Lady, and thou art of so much worth,
That whoso hopes for grace, not knowing thee,
Asks that his wish should fly without its wings.
And thy benignity not only gives
Its succor to the suppliant, but oftentimes
Will lavishly anticipate his plea.
In thee is mercy, and magnificence,
And pity, for in thee is concentrate
Whatever good there be in any creature.
"This man, who from the nethermost abyss
Of all the universe, as far as here,
Has seen the spiritual existences,
Now asks thy grace, so thou wilt grant him strength
That he may with his eyes uplift himelf
Still higher toward the ultimate salvation.
And I, who ne'er for my own vision burned
As I now burn for his, proffer to thee
All my prayers—and pray they may suffice—
That thou wilt scatter from him every cloud
Of his mortality, with thine own prayers,
So that the bliss supreme may be revealed.

And furthermore I beg of thee, O Queen
That hast the power to do whate'er thou wilt,
After his vision to keep his love still pure.
May thy protection quell his human passions!
Lo, Beatrice and many a blessed soul
Entreat thee, with clasped hands, to grant my wish!"
Those eyes so loved and reverenced by God,
Were fixed upon the suppliant, and showed
How greatly She is pleased by earnest prayers.
Then they were turned to that eternal light
Whose depth, one must believe, no other eye
Has vision clear enough to penetrate.
And I—who now was drawing near the end
Of all desires—ended, as was meet,
Within myself the ardor of my longing.
Here Bernard smiled and made a sign to me
That I should look on high; but I indeed
Was doing what he wished, of my own will,
Because my vision, being purified,
Was piercing more and more within the rays
Of light sublime, which in itself is true.
Thenceforward, no mere human speech could tell
My vision's added power: for memory
And speech are both o'ercome by such excess. . . .

JOHN DUNS SCOTUS

Duns Scotus was born in Scotland, ca. 1266. He became a Franciscan friar and both studied and taught at Oxford and Paris. His life span was relatively short, for he died in Cologne in 1308. Scotus was known as the Subtle Doctor, and, indeed, his writings are more difficult to understand than those of most of his Scholastic peers. Perhaps had he lived longer, some of the ambiguities in his work would have been clarified, although the originality of his thought often prevents any clear-cut agreement as to his intention.

Scotus was more influenced by Avicenna than by Averroës, for Avicenna's thought was more compatible with Christian theology. He did not accept, however, Avicenna's stress on necessitarianism, holding rather to a more empirical position which affirmed that the existence of necessary being (God) was demonstrated by an examination of human experience. To the contrary, Scotus affirmed the radical contingency of created being and the role of the free human will in developing the meaning of created nature, a position which followed from his intense commitment to the ongoing participation of human intelligence in the delineation of the meaning of the world. Against both Aristotle and Aquinas, Scotus held to a very radical doctrine of individuation. He contended that "things," or "particulars," are not to be known through their abstract universal representation, but rather through their individual formal qualities, that is, their "thisness." The upshot of this position is the positing of an infinitely rich panoply of differences and distinctions. This view was beautifully celebrated by the nineteenth-century English poet Gerard Manley Hopkins, who credits Scotus for his own affirmation that "there lives the dearest freshness deep down things."

Scotus developed original positions on the existence of God, the notion of being, and the activity of the human will. The selections that follow are but a hint of the rich complexity that awaits the serious student of the writings of Duns Scotus.

From Reportata Parisiensia

[BEING AS THE SUBJECT AND GOD AS THE GOAL OF METAPHYSICS]

We must first see whether metaphysics, the first and highest of the naturally acquired habits perfecting man's intellect in the present life, has God as its first object.

On this point there is a controversy between Avicenna and Averroës. Avicenna claims that God is not the subject of metaphysics, because no science proves [the existence of] its own subject. The metaphysician, however, proves that God exists. Averroës reproves Avicenna in his final comment on the *Physics*, BK. I, because he wishes, by using the same major premise against Avicenna, to prove that God and the pure spirits are the subject of metaphysics, and that God's existence is not proved in metaphysics, since it is only by means of motion, which pertains to the science of natural philosophy, that any kind of pure spirit can be proved to exist.

It seems to me, however, that of the two, Avicenna has spoken better. Wherefore I argue against Averroës as follows. The proposition they both hold, viz. "No science proves the existence of its subject" is true, because of the priority the subject holds in regard to the science. For if the subject were posterior to the science, then its existence would have to be established in some lower science, where it would be conceived under some inferior aspect which is inadequate for its role as the object [of the higher science]. Now a subject enjoys a greater priority over the lower than over the higher science. If the highest science, therefore, cannot prove that its subject exists, it is even less possible for a lower science to do so.

Or to put the argument in another way, if the philosopher of nature can prove that God exists, then God's existence is a conclusion of natural philosophy. Now if metaphysics cannot prove the existence of God in this way, then God's existence is presupposed as a principle in metaphysics. Consequently, a conclusion of natural philosophy is a principle of metaphysics, and therefore the philosophy of nature is prior to metaphysics.

Again, if a certain property can exist only in virtue of such and such a cause, from every such property that appears in the effect, we can infer the existence of the cause. Now it is not just such properties of the effect as are treated in the philosophy of nature that are possible only on condition that God exists, for the same is true of the properties treated of in metaphysics. Not only does motion presuppose a mover, but a being that is posterior presupposes one that is prior. Consequently, from the priority that exists among beings the existence of the First Being can be inferred, and this can be done in a more perfect way than the existence of a Prime Mover can be established in natural philosophy. We can infer, then, in metaphysics from act and potency, finiteness and infinity, multitude and unity, and many other such metaphysical properties, that God or the First Being exists.

So far as this article is concerned, then, I say that God is not the subject of metaphysics, because, as has been proved above in the first question, there is but one science that has God as its first subject, and this is not metaphysics. And this is proved in the following manner. Of every subject, also of a subordinate science, it is known through the senses that it is of such a nature that to exist is not repugnant to it, as is evident of the subject of optics, for the existence of a visible line is grasped immediately from the senses. Just as principles are grasped immediately once the terms are apprehended through the me-

From John Duns Scotus, *Reportata Parisiensia*, prol. qiii, art. i (VIVES, vol. xxii, 46a–47b) in *Duns Scotus Philosophical Writings*, trans. Allan Wolter (Indianapolis: Library of Liberal Arts, 1962), pp. 10–13. Originally published by Thomas Nelson and Sons Ltd., Surrey, England, and reprinted with their permission.

dium of the senses, so likewise if a subject is not to be posterior to, or less known than, its principle, it must needs be grasped through the senses. But no proper notion that we can form of God is apprehended immediately by man's intellect in this life. Therefore, we can have no naturally acquired science about God under some notion proper to Himself. Proof of the minor: The first [proper] concept we have of God is that He is the First Being. But this notion is not grasped through the senses, but we must first ascertain that the union of these two terms is compatible. Before we can know this compatibility, however, it is necessary that we demonstrate that some being is first. Therefore, etc.

Hence, I concede with Avicenna that God is not the subject of metaphysics. The Philosopher's statement, *(Metaphysics,* BK. I) that metaphysics is concerned with the highest causes, presents no difficulty. For he speaks here as he did in the *Prior Analytics,* BK. I, where he says: "First it is necessary to determine with what [Prior Analytics] is concerned and what it has to do. It is concerned with demonstration and has to do with the demonstrative branch of learning, that is with the general science of demonstrating or syllogising." Hence, "concerned with" denotes properly the circumstance of the final cause just as much as it does that of the material cause. Wherefore, metaphysics is concerned with the highest causes as its end. In knowing them, metaphysical science attains its goal.

From Concerning Human Knowledge

[*Article II. The Rejection of Scepticism*]. As regards the second article, lest the error of the Academicians be repeated in regard to any of those things which can be known, we must see what is to be said of the three types of knowledge mentioned above, viz. whether it is possible to have infallible certitude naturally: (1) of self-evident principles and conclusions, (2) of things known by experience, and (3) of our actions.

[*a. Certitude of First Principles*]. As to the certitude of principles, I have this to say. The terms of self-evident principles are so identical that it is evident that one necessarily includes the other. Consequently, the intellect uniting these terms in a proposition, from the very fact that it grasps these terms, has present to itself the necessary cause, and what is more—the evident cause, of the conformity of this proposition with the terms that compose it. This conformity, then, the evident cause of which the intellect perceives in the terms, cannot help but be evident to the intellect. That is why the intellect could not apprehend these terms and unite them in a proposition without having this relationship of conformity arise between the proposition and the terms, any more than two white objects could exist without a relationship of similarity arising between them. Now it is precisely this conformity of the proposition to the terms that constitutes the truth of a judgment. Such terms then cannot be combined in a judgment without being true, and so it is that one cannot perceive this proposition and its terms without also perceiving the conformity of the proposition to the terms, and therefore, perceiving the truth. For what is first perceived evidently includes the perception of the truth of the proposition.

In *Metaphysics,* BK. IV, the Philosopher confirms this reasoning by a simile. There he points out that the opposite of a first principle such as "It is impossible that the same thing be and not be," cannot enter the mind of anyone because then the mind would possess contrary opinions simultaneously. This is indeed true of contrary opinions, that is, propositions formally opposed to each other. For the opinions attributing existence and non-existence to one and the same thing are formally opposed. And so in the question at hand, I argue that there is some kind of repugnance existing between intellections in the mind, even though it is not exactly a formal opposition. For if the intellect possesses the knowledge of "whole" and of "part" and combines them in a proposition, since they include the necessary reason

From John Duns Scotus, *Opus Oxoniense,* I, dist. III, q. iv, in *Duns Scotus Philosophical Writings,* trans. Allan Wolter (Indianapolis: Library of Liberal Arts, 1962), pp. 114–123. Originally published by Thomas Nelson and Sons, Ltd., Surrey, England, and reprinted with their permission.

for the conformity of the proposition to the terms, if the intellect were to think this proposition false, two mutually repugnant acts of knowledge would coexist, even though the opposition is not precisely formal. The one act of knowledge would be co-present with the other even though the first is the necessary cause of the very opposite of the second, which is impossible. For just as it is impossible for white to be at the same time black because the two are formally contraries, so it is also impossible to have the white where you have the precise cause of blackness. The necessity in this case is of such a kind that it would be a contradiction to have the one [viz. the knowledge of the terms and the proposition] without the other [viz. the knowledge of the conformity between the two].

Once we have certitude of first principles, it is clear how one can be certain of the conclusions drawn from such principles, since the perfect syllogism is evident, and the certitude of the conclusion depends solely upon the certitude of the principles and the evidence of the inference.

But will the intellect not err in its knowledge of principles and conclusions, if all the senses are deceived about the terms? I reply that so far as this kind of knowledge goes, the senses are not a cause but merely an occasion of the intellect's knowledge, for the intellect cannot have any knowledge of the terms of a proposition unless it has taken them from the senses. But once it has them, the intellect by its own power can form propositions with these terms. And if a proposition be evidently true by reason of the terms involved, the intellect by its own power will assent to this proposition in virtue of the terms and not by reason of the senses from which it externally received the terms. To give an example: If the notion of "whole" and the notion of "greater than" be taken from the senses and the intellect form the proposition "Every whole is greater than its part," the intellect by its own power and in virtue of the terms will assent to this proposition without the shadow of doubt. And it does not assent to this because it sees these terms verified in some thing, as it does when it assents to the proposition "Socrates is white," because it saw the terms united in reality.

Indeed, if the senses from which these terms were received were all false, or what is more deceptive, if some were false and others true, I still maintain that the intellect would not be deceived about such principles, because the terms which are the cause of the truth would always be present to the intellect. And so it would be if the species of whiteness and blackness were impressed miraculously in sleep upon one who was blind from birth and they remained after he awoke. The intellect could abstract from these and form the proposition "White is not black." And it would not be deceived with regard to this proposition even if the terms were derived from erring senses, because the formal meaning of the terms at which the intellect has arrived is the necessary cause of this negative truth.

[*b. Experimental Knowledge*]. As for what is known by experience, I have this to say. Even though a person does not experience every single individual, but only a great many, nor does he experience them at all times, but only frequently, still he knows infallibly that it is always this way and holds for all instances. He knows this in virtue of this proposition reposing in his soul: "Whatever occurs in a great many instances by a cause that is not free, is the natural effect of that cause." This proposition is known to the intellect even if the terms are derived from erring senses, because a cause that does not act freely cannot in most instances produce an effect that is the very opposite of what it is ordained by its form to produce. The chance cause, however, is ordained either to produce or not produce the opposite of the chance effect. Consequently, if the effect occurs frequently it is not produced by chance and its cause therefore will be a natural cause if it is not a free agent. But this effect occurs through such a cause. Therefore, since the latter is not a chance cause, it is the natural cause of the effect it frequently produces.

That such an effect occurs frequently through such a cause is a fact gathered from experience. For once we find such a nature associated at one time with this accident and at another with that, we have discovered that despite the accidental differences, such an effect invariably follows from this nature. Hence, such an effect is not the result of what is merely incidental to such a nature but is rather the effect of this nature as such.

It should be noted further that at times we experience [the truth] of a conclusion, such as: "The moon is frequently eclipsed." Then, granting the validity of this conclusion because it is a fact, we proceed by the method of division to discover the reason for this. And sometimes, beginning with a conclusion thus experienced, a person arrives at self-evident principles. In such a case, the conclusion which at first was known only by experience now is known by reason of such a principle with even greater certainty, namely that characteristic of the first kind of knowledge, for it has been deduced from a self-evident principle. Thus for instance, it is a self-evident principle that when an opaque body is placed between a visible object and the source of light, the transmission of light to such an object is prevented. Now, if a person discovers by way of division that the earth is such an opaque body interposed between sun and moon, our conclusion will no longer be known merely by experience as was the case before we discovered this principle. It will be now known most certainly by a demonstration of the reasoned fact, for it is known through its cause.

Sometimes, however, we experience a principle in such a way that it is impossible to discover by further division any self-evident principle from which it could be derived. Instead we must be satisfied with a principle whose terms are known by experience to be frequently united, for example, that a certain species of herb is hot. Neither do we find any other prior means of demonstrating just why this attribute belongs to this particular subject, but must content ourselves with this as a first principle known from experience. Now even though the uncertainty and fallibility in such a case may be removed by the proposition "What occurs in most instances by means of a cause that is not free is the natural effect of such a cause," still this is the very lowest degree of scientific knowledge—and perhaps we have here no knowledge of the actual union of the terms but only a knowledge of what is apt to be the case. For if an attribute is an absolute entity other than the subject, it could be separated from its subject without involving any contradiction. Hence, the person whose knowledge is based on experience would not know whether such a thing is actually so or not, but only that by its nature is it apt to be so.

[*c. Knowledge of Our Own Acts*]. Regarding the third type of knowledge, viz. of our acts, I say that we are as certain of many of these as we are of the first and self-evident propositions, as is clear from *Metaphysics*, BK. IV. There the Philosopher says to the arguments of those who say that all that appears is true that they look for proofs of whether we are now awake or asleep. "All these doubts, however, amount to the same thing, for they all think that there is a reason for everything." And he adds: "They seek the reason for things of which there is no reason, for there is no demonstration of a principle of demonstration." According to him, then, the fact that we are awake is as self-evident as a principle of demonstration.

That such a thing is contingent matters not, for as we have pointed out elsewhere, there is an order among contingent propositions. Some proposition is first and immediate. Otherwise, we should have an infinite regress in contingent propositions or something contingent would follow from a necessary cause, both of which are impossible. And just as our certitude of being awake is like that of self-evident propositions, the same is true of many other acts in our power such as "I understand," or "I hear," and other such acts which are being performed.

For even though there is no certitude that I see white located outside, either in such a subject or at such a distance (for an illusion can be caused in the medium or in the organ or in a number of other ways), still for all that there is certitude that I see even when the illusion is in the organ itself, which seems to be the greatest of all illusions (for instance, when the same kind of act takes place in the organ without any object present as naturally should take place only when such an object is present). In such a case, if the faculty should act, that which is called vision would truly be present whether vision be action or passion or both. But if the illusion were not caused in the organ proper but in something near which seems to be the organ, for instance, if the illusion did not take place in the bundle of nerves but in the eye, a species similar to that which naturally results from a object would be impressed. In such a case there would still be an act of vision, for we would see such a species or what is to be seen therein because it is sufficiently distant from the organ of sight in the bundle of those nerves. This is evident from Augustine in *De Trinitate*, BK. XI, c. ii, because after-images of vision are seen when the eye is closed. It is also evident from the Philosopher in *De sensu et sensato*, because the flash of fire produced by violently elevating the eye and transmitted as far as the closed eyelid is seen. Although these are not the most perfect, they are true visions, for in this case a sufficient distance intervenes between the species and the principal organ of vision.

(Note: Knowledge of a principle is immutable in the sense that it cannot change from truth to falsity. It is not unchangeable in the other sense, for it is simply perishable. Thus the intelligible species, not the image, is weak. Nevertheless, it is unable to change from a true to a false representation. But the object, although perishable, cannot change from something true to something false. As a result, it is able to conform knowledge to itself or to cause knowledge or truth by being what it is, for a true entity, unable to become something false, virtually contains true knowledge immutably, that is, knowledge conformed to true entity.) (Note: According to Augustine, necessary or immutable truth is "above the mind"—understand "taken precisely as evident truth." For what is necessarily and immutably true causes this evident knowledge of itself in the mind. As evident, such a truth is not subject to the mind so that it could appear either true or false in the way that a probable truth is subject to the mind inasmuch as it is in the power of the mind to make it appear true or false by looking here or there for reasons that prove or disprove it. In this way we must understand the statement that the mind judges about other things and not about immutable truth. For it is only in the case of something probable and not in the case of something necessary that the assertion of its truth—an act of judgment—lies within the power of the mind. But this does not mean that the mind asserts the truth of a necessary proposition in a less perfect manner. According to Aristotle, the latter can be called a "judgment," whereas Augustine understands judgment as something that is in the power of the one judging and not as something that is immediately and necessarily determined by a factor beyond one's control. And so it is patent how the mind "judges" about a necessary conclusion that is not immediately evident of itself and therefore does not force itself upon the mind as something evident. The mind can even bring up sophistical reasons against the conclusion in question and on the basis of these reasons refuse its assent. But this it cannot do with something that is first known [viz. a primary principle] according to *Metaphysics*, BK. IV).

[*d. Certitude of Sense Knowledge*]. But how can a person be certain of those things which fall under the acts of the senses, for instance, that something outside is white or hot in the way that it appears to be? I reply: Regarding such an object, either the same things appear opposite to different senses or they do not appear so but rather all the senses knowing such an object judge the same about it. If the latter be the case, then we have certitude of this thing perceived by the senses in virtue of the aforementioned principle, viz. "What occurs in most instances by means of something that is not a free cause is the natural effect of this thing." Therefore, if the same change repeatedly occurs in the majority of cases when such an object is presented, it follows that the transformation or image produced is the natural effect of such a cause, and thus the external thing will be white or hot or such as it naturally appears to be according to the image so frequently produced.

But if the judgment of different senses differs in regard to what is seen outside; for instance, if sight says that the staff which is partly in the water and partly in the air is broken, or if sight says, as it invariably does, that the sun is smaller in size than it really is, or in general, that everything seen from a distance is smaller than it is in reality, in all such instances we are still certain of what is true and know which sense is in error. This we know by reason of some proposition in the soul more certain than any sense judgment together with the concurrent testimony of several of the senses. For there is always some proposition to set the mind or intellect aright regarding which acts of the senses are true and which false—a proposition, note, which the senses do not cause but merely occasion in the intellect. For instance, the intellect has this proposition reposing in it: "The harder object is not broken by the touch of something soft which gives way before it." So evident is this proposition upon analysis of its terms that the intellect could not call it in doubt, even if its terms were derived from erroneous senses. Indeed, the opposite of this proposition includes a contradiction. Now both sight and touch attest that the stick is harder than the water and that the water gives way before the stick. It follows therefore that the stick is not broken as the sense of sight judges. Hence, in the case of the "broken staff" the intellect judges by something more certain than any testimony of the sense. And so too with the other cases. Even though the terms be derived from erring senses, the intellect knows that the measure used to measure remains perfectly equal to itself. Now the sense of sight as well as that of touch tell us that the identical measure can be applied to a nearby object of vision and to a distant object. Therefore, the actual size of the object is equal whether seen from nearby or from afar. Sight errs, consequently, when it declares the size to be less. This conclusion is inferred from self-evident principles and from the repeated testimony of its truth by two senses. And so when reason judges that the senses err, it does so in virtue of two kinds of knowledge. The first is a knowledge for which the intellect requires the sense only as an occasion and not as a cause—a knowledge in which it would not be deceived even if all the senses were deceived. The other is a knowledge acquired by the oft-repeated testimony of one or more senses which are known to be true by reason of the proposition so frequently quoted, viz. "Whatever occurs in most instances, etc."

From The Oxford Commentary

BOOK II, DIST. III

Question 1

Whether Material Substance Is Individual or Singular From Itself or Its Own Nature?

. . .

It seems so. The Philosopher, in Book VII of the *Metaphysics*, proves against Plato that the substance of any kind of thing is proper to it and is not in something else. Therefore, material substance from its own nature, setting aside anything else, is proper to that in which it is, such that from its own nature it cannot be in something else. Thus it is individual from its own nature.

On the contrary: Whatever is in something intrinsically, from its nature, is in it whatever it is in. Therefore, if the nature of stone is "this" of itself, in whatever there is the nature of stone, that nature would be this stone. The consequent is unsuitable in speaking about determinate singularity, which is what the question is about.

Besides, that to which an opposite belongs of itself is of itself repugnant to the other opposite. Therefore, if a nature were of itself one in number, numerical multitude would be repugnant to it of itself.

Here it is said that just as a nature is formally a nature of itself, so is a singular of itself, so that it is not necessary to seek a cause of singularity other than the cause of the nature, as though a nature were prior in time or that a nature is a nature before it is singular and then it is made singular by something added on which contracts it. Which position is proved by an analogy, since just as a nature has true existence from itself outside the soul, but only has dependent existence in the soul—that is, dependent on the soul itself (and the reason is that true existence belongs to it unqualifiedly, but existence in the soul is derived)—so universality only belongs to a thing as it has dependent existence in the soul. But singularity belongs to a thing according to true existence, and so, from itself and unqualifiedly. What is to be sought, then, is the cause whereby a nature is universal; and the intellect should be given as the cause. But a cause does not have to be sought whereby a nature is singular, other than the nature of a thing—a cause, that is, which would mediate between the nature and its singularity. But the causes of the unity of a thing are also the causes of the singularity of a thing. Therefore, etc.

Against this it is argued thus: An object insofar as it is an object is naturally prior to its act; and according to you, an object as prior is singular of itself, since this always belongs to a nature not taken as dependent, or according to the existence it has in the soul. Therefore, the intellect knowing that object under a universal characteristic, knows it under a characteristic opposed to its own, for as it precedes the act, it is of itself determined to the opposite of that characteristic.

Besides, the real unity proper and sufficient to anything whatsoever is less than numerical unity; it is not of itself one with numerical unity, or it is not of itself "this." But the real unity proper or sufficient to the nature of stone existing in this stone is less than numerical unity. Therefore, etc. The major is obvious of itself, since nothing is of itself one with a unity greater than that sufficient to it. For if the unity which ought to be proper to something of itself is less than numerical unity, numerical unity does not

From John Duns Scotus, The Oxford Commentary on *The Four Books of the Sentences*, in James J. Walsh and Arthur Hyman, eds., *Philosophy in the Middle Ages* (Indianapolis: Hackett Publishing Co., Inc., 2d ed., 1983), pp. 624–630.

belong to it from the nature and according to itself, lest from its nature alone it should have a greater and lesser unity, which are opposites concerning and according to the same thing. For a multitude opposed to a greater unity can stand together with a lesser unity without contradiction; but that multitude cannot stand together with the greater unity because it is repugnant to it. Therefore, etc. The minor premiss is proved in that if there is no real unity of a nature less than singularity, but every unity other than singular unity is merely the unity of reason, then there will be no real unity less than numerical unity. The consequent is false, which I prove in five or six ways. Therefore, etc. . . .

Besides, secondly, I prove that the consequent is false, because according to the Philosopher in Book VII of the *Physics,* an atom is compared to a species, since it is one in nature, but not to a genus, since a genus does not have such a unity. This true unity is not a unity of reason, since the concept of a genus is just as much one in the intellect as is the concept of a species. Otherwise no concept would be definitionally predicated of many species, and so no concept would be of a genus if as many concepts were predicated of species as there are concepts of species. For then in single predications the same would be predicated of itself. Likewise, whether the unity is of a concept or not of a concept is irrelevant to the intention of the Philosopher, namely, with regard to the comparison. Therefore, the Philosopher intended the specific nature there to be one with the unity of a specific nature, but he did not intend it to be one with numerical unity, since no comparison was made to numerical unity. Therefore, etc. . . .

Again, sixthly, since if every unity is numerical, then every real diversity is numerical. But the consequent is false, since every numerical diversity insofar as it is numerical is equal; and so everything would be equally distinct, and then it follows that the intellect can no more abstract something common from Socrates and Plato than from Socrates and a line, and any universal would be a pure figment. . . .

Again, seventhly, it is not by anything existing in the intellect that fire causes fire and destroys water, and that there is a certain real unity of generator to generated according to form, because of which, generation is univocal. For intellectual consideration does not make generation to be univocal; but it knows it to be univocal.

In reply to the question, therefore, I concede the conclusion of these arguments, and I say that material substance from its own nature is not of itself "this," since then, just as the first argument concluded, the intellect could not understand it under the opposite, unless it understood under a characteristic unsuited for the understanding of such an object. As the second argument also concluded with all its proofs, there is a certain real unity in a thing apart from any operation of the intellect. This unity of a nature in itself is less than numerical unity, or the unity proper to a singular. And since a nature is not of itself one with that unity, it is according to its own proper unity indifferent to the unity of singularity.

This can also be understood through the saying of Avicenna in Book V of the *Metaphysics,* where he says that "horseness is just horseness, of itself neither one nor many, universal nor particular." One should understand that a nature is not of itself one with numerical unity, nor many with a plurality opposed to that unity. Nor is it actually universal, in the way that something is made universal by the intellect; neither is it of itself particular. Although it is never really without some of these, still, of itself it is none of them; but it is naturally prior to all. And according to this natural priority it is "that which is," and is the intrinsic object of the intellect. As such, it is considered by the metaphysician and is expressed through a definition. And propositions true in the primary way are true by reason of a quiddity so accepted, since nothing is predicated in the primary way of a quiddity that is not essentially included in it insofar as it is abstracted from everything naturally posterior to it. Not only is a nature of itself indifferent to existence in the intellect and in a particular, and hence to universal and singular existence, but also, in having existence in the intellect it does not have universality primarily from itself. For although it is understood under universality, as under the mode for understanding it, still, universality is not a part of its primary concept, since that is not a concept of the metaphysician, but rather, of the logician. For according to Avicenna himself, the logician considers second intentions applied to first intentions. Thus the primary understanding is of a nature, without any mode understood with it, neither that which belongs to it in the intellect, nor that which belongs to it outside the intellect, even though the mode of it to the intellect in understanding is universality— but it is not a mode of the intellect. And just as a nature is not of itself universal according to that existence, as though universality accrued to that nature according to its primary characteristic, but rather universality accrues to it as being an object of the intellect; so also in external reality. There, a nature exists with singularity; but the nature is not of itself limited to singularity. It is naturally prior to that characteristic contracting it to that singularity. And insofar as it is naturally prior to what contracts it, it is not repugnant to it to exist without what contracts it. And just as an object in the intellect has true intelligible existence according to that being and universality; so also in things, a nature has true real existence outside the soul according to that being. And according to that being it has a unity proportional to itself which is indifferent to singularity, so that of itself it is not repugnant to that unity, which is given with every unity of singularity.

In this way, therefore, I understand a nature to have a real unity less than numerical unity. And although it does not have numerical unity of itself, so that it would be internal to the characteristic of a nature, since "horseness is just horseness," according to Avicenna in Book V of the *Metaphysics*, still that unity is an attribute proper to a nature according to its primary being. And consequently, it is not of itself internally "this," nor is it necessarily included in a nature according to its own primary being.

But against this there seem to be two objections. One, that it seems to hold that a universal is something real in a thing, which is against the Commentator, Book I of the *De Anima*, comment 8, who says that "the intellect makes universality in things," so that universality only exists through the intellect, and so is merely a being of reason. The proof of the consequence is that this nature, as it is a being in this stone, but still naturally prior to the singularity of this stone, is being said indifferently to this singular and to that. . . .

To the first objection I say that the universal in act is that which has indifferent unity, according to which it is the same in proximate power as said of whatever individual subject, since, according to the First Book of the *Posterior Analytics*, "that is universal which is one in many and of many." For nothing according to whatever unity in a thing is such that according to just that unity it is in a proximate power to whatever subject, as said of whatever subject in a predication saying "this is this." For although to be in a singularity different from that in which it is, is not repugnant to something existing in a thing, still it cannot be truly said of just any inferior that that is it. For this is only possible of an object considered by the intellect in the same indifferent act, which object as understood also has the numerical unity of an object, according to which the same is predicable of every singular, in saying that this is this.

From this appears the disproof of that saying that the agent intellect makes universality in things, through this, that it uncovers the *that which is* existing in a phantasm. For wherever it is, before it has the existence of an object of the possible intellect, whether it is in a thing or in a phantasm, it either has certain existence or is deduced by reason. And if it is not through some illumination, but is always such a nature from itself, to which it is not repugnant to exist in another, still it is not that to which as a proximate power it belongs to be said of whatever you wish, but it is only in proximate power as it is in the possible intellect. In a thing, therefore, it is common, which is not "this" of itself, and consequently to which it is not of itself repugnant not to be "this." But such a common is not a universal in act, because there is lacking to it that differentia according to which a universal is fully universal, namely, according to which the same is predicable by some identity of whatever individual, so that the individual is it. . . .

And through this the reply is obvious to the principal argument in which he disproves that fiction which he imposes upon Plato, namely, that this intrinsically existing man, which is posited as the Idea, cannot intrinsically exist universally in every man. For every intrinsically existing substance is proper to that to which it belongs. That is, it is either from itself or it is proper through something which in contracting, makes it proper, which contracting having been posited, it cannot be in another, although it is not repugnant to it from itself to be in something else.

This gloss is also true speaking of substance as it is taken for the nature. And then it follows that the Idea will not be the substance of Socrates, since it is not the nature of Socrates either. For it is of itself neither proper to nor appropriated to Socrates, as it is merely in him, but it is also in another. But if substance is taken for first substance, then it is true that any substance is proper to that to which it belongs. And then it follows much more that that idea which is posited as substance existing intrinsically in this way cannot be the substance of Socrates or Plato. But the first member suffices for the proposed position.

For the confirmation of the opinion it is obvious that commonness and singularity are not disposed to a nature as existence in the intellect and true existence outside the soul respectively, since commonness as well as singularity belong to a nature outside the intellect. And commonness belongs to a nature of itself, whereas singularity belongs to a nature through something contracting it in the thing. But universality does not belong to a thing of itself, and hence I concede that the cause of universality is to be sought. But the cause of commonness is not to be sought, other than the nature itself. And commonness having been posited in a nature in accordance with its own being and unity, it is necessary to seek the cause of singularity, which adds something to that to which the nature belongs.

BOOK II, DIST. III

Question 4

Whether Material Substance Is Individual or Singular Through Quantity?

...

Here it is said that material substance is singular and individual through quantity, and the reason given is that what primarily and intrinsically belongs to something, belongs to anything else by reason of it. But substance and quantity do not make a one intrinsically, but only accidentally; and consequently, no one property belongs intrinsically to them at once and equally primarily, but rather, to one through the other. But to be divided into parts of the same character is a property which belongs intrinsically to quantity, from Book V of the *Metaphysics.* Thus it belongs to another, namely substance, through the characteristic of quantity. The division of a species into its individuals is of such a sort, since these divided individuals do not formally differ in character as do the species dividing a genus. . . .

Besides, this fire differs from that fire only because form differs from form; and form differs from form only because it is received in a part of matter different from another part. And a part of matter differs from another part only because it is under a part of quantity different from another part. Therefore, the entire distinction of this fire from that fire is reduced to quantity as what is primarily distinct. . . .

I argue against this conclusion in four ways. First, from the identity of numerical character, whether belonging to individuation or singularity. Second, from the order of substance to accident. Third, from the nature of predicational coordination. And these three ways together prove that no accident can be the intrinsic characteristic through which material substance is individuated. The fourth way will be especially against quantity, with regard to the conclusion of the opinion. And fifth, it will be argued especially against the arguments of the opinion.

As to the first way, I first explain what I understand by individuation, whether numerical unity or through singularity: not, indeed, the indeterminate unity according to which anything in a species is called one in number, but a unity demarkated as "this," so that, as was said before, it is impossible for an individual to be divided into subject-parts. And what is sought is the reason for this impossibility. So I say that it is impossible for an individual not to be a "this," demarkated by this singularity; and it is not the cause of singularity in general which is sought, but of this specially demarkated singularity, namely, as it is determinately "this." Understanding singularity thus, there is a two-fold argument from the first way:

First: a substance existing in act and not altered by some substantial transmutation cannot be turned from "this" to "not this," since this singularity (as was just said) cannot be in one thing and another with the same substance remaining the same and not substantially altered. But a substance existing in act with no substantial alteration can without contradiction be under one and another quantity, or any absolute accident. Therefore, this substance is in no such way formally demarkated by this singularity. The minor is obvious, since it is not a contradiction that God should conserve the same substance having this quantity and inform it with another quantity; nor would that substance existing in act be substantially altered because of this, since there would only be an alteration from quantity to quantity. Likewise, if it were altered in any accident without substantial alteration, possible or impossible, it would not on that account be formally "not this."

If you say that this is a miracle and hence is not conclusive against natural reason, my reply is that a miracle does not include contradictories, for which there is no power. But it is a contradiction for the same enduring substance to be two substances without substantial alteration, and this successively as well as simultaneously, which would follow if it were formally this substance through any accident. For then, with accident succeeding accident, the same unaltered substance would successively be two substances. . . .

Perhaps to escape these criticisms, the position that individuation is by quantity is held in this other way, namely, that just as the extension of matter is different from the quantity of that matter and adds nothing to the essence of the matter so demarkated, so the demarkation of matter, which it has causally by way of quantity, is different from the demarkation of its quantity and is naturally prior to the demarkation which it has through quantity. For substance as substance is naturally prior to quantity without any accident whatsoever. And the demarkation of matter is different from the demarkation of quantity, but it is not different from substance, so that just as matter does not have parts through the nature of quantity, since a part of matter is matter, so demarkated substance does not exist without substance. For demarkation only conveys a way of being disposed.

Against this: the position seems to include contradictories twice over. First, since it is impossible for anything naturally posterior and dependent to be the same as what is naturally prior, since then it would be prior and not prior. But substance is naturally prior to quantity. Therefore, nothing caused through quantity or in any way presupposing the nature of quantity can be the same as substance. This demarkation, therefore, is not the same as substance even though it is caused by quantity. The proof of the major is that where there is true and real identity, even though it is not formal, it is impossible for this to exist and that not, since then the same would really exist and not exist. But it is possible for what is naturally prior to exist without what is naturally posterior; consequently, much more without what is determined or caused by what is naturally posterior.

Besides, a necessary condition of a cause cannot have its existence from its result, since then the cause as sufficient for the causing would be caused by the result, and the result would be its own cause. But the singularity or demarkation of substance is a necessary condition for causing the quantity in substance, since a singular result requires a singular cause. Therefore, it is impossible for this demarkation to be derived from what is caused by substance, insofar as it is singular.

Besides, I ask what it is to determine quantity or to cause such a mode in substance. If it precedes quantity, then demarkation is in no way through quantity. But if it is anything else, I ask how it is caused by quantity, and by what type of cause? The only type of cause that it seems possible to assign here is the efficient cause, but quantity is not an active form.

SUGGESTIONS FOR FURTHER READING

Cantor, Norman F. *Medieval History.* New York: Macmillan, 1969.

Copleston, F. C. *Aquinas.* Baltimore: Penguin, 1955.

De Bruyne, Edgar. *The Esthetics of the Middle Ages.* New York: Frederick Ungar, 1969.

Erickson, Carolly, ed. *The Secrets of Medieval Europe.* New York: Doubleday–Anchor, 1971.

Gilson, Etienne. *The Christian Philosophy of St. Thomas Aquinas.* New York: Random House, 1956.

Gilson, Etienne. *History of Christian Philosophy in the Middle Ages.* New York: Random House, 1955.

Gilson, Etienne. *The Philosophy of St. Bonaventure.* Dom Illtyd Trethowan and Frank J. Sheed, trans. Paterson, N.J.: St. Anthony Guild Press, 1965.

Gilson, Etienne. *The Spirit of Medieval Philosophy.* New York: Scribner, 1940.

Grave, Leif. *Peter Abelard.* New York: Harcourt, Brace and World, 1970.

Kenny, Anthony. *Aquinas.* New York: Hill and Wang, 1980.

Kenny, Anthony, ed. *Aquinas: A Collection of Critical Essays.* New York: Doubleday–Anchor, 1969.

Knowles, David. *The Evolution of Medieval Thought.* Baltimore: Helicon Press, 1962.

Le Goff, Jacques. *Time, Work and Culture in the Middle Ages.* Chicago: University of Chicago Press, 1980.

Maurer, Armand A. *Medieval Philosophy.* New York: Random House, 1962.

McKeon, Richard, ed. *Selections from Medieval Philosophers.* 2 vols. New York: Scribner, 1929.

Ross, James Bruce, and Mary Martin McLaughlin. *The Portable Medieval Reader.* New York: Viking, 1949.

Schürmann, Reiner. *Meister Eckhart: Mystic and Philosopher.* Bloomington: Indiana University Press, 1978.

Shahan, Robert W., and Francis J. Kovach. *Bonaventure and Aquinas: Enduring Philosophers.* Norman: University of Oklahoma Press, 1976.

Shapiro, Herman, ed. *Medieval Philosophy.* New York: Modern Library, 1964.

Van Steenberghen, Fernand. *Aristotle in the West: The Origins of Latin Aristotelianism.* Louvain: E. Nauwelaerts, 1955.

Van Steenberghen, Fernand. *Thomas Aquinas and Radical Aristotelianism.* Washington, D.C.: Catholic University of America Press, 1980.

Walsh, James J., and Arthur Hyman, eds. *Philosophy in the Middle Ages.* 2d ed. Indianapolis: Hackett, 1983.

Weinberg, Julius. *A Short History of Medieval Philosophy.* Princeton: Princeton University Press, 1964.

The Fourteenth Century: Breakup of the Faith-Reason Synthesis

Philosophy at the close of the thirteenth century was characterized by a great deal of tension and confusion, largely a result of the Condemnation of 1277. In retrospect, it seems natural that the major thinkers of the thirteenth century would express considerable doubt that the philosophical injunctions of the Condemnation were as clear as the proscription claimed. In something of an effort to begin over, that is, with the new way *(via moderna)* instead of the old way *(via antiqua)*, fourteenth-century thinkers such as William of Ockham, John Buridan, and Nicolaus of Autrecourt attempted to phrase the central philosophical questions in an entirely new, and often skeptical, way. In general terms, they expressed doubt about philosophical certitude on questions pertaining to the existence of God, the immortality of the soul, and the realist claims of the existence of universals outside the mind. Some of this skepticism has a real literary bite to it, as in the writings of Francesco Petrarca.

A further development in the fourteenth-century break with the medieval synthesis of faith and reason is the appearance of powerful mystical thought and writing. This development is found in figures such as Meister Eckhart, Tauler, Henry Suso, Catherine of Siena, and Julian of Norwich. Bypassing the burdens of philosophical reasoning, the mystics boldly spoke of their experience of God, as if the conceptual latticework of the thirteenth century were merely an unnecessary encumbrance.

The following selections illustrate the complex and novel epistemology of Ockham, the skepticism of Nicolaus of Autrecourt, the irony of Francesco Petrarca, and the religious "disinterest" of Meister Eckhart. These materials can be read as symbolizing both the end of the medieval period and a darkening before the intellectual and religious storms on the horizon, namely, the Renaissance, the Reformation, and the new science, each of which heralds the birth of modern consciousness, a development that broke with both authority and inherited assumptions.

MEISTER ECKHART

Eckhart was born ca. 1260 in Hochheim, Germany. As a young man he entered the Dominican order. Despite the fact that he went on to assume a series of important administrative positions within the order, much of his teaching was condemned in 1329, approximately one year after his death.

By writing in German, Eckhart began the movement away from Latin as the language for speculative tracts. He took a radical position on the power of the soul to know God, for he believed that each of us has a divine Fünklein, *or spark, which can illuminate our soul and unite us to the Godhead. Obviously this position paid little attention to the elaborate philosophical arguments as to how the human soul knows, let alone knows the nature of God. Eckhart's preaching and teaching were very popular, for they dispensed with the prevailing intellectual apparatus, found impenetrable by many people of his time. Although Eckhart did not deny orthodox theology, it was clear that his direct and emotional appeal constituted a threat to religious authority. We include a piece from Eckhart entitled "About Disinterest," which is illustrative of both his accessibility and his attempt to transcend traditional learning.*

About Disinterest

I have read much of what has been written, both by heathen philosophers and sages and in the Old and New Testaments. I have sought earnestly and with great diligence that good and high virtue by which man may draw closest to God and through which one may best approximate the idea God had of him before he was created, when there was no separation between man and God; and having delved into all this writing, as far as my intelligence would permit, I find that [high virtue] to be pure disinterest, that is, detachment from creatures. Our Lord said to Martha: *"Unum est necessarium,"* which is to say: to be untroubled and pure, one thing is necessary and that is disinterest.

The teachers praise love, and highly too, as St. Paul did, when he said: "No matter what I do, if I have not love, I am nothing." Nevertheless, I put disinterest higher than love. My first reason is as follows. The best thing about love is that it makes me love God. Now, it is much more advantageous for me to move God toward myself than for me to move toward him, for my blessing in eternity depends on my being identified with God. He is more able to deal with me and join me than I am to join him. Disinterest brings God to me and I can demonstrate it this way: Everything likes its own habitat best; God's habitat is purity and unity, which are due to disinterest. Therefore God necessarily gives himself to the disinterested heart.

In the second place, I put disinterest above love because love compels me to suffer for God's sake, whereas disinterest makes me sensitive only to God. This ranks far above suffering for God or in God; for, when he suffers, man pays some attention to the creature from which his suffering comes, but being disinterested, he is quite detached from the creature. I demonstrate that, being disinterested, a man is sensitive only to God, in this way: Experience must always be an experience of something, but disinterest comes so close to zero that nothing but God is rarefied enough to get into it, to enter the disinterested heart. That is why a disinterested person is sensitive to nothing but God. Each person experiences things in his own way and thus every distinguishable thing is seen and understood according to the approach of the beholder and not, as it might be, from its own point of view.

The authorities also praise humility above other virtues, but I put disinterest above humility for the following reasons. There can be humility without disinterest but disinterest cannot be perfect without humility; perfect humility depends on self-denial; disinterest comes so near to zero that nothing may intervene. Thus, there cannot be disinterest without humility and, anyway, two virtues are better than one!

The second reason I put disinterest above humility is that in humility man abases himself before creatures, and in doing so pays some attention to the creatures themselves. Disinterest, however, stays within itself. No transference of attention [such as humility] can ever rank so high that being self-contained will not go higher. As the prophet puts it: "*Omnis gloria filiae regis ab intus,*" which means, "the glory of the king's daughter comes from within her." Perfectly disinterested, a man has no regard for anything, no inclination to be above this or below that, no desire to be over or under; he remains what he is, neither loving nor hating, and desiring neither likeness to this or unlikeness to that. He desires only to be one and the same; for to want to be this or that is to want something; and the disinterested person wants nothing. Thus everything remains unaffected as far as he is concerned.

Someone may say: Surely our Lady had all the virtues and therefore she must have been perfectly disinterested. If then, disinterest ranks above virtue, why did the Lady glory in her humility rather than in disinterest? She said: "*Quia respexit Dominus humilitatem ancillae suae.*" That means: "He hath regarded the low estate of his handmaiden."

I reply by saying that in God there is both disinterest and humility as well, to the extent that virtues may be attributed to God. You should know that it was loving humility that made God stoop to human nature, the same humility by which he created heaven and earth, as I shall later explain. And if our Lord, willing to become man, still remained unaffected in his disinterest, our Lady must have known that he desired this of her, too, and that therefore he would have regard to her humility rather than to her disinterest. Thus she continued, unmoved in her disinterestedness, and yet she gloried in humility.

If, however, she had said: "He hath regarded my disinterest," her disinterest would have been qualified by the thought and not perfect, for she would have departed from it. Any departure from disinterest, however small, disturbs it; and there you have the reason why our Lady gloried in humility rather than in disinterest. The prophet says: "*Audiam, qui loquatur in me Dominus Deus,*" which means "I will be silent and hear what God the Lord will utter within me"—as if to say, "If God the Lord wants to speak to me, let him come in, for I shall not go out." As Boethius puts it: "Ye people, why do you seek without for the blessing that is within you?"

I also put disinterest above mercy, for mercy is nothing but a man's going out to the want of a fellow and the heart is disturbed by it. Disinterest, however, is exempt from this, being self-contained and allowing nothing to disturb. To speak briefly: When I survey the virtues, I find none as flawless, as conducive to God as disinterest.

A philosopher named Avicenna said: "The rank of a disinterested mind is so high that what it sees is true, what it desires comes to pass, what it commands must be done." You may take this for the truth, that when a free mind is really disinterested, God is compelled to come into it; and if it could get along without contingent forms, it would then have all the properties of God himself. Of course, God cannot give his properties away and so he can do nothing for the disinterested mind except to give himself to it and it is then caught up into eternity, where transitory things no longer affect it. Then the man has no experiences of the physical order and is said to be dead to the world, since he has no appetite for any earthly thing. That is what St. Paul meant by saying: "I live; yet not I, but Christ liveth in me."

You may ask: "What is this disinterest, that it is so noble a matter?" Know, then, that a mind unmoved by any contingent affection or sorrow, or honor, or slander, or vice, is really disinterested—like a broad mountain that is not shaken by a gentle wind. Unmovable disinterest brings man into his closest resemblance to God. It gives God his status as God. His purity is derived from it, and then his simplicity and unchangeable character. If man is to be like God, to the extent that any creature may resemble him, the likeness will come through disinterest, and man proceeds from purity to simplicity and from simplicity to unchangeableness, and thus the likeness of God and man comes about. It is an achievement of the grace that allures man away from temporal things and purges him of the transitory. Keep this in mind: to be full of things is to be empty of God, while to be empty of things is to be full of God.

Bear in mind also that God has been immovably disinterested from the beginning and still is and that his creation of the heavens and the earth affected him as little as if he had not made a single creature. But I go further. All the prayers a man may offer and the good works he may do will affect the disinterested God as little as if there were neither prayers nor works, nor will God be any more compassionate or stoop down to man any more because of his prayers and works than if they were omitted.

Furthermore, I say that when the Son in the Godhead willed to be human and became so, suffering martyrdom, the immovable disinterest of God was affected as little as if the Son had never become human at all.

Perhaps, then, you will say: "I take it, therefore, that prayers and good works are so much lost motion; God pays no attention to them and will not be moved by them. And yet they say that God wants us to pray to him about everything."

Now pay close attention and understand what I mean, if you can. When God first looked out of eternity (if one may say that he ever *first* looked out), he saw everything as it would happen and at the same time he saw when and how he would create each thing. He foresaw the loving prayers and the good deeds each person might do and knew which prayers and which devotions he would heed. He foresaw that tomorrow morning you will cry out to him in earnest prayer and that tomorrow morning he will not heed you because he had already heard your prayer in his eternity, before you became a person; and if your prayer is neither honest nor earnest, he will not deny it now, for it is already denied in eternity. In that first eternal vision, God looked on each thing-to-be and therefore he does what he now does without a reason. It was all worked out beforehand.

Still, even if God remains forever unmoved, disinterested, the prayers and good works of people are not lost on that account, for well-doing is never without its reward. Philippus says: "God the Creator holds things to the course and order he ordained for them in the beginning." To God there is neither past nor future and he loves the saints, having foreseen them before ever the world began. Then, when events, foreseen by God in eternity, come to pass in time, people think that God has taken a new departure, either to anger or toward some agreeable end; but it is we who change, while he remains unchanged. Sunshine hurts ailing eyes but is agreeable to sound ones, and yet it is the same sunshine in both cases. God does not see through time, nor does anything new happen in his sight.

Isidore makes the same point in his book on the highest good. He says: "Many people ask what God was doing before he created heaven and earth. Where did he get his new impulse to make creatures? This is the answer: There never was a departure in God, nor a change of intention, and if there ever was a time when creatures did not exist as they do now, still they existed forever in God, in the mind of God." God did not make heaven and earth as our time-bound speech describes creation; they came into being when He spoke the word out of eternity. Moses said to our Lord, "Lord, if Pharaoh asks who you are, what shall I tell him?" The Lord replied: "Tell him that *he-who-is* sent you." We might say: The unchanging One hath sent me!

Someone well may ask: had Christ this unmoved disinterest when he said: "My soul is sorrowful even unto death"? Or Mary, when she stood underneath the cross? Much has been made of her lamentations. How are such things compatible with unmoved disinterest?

On this point the authorities say that a person is not one, but two people. One is called the outward man—the sensual person. He is served by the five senses, which function by means of the soul's agents. The other is the inner man—the spiritual person. But notice this, that a man who loves God prefers not to use the agents of the soul in the outward man any more than necessary and then the inner man has recourse to the five senses only to the degree to which he can guide and lead them. He guards them against animal diversions—such as people choose when they live like animals without intelligence. Such people are more properly called animals than persons.

Whatever strength the soul possesses, beyond what it devotes to the five senses, it gives to the inner man. If this inner man is devoted to some high and noble enterprise, the soul recalls its agents and the person is said to be senseless or rapt because his enterprise or object is an unintelligible idea or is unintelligible without being an idea. Remember that God requires of every spiritual person a love which includes all the agents of the soul. Thus he said: "Love your God with all your heart."

There are people who squander the strength of their souls in the outward man. These are the people, all of whose desires and thoughts turn on transient goods, since they are unaware of the inner person. Sometimes a good man robs his outward person of all the soul's agents, in order to dispatch them on some higher enterprise; so, conversely, animal people rob the inner person of the soul's agents and assign them to the outward man. A man may be ever so active outwardly and still leave the inner man unmoved and passive.

Now both in Christ and our Lady, there was an outward man and an inner person and, while they taught about external matters, they were outwardly active but inwardly unmoved and disinterested. This is how it was when Christ said: "My soul is sorrowful even unto death." And whatever the lamentations and other speeches of our Lady, inwardly she was still unmoved and disinterested. Take an illustration. A door swings to and fro through an angle. I compare the breadth of the door to the outward man and the hinge to the inner person. When the door swings to and fro, the breadth of the door moves back and forth, but the hinge is still unmoved and unchanged. It is like this here.

Now I ask what the object of pure disinterest is. I reply that it is neither this nor that. Pure disinterest is empty nothingness, for it is on that high plane on which God gives effect to his will. It is not possible for God to do his will in every heart, for even though he is almighty, he cannot act except where he finds preparations made or he makes them himself. I say "or makes them" on account of St. Paul, for God did not find him ready; he prepared St. Paul by an infusion of grace. Otherwise, I say that God acts where he finds that preparations have been made.

God's activity is not the same in a man as in a stone; and there is a simile for that, too, in nature. If a bake oven is heated and lumps of dough are put into it, some of oatmeal, some of barley, some of rye, and some of wheat, then, even though there is only one heat for all in the oven, it will not act the same way on the various doughs; for one turns into a pretty loaf, another to a rough loaf, and others still rougher. That is not due to the heat but to the material, which differs. Similarly God does not work in all hearts alike but according to the preparation and sensitivity he finds in each. In a given heart, containing this or that, there may be an item which prevents God's highest activity. Therefore if a heart is to be ready for him, it must be emptied out to nothingness, the condition of its maximum capacity. So, too, a disinterested heart, reduced to nothingness, is the optimum, the condition of maximum sensitivity.

Take an illustration from nature. If I wish to write on a white tablet, then no matter how fine the matter already written on it, it will confuse me and prevent me from writing down [my thoughts]; so that, if I still wish to use the tablet, I must erase all that is written on it, but it will never serve me as well for writing as when it is clean. Similarly, if God is to write his message about the highest matters on my heart, everything to be referred to as "this or that" must first come out and I must be disinterested. God is free to do his will on his own level when my heart, being disinterested, is bent on neither this nor that.

Then I ask: What is the prayer of the disinterested heart? I answer by saying that a disinterested man, pure in heart, has no prayer, for to pray is to want something from God, something added that one desires, or something that God is to take away. The disinterested person, however, wants nothing, and neither has he anything of which he would be rid. Therefore he has no prayer, or he prays only to be uniform with God. In this sense we may understand the comment of St. Dionysius on a text of St. Paul—"they which run in a race run all, but one receiveth the prize"—that is, all the soul's agents race for the prize but only the soul's essence receives it. Thus, Dionysius says: "This race is precisely the flight from creatures to union with the uncreated." When the soul achieves this, it loses its identity, it absorbs God and is reduced to nothing, as the dawn at the rising of the sun. Nothing helps toward this end like disinterest.

To this point we may quote a saying of St. Augustine: "There is a heavenly door for the soul into the divine nature—where somethings are reduced to nothings." On earth, this door is precisely disinterest, and when disinterest reaches its apex it will be unaware of its knowledge, it will not love its own love, and will be in the dark about its own light. Here, too, we may quote the comment of an authority: "Blessed are the pure in heart who leave everything to God now as they did before ever they existed." No one can do this without a pure, disinterested heart.

That God prefers a disinterested heart for his habitation may be seen from the question: "What is God looking for in everything?" I reply with these words from the Book of Wisdom: "I seek peace in all things." There is, however, no peace except in disinterest. Therefore God prefers it to any other condition or virtue. Remember, too, that the more his heart is trained to be sensitive to divine influences, the happier man is; the further he pushes his preparation, the higher he ascends in the scale of happiness.

But no man can be sensitive to divine influence except by conforming to God, and in proportion to his conformity he is sensitive to divine influence. Conformity comes of submission to God. The more subject to creatures a man is, the less he conforms to God, but the pure, disinterested heart, being void of creatures, is constantly worshiping God and conforming to him, and is therefore sensitive to his influence. That is what St. Paul means by saying: "Put ye on the Lord Jesus Christ"—that is, conform to Christ! Remember that when Christ became man, he was not one man but took all human nature on himself. If you get out, therefore, and clear of creatures, what Christ took on himself will be left to you and you will have put on Christ.

If any man will see the excellence and use of perfect disinterest, let him take seriously what Christ said to his disciples about his humanity: "It is expedient for you that I go away: for if I go not away, the Comforter will not come unto you"—as if he said: "You take too much pleasure in my visible form and therefore the perfect pleasure of the Holy Spirit cannot be yours." Therefore discard the form and be joined to the formless essence, for the spiritual comfort of God is very subtle and is not extended except to those who despise physical comforts.

Heed this, intelligent people: Life is good to the man who goes, on and on, disinterestedly. There is no physical or fleshly pleasure without some spiritual harm, for the desires of the flesh are contrary to those of the spirit, and the desires of the spirit are contrary to the flesh. That is why to sow the undisciplined love of the flesh is to be cut off by death, but to sow the disciplined love of the spirit is to reap of the spirit, life eternal. The less one pays attention to the creature things, the more the Creator pursues him.

Listen to this, man of intelligence: If the pleasure we take in the physical form of Christ diminishes our sensitivity to the Holy Spirit, how much more will the pleasure we take in the comfort of transitory things be a barrier against God? Disinterest is best of all, for by it the soul is unified, knowledge is made pure, the heart is kindled, the spirit wakened, the desires quickened, the virtues enhanced. Disinterest brings knowledge of God; cut off from the creature, the soul unites with God; for love apart from God is like water to a fire, while love with God is the honeycomb in the honey.

Hear this, every intelligent spirit: The steed swiftest to carry you to perfection is suffering, for none shall attain eternal life except he pass through great bitterness with Christ. Nothing pierces man like suffering and nothing is more honey sweet than to have suffered. The surest basis on which perfection rests is humility, and he whose nature kneels in deepest lowliness—*his* spirit shall rise up to the heights of divinity; for as love brings sorrow, sorrow also brings love. Human ways are various: one person lives thus and another so.

For him who wishes to attain the utmost in life in his time, I set down here several aphorisms, much abbreviated, and taken from many writings.

Among men, be aloof; do not engage yourself to any idea you get; free yourself from everything chance brings to you, things that accumulate and cumber you; set your mind in virtue to contemplation, in which the God you bear in your heart shall be your steady object, the object from which your attention never wavers; and whatever else your duty may be, whether it be fasting, watching, or praying, dedicate it all to this one end, doing each only as much as is necessary to your single end. Thus you shall come to the goal of perfection.

Someone may ask: "Who could long endure this unwavering contemplation of the divine object?" I reply: No one living in such times as these. I tell you privately about these things only to have you know what the highest is, so that you may desire it and aspire to it. And if this vision is withdrawn from you, if you are a good man, the withdrawal shall be to you as if the eternity of bliss were taken away, but you must return at once to the pursuit of it, so that it may return to you. Even so, set a perpetual watch over yourself and your thoughts and let your refuge be in this [vision], in which you abide as constantly as possible. Lord God, be thou praised forever! Amen.

WILLIAM OF OCKHAM

William of Ockham was born near London ca. 1285. He early became a Franciscan and studied at Oxford. After completing his public lectures on the Book of Sentences *of Peter Lombard, Ockham was blocked from a teaching choice in theology on charges of heresy. The major charge was that Ockham rejected the traditional medieval loyalty to philosophical realism, a position defended by the theologically orthodox work of Peter Lombard. This began a series of conflicts with the Papacy that led ultimately to his excommunication. It is believed that Ockham perished in the plague that ravaged Europe in the middle of the fourteenth century. The date of his death is set at 1349.*

Ockham's contribution to philosophy was primarily in the areas of logic, epistemology, and metaphysics. Strictly speaking he was not a nominalist, that is, he did not believe that universals were merely general names of things. Rather, he was more of a conceptualist, holding that we do experience individual things and we do apprehend this experience, so that it is not necessary to posit universals or abstract entities. This position involves the principle of parsimony, known as Ockham's razor, which although not original with Ockham, was often invoked by him—the principle that we should not posit assumptions unnecessarily in excess of what is needed for explanation.

The selection that follows shows the acuity of Ockham's thought on the important questions of "names" and "universals." It is worth noting that twentieth-century logic and epistemology are rediscovering the contribution of Ockham on these issues.

From Summa Logicae

11: ON NAMES OF FIRST AND SECOND IMPOSITION

All divisions we have considered so far apply both to terms which naturally signify and to terms which are merely conventional signs. Now we shall examine some divisions that are drawn only among terms that are conventional signs.

First of all, among names that signify conventionally, some are names of first imposition and others, names of second imposition. Names of second imposition are those which are used to signify conventional signs and all such features as pertain to conventional signs in their function as conventional signs.

The common term 'name of second imposition' has two senses however. In the broad sense names of second imposition are those which signify conventional utterances. An expression which is, in this sense, a term of second imposition may also signify intentions of the soul or natural signs; but it is only as signs of conventional utterances that they are terms of second imposition. In their application in grammar expressions like 'name', 'pronoun', 'verb', 'conjunction', 'case', 'number', 'mood', and 'tense' are all, in the broad sense, terms of second imposition. These names are called names of names; the reason for this is that they are used to signify parts of speech insofar as they are significant. Those names, on the other hand, which are predicated of verbal utterances whether or not they are significant are not called names of second imposition. Thus, although names like 'quality', 'utterance', and 'spoken word' signify conventional signs and are true of them, they also signify verbal utterances which are not significant; consequently, they are not names of second imposition. The expression 'name', however, is a name of second imposition, for the word 'man' was not some other name before it was used to signify; likewise, the expression 'of man' did not have a case before it was used to signify; the same holds true of other such expressions.

In the narrow sense expressions are names of second imposition which, while signifying only conventional signs, can never apply to intentions of the soul, natural signs. Examples are 'figure', 'conjugation', and similar expressions. All other names (i.e., those which are names of second imposition in neither the first nor second sense) are names of first imposition.

From William of Ockham, *Summa Logicae*, Part I, in Michael J. Loux, trans., *Ockham's Theory of Terms: Part I of the Summa Logicae*, pp. 72–75, 77–84, and 122–124.

However, 'name of first imposition' has two senses. In the broad sense all names which are not names of second imposition are names of first imposition. In this sense syncategorematic signs like 'every', 'no', 'some', and 'all' are names of first imposition. In the narrow sense only those categorematic names which are not names of second imposition are called names of first imposition. In this sense syncategorematic names are not names of first imposition.

Taking the expression 'name of first imposition' in the narrow sense, there are two sorts of names of first imposition; for some are names of first intention, and others are names of second intention. Names of second intention are those employed to signify intentions of the soul or natural signs, some conventional signs, and features accompanying such signs. Examples are 'genus', 'species', 'universal', 'predicable', etc. Each of these names signifies only natural or conventional signs.

But the common term 'name of second intention' has both a broad and a narrow sense. In the broad sense an expression is called a name of second intention if it signifies intentions of the soul, natural signs, whether or not it also signifies conventional signs in their capacity as signs. In this sense names of second intention can be either names of first or second imposition.

12: ON NAMES OF FIRST AND SECOND INTENTION

In the previous chapter I indicated that certain expressions are names of first intention and others, names of second intention. Ignorance of the meanings of these terms is a source of error for many; therefore, we ought to see what names of first and second intention are and how they are distinguished.

First, it should be noted that an intention of the soul is something in the soul capable of signifying something else. Earlier we indicated how the signs of writing are secondary with respect to spoken signs. Among conventional signs spoken words are primary. In the same way spoken signs are subordinated to the intentions of the soul. Whereas the former are secondary, the latter are primary. It is only for this reason that Aristotle says that spoken words are signs of the impressions of the soul. Now, that thing existing in the soul which is the sign of a thing and an element out of which a mental proposition is composed (in the same way as a spoken proposition is composed of spoken words) is called by different names. Sometimes it is called an intention of the soul; sometimes an impression of the soul; and sometimes the similitude of the thing. Boethius, in his commentary on the *De Interpretatione,* calls it an intellect. He does not, of course, mean that a mental proposition is composed of intellects in the sense of intellectual souls. He only means that a mental proposition is composed of those intellective things which are signs in the soul signifying other things. Thus, whenever anyone utters a spoken proposition, he forms beforehand a mental proposition. This proposition is internal and it belongs to no particular spoken language. But it also happens that people frequently form internal propositions which, because of the defect of their language, they do not know how to express externally. The parts of such mental propositions are called concepts, intentions, likenesses, and "intellects".

But with what items in the soul are we to identify such signs? There are a variety of opinions here. Some say a concept is something made or fashioned by the soul. Others say it is a certain quality distinct from the act of the understanding which exists in the soul as in a subject. Others say that it is simply the act of understanding. This last view gains support from the principle that one ought not postulate many items when he can get by with fewer. Moreover, all the theoretical advantages that derive from postulating entities distinct from acts of understanding can be had without making such a distinction, for an act of understanding can signify something and can supposit for some thing just as well as any sign. Therefore, there is no point in postulating anything over and above the act of understanding. But I shall have more to say about these different views later on. For the moment, we shall simply say that an intention is something in the soul which is either a sign naturally signifying something else (for which it can supposit) or a potential element in a mental proposition.

But there are two kinds of intentions. One kind is called a first intention. This is an intention which signifies something that is not itself an intention of the soul, although it may signify an intention along with this. One example is the intention of the soul predicable of all men; another is the intention that is predicable of all whitenesses, blacknesses, etc.

Hippocrates. This Byzantine miniature painting of the 14th century portrays the founder of ancient Greek medicine. (Bibliothèque Nationale, Paris)

But the expression 'first intention' can be understood in two senses. In the broad sense an intentional sign in the soul is a first intention if it does not signify only intentions or signs. In this broad sense first intentions include not only intentions which so signify that they can supposit in a proposition for their significata, but also intentions which, like syncategorematic intentions, are only signs in an extended sense. In this sense mental verbs, mental syncategorematic expressions, mental conjunctions, and similar terms are first intentions. In the narrow sense only those mental names that are capable of suppositing for their significata are called first intentions.

A second intention, on the other hand, is an intention of the soul which is a sign of first intentions. Examples are *genus, species,* and the like. One intention common to all men is predicated of all men when we say, "This man is a man; that man is a man; . . ." (and so on for all individual men). In the same way, we predicate an intention common to intentions signifying things when we say, "This species is a species; that species is a species; . . ." (and so on). Again, when we say "*Stone* is a genus," "*Animal* is a genus," and "*Color* is a genus," we predicate one intention of another just as we predicate one name of different names when we say that 'man' is a name, 'donkey' is a name, and 'whiteness' is a name. Now, just as names of second imposition conventionally signify names of first imposition, a second intention naturally signifies a first intention. And just as a name of first imposition signifies something other than names, first intentions signify things that are not themselves intentions.

Still, one could claim that in a strict sense, a second intention is an intention which signifies exclusively first intentions; whereas, in a broad sense a second intention can also be an intention signifying both intentions and conventional signs (if, indeed, there are any such intentions).

14: ON THE UNIVERSAL

It is not enough for the logician to have a merely general knowledge of terms; he needs a deep understanding of the concept of a term. Therefore, after discussing some general divisions among terms we should examine in detail the various headings under these divisions.

First, we should deal with terms of second intention and afterwards with terms of first intention. I have said that 'universal', 'genus', and 'species' are examples of terms of second intention. We must discuss those terms of second intention which are called the five universals, but first we should consider the common term 'universal'. It is predicated of every universal and is opposed to the notion of a particular.

First, it should be noted that the term 'particular' has two senses. In the first sense a particular is that which is one and not many. Those who hold that a universal is a certain quality residing in the mind which is predicable of many (not suppositing for itself, of course, but for the many of which it is predicated) must grant that, in this sense of the word, every universal is a particular. Just as a word, even if convention makes it common, is a particular, the intention of the soul signifying many is numerically one thing a particular; for although it signifies many things it is nonetheless one thing and not many.

In another sense of the word we use 'particular' to mean that which is one and not many and which cannot function as a sign of many. Taking 'particular' in this sense no universal is a particular, since every universal is capable of signifying many and of being predicated of many. Thus, if we take the term 'universal' to mean that which is not one in number, as many do, then, I want to say that nothing is a universal. One could, of course, abuse the expression and say that a population constitutes a single universal because it is not one but many. But that would be puerile.

Therefore, it ought to be said that every universal is one particular thing and that it is not a universal except in its signification, in its signifying many things. This is what Avicenna means to say in his commentary on the fifth book of the *Metaphysics.* He says, "One form in the intellect is related to many things, and in this respect it is a universal; for it is an intention of the intellect which has an invariant relationship to anything you choose." He then continues, "Although this form is a universal in its relationship to individuals, it is a particular in its relationship to the particular soul in which it resides; for it is just one form among many in the intellect." He means to say that a universal is an intention of a particular soul. Insofar as it can be predicated of many things not for itself but for these many, it is said to be a universal; but insofar as it is a particular form actually existing in the intellect, it is said to be a particular. Thus 'particular' is predicated of a universal in the first sense but not in the second. In the same way we say that the sun is a universal cause and, nevertheless, that it is really and truly a particular or individual cause. For the sun is said to be a universal cause because it is the cause of many things (i.e., every object that is generable and corruptible), but it is said to be a particular cause because it is one cause and not many. In the same way the intention of the soul is said to be a universal because it is a sign predicable of many things, but it is said to be a particular because it is one thing and not many.

But it should be noted that there are two kinds of universals. Some things are universal by nature; that is, by nature they are signs predicable of many in the same way that the smoke is by nature a sign of fire; weeping, a sign of grief; and laughter, a sign of internal joy. The intention of the soul, of course, is a universal by nature. Thus, no substance outside the soul, nor any accident outside the soul is a universal or this sort. It is of this kind of universal that I shall speak in the following chapters.

Other things are universals by convention. Thus, a spoken word, which is numerically one quality, is a universal; it is a sign conventionally appointed for the signification of many things. Thus, since the word is said to be common, it can be called a universal. But notice it is not by nature, but only by convention, that this label applies.

15: THAT THE UNIVERSAL IS NOT A THING OUTSIDE THE MIND

But it is not enough just to state one's position; one must defend it by philosophical arguments. Therefore, I shall set forth some arguments for my view, and then corroborate it by an appeal to the authorities.

That no universal is a substance existing outside the mind can be proved in a number of ways:

No universal is a particular substance, numerically one; for if this were the case, then it would follow that Socrates is a universal; for there is no good reason why one substance should be a universal rather than another. Therefore no particular substance is a universal; every substance is numerically one and a particular. For every substance is either one thing and not many or it is many things. Now, if a substance is one thing and not many, then it is numerically one; for that is what we mean by 'numerically one'. But if, on the other hand, some substance is several things, it is either several particular things or several universal things. If the first alternative is chosen, then it follows that some substance would be several particular substances; and consequently that some substance would be several men. But although the universal would be distinguished from a single particular, it would not be distinguished from several particulars. If, however, some substance were to be several universal entities, I take one of those universal entities and ask, "Is it many things or is it one and not many?" If the second is the case then it follows that the thing is particular. If the first is the case then I ask, "Is it several particular things or several universal things?" Thus, either an infinite regress will follow or it will be granted that no substance is a universal in a way that would be incompatible with its also being a particular. From this it follows that no substance is a universal.

Again, if some universal were to be one substance existing in particular substances, yet distinct from them, it would follow that it could exist without them; for everything that is naturally prior to something else can, by God's power, exist without that thing; but the consequence is absurd.

Again, if the view in question were true, no individual would be able to be created. Something of the individual would pre-exist it, for the whole individual would not take its existence from nothing if the universal which is in it were already in something else. For the same reason it would follow that God could not annihilate an individual substance without destroying the other individuals of the same kind. If He were to annihilate some individual, he would destroy the whole which is essentially that individual and, consequently, He would destroy the universal which is in that thing and in others of the same essence. Consequently, other things of the same essence would not remain, for they could not continue to exist without the universal which constitutes a part of them.

Again, such a universal could not be construed as something completely extrinsic to the essence of an individual; therefore, it would belong to the essence of the individual; and, consequently, an individual would be composed of universals, so that the individual would not be any more a particular than a universal.

Again, it follows that something of the essence of Christ would be miserable and damned, since that common nature really existing in Christ would be damned in the damned individual; for surely that essence is also in Judas. But this is absurd.

Many other arguments could be brought forth, but in the interests of brevity, I shall dispense with them. Instead, I shall corroborate my account by an appeal to authorities.

First, in the seventh book of the *Metaphysics*, Aristotle is treating the question of whether a universal is a substance. He shows that no universal is a substance. Thus, he says, "it is impossible that substance be something that can be predicated universally."

Again, in the tenth book of the *Metaphysics*, he says, "Thus, if, as we argued in the discussions on substance and being, no universal can be a substance, it is not possible that a universal be a substance in the sense of a one over and against the many."

From these remarks it is clear that, in Aristotle's view, although universals can supposit for substances, no universal is a substance.

Again, the Commentator in his forty-fourth comment on the seventh book of the *Metaphysics* says, "In the individual, the only substance is the particular form and matter out of which the individual is composed."

Again, in the forty-fifth comment, he says, "Let us say, therefore, that it is impossible that one of those things we call universals be the substance of anything, although they do express the substances of things."

And, again, in the forty-seventh comment, "It is impossible that they (universals) be parts of substances existing of and by themselves."

Again, in the second comment on the eighth book of the *Metaphysics*, he says, "No universal is either a substance or a genus."

Again, in the sixth comment on the tenth book, he says, "Since universals are not substances, it is clear that the common notion of being is not a substance existing outside the mind."

Using these and many other authorities, the general point emerges: no universal is a substance regardless of the viewpoint from which we consider the matter. Thus, the viewpoint from which we consider the matter is irrelevant to the question of whether some thing is a substance. Nevertheless, the meaning of a term is relevant to the question of whether the expression 'substance' can be predicated of the term. Thus, if the term 'dog' in the proposition 'The dog is an animal' is used to stand for the barking animal, the proposition is true; but if it is used for the celestial body which goes by that name, the proposition is false. But it is impossible that one and the same thing should be a substance from one viewpoint and not a substance from another.

Therefore, it ought to be granted that no universal is a substance regardless of how it is considered. On the contrary, every universal is an intention of the mind which, on the most probable account, is identical with the act of understanding. Thus, it is said that the act of understanding by which I grasp men is a natural sign of men in the same way that weeping is a natural sign of grief. It is a natural sign such that it can stand for men in mental propositions in the same way that a spoken word can stand for things in spoken propositions.

That the universal is an intention of the soul is clearly expressed by Avicenna in the fifth book of the *Metaphysics*, in which he comments, "I say, therefore, that there are three senses of 'universal'. For we say that something is a universal if (like 'man') it is actually predicated of many things; and we also call an intention a universal if it could be predicated of many." Then follows the remark, "An intention is also called a universal if there is nothing inconceivable in its being predicated of many."

From these remarks it is clear that the universal is an intention of the soul capable of being predicated of many. The claim can be corroborated by argument. For every one agrees that a universal is something predicable of many, but only an intention of the soul or a conventional sign is predicated. No substance is ever predicated of anything. Therefore, only an intention of the soul or a conventional sign is a universal; but I am not here using the term 'universal' for conventional signs, but only for signs that are universals by nature. That substance is not capable of functioning as predicate is clear; for if it were, it would follow that a proposition would be composed of particular substances; and, consequently, the subject would be in Rome and the predicate in England which is absurd.

Furthermore, propositions occur only in the mind, in speech, or in writing; therefore, their parts can exist only in the mind, in speech, and in writing. Particular substances, however, cannot themselves exist in the mind, in speech, or in writing. Thus, no proposition can be composed of particular substances. Propositions are, however, composed of universals; therefore, universals cannot conceivably be substances.

16: AGAINST SCOTUS' ACCOUNT OF THE UNIVERSAL

It may be clear to many that a universal is not a substance outside the mind which exists in, but is distinct from, particulars. Nevertheless, some want to claim that the universal is, in some way, outside the soul and in particulars; and while they do not want to say that a universal is really distinct from particulars, they say that it is formally distinct from particulars. Thus, they say that in Socrates there is human nature which is contracted to Socrates by an individual difference which is not really, but only formally, distinct from that nature. Thus, while there are not two things, one is not formally the other.

I do not find this view tenable:

First, in creatures there can never be any distinction outside the mind unless there are distinct things; if, therefore, there is any distinction between the nature and the difference, it is necessary that they really be distinct things. I prove my premise by the following syllogism: the nature is not formally distinct from itself; this individual difference is formally distinct from this nature; therefore, this individual difference is not this nature.

Again, the same entity is not both common and proper, but in their view the individual difference is proper and the universal is common; therefore, no universal is identical with an individual difference.

Again, opposites cannot be attributed to one and the same created thing, but *common* and *proper* are opposites; therefore, the same thing is not both common and proper. Nevertheless, that conclusion would follow if an individual difference and a common nature were the same thing.

Again, if a common nature were the same thing as an individual difference, there would be as many common natures as there are individual differences; and, consequently, none of those natures would be common, but each would be peculiar to the difference with which it is identical.

Again, whenever one thing is distinct from another it is distinguished from that thing either of and by itself or by something intrinsic to itself. Now, the humanity of Socrates is something different from the humanity of Plato; therefore, they are distinguished of and by themselves and not by differences that are added to them.

Again, according to Aristotle things differing in species also differ in number, but the nature of a man and the nature of a donkey differ in species of and by themselves; therefore, they are numerically distinguished of and by themselves; therefore, each of them is numerically one of and by itself.

Again, that which cannot belong to many cannot be predicated of many; but such a nature, if it really is the same thing as the individual difference, cannot belong to many since it cannot belong to any other particular. Thus, it cannot be predicable of many; but, then, it cannot be a universal.

Again, take an individual difference and the nature which it contracts. Either the difference between these two things is greater or less than the difference between two particulars. It is not greater because they do not differ really; particulars, however, do differ really. But neither is it less because then they would admit of one and the same definition, since two particulars, can admit of the same definition. Consequently, if one of them is, by itself, one in number, the other will also be.

Again, either the nature is the individual difference or it is not. If it is the difference I argue as follows: this individual difference is proper and not common; this individual difference is this nature; therefore this nature is proper and not common, but that is what I set out to prove. Likewise, I argue as follows: the individual difference is not formally distinct from the individual difference; the individual difference is the nature; therefore, the nature is not formally distinct from the individual difference. But if it be said that the individual difference is not the nature, my point has been proved; for it follows that if the individual difference is not the nature, the individual difference is not really the nature; for from the opposite of the consequent follows the opposite of the antecedent. Thus, if it is true that the individual difference really is the nature, then the individual difference is the nature. The inference is valid, for from a determinable taken with its determination (where the determination does not detract from or diminish the determinable) one can infer the determinable taken by itself; but 'really' does not express a determination that detracts or diminishes. Therefore, it follows that if the individual difference is really the nature, the individual difference is the nature.

Therefore, one should grant that in created things there is no such thing as a formal distinction. All things which are distinct in creatures are really distinct and, therefore, different things. In regard to creatures modes of argument like the following ought never be denied: this is *A;* this is *B;* therefore, *B* is *A;* and this is not *A;* this is *B;* therefore, *B* is not *A.* Likewise, one ought never deny that, as regards creatures, there are distinct things where contradictory notions hold. The only exception would be the case where contradictory notions hold true because of some syncategorematic element or similar determination, but in the same present case this is not so.

Therefore, we ought to say with the philosophers that in a particular substance there is nothing substantial except the particular form, the particular matter, or the composite of the two. And, therefore, no one ought to think that in Socrates there is a humanity or a human nature which is distinct from Socrates and to which there is added an individual difference which contracts that nature. The only thing in Socrates which can be construed as substantial is this particular matter, this particular form, or the composite of the two. And, therefore, every essence and quiddity and whatever belongs to substance, if it is really outside the soul, is just matter, form, or the composite of these or, following the doctrine of the Peripatetics, a separation and immaterial substance.

38: ON BEING

Having dealt with terms of second intention and second imposition we shall turn our attention to those terms of first intention that are called the categories. But first we shall consider some expressions that are common to all things, both signs and things that are not signs. 'Being' and 'one' are terms of this sort.

It should first be noted that the term 'being' has two senses. In one sense the term is used to correspond to one concept that is common to all things and is predicable *in quid* of everything in the way in which a transcendental is capable of being predicated *in quid.*

One can prove that there is one common concept predicable of everything in the following way: if there is no one such common concept, then there are different concepts for different things. Let us suppose that there are two such concepts, *A* and *B.* Following out this supposition, I can show that some concept more general than *A* and *B* is predicable of an object, *C.* Just as we can form the verbal propositions '*C* is *B*', '*C* is *A*', and '*C* is something,' we can form three corresponding mental propositions. Two of these are dubious and one is certain; for someone can doubt which of the first two is true, while knowing that the third is true. If this is granted, I argue as follows: two of the propositions are dubious and one is certain. The three propositions all have the same subject; therefore, they have different predicates. Were it not so, one and the same proposition would be both certain and dubious; for in the present case the first two are dubious. But if they have different predicates, the predicate in '*C* is something' is not the predicate in either '*C* is *B*' or '*C* is *A*'. It is, we can conclude, a different predicate. But it is clear that the relevant predicate is neither less general nor convertible with either *A* or *B*. It must therefore be more general. But this is what we set out to prove—that some concept of the mind, different from those that are logically subordinated to it, is common to everything. That must be granted. Just as one word is capable of being truly predicated of everything, there is some one concept of the mind that can be truly predicated of every object or of every pronoun referring to an object.

But while there is one concept common to everything, the term 'being' is equivocal because it is not predicated of the items logically subordinated to it according to just one concept; several different concepts correspond to the term as I have indicated in my commentary on Porphyry.

Further, it should be noted that, as the Philosopher says in the fifth book of the *Metaphysics*, "Being is said both essentially and accidentally." In drawing this distinction the Philosopher should not be understood to mean that some things are beings *per se* and others, beings *per accidens*. What he is doing on the contrary is pointing to the different ways in which one thing can be predicated of another through the mediation of 'to be'. This is clear from the examples he uses. As he notes, we say that the musical is *per accidens* just, that the musical is *per accidens* a man, and that the musical is *per accidens* a builder. It should be clear from these examples that he is only distinguishing the different ways of predicating one thing of another, viz., *per accidens* and *per se*. It is clear that there are not two kinds of being, the *per se* and the *per accidens*. Everything is either a substance or an accident, but both substances and accidents are beings *per se*. This point holds even though we have *per se* and *per accidens* predication.

Similarly, being is divided into being in potency and being in act. This should not be understood to mean that there are two kinds of beings, those which do not exist in nature but could and those which actually exist in nature. By dividing being into potency and act in the fifth book of the *Metaphysics*, Aristotle means to show that the term 'being' is predicated of some things by means of *de inesse* propositions and not by means of propositions equivalent to propositions of possibility. Thus 'Socrates is a being' and 'Whiteness is a being'. Of other things, Aristotle wants to say, 'being' is predicated only by means of a proposition of possibility or by a proposition equivalent to such. Thus 'The Anti-Christ can be' and 'The Anti-Christ is a being in potency'. He wants to say that being like knowledge and sleep, can be predicated both potentially and actually. But note: things do not sleep or have knowledge except actually.

We will talk about the other divisions in being elsewhere. In the interests of brevity these remarks will suffice for the present.

NICOLAUS OF AUTRECOURT

Nicolaus was born in Autrecourt, France, ca. 1300. After studying at the University of Paris, he became a canon at the Cathedral of Metz, where he continued his studies and writing. Nicolaus came under censure for his teachings and was summoned to the Papacy at Avignon for questioning in 1340. He was forced to burn his works in 1347 and his degrees were canceled. Still, in 1350, he became dean of the Cathedral of Metz. The date, place, and circumstances of his death are unknown.

Nicolaus went far beyond Ockham in his criticism of the accepted theological and philosophical propositions of his time. He issued trenchant critiques of the doctrine of causality and of the major tenets of natural theology. He held that the distinction between miracles and the process of natural events could not be maintained. Not until the appearance in the eighteenth century of the thought of David Hume, especially his Dialogues Concerning Natural Religion, *did philosophy have such an outspoken critic of widely held assumptions. Nicolaus can be said to be a forerunner of the bold secular thought of the fifteenth and sixteenth centuries, for he was willing to question theological orthodoxy in a direct way.*

Critique of Causality and Substance

I. FIRST LETTER TO BERNARD OF AREZZO

With all the reverence which I am obligated to show to you, most amiable Father Bernard, by reason of the worthiness of the Friars, I wish in this present communication to explain some doubts—indeed, as it seems to some of us, some obvious contradictions—which appear to follow from the things you say, so that, by their resolution, the truth may be more clearly revealed to me and to others. For I read, in a certain book on which you lectured in the Franciscan school, the following propositions which you conceded, to whoever wished to uphold them, as true. The first, which is set forth by you in the first book of the *Sentences,* Dist. 3, Qu. 4, is this: "*Clear intuitive cognition is that by which we judge a thing to exist, whether it exists or does not exist.* Your second proposition, which is set forth in the same place as above, is of this sort: *The inference,* 'An object does not exist, therefore it is not seen' *is not valid; nor does this hold,* 'This is seen, therefore this exists'; *indeed both are invalid, just as these inferences,* 'Caesar is thought of, therefore Caesar exists,' 'Caesar does not exist, therefore he is not thought of.' The third proposition, stated in that same place, is this: *Intuitive cognition does not necessarily require the existing thing.*"

From these propositions I infer a fourth, that every awareness which we have of the existence of objects outside our minds, can be false; since, according to you it [the awareness] can exist whether or not the object exists. And I infer another fifth proposition, which is this: By natural cognitive means [*in lumine naturali*] we cannot be certain when our awareness of the existence of external objects is true or false; because, as you say, it represents the thing as existing, whether or not it exists. And thus, since whoever admits the antecedent must concede the consequent which is inferred from that antecedent by a formal consequence, it follows that you do not have evident certitude of the existence of external objects. And likewise you must concede all the things which follow from this. But it is clear that you do not have evident certitude of the existence of objects of the senses, because no one has certitude of any consequent through an inference which manifestly involves a fallacy. But such is the case here; for according to you, this is a fallacy, "Whiteness is seen, therefore whiteness exists."

But you will perhaps say, as I think you wished to suggest in a certain disputation over at the Preaching Friars', that although from the fact of seeing it cannot be inferred, when that seeing is produced or conserved by a supernatural cause, that the seen object exists, nevertheless when it is produced precisely by natural causes—with only the general concurrence of the First Agent—then it can be inferred.

But to the contrary: When from some antecedent, if produced by some agent, a certain consequent cannot be inferred by a formal and evident inference, then from that antecedent, no matter by what thing it be produced, that consequent cannot be inferred. This proposition is clear, by example and by reason. By example in this way: If, whiteness being posited as existing by the agency of A, it could not be formally inferred "Whiteness exists, therefore color exists," then this could not be inferred no matter by what agency the whiteness be posited as existing. It is also clear by reason, because the antecedent is not in itself modified by whatever it is that causes it to be—nor is the fact which is signified by that antecedent.

Further, since from that antecedent it cannot be inferred evidently by way of intuitive cognition,

Nicolaus of Autrecourt, "Critique of Causality and Substance," trans. Ernest A. Moody, in Herman Shapiro, ed., *Medieval Philosophy: From Augustine to Buridan* (New York: Random House, 1964), pp. 510–526. Permission granted by Mrs. Ernest A. Moody.

"therefore whiteness exists," we must then add something to that antecedent—namely, what you suggested above, that the [vision of] whiteness is not produced or conserved in existence supernaturally. But from this my contention is clearly established. For when a person is not certain of some consequent, unless in virtue of some antecedent of which he is not evidently certain whether or not the case is as it states it to be—because it is not known by the meaning of its terms, nor by experience, nor is it inferred from such knowledge, but is only believed—such a person is not evidently certain of the consequent. It is clear that this is so, if that antecedent is considered together with its condition; therefore etc. On the other hand, according to your position, whoever makes the inference from that antecedent without adding that condition, makes an invalid inference—as was the case with the philosophers, and Aristotle, and other people who did not add this condition to the antecedent, because they did not believe that God could impede the effects of natural causes.

Again, I ask you if you are acquainted with all natural causes, and know which of them exist and which are possible, and how much they can do. And I ask how you know evidently, by evidence reducible to that of the law of contradiction, that there is anything such that its coming to pass does not involve contradiction and which nevertheless can only be brought to pass by God? On these questions I would gladly be given certitude of the kind indicated.

Again, you say that an imperfect intuitive cognition can be had in natural manner, of a non-existent thing. I now ask how you are certain (with the certitude defined above) when your intuitive cognition is of a sufficiently perfect degree such that it cannot naturally be of a non-existent thing. And I would gladly be instructed about this.

Thus, it is clear, it seems to me, that as a consequence of your statements you have to say that you are not certain of the existence of the objects of the five senses. But what is even harder to uphold, you must say that you are not certain of your own actions—e.g., that you are seeing, or hearing—indeed you must say that you are not sure that anything is perceived by you, or has been perceived by you. For, in the *Sentences, Book I, Dist. 3,* in the place above cited, you say that your intellect does not have intuitive cognition of your actions. And you prove it by this argument: Every intuitive cognition is clear; but the cognition which your intellect has of your acts, is not clear; therefore etc. Now, on this assumption, I argue thus: The intellect which is not certain of the existence of things of which it has the clearest cognition, will not be certain concerning those things of which it has a less clear cognition. But, as was said, you are not certain of the existence of objects of which you have a clearer cognition than you have of your own acts; therefore etc.

And if you say that sometimes some abstractive cognition is as clear as an intuitive cognition—e.g., that every whole is greater than its part—this will not help you, because you explicitly say that the cognition which we have of our own acts is not as clear as intuitive cognition; and yet intuitive cognition, at least that which is imperfect, is not naturally of evident certainty. This is clear from what you say. And thus it follows evidently, that you are not certain of what appears evident to you, and consequently you are not certain whether anything appears to you.

And it also follows that you are not certain whether any proposition is true or false, because you are not evidently certain whether any proposition exists, or has existed. Indeed it follows that if you were asked whether or not you believed some articles of the Faith, you would have to say, "I do not know," because, according to your position, you could not be certain of your own act of believing. And I confirm this, because, if you were certain of your act of believing, this would either be from that very act itself, in which case the direct and reflective act would be identical—which you will not admit—or else it would be by some other act, and in that case, according to your position, you would in the same way be uncertain, because there would then be no more contradiction than that the seeing of whiteness existed and the whiteness did not exist, etc.

And so, bringing all these statements together, it seems that you must say that you are not certain of those things which are outside of you. And thus you do not know if you are in the heavens or on the earth, in fire or in water; and consequently you do not know whether today's sky is the same one as yesterday's, because you do not know whether the sky exists. Just as you do not know whether the Chancellor or the Pope exists, and whether, if they exist, they are different in each moment of time. Similarly, you do not know the things within you—as, whether or not you have a beard, a head, hair, and so forth. And *a fortiori* it follows from this that you are not certain of the things which occurred in the past—as, whether you have been reading, or seeing, or hearing. Further, your position seems to lead to the destruction of social and political affairs, because if witnesses testify of what they have seen, it does not follow, "We have seen it, therefore it happened." Again, I ask how, on this view, the Apostles were certain that Christ suffered on the cross, and that He rose from the dead, and so with all the rest.

I wish that your mind would express itself on all these questions, and I wonder very much how you can say that you are evidently certain of various conclusions which are more obscure—such as concern the existence of the Prime Mover, and the like—when you are not certain about these things which I have mentioned. Again, it is strange how, on your assumptions, you believe that you have shown that a cognition is distinct from what is cognized, when you are not certain, according to your position, that any cognition exists or that any propositions exist, and consequently that any contradictory propositions exist; since, as I have shown, you do not have certainty of the existence of your own acts, or of your own mind, and do not know whether it exists. And, as it seems to me, the absurdities which follow on the position of the Academics, follow on your position. And so, in order to avoid such absurdities, I maintained in my disputation at the Sorbonne, that I am evidently certain of the objects of the five senses, and of my own acts.

I think of these objections, and of so many others, that there is no end to them, against what you say. I pray you, Father, to instruct me who, however stupid, am nevertheless desirous of reaching knowledge of the truth. May you abide in Him, who is the light, and in whom there is no darkness.

II. SECOND LETTER TO BERNARD

Reverend Father Bernard, the depth of your subtlety would truly bring forth the admiration of my mind, if I were to know that you possess evident knowledge of the separated substances—the more so if I know this, but even if I had in my mind a slight belief. And not only, if I should think that you possess true cognition of the separated substances, but even of those conjoined to matter. And so to you, Father, who assert that you have evident cognition of such lofty objects of knowledge, I wish to lay bare my doubtful and anxious mind, so that you may have the materials for leading me and other people toward acquaintance with such great things.

And the first point is, that at the foundation of discourse this principle is primary: Contradictories cannot be simultaneously true. And with respect to this, two things hold: the first is, that this is the first principle, taken negatively as that than which nothing is more primary. The second is, that this is first, taken positively, as that which is prior to every other principle.

These two statements are proved by argument, as follows: Every certitude possessed by us reduces to this principle, and it in turn is not reduced to any other in the way that a conclusion is reduced to its premise; it therefore follows that this principle is first, with the twofold primacy indicated. This consequence is known from the meaning of the term "first," according to each of the expositions given. The antecedent is proved with respect to both of its parts. And first, with respect to its first part, namely that every certitude possessed by us, short of this certitude, reduces to this principle of which you say you are certain, I set forth this consequence: It is possible, without any contradiction being implied, that something will appear to you to be so, and yet that it will not be so; therefore you are not evidently certain that it is so. It is clear to me that if I were to admit this antecedent to be true, I would concede the consequent to be true; and therefore I would not be evidently and unqualifiedly certain of that of which I was saying that I was certain.

From this it is clear that every one of our certitudes is resolved into our said principle, and that it is not resolved into another, as a conclusion into its premise. From this it is plain that all certitudes are resolved into this one, as was said, and that this consequence is valid: If this is prior to everything other than itself, then nothing is prior to it. And thus it is first, with the twofold primacy above stated.

The third point is, that a contradiction is the affirmation and negation of the same (predicate) of the same (subject), etc., as is commonly said.

From these things I infer a corollary—namely, that the certitude of evidence which we have in the natural light, is certitude in the unqualified sense; for it is the certitude which is possessed in virtue of the first principle, which neither is nor can be contradicted by any true law. And hence whatever is demonstrated in the natural light of reason, is demonstrated without qualification; and, just as there is no power which can make contradictories simultaneously true, so there is no power by which it can come to pass that the opposite of the consequent is compatible with the antecedent.

The second corollary which I infer, with regard to this, is that the certitude of evidence has no degrees. Thus, if there are two conclusions, of each of which we are evidently certain, we are not more certain of one than of the other. For as was said, every certitude is resolved into the same first principle. Either, then, those first conclusions are reduced with equal immediacy to the same first principle—in which case there is no ground for our being more certain of one than of the other; or else one is reduced mediately, and the other immediately. But this makes no difference, because, once the reduction to the first principle has been made, we are certain of the one equally with the other—just as the geometrician says that he is as certain of a second conclusion as of the first, and similarly of the third and so on, even though in his first consideration, because of the plurality of the deductions, he cannot be as certain of the fourth or third as of the first.

The third corollary which I infer, in connection with what has been said, is that with the exception of the certitude of faith, there is no other certitude except the certitude of the first principle, or the certitude which can be resolved into the first principle. For there is no certitude except that in which there is no falsity; because, if there were any in which falsity could exist, let it be supposed that falsity does exist in it—then, since the certitude itself remains, it follows that someone is certain of something whose contradictory is true, without contradiction.

The fourth corollary is this: that a syllogistic form is immediately reducible to the first principle; because, by its demonstration, the conclusion is either immediately reduced (in which case the thesis holds), or else mediately; and if mediately, then either the regress will be infinite, or else it must arrive at some conclusion which reduces immediately to the first principle.

The fifth corollary: In every consequence which reduces immediately to the first principle, the consequent, and the antecedent either as a whole or in part, are really identical; because, if this were not so, then it would not be immediately evident that the antecedent and the opposite of the consequent cannot both be true.

The sixth corollary is this: In every evident consequence reducible to the first principle by as many intermediates as you please, the consequent is really identical with the antecedent or with part of what is signified by the antecedent. This is shown because, if we suppose some conclusion to be reduced to the certitude of the first principle by three intermediates, the consequent will be really identical with its (immediate) antecedent or with part of what is signified by that antecedent, by the fifth corollary; and similarly in the second consequence, by the same reason; and thus, since in the first consequence the consequent is really identical with the antecedent or with part of what is signified by the antecedent, and likewise in the second one, and likewise in the third, it follows that in these consequences, ordered from first to last, the last consequent will be really identical with the first antecedent or with a part of what is signified by that antecedent.

On the basis of these statements, I laid down, along with other conclusions, one which was this: From the fact that some thing is known to exist, it cannot be evidently inferred, by evidence reduced to the first principle or to the certitude of the first principle, that some other thing exists.

Aside from many other arguments, I brought forth this argument. In such a consequence, in which from one thing another thing is inferred, the consequent would not be really identical with the antecedent or with part of what is signified by the antecedent; therefore it follows that such a consequence would not be evidently known with the said evidence of the first principle. The antecedent is conceded and posited by my opponent; the consequence is plain from the description of "contradiction," which is affirmation and negation of the same of the same, etc. Since therefore in this case the consequent is not really identical with the antecedent or its part, it is evident that if the opposite of the consequent, and the antecedent, be simultaneously true, this would not be a case of one thing being affirmed and denied of the same thing, etc.

But Bernard replies, saying that although in this case there is not a formal contradiction, for the reason given, yet there is a virtual contradiction; he calls a contradiction virtual, however, if from it a formal contradiction can be evidently inferred.

But against this we can argue manifestly, from the fifth and sixth of the above corollaries. For it has been shown that in every consequence reducible either immediately or mediately to the certitude of the first principle, it is necessary that the consequent—whether the first one or the last—be really identical with the first antecedent or with a part of it.

Again, we may argue conclusively from another premise. For he says that, although in a consequence in which from one thing another thing is inferred, there is not a formal contradiction, there is nevertheless a virtual one from which a formal one can be evidently inferred. Then let there be, for example, the following consequence propounded: "A exists, therefore B exists." If, then, from the propositions, "A exists," "B does not exist," a formal contradiction could be evidently inferred, this would be through a consequent of one of these propositions, or through a consequent of each of them. But whichever way it is, the thesis is not established. For these consequents would either be really identical with their antecedents, or they would not. If identical, then there will not be a formal contradiction between those consequents, since there will not then be an affirmation and a negation of the same predicate of the same subject, and hence not between the antecedents either. Just as it is not a formal contradiction to say that a rational animal exists and that a neighing animal does not exist; and for the same reason. But if it be said that these consequents differ from their antecedents, we argue the same way as before, that this is not a consequence evidently reduced to the certitude of the first principle, since the opposite of the consequent is compatible with whatever is signified by the antecedent, without contradiction. And if it be said that there is a virtual contradiction, from which a formal one can be inferred, we argue as before, either there is a regress without end, or else we must say that in a consequence evident without qualification the consequent is identical in its signification with the antecedent, or with part of what is signified by the antecedent.

And it is true that the reverend Father has said, with regard to this question, that it would not be true to say that in a consequence evident without qualification it is required that the opposite of the consequent, and the antecedent, cannot simultaneously be false, and that they are therefore not opposed as contradictories. But in actual fact this does not in any way prevent what I am maintaining. For I do not wish to say that the opposite of the consequent must be the contradictory of the antecedent—for in many consequences the antecedent can signify more than does the consequent, though the consequent signifies a part of what is signified by the antecedent—as in this consequence, "A house exists, therefore a wall exists." And on this account the opposite of the consequent, and the antecedent, can both be false. But I wish to say that in an evident consequence the opposite of the consequent, and the antecedent or a part of what it signifies, are opposed as contradictories. It is plain that this is the case in every valid syllogism; for since no term occurs in the conclusion which did not occur in the premises, the opposite of the conclusion, and something signified by the premises, are opposed as contradictories. And so it must be in every valid inference, because an enthymeme is only valid in virtue of a proposition presupposed—so that it is a kind of incomplete syllogism.

Further, I offer this argument for my main conclusion: Never, in virtue of any inference, can there be inferred a greater identity of the extreme term, than that which is between the extreme term and the middle term, because the former is only inferred in virtue of the latter. But the opposite of this will occur, if from the fact that one thing is a being, it could evidently be inferred that something else is a being; because the predicate of the conclusion, and the subject, signify what is really identical, whereas they are not really identical with the middle term which is posited as another thing.

But Bernard objects to this proposed rule, because it follows evidently, with an evidence reduced to the certitude of the first principle, "Whiteness exists, therefore something else exists"—because whiteness cannot exist unless some subject maintains it in existence. Likewise it follows, "Whiteness is not a being in the primary sense, therefore some other thing exists." Or likewise, "Fire is brought into contact with the fuel, and there is no impediment, therefore there will be heat."

To these objections I have elsewhere given many answers. But for the present I say that if a thousand such objections were adduced, either it must be said that they are irrelevant, or, if relevant, that they conclude nothing against my position. Because in these consequences which he states, if the consequent is really identical in its signification with the antecedent as a whole or with a part of the antecedent, then the argument is not to the point, because in that case I would concede the consequences to be evident, and nothing against my position would be adduced. But if it be said that the consequent is not identical with the antecedent or part of it, then, if I concede the opposite of the consequent, and the antecedent, to be simultaneously true, it is plain that I am not conceding them to be contradictories, since contradictories are of the same predicate of the same subject, etc. And thus such a consequence is not evident by the evidence of the first principle, because the evidence of the first principle was understood to be had when, if it were conceded that the opposite of the consequent is compatible with the antecedent, contradictories would be admitted as simultaneously true. For though one might concede, with respect to this consequence "A house exists, therefore a wall exists," that a house exists and a wall does not exist, he does not thereby concede contradictories to be simultaneously true, because these propositions are not contradictories. "A house exists," "A wall does not exist," since both of them may be false; yet he does concede contradictories on another ground, because to signify that a house exists is to signify that a wall exists, and then it is a contradiction that a house exists and that a wall does not exist.

From this rule, so explained to anyone having the grasp of it, I infer that Aristotle never possessed an evident cognition concerning any substance other than his own soul—taking "substance" as a thing other than the objects of the five senses, and other than our formal experiences. And this is so, because he would have had a cognition of such a thing prior to every inference—which is not true, since they (substances) are not perceived intuitively, and since (if they were) rustics would know that such things exist; nor are they known by inference, namely as inferred from things perceived to exist antecedently to discursive thought—because from one thing it cannot be inferred that another thing exists, as the above conclusion states.

And if he did not have evident cognition of conjoined (material) substances, much less did he have it of abstract substances. From which it follows, whether you like it or not, and not because I make it so but because reason determines it, that Aristotle in his whole natural philosophy and metaphysics had such certitude of scarcely two conclusions, and perhaps not even of one. And Father Bernard, who is not greater than Aristotle, has an equal amount of certitudes, or much less.

And not only did Aristotle not have evident cognition (of these things)—indeed, though I do not assert this, I have an argument which I cannot refute, to prove that he did not have probable knowledge. For a person does not have probable knowledge of any consequent, in virtue of some antecedent, when he is not evidently certain whether the consequent will at some time be true together with the antecedent. For let anyone really consider well the nature of probable knowledge—as for example that because it was at one time evident to me that when I put my hand in the fire I was hot, therefore it is probable to me that if I should put it there now I would be hot. But from the rule stated above, it follows that it was never evident to anyone that, given these things which are apparent without inference, there would exist certain other things—namely those others which are called substances. It therefore follows that of their existence we do not have probable knowledge. I do not assert this conclusion; but let this argument be resolved, for a solution will surely occur.

And that we do not possess certitude concerning any substance conjoined to matter, other than our own soul, is plain—because, pointing to a piece of wood, or a stone, this conclusion will be most clearly deduced from a belief accepted at the same time. For by the divine power it can happen, with these things which appear prior to all inference, that no substance is there; therefore in the natural light of reason it is not evidently inferred from these appearances that a substance is there. This consequence is plain from what we explained above. For it was said that a consequence is evident only if it is a contradiction for it to occur, through any power, that the opposite of the consequent is true along with the antecedent. And if it is said that the consequence is evident, if to the antecedent we add "God is not performing a miracle," this is disproved by what we have said on this point in our first letter to Bernard.

I ask, Father, that you take up these doubts and give counsel to my stupidity; and I promise that I will not be stubborn in evading the truth, to which I adhere with all my strength.

FRANCESCO PETRARCA

Petrarch, as he is known in the literature, was born in Arezzo, Italy, in 1304. Most of his middle years were spent in Avignon, France. After 1353 he returned to Italy, where he died in 1374. Petrarch is clearly a transitional figure, for he both broke with the Scholasticism of his time and anticipated the attitudes and activities of fifteenth-century Renaissance humanism.

Petrarch was clearly indebted to the ancient Roman writers, particularly Cicero and Seneca. He focused on the travails and possibilities of human life, while showing a disdain for the dialectics and abstractions of fourteenth-century philosophy. Nonetheless, Petrarch was extremely influential in his belief that the ancient philosophers, including Aristotle, should be read in the original Greek and liberated from the complex interpretations of the medieval theologians. Although we focus here on the contribution of Petrarch to the philosophical thought of the early Renaissance, it should be noted that his reputation is due as well to his poetry and literary work, particularly his autobiographical piece, The Ascent of Mont Ventoux. *The flavor of Petrarch's refreshing humanism is evident even in the brief selections that follow.*

From On the Remedies of Good and Bad Fortune

DIALOGUE 1

On the Prime of Life, and the Hope of Long Life

Joy and Hope. I am in the prime of life: I shall yet live a long time.

Reason. Lo! The first vain hope of mortal men: a hope which has already deluded many thousands, and will continue to do so.

Joy and Hope. I am in the prime of life.

Reason. A vain and short-lived joy. Even as we speak, the flower withers!

Joy and Hope. I am quite sound.

Reason. Who will call that sound which lacks much, while that which it has is uncertain?

Joy and Hope. But there is a certain law and a fixed term of living.

Reason. Who made the law? What is the fixed term of life? Surely it is a most unjust law that is not equally applied to all men; and, indeed, this one is so variable that nothing is more uncertain in the life of man than the term of his life.

Joy and Hope. Nonetheless, there is a certain term and measure of life which has been set forth by the wise.

Reason. It is not in the power of him who receives it to set the term of life. This, rather, is in the power of Him who gives it: God. But I understand: You are thinking of a term of some seventy or—if the individual be somewhat more robust—eighty years. He, however, who attains to such an age finds life to be all pain and travail. Indeed, it is possible that your hopes have been extended even further than this by him who said, *the days of a man's life are many times a hundred years.* Now this, as we know, is an age which but few attain; but granting that that which happens to few were to happen to all, what would it then profit?

Joy and Hope. A great deal, in truth; for the life of young men is the more secure the further it is from old age and death.

Reason. You deceive yourself. Nothing is safe to a man: but that which is most dangerous for him has

---

From Francesco Petrarca, *On the Remedies of Good and Bad Fortune,* in Arturo B. Fallico and Herman Shapiro, eds., *Renaissance Philosophy: The Italian Philosophers* (New York: Random House, 1967), pp. 3–7. Permission granted by Herman Shapiro.

its source in heedlessness. Nothing is closer to life than death; when they seem to be at the greatest remove, they are closest together. The one always passes, the other draws inexorably nigh. Try as you may to escape, death is ever at hand and hangs over your head.

Joy and Hope. Well, at least for now, youth is present and old age is absent.

Reason. Nothing is more fleeting than youth; nothing more treacherous than old age. Youth tarries not, but slips away in its delights; old age, following immediately after, softly, in darkness and silence, strikes men unawares; just when she is thought to be far off, she stands at the door.

Joy and Hope. My youth is in the ascendant.

Reason. You put your trust in a most treacherous thing. This "ascendancy" of which you speak is, in reality, a decline. This brief life is furtively, silently, between play and dreams, soon dissolved by unstable time. Would that God would permit us to realize in the beginning, as we do at the end, the rapidity with which time unfolds and the brevity of life! To one just commencing, it seems endless; to one who is leaving, it seems as nothing; and that which first seemed a century, is seen at the last as hardly an instant. We discover the fraud, therefore, when it is no longer possible to foil it. This is why, frequently, the counsel given to youth, which is at once incredulous and untried, is in vain; lacking in wisdom of its own, youth has contempt for the wisdom of others. And so the follies of youth, while innumerable and colossal, remain nonetheless covert and unknown to their very authors. Nothing serves better to unveil them than old age, which sets them clearly before the eyes of those who have perpetrated them and are their accomplices. Youth does not realize what it should have been, before it becomes what it has become—and then it can become nothing else. Were one able to foresee it on his own, or were one capable of believing those who instruct him, he should be one in a thousand, and would wax a happy youth. He would not drag his life along so many tortuous ways, for virtue alone provides the straight and narrow path.

Joy and Hope. My age is without fault.

Reason. How can it be faultless if from its very inception it is steadily chipped away; if it is broken up in minute fragments from the very instant in which it is given us? The sky turns with a continuous motion, the moments steal away the hours, the hours steal away the days; this day destroyed another, as that other has destroyed yet another; and so on, relentlessly. So, as Cicero affirms, pass the months; so pass the years; so time passes and hurries. It flies, as Virgil says, "without agitating its swift wings." Thus, as in sea voyages, the end arrives suddenly, without the traveler anticipating it or even thinking about it.

Joy and Hope. These are my early years, still far from the end.

Reason. Within the cramped limits of life, nothing is far off.

Joy and Hope. In every regard the beginning is farthest from the end.

Reason. Yes, in every respect: but this would be an exact observation only if everyone's life were of equal duration. Little children frequently, and in many ways, incur death. More often than not the end is close even when it seems far away.

Joy and Hope. Without doubt, these are my greenest years.

Reason. Despite the fact that few are aware of it, from the very moment that we began to speak some change has occurred; and during the very instants of syllabification some little life has passed away—something has been subtracted from the fading flower of the years. What then has the tender youth more than the old and wrinkled man, except this brief and transitory prime that we are talking about? A flower which fades a little at each instant; an age in which I find nothing sweet and joyous, since youth is aware that it will become, more swiftly than it takes to tell, what age now is and has already become. And he who closes his mind to this is demented. The only difference I would concede between youth and old age is that if both were dragged to their death, one might be considered more happy than the other: the one, that is, who is first to offer his neck to the ax. It seems to me that the one who had to wait would in some way be the more unfortunate of the two; for while their situations are thus different, the one who remains until last can hope for something which might permit him to escape the agony of his companion, and live on. Death alone can save a young man from old age. In brief: in a small space of time there can be no great felicity; and for a truly great soul, nothing that is so brief can seem desirable. Awaken, all you who sleep! The hour has come! Open your sleepy eyes! Learn, once and for all, to think of eternal things—to love them, to desire them; and yield up to time itself that which is transitory. Learn to detach yourself willingly from those things which cannot remain with us for very long, and to leave them, in spirit, before they leave us.

Joy and Hope. Mine is a green and fixed age.

Reason. Anyone who calls any age "fixed," lies. Nothing is more wanton than time. Time is the wheel of all ages. Can you conceive of it as fixed? O vanity! Nothing is fixed—in this very instant they take you away!

A Disapproval of an Unreasonable Use of the Discipline of Dialectic

TO TOMMASO OF MESSINA, AGAINST OLD DIALECTIC CAVILERS

It is a risky task to contend with an enemy who is not so eager to win as to fight. You tell me of an old dialectician who has been violently annoyed by my letter, as though I had condemned his profession. He is raging in public, you say, and threatens to assail our field of studies in a letter of his; and you have been waiting for this letter in vain for months. Do not expect it any longer. Believe me, it will never come. That much good sense is left in him. He is evidently ashamed of his stylistic capacities, or else his silence is a confession of his ignorance. Those who are implacable with their tongues do not battle with the pen. They do not like to let men know how frail their armor is. They fight after the Parthian manner, while they are fleeing; they cast their volatile words into the air, as if they were committing their darts to the wind.

As I said before, it is risky to fight with such people after their fashion, especially because they so much enjoy the combat itself. They are not set to find the truth—they want the struggle. But there is a Varronian maxim: "In too much altercation truth is lost." Do not be afraid that they will come out to the open battleground of written words and solid discussion. It is of such people that Quintilian has said in his *Instruction of Speech-making:* "You will find certain people miraculously clever in disputing. However, as soon as they must do without this kind of caviling, they are no more efficient in any serious operation than certain animals which are very nimble in narrow straits but easily caught in the open field." Therefore, they are quite right if they fear to come out. For it is true what the same Quintilian says: "The weak have recourse to crooked ways and evasive tricks, for those who do not achieve much in running away escape adroitly by their flexibility."

There is one thing, my friend, that I want to tell you: If you aim at virtue and truth, avoid this sort of men. But where can we find refuge from such mad folk if even islands are not safe from them? Not even Scylla and Charybdis prevent this pest from swimming across to Sicily. This kind of misfortune is evidently peculiar to islands, since a horde of new Cyclopes has gathered near Mount Etna, to match the host of dialectic fighters in Britain. Did I not read in Pomponius Mela's *Cosmography* that Britain resembles Sicily very much? I believed, it is true, that this resemblance consisted in the geographical situation and the almost triangular shape of the two islands and perhaps also in the ceaseless breaking of the sea against the shores of both. I had not thought of the dialecticians. I had heard that the Cyclopes were the first to live there, then the tyrants, and that both were ferocious people. However, I did not know that a new kind of monster had arrived there, armed with double-edged enthymemes, a gang more insolent than the wild breakers on the shore of Taormina. One thing I had not noticed before you brought it to my attention: They shield their sect with the splendid name of Aristotelians and pretend that Aristotle was wont to discuss in their manner. It

Francesco Petrarca, "A Disapproval of an Unreasonable Use of the Discipline of Dialectic," trans. Hans Nachod, in Ernst Cassirer, Paul Oskar Kristeller, and John Herman Randall, Jr., eds., *The Renaissance Philosophy of Man* (Chicago: University of Chicago Press, 1956), pp. 134–139.

is a kind of excuse to stick to the footsteps of famous leaders. Marcus Tullius, too, says that "not unwillingly he would commit an error," if necessary, "together with Plato." But they are mistaken: Aristotle, who was a man of fervent spirits, discussed problems of the highest order and wrote about them. How else would he have managed to write so many volumes that are composed with so much application in so many sleepless nights amid so many other occupations, particularly with his fortunate pupil, and during a life that did not last long? For we hear about him from ancient authors that he died in the ill-famed sixty-third year of his age. However, why are these people straying so far away from their leader, why are they so eager to be called Aristotelians, why are they not rather ashamed of this name? No greater contrast can be imagined than that between this great philosopher and a man who does not write anything, understands but little, and shouts much and without consequence. Who does not laugh at the insignificant little conclusions in which these highly educated people fatigue themselves and others? They waste their whole lives in such conclusions, since they are not good for anything else and especially destructive in this particular case.

Such syllogisms are very often ridiculed by Cicero and Seneca. Well known also is a repartee which Diogenes made, when a quarrelsome dialectic debater assailed him in the following manner: "What I am you are not," he began. When Diogenes admitted this statement, he went on: "But I am a man." When Diogenes did not deny this either, the caviler smuggled in the conclusion: "Thus you are not a man." It was then that Diogenes replied: "This is a wrong conclusion, and if you want it to become right, you must start with me." Many most ridiculous conclusions are like this one. These people will perhaps know what they intend to achieve by them: whether they hope to win fame or to have a pleasant time or to get counsel on how to lead a decent and happy life. I certainly do not know what they want. To noble minds profit should not appear to be a dignified reward for studies. It fits a craftsman to seek profit; generous arts know a nobler goal.

These friends of dialectic get angry when they hear what I say, for the ceaseless talking of quarrelsome persons is always liable to degenerate into an angry mood. "Thus you disapprove of the discipline of dialectic," they say. Not in the least. I know how much it was appreciated by the Stoics, this strong and masculine sect of philosophers that is so often cited by Cicero, particularly in his book *About the Ultimate Ends.* I know that it is one of the liberal arts and a stepping-stone for those who want to rise to higher grades. It is not a useless weapon in the hands of those who try to find a way through the thickets of philosophy. It sharpens the intellect, marks off the path toward truth, and teaches how to avoid fallacies. If it does not achieve anything else, it certainly gives a man a ready wit and makes him most resourceful. All this I do not deny. But where we pass with honor, we do not stay with praise. A wayfarer who forgets the goal he has set to himself because the road is so pleasant is not sound of mind. A traveler is praised if he completes a long journey quickly without ever stopping before its end. And who among us is not a traveler? All of us must cover a long and difficult road in a short set time in bad weather, almost as it were on a rainy winter day. Occupation with dialectic may cover a part of this road; it ought never to be the goal. It may be on the morning schedule but never on that of the evening. At one time we were completely right in doing many things that would turn out to be most disgraceful for us if we still did them. If we do not succeed in our old age in leaving the dialectic schools behind us, because we played in them while we were boys, we might just as well not feel ashamed to continue "playing odd and even and using a shaky reed" as a hobby horse or to start again rocking in a baby cradle.

Things are strangely different and times are changing. With most vigilant art Nature has thought out how to prevent man from being bored. Do not believe that such changes happen only within the course of a single year; many more of them will happen during a long life. Spring is charming for its blossoming flowers and trees; summer is rich in all kinds of grain, autumn in fruit, and winter brings abundance of snow. All this is not just tolerable but pleasant and agreeable. If you change one for the other, the laws of Nature will break down and everything becomes hard to bear. Just as no one would endure icy January frost all summer with even temper, or torrid summer heat if it raged in months where it does not belong, everybody without exception would become angry and laugh at an old man who did nothing else than play with little children, and everybody would be amazed at a gray-haired, gouty boy. Can you imagine anything, I ask you, that is so useful or even so necessary as the first notion of letters? They are the foundation on which all our studies rest. However, vice versa, is there anything so ridiculous as an old man who is still occupied with these elements? Therefore, stir up the pupils of that old man, quoting my words: Do not deter them, rather encourage them, not indeed to throw themselves in all haste into the study of dialectic, but to pass quickly through this discipline to better ones. And tell your old man that I do not condemn the liberal arts, but childish old people. For as there is nothing more disgraceful than "an old man in a first-grade class," as Seneca says, so there is nothing so ugly as an old man who is a dialectic debater. And if he starts to spit out syllogisms, this is my advice: Run away and let him dispute with Encheladus.

Farewell.

Avignon, March 12.

SUGGESTIONS FOR FURTHER READING

Hickman, Larry. *Modern Theories of Higher Level Predicates* [in the fourteenth and fifteenth centuries]. München: Philosophia Verlag, 1980.

Leff, Gordon. *William of Ockham: The Metamorphosis of Scholastic Discourse.* Manchester: Manchester University Press, 1975.

Sharp, Dorothea. *Franciscan Philosophy at Oxford in the Thirteenth Century.* New York: Russell and Russell, 1964.

Weinberg, Julius R. *Nicolaus of Autrecourt: A Study in Fourteenth Century Thought.* New York: Greenwood Press, 1948.

William of Ockham. *Ockham's Theory of Propositions.* A. J. Freddoso and H. Schuurman, trans. Notre Dame, Indiana: Notre Dame University Press, 1980.

William of Ockham. *Ockham's Theory of Terms.* M. Loux, trans. Notre Dame, Indiana: Notre Dame University Press, 1974.

Part 6

The Renaissance: Emergence of Modern Humanism

The Reformation: Salvation by Faith Alone

The Scientific Revolution: The Earth Moves

René Descartes: The Foundation of Modern Philosophy

The Renaissance: Emergence of Modern Humanism

The Renaissance was one of the most explosive intellectual and aesthetic periods in the history of European culture. It began in Italy and then moved to France, northern Europe, Spain, England, and finally Scandinavia. The name *Renaissance* refers to the alleged rebirth of classical learning in the fourteenth, fifteenth, and sixteenth centuries. Medievalists, however, challenge the claim that classical texts were not given their proper due before this period. Whatever the upshot of that long-standing controversy, there is no doubt that the Renaissance was characterized by an extraordinary shift of emphasis from a hierarchical schema to one in which the plights and hopes of humanity took precedence. The most telling example of this shift in social organization is the decline of medieval feudalism, which had emphasized a hierarchy of fixed places with equivalent assessments of political and economic worth. The advent of money as a replacement for the barter system, the growth of the city-states, and the commercial importance of shipping, all contributed to the demise of feudalism and the emergence of a middle class not tied to the land and its medieval structure.

The creativity of the Renaissance is made clear by an enumeration of its leading figures, who include Leonardo da Vinci, Michelangelo, Shakespeare, Erasmus, Boccaccio, Machiavelli, Rabelais, Cervantes, and Holbein. Renaissance painting and sculpture broke with the idealized style of the medieval period and emphasized more realistic renditions of human life, such as the portrait and life-size sculpture. Although the assumptions of literary work were still medieval Christian, the content focused more on the inevitable human comedy and tragedy, an emphasis lacking in earlier centuries.

The period of the Renaissance also saw the discovery of the New World, the invention of the printing press, revolutionary discoveries in science, and the Reformation. In fact, the three leading cultural assumptions of the medieval world were shattered during this period. Coming into the fourteenth century, the Christian west believed that the universe was geocentric, that there existed only one continent with three parts, Asia, Africa, and Europe, and that there was one true religion, Christianity. By the middle of the sixteenth century all of these beliefs were denied and rendered hollow. Copernicus and Galileo had demonstrated the scientific legitimacy of the heliocentric universe, the New World had been discovered, making manifest a new continent, and Protestantism had sundered the seamless garment of Christendom.

In the Renaissance, the art is magnificent, the writing superb, and the philosophy is bold, speculative, and not fully appreciated until our own time, when once again cosmological speculation is assuming a central place in our version of what it is to be human and to be in a human place.

NICHOLAS OF CUSA

Cusa, as he is known, was born in Kues, Germany, in 1401. Educated by the Brothers of the Common Life, he devoted most of his life to the Church. After many attempts to reform the monasteries and the Church at large, he died in Italy in 1464.

An opponent of the philosophy of Aristotle, Cusa was deeply influenced by Christian Neoplatonism. The Neoplatonism which influenced the Renaissance is stripped of its Augustinian re-interpretation. In fact, Renaissance Neoplatonism attempted to return to the original intentions of Plato's Academy, independent of Christian thought. Cusa's most important work was On Learned Ignorance, *in which he stressed the inevitably contradictory character of our attempts to know the ultimate nature of reality. Long before the German philosopher Hegel (1770–1831), Cusa cast doubt on the universal application of Aristotle's principle of contradiction, which held that something which is, is, and is not other at the same time. Both Cusa and Hegel held that identity or singularity was more complex than its traditional denotation and that the principle of contradiction does not do justice to the ways in which single events are actually plural in their deeper meaning. He was fond of pointing to the existence of the paradoxical presence of the "coincidence of opposites," especially as found in the attempt to discuss the nature of God.*

From On Learned Ignorance (Book 1)

CHAPTER 1

How Knowledge Is Ignorance

We see that God has endowed all existents with a natural tendency to attain the fullest degree of existence possible to them. It is to realize this end that all things are equipped with appropriate faculties and activities; and it owes to these that each thing, in accord with the end of such knowledge, is naturally able to determine that the possession of that object toward which the force of its own nature directs it will properly serve its natural tendency. If, on occasion, this does not come about, the failure is necessarily accidental: as when illness falsifies taste, or conjecture distorts precise reasoning.

So it is with the desire for truth. Truth, pursued by a natural ratiocinative movement, is that which is ceaselessly sought after in all things by the sound and unimpaired intellect. When once the intellect embraces the object of its natural desire, we say that it knows the truth. Without reservation we view the truth as that which no sound mind will fail to accept.

Now, in all investigations, men determine the uncertain by reference to some object accepted as cer-

From Nicholaus of Cusa, *On Learned Ignorance,* in Herman Shapiro and Arturo B. Fallico, eds., *Renaissance Philosophy: The Transalpine Thinkers* (New York: Random House, 1969), pp. 4–11 and 14–21. Permission granted by Herman Shapiro.

tain. Their determinations are always comparative. All investigations, thus, are relative, as they proceed by way of such comparisons.

When there obtains a relatively short span between the object of investigation and the object accepted as certain, a determination is easily arrived at; when the uncertain object can only be approached by reference to a great many intermediate objects, determination is accordingly more difficult. We see this often enough in mathematics, where the reduction of a first proposition to some well-established first principle is easily accomplished, while the more advanced propositions present greater difficulties, because it is only by way of intermediate propositions that these more remote ones are reducible to first principles. It is in this way that all investigations proceed: by a sequence of comparisons which are relatively more or less difficult to establish. This is the reason why the infinite, qua infinite, is unknown: for it is above and beyond all comparison.

Now while proportion expresses agreement in respect of some one feature, it yet expresses, at the same time, a distinction, so that it cannot be grasped without employing number. Consequently, number embraces all things capable of being compared. It is not, then, only in quantity that number produces proportion: it produces it as well in all things capable in any way—substantially or accidentally—of displaying agreement or difference. This is the reason why Pythagoras held so tenaciously to the view that all things could be understood in terms of numbers.

It is, however, so far beyond the limit of human reason to know material combinations exactly, and how to apply, with precision, what is known to what is unknown, that Socrates thought he knew nothing beyond the fact of his own ignorance, while Solomon the Wise held that there are difficulties in all things that frustrate all attempts at explanation. We have it as well from another—a divinely inspired man—that wisdom and the locus of the understanding lie forever hidden to the eyes of the living. If this is the case—and even the most sapient Aristotle affirms in his *First Philosophy* that it is true of the things most evident to us in nature—then we may be compared, in the face of such difficulties, to owls attempting to see in the sun. But our natural desire to know is not without purpose: hence, its first object must be our own ignorance. If we can gratify this natural desire fully, then we shall be in possession of learned ignorance. There could be nothing, in fact, more efficacious to even the most avid scholar than his being most learned in just that ignorance which is peculiar to him; and the more profoundly a man knows his own ignorance, the greater will be his learning. It is with this conviction that I approach the task of writing a few words on learned ignorance.

CHAPTER II

Preliminary Observations on All That Follows

As I intend to treat of ignorance as the greatest learning, I consider it requisite first to fix the precise meaning of *maximum* or *greatest*. We speak of a thing as being the greatest, or maximum, when nothing greater than it can exist. But such plenitude belongs to one being alone; consequently, unity, which is also being, and the maximum are one and the same. For if this unity in every way is itself wholly unlimited, then clearly nothing can obtain to oppose it, as it is the absolute maximum. It then follows that the absolute maximum is one and it is all. All things are in it, as it is the maximum; further, it is in all things: because the minimum cannot be in opposition to it, as it cannot be limited by anything. As absolute, it is actually all possible being: it limits all but is not limited by any.

In the present book, I shall attempt to study this maximum who is believed, properly, to be the God of all nations. It is a study that transcends reason and cannot be conducted along lines adequated to the human intellect. For my guide, I shall look to Him alone who dwells in inaccessible light.

To continue: just as there obtains the absolute maximum—the absolute entity by which all things are what they are—so there depends from it that all-encompassing unity of being which is called the maximum effect of the absolute. Consequently, the maximum's existence, qua universe, is finite; while the unity of the universe, which could not be absolute, is the relative unity of a plurality. The maximum contains all things in its all-embracing unity such that all which derives from it is in it while it is in all, yet it could not obtain outside of the plurality in which it is contained, for this limitation is an inseparable condition of its being. Concerning this maximum, which is the universe, I shall have more to say in Book II.

We shall see that there is yet another way to regard the maximum. Since its mode of subsistence in the plurality of the universe is necessarily finite, we shall study the plurality of things in order to discover that single maximum in which the universe is bound up with the absolute, for the absolute is the ultimate limit of all; and as this maximum, which is simultaneously relative and absolute, is the most perfect fulfillment of the purpose of the universe and wholly beyond our comprehension, my remarks on it will be undertaken under the aegis of Jesus himself. This maximum, indeed, bears the ever-blessed name of Jesus.

Now, to understand this matter it will be necessary to transcend the literal sense of words. We should not require that they be used according to their natural properties. These natural properties are of no efficacy in the pursuit of such mysteries. At times, we shall even use drawings to illustrate our points; but the reader must transcend what is sensible in these in order to arrive without impediment at that which is purely intelligible. It has been my aim, in adopting this approach and in attempting to avoid linguistic difficulties, to make as clear as possible to the average mind that the cornerstone for learned ignorance is the fact that absolute truth is beyond our grasp.

CHAPTER III

Absolute Truth Is Beyond Our Grasp

It is certain and obvious that there obtains no gradation from infinite to finite. Hence, it is clear that the simple maximum is not to be encountered where degrees of more or less are met with; for such degrees are finite, while the simple maximum is necessarily infinite. It follows, then, that it will always be possible to find something greater than any given, other than the simple maximum alone.

As regards equality, this too is a matter of degree. With things that are alike, one is more equal to this than to that, to the degree that they do or do not belong to the same genus or species, or to the degree that they are or are not related in time, position, or action. For this reason it is clear that there cannot be two or more things so similar and equal that an infinite number of like objects can not still be found. Hence, no matter how equal the things measured are, they will yet remain eternally different.

No finite intellect, therefore, can reach the absolute truth of things by way of comparison. Truth, being indivisible by nature, excludes any approximations of more or less, so that truth alone can be the precise measure of truth. That, for example, which is not itself a circle cannot be the measure of a circle, for the nature of a circle is one and indivisible; similarly, our intellect, which is not the truth, can never grasp the truth with such precision that it could not be grasped with infinitely greater precision. Our intellect, in relation to the truth, is as a polygon to a circle; the similarity to the circle increases directly as the multiplication of the polygon's angles. Apart, however, from its actually being made identical to the circle, no multiplication of its angles—even their infinite multiplication—could make the polygon equal the circle.

It is therefore evident that all we know of truth is that absolute truth, whatever it may be, lies forever beyond our grasp. This truth, which can admit of no more or less than it actually is, is absolute necessity, while our intellect, by contrast, is possibility. The quiddity of things, therefore—metaphysical truth—is unattainable in its totality; and though it has been sought by all philosophers, none have discovered it as it truly is. The more profoundly we learn this lesson of ignorance, the closer we approach the truth itself.

CHAPTER IV

The Absolute Maximum Is Known but Not Understood. Maximum and Minimum Are the Same.

Nothing in Existence can be greater than the simple, absolute maximum. Since, as infinite truth, it evades our power to grasp it, our knowing it does not imply that we understand it. It transcends all that we can comprehend, for its nature involves no degrees of more and less. Indeed, all things that we apprehend, whether by means of our senses, reason or intellect, are so different from one another that there obtains no precise equality between them. It follows further that the absolute maximum is most perfectly in act, since it is in act all that it can be. Being all that it can be, it is, by one and the same reason, both as great and as small as it can be. The minimum, by definition, is that which cannot be less than it is; and since this is true as well of the maximum, clearly the minimum is the same as the maximum.

When considerations of maximum and minimum are directed to quantity, this becomes even more clear. The quantitative maximum is the infinitely great, while the minimum is the infinitely small. Now if we abstract the notions of "greatness" and "smallness," there is left the maximum and the minimum without quantity, and here it becomes quite evident that the maximum and the minimum are one and the same. The minimum, in fact, is as much a superlative as the maximum. The maximum and the minimum, therefore, are equally predicable of absolute quantity, for they are identical within it.

Distinctions, then, obtain only among things which can display more or less; and among these they obtain in diverse modes. But they are not found to exist in any way in the absolute maximum, as this transcends any form of affirmation and negation. Existence and nonexistence are predicable of all that can be conceived as existing; while nonexistence cannot be affirmed any more than existence of all that is conceived as not existing. The absolute maximum, however, is all things; and although it is all of them, it is yet none of them. Stated otherwise, it is simultaneously the maximum and the minimum of being. Indeed, there is no difference between these two affirmations: "God, who is the absolute maximum itself, is light," and "God is light at its highest, therefore He is light at its lowest." Nor can it be otherwise; for, if it were not infinite, and if it were not the end to which all things are ordered while being itself subordinate to none, the absolute maximum would not be the realization of all possible perfection. In the pages that follow, we shall, with God's help, explain this.

Now this far transcends our understanding; for we are constitutionally unable, by any rational process, to reconcile contradictories. We move toward truth by means of things which are made evident to us by nature; and because this way of proceeding stops far short of the maximum's infinite power, we are unable to forge contradictories which are infinite. We know that the absolute maximum is infinite and that it is all things, as it is the same as the minimum; but actual knowledge of this, far transcends any understanding we could attain by ratiocination. Maximum and minimum, in the present book, are not to be understood as terms referring to quantity of mass or force; they are rather to be understood as an absolutely transcendent value encompassing all in absolute simplicity.

CHAPTER VII

External Unity and Trinity

There never was a nation that did not worship God and believe Him to be the absolute maximum. Marcus Varro, in his *Antiquities,* points out that the Sissennii worshiped unity as the maximum, while Pythagoras, who was an undisputed authority in his day, held that unity was trinity. If we direct our minds to a profound study of the truth of Pythagoras' contention, we may reason according to our premises thus: that which precedes all diversity is undoubtedly eternal, for diversity and mutability are synonymous; but all that precedes mutability is immutable, therefore eternal. As it takes two to manifest diversity, diversity, like number, is posterior to unity. Unity, therefore, is by nature prior to diversity; and, as a consequence of this natural priority, unity is eternal.

Further: all inequality stems from an equality with something added. Therefore, inequality is by nature posterior to equality, and this can be most validly demonstrated by reduction. All inequality reduces to an equality, since the equal lies between the greater and the lesser. If, then, we remove that which is in excess, equality will be restored; if, on the other hand, we are dealing with the lesser, we establish equality by removing from the other that which is in excess. We can proceed with this process of removal until we arrive at the simple elements. Clearly, then, in this way all inequality is reducible to equality. Equality, therefore is by nature prior to inequality.

Inequality and diversity, however, are by nature simultaneous. Where there is inequality there is necessarily diversity, and conversely. In fact, where there are at least two things there will be diversity, and because there is duplication, there will be inequality. It is precisely, therefore, because duality exhibits the first diversity and the first inequality, that inequality will naturally exist where there is diversity. Having shown that equality is prior in nature to inequality, we have established as well that it is prior by nature to diversity. It must be concluded, therefore, that equality is eternal.

Moreover, if the first of two causes naturally precedes the second, then the effect of the first will naturally precede the effect of the second. But unity is either the cause of connection or it is connection itself: indeed, this is why we say that when things are united they are connected. Duality, on the other hand, is either the cause of division or it is itself division: for duality is the first division. Hence, as unity is the cause of connection while duality is the cause of division, it follows logically that just as unity naturally precedes duality, so connection naturally precedes division. Now, as division and diversity are always found together in nature, we must conclude that since connection naturally precedes diversity, it, like unity, must be eternal.

Our proof has shown that because unity and equality are eternal, the connection is likewise eternal. But it is impossible that several eternals exist: if several existed, then, because unity is prior to all plurality, something would exist which would precede eternity, which is absurd. Besides, if there were several eternal beings, one would possess something lacking to another, and so neither would be perfect. An eternal would exist, that is to say, which, since it is imperfect, would not be eternal at all. This absurdity shows the impossibility of there being several eternals. The conclusion remains that unity, equality, and connection, which are equally eternal, are one. This is the unity which is simultaneously a trinity that Pythagoras—the first of the philosophers, and the glory of Italy and Greece—regarded as an object of worship.

We shall now proceed to a more detailed explanation of the generation of equality from unity.

CHAPTER VIII

Eternal Generation

We shall now show briefly how the equality of unity stems from unity, and how the connection derives from unity and the equality of unity.

In a manner of speaking, we get *ontas*—unity—from the Greek word *on,* from which, in turn, the Latin *ens* derives. Unity and entity may be regarded as convertible, for God is entity: He is the intrinsic principle of essence, and because of this He is the very entity of things. Equality of entity, or the uniformity of essence, (or existence, which is the same thing), may be taken as being convertible with equality of unity. Where there is uniformity of essence, there can obtain no degrees of more or less—no above or below; for if a thing possessed more than its essence provided, it would be a monster; if, on the other hand, it contained less, it could not be regarded as being equal or uniform in essence.

A clear notion of the generation of equality from unity may be gained from a study of the nature of generation. Generation is the multiplication of the same nature proceeding from father to son, or, in other words, the repetition of unity. The form of generation peculiar to finite things is of the kind where the unity is multiplied twice, thrice, or many times; but where we have unity multiplied not twice, but once, or where there is but a single repetition of unity, there we have eternal generation: the generation of unity from unity. Here we have that which can only be conceived as the formation of unity by unity: the generation of the equality of unity.

CHAPTER IX

The Eternal Procession of the Connection

As the generation of unity from unity is a single repetition of unity, so the procession from both is a repetition of the repetition of unity. Stated otherwise, it is the union of unity and the equality of unity itself. Procession is conceived as a kind of extension from one to another. For example: when two things are equal, they are conjoined and united in some manner by way of the equality which extends, so to say, from one to the other. Hence, it is correct to maintain that the connection being discussed here proceeds from unity and from the equality of unity, for there can follow no connection of one by itself. But as unity thus proceeds from unity to equality, and from equality of unity to unity since it is, so to speak, an extension of one to the other, it is correctly said to proceed from both. For the reason that this connection does not owe its existence to a repetition or multiplication of unity, we cannot say that the connection is generated by either unity or the equality of unity. Still, unity, the equality of unity, and the connection which proceeds from both, are one and the same—notwithstanding that the equality of unity is generated by unity and the connection which proceeds from both. It is, indeed, as if the words *hoc, id* and *idem* were to be used in reference to one and the same thing. What we refer to as *id* is related to the first entity, and what we call *idem* connects and unites the related to the first. If we were to employ the term *iditas,* constructed from the pronoun *id,* we should then be able to employ as well the terms *unitas, iditas* and *identitas,* which would be not inadmissible in application to the Trinity. Here, *iditas* would refer to the relation of unity, while *identitas* would denote the connection of *iditas* and unity.

It was a comparison drawn with finite things that led our saintly doctors to call the Father *Unity,* the Son *Equality,* and the Holy Ghost *Connection.* As the Father and the Son have one and the same nature in common, the Son is the equal of the Father in nature; for the human nature in them both differs in not the slightest degree, and there obtains between them a certain connection. As they share thus the same nature, they are bound to one another by the bond of natural love; and the Father loves his Son above all other men, because human nature proceeds from Him to his Son.

It was by way of this farfetched resemblance that the name *Unity* was given to the Father, *Equality* to the Son, and *Connection* or *Love* to the Holy Ghost. But such names, properly, as we shall see more clearly when we deal specifically with this question, have reference only to creatures. In thus pursuing the Pythagorean mode of investigation, we have here, as I see it, set forth a most revealing analysis of the ever-adorable Trinity in Unity, and Unity in Trinity.

CHAPTER X

How the Understanding of the Trinity in Unity Transcends All Things

Let us now attempt to understand the meaning of Marianus' contention that philosophy, in striving to attain knowledge of this trinity, rejects circles and spheres.

In the foregoing, we have demonstrated that there is but one maximum and that it is absolutely simple; that there is no figure which is such a maximum, be it the most perfect solid (like the sphere), plane (like the circle), rectilinear (like the triangle), or straight line. It so far transcends all these that, if we would reach this absolutely simple and abstract intelligence, we must reject all that the senses, imagination, or reason, with its material accretions, can yield us. For here, all things are one: the line is a triangle, circle and sphere; unity is trinity and trinity is unity; accident is substance, body and spirit; movement is rest, and so on. Our conception of unity is correct only when we understand that each thing is in unity, that unity is itself in all things, and that, consequently, each thing in unity is all things. If we fail to see that the maximum unity itself must be a trinity, it is because we have not adequately rejected the sphere, circle and all the rest; for there is one unity, and that is as a trinity.

Let us attempt now to stress this truth by way of an appropriate illustration. It is apparent that the unity of the understanding involves necessarily the intelligent being, the intelligible object, and the act of understanding. Now, suppose that you want to proceed from intelligent being to the Absolute Intelligent Being. Here you would say that the Absolute is the absolutely Supreme Intelligent Being. But you would not have a correct conception of the absolute and most perfect Unity unless you added that He is also the absolutely Supreme Intelligible as well as the absolutely Supreme Act of Understanding. For if unity is understanding at its highest and most perfect, and if understanding necessarily involves the three correlates—intelligent being, intelligible object, and act of understanding—then it follows that the correct idea of unity must be of three in one.

Unity, indeed, is a trinity: for unity means nondivision, distinction, and connection, or union. These three—nondivision, distinction, and connection—originate in unity; it is then necessary that the Absolute Unity will be nondivision, distinction, and connection. Just as the eternal is that which is not separated from anything, so the Absolute Unity is eternity, or without beginning, because it is nondivision; it is from unchangeable eternity, because it is distinction; and it proceeds from both nondivision and distinction, because it is connection or union.

Moreover, when I say "Unity is the maximum," I am calling it a trinity: indeed, when I speak of unity, I am speaking of a beginning without a beginning; when I use the word "maximum," I refer to a beginning from a principle; and when I combine and write these with the verb "to be," I am speaking of a procession from both. It has already been quite clearly shown that the maximum is one: for the minimum, maximum, and connection are one; unity is itself the minimum, the maximum, and the connection; and as this is so, it is obvious that a philosophy which would grasp the necessity of the maximum unity's being a trinity could do so only by means of a simple intuition: for here any aid supplied by the imagination and reason is of no efficacy.

Such statements as: "He must transcend the differences and diversities of things, and above all mathematical figures, who would grasp the maximum in a simple intuition," and: "In the maximum the line is a surface, a circle and a sphere," may have surprised you greatly. In order to more easily enable your intellect to approach and grasp the truth and necessity of such statements, I shall employ an illustrative example: if, by correctly interpreting this example, you attain the truth and grasp these statements, you will undergo a wonderful experience—for you will, in this way, have advanced in learned ignorance and have come to comprehend, so far as this is possible to the human intellect, that the one incomprehensible Absolute is the ever-blessed, triune God.

MARSILIO FICINO

Ficino was born near Florence, Italy, in 1433. He devoted his life to scholarship and particularly to translating and writing commentaries on the works of Plato. Because of the largesse of Cosimo de' Medici, he was able to found a Platonic Academy in Florence. He was the first to translate a complete edition of Plato's writings in a western language, and it is to Ficino that we owe the central importance of Platonism in the Renaissance. Platonism gave philosophical dignity to the emerging secular thought of the fifteenth century, thought which was increasingly independent of the influence and power of the medieval church.

Profoundly influenced by Augustine, Ficino made Plato into an even more significant figure than was characteristic of Christian Neoplatonism. He was convinced that Plato's philosophical doctrine was a perfect parallel to Christian thought, especially in its cosmology, its emphasis on the immortality of the soul, and its emphasis on love, as found in the Symposium. *The Platonism of Ficino, because of his translations and commentaries, persisted after his death in 1499 and exerted an influence as late as the seventeenth century, for example, in the thought of Descartes.*

Five Questions Concerning the Mind

Five questions concerning the mind: first, whether or not the motion of the mind is directed toward some definite end; second, whether the end of this motion of the mind is motion or rest; third, whether this [end] is something particular or universal; fourth, whether the mind is ever able to attain its desired end; fifth, whether, after it has obtained the end, it ever loses it.

From Marsilio Ficino, "Five Questions Concerning the Mind," trans. Josephine L. Burroughs, in Ernst Cassirer, Paul Oskar Kristeller, and John Herman Randall, Jr., eds., *The Renaissance Philosophy of Man* (Chicago: University of Chicago Press, 1956), pp. 193–212. Published 1948. Fourth impression 1956. Composed and printed by the University of Chicago Press, Chicago, Ill., U.S.A.

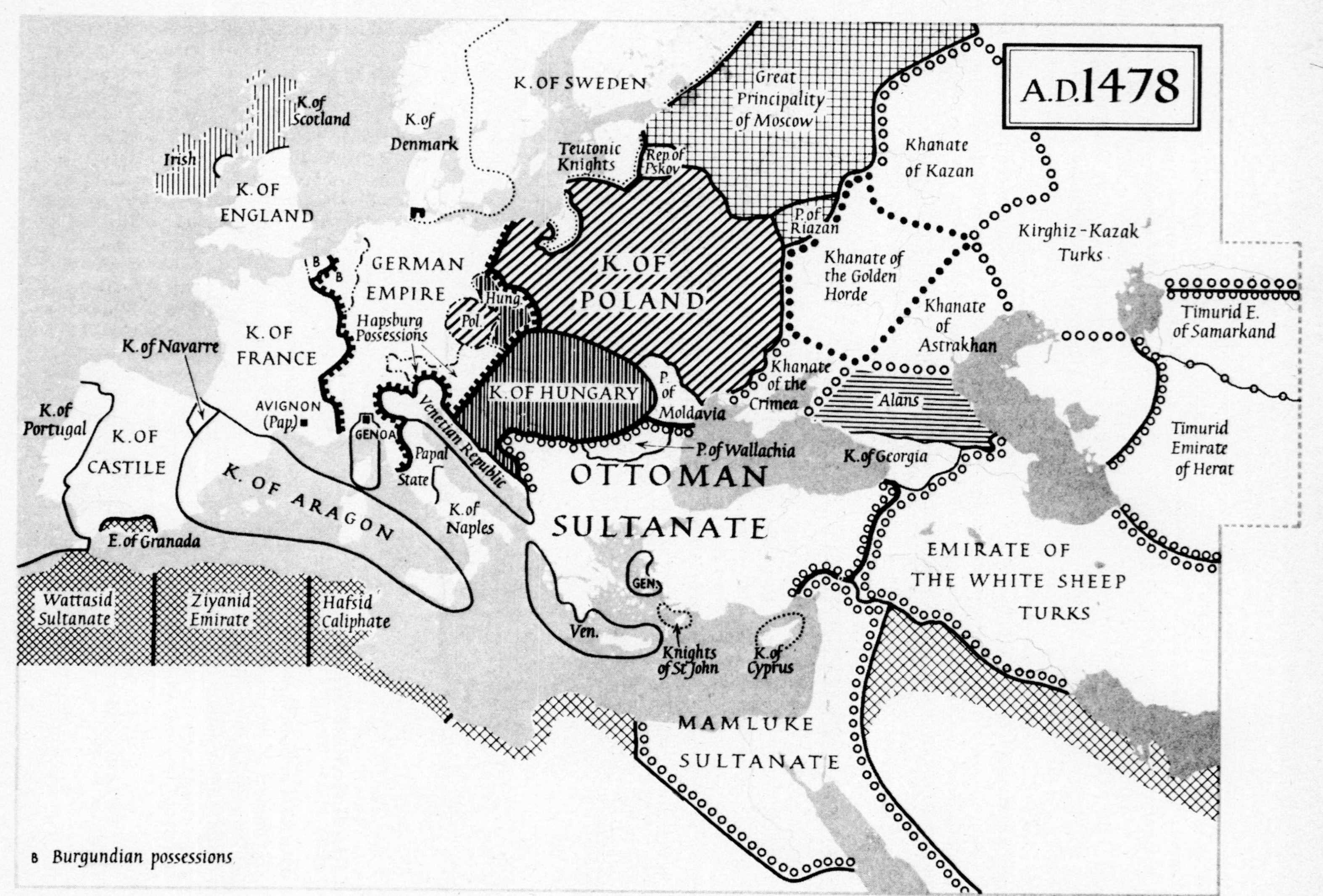
A.D. 1478
K. OF SWEDEN
Great Principality of Moscow
K. of Scotland
Irish
K. OF ENGLAND
K. of Denmark
Teutonic Knights
Rep. of Pskov
Khanate of Kazan
P. of Riazan
Kirghiz-Kazak Turks
K. OF POLAND
Khanate of the Golden Horde
Khanate of Astrakhan
Timurid E. of Samarkand
GERMAN EMPIRE
Hung.
Pol.
Hapsburg Possessions
K. OF FRANCE
K. of Navarre
AVIGNON (Pap.)
K. OF HUNGARY
P. of Moldavia
Khanate of the Crimea
Alans
Timurid Emirate of Herat
K. of Portugal
K. OF CASTILE
GENOA
Venetian Republic
Papal State
K. of Naples
K. OF ARAGON
P. of Wallachia
K. of Georgia
OTTOMAN SULTANATE
E. of Granada
EMIRATE OF THE WHITE SHEEP TURKS
GEN.
Wattasid Sultanate
Ziyanid Emirate
Hafsid Caliphate
Ven.
Knights of St John
K. of Cyprus
MAMLUKE SULTANATE
B Burgundian possessions

Europe, A.D. *1478*

Marsilio Ficino to His Fellow-Philosophers Sends Greeting

Wisdom, sprung from the crown of the head of Jove, creator of all, warns her philosophical lovers that if they truly desire ever to gain possession of their beloved, they should always seek the highest summits of things rather than the lowest places; for Pallas, the divine offspring sent down from the high heavens, herself frequents the high citadels which she has established. She shows, furthermore, that we cannot reach the highest summits of things unless, first, taking less account of the inferior parts of the soul, we ascend to the highest part, the mind. She promises, finally, that if we have concentrated our powers in this most fruitful part of the soul, then without doubt by means of this highest part itself, that is, by means of mind, we shall ourselves have the power of creating mind; mind which, I say, is the companion of Minerva herself and the foster-child of highest Jove. So then, O best of my fellow-philosophers, not long ago on Monte Cellano I may perhaps have created, in a night's work, a mind of this kind, by means of mind; and this mind I would now introduce among you in order that you yourselves, who are far more fruitful than Marsilio, prompted by a kind of rivalry, as I might say, may at some time bring forth an offspring more worthy of the sight of Jove and Pallas.

The Motion of Each Natural Species, Because It Is Driven in a Certain Orderly Manner, Is Known to Be Directed and to Proceed From Some Definite Origin to Some Certain End

The motion of each of all the natural species proceeds according to a certain principle. Different species are moved in different ways, and each species always preserves the same course in its motion so that it always proceeds from this place to that place and, in turn, recedes from the latter to the former, in a certain most harmonious manner. We inquire particularly from what source motion receives order of this kind.

According to the philosophers, the limits of motion are two, namely, that from which it flows and that to which it flows. From these limits motion obtains its order. Therefore, a motion does not wander from one uncertain and disorderly state to another but is directed from a certain and orderly state [its origin] to a certain and orderly state [its end], harmonizing with that origin. Certainly, everything returns to its own place rather than to that which belongs to another. If this were not so, different species of things would sometimes move in the same manner, and the same species in a different manner; and, similarly, the same species would be set in motion in different ways at different times, and different species often in the same way. Further, if this were not the case, the orderly sequence of motion would have been destroyed—the sequence by which a motion gradually flows forth at a certain time through many appropriate steps and seemly forms and, by turns, flows back after a definite interval of time. Add to this that, if each motion did not proceed according to a certain principle, it would not be directed to one determined region, or quality, or substance, rather than to any other whatsoever.

The Most Orderly Motion of the Cosmos Is Directed by Divine Providence to a Determined End

If individual motions are brought to completion according to such a wonderful order, then certainly the universal motion of the cosmos itself cannot be lacking in perfect order. Indeed, just as the individual motions are derived from and contribute to universal motion, so from the order of universal motion they receive order and to the order of universal motion they contribute order. In this common order of the whole, all things, no matter how diverse, are brought back to unity according to a single determined harmony and rational plan. Therefore, we conclude that all things are led by one certain orderer who is most full of reason. Indeed, a supremely rational order flows from the highest reason and wisdom of a mind; and the particular ends to which single things are directed have been prescribed by that mind; certainly, the common end of the whole to which the single ends are led must also be prescribed by that mind.

Concerning the Ends of the Motion of the Elements, of Plants, and of Brutes

We are not in doubt concerning the ends of the motion of the elements and plants and irrational animals. Certainly, some elements, because of a certain heaviness, descend to the center of the universe; while others, because of their lightness, ascend to the vault of the superior sphere. It is clear also that the motion of plants originates from the powers of nutrition and generation and is terminated in the sufficient nourishment of the plant itself and reproduction of its kind. The same is true of the powers which we and the brutes have in common with the plants. The motion of irrational animals, which characteristically pertains to sense, arises from the sensible form and the need of nature and, by means of that which is perceived from without, moves toward the fulfilment of bodily needs. The same is true of that nature which we ourselves have in common with all animals. Certainly, it must be recognized that all these motions which we have just mentioned, because they strive toward some particular thing, are the result of a particular power and, further, that in those ends which we have described they achieve sufficient rest and are perfected as much as their natures require.

Five Questions Concerning the Motion of the Mind

It remains for us to inquire concerning the motion of the human mind: first, whether or not the mind strives toward some end; second, whether the end of its motion is motion or rest; third, whether this good [toward which the mind strives] is something particular or something universal; fourth, whether the mind is strong enough eventually to attain its desired end, that is, the highest good; fifth, whether, after it has attained the perfect end, it ever loses it.

The Motion of the Mind Looks Toward a Certain End

If other things do not wander upward and downward in a foolish accidental way but are directed according to a certain rational order toward something which is in the highest degree peculiar and appropriate to them and in which they are entirely perfected, then certainly mind, which is the receptacle of wisdom, which comprehends the order and ends of natural things, which orders its daily affairs in a rational manner to a certain end, and which is more perfect than all the others we have mentioned; mind, I say, must be directed in a far greater degree to some ordered end in which it is perfected according to its earnest desire. Just as the single parts of life [of man], that is, deliberations, choices, and abilities, refer to single ends (for any one of these looks toward its own end, as it were, its own good); so in like manner the whole life [of man] looks toward the universal end and good. Now, since the parts of anything serve the whole, it follows that the order which is inherent in them in relation to each other is subordinate to their order in relation to the whole. It follows further that their order in relation to particular ends depends upon a certain common order of the whole—an order which especially contributes to the common end of the whole. Indeed, if any mover whatsoever moves for its own benefit, then it is reasonable to suppose that mind brings any of its own [parts] to their proper ends only because they contribute to the common end and good of the mind. Finally, who is so weak in mind that he believes it possible for the mind to strive, both by nature and by plan, to give diverse and single things an order in relation to one thing, without the mind itself having an order in relation to one thing? Furthermore, the ultimate common end moves the rest everywhere (for all other things are desired for the sake of that which is desired first). Therefore, it would not be extraordinary if, the ultimate and common end itself being absent, the rest could not be present at all. In the same way, unless the perfect form of an edifice is prescribed by the architect, the different workmen will never be moved to particular tasks which accord with the plan of the whole itself. Nay, truly, by no means will they be moved to their prescribed occupations by anyone who does not first possess the common prescribed end of the whole work.

The End of Intellectual Motion Is Not Motion but Rest

If the end of intellectual motion is itself motion, then certainly the intellect is moved in order that it may be further moved, and again is moved in order that it may be moved yet further, and so on without end. From this it is brought about that, persevering in its own motion, the intellect does not cease to be moved and on that account does not at any time cease to live and to know. Perhaps this is that continuous motion of the soul by which, in the opinion of some Platonists, the soul is always set in motion and always lives. I believe, however, that the mind, because it knows rest and judges rest itself to be more excellent than change, and because it naturally desires rest beyond motion, desires and finally attains its end and good in a certain condition of rest rather than of motion. For this there is the following evidence: the mind makes more progress at rest than in motion; the familiar objects of the mind are the eternal reasons of things, not the changeable passions of matter; just as the characteristic power or excellence of life, namely, intelligence and will, proceeds beyond the ends of mobile things to those things which are stable and eternal, so life itself certainly reaches beyond any temporal change to its end and good in eternity; indeed the soul could never pass beyond the limits of mobile things, either by understanding or by willing, unless it could transcend them by living; finally, motion is always incomplete and strives toward something else, while the nature of an end, especially the highest, is above all such that it is neither imperfect nor proceeds toward some other thing.

The Object and End of the Mind Is Universal Truth and Goodness

Now it is asked whether the end of intelligence and will is some particular truth and goodness or universal truth and goodness. It is universal, certainly, for the following reasons. The intellect grasps a certain fullest notion of that which the philosophers call being and truth and goodness, a notion under which everything that either is or is possible is completely comprehended. That which is itself called being and truth and goodness, and which contains all things, the Peripatetics think is the common object of the human intellect, because just as the object of sense is said to be the sensible, so the object of intellect itself is the intelligible. The intelligible, moreover, comprehends all in its fulness. Again, the intellect is prompted by nature to comprehend the whole breadth of being; in its notion it perceives all, and, in the notion of all, it contemplates itself; under the concept of truth it knows all, and under the concept of the good it desires all. The Peripatetics refer both of these to the concept of being, while the Platonists think that goodness is fuller than being. This question, however, clearly has no bearing on the problem in hand, and we shall for the present use these three names, that is, being and truth and goodness, as if they were synonymous. (In the commentary on the *Philebus* we have discussed this very matter more diligently.)

The first question appears to be whether or not the intellect can attain a clear understanding of everything which is included under being. Certainly it can. The intellect divides being into ten most universal genera, and these ten by degrees into as many subordinate genera as possible. It then arranges certain ultimate species under the subordinate genera; and, finally, it places single things, without end, as it were, under the species in the manner we have described. If the intellect can comprehend being itself as a definite whole, and, as it were, divide it by degrees into all its members, diligently comparing these members in turn both to each other and to the whole, then who can deny that by nature it is able to grasp universal Being itself? Surely that which sees the form of the whole itself, and which, from any point, beholds the limits of the whole, and the gradations through which it extends, can comprehend as middle points the particular things which are included under these limits. Now, it goes without saying that since the intellect, according to the Platonists, can devise the one and the good above being and below being, how much more will it be able to run discursively through the broad whole of being! Certainly, next to the notion of being (the name of which we have already repeated many times), the intellect can at its pleasure think of that which is most different from being, that is, nonbeing. If it can go from being to that which is infinitely far from being, then how much more must it be able to run through those things which are contained under being as middle points! For this reason Aristotle says: just as matter, which is the lowest of natural things, can put on all corporeal forms and by this means become all corporeal things, so the intellect, which is, as it were, the lowest of all supernatural things and the highest of natural things, can take on the spiritual forms of all things and become all. In this manner the universe, under the concept of being and truth, is the object of the intellect; and similarly, under the concept of goodness, it is the object of the will. What, then, does the intellect seek if not to transform all things into itself by depicting all things in the intellect according to the nature of the intellect? And what does the will strive to do if not to transform itself into all things by enjoying all things according to the nature of each? The former strives to bring it about that the universe, in a certain manner, should become intellect; the latter, that the will should become the universe. In both respects therefore, with regard to the intellect and with regard to the will, the effort of the soul is directed (as it is said in the metaphysics of Avicenna) toward this end: that the soul in its own way will become the whole universe. Thus we see that by a natural instinct every soul strives in a continuous effort both to know all truths by the intellect and to enjoy all good things by the will.

The Origin and End of the Soul Is None Other Than Infinite Truth and Goodness

It is indeed necessary to remember that the universe, which we say is the end of the soul, is entirely infinite. We reckon to be peculiar and proper to each thing an end for which that thing characteristically feels a very strong desire, as if this end were the highest good for it; an end, moreover, for whose sake it desires and does everything else; and in which at length that thing rests completely, so much so that it now puts an end to the impulses of nature and desire. Surely, the condition natural to our intellect is that it should inquire into the cause of each thing and, in turn, into the cause of the cause. For this reason the inquiry of the intellect never ceases until it finds that cause of which nothing is the cause but which is itself the cause of causes. This cause is none other than the boundless God. Similarly, the desire of the will is not satisfied by any good, as long as we believe that there is yet another beyond it. Therefore, the will is satisfied only by that one good beyond which there is no further good. What can this good be except the boundless God? As long as any truth or goodness is presented which has distinct gradations, no matter how many, you inquire after more by the intellect and desire further by the will. Nowhere can you rest except in boundless truth and goodness, nor find an end except in the infinite. Now, since each thing rests in its own especial origin, from which it is produced and where it is perfected, and since our soul is able to rest only in the infinite, it follows that that which is infinite must alone be its especial origin. Indeed, this should properly be called infinity itself and eternity itself rather than something eternal and infinite. Certainly, the effect nearest to the cause becomes most similar to the cause. Consequently, the rational soul in a certain manner possesses the excellence of infinity and eternity. If this were not the case, it would never characteristically incline toward the infinite. Undoubtedly this is the reason that there are none among men who live contentedly on earth and are satisfied with merely temporal possessions.

At Some Time the Soul Can Attain Its Desired End and Good

Surely the rational soul can at some time reach its perfect end. If those things which are less perfect in nature attain their natural perfection in the possession of their desired ends, how much more will the soul, which is both most perfect and the end of all natural things! If those things which do not prescribe an end either to themselves or to others, at some time attain an appropriate end, how much more will the mind, which seeks and discovers its own end and, further, determines the end of many things, foreknows the end of many, and sees the end of all! If natural power is not ineffectual in the lowest things, certainly it is not ineffectual in the soul, for the soul is so great a thing that it can accurately measure by how great an interval every smallest thing is exceeded by the greatest things. Moreover, the soul would never naturally follow a certain end unless it were able to attain it, for by what other power is it moved to it [a certain end] except by that by which it can attain it? Further, we see that when it [the soul] strives very eagerly, in motion toward a certain end, it makes great progress; assuredly, in so far as it makes progress by a certain power, by that same power it is at some time perfected. Finally, we see that the soul is gradually moved more and more rapidly, just as any element moves faster and faster toward its natural goal the closer it comes to it. Therefore, the mind, like the element, does not forever proceed in vain from one point to another without end but at some time or other attains an end which is desired for the sake of itself alone.

Further, there are in things and actions, both natural and human, certain beginnings and ends. It is contrary to nature itself and to the rationality of a beginning for anything to ascend continually from one beginning to another without a [first] beginning. It is contrary to the rationality of an end for anything to descend successively from one end to another without a [last] end. All action takes its beginning from the highest agent. All desire takes its beginning from the highest end. All things which have a certain characteristic because of something else are necessarily related to that very thing which has that characteristic through its own nature. Therefore, if there were no extremes on both sides [i.e., a first beginning and a last end], absolutely no action would commence nor any appetite be aroused. Finally, since any mover moves for its own benefit, where the highest mover is, there is also found the highest end. This is the case in every order of things. Truly, this is the case in the order of the universe.

But it might be well to expand further the above argument concerning the mind. If someone asks us which of these is more perfect, intellect or sense, the intelligible or the sensible, we shall promise to answer promptly if he will first give us an answer to the following question. You know, my inquiring friend, that there is some power in you which has a notion of each of these things—a notion, I say, of intellect itself and of sense, of the intelligible and of the sensible. This is evident, for the same power which compares these to each other must at that time in a certain manner see both. Tell me, then, whether a power of this kind belongs to intellect or to sense. Tell me, I entreat you, without hesitation, so that with the help of what you say I may soon answer the question which you asked. Now, then, I hear you answering thus: a power of this kind does not belong to sense. Certainly we all continually make very active use of the senses. If, then, sense were able to perceive both itself and these other things, all men, or at least most men, would clearly and easily know the very power of perceiving and of knowing, and intelligible and sensible things. Since, however, those who know all these are very few in number, and indeed those few gain this knowledge only with effort and after a long, hard process of logical reasoning on the part of intelligence, it is certain that sense has no power to know either itself or intellect and the objects of intellect. Nay, indeed, all this remains for the intellect to know. Further, the power which inquires earnestly concerning both intellect and sense is the same as that which discovers these by argumentation, and which by reason decides which is more perfect. Because this power inquires by reasoning and assigns a reason for its decision, it is reason, not sense. Therefore, intellect alone is that which knows all things.

To that original question of yours I now give the following answer. Intellect is at least as much more perfect than sense, as its power is extended in its action more widely and more perfectly than that of sense. Sense, as you yourself have shown, can perceive neither itself nor intellect and the objects of intellect; whereas intellect knows both. Moreover, another certain degree of perfection may be attributed to intellect. Certainly, when intellect successively compares itself and sense and the rest with respect to their degrees of perfection, it has the highest form of perfection itself, before its eyes, as it were; and, bringing each near to this form, it judges that one which comes nearest to it to be the more perfect. If intellect thus touches upon the highest form of perfection, it does so undoubtedly because of a certain highest affinity between that highest form and itself. Therefore, intellect is not only more perfect than sense but is also, after perfection itself, in the highest degree perfect. I see, in addition, a third degree of perfection belonging to intelligence. Since the intellect inquires into and judges itself, it is certainly reflected into itself. Moreover, that which has this characteristic [of being reflected into itself] exists and remains within itself. It is, furthermore, entirely incorporeal and simple. Finally, since it goes forth from itself to itself in a circular motion, it can be perpetually moved, that is, it can always act and be alive. It goes without saying that intellect, as if more perfect, is characteristic of fewer men and is perfectly employed much later in life and much more seldom. Indeed, as if it were an end, it is granted [to us] only after the vegetable powers and senses have been excercised. To sense the intellect gives guidance and laws, and for sense it prescribes an end. Intellect, when it argues and ponders, guides its own motion according to free choice. Sense, however, when reason does not resist, is always driven by the instinct of nature. It goes without saying that reason often chooses in a way different from that which sense and the need of the body demand, for clearly the beginning of the choice does not depend on the body. Otherwise, the end of the choice would always have a regard for the body. It is seen from this that reason is never subjected to bodily things in its motion, because in its speculations it transcends bodily things, in its pondering it extends itself to things diverse and opposite, and in its choice it often opposes the inclination of the body. Therefore, we say that intellect is much less subjected to any corporeal substance, in essence and in life. Moreover, sense seems to be dulled in a certain manner by advancing age, whereas intellect is certainly by no means dulled. Intellect can, however, be diverted from its speculative intention when it occupies itself excessively with the care and cultivation of the body. Moreover, when the object of sense is very violent, it injures sense at once, so that sense, after its occurrence, cannot immediately discern its weaker objects. Thus extreme brightness offends the eye, and a very loud noise offends the ears. Mind, however, is otherwise; by its most excellent object it is neither injured nor ever confused. Nay, rather, after this object is known, it distinguishes inferior things at once more clearly and more truly. This indicates that the nature of the mind is exceedingly spiritual and excellent. Moreover, sense is limited to corporeal objects; the intellect, in its inmost action, frees itself from all corporeal things, seeing that in its essence and life it has not been submerged. It separates the corporeal forms from the passions of matter. It also distinguishes from the corporeal forms those which through their own nature are completely incorporeal. Certainly it has itself been separated from the passions of matter and the conditions of corporeal forms. Further, sense is satisfied with particular objects alone, whereas the familiar objects of the intellect are the universal and everlasting reasons of things. With these it could never become familiar unless it were in a peculiar way similar to them. In this way, intellect shows itself, also, to be absolute and everlasting.

Finally, we say this especially because it [intellect] reaches reasons of such a kind through certain species which it both makes and receives itself. These must necessarily be unconditioned by the passions of matter, otherwise they could not refer to those reasons and ideas. Furthermore, unless intellect itself were free from the passions of matter, it could neither create species of this kind nor receive them in this way.

The Mind Is Much Better Able Than Sense to Attain Its Desired End

Reason is certainly peculiar to us. God has not bestowed it upon the beasts, otherwise he would have given them discourse which is, as it were, the messenger of reason. [He also would have given them] the hand, the minister and instrument of reason. [If the beasts possessed reason,] we would also have seen in them some indications of deliberation and of versatility. On the contrary, we now observe that they never act except in so far as they are driven by a natural impulse toward a necessity of nature. Thus all spiders weave their webs in a similar manner; they neither learn to weave nor become more proficient through practice, no matter how long. Lastly, if the beasts possessed reason, definite indications and works of religion manifest to all would have appeared among them. Where intellect is present, intellect which is, as it were, a kind of eye turned toward the intelligible light, there also the intelligible light which is God shines and is honored and loved and worshiped.

As intellect is more perfect than sense, man is more perfect than the brutes. Because of this very thing, he is more perfect: he has a characteristic not shared by the beasts. Thus on account of his intelligence alone man is judged to be more perfect, especially since, by means of the function of intelligence, he approaches the infinite perfection which is God, through love, thought, and worship. Moreover, the especial perfection of each thing consists in the possession of its appropriate end. The attainment of this end is easier and more abundant in proportion to the richness of the innate perfection of that thing; for where that formal perfection which is innate from the beginning is more strong, at that very place final perfection, according to the order of nature, is granted more easily, more abundantly, and with greater felicity, for the latter [final perfection] obeys the former [formal perfection] yet does not result from its obedience. From this we conclude that reason can attain its wished-for and appropriate end more easily than sense; man, more easily than the beasts.

The Immortal Soul Is Always Miserable in Its Mortal Body

We know by experience that the beast in us, that is, sense, most often attains its end and good. This is the case, for instance, when sense, so far as pertains to itself, is entirely satisfied with the attainment of its adequate object. We do not, however, know by experience that the man in us, that is, reason, attains its desired end. On the contrary, when sense itself, in the greatest delights of the body, is as much satisfied as is possible to it, reason is still violently agitated and agitates sense. If it chooses to obey the senses, it always makes a conjecture about something; it invents new delights; it continually seeks something further, I know not what. If, on the other hand, it strives to resist the senses, it renders life laborious. Therefore, in both cases reason not only is unhappy but also entirely disturbs the happiness of sense itself. Yet if reason tames sense, and concentrates itself in itself, then, driven by nature, it searches eagerly for the reasons and causes of things. In this search it often finds what it does not want, or does not find what it does want, or, by chance, does not understand as much as it desires and is able to. Truly, reason is always uncertain, vacillating and distressed; and since it is nowhere at rest while thus affected, it certainly never gains possession of its desired end or permits sense to take possession of its proper end which is already present.

Nothing indeed can be imagined more unreasonable than that man, who through reason is the most perfect of all animals, nay, of all things under heaven, most perfect, I say, with regard to that formal perfection which is bestowed upon us from the beginning, that man, also through reason, should be the least perfect of all with regard to that final perfection for the sake of which the first perfection is given. This seems to be that most unfortunate Prometheus. Instructed by the divine wisdom of Pallas, he gained possession of the heavenly fire, that is, reason. Because of this very possession, on the highest peak of the mountain, that is, at the very height of contemplation, he is rightly judged most miserable of all, for he is made wretched by the continual gnawing of the most ravenous of vultures, that is, by the torment of inquiry. This will be the case, until the time comes when he is carried back to that same place from which he received the fire, so that, just as he is now urged on to seek the whole by that one beam of celestial light, he will then be entirely filled with the whole light.

Man, the More Laboriously He Follows Happiness When He Is Placed Outside His Natural Condition, the More Easily He Reaches It When Restored to That Natural Condition

The reasons we previously offered for the facility with which human happiness may be attained plainly seemed to show the truth itself according to a certain natural order. For what reason then is so much difficulty, as experience teaches, placed in the way of our strivings, so that we seem to be rolling the great stone of Sisyphus up the steep slopes of the mountain? What wonder? We seek the highest summits of Mount Olympus. We inhabit the abyss of the lowest valley. We are weighted down by the burden of a most troublesome body. Panting toward the steep places, we often slide back to a sudden precipice because of this burden itself and because of the overhanging rocks on both sides. Moreover, from one side as many dangers and obstacles as possible detain us, while from the other the harmful blandishments of certain meadows delay us. Thus, alas, outside the sublime fatherland, we, unhappy people, are confined to the lowest places, where nothing presents itself which is not exceedingly difficult, where nothing happens which is not lamentable.

How, then, shall we reply to a contradiction of this kind? On the one hand, the argument promised the greatest ease; on the other, experience shows in an equal degree, the greatest difficulty. Only the law of Moses will solve this conflict for us. Indeed, we have been placed outside the order of first nature, and—O sorrow!—live and suffer contrary to the order of nature. The more easily the first man was able to receive happiness when in the beginning he was entirely devoted to God, the more easily he has lost ease itself when thereafter he turned against God. Therefore, the greater the difficulty with which all the descendants of the first parent receive blessedness when placed outside the order of nature, the greater the ease with which they would receive it if restored to that very order.

What do the philosophers say to these things? Certainly the Magi, followers of Zoroaster and Hostanes, assert something similar. They say that, because of a certain old disease of the human mind, everything that is very unhealthy and difficult befalls us; but, if anyone should restore the soul to its previous condition, then immediately all will be set in order. Neither does the opinion of the Pythagoreans and Platonists disagree with this. They say that the soul is manifestly afflicted in the sensible world by so many ills because, seduced by an excessive desire for sensible goods, it has imprudently lost the goods of the intelligible world. The Peripatetics perhaps will say that man wanders from his appropriate end more than the brutes because he is moved by free will. For this reason, as he makes use of various conjectures in deliberating, man subsequently strays on this side or on that side. The irrational animal, on the contrary, is not led by its own will but is directed to the end appropriate for it by the very providence of nature, which never strays, just as the arrow is directed to the target. However, since our error and violation of duty result not from a defect of nature but rather from the variety of the opinions of reason and the divergence of resolution from the straight way, they by no means destroy the natural power but rather throw the will into turmoil. Just as, even when an element is situated outside its proper location, its power and natural inclination toward that natural place are preserved together with its nature, in so far as it is able at some time to return to its own region; so, they think, even after man has wandered from the right way, the natural power remains to him of returning first to the path, then to the end.

Finally, the most precise investigations of the theologians briefly sum up the whole matter in the following way. There can be no inclination toward any motion greater than the moving power. Since the inclination of the soul is clearly directed toward the infinite, it undoubtedly depends solely upon the infinite. If, on the contrary, the inclination of the soul had resulted immediately from some limited cause which moved the soul besides God, then it would also have been directed in like measure to a limited end. The reason for this is that, however much the power of moving were infinite in its infinite origin, it would be limited in a subsequent cause which is limited. Motion follows the quality of the most immediate rather than of the remote moving power. The mover which alone turns the soul toward the infinite is therefore none other than infinite power itself. This power, conformably with the free nature of the will, moves the mind in a certain manner which is in the highest degree free toward the paths to be chosen; while conformably with the infinite power of the moving cause, it urges the mind toward the desired end, so much so that the mind cannot fail to strive after that end. If motion of this kind could not reach the end to which it is directed, certainly none could. Where infinite power is active, in that very place infinite wisdom and goodness rule. This power, moreover, neither moves anything in vain nor denies to anything a good which that thing could and should receive. Accordingly, since man, on the one hand, because of the use of reason and contemplation, comes much nearer to the blessed angels than do the brutes, and, on the other hand, because of divine worship, comes much nearer than they to God, the fountain of blessedness, it is necessary that he can at some time be much more blessed than they in the possession of his desired end. This is necessary in order that he who is more similar to the celestial beings, both because of the ardor of the will and because of the light of intelligence, may be, in like manner, more similar to them in happiness of life, for the power and excellence of thinking and willing originate from the power of life.

Now, in the body the soul is truly far more miserable, both because of the weakness and infirmity of the body itself and its want of all things and because of the continual anxiety of the mind; therefore, the more laborious it is for the celestial and immortal soul continually to follow its happiness, while fallen into an intemperate earthly destructible body, the more easily it obtains it when it is either free from the body or in a temperate immortal celestial body. The natural end itself, moreover, seems to exist only in a natural condition. The condition of the everlasting soul which seems to be in the highest degree natural is that it should continue to live in its own body made everlasting. Therefore, it is concluded by necessary reasoning that the immortality and brightness of the soul can and must at some time shine forth into its own body and that, in this condition alone, the highest blessedness of man is indeed perfected. Certainly, this doctrine of the prophets and theologians is confirmed by the Persian wise men and by the Hermetic and the Platonic philosophers.

The Mind Which Has Attained Blessedness Never Loses It

When, indeed, the soul attains the infinite end, it certainly attains it without end, for it attains it in the same manner in which it is influenced, drawn along, and led by it [the end]. If the soul has been able at some time to rise up again to immensity from a certain finite condition infinitely distant from immensity, then certainly it can remain infinitely steadfast in immensity itself. This must indeed be true, for the same infinite power which attracted the soul to itself from afar will, when close by, hold it fast within itself with indescribable power. Finally, in the infinite good nothing evil can be imagined, and whatever good can be imagined or desired is most abundantly found there. Therefore, at that place [shall be found] eternal life and the brightest light of knowledge, rest without change, a positive condition free from privation, tranquil and secure possession of all good, and everywhere perfect joy.

GIOVANNI PICO DELLA MIRANDOLA

Pico was born in 1463, in Mirandola, Italy. At an early age he became fluent in Latin and Greek, and he later acquired a knowledge of Hebrew and Arabic. In 1486, Pico offered to defend in public some 900 theses. Unfortunately 13 of them were considered either unorthodox or of doubtful worth by a commission appointed by Pope Innocent

VIII. The public defense was canceled and Pico left for France. In preparation for discussion of the theses, Pico wrote an "Oration." This is a remarkable document for its time in that it emphasizes the creative flexibility of the human being and rejects the classical position that human dignity proceeds from a fixed place in either the natural or divine scheme. Although it is anachronistic to claim that Pico's position resembles the existentialism of the twentieth century, nonetheless, his stress on human capacity and human freedom is clearly anticipatory of major strands in contemporary thought.

Pico's form of humanism was influenced by Ficino and the Platonic Academy, as well as by the rich reservoir of Arabic, Jewish, and Oriental thought. He spent his last years in Italy under the protection of Lorenzo de' Medici. Although he was finally released from Church sanctions in 1493, he died in Florence just a year later.

Oration on the Dignity of Man

I have read, most reverend Fathers, in ancient Arabic writings, that upon being asked what it was that seemed to him most marvelous upon the world stage, as one might call it, Abdala the Saracen replied that nothing to be seen was more wonderful than man. This opinion is echoed, as well, in that famous remark of Hermes Trismegistus: "What a great miracle is man, Asclepius."

Still, as I pondered upon the grounds given for these estimates, I was not particularly struck by the different reasons advanced by different people for the assignment of such pre-eminence to human nature. It is said, for example, that man is intermediate among creatures; that he is the equal of the gods above as he is master over the beings beneath; that he, set midway between the eternal and the temporal, is the interpreter of nature by reason of the acuity of his sense, the light of his intellect, and the probing of his reason; that he, as the Persians have it, is a living unity, the world's very marriage hymn; and but a bit below the angels, according to David.

Now without doubt these statements are all quite powerful; still, they do not go to the core of the matter to touch upon the principal gounds which might justify man's unique right to such boundless praise. I asked, why should we not admire the angels and the heavenly choir more than man?

At last I feel that I have come to understand why it is that man, the most fortunate of all living things, deserves universal admiration; of what his proper place is in the hierarchy of beings that makes him the envy not only of brutes, but as well of the astral beings and the very intelligences which inhabit the world's outer limits—a being beggaring belief and smiting the soul with awe.

And why should this not be so? Is it not precisely on this ground that man, with full justification is considered to be, as he is called, a great miracle? Hear then, O Fathers, just what the condition of man is; and grant me, in the name of your humanity, your gracious hearing, as I develop this theme.

God the Father, Almighty Architect, in accord with His mysterious Wisdom had already created this sensible world, this cosmic habitation of divinity, this most revered temple; He had already dressed the supercelestial arena with intelligences, informed the celestial spheres with the life of immortal souls, and set the dung-heap of the inferior world into ferment, swarming with every form of animal life; but when all this was accomplished, The divine Artificer still felt the lack of some creature capable of comprehending the meaning of so great an achievement—a creature which might be stirred with love at its beauty, and struck with awe at its

Giovanni Pico della Mirandola, "On the Dignity of Man," Arturo B. Fallico and Herman Shapiro, eds., in *Renaissance Philosophy: The Italian Philosophers* (New York: Random House, 1967), pp. 141–171. Permission granted by Herman Shapiro.

grandeur. Thus, after the completion of all else—as both Moses and Timaeus witness—finally, He conceived of man's creation.

However, in truth, there was left to Him no archetype according to which He might form this new being. His treasures, all but spent, contained nothing fit with which to endow a new son; nor among the seats of the universe was there left a place from which this new creature might comprehend the world. All space was already taken; all beings had been relegated to their proper high, middle, or low order. But the Father's Power was such that it would not falter in this last creative urge; nor was it in the nature of the Supreme Wisdom to fail through lack of counsel in this matter; nor, finally, was it in the nature of His Beneficent Love to create a creature destined to praise the divine Generosity in all other things, who lacked it in himself.

The Super Maker, at last, decreed that this creature to whom He could give nothing uniquely his own, should share in the heritage of all other creatures. Taking this creature of indeterminate image, man, He therefore set him in the center of the world and spoke to him thus:

O Adam, We have given you neither visage nor endowment uniquely your own, so that whatever place, form, or gifts you may select after pondering the matter, you may have and keep through your own judgment and decision. All other creatures have their natures defined and limited by laws which We have established; you, by contrast, unimpeded by any such limits, may, by your own free choice, to whose custody We have assigned you, establish the features of your own nature. I have set you at the center of the world so that from that position you may search about you with the greater ease upon all that is in the world contained. We have made you a creature neither of heaven nor of earth, neither mortal nor immortal, so that you may freely and proudly make yourself in the form which you wish. It will be in the orbit of your power to descend to the inferior and brutish form of life, just as it will be within your power to rise, through your own choice, to the superior orders of divine life.

O boundless generosity of God the Father! O admirable and unsurpassable happiness of man to whom it is given to have what he chooses, and to be what he wills to be! From the moment of their birth, or, to quote Lucilius, "from their mother's womb," the brute creatures carry with them all that they will ever possess. Again, the highest spiritual beings, from the moment of their creation, or soon thereafter, were fixed in the mode of being which would be theirs throughout eternity. But it was to man alone, at the moment of his creation, that God bequeathed seeds laden with all potentialities—the germs of every form of life. Whichsoever of these a man cultivates will mature and bear fruit within him; if vegetative, he will become a plant; if sensitive, a brute; if rational, he will discover himself a heavenly being; if intellectual, he will be an angel and the son of God. Again, if he should draw himself to himself alone, because of dissatisfaction with the lot of all creatures, he will there find and become united in spirit with God: and within the solitary darkness of the Father who is above all, he will himself transcend all.

Who then will fail to look with awe or will look with greater admiration upon any being other than this, our chameleon? For man is the creature whom Asclepius the Athenian correctly observed to be symbolized in the Mysteries by the figure of Proteus because of his mutability—his nature capable of self-transformation. This is the origin of those metamorphoses or transformations so celebrated among the Hebrews and the Pythagoreans. For in the hidden theological teachings of the Hebrews, holy Enoch at times is transformed into that divine angel which is sometimes called *Mal 'akh Adonay Shebaoth,* while at other times other personages are transformed into other named divinities. The Pythagoreans transform men found guilty of crimes into brutes, or—if we are to believe Empedocles—even into plants; while Mohammed, following them, was known to have said on many occasions that the man who forsakes divine Law becomes a brute. What is more, he was right; for it is not the bark that makes the tree, but rather its nonsensitive and unresponsive nature. Neither is it the hide that makes the beast of burden, but rather its brute and sensitive soul; nor is it the bowl-like form which makes the heavens, but rather their harmonious order. Finally, it is its spiritual intelligence, rather than its freedom from a body, which makes the angel.

Should you see a man devoted to his appetites crawling along the ground, you see then a plant and not a man. And should you see a man enchanted by the vain forms of imagery, as if by the spells of Calypso, and seduced through these empty wiles into becoming slave to his own senses, you see then a brute and not a man. If, however, you see a philosopher, judging and considering all things according to the rule of reason, you see then a creature worthy of veneration—for he is a creature of heaven and not of earth. And if, finally, you observe a pure knower—one who, unmindful of the body, is wholly withdrawn into the inner chambers of the mind—here, indeed, is one who is creature of neither heaven nor earth, but some higher divinity draped about in human flesh.

Who now will not look with wonder upon man? Upon man who, with good reason, is sometimes called "all flesh" and sometimes "every creature" in the holy Mosaic and Christian writings, because he shapes, forms, and transforms himself into the likeness of all flesh and takes on the characteristics of every creature. This is the reason why Euanthes the Persian writes in his exposition of the Chaldean theology that man has no single innate and fixed nature but, rather, many which are external and contingent. Hence, the Chaldean maxim: *Hanorish tharah sharinas*—"Man is a being of varied, manifold and ever-changing nature."

What is the point of all this? That we may understand that since we are born creatures who may be what we choose ourselves to be, we are responsible, above all, for seeing that it could never be said of us that being born to this high estate we failed to recognize it and descended to the condition of brutes and stolid beasts of burden; and for seeing, as well, that we verify the saying of Asaph the prophet: "You are all gods and sons of the Most High"; and, finally, that we may not, through abuse of the Most Indulgent father's generosity, pervert the free choice which He has granted us by forging a tool of damnation out of His gift of salvation.

Let a species of holy ambition capture our souls, so that, disdainful of mediocrity, we burn after superior things and—since it is in our power to do so—direct all of our energies to their acquisition. Let us despise the things of earth; let us not overevaluate even the astral; let us, putting all the things of this world behind us, hasten to that arena beyond the world which is closest to the Most Exalted Godhead. There, as the sacred mysteries have it, the Seraphim, Cherubim, and Thrones occupy the first places; still, while contemptuous of any secondary place and unable to yield first to them, let us emulate their dignity and glory. In this way, by willing it, we shall be lesser than they in nothing.

How are we to proceed, and what shall we do in order to realize this ambition? Let us see what they do; what sort of life they lead. For if we lead this kind of life—as it is in our power to do—we shall then attain the same noble estate as they. The Seraphim burns with the fire of love; from the Cherubim there bursts forth the brilliance of intelligence; and the Throne is resolute with the steadfastness of justice. So, in our lives, if we rule over our inferiors with justice we shall be as firm as Thrones. If, devoting ourselves to intellect we meditate upon the Creator in His creature and the creature in its Creator, and free ourselves from external activity, we shall burn with the light of the Cherubim. And if we are consumed with love for the Creator only, His all-embracing fire will at once transform us into the fiery likeness of the Seraphim. God, Judge of Ages, is above the just judge—above the Throne, that is. Higher than the Cherub—he who contemplates, that is—God flies and cherishes him in watching over him. For the spirit of the Lord moves upon the waters—those waters, which are above the Firmament and which, according to Job, praise the Lord with hymns before the dawn. Whoever is a Seraph—a lover—is in God, and God is in him; it may even be said that God and he are one. Great is the power of Thrones, which we attain by using judgment; and most high the sublimity of Seraphim, which we attain by loving.

But how is it possible for one to judge or to love that which he does not know? Moses loved a God whom he saw and, as judge of his people, he administered among them that which he had first seen upon the mountain. The Cherub is, therefore, intermediary, and by his light prepares us equally for the fire of the Seraphim and the judgment of Thrones. This is the bond which binds the first minds, the Palladian order, the master of contemplative philosophy. This, then, is the bond which we must emulate, embrace, and understand above all else; the bond by means of which we may ascend to the heights of love, or descend, well instructed and ready, to the tasks of the practical life. But surely, if we are to pattern our life on the model provided by the Cherubim, it is worth the effort to have constantly before our eyes both its nature and quality, as well as its offices and functions. Since, flesh as we are, and in possession only of knowledge touching on earthly things, it is not granted us to acquire such knowledge by our own efforts; let us seek the counsel of the ancient Fathers. They can provide us the fullest and most authentic testimony concerning these matters because they were familiar and conversant with them.

Let us ask the apostle Paul, the chosen vessel, in what activity he saw the armies of the Cherubim engaged when he was transported to the third heaven. According to the interpretation of Dionysius, he will answer that he saw them first being purified, then illuminated, then, at the last, made perfect. We, therefore, emulating the life of the Cherub here on earth, may likewise purify our souls so that her passions may not rave at random or her reason be deranged by restraining the impulses of our passions through moral science; and by dissipating the darkness of reason through dialectic, thus washing away, so to say, the filth of ignorance and vice. Next, let us fill our purified souls with the light of natural philosophy so that it may be brought, at the last, to final perfection by knowledge of things divine.

But lest we be satisfied to consult with those of our faith only, let us have recourse to the patriarch Jacob, whose likeness, carved on the throne of glory, shines out before us. This wisest of the Fathers, who, though asleep in the lower world keeps watch on the upper, will guide us. He will advise us, however, in a figure: for all things appeared in figures to the men of those times. A ladder rises by many rungs from earth to the peaks of heaven, and at its summit sits the Lord; over its rungs move the contemplative angels, descending and ascending by turn.

Now, if this is what we who wish to emulate the life of the angels must do, then who, I ask, would dare place filthy feet or soiled hands to the ladder of the Lord? As the mysteries teach, it is forbidden for the impure to handle what is pure. But these hands and feet of which we speak—what are they? The feet of the soul, to be sure: the soul's most despicable part—that by which the soul is held to the earth as a root to the ground. Its nourishing and feeding part, that is, where lust boils and voluptuous softness is fostered. And is not the hand of which we spoke the soul's irascible power? That which struggles in its behalf, fighting and foraging for it in the filth and in the sun, seizing for it all the things which it will devour while slumbering in the shade? Let us purify ourselves—our hands—in moral philosophy as in a living stream: the whole sentient part, that is, in which the body's lusts are seated and which, as the saying goes, holds the soul by the scruff of the neck—lest we be flung from the ladder as profane and unclean. But even this, if we wish to be the familiar of the angels who climb the ladder of Jacob, will not be enough unless we are first taught and rendered able to advance, step by step, on that ladder without deviating and without failing to complete the ascents and descents in their proper turn. When by the art of discourse or reason we shall have been properly prepared, then, inspired by the Cherubic spirit, employing philosophy through the steps of the ladder—the ladder, that is, of nature—we shall penetrate all things from center to center. We shall at one instant descend, sundering the unity of the many, like the limbs of Osiris, with Titanic power; at another instant, we shall ascend, collecting by the power of Phoebus those same limbs into their original unity. At the last, in the bosom of the Father who reigns above the ladder, we shall find perfection and peace through the felicity of theology.

Of just Job who made his covenant with God even before he was born, let us also inquire what it is, above all else, that the Supreme God wishes of those scores of beings which surround Him. Without a doubt he will answer, "Peace." For, as is written in Job, "He establishes peace in the high vaults of heaven." And just as the middle order interprets the warnings of the higher for the lower orders, so the words of Job the theologian may well be interpreted for us by Empedocles the philosopher. Empedocles teaches that there is a dual nature to our souls: one bears us upward to the heavenly reaches, while the other drags us to the nether regions, through friendship and discord, war and peace, as he testifies in those verses in which he makes complaint that he is being driven into the sea-depths, goaded as he is by strife and discord into the semblance of a lunatic and a refugee from the gods.

It is clear, Fathers, that many forces contend within us in deadly intestine war, worse than the civil wars of states. It is equally clear that if we bring about that peace which will place us at last among the elect of God, this will have been accomplished through philosophy alone. To begin with, if we seek only a truce with our enemies, moral philosophy will halt the unreasoning drives of the many-sided brute, the passionate violence and anger of the lion within us. If, acting on wiser counsel, we seek to achieve a lasting peace, moral philosophy will still be available to abundantly fulfill our wants. After both beasts are felled, like a sacrificed sow, an inviolable covenant of peace between flesh and spirit will have been accomplished. Dialectic will soothe those disorders of reason engendered by the anxiety and uncertainty of conflicting hordes of words and captious reasoning; natural philosophy will compose the conflict of opinions and the endless disputes which vex, distract, and tear at the spirit from all sides. Natural philosophy will assuage this conflict, however, in such a way as to remind us that nature, as Heraclitus wrote, is generated by war, and, for this reason, is repeatedly called "strife" by Homer. Natural philosophy, therefore, cannot assure us a true and inviolable peace; the bestowal of such a peace is rather the privilege and office of the Queen of the Sciences, most holy theology. At best, moral philosophy only points the way to theology—it may even accompany us along the path—but theology, seeing us hastening to draw near to her from afar, calls out: "Come to me ye who have labored and I will restore you; come to me and I shall give you the peace which the world and nature cannot give."

Summoned so comfortingly, and invited with such kindness, we shall fly, like earthly Mercurys, on winged feet to greet that most blessed mother, and there enjoy the peace for which we have yearned: that unbounded friendship through which all souls will be at one in that one Mind which transcends all others; and, in a manner which beggars description, we shall attain true unity in the most profound depths of being. It is the attainment of this friendship that, as the Pythagoreans say, is the aim of all philosophy. It is this peace that God established in the high places of heaven, and which the angels, descending to earth, proclaimed to men of good will, so that men, ascending by means of this peace to heaven, might become angels. This is the peace that we would wish for our friends, for our age, for every home into which we enter, and for our own soul, so that it may, through this peace, become the dwelling place of God. So also, when the soul shall have purged herself of all stain by means of moral philosophy and dialectic, and adorned herself with the many disciplines of philosophy as with princely raiment, and crowned her portals with the wreaths of theology, the King of Glory may descend and, entering with the Father, domicile with her. Should she prove worthy of so magnificent a Visitor, she will, through His boundless clemency, draped in the golden gown of the many sciences as in bridal vesture, welcome Him, not as a guest but as a spouse from whom she will never be parted. Indeed, rather than part with Him, she will prefer to leave her own people and her father's home. Mindless of her very self, she will wish to be dead to herself in order to live in her spouse, in whose eyes the death of His saints is infinitely precious: I mean that death—if the very fullness of life may be so called—the consideration of which wise men have asserted to be the end of philosophy.

Let us cite, as well, Moses himself, who is but at a little remove from the living fountain of the holy and unutterable wisdom with whose nectar the angels are drunk. Let us harken to the venerable judges as he proclaims his laws to us who live in the arid loneliness of the body: "Let those who, still profane, have need of moral philosophy, dwell with the herd outside the tabernacle under the open sky until, like the priests of Thessaly, they shall have purified themselves. Those who have already ordered their conduct may enter into the tabernacle: but they may not yet touch the sacred vessels. Let them first, as zealous Levites, in the service of dialectic, minister to the holy offices of philosophy. When they shall have been admitted to those offices they may, as priests of philosophy, gaze upon the multicolored throne of the higher God: the stars. Let them then behold the heavenly candelabra aflame with its seven lights. Let them then behold the fur tent, that is, the elements, in the priesthood of philosophy, so that, at last, having been granted entry to the innermost bosom of the temple through divine theology, they may be made glad in the glory of the Godhead, viewed with no veil before His image." Clearly, this is what Moses commands: admonishing, urging, and summoning us to prepare for ourselves, while we may, by means of philosophy, a path to heavenly glory to come.

Now the dignity of the liberal arts, which I am about to discuss, and the value that they have for us, is testified to in the Mosaic and Christian religions as well as in the most ancient theologies. What else can we understand by the degrees through which the initiates must pass in the mysteries of the Greeks? These neophytes, after their purification by the sciences which we might refer to as expiatory—moral philosophy and dialectic, that is—were granted admission to the mysteries. What else could such admission portend but the interpretation of occult nature by philosophy? Only after they had been prepared thus, did they receive *epopteia*—the direct vision of divine things by the light of theology. Who would not wish to be initiated into such mysteries?

Who could not consent to put behind him all human concerns, scorn the gifts of fortune and reject the goods of the body, in order thus to become a guest of the gods, drunk with the nectar of eternity, and receive the gift of immortality while still an earthbound mortal? Who would refuse to be so inspired by those Socratic frenzies celebrated by Plato in the *Phaedrus,* that swiftly fleeing this place, this evil world, by the oars, so to say, of both feet and wings, he might attain swiftly to the heavenly Jerusalem? Let us, O Fathers, be thus driven: driven by those Socratic frenzies which elevate us to such ecstasy that our intellect and our very being become one with God. Indeed, this will be our lot if we have previously done all that lies within us to do. If we shall have restrained our passions with proper controls—moral philosophy—so that they achieve harmonious accord; and if—by dialectic—our reason shall have progressed by rhythmic measures, then, stirred by the frenzy of the Muses, we shall drink in the heavenly harmony with the ears of the spirit. Then Bacchus, leader of the Muses, revealing to us in our study of philosophy, through his mysteries—the visible signs of nature—the invisible things of God, will dazzle us with the richness of the house of God; and there, if like Moses we prove wholly faithful, most sacred theology will supervene to swell our ecstasy. For, risen to her lofty height, we shall from that vantage survey all that is, shall be, and has been in seamless eternity; and marveling at their pristine loveliness, like the seers of Phoebus, we shall become her winged lovers. Finally, roused by ineffable love as by a sting, and, like the Seraphim, born outside ourselves, drunk with the Godhead, we shall be, no longer ourselves, but He himself who made us.

To anyone who grasps their meanings and the mysteries involved in them, the sacred names of Apollo clearly show that God is a philosopher as well as a seer. Ammonius has amply discussed this theme, however, and there is no need for me to develop it anew. Yet, O Fathers, we cannot fail to remark those three Delphic teachings which are so basic for one about to enter the most holy and august temple of the true Apollo who illumines every soul as it enters this world. These, you shall see, give us no advice other than that we should with all our might embrace this tripartite philosophy which we are here discussing. The saying *meden agan,* that is, "Nothing too much," prescribes a standard for all the virtues through the Doctrine of the Mean, which is that of which moral philosophy treats. Again, that other saying, *gnothi seauton,* that is, "Know thyself," urges and encourages us to the study of all nature, of which the nature of man is both connecting link and, so to speak, the "mixed potion"; for he who knows himself knows all things in himself, as first Zoroaster, and then Plato in the *Alcibiades,* wrote. At last, lighted in this knowledge through the aid of natural philosophy, being already close to God, employing the theological greeting *ei,* that is, "Thou art," we shall blissfully address the true Apollo on intimate terms.

Let us seek also the opinion of Pythagoras, that most sage of men, known as a sage precisely because he never deemed himself worthy to be so called. He will first advise us "Never to sit on a bushel"—never, that is, through disuse to lose our reasoning power, that faculty by which the mind proves, judges, and measures all things, but, rather, by the constant use of dialectic to guide and keep that faculty vital. Then he will admonish us concerning the two things which are to be eschewed at all costs: neither to make water facing the sun, not to pare our nails while offering sacrifice. But only after we have, through the agency of moral philosophy, both voided the debilitating appetite of our too abundant pleasures, and cut away, like nail-clippings, the prickly points of anger and wrath in our souls, can we finally begin to take part in the sacred rites, that is, the mysteries of Bacchus of which we have spoken, and to dedicate ourselves to that contemplation of which the Sun is correctly named father and guide. Finally, Pythagoras commands us to "Feed the cock": to nourish, that is, the divine part of our soul on knowledge of divine things, as if on solid food and heavenly ambrosia. This is the cock at whose sight the lion—all earthly power, that is—cowers in fear and awe. It is this cock to whom, as we read in Job, intelligence was given. At the crowing of this cock, erring man comes to his senses. This is the cock which, in the morning twilight of each day, raises a *Te Deum* to heaven along with the morning stars. This is the cock which Socrates, at the time of his death, when he hoped that he was about to merge the divinity of his spirit with the divinity of the higher world, and when all thought of any bodily illness was gone, said that he owed to Aesculapius, that is, to the physician of souls.

Let us also review the records of the Chaldeans and, if we can trust them, we shall see the road to felicity opened up for mortals through these same arts. The Chaldean interpreters tell us that it was a saying of Zoroaster that the soul is a winged being, and that when her wings are shed, she is plummeted into the body; but when they have grown again, she departs for the heavenly regions. And when his disciples inquired of him how they might obtain well-plumed and swift-flying souls, he is said to have replied: "Refresh ye your wings with the waters of life." And when they pressed him concerning whence they might obtain these waters of life, he replied, as was his custom, in a parable: "God's paradise is washed and watered by four rivers. From these founts you may draw the waters which will be your salvation. The river which flows from the north is called *Pischon,* which means 'The Right'; that which flows from the west is *Gichon,* that is, 'Expiation'; the river which flows from the east is called *Chiddekel,* that is, 'Light'; while the last one, flowing from the south, is *Perath,* which may be understood as 'Piety.'"

Now consider, O Fathers, what these doctrines of Zoroaster might mean. Clearly they mean that we should wash the filth from our eyes by moral science as by western waves; and that our aim must be correctly directed by dialectic as by a sighting taken on the North Star. Then, that we should develop the habit of bearing, in the contemplation of nature, the still feeble light of truth, like unto the first rays of the rising sun, so that finally we may, through theological piety and the most holy worship of God, be enabled, as heavenly eagles, to bear the most dazzling splendor of the noonday sun. It is these, perhaps, which are the "morning, midday, and evening thoughts," which David first sang and St. Augustine later developed. This is the noonday light that inspires the Seraphim toward their goal and illumines, as well, the Cherubim. This is the promised land toward which our ancient father, Abraham, was ever journeying; this is no place for impure spirits. And, if it be permissible to say anything in public about the deeper mysteries, even in the guise of a riddle—since man's sudden fall from heaven has left his mind in a dizzy whirl, and since, according to Jeremiah, death has come in through the windows to plague our hearts and vitals with evil—let us implore Raphael, the heavenly healer, to release us by moral science and dialectic, as with heavenly drugs. When we shall have once again attained health, Gabriel—the strength of God—will dwell within us. Guiding us through the marvels of nature and showing us the power and goodness of God in everything, he will consign us at last to the high priest Michael who, in turn, will reward those who have successfully completed their term in philosophy's service, with the holy office of theology, as with a crown of precious stones.

These, most reverend Fathers, are the reasons which led—nay, compelled—me to the study of philosophy. I set them forth only to reply to those who would condemn its study: not only those in high office, but those, as well, in modest situation. For the whole study of philosophy—and it is the misfortune of our time—is now regarded as contemptible and vicious rather than honorable and glorious. This lethal and monstrous conviction—that philosophy ought not be studied at all, or, at best, by very few—has taken over practically all minds; as though it were valueless to have before our eyes and at our disposal the causes of things, the ways of nature, the plan of the universe, God's counsels, and the mysteries of heaven and earth, unless by such knowledge one might procure some profit or benefit. We have reached, thus, the point, alas, where no one is deemed wise unless he can prostitute the pursuit of wisdom; and chaste Pallas, who dwells among men only by the generosity of the gods, is scorned, derided, and whistled off the scene, with no one to love or befriend her unless, by making money, she is able to recompense her lover with the foully procured price of her deflowerment.

I direct all these complaints, with the most profound disgust and indignation, not against the princes of our times, but against the philosophers, who believe and insist that philosophy should not be pursued because it brings no material reward. They are mindless that by this alone they disqualify themselves as philosophers. As their whole life is dedicated to gain and the fulfilment of worldly ambitions, they never embrace the knowledge of the truth for its own sake. This much I will say for myself—and I feel no embarrassment for praising myself on this point: I have never studied philosophy except for the sake of philosophy; nor have I ever desired or hoped to secure any profit or fruit from my studies and lamplighted researches other than the cultivation of my mind and knowledge of the truth—things I value more and more with the passage of time. I have been so keen for this knowledge, and so in love with it, that I have neglected all my private and public affairs to spend myself fully on contemplation, from which no disparagements of those who hate me, no curses of the enemies of wisdom, have ever been or will be able to divert me. Philosophy has taught me to depend on my own convictions rather than on the opinions of others, and to be less concerned with whether I am well thought of than whether what I do or say is evil.

I was not unaware, reverend Fathers, that this disputation of mine would be as acceptable and pleasing to you who favor all good sciences and who have consented to honor it with your presence, as it would be annoying and displeasing to many others. I am aware, as well, that there are many who have condemned my project before this, and continue to do so, for a number of reasons. But it has always been so: well-meant works, those genuinely intended for virtuous ends, have always had rather more than fewer detractors as compared to those works directed at questionable ends and undertaken for devious reasons. Some persons disapprove of the present species of disputation in general, as well as the method of publicly arguing learned matters; they hold that they serve only to exhibit cleverness and biases rather than to add to the stock of knowledge. Others, while not disapproving disputations in general, resent the fact that at my age, a mere twenty-four years, I have presumed in proposing a disputation dealing with the most abstruse mysteries of Christian theology, the most subtle points of philosophy, and the most exotic branches of learning; and that I have done so here, in this most celebrated of cities, before a large body of the most learned men, in the presence of the Apostolic Senate. Yet others have yielded that I have the right to dispute, but not nine hundred theses; for they hold that such an undertaking is too much, overambitious, and well beyond my powers. To these objections I should have bowed willingly, and at once, if the philosophy which I espouse would have permitted me to do so. Further, if I believed that this disputation were motivated by mere purposes of altercation and litigation, I should not here have undertaken to respond to them, as my philosophy urges me to do. Therefore, let all intention of denigration and annoyance be cleansed from our minds, and with it that malice which, as Plato says, is wholly absent in the heavenly choir. Let us decide, as friends, whether I am to be allowed to proceed with my disputation and whether I may venture to treat of so great a multitude of theses.

To begin with, I shall not have much to say against those who disapprove this species of public disputation. If it be criminal, it is a crime in which I participate with all of you, most excellent Doctors, who have yourselves engaged in such bouts on many occasions to the glory of your reputation, as well as with Plato and Aristotle and all of the most respected philosophers of every age. Philosophers of the past thought that naught would repay them more in their search for wisdom than frequent participation in public disputation. Just as the body's powers are strengthened through gymnastic, so the powers of the mind wax in strength and vigor by this manner of learning. I am inclined to the belief that when the poets sang of the arms of Pallas, and that when the Hebrews called the *barzel,* that is, the sword, the symbol of men of wisdom, meant nothing else by these symbols than this species of combat, so honorable and so necessary for the attainment of wisdom. Possibly this is also the reason why the Chaldeans cast a horoscope in which Mars confronted Mercury from three distinct angles at the birth of a man who was to be a philosopher: as if, that is, they wished to say "if these assemblies, these disputations, should be discontinued, all philosophy would become lethargic and dormant."

Now against those who claim that I am unequal to this task, I have a more difficult time defending myself. If I maintain that I am equal to it, I shall appear to entertain an immoderately high opinion of myself. If I admit that I am unequal to it, while yet persisting, I shall certainly merit the charge of being rash and imprudent. You see the difficulty of my position: I cannot, without censure, promise something about myself; nor can I, without equal censure, fail in what I promise. Perhaps I can remark the saying of Job: "The spirit is in all men"; or take consolation in what is said to Timothy: "Let no man despise your youth." But to speak out of my own conscience, I might say that there is nothing either outstanding or singular about me. I am, I admit, wedded to study and avid after the good sciences. Still I neither assume nor arrogate to myself the title of "learned." Consequently, if it is the case that I have assumed such a tremendous burden, it is not owing to ignorance of my own limitations. It is, rather, the case that I understand that in this kind of learned contest the real victory lies in being defeated. Hence even the weakest ought not to shun them, but should, indeed, seek them out as best they are able. For he who is overcome receives a benefit, and not an injury, from his conqueror. He returns home richer than he left—more learned, that is, and better armed for future combat. Inspired by such hope, though myself but a feeble soldier, I have never feared to enter so dangerous a contest against even the most strong and vigorous man. Whether, by acting so, I have been foolish, or not, may be judged best from the outcome of the battle and not from my age.

Third, I must respond to those who are shocked by the large number of theses and the variety of topics I have proposed for dispute, as though the onus, however great, rested on their shoulders and not, as it does, on mine. Surely it is unbecoming and immeasurably captious to want to set the limits for another's endeavor and, as Cicero says: "To desire moderation in a matter which is the better for being on a large scale." In undertaking this venture, but one alternative confronts me: success or failure. If I succeed, I do not see how it would be more honorable to succeed in defending ten theses than in defending nine hundred. If I fail, those who hate me will have proper grounds for disparagement, while those who love me will have occasion enough to forgive me. In so grand and important an undertaking it appears that a young man who fails through paucity of talent or learning deserves indulgence rather than chastisement. For, according to the poets: "If strength fails, surely there shall be praise for daring; and it is enough to have striven for great things." And if in our time many, in imitation of Gorgias of Leontini, have been accustomed to dispute not merely nine hundred questions, but the whole range of questions concerning all the branches of knowledge, and have incurred praise for doing so, why should I not, then, without incurring criticism, be permitted to discuss a large number of questions indeed, but questions which are at least clear and well defined? This, they answer, is unnecessary and ostentatious; I reply that in my case no superfluity is involved, but that all is necessary. If they consider the purpose of philosophy, they will then feel compelled, even against their instincts, to recognize this necessity. Those who are disciples of one or another of the philosophers—of Thomas or Scotus, for example, who today have the widest following—can indeed make trial of their particular doctrines with a few questions. I, by contrast, have trained myself so that I am the disciple of no one man. I have examined all the masters of philosophy; perused all their works; become acquainted with all schools. Consequently, I had to speak of them all in order that while defending the beliefs of one I might not seem committed to him at the cost of deprecating the rest; thus, while setting forth a few theses from some one school, I was led inevitably to set forth a great number concerning all the schools together. Nor am I to be held culpable because "wherever the gale blows me, there I remain as guest." For it was a practice among all the ancient writers never to leave unread any commentaries which might be available. Aristotle, in particular, observed this so religiously that Plato called him *anagnostes*, that is, "the reader." Clearly, it is a mark of mental narrowness to restrict oneself to a Porch or an Academy; nor is anyone justified in being the disciple of one school or philosopher unless he has first acquainted himself with them all. There is, further, in each school some unique position which is not shared by others.

Now when we turn to the men of our own faith, to whom philosophy came after all the others, we find in John Scotus both vigor and subtlety; in Thomas, solidity and consistency; in Aegidius, clarity and precision; in Francis, depth and penetration; in Albert, a sweeping sense for ultimate issues; in Henry, as it seems to me, a sublimity which inspires reverence. Among the Arabs, there is something solid and deep-rooted in Averroës; in Avempace, as well as Alfarabi, something serious and profound; in Avicenna, something divine and Platonic. Among the Greeks, philosophy was always brilliant and, above all, pure: in Simplicius, it is rich and overflowing; in Themistius, elegant and comprehensive; in Alexander, learned and consistent; in Theophrastus, well thought-out; in Ammonius, graceful and pleasing. If you look to the Platonists, to name but a few, you will, in Porphyry, be charmed by the wealth of material and by his preoccupation with things religious; in Iamblichus, you will be awed by his knowledge of occult philosophy and barbarian mysteries; in Plotinus, you will find it impossible to point to any one admirable thing, since all is admirable. The Platonists themselves, laboring over his writings, understand him only with great difficulty when, in his abstruse style, he speaks divinely about divine things, and far more than humanly of human things. I shall not remark the more recent figures, Proclus and those others who follow him, Hermias, Damascius, Olympiodorus, and several more in whom there flame that *to theion*, that is, "the divine," something which is the special mark of the Platonists.

It should be added that any school which attacks the true doctrines, and makes sport of true causes by means of clever slander, strengthens rather than weakens the truth itself, which like a glowing ember is encouraged to flame rather than die, by being thus agitated. These considerations have motivated me in my determination to bring the opinions of all schools, rather than, as some might have preferred, those of any particular coterie, to the attention of mankind. For it appeared to me that by the presentation of many schools, and the argument of many philosophical systems, that "effulgence of truth" of which Plato speaks in his *Epistles* might illumine our minds the more clearly, like the sun rising over the sea. What should our plight have been if only the philosophy of the Latins—say, Albert, Thomas, Scotus, Aegidius, Francis, and Henry—had been broadcast, while that of the Greeks and the Arabs was neglected, as all the thought of the barbarian nations was inherited by the Greeks and from the Greeks transmitted to us? In philosophy our Latins have always based themselves on the thought of foreigners, and simply perfected their work. What value would there have been in discussing natural philosophy with the Peripatetics if the Platonic Academy had not also taken part in the exchange? Indeed, the Academy's philosophy, even where it touched on divine matters, has always been esteemed as the most lofty of all philosophies, as St. Augustine bears witness. And now, for the first time, so far as I am aware—and there is nothing invidious in my saying so—this philosophy has been brought by me, after so many centuries, to the test of public disputation. And what would be the worth of all this if, having simply discussed the opinions of innumerable authors, we—like free-loaders at a banquet of wise men—should contribute nothing of our own: nothing conceived and worked out by our own mind? It is, indeed, the earmark of the impotent, as Seneca writes, to have all their learning inscribed in notebooks, as though the discoveries of our predecessors had blocked the road to us, as though the power of nature were lacking to us and could bring nothing forth which, if not capable of demonstrating the truth, might at least point to it from afar. The rustic hates sterility in his field; the husband, in his wife: much more, then, must the divine mind hate the sterile mind to which it is yoked, because it desires in vain from that dam to have noble offspring.

These are the reasons why I have not been satisfied to mouth well-worn doctrines, but have proposed for disputation, instead, many points of the early theology of Hermes Trismegistus, many theses drawn from the doctrines of the Chaldeans, Pythagoreans, the occult mysteries of the Hebrews, and finally, a large number of propositions concerning both natural philosophy and God, which were discovered and studied by me. First, I have proposed a harmony between Plato and Aristotle. Many before have believed this harmony to obtain, but no one has ever established it. Among the Latins, Boethius promised to establish such a harmony, but he never carried his proposal to the end. Among the Greeks, Simplicius made the same promise, with like outcome. St. Augustine also writes, in his *Contra academicos*, that others had attempted to prove it, and with the most subtle arguments. John the Grammarian, for example, held that Plato differed from Aristotle only for those who did not understand Plato—but he left it to posterity to prove that their philosophies were identical. I cite, moreover, a great number of passages drawn from Scotus' and Thomas' writings, as well as from Averroës' and Avicenna's, which, traditionally regarded as irreconcilable, I prove to be wholly in accord with one another.

In the second place, along with my own expansion of both the Platonic and the Aristotelian philosophies, I have set forth seventy-two theses in physics and metaphysics such that, if I am not completely wrong—and this will become clear in the course of the disputation—anyone who subscribes to them will be able to answer any question put to him on the subject of natural philosophy or theology: and this based upon a principle entirely different from any contained in the philosophy that is current in the schools or taught by any contemporary master. Nor should anyone be surprised that I, in my early youth, at such a tender age that I should barely be permitted to read the works of others, as some have hinted, should wish to propose a new philosophy. Rather, if it is well defended, they ought to praise this new philosophy; or if it is refuted, reject it.

Finally, since it will be their duty to evaluate my discoveries and my scholarship, they ought to look to the merit or fault which these show, rather than to the number of their author's years.

In addition, I have introduced a new method of doing philosophy—a method based on numbers. This approach, in truth, is very old, having been cultivated by the ancient theologians: first by Pythagoras, and then by Aglaophamos, Philolaus, Plato, and the earliest Platonists. However, like so many other noteworthy achievements of the past, it has fallen into such disuse, owing to the carelessness of subsequent generations, that hardly any traces of it are to be found. Plato writes, in the *Epinomis,* that the science of numbering is supreme, and the most divine among all the liberal arts and theoretical sciences. In another place, asking why man is the wisest of animals, he replies: "Because he knows how to count"—a view in which Aristotle, in his *Problems,* concurs. Albumazar writes that a favorite saying of Avenzoar of Babylon was: "He knows all things who knows how to count." These opinions are devoid of any truth if, by the art of number, they intend that art in which merchants are most proficient. Plato confirms this, warning us emphatically not to confuse divine arithmetic with the arithmetic of the marketplace. I therefore promised, when I appeared, after many long nights of study, to have discovered that arithmetic which is so highly regarded, that I would myself, in order to put it to the test, respond in public through the art of number to seventy-four questions considered of prime importance in physics and metaphysics.

I have proposed, as well, certain theses concerning magic, in which I have indicated that magic has two forms: one consists entirely in the operations and powers of demons, which, as God is my witness, appears to me to be a distorted and monstrous business; and the other, as it proves when thoroughly investigated, is nothing other than the highest realization of natural philosophy. The Greeks knew both these forms. But as they considered the first form to be wholly an aberration, they named it *goeteia,* reserving the term *mageia* for the second form, and understanding by it the highest and most perfect wisdom. The Persian term, *magus,* according to Porphyry, means "interpreter" and "worshiper of the divine" in our tongue. What is more, Fathers, the disparity and dissimilarity between these arts is as great as one could possibly imagine. Not only the Christian but all religions and every well-structured state despises and condemns the first; while the second, by contrast, is approved and respected by all the wise and by all peoples solicitous of heavenly and divine things. The first is the most meretricious of arts; the second, an exalted and holy philosophy. The first is empty and frustrating; the second, firm, well founded, and gratifying. The disciple of the first tries to conceal his practices because they are shameful and unholy; while cultivation of the second has always been the source of highest glory and renown in the arena of knowledge. No philosopher of merit, eager in the study of the beneficial arts, ever devoted himself to the first; but to command the second, Pythagoras, Empedocles, Plato, and Democritus crossed the seas. They, in turn, returning to their homeland, taught it to others and deemed it a priceless possession, well worth watching over. As the first can be supported by no true arguments, it is never defended by reputable thinkers; the second, esteemed by the most celebrated fathers, so to say, has in particular two proponents: Zamolxis, who was imitated by Aboris the Hyperborean, and Zoroaster—not him of whom, perhaps, you are thinking, but he who is the son of Oromasior.

Should we turn to Plato and inquire after the nature of each of these magic forms, he will reply, in his *Alcibiades,* that Zoroaster's magic is naught else but that science of divine things in which the Persian kings had their sons educated so that they might learn to rule their state on the model of the universe-state. In the *Charmides,* he will reply further that Zamolxis' magic is the medicine of the soul through which temperance is brought about in the soul, just as through temperance health is brought about in the body. In the footsteps of these men, there followed Charondas, Damigeron, Apollonius, Osthanes, and Dardanus, as also Homer—of whom I shall prove at some time in a *Poetic Theology* which I plan to write—who concealed this doctrine along with other doctrines, symbolically, in the wanderings of his Ulysses. These same two men were followed also by Eudoxus, Hermippus, and practically all those who delved into the Pythagorean and Platonic mysteries. Of later philosophers, I find three who had ferreted it out—the Arab, al-Kindi, Roger Bacon, and William of Paris. Plotinus gives certain signs that he was not unaware of it: particularly in the passage where he shows that the magician is a *magus* of nature, and not merely a charlatan. This most wise man lauds and supports this kind of magic, while so detesting the other, that once, when asked to participate in rites involving evil spirits, he replied that they ought rather to come to him than he to them. Surely he spoke well: for just as that first form of magic makes man a slave and a pawn of evil powers, so the second form makes him their ruler and lord. That first form cannot lay claim to being either an art or a science; while the second, filled as it is with mysteries, comprehends the most profound contemplation of the deepest secrets of things and, ultimately, the knowledge of the whole of nature. This beneficial magic, in coaxing, so to speak, the powers which God's generosity has sown and planted in the world from their hiding places into the light, does not so much perform wonders of itself as serve a wonder-working nature. Gazing, with keen insight, upon that universal harmony which the Greeks, with their rare facility for such terms, called *sumpatheia,* and seizing upon the mutual affinity of natures, this second form allows us to apply to each thing those inducements—called the *iugges* of the magicians—most suitable to its nature. Thus it draws forth for public scrutiny the miracles which lie hidden in the secret recesses of the world, in the womb of nature, in the storehouse and secret vaults of God, as though it were itself their creator. As the farmer weds his elms to the vines, so the *magus* weds earth to heaven—the lower orders, that is, to the endowments and powers of the higher. Hence it is that the second form of magic is as divine and beneficial as the first is monstrous and harmful. But the most profound ground of the difference between them is the fact that the first, delivering man over to the foes of God, separates him from God; while the second, benevolent magic, rouses him to an admiration of God's works which becomes, quite naturally, faith, hope, and charity. Nothing so surely directs us, that is, to religion and the worship of God, as the diligent contemplation of His miracles; and when, by means of this natural magic, we shall have profoundly scrutinized these works, we shall all the more avidly be led to love and worship Him in His works until, at the last, we are compelled to give voice to the paean: "The heavens and all of the earth are filled with the majesty of Thy glory." So much of magic: I felt it necessary to say even this much because I know that there are many who—just as dogs always bark at strangers—condemn and despise it despite the fact that they do not understand it.

I come now to those matters which I have elicited from the ancient mysteries of the Hebrews and have cited to confirm the inviolable Catholic faith. Lest these matters be thought mere fancy and charlatanry by those who are not conversant with them, I want everyone to understand what they are; what their true nature is; whence they came; who the famed writers are who testify to them; and how mysterious, divine, and necessary they are to men of our faith for the defense of our religion against the gross misrepresentations of the Hebrews. Not only famous Hebrew masters, but such men of our faith as Esdras, Hilary, and Origen, write that Moses, when on the Mount, received from God a more secret and true explanation of the Law than is contained in the five Books which he handed down to posterity. They write further, that God directed Moses to make the Law known to the people, but not to write its interpretation down or to divulge it to any but Jesu Nave who, in turn, was to reveal it to succeeding high priests, all of whom were to be similarly pledged to silence. It was sufficient to relate, through simple historical narrative, God's power, His wrath against the wicked, His mercy toward the good, His justice toward all; and to enlighten the people, by divine and benign commands, to live well and happily, and to worship in the true religion. To have explicitly revealed to the people the hidden mysteries and the secret plans of the highest divinity, which lay hidden under the shell of the Law and the rough garb of language—would this not be tantamount to casting holy things to dogs, or pearls among swine? Consequently, the decision to keep such things hidden from the rabble and to make them known but to a chosen few, among whom alone, as Paul says, wisdom speaks, was not a decision made by human prudence, but by divine fiat. And the philosophers of antiquity maintained this safeguard: Pythagoras confided but a few trifles to his daughter, Dama, on his deathbed. The Sphinxes, carved on the Egyptian temples, reminded them that the occult doctrines should be kept inviolable from the vulgar by means of the knots of riddles. Plato, writing to Dion concerning the most divine substances, explained that he had to write in riddles "Because the letter might fall into other hands, and others come to know the things I have meant for you." Aristotle used to say that the books of the *Metaphysics* in which he treats of divine matters were both published and unpublished. But need I multiply instances? Origen maintains that Jesus Christ, the Teacher of Life, revealed much to His disciples which they feared to commit to writing lest the vulgar come into possession of it. Dionysius the Areopagite gives strong support to this when he writes that the most secret of mysteries were transmitted by the founders of our religion *ex nou eis moun dia meson logou*—that is, by rote learning, without any writing, through the medium of the spoken word alone. As the true interpretation of the Law given to Moses was, by God's fiat, revealed in precisely this same way, it was called *cabala*, which in Hebrew means "reception." The point is that the doctrine was received from one man by another as a hereditary right, not through written records but through a regular succession of revelations.

Now after the Hebrews had been released by Cyrus from their Babylonian captivity, and after re-establishment of the temple under Zerubbabel, the Hebrews directed themselves to the restoration of the Law. Esdras, then head of the church, amended the Book of Moses. He says clearly that because of the exiles, massacres, flights, and captivities of the Israelites, the practice of transmitting the doctrine by word of mouth, which had been established by the ancients, could not be continued. They had to be committed to writing, or else these heavenly teachings, divinely revealed, must surely perish, as the memory of them was rapidly dwindling. Hence he decided that all of the sages who were still alive should be convened, and that each should communicate to the assembled body all that he remembered of the mysteries of the Law. These communications were then to be inscribed in seventy volumes—about the number of elders in the Sanhedrin. But, Fathers, there is no need to take my word alone for all this; listen to Esdras: "After forty days had passed, the Most High spake unto me, saying, 'the first things which thou hast written, publish openly, and let the worthy and unworthy alike read it: but keep ye the seventy last books, that thou may deliver them over to such as be wise among the people: for in them is the fount of understanding, the stream of wisdom, and the river of knowledge.' And thus did I." These are Esdras' words to the letter. These are the books of cabalistic lore. In these books, as Esdras clearly tells us, there dwells "the fount of understanding"—that is, the ineffable theology of the supersubstantial deity; "the stream of wisdom"—that is, the precise metaphysical doctrine concerning intelligible and angelic forms; and "the river of knowledge"—that is, the best-grounded philosophy of nature. Pope Sixtus IV, the immediate predecessor of our present pope, Innocent VIII, under whose reign we are fortunate, indeed, to be living, took all possible steps to guarantee that these books would be translated into Latin for the general good of our own faith. By the time of his death, indeed, three had already appeared. Among the Hebrews of today, these books are treasured with such reverence that no man is so much as permitted to touch them who has not attained his fortieth year.

When I purchased these books, at no small expense, and had read them through from cover to cover with the most rapt attention and unwearying labor, I discovered in them—as God is my witness—not so much the Mosaic as the Christian religion. Therein I found the mystery of the Trinity; the Incarnation of the Word; the divinity of the Messiah. Therein one may read as well of original sin; of its expiation by Christ; of the heavenly Jerusalem; of the fall of the devils; of the pains of purgatory and of hell. Therein I encountered the same things which we read every day in Paul, Dionysius, Jerome, and Augustine. As for philosophy, it is as though one were listening to Pythagoras and Plato, whose doctrines are so closely related to the Christian faith that our Augustine offered infinite thanks to God that the books of the Platonists had fallen into his hands. In brief, there is absolutely no controversy between ourselves and the Hebrews, on any matter, with regard to which they cannot be refuted and convinced out of the cabalistic writings, so that no corner is left for them to retreat to. With regard to this, I can cite a witness of unimpeachable authority: the most learned Antonius Chromicus. On the occasion of a banquet at his home, which I attended, he heard, with his own ears, the Hebrew, Dactylus, a profound cabalistic scholar, come over completely to the Christian doctrine of the Trinity.

But let me return to reviewing the chapters of my disputation. I have also set forth my conception of the way in which the poems of Orpheus and Zoroaster should be interpreted. Orpheus is read by the Greeks in an almost complete text; Zoroaster they know in a corrupt text, while in Chaldea he is read in a form more nearly complete; and both these men are considered as the authors and fathers of ancient wisdom. I shall pass over Zoroaster, who is cited frequently by the Platonists, and always with the most profound respect. But of Pythagoras, Iamblichus the Chaldean writes that he took the Orphic theology as the archetypal model after which he shaped and formed his own philosophy. It is for this reason that the Pythagorean maxims are called holy—because, that is, they derive from the Orphic. For it is from this original source that there followed that occult doctrine of numbers, and everything else that the Greek philosophy has of greatness and sublimity. Orpheus, however—as was the case with all the ancient theologians—so interwove the mysteries of his doctrine with the veil of poetry that one reading his hymns might well take them to be but vain fables and the veriest commonplaces. I say this so that one might appreciate what labor and difficulty was involved in my ferreting out the occult meanings of the hidden philosophy from the intentional knots of riddles and the obscurity of fables in which they were submerged. This task was made all the more difficult by the fact that in a matter so profound, abstruse, and unplumbed, I could look for aid to the work of no other interpreter. And still, like dogs, some growl that I have heaped together a great quantity of pointless drivelings in order to make my display impressive by sheer numerical weight. As though all did not concern subtle questions, subjects of vicious controversy, over which the principal schools confront each other like gladiators—at dagger's point. As though I had not contributed many things heretofore unknown and unsuspected by the very men who are even now striking at my repute while styling themselves the masters in philosophy. I am, in truth, so innocent of the fault with which they charge me that I have striven to limit the disputation to as few chapters as I could; had I wished—as others are wont—to divide it into parts, and to cut these into bits, their number might well have increased to infinity.

To pass in silence over other things that I might mention, who is not aware that one alone among my nine hundred theses—namely, that concerning the reconciliation of the philosophies of Plato and Aristotle—might easily have been expanded, without anyone suspecting that I was seeking mere quantity, into six hundred or more chapters? How? By simply enumerating, one after another, in proper order, those points on which others think that these philosophies differ, and I that they agree. But speak out I shall—though in a manner which is neither modest in itself nor truly characteristic of me—because my detractors, those who envy me, force me so to speak out. I wished to make clear in this disputation, not so much that I know a great deal, but that I know a great deal which others do not. And now, reverend Fathers, in order that this claim may be verified by the fact; and, in order that my oration may no longer delay the gratification of your desire—for I see, excellent Doctors, that you are prepared, girded up, and even pleasured in anticipation of the contest—let us now, with the hope that the outcome may be fortunate and favorable, as to the sound of war trumpet, join in battle.

PIETRO POMPONAZZI

Although Renaissance humanism was dominated by the tradition of Neoplatonism, Aristotle found an able defender in Pietro Pomponazzi, of Mantua, Italy (1462–1525). After studying medicine and philosophy at the University of Padua, Pomponazzi taught at both Padua and Bologna until his death. His most important and controversial work was his treatise On the Immortality of the Soul. *Opposing both Thomas Aquinas and Averroës, Pomponazzi held that philosophical reasoning could not prove the individual soul to be immortal. With learning and excellent dialectical skill, he defended an Aristotelian naturalism unencumbered by later Arabic or Christian accretions. In the long and still-active philosophical debate on the immortality of the soul, Pomponazzi's treatise remains one of the classic arguments.*

From On the Immortality of the Soul

CHAPTER XIV

In Which the Objections Are Answered

It seems to me arduous indeed and burdensome to satisfy these arguments, and especially since it is common repute that souls remain after death; and, as it is written in *Metaphysica* ii, it is difficult to speak against common custom. But so far as we are given power we shall endeavor to speak in this matter with probability at least.

For answer then to the first objection, it must be known that each thing, at least each complete thing, has some end. And although the end has the nature of good, as is said in *Metaphysica* ii, nevertheless there must be assigned to each thing as its end not what is good to a greater degree, but only according to what suits its nature, and has a due proportion to it. For although it is better to sense than not to sense, it does not suit a stone to sense, nor would it be the good of the stone; for then it would no longer be a stone. Whence also in assigning an end to man, if it were such as we should assign to God and the Intelligences, that would not be fitting, since he would thus not be man.

Secondly, it must be accepted and particularly committed to memory that the whole human race can be compared to one single man. But in one human individual there are multiple and divers members, ordered to divers offices or to divers proximate ends; yet all are also directed to a single end, whence they must all share in some things. Now if that order were violated either he would not be a man or would be so with great difficulty. But all the members are ordered to the common advantage of that man, and the one is either necessary to the other and vice versa, or at least useful, though at times one more, and another less. Whence the heart is necessary to the brain, and the brain to the heart, and the heart is necessary to the hand while the hand is useful for the heart; and the right hand is useful to the left, and the left to the right, and all the members share in life and natural heat, and need spirits and blood, as is plain to see from the *De animalibus*. And besides what they share in, each single member has a single function; for the heart has one, the brain another, the liver a third, and so of the rest, as Aristotle declares in the same *De animalibus*, and Galen more fully in his *De utilitate particularum*. Moreover, these functions or operations are not equal, but one is prior and the other posterior, one is more perfect and the other less perfect. For, according to Aristotle, since the heart is the noblest and the first, so also is its function the noblest and the first. And so of the rest in order. And although the brain, for instance, is not so perfect as the heart, still in its kind it can be perfect. Wherefore, just as all the members have latitude and diversity among themselves, so also each genus of member, yet within fixed limits. For neither are all hearts equally great nor similarly warm; and so of the other members. This, too, is to be observed, that, although among these members there may exist so great a diversity, yet it is not such as to produce discord; but it must be a commensurate diversity. But if it becomes beyond measure, either the destruction of the individual or sickness will follow. If indeed there were not that commensurate diversity, the individual could in no way endure. For if all the members were either heart or eye, there would be no animal; just as in instrumental and vocal music, if all the voices were of a single order, no harmony and pleasure would be caused. And they are so disposed that neither the whole individual nor any part of it can be disposed in a better way than it is. Just as Plato says in the *Timaeus* that God gave to each what is best for it and for the whole, in the same way we must think of the whole human race.

For the whole human race is like a single body composed of different members, also with different

Pietro Pomponazzi, *On the Immortality of the Soul*, trans. William Henry Hay II, rev. John Herman Randall, Jr., in Ernst Cassirer, Paul Oskar Kristeller, and John Herman Randall, Jr., eds., *The Renaissance Philosophy of Man* (Chicago: University of Chicago Press, 1956), pp. 350–381. Published 1948. Fourth impression 1956. Composed and printed by the University of Chicago Press, Chicago, Ill., U.S.A.

functions, yet ordered to the common advantage of the human race. And each gives to the other, and receives from him to whom he gives, and they have reciprocal functions. Nor can all be of equal perfection, but to some are given functions more perfect, to some less perfect. And were this inequality destroyed, either the human race would perish or it would persist with great difficulty. Yet there are some things in which all or almost all share. For otherwise they would not be parts of one genus and with a tendency toward a single common good, just as was said of the members of a single individual man. Nor ought the inequality among men, provided it be commensurate, to produce discord. Indeed, just as in a musical group a commensurate diversity of voices makes a delightful harmony, so a commensurate diversity among men generates the perfect, the beautiful, the suitable, and the delightful; but an incommensurate diversity the contrary.

Therefore, having thus disposed of these things, let us say that all men in pursuing this sort of common end must share in three intellects: the theoretical, the practical or operative, and the productive. For no man who is sound and of due age fails to possess something of these three intellects, just as there is no member which does not participate in blood and natural heat. For each man has something of speculation, and perhaps in each theoretical science. Because he knows the principles at least, as is said in *Metaphysica* ii, which are as the doors of the house, which no one does not know. For who is there who does not know first principles like "Of anything it is said to be or not to be," "It does not happen that the same thing at the same time both is and is not"? Who is altogether ignorant of God? Of being, of one, of true, of good? And so of the rest, which it would be too burdensome to run through. But these things belong to metaphysics. It is also clear to natural philosophy, since those things are subject to the senses which first meet the intellect. In mathematics also it is clear to see, since human life could not be carried on without numbers and figures; and all men know hours, days, months, and years and many other things which are the business of astronomy. And no less, unless he be blind, does he know something of sight, which is the task of optics; and unless he be deaf, of harmonies, which belong to music. What shall I say, moreover, of rhetoric and dialectic, since Aristotle in the Preface to the *Rhetoric* says "wherefore and in a certain fashion all participate in both"?

Now in regard to the operative intellect, which is concerned with morals, public and private affairs, it is very clear, since to each it is given to know good and evil, to be part of the state and the family. For intellect of this sort is truly and properly called human, as Plato in the *Republic* and Aristotle in the *Ethics* testify. And as regards the productive intellect, it is plain, since no man can maintain life without it. For without things mechanical and necessary to life man could not endure.

But it must be known that, although no man is completely deprived of these three intellects, yet man is not equally related to them. For the theoretical intellect is not of man but of the gods, as Aristotle teaches in *Ethics* x. And Plato in the *Timaeus;* "The greatest gift of the Gods is philosophy." Wherefore man in no way shares it with other creatures. Hence even if all men possess something of it, yet very few have it and can have it exactly and perfectly. Wherefore it happens that that part of the human race which gives itself wholly to speculation holds that proportion in the race of men which the heart holds in the genus of members; although there is also latitude for some to be mathematicians, some to be physicists, and some metaphysicians. Among all these ways there is latitude, as is clear enough. But the productive intellect, which is lowest and mechanical, is common to all men; nay, even beasts participate in it, as Aristotle teaches in *De historiis,* since many beasts build houses, and many other things which indicate the productive intellect. And this is most necessary, inasmuch as the greater part of men have been occupied with it. Whence the female sex apply themselves almost completely to it, as in weaving, spinning, sewing, etc. And the greatest part of men spend their time in agriculture, then in the different crafts. Nor can he who applies himself to one craft easily apply himself to another. Wherefore Plato in the *Republic* and Aristotle in the *Politics* ordered that, just as one member does not easily perform different functions, so one artisan ought not to spend his time at different crafts. For he will master neither. Yet the practical or operative intellect is truly fitting for man. And every man not incapacitated can pursue it perfectly. And according to it man is called unqualifiedly and absolutely good and evil, but according to the theoretical and the productive intellects only relatively and within limits. For according to his virtues and vices a man is called a good man or a bad; but a good metaphysician is not called a good man but a good metaphysician, and a good builder is not called good absolutely but a good builder. Wherefore a man submits without offense if he is not called a metaphysician, a philosopher, or a smith; but if he is called a thief, intemperate, unjust, imprudent, or something vicious of this sort, he is much offended and gets excited, since being righteous or vicious is human and is in our power, but being a philosopher or a builder is not our task, nor is it necessary to man. Whence it is that all men can and ought to be of good character, but not all philosophers, mathematicians, builders, and the rest. For mankind would not endure if there were not such diversity, as was said above about the members.

Returning then to the proposition, we say that the end of the human race in general is to participate in these three intellects, by which men communicate with each other and live together; and one is either useful or necessary to the other, just as all the members in a single man share in vital spirits and have mutual operations together. And from this end man cannot be absolved. But as to the practical intellect, which is proper to man, every man should possess it perfectly. For in order that the human race be rightly preserved, every man must be morally virtuous and as far as possible lack vice; and a vice is imputed to him as his, in whatever condition he be found, whether destitute or poor or rich or moderately wealthy or quite wealthy. With the other intellects this is not necessary, nor is it possible. Nor does it suit the human race; for the world would not endure if everyone were theoretical, nor would he himself, for it is impossible for one kind of men, like philosophers, to be self-sufficient; nor for a race of builders alone, or anything of this sort. Nor can it be that one should perfectly perform the functions of another, still less of all, just as happens in the members.

Wherefore the universal end of the human race is to participate relatively in the speculative and the productive intellects but perfectly in the practical. For the whole would be most perfectly preserved if all men were righteous and good, but not if all were philosophers or smiths or builders. Nor is it thus in the moral virtues as in the arts and sciences, that one hinders another, and applying one's self to one prevents applying one's self to another. Indeed, as is said in the *Ethics*, the moral virtues are bound up together, and he who possesses one perfectly possesses them all. Wherefore all ought to be righteous and good. But to be a philosopher, a mathematician, or an architect is a particular end; just as the brain has its own function and the liver its. Nor ought that inequality in the human race to beget envy and quarrels among them, just as the diversity in the members does not; nay rather union and peace, especially since every man ought to be moral, by which such things are expelled. And as each element has its proper place in the whole categorematically, yet some part of it is better than another; for not every part of fire touches the sphere of the moon unless as it is joined to the whole, nor is every part of earth the center of the world, except by reason of the whole; so not every man has the final end which suits the part, except as part of the human race. It is enough that he have the common human end.

Wherefore it is said to the argument, that if man is mortal, every man can have the end which suits man universally; the end that belongs to the most perfect part he cannot, nor is it fitting. Just as not every member can have the perfection of the heart or the eye, indeed, the animal would not persist; so, if every man were theoretical, the human

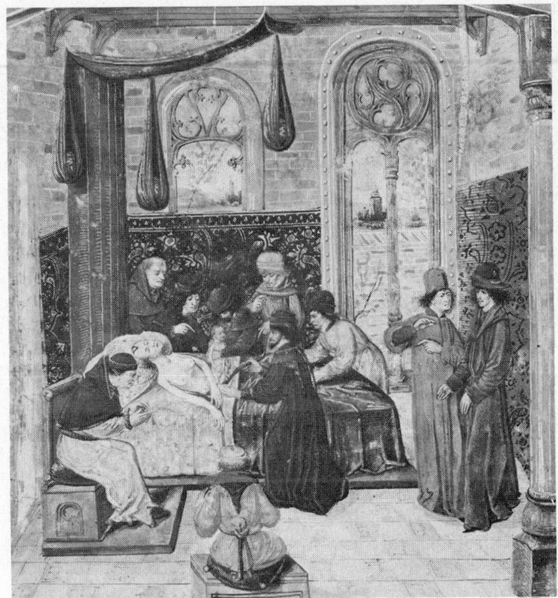

Delivery of a Baby. Both the secular, non-religious setting and the attention given to the face are Renaissance elements in this 15th-century manuscript illustration. (Bibliothèque Nationale, Paris)

community would not persist. Whence many climates and different regions are necessary. Happiness then does not consist in the theoretical power of demonstration, as suitable for the whole human race, but as suiting its first principal part. And though the other parts cannot arrive at such happiness, they are still not wholly deprived of all happiness, since they can possess something of the theoretical and something of the productive, and the practical perfectly. This power can make almost everyone blessed. For farmer or smith, destitute or rich, if his life be moral, can be called happy, and truly so called, and can depart contented with his lot. In addition, besides moral happiness he can be called a happy farmer or a happy builder, if he operates successfully in agriculture or in house-building, although he is not on this account so properly called happy. For these things are not in human power, like the virtues and vices. Hence the human race is not frustrated in its end, unless it make itself so.

And what was added further, that such speculation does not seem to be able to make man happy, since it is very weak and obscure; to this I say that, although it is of this sort in relation to eternal things and to that of the Intelligences, yet among mortal things nothing can be found more excellent, as Plato says in the *Timaeus.* Nor ought a mortal to desire immortal happiness, since the immortal is not fitting for the mortal: just as immortal wrath is not fitting for mortal man, as Aristotle says in *Rhetoric* ii. Whence we first suppose that to each thing a proportionate end is assigned. For if man will be moderate, he will not desire the impossible, nor does it suit him. For to have such happiness is proper to the gods, who are in no wise dependent on matter and change. The opposite of this occurs in the human race, which is a mean between the mortal and the immortal.

And when it was further said, that the end ought to bring peace but this does not set man's intellect and will at rest; to this I say that Aristotle at the end of *Ethica* i does not assert human happiness as perfect peace; nay, he holds that no matter how happy a man be, yet he is not so steadfast that many things do not disturb him (for he would not be man), but they do not remove him from happiness; just as every wind does not strip a tree, though it moves the leaves. Whence in human happiness a steadfastness that cannot be destroyed is enough, although it may be disturbed somewhat; nay, what is more, also at any age: for in youth, if he does not have exact knowledge, which belongs to manhood, provided he have what belongs to youth he is content for that age; nor does he desire more than suits him. Wherefore he will not be perturbed, as was said.

And when it proceeded further, that man never knows as much as he can know, nor so clearly but that it might be more clear; I say that this does not destroy his happiness, so long as he have as much as suits his condition, and that he is not deficient on his part. For it is characteristic of a temperate appetite to desire as much as it can digest; so it is characteristic of the temperate man to be content with what suits him and what he can have.

And when it was further added, since man knows he will soon lose this happiness, and that it can be destroyed in many ways, he will have more misery than happiness; to this I say that it belongs to an illiberal man not to wish to give back what he has received freely, when man is assumed to be mortal; for the ancients also called life a purgatory, since man receives it with the provision that he knows he must give it back to nature. He will give thanks to God and nature, and will always be ready to die, nor will he fear death, since fear of the inevitable is vain; and he will see nothing evil in death.

And when further it was inferred that the condition of man would be far worse than that of any brute, surely in my opinion this is not said philosophically, since the works of beasts, though they bring content to their kind, are here preferred to the restless works of the intellect. Who would prefer to be a stone or a stag of long life, rather than a man of however low degree? Inasmuch as a prudent man can maintain a contented mind in any condition or time, though he be troubled by bodily distresses. Indeed the wise man would much prefer to be in extreme necessity and the greatest troubles rather than to be stupid, cowardly, and vicious under the opposite conditions.

Nor is it true that one who sees immense labors, withdrawal from bodily pleasures, obscure knowledge of things, the easy loss of what has been acquired, would turn aside to vice and bodily things rather than be moved to acquire knowledge, if that man acts according to reason. For the slightest modicum of knowledge and virtue is to be preferred to all bodily delights, nay, to kingdoms themselves, in which abound tyrannies and vices. Wherefore the first argument seems in no way to prove that the soul is immortal.

But in answer to the second objection, which asserted that if the mortality of the soul is established, then we ought never to choose death, I say that it on no account follows but rather the opposite. For in *Topica* iii it is said: "Of two evils the lesser is to be chosen." And in *Ethica* iii: "Choice is of goods, rejection of evils." Since then in choosing death for the sake of country, of friends, and of avoiding sin the greatest virtue is acquired, and it is greatly to the advantage of others, since men naturally praise an act of this sort, and nothing is more precious and more happy than virtue itself, it is above all things to be chosen. But, in committing a crime, a man very greatly harms the community, and hence also himself, since he is part of the community. And he falls into vice, than which there is nothing more unhappy, since he ceases to be a man, as Plato says in so many places in the *Republic;* and therefore this has the nature of a thing to be avoided. And happiness follows the attainment of that virtue, or a great part of happiness, even though it be of short duration. But misery follows sin, for, as Plato witnesses, sin is misery and in the end death, since immortality may not follow on account of the crime committed, except perhaps through infamy and vituperation. But it is plain that the former rather than the latter is the lesser evil. Nor is living long with infamy to be put above living a brief time with praise, just as the life of man however brief is to be set above the life of beasts however long. For Aristotle, in *Ethica* i, says: "A long life is not to be preferred to a short life, unless other things are equal."

Nor is death chosen in such a case for itself, since it is nothing; but rather a righteous act, though death follow it; just as in not committing a sin life is not refused, since life is good in itself, but the sin is refused whose consequence is life. But as to the objection based on the statement in the *Phaedo,* Plato holds in the *Republic* and the *Crito,* just as life with an incurable infirmity ought to be rejected, nay, even taken from the living, so the soul with sin ought to be eradicated; and the soul, were it to live forever in sin, is the highest misery, since there is nothing worse for the soul than sin itself. But Plato said this in regard to what would actually happen. For if men hoped for no better life after death, they would doubtless endure this one uneasily, because they do not know the excellence of virtue and the ignobility of vice. For only the philosophers and the righteous, as Plato says in the *Republic* and Aristotle in *Ethica* ix, know how much delight the virtues produce and how much misery ignorance and vice. Nay, Socrates, in Plato's *Apology,* says: "Whether the soul be mortal or immortal, death is nonetheless to be despised." Nor ought we in any way to turn aside from virtue, whatever may happen after death. I think in the same way also the words of St. Thomas in *On the Apostles' Creed* are to be interpreted, not that crimes ought to be committed rather than to suffer death, if the soul were mortal—for that I judge to be said neither wisely nor in accordance with theology—but that men who did not know the excellence of virtue and the foulness of vice would commit every crime rather than die. Wherefore to restrain the abominable desires of men there is given the hope of reward and the fear of punishment.

That also, if the mortality of the soul be assumed, death is in some cases to be suffered, is clear from many actions of beasts, in which there is no doubt that the souls are mortal and guided by natural instinct. For Aristotle tells, in *De historiis* ix, chapter 30, which our Vergil recalls in *Georgics* iv, that bees risk death to protect their ruler and their community. And he writes in the same place that the male cuttlefish suffers death to save his mate. And he tells in *De historiis* ix, chapter 37, that a camel killed a cameldriver with a piercing bite, because he compelled it by a trick to couple with its mother; and a horse, deceived in the same way, committed the same crime; but when it recognized what it had done, suddenly killed itself. Now since these things were done by nature, they were done according to reason, inasmuch as in the opinion of Themistius and Averroes nature is directed by an unerring intelligence. Hence in man also this is not contrary to reason.

But to the third principal objection, which asserted that either God is not the governor of the universe or he is unjust; to this I say that neither follows. And, I say, no evil remains in essence unpunished, nor any good in essence unrewarded. In proof it must be known that reward and punishment have two meanings: one is essential and inseparable, the other accidental and separable. The essential reward of virtue is virtue itself, which makes man happy. For human nature can possess nothing greater than virtue itself, since it alone makes man secure and removed from every perturbation. For all things work together for him who loves the good: fearing nothing, hoping for nothing, but in prosperity and adversity ever the same, as is said in the end of *Ethica* i. And Plato says in the *Crito:* "To the good man neither alive nor dead can any evil happen." But it is the opposite with vice. For the punishment of the vicious is vice itself, than which nothing can be more miserable, nothing more unhappy. But how perverted is the life of the vicious man, and how greatly it is to be shunned, Aristotle makes clear in *Ethica* vii, where he shows that for the vicious man all things are discordant. Faithful to no one, not even to himself, neither awake nor asleep is he at peace; he is beset by horrible tortures of body and soul: a most unhappy life. So that no wise man, however destitute, infirm in body, deprived of the goods of fortune, would choose the life of a tyrant or of some vicious ruler, and the wise man would prefer to remain in his own condition. And so every virtuous man is rewarded by his virtue and happiness. Wherefore Aristotle, in *Problemata* 30, problem 10, when he asks why rewards are set for contests, but not for virtues and knowledge, says that this is because virtue is its own reward. For since the reward ought to be more excellent than the contest, and since nothing is more excellent than prudence, it is thus its own reward. But the contrary takes place with vice. Hence no vicious man is left unpunished, since vice itself is the punishment of the vicious man.

Moreover, accidental reward or punishment is what can be separated, like gold, or penalties of any sort. And not every good is rewarded thus nor is all evil punished. Nor is this unfitting, since they are accidents. These two things should be known: first, that accidental reward is far more imperfect than essential reward, for gold is more imperfect than virtue. And accidental punishment is far less than essential punishment; for accidental punishment is the punishment of a penalty, but essential, that of guilt. But the punishment of guilt is far worse than the punishment of a penalty. Whence it does not matter if sometimes the accidental is lacking, provided the essential remains. Secondly, in addition it should be known, that when good is accidentally rewarded, essential good seems to be diminished, nor does it remain in its perfection. For example, if one man acts virtuously without hope of reward, and another with hope of reward, the act of the second is not considered as virtuous as that of the first. Whence he is rewarded more essentially who is not rewarded accidentally than he who is rewarded accidentally. Likewise, he who acts viciously and is punished accidentally, seems to be punished less than he who is not punished accidentally; for the punishment of guilt is greater and worse than the punishment of a penalty; and when the punishment of a penalty is added to guilt, it diminishes the guilt. Whence he who is not punished accidentally is punished more essentially than he who is punished accidentally. Witness also on this what Laertius wrote of Aristotle: for when Aristotle was asked what he had acquired from philosophy, he answered, "What you do from the hope of reward and shun from fear of punishment, I do from love and nobility of virtue, and shun from hatred of vice." But why some are rewarded or punished accidentally, and others not, does not concern the present proposition.

But in answer to the fourth objection, that almost the whole world would be deceived, since all religions hold the soul to be immortal, I say that if the whole is nothing but its parts, as many think, since there is no man who is not deceived, as Plato says in the *Republic,* it is not wrong, nay, it is necessary to admit that either the whole world is deceived or at least the greater part. For assuming that there are only three religions, those of Christ, of Moses, and of Mohammed; then either they are all false, and thus the whole world is deceived; or at least two of them, and thus the greater part is deceived.

But it must be known that, as Plato and Aristotle say, the statesman is the physician of souls, and the purpose of the statesman is to make man righteous rather than learned. Now, according to the diversity of men, one must proceed by different devices to attain this end. For some are men of ability and of a nature well formed by God, who are led to the virtues by the nobility of the virtues alone, and are restrained from vices by their foulness alone. And these are of the best nature, though they are very few. Some, however, have a nature less well ordered, and these, besides the nobility of virtue and the foulness of vice, perform righteous acts and shun vice from rewards, praise, and honors, from punishments like censure and infamy. And these are on the second level. Some, however, are made righteous on account of the hope of some good and the fear of bodily punishment. Wherefore, so that they may attain such virtue, statesmen establish either gold or dignity or some other such thing; and that they may shun vice, they establish that they shall be punished in money, or in honor, or in body, either by mutilating a member or by killing. But some from the fierceness and perversity of their nature are moved by none of these, as daily experience teaches. Therefore they have set up for the virtuous eternal rewards in another life, and for the vicious, eternal punishments, which frighten greatly. And the greater part of men, if they do good, do it more from fear of eternal punishment than from hope of eternal good, since punishments are better known to us than that eternal good. And since this last device can benefit all men, of whatever degree, the lawgiver regarding the proneness of men to evil, intending the common good, has decreed that the soul is immortal, not caring for truth but only for righteousness, that he may lead men to virtue.

Nor is the statesman to be blamed. For just as the physician feigns many things to restore a sick man to health, so the statesman composes fables to keep the citizens in the right path. But in these fables, as says Averroes in the prologue to *Physica* iii, there is, properly speaking, neither truth nor falsity. So also nurses bring their charges to what they know to benefit children. But if a man were healthy or of sound mind, neither physician nor nurse would need such fictions. Wherefore if all men were on the first level mentioned, even granting the mortality of the soul, they would be righteous. But almost none are of that nature. Whence it has been necessary to proceed by other devices. Nor is this unfitting, since human nature is almost entirely immersed in matter, and participates very little in intellect; whence man is farther from the Intelligences than a sick man from a healthy one, a boy from a man, and a fool from a wise man. Wherefore it is not strange that the statesman uses such devices, etc.

In the fifth principal objection two points were touched upon: one concerning the things that have been seen in tombs, and the other concerning dreams. To the first of these I say, first, that many things are counted among histories which nevertheless are mere fables. Secondly, it is said that in the neighborhood of tombs, as in many places, the air is rather heavy, partly from the evaporation of the corpses, partly from the coldness of the stones, and from many other reasons which cause density of the air. But as is said in *Meteora* iii, in the chapter on the rainbow, "Such air easily receives the image of the things near by, just as a mirror receives figures." Whence things seen in air so disposed are thought by simple men to be the things which seem to be there, just as children looking in a mirror or in water believe that the things seen in them are really there. For Aristotle tells of a certain man of weak sight who, seeing his shadow at night, thought it was a man following him. Whence it is that simple men on account of such incidents think that those things are the souls of the dead. Imagination and universal repute also help. Wherefore, as Aristotle tells in *De somno et vigilia*, chapter 2, many things are thought to be seen by those living in fear or other passions, even though they be awake, which yet do not exist; just as happens to those ill.

Thirdly, it is said that this happens often because of the illusions and tricks of wicked priests, as is said in the last chapter of Daniel of the idol Bel. For many priests and guardians of temples have changed the four cardinal virtues into ambition, avarice, gluttony, and riotous living. And upon these sins all others follow. Wherefore that they may fulfil their desires they employ these frauds and fictions; just as in our time we know to have happened occasionally. Fourthly, it is said because many histories of the Greeks and the Romans recount marvels. For on the birth and death of men worthy of record it is most certain that portents appeared. For Suetonius Tranquillus in his *On the Twelve Caesars* tells of great signs both by birds and by answer of the gods, and many others. No less does Plutarch in his *Lives of Illustrious Men*. And our Vergil at the end of the first *Georgic* sang these verses:

> But at the time the earth and sea besides,
> Unseasonable birds and hell-sent dogs,
> Gave portents. Often Etna 'neath our gaze
> Burst her great furnaces and shed her heart
> O'er Cyclopean fields, a boiling flood
> Of liquid rocks and solid balls of flame!
> The Germans heard the din of heavenly wars;
> Unwonted tremors shook the Alps; a voice
> Of awful power rang through the silent
> groves;
> Pale phantoms of strange aspect were espied
> Through the night shadows; beasts were
> heard to speak,
> O horror! rivers stood, earth oped her mouth,
> Bronze statues sweated, ivory shed tears.

No less does Lucan relate many things. In Maccabees ii, chapter 5, also, it is written thus: "At the same time Antiochus prepared a second journey into Egypt. And it came to pass that through the whole city of Jerusalem for the space of forty days there were seen horsemen running in the air, in gilded raiment, and armed with spears, like bands of soldiers, and horses set in order by ranks, running one against another, with the shakings of shields, and a multitude of men in helmets with drawn swords, and casting of darts, and glittering of golden armor, and of harnesses of all sorts. Wherefore all men prayed that these prodigies might turn to good."

Wherefore the oracular responses of old do not seem to be wholly without meaning. To deny such things, moreover, seems great obstinacy and impudence. Wherefore we must speak otherwise. Granted that they are not fictions or illusions or our imaginings, we must say that Christians, and almost universally all religions, and Plato and Avicenna and many others hold that these things are done either by God or by his servants, whom we call angels if they are good, and demons if they are bad. It is true that there is some difference between the two, with which we are not now concerned.

And these men grant that the human soul is unqualifiedly immortal and multiple, as is well known. But this clearly contradicts the words of Aristotle, since there is no immaterial substance which does not move a sphere; for in *Metaphysica* xii he holds that the number of Intelligences corresponds to the number of spheres. Nor is there any effect here below which is not reducible, in his opinion, to first motion, as appears in *Physica* viii and *Meteora* i. Further, because it seems to me this cannot be demonstrated by conclusive natural reason. Whence we shall not remain within natural limits, which we nevertheless promised in the beginning. Hence Alexander of Aphrodisias, as St. Thomas relates in the disputed question *About Miracles,* Articles III and X, in the body of the question, says that these things are produced by separated substances, by means of heavenly bodies, according to the powers of the stars, according to their conjunctions and oppositions. And truly if these effects are granted, according to the Peripatetics, it cannot be said otherwise; since the whole world here below borders on that above, so that every power is governed from there, as is said in the beginning of the *Meteora.* And this also does not seem to be unreasonably said. For Alexander holds that God and the Intelligences exercise providence over things below, as St. Thomas notes as his opinion in the exposition of *De caelo* ii, text 56. And Alexander expressly admits it in *De fato.* Wherefore according to the conditions of time and place he rules things below, both kings and prophets, and other events. Therefore that at times such things have appeared as is said in *Maccabees,* marked future wars as the event made plain; although perhaps these too could have been avoided, according to Alexander, since he holds in *De fato* to free will. Nor is it strange if such things can be shadowed forth by the heavenly bodies, since they are animated by a most noble soul and generate and govern all things below.

The same may be said of those things which Titus Livy, Suetonius, Vergil, Plutarch, and Lucan relate. For if signs precede spring, summer, and the other seasons, as is obvious, how much more ought those Intelligences to be solicitous for human nature! This is indeed very clear to see. For I do not remember having read the life of any man excelling in anything whatever, whose birth and death were not heralded by many signs, nay, many of his acts. And what the Platonists call the genius or familiar demon, is with the Peripatetics his natal star; because such a man is born under such a constellation, but another under another. If we can do without that multiplication of demons and genii, it seems superfluous to assume them; besides the fact that it is also contrary to reason.

Therefore the heavenly bodies according to their powers produce these marvels for the advantage of mortals, and especially of men, since human nature partakes of divinity.

For Aristotle relates in *De historiis* iii, chapter 20, that on the island of Lemnos so much milk had been drawn from the dugs of a he-goat—it had twin ones close to the genitals—that they made cheese from it; and when the master of the animal consulted an oracle, he received the answer that there would be a further increase of his cattle; which was discovered to be so. If therefore they give portents about cattle, how much more about men!

But St. Thomas attacks this opinion with many subtle arguments. First, because such events take place in irregular fashion; but what takes place by nature takes place regularly, in *Physica* ii and viii. Secondly, because there are some effects in apparitions of this sort which cannot be traced back to the heavenly bodies, like sayings and especially predictions about the future, since such things cannot be done except by one who possesses intellect. But such things are very often inanimate, or lacking in intellect, as when beasts speak, or when in the air human voices are heard, or something else like that. Thirdly, because some things take place that cannot be done by the power of the heavenly bodies, as that branches are turned into serpents. Whence there seems to be no answer.

But these things do not seem to me to prove the conclusion. For the first is answered, that on the contrary such things occur in a regular manner, both as to time and to place, and by determinate causes, etc. The proof is that many astrologers know how to predict them, and future prodigies, changes in states, and in determinate places, as has often been seen. But that to us they seem indeterminate is due to our ignorance. And in regard to the second point, so emphasized by St. Thomas, I do not wish to say that I marvel, but that I do not rightly understand. For according to him effects and sayings of this sort are accomplished by Intelligences, sometimes good and sometimes evil, and by divine permission, sometimes by human souls now separated from the body. But all such things are then not forms of those bodies, whether animate or inaminate, which are heard to speak thus. Hence they are only movers. Why then cannot the Intelligences moving the heavenly bodies do this by means of their instruments, which accomplish so many and such great things, make parrots, magpies, crows, blackbirds, and so on speak? I do not see why he denies these so flatly, especially since he holds, in the *Summa*, Part 1, question 51, that an angel speaks or makes some other sound by means of an aerial body condensed and shaped. Now the heavenly bodies accomplish these and much greater things by means of their powers and the conjunctions of the stars, because they make animals and other amazing things, as appears from stones and plants; whence they can accomplish these things also.

And this is confirmed by the Conciliator, in expounding the twenty-sixth problem of the eleventh part, "The problem is, why some speak as soon as they are born." He says, "Haly ben Ragel writes *De nativitatibus:* 'Our king called us because one of his wives bore a son, and the ascendent was 8 degrees of Libra, the terminus of Mercury, and in it were Jupiter, Venus, Mars and Mercury. And a group of astrologers gathered there, each one of whom gave his opinion. And I kept silent. Then the king said to me, What is the matter? Why do you not speak? I answered, Give me a limit of three days; because if your son survives the third day a great miracle will occur. And when the child completed twenty-four hours he began to speak and to make signs with his hands. And the king grew much frightened; wherefore I said, It is possible that he may say some prophecy and some miracle. And then we were with the king at the child's side. And the child said, I am born unfortunate, and I am born to foretell the loss of the kingdom of Agedeir and the destruction of the house of Almann. He at once fell back and was dead.' " And it was discovered to be as he said. Now this child either spoke by a spirit or of himself. Not the first, because Haly would not have known by astrology how to predict what he said; hence of himself, that is, from within, and not from any knowledge he had from any man; hence from the power of the Intelligences and the heavenly bodies. Wherefore it can happen thus in other things as well.

But if it be said that all teaching and instruction comes from pre-existing knowledge, I answer that this is not teaching or instruction, nor knowledge properly speaking. The mark of this can be that those soothsayers, when they have recovered from the madness, recall nothing, nay, deny that they have said those things. But they are moved by a heavenly impulse. Whence Plato says in the *Meno* and in many other places, "Soothsayers announce very many true things, yet understand nothing of what they say." And in *Problemata* xxx, problem I, "Sybils and seers and all who are believed to be stirred up by a divine inspiration, are directed by impulse." And the Conciliator in that passage says, "I heard from a faithful physician that a certain illiterate woman spoke coherent Latin while she was delirious; when she was recovered it disappeared." This does not seem to take place except from the disposition of the body with the motion of the stars.

Now to St. Thomas' third objection it is answered that the Peripatetics would say that such things are illusions, such as many produce by alteration of the medium or of the eyes. Or, if it was true, we are not within natural limits, because we exclude miracles. What was further added about dreams, those and greater things we grant. For Averroes, who did not hold that souls are multiplied, in the chapter *On the Divination of Dreams* fully concedes it; and Galen, who thought the soul mortal. Nay, many things are accomplished in medicine by dreams. But this does not prove that the soul is unqualifiedly immortal, but that the gods concern themselves with things below. Wherefore by signs in waking and by dreams they teach many things and exercise providence over human affairs; as Averroes fully says there. And what is said of those Arcadians is not strange since Plato says in the *Republic* v, "God is the avenger of those who do wrong to strangers." What is adduced about the Pamphylian is a fable for restraining the citizens.

But why some are left unpunished or even others on the contrary rewarded does not belong to the present consideration. And the Commentator there touches upon many beautiful and difficult things, which are not in accordance with our intention.

Now to the fifth point concerning those possessed by demons, the answer can be clear through what has been said. For all such men are suffering either from black bile or insanity, or from a trance or are near to death and far from human thoughts; whence it is that they become almost lifeless and irrational. Hence they can receive the heavenly motions and are driven and led by the lymphatic impulse rather than act or lead themselves. The conclusive mark of which is that, as Plato says and Aristotle agrees, they do not understand what they are saying but are moved like beasts by another. Whence the proverb has it that children and fools prophesy, while wise and sane men are strange to this sort of thing. Nor should anyone wonder at this, inasmuch as Aristotle writes in *De historiis* ix, chapter 31, "At the time when the Median enemies were attacking at Pharsalus, there were no crows in the places of Athens and the Peloponnesus, as if they had some sense by which they made known to each other, and were moved by, the outcome of things." For if crows sensed such future events from the heavens, why not those men too, who stand hardly above crows, since they have very little intellect. Let him who thus objects then consider the beasts from which augurs also derive their predictions. Now that the art of augury is not entirely without value, the histories of the Greeks and Romans make clear; and Plato establishes in the *Laws* that in a well-ordered city the art of augury must not be overlooked. Aristotle also, in *De historiis* i, chapter 10, and also vi, chapter 2, and ix, chapter 1, recalls some things about the art of augury. But if birds and many creatures lacking reason can foretell by the impression of the heavens, why not also men who are like them? This is also confirmed, since otherwise astrologers could not make such certain predictions, as has been seen, unless the heavenly powers act on things below. But if they sometimes seem to lie, it is because they are either unskilled or have not correctly taken the horoscope, or else it happens because free will is overcoming heavenly powers.

Now to the seventh objection it is answered that Aristotle in no wise believes that the soul remains after death but believes the opposite. And as to that passage in *Ethica* i it is plain enough, since he says that it neither profits nor harms them, since they are nothing, but only the opinion held of them. For the kind of existence that Homer has in the mind the dead also have. As for the second passage in *Oeconomica* ii, it is replied that either these women were rewarded by the gods in their lifetime, for it is not said there that it was after death, or if after death, this is understood as referring to the opinion held of them, or that it may induce other women to like performances.

Now to the eighth and last objection, in which it was said that men impure and sinful and conscious of their crimes assert that the soul is mortal, while those who are holy and just hold it immortal; to this it is answered that neither do impure men universally maintain mortality nor do the temperate universally maintain immortality. For obviously we see that many wicked men believe in religion but are seduced by the passions. And we also know that many holy and just men have maintained the mortality of the soul. For Plato in the *Republic* i says that Simonides the poet was a divine and very good man, who nevertheless asserted it to be mortal. And Homer also, as Aristotle relates in *De anima* ii, thought that sense does not differ from intellect. But who does not know Homer's worth? Hippocrates also and Galen, most learned and good men, are reputed to have been of this opinion. Alexander of Aphrodisias, the great Alfarabi, Abubacher, Avempace, and of our countrymen also Pliny the Elder, Seneca and numberless others thought so. For Seneca, in the *Epistles to Lucilius* vii, epistle 54, which begins, "Ill health had given me long companionship," and more clearly in *On Consolation to Martia*, asserts that the soul is mortal, and he numbers many other upright and most learned men as being of the same opinion. And for this reason, that they thought that virtue alone is happiness, and vice misery, and neglected the other remaining goods except as they serve virtue, and cast from themselves those which hinder virtue.

And it must be considered that many men have thought the soul mortal, who nevertheless have written that it is immortal. But they did so on account of the proneness to evil of men who have little or no intellect, and neither knowing nor loving the goods of the soul devote themselves to bodily things alone. Whence it is necessary to cure them by devices of this sort, just as the physician acts toward the sick man and the nurse toward the child lacking reason.

By these reasons, I think, other points also can be resolved. For although it is commonly said that, if the soul is mortal, man ought to give himself over completely to bodily pleasures, commit all evils for his own advantage, and that it would be vain to worship God, to honor the divine, to pour forth prayers to God, to make sacrifices, and do other things of this sort, the answer is clear enough from what has been said. For since happiness is naturally desired and misery shunned, and by what has been said happiness consists in virtuous action, but misery in vicious action, since to worship God with the whole mind, to honor the divine, to raise prayers to God, to sacrifice are actions in the highest degree virtuous, we ought hence to strive with all our powers to acquire them. But on the contrary, thefts, robberies, murders, a life of pleasures are vices, which make man turn into a beast and cease to be a man; hence we ought to abstain from them. And note that one who acts conscientiously, expecting no other reward than virtue, seems to act far more virtuously and purely than he who expects some reward beyond virtue. And he who shuns vice on account of the foulness of vice, not because of the fear of due punishment for vice, seems more to be praised than he who avoids vice on account of the fear of punishment, as in the verses:

> The good hate sin from love of virtue,
> The evil hate sin from fear of punishment.

Wherefore those who claim that the soul is mortal seem better to save the grounds of virtue than those who claim it to be immortal. For the hope of reward and the fear of punishment seem to suggest a certain servility, which is contrary to the grounds of virtue, etc.

To complete this opinion it must be known that, as Aristotle teaches in *De generatione animalium*, nature proceeds by degrees and in orderly fashion, so that it does not join an extreme immediately with an extreme, but an extreme with a mean. For we see that shrubs serve as a mean between grasses and trees; between vegetables and animals are unmoving animal things, like oysters and the rest of this sort; and so on ascending further. The Blessed Dionysius also suggests this in *De divinis nominibus*, chapter 7, when he says that the divine wisdom joins the ends of higher things to the beginning of lower things. But man, as has been said, is the most perfect of the animals. Wherefore since among material things the human soul holds first place, it will hence be joined to the immaterial, and is a mean between the material and the immaterial. But a mean compared to the extremes is called the other of the extremes; whence compared to the immaterial the soul can be called material, and with respect to the material, immaterial. Nor is it only those names that it deserves; indeed, it participates in the properties of the extremes. For green compared to white is not only called black; it truly gathers sight like black, though not so intensely.

Wherefore also the human soul has some of the properties of the Intelligences and some of the properties of all material things; whence it is that when it performs functions through which it agrees with the Intelligences, it is said to be divine and to be changed into a God; but when it performs the functions of beasts, it is said to be changed into a beast; for because of malice it is said to be a serpent or a fox, because of cruelty a tiger, and so on. For there is nothing in the world which because of some property cannot agree with man himself; wherefore man is not undeservedly called a microcosm, or little world. Therefore some have said that man is a great marvel, since he is the whole world and can change into every nature, since to him is given the power to follow whatever property of things he may prefer. Therefore the ancients were telling the right fable when they said that some men had been made into gods, some into lions, some into wolves, some into eagles, some into fish, some into plants, some into stones, and so on; since some men have attained intellect, some sense, some the powers of the vegetative soul, and so on.

Therefore those who place bodily pleasures above moral or intellectual virtues rather produce a beast than a god; those who put riches first, rather gold; whence the former are to be called beasts, the latter insensate. Therefore, though the soul is mortal, the virtues are not to be despised, and pleasures sought, unless one prefers to be a beast rather than a man, and insensate rather than sensate or knowing. For we must know that however much man thus participates in the material and in the immaterial, yet he is properly said to participate in the immaterial, because he lacks much of immateriality; but he is not properly said to participate in the brute and the vegetable, but rather to contain them, for he is below the immaterial and above the material. Wherefore he cannot arrive at the perfection of the immaterial, whence men are not to be called gods, but godlike or divine. But man cannot only make himself equal to the beast, nay exceed the beast; for there are some men far crueler than any beast, as Aristotle says in *Ethica* vii: "An evil man is ten thousand times worse than a beast." And just as it was said of cruelty, so of the other vices. Since, therefore, vice is so foul, and so unjust the life of a vicious man, but the contrary of virtue, who then, even if the soul be mortal, would prefer vice rather than virtue, unless he preferred to be a beast or worse than a beast, rather than to be a man? Wherefore, etc.

CHAPTER XV AND LAST

In Which Is Affirmed the Final Conclusion in This Matter, Which in My Opinion Must be Maintained as Beyond Doubt

Now since these things are so, it seems to me that in this matter, keeping the saner view, we must say that the question of the immortality of the soul is a neutral problem, like that of the eternity of the world. For it seems to me that no natural reasons can be brought forth proving that the soul is immortal, and still less any proving that the soul is mortal, as very many scholars who hold it immortal declare. Wherefore I do not want to make answer to the other side, since others do so, St. Thomas in particular, clearly, fully, and weightily. Wherefore we shall say, as Plato said in the *Laws* i, that to be certain of anything, when many are in doubt, is for God alone. Since therefore such famous men disagree with each other, I think that this can be made certain only through God.

But it does not seem to be fitting or expedient for man to lack such certainty. For if he were in doubt on this matter, he would have actions uncertain and without any end; since if the end be unknown, the means thereto would also be necessarily unknown. Whence if the soul is immortal, earthly things are to be despised, and eternal things to be pursued; but if its existence is mortal, a contrary way is to be pursued. But if other things besides man have their own determinate ends, how much more man himself, since man is the most perfect of mortals, and the only one, as Plato says in the *Republic,* who worships God and justice! Wherefore I say, that before the gift or advent of grace "in many places and in many ways by the prophets" and by supernatural signs God himself settled this question, as is plain to see in the Old Testament. But "most recently by the Son whom he made the heir of all, through whom he also made the ages," he has made clear this question, as the Apostle says in the *Epistle to the Hebrews.* That he is truly the Son of God, true God and true man, most fittingly and without doubt, the light of the Christian name, St. Thomas Aquinas, declares in *Contra Gentiles* i, chapter 6. Which points John Scotus, in my opinion most subtle of all and a man above all most religious, reducing them to the number of eight enumerates in the prologue to the *Sentences.* And indeed so clearly do these eight points set it forth that unless demented or stubborn no one could deny it. Since therefore he is the true God, he alone is truly that light by which all things are seen, as in *John* i, and he alone also is the truth by which other things are true, as in *John* xiv: "I am the way, the truth and the life." But since he himself has made manifest in word and deed that the soul is immortal, in word when he threatens the evil with eternal fire, but to the good promises eternal life; for he says, "Come, blessed of my Father, etc.," and it follows, "Go, accursed ones, into eternal fires, etc."; in deed, when he rose on the third day from the dead. But as far as the light differs from the lucid and truth from the true, and as much as the infinite cause is more powerful than the finite effect, the more efficaciously does this demonstrate the immortality of the soul.

Wherefore, if any arguments seem to prove the mortality of the soul, they are false and merely seeming, since the first light and the first truth show the opposite. But if any seem to prove its immortality, they are true and clear, but not light and truth. Wherefore this way alone is most firm, unshaken, and lasting; the rest are untrustworthy.

Moreover, every art ought to proceed by things proper and fitting to that art; for otherwise it errs and does not proceed according to the rule of art, as Aristotle says in *Posteriora* and *Ethica* i. But that the soul is immortal is an article of faith, as appears from the Apostles' Creed and the Athanasian Creed; hence it ought to be proved by what is proper to faith. But the means on which faith relies is revelation and canonical Scripture. Hence it is proved truly and properly only by them; but other reasons are foreign, and rely on a means that does not prove what is intended. Hence it is not surprising if philosophers disagree among themselves about the immortality of the soul, when they rely on arguments foreign to the conclusion and fallacious; but all followers of Christ agree, since they proceed by what is proper and infallible, since matters cannot be except in one way.

Further, he who is ill is concerned for health. Yet let no one be physician to himself, since it is said in *Politics* iii: "In his own affairs no one judges rightly, since he is in a state of passion. Let him therefore ask another. But the good physician ought to be skilled

The School of Athens, by Raphael. This masterpiece pays homage to the Academy of Plato, illustrating the Renaissance attempt to recover the world of classical learning. (Art Resource)

in his art, and of good character, since neither the first without the second nor the second without the first suffices. But as Plato says, just as distemper in the humors is sickness of the body, so ignorance is sickness of the soul. Therefore not knowing whether the soul is immortal or not, let him seek a man well informed and good. Yet two classes of men profess to know this: infidels and Christians. Now there have been many very learned men among the infidels, but almost all of spotted life. Not to speak of other things, at least of empty glory, they have understood only natural things, which produce an obscure and infirm knowledge. But many Christians, unless I am mistaken, have known no less than they in natural philosophy: like Paul, Dionysius, Basil, Athanasius, Origen, and two Gregories, of Nazianzus and of Nyssa, Augustine, Jerome, Ambrose, Gregory and countless others; and besides a knowledge of natural things they have also had a knowledge of divinity. Which things, as Jerome says, "learned Plato did not know, and eloquent Demosthenes was ignorant of," and they led most spotless lives. But who except a madman would rather believe infidels thus ignorant than Christians so well endowed? And to me it makes faith firm that Augustine, in my opinion second to none in learning (for I do not judge him less than Plato or Aristotle), first hostile to the Christian name, having become so virtuous of life, writes in the end of the *City of God* that he had seen made visible by faith so many miracles, which shows a faith unlimited, inviolable, and most firm. And Pope Gregory also, comparable in learning and holiness with any man, adduces so many and such great things in his *Dialogues*, that all doubt is completely removed.

Wherefore we must assert that beyond doubt the soul is immortal. But we must not go the way the wise men of this age have gone, who, when they call themselves wise, have become fools. For whoever goes this way, I think, will waver always uncertain and wandering. Wherefore I believe that even though Plato wrote so many and such great things about the immortality of the soul, yet I think that he did not possess certainty. This I conjecture from the end of the *Apology*, for there it seems to be left in doubt. In the *Timaeus* also, when he was about to discuss the matter, he said that for him it would be enough if in so difficult a matter he should speak in probabilities. Wherefore, comparing everything he says, he seems to me to speak more as in opinion than in assertion. And it is his endeavor to make good citizens but not learned ones. Indeed, as says St. Thomas, in *Summa* ii a ii ae, question I, article 3, the act remains moral even with a false opinion. But those that go the way of the faithful remain firm and unshaken. This their contempt of riches, honors, pleasures, and all things worldly makes clear, and finally the martyr's crown, which they ardently strove after, and when striven for attained with the highest joy.

And therefore these are the things that seem to me must be said in this matter, yet always submitting myself in this and in other matters to the Apostolic See. Wherefore, etc.

The end has been put to this treatise by me, Peter, son of John Nicholas Pomponazzi of Mantua, the twenty-fourth day of the month of September, 1516.

At Bologna, in the fourth year of the Pontificate of Leo X. To the praise of the indivisible Trinity, etc.

NICCOLO MACHIAVELLI

Born in Florence, Italy, in 1469, Machiavelli had a career as a civil servant. After the overthrow of the republican regime and the return to power of the Medici, Machiavelli fell into deep disfavor. He spent his last years writing and in economic distress. He died in 1527.

Although Machiavelli wrote several important works in political theory and history, he is best known for his controversial book The Prince, *which he wrote to regain political favor. This book takes its place with Aristotle's* Politics *and the* Leviathan *of Hobbes as one of the classics of western political philosophy, a tradition with a variety of viewpoints, mostly anti-Machiavellian in their basic outlook, and continued by John*

Locke, Jean Jacques Rousseau, and John Dewey, among others. Political theory and political philosophy in the last half of the twentieth century have become overrun by quantitative methods, thereby rendering philosophical theory on political issues less prominent. This development is most unfortunate, for as a reading of Machiavelli will demonstrate, political wisdom cannot be confined to mere collection of data. Interpretations of The Prince *abound; it has been read as a satire on the Medici and, alternatively, as a masterpiece of cunning and amorality. Whatever the actual intention, the term "Machiavellian" refers to one who manipulates others for personal gain. The following selection reveals Machiavelli to be astute in his judgment of how to gain and maintain power. (Note that the last paragraph of the intriguing chapter on fortune is a cameo presentation of the male chauvinism that has unfortunately dominated the history of western culture.)*

From The Prince

CHAPTER XV

Of the Things for Which Men, and Especially Princes, Are Praised or Blamed

It now remains to be seen what are the methods and rules for a prince as regards his subjects and friends. And as I know that many have written of this, I fear that my writing about it may be deemed presumptuous, differing as I do, especially in this matter, from the opinions of others. But my intention being to write something of use to those who understand, it appears to me more proper to go to the real truth of the matter than to its imagination; and many have imagined republics and principalities which have never been seen or known to exist in reality; for how we live is so far removed from how we ought to live, that he who abandons what is done for what ought to be done, will rather learn to bring about his own ruin than his preservation. A man who wishes to make a profession of goodness in everything must necessarily come to grief among so many who are not good. Therefore it is necessary for a prince, who wishes to maintain himself, to learn how not to be good, and to use this knowledge and not use it, according to the necessity of the case.

Leaving on one side, then, those things which concern only an imaginary prince, and speaking of those that are real, I state that all men, and especially princes, who are placed at a greater height, are reputed for certain qualities which bring them either praise or blame. Thus one is considered liberal, another *misero* or miserly (using a Tuscan term, seeing that *avaro* with us still means one who is rapaciously acquisitive and *misero* one who makes grudging use of his own); one a free giver, another rapacious; one cruel, another merciful; one a breaker of his word, another trustworthy; one effeminate and pusillanimous, another fierce and high-spirited; one humane, another haughty; one lascivious, another chaste; one frank, another astute; one hard, another easy; one serious, another frivolous; one religious, another an unbeliever, and so on. I know that every one will admit that it would be highly praiseworthy in a prince to possess all the above-named qualities that are reputed good, but as they cannot all be possessed or observed, human conditions not permitting of it, it is necessary that he should be prudent enough to avoid the scandal of those vices which would lose him the state and guard himself if possible against those which will not lose it him, but if not able to, he can indulge them with less scruple. And yet he must not mind incurring the scandal of those vices,

---

From Niccolo Machiavelli, *The Prince,* translated by Luigi Ricci, revised by E. R. P. Vincent, *The Prince and the Discourses* (New York: Random House, 1950), pp. 56–66 and 91–94. Originally published by Oxford University Press in 1935. Reprinted by permission of Oxford University Press.

without which it would be difficult to save the state, for if one considers well, it will be found that some things which seem virtues would, if followed, lead to one's ruin, and some others which appear vices result in one's greater security and wellbeing.

CHAPTER XVI

Of Liberality and Niggardliness

Beginning now with the first qualities above named, I say that it would be well to be considered liberal; nevertheless liberality such as the world understands it will injure you, because if used virtuously and in the proper way, it will not be known, and you will incur the disgrace of the contrary vice. But one who wishes to obtain the reputation of liberality among men, must not omit every kind of sumptuous display, and to such an extent that a prince of this character will consume by such means all his resources, and will be at last compelled, if he wishes to maintain his name for liberality, to impose heavy taxes on his people, become extortionate, and do everything possible to obtain money. This will make his subjects begin to hate him, and he will be little esteemed being poor, so that having by this liberality injured many and benefited but few, he will feel the first little disturbance and be endangered by every peril. If he recognises this and wishes to change his system, he incurs at once the charge of niggardliness.

A prince, therefore, not being able to exercise this virtue of liberality without risk if it be known, must not, if he be prudent, object to be called miserly. In course of time he will be thought more liberal, when it is seen that by his parsimony his revenue is sufficient, that he can defend himself against those who make war on him, and undertake enterprises without burdening his people, so that he is really liberal to all those from whom he does not take, who are infinite in number, and niggardly to all to whom he does not give, who are few. In our times we have seen nothing great done except by those who have been esteemed niggardly; the others have all been ruined. Pope Julius II, although he had made use of a reputation for liberality in order to attain the papacy, did not seek to retain it afterwards, so that he might be able to wage war. The present King of France has carried on so many wars without imposing an extraordinary tax, because his extra expenses were covered by the parsimony he had so long practised. The present King of Spain, if he had been thought liberal, would not have engaged in and been successful in so many enterprises.

For these reasons a prince must care little for the reputation of being a miser, if he wishes to avoid robbing his subjects, if he wishes to be able to defend himself, to avoid becoming poor and contemptible, and not to be forced to become rapacious; this niggardliness is one of those vices which enable him to reign. If it is said that Cæsar attained the empire through liberality, and that many others have reached the highest positions through being liberal or being thought so, I would reply that you are either a prince already or else on the way to become one. In the first case, this liberality is harmful; in the second, it is certainly necessary to be considered liberal. Cæsar was one of those who wished to attain the mastery over Rome, but if after attaining it he had lived and had not moderated his expenses, he would have destroyed that empire. And should any one reply that there have been many princes, who have done great things with their armies, who have been thought extremely liberal, I would answer by saying that the prince may either spend his own wealth and that of his subjects or the wealth of others. In the first case he must be sparing, but for the rest he must not neglect to be very liberal. The liberality is very necessary to a prince who marches with his armies, and lives by plunder, sack and ransom, and is dealing with the wealth of others, for without it he would not be followed by his soldiers. And you may be very generous indeed with what is not the property of yourself or your subjects, as were Cyrus, Cæsar, and Alexander; for spending the wealth of others will not diminish your reputation, but increase it, only spending your own resources will injure you. There is nothing which destroys itself so much as liberality, for by using it you lose the power of using it, and become either poor and despicable, or, to escape poverty, rapacious and hated. And of all things that a prince must guard against, the most important are being despicable or hated, and liberality will lead you to one or other of these conditions. It is, therefore, wiser to have the name of a miser, which produces disgrace without hatred, than to incur of necessity the name of being rapacious, which produces both disgrace and hatred.

CHAPTER XVII

Of Cruelty and Clemency, and Whether It Is Better to Be Loved or Feared

Proceeding to the other qualities before named, I say that every prince must desire to be considered merciful and not cruel. He must, however, take care not to misuse this mercifulness. Cesare Borgia was considered cruel, but his cruelty had brought order to the Romagna, united it, and reduced it to peace and fealty. If this is considered well, it will be seen that he was really much more merciful than the Florentine people, who, to avoid the name of cruelty, allowed Pistoia to be destroyed. A prince, therefore, must not mind incurring the charge of cruelty for the purpose of keeping his subjects united and faithful; for, with a very few examples, he will be more merciful than those who, from excess of tenderness, allow disorders to arise, from whence spring bloodshed and rapine; for these as a rule injure the whole community, while the executions carried out by the prince injure only individuals. And of all princes, it is impossible for a new prince to escape the reputation of cruelty, new states being always full of dangers. Wherefore Virgil through the mouth of Dido says:

> Res dura, et regni novitas me talia cogunt
> Moliri, et late fines custode tueri.

Nevertheless, he must be cautious in believing and acting, and must not be afraid of his own shadow, and must proceed in a temperate manner with prudence and humanity, so that too much confidence does not render him incautious, and too much diffidence does not render him intolerant.

From this arises the question whether it is better to be loved more than feared, or feared more than loved. The reply is, that one ought to be both feared and loved, but as it is difficult for the two to go together, it is much safer to be feared than loved, if one of the two has to be wanting. For it may be said of men in general that they are ungrateful, voluble, dissemblers, anxious to avoid danger, and covetous of gain; as long as you benefit them, they are entirely yours; they offer you their blood, their goods, their life, and their children, as I have before said, when the necessity is remote; but when it approaches, they revolt. And the prince who has relied solely on their words, without making other preparations, is ruined; for the friendship which is gained by purchase and not through grandeur and nobility of spirit is bought but not secured, and at a pinch is not to be expended in your service. And men have less scruple in offending one who makes himself loved than one who makes himself feared; for love is held by a chain of obligation which, men being selfish, is broken whenever it serves their purpose; but fear is maintained by a dread of punishment which never fails.

Still, a prince should make himself feared in such a way that if he does not gain love, he at any rate avoids hatred: for fear and the absence of hatred may well go together, and will be always attained by one who abstains from interfering with the property of his citizens and subjects or with their women. And when he is obliged to take the life of any one, let him do so when there is a proper justification and manifest reason for it; but above all he must abstain from taking the property of others, for men forget more easily the death of their father than the loss of their patrimony. Then also pretexts for seizing property are never wanting, and one who begins to live by rapine will always find some reason for taking the goods of others, whereas causes for taking life are rarer and more fleeting.

But when the prince is with his army and has a large number of soldiers under his control, then it is extremely necessary that he should not mind being thought cruel; for without this reputation he could not keep an army united or disposed to any duty. Among the noteworthy actions of Hannibal is numbered this, that although he had an enormous army, composed of men of all nations and fighting in foreign countries, there never arose any dissension either among them or against the prince, either in good fortune or in bad. This could not be due to anything but his inhuman cruelty, which together with his infinite other virtues, made him always venerated and terrible in the sight of his soldiers, and without it his other virtues would not have sufficed to produce that effect. Thoughtless writers admire on the one hand his actions, and on the other blame the principal cause of them.

And that it is true that his other virtues would not have sufficed may be seen from the case of Scipio (famous not only in regard to his own times, but all times of which memory remains), whose armies rebelled against him in Spain, which arose from nothing but his excessive kindness, which allowed more licence to the soldiers than was consonant with military discipline. He was reproached with this in the senate by Fabius Maximus, who called him a corrupter of the Roman militia. Locri having been destroyed by one of Scipio's officers was not revenged by him, nor was the insolence of that officer punished, simply by reason of his easy nature; so much so, that some one wishing to excuse him in the senate, said that there were many men who knew rather how not to err, than how to correct the errors of others. This disposition would in time have tarnished the fame and glory of Scipio had he persevered in it under the empire, but living under the rule of the senate this harmful quality was not only concealed but became a glory to him.

I conclude, therefore, with regard to being feared and loved, that men love at their own free will, but fear at the will of the prince, and that a wise prince must rely on what is in his power and not on what is in the power of others, and he must only contrive to avoid incurring hatred, as has been explained.

CHAPTER XVIII

In What Way Princes Must Keep Faith

How laudable it is for a prince to keep good faith and live with integrity, and not with astuteness, every one knows. Still the experience of our times shows those princes to have done great things who have had little regard for good faith, and have been able by astuteness to confuse men's brains, and who have ultimately overcome those who have made loyalty their foundation.

You must know, then, that there are two methods of fighting, the one by law, the other by force: the first method is that of men, the second of beasts; but as the first method is often insufficient, one must have recourse to the second. It is therefore necessary for a prince to know well how to use both the beast and the man. This was covertly taught to rulers by ancient writers, who relate how Achilles and many others of those ancient princes were given to Chiron the centaur to be brought up and educated under his discipline. The parable of this semi-animal, semi-human teacher is meant to indicate that a prince must know how to use both natures, and that the one without the other is not durable.

A prince being thus obliged to know well how to act as a beast must imitate the fox and the lion, for the lion cannot protect himself from traps, and the fox cannot defend himself from wolves. One must therefore be a fox to recognise traps, and a lion to frighten wolves. Those that wish to be only lions do not understand this. Therefore, a prudent ruler ought not to keep faith when by so doing it would be against his interest, and when the reasons which made him bind himself no longer exist. If men were all good, this precept would not be a good one; but as they are bad, and would not observe their faith with you, so you are not bound to keep faith with them. Nor have legitimate grounds ever failed a prince who wished to show colourable excuse for the non-fulfillment of his promise. Of this one could furnish an infinite number of modern examples, and show how many times peace has been broken, and how many promises rendered worthless, by the faithlessness of princes, and those that have been best able to imitate the fox have succeeded best. But it is necessary to be able to disguise this character well, and to be a great feigner and dissembler; and men are so simple and so ready to obey present necessities, that one who deceives will always find those who allow themselves to be deceived.

I will only mention one modern instance. Alexander VI did nothing else but deceive men, he thought of nothing else, and found the occasion for it; no man was ever more able to give assurances, or affirmed things with stronger oaths, and no man observed them less; however, he always succeeded in his deceptions, as he well knew this aspect of things.

It is not, therefore, necessary for a prince to have all the above-named qualities, but it is very necessary to seem to have them. I would even be bold to say that to possess them and always to observe them is dangerous, but to appear to possess them is useful. Thus it is well to seem merciful, faithful, humane, sincere, religious, and also to be so; but you must have the mind so disposed that when it is needful to be otherwise you may be able to change to the opposite qualities. And it must be understood that a prince, and especially a new prince, cannot observe all those things which are considered good in men, being often obliged, in order to maintain the state, to act against faith, against charity, against humanity, and against religion. And, therefore, he must have a mind disposed to adapt itself according to the wind, and as the variations of fortune dictate, and, as I said before, not deviate from what is good, if possible, but be able to do evil if constrained.

A prince must take great care that nothing goes out of his mouth which is not full of the above-named five qualities, and, to see and hear him, he should seem to be all mercy, faith, integrity, humanity, and religion. And nothing is more necessary than to seem to have this last quality, for men in general judge more by the eyes than by the hands, for every one can see, but very few have to feel. Everybody sees what you appear to be, few feel what you are, and those few will not dare to oppose themselves to the many, who have the majesty of the state to defend them; and in the actions of men, and especially of princes, from which there is no appeal, the end justifies the means. Let a prince therefore aim at conquering and maintaining the state, and the means will always be judged honourable and praised by every one, for the vulgar is always taken by appearances and the issue of the event; and the world consists only of the vulgar, and the few who are not vulgar are isolated when the many have a rallying point in the prince. A certain prince of the present time, whom it is well not to name, never does anything but preach peace and good faith, but he is really a great enemy to both, and either of them, had he observed them, would have lost him state or reputation on many occasions.

CHAPTER XXV

How Much Fortune Can Do in Human Affairs and How It May Be Opposed

It is not unknown to me how many have been and are of opinion that worldly events are so governed by fortune and by God, that men cannot by their prudence change them, and that on the contrary there is no remedy whatever, and for this they may judge it to be useless to toil much about them, but let things be ruled by chance. This opinion has been more held in our day, from the great changes that have been seen, and are daily seen, beyond every human conjecture. When I think about them, at times I am partly inclined to share this opinion. Nevertheless, that our free-will may not be altogether extinguished, I think it may be true that fortune is the ruler of half our actions, but that she allows the other half or thereabouts to be governed by us. I would compare her to an impetuous river that, when turbulent, inundates the plains, casts down trees and buildings, removes earth from this side and places it on the other; every one flees before it, and everything yields to its fury without being able to oppose it; and yet though it is of such a kind, still when it is quiet, men can make provision against it by dykes and banks, so that when it rises it will either go into a canal or its rush will not be so wild and dangerous. So it is with fortune, which shows her power where no measures have been taken to resist her, and directs her fury where she knows that no dykes or barriers have been made to hold her. And if you regard Italy, which has been the seat of these changes, and who has given the impulse to them, you will see her to be a country without dykes or banks of any kind. If she had been protected by proper measures, like Germany, Spain, and France, this inundation would not have caused the great changes that it has, or would not have happened at all.

This must suffice as regards opposition to fortune in general. But limiting myself more to particular cases, I would point out how one sees a certain prince to-day fortunate and to-morrow ruined, without seeing that he has changed in character or otherwise. I believe this arises in the first place from the causes that we have already discussed at length; that is to say, because the prince who bases himself entirely on fortune is ruined when fortune changes. I also believe that he is happy whose mode of procedure accords with the needs of the times, and similarly he is unfortunate whose mode of procedure is opposed to the times. For one sees that men in those things which lead them to the aim that each one has in view, namely, glory and riches, proceed in various ways; one with circumspection, another with impetuosity, one by violence, another by cunning, one with patience, another with the reverse; and each by these diverse ways may arrive at his aim. One sees also two cautious men, one of whom succeeds in his designs, and the other not, and in the same way two men succeed equally by different methods, one being cautious, the other impetuous, which arises only from the nature of the times, which does or does not conform to their method of procedure. From this it results, as I have said, that two men, acting differently, attain the same effect, and of two others acting in the same way, one attains his goal and not the other. On this depend also the changes in prosperity, for if it happens that time and circumstances are favourable to one who acts with caution and prudence he will be successful, but if time and circumstances change he will be ruined, because he does not change his mode of procedure. No man is found so prudent as to be able to adapt himself to this, either because he cannot deviate from that to which his nature disposes him, or else because having always prospered by walking in one path, he cannot persuade himself that it is well to leave it; and therefore the cautious man, when it is time to act suddenly, does not know how to do so and is consequently ruined, for if one could change one's nature with time and circumstances, fortune would never change.

Pope Julius II acted impetuously in everything he did and found the times and conditions so in conformity with that mode of procedure, that he always obtained a good result. Consider the first war that he made against Bologna while Messer Giovanni Bentivogli was still living. The Venetians were not pleased with it, neither was the King of Spain. France was conferring with him over the enterprise, notwithstanding which, owing to his fierce and impetuous disposition, he engaged personally in the expedition. This move caused both Spain and the Venetians to halt and hesitate, the latter through fear, the former through the desire to recover the entire kingdom of Naples. On the other hand, he engaged with him the King of France, because seeing him make this move and desiring his friendship in order to put down the Venetians, that king judged that he could not refuse him his troops without manifest injury. Thus Julius by his impetuous move achieved what no other pontiff with the utmost human prudence would have succeeded in doing, because, if he had waited till all arrangements had been made and everything settled before leaving Rome, as any other pontiff would have done, it would never have succeeded. For the King of France would have found a thousand excuses, and the others would have inspired him with a thousand fears. I will omit his other actions, which were all of this kind and which all succeeded well, and the shortness of his life did not suffer him to experience the contrary, for had times followed in which it was necessary to act with caution, his ruin would have resulted, for he would never have deviated from these methods to which his nature disposed him. . . .

I conclude then that fortune varying and men remaining fixed in their ways, they are successful so long as these ways conform to circumstances, but when they are opposed then they are unsuccessful. I certainly think that it is better to be impetuous than cautious, for fortune is a woman, and it is necessary, if you wish to master her, to conquer her by force; and it can be seen that she lets herself be overcome by the bold rather than by those who proceed coldly. And therefore, like a woman, she is always a friend to the young, because they are less cautious, fiercer, and master her with greater audacity.

SUGGESTIONS FOR FURTHER READING

Burckhardt, Jacob. *The Civilization of the Renaissance in Italy.* 2 vols. New York: Harper Torchbooks, 1958.

Cassirer, Ernst. *The Individual and the Cosmos in Renaissance Philosophy.* New York: Harper Torchbooks, 1963.

Fallico, Arturo B., and Herman Shapiro. *Renaissance Philosophy.* 2 vols. New York: Modern Library, 1967, 1969.

Jaspers, Karl. *Anselm and Nicholas of Cusa.* Hannah Arendt, ed. Ralph Manheim, trans. New York: Harcourt Brace Jovanovich, 1966.

Kristeller, Paul Oskar. *Eight Philosophers of the Italian Renaissance.* Stanford: Stanford University Press, 1964.

Kristeller, Paul Oskar. *Renaissance Thought: The Classic, Scholastic and Humanist Strains.* New York: Harper Torchbooks, 1961.

Mahoney, Edward P., ed. *Philosophy and Humanism.* New York: Columbia University Press, 1976.

Pater, Walter. *The Renaissance.* New York: New American Library, 1959.

Ross, James Bruce, and Mary Martin McLaughlin. *The Portable Renaissance Reader.* New York: Viking, 1953.

Trinkaus, Charles Edward. *In Our Image and Likeness: Humanity and Divinity in Italian Humanist Thought.* 2 vols. Chicago: University of Chicago Press, 1970.

von Martin, Alfred. *Sociology of the Renaissance.* New York: Harper Torchbooks, 1963.

The Reformation: Salvation by Faith Alone

As the sixteenth century opened, the vaunted power of the Roman Church seemed impervious to major change. True, earlier movements of protest such as the Hussites in Bohemia and the followers of John Wycliffe in England had given cause for concern, but they were quickly suppressed. Yet, the vulnerability of the Church to movements of protest became apparent early in the sixteenth century, and by 1648, with the end of the religious wars, Europe was as Protestant as it was Catholic.

The reasons for this startling development are very complex; they involve not only theological and philosophical conflicts but also profound shifts in economic and political strategies. In sociological terms, the cause of the Reformation lay in the flaunted opulence of the Roman Church, unfortunately combined with ecclesiastical corruption. This corruption was manifest in the selling of church offices, simony, and the use of indulgences to reward vain and wealthy donors to the Church. Indulgences were intended to remit punishment for sin; theologically, they could not be awarded to anyone not in the state of grace. Unfortunately, this requirement was frequently bypassed such that the immoral wealthy seemed to receive undeserved spiritual reward. Infuriated at this situation, an Augustinian friar, Martin Luther, issued a protest. In 1517, he posted 95 contentious theses on the door of the Castle Church in Wittenberg, Germany.

The Roman Church did not respond to this protest with the seriousness it deserved. Furthermore, the Church underestimated the broad support for Luther's position. The eventual result was a series of conflicts on every level, including political and military. An extraordinary number of variations of Luther's radical theology soon gave rise to many Protestant sects, decisively changing the religious map of Europe. The Roman Church finally responded at the Council of Trent, which met periodically from 1545 to 1563. Abuses were corrected and Catholic doctrine was clarified, but it was too late to stem the tide of a new approach to Christianity. The significance of the Reformation for philosophy is clear. First, Luther's view of salvation (justification in Protestant terms) gave to the individual person a profound sense of personal liberation, independent of the authority of the Church and the priest as the intercessory with God *(mediator Dei)*. Second, justification took place in the present rather than after death, as in the tradition of medieval Christendom. These two factors intensified both the social and political importance of the Reformation, for they awarded to the individual a sense of personal importance which was in time to translate into political rights. After the early seventeenth century, virtually every major philosopher until the twentieth century proceeded from a Protestant rather than a Roman Catholic experience.

MARTIN LUTHER

Born in Eisleben, Saxony, in 1483, Martin Luther became an Augustinian friar. During his early years he suffered from extreme scruples about his spiritual worth and lived an intense, self-deprecating religious life. Upon visiting Rome in 1510, Luther was scandalized by the lack of spiritual conduct among leaders of the Church. A careful reading of the Epistles of St. Paul, coupled with the controversy over illicit indulgences, led him to post his theses in 1517. When efforts at reconciliation failed, Luther widened his critique of the Church, and he was excommunicated in 1521. Subsequent years found him in conflict with the Church, with philosophy, especially that of Aristotle and Aquinas, with other reformers who departed from his position, and finally with the peasants, whom he refused to support in their revolt against the Princes in 1524 to 1525. He died in Eisleben in 1546.

Luther's main doctrines constituted an obvious threat to the medieval Church. He denied the role of the priest as the mediator between God and the believer, and he stressed that justification (salvation) was due to faith, thereby obviating the equivalent importance of "good works." In theological terms, this position of Luther began the distinction between the experience of justification as an encounter with the grace of God through Jesus and the attempt to save oneself by doing good works, such as visiting the sick, caring for the poor, and grieving for the dead—acts of free will in which the person was responsible for his or her decisions. The medieval Church stipulated that if one were to be in the state of grace, by virtue of receiving one of the seven sacraments (Baptism, Penance, Holy Eucharist, Confirmation, Marriage, Holy Orders, or Extreme Unction as given to the dying), then a person could obtain further grace for doing good works. For Luther, however, salvation was predestined by the will of God. The possibility of salvation was circumscribed by the acknowledgment of sin and the direct appeal to God for forgiveness. The implication was clear; the Church and its priests were no longer necessary for salvation, and European Christianity was profoundly changed.

Preface to the Complete Edition of Luther's Latin Writings

WITTENBERG, 1545

Martin Luther wishes the sincere reader salvation!

For a long time I strenuously resisted those who wanted my books, or more correctly my confused lucubrations, published. I did not want the labors of the ancients to be buried by my new works and the reader kept from reading them. Then, too, by God's

Martin Luther, "Preface to the Complete Edition of Luther's Latin Writings," trans. Lewis W. Spitz, in John Dillenberger, ed., *Martin Luther: Selections from His Writings* (Garden City, New York: Doubleday & Co., 1961), pp. 3–12, originally found in *Luther's Works*, vol. 34, *Career of the Reformer: IV*, edited and translated by Lewis W. Spitz (Philadelphia: Muhlenberg Press, 1960), pp. 327–338,

Martin Luther, by Lucas Cranach. Luther was the founder of the Protestant Reformation in the 16th century. (Germanisches Nationalmuseum)

grace a great many systematic books now exist, among which the *Loci communes* of Philip excel, with which a theologian and a bishop can be beautifully and abundantly prepared to be mighty in preaching the doctrine of piety, especially since the Holy Bible itself can now be had in nearly every language. But my books, as it happened, yes, as the lack of order in which the events transpired made it necessary, are accordingly crude and disordered chaos, which is now not easy to arrange even for me.

Persuaded by these reasons, I wished that all my books were buried in perpetual oblivion, so that there might be room for better ones. But the boldness and bothersome perseverance of others daily filled my ears with complaints that it would come to pass, that if I did not permit their publication in my lifetime, men wholly ignorant of the causes and the time of the events would nevertheless most certainly publish them, and so out of one confusion many would arise. Their boldness, I say, prevailed and so I permitted them to be published. At the same time the wish and command of our most illustrious Prince, Elector, etc., John Frederick was added. He commanded, yes, compelled the printers not only to print, but to speed up the publication.

But above all else, I beg the sincere reader, and I beg for the sake of our Lord Jesus Christ himself, to read those things judiciously, yes, with great commiseration. May he be mindful of the fact that I was once a monk and a most enthusiastic papist when I bagan that cause. I was so drunk, yes, submerged in the pope's dogmas, that I would have been ready to murder all, if I could have, or to co-operate willingly with the murderers of all who would take but a syllable from obedience to the pope. So great a Saul was I, as are many to this day. I was not such a lump of frigid ice in defending the papacy as Eck and his like were, who appeared to me actually to defend the pope more for their own belly's sake than to pursue the matter seriously. To me, indeed, they seem to laugh at the pope to this day, like Epicureans! I pursued the matter with all seriousness, as one, who in dread of the last day, nevertheless from the depth of my heart wanted to be saved.

So you will find how much and what important matters I humbly conceded to the pope in my earlier writings, which I later and now hold and execrate as the worst blasphemies and abomination. You will, therefore, sincere reader, ascribe this error, or, as they slander, contradiction, to the time and my inexperience. At first I was all alone and certainly very inept and unskilled in conducting such great affairs. For I got into these turmoils by accident and not by will or intention. I call upon God himself as witness.

Hence, when in the year 1517 indulgences were sold (I wanted to say promoted) in these regions for most shameful gain—I was then a preacher, a young doctor of theology, so to speak—and I began to dissuade the people and to urge them not to listen to the clamors of the indulgence hawkers; they had better things to do. I certainly thought that in this case I should have a protector in the pope, on whose trustworthiness I then leaned strongly, for in his decrees he most clearly damned the immoderation of the quaestors, as he called the indulgence preachers.

Soon afterward I wrote two letters, one to Albrecht, the archbishop of Mainz, who got half of the money from the indulgences, the pope the other half—something I did not know at the time—the other to the ordinary (as they call them) Jerome, the bishop of Brandenburg. I begged them to stop the shameless blasphemy of the quaestors. But the poor little brother was despised. Despised, I published the *Theses* and at the same time a German *Sermon on Indulgences,* shortly thereafter also the *Explanations,* in which, to the pope's honor, I developed the idea that indulgences should indeed not be condemned, but that good works of love should be preferred to them.

This was demolishing heaven and consuming the earth with fire. I am accused by the pope, am cited to Rome, and the whole papacy rises up against me alone. All this happened in the year 1518, when Maximilian held the diet at Augsburg. In it, Cardinal Cajetan served as the pope's Lateran legate. The most illustrious Duke Frederick of Saxony, Elector Prince, approached him on my behalf and brought it about that I was not compelled to go to Rome, but that he himself should summon me to examine and compose the matter. Soon the diet adjourned.

The Germans in the meantime, all tired of suffering the pillagings, traffickings, and endless impostures of Roman rascals, awaited with bated breath the outcome of so great a matter, which no one before, neither bishop nor theologian, had dared to touch. In any case that popular breeze favored me, because those practices and "Romanations," with which they had filled and tired the whole earth, were already hateful to all.

So I came to Augsburg, afoot and poor, supplied with food and letters of commendation from Prince Frederick to the senate and to certain good men. I was there three days before I went to the cardinal, though he cited me day by day through a certain orator, for those excellent men forbade and dissuaded me most strenuously, not to go to the cardinal without a safe conduct from the emperor. The orator was rather troublesome to me, urging that if I should only revoke, everything would be all right! But as great as the wrong, so long is the detour to its correction.

Finally, on the third day he came demanding to know why I did not come to the cardinal, who expected me most benignly. I replied that I had to respect the advice of those very fine men to whom I had been commended by Prince Frederick, but it was their advice by no means to go to the cardinal without the emperor's protection or safe conduct. Having obtained this (but they took action on the part of the imperial senate to obtain it), I would come at once. At this point he blew up. "What?" he said, "Do you suppose Prince Frederick will take up arms for your sake?" I said, "This I do not at all desire." And where will you stay?" I replied, "Under heaven." Then he, "If you had the pope and the cardinals in your power, what would you do?" "I would," said I, "show them all respect and honor." Thereupon he, wagging his finger with an Italian gesture, said, "Hem!" And so he left, nor did he return.

On that day the imperial senate informed the cardinal that the emperor's protection or a safe conduct had been granted me and admonished him that he should not design anything too severe against me. He is said to have replied, "It is well. I shall nevertheless do whatever my duty demands." These things were the start of that tumult. The rest can be learned from the accounts included later.

Master Philip Melanchthon had already been called here that same year by Prince Frederick to teach Greek literature, doubtless so that I should have an associate in the work of theology. His works attest sufficiently what the Lord has performed through this instrument, not only in literature but also in theology, though Satan is mad and all his adherents.

Maximilian died, in the following year, '19, in February, and according to the law of the empire Duke Frederick was made deputy. Thereupon the storm ceased to rage a bit, and gradually contempt of excommunication or papal thunderbolts arose. For when Eck and Caraccioli brought a bull from Rome condemning Luther and revealed it, the former here, the latter there to Duke Frederick, who was at Cologne at the time together with other princes in order to meet Charles who had been recently elected, Frederick was most indignant. He reproved that papal rascal with great courage and constancy, because in his absence he and Eck had disturbed his and his brother John's dominion. He jarred them so magnificently that they left him in shame and disgrace. The prince, endowed with incredible insight, caught on to the devices of the Roman Curia and knew how to deal with them in a becoming manner, for he had a keen nose and smelled more and farther than the Romanists could hope or fear.

Hence they refrained from putting him to a test. For he did not dignify with the least respect the Rose, which they call "golden," sent him that same year by Leo X, indeed ridiculed it. So the Romanists were forced to despair of their attempts to deceive so great a prince. The gospel advanced happily under the shadow of that prince and was widely propagated. His authority influenced very many, for since he was a very wise and most keen-sighted prince, he could incur the suspicion only among the hateful that he wanted to nourish and protect heresy and heretics. This did the papacy great harm.

That same year the Leipzig debate was held, to which Eck had challenged us two, Karlstadt and me. But I could not, in spite of all my letters, get a safe conduct from Duke George. Accordingly, I came to Leipzig not as a prospective debater, but as a spectator under the safe conduct granted to Karlstadt. Who stood in my way I do not know, for till then Duke George was not against me. This I know for certain.

Here Eck came to me in my lodging and said he had heard that I refused to debate. I replied, "How can I debate, since I cannot get a safe conduct from Duke George?" "If I cannot debate with you," he said, "neither do I want to with Karlstadt, for I have come here on your account. What if I obtain a safe conduct for you? Would you then debate with me?" "Obtain," said I, "and it shall be." He left and soon a safe conduct was given me too and the opportunity to debate.

Eck did this because he discerned the certain glory that was set before him on account of my proposition in which I denied that the pope is the head of the church by divine right. Here a wide field was open to him and a supreme occasion to flatter in praiseworthy manner the pope and to merit his favor, also to ruin me with hate and envy. He did this vigorously throughout the entire debate. But he neither proved his own position nor refuted mine, so that even Duke George said to Eck and me at the morning meal, "Whether he be pope by human or divine right, yet he is pope." He would in no case have said this had he not been influenced by the arguments, but would have approved of Eck only.

Here, in my case, you may also see how hard it is to struggle out of and emerge from errors which have been confirmed by the example of the whole world and have by long habit become a part of nature, as it were. How true is the proverb, "It is hard to give up the accustomed," and, "Custom is second nature." How truly Augustine says, "If one does not resist custom, it becomes a necessity." I had then already read and taught the sacred Scriptures most diligently privately and publicly for seven years, so that I knew them nearly all by memory. I had also acquired the beginning of the knowledge of Christ and faith in him, i.e., not by works but by faith in Christ are we made righteous and saved. Finally, regarding that of which I speak, I had already defended the proposition publicly that the pope is not the head of the church by divine right. Nevertheless, I did not draw the conclusion, namely, that the pope must be of the devil. For what is not of God must of necessity be of the devil.

So absorbed was I, as I have said, by the example and the title of the holy church as well as my own habit, that I conceded human right to the pope, which nevertheless, unless it is founded on divine authority, is a diabolical lie. For we obey parents and magistrates not because they themselves command it, but because it is God's will, I Peter 3 [2:13]. For that reason I can bear with a less hateful spirit those who cling too pertinaciously to the papacy, particularly those who have not read the sacred Scriptures, or also the profane, since I, who read the sacred Scriptures most diligently so many years, still cling to it so tenaciously.

In the year 1519, Leo X, as I have said, sent the Rose with Karl von Miltitz, who urged me profusely to be reconciled with the pope. He had seventy apostolic briefs that if Prince Frederick would turn me over to him, as the pope requested by means of the Rose, he should tack one up in each city and so transfer me safely to Rome. But he betrayed the counsel of his heart toward me when he said, "O Martin, I believed you were some aged theologian who, sitting behind the stove, disputed thus with himself; now I see you are still young and strong. If I had twenty-five thousand armed men, I do not believe I could take you to Rome, for I have sounded out the people's mind all along the way to learn what they thought of you. Behold, where I found one standing for the pope, three stood for you against the pope." But that was ridiculous! He had also asked simple little women and girls in the hostelries, what they thought of the Roman chair. Ignorant of this term and thinking of a domestic chair, they replied, "How can we know what kind of chairs you have in Rome, wood or stone?"

Therefore he begged me to seek the things which

made for peace. He would put forth every effort to have the pope do the same. I also promised everything abundantly. Whatever I could do with a good conscience with respect to the truth, I would do most promptly. I, too, desired and was eager for peace. Having been drawn into these disturbances by force and driven by necessity, I had done all I did: the guilt was not mine.

But he had summoned Johann Tetzel of the preaching order, the primary author of this tragedy, and had with verbose threats from the pope so broken the man, till then so terrible to all, a fearless crier, that from that time on he wasted away and was finally consumed by illness of mind. When I found this out before his death, I comforted him with a letter, written benignly, asking him to be of good cheer and not to fear my memory. But perhaps he succumbed a victim of his conscience and of the pope's indignation.

Karl von Miltitz was regarded as vain and his advice as vain. But, in my opinion, if the man at Mainz had from the start, when I admonished him, and, finally, if the pope, before he condemned me unheard and raged with his bulls, had taken this advice, which Karl took although too late, and had at once quenched Tetzel's fury, the matter would not have come to so great a tumult. The entire guilt belongs to the one at Mainz, whose smartness and cleverness fooled him, with which he wanted to suppress my doctrine and have his money, acquired by the indulgences, saved. Now counsels are sought in vain; in vain efforts are made. The Lord has awakened and stands to judge the people. Though they could kill us, they still do not have what they want, yes, have less than they have, while we live in safety. This some of them who are not entirely of a dull nose smell quite enough.

Meanwhile, I had already during that year returned to interpret the Psalter anew. I had confidence in the fact that I was more skilful, after I had lectured in the university on St. Paul's epistles to the Romans, to the Galatians, and the one to the Hebrews. I had indeed been captivated with an extraordinary ardor for understanding Paul in the Epistle to the Romans. But up till then it was not the cold blood about the heart, but a single word in Chapter 1 [:17], "In it the righteousness of God is revealed," that had stood in my way. For I hated that word "righteousness of God," which, according to the use and custom of all the teachers, I had been taught to understand philosophically regarding the formal or active righteousness, as they called it, with which God is righteous and punishes the unrighteous sinner.

Though I lived as a monk without reproach, I felt that I was a sinner before God with an extremely disturbed conscience. I could not believe that he was placated by my satisfaction. I did not love, yes, I hated the righteous God who punishes sinners, and secretly, if not blasphemously, certainly murmuring greatly, I was angry with God, and said, "As if, indeed, it is not enough, that miserable sinners, eternally lost through original sin, are crushed by every kind of calamity by the law of the decalogue, without having God add pain to pain by the gospel and also by the gospel threatening us with his righteousness and wrath!" Thus I raged with a fierce and troubled conscience. Nevertheless, I beat importunately upon Paul at that place, most ardently desiring to know what St. Paul wanted.

At last, by the mercy of God, meditating day and night, I gave heed to the context of the words, namely, "In it the righteousness of God is revealed, as it is written, 'He who through faith is righteous shall live.'" There I began to understand that the righteousness of God is that by which the righteous lives by a gift of God, namely by faith. And this is the meaning: the righteousness of God is revealed by the gospel, namely, the passive righteousness with which merciful God justifies us by faith, as it is written, "He who through faith is righteous shall live." Here I felt that I was altogether born again and had entered paradise itself through open gates. There a totally other face of the entire Scripture showed itself to me. Thereupon I ran through the Scriptures from memory. I also found in other terms an analogy, as, the work of God, that is, what God does in us, the power of God, with which he makes us strong, the wisdom of God, with which he makes us wise, the strength of God, the salvation of God, the glory of God.

And I extolled my sweetest word with a love as great as the hatred with which I had before hated the word "righteousness of God." Thus that place in Paul was for me truly the gate to paradise. Later I read Augustine's *The Spirit and the Letter*, where contrary to hope I found that he, too, interpreted God's righteousness in a similar way, as the righteousness with which God clothes us when he justifies us. Although this was heretofore said imperfectly and he did not explain all things concerning imputation clearly, it nevertheless was pleasing that God's righteousness with which we are justified was taught. Armed more fully with these thoughts, I began a second time to interpret the Psalter. And the work would have grown into a large commentary, if I had not again been compelled to leave the work begun, because Emperor Charles V in the following year convened the diet at Worms.

I relate these things, good reader, so that, if you are a reader of my puny works, you may keep in mind, that, as I said above, I was all alone and one of those who, as Augustine says of himself, have become proficient by writing and teaching. I was not one of those who from nothing suddenly become the topmost, though they are nothing, neither have labored, nor been tempted, nor become experienced, but have with one look at the Scriptures exhausted their entire spirit.

To this point, to the year 1520 and 21, the indulgence matter proceeded. Upon that followed the sacramentarian and the Anabaptist affairs. Regarding these a preface shall be written to other tomes, if I live.

Farewell in the Lord, reader, and pray for the growth of the Word against Satan. Strong and evil, now also very furious and savage, he knows his time is short and the kingdom of his pope is in danger. But may God confirm in us what he has accomplished and perfect his work which he began in us, to his glory, Amen. March 5, in the year 1545.

The Ninety-Five Theses

Out of love and concern for the truth, and with the object of eliciting it, the following heads will be the subject of a public discussion at Wittenberg under the presidency of the reverend father, Martin Luther, Augustinian, Master of Arts and Sacred Theology, and duly appointed Lecturer on these subjects in that place. He requests that whoever cannot be present personally to debate the matter orally will do so in absence in writing.

1. When our Lord and Master, Jesus Christ, said "Repent," He called for the entire life of believers to be one of penitence.
2. The word cannot be properly understood as referring to the sacrament of penance, i.e., confession and satisfaction, as administered by the clergy.
3. Yet its meaning is not restricted to penitence in one's heart; for such penitence is null unless it produces outward signs in various mortifications of the flesh.
4. As long as hatred of self abides (i.e., true inward penitence) the penalty of sin abides, viz., until we enter the kingdom of heaven.
5. The pope has neither the will nor the power to remit any penalties beyond those imposed either at his own discretion or by canon law.
6. The pope himself cannot remit guilt, but only declare and confirm that it has been remitted by God; or, at most, he can remit it in cases reserved to his discretion. Except for these cases, the guilt remains untouched.
7. God never remits guilt to anyone without, at the same time, making him humbly submissive to the priest, His representative.

Martin Luther, "The Ninety-Five Theses," John Dillenberger, ed., translated by Bertram Lee Woolf, in *Martin Luther: Selections from his Writings* (Garden City, New York: Doubleday, 1961), pp. 490–500. Originally found in *The Reformation Writings of Martin Luther*, vol. I, *The Basis of the Protestant Reformation*, translated and edited by Bertram Lee Woolf (London: Lutterworth Press, 1953), pp. 32–42. Reprinted by permission of Lutterworth Press.

8. The penitential canons apply only to men who are still alive, and, according to the canons themselves, none applies to the dead.

9. Accordingly, the Holy Spirit, acting in the person of the pope, manifests grace to us, by the fact that the papal regulations always cease to apply at death, or in any hard case.

10. It is a wrongful act, due to ignorance, when priests retain the canonical penalties on the dead in purgatory.

11. When canonical penalties were changed and made to apply to purgatory, surely it would seem that tares were sown while the bishops were asleep.

12. In former days, the canonical penalties were imposed, not after, but before absolution was pronounced; and were intended to be tests of true contrition.

13. Death puts an end to all the claims of the church; even the dying are already dead to the canon laws, and are no longer bound by them.

14. Defective piety or love in a dying person is necessarily accompanied by great fear, which is greatest where the piety or love is least.

15. This fear or horror is sufficient in itself, whatever else might be said, to constitute the pain of purgatory, since it approaches very closely to the horror of despair.

16. There seems to be the same difference between hell, purgatory, and heaven as between despair, uncertainty, and assurance.

17. Of a truth, the pains of souls in purgatory ought to be abated, and charity ought to be proportionately increased.

18. Moreover, it does not seem proved, on any grounds of reason or Scripture, that these souls are outside the state of merit, or unable to grow in grace;

19. Nor does it seem proved to be always the case that they are certain and assured of salvation, even if we are very certain of it ourselves.

20. Therefore the pope, in speaking of the plenary remission of all penalties, does not mean "all" in the strict sense, but only those imposed by himself.

21. Hence those who preach indulgences are in error when they say that a man is absolved and saved from every penalty by the pope's indulgences;

22. Indeed, he cannot remit to souls in purgatory and penalty which canon law declares should be suffered in the present life.

23. If plenary remission could be granted to anyone at all, it would be only in the cases of the most perfect, i.e., to very few.

24. It must therefore be the case that the major part of the people are deceived by that indiscriminate and high-sounding promise of relief from penalty.

25. The same power as the pope exercises in general over purgatory is exercised in particular by every single bishop in his bishopric and priest in his parish.

26. The pope does excellently when he grants remission to the souls in purgatory on account of intercessions made on their behalf, and not by the power of the keys (which he cannot exercise for them).

Henry VIII, 1542, by Hans Holbein. Henry VIII was awarded a papal honor as defender of the faith against the Lutheran Reformation. Due to marital problems, he then broke with the Roman Church and began the Anglican or English Catholic Church, placing himself at its head. (George Howard Collection, Castle Howard)

27. There is no divine authority for preaching that the soul flies out of purgatory immediately the money clinks in the bottom of the chest.

28. It is certainly possible that when the money clinks in the bottom of the chest avarice and greed increase; but when the church offers intercession, all depends on the will of God.

29. Who knows whether all souls in purgatory wish to be redeemed in view of what is said of St. Severinus and St. Paschal?

30. No one is sure of the reality of his own contrition, much less of receiving plenary forgiveness.

31. One who *bona fide* buys indulgences is as rare as a *bona fide* penitent man, i.e., very rare indeed.

32. All those who believe themselves certain of their own salvation by means of letters of indulgence, will be eternally damned, together with their teachers.

Sir Thomas More, by Hans Holbein. Churchman and statesman, More was beheaded because he refused to acknowledge the authority of Henry VIII rather than the authority of the Church of Rome. (The Frick Collection)

33. We should be most carefully on our guard against those who say that the papal indulgences are an inestimable divine gift, and that a man is reconciled to God by them.

34. For the grace conveyed by these indulgences relates simply to the penalties of the sacramental "satisfactions" decreed merely by man.

35. It is not in accordance with Christian doctrine to preach and teach that those who buy off souls, or purchase confessional licences, have no need to repent of their own sins.

36. Any Christian whatsoever, who is truly repentant, enjoys plenary remission from penalty and guilt, and this is given him without letters of indulgence.

37. Any true Christian whatsover, living or dead, participates in all the benefits of Christ and the Church; and this participation is granted to him by God without letters of indulgence.

38. Yet the pope's remission and dispensation are in no way to be despised, for, as already said, they proclaim the divine remission.

39. It is very difficult, even for the most learned theologians, to extol to the people the great bounty contained in the indulgences, while, at the same time, praising contrition as a virtue.

40. A truly contrite sinner seeks out, and loves to pay, the penalties of his sins; whereas the very multitude of indulgences dulls men's consciences, and tends to make them hate the penalties.

41. Papal indulgences should only be preached with caution; lest people gain a wrong understanding, and think that they are preferable to other good works: those of love.

42. Christians should be taught that the pope does not at all intend that the purchase of indulgences should be understood as at all comparable with works of mercy.

43. Christians should be taught that one who gives to the poor, or lends to the needy, does a better action than if he purchases indulgences;

44. Because, by works of love, love grows and a man becomes a better man; whereas, by indulgences, he does not become a better man, but only escapes certain penalties.

45. Christians should be taught that he who sees a needy person, but passes him by although he gives money for indulgences, gains no benefit from the pope's pardon, but only incurs the wrath of God.

46. Christians should be taught that, unless they have more than they need, they are bound to retain

what is necessary for the upkeep of their home, and should in no way squander it on indulgences.

47. Christians should be taught that they purchase indulgences voluntarily, and are not under obligation to do so.

48. Christians should be taught that, in granting indulgences, the pope has more need, and more desire, for devout prayer on his own behalf than for ready money.

49. Christians should be taught that the pope's indulgences are useful only if one does not rely on them, but most harmful if one loses the fear of God through them.

50. Christians should be taught that, if the pope knew the exactions of the indulgence-preachers, he would rather the church of St. Peter were reduced to ashes than be built with the skin, flesh, and bones of his sheep.

51. Christians should be taught that the pope would be willing, as he ought if necessity should arise, to sell the church of St. Peter, and give, too, his own money to many of those from whom the pardon-merchants conjure money.

52. It is vain to rely on salvation by letters of indulgence, even if the commissary, or indeed the pope himself, were to pledge his own soul for their validity.

53. Those are enemies of Christ and the pope who forbid the word of God to be preached at all in some churches, in order that indulgences may be preached in others.

54. The word of God suffers injury if, in the same sermon, an equal or longer time is devoted to indulgences than to that word.

55. The pope cannot help taking the view that if indulgences (very small matters) are celebrated by one bell, one pageant, or one ceremony, the gospel (a very great matter) should be preached to the accompaniment of a hundred bells, a hundred processions, a hundred ceremonies.

56. The treasures of the church, out of which the pope dispenses indulgences, are not sufficiently spoken of or known among the people of Christ.

57. That these treasures are not temporal is clear from the fact that many of the merchants do not grant them freely, but only collect them;

58. Nor are they the merits of Christ and the saints, because, even apart from the pope, these merits are always working grace in the inner man, and working the cross, death, and hell in the outer man.

59. St. Laurence said that the poor were the treasures of the church, but he used the term in accordance with the custom of his own time.

60. We do not speak rashly in saying that the treasures of the church are the keys of the church, and are bestowed by the merits of Christ;

61. For it is clear that the power of the pope suffices, by itself, for the remission of penalties and reserved cases.

62. The true treasure of the church is the Holy Gospel of the glory and the grace of God.

63. It is right to regard this treasure as most odious, for it makes the first to be the last.

64. On the other hand, the treasure of indulgences is most acceptable, for it makes the last to be the first.

65. Therefore the treasures of the gospel are nets which, in former times, they used to fish for men of wealth.

66. The treasures of the indulgences are the nets to-day which they use to fish for men of wealth.

67. The indulgences, which the merchants extol as the greatest of favours, are seen to be, in fact, a favourite means for money-getting;

68. Nevertheless, they are not to be compared with the grace of God and the compassion shown in the Cross.

69. Bishops and curates, in duty bound, must receive the commissaries of the papal indulgences with all reverence;

70. But they are under a much greater obligation to watch closely and attend carefully lest these men preach their own fancies instead of what the pope commissioned.

71. Let him be anathema and accursed who denies the apostolic character of the indulgences;

72. On the other hand, let him be blessed who is on his guard against the wantonness and licence of the pardon-merchants' words.

73. In the same way, the pope rightly excommunicates those who make any plans to the detriment of the trade in indulgences.

74. It is much more in keeping with his views to excommunicate those who use the pretext of indulgences to plot anything to the detriment of holy love and truth.

75. It is foolish to think that papal indulgences have so much power that they can absolve a man even if he has done the impossible and violated the mother of God.

76. We assert the contrary, and say that the pope's

pardons are not able to remove the least venial of sins as far as their guilt is concerned.

77. When it is said that not even St. Peter, if he were now pope, could grant a greater grace, it is blasphemy against St. Peter and the pope.

78. We assert the contrary, and say that he, and any pope whatever, possesses greater graces, viz., the gospel, spiritual powers, gifts of healing, etc., as is declared in I Corinthians 12 [:28].

79. It is blasphemy to say that the insignia of the cross with the papal arms are of equal value to the cross on which Christ died.

80. The bishops, curates, and theologians, who permit assertions of that kind to be made to the people without let or hindrance, will have to answer for it.

81. This unbridled preaching of indulgences makes it difficult for learned men to guard the respect due to the pope against false accusations, or at least from the keen criticisms of the laity;

82. They ask, e.g.: Why does not the pope liberate everyone from purgatory for the sake of love (a most holy thing) and because of the supreme necessity of their souls? This would be morally the best of all reasons. Meanwhile he redeems innumerable souls for money, a most perishable thing, with which to build St. Peter's church, a very minor purpose.

83. Again: Why should funeral and anniversary masses for the dead continue to be said? And why does not the pope repay, or permit to be repaid, the benefactions instituted for those purposes, since it is wrong to pray for those souls who are now redeemed?

84. Again: Surely this is a new sort of compassion, on the part of God and the pope, when an impious man, an enemy of God, is allowed to pay money to redeem a devout soul, a friend of God; while yet that devout and beloved soul is not allowed to be redeemed without payment, for love's sake, and just because of its need of redemption.

85. Again: Why are the penitential canon laws, which in fact, if not in practice, have long been obsolete and dead in themselves,—why are they, to-day, still used in imposing fines in money, through the granting of indulgences, as if all the penitential canons were fully operative?

86. Again: Since the pope's income to-day is larger than that of the wealthiest of wealthy men, why does he not build this one church of St. Peter with his own money, rather than with the money of indigent believers?

87. Again: What does the pope remit or dispense to people who, by their perfect penitence, have a right to plenary remission or dispensation?

88. Again: Surely greater good could be done to the church if the pope were to bestow these remissions and dispensations, not once, as now, but a hundred times a day, for the benefit of any believer whatever.

89. What the pope seeks by indulgences is not money, but rather the salvation of souls; why then does he not suspend the letters and indulgences formerly conceded, and still as efficacious as ever?

90. These questions are serious matters of conscience to the laity. To suppress them by force alone, and not to refute them by giving reasons, is to expose the church and the pope to the ridicule of their enemies, and to make Christian people unhappy.

91. If, therefore, indulgences were preached in accordance with the spirit and mind of the pope, all these difficulties would be easily overcome, and, indeed, cease to exist.

92. Away, then, with those prophets who say to Christ's people, "Peace, peace," where there is no peace.

93. Hail, hail to all those prophets who say to Christ's people, "The cross, the cross," where there is no cross.

94. Christians should be exhorted to be zealous to follow Christ, their Head, through penalties, deaths, and hells;

95. And let them thus be more confident of entering heaven through many tribulations rather than through a false assurance of peace.

JOHN CALVIN

Calvin was born in Noyon, France, in 1509. He prepared for an ecclesiastical career and later studied law, as well as Hebrew and the classics. After experiencing a "conversion," he broke with the Roman Church and became a principal spokesman for the

Reformation. Most of his life was spent in Geneva, Switzerland, where he established a theocracy in which the state was subordinate to the church. He died in Geneva in 1564.

Calvin was a more radical thinker than Luther. In addition to holding the doctrine of justification by faith alone and denying papal authority, Calvin believed that the reception of grace resulted from the arbitrary will of God and could not be earned by either good works, goodwill, or a direct appeal to God for forgiveness. This religious austerity and total dependence on the will of God is the most demanding interpretation of biblical Christianity. For Calvin, all human beings are depraved and can be saved only if God so chooses, a choice made by God independent of any human effort. In orthodox Calvinist theology, one can say that it is better to be born and damned, than not to be born at all, for our very dependence on God awards glory to God. Its most loyal and intense formulation was to be found in the American Puritans of the seventeenth century and in the thought of the eighteenth-century American philosopher-theologian Jonathan Edwards.

From Institutes of the Christian Religion

THE KNOWLEDGE OF GOD AND THAT OF OURSELVES ARE CONNECTED. HOW THEY ARE INTERRELATED

1. Without Knowledge of Self There Is No Knowledge of God

Nearly all the wisdom we possess, that is to say, true and sound wisdom, consists of two parts: the knowledge of God and of ourselves. But, while joined by many bonds, which one precedes and brings forth the other is not easy to discern. In the first place, no one can look upon himself without immediately turning his thoughts to the contemplation of God, in whom he "lives and moves" (Acts 17:28). For, quite clearly, the mighty gifts with which we are endowed are hardly from ourselves; indeed, our very being is nothing but subsistence in the one God. Then, by these benefits shed like dew from heaven upon us, we are led as by rivulets to the spring itself. Indeed, our very poverty better discloses the infinitude of benefits reposing in God. The miserable ruin, into which the rebellion of the first man cast us, especially compels us to look upward. Thus, not only will we, in fasting and hungering, seek thence what we lack; but, in being aroused by fear, we shall learn humility. For, as a veritable world of miseries is to be found in mankind, and we are thereby despoiled of divine raiment, our shameful nakedness exposes a teeming horde of infamies. Each of us must, then, be so stung by the consciousness of his own unhappiness as to attain at least some knowledge of God. Thus, from the feeling of our own ignorance, vanity, poverty, infirmity, and—what is more—depravity and corruption, we recognize that the true light of wisdom, sound virtue, full abundance of every good, and purity of righteousness rest in the Lord alone. To this extent we are prompted by our own ills to contemplate the good things of God; and we cannot seriously aspire to him before we begin to become displeased with ourselves. For what man in all the world would not gladly remain as he is—what man does not remain as he is—so long as he does not know himself, that is, while content with his own gifts, and either ignorant or unmindful of his own misery? Accordingly, the knowledge of ourselves not only arouses us to seek God, but also, as it were, leads us by the hand to find him.

2. Without Knowledge of God There Is No Knowledge of Self

Again, it is certain that man never achieves a clear knowledge of himself unless he has first looked upon God's face, and then descends from contemplating him to scrutinize himself. For we always seem to ourselves righteous and upright and wise and holy—this pride is innate in all of us—unless by clear proofs we stand convinced of our own unrighteousness, foulness, folly, and impurity. Moreover, we are not thus convinced if we look merely to ourselves and not also to the Lord, who is the sole standard by which this judgment must be measured. For, because all of us are inclined by nature to hypocrisy, a kind of empty image of righteousness in place of righteousness itself abundantly satisfies us. And because nothing appears within or around us that has not been contaminated by great immorality, what is a little less vile pleases us as a thing most pure—so long as we confine our minds within the limits of human corruption. Just so, an eye to which nothing is shown but black objects judges something dirty white or even rather darkly mottled to be whiteness itself. Indeed, we can discern still more clearly from the bodily senses how much we are deluded in estimating the powers of the soul. For if in broad daylight we either look down upon the ground and survey whatever meets our view round about, we seem to ourselves endowed with the strongest and keenest sight; yet when we look up to the sun and gaze straight at it, that power of sight which was particularly strong on earth is at once blunted and confused by a great brilliance, and thus we are compelled to admit that our keenness in looking upon things earthly is sheer dullness when it comes to the sun. So it happens in estimating our spiritual goods. As long as we do not look beyond the earth, being quite content with our own righteousness, wisdom, and virtue, we flatter ourselves most sweetly, and fancy ourselves all but demigods. Suppose we but once begin to raise our thoughts to God, and to ponder his nature, and how completely perfect are his righteousness, wisdom, and power—the straightedge to which we must be shaped. Then, what masquerading earlier as righteousness was pleasing in us will soon grow filthy in its consummate wickedness. What wonderfully impressed us under the name of wisdom will stink in its very foolishness. What wore the face of power will prove itself the most miserable weakness. That is, what in us seems perfection itself corresponds ill to the purity of God.

3. Man Before God's Majesty

Hence that dread and wonder with which Scripture commonly represents the saints as stricken and overcome whenever they felt the presence of God. Thus it comes about that we see men who in his absence normally remained firm and constant, but who, when he manifests his glory, are so shaken and struck dumb as to be laid low by the dread of death—are in fact overwhelmed by it and almost annihilated. As a consequence, we must infer that man is never sufficiently touched and affected by the awareness of his lowly state until he has compared himself with God's majesty. Moreover, we have numerous examples of this consternation both in The Book of Judges and in the Prophets. So frequent was it that this expression was common among God's people: "We shall die, for the Lord has appeared to us" (Judg. 13:22; Isa. 6:5; Ezek. 2:1; 1:28; Judg. 6:22–23; and elsewhere). The story of Job, in its description of God's wisdom, power, and purity, always expresses a powerful argument that overwhelms men with the realization of their own stupidity, impotence, and corruption (cf. Job 38:1 ff.). And not without cause: for we see how Abraham recognizes more clearly that he is earth and dust (Gen. 18:27) when once he had come nearer to beholding God's glory; and how Elijah, with uncovered face, cannot bear to await his approach, such is the awesomeness of his appearance (I Kings 19:13). And what can man do, who is rottenness itself (Job 13:28) and a worm (Job 7:5; Ps. 22:6), when even the very cherubim must veil their faces out of fear (Isa. 6:2)? It is this indeed of which the prophet Isaiah speaks: "The sun will blush and the moon be confounded when the Lord of Hosts shall reign" (Isa. 24:23); that is, when he shall bring forth his splendor and cause it to draw nearer, the brightest thing will become darkness before it (Isa. 2:10, 19 p.).

Yet, however the knowledge of God and of ourselves may be mutually connected, the order of right teaching requires that we discuss the former first, then proceed afterward to treat the latter.

JUSTIFICATION BY FAITH: FIRST THE DEFINITION OF THE WORD AND OF THE MATTER

(Justification and Regeneration, the Terms Defined, 1–4)
1. Place and Meaning of the Doctrine of "Justification"

I believe I have already explained above, with sufficient care, how for men cursed under the law, there remains, in faith, one sole means of recovering salvation. I believe I have also explained what faith itself is, and those benefits of God which it confers upon man, and the fruits it brings forth in him. Let us sum these up. Christ was given to us by God's generosity, to be grasped and possessed by us in faith. By partaking of him, we principally receive a double grace: namely, that being reconciled to God through Christ's blamelessness, we may have in heaven instead of a Judge a gracious Father; and secondly, that sanctified by Christ's spirit we may cultivate blamelessness and purity of life. Of regeneration, indeed, the second of these gifts, I have said what seemed sufficient. The theme of justification was therefore more lightly touched upon because it was more to the point to understand first how little devoid of good works is the faith, through which alone we obtain free righteousness by the mercy of God; and what is the nature of the good works of the saints, with which part of this question is concerned. Therefore we must now discuss these matters thoroughly. And we must so discuss them as to bear in mind that this is the main hinge on which religion turns, so that we devote the greater attention and care to it. For unless you first of all grasp what your relationship to God is, and the nature of his judgment concerning you, you have neither a foundation on which to establish your salvation nor one on which to build piety toward God. But the need to know this will better appear from the knowledge itself.

2. The Concept of Justification

But that we may not stumble on the very threshold—and this would happen if we should enter upon a discussion of a thing unknown—first let us explain what these expressions mean: that man is justified in God's sight, and that he is justified by faith or works. He is said to be justified in God's sight who is both reckoned righteous in God's judgment and has been accepted on account of his righteousness. Indeed, as iniquity is abominable to God, so no sinner can find favor in his eyes in so far as he is a sinner and so long as he is reckoned as such. Accordingly, wherever there is sin, there also the wrath and vengeance of God show themselves. Now he is justified who is reckoned in the condition not of a sinner, but of a righteous man; and for that reason, he stands firm before God's judgment seat while all sinners fall. If an innocent accused person be summoned before the judgment seat of a fair judge, where he will be judged according to his innocence, he is said to be "justified" before the judge. Thus, justified before God is the man who, freed from the company of sinners, has God to witness and affirm his righteousness. In the same way, therefore, he in whose life that purity and holiness will be found which deserves a testimony of righteousness before God's throne will be said to be justified by works, or else he who, by the wholeness of his works, can meet and satisfy God's judgment. On the contrary, justified by faith is he who, excluded from the righteousness of works, grasps the righteousness of Christ through faith, and clothed in it, appears in God's sight not as a sinner but as a righteous man.

Therefore, we explain justification simply as the acceptance with which God receives us into his favor as righteous men. And we say that it consists in the remission of sins and the imputation of Christ's righteousness.

4. Justification as Gracious Acceptance by God and as Forgiveness of Sins

And to avoid contention over a word, if we look upon the thing itself as described to us, no misgiving will remain. For Paul surely refers to justification by the word "acceptance" when in Eph. 1:5–6 he says: "We are destined for adoption through Christ according to God's good pleasure, to the praise of his glorious grace by which he has accounted us acceptable and beloved" (Eph. 1:5–6 p.). That means the very thing that he commonly says elsewhere, that "God justifies us freely" (Rom. 3:24). Moreover, in the fourth chapter of Romans he first calls justification "imputation of righteousness." And he does not hesitate to include it within forgiveness of sins. Paul says: "That man is declared blessed by David whom God renders acceptable or to whom he imputes righteousness apart from works, as it is written: 'Blessed are they whose transgressions have been forgiven'" (Rom 4:6–7 p.; Ps. 32:1). There he is obviously discussing not a part of justification but the whole of it. Further, he approves the definition of it set forth by David when he declares those men blessed to whom free pardon of sins is given (Ps. 32:1–2). From this it is clear that the righteousness of which he speaks is simply set in opposition to guilt. But the best passage of all on this matter is the one in which he teaches that the sum of the gospel embassy is to reconcile us to God, since God is willing to receive us into grace through Christ, not counting our sins against us (II Cor. 5:18–20). Let my readers carefully ponder the whole passage. For a little later Paul adds by way of explanation: "Christ, who was without sin, was made sin for us" (II Cor. 5:21), to designate the means of reconciliation (cf. vs. 18–19). Doubtless, he means by the word "reconciled" nothing but "justified." And surely, what he teaches elsewhere—that "we are made righteous by Christ's obedience" (Rom. 5:19 p.)—could not stand unless we are reckoned righteous before God in Christ and apart from ourselves.

13. Righteousness by Faith and Righteousness by Works

But a great part of mankind imagine that righteousness is composed of faith and works. Let us also, to begin with, show that faith righteousness so differs from works righteousness that when one is established the other has to be overthrown. The apostle says that he "counts everything as dross" that he "may gain Christ and be found in him, . . . not having a righteousness of (his) own, based on law, but one that is through faith in Jesus Christ, the righteousness from God through faith" (Phil. 3:8–9 p.). You see here both a comparison of opposites and an indication that a man who wishes to obtain Christ's righteousness must abandon his own righteousness. Therefore, he states elsewhere that this was the cause of the Jews' downfall: "Wishing to establish their own righteousness, they did not submit to God's righteousness" (Rom. 10:3 p.). If by establishing our own righteousness we shake off the righteousness of God, to attain the latter we must indeed completely do away with the former. He also shows this very thing when he states that our boasting is not excluded by law but by faith (Rom. 3:27). From this it follows that so long as any particle of works righteousness remains some occasion for boasting remains with us. Now, if faith excludes all boasting, works righteousness can in no way be associated with faith righteousness. In this sense he speaks so clearly in the fourth chapter of Romans that no place is left for cavils or shifts: "If Abraham," says Paul, "was justified by works, he has something to boast about." He adds, "Yet he has no reason to boast before God" (Rom. 4:2). It follows, therefore, that he was not justified by works. Then Paul sets forth another argument from contraries. When reward is made for works it is done out of debt, not of grace (Rom. 4:4). But righteousness according to grace is owed to faith. Therefore it does not arise from the merits of works. Farewell, then, to the dream of those who think up a righteousness flowing together out of faith and works.

14. Likewise, the Works of the Regenerated Can Procure No Justification

The Sophists, who make game and sport in their corrupting of Scripture and their empty caviling, think they have a subtle evasion. For they explain "works" as meaning those which men not yet reborn do only according to the letter by the effort of their own free will, apart from Christ's grace. But they deny that these refer to spiritual works. For, according to them, man is justified by both faith and works provided they are not his own works but the gifts of Christ and the fruit of regeneration. For they say that Paul so spoke for no other reason than to convince the Jews, who were relying upon their own strength, that they were foolish to arrogate righteousness to themselves, since the Spirit of Christ alone bestows it upon us not through any effort arising from our own nature. Still they do not observe that in the contrast between the righteousness of the law and of the gospel, which Paul elsewhere introduces, all works are excluded, whatever title may grace them (Gal. 3:11–12). For he teaches that this is the righteousness of the law, that he who has fulfilled what the law commands should obtain salvation; but this is the righteousness of faith, to believe that Christ died and rose again (Rom. 10:5, 9).

Moreover, we shall see afterward, in its proper place, that the benefits of Christ—sanctification and righteousness—are different. From this it follows that not even spiritual works come into account when the power of justifying is ascribed to faith. The statement of Paul where he denies that Abraham had any reason to boast before God—a passage that we have just cited—because he was not righteous by his works, ought not to be restricted to a literal and outward appearance of virtues or to the effort of free will. But even though the life of the patriarch was spiritual and well-nigh angelic, he did not have sufficient merit of works to acquire righteousness before God.

15. The Roman Doctrine of Grace and Good Works

Somewhat too gross are the Schoolmen, who mingle their concoctions. Yet these men infect the simple-minded and unwary with a doctrine no less depraved, cloaking under the disguise of "spirit" and "grace" even the mercy of God, which alone can set fearful souls at rest. Now we confess with Paul that the doers of the law are justified before God; but, because we are all far from observing the law, we infer from this that those works which ought especially to avail for righteousness give us no help because we are destitute of them.

As regards the rank and file of the papists or Schoolmen, they are doubly deceived here both because they call faith an assurance of conscience in awaiting from God their reward for merits and because they interpret the grace of God not as the imputation of free righteousness but as the Spirit helping in the pursuit of holiness. They read in the apostle: "Whoever would draw near to God must first believe that he exists and then that he rewards those who seek him" (Heb. 11:6). But they pay no attention to the way in which he is to be sought. It is clear from their own writings that in using the term "grace" they are deluded. For Lombard explains that justification is given to us through Christ in two ways. First, he says, Christ's death justifies us, while love is aroused through it in our hearts and makes us righteous. Second, because through the same love, sin is extinguished by which the devil held us captive, so that he no longer has the wherewithal to condemn us. You see how he views God's grace especially in justification, in so far as we are directed through the grace of the Holy Spirit to good works. Obviously, he intended to follow Augustine's opinion, but he follows it at a distance and even departs considerably from the right imitation of it. For when Augustine says anything clearly, Lombard obscures it, and if there was anything slightly contaminated in Augustine, he corrupts it. The schools have gone continually from bad to worse until, in headlong ruin, they have plunged into a sort of Pelagianism. For that matter, Augustine's view, or at any rate his manner of stating it, we must not entirely accept. For even though he admirably deprives man of all credit for righteousness and transfers it to God's grace, he still subsumes grace under sanctification, by which we are reborn in newness of life through the Spirit.

18. Justification Not the Wages of Works, but a Free Gift

The second passage is this: "It is evident that no man is justified before God by the law. For the righteous shall live by faith (cf. Hab. 2:4). But the law is not of faith; rather, the man who does these things shall live in them" (Gal. 3:11–12, Comm., cf. Vg.). How would this argument be maintained otherwise than by agreeing that works do not enter the account of faith but must be utterly separated? The law, he says, is different from faith. Why? Because works are required for law righteousness. Therefore it follows that they are not required for faith righteousness. From this relation it is clear that those who are justified by faith are justified apart from the merit of works—in fact, without the merit of works. For faith receives that righteousness which the gospel bestows. Now the gospel differs from the law in that it does not link righteousness to works but lodges it solely in God's mercy. Paul's contention in Romans is similar to this: that Abraham had no occasion to boast, for faith was reckoned as righteousness for him (Rom. 4:2–3); and he adds as confirmation that the righteousness of faith has a place in circumstances where there are no works for which a reward is due. "Where," he says, "there are works, wages are paid as a debt; what is given to faith is free." (Rom. 4:4–5 p.) Indeed, the meaning of the words he uses there applies also to this passage. He adds a little later that we on this account obtain the inheritance from faith, as according to grace. Hence he infers that this inheritance is free, for it is received by faith (cf. Rom. 4:16). How is this so except that faith rests entirely upon God's mercy without the assistance of works? And in another passage he teaches, doubtless in the same sense that "the righteousness of God has been manifested apart from law, although it is attested by the Law and the "Prophets" (Rom. 3:21 p.). For, excluding the law, he denies that we are aided by works and that we attain righteousness by working; instead, we come empty to receive it.

19. Through "Faith Alone"

Now the reader sess how fairly the Sophists today cavil against our doctrine when we say that man is justified by faith alone (Rom. 3:28). They dare not deny that man is justified by faith because it recurs so often in Scripture. But since the word "alone" is nowhere expressed, they do not allow this addition to be made. Is it so? But what will they reply to these words of Paul where he contends that righteousness cannot be of faith unless it be free (Rom. 4:2 ff.)? How will a free gift agree with works? With what chicaneries will they elude what he says in another passage, that God's righteousness is revealed in the gospel (Rom. 1:17)? If righteousness is revealed in the gospel, surely no mutilated or half righteousness but a full and perfect righteousness is contained there. The law therefore has no place in it. Not only by a false but by an obviously ridiculous shift they insist upon excluding this adjective. Does not he who takes everything from works firmly enough ascribe everything to faith alone? What, I pray, do these expressions mean: "His righteousness has been manifested apart from the law" (Rom. 3:21 p.); and, "Man is freely justified" (Rom. 3:24 p.); and, "Apart from the works of the law" (Rom. 3:28)?

Here they have an ingenious subterfuge: even though they have not devised it themselves but have borrowed it from Origen and certain other ancient writers, it is still utterly silly. They prate that the ceremonial works of the law are excluded, not the moral works. They become so proficient by continual wrangling that they do not even grasp the first elements of logic. Do they think that the apostle was raving when he brought forward these passages to prove his opinion? "The man who does these things will live in them" (Gal. 3:12), and, "Cursed be every one who does not fulfill all things written in the book of the law" (Gal. 3:10 p.). Unless they have gone mad they will not say that life was promised to keepers of ceremonies or the curse announced only to those who transgress the ceremonies. If these passages are to be understood of the moral law, there is no doubt that moral works are also excluded from the power of justifying. These arguments which Paul uses look to the same end: "Since through the law comes knowledge of sin" (Rom. 3:20), therefore not righteousness. Because "the law works wrath" (Rom. 4:15), hence not righteousness. Because the law does not make conscience certain, it cannot confer righteousness either. Because faith is imputed as righteousness, righteousness is therefore not the reward of works but is given unearned (Rom. 4:4–5). Because we are justified by faith, our boasting is cut off (Rom. 3:27 p.). "If a law had been given that could make alive, then righteousness would indeed be by the law. But God consigned all things to sin that the promise might be given to those who believe." (Gal. 3:21–22 p.) Let them now babble, if they dare, that these statements apply to ceremonies, not to morals. Even schoolboys would hoot at such impudence. Therefore, let us hold as certain that when the ability to justify is denied to the law, these words refer to the whole law.

20. "Works of the Law"

If anyone should wonder why the apostle, not content with naming works, uses such a qualification, there is a ready explanation. Though works are highly esteemed, they have their value from God's approval rather than from their own worth. For who would dare recommend works righteousness to God unless God himself approved? Who would dare demand a reward due unless he promised it? Therefore, it is from God's beneficence that they are considered worthy both of the name of righteousness and of the reward thereof. And so, for this one reason, works have value, because through them man intends to show obedience to God. Therefore, to prove that Abraham could not be justified by works, the apostle declares in another place that the law was given fully four hundred and thirty years after the covenant was made (Gal. 3:17). The ignorant would laugh at this sort of argument, on the ground that before the promulgation of the law there could have been righteous works. But because he knew that works could have such great value only by the testimony and vouchsafing of God, he took as a fact that previous to the law they had no power to justify. We have the reason why he expressly mentions the works of the law when he wants to take justification away from them, for it is clearly because a controversy can be raised only over them.

Yet he sometimes excepts all works without any qualification, as when on David's testimony he states that blessedness is imparted to that man to whom God reckons righteousness apart from works (Rom. 4:6; Ps. 32:1–2). Therefore no cavils of theirs can prevent us from holding to the exclusive expression as a general principle.

Also, they pointlessly strive after the foolish subtlety that we are justified by faith alone, which acts through love, so that righteousness depends upon love. Indeed, we confess with Paul that no other faith justifies "but faith working through love" (Gal. 5:6). But it does not take its power to justify from that working of love. Indeed, it justifies in no other way but in that it leads us into fellowship with the righteousness of Christ. Otherwise, everything that the apostle insists upon so vigorously would fall. "Now to him who works the pay is not considered a gift but his due," says he. (Rom. 4:4) "But to one who does not work but believes in him who justifies the ungodly, his faith is reckoned as righteousness." (Rom. 4:5) Could he have spoken more clearly than in contending thus: that there is no righteousness of faith except where there are no works for which a reward is due? And then that faith is reckoned as righteousness only where righteousness is bestowed through a grace not owed?

DESIDERIUS ERASMUS

Erasmus was born in Rotterdam, Holland, in 1466, the illegitimate son of a priest. Like his father, Erasmus took holy orders, but became an Augustinian friar. Most of his life, however, was spent outside the monastery. A classical scholar, Erasmus was the central figure in the development of the northern Renaissance. He was a close friend of the English humanists John Colet and Thomas More. One of Erasmus' most significant scholarly contributions was his edition of the New Testament, in both Greek and Latin. He also provided commentaries on the Fathers of the Church as an aspect of his denigration of medieval Scholasticism.

Erasmus' most important and trying role, however, was as a frustrated mediator following the Lutheran Reformation. Long a biting critic of the pompous intellectual and personal excesses of the Church hierarchy, Erasmus found himself counted on the side of the Reformers. His critique of the Church notwithstanding, Erasmus remained loyal to his Catholic heritage and broke with Luther by holding to the doctrine of free will and opposing Luther's doctrine of predestination. He wrote in a conciliatory manner, continuing his attempt to bridge the growing chasm between Protestants and Catholics. Erasmus died in Basel, Switzerland, in 1536.

As the following selection from his Colloquies *demonstrates, Erasmus was a superb satirist. His tolerance, wit, irony, and satire caused him to be rejected by both Catholic and Protestant establishments. He was in essence a Renaissance humanist and, as such, out of step in the time of early sixteenth-century religious strife. It is in the modern era that an appreciation has developed for the wisdom and forbearance of the person and work of Erasmus.*

Alchemy

*Philecous.** What's happened to amuse Lalus so? He's nearly bursting with laughter, and he crosses himself again and again. I'll interrupt the man's bliss.—Greetings, my dear Lalus! You seem very happy.

Lalus. But I'll be happier if I share this pleasure with you.

Phil. Then do me the favor as soon as you can.

Lal. You know Balbinus?

Desiderius Erasmus, by Hans Holbein, the Younger. The illustrator of Erasmus' Praise of Folly, *Holbein, the Younger, was a master draftsman of the 16th century. (The Granger Collection)*

Phil. That learned, much-esteemed gentleman?

Lal. Just as you say, but no mortal is wise at all times, or perfect in every respect. Along with many brilliant gifts, the gentleman has this slight blemish: that for a long while he's been mad about the art called alchemy.

Phil. What you refer to is not a blemish, surely, but a notorious disease.

Lal. However that may be, Balbinus, often as he's been taken in by this class of men, nevertheless allowed himself to be marvelously cheated a little while ago.

Phil. How?

Lal. A certain priest came to him, greeted him deferentially, and soon began thus: "Most learned Balbinus, you wonder perhaps why an ignorant creature like me should interrupt you in this fashion, when I know you never rest a moment from your most sacred studies." Balbinus nodded, as is his custom, for he's remarkably sparing of words.

Phil. That's proof of shrewdness.

Lal. But the other, who was shrewder, continued: "Yet you'll forgive this impertinence of mine when you learn my reason for coming to you." "Tell it," says Balbinus, "but in few words if possible." "I'll tell it as briefly as I can," says he. "You know, most learned of men, that mortals have different destinies. I'm uncertain whether to include myself among the happy or the unhappy. For if I consider my fate from one standpoint, I think I'm very lucky; but if from another, no one seems less lucky than I." When Balbinus urged him to cut it short, "I'll finish, most learned Balbinus," he says. "It will be all the easier for me to address a man whose knowledge of this whole business is unexcelled."

Phil. You're describing a rhetorician to me, not an alchemist.

Lal. You'll hear the alchemist in a moment. "From boyhood," he says, "I've had the good fortune to learn by far the most eagerly sought of all arts, that core of all philosophy, I say—alchemy." At the word "alchemy" Balbinus started somewhat—a mere ges-

---

Reprinted with permission of The Bobbs-Merrill Company, Inc., © 1957 (Liberal Arts Press), Erasmus, "Ten Colloquies of Erasmus," trans. by Craig R. Thompson. (pp. 47–55)

* *Philecous* means "a good listener"; *Lalus* means "one who is talkative."

ture—but uttering a groan, bade him continue. Then says the other, "But O wretched me! I did not follow the right path." When Balbinus asked him what paths he was talking about, he replied, "You know, Excellency—for what escapes you, Balbinus, a man most learned in every respect?—that there is a twofold path in this art: one named longation, the other curtation. But I had the misfortune to fall into longation." When Balbinus inquired what the difference was between the two ways, he replied, "It's presumptuous of me to speak of these matters in your presence when I know that your familiarity with them is unsurpassed. And so I've hurried here to you in hopes that you might take pity on me and deign to share with me that most blessed way of curtation. The more learned you are in this science, the less trouble it will be for you to impart it to me. Do not conceal so great a gift of God from a brother who is about to die of grief. So may Jesus Christ ever enrich you with greater gifts!"

Since he made no end of entreaties, Balbinus was forced to confess that he simply didn't know what longation or curtation was. He bids the man explain the meaning of these terms. Then says the other, "Although I know I'm talking to a man of superior learning, nevertheless I'll do as you command. Those who have spent an entire lifetime on this sacred science transmute species of things by two methods. One is shorter but a little more risky; the other takes longer but is safer. I regard myself as unlucky: up to now I've toiled in this latter path, which does not please me, and I've been unable to find anyone willing to show me the other path that I'm dying to find. At last God put it into my mind to come to you, a man as good as you are learned. Knowledge enables you to grant my request without trouble; goodness will move you to take compassion on a brother whose welfare is in your power."

In brief, after the sly old rascal, by this kind of talk, had dispelled suspicion of fraud and had convinced Balbinus of his perfect understanding of the other way, Balbinus was already itching with impatience. Finally, unable to restrain himself, he says, "Away with that curtation! I've never even heard of it, let alone mastered it. Tell me straight, do you understand longation well?" "Pooh!" says the other, "To a T. But the length I don't care for." When Balbinus asked him how much time it took, he replied, "Too much—almost a whole year. It's the safest way though." "Don't worry even if the job takes two years," says Balbinus, "provided you're sure of your skill." To make a long story short, they reach an agreement to undertake the business secretly in Balbinus' house, on condition that the priest do the work and Balbinus put up the money. The profit was to be divided half and half, although the swindler—modest fellow!—voluntarily assigned all anticipated profit to Balbinus. And each swears an oath of secrecy, like persons initiated into secret rites. Money is counted out then and there for the operator to buy pots, glasses, charcoal, and other equipment needed for the laboratory. This money our alchemist promptly and enjoyably squanders on whores, dice, and drink.

Phil. That's changing the species of things, all right!

Lal. To Balbinus' urging that they get to work, he replied, "Don't you agree with the saying that 'Well begun is half done'? It's a big job to prepare the material properly." At last he began fitting up the furnace. Here again more gold was needed: a lure to catch later gold, as it were. As a fish isn't landed without bait, so an alchemist produces no gold unless he has some to begin with.

Meanwhile Balbinus devoted all his time to calculations. He was figuring how much profit, if one ounce yielded fifteen, would be made from two thousand ounces; for so much had he determined to invest. After the alchemist had run through this money, too, and already had pretended for a month or so to be busy with bellows and charcoal, Balbinus asked him how the work was coming along. At first he was silent. Finally, when Balbinus pressed him, he answered, "Just as important projects generally come along—they're always hard to get under way." He gave as the reason a mistake in buying charcoal: he had bought some made from oak when fir or hazel was required. There went a hundred gold crowns—and the dice went rolling just as promptly!

With the new grant of money the charcoal was replaced. Now the work was started more earnestly than before: as, in a war, if soldiers suffer a setback, they make up for it by valor. When the laboratory had glowed for some months now, and the golden fruit was expected, and not a bit of gold was left in the vessels (for by this time the alchemist had squandered all that too), another excuse was alleged: the glasses used had not been heated properly. For as a likeness of Mercury isn't fashioned from just any kind of wood, so gold isn't made in glasses of just any kind. The greater the investment, the slighter was the inclination to give up.

Phil. That's like gamblers. As if it weren't much better to cut your losses than to lose everything!

Lal. So it is. The alchemist swore he'd never been so cheated. Now that the error was corrected, the rest would be quite safe, and this loss would be made good, with a large amount of interest besides.

After the glasses were changed, the laboratory was set up for the third time. The alchemist suggested that their business would succeed better if he sent some gold crowns as an offering to the Virgin Mother who, as you know, is worshiped at Paralia. For the art is a sacred one, and cannot prosper without the blessing of heaven. This advice was most acceptable to Balbinus, since he was a devout man who would not let a day go by without attending divine service. The alchemist set out on his pious journey—to the next village, that is, and there spent the votive money in riotous living. Home again, he announces he has the highest hopes that their enterprise will prosper in accordance with their wishes, so pleased did the Holy Virgin seem with his offering.

Ship of Fools, by Hieronymus Bosch. This painting illustrates the long-standing artistic and literary theme of the search for pleasure while on the brink of disaster. (Bibliothèque Nationale, Paris)

When, after much time and toil, not even a grain of gold had been produced, the alchemist, in reply to Balbinus' complaint, declared he had never had such an experience in his life, expert though he was in this art: he couldn't guess what the trouble was. Finally, after much pondering, it occurred to Balbinus to wonder if the alchemist had missed hearing mass on any day, or failed to say his rosary, as they call it; for nothing succeeds if these are neglected. Thereupon the swindler replies, "You've hit the nail on the head. Wretched me! I did forget to do that once or twice, and lately I forgot to salute the Virgin on rising from a long-drawn-out dinner party." "No wonder," says Balbinus then, "that so important a matter doesn't succeed." The expert undertook to hear twelve masses for the two he had missed, and in place of a single salutation to make ten.

When the spendthrift alchemist had gone broke time after time, and no excuses for demanding money presented themselves, he finally thought up this trick. He arrived home out of breath and moaned, "I'm done for, Balbinus, done for; I'll swing for this!" Balbinus was amazed and impatient to learn the cause of so great a disaster. "Some officials at court got word of what we're up to," he says, "and I fully expect to be dragged off to jail any minute." At this speech Balbinus turned pale in earnest, for you know that to practice alchemy without royal permission is a capital crime in these parts. The other continues, "I'm not afraid of death; I only hope that's what I get. I'm afraid of something more cruel." To the question of what this was, he answers, "That I'll be carried off to a tower somewhere and forced to slave there all my life for persons against my will. Is there any death not preferable to such a life?"

Then and there they examined the matter from every angle. Balbinus, since he was a master of rhetoric, hammered away at every position, seeking an escape from the danger. "Can't you deny the crime?" he says. "By no means," says the other. "The affair is common knowledge among the king's men, and they have evidence that can't be brushed aside." So plain was the law that they could put up no defense. After many possibilities had been weighed and nothing very reassuring appeared, the alchemist, who was now sorely in need of cash finally said, "Balbinus, we take our time discussing it, but the problem demands an immediate solution. I think they're coming very soon to arrest me." In the end, when Balbinus could think of nothing by way of reply, the alchemist said, "I can't think of anything either, nor do I see anything left to do except die bravely. Unless, perhaps, this one remaining possibility appeals to you. It's a useful rather than honorable one, except that necessity is a cruel goad. You know," says he, "that men of this sort are greedy of money, and therefore it's rather easy to bribe them to keep their mouths shut. However hard it may be to give those rascals money to throw away, still, as things now stand, I see no better remedy." Balbinus agreed, and counted out thirty gold crowns to stop their tongues.

Phil. That's wonderful generosity on Balbinus' part.

Lal. Oh, no; in any honest business you would sooner have drawn a tooth from him than a farthing. Thus the alchemist was provided for. He was in no danger except that of having no money to give to his mistress.

Phil. I'm surprised Balbinus wasn't alert in such an important matter.

Lal. Only in this is he gullible. In others he's extremely alert. With fresh funds the furnace was set up once more, but first brief prayers were made to the Virgin Mother, to win her favor for the undertaking. Already a whole year had passed, while the alchemist made up one excuse after another; the labor was lost and the investment wasted. Meantime an absurd accident occurred.

Phil. What was it?

Lal. The alchemist was having a secret affair with the wife of a courtier. Her husband, his suspicions aroused, began to keep an eye on the man. At last, when he was informed that the priest was in the bedroom, he returned home unexpectedly and pounded on the door.

Phil. What was he going to do to the fellow?

Lal. What? Nothing pleasant—either kill him or castrate him. When the husband, insistent, threatened to break down the door if his wife didn't open it, a great commotion resulted. Some instant remedy was sought. There was none but that offered by the situation itself. The man threw off his cloak, lowered himself through a narrow window—not without risk or injury—and fled. Such stories get around quickly, you know. So the word reached Balbinus too, as the alchemist foresaw it would.

Phil. And thus he's caught in the middle.

Lal. On the contrary, he got out of this more luckily than from the bedroom. Mark the fellow's trick. Balbinus did not protest, but showed well enough by his stern expression that he was not unaware of the gossip. The alchemist knew that Balbinus was strait-laced—I might almost say superstitious—in some things. Such men readily forgive an offender, no matter how serious his fault. So the other purposely brings up the success of the business. He complains that he's not getting along as well as usual, or as he would like, adding emphatically that he wonders what the reason is. Balbinus, who otherwise seemed resolved upon silence, was aroused at once by this opportunity; and he was a man easily aroused. "There's no mystery about what the trouble is," he says. "Your sins block the success of what should be handled by pure men in a pure way." At this word the alchemist dropped to his knees, beating his breast repeatedly, and with tearful looks and tone said, "Balbinus, you've spoken the absolute truth. My sins, I admit, are the hindrance. But they're my sins, not yours, for I shan't be ashamed to confess my disgrace before you, as before the holiest priest. Weakness of the flesh overcame me; Satan drew me into his snares, and—O wretched me!—from priest I am become an adulterer. Yet the offering we made to the Virgin Mother was not altogether wasted. I would certainly have been killed if she had not come to my rescue. The husband was breaking down the door; the window was too narrow for me to slip through. In so imminent a danger I thought of the Most Holy Virgin. I fell on my knees and implored her, if the gift had been acceptable, to help me. Without further delay I tried the window again—my plight forced me to do so—and found it was wide enough for my escape.

Phil. Balbinus believed this?

Lal. Believed it? More than that, he forgave him, and piously warned him not to show himself ungrateful to the Most Blessed Virgin. Once more money was paid out to the alchemist, who promised that hereafter his conduct in this solemn business would be above reproach.

Phil. How did it turn out?

Lal. It's a long story, but I'll finish it in few words. After he had made a fool of the man for a long time by tricks of this sort, and fleeced him of no mean sum of money, the affair finally came to the ears of one who had known the rascal from boyhood. Readily guessing that the fellow was doing the same thing in Balbinus' house that he had done everywhere, he visits Balbinus secretly, explains what kind of "expert" he shelters in his house, and warns him to get rid of the man as quickly as possible unless he wants that same expert to make off sometime after robbing Balbinus' desk.

Phil. What did Balbinus do at this? He had him thrown into jail, surely?

Lal. Jail? Oh, no: he gave him travel money, imploring him by everything sacred not to blab about what had happened. And in my opinion he was wise to prefer this to having the story become the talk of the town, and, in the second place, to risking confiscation of his property. The impostor was in no danger. He understood the "art" about as well as an ass does, and in an affair of this kind swindling is regarded leniently. Besides, if he had attempted robbery, benefit of clergy would have saved him from hanging. Nor would anyone willingly be at the expense of keeping him in jail.

Phil. I might feel sorry for Balbinus if he himself didn't enjoy being gulled.

Lal. I must hurry to court now. Some other time I'll tell you far more foolish tales.

Phil. I'll be glad to hear them when I have time, and I'll match you story for story.

An Inquiry Concerning Faith (Inquisitio De Fide)

Aulus. Saluta libenter is a book of Latin poems for young boys, but I question whether it is all right for me to wish you well!

Barbatius. Frankly, I would rather have you make me well than wish me well. But why do you say that, Aulus?

Aul. Why? Well, if you must know, you smell of brimstone or Jupiter's thunderbolt.

Bar. They are malevolent gods, and there are senseless thunderbolts that differ greatly in origin from those that are ominous. I suspect you are thinking about excommunication.

Aul. Exactly.

Bar. I have heard the thunder but never felt the bolt.

Aul. How so?

Bar. Because I do not suffer from indigestion and can sleep soundly.

Aul. But sickness is generally so much more dangerous the less it is felt. And as for these so-called senseless thunderbolts, why, they strike even the mountains and the seas.

Bar. True, but they have no effect there. But there is lightning that comes from a glass or a vessel of brass.

Aul. And that, too, is frightening.

Bar. Yes, but only to children. Only God has thunderbolts that strike the soul.

Aul. But suppose God is in His vicar?

Bar. I wish that He were!

Aul. Many are amazed that you have not already been reduced to ashes.

Bar. Suppose I was. Then according to the gospel my salvation would be much more desired.

Aul. We should not speak of such things but, rather, hope for them.

Bar. And why?

Aul. So he who has been struck may be ashamed and repent.

Bar. If God had done this, we would have all been lost.

Aul. I don't follow you.

Bar. Because when we were enemies to God, and worshippers of idols, soldiers in Satan's camp, that is

---

to say, most excommunicated, then in a special manner He spoke to us by His Son, and by His speech restored us to life when we were dead.

Aul. What you say is true.

Bar. It would be very hard on a sick person if a doctor would only examine him when he was well, for he doesn't need a doctor when he is well.

Aul. But I am afraid that you will infect me with your disease before I shall cure you of it. It sometimes happens that he who visits a sick man is forced to be a fighter instead of a physician.

Bar. Indeed it sometimes so happens in physical illness; but in the diseases of the mind you have an antidote ready against every contagion.

Aul. What's that?

Bar. A strong resolution to stick to your opinion. And besides, why do you fear fighting when this business is managed by words?

Aul. There is something in what you say, if there is any hope of doing good.

Bar. It is said in the proverb that, "While there's life, there's hope"; and according to St. Paul, charity cannot despair, because it "hopeth all things."

Aul. Your admonition is not ill advised, and with this in mind I will carry on this discussion with you a little; and if you'll permit me, I'll be a physician to you.

Bar. Do.

Aul. Inquisitive persons are commonly hated, yet physicians are allowed to inquire after every particular.

Bar. Ask me what you will; the sky's the limit.

Aul. I'll try. But you must promise you'll answer me sincerely.

Bar. I promise. But let me know what you'll ask me about.

Aul. The Apostles' Creed.

Bar. I hear a military word. I will be content to be looked upon as an enemy of Christ if I shall deceive you in this matter.

Aul. Do you believe in God the Father Almighty, who made heaven and earth?

Bar. Yes, and whatever is contained in heaven and earth; as well as the angelic minds.

Aul. When you say God, what do you understand by this?

Bar. I understand a certain eternal mind, which neither had beginning nor shall have any end, than which nothing can be either greater, wiser, or better.

Aul. You believe indeed like a good Christian.

Bar. Who by His omnipotent nod made all things visible or invisible; who by His wonderful wisdom orders and governs all things and by His goodness feeds and maintains all things; and who freely restored fallen mankind.

Aul. These are indeed three special attributes in God; but what benefit do you receive by a knowledge of them?

Bar. When I conceive Him to be omnipotent, I submit myself wholly to Him, in comparison with whose majesty and excellence of men and angels is nothing. Moreover, I firmly believe whatever the Holy Scriptures teach to have been accomplished by Him, and also that what He has promised shall be done, since He can by His will do whatever He pleases, however impossible it may seem to man. And therefore, distrusting my own strength, I depend wholly upon Him who can do all things. When I consider His wisdom, I attribute nothing at all to my own, but believe all things are done by Him righteously and justly, although they may seem to our way of thinking absurd or unjust. When I consider His goodness, I see nothing in myself that I do not owe to His free grace, and I think there is no sin so great but that He is willing to forgive a true penitent, nor nothing that He will not freely bestow on him who asks in faith.

Aul. Do you think that this is a sufficient belief?

Bar. By no means. But with a sincere affection I put my whole trust and confidence in Him alone, detesting Satan and all idolatry and magic arts. I worship Him alone, preferring nothing to Him, nor equating anything to Him, neither angel, nor parents, nor children, nor wife, nor prince, nor riches, nor honors, nor pleasures. For this I am prepared to lay down my life if He demands it, assured that one cannot possibly perish who commits himself wholly to Him.

Aul. Then you worship nothing, fear nothing, love nothing but God alone?

Bar. If I reverence anything, fear anything, or love anything besides Him, it for His sake I love it, fear it, and reverence it, referring all things to His glory, always giving thanks to Him for whatever happens, whether prosperous or adverse, life or death.

Aul. Certainly your confession is very sound so far. What do you think about the Second Person?

Bar. Try me.

Aul. Do you believe Jesus was God and man?

Bar. Yes.

Aul. How could it be that the same should be both immortal God and mortal man?

Bar. That was an easy thing for Him to do who can do what He will. And by reason of His divine nature, which is common to Him with the Father, whatever greatness, wisdom, and goodness I attribute to the Father I attribute the same to the Son; and whatever I owe to the Father, I owe also to the Son, except that it seemed good to the Father to create all things and bestow all things on us through the Son.

Aul. Why then do the Holy Scriptures more frequently call the Son Lord than God?

Bar. Because God is a name of authority, that is to say, of sovereignty, which in a special manner belongs to the Father, who is absolutely the origin of all things, and the fountain even of the Godhead itself. Lord is the name of a redeemer and deliverer, although the Father also redeemed us by His Son, and the Son is God, but of God the Father. But the Father alone is from no other and obtains the first place among the divine persons.

The Hay Wain, by Hieronymus Bosch (1485). Depicted here is the folly of humankind as it frolics in the everyday world, heedless of the watchful eye of the eternal. (Scala/ Art Resource)

Aul. Then do you put your confidence in Jesus?

Bar. Why not?

Aul. But the Prophet says he is accursed who puts his trust in man.

Bar. But to this Man alone has all the power in heaven and earth been given, that at His name every knee should bow, both of things in heaven, things in earth, and things under the earth. Unless He were God, I would not, as they say, make Him the sacred anchor of my faith and hope.

Aul. Why is He called Son?

Bar. So that no one would imagine Him to be a creature.

Aul. Why an only Son?

Bar. To distinguish the natural Son from the sons by adoption, the honor of which surname God imputes to us also, that we may look for no other besides this Son.

Aul. Why would He have Him who was God become man?

Bar. That being man, He might reconcile men to God.

Aul. Do you believe He was conceived without the help of man, by the operation of the Holy Spirit, and born of the undefiled Virgin Mary, taking a mortal body of her substance?

Bar. Yes.

Aul. Why did He wish to be born in this way?

Bar. Because it so behooved God to be born. It behooved Him to be born in this manner Who was to cleanse away the filthiness of our conception and birth. God was willing to be born the Son of man that we, being regenerated in Him, might be made the sons of God.

Aul. Do you believe that He lived upon earth, performed those miracles, taught those things revealed in the Gospel?

Bar. Yes, more certainly than I believe you to be a man.

Aul. I am not an Apuleius turned inside out, that you should suspect that an ass lies hidden under the form of a man. But do you believe this very person to be that Messiah whom the prototypes of the law delineated, whom the oracles of the prophets promised, whom the Jews expected for so many ages?

Bar. I believe nothing more firmly.

Aul. Do you believe His doctrine and life are sufficient for perfect piety?

Bar. Yes, perfectly sufficient.

Aul. Do you believe that He was really apprehended by the Jews, bound buffeted, beaten, spit upon, mocked, scourged under Pontius Pilate, and finally nailed to the cross, and there died?

Bar. Yes, I do.

Aul. Do you believe Him to have been free from all sin?

Bar. Yes, why should I not? A lamb without spot.

Aul. Do you believe He suffered all these things of His own accord?

Bar. Not only willingly, but even with great desire; and according to the will of His Father.

Aul. Why would the Father have His only Son, innocent and most dear to Him, suffer all these horrible things?

Bar. That by this sacrifice He might reconcile to Himself us who were guilty, we putting our confidence and hope in His name.

Aul. Why did God allow all mankind so to fall? And if He did allow them, was there no other way possible to repair our fall?

Bar. Not human reason but faith has persuaded me that it could be done in no better way nor more beneficially for our salvation.

Aul. Why did this kind of death please Him best?

Bar. Because in the estimate of the world it was the most disgraceful; its torment was cruel and lingering. It was appropriate for Him who would invite all the nations of the world to salvation to stretch Himself out toward every region on the earth. To summon men, attached to earthly cares, to heavenly things. Finally He did this that He might represent the brazen serpent that Moses erected, that whoever should fix his eyes upon it should be healed of the wound of the serpent and thus fulfill the Prophet's promise, "Proclaim to the nations, God hath reigned from a tree."

Aul. Why was He buried also, and so carefully anointed with myrrh and ointments, enclosed in a new tomb cut out of hard and living rock, the door being sealed, and public guards being placed there?

Bar. That it might be more apparent that He was dead.

Aul. Why did He not rise again at once?

Bar. For the very same reason: for if His death had been doubtful, His resurrection would have been doubtful, too; but He wanted that to be as certain as possible.

Aul. Do you believe His soul descended into hell?

Bar. St. Cyprian affirms that this clause was not formerly inserted either in the Roman creed or in the creed of the Eastern churches; neither is it recorded in Tertullian, a very ancient writer. And yet I do firmly believe it both because it agrees with the prophecy of the psalm, "Thou wilt not leave my soul in hell," and again, "O Lord, thou hast brought up my soul from the grave"; and also because the Apostle Peter, in the third chapter of his first epistle (whose authorship has never been doubted), writes in this manner: " . . . being put to death in the flesh, but vivified by the Spirit, by which also He went and preached unto the spirits in prison." But I believe He descended not to be there tormented, but that He might destroy for us the kingdom of Satan.

Aul. Well I hear nothing yet that is impious; but He died that He might restore us to life again who were dead in sin. Why did He rise to live again?

Bar. For three reasons particularly.

Aul. What are they?

Bar. First of all, to give us a certain hope of our resurrection. Secondly, that we might know that He in whom we have placed the safety of our resurrection is immortal and shall never die. Finally, that we being dead to sin by repentance, and buried together with Him by baptism, should by His grace be raised up again to newness of life.

Aul. Do you believe that the very same body that died upon the cross, that revived in the grave, that was seen and touched by the disciples, ascended into heaven?

Bar. Yes, most certainly.

Aul. Why did He leave the earth?

Bar. That we might all love Him spiritually, and that no man should appropriate Christ to himself upon the earth, but that we should all equally lift up our minds to heaven, knowing that our Head is there. For if men now take such pleasure in the color and the shape of garments, and boast so much of the blood or the foreskin of Christ, and the milk of the Virgin Mary, what do you think would have happened had He abode on the earth clothed, eating and discoursing? What dissensions would those peculiarities of His body have not occasioned?

Aul. Do you believe that He, being made immortal, sits at the right hand of the Father?

Bar. Yes, as Lord of all things, and partaker of His Father's kingdom. He promised His disciples that this should be, and He presented this vision to His martyr Stephen.

Aul. Why did He show this?

Bar. That we may not be discouraged in anything, knowing what a powerful defender and Lord we have in heaven.

Aul. Do you believe that He will come again in the same body to judge the living and the dead?

Bar. As certain as I am that those things the prophets have foretold concerning Christ have come to pass, so certain I am that whatever He would have us expect for the future shall come to pass. We have seen His first coming, according to the predictions of the prophets, wherein He came in humility to instruct and save us. We shall also see His second coming, when He will come on high, in the glory of His Father, before whose judgment seat all men of every nation and of every condition, whether kings or peasants, Greeks or Scythians, shall be compelled to appear; and not only those whom at that coming He shall find alive but also all those who have died from the beginning of the world, everyone in his own body. The blessed angels also shall be there as faithful servants, and the devils who are to be judged. Then from on high He will pronounce that unavoidable sentence that will cast the devil, together with those that have taken his part, into eternal punishments, that they may not afterward be able to harm anyone. He will translate the godly, freed from all trouble, to the company of His heavenly kingdom; although He wishes the day of His coming to remain unknown.

Aul. I hear no error yet. Let us now come to the Third Person.

Bar. As you please.

Aul. Do you believe in the Holy Spirit?

Bar. I do believe that It is true God, together with the Father and the Son. I believe those who wrote the books of the Old and New Testaments were inspired by It, without whose help no man attains salvation.

Aul. Why is He called Spirit?

Bar. Because as our bodies live by breath so our minds are vivified by the secret inspiration of the Holy Spirit.

Aul. Is it not lawful to call the Father Spirit?

Bar. Why not?

Aul. Are not the persons confounded?

Bar. No, not at all, for the Father is called Spirit because He is without a body, which is common to all the persons according to their divine nature. But the Third Person is called Spirit because He breathes out and transfuses Himself insensibly into our minds, even as the air breathes from the land or the rivers.

Aul. Why is the name of Son given to the Second Person?

Bar. Because of His perfect similarity of nature and will.

Aul. Is the Son more like the Father than the Holy Spirit is?

Bar. Not according to the divine nature, except that He resembles the property of the Father the more in this, that the Holy Spirit proceeds from Him also.

Aul. What, then, hinders, the Holy Spirit from being called Son?

Bar. Because, as St. Hilary says, "I have read nowhere that He was begotten; neither do I read this of His Father; I read of the Spirit, that He proceeds from!"

Aul. Why is the Father alone called God in the Creed?

Bar. Because, as I have said before, He is simply the author of all things that are, and the fountain of the whole Deity.

Aul. Would you clarify that?

Bar. Because there is nothing one can name that has not its origin from the Father. For in this very fact, that the Son and Holy Spirit is God, they acknowledge they receive from the Father. Therefore the chief authority, that is to say, the cause of beginning, is the Father alone, because He alone is of nothing. But yet in the Creed it may be so interpreted that the name of God may not be proper to one person but used in general, since it is distinguished afterward by the terms of Father, Son, and Holy Spirit into one God, which expression includes the Father, Son, and Holy Spirit; that is to say, the Three Persons.

Aul. Do you believe in the Holy Church?

Bar. No!

Aul. What? Don't you believe in it?

Bar. I believe the Holy Church, which is the body of Christ, that is to say, a certain congregation of all men throughout the whole world who agree in the faith of the Gospel, who worship one God the Father, who put their whole confidence in His Son, who are guided by the same Spirit of Him; from whose fellowship he is cut off who commits a mortal sin.

Aul. But why do you shrink from saying, "I believe in the Holy Church"?

Bar. Because St. Cyprian has taught me that we

must believe in God alone, in whom we absolutely put all our confidence. Whereas the Church, properly so called, although it consists of none but good men, yet consists of men, who may become bad, who may be deceived and deceive others.

Aul. What do you think of the communion of saints?

Bar. This article is not touched on at all by Cyprian when he particularly shows what in such and such churches is more or less used. For he thus connects them: "For there follows after this saying, 'the Holy Church, the forgiveness of sins, the resurrection of this flesh,' and some are of the opinion that this part does not differ from the former, but that it explains and enforces what previously was called the Holy Church, so that the Church is nothing else but the profession of one God, one gospel, one faith, one hope; the participation of the same Spirit and the same sacraments, in short, a kind of communion of all good things, among all pious men from the beginning of the world to the end, just as the fellowship of the members of the body is between one another. So that the good deeds of one may help another so long as they are living members of the body. But in this society even one's own good works do not further his salvation, unless he be reconciled to the holy congregation; and therefore follows, 'the forgiveness of sins,' because outside of the Church there is no remission of sins, though a man should pine himself away with repentance and perform works of charity. In the Church, I say, not of heretics, but the Holy Church, that is to say, gathered by the Spirit of Christ, there is forgiveness of sins by baptism, and after baptism by repentance and the keys given to the Church."

Aul. Thus far those are the words of a man who is sound. Do you believe that there will be a resurrection of the flesh?

Bar. I should believe all the rest to no purpose if I did not believe this, which is the most important of all.

Aul. What do you mean when you say the flesh?

Bar. A human body, animated with a human soul.

Aul. Shall every soul receive its own body that it left dead?

Bar. The very same from which it left, and, therefore, in Cyprian's Creed it is added, "of this flesh."

Aul. How can it be that the body, which has now been so often changed out of one thing into another, can rise again the same?

Bar. For Him who could create whatever He would out of nothing, is it a hard thing to restore to its former nature that which has been changed in its form? I don't dispute anxiously how it can be done; it is sufficient to me that He who has promised that it shall be so is so truthful that He cannot lie, and so powerful as to be able to accomplish with a nod whatever He pleases.

Aul. What need will there be of a body, then?

Bar. That the whole man may be glorified with Christ, who in this world was wholly afflicted for Christ.

Aul. What does the addition of "and life everlasting" mean?

Bar. That no one should think that we shall so rise again as the frogs revive at the beginning of the spring, to die again. For here is a twofold death: of the body, that is common to all men, both good and bad; and of the soul. And the death of the soul is sin. But after the resurrection the pious shall have everlasting life, both of body and soul. Nor shall the body then be subject again to diseases, old age, hunger, thirst, pain, weariness, death, or any inconvenience, but being made spiritual it shall be moved as the spirit will have it; nor shall the soul be any more perplexed with any vices or sorrows, but shall forever enjoy the greatest good, which is God Himself. On the contrary, eternal death both of body and soul shall seize upon the wicked. For their bodies shall be made immortal, for everlasting torments; and their souls forever distressed by the torments of their sins, without any hope of pardon.

Aul. Do you believe these things from your very heart, and truthfully?

Bar. I believe them with greater certainty than that I am now talking with you.

Aul. When I was at Rome, I did not find all believing with equal sincerity.

Bar. No, but if you look about more thoroughly, you'll find a great many others in other places, too, who do not firmly believe these things.

Aul. Well, then, since you agree with us in so many important points, what keeps you from joining completely with us?

Bar. I thought that you would ask that. I believe I am orthodox. Although I will not risk my life for it yet, I endeavor at all times to fulfill the obligation of my profession.

Aul. Why, then, is there so great a war between you and the orthodox?

Bar. Do inquire into that. But listen, Doctor, if you are not displeased with this introduction, have lunch with me, and after dining you may inquire of everything at leisure. I'll give you both arms to feel my pulse, and you shall see both stool and urine; and after that, if you please, you shall anatomize this whole chest of mine, that you may make a better judgment of me.

Aul. But I make eating with you a matter of religion.

Bar. Physicians are accustomed to do so, that they may better observe their patients and study their ailments.

Aul. I am afraid lest I should seem to favor heretics.

Bar. No, there is nothing more religious than to favor heretics.

Aul. How so?

Bar. Did not Paul wish to be made anathema to the Jews, who were worse than heretics? Doesn't he who attempts to improve a bad man and revive a dead man help him?

Aul. Yes, he certainly does.

Bar. Well, then, do me the same favor and you need not fear anything.

Aul. I've never heard a sick man answer more to the purpose. Well, come on, let me dine with you, then.

Bar. You shall be entertained in a medical way and as it befits a patient to entertain; and we will refresh our bodies with food that the mind shall be nevertheless fit for disputation.

Aul. Yes, let it be so, we shall dine on good birds.

Bar. You had better make that bad fish, unless you have forgotten that it is Friday.

Aul. That is something outside our creed.

MICHEL DE MONTAIGNE

Born in Périgord, France, in 1533, Montaigne mastered Latin as a child. In his studies he was influenced by the Renaissance humanists and by the unorthodox religious ideas of thinkers at the University of Toulouse. He later became a member of the parlement *at Bordeaux. Montaigne was a superb essayist. He defended scepticism in his extremely influential "Apology for Raymond Sebond." Continuing the ancient tradition of the sceptic Sextus Empiricus, Montaigne addressed the claims of science, religion, and morals with equal dubiety. Always a man of toleration and good sense, he, like Erasmus, tried to mediate the Catholic–Protestant conflict. Montaigne constantly revised his* Essays, *finishing a complete edition in 1588, only four years before his death.*

We reprint Montaigne's essay "That to Philosophize Is to Learn to Die," in which the experience of death is filtered through the wisdom of ancient authors. As in most of Montaigne's essays, antiquity is brought to bear on the contemporary scene, yielding a richness of insight that is too often forgotten in our own time.

That to Philosophize Is to Learn to Die

Cicero says that to philosophize is nothing else but to prepare for death. This is because study and contemplation draw our soul out of us to some extent and keep it busy outside the body; which is a sort of apprenticeship and semblance of death. Or else it is because all the wisdom and reasoning in the world boils down finally to this point: to teach us not to be afraid to die. In truth, either reason is a mockery, or

---

it must aim solely at our contentment, and the sum of its labors must tend to make us live well and at our ease, as Holy Scripture says. All the opinions in the world agree on this—that pleasure is our goal—though they choose different means to it. Otherwise they would be thrown out right away; for who would listen to a man who would set up our pain and discomfort as his goal?

The dissensions of the philosophic sects in this matter are merely verbal. *Let us skip over such frivolous subtleties* [Seneca]. There is more stubbornness and wrangling than befits such a sacred profession. But whatever role man undertakes to play, he always plays his own at the same time. Whatever they say, in virtue itself the ultimate goal we aim at is voluptuousness. I like to beat their ears with that word, which so goes against their grain. And if it means a certain supreme pleasure and excessive contentment, this is due more to the assistance of virtue than to any other assistance. This voluptuousness, for being more lusty, sinewy, robust, and manly, is only the more seriously voluptuous. And we should have given virtue the name of pleasure, a name more favorable, sweet, and natural; not that of vigor, as we have named it. That other baser sort of voluptuousness, if it deserved that beautiful name, should have acquired it in competition, not as a privilege. I find it less free of inconveniences and obstacles than virtue. Besides the fact that its enjoyment is more momentary, watery, and weak, it has its vigils, its fasts, and its hardships, its sweat and blood; and, more particularly its poignant sufferings of so many kinds, and an accompanying satiety so heavy that it is the equivalent of penance. We are very wrong to suppose that these disadvantages act as a spur and a spice to its sweetness, as in nature a thing is enlivened by its opposite, and to say, when we come to virtue, that similar consequences and difficulties oppress it, make it austere and inaccessible; whereas, much more than in the case of voluptuousness, they ennoble, whet, and heighten the divine and perfect pleasure that virtue affords us. That man is surely very unworthy of its acquaintance who balances its cost against its fruits; he knows neither its graces nor its use. Those who go on teaching us that the quest of it is rugged and laborious, though the enjoyment of it is agreeable, what are they doing but telling us that it is always disagreeable? For what human means ever attained the enjoyment of virtue? The most perfect have been quite content to aspire to it and to approach it, without possessing it. But those others are wrong; since in all the pleasures that we know, even the pursuit is pleasant. The attempt is made fragrant by the quality of the thing it aims at, for it is a good part of the effect, and consubstantial with it. The happiness and blessedness that shines in virtue fills all its appurtenances and approaches even to the first entrance and the utmost barrier.

Now among the principal benefits of virtue is disdain for death, a means that furnishes our life with a soft tranquillity and gives us a pure and pleasant enjoyment of it, without which all other pleasures are extinguished. That is why all rules meet and agree at this point. And though they all with one accord lead us also to scorn pain, poverty, and other accidents to which human life is subject, it is not with equal insistence; partly because these accidents are not so inevitable (most men spend their life without tasting poverty, and some also without feeling pain and illness, like Xenophilus the musician, who lived a hundred and six years in complete health), and also because at worst, whenever we please, death can put an end, and deny access, to all our other woes. But as for death itself, it is inevitable.

> We are all forced down the same road. Our
> fate,
> Tossed in the urn, will spring out soon or
> late,
> And force us helpless into Charon's bark,
> Passengers destined for eternal dark. (*Horace*)

And consequently, if it frightens us, it is a continual source of torment which cannot be alleviated at all. There is no place from which it may not come to us; we may turn our heads constantly this way and that as in a suspicious country: *death always hangs over us, like the stone over Tantalus* [Cicero]. Our law courts often send criminals to be executed at the place where the crime was committed. On the way, take them past beautiful houses, give them as good a time as you like—

> Not even a Sicilian feast
> Can now produce for him a pleasant taste,
> Nor song of birds, nor music of the lyre
> Restore his sleep (*Horace*)

—do you think that they can rejoice in these things, and that the final purpose of their trip, being steadily before their eyes, will not have changed and spoiled their taste for all these pleasures?

He hears it as it comes, counts days, measures the breath
Of life upon their length, tortured by coming death. (*Claudian*)

The goal of our career is death. It is the necessary object of our aim. If it frightens us, how is it possible to go a step forward without feverishness? The remedy of the common herd is not to think about it. But from what brutish stupidity can come so gross a blindness! They have to bridle the ass by the tail,

Who sets his mind on moving only backward. (*Lucretius*)

It is no wonder they are so often caught in the trap. These people take fright at the mere mention of death, and most of them cross themselves at that name, as at the name of the devil. And because death is mentioned in wills, don't expect them to set about writing a will until the doctor has given them their final sentence; and then, between the pain and the fright, Lord knows with what fine judgment they will concoct it.

Because this syllable struck their ears too harshly and seemed to them unlucky, the Romans learned to soften it or to spread it out into a periphrasis. Instead of saying "He is dead," they say "He has ceased to live." "He has lived." Provided it is life, even past life, they take comfort. We have borrowed from them our "late Mr. John."

Perhaps it is true that, as the saying goes, the delay is worth the money. I was born between eleven o'clock and noon on the last day of February, 1533, as we reckon time now, beginning the year in January. It was only just two weeks ago that I passed the age of thirty-nine years, and I need at least that many more; but to be bothered meanwhile by the thought of a thing so far off would be folly. After all, young and old leave life on the same terms. None goes out of it otherwise than as if he had just entered it. And besides, there is no man so decrepit that as long as he sees Methuselah ahead of him, he does not think he has another twenty years left in his body. Furthermore, poor fool that you are, who has assured you the term of your life? You are building on the tales of doctors. Look rather at facts and experience. By the ordinary run of things, you have been living a long time now by extraordinary favor. You have passed the accustomed limits of life. And to prove this, count how many more of your acquaintances have died before your age than have attained it. And even for those who have glorified their lives by renown, make a list, and I'll wager I'll find more of them who died before thirty-five than after. It is completely reasonable and pious to take our example from the humanity of Jesus Christ himself; now he finished his life at thirty-three. The greatest man that was simply a man, Alexander, also died at that age.

How many ways has death to surprise us!

Man never can plan fully to avoid
What any hour may bring. (*Horace*)

I leave aside fevers and pleurisies. Who would ever have thought that a duke of Brittany would be stifled to death by a crowd, as that duke was at the entrance of Pope Clement, my neighbor, into Lyons? Haven't you seen one of our kings killed at play? And did not one of his ancestors die from the charge of a hog? Aeschylus, threatened with the fall of a house, takes every precaution—in vain: he gets himself killed by a sort of roof, the shell of a tortoise dropped by a flying eagle. Another dies from a grape seed; an emperor from the scratch of a comb, while combing his hair; Aemilius Lepidus through stumbling against his threshold, and Aufidius through bumping against the door of the council chamber on his way in; and between women's thighs, Cornelius Gallus the praetor, Tigillinus, captain of the watch at Rome, Ludovico, son of Guido de Gonzaga, marquis of Mantua—and still worse, the Platonic philosopher Speusippus, and one of our Popes. Poor Bebius, a judge, in the act of granting a week's postponement to a litigant, has a seizure, his own term of living having expired; and Caius Julius, a doctor, is anointing the eyes of a patient, when along comes death and closes his. And, if I must bring myself into this, a brother of mine, Captain Saint-Martin, twenty-three years old, who had already given pretty good proof of his valor, while playing tennis was struck by a ball a little above the right ear, with no sign of contusion or wound. He did not sit down or rest, but five or six hours later he died of an apoplexy that this blow gave him. With such frequent and ordinary examples passing before our eyes, how can we possibly rid ourselves of the thought of death and of the idea that at every moment it is gripping us by the throat?

What does it matter, you will tell me, how it happens, provided we do not worry about it? I am of that opinion; and in whatever way we can put ourselves in shelter from blows, even under a calf's skin, I am not the man to shrink from it. For it is enough for me to spend my life comfortably; and the best game I can give myself I'll take, though it be as little glorious and exemplary as you like:

> If but my faults could trick and please
> My wits, I'd rather seem a fool at ease,
> Than to be wise and rage. (*Horace*)

But it is folly to expect to get there that way. They go, they come, they trot, they dance—of death no news. All that is fine. But when it comes, either to them or to their wives, children, or friends, surprising them unprepared and defenseless, what torments, what cries, what frenzy, what despair overwhelms them! Did you ever see anything so dejected, so changed, so upset? We must provide for this earlier; and this brutish nonchalance, even if it could lodge in the head of a man of understanding—which I consider entirely impossible—sells us its wares too dear. If it were an enemy we could avoid, I would advise us to borrow the arms of cowardice. But since that cannot be, since it catches you just the same, whether you flee like a coward or act like a man—

> As surely it pursues the man that flees,
> Nor does it spare the haunches slack
> Of warless youth, or its timid back (*Horace*)

—and since no kind of armor protects you—

> Hide as he will, cautious, in steel and brass,
> Still death will drag his head outside at last
> (*Propertius*)

—let us learn to meet it steadfastly and to combat it. And to begin to strip it of its greatest advantage against us, let us take an entirely different way from the usual one. Let us rid it of its strangeness, come to know it, get used to it. Let us have nothing on our minds as often as death. At every moment let us picture it in our imagination in all its aspects. At the stumbling of a horse, the fall of a tile, the slightest pin prick, let us promptly chew on this: Well, what if it were death itself? And thereupon let us tense ourselves and make an effort. Amid feasting and gaiety let us ever keep in mind this refrain, the memory of our condition; and let us never allow ourselves to be so carried away by pleasure that we do not sometimes remember in how many ways this happiness of ours is a prey to death, and how death's clutches threaten it. Thus did the Egyptians, who, in the midst of their feasts and their greatest pleasures, had the skeleton of a dead man brought before them, to serve as a reminder to the guests.

> Look on each day as if it were your last,
> And each unlooked-for hour will seem a
> boon. (*Horace*)

It is uncertain where death awaits us; let us await it everywhere. Premeditation of death is premeditation of freedom. He who has learned how to die has unlearned how to be a slave. Knowing how to die frees us from all subjection and constraint. There is nothing evil in life for the man who has thoroughly grasped the fact that to be deprived of life is not an evil. Aemilius Paulus replied to the messenger sent by that miserable king of Macedon, his prisoner, to beg him not to lead him in his triumph: "Let him make that request of himself."

In truth, in all things, unless nature lends a hand, it is hard for art and industry to get very far. I am by nature not melancholy, but dreamy. Since my earliest days, there is nothing with which I have occupied my mind more than with images of death. Even in the most licentious season of my life,

> When blooming youth enjoyed a gladsome
> spring, (*Catullus*)

amid ladies and games, someone would think me involved in digesting some jealousy by myself, or the uncertainty of some hope, while I was thinking about I don't remember whom, who had been overtaken a few days before by a hot fever and by death, on leaving a similar feast, his head full of idleness, love, and a good time, like myself; and thinking that the same chance was hanging from my ear:

> And soon it will have been, past any man's
> recall. (*Lucretius*)

I did not wrinkle my forehead any more over that thought than any other. It is impossible that we should fail to feel the sting of such notions at first. But by handling them and going over them, in the long run we tame them beyond question. Otherwise for my part I should be in continual fright and frenzy; for never did a man so distrust his life, never did a man set less faith in his duration. Neither does health, which thus far I have enjoyed in great vigor and with little interruption, lengthen my hope of life, nor do illnesses shorten it. Every minute I seem to be slipping away from myself. And I constantly sing myself this refrain: Whatever can be done another day can be done today. Truly risks and dangers bring us little or no nearer our end; and if we think how many million accidents remain hanging over our heads, not to mention this one that seems to threaten us most, we shall conclude that lusty or feverish, on sea or in our houses, in battle or in rest, death is equally near us. *No man is frailer than another, no man more certain of the morrow* [Seneca]. To finish what I have to do before I die, even if it were one hour's work, any leisure seems short to me.

Someone, looking through my tablets the other day, found a memorandum about something I wanted done after my death. I told him what was true, that although only a league away from my house, and hale and hearty, I had hastened to write it there, since I could not be certain of reaching home. Since I am constantly brooding over my thoughts and settling them within me, I am at all times about as well prepared as I can be. And the coming of death will teach me nothing new.

We must be always booted and ready to go, so far as it is in our power, and take especial care to have only ourselves to deal with then:

> Why aim so stoutly at so many things
> In our short life? (*Horace*)

For we shall have enough trouble without adding any. One man complains not so much of death as that it interrupts the course of a glorious victory; another, that he must move out before he has married off his daughter or supervised the education of his children; one laments losing the company of his wife, another of his son, as the principal comforts of his life.

I am at this moment in such a condition, thank God, that I can move out when he chooses, without regret for anything at all, unless for life, if I find that the loss of it weighs on me. I unbind myself on all sides; my farewells are already half made to everyone except myself. Never did a man prepare to leave the world more utterly and completely, nor detach himself from it more universally, than I propose to do.

> "Wretch that I am," they say, "one all-destroying day
> Takes every last reward of all my life away!"
> (*Lucretius*)

And the builder says:

> The works remain suspended,
> And the high looming walls. (*Virgil*)

We must not plan anything that takes so long, or at least not with the idea of flying into a passion if we cannot see it accomplished. We are born to act:

> When death comes, let it find me at my work.
> (*Ovid*)

I want a man to act, and to prolong the functions of life as long as he can; and I want death to find me planting my cabbages, but careless of death, and still more of my unfinished garden. I saw a man die who, in his last extremity, complained constantly that destiny was cutting short the history, on which he was at work, of the fifteenth or sixteenth of our kings.

> But this they fail to add: that after you expire
> Not one of all these things will fill you with desire. (*Lucretius*)

We must rid ourselves of these vulgar and harmful humors. Just as we plant our cemeteries next to churches, and in the most frequented parts of town, in order (says Lycurgus) to accustom the common people, women and children, not to grow panicky at the sight of a dead man, and so that the constant sight of bones, tombs, and funeral processions should remind us of our condition—

> To feasts, it once was thought, slaughter lent added charms,
> Mingling with foods the sight of combatants in arms,
> And gladiators fell amid the cups, to pour
> Onto the very tables their abundant gore.
> (*Silius Italicus*)

—and as the Egyptians, after their feasts, had a large image of death shown to the guests by a man who called out to them: "Drink and be merry, for when you are dead you will be like this"; so I have formed the habit of having death continually present, not merely in my imagination, but in my mouth. And there is nothing that I investigate so eagerly as the death of men: what words, what look, what bearing they maintained at that time; nor is there a place in the histories that I note so attentively. This shows in the abundance of my illustrative examples; I have indeed a particular fondness for this subject. If I were a maker of books, I would make a register, with comments, of various deaths. He who would teach men to die would teach them to live. Dicearchus made a book with such a title, but with a different and less useful purpose.

People will tell me that the reality of death so far exceeds the image we form of it that, when a man is faced with it, even the most skillful fencing will do him no good. Let them talk; beyond question forethought is a great advantage. And then, is it nothing to go at least that far without disturbance and fever? What is more, Nature herself lends us her hand and gives us courage. If it is a quick and violent death, we have no leisure to fear it; if it is otherwise, I notice that in proportion as I sink into sickness, I naturally enter into a certain disdain for life. I find that I have much more trouble digesting this resolution to die when I am in health than when I have a fever. Inasmuch as I no longer cling so hard to the good things of life when I begin to lose the use and pleasure of them, I come to view death with much less frightened eyes. This makes me hope that the farther I get from life and the nearer to death, the more easily I shall accept the exchange. Even as I have experienced in many other occasions what Caesar says, that things often appear greater to us from a distance than near, so I have found that when I was healthy I had a much greater horror of sicknesses than when I felt them.

The good spirits, pleasure, and strength I now enjoy make the other state appear to me so disproportionate to this one, that by imagination I magnify those inconveniences by half, and think of them as much heavier than I find they are when I have them on my shoulders. I hope I shall have the same experience with death.

Let us see how, in those ordinary changes and declines that we suffer, nature hides from us the sense of our loss and decay. What has an old man left of the vigor of his youth, and of his past life?

> Alas! how scant a share of life the old have left! (*Maximianus*)

Caesar, observing the decrepit appearance of a soldier of his guard, an exhausted and broken man, who came to him in the street to ask leave to kill himself, replied humorously: "So you think you're alive." If we fell into such a change suddenly, I don't think we could endure it. But, when we are led by Nature's hand down a gentle and virtually imperceptible slope, bit by bit, one step at a time, she rolls us into this wretched state and makes us familiar with it; so that we feel no shock when youth dies within us, which in essence and in truth is a harder death than the complete death of a languishing life or the death of old age; inasmuch as the leap is not so cruel from a painful life to no life as from a sweet and flourishing life to a grievous and painful one.

The body, when bent and bowed, has less strength to support a burden, and so has the soul; we must raise and straighten her against the assault of this adversary. For as it is impossible for the soul to be at rest while she fears death, so, if she can gain assurance against it, she can boast of a thing as it were beyond man's estate: that it is impossible for worry, torment, fear, or even the slightest displeasure to dwell in her:

> The fierce look of a tyrant brings no fright
> To his firm mind, nor yet the south wind's
> might,
> That drives the Adriatic on command,
> Nor Jupiter's great thunder-hurling hand.
> (*Horace*)

She is made mistress of her passions and lusts, mistress over indigence, shame, poverty, and all other wounds of fortune. Let us gain this advantage, those of us who can; this is the true and sovereign liberty, which enables us to thumb our noses at force and injustice and to laugh at prisons and chains:

> "I'll keep you bound
> Both hand and foot, in savage custody."
> —"Whene'er I please, a god will set me free."
> I think he meant: I'll die. For death is final.
> (*Horace*)

Our religion has no surer human foundation than contempt for life. Not only do the arguments of reason invite us to it; for why should we fear to lose a thing which once lost cannot be regretted? And since we are threatened by so many kinds of death, is there not more pain in fearing them all than in enduring one?

What does it matter when it comes, since it is inevitable? To the man who told Socrates, "The thirty tyrants have condemned you to death," he replied: "And nature, them."

What stupidity to torment ourselves about passing into exemption from all torment! As our birth brought us the birth of all things, so will our death bring us the death of all things. Wherefore it is as foolish to lament that we shall not be alive a hundred years from now as it is to lament that we were not alive a hundred years ago. Death is the origin of another life. Just so did we weep, just so did we struggle against entering this life, just so did we strip off our former veil when we entered it.

Nothing can be grievous that happens only once. Is it reasonable so long to fear a thing so short? Long life and short life are made all one by death. For there is no long or short for things that are no more. Aristotle says that there are little animals by the river Hypanis that live only a day. The one that dies at eight o'clock in the morning dies in its youth; the one that dies at five in the afternoon dies in its decrepitude. Which of us does not laugh to see this moment of duration considered in terms of happiness or unhappiness? The length or shortness of our duration, if we compare it with eternity, or yet with the duration of mountains, rivers, stars, trees, and even of some animals, is no less ridiculous.

But Nature forces us to it. Go out of this world, she says, as you entered it. The same passage that you made from death to life, without feeling or fright, make it again from life to death. Your death is a part of the order of the universe; it is a part of the life of the world.

> Our lives we borrow from each other . . .
> And men, like runners, pass along the torch
> of life. (*Lucretius*)

Shall I change for you this beautiful contexture of things? Death is the condition of your creation, it is a part of you; you are fleeing from your own selves. This being of yours that you enjoy is equally divided between death and life. The first day of your birth leads you toward death as toward life:

> The hour which gave us life led to its
> end. (*Seneca*)

> Even in birth we die; the end is there from
> the start. (*Manilius*)

All the time you live you steal from life; living is at life's expense. The constant work of your life is to build death. You are in death while you are in life; for you are after death when you are no longer in life. Or, if you prefer it this way, you are dead after life; but during life you are dying; and death affects the dying much more roughly than the dead, and more keenly and essentially.

If you have made your profit of life, you have had your fill of it; go your way satisfied:

> Why, like a well-filled guest, not leave the
> feast of life? (*Lucretius*)

If you have not known how to make good use of it, if it was useless to you, what do you care that you have lost it, what do you still want it for?

> Why do you seek to add more years
> Which too would pass but ill, and vanish
> unawares? (*Lucretius*)

Life is neither good nor evil in itself: it is the scene of good and evil according as you give them room.

And if you have lived a day, you have seen everything. One day is equal to all days. There is no other light, no other night. This sun, this moon, these stars, the way they are arranged, all is the very same your ancestors enjoyed and that will entertain your grandchildren:

> Your ancestors beheld no other one, nor shall
> Your nephews see another. (*Manilius*)

And at worst, the distribution and variety of all the acts of my comedy runs its course in a year. If you have taken note of the revolution of my four seasons, they embrace the infancy, the youth, the manhood, and the old age of the world. It has played its part. It knows no other trick than to begin again. It will always be just this:

> We turn in the same circle, and never
> leave; (*Lucretius*)
> And on itself the year revolves along its
> track. (*Virgil*)

I am not minded to make you any other new pastimes:

> I can contrive, to please you, nothing more;
> All things remain as they have been before.
> (*Lucretius*)

Make room for others, as others have for you. Equality is the principal part of equity. Who can complain of being included where all are included? And so, live as long as you please, you will strike nothing off the time you will have to spend dead; it is no use; you shall be as long in that state which you fear as if you had died nursing:

> So live victorious, live long as you will,
> Eternal death shall be there waiting still.
> (*Lucretius*)

And furthermore, I shall put you in such a condition as will give you no cause for complaint:

> Do you not know that when death comes, there'll be
> No other you to mourn your memory,
> And stand above you prostrate? (*Lucretius*)

Nor will you wish for the life you now lament so much:

> Then none shall mourn their person or their life . . .
> And all regret of self shall cease to be.
> (*Lucretius*)

Death is to be feared less than nothing, if there is anything less than nothing:

> For us far less a thing must death be thought,
> If ought there be that can be less than nought. (*Lucretius*)

It does not concern you dead or alive: alive, because you are; dead, because you are no more.

No one dies before his time. The time you leave behind was no more yours than that which passed before your birth, and it concerns you no more.

> Look back and see how past eternities of time
> Are nothing to us. (*Lucretius*)

Wherever your life ends, it is all there. The advantage of living is not measured by length, but by use; some men have lived long, and lived little; attend to it while you are in it. It lies in your will, not in the number of years, for you to have lived enough. Did you think you would never arrive where you never ceased going? Yet there is no road but has its end. And if company can comfort you, does not the world keep pace with you?

> All things, their life being done, will follow you. (*Lucretius*)

Does not everything move with your movement? Is there anything that does not grow old along with you? A thousand men, a thousand animals, and a thousand other creatures die at the very moment when you die:

> No night has ever followed day, no day the night,
> That has not heard, amid the newborn infants' squalls,
> The wild laments that go with death and funerals. (*Lucretius*)

Why do you recoil, if you cannot draw back? You have seen enough men who were better off for dying, thereby avoiding great miseries. Have you found any man that was worse off? How simple-minded it is to condemn a thing that you have not experienced yourself or through anyone else. Why do you complain of me and of destiny? Do we wrong you? Is it for you to govern us, or us you? Though your age is not full-grown, your life is. A little man is a whole man, just like a big one. Neither men nor their lives are measured by the ell.

Chiron refused immortality when informed of its conditions by the very god of time and duration, his father Saturn. Imagine honestly how much less bearable and more painful to man would be an ever-lasting life than the life I have given him. If you did not have death, you would curse me incessantly for having deprived you of it. I have deliberately mixed with it a little bitterness to keep you, seeing the convenience of it, from embracing it too greedily and intemperately. To lodge you in that moderate state that I ask of you, of neither fleeing life nor fleeing back from death, I have tempered both of them between sweetness and bitterness.

I taught Thales, the first of your sages, that life and death were matters of indifference; wherefore, to the man who asked him why then he did not die, he replied very wisely: "Because it is indifferent."

Water, earth, air, fire, and the other parts of this structure of mine are no more instruments of your life than instruments of your death. Why do you fear your last day? It contributes no more to your death than each of the others. The last step does not cause the fatigue, but reveals it. All days travel toward death, the last one reaches it.

Such are the good counsels of our mother Nature. Now I have often pondered how it happens that in wars the face of death, whether we see it in ourselves or in others, seems to us incomparably less terrifying than in our houses—otherwise you would have an army of doctors and snivelers—and, since death is always the same, why nevertheless there is much more assurance against it among villagers and humble folk than among others. I truly think it is those dreadful faces and trappings with which we surround it, that frighten us more than death itself: an entirely new way of living; the cries of mothers, wives, and children; the visits of people dazed and benumbed by grief; the presence of a number of pale and weeping servants; a darkened room; lighted candles; our bedside besieged by doctors and preachers; in short, everything horror and fright around us. There we are already shrouded and buried. Children fear even their friends when they see them masked, and so do we ours. We must strip the mask from things as well as from persons; when it is off, we shall find beneath only that same death which a valet or a mere chambermaid passed through not long ago without fear. Happy the death that leaves no leisure for preparing such ceremonies!

SUGGESTIONS FOR FURTHER READING

Bainton, Roland H. *The Reformation of the Sixteenth Century.* Boston: Beacon Press, 1952.

Dillenberger, John, ed. *John Calvin.* New York: Doubleday-Anchor, 1971.

Dolan, John P. *History of the Reformation.* New York: New American Library, 1967.

Elton, G. R. *Reformation Europe: 1517–1559.* New York: Meridian, 1964.

Harbison, E. Harris. *The Age of Reformation.* Ithaca: Cornell University Press, 1955.

Manns, Peter. *Martin Luther.* New York: Crossroad, 1982.

Ong, Walter J. *Ramus.* Cambridge, Massachusetts: Harvard University Press, 1958.

Popkin, Richard H. *The History of Scepticism from Erasmus to Descartes.* New York: Harper Torchbooks, 1964.

Rabil, Albert, Jr. *Erasmus and the New Testament: The Mind of a Christian Humanist.* San Antonio: Trinity University Press, 1972.

Whale, G. S. *The Protestant Tradition.* Cambridge: Cambridge University Press, 1959.

The Scientific Revolution: The Earth Moves

It would be impossible to overestimate the importance of the Scientific Revolution for the subsequent history of civilization. This intellectual explosion of the sixteenth and seventeenth centuries gave birth to modern science, modern technology, and the Industrial Revolution. Together, these transformed western civilization and by the twentieth century spread throughout the planet earth.

The key events triggering the Scientific Revolution were the claim of Copernicus that the earth revolved about the sun and its subsequent verification by Tycho Brahe, Johannes Kepler, and Galileo Galilei. The stern opposition of the Roman Church and general incredulity were soon overcome by the development of an empirical scientific method and especially by the invention of the telescope. In short, the time-honored geocentric contention of Ptolemy and Aristotle was shattered. Experimental science, pioneered by Galileo and furthered by Francis Bacon, took the center of the philosophical stage. By virtue of the experimental method, philosophical speculation was forced to acknowledge the priority of the observation, collection, and quantification of data.

Parallel breakthroughs in scientific method and experimentally verified results were found in the anatomical studies of Andreas Vesalius, the physiology of William Harvey, and the chemistry of Robert Boyle. Along with the telescope, the invention of the microscope and the mechanical clock greatly furthered the accuracy of human observation. Science needed only a universal method *(universalis mathesis)* in order to combine bold speculation with empirical observation, so as to account for all data, all change, and all natural laws. In the succeeding volume we shall see that such a method was forthcoming in the independent creation of the calculus by Isaac Newton and Gottfried Leibniz.

The sixteenth century was characterized by profound breaks with the past—a new universe, a new world, a new religion, and a new way of knowing. In global terms, the most influential of these was the birth of modern science, which for better or worse, provided the gateway to the twentieth century.

Nicholaus Copernicus

Copernicus was born in Torun, Poland, in 1473. Although he performed a multiplicity of roles—he was a physician, a canon at the Cathedral of Frauenberg, and a translator of Greek texts—it was as an astronomer that he achieved lasting fame. After studying ancient manuscripts, Copernicus concluded that the classical geocentric assumption was incorrect. Copernicus reached this conclusion as early as 1530 but did not publish his work, On the Revolutions of the Heavenly Spheres, *until 1543, when he was on his deathbed. Although he had predecessors, Nicholas of Cusa, for example, Copernicus was the first to stress the earth's rotation around the sun and made it possible for Kepler's theory of planetary motion to provide an accurate defense of heliocentrism.*

Copernicanism—that is, the contributions of Copernicus, Brahe, Kepler, and Galileo—not only defied sense experience of a stable earth and a setting sun, but also destroyed the Aristotelian doctrine of natural place. No longer was the earth fixed, and therefore no longer was there a fixed human place. It is thus that John Donne could write "new Philosophy calls all in doubt, . . . 'Til all in pieces, all coherence gone." Not until the thought of René Descartes and Isaac Newton was a semblance of order to be restored, although such order was to prove temporary, for the work of Einstein on relativity and Heisenberg on indeterminacy was to appear in the twentieth century.

Preface to On the Revolutions of the Heavenly Spheres

TO THE MOST HOLY LORD, POPE PAUL III

The Preface of Nicholaus Copernicus to the Books of the Revolutions

I may well presume, most Holy Father, that certain people, as soon as they hear that in this book *On the Revolutions of the Spheres of the Universe* I ascribe movement to the earthly globe, will cry out that, holding such views, I should at once be hissed off the stage. For I am not so pleased with my own work that I should fail duly to weigh the judgment which others may pass thereon; and though I know that the speculations of a philosopher are far removed from the judgment of the multitude—for his aim is to seek truth in all things as far as God has permitted human reason so to do—yet I hold that opinions which are quite erroneous should be avoided.

Thinking therefore within myself that to ascribe movement to the Earth must indeed seem an absurd performance on my part to those who know that many centuries have consented to the establishment of the contrary judgment, namely that the Earth is placed immovably as the central point in the middle of the Universe, I hesitated long whether, on the one hand, I should give to the light these my Commentaries written to prove the Earth's motion, or whether, on the other hand, it were better to follow the example of the Pythagoreans and others who were wont to impart their philosophic mysteries only to intimates and friends, and then not in writing but by word of mouth, as the letter of Lysis to Hipparchus witnesses. In my judgment they did so not, as some would have it, through jealousy of sharing their doctrines, but as fearing lest these so noble and hardly won discoveries of the learned should be despised by such as either care not to study aught save for gain, or—if by the encouragement and example of others they are stimulated to philosophic liberal pursuits—yet by reason of the dulness of their wits are in the company of philosophers as drones among bees. Reflecting thus, the thought of the scorn which I had to fear on account of the novelty and incongruity of my theory, well-nigh induced me to abandon my project.

These misgivings and actual protests have been overcome by my friends. First among these was Nicolaus Schönberg, Cardinal of Capua, a man renowned in every department of learning. Next was one who loved me well, Tiedemann Giese, Bishop of

---

Nicholaus Copernicus, Preface to *De Revolutionibus,* trans. John F. Dobson and Selig Brodetsky, in Milton K. Munitz, ed., *Theories of the Universe: From Babylonian Myth to Modern Science* (Glencoe, Ill.: Free Press, 1957), pp. 149–152. Originally published in *Occasional Notes,* No. 10, 1947, and reprinted with the permission of the Royal Astronomical Society.

Kulm, a devoted student of sacred and all other good literature, who often urged and even importuned me to publish this work which I had kept in store not for nine years only, but to a fourth period of nine years. The same request was made to me by many other eminent and learned men. They urged that I should not, on account of my fears, refuse any longer to contribute the fruits of my labours to the common advantage of those interested in mathematics. They insisted that, though my theory of the Earth's movement might at first seem strange, yet it would appear admirable and acceptable when the publication of my elucidatory comments should dispel the mists of paradox. Yielding then to their persuasion I at last permitted my friends to publish that work which they have so long demanded.

That I allow the publication of these my studies may surprise your Holiness the less in that, having been at such travail to attain them, I had already not scrupled to commit to writing my thoughts upon the motion of the Earth. How I came to dare to conceive such motion of the Earth, contrary to the received opinion of the Mathematicians and indeed contrary to the impression of the senses, is what your Holiness will rather expect to hear. So I should like your Holiness to know that I was induced to think of a method of computing the motions of the spheres by nothing else than the knowledge that the Mathematicians are inconsistent in these investigations.

Nicholaus Copernicus, by P. Gassendi, in N. Copernici vita *(1654). In 1543 Copernicus published the first extensive work to cast doubt on the belief that the earth was the stable center of the universe. (Armitage, frontispiece)*

For, first, the mathematicians are so unsure of the movements of the Sun and Moon that they cannot even explain or observe the constant length of the seasonal year. Secondly, in determining the motions of these and of the other five planets, they do not even use the same principles and hypotheses as in their proofs of seeming revolutions and motions. So some use only concentric circles, while others eccentrics and epicycles. Yet even by these means they do not completely attain their ends. Those who have relied on concentrics, though they have proven that some different motions can be compounded therefrom, have not thereby been able fully to establish a system which agrees with the phenomena. Those again who have devised eccentric systems, though they appear to have well-nigh established the seeming motions by calculations agreeable to their assumptions, have yet made many admissions which seem to violate the first principle of uniformity in motion. Nor have they been able thereby to discern or deduce the principal thing—namely the shape of the Universe and the unchangeable symmetry of its parts. With them it is as though an artist were to gather the hands, feet, head and other members for his images from divers models, each part excellently drawn, but not related to a single body, and since they in no way match each other, the result would be monster rather than man. So in the course of their exposition, which the mathematicians call their system (μέθοδος) we find that they have either omitted some indispensable detail or introduced something foreign and wholly irrelevant. This would of a surety not have been so had they followed fixed principles; for if their hypotheses were not misleading, all inferences based thereon might be surely verified. Though my present assertions are obscure, they will be made clear in due course.

I pondered long upon this uncertainty of mathematical tradition in establishing the motions of the system of the spheres. At last I began to chafe that philosophers could by no means agree on any one certain theory of the mechanism of the Universe, wrought for us by a supremely good and orderly Creator, though in other respects they investigated with meticulous care the minutest points relating to its orbits. I therefore took pains to read again the works of all the philosophers on whom I could lay hand to seek out whether any of them had ever supposed that the motions of the spheres were other than those demanded by the mathematical schools. I found first in Cicero that Hicetas had realized that the Earth moved. Afterwards I found in Plutarch that certain others had held the like opinion. I think fit here to add Plutarch's own words, to make them accessible to all:—

> The rest hold the Earth to be stationary, but Philolaus the Pythagorean says that she moves around the (central) fire on an oblique circle like the Sun and Moon. Heraclides of Pontus and Ecphantus the Pythagorean also make the Earth to move, not indeed through space but by rotating round her own centre as a wheel on an axle from West to East.

Taking advantage of this I too began to think of the mobility of the Earth; and though the opinion seemed absurd, yet knowing now that others before me had been granted freedom to imagine such circles as they chose to explain the phenomena of the stars, I considered that I also might easily be allowed to try whether, by assuming some motion of the Earth, sounder explanations than theirs for the revolution of the celestial spheres might so be discovered.

Thus assuming motions, which in my work I ascribe to the Earth, by long and frequent observations I have at last discovered that, if the motions of the rest of the planets be brought into relation with the circulation of the Earth and be reckoned in proportion to the orbit of each planet, not only do their phenomena presently ensue, but the orders and magnitudes of all stars and spheres, nay the heavens themselves, become so bound together that nothing in any part thereof could be moved from its place without producing confusion of all the other parts and of the Universe as a whole.

In the course of the work the order which I have pursued is as here follows. In the first book I describe all positions of the spheres together with such movements as I ascribe to Earth; so that this book contains, as it were, the general system of the Universe. Afterwards, in the remaining books, I relate the motions of the other planets and all the spheres to the mobility of Earth, that we may gather thereby how far the motions and appearances of the rest of the planets and spheres may be preserved, if related to the motions of the Earth.

I doubt not that gifted and learned mathematicians will agree with me if they are willing to comprehend and appreciate, not superficially but thoroughly, according to the demands of this science, such reasoning as I bring to bear in support of my judgment. But that learned and unlearned alike may see that I shrink not from any man's criticism, it is to your Holiness rather than anyone else that I have chosen to dedicate these studies of mine, since in this remote corner of Earth in which I live you are regarded as the most eminent by virtue alike of the dignity of your Office and of your love of letters and science. You by your influence and judgment can readily hold the slanderers from biting, though the proverb hath it that there is no remedy against a sycophant's tooth. It may fall out, too, that idle babblers, ignorant of mathematics, may claim a right to pronounce a judgment on my work, by reason of a certain passage of Scripture basely twisted to suit their purpose. Should any such venture to criticize and carp at my project, I make no account of them; I consider their judgment rash, and utterly despise it. I well know that even Lactantius, a writer in other ways distinguished but in no sense a mathematician, discourses in a most childish fashion touching the shape of the Earth, ridiculing even those who have stated the Earth to be a sphere. Thus my supporters need not be amazed if some people of like sort ridicule me too.

Mathematics are for mathematicians, and they, if I be not wholly deceived, will hold that these my labours contribute somewhat even to the Commonwealth of the Church, of which your Holiness is now Prince. For not long since, under Leo X, the question of correcting the ecclesiastical calendar was debated in the Council of the Lateran. It was left undecided for the sole cause that the lengths of the years and months and the motions of the Sun and Moon were not held to have been yet determined with sufficient exactness. From that time on I have given thought to their more accurate observation, by the advice of that eminent man Paul, Lord Bishop of Sempronia, sometime in charge of that business of the calendar. What results I have achieved therein, I leave to the judgment of learned mathematicians and of your Holiness in particular. And now, not to seem to promise your Holiness more than I can perform with regard to the usefulness of the work, I pass to my appointed task.

JOHN DONNE

John Donne was born in England in 1572 and lived until 1631. He is one of the great poets of the English language and has significantly influenced twentieth-century poetry. In the following brief selection from his poem "An Anatomy of the World," Donne lays bare the deep frustration and bewilderment attendant upon the Copernican revolution. His lamentation that each of us thinks he must be a "Phenix" and rise anew from the ashes of the world presages the appearance of post-Copernican religious, social, philosophical, and political individuality.

From An Anatomy of the World

. . . new Philosophy calls all in doubt,
The Element of fire is quite put out;
The Sun is lost, and the earth, and no man's wit
Can well direct him where to look for it.
And freely men confess that this world's spent,
When in the Planets, and the Firmament
They seek so many new; then see that this
Is crumbled out again to his Atomies.
'Til all in pieces, all coherence gone;
All just supply, and all Relation:
Prince, Subject, Father, Son, are things forgot,
For every man alone thinks he hath got
To be a Phenix, and that then can be
None of that kind, of which he is, but he.

AMERIGO VESPUCCI

Long overlooked because of his humble beginning and the publicity given to Columbus, who, nevertheless, could not admit to the existence of a new continent, Vespucci is now regarded as the true discoverer of the New World. Born in Florence in 1454, he sailed under the Portuguese flag in 1501, when he explored the coast of Latin America. On the basis of Vespucci's claim, a map was published which featured the presence of America. The Waldseemüller map accompanied the publication of The Cosmographiae Introductio. *This map added another continent, America, to the single continent with the three "parts" of Asia, Africa, and Europa.*

From John Donne, "An Anatomy of the World," in *The Complete Poetry and Selected Prose of John Donne* (New York: Modern Library, 1952), p. 191.

Sixteenth-Century Map of the World by Robert Thorne, A.D. *1527*

Although in the long run this discovery may not seem as surprising as that of Copernicus, nonetheless sixteenth-century Europe was flabbergasted. The discovery of another continent caused havoc not only with classical cartography but with the belief in the Bible as well. Who, after all, were these new people? If they were not descendants of Adam, what was their place, their meaning, in the scheme of Christian theology?

As is now well documented, the answers given to these questions were to have pernicious consequences. The Protestant settlers of North America, clinging to a literal

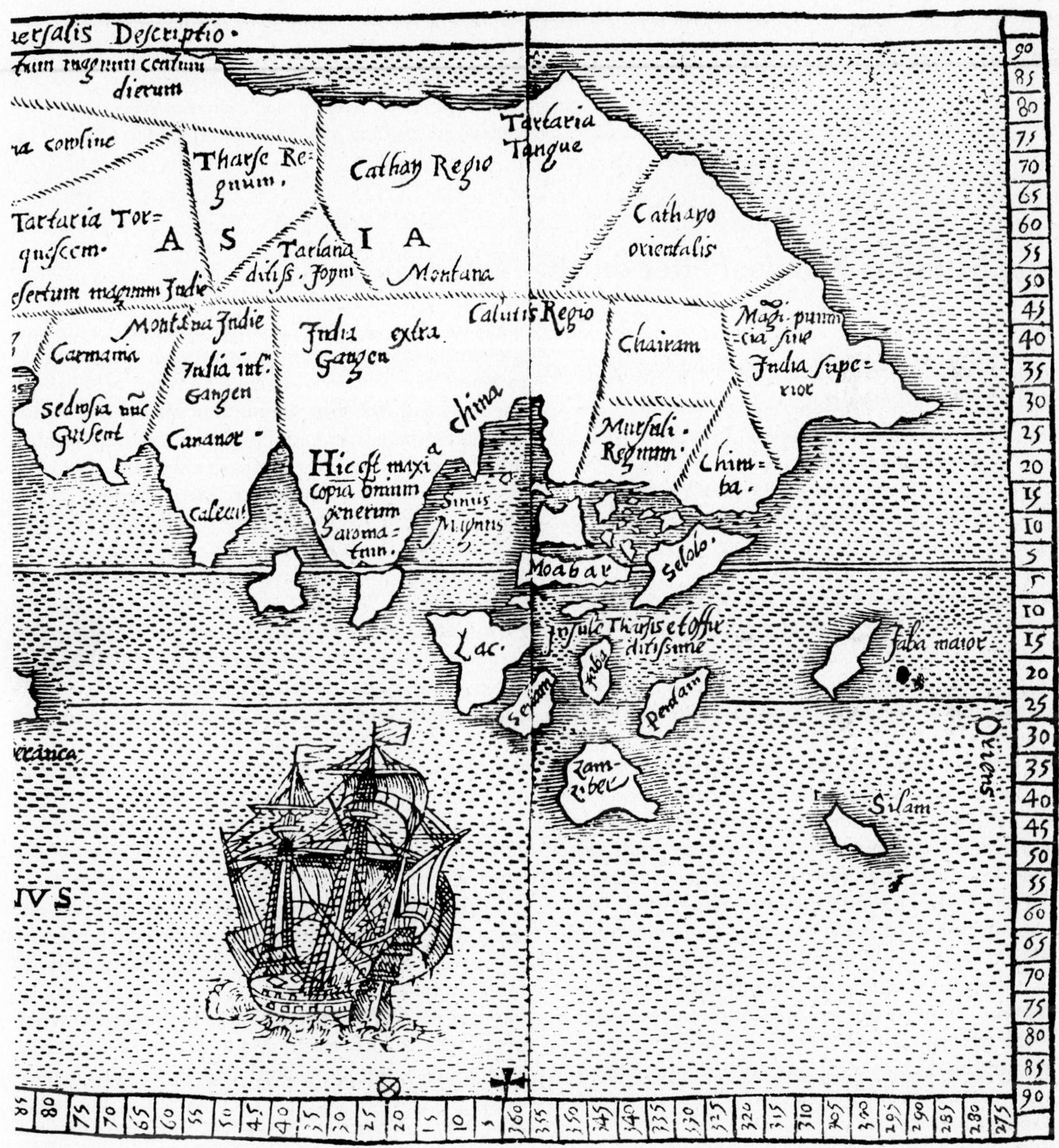

interpretation of the Bible, regarded the Amerindians as nonpersons and treated them as such. The Catholic settlers of Latin America, less bound by the Bible and more colonially inclined, were less ideological and therefore more amenable to intermarriage and partial preservation of the native traditions. On both continents, however, European culture sought to dominate for reasons of King, Queen, or religion. The irony, of course, is that if Europe proclaimed the existence of a New World, it had no choice but to accept the unflattering appellation of an Old World, or to view itself as a parent, a mother *country. In turn, the relationship between Europe and colonial America was to alternate between fascination and condescension. The insulated, provincial character of European civilization was severely challenged by the explorations. Civilization was moving to the west. More than any other single figure, this extraordinary development is attributable to Amerigo Vespucci, whose voyages were epoch-making and whose travels caused his death by malaria in 1512.*

From Mundus Novus: Letter on the New World

1503

Amerigo Vespucci Offers His Best Compliments to Lorenzo Pietro di Medici

On a former occasion I wrote to you at some length concerning my return from those new regions which we found and explored with the fleet, at the cost, and by the command of this Most Serene King of Portugal. And these we may rightly call a new world.

Because our ancestors had no knowledge of them, and it will be a matter wholly new to all those who hear about them. For this transcends the view held by our ancients, inasmuch as most of them hold that there is no continent to the south beyond the equator, but only the sea which they named the Atlantic; and if some of them did aver that a continent there was, they denied with abundant argument that it was a habitable land. But that this their opinion is false and utterly opposed to the truth, this my last voyage has made manifest; for in those southern parts I have found a continent more densely peopled and abounding in animals than our Europe or Asia or Africa, and, in addition, a climate milder and more delightful than in any other region known to us, as you shall learn in the following account wherein we shall set succinctly down only capital matters and the things more worthy of comment and memory seen or heard by me in this new world, as will appear below.

On the fourteenth of the month of May, one thousand five hundred and one we set sail from Lisbon under fair sailing conditions, in compliance with the commands of the aforementioned king, with these ships for the purpose of seeking new regions toward the south; and for twenty months we continuously pursued this southern course. The route of this voyage is as follows: Our course was set for the Fortunate Isles, once so called, but which are now termed the Grand Canary Islands; these are in the third climate and on the border of the inhabited west. Thence by sea we skirted the whole African coast and part of Ethiopia as far as the Ethiopic Promontory, so called by Ptolemy, which we now call Cape Verde and the Ethiopians Beseghice. And that region, Mandingha, lies within the torrid zone fourteen degrees north of the equator; it is inhabited by tribes and nations of blacks. Having there recovered our strength and taken on all that our voyage required, we weighed anchor and made sail. And directing our course over the vast ocean toward the Antarctic, we for a time bent westward, owing to the wind called Vulturnus; and from the day when we set sail from the said promontory we cruised for the space of two months and three days, before any land appeared to us. But what we suffered on that vast expanse of sea, what perils of shipwreck, what discomforts of the body we endured, with what anxiety of mind we toiled, this I leave to the judgment of those who out of rich experience have well learned what it is to seek the uncertain and to attempt discoveries even though ignorant. And that in a word I may briefly narrate all, you must know that of the sixty-seven days of our sailing we had forty-four of constant rain, thunder and lightning—so dark that never did we see sun by day or fair sky by night. By reason of this such fear invaded us that we soon abandoned almost all hope of life. But during these

Reprinted with permission of The Free Press, a Division of Macmillan, Inc., from *The Philosophy of the Sixteenth and Seventeenth Centuries,* edited by Richard H. Popkin. (pp. 24–30)

tempests of sea and sky, so numerous and so violent, the Most High was pleased to display before us a continent, new lands, and an unknown world. At sight of these things we were filled with as much joy as anyone can imagine usually falls to those who have gained refuge from varied calamity and hostile fortune. It was on the seventh day of August, one thousand five hundred and one that we anchored off the shores of those parts, thanking our God with formal ceremonial and with the celebration of a choral mass. We knew that land to be a continent and not an island both because it stretches forth in the form of a very long and unbending coast, and because it is replete with infinite inhabitants. For in it we found innumerable tribes and peoples and species of all manner of wild beasts which are found in our lands and many others never seen by us concerning which it would take long to tell in detail. God's mercy shone upon us much when we landed at that spot, for there had come a shortage of fire-wood and water; and in a few days we might have ended our lives at sea. To Him the honor, glory, and thanksgiving.

We adopted the plan of following the coast of this continent toward the east and never losing sight of it. We sailed along until at length we reached a bend where the shore made a turn to the south; and from that point where we first touched land to that corner it was about three hundred leagues, in which sailing distance we frequently landed and had friendly relations with those people, as you will hear below. I had forgotten to write you that from the promontory of Cape Verde to the nearest part of that continent is about seven hundred leagues, although I should estimate that we sailed more than eighteen hundred, partly through ignorance of the route and the ship-master's want of knowledge, partly owing to tempests and winds which kept us from the proper course and compelled us to put about frequently. Because, if my companions had not heeded me, who had knowledge of cosmography, there would have been no ship-master, nay not the leader of our expedition himself, who would have known where we were within five hundred leagues. For we were wandering and uncertain in our course, and only the instruments for taking the altitudes of the heavenly bodies showed us our true course precisely; and these were the quadrant and the astrolabe, which all men have come to know. For this reason they subsequently made me the object of great honor; for I showed them that though a man without practical experience, yet through the teaching of the marine chart for navigators I was more skilled than all the ship-masters of the whole world. For these have no knowledge except of those waters to which they often sailed. Now, where the said corner of land showed us southern trend of the coast we agreed to sail beyond it and inquire what there might be in those parts. So we sailed along the coast about six hundred leagues, and often landed and mingled and associated with the natives of those regions, and by them we were received in brotherly fashion; and we would dwell with them too, for fifteen or twenty days continuously, maintaining amicable and hospitable relations, as you shall learn below. Part of this new continent lies in the torrid zone beyond the equator toward the Antarctic pole, for it begins eight degrees beyond the equator. We sailed along this coast until we passed the tropic of Capricorn and found the Antarctic pole fifty degrees higher than that horizon. We advanced to within seventeen and a half degrees of the Antarctic circle, and what I there have seen and learned concerning the nature of those races, their manners, their tractability and the fertility of the soil, the salubrity of the climate, the position of the heavenly bodies in the sky, and especially concerning the fixed stars of the eighth sphere, never seen or studied by our ancestors, these things I shall relate in order.

First then as to the people. We found in those parts such a multitude of people as nobody could enumerate (as we read in the Apocalypse), a race I say gentle and amenable. All of both sexes go about naked, covering no part of their bodies; and just as they spring from their mothers' wombs so they go until death. They have indeed large square-built bodies, well formed and proportioned, and in color verging upon reddish. This I think has come to them, because, going about naked, they are colored by the sun. They have, too, hair plentiful and black. In their gait and when playing their games they are agile and dignified. They are comely, too, of countenance which they nevertheless themselves destroy; for they bore their cheeks, lips, noses and ears. Nor think those holes small or that they have one only. For some I have seen having in a single face seven borings any one of which was capable of holding a plum. They stop up these holes of theirs with blue stones, bits of marble, very beautiful crystals of alabaster, very white bones, and other things artificially

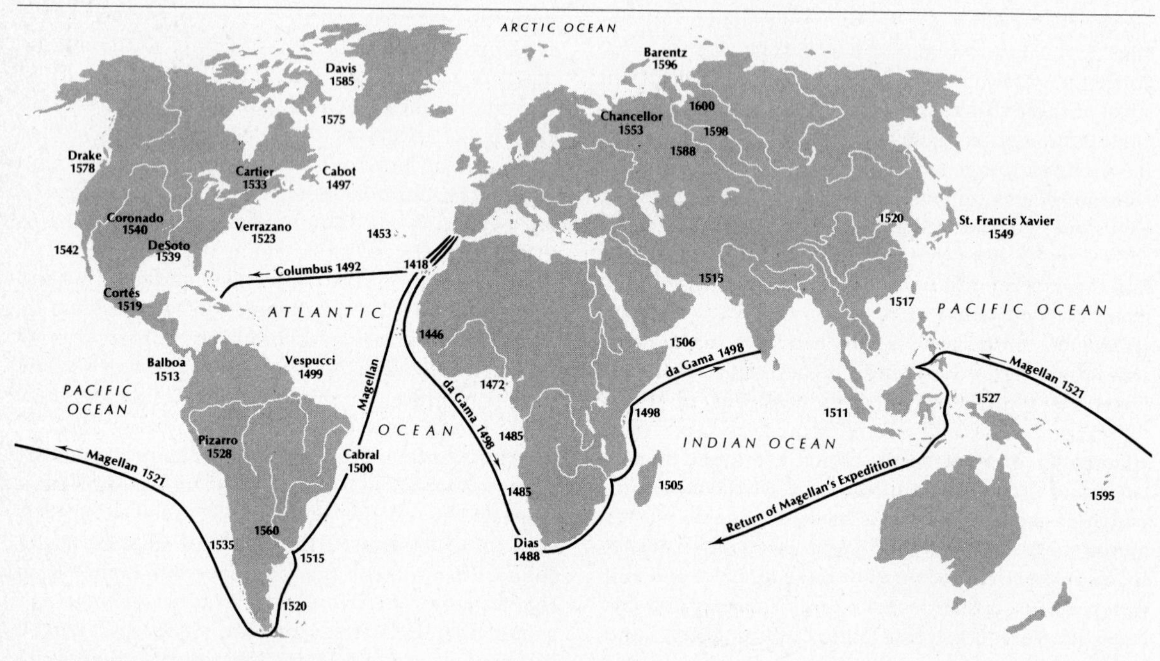

European Discoveries, A.D. 1450–1600

prepared according to their customs. But if you could see a thing so unwonted and monstrous, that is to say a man having in his cheeks and lips alone seven stones some of which are a span and a half in length, you would not be without wonder. For I frequently observed and discovered that seven such stones weighed sixteen ounces aside from the fact that in their ears, each perforated with three holes, they have other stones dangling on rings; and this usage applies to the men alone. For women do not bore their faces, but their ears only. They have another custom, very shameful and beyond all human belief. For their women, being very lustful, cause the private parts of their husbands to swell up to such a huge size that they appear deformed and disgusting; and this is accomplished by a certain device of theirs, the biting of certain poisonous animals. And in consequence of this many lose their organs which break through lack of attention, and they remain eunuchs. They have no cloth either of wool, linen or cotton, since they need it not; neither do they have goods of their own, but all things are held in common. They live together without king, without government, and each is his own master. They marry as many wives as they please; and son cohabits with mother, brother with sister, male cousin with female, and any man with the first woman he meets. They dissolve their marriages as often as they please, and observe no sort of law with respect to them. Beyond the fact that they have no church, no religion and are not idolaters, what more can I say? They live according to nature, and may be called Epicureans rather than Stoics. There are no merchants among their number, nor is there barter. The nations wage war upon one another without art or order. The elders by means of certain harangues of theirs bend the youths to their will and inflame them to wars in which they cruelly kill one another, and those whom they bring home captives from war they preserve, not to spare their lives, but that they may be slain for food; for they eat one another, the victors the vanquished, and among other kinds of meat human flesh is a common article of diet with them. Nay be the more assured of this fact because the father has already been seen to eat children and wife, and I knew a man whom I also spoke to who was reputed to have eaten more than three hundred human bodies. And I likewise remained twenty-seven days in a certain city where I saw salted human flesh suspended from beams between the houses, just as with us it is the custom to hang pork. I say further: they themselves wonder why we do not eat our enemies and do not use as food their flesh which they say is most savory. Their weapons are bows and arrows, and when they advance to war they cover no part of their bodies for the sake of protection, so like beasts are they in this matter. We endeavored to the extent of our power to dissuade them and persuade them to desist from these depraved customs, and they did promise us that they would leave off. The women as I have said go about naked and are very libidinous; yet they have bodies which are tolerably beautiful and cleanly. Nor are they so unsightly as one perchance might imagine; for, inasmuch as they are plump, their ugliness is the less apparent which indeed is for the most part concealed by the excellence of their bodily structure. It was to us a matter of astonishment that none was to be seen among them who had a flabby breast, and those who had borne children were not to be distinguished from virgins by the shape and shrinking of the womb; and in the other parts of the body similar things were seen of which in the interest of modesty I make no mention. When they had the opportunity of copulating with Christians, urged by excessive lust, they defiled and prostituted themselves. They live one hundred and fifty years, and rarely fall ill, and if they do fall victims to any disease, they cure themselves with certain roots and herbs. These are the most noteworthy things I know about them. The climate there was very temperate and good, and as I was able to learn from their accounts, there was never there any pest or epidemic caused by corruption of the air; and unless they die a violent death they live long. This I take to be because the south winds are ever blowing there, and especially that which we call Eurus, which is the same to them as the Aquilo is to us. They are zealous in the art of fishing, and that sea is replete and abounding in every kind of fish. They are not hunters. This I deem to be because there are there many sorts of wild animals, and especially lions and bears and innumerable serpents and other horrid and ugly beasts, and also because forests and trees of huge size there extend far and wide; and they dare not, naked and without covering and arms, expose themselves to such hazards. The land in those parts is very fertile and pleasing, abounding in numerous hills and mountains, boundless valleys and mighty rivers, watered by refreshing springs, and filled with broad, dense and well-nigh impenetrable forests full of every sort of wild animal. Trees grow to immense size without cultivation. Many of these yield fruits delectable to the taste and beneficial to the human body; some indeed do not, and no fruits there are like those of ours. Innumerable species of herbs and roots grow there too, of which they make bread and excellent food. They have, too, many seeds altogether unlike these of ours. They have there no metals of any description except gold, of which those regions have a great plenty, although to be sure we have brought none thence on this our first voyage. This the natives called to our attention, who averred that in the districts remote from the coast there is a great abundance of gold, and by them it is in no respect esteemed or valued. They are rich in pearls as I wrote you before. If I were to seek to recount in detail what things are there and to write concerning the numerous species of animals and the great number of them, it would be a matter all too prolix and vast. And I truly believe that our Pliny did not touch upon a thousandth part of the species of parrots and other birds and the animals, too, which exist in those same regions so diverse as to form and color; because Policleitus, the master of painting in all its perfection would have fallen short in depicting them. There all trees are fragrant and they emit each and all gum, oil, or some sort of sap. If the properties of these were known to us, I doubt not but that they would be salutary to the human body. And surely if the terrestrial paradise be in any part of this earth, I esteem that it is not far distant from those parts. Its situation, as I have related, lies toward the south in such a temperate climate that icy winters and fiery summers alike are never there experienced. . . .

I observed many other very beautiful stars, the movements of which I have diligently noted down and have described beautiful with diagrams in a certain little book of mine treating of this my voyage. But at present this Most Serene King has it, which I hope he will restore to me. In that hemisphere I saw things incompatible with the opinions of philosophers. A white rainbow was twice seen about midnight, not only by me but by all the sailors. Likewise we have frequently seen the new moon on that day when it was in conjunction with the sun. Every night in that part of the sky innumerable vapors and glowing meteors fly about. I said a little while ago respecting that hemisphere that it really cannot properly be spoken of as a complete hemisphere comparing it to ours, yet since it approaches such a form, such may we be permitted to call it. . . .

These have been the more noteworthy things which I have seen in this my last voyage which I call my third chapter. For two other chapters consisted of two other voyages which I made to the west by command of the most Serene King of the Spains, during which I noted down the marvellous works wrought by that sublime creator of all things, our God. I kept a diary of noteworthy things that if sometime I am granted leisure I may bring together these singular and wonderful things and write a cosmographical or geographical work so that I may live with posterity and that the immense work of almighty God, partly unknown to the ancients, but known to us, may be understood. Accordingly I pray the most merciful God to prolong the days of my life that with His good favour and the salvation of my soul I may carry out in the best possible manner this my will. . . .

Jocundus, the translator, is turning this epistle from the Italian into the Latin tongue, that Latinists may know how many wonderful things are daily being discovered, and that the audacity of those who seek to scrutinize heaven and sovereignty and to know more than it is licit to know may be held in check inasmuch as ever since that remote time when the world began the vastness of the earth and what therein is contained has been unknown.

GIORDANO BRUNO

A restless and idiosyncratic thinker, Bruno was born in Nola, Italy, in 1548. He was a Dominican until 1576, when he left the order after having been charged with heresy. Bruno was interested in the occult and continued the speculative philosophy of Ficino. He had little patience with any form of traditional thought and even went beyond the radical premises of Copernicanism. Something of a wanderer, Bruno made his mark at Oxford, Paris, and Wittenberg.

Upon returning to Venice in 1591, Bruno was arrested by the Inquisition. The charges were complex, but his reputation as one who was interested in the superiority of the personal results of ancient magic to those of Christianity did not help him. He recanted after his trial in Venice but was later sentenced to jail in Rome. After eight years of imprisonment, he refused to acknowledge his alleged errors and was burned alive in 1600, ironically the first year of the seventeenth century, which century was to bring forth the birth of modern scientific philosophy. Bruno's thought influenced Baruch Spinoza and Liebniz. Of significance to the twentieth century is his fascination with the infinite and with the relativity of all knowledge.

From On the Infinite, the Universe, and Worlds

THE FIFTH DIALOGUE

Participants in the Dialogue are Elpino, Fracastoro, Filotheo, Burchio and Albertino. Albertino has just entered and speaks first.

Albertino. Just what, I should like to know, is this ghost, this incredible monster, this living prophet, this extraordinary mind? What message does he bring to the world? Or, better, just what are these reborn ancient and obsolete views? What are these

From Giordano Bruno, *On the Infinite, the Universe and Worlds*, The Fifth Dialogue, in Arturo B. Fallico and Herman Shapiro, eds., *Renaissance Philosophy: The Italian Philosophers* (New York: Random House, 1967), pp. 392–423. Permission granted by Herman Shapiro.

truncated roots which are growing fresh shoots in this, our age?

Elpino. They are truncated, but fruitful roots; ancient views which have returned; occult truths which are made manifest. It is a new light which rises over the horizon in the hemisphere of our knowledge and little by little approaches the zenith of our intelligence.

Alb. If I didn't know you, Elpino, I know what I should say.

Elp. Say what you will. If you are as wise as I think you are, you will agree with him even as I do. If your perspicuity is greater, you will, as I expect, agree all the more rapidly and completely. Those who find the current philosophy and ordinary knowledge difficult, and those who subscribe to these current and ordinary views even though they are themselves not too bright (as is often the case although they are not aware of it), will not be easily converted to our view. To them, universal consent is the most powerful argument; and they are so awed by the reputation of those authors whom they read that they seek for nothing else than to be reputed expositors and commentators. Some, however, who fully comprehend the transmitted philosophy, have reached the point where they no longer choose to spend the rest of their lives listening to others; they see by their own light and penetrate every cranny with the power of their mind's eye—Arguslike with the eyes of their knowledge, they gaze at this philosophy, unveiled, through a thousand doorways. In this way they are able, upon coming closer, to distinguish matters of belief accepted as truth by habit and universal consent, from that which truly is and must be accepted as certain: as obtaining in the very nature and substance of things. It is true, I hold, that those who have not had the fortune to be blessed by nature with intelligence, or are not at least somewhat familiar with the different branches of knowledge, will not be able to accept our philosophy. Those who are able to do so must have the power of intellectual reflection by means of which they can distinguish between belief based on faith and belief based on the evidence of true principles.

Quite often an opinion is accepted as a principle which, if carefully scrutinized, would be found to lead to an incredible and unnatural conclusion. I say nothing of those mean and mercenary minds that contain no, or little, desire to attain truth, contenting themselves with what passes generally for knowledge: not friends of true wisdom, but greedy for the fame and reputation bestowed upon those who give the appearance of possessing knowledge. I hold him to be poorly equipped to choose between diverse opinions and contradictory statements who lacks soundness and judgment on these matters. He who lacks the ability to compare them will find it difficult to decide, when the differences that distinguish them are beyond his ken. Indeed, it is for him difficult even to understand how such positions differ, since the substance and being of each remains hidden from him. And their differences can never be evident except through a clear grasp of the reasons and principles upon which each is based. After you have looked with the mind's eye, and considered with disciplined sensibilities the foundations, principles and reasons on which diverse and opposed philosophies are based: after you have examined the nature, substance, and peculiarities of each, and weighed one argument against the other on the scales of the intellect: after you have distinguished their differences and compared and judged rightly between them: then, without delay, you will immediately choose to yield your assent to the truth.

Alb. Aristotle, the prince of philosophers, maintains that it is vain and foolish to waste time in fighting foolish opinions.

Elp. True: but if you look closely this advice applies against his own opinions too when they are vain and foolish. He who would judge perfectly must, as I said, be able to abstain from the habit of belief. He must regard two opposed views as equally plausible, and must dismiss all prejudice inculcated from birth: prejudice which is encountered in general conversation as well as that by which we are (as if dying to the mass of men) reborn through philosophy among those scholars who are held by the majority of their contemporaries to be wise. When there arises controversy between different persons held by their contemporaries and countrymen to be wise, I would say that if we would judge rightly we must recall the warning issued by this same Aristotle; who says that we may sometimes too quickly assent to opinions because we focus too narrowly upon an inadequate number of facts. Sometimes, too, an opinion too quickly captures our assent because of custom, so that something appears to us to be necessary which actually is impossible; or we perceive and learn that to be impossible which is actually most true and necessary. And if this can happen with respect to the most obvious things, what must happen in those matters which are somewhat unique, which yet depend upon well-grounded principles and solid foundations?

Alb. It is the opinion of the commentator, Averroës, and of many others, that that which Aristotle did not know cannot be known.

Elp. Both he and the mass of his followers had so little genius and were in such profound darkness, that they could see nothing higher and more brilliant than Aristotle. In truth, if he and others when they let fall such opinions were to speak with strict accuracy, they would say that for them Aristotle is a god. In this way they would not so much exalt Aristotle as show their own worthlessness. For to them the matter seems even as it does to the ape, to whom her own children appear the most beautiful creatures in the world, and her own ape husband the most handsome of consorts.

Alb. "The mountains do bring forth."

Elp. You will see it is no mouse which they bring forth.

Alb. Many have crossed swords with Aristotle, but it is their own castles which have fallen, their arrows have been blunted, and their bows broken.

Elp. What happens when one useless thing makes war against another? One is completely victorious, but remains nonetheless useless; and will it not, in its turn, finally be discovered and overcome by truth?

Alb. It is impossible, as I see it, to prove that Aristotle is in error.

Elp. That is much too rash a statement.

Alb. I say it because I have fully considered and carefully examined what Aristotle has to say, and have never found him to be in error. Indeed, I can discover nothing concerning divinity which he did not know; and I feel that I must insist that no other man can find that which I have not been able to find in his writings.

Elp. You gauge the stomach and brain of others, then by your own, and hold that which you cannot do to be impossible for others. In this world there are some not only so unfortunate and unhappy as to be deprived of every good, but who have been selected in addition, to live forever with that Erinnys and infernal Fury which impels them voluntarily to cover their eyes with the black veil of corrosive jealousy so that they may see neither their own nakedness, poverty, and misery, nor the ornaments, riches, and delights of others. It is their preference to pine away in filth, pride, and penury and to remain buried under the dung of stubborn ignorance rather than be discovered turning to a new discipline or appearing to yield that they had previously been ignorant, and guided by an ignorant man.

Alb. Are you then suggesting that I become a disciple of this man (Filotheo)? I—a doctor, approved by a thousand Academies of the world—am I now to reject Aristotle and beg to learn philosophy from such as he?

Elp. As I see it, I would learn not as a doctor, but as a neophyte. I would learn not because I ought to, but because of my lack. I would choose as a master not only this man, but any others whom the gods have selected for that function; for they enable me to understand that which I do not now understand.

Alb. You would make me a child again?

Elp. Only so that you may discard childishness.

Alb. I thank you for your kindness. You do me too much honor in allowing me to listen to this miserable wanderer. Everyone knows how he detests the Academies; all know how he impugns every traditional doctrine. He is praised by few, approved by none, and persecuted by all.

Elp. True, he is persecuted by all—but what sort of people are they? He is praised by few—but these are the best, the heroes. He opposes traditional doctrine not as doctrine, nor as traditional, but because it is false. He is hated by the Academies, because wherever there is disagreement there is no love. He is in distress because the mass oppose all independents, and he who thus enjoys an exalted position is always a target for the many. To characterize his mind as concerns speculative matters, I should say that he is not so anxious to teach as he is to learn. He will regard it as good news and be quite pleased when he hears that you want to teach him; for his wish is to learn rather than teach, and he regards himself as better equipped to be a student than a master.

Alb. Welcome most heartily, Filotheo.

Filotheo. And you sir, not less.

Alb. "If in the forest I chew straw with the ox, the sheep, the goat, the ass and the horse, then, to improve my livelihood, without sin do I come hither to make myself a disciple."

Fracastoro. You are welcome, indeed.

Alb. I have till now regarded your views unworthy of being heard, let alone worthy of answer.

Filo. As a youth, up to a certain age, I too felt as you do, being then entirely captivated by Aristotle. Now, however, that I have seen more and meditated more and have matured, I should be able to judge matters more ably—although, to tell the truth, I may have become foolish and witless. As this is a malady that none can see better than the sick one himself, I am even more inclined to suspect that I have passed from wisdom to ignorance: I am, consequently, most happy to have discovered a physician regarded by all as competent to cure my mania.

Alb. Neither nature nor I can help if the disease has penetrated to the bone.

Fra. Please, sir, first feel his pulse and examine his urine. Afterwards, if no cure is effected, we'll all be wary of him.

Alb. The "pulse feeling" which I have in mind is to see whether you can resolve and extricate yourself from certain arguments which I will now set forth. These will prove conclusively that a plurality of worlds is impossible, not to speak of an infinity of such.

Filo. When you have taught me this, I shall be greatly in your debt. And if you do not fulfill your intention, I shall still be in your debt for having thus indirectly confirmed my views. Indeed, it seems to me that I shall receive from you the full force of those arguments which are in opposition to my views; and as you are an expert in the traditional sciences, you will be able clearly to exhibit the solidity of the foundation and the whole structure of these sciences as a function of their differences from my own principles. In order that the discussion proceed without interruption, and that each of us may have an equal opportunity to explain his own position, please set forth those arguments which you regard as the most impregnable, significant, and conclusive.

Alb. Yes. Here they are:

(1) Beyond this world there is believed to be neither time nor space. For there is supposed to be but one primal heaven, a body most distant from us—the Primum Mobile. Thus, we customarily call "heaven" that which is on the farthest horizon of the world. On this are all the still, motionless, fixed, and quiet bodies: the intelligences, which endow the orbs with motion.

The world is divided into a celestial and an elemental body. The latter is bounded and contained, the former the containing limit. This world is ordered hierarchically: from the most dense to the most subtle which obtains above the convex of fire. On this, which constitutes the fifth essence, the sun, moon, and other stars are fixed. The nature of this fifth essence is such that it does not stray into the infinite; because it could not be conjoined with the Primum Mobile. Nor does it meet the other elements; because these would then envelop it causing the incorruptible and divine to be contained and surrounded by the corruptible, which is not appropriate. To the divine there belongs a nature conditioned to form and act, and therefore to the function of containing and endowing others with defining form and limit, being itself without limit, form, or substance.

Having stated this, we now proceed to argue, with Aristotle, that if there is a body beyond this heaven, it must be either simple or compound. No matter which of these you choose, I ask further: will this body occupy a position determined by its inner nature, or by the accident of position and external constraint? We will show that there can be no simple body beyond the heaven, as it is impossible for a perfect sphere to alter its position. Since the center of such a sphere is immutable, its position cannot change, for only by constraint can it change to any but its own proper position—and a sphere can undergo no constraint, active or passive.

Similarly, outside the heavens it is impossible that there be a simple body which moves rectilinearly. Whether this simple body is heavy or light, it cannot be outside the heaven, since the natural place of simple bodies is not beyond the world. Nor can it be held that these bodies are beyond the world by accident or constraint, for in that case other bodies would, of their own nature, already be there.

It is proved then, that there are no simple bodies other than those which make up our own world, and these bodies are endowed with three kinds of local motion. Therefore, no other simple body can exist beyond the world. Therefore also, no compound body can exist beyond the world, since the latter is a compound of the simples and reducible to them. Consequently, it is clear that many worlds do not exist, as there can be but one heaven, since it is unique, perfect, and complete.

From this it follows that there can be neither space, plenum, void, nor time outside of our world. Space could not be there—for if it were a plenum it would contain either a simple or a compound body. If it were void, then, according to the nature of a void which is defined as space capable of containing body, it would be possible for a body to obtain there—but we have already shown that no body can exist beyond the heaven. Time could not obtain there, for time is the number of motion, and motion can only be postulated of a body. Hence where there is no body, there is no motion and, as a consequence, no measurement of motion—*ergo,* no time. Further, since we have already proved that no body exists beyond this world, we have simultaneously demonstrated that there is neither motion, time, nor anything temporal or movable beyond it. Therefore, there exists only one world.

(2) The unicity of the world may be inferred from the unicity of the moving body, the Primum Mobile. Circular motion, it is agreed, is truly one, uniform and without beginning or end. If it be thus one, then it can be the effect of but one cause. If then, there is but one primal heaven below which all the lower heavens are subsumed to make up a single order, then there can be but one guiding or motive power. This cannot be multiplied by the addition of matter, since it is incorporeal. Now if the moving power is one; and if a single moving power can bring only one kind of motion into being; and if motion, whether simple or complex, can occur only within a simple or compound mobile body; it must follow that the mobile world is one. Therefore, there can be no other worlds.

(3) It follows from the positions occupied by bodies in motion that there can be only one world. There are three kinds of mobiles; the heavy, the light, and that which is neither heavy nor light. Earth and water are examples of the heavy; air and fire of the light; and the heavens of the third kind of mobile. Similarly, there are three different regions for moving bodies: the lowest and central, occupied by heavy bodies; the uppermost, at the furthest remove from the lowest; and the middle region, between the central and the uppermost. Thus the first kind of mobile, the heavy, belongs properly to the center; those which are neither heavy nor light belong to the outer circumference; while the light belongs to the space between. There is, consequently, a lowest region to which all heavy objects from any world will tend to move; there is also an upper region toward which all light objects from any world would move; and there is also a region in which the heaven moves, no matter what world it belongs to. Hence, if there is but one space, there is also one world and not many.

(4) If there were more than one world, I say that there would be various centers toward which the heavy objects of these worlds would move, as well as several horizons toward which light objects would move. In different worlds these positions would not differ in kind but only in number. In this way the center of one world would be more distant from the center of another world than it would from its own horizon. But such centers would be similar in kind, while center and horizon are of opposite natures. Hence the spatial distance between things similar in kind would be greater than the distance between opposed things. But this is contrary to the nature of opposites: for when it is said that contraries are at the greatest remove from one another, this should be understood to refer to distance in the same space. You can see then what follows from postulating more than one world. It is clear that such a hypothesis is not only incorrect but impossible.

(5) If there were more worlds possessed of natures similar to this one, they must be equal, or at least proportional in size to this one—which is to say that they would be equal to one another. If this is the case, then no more than six worlds can adjoin this one. For it is impossible for more than six spheres to touch a single sphere without interpenetrating—just as it is impossible that more than six equal circles can touch one another without their lines intersecting. If this is the case, then six horizons will be grouped around a single center—i.e., at the points where the six worlds touch each other or our world. But as the virtue of two opposed elements should be equal in power, and as a lack of equality follows from the arrangement here being hypothesized, the fact that the upper elements are stronger than the lower will result in making the upper victorious over the lower, thus destroying the totality.

(6) Now if the circular surfaces of different worlds touch only at a point, then there must of necessity remain a space between the convex circumference of one sphere and that of another. Either there is something in this space which fills it, or there is nothing.

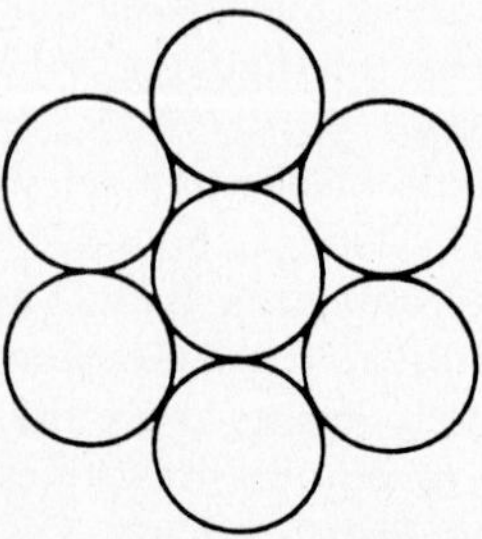

If there is something, then clearly it will not have the nature of an element distant as it will be from the convex surface of a sphere, because, as is quite obvious, this space will be triangular in shape and enclosed within the three arcs that form part of the circumferential surface of three worlds; and in this way the (triangle's) center will be located at some distance from the parts nearest the angles but most distant from the spheres. It then becomes necessary to hypothesize new elements and a new world filling that space—wholly different from our elements and our world. Were this not so, it would be necessary to hypothesize a vacuum in the triangular space, and this, as we see it, is impossible.

(7) If there were other worlds, they would be either finite or infinite. If infinite, then the infinite would have come about as the result of a determined action. For many reasons this is held to be impossible. If finite, they must be a definite number. And then we ask: Why just this many and neither more nor less? Why not one more? What would happen if there were this or that world in addition? Whether even or uneven in number, why should they be of this kind rather than some other? Why is all this matter split into so many worlds rather than unified in a single globe? As unity is better than plurality, *ceteris paribus,* why divide substance among four or six or even ten earths, rather than making a single, great, and perfect globe? Indeed, just as from the possible and impossible there arises a finite rather than an infinite number, so, in choosing between the consistent and the inconsistent, unity is more rational and natural than multiplicity or plurality.

(8) In all things we observe nature to accomplish her ends with the greatest efficacy: just as she does not lack the necessary, she eschews the superfluous. Since she can, then, produce all of her effects with just that which obtains in this world, it would not be reasonable to assume that there are more worlds.

(9) If an infinity of worlds or, indeed, more than one world existed, this would be so principally because God could make them—or rather because they would depend on God. But as true as this may be, it does not follow that these worlds do exist, for besides God's active power, the passive power of things must also obtain. That which can be created in nature does not depend (solely) upon the absolute divine power, as not every active power transforms itself into passive, but only that which has a subject adequate to itself—i.e., a subject able to receive the efficient act in its completeness. But nothing has such a relationship to the Prime Cause; hence, insofar as the nature of the world is concerned, there cannot be more than one, even though God is capable of making more.

(10) The plurality of worlds is not consonant with reason, for they would contain no civil virtue, which consists in civil intercourse. And had the gods created diverse worlds they would have acted badly in that they had not arranged for the citizens of these worlds to have commerce with one another.

(11) Were there a plurality of worlds they would place barriers in the path of every motive force or divinity. For since the spheres must touch at certain points, one would block the movement of another and the gods could then scarcely control the world through motion.

(12) The only way that a plurality of individuals can arise from a single one is by nature's process of multiplication by substantial division—i.e., generation. Aristotle and the Peripatetics tell us that individuals of a single species multiply only by the act of generation. Those, however, who hold to the existence of a plurality of worlds made up of the same matter and form do not assert that one is converted into, or generated from, another.

(13) Nothing can be added to perfection. If this world is perfect, then clearly there is no need for another to be added to it. The world is perfect: it is a sort of continuum not bounded by another sort of continuum. An indivisible mathematical point culminates mathematically in a line which is a kind of continuum; the line culminates in a surface which is a second kind of continuum; the surface, in a solid body which is a third kind of continuum. No body migrates or moves to another kind of continuum. But if it is part of the universe, it is bounded by another body; while if it is the universe itself, it is perfect and bounded by itself only. Thus the universe must be one if it is to be perfect. And here are the thirteen arguments which I want, for now, to put before you. If you satisfy me with respect to these, then I shall be completely satisfied.

Filo. But Albertino, anyone who proposes to defend a proposition must first (unless he is a fool) have examined the contrary arguments. The case is the same as with a soldier who would indeed be foolish if he attempted to defend a castle without having investigated the circumstances and places from which it may be attacked. Your arguments—if, indeed, they are arguments at all—are quite well known and oft repeated. The most effective way to respond to them consists in considering, on the one hand, their origin and, on the other, how they stand up to our own assertions. I will make both clear to you in the course of my reply. I shall make my reply brief, and if you require further amplification or clarification I shall refer you to Elpino, who will repeat that which he has previously heard from me.

Alb. Please, first show me that this method will not be fruitless or lacking in satisfaction to one who wants to learn, and that listening first to you and then to him will not weary me.

Filo. To the wise and judicious, among whom I count you, it is sufficient to show the direction of our considerations. They themselves will then be able to proceed deeper into an appraisal of the means by which one or the other of opposing views is to be reached.

Now as regards your Argument (1), we say that your whole system falls because the differences which you mark as obtaining between the various orbs and heavens do not exist; further the stars move through this vast, ethereal space because of their own nature, each revolving about its own and another center. In fact, there is no Primum Mobile that draws the many bodies around ourselves as center. Rather, our globe causes it to appear that this is happening for reasons that Elpino will explain to you.

Alb. I will listen to him willingly.

Filo. And when you have heard him, and noted that such an opinion is contrary to nature while ours is consonant with reason, sense, and verification in nature, you will no longer say that there is a boundary or limit either to the extent or to the motion of the universe. You will then judge the belief in a Primum Mobile—a highest and all-containing heaven—to be an empty fantasy. Rather, you will begin to conceive of a universal field in which all worlds are alike situated, even as this globe, in this our local space, is enveloped by our atmosphere and is in no way fixed or attached to any other body and has no fixed point other than its own center. And should it be discovered that the constitution of our globe differs in no way from that of the surrounding stars, since it contains no accidents different from theirs, then it will become clear that it no more occupies the central place in the universe than any of them, nor is it any more fixed than they, nor will they appear to revolve around it rather than it around them. Since this implies an utter indifference on the part of nature, we must conclude the emptiness of (alleged) inferior orbs; and we must accept the internal impulse toward motion which is implanted in the souls of these globes, the lack of difference throughout the vast space of the universe, and the irrationality of conceiving any boundary or external shape to the universe.

Alb. But these are views which, although not repugnant to nature and perhaps even quite consistent, are still difficult to prove. Great skill would be required to disprove the contrary view and arguments.

Filo. But once the end of the thread is discovered, the tangle is easily unraveled. The difficulty issues from an unsuitable method and presupposition: namely, the weight and immobility of the earth: the position of the Primum Mobile together with the other seven, eight, nine, or more (spheres) on which the stars are implanted, stuck, nailed, knotted, glued, sculptured, or painted: and that these do not reside in the same space as our own star, called by us the earth. But you will hear that her space, figure, and nature are neither more nor less fundamental than those of the other stars, nor is her nature any less adapted to motion than each of these other divine animals.

Alb. True, if this is once fixed in my mind, everything else which you propose will be easily accepted in its turn. You will at once have severed the roots of one philosophy and implanted those of another.

Filo. And you will thereafter refuse, with good reason, to accept common opinions based upon general consensus, such as the existence of a furthest horizon, most lofty and noble, the frontier of the divine, motionless substances which are the movers of these finite orbs. You will then admit that it is at least plausible that this earth, as all the others, is an animal which moves and travels by virtue of her own intrinsic nature. You will regard as mere fable, incapable of any proof, the view that these bodies derive their motion from that of a body which lacks all holding power and resistance—a body more rare and subtle than the air we breathe. You will further see that our view conforms to good sense as well as sound reasoning. You will no longer hold as true the notion of spheres with concave and convex surfaces moving and drawing the stars with them. You will rather see as true, consonant with reason and natural consistency, the view that the stars follow, in conformity with their own intrinsic nature and life—as you shall soon hear—their circular courses around and toward one another without fear of either rising or falling, since in the immensity of space there is no up or down, no right or left, no forward or backward. You will see that beyond the alleged circumference of the heaven there can be a body—either simple or composite—moving in a straight line; for just as the parts of this globe move in a straight line, so also and with similar ease the parts of other bodies can do so. Our own globe is not composed of material different from those beyond our globe; nor does our globe appear to revolve around them any less than they appear to revolve around us.

Alb. I now see more clearly than ever before that the smallest error at the start may cause the greatest difference and danger of errors at the conclusion. A single, simple mistake will multiply little by little and swell into an infinity of others—even as a great plant with numberless branches may grow from a tiny root. On my life, Filotheo, I strongly desire that you prove all of this to me. I do regard your views as both likely and worthy and I wish that you would also show me their truth.

Filo. I will do as much as time and the occasion permit, submitting many things to your judgment which have been previously kept from you not because of your incapacity but because of inadvertence.

Alb. Put the whole matter before me in the form of premise and conclusion. I know that before you came to embrace your present views you carefully examined everything which suggested contrary conclusions, and I am certain that the secrets of the currently accepted philosophy are as well known to you as they are to me. Please then, proceed.

Filo. It is then unnecessary to inquire whether there is space, void, or time beyond the heaven. For there obtains a single, universal space, a single vast immensity which we may freely call *void.* In it are infinite globes like this one on which we live and flourish. This space we declare to be infinite—since neither reason, consistency, possibility, sense, or nature assign any limit to it. In it there are an infinity of worlds, similar to our own and of the same kind. For there is no reason or defect of nature's powers—either active or passive power—that prevents their existence in all the rest of space, which is identical in natural character to our own, just as they exist in the space around us.

Alb. If what you said at the outset is true (and to this point it appears to be quite as likely as the opposite view), then this which you now state follows necessarily.

Filo. Time obtains beyond the alleged convex circumference of the world. For there is found the measure and true nature of motion, since there are similar moving bodies there. Accept this in part as having been proved, and in part as proposed in regard to what you have said in your Argument (1) for a single world. But let me now turn to your Argument (2).

Concerning your Argument (2), I say that there is but one prime and principal motive power. But not that it is prime and principal relative to a second, third, or other motive power in a scale descending to the middle and last, since no such motive powers can or do exist. For where infinite number obtains, there can be neither rank nor numerical order, although rank and order there is according to the nature and value of either different species and kinds, or of diverse grades of the same species and kind. There are, as I see it, an infinity of motive powers, just as there are an infinity of souls inhabiting the infinite spheres. And since these consist of form and intrinsic action, there is relative to them all a governing principle upon which all depends—a first principle which endows spirits, gods, heavenly powers, and motive power with the ability to move. It sets into motion matter, body, animated being, lower orders of nature, and anything which can move. There are, that is to say, an infinity of mobile bodies and motive forces, all of which are reducible to a single passive and active principle, in the same way in which every number reduces to unity, and as an infinite number coincides with unity, and just as the supreme agent and supreme active power coincide in a single principle with all that is possible, as was shown at the end of our book *On Cause, Origin and the One.* In number then, and in magnitude, there is an infinite possibility of motion and movers. In unity and singularity, however, the whole is infinite unmoved mover: an infinite motionless universe. And the infinite number and magnitude coincides with the infinite unity and simplicity in a single, utterly simple and indivisible principle, which is truth and being. Thus there is no Primum Mobile, no order descending from it of second and other mobile bodies, either to a last body or to infinity. But all moving bodies are equally near and far from the prime and universal mover just as (in logical terms) all species are equally related to the same genus, and all individuals to the same species. Thus from a single, infinite, and universal motive force in a single, infinite space, there issues only one infinite universal motion on which an infinite number of mobile bodies and forces depend, each of which is finite in both magnitude and power.

As for your Argument (3), I say that there is no privileged point, no center, in ethereal space toward which heavy objects move and from which all light bodies leave in their search for a circumference. In the universe there is neither center nor circumference; but, rather, the whole is central and every point may be seen as a part of the circumference in relation to some other central point. As concerns us, that object which we regard as being heavy is any object which moves from the circumference to the center of our own globe. We regard as being light that object which moves in the opposite direction—toward the opposite goal. But we shall see that nothing is heavy which is not also light; for every part of the earth changes, in turn, both place, position, and also composition, so that during the long course of centuries no particle in the center fails to reach the circumference, and no particle on the circumference fails to reach the center. We shall see also that weight and lightness are nothing else than the drive of a body's particles to their own containing region, wherever that may be, in which they are best conserved. There are no differences of position, therefore, which attract or repel different parts. But the desire for self-preservation is an inner drive impelling every object—provided that no obstacle intervenes—to fly as far away from contrary matter as possible, and to join with a close neighbor. In this way, then, the particles from the circumference of the moon and of other worlds similar in species and kind to our own, tend to unite in the center of their own globe as though compelled by their own weight, while the more subtle particles, as though compelled by their own lightness, remove themselves to the circumference. This is not a function of the particles taking flight to or from the circumference (because of attraction or repulsion), because if this were the case then the nearer they approached, or the further they went away from the circumference, the more rapid and powerful their motion would become, and observation gives this the lie; for if they are impelled beyond the terrestrial region, they remain balanced in the air and neither ascend nor descend until they either gain more weight by accretion of parts, or increased density because of the cold, in which case they descend, or else they become more rarefied and heat-dissolved, in which case they disperse into atoms.

Alb. I shall be much easier in mind when you have more fully shown me that the stars do not differ in nature from this earthly sphere.

Filo. Elpino will easily make this known to you as he has heard it from me. He will also make you see most clearly that no object is heavy or light in respect to the universe, but only in respect to its own region and the body which contains and maintains it. It is the tendency, you see, to maintain an existing condition which brings about every change of position; as seas, for example, and even drops of water become united, or disperse, as all liquids do when exposed to the sun or other heat. All natural motion, brought about by a body's own internal impulsion, is nothing but an attempt to either escape an inimical or opposed body, or to pursue a friendly and compatible one. Whence nothing changes position unless driven to do so by its contrary. Nothing in its natural position is either heavy or light; but the earthy matter, when it is raised up into the air, strives for its natural position and is felt thus to be heavy, just as water is heavy when suspended in air, though it is not when it is in its own region. In this way, to anyone who is submerged, the whole of the water is not at all heavy, while a little vase full of water will become quite heavy if placed above the air beyond the dry surface. The head on a man's body is not heavy, but if the head of another man is placed on his own it will be heavy—because the latter is not in its natural position. If then, weight and lightness are merely an impulse to a position of safety and escape from a contrary position, it follows that nothing is by nature either heavy or light; and that nothing is endowed with either weight or lightness if it is so far away from its preserving (environment), or so far removed from its contrary as not to be affected by the aid of the one or the harm of the other. If, however, it becomes aware of an inimical environment, and then grows hopeless, perplexed, and irresolute, it will be vanquished by its contrary.

Alb. You promised, and in part you have accomplished great things.

Filo. To avoid repetition, I will now turn you over to Elpino, who will continue with the remainder.

Alb. It seems to me that I understand it all. Just as one doubt fosters another, so one truth demonstrates another. I begin to understand more than I can explain, and I now doubt many things which I had previously held to be certain. In this way, little by little, I feel myself ready to agree with you.

Filo. When you have heard me out, you will yield

your full assent. For now, bear this in mind—or at least do not be quite as solidly convinced of the contrary opinion as you were when you first entered the discussion. For little by little, as the opportunity arises, we shall complete the exposition of this subject—a subject which depends, to be sure, on several principles and arguments. For just as one error leads to another, so one uncovered truth is followed by another.

As regards your Argument (4), I say that although there are as many centers as there are individual globes, spheres, or worlds, yet it does not follow that the particles of each are related to any center but their own; nor does it follow that they fly to any circumference but that of their own region. Just as the particles of our earth do not seek any but their own center, nor do they attempt to unite with any but that of their own globe, so it is also that the humors and parts of an animal ebb and flow in their own subject, and do not relate to some other animal.

As regards that which you think unfitting, namely, that a center would become further removed from another center than it would from the circumference of its own globe, although centers are of the same species while centers and circumferences are contraries and should therefore be at the furthest distance from one another, I reply as follows: contraries need not be at the furthest distance from one another, inasmuch as one may either influence or be influenced by the other. We see, for example, that the sun is very close to us among the earths which encircle it, since the order of nature requires an object to subsist, live, and be nurtured by its contrary, while it becomes affected, altered, overcome, and changed by the first.

Further, a short while back we discussed with Elpino the arrangement of the four elements which all contribute particles in the composition of each globe, one particle being placed within another, and one mixed with another. And these are not respectively distinguished as a containing and a contained body. For where there is dry earth, so also there is water, air, and fire, either manifest or latent. The distinction which we made concerning globes—some, like the sun, being fiery, while others, as the moon and earth, being watery—does not depend upon these bodies consisting solely of a single element, but merely on the predominance of one element in the mixed substance.

Furthermore, it is false that contraries are situated at the furthest remove from one another. For the elements have naturally combined and mixed in all objects. The whole universe, indeed, consists solely—both in the principal and secondary parts—of such conjunction and union, as there is no portion of the earth which is not intimately mixed with water. For without water the earth would have neither density, connections between its composite atoms, nor solidity.

Again, what terrestrial body is so dense as to lack insensible openings? Lacking these, such bodies would be indivisible and incapable of penetration by fire or its heat, which latter is, however, sensibly perceived to issue from the substance of these bodies. Where, in this your body, is there any cold, dry segment which is not joined to a moist and warm part of your body? This distinction of elements is a logical, not a natural distinction. If the sun is in a region far removed from that of our earth, yet neither air nor dry land nor water is further removed from it than from our own globe. For the sun, like our earth, is a composite body, though in it a certain one of the four above-mentioned elements predominates, while another is predominant in our earth.

Moreover, if we insist that nature conform to that logic which insists that the greatest distance obtain between contrary bodies, then, between your fire—which is light—and the heavy earth, heaven—which is neither heavy nor light—must be interposed. Or if you would limit your proposition by saying that this order pertains only in respect of the four elements, still you would be forced to arrange them in a different order. Water, I mean, must occupy the central position of the heaviest element if fire, as the lightest element, is on the circumference of the elemental region; for water, which is cold and moist, is opposed to fire in both of these qualities and must, consequently, be at the greatest distance from the hot and dry element; while air, which you hold to be hot and moist, should be at the furthest distance from the cold and dry earth. You see, then, how this Peripatetic proposition falters, whether it is tested according to the truth of nature or according to the Peripatetics' own logical principles and foundations.

Alb. I see it most clearly.

Filo. What is more, you see that our philosophy is not at all contrary to reason. It reduces everything to a single origin and relates everything to a single end; it makes contraries coincide so that there is one primal basis of both origin and end. From this coincidence of contraries we deduce that it is ultimately and divinely right to hold that contraries are within contraries, for which reason it is not difficult to comprehend that each thing is within every other thing—which Aristotle and the other Sophists could not comprehend.

Alb. I listen to you most willingly. I know that so much material and such diverse positions cannot all be demonstrated at once upon a single occasion. But since you have shown me the untenability of those beliefs which I had once regarded as certain, I have been doubtful of all others which for the same, or similar reasons, I would now regard as certain. Therefore, I am prepared to listen to the foundations of your philosophy, your principles and reasons, with rapt attention.

Elp. You will see that Aristotle brought no golden age to philosophy. For now let us dispel your further doubts.

Alb. I am not so curious about those—I am, however, quite eager to understand the doctrine and principles by means of which these and other doubts are resolved in your philosophy.

Filo. We shall turn to those soon. As for your Argument (5), you ought to know that if we conceive of an infinity of worlds possessed of a nature and composition such as you are accustomed to imagine, it would be as if besides a spherical world containing the four elements arranged in the traditional order, and the eight, nine, or ten other heavens of a different nature and substance encircling and rapidly revolving around these, we should then imagine innumerable other worlds also spherical and endowed with motion like ours. But if we conceived of them thus, then we should have to produce arguments and invent ways to explain how one of these worlds could touch or be continuous with the others; we should then proceed with fantastic imaginings to discuss at how many points the circumference of one world may touch those of the surrounding worlds. You would then see that however numerous the horizons around a world, they would not belong to one world, but each one would have the same relation to its own center. For their influence is exerted there where they revolve, and at the center about which they spin in the same way that a number of animals, if bound together and touching one another, would not interchange limbs in such a manner that one or each of them could possess several hands or bodies. We, however—thanks to the gods—are free of the need to employ such explanations. Because instead of these numerous heavens—these many swift, stubborn, and mobile bodies, straight and oblique, to the east and west, on the axis of the world, on the axis of the zodiac, in so far and so much, in greater and lesser declination—we have but one single heaven, a single space through which our own star on which we live, and all other stars, each run their own circuits and courses. These are the infinite worlds, the innumerable stars; this is the infinite space, this heaven embracing all, traversed by all. Gone forever is the fable that the whole revolves around us as the center; for we now know that it is our earth which revolves; and that our earth, spinning about her own center, speeds every twenty-four hours to the successive places of the surrounding luminaries. Gone also is the notion of orbs encircling our own space in which the stars are fixed. To each star we attribute its own motion—named *epicycle*—differing from that of each of the other mobile bodies. These orbs—directed by no motive force other than the spontaneous impulse of the spirit within each—follow, as our own earth, their own course about their own center and around the fiery element, during long centuries if not, indeed, to eternity. Here then is the true nature of the worlds and of heaven. Heaven is just as we see it surrounding our own globe which is, like all the other globes, a luminous and noble star. The worlds are those whose brilliant shining surfaces are clearly visible to us, and they are located at specific distances from one another. But none of them is closer to one another than the moon is to our earth, or our planets to our sun; in this way, those of contrary nature do not destroy but, rather, nourish one another, while those of similar nature do not impede but, rather, give each other space. Thus, from one position to another, little by little, from season to season, our frigid globe is heated by the sun, now from this side, now from that, now on this part, now on that; and by certain changes she first yields, and then takes place from the neighboring earth which we call the moon, so that first one and then the other body is respectively nearer to or further from the sun—for which reason the moon is called the counterearth by Timaeus and other Pythagoreans. These then are the world; each inhabited and cultivated by their own living beings: each the principal and most divine of all living beings in the universe: and each composed, no less than this earth on which we find ourselves, of four elements, although some may be predominantly activated by one active quality, while others are predominantly activated by another, so that some of these are perceptible to us by means of their water and others by their fire.

In addition to the four elements which compose the heavenly bodies there is, as we have said, a vast and ethereal region in which they all move, live and grow—the ether, which both envelops and penetrates all things. To the degree that this ether enters into and forms part of the mixture of the elements, it is commonly called *air*—the term applying to that misty layer around the waters and within the land, enclosed between the highest mountains, capable of holding thick clouds and strong winds from north and south. To the degree that it remains pure and does not enter into composites, but forms the locale and the enveloping space through which the compound body moves on its course, we call it properly, *ether*—a term which means *course.* This ether, although identical in substance with the air which is stirred within the earth's bowels, is nonetheless differently named; just as that which surrounds us is called *air,* although when it is in some part of us or has a part in our composition—as when it is in our lungs, arteries, and other cavities and lacunae of the body—it is called spirit. Similarly, the ether, when surrounding a cold body, condenses into vapor; while around a hot body it is attenuated like a flame which becomes sensible only when it is joined to a denser body which then ignites. Thus the ether is of its own nature: it lacks all determinate quality, but takes on all the qualities offered by neighboring bodies and carries them by means of its own motion to the furthest limits of the horizon where such active principles have efficacy.

Now the nature of the worlds and the heavens have been demonstrated to you, so that not only can your present doubt be resolved, but innumerable others. You are now provided with the basis for many true physical conclusions. If some proposition has up to here seemed to you to have been stated but not proved, I shall leave it for the time being to your own discretion and, if you are judicious, then even before you actually discover the supreme truth of such a proposition, you will hold it far more probable than the contrary views.

Alb. Continue, Filotheo, so that I may hear more from you.

Filo. We have already resolved your Argument (6). In that Argument, considering the contact of worlds at a single point, you asked what object could fill those triangular spaces so that it be neither an element nor of a heavenly nature. We, however, posit a single heaven in which each world has its own space, region, and correct area. It diffuses through all, penetrates and envelops all, touches and is closely attached to all, leaving no place vacant—unless, that is, like so many others you prefer to call *void* this site and locale of all motion, this space in which all have their course. Or you may call it the primal subject denoted by the term *space,* in order not to ascribe to it a limited locale, if you wish, by this omission logically to regard it as something existing in the mind not derived, in nature and substance, from being and body; this may satisfy one's insistence that nothing exists which has no position, finite or infinite, corporeal or incorporeal, either as a whole or by means of its parts. Such a subject, in the last analysis, can be nothing else but space; and this space, nothing else but void. If then, we regard this space or void as obtaining, we call it the ethereal field which contains all worlds; if we regard it as an underlying substance, we call it the space within which there obtains the ethereal field with the worlds; and this space cannot be conceived as existing within another space. Observe then, that it is not necessary for us to postulate new elements and worlds—unlike those who begin to designate, upon the slightest pretext, inferior orbs, divine substances, rarer and denser parts of celestial nature, quintessences, and other such fantastic names utterly lacking any meaning or truth.

To your Argument (7), I say that the infinite universe is one: a single continuum: a compound of ethereal regions and worlds. The worlds are innumerable, and they should be understood to reside in diverse regions of the single universe and to exist according to the same law of nature as this world which we inhabit is understood and does reside in its own space and region. I have been telling all this to Elpino during the past days; approving and affirming that which has been expounded by Democritus, Epicurus, and many others who kept their eyes and ears directed always to nature.

> Then, spew not reason from thy mind away,
> Beside thyself because the matter's new,
> But rather with keen judgment nicely weigh;
> And if to thee it then appeareth true,
> Render thy hands, or, if 'tis false at last,
> Gird thee to combat. For my mind-of-man
> Now seeks the nature of the vast Beyond
> There on the other side, that boundless sum
> Which lies without the ramparts of the world,

Toward which the spirit longs to peer afar,
Toward which indeed the swift élan of
 thought
Flies unencumbered forth
 Firstly, we find,
Off to all regions round, on either side,
Above, beneath, throughout the universe
End there is none—as I have taught, as too
The very thing of itself declares aloud,
And as from nature of the unbottomed deep
Shines clearly forth. . . .

Lucretius rejects your Argument (8), which held that nature should include herself. Although this has been tested in great and small worlds, it is yet never observed to be the case in any. Our eye never discovers an end, but is overcome by the immensity of space spread before it. Confused and bewildered by the myriad of ever multiplying stars, our perception falters and reason is then forced to add space to space, region to region, world to world.

. . . Nor can we once suppose
In any way 'tis likely, (seeing that space
To all sides stretches infinite and free,
And seeds, innumerable in number, in sum
Bottomless, there in many a manner fly,
Bestirred in everlasting motion there),
That only this one earth and sky of ours
Hath been create . . .
 Thus, I say,
Again, again, 'tmust be confessed there are
Such congregations of matter otherwhere,
Like this our world which vasty ether holds
In huge embrace. . . .

Lucretius complains too against your Argument (9) which assumes, without proof, that there is no infinite passive power which corresponds with infinite active power; and that infinite matter cannot be patient and infinite space cannot make a field to itself; and that, as a consequence, act and action cannot become comformable to the agent so that it may happen that even though the agent imparts the entire act, yet the whole act cannot be imparted. This latter view clearly and entirely contradicts the former observation. Wisely has it been remarked:

. . . Besides, when matter abundant
Is ready there, when space on hand, nor
 object
Nor any cause retards, no marvel 'tis
That things are carried on and made
 complete,
Perforce. And now, if store of seeds there is
So great that not whole life-times of the
 living
Can count the tale. . . .
And if their force and nature abide the same,
Able to throw the seeds of things together
Into their places, even as here are thrown
The seeds together in this world of ours,
'Tmust be confessed in other realms there are
Still other worlds, still other breeds of men
And other generations of the wild.

To your Argument (10), we say that there is no need of this pleasant exchange between the various worlds any more than it is necessary that all men should be one man, or all animals one animal. I do not here even consider what we learn about this from experience—i.e., that it is best for all living creatures of this world that nature has distributed their different kinds throughout the seas and mountains. If it had been the case that, by human devices, they were to traffic together, good is not thereby added to them but, rather, removed; since such traffic tends rather to redouble vices than to augment virtues. Rightly, then, the Tragic Muse laments:

The lands, well separated before by Nature's
laws, the Thessalian ship made one, bade the
deep suffer blows and the sequestered sea
become a part of our human fear.

To your Argument (11) I reply as to your Argument (5). Each world in the ethereal field occupies its own space so that one neither thrusts against nor touches another. Each pursues its own course and is set at such a distance that the contraries do not destroy, but rather complement one another.

Your Argument (12) asserts that nature, having multiplied by defining and dividing matter, accomplishes this only by way of generation—i.e., when an individual, as parent, produces another individual. But this, we say, is not universally true. For by the act of a single efficient cause there may be produced from one mass many and diverse vessels of various forms and shapes. I mention in passing the fact that if the destruction of a world, followed by its renewal, should come to pass, the production of animals in it—perfect and imperfect—would come about without an original act of generation: and this by the sole force and innate power of nature herself.

Your final argument, Argument (13), holds that because this or some other world is perfect, no further worlds are requisite. I reply that certainly they are not requisite for the perfection and subsistence of our own world; but in order that the subsistence and perfection of the whole universe obtains, an infinity of worlds is indeed requisite. It follows therefore, not from the perfection of this or of those that they, or this, be less perfect; for this world, as those others, and they even as this, consist in their parts, and each is a single totality in virtue of its members.

Alb. The voice of the mob, Filotheo, shall not deny your noble countenance to me. Nor shall I be deprived of your divine conversation by the indignation of the vulgar, the foolishness of the mentally deficient, the displeasure of sycophants, the emptiness of blockheads, the betrayal of liars, the complaints of the malicious, not the sniping of the envious. Continue, Filotheo, persevere; do not lose heart or quit the field even though the great and dignified conference of ignorant fools threatens you with many traps and devious devices and tries to destroy your divine task—your exalted task. Rest assured that all will finally see as I now see: that all will agree that it is as easy for everyone to praise you as it is difficult for them all to instruct you. All of them (if they are not wholly perverse) will, when they properly understand you, deliver a favorable verdict of you, just as everyone, at the last, comes to be taught through the kindly mastery of the mind; for only by dint of our own mind can we attain to the treasures of the mind. And since a certain natural holiness is enthroned in the court of the intellect which exercises judgment between good and evil, light and darkness, so it will come about that each individual, by his own private meditation, shall come to your case as just witnesses and defenders. And they who do not make themselves your friend, but stolidly seek the defense of shadowy ignorance, and remain your stubborn and steadfast enemies, will feel the hangman and executioner—your avenger—within themselves; for the more they hide him within the depth of their thought, the more he will torture them. In just this way the Hellish worm dwelling on the bristling hair of the Furies, seeing that his plan against you has failed, will furiously turn on the hand and breast of his unbelieving host and bring him that death which he spreads who disseminates the Stygian poison.

Commence to tell us what is, in truth, in the heavens: what, in truth, the planets and all the stars are: how the infinite space—far from being impossible—is necessary: how such an infinite effect is seemly in the infinite cause. Tell us the true substance, matter, act, and efficient cause of the whole: how every sensible and composite thing is built up from the same origin and elements. Instruct our minds on the infinite universe. Tear to bits the concave and convex surfaces which would limit and separate so many elements and heavens: pour ridicule on inferior orbs and fixed stars: break and fling to earth with the resounding whirlwind of active reasoning those fortresses of the blind and vulgar masses, the adamantine walls of the Primum Mobile and the ultimate sphere: disperse the ideas that our earth is the one and only center of the universe: destroy the ignoble belief in that fifth essence. Make known to us that the composition of our own star and world is the same as that of the many other stars and worlds that are visible to us. Each of the infinity of great and vast worlds, each of the infinity of lesser worlds, is equally sustained and nourished anew through the succession of its ordered phases. Destroy the notion of external motive forces together with that of a limited, bounded, heaven. Open wide to us the gate through which we may mark the lack of difference between our own and all the other stars. Show us that the substance of the other worlds throughout the ether is the same as that of our own world. Make us see clearly that the motion of all of them stems from the impulsion of the inward soul, so that we, illumined by such thoughts, may proceed all the more surely toward a knowledge of nature.

Filo. Elpino, what is the significance of Doctor Burchio's reluctance to consent to what we have said?

Elp. It is typical of an alert mind, that although seeing and hearing little, it yet considers and understands much.

Alb. Although I have not yet seen the whole body of the shining planet, I can yet see by the rays shimmering through the narrow chinks in the closed windows of my mind that this is no meretricious brightness or Sophist's lamp. Nor does it proceed from the moon or any minor star. I anticipate still greater enlightenment in the future.

Filo. Your continuing friendship will be most welcome.

Elp. Let us now go to supper.

GALILEO GALILEI

Galileo was born in Pisa, Italy, in 1564. He studied medicine and then mathematics, which he taught at the Universities of Pisa and Padua. His claim to fame, however, rests with his pioneering work in experimental method, his perfecting of the just-invented telescope, and his stress on the necessity of careful observation and measurement.

The reputation and publishing privileges of Galileo ebbed and flowed with the alternating influence of the Inquisition and his Church protectors. Periodically, Galileo would issue a work that would oppose Aristotle, as in "The Discourse on Bodies in Water," or take an aggressively pro-Copernican position, as in "Letters on Sunspots." Far more than previous thinkers, Galileo had the experimental evidence to support his position. He made significant contributions in distinguishing between subjective and objective qualities in scientific observation. After the appearance of his Dialogue Concerning the Two Chief World Systems, *Galileo was summoned to a hearing before the Inquisition. He was remanded to house arrest in 1633. Most present-day scholarship affirms that at his sentencing, despite his recantation, he was heard to say* "E pur si muove" *(nevertheless, it does move). Galileo died in 1642 and is known today as one of the founders of modern scientific method as well as a man of courage, impervious to the centuries-long effort to stifle freedom of thought.*

From The Assayer

In which with a most just and accurate balance
there are weighed the things contained in
THE ASTRONOMICAL AND PHILOSOPHICAL BALANCE
OF LOTHARIO SARSI OF SIGUENZA
Written in the form of a letter
To the Illustrious and Very Reverend
Monsignor DON VIRGINIO CESARINI
Lincean Academician, and Chamberlain to His Holiness
By Signor
GALILEO GALILEI
Lincean Academician, Gentleman of Florence,
Chief Philosopher
and Mathematician to the
Most Serene Grand Duke of Tuscany

ROME
1623

I have never understood, Your Excellency, why it is that every one of the studies I have published in order to please or to serve other people has aroused in some men a certain perverse urge to detract, steal, or deprecate that modicum of merit which I thought I had earned, if not for my work, at least for its intention. In my *Starry Messenger* there were revealed many new and marvelous discoveries in the heavens that should have gratified all lovers of true science; yet scarcely had it been printed when men sprang up everywhere who envied the praises belonging to the discoveries there revealed. Some, merely to contradict what I had said, did not scruple to cast doubt upon things they had seen with their own eyes again and again.

My lord the Grand Duke Cosimo II, of glorious memory, once ordered me to write down my opinions about the causes of things floating or sinking in water, and in order to comply with that command I put on paper everything I could think of beyond the teachings of Archimedes, which perhaps is as much as may truly be said on this subject. Immediately the entire press was filled with attacks against my *Discourse.* My opinions were contradicted without the least regard for the fact that what I had set forth was supported and proved by geometrical demonstrations; and such is the strength of men's passion that they failed to notice how the contradiction of geometry is a bald denial of truth.

How many men attacked my *Letters on Sunspots,* and under what disguises! The material contained therein ought to have opened to the mind's eye much room for admirable speculation; instead it met with scorn and derision. Many people disbelieved it or failed to appreciate it. Others, not wanting to agree with my ideas, advanced ridiculous and impossible opinions against me; and some, overwhelmed and convinced by my arguments, attempted to rob me of that glory which was mine, pretending not to have seen my writings and trying to represent themselves as the original discoverers of these impressive marvels.

I say nothing of certain unpublished private discussions, demonstrations, and propositions of mine which have been impugned or called worthless; yet even these have sometimes been stumbled upon by other men who with admirable dexterity have exerted themselves to appropriate these as inventions of their own ingenuity. Of such usurpers I might name not a few. I shall pass over first offenders in silence, as they customarily receive less severe punishment than repeaters. But I shall no longer hold my peace about one of the latter, who has too boldly tried once more to do the very same thing he did many years ago when he appropriated the invention of my geometric compass, after I had shown it to and discussed it with many gentlemen years before, and had finally published a book about it. May I be pardoned if on this occasion—against my nature, my custom, and my present purpose—I show resentment and protest (perhaps too bitterly) about something I have kept to myself all these years.

I speak of Simon Mayr of Guntzenhausen. He it was in Padua, where I resided at the time, who set forth in Latin the uses of my compass and had one of his pupils publish this and sign it. Then, perhaps to escape punishment, he departed immediately for his native land and left his pupil in the lurch. In Simon Mayr's absence I was obliged to proceed against his pupil, in the manner described in the *Defense* which I published at the time.

Now four years after my *Starry Messenger* appeared, this same fellow (in the habit of trying to ornament himself with other people's works) unblushingly made himself the author of the things I had discovered and printed in that book. Publishing under the title of *The World of Jupiter,* he had the gall to claim that he had observed the Medicean planets which revolve about Jupiter before I had. . . . But note his sly way of attempting to establish his priority. I had written of making my first observation on the seventh of January, 1610. Along comes Mayr, and, appropriating my very observations, he prints on the title page of his book (as well as in the opening pages) that he had made his observations in the year 1609. But he neglects to warn the reader that he is a Protestant, and hence had not accepted the Gregorian calendar. Now the seventh day of January, 1610, for us Catholics, is the same as the twenty-eighth day of December, 1609, for those heretics. And so much for his pretended priority of observation. . . .

It now remains for me to tell Your Excellency, as I promised, some thoughts of mine about the proposition "motion is the cause of heat," and to show in what sense this may be true. But first I must consider what it is that we call heat, as I suspect that people in general have a concept of this which is very remote from the truth. For they believe that heat is a real phenomenon, or property, or quality, which actually resides in the material by which we feel ourselves warmed. Now I say that whenever I conceive any material or corporeal substance, I immediately feel the need to think of it as bounded, and as having this or that shape; as being large or small in relation to other things, and in some specific place at any given time; as being in motion or at rest; as touching or not touching some other body; and as being one in number, or few, or many. From these conditions I cannot separate such a substance by any stretch of my imagination. But that it must be white or red, bitter or sweet, noisy or silent, and of sweet or foul odor, my mind does not feel compelled to bring in as necessary accompaniments. Without the senses as our guides, reason or imagination unaided would probably never arrive at qualities like these. Hence I think that tastes, odors, colors, and so on are no more than mere names so far as the object in which we place them is concerned, and that they reside only in the consciousness. Hence if the living creature were removed, all these qualities would be wiped away and annihilated. But since we have imposed upon them special names, distinct from those of the other and real qualities mentioned previously, we wish to believe that they really exist as actually different from those.

I may be able to make my notion clearer by means of some examples. I move my hand first over a marble statue and then over a living man. As to the effect flowing from my hand, this is the same with regard to both objects and my hand; it consists of the primary phenomena of motion and touch, for which we have no further names. But the live body which receives these operations feels different sensations according to the various places touched. When touched upon the soles of the feet, for example, or under the knee or armpit, it feels in addition to the common sensation of touch a sensation on which we have imposed a special name, "tickling." This sensation belongs to us and not to the hand. Anyone would make a serious error if he said that the hand, in addition to the properties of moving and touching, possessed another faculty of "tickling," as if tickling were a phenomenon that resided in the hand that tickled. A piece of paper or a feather drawn lightly over any part of our bodies performs intrinsically the same operations of moving and touching, but by touching the eye, the nose, or the upper lip it excites in us an almost intolerable titillation, even though elsewhere it is scarcely felt. This titillation belongs entirely to us and not to the feather; if the live and sensitive body were removed it would remain no more than a mere word. I believe that no more solid an existence belongs to many qualities which we have come to attribute to physical bodies—tastes, odors, colors, and many more.

A body which is solid and, so to speak, quite material, when moved in contact with any part of my person produces in me the sensation we call touch. This, though it exists over my entire body, seems to reside principally in the palms of the hands and in the finger tips, by whose means we sense the most minute differences in texture that are not easily distinguished by other parts of our bodies. Some of these sensations are more pleasant to us than others. . . . The sense of touch is more material than the other sense; and, as it arises from the solidity of matter, it seems to be related to the earthly element.

Perhaps the origin of two other senses lies in the fact that there are bodies which constantly dissolve into minute particles, some of which are heavier than air and descend, while others are lighter and rise up. The former may strike upon a certain part of our bodies that is much more sensitive than the skin, which does not feel the invasion of such subtle matter. This is the upper surface of the tongue; here the tiny particles are received, and mixing with and penetrating its moisture, they give rise to tastes, which are sweet or unsavory according to the various shapes, numbers, and speeds of the particles. And those minute particles which rise up may enter by our nostrils and strike upon some small protuberances which are the instrument of smelling; here likewise their touch and passage is received to our like or dislike according as they have this or that shape, are fast or slow, and are numerous or few. The tongue and nasal passages are providently arranged for these things, as the one extends from below to receive descending particles, and the other is adapted to those which ascend. Perhaps the excitation of tastes may be given a certain analogy to fluids, which descend through air, and odors to fires, which ascend.

Then there remains the air itself, an element available for sounds, which come to us indifferently from below, above, and all sides—for we reside in the air and its movements displace it equally in all directions. The location of the ear is most fittingly accommodated to all positions in space. Sounds are made and heard by us when the air—without any special property of "sonority" or "transonority"—is ruffled by a rapid tremor into very minute waves and moves certain cartilages of a tympanum in our ear. External means capable of thus ruffling the air are very numerous, but for the most part they may be reduced to the trembling of some body which pushes the air and disturbs it. Waves are propagated very rapidly in this way, and high tones are produced by frequent waves and low tones by sparse ones.

To excite in us tastes, odors, and sounds I believe that nothing is required in external bodies except shapes, numbers, and slow or rapid movements. I think that if ears, tongues, and noses were removed, shapes and numbers and motions would remain, but not odors or tastes or sounds. The latter, I believe, are nothing more than names when separated from living beings, just as tickling and titillation are nothing but names in the absence of such things as noses and armpits. And as these four senses are related to the four elements, so I believe that vision, the sense eminent above all others in the proportion of the finite to the infinite, the temporal to the instantaneous, the quantitative to the indivisible, the illuminated to the obscure—that vision, I say, is related to light itself. But of this sensation and the things pertaining to it I pretend to understand but little; and since even a long time would not suffice to explain that trifle, or even to hint at an explanation, I pass this over in silence.

Having shown that many sensations which are supposed to be qualities residing in external objects have no real existence save in us, and outside ourselves are mere names, I now say that I am inclined to believe heat to be of this character. Those materials which produce heat in us and make us feel warmth, which are known by the general name of "fire," would then be a multitude of minute particles having certain shapes and moving with certain velocities. Meeting with our bodies, they penetrate by means of their extreme subtlety, and their touch as felt by us when they pass through our substance is the sensation we call "heat." This is pleasant or unpleasant according to the greater or smaller speed of these particles as they go pricking and penetrating; pleasant when this assists our necessary transpiration, and obnoxious when it causes too great a separation and dissolution of our substance. The operation of fire by means of its particles is merely that in moving it penetrates all bodies, causing their speedy or slow dissolution in proportion to the number and velocity of the fire-corpuscles and the density or tenuity of the bodies. Many materials are such that in their decomposition the greater part of them passes over into additional tiny corpuscles, and this dissolution continues so long as these continue to meet with further matter capable of being so resolved. I do not believe that in addition to shape, number, motion, penetration, and touch there is any other quality in fire corresponding to "heat"; this belongs so intimately to us that when the live body is taken away, heat becomes no more than a simple name. . . .

Since the presence of fire-corpuscles alone does not suffice to excite heat, but their motion is needed also, it seems to me that one may very reasonably say that motion is the cause of heat. . . . But I hold it to be silly to accept that proposition in the ordinary way, as if a stone or piece of iron or a stick must heat up when moved. The rubbing together and friction of two hard bodies, either by resolving their parts into very subtle flying particles or by opening an exit for the tiny fire-corpuscles within, ultimately sets these in motion; and when they meet our bodies and penetrate them, our conscious mind feels those pleasant or unpleasant sensations which we have named heat, burning, and scalding. And perhaps when such attrition stops at or is confined to the smallest quanta, their motion is temporal and their action calorific only; but when their ultimate and highest resolution into truly indivisible atoms is arrived at, light is created. This may have an instantaneous motion, or rather an instantaneous expansion and diffusion, rendering it capable of occupying immense spaces by its—I know not whether to say its subtlety, its rarity, its immateriality, or some other property which differs from all these and is nameless.

I do not wish, Your Excellency, to engulf myself inadvertently in a boundless sea from which I might never get back to port, nor in trying to solve one difficulty do I wish to give rise to a hundred more, as I fear may have already happened in sailing but this little way from shore. Therefore I shall desist until some more opportune occasion.

From Dialogue Concerning the Two Chief World Systems – Ptolemaic and Copernican

TO THE DISCERNING READER

Several years ago there was published in Rome a salutary edict which, in order to obviate the dangerous tendencies of our present age, imposed a seasonable silence upon the Pythagorean opinion that the earth moves. There were those who impudently asserted that this decree had its origin not in judicious inquiry, but in passion none too well informed. Complaints were to be heard that advisers who were totally unskilled at astronomical observations ought not to clip the wings of reflective intellects by means of rash prohibitions.

Upon hearing such carping insolence, my zeal could not be contained. Being thoroughly informed about that prudent determination, I decided to appear openly in the theater of the world as a witness of the sober truth. I was at that time in Rome; I was not only received by the most eminent prelates of that Court, but had their applause; indeed, this decree was not published without some previous notice of it having been given to me. Therefore I propose in the present work to show to foreign nations that as much is understood of this matter in Italy, and particularly in Rome, as transalpine diligence can ever have imagined. Collecting all the reflections that properly concern the Copernican system, I shall make it known that everything was brought before the attention of the Roman censorship, and that there proceed from this clime not only dogmas for the welfare of the soul, but ingenious discoveries for the delight of the mind as well.

To this end I have taken the Copernican side in the discourse, proceeding as with a pure mathematical hypothesis and striving by every artifice to represent it as superior to supposing the earth motionless—not, indeed, absolutely, but as against the arguments of some professed Peripatetics. These men indeed deserve not even that name, for they do not walk about; they are content to adore the shadows, philosophizing not with due circumspection but merely from having memorized a few ill-understood principles.

Three principal headings are treated. First, I shall try to show that all experiments practicable upon the earth are insufficient measures for proving its mobility, since they are indifferently adaptable to an earth in motion or at rest. I hope in so doing to reveal many observations unknown to the ancients. Secondly, the celestial phenomena will be examined, strengthening the Copernican hypothesis until it might seem that this must triumph absolutely. Here new reflections are adjoined which might be used in order to simplify astronomy, though not because of any necessity imposed by nature. In the third place, I shall propose an ingenious speculation. It happens that long ago I said that the unsolved problem of the ocean tides might receive some light from assuming the motion of the earth. This assertion of mine, passing by word of mouth, found loving fathers who adopted it as a child of their own ingenuity. Now, so that no stranger may ever appear who, arming himself with our weapons, shall charge us with want of attention to such an important matter, I have thought it good to reveal those probabilities which might render this plausible, given that the earth moves.

I hope that from these considerations the world will come to know that if other nations have navigated more, we have not theorized less. It is not from failing to take count of what others have thought that we have yielded to asserting that the earth is motionless, and holding the contrary to be a mere

---

From Galileo Galilei, *Dialogue Concerning the Two Chief World Systems—Ptolemaic and Copernican,* trans. Stillman Drake (Berkeley: University of California Press, 1962), pp. 5–7 and 318–328.

mathematical caprice, but (if for nothing else) for those reasons that are supplied by piety, religion, the knowledge of Divine Omnipotence, and a consciousness of the limitations of the human mind.

I have thought it most appropriate to explain these concepts in the form of dialogues, which, not being restricted to the rigorous observance of mathematical laws, make room also for digressions which are sometimes no less interesting than the principal argument.

Many years ago I was often to be found in the marvelous city of Venice, in discussions with Signore Giovanni Francesco Sagredo, a man of noble extraction and trenchant wit. From Florence came Signore Filippo Salviati, the least of whose glories were the eminence of his blood and the magnificence of his fortune. His was a sublime intellect which fed no more hungrily upon any pleasure than it did upon fine meditations. I often talked with these two of such matters in the presence of a certain Peripatetic philosopher whose greatest obstacle in apprehending the truth seemed to be the reputation he had acquired by his interpretations of Aristotle.

Now, since bitter death has deprived Venice and Florence of those two great luminaries in the very meridian of their years, I have resolved to make their fame live on in these pages, so far as my poor abilities will permit, by introducing them as interlocutors in the present argument. (Nor shall the good Peripatetic lack a place; because of his excessive affection toward the *Commentaries* of Simplicius, I have thought fit to leave him under the name of the author he so much revered, without mentioning his own.) May it please those two great souls, ever venerable to my heart, to accept this public monument of my undying love. And may the memory of their eloquence assist me in delivering to posterity the promised reflections.

It happened that several discussions had taken place casually at various times among these gentlemen, and had rather whetted than satisfied their thirst for learning. Hence very wisely they resolved to meet together on certain days during which, setting aside all other business, they might apply themselves more methodically to the contemplation of the wonders of God in the heavens and upon the earth. They met in the palace of the illustrious Sagredo; and, after the customary but brief exchange of compliments, Salviati commenced as follows.

THE THIRD DAY

Now, since the great difference between the arguments of the astronomers and of this opponent of theirs seems to me to have been very clearly demonstrated, we may as well leave this point and return to our main subject. We shall next consider the annual movement generally attributed to the sun, but then, first by Aristarchus of Samos and later by Copernicus, removed from the sun and transferred to the earth. Against this position I know that Simplicio comes strongly armed, in particular with the sword and buckler of his booklet of theses or mathematical disquisitions. It will be good to commence by producing the objections from this booklet.

Simplicio. If you don't mind, I am going to leave those for the last, since they were the most recently discovered.

Salviati. Then you had better take up in order, in accordance with our previous procedure, the contrary arguments by Aristotle and the other ancients. I also shall do so, in order that nothing shall be left out or escape careful consideration and examination. Likewise Sagredo, with his quick wit, shall interpose his thoughts as the spirit moves him.

Sagredo. I shall do so with my customary lack of tact; and since you have asked for this, you will be obliged to pardon it.

Salv. This favor will oblige me to thank and not to pardon you. But now let Simplicio begin to set forth those objections which restrain him from believing that the earth, like the other planets, may revolve about a fixed center.

Simp. The first and greatest difficulty is the repugnance and incompatibility between being at the center and being distant from it. For if the terrestrial globe must move in a year around the circumference of a circle—that is, around the zodiac—it is impossible for it at the same time to be in the center of the zodiac. But the earth is at that center, as is proved in many ways by Aristotle, Ptolemy, and others.

Salv. Very well argued. There can be no doubt that anyone who wants to have the earth move along the circumference of a circle must first prove that it is not at the center of that circle. The next thing is for us to see whether the earth is or is not at that center around which I say it turns, and in which you say it is situated. And prior to this, it is necessary that we declare ourselves as to whether or not you and I have the same concept of this center. Therefore tell me what and where this center is that you mean.

Simp. I mean by "center," that of the universe; that of the world; that of the stellar sphere; that of the heavens.

Salv. I might very reasonably dispute whether there is in nature such a center, seeing that neither you nor anyone else has so far proved whether the universe is finite and has a shape, or whether it is infinite and unbounded. Still, conceding to you for the moment that it is finite and of bounded spherical shape, and therefore has its center, it remains to be seen how credible it is that the earth rather than some other body is to be found at that center.

Simp. Aristotle gives a hundred proofs that the universe is finite, bounded, and spherical.

Salv. Which are later all reduced to one, and that one to none at all. For if I deny him his assumption that the universe is movable all his proofs fall to the gound, since he proves it to be finite and bounded only if the universe is movable. But in order not to multiply our disputes, I shall concede to you for the time being that the universe is finite, spherical, and has a center. And since such a shape and center are deduced from mobility, it will be the more reasonable for us to proceed from this same circular motion of world bodies to a detailed investigation of the proper position of the center. Even Aristotle himself reasoned about and decided this in the same way, making that point the center of the universe about which all the celestial spheres revolve, and at which he believed the terrestrial globe to be situated. Now tell me, Simplicio: if Aristotle had found himself forced by the most palpable experiences to rearrange in part this order and disposition of the universe, and to confess himself to have been mistaken about one of these two propositions—that is, mistaken either about putting the earth in the center, or about saying that the celestial spheres move around such a center—which of these admissions do you think that he would choose?

Simp. I think that if that should happen, the Peripatetics . . .

Salv. I am not asking the Peripatetics; I am asking Aristotle himself. As for the former, I know very well what they would reply. They, as most reverent and most humble slaves of Aristotle, would deny all the experiences and observations in the world, and would even refuse to look at them in order not to have to admit them, and they would say that the universe remains just as Aristotle has written; not as nature would have it. For take away the prop of his authority, and with what would you have them appear in the field? So now tell me what you think Aristotle himself would do.

Simp. Really, I cannot make up my mind which of these two difficulties he would have regarded as the lesser.

Salv. Please, do not apply this term "difficulty" to something that may necessarily be so; wishing to put the earth in the center of the celestial revolutions was a "difficulty." But since you do not know to which side he would have leaned, and considering him as I do a man of brilliant intellect, let us set about examining which of the two choices is the more reasonable, and let us take that as the one which Aristotle would have embraced. So, resuming our reasoning once more from the beginning, let us assume out of respect for Aristotle that the universe (of the magnitude of which we have no sensible information beyond the fixed stars), like anything that is spherical in shape and moves circularly, has necessarily a center for its shape and for its motion. Being certain, moreover, that within the stellar sphere there are many orbs one inside another, with their stars which also move circularly, our question is this: Which is it more reasonable to believe and to say; that these included orbs move around the same center as the universe does, or around some other one which is removed from that? Now you, Simplicio, say what you think about this matter.

Simp. If we could stop with this one assumption and were sure of not running into something else that would disturb us, I should think it would be much more reasonable to say that the container and the things it contained all moved around one common center rather than different ones.

Salv. Now if it is true that the center of the universe is that point around which all the orbs and world bodies (that is, the planets) move, it is quite certain that not the earth, but the sun, is to be found at the center of the universe. Hence, as for this first general conception, the central place is the sun's, and the earth is to be found as far away from the center as it is from the sun.

Simp. How do you deduce that it is not the earth, but the sun, which is at the center of the revolutions of the planets?

Salv. This is deduced from most obvious and therefore most powerfully convincing observations. The most palpable of these, which excludes the earth from the center and places the sun there, is that we find all the planets closer to the earth at one time and farther from it at another. The differences are so great that Venus, for example, is six times as distant from us at its farthest as at its closest, and Mars soars nearly eight times as high in the one state as in the other. You may thus see whether Aristotle was not some trifle deceived in believing that they were always equally distant from us.

Simp. But what are the signs that they move around the sun?

Salv. This is reasoned out from finding the three outer planets—Mars, Jupiter, and Saturn—always quite close to the earth when they are in opposition to the sun, and very distant when they are in conjunction with it. This approach and recession is of such moment that Mars when close looks sixty times as large as when it is most distant. Next, it is certain that Venus and Mercury must revolve around the sun, because of their never moving far away from it, and because of their being seen now beyond it and now on this side of it, as Venus's changes of shape conclusively prove. As to the moon, it is true that this can never separate from the earth in any way, for reasons that will be set forth more specifically as we proceed.

Sagr. I have hopes of hearing still more remarkable things arising from this annual motion of the earth than were those which depended upon its diurnal rotation.

Salv. You will not be disappointed, for as to the action of the diurnal motion upon celestial bodies, it was not and could not be anything different from what would appear if the universe were to rush speedily in the opposite direction. But this annual motion, mixing with the individual motions of all the planets, produces a great many oddities which in the past have baffled all the greatest men in the world.

Now returning to these first general conceptions, I repeat that the center of the celestial rotation for the five planets, Saturn, Jupiter, Mars, Venus, and Mercury, is the sun; this will hold for the earth too, if we are successful in placing that in the heavens. Then as to the moon, it has a circular motion around the earth, from which as I have already said it cannot be separated; but this does not keep it from going around the sun along with the earth in its annual movement.

Simp. I am not yet convinced of this arrangement at all. Perhaps I should understand it better from the drawing of a diagram, which might make it easier to discuss.

Salv. That shall be done. But for your greater satisfaction and your astonishment, too, I want you to draw it yourself. You will see that however firmly you may believe yourself not to understand it, you do so perfectly, and just by answering my questions you will describe it exactly. So take a sheet of paper and the compasses; let this page be the enormous expanse of the universe, in which you have to distribute and arrange its parts as reason shall direct you. And first, since you are sure without my telling you that the earth is located in this universe, mark some point at your pleasure where you intend this to be located, and designate it by means of some letter.

Simp. Let this be the place of the terrestrial globe, marked A.

Salv. Very well. I know in the second place that you are aware that this earth is not inside the body of the sun, nor even contiguous to it, but is distant from it by a certain space. Therefore assign to the sun some other place of your choosing, as far from the earth as you like, and designate that also.

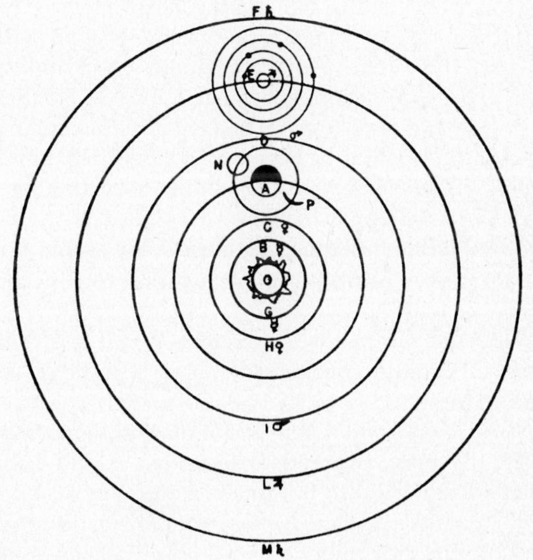

Simp. Here I have done it; let this be the sun's position, marked O.

Salv. These two established, I want you to think about placing Venus in such a way that its position and movement can conform to what sensible experience shows us about it. Hence you must call to mind, either from past discussions or from your own observations, what you know happens with this star. Then assign it whatever place seems suitable for it to you.

Simp. I shall assume that those appearances are correct which you have related and which I have read also in the booklet of theses; that is, that this star never recedes from the sun beyond a certain definite interval of forty degrees or so; hence it not only never reaches opposition to the sun, but not even quadrature, nor so much as a sextile aspect. Moreover, I shall assume that it displays itself to us about forty times as large at one time than at another; greater when, being retrograde, it is approaching evening conjunction with the sun, and very small when it is moving forward toward morning conjunction, and furthermore that when it appears very large, it reveals itself in a horned shape, and when it looks very small it appears perfectly round.

These appearances being correct, I say, I do not see how to escape affirming that this star revolves in a circle around the sun, in such a way that this circle cannot possibly be said to embrace and contain within itself the earth, nor to be beneath the sun (that is, between the sun and the earth), nor yet beyond the sun. Such a circle cannot embrace the earth because then Venus would sometimes be in opposition to the sun; it cannot be beneath the sun, for then Venus would appear sickle-shaped at both conjunctions; and it cannot be beyond the sun, since then it would always look round and never horned. Therefore for its lodging I shall draw the circle CH around the sun, without having this include the earth.

Salv. Venus provided for, it is fitting to consider Mercury, which, as you know, keeping itself always around the sun, recedes therefrom much less than Venus. Therefore consider what place you should assign to it.

Simp. There is no doubt that, imitating Venus as it does, the most appropriate place for it will be a smaller circle, within this one of Venus and also described about the sun. A reason for this, and especially for its proximity to the sun, is the vividness of Mercury's splendor surpassing that of Venus and all the other planets. Hence on this basis we may draw its circle here and mark it with the letters BG.

Salv. Next, where shall we put Mars?

Simp. Mars, since it does come into opposition with the sun, must embrace the earth with its circle. And I see that it must also embrace the sun; for, coming into conjunction with the sun, if it did not pass beyond it but fell short of it, it would appear horned as Venus and the moon do. But it always looks round; therefore its circle must include the sun as well as the earth. And since I remember your having said that when it is in opposition to the sun it looks sixty times as large as when in conjunction, it seems to me that this phenomenon will be well provided for by a circle around the sun embracing the earth, which I draw here and mark DI. When Mars is at the point D, it is very near the earth and in opposition to the sun, but when it is at the point I, it is in conjunction with the sun and very distant from the earth.

And since the same appearances are observed with regard to Jupiter and Saturn (although with less variation in Jupiter than in Mars, and with still less in Saturn than in Jupiter), it seems clear to me that we can also accommodate these two planets very neatly with two circles, still around the sun. This first one, for Jupiter, I mark EL; the other, higher, for Saturn, is called FM.

Salv. So far you have comported yourself uncommonly well. And since, as you see, the approach and recession of the three outer planets is measured by double the distance between the earth and the sun, this makes a greater variation in Mars than in Jupiter because the circle DI of Mars is smaller than the circle EL of Jupiter. Similarly, EL here is smaller than the circle FM of Saturn, so the variation is still less in Saturn than in Jupiter, and this corresponds exactly to the appearances. It now remains for you to think about a place for the moon.

Simp. Following the same method (which seems to me very convincing), since we see the moon come into conjunction and opposition with the sun, it must be admitted that its circle embraces the earth. But it must not embrace the sun also, or else when it was in conjunction it would not look horned but always round and full of light. Besides, it would never cause an eclipse of the sun for us, as it frequently does, by getting in between us and the sun. Thus one must assign to it a circle around the earth, which shall be this one, NP, in such a way that when at P it appears to us here on the earth A as in conjunction with the sun, which sometimes it will eclipse in this position. Placed at N, it is seen in opposition to the sun, and in that position it may fall under the earth's shadow and be eclipsed.

Salv. Now what shall we do, Simplicio, with the fixed stars? Do we want to sprinkle them through the immense abyss of the universe, at various distances from any predetermined point, or place them on a spherical surface extending around a center of their own so that each of them will be the same distance from that center?

Simp. I had rather take a middle course, and assign to them an orb described around a definite center and included between two spherical surfaces—a very distant concave one, and another closer and convex, between which are placed at various altitudes the innumerable host of stars. This might be called the universal sphere, containing within it the spheres of the planets which we have already designated.

Salv. Well, Simplicio, what we have been doing all this while is arranging the world bodies according to the Copernican distribution, and this has now been done by your own hand. Moreover, you have assigned their proper movements to them all except the sun, the earth, and the stellar sphere. To Mercury and Venus you have attributed a circular motion around the sun without embracing the earth. Around the same sun you have caused the three outer planets, Mars, Jupiter, and Saturn, to move, embracing the earth within their circles. Next, the moon cannot move in any way except around the earth and without embracing the sun. And in all these movements you likewise agree with Copernicus himself. It now remains to apportion three things among the sun, the earth, and the stellar sphere: the state of rest, which appears to belong to the earth; the annual motion through the zodiac, which appears to belong to the sun; and the diurnal movement, which appears to belong to the stellar sphere, with all the rest of the universe sharing in it except the earth. And since it is true that all the planetary orbs (I mean Mercury, Venus, Mars, Jupiter, and Saturn) move around the sun as a center, it seems most reasonable for the state of rest to belong to the sun rather than to the earth—just as it does for the center of any movable sphere to remain fixed, rather than some other point of it remote from the center.

Next as to the earth, which is placed in the midst of moving objects—I mean between Venus and Mars, one of which makes its revolution in nine months and the other in two years—a motion requiring one year may be attributed to it much more elegantly than a state of rest, leaving the latter for the sun. And such being the case, it necessarily follows that the diurnal motion, too, belongs to the earth. For if the sun stood still, and the earth did not revolve upon itself but merely had the annual movement around the sun, our year would consist of no more than one day and one night; that is, six months of day and six months of night, as was remarked once previously.

See, then, how neatly the precipitous motion of each twenty-four hours is taken away from the universe, and how the fixed stars (which are so many suns) agree with our sun in enjoying perpetual rest. See also what great simplicity is to be found in this rough sketch, yielding the reasons for so many weighty phenomena in the heavenly bodies.

Sagr. I see this very well indeed. But just as you deduce from this simplicity a large probability of truth in this system, others may on the contrary make the opposite deduction from it. If this very ancient arrangement of the Pythagoreans is so well accommodated to the appearances, they may ask (and not unreasonably) why it has found so few followers in the course of centuries; why it has been refuted by Aristotle himself, and why even Copernicus is not having any better luck with it in these latter days.

Salv. Sagredo, if you had suffered even a few times, as I have so often, from hearing the sort of follies that are designed to make the common people contumacious and unwilling to listen to this innovation (let alone assent to it), then I think your astonishment at finding so few men holding this opinion would dwindle a good deal. It seems to me that we can have little regard for imbeciles who take it as a conclusive proof in confirmation of the earth's motionlessness, holding them firmly in this belief, when they observe that they cannot dine today at Constantinople and sup in Japan, or for those who are positive that the earth is too heavy to climb up over the sun and then fall headlong back down again. There is no need to bother about such men as these, whose name is legion, or to take notice of their fooleries. Neither need we try to convert men who define by generalizing and cannot make room for distinctions, just in order to have such fellows for our company in very subtle and delicate doctrines. Besides, with all the proofs in the world what would you expect to accomplish in the minds of people who are too stupid to recognize their own limitations?

No, Sagredo, my surprise is very different from yours. You wonder that there are so few followers of the Pythagorean opinion, whereas I am astonished that there have been any up to this day who have embraced and followed it. Nor can I ever sufficiently admire the outstanding acumen of those who have taken hold of this opinion and accepted it as true; they have through sheer force of intellect done such violence to their own senses as to prefer what reason told them over that which sensible experience plainly showed them to the contrary. For the arguments against the whirling of the earth which we have already examined are very plausible, as we have seen; and the fact that the Ptolemaics and Aristotelians and all their disciples took them to be conclusive is indeed a strong argument of their effectiveness. But the experiences which overtly contradict the annual movement are indeed so much greater in their apparent force that, I repeat, there is no limit to my astonishment when I reflect that Aristarchus and Copernicus were able to make reason so conquer sense that, in defiance of the latter, the former became mistress of their belief.

The Trial of Galileo

ACCUSATION

We, Gaspar, of the title of Holy Cross of Jerusalem, Borgia, brother Felix Certinus of the title of St. Anastatia, surnamed of Asculum.

Guidus, of the title of St. Mary of the People, Bentivolus, brother Desiderius Scaglia, of the title of St. Charles, surnamed of Cremona.

Brother Antonius Barbarinus, surnamed of St. Onuphrius, Laudivius Zacchis, of the title of St. Peter, in vinculis, surnamed of St. Sixtus.

Berlingerius, of the title of St. Augustin Gyposius.

Fabricius of St. Lawrence.

Francis of St. Lawrence.

Martin, of the new St. Mary and Ginethis, Deacons, by the mercy of God, Cardinals of the Holy Roman Catholic Church, and specially deputed by the Holy Apostolical seat as Inquisitors General against heretical perverseness throughout the whole Christian common-wealth.

Whereas you, Galileo, son of the late Vincent Galileo of Florence, being 70 years of age, had a charge brought against you in the year 1615, in this Holy Office, that you held as true, an erroneous opinion held by many; namely, *that the Sun is the centre of the World, and immoveable,* and that the *Earth* moves even with a *diurnal motion:* also that you had certain scholars into whom you instilled the same doctrine: also that you maintained a correspondence on this point, with certain Mathematicians of Germany: also that you published certain Epistles, treating of the *solar spots,* in which you explained the same doctrine, *as true,* because you answered to the objections, which from time to time were brought against you, taken from the Holy Scripture, by glossing over the said Scripture according to *your own sense;* and that afterwards when a copy of a writing in the form of an Epistle, written by you to a certain late scholar of yours, was presented to you, (it following the hypothesis of Copernicus) you stood up for, and de-

---

Galileo Galilei, "The Trial of Galileo," in Justus Buchler et al., eds., *Introduction to Contemporary Civilization in the West,* vol. 1 (New York: Columbia University Press, 1960), pp. 799–804.

The Parable of the Blind, by Pieter Brueghel, the Elder. The persistence of affliction, relieved only by the possible peace of future salvation, as found in the distant, tranquil church. (Alinari/Art Resource)

fended certain propositions in it, which are against the true sense, and authority of Holy Scripture.

This Holy Tribunal, desiring, therefore, to provide against the inconveniences and mischiefs which have issued hence, and increased to the danger of our Holy Faith; agreeably to the mandate of Lord N——— and the very eminent Doctors, Cardinals of this supreme and universal inquisition: to propositions respecting the immobility of the Sun, and the motion of the Earth, have been adopted and pronounced, as under.

That the Sun is the centre of the World, and immoveable, in respect of local motion, is an absurd proposition, false in philosophy and formally heretical; seeing it is expressly contrary to Holy Scripture.

That the Earth is not the centre of the World, nor immoveable, but moves even with a diurnal motion, is also an absurd proposition, false in Philosophy, and considered Theologically, is at least an error in Faith.

But whereas we have thought fit in the interim to proceed gently with you, it has been agreed upon in the Holy Congregation held before D.N. on the 25th day of Feb. 1616, that the most Eminent Lord Cardinal Bellarmine should enjoin you entirely to recede from the aforesaid false doctrine; and, on your refusal, it was commanded by the Commissary of the Holy Office, that you should recant the said false doctrine, and should not teach it to others, nor defend it, nor dispute concerning it: to which command if you would not submit, that you should be cast into prison: and in order to put in execution the same decree, on the following day you were gently admonished in the Palace before the abovesaid most eminent Lord Cardinal Bellarmine, and afterwards by the same Lord Cardinal: and by the Commissary of the Holy Office, a notary and witnesses being present, entirely to desist from the said erroneous opinion; and that thereafter it should not be permitted you to defend it, or teach it in any manner, either by speaking, or writing; and whereas you promised obedience, you were at that time dismissed.

And to the end, such a *pernicious doctrine* may be entirely extirpated away, and spread no farther, to the grievous detriment of the Catholic verity, a decree was issued by the Holy Congregation *indicis*, prohibiting the printing of books, which treat of such sort of doctrine, which was therein pronounced false, and altogether contrary to Holy and Divine Scripture. And the same book has since appeared at Florence, published in the year last past, the inscription of which, shewed that you were its author, as the title was, *"A Dialogue of Galileo Galilei,"* concerning the two principal systems of the World, the Ptolemaic and the Copernican, as the Holy Congregation, recognizing from the expression of the aforesaid book, that the false opinion concerning the motion of the Earth, and the immobility of the Sun prevailed daily more and more: the aforesaid book, was diligently examined, when we openly discovered the transgression of the aforesaid command, before injoined you; seeing that in the same book you had resumed and defended the aforesaid opinion already condemned, and in your presence declared to be erroneous, because in the said book by various circumlocutions, you earnestly endeavour to persuade, that it is left by you undecided, and at the least probable which must necessarily be a grievous error, since an opinion can by no means be probable, which hath already been declared and adjudged contrary to divine Scripture.

Wherefore you have by our authority been summoned to this our Holy Office, in which being examined you have on oath acknowledged the said book was written and printed by you. And have also confessed, that about tcn or twelve years ago, after the injunction had been given you as above, that the said book was begun to be written by you. Also that you petitioned for licence to publish it, but without signifying to those who gave you such licence, that it had been prohibited you, not by any means to maintain, defend, or teach such doctrine.

You likewise confessed, that the writing of the aforesaid book was so composed in many places, that the reader might think, that arguments adduced on the false part, calculated rather to perplex the understanding by their weight, than be easily resolved; excusing yourself, by saying you had fallen into an error so foreign from your intention, (as you declared) because you had handled the subject in the form of a dialogue, and because of the natural complacence which every one hath in maintaining his own arguments, and in shewing himself more acute than others in defending even false propositions by ingenious deductions, and of apparent probability

And, when a time was assigned you for making your defence, you produced a certificate under the hand-writing of the most eminent Lord Cardinal Bellarmine, procured as you said, in order to defend yourself against the calumnies of our enemies, who everywhere gave it out, that you had abjured, and had been punished by the Holy Office: in which certificate it is said, that you had not abjured, nor had been punished, but only that a declaration had been filed against you, drawn up by the said Lord, and formally issued by the Holy Congregation *Indicis,* in which it is declared that the doctrine concerning the motion of the Earth, and the immobility of the Sun, is contrary to the Holy Scriptures, and therefore can neither be defended or maintained. Wherefore seeing no mention was then made of two particulars of the mandate; namely, *(docere & quovis modo) teaching, and by any means,* we judge that in the course of fourteen or sixteen years they had slipped out of your memory, and for the same reason you were silent respecting the mandate, when you petitioned for a licence to print your book, and yet this was said by you not to maintain, or obstinately persist in your error, but as proceeding from vain ambition, and not perverseness. But this very certificate produced in your defence, rather tends to make your excuse look worse, because in it is declared, that the aforesaid opinion is contrary to the Holy Scripture, and yet you have dared to treat of it as a matter of dispute, and defend, and teach it as probable: nor does the licence itself favour you, seeing it was deceitfully and artfully extorted by you, as you did not produce the mandate imposed upon you.

And whereas it appeared to us, that the whole truth was not expressed by you, respecting your intention: we have judged it necessary to come to a more accurate examination of the business, in which (without prejudice to those things which you have confessed, and which have been brought against you as above, respecting your said intention) you have answered as a penitent, and good Catholic. Wherefore we having maturely considered the merits of your cause, together with your abovesaid confessions, and defence, and are come to the underwritten definitive sentence against you.

Having invoked the most holy name of our Lord Jesus Christ, and of his most glorious mother the ever blessed Virgin Mary, we, by this our definitive sentence, by the advice and judgment of the most Reverend Masters of Holy Theology, and the Doctors of both Laws, our Counsellors respecting the cause and causes controverted before us, between the magnificent Charles Sincerus, Dr. of both Laws, Fiscal Procurator of this Holy Office on the one part, and you, Galileo Galilei defendant, question examined, and having confessed, as above on the other part, we say, judge and declare, by the present processional writing, you, the abovesaid Galileo, on account of those things, which have been adduced in the written process, and which you have confessed, as above, that you have rendered yourself liable to the suspicion of heresy by this office, that is, you have believed and maintained a false doctrine, and contrary to the Holy and Divine Scriptures, namely, that the Sun is the centre of the orb of the Earth, and that it does not move from the East to the West, and that the Earth moves and is not the centre of the World; and that this position may be held and defended as a probable opinion, after it had been declared and defined to be contrary to Holy Scriptures, and consequently that you have incurred all the censures and penalties of the Holy Canons, and other Constitutions general and particular, enacted and promulgated against such delinquents from which it is our pleasure to absolve you, on condition that first, with sincere heart and faith unfeigned, you abjure, execrate, and detest the above errors and heresies, and every other error and heresy, contrary to the Catholic and Apostolical Roman Church, in our presence, in that formula which is hereby exhibited to you.

But that your grievous and pernicious error and transgression may not remain altogether unpunished, and that you may hereafter be more cautious, serving as an example to others, that they may abstain from the like offences, we decree, that the book of the Dialogue of Galileo, be prohibited by public edict, *and we condemn yourself to the prison of this Holy Office, to a time to be limited by our discretion; and we enjoin under the title of salutary penitence, that during three years to come you recite once a week the seven penitential Psalms,* reserving to ourselves the power of moderating, changing, or taking away entirely, or in part, the aforesaid penalties and penitences.

And so we say, pronounce, and by our sentence declare, enact, condemn, and reserve, by this and every other better mode or formula, by which of right we can and ought.

So we, the underwritten Cardinals pronounce, F. Cardinal de Asculo, G. Cardinal Bentivolus, F. Cardinal de Cremona, Fr. Antony Cardinal S. Onuphrii, B. Cardinal Gypsius, F. Cardinal Verospius, M. Cardinal Ginettus.

THE ABJURATION OF GALILEO

I, Galileo Galilei, son of the late Vincent Galileo, a Florentine, of the age of 70, appearing personally in judgment, and being on my knees in the presence of you, most eminent and most reverend Lords Cardinals of the Universal Christian Commonwealth, Inquisitors General against heretical depravity, having before my eyes the holy Gospels, on which I now lay my hands, swear that I have always believed, and now believe, and God helping, that I shall for the future always believe, whatever the Holy Catholic and Apostolic Roman Church holds, preaches, and teaches. But because this Holy Office had enjoined me by precept, entirely to relinquish the false dogma which maintains that the Sun is the centre of the world, and immoveable, and that the Earth is not the centre, and moves; not to hold, defend, or teach by any means, or by writing, the aforesaid false doctrine; and after it had been notified to me that the aforesaid doctrine is repugnant to the Holy Scripture, I have written and printed a book, in which I treat of the same doctrine already condemned, and adduce reasons with great efficacy in favour of it, not offering any solution of them; therefore I have been adjudged and vehemently suspected of heresy, namely, that I maintained and believed that the Sun is the centre of the world, and immoveable, and that the Earth is not the centre, and moves.

Therefore, being willing to take out of the minds of your eminences, and of every Catholic Christian, this vehement suspicion of right conceived against me, I with sincere heart, and faith unfeigned, abjure, execrate, and detest the aforesaid errors and heresies, and generally every other sect contrary to the above said Holy Church; and I swear that I will never any more hereafter say or assert, by speech or writing, any thing through which the like suspicion may be had of me; but if I shall know any one heretical, or suspected of heresy, I will denounce him to this Holy Office, or to the Inquisitor, and Ordinary of the place in which I shall be. I moreover swear and promise, that I will fulfil and observe entirely all the penitences which have been imposed upon me, or which shall be imposed by this Holy Office. But if it shall happen that I shall go contrary (which God avert) to any of my words, promises, protestations, and oaths, I subject myself to all the penalties and punishments, which, by the Holy Canons, and other Constitutions, general and particular, have been enacted and promulgated against such delinquents: So help me God, and his Holy Gospels, on which I now lay my hands.

I, the aforesaid Galileo Galilei, have abjured, sworn, promise, and have bound myself as above, and in the fidelity of those with my own hands, and have subscribed to this present writing of my abjuration, which I have recited word by word. At Rome, in the Convent of Minerva, this 22d of June, of the year 1633.

I, Galileo Galilei, have abjured as above, with my own hand.

JOHANNES KEPLER

The revolutionary cosmology and astronomy of Copernicus would have been stillborn had it not been for the work of Tycho Brahe (1546–1601) and his more famous assistant Johannes Kepler (1571–1630). The accurate observations of Brahe enabled Kepler to formulate his three laws pertaining to the planets' revolution around the sun. Kepler's most important discovery was that the orbit of a planet around the sun was an ellipse rather than a circle. This discovery made it possible for Kepler to develop a highly sophisticated mathematical version of celestial mechanics. He correctly saw the sun as exercising power in the control of these orbits and thus prepared the way for Newton's laws of gravitation. In fact, Kepler was a forerunner of the inductive scientific method, by which hypotheses unlock subsequent data, otherwise unexamined.

From The Harmonies of the World

Concerning the very perfect harmony of the celestial movements, and the genesis of eccentricities and the semidiameters, and the periodic times from the same.

After the model of the most correct astronomical doctrine of today, and the hypothesis not only of Copernicus but also of Tycho Brahe, whereof either hypotheses are today publicly accepted as most true, and the Ptolemaic as outmoded.

> I commence a sacred discourse, a most true hymn to God the Founder, and I judge it to be piety, not to sacrifice many hecatombs of bulls to Him and to burn incense of innumerable perfumes and cassia, but first to learn myself, and afterwards to teach others too, how great He is in wisdom, how great in power, and of what sort in goodness. For to wish to adorn in every way possible the things that should receive adornment and to envy no thing its goods—this I put down as the sign of the greatest goodness, and in this respect I praise Him as good that in the heights of His wisdom He finds everything whereby each thing may be adorned to the utmost and that He can do by his unconquerable power all that he has decreed.
> (GALEN, on the Use of Parts. BOOK III)

PROEM

[268] As regards that which I prophesied two and twenty years ago (especially that the five regular solids are found between the celestial spheres), as re-

From Johannes Kepler, "The Harmonies of the World," Robert Hutchins, ed., *Great Books of the Western World*, vol. 16 (Chicago: Encyclopaedia Britannica, 1952), pp. 1009–1010; 1014–1018.

gards that of which I was firmly persuaded in my own mind before I had seen Ptolemy's *Harmonies*, as regards that which I promised my friends in the title of this fifth book before I was sure of the thing itself, that which, sixteen years ago, in a published statement, I insisted must be investigated, for the sake of which I spent the best part of my life in astronomical speculations, visited Tycho Brahe, [269] and took up residence at Prague: finally, as God the Best and Greatest, Who had inspired my mind and aroused my great desire, prolonged my life and strength of mind and furnished the other means through the liberality of the two Emperors and the nobles of this province of Austria-on-the Anisana: after I had discharged my astronomical duties as much as sufficed, finally, I say, I brought it to light and found it to be truer than I had even hoped, and I discovered among the celestial movements the full nature of harmony, in its due measure, together with all its parts unfolded in Book III—not in that mode wherein I had conceived it in my mind (this is not last in my joy) but in a very different mode which is also very excellent and very perfect. There took place in this intervening time, wherein the very laborious reconstruction of the movements held me in suspense, an extraordinary augmentation of my desire and incentive for the job, a reading of the *Harmonies* of Ptolemy, which had been sent to me in manuscript by John George Herward, Chancellor of Bavaria, a very distinguished man and of a nature to advance philosophy and every type of learning. There, beyond my expectations and with the greatest wonder, I found approximately the whole third book given over to the same consideration of celestial harmony, fifteen hundred years ago. But indeed astronomy was far from being of age as yet; and Ptolemy, in an unfortunate attempt, could make others subject to despair, as being one who, like Scipio in Cicero, seemed to have recited a pleasant Pythagorean dream rather than to have aided philosophy. But both the crudeness of the ancient philosophy and this exact agreement in our meditations, down to the last hair, over an interval of fifteen centuries, greatly strengthened me in getting on with the job. For what need is there of many men? The very nature of things, in order to reveal herself to mankind, was at work in the different interpreters of different ages, and was the finger of God—to use the Hebrew expression; and here, in the minds of two men, who had wholly given themselves up to the contemplation of nature, there was the same conception as to the configuration of the world, although neither had been the other's guide in taking this route. But now since the first light eight months ago, since broad day three months ago, and since the sun of my wonderful speculation has shone fully a very few days ago: nothing holds me back. I am free to give myself up to the sacred madness, I am free to taunt mortals with the frank confession that I am stealing the golden vessels of the Egyptians, in order to build of them a temple for my God, far from the territory of Egypt. If you pardon me, I shall rejoice; if you are enraged, I shall bear up. The die is cast, and I am writing the book—whether to be read by my contemporaries or by posterity matters not. Let it await its reader for a hundred years, if God Himself has been ready for His contemplator for six thousand years. . . .

3. A Summary of Astronomical Doctrine Necessary for Speculation into the Celestial Harmonies

First of all, my readers should know that the ancient astronomical hypotheses of Ptolemy, in the fashion in which they have been unfolded in the *Theoricae* of Peurbach and by the other writers of epitomes, are to be completely removed from this discussion and cast out of [275] the mind. For they do not convey the true lay out of the bodies of the world and the polity of the movements.

Although I cannot do otherwise than to put solely Copernicus' opinion concerning the world in the place of those hypotheses and, if that were possible, to persuade everyone of it; but because the thing is still new among the mass of the intelligentsia [*apud vulgus studiosorum*], and the doctrine that the Earth is one of the planets and moves among the stars around a motionless sun sounds very absurd to the ears of most of them: therefore those who are shocked by the unfamiliarity of this opinion should know that these harmonical speculations are possible even with the hypotheses of Tycho Brahe—because that author holds, in common with Copernicus, everything else which pertains to the layout of the bodies and the tempering of the movements, and transfers solely the Copernican annual movement of the Earth to the whole system of planetary spheres and to the sun, which occupies the centre of that system, in the opinion of both authors. For after this transference of movement it is nevertheless true that in Brahe the Earth occupies at any time the same place that Copernicus gives it, if not in the very vast and measureless region of the fixed stars, at least in the system of the planetary world. And accordingly, just as he who draws a circle on paper makes the writing-foot of the compass revolve, while he who fastens the paper or tablet to a turning lathe draws the same circle on the revolving tablet with the foot of the compass or stylus motionless; so too, in the case of Copernicus the Earth, by the real movement of its body, measures out a circle revolving midway between the circle of Mars on the outside and that of Venus on the inside; but in the case of Tycho Brahe the whole planetary system (wherein among the rest the circles of Mars and Venus are found) revolves like a tablet on a lathe and applies to the motionless Earth, or to the stylus on the lathe, the mid-space between the circles of Mars and Venus; and it comes about from this movement of the system that the Earth within it, although remaining motionless, marks out the same circle around the sun and midway between Mars and Venus, which in Copernicus it marks out by the real movement of its body while the system is at rest. Therefore, since harmonic speculation considers the eccentric movements of the planets, as if seen from the sun, you may easily understand that if any observer were stationed on a sun as much in motion as you please, nevertheless for him the Earth, although at rest (as a concession to Brahe), would seem to describe the annual circle midway between the planets and in an intermediate length of time. Wherefore, if there is any man of such feeble wit that he cannot grasp the movement of the earth among the stars, nevertheless he can take pleasure in the most excellent spectacle of this most divine construction, if he applies to their image in the sun whatever he hears concerning the daily movements of the Earth in its eccentric—such an image as Tycho Brahe exhibits, with the Earth at rest.

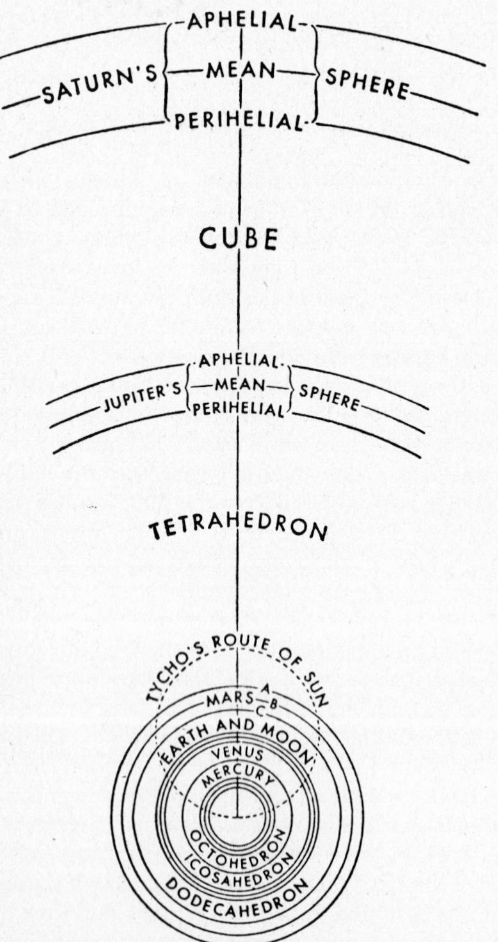

And nevertheless the followers of the true Samian philosophy have no just cause to be jealous of sharing this delightful speculation with such persons, because their joy will be in many ways more perfect, as due to the consummate perfection of speculation, if they have accepted the immobility of the sun and the movement of the earth.

Firstly [I], therefore, let my readers grasp that today it is absolutely certain among all astronomers that all the planets revolve around the sun, with the exception of the moon, which alone has the Earth as its centre: the magnitude of the moon's sphere or orbit is not great enough for it to be delineated in this diagram in a just ratio to the rest. Therefore, to the other five planets, a sixth, the Earth, is added, which traces a sixth circle around the sun, whether by its own proper movement with the sun at rest, or motionless itself and with the whole planetary system revolving.

Secondly [II]: It is also certain that all the planets are eccentric, *i.e.*, they change their distances from the sun, in such fashion that in one part of their circle they become farthest away from the sun, [276] and in the opposite part they come nearest to the sun. In the accompanying diagram three circles apiece have been drawn for the single planets: none of them indicate the eccentric route of the planet itself; but the mean circle, such as *BE* in the case of Mars, is equal to the eccentric orbit, with respect to its longer diameter. But the orbit itself, such as *AD*, touches *AF*, the upper of the three, in one place *A*, and the lower circle *CD*, in the opposite place *D*. The circle *GH* made with dots and described through the centre of the sun indicates the route of the sun according to Tycho Brahe. And if the sun moves on this route, then absolutely all the points in this whole planetary system here depicted advance upon an equal route, each upon his own. And with one point of it (namely, the centre of the sun) stationed at one point of its circle, as here at the lowest, absolutely each and every point of the system will be stationed at the lowest part of its circle. However, on account of the smallness of the space the three circles of Venus unite in one, contrary to my intention.

Thirdly [III]: Let the reader recall from my *Mysterium Cosmographicum*, which I published twenty-two years ago, that the number of the planets or circular routes around the sun was taken by the very wise Founder from the five regular solids, concerning which Euclid, so many ages ago, wrote his book which is called the *Elements* in that it is built up out of a series of propositions. But it has been made clear in the second book of this work that there cannot be more regular bodies, *i.e.*, that regular plane figures cannot fit together in a solid more than five times.

Fourthly [IV]: As regards the ratio of the planetary orbits, the ratio between two neighbouring planetary orbits is always of such a magnitude that it is easily apparent that each and every one of them approaches the single ratio of the spheres of one of the five regular solids, namely, that of the sphere circumscribing to the sphere inscribed in the figure. Nevertheless it is not wholly equal, as I once dared to promise concerning the final perfection of astronomy. For, after completing the demonstration of the intervals from Brahe's observations, I discovered the following: if the angles of the cube [277] are applied to the inmost circle of Saturn, the centres of the planes are approximately tangent to the middle circle of Jupiter; and if the angles of the tetrahedron are placed against the inmost circle of Jupiter, the centres of the planes of the tetrahedron are approximately tangent to the outmost circle of Mars; thus if the angles of the octahedron are placed against any circle of Venus (for the total interval between the three has been very much reduced), the centres of the planes of the octahedron penetrate and descend deeply within the outmost circle of Mercury, but nonetheless do not reach as far as the middle circle of Mercury; and finally, closest of all to the ratios of the dodecahedral and icosahedral spheres—which ratios are equal to one another—are the ratios or intervals between the circles of Mars and the Earth, and the Earth and Venus; and those intervals are similarly equal, if we compute from the inmost circle of Mars to the middle circle of the Earth, but from the middle circle of the Earth to the middle circle of Venus. For the middle distance of the Earth is a mean proportional between the least distance of Mars and the middle distance of Venus. However, these two ratios between the planetary circles are still greater than the ratios of those two pairs of spheres in the figures, in such fashion that the centres of the dodecahedral planes are not tangent to the outmost circle of the Earth, and the centres of the icosahedral planes are not tangent to the outmost circle of Venus; nor, however, can this gap be filled by the semidiameter of the lunar sphere, by adding it, on the upper side, to the greatest distance of the Earth and subtracting it, on the lower, from the least distance of the same. But I find a certain other ratio of figures—namely, if I take the augmented dodecahedron, to which I have given the name of echinus, (as being fashioned from twelve quinquangular stars and thereby very close to the five regular solids), if I take it, I say, and place its twelve points in the inmost circle of Mars, then the sides of the pentagons, which are the bases of the single rays or points, touch the middle circle of Venus. In short: the cube and the octahedron, which are consorts, do not penetrate their planetary spheres at all; the dodecahedron and the icosahedron, which are consorts, do not wholly reach to theirs, the tetrahedron exactly touches both: in the first case there is falling short; in the second, excess; and in the third, equality, with respect to the planetary intervals.

Wherefore it is clear that the very ratios of the planetary intervals from the sun have not been taken from the regular solids alone. For the Creator, who is the very source of geometry and, as Plato wrote, "practices eternal geometry," does not stray from his own archetype. And indeed that very thing could be inferred from the fact that all the planets change their intervals throughout fixed periods of time, in such fashion that each has two marked intervals from the sun, a greatest and a least; and a fourfold comparison of the intervals from the sun is possible between two planets: the comparison can be made between either the greatest, or the least, or the contrary intervals most remote from one another, or the contrary intervals nearest together. In this way the comparisons made two by two between neighbouring planets are twenty in number, although on the contrary there are only five regular solids. But it is consonant that if the Creator had any concern for the ratio of the spheres in general, He would also have had concern for the ratio which exists between the varying intervals of the single planets specifically and that the concern is the same in both cases and the one is bound up with the other. If we ponder that, we will comprehend that for setting up the diameters and eccentricities conjointly, there is need of more principles, outside of the five regular solids.

Fifthly [V]: To arrive at the movements between which the consonances have been set up, once more I impress upon the reader that in the *Commentaries on Mars* I have demonstrated from the sure observations of Brahe that daily arcs, which are equal in one and the same eccentric circle, are not traversed with equal speed; but that these differing *delays in equal parts of the eccentric observe the ratio of their distances from the sun,* the source of movement; and conversely, that if equal times are assumed, namely, one natural day in both cases, the corresponding *true diurnal arcs* [278] *of one eccentric orbit have to one another the ratio which is the inverse of the ratio of the two distances from the sun.* Moreover, I demonstrated at the same time that *the planetary orbit is elliptical and the sun, the source of movement, is at one of the foci of this ellipse; and so, when the planet has completed a quarter of its total circuit from its aphelion, then it is exactly at its mean distance from the sun, midway between its greatest distance of the aphelion and its least at the perihelion.* But from these two axioms it results *that the diurnal mean movement of the planet in its eccentric is the same as the true diurnal arc of its eccentric at those moments wherein the planet is at the end of the quadrant of the eccentric measured from the aphelion, although that true quadrant appears still smaller than the just quadrant.* Furthermore, it follows *that the sum of any two true diurnal eccentric arcs, one of which is at the same distance from the aphelion that the other is from the perihelion, is equal to the sum of the two mean diurnal arcs.* And as a consequence, *since the ratio of circles is the same as that of the diameters, the ratio of one mean diurnal arc to the sum of all the mean and equal arcs in the total circuit is the same as the ratio of the mean diurnal arc to the sum of all the true eccentric arcs, which are the same in number but unequal to one another.* And those things should first be known concerning the true diurnal arcs of the eccentric and the true movements, so that by means of them we may understand the movements which would be apparent if we were to suppose an eye at the sun.

FRANCIS BACON

If many of our previous philosophers were persons of courage, even to the death, we lament that Francis Bacon was an exception. Born in London in 1561, Bacon made his way up the royal hierarchy, largely through the beneficence of the Earl of Essex. When Essex fell out of favor with Queen Elizabeth, it was Bacon who prosecuted him and presided over his hanging. Bacon continued to prosper in the service of King James I, until 1621 when he was accused and convicted of taking bribes. Banished from office and publicly disgraced, Bacon retired to a life of writing until his death in 1626.

Francis Bacon was not an original philosopher, but he had an uncanny sense of his times. He was a founder of the modern inductive scientific method, and his writings are funds of wise advice about the method of inquiry. His own situation notwithstanding, Bacon made important comments regarding what is called in the twentieth century the snare of self-deception. The following selection on the dangers that "Idols" pose to free and creative inquiry is as true today as when it was published, in 1620.

The Idols, *from* The New Organon

XXXIX

There are four classes of Idols which beset men's minds. To these for distinction's sake I have assigned names,—calling the first class *Idols of the Tribe;* the second, *Idols of the Cave;* the third, *Idols of the Market-place;* the fourth, *Idols of the Theatre.*

XL

The formation of ideas and axioms by true induction is no doubt the proper remedy to be applied for the keeping off and clearing away of idols. To point them out, however, is of great use; for the doctrine of Idols is to the Interpretation of Nature what the doctrine of the refutation of Sophisms is to common Logic.

XLI

The Idols of the Tribe have their foundation in human nature itself, and in the tribe or race of men. For it is a false assertion that the sense of man is the measure of things. On the contrary, all perceptions as well of the sense as of the mind are according to the measure of the individual and not according to the measure of the universe. And the human understanding is like a false mirror, which, receiving rays irregularly, distorts and discolours the nature of things by mingling its own nature with it.

XLII

The Idols of the Cave are the idols of the individual man. For every one (besides the errors common to human nature in general) has a cave or den of his own, which refracts and discolours the light of nature; owing either to his own proper and peculiar nature; or to his education and conversation with others; or to the reading of books, and the authority of those whom he esteems and admires; or to the differences of impressions, accordingly as they take place in a mind preoccupied and predisposed or in a mind indifferent and settled; or the like. So that the spirit of man (according as it is meted out to different individuals) is in fact a thing variable and full of perturbation, and governed as it were by chance. Whence it was well observed by Heraclitus that men look for sciences in their own lesser worlds, and not in the greater or common world.

XLIII

There are also Idols formed by the intercourse and association of men with each other, which I call Idols of the Market-place, on account of the commerce and consort of men there. For it is by discourse that men associate; and words are imposed according to the apprehension of the vulgar. And therefore the ill and unfit choice of words wonderfully obstructs the understanding. Nor do the definitions or explanations wherewith in some things learned men are wont to guard and defend themselves, by any means set the matter right. But words plainly force and overrule the understanding, and throw all into confusion, and lead men away into numberless empty controversies and idle fancies.

XLIV

Lastly, there are Idols which have immigrated into men's minds from the various dogmas of philosophies, and also from wrong laws of demonstration. These I call Idols of the Theatre; because in my judgment all the received systems are but so many stage-plays, representing worlds of their own creation after an unreal and scenic fashion. Nor is it only of the systems now in vogue, or only of the ancient sects and philosophies, that I speak; for many more plays of the same kind may yet be composed and in like artificial manner set forth; seeing that errors the most widely different have nevertheless causes for the most part alike. Neither again do I mean this only of entire systems, but also of many principles

---

From Francis Bacon, *The New Organon,* James Spedding, Robert Leslie Ellis, and Douglas Denning Heath, eds., *The Works of Francis Bacon* (New York: Hurd and Houghton, 1878), pp. 76–99.

and axioms in science, which by tradition, credulity, and negligence have come to be received.

But of these several kinds of Idols I must speak more largely and exactly, that the understanding may be duly cautioned.

XLV

The human understanding is of its own nature prone to suppose the existence of more order and regularity in the world than it finds. And though there be many things in nature which are singular and unmatched, yet it devises for them parallels and conjugates and relatives which do not exist. Hence the fiction that all celestial bodies move in perfect circles; spirals and dragons being (except in name) utterly rejected. Hence too the element of Fire with its orb is brought in, to make up the square with the other three which the sense perceives. Hence also the ratio of density of the so-called elements is arbitrarily fixed at ten to one. And so on of other dreams. And these fancies affect not dogmas only, but simple notions also.

XLVI

The human understanding when it has once adopted an opinion (either as being the received opinion or as being agreeable to itself) draws all things else to support and agree with it. And though there be a greater number and weight of instances to be found on the other side, yet these it either neglects and despises, or else by some distinction sets aside and rejects; in order that by this great and pernicious predetermination the authority of its former conclusions may remain inviolate. And therefore it was a good answer that was made by one who when they showed him hanging in a temple a picture of those who had paid their vows as having escaped shipwreck, and would have him say whether he did not now acknowledge the power of the gods,—"Aye," asked he again, "but where are they painted that were drowned after their vows?" And such is the way of all superstition, whether in astrology, dreams, omens, divine judgments, or the like; wherein men, having a delight in such vanities, mark the events where they are fulfilled, but where they fail, though this happen much oftener, neglect and pass them by. But with far more subtlety does this mischief insinuate itself into philosophy and the sciences; in which the first conclusion colours and brings into conformity with itself all that come after, though far sounder and better. Besides, independently of that delight and vanity which I have described, it is the peculiar and perpetual error of the human intellect to be more moved and excited by affirmatives than by negatives; whereas it ought properly to hold itself indifferently disposed towards both alike. Indeed in the establishment of any true axiom, the negative instance is the more forcible of the two.

XLVII

The human understanding is moved by those things most which strike and enter the mind simultaneously and suddenly, and so fill the imagination; and then it feigns and supposes all other things to be somehow, though it cannot see how, similar to those few things by which it is surrounded. But for that going to and fro to remote and heterogeneous instances, by which axioms are tried as in the fire, the intellect is altogether slow and unfit, unless it be forced thereto by severe laws and overruling authority.

XLVIII

The human understanding is unquiet; it cannot stop or rest, and still presses onward, but in vain. Therefore it is that we cannot conceive of any end or limit to the world; but always as of necessity it occurs to us that there is something beyond. Neither again can it be conceived how eternity has flowed down to the present day; for that distinction which is commonly received of infinity in time past and in time to come can by no means hold; for it would thence follow that one infinity is greater than another, and that infinity is wasting away and tending to become finite. The like subtlety arises touching the infinite divisibility of lines, from the same inability of thought to stop. But this inability interferes more mischievously in the discovery of causes: for although the most general principles in nature ought to be held merely positive, as they are discovered, and cannot with truth be referred to a cause; nevertheless the human understanding being unable to rest still seeks something prior in the order of nature. And then it is that in struggling towards that which is further off it falls back upon that which is more nigh at hand; namely, on final causes: which have relation clearly to the nature of man rather than to the nature of the universe; and from this source have strangely defiled philosophy. But he is no less an unskilled and shallow philosopher who seeks causes of that which is most general, than he who in things subordinate and subaltern omits to do so.

XLIX

The human understanding is no dry light, but receives an infusion from the will and affections; whence proceed sciences which may be called "sciences as one would." For what a man had rather were true he more readily believes. Therefore he rejects difficult things from impatience of research; sober things, because they narrow hope; the deeper things of nature, from superstition; the light of experience, from arrogance and pride, lest his mind should seem to be occupied with things mean and transitory; things not commonly believed, out of deference to the opinion of the vulgar. Numberless in short are the ways, and sometimes imperceptible, in which the affections colour and infect the understanding.

L

But by far the greatest hindrance and aberration of the human understanding proceeds from the dullness, incompetency, and deceptions of the senses; in that things which strike the sense outweigh things which do not immediately strike it, though they be more important. Hence it is that speculation commonly ceases where sight ceases; insomuch that of things invisible there is little or no observation. Hence all the working of the spirits inclosed in tangible bodies lies hid and unobserved of men. So also all the more subtle changes of form in the parts of coarser substances (which they commonly call alteration, though it is in truth local motion through exceedingly small spaces) is in like manner unobserved. And yet unless these two things just mentioned be searched out and brought to light, nothing great can be achieved in nature, as far as the production of works is concerned. So again the essential nature of our common air, and of all bodies less dense than air (which are very many), is almost unknown. For the sense by itself is a thing infirm and erring; neither can instruments for enlarging or sharpening the senses do much; but all the truer kind of interpretation of nature is effected by instances and experiments fit and apposite; wherein the sense decides touching the experiment only, and the experiment touching the point in nature and the thing itself.

LI

The human understanding is of its own nature prone to abstractions and gives a substance and reality to things which are fleeting. But to resolve nature into abstractions is less to our purpose than to dissect her into parts; as did the school of Democritus, which went further into nature than the rest. Matter rather than forms should be the object of our attention, its configurations and changes of configuration, and simple action, and law of action or motion; for forms are figments of the human mind, unless you will call those laws of action forms.

LII

Such then are the idols which I call *Idols of the Tribe;* and which take their rise either from the homogeneity of the substance of the human spirit, or from its preoccupation, or from its narrowness, or from its restless motion, or from an infusion of the affections, or from the incompetency of the senses, or from the mode of impression.

LIII

The *Idols of the Cave* take their rise in the peculiar constitution, mental or bodily, of each individual; and also in education, habit, and accident. Of this kind there is a great number and variety; but I will instance those the pointing out of which contains the most important caution, and which have most effect in disturbing the clearness of the understanding.

LIV

Men become attached to certain particular sciences and speculations, either because they fancy themselves the authors and inventors thereof, or because they have bestowed the greatest pains upon them and become most habituated to them. But men of this kind, if they betake themselves to philosophy and contemplations of a general character, distort and colour them in obedience to their former fancies; a thing especially to be noticed in Aristotle, who made his natural philosophy a mere bond-servant to his logic, thereby rendering it contentious and well nigh useless. The race of chemists again out of a few experiments of the furnace have built up a fantastic philosophy, framed with reference to a few things; and Gilbert also, after he had employed himself most laboriously in the study and observation of the loadstone, proceeded at once to construct an entire system in accordance with his favourite subject.

LV

There is one principle and as it were radical distinction between different minds, in respect of philosophy and the sciences; which is this: that some minds are stronger and apter to mark the differences of things, others to mark their resemblances. The steady and acute mind can fix its contemplations and dwell and fasten on the subtlest distinctions: the lofty and discursive mind recognises and puts together the finest and most general resemblances. Both kinds however easily err in excess, by catching the one at gradations, the other at shadows.

LVI

There are found some minds given to an extreme admiration of antiquity, others to an extreme love and appetite for novelty; but few so duly tempered that they can hold the mean, neither carping at what has been well laid down by the ancients, nor despising what is well introduced by the moderns. This however turns to the great injury of the sciences and philosophy; since these affectations of antiquity and novelty are the humours of partisans rather than judgments; and truth is to be sought for not in the felicity of any age, which is an unstable thing, but in the light of nature and experience, which is eternal. These factions therefore must be abjured, and care must be taken that the intellect be not hurried by them into assent.

LVII

Contemplations of nature and of bodies in their simple form break up and distract the understanding, while contemplations of nature and bodies in their composition and configuration overpower and dissolve the understanding: a distinction well seen in the school of Leucippus and Democritus as compared with the other philosophies. For that school is so busied with the particles that it hardly attends to the structure, while the others are so lost in admiration of the structure that they do not penetrate to the simplicity of nature. These kinds of contemplation should therefore be alternated and taken by turns; that so the understanding may be rendered at once penetrating and comprehensive, and the inconveniences above mentioned, with the idols which proceed from them, may be avoided.

LVIII

Let such then be our provision and contemplative prudence for keeping off and dislodging the *Idols of the Cave,* which grow for the most part either out of the predominance of a favourite subject, or out of an excessive tendency to compare or to distinguish, or out of partiality for particular ages, or out of the largeness or minuteness of the objects contemplated. And generally let every student of nature take this as a rule,—that whatever his mind seizes and dwells upon with peculiar satisfaction is to be held in suspicion, and that so much the more care is to be taken in dealing with such questions to keep the understanding even and clear.

LIX

But the *Idols of the Market-place* are the most troublesome of all: idols which have crept into the understanding through the alliances of words and names. For men believe that their reason governs words; but it is also true that words react on the understanding; and this it is that has rendered philosophy and the sciences sophistical and inactive. Now words, being commonly framed and applied according to the capacity of the vulgar, follow those lines of division which are most obvious to the vulgar understanding. And whenever an understanding of greater acuteness or a more diligent observation would alter those lines to suit the true divisions of nature, words stand in the way and resist the change. Whence it comes to pass that the high and formal discussions of learned men end oftentimes in disputes about words and names; with which (according to the use and wisdom of the mathematicians) it would be more prudent to begin, and so by means of definitions reduce them to order. Yet even definitions cannot cure this evil in dealing with natural and material things; since the definitions themselves consist of words, and those words beget others: so that it is necessary to recur to individual instances, and those in due series and order; as I shall say presently when I come to the method and scheme for the formation of notions and axioms.

LX

The idols imposed by words on the understanding are of two kinds. They are either names of things which do not exist (for as there are things left unnamed through lack of observation, so likewise are there names which result from fantastic suppositions and to which nothing in reality corresponds), or they are names of things which exist, but yet confused and ill-defined, and hastily and irregularly derived from realities. Of the former kind are Fortune, the Prime Mover, Planetary Orbits, Element of Fire, and like fictions which owe their origin to false and idle theories. And this class of idols is more easily expelled, because to get rid of them it is only necessary that all theories should be steadily rejected and dismissed as obsolete.

But the other class, which springs out of a faulty and unskillful abstraction, is intricate and deeply rooted. Let us take for example such a word as *humid;* and see how far the several things which the word is used to signify agree with each other; and we shall find the word *humid* to be nothing else than a mark loosely and confusedly applied to denote a variety of actions which will not bear to be reduced to any constant meaning. For it both signifies that which easily spreads itself round any other body; and that which in itself is indeterminate and cannot solidise; and that which readily yields in every direction; and that which easily divides and scatters itself; and that which easily unites and collects itself; and that which readily flows and is put in motion; and that which readily clings to another body and wets it; and that which is easily reduced to a liquid, or being solid easily melts. Accordingly when you come to apply the word,—if you take it in one sense, flame is humid; if in another, air is not humid; if in another, fine dust is humid; if in another, glass is humid. So that it is easy to see that the notion is taken by abstraction only from water and common and ordinary liquids, without any due verification.

There are however in words certain degrees of distortion and error. One of the least faulty kinds is that of names of substances, especially of lowest species and well-deduced (for the notion of *chalk* and of *mud* is good, of *earth* bad); a more faulty kind is that of actions, as *to generate, to corrupt, to alter;* the most faulty is of qualities (except such as are the immediate objects of the sense) as *heavy, light, rare, dense,* and the like. Yet in all these cases some notions are of necessity a little better than others, in proportion to the greater variety of subjects that fall within the range of the human sense.

LXI

But the *Idols of the Theatre* are not innate, nor do they steal into the understanding secretly, but are plainly impressed and received into the mind from the play-books of philosophical systems and the perverted rules of demonstration. To attempt refutations in this case would be merely inconsistent with what I have already said; for since we agree neither upon principles nor upon demonstrations there is no place for argument. And this is so far well, inasmuch as it leaves the honour of the ancients untouched. For they are no wise disparaged—the question between them and me being only as to the way. For as the saying is, the lame man who keeps the right road outstrips the runner who takes a wrong one. Nay it is obvious that when a man runs the wrong way, the more active and swift he is the further he will go astray.

But the course I propose for the discovery of sciences is such as leaves but little to the acuteness and strength of wits, but places all wits and understandings nearly on a level. For as in the drawing of a straight line or a perfect circle, much depends on the steadiness and practice of the hand, if it be done by aim of hand only, but if with the aid of rule or compass, little or nothing; so is it exactly with my plan. But though particular confutations would be of no avail, yet touching the sects and general divisions of such systems I must say something; something also touching the external signs which show that they are unsound; and finally something touching the causes of such great infelicity and of such lasting and general agreement in error; that so the access to truth may be made less difficult, and the human understanding may the more willingly submit to its purgation and dismiss its idols.

LXII

Idols of the Theatre, or of Systems, are many, and there can be and perhaps will be yet many more. For were it not that now for many ages men's minds have been busied with religion and theology; and were it not that civil governments, especially monarchies, have been averse to such novelties, even in matters speculative; so that men labour therein to the peril and harming of their fortunes,—not only unrewarded, but exposed also to contempt and envy; doubtless there would have arisen many other philosophical sects like to those which in great variety flourished once among the Greeks. For as on the phenomena of the heavens many hypotheses may be constructed, so likewise (and more also) many various dogmas may be set up and established on the phenomena of philosophy. And in the plays of this philosophical theatre you may observe the same thing which is found in the theatre of the poets, that stories invented for the stage are more compact and elegant, and more as one would wish them to be, than true stories out of history.

In general however there is taken for the material of philosophy either a great deal out of a few things, or a very little out of many things; so that on both sides philosophy is based on too narrow a foundation of experiment and natural history, and decides on the authority of too few cases. For the Rational School of philosophers snatches from experience a variety of common instances, neither duly ascertained nor diligently examined and weighed, and leaves all the rest to meditation and agitation of wit.

There is also another class of philosophers, who having bestowed much diligent and careful labour on a few experiments, have thence made bold to educe and construct systems; wresting all other facts in a strange fashion to conformity therewith.

And there is yet a third class, consisting of those who out of faith and veneration mix their philosophy with theology and traditions; among whom the vanity of some has gone so far aside as to seek the origin of sciences among spirits and genii. So that this parent stock of errors—this false philosophy—is of three kinds; the Sophistical, the Empirical, and the Superstitious.

LXIII

The most conspicuous example of the first class was Aristotle, who corrupted natural philosophy by his logic: fashioning the world out of categories; assigning to the human soul, the noblest of substances, a genus from words of the second intention; doing the business of density and rarity (which is to make bodies of greater or less dimensions, that is, occupy greater or less spaces), by the frigid distinction of act and power; asserting that single bodies have each a single and proper motion, and that if they participate in any other then this results from an external cause; and imposing countless other arbitrary restrictions on the nature of things; being always more solicitous to provide an answer to the question and affirm something positive in words, than about the inner truth of things; a failing best shown when his philosophy is compared with other systems of note among the Greeks. For the Homoeomera of Anaxagoras; the Atoms of Leucippus and Democritus; the Heaven and Earth of Parmenides; the Strife and Friendship of Empedocles; Heraclitus's doctrine how bodies are resolved into the indifferent nature of fire, and remoulded into solids; have all of them some taste of the natural philosopher,—some savour of the nature of things, and experience, and bodies; whereas in the physics of Aristotle you hear hardly anything but the words of logic; which in his metaphysics also, under a more imposing name, and more forsooth as a realist than a nominalist, he has handled over again. Nor let any weight be given to the fact, that in his books on animals and his problems, and other of his treatises, there is frequent dealing with experiments. For he had come to his conclusion before; he did not consult experience, as he should have done, in order to the framing of his decisions and axioms; but having first determined the question according to his will, he then resorts to experience, and bending her into conformity with his placets leads her about like a captive in a procession; so that even on this count he is more guilty than his modern followers, the schoolmen, who have abandoned experience altogether.

LXIV

But the Empirical school of philosophy gives birth to dogmas more deformed and monstrous than the

Sophistical or Rational school. For it has its foundations not in the light of common notions, (which though it be a faint and superficial light, is yet in a manner universal, and has reference to many things,) but in the narrowness and darkness of a few experiments. To those therefore who are daily busied with these experiments, and have infected their imagination with them, such a philosophy seems probable and all but certain; to all men else incredible and vain. Of this there is a notable instance in the alchemists and their dogmas; though it is hardly to be found elsewhere in these times, except perhaps in the philosophy of Gilbert. Nevertheless with regard to philosophies of this kind there is one caution not to be omitted; for I foresee that if ever men are roused by my admonitions to betake themselves seriously to experiment and bid farewell to sophistical doctrines, then indeed through the premature hurry of the understanding to leap or fly to universals and principles of things, great danger may be apprehended from philosophies of this kind; against which evil we ought even now to prepare.

LXV

But the corruption of philosophy by superstition and an admixture of theology is far more widely spread, and does the greatest harm, whether to entire systems or to their parts. For the human understanding is obnoxious to the influence of the imagination no less than to the influence of common notions. For the contentious and sophistical kind of philosophy ensnares the understanding; but this kind, being fanciful and tumid and half poetical, misleads it more by flattery. For there is in man an ambition of the understanding, no less than of the will, especially in high and lofty spirits.

Of this kind we have among the Greeks a striking example in Pythagoras, though he united with it a coarser and more cumbrous superstition; another in Plato and his school, more dangerous and subtle. It shows itself likewise in parts of other philosophies, in the introduction of abstract forms and final causes and first causes, with the omission in most cases of causes intermediate, and the like. Upon this point the greatest caution should be used. For nothing is so mischievous as the apotheosis of error; and it is a very plague of the understanding for vanity to become the object of veneration. Yet in this vanity some of the moderns have with extreme levity indulged so far as to attempt to found a system of natural philosophy on the first chapter of Genesis, on the book of Job, and other parts of the sacred writings; seeking for the dead among the living; which also makes the inhibition and repression of it the more important, because from this unwholesome mixture of things human and divine there arises not only a fantastic philosophy but also an heretical religion. Very meet it is therefore that we be soberminded, and give to faith that only which is faith's.

LXVI

So much then for the mischievous authorities of systems, which are founded either on common notions, or on a few experiments, or on superstition. It remains to speak of the faulty subject-matter of contemplations, especially in natural philosophy. Now the human understanding is infected by the sight of what takes place in the mechanical arts, in which the alteration of bodies proceeds chiefly by composition or separation, and so imagines that something similar goes on in the universal nature of things. From this source has flowed the fiction of elements, and of their concourse for the formation of natural bodies. Again, when man contemplates nature working freely, he meets with different species of things, of animals, of plants, of minerals; whence he readily passes into the opinion that there are in nature certain primary forms which nature intends to educe, and that the remaining variety proceeds from hindrances and aberrations of nature in the fulfilment of her work, or from the collision of different species and the transplanting of one into another. To the first of these speculations we owe our primary qualities of the elements; to the other our occult properties and specific virtues; and both of them belong to those empty *compendia* of thought wherein the mind rests, and whereby it is diverted from more solid pursuits. It is to better purpose that the physicians bestow their labour on the secondary qualities of matter, and the operations of attraction, repulsion, attenuation, conspissation, dilatation, astriction, dissipation, maturation, and the like; and were it not that by those two compendia which I have mentioned (elementary qualities, to wit, and specific virtues) they corrupted their correct observations in these other matters,—either reducing them to first qualities and their subtle and incommensurable mixtures, or not following them out with greater and more diligent observation to third and fourth qualities, but breaking off the scrutiny prematurely,—they had made much greater progress. Nor are powers of this kind (I do not say the same, but similar) to be sought for only in the medicines of the human body, but also in the changes of all other bodies.

But it is a far greater evil that they make the quiescent principles, *wherefrom,* and not the moving principles, *whereby,* things are produced, the object of their contemplation and inquiry. For the former tend to discourse, the latter to works. Nor is there any value in those vulgar distinctions of motion which are observed in the received system of natural philosophy, as generation, corruption, augmentation, diminution, alteration, and local motion. What they mean no doubt is this:—If a body in other respects not changed, be moved from its place, *this is local motion;* if without change of place or essence, it be changed in quality this is *alteration;* if by reason of the change the mass and quantity of the body do not remain the same, this is *augmentation* or *diminution;* if they be changed to such a degree that they change their very essence and substance and turn to something else, this is *generation* and *corruption.* But all this is merely popular, and does not at all go deep into nature; for these are only measures and limits, not kinds of motion. What they intimate is *how far,* not *by what means,* or *from what source.* For they do not suggest anything with regard either to the desires of bodies or to the development of their parts: it is only when that motion presents the thing grossly and palpably to the sense as different from what it was, that they begin to mark the division. Even when they wish to suggest something with regard to the causes of motion, and to establish a division with reference to them, they introduce with the greatest negligence a distinction between motion natural and violent; a distinction which is itself drawn entirely from a vulgar notion, since all violent motion is also in fact natural; the external efficient simply setting nature working otherwise than it was before. But if, leaving all this, any one shall observe (for instance) that there is in bodies a desire of mutual contact, so as not to suffer the unity of nature to be quite separated or broken and a vacuum thus made; or if any one say that there is in bodies a desire of resuming their natural dimensions or tension, so that if compressed within or extended beyond them, they immediately strive to recover themselves, and fall back to their old volume and extent; or if any one say that there is in bodies a desire of congregating towards masses of kindred nature,—of dense bodies, for instance, towards the globe of the earth, of thin and rare bodies towards the compass of the sky; all these and the like are truly physical kinds of motion;—but those others are entirely logical and scholastic, as is abundantly manifest from this comparison.

Nor again is it a less evil, that in their philosophies and contemplations their labour is spent in investigating and handling the first principles of things and the highest generalities of nature; whereas utility and the means of working result entirely from things intermediate. Hence it is that men cease not from abstracting nature till they come to potential and uninformed matter, nor on the other hand from dissecting nature till they reach the atom; things which, even if true, can do but little for the welfare of mankind.

LXVII

A caution must also be given to the understanding against the intemperance which systems of philosophy manifest in giving or withholding assent; because intemperance of this kind seems to establish Idols and in some sort to perpetuate them, leaving no way open to reach and dislodge them.

This excess is of two kinds: the first being manifest in those who are ready in deciding, and render sciences dogmatic and magisterial; the other in those who deny that we can know anything, and so introduce a wandering kind of inquiry that leads to nothing; of which kinds the former subdues, the latter weakens the understanding. For the philosophy of Aristotle, after having by hostile confutations destroyed all the rest (as the Ottomans serve their brothers), has laid down the law on all points; which done, he proceeds himself to raise new questions of his own suggestion, and dispose of them likewise; so that nothing may remain that is not certain and decided: a practice which holds and is in use among his successors.

The school of Plato, on the other hand, introduced *Acatalepsia,* at first in jest and irony, and in disdain of the older sophists, Protagoras, Hippias, and the rest, who were of nothing else so much ashamed as of seeming to doubt about anything. But the New

Academy made a dogma of it, and held it as a tenet. And though theirs is a fairer seeming way than arbitrary decisions; since they say that they by no means destroy all investigation, like Pyrrho and his Refrainers, but allow of some things to be followed as probable, though of none to be maintained as true; yet still when the human mind has once despaired of finding truth, its interest in all things grows fainter; and the result is that men turn aside to pleasant disputations and discourses and roam as it were from object to object, rather than keep on a course of severe inquisition. But, as I said at the beginning and am ever urging, the human senses and understanding, weak as they are, are not to be deprived of their authority, but to be supplied with helps.

LXVIII

So much concerning the several classes of Idols, and their equipage: all of which must be renounced and put away with a fixed and solemn determination, and the understanding thoroughly freed and cleansed; the entrance into the kingdom of man, founded on the sciences, being not much other than the entrance into the kingdom of heaven, whereinto none may enter except as a little child.

WILLIAM HARVEY

Harvey was born in Folkstone, England, in 1578. After completing studies at Cambridge and taking his medical degree at Padua, he became a physician at St. Bartholomew's Hospital. With the exception of some problems his Royalist sympathies occasioned during the Puritan revolution in 1642, Harvey concentrated on medicine and writing.

Vesalius, among others, had approached the modern theory of the circulation of the blood, but it was Harvey, disproving the ancient assumption traced to Galen in the second century A.D., *who provided the first systematic empirical evidence that the power to move blood comes from the heart rather than from the arteries. More generally, Harvey brought the method of observation to the center of biology and physiology, which had been characterized by speculative and even occult approaches. It was all the more remarkable an achievement because he made his discoveries before the perfection of the microscope, which occurred after his death in 1657.*

From The Circulation of the Blood

INTRODUCTION

In which Is Shown the Relative Weakness of Previous Accounts of the Movement and Function of the Heart and Arteries

It profits one who is pondering on the movement, pulsation, performance, function, and services of the heart and arteries to read what his predecessors have written, and to note the general trend of opinion handed on by them. For by so doing he can confirm their correct statements, and through anatomical dissection, manifold experiments, and persistent careful observation emend their wrong ones.

Almost all anatomists, physicians, and naturalists hitherto suppose, with Galen, that pulsation and respiration have the same function, and differ only in

William Harvey, "Introduction" to *The Circulation of the Blood and Other Writings*, Kenneth J. Franklin, translator (London: Dent, 1963), pp. 9–21. Originally published by Blackwell Scientific Publications, Ltd.

that the former derives from the psychic faculty, the latter from the vital one, while in all other respects they are alike, both in the service they render and in the nature of their movement. Hence these authors assert (as, for instance, does Girolamo Fabrizzi d'Acquapendente in his very recently published book on *Respiration*) that, since the pulsation of the heart and arteries is inadequate for the fanning and cooling of the blood, nature has fashioned the lungs around the heart. Thus it is clear that whatever these earlier writers have noted about systole and diastole, in connection with the movement of the heart and arteries, has all been penned with an eye upon the lungs.

As, however, the movement and constitution of the heart are other than those of the lungs, and of the arteries than those of the chest, it is probable that their respective functions and services are equally otherwise, and that the pulsations and functions of the heart and likewise of the arteries differ very greatly from those of the chest and lungs. For, if pulsation and respiration serve the same purposes, and if (as is commonly stated) in diastole the arteries take air into their cavities and in systole expel sooty vapours through the same pores of flesh and skin; further, if between systole and diastole they contain air, and at any given time air or spirits or sooty vapours, what answer can those holding such views make to Galen, who wrote in his book that the arteries normally contain blood and nothing but blood, certainly no spirits or air, as one can readily ascertain from his experiments, and from his arguments in that book? And, if in diastole the arteries are filled by the intake of air (the greater the pulsation the greater the intake), then should you, with a large pulsation obtaining, immerse the whole body in a bath of water or of oil, the pulsation must at once be either much smaller or much slower, since passage of air into the arteries is made more difficult, if not impossible, through the surrounding mass of bath fluid. Likewise, as all arteries, deep as well as cutaneous, are distended simultaneously and at equal speed, how will air be able to pass so freely and rapidly through skin, flesh and body fabric into the depths as it will through the skin alone? And how can the arteries of embryos draw external air into their cavities through the maternal belly and the substance of the womb? Or how do seals, whales, dolphins and the whole cetacean tribe, and all the fishes in the depth of the sea, by the diastole and systole of their arteries take in and emit air in rapid succession across the immense mass of water? To say that they suck in the air embedded in the water and return into it their sooty vapours is not unlike a fiction. And, if in systole the arteries expel sooty vapours from their cavities through the pores of the flesh and skin, why not also spirits, which they say are contained in these vessels? For spirits are much more rarefied than sooty vapours. And, if the arteries receive and give out air in systole and diastole, as the lungs do in respiration, why do they not also do so when cut across in a wounding? When the trachea is so severed, the successive in and out movements of air are obvious. When, however, an artery is severed, one sees an immediate and continuous expulsion of blood, and no in and out movement of air. If the arterial pulsations cool and fan the parts of the body as the lungs do the heart itself, how is it commonly stated that the arteries distribute from the heart to the individual parts blood packed with the spirits of life, which foster the heat of the parts, rouse it when torpid, and so to speak restock it when it is low? And how, if you ligate the arteries, do the parts not only straightway become sluggish, cool, and turn somewhat pale, but also finally cease to be nourished? According to Galen, this is because they have been deprived of the heat which had previously flowed to all parts from the heart, since it is clear that the arteries transmit heat rather than cooling and ventilation from the heart to the parts. Moreover, how in

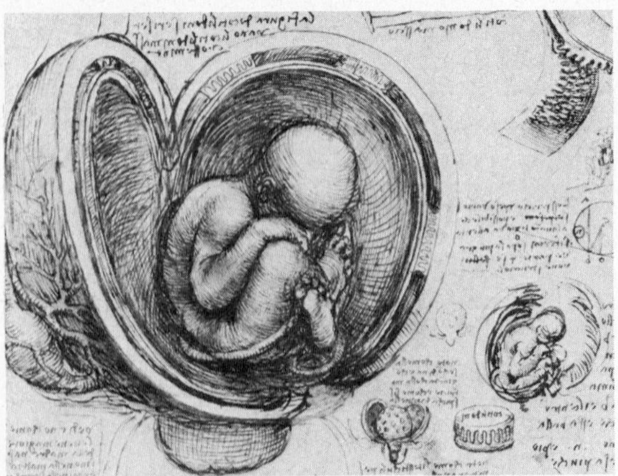

Embryo in the Womb, by Leonardo da Vinci. Painter, sculptor, architect, musician, engineer, mathematician, and scientist, da Vinci was the master of the Renaissance synthesis of art and science. (Royal Library, Windsor Castle)

diastole can there simultaneously be drawn spirits from the heart to warm the parts, and from outside means for their cooling? Further, though some assert that the lungs, arteries, and heart subserve the same functions, they also say that the heart is the laboratory of spirits and the arteries their containers and transmitters, but deny, in opposition to Colombo's view, that the lungs either make or retain spirits. In addition, with Galen, and in opposition to Erasistratus, they stress that blood, and not spirit, is the content of arteries. Such views are clearly mutually conflicting and contradictory, with the result that all are deservedly suspect. That the arteries contain blood and transport blood alone is obvious from Galen's experiment, and in arterial section, and in woundings. For Galen asserts in very many places that in the space of half an hour, from the opening up of a single artery, the whole of the blood will be drained off from every part of the body in a large, torrential outflow. Galen's experiment is as follows. 'If,' he says, 'you tie an artery in two places with a fine cord and cut the part lying between the two ligatures along its length, you will find nothing but blood inside.' And so he proves that it contains blood alone. From which we can argue in like manner as follows. If you find in the arteries (an experiment I have fairly often done in dead human beings and in other animals) the same blood as in the similarly ligated and opened-up veins, we can by the same argument similarly conclude that the arteries contain the same blood as do the veins, and nothing beyond that same blood. Some, while attempting to resolve the difficulty by stating that the blood is spirituous *and* arterial, tacitly concede that the office of the arteries is to distribute blood from the heart to the whole of the body, and that these vessels are full of blood. For spirituous blood is none the less blood. Indeed, no one denies that blood as blood, even that which flows in the veins, is imbued with spirits. Nay, if the blood that is in the arteries is turgid with a more copious amount of spirits, one must nevertheless regard these spirits as being equally inseparable from the blood as are those in the veins. And, as to the idea that the blood and spirits form one fluid (as do whey and butter in milk, or heat [and water] in hot water), with which the arteries are filled and over the distribution of which from the heart they preside, why, even this fluid is nothing other than blood. Moreover, if they say that the blood in the arteries is drawn from the heart through the diastole of these vessels, they appear to impute the filling of the expanding arteries to the blood in question and not, as earlier, to the surrounding air. For, if they say they are filled from this latter, how and when do they receive blood from the heart? If the suggestion is that it happens in [arterial] systole, the impossible will come to pass, namely, arteries filling while they are contracting, or filling and not increasing in volume. If on the other hand the suggestion is that it occurs in diastole, they will receive at one and the same time for two opposing purposes both blood and air, both warmth and cooling; which is improbable. Further, the diastole of the heart and of the arteries cannot be simultaneous, as they state; nor can the systole. For how can one of two so conjoined bodies, when they are simultaneously increasing in volume, draw from the other; or, when they are simultaneously contracting, receive from the other? In addition it is perhaps not possible for something to dilate (dilation being a passive process) while drawing another substance into itself unless it does so in the manner of a sponge, squeezed from outside, during its return to its natural shape. It is, however, difficult to imagine such a happening being possible in arteries. On the other hand, I think that I can readily and openly show, and have before this publicly shown, that arteries increase in volume because they fill up like bags or leather bottles, and are not filled up

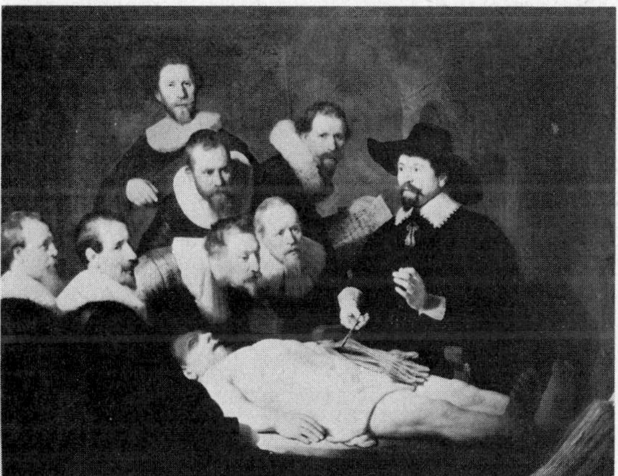

Professor Tulp's Anatomy Lesson, by Rembrandt van Rijn. After more than a thousand years' lapse, Vesalius returned anatomy to public analysis in the sixteenth century. Here, the marvelous intensity of the human face illustrates the new seriousness of anatomy. (Art Resource)

because they increase in volume like bellows. This, it is true, goes contrary to the experiment described by Galen in his book under the heading, 'That the arteries contain blood'. He exposes an artery, incises it along its length, and inserts a reed (or hollow pervious tube), thus ensuring that the blood cannot escape and closing the wound. 'So long', he says, 'as matters stay thus, the whole of the artery will pulsate. So soon, however, as you pass a ligature and knot it over the artery and the tube, thus clamping the arterial coats to the reed, you will cease to observe arterial pulsation beyond the knot.' I have not done Galen's experiment and I do not think it could well be performed in a living subject, because the blood would erupt too forcibly from the arteries; the reed, too, without a ligature will not close the wound, and I have no doubt the blood will leap out through the reed and beyond it. By this experiment, however, Galen seems to prove that the pulsatile power spreads from the heart through the arterial coats, and that the arteries during their dilation are filled by that pulsatile force because they dilate like bellows, and do not dilate because they are filled like leather bottles. The opposite to this is, in fact, apparent both in arterial section and in woundings. For the blood escapes from the arteries in forcible spurts and, even if the distance it travels is now greater and now lesser, the spurt is always in the diastole of the artery and never in its systole. From which it is clear that it is the force of the blood which causes dilation of the artery. For it cannot itself, while dilating, project the blood with such force, it ought rather to draw air into itself through the wound according to common statements about the function of arteries. And let not the thickness of the arterial coats mislead us into thinking that the pulsatile force comes from the heart through those very coats. For in some animals the arteries are no different from veins; and in the most peripheral parts of the human body, with the arteries finely subdivided (as in the brain, hand, etc.), no one will be able by looking at their coats to distinguish arteries from veins, for the coat of each is identical. Again, in an aneurysm resulting from wounding or erosion of an artery, the pulsation is exactly the same as in the remaining arteries, though the arterial coat is missing. The learned Riolan, in his Seventh Book, concurs with me in this. And let no one think that the function of the pulse and of respiration is the same merely because he sees the pulsations get more frequent, larger, and more rapid for the same reasons as does respiration, e.g. running, anger, bathing, or anything heating, as Galen states. For not only is the very finding (which Galen attempts to explain away) opposed to such a view, since immoderate feeding causes increase in size of pulsations with decrease in size of respirations, but in addition children exhibit frequent pulsations simultaneously with infrequent respiration. Similarly in fear, cares, anxiety of mind, and even in some fevers, the pulsations are rapid and frequent, but respirations slower. These difficulties and others of similar sort follow on accepted views of arterial pulsation and function; equally, perhaps, are statements about cardiac function and pulsation a complex of very many problems which it is not easy to disentangle. The heart is usually called the source and laboratory of the spirits of life, by means of which it dispenses life to the individual parts. They say, however, that the right ventricle does not make spirits, but is merely concerned with the nourishment of the lungs. Hence they explain the absence of a right ventricle of the heart from fishes (and, indeed, it is absent from all lungless animals) and assert that the right ventricle of the heart is there for the sake of the lungs.

1. How, I ask, when the structure of the two ventricles is almost identical, with the same make-up of fibres, 'armlets' of muscle, valves, vessels, and auricles, and in our dissection-subjects with similar dark, coagulated blood filling each; how, I say, when each behaves, moves, and pulsates in the same way, can we regard them as having been designed for such very different functions? If the three tricuspid valves at the entry into the right ventricle hinder return of blood into the vena cava, and if the three semilunar ones at the opening into the artery-like vein have been made to hinder return of blood; how, when a similar arrangement holds in the left ventricle, can we say that these valves have not been made similarly to hinder forward or backward movement of blood?

2. And as the valves are almost identically arranged in respect of size, form, and position in the left ventricle and in the right one, why do they say that they hinder egress and regress of spirits in the former, but of blood in the latter? The same sort of mechanism does not seem calculated to prevent equally effectively movements of blood and of spirits.

3. And as the respective paths and vessels correspond in size, that is, the artery-like vein and the vein-like artery, why may the one be regarded as

having a private function, namely, nourishment of the lungs, and the other a public one?

4. And how is it likely (as Realdo Colombo noted) that so much blood is needed for the nourishment of the lungs? Since this vessel, that is, the artery-like vein, exceeds in size both femoral distribution branches of the descending vena cava, taken together.

5. And, I ask, as the lungs are so close, and so large a vessel is available, and the lungs themselves are in continual movement, what reason can there be for pulsation of the right ventricle? And what need for nature to add a second ventricle to the heart for the sake of nourishing the lungs?

When they say that the left ventricle draws material, namely air and blood, from the lungs and the right sinus of the heart for the formation of spirits, and likewise distributes spirituous blood into the aorta; that sooty vapours are sent back to the lungs through the vein-like artery and spirit forwards into the aorta; what is it that keeps the two streams separate? And how do the spirits and the sooty vapours pass in opposite directions without mixing or getting into disorder? If the mitral valves do not hinder exit of sooty vapours into the lungs, how will they hinder exit of air? And how will the semilunar [aortic] valves prevent backflow of spirits (in the subsequent diastole of the heart) from the aorta? And in general, how do they say that the spirituous blood is distributed from the left ventricle through the vein-like artery to the lungs without the mitral valves meanwhile hindering such movement? For they have stated that air enters the left ventricle from the lungs through the same vessel, but would have it that the mitral valves should hinder its return. Good God! How do the mitral valves hinder the return of air, and not of blood?

Further, as they have assigned a single, purely private function (that is, nourishment of the lungs) to the artery-like vein, which is a wide and big vessel, fashioned with an arterial coat, why do they strongly assert that the vein-like artery, with the coat of a vein, soft and lax, has been made for several functions (three or four, to wit)? For they will have it that the air passes through that vessel from the lungs into the left ventricle: they will similarly have sooty vapours pass back through it from the heart into the lungs: and they will have a portion of spirituous blood distributed through it from the heart to the lungs for their revivification.

If they will have sooty vapours and air (the former from the heart, the latter to it) transmitted through the same tube, I must reply that nature is not wont to fashion one vessel and one route for movements and functions so opposite, and that I have never seen such anywhere.

If they claim that sooty vapours and air respectively pass out and in by this route as they do through the bronchial tubes of the lungs, why, when we cut out or open up the vein-like artery, can we never find air or sooty vapours in our dissection subjects? And whence comes it that we always see that vein-like artery packed full of blood, and never of air, while we perceive air still present in the lungs?

If one performed Galen's experiment, and incised the trachea of a still living dog, forcibly filled its lungs with air by means of bellows, and ligated them strongly in the distended position, one would find, on rapidly opening up the chest, a great deal of air in the lungs right out to their outermost coat, but no trace of such in the vein-like artery or in the left ventricle of the heart. If in the living dog either the heart drew air from the lungs, or the lungs transmitted air to the heart, they should do so much more in this experiment. Indeed, were the lungs of the cadaver inflated in an anatomical demonstration, who would doubt that air would at once enter the vein-like artery and left ventricle were any passages available for it? So highly, however, do they rate this function of the vein-like artery, namely, the transfer of air from the lungs to the heart, that Girolamo Fabrizzi d'Acquapendente claims that the lungs were made for the sake of this vessel, and that this is their chief role.

But why, will you please tell me, is the vein-like artery venous in structure if it has been fashioned for the transport of air? Nature should rather use tubes, and ringed ones at that (like those of the bronchi), so that they always stay open and never collapse, and so that they remain completely empty of blood, and fluid causes no hindrance to the passage of air, as it obviously does when the lungs are in difficulties with their tubes packed or moderately filled with phlegm, giving rise to whistling and rustling sounds during our breathing.

Even less acceptable is the opinion which supposes that two sources of raw material (air and blood) are required for making the spirits of life, and claims that the blood oozes from the right to the left ventricle through invisible pores in the cardiac septum while the air is drawn from the lungs through a large vessel, the vein-like artery; that, accordingly, fairly large numbers of pores have been provided in the cardiac septum for the onward transmission of the blood. But, damme, there are no pores and it is not possible to show such.

For the substance of the cardiac septum is denser and more compact than any other part of the body except the bones and tendons. Assuming, however, the presence of openings, how (since both ventricles distend and dilate simultaneously) is it possible for one of them to suck something from the other, or—specifically—for the left ventricle to suck blood from the right one? And why should I not believe that the right ventricle calls spirits from the left one through the aforesaid openings rather than that the left ventricle calls blood from the right one? It is certainly strange and inconsistent that in the same instant blood is more fittingly drawn through obscure invisible channels and air through very widely open ones. And why, I ask, for the transit of the blood to the left ventricle do they have recourse to concealed invisible pores that are ill-defined and obscure, when there is so open a way through the vein-like artery? It is certainly a cause of wonder to me that they have preferred to make or invent a way through the solid, hard, dense, and extremely compact septum cordis rather than through the open vein-like artery, or even through the tenuous, lax, very soft, and spongy substance of the lungs. Moreover, had the blood been able to pass through the substance of the septum or to be imbibed from the ventricles, what need would there be for the small branches of the coronary vein and artery to be spread about for the nutrition of the septum itself? Most noteworthy of all is the following. If in foetal life (when everything is more tenuous and soft) nature has been forced to take blood across through the foramen ovale into the left ventricle [and] from the vena cava through the artery-like vein, how can it be likely that she transfers it so readily and easily in the adult through the cardiac septum, now denser with age?

André du Laurens (in his Book IX, Chapter XI, Question 12), relying on the authority of Galen (*De locis affectis*, Book VI, Chapter VII) and the experience of Holler, asserts and claims to prove that the watery fluids and pus of patients suffering from abscesses can be absorbed from the chest-cavity into the vein-like artery, pass to the left ventricle and arteries, and be expelled with the urine or the faeces of the bowels. Indeed, he recounts in confirmation the case of a person affected with melancholia who, after many fainting fits, was relieved of a paroxysm by the passing of turbid, foetid, and sharp-smelling urine. He finally succumbed to this sort of illness and, when his body was dissected, nothing comparable to the urine he used to pass was found in his bladder or anywhere in his kidneys. In the left ventricle and chest-cavity, however, it was present in abundance, and du Laurens claims that he had foretold such a cause of the affections mentioned. For my part, however, I cannot help but be surprised that, as he had divined and predicted that heterogeneous matter could be evacuated by the route in question, he could not or would not readily perceive or stress that blood could naturally be carried by the same routes from the lungs to the left ventricle.

From these and very many other arguments it is clear that the statements made hitherto by earlier writers about the movement and function of the heart and arteries appear incongruous or obscure or impossible when submitted to specially careful consideration. It will therefore be very useful to look a little more deeply into the matter; to contemplate the movements of the arteries and of the heart not only in man, but also in all other animals with hearts; moveover, by frequent experiments on animals and much use of one's own eyes, to discern and investigate the truth.

SUGGESTIONS FOR FURTHER READING

Burtt, Edwin Arthur. *The Metaphysical Foundations of Modern Science.* New York: Doubleday–Anchor, 1955.

Butterfield, Herbert. *The Origins of Modern Science.* New York: Collier, 1967.

Clavelin, Maurice. *The Natural Philosophy of Galileo.* Cambridge, Mass.: MIT Press, 1974.

Crombie, A. C. *Medieval and Early Modern Science.* 2 vols. New York: Doubleday–Anchor, 1959.

Drake, Stillman. *Copernicus, Philosophy and Science: Bruno–Kepler–Galileo.* Norwalk, Conn.: Burndy Library, 1973.

Dreye, J. L. E. *Tycho Brahe.* New York: Dover, 1963.

Hall, A. R. *The Scientific Revolution.* Boston: Beacon Press, 1954.

Koestler, Arthur. *The Watershed: A Biography of Johannes Kepler.* New York: Doubleday–Anchor, 1960.

Koyre, Alexandre. *From the Closed World to the Infinite Universe.* New York: Harper Torchbooks, 1958.

Kuhn, Thomas S. *The Copernican Revolution.* Cambridge, Mass.: Harvard University Press, 1957.

Morison, Samuel Eliot. *The European Discovery of America.* 2 vols. New York: Oxford University Press, 1971.

Munitz, Milton, ed. *Theories of the Universe.* Glencoe, Ill.: Free Press, 1957.

Sarton, George. *Appreciation of Ancient and Medieval Science During the Renaissance.* Philadelphia: University of Pennsylvania Press, 1955.

Sarton, George. *Six Wings: Men of Science in the Renaissance.* Bloomington: Indiana University Press, 1957.

René Descartes: The Foundation of Modern Philosophy

The chronological distance traversed by the selections in this volume is, by earth history standards, enormous. Some 2500 years have elasped between the writing of the *Odyssey*, the Hebrew *Bible*, and the *Egyptian Book of the Dead* and the work of René Descartes, who lived from 1596 to 1650 A.D. By the beginning of the seventeenth century, modern European civilization had come to the center of the stage, fortified by the discovery and settling of the New World. And by this time, Copernicanism and the Scientific Revolution had foretold still another chapter in the history of western civilization, the upshot of which will not be acknowledged until our own time, when recent cosmology and astral physics have pressed upon us the dramatic significance of the Copernican revolution, namely, that our cosmic environment is infinite and perhaps ultimately unintelligible.

Educated by the Jesuits, a Roman Catholic religious order founded to combat the Reformation, René Descartes was singularly unimpressed by his exposure to philosophy, poetry, history, and theology. Only his work in mathematics gave him confidence. After having a prophetic dream in 1618, Descartes set out to put philosophy on a basis of certitude equivalent to that which he found in mathematics. The founder of analytic geometry, Descartes was prepared to bring seventeenth-century mathematics to bear on the problems of knowledge, the existence of God, and the activity of the physical world.

The methodological approach of Descartes to these thorny issues was original and has generated controversy ever since. Invoking what he referred to as methodic doubt, Descartes offers that it is conceivable to doubt the existence of God. If it is possible that God does not exist, then it is possible that the external world, as we know it, does not exist, for God is the guarantor of the truth of our perceptions. Descartes then takes the third step in his application of methodic doubt—he doubts the existence of the knowing self. This step, however, is fraught with a basic contradiction, for to doubt is to acknowledge the existence of the self. Thus Descartes arrives at one of the most famous phrases in the history of philosophy, *cogito ergo sum*. Translated idiomatically, this phrase tells us that in that I am thinking, therefore I must be. The thinking self *(res cogitans)* then becomes for Descartes the source of innate ideas, one of which is the idea of a perfect being. Invoking the scholastic principle that the cause must be equal to or greater than its effect, Descartes concludes that a perfect being must exist as the cause of this innate idea. It follows that the perfect being, which exists, is veracious and therefore guarantees our perception of the external world. The original classical scheme of God, world, and self is once again intact, although with the radical difference that the source of certitude is no longer either our perception of the external world or the message of revelation, but rather the intuitive power of the human mind. Modern continental philosophy had begun, with the human mind at the center of the stage.

In 1634, frightened by the Church's censure of Galileo, Descartes suppressed his pro-Copernican work, *Le Monde.* Subsequently, his writings were circulated surreptitiously and he tended to mask his more advanced thought on the issues in question. He remained, however, a scientifically creative and philosophically original thinker. Despite his debt to his Scholastic forebears, Descartes deserves the title of the founder of modern philosophy, for it was he who broke with the past and attempted to use mathematics, physics, and the new scientific method to place philosophical speculation on a sure, that is, scientific, footing. The selections that follow, from *The Discourse on Method* (1637) and *The Meditations* (1641), will sustain this judgment.

In 1649, called by Queen Christina of Sweden to instruct her in philosophy, Descartes obliged, only to die the following year of pneumonia, brought on by a hostile climate and having to teach the Queen in the damp early hours of the morning.

Discourse Concerning the Method for Conducting His Reason Well and for Seeking the Truth in the Sciences

If this discourse seems too long to be read entirely at one sitting, it can be divided into six parts. And in the first will be found different considerations bearing upon the sciences. In the second the principal rules of the method that the author has cultivated. In the third particular rules of morality that he has extracted from this method. In the fourth the reasons by which he proves the existence of God and of the human soul—which are the foundations of his metaphysics. And in the fifth the order of questions belonging to physics that he has researched, and particularly the explanation of the movement of the heart and of some other difficulties that pertain to medicine, as well as the explanation of the difference that exists between our soul and the soul of beasts. And in the last certain things he believes required in order to advance beyond what has been accomplished in the research into nature, as well as the reasons that have persuaded him to write.

FIRST PART

Good sense is the best distributed thing in the world; for everyone thinks himself so well endowed with it that even those most difficult to satisfy in every other matter do not usually desire more of it than they have. It is not likely that everyone is mistaken about this; it rather testifies to the fact that the

Pages 114–164 from *René Descartes: The Essential Writings*, translated by John J. Blom.

ability of judging well and of distinguishing the true from the false, which is what is properly called good sense or reason, is naturally equal in all men; and thus the diversity of our opinions does not derive from the fact that some people are more reasonable than others, but only from the fact that we direct our thinking along different paths and do not consider the same things. For it is not enough to have a good wit, but the principal thing is to apply it well. The greatest souls are capable of the greatest vices as well as the greatest virtues; and if they always follow the right path, those who march only very slowly can advance further than those who run but go astray.

As for myself, I have never presumed my wit in any respect more perfect than that of ordinary men; indeed, I have often wished for thought as prompt, or an imagination as precise and distinct, or a memory as ample or quick, as some other men have. And I know no qualities but these that contribute to the perfection of our wit: for, as regards reason or sense, inasmuch as it is the only thing that makes us men and distinguishes us from the beasts, I wish to believe that it exists complete and entire in each of us; and in this matter I follow the common opinion of the philosophers who say that there is no place for more or less except among the *accidents,* and certainly not among the *forms,* or natures, of *individuals* of the same *kind.*

But I shall not hesitate to say that I think I have had great luck to discover myself ever since youth on particular paths that have led me to certain considerations and maxims out of which I have formed a method; and with this method it seems to me that I have a means of increasing my knowledge by degrees, and of raising it little by little to as high a point as the moderate character of my wit and the brief duration of my life will allow. Now, although in judgments about myself I try always to lean toward the side of caution rather than presumption, and although in looking at the different activities and undertakings of all men with the eye of a philosopher, I find hardly any that do not seem to me vain and useless—nevertheless I have already derived such fruits from this method that I do not fail to receive an extreme satisfaction in the progress I think I have already made in the search for truth. And I conceive such prospects for the future that, if there is any occupation solidly good and important among the occupations of men purely as men, I dare to believe it is the one I have chosen.

All the same, perhaps I am deceived, and possibly it is only a bit of copper and glass that I am mistaking for gold and diamonds. I know how much we are prone to fool ourselves in vital matters; and I know also how often the judgments of our friends, if those judgments run in our favor, should be held suspect. However, I will be very agreeable to showing in this discourse what paths I have followed, and to represent herein my life like a painting, so that everyone can judge it; and thus by gathering from the general response the opinions that readers shall form about this discourse, I will have a new means of instructing myself, which I shall add to those I customarily use.

Thus my design is not to teach here the method everyone should follow to conduct his reason well, but only to explain the manner in which I have tried to conduct my own. Those who involve themselves in laying down precepts should consider themselves abler than those to whom they give them; and such people, if they are lacking in the least thing, are blameworthy. But since I offer this essay only as an autobiography, or, if you prefer, as a fable, in which, among some examples a reader can imitate, he will perhaps find very many others he will be right not to follow, I hope that the essay will be useful to some without being harmful to anyone, and that everyone will recognize that I am inclined to be candid.

I was nourished on letters from my childhood, and because I was persuaded that by their means one could acquire a clear and assured knowledge of everything useful for life, I had a great desire to learn them. But as soon as I had finished the entire course of study at the end of which one is customarily received into the ranks of the learned, I changed my opinion completely. For I found myself embarrassed by so many doubts and errors that it seemed I had derived no other profit in trying to instruct myself except that I had more and more discovered my ignorance. And nevertheless I was in one of the most celebrated schools of Europe, where I thought there ought to be other knowledgeable men, if any are to be found on this earth. I had learned at school everything the others learned there; moreover, not being content with the sciences taught to us, I surveyed all the books I could manage to lay hands upon that treat of things deemed most curious and most rare. Furthermore, I knew the evaluations others made of me; and I did not notice that they esteemed me inferior to my fellow students, although there were already some among them who were destined to fill the places of our teachers. And finally our century seemed to me as flourishing and as fertile with good wits as any preceding century had been. This made me exercise the liberty of judging on my own about all previous times and of thinking that no doctrine in the world was such as I had previously been made to expect.

I did not completely cease to esteem the exercises with which one occupies oneself in the schools. I knew that the languages one learns there are necessary to understand the ancient books; that the gracefulness of the stories awakens our wits, and that when such actions are praised with discretion, they help to form the judgment; that the reading of all good books is like a conversation with the most virtuous people of past ages who have authored them, or even like a considered conversation in which they reveal to us only the best of their thoughts; that eloquence has powers and incomparable beauties; that poetry has delicacies and delights that are very ravishing; that mathematics contains very subtle discoveries that can offer a great deal, as much to content the curious as to facilitate all the arts and diminish the work of men; that the writings that treat of customs contain very many teachings and very many exhortations to virtue that are very useful; that theology teaches how to gain heaven; that philosophy provides a means of speaking with probability about everything, and of eliciting the admiration of the less learned; that jurisprudence, medicine, and the other sciences bring honors and riches to those who cultivate them; and finally that it is good to have examined all of them, even the most superstitious and most false, in order to know their just value and to guard against being deceived by them.

But I believed that I had already devoted enough time to languages, and also even to the reading of ancient books and to their histories and fables. For to converse with the people of other centuries is nearly the same as to take a journey. It is good to know something about the customs of different peoples in order to judge our own more sanely and to guard against thinking that everything contrary to our own is ridiculous and irrational, such as those who have seen nothing customarily believe. Yet when one spends too much time journeying, one finally becomes a stranger in his own country; and when one is too curious about things practiced in past centuries, one ordinarily remains very ignorant of those practiced in this century. Besides, fables make one imagine very many things to be possible that are not possible; and the most faithful histories, even if they do not change or augment the value of things to make them more worthy of praise, at least nearly always omit the most base and the least renowned circumstances: and from this it arises that the rest does not seem such as it is; and those people who direct their customs by the examples they select out are subject to fall into the extravagances of the knights-errant of our novels, and to conceive designs that surpass their powers.

I esteemed eloquence very much, and I was enamored of poetry; but I thought that both were gifts of wit more than the fruits of study. People who have the strongest power of reasoning, and who direct their thoughts in the best manner to render them clear and intelligible, are always best able to persuade us of what they propose, even if they speak only low Breton and have never learned rhetoric. And those with the most agreeable fancies, and who know how to explain them with the most embellishment and grace, would not fail to be the best poets, even though the art of poetry were unknown to them.

I was pleased most of all by the mathematical [disciplines] because of the certitude and evidence of their reasonings; but as yet I did not at all notice their true usage; and thinking they served only in the mechanical arts, I was astonished that, since their foundations were so firm and solid, nothing more dignified had been built upon them. However, on the other hand, I compared those writings of the ancient pagans that treat of customs to those very imposing and very magnificent palaces built only upon sand and mud. These writings elevate the virtues to a high degree, and they make them appear estimable in relation to all the things in the world; but they do not teach us well enough to come to recognize the virtues, and often what they call by so beautiful a name is only an insensibility, or pride, or despair, or parricide.

I revered our theology, and intended as much as any other person to gain heaven; but having learned, as something very assured, that the path to heaven is not less open to the most ignorant than to the most instructed person, and that the revealed truths that lead to heaven are above our intelligence, I did not dare to submit them to the weakness of my reasonings; and I thought that to attempt to examine them and be successful at it required some extraordinary assistance from heaven, and that one be more than man.

I will say nothing about philosophy except, seeing that for many centuries it has been cultivated by the most excellent wits who have lived, and yet still contains nothing that is undisputed, and as a consequence, is not doubtful, I did not have enough presumption to expect to discover more in it than others did; and considering how many different opinions touching on the same matter can exist and be maintained by learned people, even though there cannot be more than one opinion that is true, I regarded as all but false everything that was only probable.

Then, as regards the other sciences, inasmuch as they borrow their principles from philosophy, I judged that one could not have built anything solid on foundations so little secure. And neither the honor nor the gain they promise were sufficient to urge me to learn them; for I did not find myself, thanks to God, in a condition that obliged me to make a profession of science in order to augment my riches. And although I did not make a profession of disdaining glory as the cynics do, I nevertheless placed little importance upon what I could only hope to acquire by false titles. And finally, as for wrong doctrines, I thought that I already sufficiently knew their worth so as to be no longer subject to deception by either the promises of an alchemist, or the predictions of an astrologer, or the impostures of a magician, or the devices or windy claims of those who make a profession of knowing what they do not know.

That is why, as soon as my age permitted me to quit the direction of my teachers, I entirely abandoned the study of letters. And resolving to seek no longer for any science other than that which could be found in myself, or else in the great book of the world, I employed the rest of my youth voyaging, in seeing courts and armies, in making contact with people of different temperaments and conditions, in cultivating different experiences, in testing myself in the situations fortune held out to me, and in every situation devoting such reflection to the things that presented themselves that I would be able to extract some profit from them. For it seemed to me that I should be able to encounter very much more truth in the reasonings everyone makes about things that concern them, and whose outcome, if they judge badly, would punish them, than in those reasonings a man of letters makes in his study regarding speculations that produce no effect and involve no further consequence for him—excepting perhaps that he will derive a greater vanity the more they are removed from common sense, since he will have to employ so much more ingenuity and inventiveness to try to render them probable. And I always had an extreme desire to learn to distinguish the true from the false, in order to see clearly in my actions, and to walk with assurance in this life.

It is true that, while I did nothing but consider the customs of other men, I found hardly anything there to provide me with assurance; and I noticed almost as much diversity among these customs as I had previously noticed among the opinions of the philosophers. Thus the greatest profit I derived from it was, seeing very many things that, although they seem very extravagant and ridiculous to us, are nevertheless commonly received and approved by other large nations, I learned not to believe too firmly any of those things I had been persuaded of only by example and custom; and so I delivered myself, little by little, from very many errors that can obfuscate our natural light and render us less capable of listening to reason. But after I had spent a few years studying the book of the world, and in trying to acquire some experience, one day I made a resolution to also study of myself and to employ all the forces of my wits in choosing the paths I ought to follow. This succeeded for me very much more than if I had never separated myself from my country or my books.

SECOND PART

At that time I was in Germany, where I had been attracted because of the wars that are still not finished there; and as I was returning to the army from the coronation of the emperor, the beginning of winter caused me to put up in a place where, finding no conversation that diverted me, and fortunately having no cares or passions that disturbed me, I remained all day near a stove, where I had complete freedom to weigh my thoughts. Among my thoughts one of the first I undertook to consider was that often there is not as much perfection in works composed of many parts and made by the hands of different masters as in those upon which one person has labored. Thus one sees that the buildings a single architect has undertaken and completed are ordinarily more beautiful and better ordered than those that several persons have tried to renovate by making use of old walls built for other purposes. Thus those ancient cities, initially only small market towns, that finally became large cities after periods of time, are ordinarily badly organized in comparison with the regular places an engineer lays out as suits his fancy upon a plain; for although in considering their edifices individually, one finds in them as much or more artistry, still, seeing their arrangement, with a large edifice here and a small one there, and how they cause the streets to be curved and unequal, one would say that it is more luck than the will of men employing their reason that has arranged them thus. Moreover, if one considers that, despite all this, there have always been certain officers in charge of taking care of particular buildings in order to make them serve as public ornaments, one will certainly recognize that it is difficult, in laboring only upon the works of another, to produce results that are very accomplished. And so I imagined that peoples who, having been formerly half savage and having civilized themselves little by little, thus made their laws only in proportion as the inconvenience of crimes and feuds forced them to do so, could not be so well regulated as those who, from the time they assembled, have observed the constitutions of some prudent legislator. Similarly, it is very certain that the state of true religion, whose ordinances God alone has laid down, ought to be incomparably better regulated than all others. And to speak of human affairs, I believe that if Sparta was very flourishing in former times, it was not because of the goodness of each of its laws in particular, seeing that some were very strange and contrary to good customs; rather it was because the laws, having been devised by a single person, all tended to the same end. And thus I thought that the sciences found in books—at least in those whose reasonings are only probable, and that, since they have been put together and have grown little by little from the opinions of many different persons, contain no demonstrations—are not at all so close to the truth as are the simple reasonings that a man of good sense can naturally make in regard to things that present themselves. Likewise, I thought that because we were all children before being men, and because we had to be directed for a long time by our appetites and teachers—who often contradicted one another, and who perhaps, neither one nor the other, always counseled us for the best—it is almost impossible that our judgments be so pure or so solid as they would have been if we had had the complete use of our reason from the time of our birth, and had been led only by reason.

It is true that we do not find anyone completely razing all the houses of a village solely to make them over anew in another fashion and to render the streets more beautiful; but one certainly sees some people pulling down their own houses in order to rebuild them; one even finds people who are forced to do so when their houses are in danger of falling down themselves and the foundations are not entirely firm. In imitation of this, I persuaded myself that there certainly would be no plausibility in an individual undertaking to reform a state by changing all its foundations, and by turning them upside down to straighten them out; I was also persuaded that one would not even undertake to reform the body of the sciences, or the order established in the schools for teaching them; however, as for all the opinions I had accepted among my beliefs until this time, I was persuaded that I could not do better than to undertake, once and for all, to reject them, in order to replace them afterward, either by better beliefs, or perhaps even with themselves, when I had made them conform to the standard of reason. And I firmly believed that by this means I would succeed in conducting my life very much better than if I built only upon old foundations and relied only upon principles I had allowed to persuade me in my youth, without ever having examined whether they were true. For although I noticed diverse difficulties in this undertaking, they were not, however, such as have no remedy; nor were they comparable to those involved in reforming even the slightest matters that have reference to the public. These large bodies are too difficult to build anew once they have been built; indeed, they are too difficult to hold up once they are disturbed; and their falls can only be very violent. Moreover, as regards the imperfections of states, if such imperfections exist—and the single fact of diversity among states suffices to assure us that some states are imperfect—they undoubtedly are very much tempered by customs; and custom has even avoided or corrected in an imperceptible amount imperfections that one could not so well foresee by prudence. And finally, these imperfections are nearly always more bearable than their changes would be: just as the great paths that wander through the mountains little by little become so connected and so convenient, simply because they are used, that it is very much better to follow them than to proceed straight ahead, jumping over rocks and descending to the bottom of precipices.

This is why I cannot at all approve those persons with mischief-making and unquiet temperaments who, being called neither by birth nor fortune to the management of public affairs, do not hesitate always to conjure up some new reform in their minds. And if I thought this essay had contained anything whatever on the basis of which anyone could have suspected me of this folly, I should be very grieved to have allowed it to be published. My goal has never extended further than to try to reform my own thoughts and to build upon a foundation entirely my own. But if, because my work has pleased me so, I wish to make you see here the model for it, I do not for all that wish to counsel anyone to imitate the model. Those upon whom God has bestowed his graces more abundantly will perhaps have grander goals; but my fear is that the goals set out [in this discourse] are already too venturesome for some people. The single resolve to rid oneself of all the opinions one has hitherto accepted among one's beliefs is not an example everyone ought to follow; the world is, as it were, composed of two sorts of wits for whom such a design is not at all fitting. There are those who, believing themselves abler than they are, cannot prevent themselves from precipitously forming judgments, and lack sufficient patience for conducting their thoughts in an orderly manner: from which it follows that, if once they had taken the liberty of doubting the principles they formerly accepted and of deviating from the common path, they could never stick to the route it is necessary to take to proceed straight ahead, and they would remain astray all their lives. Then there are those who have the reason, or modesty, to judge that they are less capable of distinguishing the true from the false than are some others by whom they can be instructed—these less capable persons ought certainly to content themselves in following the opinions of these others rather than to seek to form better opinions on their own.

As for myself, I undoubtedly would have been numbered among this last group had I had only one teacher, or had I never known the differences that have always existed among the opinions of the most learned. But having learned at college that one could imagine nothing so strange or so incredible that it has not been maintained by one of the philosophers; and having recognized in journeying that everyone who has sentiments contrary to our own is not on that account barbarous or savage, but that some of them use as much, or more, reason than us; and having considered how often the same man, with the same wits, in being reared from childhood among the French or Germans turns out differently than he would have had he always lived among the Chinese or the cannibals; and realizing how, even as regards the fashions in our own customs, the same thing that has pleased us for ten years, and perhaps will again please us before ten years hence, now seems to us extravagant and ridiculous: I accordingly discovered that we are persuaded very much more by custom and example than by any certain knowledge, and that, nevertheless, a plurality of voices constitutes no proof of any value in regard to truths somewhat difficult to discern, because it is certainly more probable that a single man has discovered them rather than an entire nation. And since I was unable to select anyone whose opinions seemed to me preferable to those of others, I found myself, as it were, forced to assume the direction of my own studies.

But like a man who walks alone and in the darkness, I resolved to proceed so slowly, and to use so much circumspection in every matter, that however small my advance, I would at least protect myself from falling. Accordingly, I did not wish to begin to reject entirely any of the opinions that formerly were able to slip into my belief without having been placed there by reason until I had first employed sufficient time to establish the design of the task I was undertaking, and to seek the true method for arriving at the knowledge of everything of which my wit would be capable.

When younger I had studied a little logic from among the parts of philosophy, and a little of the analysis of the geometers and a little algebra from among the parts of mathematics. It seemed to me that these three arts or sciences ought to contribute something to my goal. However, in examining them I noticed that, as regards logic, its syllogism and the greater part of its other instructions, rather than helping one learn things, serve more to explain to another the things one knows, or even, like the art of Lully, to make one speak without judgment about things of which one is ignorant. And although logic in effect contains many very true and good precepts, there are always so many harmful or superfluous precepts mixed among them that to separate the two is nearly as difficult as to extract a Diana or a Minerva out of a block of marble upon which no design has yet been sketched. Then, as regards the analysis of the ancients and the algebra of the moderns, besides the fact that these extend only to very abstract matters that seem to have no application, the former is always so bound to the consideration of figures that it cannot exercise the understanding without very much fatiguing the imagination; and in the latter discipline one is so subjected to certain rules and notations that, instead of a science that cultivates the wits, one produces from all of it only a confused and obscure art that embarrasses one's wits. This was the reason why I thought it necessary to seek some method that would comprise the advantages of these three but be exempt from their defects. And as the multiplicity of laws often furnishes excuses for vices, so that a state is better regulated when, having only very few laws, they are observed very strictly; so also, in place of the great number of precepts composing logic, I believed that the four following rules would suffice, provided I took a firm and constant resolution not to fail even once to observe them.

The first rule was never to receive anything as true unless I knew it evidently to be such—that is to say, to avoid assiduously precipitation and obstinacy—and to include nothing among my judgments except what presented itself so clearly and so distinctly to my mind that I would have no occasion to place it in doubt.

The second rule was to divide each of the difficulties I would examine in as many parts as would be possible, and as would be required in order to solve them better.

The third rule was to direct my thoughts according to an order, beginning with the simplest objects, and those easiest to know, in order to lead up little by little, as by degrees, to the knowledge of the most composite objects, supposing an order even among those that have no natural precedence one over the other.

The last rule was in every case to make such complete enumerations and such general reviews that I would be assured of omitting nothing.

Those long chains of reasonings, all simple and easy, that the geometers are accustomed to use in order to arrive at their more difficult demonstrations had given me occasion to imagine that everything that can fall within the knowledge of men follows each other in that same fashion, and—provided only one abstains from accepting anything as true that is not true, and heeds the order required for deducing one thing from the others—there can be nothing so distant that one may not reach it, or nothing so hidden that one may not discover it. And it was not difficult to discover where to begin: for I already knew that it was necessary to begin with the simplest and easiest objects to know; and considering that, among those who previously sought for truth in the sciences, only the mathematicians had been able to find any demonstrations—that is to say, any certain and evident reasons—I did not doubt that they conducted their examinations by the same means; however, I hoped for no other advantage from these mathematical exercises except that they would accustom my mind to delight in truths, and not to satisfy itself at all with false reasons. But for all that, I did not set it as my goal to try to learn all the particular sciences commonly called mathematics; and seeing that although the objects of these sciences differ, all these sciences nevertheless accord in the respect that they consider only the different relations or proportions in their objects, I thought it would be more worthwhile to examine these proportions only in general, and without supposing them except in subjects that serve to render knowledge of them easier for me; and I also decided not to bind these proportions in any way to such objects, in order that I could more easily apply them afterward to all the other subjects upon which they have a bearing. Then, having noted that to know them I would sometimes need to consider each individually, and sometimes merely to retain them or comprehend them severally together, I thought that to consider them better individually I ought to suppose them in lines, because I found nothing simpler and nothing that I could more distinctly represent to my imagination and my senses; but to retain them, or to comprehend many of them together, it was necessary that I explain them by certain notations, as concise as would be possible; and thus in this way I would borrow everything good in geometrical analysis and algebra, and would correct all the faults of the one by the other. And in effect, I dare to say that the exact observance of these few precepts that I had chosen gave me such facility at disentangling all the questions to which these two sciences extend that in the two or three months I employed to examine these questions—having begun with the simplest and most general, and using each truth I discovered as a rule to serve me afterward in discovering other truths—I not only came to the resolution of many questions I formerly judged very difficult, but it also seemed to me toward the end that, even as regards unsolved questions, I could determine by what means and to what extent it was possible to resolve them. Perhaps I will not appear very vain in my claims if you consider that, since there is only one truth about each matter, whoever discovers it knows as much as one can know about it; thus, for example, a child instructed in arithmetic who has performed an addition according to arithmetical rules can be assured to have found, in regard to the sum he examined, everything the human mind can find out. For the method that teaches us to follow the true order, and to enumerate exactly all the conditions of what one seeks after, contains everything that gives certitude to the rules of arithmetic.

But what contented me the most with this method was that it assured me of using my reason in every matter, if not perfectly, at least as well as was in my power; besides, I felt that in practicing this method my mind was accustoming itself little by little to conceive its objects more plainly and distinctly; and not having restricted this method to a particular matter, I promised myself to apply it as usefully to the difficulties of the other sciences as I had applied it to those of algebra. However, I did not on that account immediately dare to undertake to examine all the difficulties that would arise; for that itself would have been contrary to the order the method prescribes. But having noticed that their principles ought all to be borrowed from philosophy, in which I as yet found nothing certain, I thought it necessary before anything else to try to establish something certain in philosophy. And yet, since this is the most important thing in the world, and the place where precipitation and obstinacy were most to be feared, I thought I ought not undertake to solve the matter until I had attained an age far more mature than twenty-three years, which was my age at that time. Likewise, I thought I could not employ too much time beforehand in preparing myself for the task, as much in uprooting from my mind the wrong opinions I had hitherto accepted as in making an accumulation of experiments that afterward would constitute the matter for my reasonings, and by constantly exercising myself in the method I had prescribed for myself in order to become more and more adept at its use.

THIRD PART

And finally, just as it does not suffice, before beginning to rebuild the house in which one dwells, to rip it down and to supply oneself with materials and architects, or to practice architecture oneself, and, indeed, to have a plan painstakingly worked out; but as it is also necessary to be provided with another house where one can be lodged comfortably during the time one will work on the new dwelling; so too, in order that I should not remain irresolute in my actions while reason would oblige me to be so in my judgments, and in order that I should not fail to live from that point on as happily as possible, I formed for myself a provisional morality consisting of only three or four maxims that I very much wish to share with you.

The first was to obey the laws and customs of my country, retaining constantly the religion in which God gave me the grace to be instructed since my childhood, and governing myself in every other matter according to the most reasonable and least excessive opinions commonly received in practice by the more judicious of those with whom I would have to live. For beginning from then onward to esteem my own opinions as nothing, since I wished to subject all of them to examination, I was assured I could not do better than to follow the opinions of the more judicious of people. And although among the Persians or the Chinese there are perhaps people as judicious as among us, it seemed to me the most useful thing was to regulate myself according to those with whom I would have to live; moreover, it seemed to me that to know what their opinions really were, I was to take notice of what they practiced rather than what they said; and this, not just because in the corrupt state of our customs few wish to say everything they believe, but also because many people are not aware of their own beliefs; for the action of thought by which one believes a thing being different from that by which one knows that one believes it, these actions often occur the one without the other. And among several opinions equally received, I chose only the most moderate: I did this because such opinions are always the most convenient as regards practice, and are probably best, since all excess is customarily bad; and I did this equally so that, in case I erred, I would turn myself away from the true path to a lesser extent than if, having chosen one of the extreme opinions, it had been the other extreme that it had been necessary to follow. And, in particular, I placed among excesses all the promises by which one diminishes something of one's liberty. It was not that I disapproved of the laws that, to remedy the fickleness of feeble minds, permit one to make vows or contracts obliging one to persevere in some good design, or even, for the security of commerce, in a design that is only indifferent. But because I did not see anything in the world that always remained in the same condition, and because, as my particular goal, I promised myself to perfect my judgments more and more and not to render them worse, I would have thought myself as committing a great breach of good sense if, because I approved something up until that time, I obliged myself to consider it as good even afterward, when perhaps it would have ceased to be good or I would have ceased to deem it such.

My second maxim was to be as firm and resolute in my actions as I could be, and when once I decided on them, to follow doubtful opinions no less constantly than if they had been very assured. In this matter I would imitate those travelers who, finding themselves lost in some forest, should not wander about by heading first this way and then another way, nor still less remain in one place, but should instead always walk as straight as they can in the same direction, and certainly not change their direction for petty reasons, despite the fact that at the beginning it has perhaps been chance alone that determined them to choose that direction; for by this means, if they do not come exactly to the place they wish, they at least will arrive at the end of some part of the forest, where probably they will be better off than in the middle. And so the actions of life often permitting no delay, it is a very certain rule that when it is not in our power to discern the truest opinions, we ought to follow the most probable ones; furthermore, even if we do not notice more probability in some opinions than in others, we ought nevertheless to choose certain ones, and afterward no longer consider them as doubtful in respect to their relation to action; we ought rather to consider them as very true and very certain, because the reason that has determined us to do so is very true and very certain. And this maxim was henceforth capable of sparing me all the repentances and remorse that customarily disturb the consciences of those feeble and vacillating minds who with wavering resolution allow themselves to practice as good things they afterward judge to be bad.

My third maxim was to try always to control myself rather than fortune, and to change my desires rather than the order of the world; and generally to accustom myself to believe that nothing is entirely in our power except our thoughts, so that after we have done our best regarding things lying outside us, everything that fails to happen, and yet is required for success, is, from the point of view of what we can do, absolutely impossible. And this alone seemed to me sufficient to prevent me from desiring in the future anything I do not acquire, and thus to render me content. For since our will naturally inclines to desire only those things our understanding represents to it as possible, it is certain that if we consider all the goods lying outside us as equally beyond our power, we will no more regret lacking those things that seem owed to us at birth, when we shall be deprived of them by no fault of our own, than we regret not possessing the kingdoms of China or Mexico; and making, as it is said, a virtue of necessity, we will no more desire to be well when we are sick, or free when we are in prison, than we now desire to have a body made of a matter as incorruptible as diamonds, or wings to fly like the birds. But I admit it requires long practice and oft-repeated meditation to accustom oneself to view everything from this point of view; and I believe it is principally in this that the secret of those philosophers consisted who in former times were able to free themselves from the dominion of fortune, and despite hardships and poverty, to rival their gods in happiness. For by constantly directing their attention to a consideration of the limits prescribed for them by nature, they persuaded themselves so perfectly that nothing was in their power except their thoughts that this was sufficient to prevent them from having any affection for other things; and they ordered their thoughts so absolutely that it gave them a reason to consider themselves richer, more powerful, more free, and happier than any of those other men (however much favored by nature and fortune they might be) who, not having any of this philosophy, never rank everything they desire in this manner.

Finally, as a conclusion to this morality, I took it upon myself to make a review of the different occupations men hold in this life in order to choose the best; and without wishing to say anything about the occupations of others, I thought I could not do better than to continue in the same occupation I found myself engaged in, that is to say, to employ all my life to cultivate my reason, and to advance myself as much as I could in the knowledge of the truth, following the method I prescribed for myself. I had found such great satisfactions since I had begun to avail myself of this method that I did not believe one could have received sweeter or more innocent satisfactions in this life; and discovering each day by this means some truths that seemed to me sufficiently important and yet commonly unknown to other men, the satisfaction I had from it so filled my mind that everything else had no effect upon me. But very importantly, the three preceding maxims had been built only upon the plan I had of continuing to instruct myself; for since God has given each person some light by which to distinguish the true from the false, I would not have believed I ought to content myself with the opinions of another even for a moment unless I intended to employ my own judgment to examine those opinions when there should be time; and I would not have known how to relieve myself of scruples in following the opinions of others had I not hoped, for all that, to lose no opportunity to find better opinions in the event that there might have been such. And finally, I would not have known how to limit my desires or to rest content if I had not followed a single path by which I thought myself assured of acquiring not only all the knowledge of which I would be capable, but also all the true goods that would be in my power; and inasmuch as the will does not incline to pursue or avoid anything except according as our understanding represents the thing to it as good or bad, it follows that in order to do well it suffices to judge well, and in order to do one's very best, it suffices to judge the best one can—which is to say, to acquire all the virtues together with all the other goods one can acquire; and when one is certain that one has done that, one could not lack contentment.

After having thus assured myself of these maxims, and having placed them to one side together with truths of faith, which have always been the foremost elements of my belief, I judged that as far as all the rest of my opinions were concerned, I could freely undertake to forsake them. And seeing that I hoped to be better able to achieve my goal by conversing with other men than by remaining any longer near the stove where I had all these thoughts, I began again to journey before the winter was long gone. And throughout all the nine years that followed I did nothing but roam here and there in the world, trying to be a spectator rather than an actor in all the comedies that take place there; and particularly by giving reflection in every subject matter to what could render it suspect and provide an occasion for making a mistake, I uprooted from my mind all the errors that previously had been able to pass into it. I did not do so to imitate the skeptics, who doubt only for the sake of doubting, and who pretend always to be irresolute: for, on the contrary, my whole plan was directed only to convince myself, and to cast away the shifting earth and sand in order to find rock or clay. It seems to me that this was succeeding well enough, since in trying to discover the falsity or uncertainty of the propositions I was examining (and this I did not by weak conjectures, but by clear and assured reasonings), I did not encounter any proposition so doubtful that I would not extract some sufficiently certain conclusion from it, even if the conclusion was only that the proposition contained nothing certain. And as in pulling down an old house one ordinarily preserves its materials to use them in building a new house; so also in abolishing all my opinions that I had judged ill founded, I made various observations and acquired many experiences that have served me since in establishing more certain opinions. And furthermore, I continued to exercise myself in the method I had prescribed for myself; for beyond the fact that I had taken care generally to direct all my thoughts according to its rules, I reserved some hours for myself from time to time that I particularly employed in applying the method to the difficulties of mathematics, and also even to some other difficulties that, by detaching them from all the principles of the other sciences that I did not find sufficiently firm, I was able to express as if similar to the difficulties of mathematics—as you will see I have done with many of the difficulties explained in this volume. And so while appearing like those who, having no occupation except to pass a calm and innocent life, study how to separate pleasures from vices, and occupy themselves with honorable amusements to enjoy their leisure without boredom, I was not remiss about pursuing my plan. And I did not fail to make advances in the knowledge of the truth—perhaps more advances than if I had only read books or associated with men of letters.

However, these nine years passed away before I had again taken any part in the difficulties customarily disputed among the learned, or had begun to seek the foundations of any philosophy more certain than the common one. And the example of many excellent minds who previously had this goal, but seemed to me not to have succeeded, made me imagine so great a difficulty in erecting a philosophy that perhaps I would still not as yet have dared to undertake to erect one had I not observed that some people were already spreading the rumor that I had succeeded. I could not say upon what they based this opinion; and if I had contributed something to it by my discussions, it was bound to have been by confessing more truthfully the things of which I was ignorant than is typical of those who have studied only a little, and perhaps also by making plain the reasons I had for doubting very many things others deem certain, rather than by flaunting any doctrine of my own. But since my heart was sincere enough not to wish that anyone mistook me for something different than I was, I thought it necessary to try by every means to make myself worthy of the reputation bestowed upon me; and it has been exactly eight years since this desire made me resolve to remove myself from every location where I could have acquaintances, and to retire here, in a country where the long duration of the war has caused such order to be established that the armies maintained here seem only to allow one to delight in the fruits of peace with so much the more security; in a country where, among the mass of a great and very active people who are more concerned with their own affairs than curious about those of others, I have been able to live in as much solitude and retirement as in the most isolated desert, and yet without lacking any of the conveniences of the busiest cities.

FOURTH PART

I do not know whether I ought to share with you the first meditations I made here; for they are so metaphysical and so uncommon that perhaps they will not be to everyone's taste. And yet in order that one may judge whether the foundations I have employed are sufficiently firm, I find myself in some way constrained to speak of these first meditations. I had been aware for many years that in respect to customs it is sometimes necessary to follow opinions one knows to be very uncertain just as if they were indubitable, as has been said above; but because at that time I desired to attend only to the search for truth, I thought it necessary to do exactly the contrary, and to reject, as if absolutely false, everything in which I could imagine the least doubt, in order to see if there would not afterward remain among my beliefs something entirely indubitable. Thus because our senses sometimes deceive us, I wished to suppose there was nothing such as they make us imagine it. And because there are men who make a mistake in reasoning even regarding the most simple matters of geometry, and form paralogisms, I, judging myself subject to error as much as any other man, rejected as false all the reasons I had previously taken as demonstrations. And finally, considering that all the same thoughts we have when awake can also come to us when we are sleeping without any of them being true at that time, I resolved to suppose that all the things that had ever entered my mind were no more true than the illusions of my dreams. But immediately afterward I noticed that, while I thus wished to think that everything was false, it was necessary that I who was thinking be something. And noting that this truth, *I think, therefore I am,* was so firm and so assured that all the most extravagant suppositions of the skeptics were not capable of disturbing it, I judged that I could receive it, without scruple, as the first principle of the philosophy I was seeking.

Then, examining with attention what I was, and seeing that I was able to suppose I had no body, and that there was no world nor any place where I might be; and seeing also that, for all of that, I was not able to suppose that I was not; but seeing, on the contrary, that, from the very fact that I was thinking of doubting the truth of other things, it followed very evidently and very certainly that I was; whereas had I only ceased to think, even if all the rest of what I had ever imagined had been true, I should have no reason to believe that I had been: from that I knew that I was a substance whose entire essence or nature is only to think, and which, in order to exist, has no need of a place nor depends upon any material thing. So that this I, that is to say, the soul by which I am what I am, is entirely distinct from the body, and is even easier to know than the body, and even if the body had never been, the soul would not fail to be everything that it is.

After that I considered in general what is required for a proposition to be true and certain; for since I came to find one which I knew to be such, I thought I must also know in what this certitude consists. And having noticed that there is nothing at all in this *I think, therefore I am* that assures me I am speaking the truth except that I see very clearly that in order to think it is necessary to exist, I judged that I could take it as a general rule that things we conceive very clearly and very distinctly are all true; but there is only some difficulty to note well the things that we conceive distinctly.

Following this, in reflecting upon the fact that I doubted, and that consequently my being was not completely perfect—since I saw clearly that it was a greater perfection to know than to doubt—I resolved to inquire whence I had learned to think of something more perfect than I was; and I recognized evidently that this ought to be from some nature that was in fact more perfect than myself. For as regards the thoughts I had of things outside me—such as of heaven, earth, light, heat, and a thousand other things—I was not very hard pressed to know whence they came; because, not noticing anything in them that seemed to render them superior to myself, I was able to believe that if they were true, they were dependent upon my nature inasmuch as it had some perfection; and if they were not true, that I derived them from nothingness, that is to say, they were in me because I had some defect. But it could not be the same as regards the idea of a more perfect being than my own; for to derive that idea from nothingness was something manifestly impossible; and because for the more perfect to be a consequence of, and dependent on, the less perfect is no less contradictory than that nothing proceed from something, I was not able to maintain that that idea derived from myself. Thus it remained that that idea had been placed in me by a nature that was truly more perfect than I was, and that had in itself all the perfections of which I could have some idea, that is to say, to explain myself in a word, who was God. To which I added that, since I knew of some perfections I did not have, I was not the only being who existed (if you please, I shall here make free use of the words of the school), but that it followed of necessity that there was another more perfect being upon which I was dependent, and from which I had acquired everything that I had. For if I had been alone and independent of every other thing, in such a way that I had had from myself all this meager amount of perfect being in which I participate, by the same reasoning I would have been able to derive from myself all the other perfections I recognized myself to lack, and thus to be myself infinite, eternal, immutable, all-knowing, all-powerful, and lastly, to have all the perfections I was able to distinguish to be in God. For according to the reasonings I used in order to know the nature of God, insofar as I was capable of knowing it, I had only to consider, in respect of all things of which I found an idea in myself, whether it was or was not a perfection to possess these things; and I was assured that none of those things that indicated some imperfection was in God, but that all the other things were in him. Thus I saw that doubt, inconstancy, sadness, and similar things could not be there, since I saw that I myself would have been very comfortable in being rid of them. Then, besides that, I had ideas of many sensible and corporeal things: for although I supposed I was dreaming, and that all I saw or imagined was false, I was nevertheless unable to deny that these ideas were truly in my thought. But because I had already recognized very clearly in myself that the intellectual nature is distinct from the corporeal, and because I recognized that all composition testifies to dependency, and that dependency is manifestly a defect, I judged from that that it couldn't be a perfection in God to be composed of these two natures, and that, as a consequence, he was not so composed; but I judged that if there were some bodies in the world, or even some intelligences or other natures that were not all perfect, their being ought to depend upon his power in such a way that they could not subsist without him for a single moment.

After that I wished to seek out other truths. I proposed to my study the object of the geometers, which I conceived as a continuous body, or as a space indefinitely extended in length, breadth, altitude or depth, and which is divisible into different parts that could have different figures and sizes, and be moved or transported in all sorts of ways—for the geometers assume all these things in their object. I then ran through some of their most simple demonstrations. And having noticed that this great certitude that everyone attributes to the demonstrations of geometry is founded only on the fact that one conceives them evidently, following the rule I a little while ago laid down, I also noted that there was nothing at all in these demonstrations to assure me of the existence of their object. For example, I saw indeed that, in supposing a triangle, it was necessary that its three angles be equal to two right angles; but I did not on that account see anything that assured me there was any triangle in the world; whereas returning to examine the idea I had of a perfect being, I found that existence was included there in the same way as, or even still more evidently than, the equality of its three angles to two right angles is included in the idea of a triangle, or the equality of distance of all its parts from its center is included in the idea of a sphere; and therefore I concluded that it is at least as certain as any of the demonstrations of geometry could be, that God, who is this perfect being, is or exists.

But what makes many people persuade themselves there is difficulty in recognizing God, and also even in recognizing what their soul is, is that they never elevate their mind above sensible things, and they are so accustomed to consider nothing except by imagining it, which is a manner of thought specifically appropriate to thinking of material things, that everything that cannot be imagined seems to them unintelligible. This is sufficiently manifest from the fact that even the philosophers in the schools espouse as a maxim that there is nothing in the understanding that has not initially been in the senses, when nevertheless it is certain that the ideas of God and of the soul have never been in the senses. And it seems to me that those who wish to use their imagination to comprehend the ideas of God and the soul act just like those who wish to use their eyes to hear sounds or smell odors: unless there is yet this difference, that the sense of sight does not assure us any less concerning the truth of its objects than the senses of smell and hearing assure us concerning theirs; whereas neither our imagination nor our senses could ever assure us of anything unless our understanding intervened.

Finally, if there are men who are still not sufficiently persuaded of the existence of God and their soul by the reasons brought forward, I strongly wish that they may know that every other thing of which they think themselves perhaps more assured, such as the fact that they have a body, and that there are stars and an earth and similar things, is less certain. For although one has a moral assurance of these things such that one cannot doubt them without being extravagant, nevertheless unless one is to be unreasonable when it is a question of metaphysical certitude, one cannot deny there are grounds enough for not being entirely assured of them if only one attends to the fact that while sleeping one can in the same way imagine that one has another body, that one sees other stars, another earth, without any of these things existing. For on what basis does one know that the thoughts that come during dreams are false rather than the others, having seen that often they are not less vivid and expressive? And were the best minds to study this matter as much as it pleases them to do so, I do not believe they could give any reason sufficient to banish this doubt unless they presuppose the existence of God. For in the first place what I recently took as a rule—namely, that the things we conceive very clearly and very distinctly are all true—is assured only because God is or exists and is a perfect being, and because everything in us comes from him. From which it follows that our ideas or notions, being real things and things that come from God, must be true as regards everything in which they are clear and distinct. Thus if often enough we have ideas that contain falsity, this falsity can only be in those ideas that contain something confused and obscure, because insofar as they are confused and obscure, they participate in nothingness—which is to say, they are in us in a confused manner only because we are not completely perfect. And it is evident that it is not less contradictory that falsity *qua* falsity or imperfection *qua* imperfection proceed from God than that truth or perfection proceed from nothingness. But if we do not know that everything in us that is real and true comes from a perfect and infinite being, no matter how clear and distinct our ideas would be, we would have no reason that assured us that they have the perfection of being true.

But, now, after the knowledge of God and of the soul has thus rendered us certain of this rule, it is very easy to recognize that the reveries we imagine when asleep should not make us doubt at all the truth of the thoughts we have while awake. For if it happened even while sleeping that one had some very distinct idea, as if, for example, a geometer discovered some new demonstration, his sleeping would not prevent that demonstration from being true. And as for the most ordinary error of our dreams, which consists in that they represent various objects to us in the same fashion as do our external senses, it makes no difference that they provide us with an occasion to be distrustful of the truth of such ideas, because the senses can also trick us often enough when we are not sleeping: as when those who have jaundice always see the color yellow, or as when the stars or other very distant bodies seem very much smaller than they are. For finally, whether we are sleeping or waking, we should never allow ourselves to be persuaded except by the evidence of our reason. And it is to be noted that I say of our reason, and not of our imagination or senses. Consider the following cases. When we see the sun very clearly we ought not to judge on that account that it is only the size we see it to be; and certainly we can distinctly imagine the head of a lion placed upon the body of a goat without it being necessary to conclude that there exists a Chimera in the world—in such cases reason does not tell us that what we thus see or imagine is genuine. However, reason certainly does tell us that all our ideas or notions have to have some foundation in the truth; for it would not be possible that God, who is all-perfect and all-truthful, had placed them in us without that being so. And since our reasonings are never so evident nor so complete during sleep as during waking—although our imaginations may be equally or more vivid and expressive—reason tells us also that our thoughts cannot all be true, because we are not all-perfect, and that what truth is in them should without question be discovered in those we have while awake, rather than in our dreams.

FIFTH PART

I should be very pleased to continue and to display here the entire chain of other truths I have deduced from these first truths. But since to do this it would be necessary for me to speak here of many questions that are disputed among the learned (with whom I do not wish to enter into controversy), I believe it better to abstain from the details and say only in general what are the truths I have deduced, in order to leave it to the wiser to judge whether it would be useful for the public to be more particularly informed about them. I always lived attached to the resolve I had taken to suppose no other principle except that which I just used to demonstrate the existence of God and the soul, and to accept nothing as true that did not seem to me more clear and more certain than the demonstrations of the geometers had formerly seemed. And nevertheless I dare to say that not only have I found a means of satisfying myself in a short time concerning all the principal difficulties customarily treated in philosophy; but also I have noted certain laws that God has so established in nature, and of which he has impressed such notions in our soul, that after having devoted sufficient reflection to them, we could not doubt that they are exactly observed in everything that is or that happens in the world. Then, in considering what follows from these laws, it seems I discovered many truths more useful and more important than everything I had previously learned or even hoped to learn.

But because I tried to explain the principles in a treatise that certain considerations prevent me from publishing, I cannot reveal these principles any better than by saying here in summary fashion what that treatise contains. It was my goal to include in it everything I thought I knew before writing it concerning the nature of material things. However, just as painters, finding themselves unable to represent on a flat board all the different sides of a solid body, choose one of its principal sides, which is the only one they position squarely in daylight, while they shadow the others and so make them appear only as seen by looking at the former: well, in this same manner, fearing myself unable to place in that discourse everything I had thought about, I undertook to explain there very amply only what I conceived to be the nature of light. I resolved to add, in their turn, something concerning the sun and the fixed stars, because light proceeds nearly completely from them; next, to treat of the heavens, because they transmit light; next, to treat of the planets, comets, and the earth, because they cause light to reflect; next, to treat particularly of all the bodies on the earth, because they are either colored, or transparent, or luminous; and finally, to treat of man, because he views light. However, to fill in these matters a little better, and to say more freely what I judged about them, without being obliged to follow or refute the opinions held among the learned, I resolved to consign this entire world to their disputes, and to speak only about what would come about in a new world if God created someplace in imaginary spaces enough matter to compose such a world, and agitated its different parts without any order so as to compose a chaos as confused as the poets could imagine, and afterward did nothing but impart his ordinary operation on nature, and allow her to act following the laws he established. Thus, first of all, I described this matter and tried to represent it such that there is nothing in the world, it seems to me, clearer or more intelligible, except what has already been said of God and of the soul: for in the same manner I expressly supposed that this matter did not have within it any of those forms or qualities disputed about in the schools, and I supposed generally that it contained nothing whose knowledge was not so natural to our souls that anyone could even feign ignorance of it. Furthermore, I made it manifest what the laws of nature were, and without resting my reasons on any other principle except the infinite perfections of God, I tried to demonstrate everything about which one could have had some doubt, and to make it clear that the laws of nature are such that, even if God had created many worlds, there could not be any in which these laws failed to be observed. After that I showed how the greatest part of the matter of this chaos ought, as a consequence of these laws, to dispose itself and arrange itself in a certain fashion that rendered it similar to our heavens; and how, meanwhile, certain of these parts of matter ought to have composed an earth and some planets and comets, and why still other parts ought to have composed a sun and fixed stars. And here, pursuing the subject of light, I explained in long detail what this light was that ought to be found in the sun and stars; and how, from these places, it traversed in an instant the immense spaces of the heavens; and how it reflected from the planets and the comets toward the earth. And there I also added many things regarding the substance, the situation, the movements, and all the different qualities of these heavens and stars, in such a way that I thought I said enough to make one recognize that one notices nothing as regards the heavens and the stars of this world that would not have, or at least could not have, appeared completely similar in those of the world I described. After that I came to speak particularly about the earth: how, even though I expressly supposed that God had not placed any weight in the matter from which it was composed, nevertheless all its parts would not fail to tend exactly toward its center; how, with water and air on the superficies of the earth, the disposition of the heavens and the stars, and principally of the moon, would cause a certain rising and ebbing on the superficies of the earth, which it seemed to me was similar in all circumstances to that which we notice upon our seas; and moreover, how this would cause a certain flow not only of water, but also of air, from east to west, such as one also notices between the tropics; how the mountains, the seas and the fountains, and the rivers were able to form naturally; and how the metals came to exist in the rivers, and the plants to grow upon the fields, and generally how all the bodies that are called mixed or composed are formed on earth. And regarding the other things, since other than the stars I knew nothing in the world that produces light except fire, I studied how to understand very clearly everything that pertains to the nature of fire: how it is made; how it nourishes itself; how there is only sometimes heat without light and sometimes light without heat; how fire can introduce different colors into different bodies as well as other different qualities; how fire can melt certain bodies and harden others; how it can nearly completely consume bodies, or change them into cinders and smoke; and finally how from these cinders, by the mere violence of its action, fire forms glass—for since this transmutation of cinders into glass seems to me to be as admirable as anything else that appears in nature, I took particular pleasure in describing it.

Nevertheless, I did not wish to infer from all these things that this world had been created in the fashion I proposed; for it is very much more probable that from the beginning God formed it such as it ought to be. But it is certain, and an opinion commonly received among the theologians, that the action by which he now conserves this world is entirely the same as that by which he has created it; and this in such a way that even if God would not have bestowed upon it in the beginning any other form but that of chaos, still, provided after he established the laws of nature he imparted to this chaos his support, so as to make it operate in its customary manner, one can believe, without committing an error as regards the miracle of creation, that by this alone all the things that are purely material could have with the passage of time disposed themselves such as we see them at present. And their nature is very much easier to conceive when one sees them born little by little in this manner than when one considers them only as completely formed.

From the description of inanimate bodies and plants, I passed to the description of animals, and particularly to that of men. But because I did not as yet have enough knowledge to speak of them in the same style as of the rest—that is to say, to demonstrate the effects by causes, and to make obvious from what seeds, and in what manner, nature ought to produce them—I contented myself with assuming that God formed the body of man entirely similar to our body, as much in the exterior figure of its members as in the conformity of its interior organs; and that he composed this body only from the matter I had described, and without placing in it, in the beginning, any reasoning soul, or any other thing to serve therein as a vegetative or sensitive soul, except that he excited in its heart one of those fires without light that I had already explained and conceived as having the same nature as the fire that heats hay when one has stored it away before it was dry, or that activates new wines when one allows them to ferment over sediment. For in examining the functions that could be in this body as a result of that, I found there exactly all those functions that can be in us without our thinking of them, and consequently without our soul contributing anything to them—that is to say, without this part distinct from the body, of which it has been said above that its nature is only to think, contributing anything to them. And these functions are exactly those in which one can say the animals without reason resemble us. However, for all this, I could not find any of those functions that, being dependent upon thought, are the only ones that pertain to us insofar as we are men; and yet I found all of them afterward, when once I supposed that God created a reasoning soul and joined it to his body in a certain manner that I described.

But in order that one can see in what manner I treated this matter, I wish to present here the explanation of the movement of the heart and arteries: since it is the principal and most general movement that one observes in the animals, one will easily judge from it what one ought to think of all the other movements. And in order that there may be less difficulty in understanding what I will say about it, I should wish that those who are not versed in anatomy would take the trouble before reading this to cut up in front of themselves the heart of some large animal that has lungs, because such an animal is in all respects sufficiently similar to man; and I should wish them to expose the two chambers or cavities within the heart. Firstly, there is that cavity in the right side of the heart to which correspond two very large tubes: they are, namely, the vena cava, which is the principal receptacle of the blood, and is like the trunk of a tree of which all the other veins are the branches; and the arterial vein, which has been inappropriately called by this name, because in fact it is an artery that, after taking its origin from the heart, divides into many branches that spread throughout the lungs. Secondly, there is that cavity in the left side of the heart to which in the same fashion correspond two tubes, and these are as large or larger than the preceding: they are, namely, the venous artery, which also has been badly named, since it is only a vein that comes from the lungs, where it is divided into many branches interlaced with those of the arterial vein, and with those of that passageway one calls the windpipe, through which the air enters during respiration; and then there is the grand artery, which, coming from the heart, distributes its branches throughout the entire body. I should also like one to observe carefully the eleven small skins that, acting like as many small doors, open and close the four openings in these two cavities of the heart: namely, the three small skins at the entrance of the vena cava, where they are so disposed that they can in no way prevent the blood it contains from running into the right cavity of the heart, but furthermore, perfectly prevent the blood in the heart from running out; the three small skins at the entrance to the arterial vein that, being disposed in a completely contrary manner, easily permit the blood in this cavity to pass into the lungs, but prevent that which is in the lungs from returning into this cavity; and also the two other skins at the entrance to the venous artery that allow the blood from the lungs to flow toward the left cavity of the heart, but oppose any motion of that blood back into the cavity; and finally, the three skins at the entrance of the grand artery that permit the blood to leave the heart, but prevent it from returning. And it is not necessary to seek any other reason for the number of these skins beyond the fact that the opening of the venous artery, being oval in shape because of the conditions it encounters where it is located, can easily be closed by two skins, whereas the other openings, because they are round, are more easily closed by three skins. Furthermore, I would like one to consider that the grand artery and the arterial vein are of a composition very much harder and firmer than are the venous artery and the vena cava, and that these last two enlarge before entering the heart and form there, as it were, two sacks, called the ears of the heart, which are composed of flesh similar to the flesh of the heart; and I would

Portrait of Rembrandt van Rijn. The portrait and the self-portrait symbolized the increasing importance of the individual in the Renaissance. (Alinari/Art Resource)

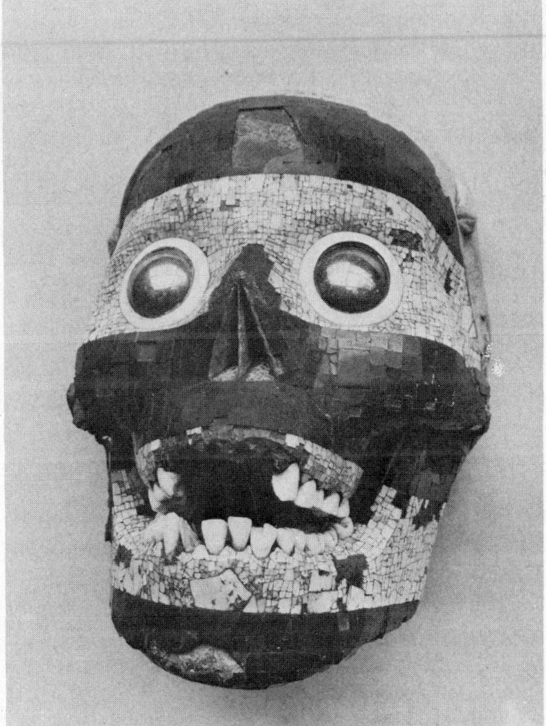

Aztec Skull (14th–15th centuries, A.D.). Sometimes called the "Romans of the New World," the Aztecs built a highly sophisticated civilization in Mexico. The contrast between this skull and the Rembrandt portrait provides a hint as to the vast variety of facial images in world art throughout the centuries. (British Museum)

like one to consider that there is always more heat in the heart than in any other place in the body, and finally that this heat is capable of bringing it about that, when some drop of blood enters into its cavities, the heart promptly inflates and dilates, just as generally all liquids do when one allows them to fall drop by drop into some very hot vessel.

After this I have no need to speak of anything else in order to explain the movement of the heart, except that when its cavities are not filled with blood, then blood necessarily flows from the vena cava into the right cavity and from the venous artery into the left cavity, and this occurs because these two vessels are always filled with blood, and their openings, which face the heart, cannot be closed when the cavities are not filled by blood; but as soon as two drops of blood enter into the heart, one into each of its cavities, these drops—which can only be very large because the openings by which they enter the cavities are very large, and the vessels from which they come are very filled with blood—rarify and dilate because of the heat they encounter there, by means of which heat they inflate all the heart and push and close the five little skins at the entrances of the two vessels from which they come, thus preventing more blood from descending into the heart; and continuing to rarify more and more, they push and open the six other small skins at the entrance of the two other vessels through which they leave, and by this means they inflate all the branches of the arterial vein and of the grand artery at about the same time as they inflate the heart; immediately afterward the heart deflates, as also do these arteries, because the blood that entered them has cooled; the six small skins of these arteries close and the five small skins of the vena cava and the venous artery open and allow passage to two other drops of blood that again make the heart and the arteries inflate in the same manner as before. And because the blood that thus enters into the heart passes through those two sacks called the ears of the heart, from this it comes about that the movement of these ears is contrary to that of the heart, and that these ears deflate when the heart inflates. Moreover, in order that those who do not know the force of mathematical demonstrations, and are unaccustomed to distinguish true reasons from probabilities, will not venture to deny this account without examining it, I wish to alert them that this movement I am explaining follows just as necessarily from the combination of, first, the disposition of the organs of the heart that one can see with the human eye; second, the heat one can feel in the heart with one's finger; and third, the nature of the blood one can know by experience—it follows just as necessarily from this combination as the movement of a clock follows from the force, situation, and figure of its counterweights and wheels.

But if one asks why the blood in the veins is not dissipated in thus continually flowing into the heart, and why the arteries are not too filled, since all the blood that passes through the heart collects there, I have no need to say anything different concerning this matter than what has already been said by a medical physician from England, upon whom it is necessary to bestow praise for having broken the ice on this matter, and who is the first to have taught that there are many small passages at the extremities of the arteries by which the blood they receive from the heart enters into the small branches of the veins from where it flows to collect anew in the heart, in such a way that its motion is nothing else than a perpetual circulation. And this he proves very well, based upon the ordinary experience of surgeons who, having bound the arm moderately tightly above the place where they open the vein, make the blood flow out more abundantly than if they had not made the tie. But the opposite would occur if they tied the arm below, that is, between the hand and the opening in the vein, or indeed, if they tied the arm very tightly above the opening. For it is manifest that the tie moderately tightened, being able to prevent the blood already in the arm from returning toward the heart by the veins, does not, on that account, prevent the blood from always coming again by the arteries, because the arteries are situated below the veins and their skins, being harder, are less easy to compress; nor does such a tie prevent the blood that comes from the heart from tending to pass by means of the arteries toward the hand with more force than it tends to return from the hand to the heart by means of the veins. And since this blood leaves the arm by the opening in one of the veins, there ought necessarily to be some passages in the arm below the tie, that is to say, near the extremities of the arm, by which the blood can come from the arteries. He also proves very well what he said about the course of the blood by referring to certain small skins that are so disposed in different places along the veins that they do not permit the blood to pass from the middle of the body toward the extremities, but only to return from the extremities toward the heart; and furthermore he proves this by the experiment that shows that all the blood in the body can leave in a short amount of time by one artery alone when it is cut—and this is true even when the artery has been tightly tied very close to the heart, with the cut in the artery made between the heart and the tie, in such a way that there is no reason to imagine that the blood that runs out comes from some place other than the heart.

But very many other things testify to the fact that the true cause of this movement is what I have said. For, firstly, the difference one notices between the blood that leaves by the veins and that which leaves by the arteries could derive only from the fact that, being rarefied and as it were distilled in passing through the heart, the blood is subtler, more forceful, and warmer immediately after leaving the heart, that is to say, when in the arteries, than a little while before entering the heart, that is to say, when in the veins. And if one takes notice of this, one will find that this difference clearly appears only near the heart, and not in places that are farthest away. Moreover, the hardness of the skins from which the arterial vein and the grand artery are composed show sufficiently well that the blood strikes against them with more force than against the veins. Why else would the right cavity of the heart and the grand artery be wider and larger than the left cavity and the arterial vein if it is not that the blood from the venous artery, which has been only in the lungs since passing through the heart, is subtler and rarefies more forcefully and easily than that which comes immediately from the vena cava? And what can the medical physicians conclude by feeling the pulse unless they know that, according as the blood changes nature, it can be rarefied by the heat of the heart more or less forcefully and more or less quickly than beforehand? And if one examines how this heat communicates itself to the other members of the body, must not one admit that it happens by means of the blood that is reheated in passing through the heart and that spreads out from there throughout the body? From this it results that if one removes the blood from some part of the body, by the same means one also removes the heat; and although the heart were as hot as red-hot iron, it would not suffice to warm the feet and the hands as much as it does if it did not continually send new blood there. Then one also recognizes from this that the true usage of respiration is to deliver enough fresh air into the lungs to make the blood that comes there from the right cavity of the heart, where it has been rarefied and as it were changed into vapors, thicken and change into blood again before falling back into the left cavity, without which process it could not be suited to serve as nourishment for the fire that is in the left cavity of the heart. This is confirmed by the fact that one sees that animals without lungs also have only one cavity in the heart and that infants, who cannot use their lungs when they are enclosed in their mother's womb, have one opening by which the blood runs from the vena cava into the left cavity of the heart, and a passage by which the blood comes from the arterial vein into the grand artery without passing through the lungs. Then, as regards digestion, how would it take place in the stomach unless the heart sent heat there by means of the arteries, as well as some more motile parts of the blood that aid in dissolving the foods that have passed there? And as regards the action that changed the juice from these foods into blood, is it not easy to recognize what it is if one considers that this juice is distilled by passing and repassing through the heart, perhaps more than a hundred or two hundred times each day? And what need is there of anything else to explain nutrition and the production of the different humors in the body, except to say that the force with which the blood in rarifying passes from the heart to extremities of the arteries makes some of its parts stop among some of the bodily members they encounter and supplant other parts they eject; and that, according to the situation, or the figure, or the smallness of the pores they encounter, some of these parts collect in certain places rather than in others, in the same manner as each of us has seen different sieves that, when pierced in various ways, serve to separate different grains each from the other? And finally, what is most remarkable in all this is the generation of animal spirits, which are like a very subtle wind, or rather like a very pure and very lively flame that, continually rising up in great abundance from the heart into the brain, proceed from there by means of the veins into the muscles and provide movement to all the bodily members. And as to why those parts of the blood—which being the most agitated and penetrating are most fitted to compose these spirits—will gather in the brain rather than in other areas of the body, there is no need to imagine any other cause than as follows. First of all, the arteries that carry them proceed from the heart in the straightest line of all. Moreover, according to the rules of mechanics, which are the same as the rules of nature, when many parts tend together to move toward the same side, but there is not enough room for all—which is the case with the parts of the blood that in leaving the left cavity of the heart will tend toward the brain—then the weakest and least agitated parts ought to be deflected by the most forceful. Thus in this way the most forceful parts of the blood will gather together in isolation in the brain.

I sufficiently explained all these matters in the treatise I hitherto had in mind to publish. And after these matters, I showed what the structure of the nerves and muscles of the human body ought to be to allow the animal spirits, once within them, to have the force to move the bodily members—just as one sees that heads, a little while after decapitation, still move and bite the earth, although they are no longer animated. I also showed what changes ought to take place in the brain to cause the waking state, sleep, and dreams; how light, odors, tastes, heat, and all the other qualities of exterior objects can implant different ideas in the brain by means of the senses; how hunger, thirst, and the other interior passions can also send their own ideas to the brain. I showed what should be considered as the common sense where these ideas are received. And I showed what should be considered as the memory that conserves ideas and as the fantasy that can change them in diverse ways to compose new ideas and by the same means to distribute the animal spirits into the muscles so as to make the body move in as many different fashions and ways—all apropos in relation to the objects that its senses present or that come to it from the interior passions—as our bodies can move without the will directing them. This shall not seem at all strange to those who, knowing how many different automata, or moving machines, the industry of men can make by using only very few parts in comparison with the great number of bones, muscles, nerves, arteries, veins, and all the other parts in the body of each animal, will consider the body as a machine that, having been made by the hands of God, is incomparably better ordered and has in it movements more noteworthy than any of those that can be invented by men.

And I stopped here particularly to make it clear that, if such machines had the organs and figure of a monkey or some other animal lacking reason, we would have no means of recognizing that they were not of exactly the same nature as these animals; whereas if there were machines that had a resemblance to our bodies and imitated as many of our actions as would be morally possible, we would always have two very certain means of recognizing that they would not be, for all that, real men. Firstly, these machines could never use words or other signs to compose words as we do in order to declare our thoughts to others. For one can well conceive a machine made in such a way that it produces words, and even some words that are fitting as regards the corporeal actions that cause some change in its organs: as if, when one touched it in a particular place, it asked what one wished to say to it; and as if, when one touched it in another place, it cried out that one was hurting it, and similar things. But one could not conceive that such a machine would arrange its words in different ways to respond to the meaning of everything one shall say in its presence, as even the most primitive men can do. Secondly, although these machines would do many things as well, or perhaps even better than any of us, they would unfailingly lack in some other things; and because of this one would discover that they act, not by means of knowledge, but only by the disposition of their organs. For whereas reason is a universal instrument that can serve in all sorts of situations, these organs require some particular disposition for each particular action; from this it follows that it is morally impossible that there be enough diversities in a machine to make it act in all the occurrences of life in the same manner as our reason makes us act.

Well, then, by these same two means one can also know the difference between men and the beasts. For it is a very remarkable thing that there are no men so primitive or so stupid, not excepting even the most insane, that they are not capable of arranging different words together and composing from them discourse by means of which they make us understand their thoughts; but, on the contrary, there is no other animal, however perfect and well born it be, who does something similar. This does not occur because they lack organs, since one observes that magpies and parrots can produce words just as we do, and nevertheless they cannot speak as we do, that is to say, by giving evidence that they think what they say. However, even men born deaf and dumb, who are as much or more deprived than the beasts of the organs that serve others for speaking, will usually invent of themselves certain signs by which they make themselves understood to those who, because they are customarily with them, have the time to learn their language. And this does not signify merely that the beasts have less reason than men, but that they have no reason at all. For one sees that only very little reason is required to learn to speak; and inasmuch as one notes the inequality between animals of the same species as well as between men, and observes that some beasts and men are easier to train than others, it is unbelievable that a monkey or a parrot considered one of the most perfect of its species has not equaled in this matter of language the most stupid of children, or at least a child with a troubled brain—unless the soul of these beasts is of a nature completely different from our own. And one should not confuse words with natural movements, which are evidence of the passions, and which can be imitated by machines as well as by other animals; nor should one think, as some ancients thought, that the beasts speak even though we do not understand their language: for if that were true, since the beasts have many organs related to ours, they should also be able to make themselves understood by us as well as by their own kind. It is also very noteworthy that, although there are many animals who give evidence of more skill in certain of their actions than we do, one nevertheless notices that the same animals do not manifest any skill whatever in very many other actions: thus what they do better than us does not prove that they have a mind; for if this tale were true they should have more of a mind than we have and should be better at everything; but rather the beasts have no mind at all, and it is nature that acts in them according to the dispositions of their organs—just as one sees that a clock, which is composed only of wheels and springs, can count the hours and measure the time more accurately than we can with all our foresight.

After that I described the rational soul, and I showed that it can in no way be derived from the power of matter, as could the other things of which I spoke, but that instead it must be expressly created; and I showed why it is not sufficient for it to be lodged in the human body like a pilot in his ship—unless perhaps to move the bodily members—but that it is necessary that it be joined and united more intimately with the body in order to have, beyond the ability to move the bodily members, feelings and appetites similar to ours, and thus to compose a genuine man. I have just here lingered somewhat over this subject of the soul because it is one of the most important; for after the error of those who deny God, which I think that I have sufficiently refuted above, there is nothing that more readily leads feeble minds away from the path of virtue than to imagine that the soul of beasts is of the same nature as ours, and that consequently we have nothing more to fear or hope for after this life than do the flies and ants: whereas when one knows how much the souls of beasts differ from our souls, one understands very much better the reasons that prove that our soul is of a nature entirely independent of the body, and consequently that it isn't subjected to die with the body; then, inasmuch as one doesn't see other causes that would destroy it, one is naturally inclined to judge that it is immortal.

SIXTH PART

It is now three years since I came to the end of the treatise containing all these matters, and was beginning to review it to place it in the hands of a printer. But then I learned that certain persons, to whom I defer, and whose authority over my actions can hardly be less than that of my own reason, had disapproved of an opinion in physics published a little while beforehand by someone else. I do not wish to say that I held this opinion, but certainly I had noticed nothing in the opinion, before their censure, that I could imagine to be prejudicial either to religion or to the state, or that consequently might have prevented me from writing it had reason persuaded me of it. And this circumstance made me fear that in just the same way there would be found among my own opinions one in which I would be mistaken, despite the great care I have always exercised to receive nothing new into my belief without very certain demonstrations, and to write nothing that could turn out to be to anyone's disadvantage. This was sufficient to oblige me to change the resolve I had had to publish those opinions. For although the reasons why I had held them beforehand were very strong, my inclination, which has always been to hate the profession of writing books, made me at once find enough other reasons to excuse myself from the task of writing. And all these reasons are such that not only have I some interest in stating them here, but perhaps it is also in the public's interest to know them.

I have never had a great opinion of the things that came from my hand; and as long as I received no other fruits from the method which I was using except the satisfaction it gave me in regard to some difficulties pertaining to speculative science, or when I tried to regulate my customs by the reasons it taught me, I did not believe myself obliged to write anything about the method. For regarding customs, everybody readily and so confidently offers his opinions that one would find as many reformers as heads were it permitted to others than those whom God has either established as sovereigns over the nations, or given sufficient grace and zeal to be prophets, to undertake to change anything; and although my speculations strongly pleased me, I believed that other people also made speculations that pleased them perhaps even more. But as soon as I had acquired some general notions about physics, and began to test them in different specific problems, I noted how far these notions can take one, and how much they differ from the principles that have been used until the present time; thus I believed that I could not hide these notions without sinning greatly against the law that obliges us to procure, as much as we can, the general good of all men. For these notions have made me see that it is possible to reach various knowledge very useful to life, and that, instead of the speculative philosophy taught in the schools, one can find another practical philosophy by which we can know—as distinctly as we now know the different professions of our artisans—the force and action of fire, water, air, the stars, the heavens, and all the other bodies that surround us; and thus, in the same way that we employ artisans, we could also employ all these things for all the uses for which they are fit, thereby rendering ourselves like masters and possessors of nature. And this is to be desired not only in order to discover an infinity of devices that would allow one to enjoy without difficulty the fruits of the earth, and all the conveniences involved in that; rather it is principally to be desired to preserve health, which is without a doubt the first good, and the foundation of all the other goods of this life; for even the mind is so much dependent upon the temperament of the body and the disposition of its organs, that if any means can be found to generally render men wiser and abler than they have been until now, I believe that it ought to be sought after in medicine. It is true that the medicine now practiced contains few things whose utility is noteworthy; but without having any wish to disparage it, I am assured there is hardly anyone, not even among those whose profession is medicine, who does not admit that what is known in it is nearly nothing in comparison with what remains to be known and that one could eliminate an infinity of illnesses, both of the body and of the mind, and perhaps also the weakening that comes with old age, if one had enough knowledge of their causes, and of all the remedies nature has provided to us. Thus, since my goal was to employ all my life in the quest of so necessary a science, and since I encountered a path that, it seems, must unfailingly lead to its discovery if one pursues it and is not prevented either by the brevity of life or by the lack of experiments, I judged that there was no better remedy against these two impediments than to communicate faithfully to the public all the few things I had found, and to urge good minds to advance further, each contributing according to his inclination and abilities to the experiments it would be necessary to perform, and also communicating publicly all the things he would learn; so that, with the last researcher beginning where the preceding ones left off, thus joining together the lives and works of many, we would all progress very much further than each person working alone could do.

I even noticed, as regards experiments, that they are more necessary the more one has progressed in knowledge. For in the beginning it is preferable to use only those experiences that present themselves of their own accord to our senses—for of these we could not be ignorant provided we devote a little reflection to them—rather than to seek out the more unusual and studied experiences. The reason for this is that the more unusual experiences are often deceptive when one does not as yet know the causes of the most ordinary—for the circumstances upon which these more unusual experiences depend are nearly always so particular and detailed that it is very difficult to take note of them. The order I employed in this matter has been as follows. First, I tried to find in general the principles or first causes of everything that is or can be in the world, without considering anything for this purpose except God alone, who created the world; and I did not attempt to understand these principles except by extracting them from certain seeds of truths naturally in our souls. After that I examined what were the first and more ordinary effects one could deduce from these causes: and it seems to me that by doing this I discovered the heavens, the stars, and earth, and also on the earth, water, air, fire, minerals, and some other such things that are the most common and simplest of all, and consequently the easiest to know. Next, when I wished to descend to things more particular, so many different things presented themselves to me that I did not believe it possible for the human mind to distinguish the forms or kinds of bodies that are on the earth from an infinity of others that could be there had God willed it so; and consequently I did not think it possible to relate such things to our practice unless one proceeds to causes by way of effects and makes use of many particular experiments. In consequence of this, upon reviewing with my mind all the objects that had ever been presented to my senses, I venture to say definitely that I never noticed anything I could not explain easily enough by the principles I had found. But it is also necessary for me to admit that the power of nature is so great and vast, and these principles so simple and general, that scarcely did I notice a particular effect before I immediately recognized that it could be deduced in many different ways from these principles; and my greatest difficulty ordinarily consists in discovering the specific way in which an effect does depend upon principles. In regard to this matter I do not know any other technique but to seek afresh for certain experiments that are such that their outcome is not the same if the effect ought to be explained in one of these ways rather than in another of these ways. Moreover, I have now reached the point where it seems to me that I see well enough on what basis one ought to rely to devise the greatest part of those experiments that can serve this purpose; but I see also that these experiments are such, and so great in number, that neither my hands nor funds, although I were to have a thousand times more of them than I have, would suffice to perform all of them; so that, according as I will henceforth have the opportunity to perform more or less of these experiments, I will advance the more or the less in the knowledge of nature. This is what I promised myself to make known in the treatise I had written, and therein to manifest so clearly the utility the public can derive from such experiments, that I would oblige all those who desire the general good of men—that is to say, oblige all those who are in effect virtuous, and not by false pretense or only by opinion—both to communicate to me those experiments that they had already made, and to assist me in researching those that remain to be performed.

But since that time I have found other reasons that made me change my opinion and think that I ought to continue to write about all the things I judge of some importance insofar as I discover the truth about them, devoting the same care to this as if I wished to have the matter published: I chose to do this, first, to have so much the more opportunity to examine them well, since undoubtedly one always looks more closely at what one believes bound to be seen by many people than at what one prepares only for oneself, and because often things that have seemed true when I began to conceive them have seemed false when I wished to put them down on paper; second, to lose no occasion to benefit the public, if I can do so, and in order that, if my writings are worth something, those who will have them after my death can use them in whatever way will be most proper. But it was my choice that I should not at all consent to have my writings published during my life, so that neither the oppositions and the controversies to which they would be subject during my life, nor even such reputation as I would be able to gain, would give me any occasion to lose the time I had planned to employ instructing myself. For although it is true that every man is obliged to procure, as much as he is able, the good of others, and although it is truly of no value to be useful to nobody, nevertheless it is also true that our concerns ought to extend further than the present time, and that it is good to omit things that perhaps would bring some profit to those who are alive when the goal is to produce other advantages that pertain more to our posterity. In fact, I certainly wish that everyone realize that the little bit I have learned until this time is hardly anything in comparison with that of which I am ignorant and hope to learn; for the situation of those who discover the truth little by little in the sciences is nearly the same as the situation of those who, beginning to become rich, have less difficulty making great acquisitions than they previously had when poor in making very much lesser acquisitions. Or else one can compare those in the sciences with the leaders of an army, whose forces customarily grow in proportion to their victories, and who require more leadership to maintain themselves when they have lost a battle than to take cities and provinces after they have won a battle. For it is truly to undertake battles when one tries to vanquish all the difficulties and errors that prevent us from arriving at a knowledge of the truth, and it is the same as losing a battle when one accepts some false opinion respecting a matter somewhat general and important; for afterward, to put oneself back on the same footing as before requires very much more cleverness than is required to make great progress when one already has principles that are assured. For me, if I have hitherto found some truths in the sciences (and I hope that the things contained in this volume will serve to make others judge that I have found some), I can say that these truths are only the consequences dependent upon five or six principal difficulties that I have overcome, and that I consider to be as many battles where the hour fell to my side. Moreover, I will not fear to say that I think I do not need to gain more than two or three similar battles to achieve my goals entirely; and my age is not so advanced that, according to the ordinary course of nature, I may not still have sufficient opportunity to do so. But I believe myself the more bound to manage the time remaining to me, the more I hope to be able to use it well; and without a doubt I would have many occasions to waste that time if I published the foundations of my physics. For although they are nearly all so evident that it is necessary only to understand them to believe them, and although there is not one of them of which I think myself unable to give demonstrations, nevertheless because it is impossible that they accord with all the different opinions of other men, I foresee that I would often be diverted by the oppositions to which they will give birth.

One can say that such oppositions would be useful to make me recognize my mistakes, and in order that, if I had something good, others might gain more knowledge by means of these oppositions; and moreover, it can be said that, since many can see more than one man alone, by beginning to make use of what is good in my work, others might also assist me with their discoveries. But although I recognize that I am extremely subject to mistake, and that I hardly ever trust the first thoughts that come to me, nevertheless the experience I have had of objections that can be made to me prevents me from expecting any profit from such objections: for I have already often tested the judgments of those whom I considered my friends, of some others to whom I thought myself to be indifferent, and also even of certain people whose ill will and envy I knew would cause them to try hard enough to discover what the good will of my friends would hide from them; but it has rarely happened that anyone has made some objection I did not foresee at all, unless it was something very far removed from my subject; thus I hardly ever encountered any critic of my opinions who did not seem to me less rigorous or less fair than myself. And furthermore, I never noticed that one discovered any truth of which he was hitherto ignorant by means of the disputes practiced in the schools; for as long as each participant aims at victory, he occupies himself much more in defending a probability than in weighing the reasons on all sides of a matter; and one who has for a long time been a good pleader is not, on that account, afterward a good judge.

As for the utility others would receive from the communication of my thoughts, it could not be very great inasmuch as I have not yet carried them so far that very many things need not be added before applying them in practice. And I think that I can say without vanity that if there is anyone able to add them, it is me rather than anyone else: not that there may not be many more minds in the world incomparably better than mine; but because one cannot conceive something so well, nor make it his own, except when he invents it himself. This is so true as regards this matter that, although I have often explained some of my opinions to persons with very good minds who, while I spoke with them, seemed to understand them very distinctly, nevertheless when these people repeated them, I noticed that they had changed them nearly all the time in such a way that I could no longer admit them as my own. On this account I feel very free in here asking posterity never to believe things that others will say issue from me when I myself shall not have divulged them. And I am not all astonished by the extravagances that are attributed to all those ancient philosophers whose writings we lack; and for all that is said about them, I do not judge that their thoughts were so unreasonable, seeing that they were the best minds of their times; I judge only that their thoughts have been badly related to us. Thus one also sees that hardly ever has any of their followers surpassed them; and I am assured that the most passionate of those who follow Aristotle would believe themselves happy if they had as much knowledge about nature as he had, even though it was on the condition that they would never have more. They are like the ivy that does not tend to rise higher than the trees that support it, and that often goes back downward if it has arrived at the summit. For it seems to me that they do go back downward—which is to say, they render themselves less knowledgeable than if they abstained from studying—when, not contented with knowing everything intelligibly explained in their author, they wish also to find the solution of many difficulties about which he says nothing and about which he perhaps never thought. Nevertheless, their manner of philosophizing is very convenient for those who have only very mediocre minds; for the obscurity of the distinctions and the principles that they use is the reason why they can speak of all things as boldly as if they knew about them, and sustain everything they say about them against subtler and abler minds without anyone having a means of convincing them. And in this respect they seem to me to be the same as a blind man who, in order to fight without disadvantage an opponent who is able to see, lures him into the depths of some very dark cave; and I can say that it is to the interest of such as these that I abstain from publishing the principles of the philosophy of which I make use; for since these principles are very simple and very evident, I would do nearly the same thing in publishing them as if I opened some windows and allowed the daylight to enter the cave where they have descended to do battle. Moreover, the best minds have no reason to wish to know these principles of mine. For if they wish to know how to speak of all things and to acquire the reputation of being learned, they will achieve their goal more easily by contenting themselves with probability. This can be found without great difficulty in all sorts of subject matters, whereas truth is discovered only little by little in a few subject matters; and when it is a question of speaking about others, it obliges one to admit frankly that one is ignorant about them. However, if the best minds do prefer the knowledge of a few truths to the vanity of seeming to be ignorant of none, which undoubtedly is preferable, and if they wish to follow a plan similar to my own, they have no need on that account that I say to them anything more than what I have already said in this discourse. For if they are capable of advancing further than I have done, it follows that they will by themselves find all that I think I have found. And, inasmuch as I have never examined anything except in an orderly manner, it is certain that what yet remains for me to discover is in itself more difficult and hidden than what I have been previously able to find, and others would have much less pleasure in learning about it from me than from themselves; besides, the habit they will acquire in first seeking easy things, and in passing little by little by degrees to things more difficult, will serve them better than could all my instructions. As for myself, I am persuaded that if I had been taught from my youth all the truths for which I have since sought the demonstrations, and if I had no difficulty in learning them, I would perhaps never have known any others and never have acquired the habit and the facility that I think myself to have in always finding new truths in proportion to the application I devote to finding them. And in a word, if there is any work in this world that cannot be so well achieved by anyone other than he who began it, it is the work at which I labor.

It is true that, as regards the experiments that can be of use in this project, one man alone could not perform all of them; but he also could not usefully employ any hands but his own, except those of artisans or such people as he could pay—people to whom the prospect of payment, which is a very efficient means, would make them do exactly everything prescribed for them to do. As for volunteers, who out of curiosity or a desire to learn would perhaps offer to aid him, besides the fact that they ordinarily promise more than they perform, thus making only fine-sounding proposals whose issue is nothing, such people invariably would want to be paid by an explanation of certain difficulties, or at least by compliments and useless conversations, which would mean the loss of more of his time than he saves. And as regards the experiments others have already performed, even when they would wish to communicate them to him (which is something those people who call experiments secrets would never do), the experiments are, for the most part, dependent on so many circumstances or superfluous ingredients that it would be very difficult for him to decipher the truth; beyond this, he would find all of them so badly explained or even so false, because those who have made them have forced themselves to make them appear in conformity with their principles, that as a result, if there had been some of them that might serve his purpose, they would not be worth the time required for him to select them out. In this way, if somewhere in the world there were a person that one assuredly knew to be capable of finding out the greatest things, and things as useful to the public as is possible, and if for this reason other men would be forced to help him by every means to achieve his goals, I do not see that they could do anything for him except to furnish the moneys for the experiments he would require, and beyond this to prevent him from being deprived of his leisure by anyone's importunities. But besides the fact that I am not so presumptuous as to wish to promise anything extraordinary, nor to feed myself on thoughts so vain as to imagine that the public ought to interest itself very much in my plan, I also do not have a soul so base that I ever wished to accept from anyone any favor that one could believe I did not merit.

All these considerations joined together were the reason why three years ago I did not wish to divulge the treatise I had in my hands, and why I made a resolve not to bring into light of day during my lifetime any other treatise that might be so general, or such that one could understand the foundations of my physics. But since that time I again have had two other reasons that have obliged me to present here some particular essays and to provide the public with some account of my actions and my goals. The first is that, if I failed to do so, some who have known the intention I have previously had to publish certain wriings would imagine that the reasons for my abstaining would be more to my disadvantage than they are. For although I do not love excessive glory, or even, if I dare say, hate it, because I consider it contrary to leisure, which I value above everything; nevertheless I have also never tried to hide my actions like crimes, nor have I used very many precautions to keep them unknown. Not only would I have thought it wrong for me to do that, but also it would have brought me some sort of inquietude, which again might have been contrary to the perfect repose of mind for which I seek. And since being thus indifferent—between exercising care that I be recognized or remain unknown, I have not been able to prevent myself from acquiring some sort of reputation, I thought I ought to do my best at least to prevent myself from developing a bad one. The other reason that has obliged me to write this is that, seeing the goal I previously had of instructing myself daily set back more and more because of an infinity of experiments I require, and realizing I cannot perform them without the aid of others, even though I do not flatter myself that the public will participate in a large degree in my interests, nevertheless I also do not wish to withdraw so much into myself as to provide to those who will follow a reason for reproaching me someday that I could have left them many very much better things had I not excessively neglected making them understand how they could contribute to my goals.

And I thought that it was easy to choose certain matters that, without being subject to very much controversy or obliging me to declare more of my principles than I desire, would not fail to manifest clearly enough what I can and cannot do in the sciences. In this I could not say if I have succeeded; I do not wish to anticipate the judgments of anyone when I myself am speaking of my writings; but I would be happy if others examined them; and in order that they may have more opportunity of doing so, I urge everyone who will have some objections to make to these essays to take the trouble to send them to my publisher; and when he brings them to my attention I will try to make my replies at the same time; and by this means readers, seeing together the objections and replies, will judge so much the more easily about the truth. I do not promise ever to make long responses, but only to admit my mistakes very frankly if I have recognized them, or if I cannot perceive them, to say simply what I shall believe to be required for the defense of the things I have written, without introducing an explanation of any new subject matters in order to avoid involving myself endlessly in one thing and then another.

If some of the things about which I have spoken at the beginning of the *Dioptrics* and *Meteors* displease at first glance, because I call them suppositions and do not seem to have any desire to prove them, let the reader have the patience to read through the whole with attention, and I hope he will find himself satisfied. For it seems to me that the reasons are interdependent in such a way that just as the last are demonstrated by the first, which are their causes, so these first are reciprocally demonstrated by the last, which are their effects. And one should not imagine that I commit in this matter the mistake logicians call a circle; for since experience renders the greatest part of these effects very certain, the causes from which I have deduced them do not serve so much to prove them as to explain them; indeed, the very opposite is the case, namely, the causes from which I have deduced these effects are proved by the effects. And I have called them suppositions only so that one may know that while I think I can deduce them from those first truths explained above, I have expressly chosen not to do so in order to prevent certain minds from taking the opportunity to erect some extravagant philosophy, for which I will be blamed, upon what they will believe to be my principles. I refer to those who imagine that they can know in a day everything someone else has thought throughout twenty years once they have heard two or three words about his thoughts. Such people are the more likely to go wrong and the less capable of arriving at the truth, the more they are penetrating and precipitous. But as for opinions that are truly mine, I ask no pardon for their novelty, inasmuch as if one considers thoroughly the reasons for them, I am assured they will be found so simple and consonant with common sense that they will seem less extraordinary and strange than any other opinions that can be held on the same subject matters. And also I do not flatter myself with being the first discoverer of any of them. I take this attitude not because I have ever received them from anyone—that is, neither because others have said them nor because others have not said them—but only because reason has persuaded me of them.

If artisans are not soon able to build the invention explained in the *Dioptrics,* I do not believe on that account one can say it is difficult: for since skill and practice are required to make and adjust the machines I have described, even if no other requirement were lacking, I would be no less astonished if artisans would hit the mark at the first try than if someone could learn to play the lute excellently in one day just because he had been given a good score. And if I write in French, which is the language of my country, rather than in Latin, which is the language of my teachers, it is because I hope that those who make use only of their pure natural reason will judge better concerning my opinions than those who believe only in ancient books. And for those who join good sense to duty, who alone I desire as my judges, I am assured that they will not be so partial to Latin as to refuse to understand my reasons because I explain them in a common language.

I do not wish to speak here in detail of the progress I hope to make in the sciences in the future, nor do I wish to involve myself in any promises to the public that I am not assured I will fulfill; but I shall say only that I have resolved not to employ the time that remains to me in life at any other endeavor than to try to acquire such a knowledge of nature that one can extract from it rules of medicine more assured than those that have been followed up until the present. My inclination so strongly turns me from every other sort of goal, and principally from those that could not be useful to some without being harmful to others, that if circumstances constrained me to engage myself in such activities, I do not believe that I would be capable of succeeding at them. And as far as this is concerned, I here declare that not only do I recognize that in this way I cannot serve to establish by renown throughout the world, but also that I have no desire to be renowned; and I will always hold myself more obliged to those by whose thoughtfulness I shall enjoy my leisure without impediment than to those would offer me the most honorable offices on the earth.

Meditations Concerning First Philosophy

To Those Most Wise and Very Distinguished Men of the Faculty of Sacred Theology at Paris

To the Dean and the Doctors

The motive that persuades me to present this treatise to you is so worthy—and I am confident that after you have understood the rationale of my undertaking you too will have so worthy a motive for undertaking its defense—that I can do nothing better here to procure your favor for the treatise than to state briefly what I have sought to ascertain in it.

I have always considered that two questions, namely, those of God and the soul, are the foremost of all those that ought to be demonstrated by philosophy rather than by theology: for although it suffices for us faithful ones to believe by faith that the human soul does not perish with the body and that God exists, certainly it seems that those without faith cannot be persuaded of any religion, nor usually even of any moral virtue, unless these two things are proved to them beforehand by natural reason: and since often in this life greater rewards are offered for vices than for virtues, few persons would prefer what is right to what is useful if they did not fear God or expect another life. And although it is indeed true that the existence of God ought to be believed because it is taught in the sacred Scriptures, and vice versa, that the sacred Scriptures are to be believed because we receive them from God—the reason being that, since faith is a gift of God, the same God who gives grace for believing other things can also give the grace that we may believe in His existence—nevertheless this cannot be proposed to those without faith, because they would judge it a circle. And certainly, not only have I noticed that all of you and other theologians affirm that the existence of God can be proved by natural reason, but also I have noticed that we can infer from sacred Scripture that a knowledge of God is easier than knowledge of the many things we know about created things, and indeed so easy that those who do not have it are blameworthy. This is evident from these words in Wisdom, 13: *Neither should they be pardoned. For if they could know so much as to be able to render a judgment about the world, how is it that they did not more easily discover its lord?* And in Romans, chapter 1, it is said that they are *not to be excused.* And again, in the same place, through these words, *What is known of God is manifest in them,* we seem to be admonished that everything that can be known about God can be made manifest from reasons drawn from no other source but our very own mind. Accordingly, I did not think it outside my prerogative to inquire how to do this, and into the manner in which God is known more easily and certainly than the things of the world.

And as regards the soul, although many have judged that it is not easy to investigate its nature, and some have even dared to say that human reasonings persuade us that it perishes at the same time as the body, and that the contrary is held only on the basis of faith, nevertheless because the Lateran Council, held under Leo X, session 8, condemns such people, and expressly orders Christian philosophers to destroy their arguments and to show the truth to be stronger, I did not hesitate to attempt this also.

Moreover, I know that very many of the impious do not believe in God, and in the distinction of the human mind from the body, for no other reason than because they say that up until the present nobody has been able to demonstrate these two things: although I in no way agree with them, but, on the contrary, think that nearly all the reasonings that have been brought forth by great men concerning these two questions have the force of demonstrations when properly understood; and although I am persuaded that hardly any other reasonings can be given that have not been discovered previously by others; nevertheless I believe that nothing can prove more useful in philosophy than for once studiously to seek after the best of all these arguments, and to explain them so accurately and perspicuously that afterward they are received by everyone as demonstrations. And finally, I am entreated to consider it of the greatest importance that I undertake to do this. This entreaty comes from people to whom it is known that I have cultivated a particular method for resolving certain difficulties in the sciences, not indeed that this method is new, since nothing is older than the truth, but they have often seen me use it with fortunate results in other subject matters. Accordingly, I thought it my obligation to attempt something in this matter.

Whatever I have been able to achieve is completely contained in this treatise. Not that I have attempted to gather here all those different reasonings that can be brought forward to prove these same matters, for that seems required only in those undertakings where there are no sufficiently certain reasonings; rather I have pursued only the primary and principal reasonings in such a way that I now dare to propose them as most certain and most evident demonstrations. And I may also add that they are such that I think there is no way open to human wits by which better reasonings can ever be discoverd: for the gravity of the subject, and the glory of God, to which all this relates, compel me to speak here somewhat more freely of myself than I am ordinarily inclined to do. But notwithstanding the fact that I think these reasonings certain and evident, I am nevertheless not on that account persuaded that they are suited to everyone's grasp: but just as there are many demonstrations in geometry laid down by Archimedes, Apollonius, Pappus, and other writers, which, although they are considered by everyone as also evident and certain, because they manifestly contain nothing that individually considered is not easily known and nothing in which what follows does not accurately cohere with the antecedents, nevertheless they are not understood except by very few persons because they are lengthy and demand a truly attentive reader: and so too, although I judge those reasonings I use here to equal or even to surpass geometrical reasonings in certainty and evidence, nevertheless I fear they cannot be sufficiently perceived by many people, both because they are long and depend the ones upon the others, but also and principally because they require a mind clearly free from prejudices and a mind that leads itself away from any dependence upon the senses. And to be sure, one cannot find more people suited to metaphysical than to geometrical studies. And besides, there is this difference: that in geometry, since everyone is persuaded nothing is ordinarily written for which there is no certain demonstration, the inexperienced more often err by accepting falsities, which they wish to seem to understand, than by refuting the truth; in philosophy the situation is indeed the opposite—because it is believed there is nothing that cannot be argued either way in philosophy, few investigate the truth, and many more people, by daring to challenge every very good truth, strive to make themselves renowned for their wits.

Accordingly, whatever the quality of my reasonings, nevertheless because they pertain to philosophy, I do not hope to effect a great reception for my work by sheer force of these reasonings alone, unless you help me by your protection. For there is fixed so high a regard in everyone's mind for your faculty, and the name of SORBONNE is of such great authority that, not only in matters of faith has no other society, except the Sacred Councils, been as trusted as yours, but also, as regards human philosophy, there is nowhere else thought to be greater perspicuity and solidity, nor greater integrity and wisdom, in making judgments. And thus I have no doubt that if you deign to undertake such concern for this treatise as, *firstly*, to correct it—for mindful not only of my humanity but most especially of my ignorance, I do not affirm that it is free of errors; and *secondly*, to see to it that either you yourselves, or I, after being admonished by you, add, complete, or elucidate whatever is lacking to it, or insufficiently complete in it, or requiring of greater explanation; and *finally*, if after the reasons contained in it, which prove that God exists and that the mind is something other than the body, shall have been rendered so perspicuous that they ought to be received as most accurate demonstrations, as I am confident can be accomplished—if then you would wish to declare this fact and publicly testify to it, I say to you, I have no doubts that, if you do this, all the error that ever existed concerning these questions would, in a brief period of time, be removed from the minds of men. For the truth itself will bring it about that other men of native talent and learning will subscribe to your opinion; and this authority will bring it about that the atheists, who are ordinarily sophomoric rather than natively talented or learned, will leave off their spirit of contradiction, and perhaps even defend reasonings that they will know are accepted as demonstrations by all those endowed with native wit, lest they themselves seem not to understand them. And finally, everyone else will easily believe such numbers of witnesses that there will be no one left in the world who dares to call into doubt either the existence of God or the real distinction of the human soul from the body. How useful this would be, you yourselves, in your singular wisdom, can judge best of all; nor would it be fitting for me to commend further the cause of God and of religion to you, who have always been the greatest support of the Catholic Church.

PREFACE TO THE READER

I have previously touched on a few matters concerning the questions of God and the human mind in *The Discourse concerning the Method of correctly conducting reason and of investigating truth in the sciences,* published in French in the year 1637. Indeed, I did not intend to treat these questions thoroughly in that work, but only to lay down the beginnings, and to learn from the judgments of readers the way in which they ought to be treated afterward. These questions seemed to me of such importance that I judged they should be treated in more than one place; and the path I follow to explain them is so little traveled, and so remote from the common practice, that I have decided it would not be useful to set forth the more detailed explanation in a French treatise that might be read at random by everyone, lest even people of weaker talents be led to believe this path is intended for them.

However, although I there asked everyone to whom anything in my writings appeared deserving of rebuttal please to advise me of it, only two objections were worthy of note as regards what I said touching on these questions [of God and the mind]. I will here respond to these objections in a few words before entering upon a complete explanation of them.

The first objection is that from the fact that the human mind in turning its attention toward itself does not perceive itself to be something other than a thinking thing, it does not follow that its nature or *essence* consists *only* in the fact that it is a thinking thing; thus the word *only* excludes everything else that perhaps can also be said to pertain to the nature of the soul. To this objection I respond that at that place [in the *Discourse*] I did not wish to exclude those other things as far as the order that pertains to the very truth about the thing is concerned, for I was not dealing with this at that place; rather I merely wished to exclude those other things as far as the order of my perception was concerned, and thus my meaning was that there was nothing I plainly recognized to pertain to my essence except the fact that I was a thinking thing, or a thing having in itself the faculty of thinking. However, in what is to follow I will show the manner in which, from the fact that I know nothing else to pertain to my essence, it also follows that in reality nothing else does pertain to it.

The other objection is that, from the fact that I have in me the idea of a more perfect thing, it does not follow that this idea is more perfect than myself, and much less does it follow that what is represented by this idea exists. But I here respond that an equivocation is concealed in the word "idea": for it can be understood either materially, as an operation of the intellect, in which meaning it cannot be said to be more perfect than myself; or it can be understood objectively, that is, for the thing represented through this very operation—which thing, even though it is not assumed to exist outside my intellect, can nevertheless be more perfect than myself by reason of its essence. To be sure, it will be explained at length in the present treatise how, from the mere fact that there is in me the idea of a thing more perfect than me, it follows that the thing truly exists.

Moreover, I did indeed also see two rather lengthy works that were less attacks on my reasonings than on my conclusions concerning these matters; and they were based on arguments commonly employed by the atheists. Since arguments of this kind can have no force among those who understand my reasonings, and because the judgments of many men are so disordered and feeble that they are persuaded more by the opinions they have first accepted than by true and firm opinions heard later on, I do not wish to respond to these arguments here by way of refuting them, lest I have to first relate them. I will only say generally that everything ordinarily hurled forth by the atheists to attack the existence of God always assumes either that human affections are ascribed to God or that such a great power and wisdom may be arrogated to our minds that we may attempt to determine and to comprehend what God can and ought to do; thus these matters will occasion no difficulty for us, provided only we are mindful that our minds must be considered as finite, whereas God is incomprehensible and infinite.

Now, indeed, having once freely tested the judgments of other men, I here again enter into the same two questions of God and the human mind, and at the same time treat of the beginnings of first philosophy; however, I do so expecting no praise from the vulgar nor a great number of readers; rather I am an author suited only to those who will read this treatise to meditate in earnest along with me, and who are able and willing to lead the mind away from the senses and at the same time away from all prejudices. I know well enough that only a very few readers of this kind are to be found. However, as for those who, taking no care to comprehend the order and connection of my reasonings, will study them to dispute isolated parts of them, as is the custom among many, they will not derive much fruit from reading this treatise; and although they may accidentally discover opportunity for caviling on many points, nevertheless it will not be easy for them to make any objection that is urgent or worthy of response.

Because I cannot indeed promise to satisfy others in all details on first showing, and because I am not so presumptuous as to believe that I can foresee everything that will seem difficult to anyone, I will first explain in the Meditations those very thoughts by means of which I believe myself to have arrived at certain and evident knowledge of the truth, so that I may test whether perhaps I can also persuade others by those same reasons by which I have been persuaded. Afterward, I will respond to the objections of several men of surpassing native talent and learning to whom these Meditations have been sent for examination before being consigned to print. Their objections have been sufficiently many and varied that I dare to hope it is not easy for any objection, at least of any importance, to come to the minds of others that these men have not already touched upon. And accordingly, I also ask the readers not to render a judgment about the Meditations until they have read through these objections and all the solutions to them.

A SYNOPSIS OF THE SIX FOLLOWING MEDITATIONS

In the First Meditation, the reasons are explained why we can doubt all things, especially material things—that is, until we have other foundations for the sciences than those we had up to that time. However, although the usefulness of this large doubt is not obvious on first appearance, nevertheless it is very great—for it frees us from all prejudices and opens up a very easy path for leading the mind away from the senses; and it brings it about that we can finally no longer doubt those things we shall afterward accurately ascertain to be true.

In the Second Meditation, the mind, using its proper liberty, supposes that nothing exists about whose existence it can doubt in the least degree; and it notices that it is impossible but that it exists. This also is of the greatest usefulness, because in this manner the mind easily distinguishes between what pertains to itself, that is, to its intellectual nature, and what pertains to the body. But since at this point some will perhaps expect to find reasonings about the immortality of the soul, I warn them right now that I view myself as inclined to write down nothing

I have not accurately demonstrated; and accordingly I have been able to follow no order except that used by geometers—that is, I would set out in advance all those things on which the proposition I wished to prove depends before drawing any conclusion concerning the proposition. But now, the first and principal thing prerequisite to knowing the immortality of the soul is for us to form as perspicuous a conception of it as possible, and one manifestly distinct from every conception of body; and this has been done here. Furthermore, we must certainly also know that everything clearly and distinctly understood by us is true in the very same way in which we understand it, which could not be established before the Fourth Meditation; and moreover, we must have a distinct conception of corporeal nature, which is formed partially in this Second Meditation and also partially in the Fifth and Sixth Meditations; and from all the foregoing it should be concluded that everything clearly and distinctly conceived to be different substances, just as mind and body are conceived to be, are in truth substances really distinct from one another; and this I concluded in the Sixth Meditation. This same conclusion is also confirmed in the Sixth Meditation by the fact that we understand no body unless it is divisible, whereas, on the contrary, we understand no mind unless it is indivisible: for we cannot conceive a half part of any mind as we can of any body however small; thus, in the same manner, the natures of mind and body are recognized as not merely different, but even as in a certain way contrary. However, I have dealt no further with this matter in this treatise; not only because what I have said suffices to show that the perishing of the mind does not follow from the corruption of the body, and thus to provide mortals with a hope for another life; but also because the premises from which this immortality of the mind can be concluded depend upon the explanation of all of physics: for, first, it would have to be made known that all substances generally—that is, things that must be created by God in order to exist—are incorruptible from their nature and can never cease to exist unless they are reduced to nothing by that same God refusing them his support; and next, it would have to be noted that certainly body considered in general is a substance, and accordingly also never perishes. However, the human body differs from other bodies only insofar as it is constituted from a specific configuration of members and other accidents of this kind; but indeed the human mind is not in this way constituted from any accidents; rather it is a pure substance, because even if all its accidents are changed, so that it understands other things, wills other things, senses other things, and so on, this very mind does not, on that account, become something else; yet the human body does become something else from the mere fact that the figure of some part of it is changed: from all this it follows that the body indeed perishes very easily, but, on the contrary, the mind is immortal from its very nature.

In the Third Meditation, it seems to me I explained at sufficient length my principal argument for proving the existence of God. Nevertheless, since I have chosen not to employ there any comparisons drawn from material things, in order to lead the minds of the readers as far as possible away from the senses, perhaps many obscurities have remained that I hope are afterward, however, completely removed in the responses to the objections; as, among others, how the idea of a most perfect entity—which idea is in us—has so much objective reality that it cannot fail to be from a most perfect cause; and this I illustrate in this same Third Meditation by a comparison to an exceedingly perfect machine, the idea of which is in the mind of some artisan; for as the objective inventiveness of this idea must have some cause, namely, the knowledge of this artisan or of someone else from whom he received the idea, so also the idea of God, which is in us, can only have God Himself as its cause.

In the Fourth Meditation, it is proved that everything is true that we perceive clearly and distinctly, and at the same time the cause in which falsity consists is explained: these things must necessarily be known, as much to strengthen what preceded as to understand what remains. (But nevertheless, it must be noted that in this Fourth Meditation I in no way treat of sin, or of the error that is committed in pursuing good and evil; rather I treat only of such errors as occur in judgment about the true and the false. Neither am I concerned with matters pertaining to faith nor with matters related to the conduct of our lives, but only with speculative truths known solely by means of the natural light.)

In the Fifth Meditation, beyond an explanation of corporeal nature generally considered, the existence of God is demonstrated by a new argument; but here again perhaps some difficulties occur that will be resolved in the responses to the objections; and finally,

I show the manner in which it is true that the certainty of the very demonstrations of geometry depends upon the knowledge of God.

Lastly, in the Sixth Meditation, the intellect is distinguished from the imagination; the signs of the distinctions are described; the mind is proved to be really distinguished from the body; nonetheless, it is shown that the mind is so intimately joined to the body that it forms the body into a single thing with itself; all the errors that are wont to arise from the senses are examined; the ways in which they can be avoided are explained; and finally, all the reasons are set forth by which the existence of material things can be concluded. I set them forth not because I deemed them very useful for proving what they do prove, namely, that there is in truth some world, that men have bodies, and similar things concerning which no one of healthy mind ever seriously doubted; but because, by considering them, one recognizes that these reasons are not so firm nor perspicuous as those by which we arrive at a knowledge of our mind and of God; hence our mind and God are the most certain and most evident things that can be known by means of our native talents. The proof of this one thing is what I proposed for myself as the goal in these Meditations. Accordingly, I do not here enumerate other questions that it is also out of place to consider in these Meditations.

Of the Meditations Concerning First Philosophy

In Which the Existence of God and the Distinction of the Soul from the Body Are Demonstrated

THE FIRST

Concerning Those Things That Can Be Called Back into Doubt

It is now some years since I noticed that, starting from the beginning of life, I had embraced very many falsities for truths, and that whatever I afterward erected upon them is equally dubious; accordingly I noticed that were I at any time to wish to establish something firm and lasting in the sciences, then once in my life everything would have to be overturned right from the bottom and built up anew from the first foundations. However, the task seemed monumental, and I looked forward to a time of life so mature that none would follow it more suited to the goal because of my accumulation of learning. Wherefore have I delayed so long that hereafter I would be guilty were I to consume in deliberation the time that remains to me for action. Fortunately therefore, I have today released my mind from all cares and arranged an untroubled leisure for myself. I withdraw alone, and at last I shall freely and earnestly devote myself to this completely general overthrowing of my opinions.

However, to accomplish this it will not be necessary to show all these opinions false, which perhaps I can never do; rather, since even now reason persuades me that assent ought to be withheld no less carefully from things not manifestly certain and indubitable than from things obviously false, it will suffice to reject all my opinions if I might find some reason for doubting each of them. And to do this it is likewise unnecessary to run through them individually, which would be an infinite task; rather, since once the foundations are undermined, whatever has been built upon them will automatically collapse, I shall immediately consider the very principles upon which everything I formerly believed depended.

Indeed, whatever I accepted as most true up until this time, I accepted either from the senses or on the basis of the senses; however, I have discerned that they occasionally deceive, and it is prudent never to quite trust things that have deceived us even once.

But although the senses occasionally deceive us concerning certain small objects or those farther away, perhaps there are very many other things about which it is manifestly impossible to doubt even though they are drawn from the senses: for example, that I am now here, seated in this place, clothed in a winter garment, holding this sheet of paper in my hands, and similar things. Indeed, by what reasoning could it be denied that these very hands and this entire body exist? Unless, perhaps, I were comparing myself to some insane people whose brains are injured by so exceedingly unyielding a vapor from the black bile that they constantly maintain that they are kings when they are very poor, or that they are clothed in purple when they are naked, or that they have a head of clay, or are completely pumpkins, or composed of glass—but such people are out of their minds, nor would I seem any less demented were I to apply to myself an example drawn from them.

All this seems magnificently sane, just as though I were not a man who is accustomed to sleep at night and to undergo in dreams all those same things, or even on occasion things less probable than what these insane people undergo while awake. How often indeed does the quiet of night persuade me of these ordinary things—that I am here, dressed in a garment, seated in this place—when I am nevertheless lying nude between the bed covers. But, on the contrary, I am now certainly intuiting this paper with waking eyes, this head I move to and fro is not lulled to sleep, it is adroitly and knowingly that I extend and sense this hand; things so distinct would not occur to one who is sleeping. As though I do not remember having been deluded even by similar thoughts at other times; in dwelling on these matters more attentively, I so manifestly see that waking can never be distinguished from sleeping by signs that are certain that I become bewildered—and this very stupor is nearly enough to confirm me in the opinion that I am sleeping.

Therefore, let us act as though we are dreaming and none of these particulars are true: that we open our eyes, move our head, extend our hands, or perhaps even that we have hands or an entire body that are such [as they seem]. Nevertheless it must indeed be acknowledged that appearances occurring in sleep are, as it were, certain painted pictures that could only have been fashioned in the likeness of true things. Accordingly at least these general things—eyes, head, hands, the entire body—are not imaginary, but truly exist. For, to be sure, painters themselves, even when they strive to fashion Sirens and Satyrs with the most extraordinary forms, cannot assign them natures new in every detail; rather they merely intermingle the members of different animals; or if perchance they do think up something so new that nothing at all similar to it shall have been seen, nevertheless at least the colors out of which they form it must certainly be true. By similar reasoning, even if these general things—eyes, head, hands, and so on—could also be imaginary, it is at least necessary that some other still more simple and universal things be acknowledged as true, which, like true colors, are the sources from which are fashioned all these images of things, whether true or false, that exist in our thinking.

Corporeal nature in general and its extension seem to be of this simple and universal kind; and so also does the shape of extended things; and so also does quantity, which is the magnitude and number of extended things; and so also do place, in which extended things exist, time, throughout which they endure, and the like.

For this reason perhaps, from what has been said above, we shall not unreasonably conclude that physics, astronomy, medicine and all the other disciplines that depend upon a consideration of composite things are indeed dubious, whereas there is something certain and indubitable in arithmetic, geometry, and other disciplines of this kind that treat only of very simple and most general things, and are not particularly concerned whether or not they exist in nature. For whether I am awake or asleep, 2 and 3 joined together is 5, the square does not have more than four sides; nor does it seem possible that truths so perspicuous may incur any suspicion of falsity.

Nevertheless, there is a certain age-old opinion ingrained in my mind that a God exists who is able to do everything, by whom I, with such a nature as I presently exist, have been created. But now how do I know he has not arranged things such that there is definitely no earth, no heaven, no extended thing, no figure, no magnitude, no place, and nevertheless all these things appear to me to exist just as at present? In fact, the same way I judge that other people occasionally err about things they think they know most perfectly, may it not happen that I am deceived each time I add 2 and 3 together, or number the sides of a square, or anything else, if anything easier can be thought? On the other hand, perhaps God has not wished to deceive me, for he is said to be exceedingly good; but were it inconsistent with his goodness to have created me such that I am always deceived, by the same reasoning it would also appear inconsistent with his nature to allow me to be occasionally deceived; but it cannot be said that he does not allow me to be occasionally deceived.

Perhaps indeed there are some people who, rather than believe everything else uncertain, would prefer to deny the existence of so powerful a God. But let us not contradict them, and let us grant them that everything said about God is fictitious; then, in whatever way they suppose that I have become what I presently am—be it by some fate, chance, or a continuous series of events, or in any other manner—still, because to be deceived and to err seems to constitute some imperfection, it will be more probable that I am so imperfect as always to err, the less perfect the author they assign to my origins. And to these arguments I indeed have nothing I may use in reply, but at last I am forced to confess that nothing I formerly believed true is such that one cannot doubt it for strong and well-thought-out reasons, and not just because of lack of consideration or flippancy; accordingly if I wish to discover anything that is certain, my assent must hereafter be carefully withheld from all these former beliefs no less than from what is manifestly false.

But it does not yet suffice to have noticed this; care must be taken to remember it. My customary opinions still relentlessly recur, and almost as though I invite them, they lay hold upon my belief. Because, as it were, of a long-time use of them and the right of familiarity, my beliefs have become resistant to change. I will never disaccustom myself to assenting to them and to placing trust in them as long as I shall suppose them of the sort they really are—namely, in some way dubious indeed, as has already been shown, but nevertheless exceedingly probable, such that it is much more consonant with reason to be-

The Philistines Stricken with the Plague, by Nicholas Poussin. The plague of the 14th century resulted in the death of 75 percent of the population of Europe and Asia. Poussin died in 1665, just as the plague returned to London. (Bibliothèque Nationale, Paris)

lieve them than to deny them. Accordingly, it is my opinion that I shall not act improperly if, with a will turned completely toward the opposite, I shall deceive my own self and shall pretend for some period of time that these beliefs are altogether false and imaginary, until finally, because, as it were, of the equal weights of the prejudices on both sides, my perverse habit will not longer divert my judgment from the right perception of things. I know that by acting in this way no danger or error will arise in the meanwhile, and that it is no longer possible for me calmly to give way to diffidence, since I am not turning my attention toward doing things but only toward understanding them.

Accordingly, I will suppose not that God, who is most good and the fountain of truth, but rather that some evil genius, at once very powerful and cunning, has bent all his efforts to deceive me. I will suppose heaven, air, earth, colors, shapes, sounds and everything external are nothing but the delusions of dreams that he has contrived to lure me into belief. I will consider myself not to have hands, eyes, flesh, blood, or any senses, but as falsely thinking myself to have all these things. I will remain obstinately attached to this point of view, and thus, if indeed it is not in my power to know anything of the truth, still, in virtue of a power I certainly do have, I will resolutely guard against assenting to falsities and against whatever this deceiver can employ to trick me. But this project is laborious and a certain slothfulness draws me back to my customary manner of life. I am like a prisoner who by chance was enjoying an imaginary liberty in his dreams, and at the very moment when he later on begins to suspect that he is sleeping, fears being awakened, and persistently fails to notice his agreeable illusions for what they are: thus I spontaneously relapse into my old opinions, and fear to be awakened lest the labors of that waking life that follow on this calm repose have to be spent, not amidst the light, but among the labyrinthine obscurities of those constantly elusive difficulties already discussed.

MEDITATION II

On the Nature of the Human Mind: That It Is Better Known Than the Body

I have been thrown into such great doubts by yesterday's meditation that I can no longer forget them; nor do I see by what argument they are to be resolved. Rather, just as though I fell unexpectedly into a whirlpool, I have been so battered about that I cannot get a foothold on the bottom or swim up and out of it. Nevertheless, I shall rally my energies and again try the same path I had entered upon yesterday, namely, removing everything that admits of the slightest doubt, just as if I had learned it to be altogether false; and I will proceed onward until at length I shall know something certain, or if nothing else, at least know this for certain, namely, that nothing is certain. To move the earth from its place, Archimedes asked for nothing but one small spot that should be firm and stable; similarly, great things are to be hoped for if I shall find at least one thing that is certain and unshaken.

I suppose therefore that everything I see is false; I believe that nothing that my deceptive memory represents has existed; I manifestly have no senses; body, shape, extension, motion, and place are chimerical. What then will be true? Perhaps this one thing, that nothing is certain.

But on what basis do I know there is not something—different from everything I have just now enumerated—about which there is not even the slightest occasion for doubting? Is there not some God, or by whatever other name I may call him, who sends me these very thoughts? Yet on what grounds may I assuredly believe this, since perhaps I myself can be their author? Therefore am I at least not something? But I have already denied I have any senses and any body. Nevertheless, I stick to this point; for what follows from the fact that I have already denied I have any senses and any body? Am I so bound to the body and senses that I cannot exist without them? I have persuaded myself that there is manifestly nothing in the world—no heaven, no earth, no minds, no bodies. Does it not accordingly follow that I also do not exist? On the contrary, I certainly existed if I persuaded myself of something. But there is that deceiver—I know not exactly who—who is very powerful and very cunning and always purposefully deceives me. Beyond a doubt therefore I also exist if he deceives me; and let him deceive as much as he can, nevertheless he will never bring it about that I am nothing as long as I shall think myself to be something. Accordingly, with everything above having been sufficiently thought out, it must finally be concluded that this axiom, *I am, I exist,* every time it is pronounced by me, or mentally conceived, necessarily is true.

However I do not yet sufficiently understand what

it is that I may be, I who now necessarily am; and next, care must be taken lest by chance I imprudently take something else in place of myself and thus go astray even as regards that cognition which I contend is the most certain and most evident of all. For this reason I will now ponder anew what I formerly believed myself to be before I had launched on these reflections. Afterward I will remove from this whatever can have been weakened, even in the least degree, by the arguments that have been brought forth; thus, finally, there will remain only what is certain and unshaken.

Accordingly, what did I formerly consider myself to be? Namely this—a man. But what is a man? Shall I say a rational animal? No, because afterward it should have to be determined what "animal" is, what "rational" is, and thus from one question I would have slipped into many others more difficult; moreover, I do not now have so much leisure as to wish to waste it upon subtleties of this kind. Rather I will here direct attention to what formerly occurred spontaneously to my thought each time I considered what I was. First, that I have a face, hands, arms, and this entire contrivance of members such as is discerned in a corpse: and this I called by the name of "body." Furthermore, that I am nourished, that I walk, sense, and think: which actions I indeed referred to the soul. But either I did not notice what this soul was, or I vaguely imagined it as something subtle—resembling wind, fire, or ether—diffused through my more solid parts. As far as the body is concerned, I certainly did not doubt about it, but thought I knew its nature distinctly—a nature that, had perchance I tried to describe it such as I considered it in my mind, I would have explained as follows: by "body" I understand everything capable of being bounded by some shape, circumscribed in some place, and filling a space in such a way as to exclude from it every other body; moreover, it is capable of being perceived by touch, sight, hearing, taste, or smell, and of being moved in many ways, not indeed by itself, but by some other body by which it is touched at any place; for I judged that to have the force of moving itself, and likewise of sensing or thinking, in no way pertains to the nature of body; to be sure I was rather astonished that such faculties are found in certain bodies.

What, however, do I now think myself to be, since I am supposing some very powerful—and if it is not impious to say so—evil deceiver has employed every effort in his power in order to delude me? Can I affirm I have even the least of those things I already said pertain to the nature of body? I consider this matter, think about it, and go over it again—but nothing qualifies. Which of those things I attributed to the soul can I now truly affirm to belong to me? To be nourished or to walk? Since indeed I do not now have a body, these too are only figments [of my imagination]. To sense? To be sure even this does not exist without a body, and I seemed to sense very many things in dreams that I afterward noticed I had not sensed. To think? Here I hit upon it: it is thinking; this alone cannot be separated from me. I am, I exist: it is certain. For how long however? Well, for as long as I think; for perhaps it could even happen that, were I to stop all thinking, I would with that completely cease to be. Now, I admit nothing but what necessarily is true; I am, accordingly, precisely only a thinking thing, that is, a mind, or soul, or intellect, or reason—words whose signification was previously unknown to me. I am however a true thing, and truly existing; but what sort of thing? I have said so—a thinking thing.

What else am I? I will imagine: I am not that network of members called the human body; I am not even some subtle air dispersed through these members, not a wind, nor a fire, nor a vapor, nor an exhalation, nor anything I imagine to myself—for I have supposed all these to be nothing. The situation remains, however, I am nonetheless something. Indeed, perhaps it is the case that all these things that I suppose are nothing because they are unknown to me nevertheless do not really differ from that which I have come to acknowledge as myself. This I do not know, and I am not now disputing about this matter; I can make a judgment only about those things that are known to me. I have come to acknowledge that I exist; I seek to learn what I am—this "I" that I have acknowledged. It is most certain that thus precisely taken, the notion of this "I" does not depend on those things I have not yet recognized to exist; and accordingly it does not depend on any of these things I portray in the imagination. And these words, "I portray," warn me of my error: for I would truly be portraying myself were I to imagine myself to be something, since to imagine is nothing else than to contemplate the shape or image of some bodily thing. However, I now certainly know that I exist and at the same time know it possible that all these images, and generally whatever is related to the nature of body, may be nothing more than dreams. Having noticed all this, I seem no less foolish in saying: I will use my imagination in order to recognize more distinctly what I am, than if I should say: I am now indeed awake and see something of the truth, but because I do not yet see it sufficiently evidently, I will purposefully fall asleep so that dreams may represent it to me more truly and evidently. And so I know that none of those things I can comprehend by the use of the imagination pertain to that notion I have of myself, and I know that my mind must most carefully be called back from those things in order that it may perceive its own nature as distinctly as possible.

But what then am I? A thinking thing. What is that? It is something doubting, understanding, affirming, denying, wishing for, wishing not, imagining as well, and sensing. To be sure, these are not just a few things, if they all pertain to me. But for what reason should they not pertain to me? Am I not the very one who now doubts about nearly everything, who nevertheless understands some things, who affirms this one thing to be true, who denies other things, desires to know many others, is unwilling to be deceived, and who also notices many things as if coming from the senses? Even though I may always be sleeping, or even though he who created me deludes me as much as he can, which of these things is not just as true as that I exist? Which of these things is such as may be distinguished from my thinking? Which of these things is such as can be said to be separated from myself? For that I am the one who doubts, understands, and wills is so manifest that nothing could happen by which it may be explained more evidently. And indeed I am also the same one who imagines; for although perhaps, as I have supposed, none of the things imagined by me are true, nevertheless this very force of imagining truly exists and constitutes a part of my thinking. Finally, I am the same one who senses or notices corporeal things, as it were, through the senses. For it is manifest that I now see light, hear noise, feel heat. Yet these are false, for I am sleeping. But on the other hand, I certainly seem to see, hear, grow warm. This cannot be false; this is what in me is properly called "to sense"; and this, thus precisely taken, is nothing but to think.

From these things I certainly begin to recognize a little better what I am; but it still nevertheless seems, nor can I keep from believing, that corporeal things, whose images are formed in thinking, and which these very senses explore, are much more distinctly recognized than this something I know not what of me that does not come under the imagination: but this would indeed be truly marvelous if things that I recognize are unknown and foreign to myself are comprehended by me more distinctly than what is true, known, or in a few words, more distinctly than my very self. But I see what the problem is: my mind likes to wander and as yet refuses to allow itself to be restrained within the limits of the truth. Very well, let us continue to give it once and for all very free rein, so that somewhat later, having pulled back those reins at the opportune time, the mind will allow itself to be governed more easily.

Let us consider those things ordinarily thought the most distinctly comprehended of all, namely, the bodies we touch and see; not indeed bodies in general, because these general perceptions are usually somewhat more confused, but one body in particular. Let us take as an example this wax: it has been very recently taken from the honeycombs; it has not yet entirely lost the taste of its honey; it retains something of the odor of the flowers from which it has been collected; its color, figure, magnitude, are manifest; it is hard, cold, easily touched, and if you strike it with a finger, it will emit a sound; in short, it has everything that seems required for a particular body to be very distinctly known. But behold, while I am speaking, this wax is moved toward the fire: what remains of its flavor is lost, its odor ceases, its color is changed, its shape is taken away, its size increases, it becomes liquified, hot, scarcely capable of being touched, and now, if you hit upon it, it will not emit a sound. Does not the same wax still remain? It must be admitted that it does remain; nobody denies it, nobody thinks otherwise. Therefore what in the wax was so distinctly comprehended? Certainly none of those things with which I came in contact by the senses; for whatever came under taste, or odor, or sight, or touch has by this time been changed: yet the wax remains.

Perhaps this wax was what I now think: namely, this same wax was never that sweetness of honey, nor that fragrance of flowers, nor that whiteness, nor shape, nor sound; rather it is a body that appeared to me a little beforehand quite obviously in those ways and now appears to me in different ways. However, what exactly is this body that I thus imagine. Let us attend, and having removed those things that do not pertain to the wax, let us see what remains: namely, nothing other than an extended something, flexible, changeable. What truly is this being flexible and changeable? Is it that I imagine this wax can be changed from a round shape into a square shape, or from a square into a triangle? In no way; for I comprehend that this wax is capable of innumerable changes of this kind, and nevertheless I am unable to run through them by imagining them; therefore this comprehension is not entirely carried out by the faculty of imagining. And what is something extended? Isn't its very extension likewise unknown? For in the liquefying wax its extension becomes greater, greater again in the burning wax, and yet still greater if the heat is augmented; and I would not judge correctly what this wax is unless I would think it admits of even more differences in extension than I have ever encompassed by imagining them. Therefore it remains for me to concede that I do not at all imagine what this wax is, but perceive what it is by the mind alone; I speak of this wax in particular; as for wax in general it is even clearer. And what in truth is this wax perceived only by the mind? It is without a doubt the same wax as I see, touch, imagine, and lastly, the same as I thought it to be from the beginning. However, what must be noticed is that the perception of it is not a seeing, tasting, or imagining, and never has been, although previously it seemed so; rather it is an inspection of the mind alone, which can be either imperfect and confused as previously, or clear and distinct as it now is, depending upon whether I attend less or more to those things from which it is composed.

I am truly astonished how, despite all this, my mind is prone toward errors; for although I was silently considering this to myself and without words, I am nevertheless saddled by these very words I am using, and almost deceived by this very manner of speaking. For we say we see this very wax when it is present; we do not say we judge it to be present from its color or shape. Because of this I would have forthwith concluded that therefore the wax is known by the vision of the eye rather than by an inspection of the mind alone—except that by chance I had then turned and glanced from my window upon men passing in the square, men whom it is just as customary for me to say I see as to say I see wax. But nevertheless, what do I see except hats and coats under which there could be automata? But I judge them to be men. And thus what I was supposing I saw with the eyes, I comprehend with the faculty of judging alone, which is in my mind.

But it is shameful that one who aspires to a discernment higher than that of ordinary people has rested his reason for doubt on the forms of speech common people have fallen into. So let us proceed onward in an orderly fashion. Did I more perfectly and evidently perceive what wax is when, in first seeing it, I believed myself to know it either by the external sense of sight, or at least by what they call common sense—that is, by the power of imagining? Or, indeed, is it rather the case that I now perceive more perfectly and evidently what wax is, after I have more diligently investigated both what it is and the manner in which it is known? Certainly it would be silly to hesitate about this matter. For what was distinct in the first perception of the wax? What was included there that, it would have seemed, cannot be had by any animal? On the other hand, indeed, when I distinguish the wax from external forms, and so to speak, by stripping off its garments, consider it naked, that is, as it truly is—when I do this, although there can still be an error in my judgment, nevertheless I cannot perceive it without a human mind.

Now, what shall we say of this very mind, that is, of me myself? For at present I am admitting nothing in me except the mind. What, I ask, am I who seem to perceive this wax so distinctly? Do I not know myself not only much more truly, much more certainly, but also much more distinctly and evidently? For if I judge that wax exists from the fact that I see this, certainly, from the very fact that I see this, it is much more evidently proved that I myself also exist. For it can be that what I am seeing is not truly wax; indeed, it can be that I have no eyes with which to see anything; but it manifestly cannot be that, when I see, or (what I do not now distinguish) when I think I see, this very thinking "I" is not something. By similar reasoning, if I judge that wax exists from the fact that I touch this, it likewise will again be proved that manifestly I exist. If I judge that wax exists from the fact that I imagine it, or from whatever other cause, manifestly the same conclusion follows. And the same thing I notice concerning the wax can also be applied to all the remaining things posited outside me. But furthermore, if the perception of the wax has seemed more distinct after it became known to me, not only by sight or touch alone, but by many other causes, it must be conceded how much more distinctly I myself am now known by myself, since no reasons can assist my perception of the wax, or of any other body, without all these same reasons better proving the nature of my mind! But there are so many other things besides in this very mind from which the notion of it can be rendered more distinct than those things that come to it from the body seem hardly worth enumerating.

And behold, I have finally spontaneously come back to where I wished to be; for since it is now manifest to me that even bodies are not properly perceived by the senses or by the faculty of imagining but by the intellect alone, and since bodies are not perceived because they are touched or seen, but only because they are understood, I manifestly know that I can perceive nothing more easily or evidently than my mind. Yet because the inclination to an old opinion cannot be so readily cast off, it is fitting to halt at this point so that by prolonged meditation this new knowledge may be more deeply ingrained on my memory.

MEDITATION III

Concerning God, That He Exists

I will now close my eyes, stop my ears, call back my senses, and even extinguish from my thinking all images of corporeal things, or because this is hardly possible to do, I will consider these images as empty and false things of no value; and by addressing myself alone, and by examining myself from my most inward depths, I will try to render myself gradually more known and familiar to myself. I am a thinking thing: that is, I am a thing that is doubting, affirming, denying, understanding a few matters, ignorant of many things, wishing for and wishing not, and even imagining and sensing; for as I noted before, although those things I sense or imagine outside me are perhaps nothing, I am nevertheless certain that those modes of thinking I call senses and imaginations are in me insofar as they are only particular modes of thinking.

In these few remarks I have recounted everything I truly know, or at least everything I have thus far noticed that I know. Now I will more diligently seek to find whether there are still other things in me to which I have not as yet attended. I am certain that I am a thinking thing. Do I not therefore also know what is required in order to be certain of something? Undoubtedly in this first cognition it is nothing but the particular clear and distinct perception of what I affirm; but this indeed would not suffice to make me certain of the truth of the matter if it could ever occur that anything I were to perceive just as clearly and distinctly would be false; and accordingly I now seem able to lay down as a general rule that everything is true that I perceive very clearly and distinctly.

But yet I formerly admitted many things as altogether certain and manifest that afterward I nevertheless recognized as doubtful. Well, then, what sorts of things were they? The earth, the heaven, the constellations of stars, and all the other things I appropriated from the senses. What, however, did I clearly perceive about them? That the very ideas of these things, or the thoughts of them, are noticed by my mind. But indeed I do not now deny that these ideas are in me. However, I affirmed something else that, because of my habits of belief, I likewise believed I clearly perceived, although I did not truly perceive it—namely, that certain things exist outside me from which these very ideas proceed, and to which they are similar. And in this either I was deceived, or if I did judge truly, it certainly did not result from the force of my perception.

What then do I perceive to be true? When I considered anything exceedingly simple and easy in regard to arithmetical and geometrical matters, such as that 2 and 3 joined together is 5, or similar things, didn't I at least intuit those things perspicuously enough to affirm them true? Indeed, I afterward judged they should be doubted only because the thought came to my mind that perhaps some God has been able to make my nature such that I would be deceived even about those things that seem most manifest. Every time this preconceived opinion about the very great power of God occurs to me, I cannot but confess that, if he wishes, it is easy for him to bring it about that I err even in the things I consider myself to intuit as evidently as possible with the eyes of the mind. Similarly, every time I turn my attention to those things themselves that I think I perceive very clearly, I am so obviously persuaded by them that I spontaneously break forth saying: let him deceive me who can, nevertheless he will never bring it about that I am nothing as long as I shall think myself to be something; neither will he ever bring it about hereafter that I have never been, since it is now true that I exist; also, he will never bring about that 2 and 3 joined together is more or less than 5, or any similar things—that is, things in which I recognize a manifest contradiction. And certainly, since I have no occasion for thinking there is some deceiving God, and indeed, since I do not as yet well enough know whether there is any God at all, the reason for doubting that depends only on this opinion is certainly tenuous, and such as I may call metaphysical. However, in order now to remove even this reason for doubting, as soon as the first opportunity arises I ought to examine whether there is a God, and if there is one, whether he can be a deceiver; for as long as this is unknown, I seem unable ever to be manifestly certain about any other thing.

Now, indeed, order seems to require that I shall first distribute all my thoughts into certain kinds and inquire in which of these kinds truth or falsity resides. Certain of these thoughts are, as it were, images of things, and to these alone the name of "idea" accurately applies: as when I think of a man, or of a Chimera, or heaven, or an angel, or of God. To be sure, other thoughts have particular forms beyond this: thus when I will, fear, affirm, deny, I always do indeed apprehend something as the subject of my thinking, but I also include in my thinking something more than the similitude of this very subject; and as regards these other things included in such thinking, some of them are named volitions or affections; others, however, are called judgments.

Now, as far as ideas are concerned, if they are regarded alone and in themselves, and if I do not refer them to anything else, they cannot properly [speaking] be false; for whether I imagine a she goat or a Chimera, it is no less true that I imagine the one rather than the other. Also, falsity is not to be feared in willing itself or in the affections; for although I can wish for bad things, and even for things that never exist, it is nevertheless still true that I wish for them. And accordingly only judgments remain, and in these care must be taken so that I am not deceived. Moreover, the principal and most frequent error that can be found in them consists in the fact that I judge the ideas in me are similar to, or conform to, certain things situated outside me; for certainly were I to consider these very ideas only as particular modes of my thinking, and not refer them to any other thing, they could scarcely provide any matter for error.

Furthermore, among these ideas some seem innate, some seem adventitious, and some seem made by me myself: for I seem to obtain my understanding of what a thing is, what truth is, and what thinking is from no other source than my very nature; moreover, until this time I have judged that the noise I now hear, the sun I see, the fire I feel, proceed from particular things situated outside me; finally, until this time I judged that Sirens, Hippogriffs, and similar things are formed by me. I am able to suspect that perhaps these ideas are all adventitious, or all innate, or all made by me: for I have not yet clearly seen through to their true origin.

But here I must principally inquire what particular reason leads me to suppose that the ideas I consider taken from things existing outside me are similar to those things. Certainly, nature seems to teach me so. And besides, I experience that they do not depend upon my willing, and thus not upon my own self; for often these ideas are present when unwanted—just as now, whether I will it or will the opposite, I still feel heat and therefore suspect that this feeling, or the idea of heat, comes to me from something different from myself, namely, from the heat of the fire near which I am sitting. And nothing is more obvious than for me to judge that this thing sends into me its likeness rather than something else.

I will now see whether these reasonings are sufficiently firm. When just above I say I am taught so by nature, I understand only that I feel moved to believe this by some spontaneous impulse, not that some natural light shows me it is true. These two things greatly differ; for whatever the natural light shows me—for example, that from the fact that I doubt, it follows that I exist, and similar things—can in no way be dubious; for there is no other faculty so trustworthy as this natural light that can teach me that the things shown me by it are not true; but as for natural impulses, I have already often judged that I was pushed by them in the worse direction when it was a question of choosing the good, and I do not see why I may place more trust in them as regards any other matter.

Next, although these ideas do not depend upon my willing, it is not therefore established that they necessarily proceed from things situated outside me: for those impulses about which I was just speaking, although they are in me, nevertheless seem different from my will; so too, perhaps some other faculty, not yet sufficiently known, is also in me and produces these ideas, in the same way as up until this time it has always seemed that while I sleep ideas are formed in me without any need of external things.

And lastly, even if they were to proceed from things different from myself, it does not thereby follow that they must be similar to those things. On the contrary, I seem to have often noticed a great crucial difference in many cases. For example, I find in myself two different ideas of the sun: one idea has, as it were, been drawn from the senses, and I judge that it must by all means be included among those ideas that are adventitious, and through it the sun appears to me to be very small; the other idea is certainly derived from the reasonings of astronomy—that is, elicited from certain notions innate in me or made in some other way—and through it the sun is represented to be several times larger than the earth. Undoubtedly both these ideas cannot be similar to the same sun existing outside me, and reason persuades me that the former idea, which seems to have most closely originated from the sun, is most dissimilar to it.

All these things sufficiently demonstrate that up until now it has not been out of a judgment that is certain, but merely from some blind impulse, that I believed in the existence of particular things different from myself that send me into their ideas, or images, through the organs of the senses or by whatever other means it be.

But it occurs to me there is yet another particular way of inquiring whether any of those things whose ideas are in me exist outside me. To be sure, inasmuch as these ideas are only particular modes of thinking, I recognize no inequality among them, and they all seem to proceed from me in the same manner; but insofar as one idea represents one thing and another idea represents something else, it is manifest that they are indeed different from each other. Beyond a doubt, those ideas that represent substances to me are something greater, and as I may say, contain in themselves more objective reality than those representing only modes or accidents; and furthermore that idea through which I understand a supreme God—eternal, infinite, omniscient, omnipotent, and creator of all things other than himself—certainly has in it more objective reality than those through which finite substances are represented.

Now, it is truly manifest by the natural light that at least as much [reality] must be in the efficient and total cause as is in the effect of this same cause. For, I ask, whence could the effect receive its reality if not from the cause? And how could the cause give this reality to the effect unless it has it? Moreover, from this it follows that it is impossible both that anything come from nothing and also that what is more perfect—that is, what contains more reality in itself—come from what contains less reality in itself. And this is not only perspicuously true of those effects whose reality is actual or formal, but also of ideas in which objective reality only is considered. To take some examples, not only is it impossible for a stone that had not previously existed to now begin to exist, unless it is produced by something in which there exists either formally or eminently everything posited in the stone; or for heat to be produced in a subject previously not warm; and so forth; but furthermore, it is also impossible that the idea of heat or the idea of a stone exist in me, unless it is placed in me by some cause in which there is at least as much reality as I conceive in heat or a stone. For although that particular cause transfers nothing of its actual or formal reality into my idea, I should not on that account suppose it is a less real cause, but only that the nature of this idea is such that of itself it requires no other formal reality beyond that which it borrows from my thinking, of which it is a mode. But now, the fact that an idea contains this or that objective reality rather than some other must indeed be due to some cause in which there is at least as much of formal reality as the idea itself has of objective reality. For if we suppose that anything is to be discovered in the idea that did not exist in the cause of the idea, this thing accordingly derives from nothing; but now, however imperfect this manner of being by which a thing is objectively in the intellect by means of an idea, it nevertheless indeed is manifestly not nothing. Also, I should not suspect that, because the reality I consider in my ideas is only objective, this same reality need not exist formally in the causes of these ideas, but that it suffices if it is also objectively in them. For just as this objective mode of being belongs to ideas from their own nature, so also the formal mode of being belongs to the causes of ideas from their very nature, or at least to the first and principal causes. And although perhaps one idea can be born from another, nevertheless an infinite regress is not allowed here; rather I must finally come to some first idea whose cause is like an archetype, which contains formally all the reality that is in the idea only objectively. Thus it is perspicuous to me by the natural light that the ideas in me are, as it were, particular images, which can indeed easily fall short of the perfection of the things from which they are taken, but cannot, however, contain anything at all that is greater or more perfect.

The longer and more painstakingly I examine all these things, so much the more clearly and more distinctly do I know that they are true. But what then should I finally conclude from them? Namely this: if the objective reality of some one of my ideas is so great that I am certain the same reality is not in me either formally or eminently, and consequently that it is impossible that I myself am the cause of this idea, then it necessarily follows that I do not exist alone in the world but that some other thing, which is the cause of this particular idea, also exists. If indeed no such idea shall be found within me, then I will manifestly have no argument that renders me certain concerning the existence of anything different from myself; for I have most diligently inquired into every other kind of argument, and until this day have been unable to find any other.

Now, of my ideas, beyond that which represents my own self to me—about which there can be no difficulty here—one idea represents God, others represent things corporeal and inanimate, others represent angels, others represent animals, and finally, others represent men similar to myself.

And as for ideas representing other men, or animals, or angels, I easily understand that they can be composed from those I have of my own self and corporeal things—even if there were no other men but me, nor animals, nor angels, in the world.

Moreover, as regards the ideas of corporeal things, nothing occurs in them so great that it seems it could not have originated from my own self. For if I consider them more thoroughly and examine them individually in the way I examined the idea of the wax yesterday, I notice there are but very few things in them that I perceive clearly and distinctly: namely, magnitude, or extension in length, breadth, and depth; shape, which arises from the fixing of a boundary of this same extension; position, which the diversely shaped bodies possess in relation to one another; and motion, or the change of this position; to which can be added substance, duration, and number. The other things, such as light and colors, sounds, odors, flavors, heat, and cold, as well as the other tactile qualities, are thought of by me only very confusedly and obscurely, so that I also do not know whether they are true or false, that is, whether the ideas I have of them are ideas of particular things or not ideas of things. For as I noted a little way back, although falsity properly so-called—that is, formal falsity—can be found only in judgments, nevertheless there is indeed a certain other material falsity in ideas when they represent what is not a thing as though it is a thing: thus the ideas I have of heat and cold are so little clear and distinct that I cannot say regarding them whether cold is only a privation of heat, or whether it is a real quality, or neither. And since there can be no ideas unless they are, as it were, of things, if it be true the cold is nothing other than the privation of heat, the idea that represents it to me as something real and positive is not unreasonably called false, and so too with the other ideas—that is, the ideas of light, colors, sounds, and so on.

With these things established, I need not assign these ideas of heat, light, colors, and so on, any author different from myself: for if they are indeed false, that is, if they represent no things, it is known to me by the natural light that they proceed from nothing—that is, they are in me only because something is lacking in my nature or because my nature is not manifestly perfect; if, however, they are true, nevertheless, since they display to me so little reality that I cannot distinguish that little amount of reality from what is not a thing, I do not see why they cannot be from my own self.

To be sure, as regards those things that are clear and distinct in the ideas of corporeal things, I seem able to have borrowed certain of them from the idea of my own self, namely, the ideas of substance, duration, number, and whatever else is of this sort: for when I think that a stone is a substance, or a thing suited to exist through itself, and when I likewise think that I am a substance—despite the fact that I conceive myself as a thinking and nonextended thing, and certainly conceive a stone as an extended and nonthinking thing, so that the greatest diversity is conceived between both of them—both nevertheless seem to accord as regards the aspect of substance; and in a corresponding way, when I perceive that I exist now and recall that I have also existed for some period of time beforehand, and when I have various thoughts whose number I understand, I acquire the ideas of duration and number, which I can then transfer from this source to various and sundry things. However, all the other things from which the ideas of corporeal things are composed—namely, extension, shape, position, and motion—are certainly not contained in me formally, since I am nothing but a thinking thing; yet because they are only particular modes of a substance, and I also am a substance, they seem able to be contained in me eminently.

And so the idea of God alone remains, and I must consider whether there is anything in it that could not have proceeded from my very self. By the name of God I understand a particular infinite, independent, omniscient, omnipotent substance by whom not only I myself, but also every other thing of whatever sort, if any other thing does exist, is created. Undoubtedly, all these things are such that, the more diligently I consider them, the less they seem able to originate from me alone. Accordingly, from what has been said above it must be concluded that God necessarily exists.

Indeed, although the idea of a substance is in me from this very fact that I am a substance, nevertheless, since I am finite, the idea of an infinite substance would not therefore have been in me unless it proceeded from some substance that really is infinite.

I should not suppose that I do not perceive infinity by a true idea, but merely by negation of the finite, in the way that I perceive rest and darkness by the negation of motion and of light; for, on the contrary, I manifestly understand that there is more reality in infinite substance than in finite substance, and hence that the perception of the infinite is somehow prior in me to that of the finite—that is, the perception of God is in some way prior to the perception of my very self. For by what standard would I understand that I doubt, that I desire—that is, that something is lacking to me and that I am not altogether perfect—unless there were in me the idea of a more perfect being by comparison with which I recognized my defects?

Neither can it be said that this idea is perhaps materially false, and therefore can be from nothing, as I noted a little way back in regard to the ideas of heat and cold; for, on the contrary, since this idea is the most clear and distinct, and since it contains more objective reality than any other idea, no idea is in itself more true or less suspect of falsity. I say that this idea of the most perfect and infinite being is most true; for although it can perhaps be supposed that such a being does not exist, nevertheless it cannot be supposed that the idea of it displays nothing real to me, as I previously said concerning the idea of cold. For it is most clear and distinct; indeed, whatever I clearly and distinctly perceive, because it is real and true, and because it involves some perfection, is totally contained in it. None of this is impugned either by the fact that I do not comprehend infinity or because there are innumerable other things in God that I can in no way comprehend, or perhaps even approach by thinking; for it is the character of infinity that it is not comprehended by me who am finite; and it suffices that I understand this very fact and judge that all those things that I clearly perceive and know to involve some perfections, and also perhaps innumerable other things of which I am ignorant, are either in God formally or eminently, so that the idea I have of him is the most true, and most clear and distinct, of all the ideas in me.

But perhaps I am something greater than I myself understand, and perhaps all those perfections I attribute to God are in a certain manner in me by means of a power, even if they do not as yet reveal themselves or are not as yet reduced to act. For I now experience that my knowledge is gradually increased; neither do I see anything to prevent my knowledge, starting from less, from thus being more and more increased to infinity; nor do I see any reason why, with my thinking thus increased, I could not by means of it reach all the remaining perfections of God; finally, I do not see why the power for such perfections, if it is already in me, may not suffice to produce the idea of those perfections.

But, on the contrary, none of these things is possible. Firstly, although it is true that my knowledge is gradually increased and that many things are in me potentially that are not yet in act, nevertheless none of these things pertains to the idea of God, in which, namely, nothing at all is potential; for this very fact—that my knowledge is gradually increased—is a very certain proof of my imperfection. Furthermore, even if my knowledge is always more and more increased, nonetheless I understand that it will never therefore be infinite in act, because it will never arrive at a point such that it is not still capable of an increment; however, I judge God to be infinite in act in such a way that nothing can be added to his perfection. And finally, I perceive that the objective being of an idea cannot be produced from a mere potential being, which, properly speaking, is nothing, but only by an actual or formal being.

There is certainly nothing in all this that is not manifest by the natural light to one exercising diligent attention; but because when I am less attentive and the images of sensible things blind the sharp vision of my mind, it is not so easy for me to recall why the idea of an entity more perfect than myself necessarily proceeds from some being that really is more perfect, it is desirable to inquire further whether I myself could exist having this idea if no such being were to exist.

Indeed, where would I be from? Undoubtedly, either from myself, or from parents, or from sundry other things less perfect than God; for it is impossible to think of anything more perfect than God, or even equally perfect.

And yet were I to be from myself, I would neither doubt nor desire, nor would anything at all be lacking to me. I would also have given myself all the perfections of which I had any idea, and so I myself would be God. Neither ought I to suppose that perhaps those perfections that are lacking to me can be acquired with more difficulty than those already in me; for, on the contrary, it is manifest that it would have been far more difficult for me, that is, for a thinking thing or substance, to emerge from nothing than to acquire the cognitions of many things of which I am now ignorant—cognitions that are only accidents of this substance. And certainly, if of my own accord I might have what is greater, I would not have denied myself what is more easily had, and moreover, I would not in the least have denied myself any of those other things I perceive to be contained in the idea of God; and this is so because none of them seems to me more difficult to bring about; and were they more difficult to bring about, then assuming I were to have the perfections I do have from myself, they certainly would also seem so to me—for then I would experience my power to be limited by them.

Neither do I escape the force of these reasonings if I suppose that perhaps I have always been as I now am, as though it would follow from that that no author of my existence need be sought after. For since all the time of my life can be divided into innumerable parts, each of which in no way depends on the others, from the fact that I had existed a little beforehand, it does not follow that I must now exist, unless some cause creates me, as it were, anew at this moment—that is, unless some cause conserves me. For it is perspicuous to one who is attending to the nature of time that manifestly the same force and action is required to conserve any particular thing whatever in the single moments in which it lasts as would be required to create that thing de novo were it not yet to exist; thus one of the things manifest by the natural light is that conservation differs from creation only as regards our viewpoint.

Accordingly, I should now inquire as regards my own self, whether I have some force by which I can bring it about that this "I" who now exists will also exist a little afterward in the future: for since I am nothing but a thinking thing, or at least since I am now concerned only with precisely that part of myself that is a thinking thing, were such a force in me, I would undoubtedly be conscious of it. But I experience no such force, and from this very fact I know most evidently that I depend upon another entity different from myself.

Perhaps this being is not God, and I am produced either from parents or some other cause less perfect than God. On the contrary, as I already said before, it is perspicuous that there ought to be at least as much [reality] in the cause as in the effect; and therefore, since I am a thinking thing having in me a particular idea of God, whatever the cause finally assigned to me, it must be admitted that it too is a thinking thing having an idea of all the perfections I attribute to God. It is again possible to investigate whether that cause is from itself or from another. For if it is from itself, it is manifest from what has been said that it is God, because since it has a force of existing through itself, it undoubtedly also has a force of possessing in act all the perfections of which it has an idea in itself—that is, all the perfections I conceive to be in God. If, however, it is from another, in the same way it again may be asked of this latter whether it is from itself or from another, until finally the ultimate cause, which will be God, is reached.

For it is sufficiently apparent that there can be no progressing to infinity in this matter, particularly since I am here concerned not only with the cause that formerly produced me, but most especially also with the cause that conserves me at the present time.

Neither can it be supposed that many partial causes have come together with the result of producing me, and that I have received from one of these causes the idea of one of the perfections I attribute to God, and from another the idea of another perfection attributed to God, so that all the perfections are indeed found somewhere in the universe, but are not all joined together in any one thing that is God. On the contrary, the unity, simplicity, or inseparability of all the perfections in God is one of the principal perfections I understand to be in him. And certainly the idea of the unity of all of these perfections of his could not be placed in me by any cause from which I did not also have the ideas of the other perfections: for no cause could have brought it about that I would understand them to be joined together and inseparable unless it at the same time brought it about that I would recognize which perfections they were.

Finally, as regards my parents, if everything I every thought about them were true, nevertheless they certainly do not conserve me, nor have they in any way produced me insofar as I am a thinking thing; rather they have merely placed arrangements in that matter to which I—that is, the mind, which I now alone accept as myself—have judged myself to belong. Accordingly, there can be no difficulty here concerning them; rather it is by all means to be concluded that, from the mere fact that I exist and that the idea of a most perfect being, that is, of God, is in me, God's existence is also most evidently demonstrated.

It remains only for me to examine the way in which I received this idea of God; for I have not drawn it from the senses, nor does it ever come to me when I am not seeking for it, as the ideas of sensible things are wont to do when these things are present to the external organs of the senses, or seem present; also, neither has this idea of God been put together by me, for I am manifestly unable to take anything away from it or to add anything to it; consequently, it remains that the idea of God is innate in me, in the manner in which the idea of my own self is also innate in me.

And truly it is not astonishing that God, in creating me, has placed that idea in me, so that it would be, as it were, the sign of the craftsman impressed upon his work. And neither is it necessary that this sign be something different from his very work. Rather, from the mere fact that God created me, it is exceedingly credible that I have been made in some way to his image and likeness, and that this likeness to God, which involves the fact that I have the idea of him, is perceived by me through the same faculty through which I myself am perceived by myself: that is, when I turn the sharp vision of my mind upon my own self, I do not merely understand that I am an incomplete thing who is dependent upon another and who indefinitely aspires to greater and greater or better and better things; but also, at the same time I understand that he upon whom I depend has in himself all those greater perfections, not indefinitely and merely potentially, but rather has each perfection infinitely and thus is God. And the entire force of the argument lies here: I recognize that it is not possible for me to exist constituted of such a nature as I have, namely, having the idea of God in me, unless there also exists in reality the God whose idea is in me—that is, God manifestly subject to no defects, and having all those perfections that I am not able to comprehend, but can only to some extent approach by thinking. From these perfections of God it is sufficiently manifest that he cannot be deceitful; for it is manifest by the natural light that all fraud and deception depends on some defect.

But before I examine this more diligently and at the same time inquire into other truths that can be gathered from it, it is edifying to rest here for some time in the contemplation of this God, to ponder his attributes, and as far as the vision of my dull wits permits me to endure, to intuit, admire, and adore the beauty of his immense light. For as we believe by faith that the greatest happiness of the next life consists solely in the contemplation of the divine majesty, so even now, although much less perfectly, we experience that in this same contemplation can be perceived the greatest delight of which we are capable in this life.

MEDITATION IV

On the True and the False

During these days I have so accustomed myself to leading my mind away from the senses, and I have so carefully noticed that very little is truly perceived concerning material things, and that much more is known concerning the human mind, and more still concerning God, that now, without any difficulty, I turn my thought from imaginable to solely intelligible things separated from all matter. And indeed I have an idea of the human mind insofar as it is a thinking thing not extended in length, breadth, and depth, nor having anything else that pertains to body; and this idea is much more distinct than my ideas of any corporeal thing. And when I consider that I doubt, or that I am an incomplete and dependent thing, so much the more clear and distinct an idea of an independent and complete entity, that is, of God, also presents itself to me; and from this one thing, that such an idea is in me, or that I exist having that idea, I so much the more manifestly conclude that God also exists, and that my entire existence depends on him at every moment, that I am firmly assured that nothing more evident, nothing more certain, can be known by human wits. And already I seem to see another way through which, by contemplating the true God in whom lies hidden all the treasures of the sciences and of wisdom, to reach a cognition of other things.

First, to be sure, I recognize that it is impossible for him ever to deceive me; for in all deceit or deception some imperfection is found; and although to be able to deceive seems some proof of shrewdness or power, undoubtedly to wish to deceive attests to either ill will or weakness, and hence does not accord with God.

Next I experience that there is in me a particular faculty of judging, which I certainly received from God, just as I received from him everything else that is in me; and since he does not wish to deceive me, he assuredly bestowed this faculty upon me in such a way that when I use it rightly I can never err.

Nothing doubtful would remain regarding this matter if it did not seem that as a consequence I could never err; for if everything in me is from God, and he has not given me any faculty of erring, it seems I can never err. And so, in short, as long as I think only of God and totally turn my attention to him alone, I discover no cause of error or falsity; but afterward, having turned my attention back upon myself, I experience that I am nevertheless subject to innumerable errors. Inquiring into the cause of these errors, I notice that there is present to me not only the real and positive idea of God, or of a most perfect being, but also a certain negative idea, as I may say, of nothing, or of that which is furthest removed from all perfection. Moreover, I notice that I am placed, as it were, as something between God and nothing, or between the greatest being and nonbeing; so that, to the extent that I am created by the greatest being, there is indeed nothing in me through which I will be deceived or led into error; but inasmuch as I participate in some manner in nothingness or in nonbeing, that is, inasmuch as I am not this same highest being, and so very many things are lacking to me, it is not so astonishing that I will be deceived. And thus I certainly understand that error, inasmuch as it is error, is not something real that depends upon God but is rather only a defect; accordingly my errors do not require any faculty given by God for that purpose; rather I err because the faculty of judging the truth that I have from God is not infinite in me.

Nonetheless, this is not yet entirely satisfactory; for error is not a pure negation, but rather a privation or the absence of such cognitions as ought in some manner to have been in me; and to one attending to the nature of God, it does not seem possible that he has placed any faculty in me that is not perfect in its kind or that is deprived of any perfection owed to it. For if the more expert the artisan, the more perfect the works produced by him, what can that most great builder of all things make that is not perfect at every level? There is no doubt that God was able to create me such that I would never err; moreover, there is no doubt that he always wishes what is best. Is it therefore better that I am deceived rather than not?

While I ponder this matter more attentively, it occurs to me that first of all it is not astonishing if God had certain reasons that I do not understand; thus, because I will perhaps find some other things that I do not comprehend as to why or how God has made them, God's existence must not therefore be doubted. I already know my nature is very weak and limited, and that by contrast the nature of God is immense, incomprehensible, infinite; moreover, from this very fact I also sufficiently well know that God can do innumerable things, the causes of which I am ignorant; and because of this single reason, I consider that the entire genus of causes customarily taken from the end have no use in the matters of physics; for it would be rash of me to think I can investigate the ends of God.

It also occurs to me that we should regard not any one creature separately, but the entire universe of things, each time we inquire whether the works of God are perfect; for a single creature, were it alone in the universe, thus holding the place of the most perfect thing in the world, would perhaps quite justifiably seem exceedingly imperfect; and although, from the fact that I wished to doubt everything, I have as yet come to know the existence of nothing except myself and God, nevertheless, from the fact that I have noticed the immense power of God, I cannot deny that many other things have been made by him, or at least can be made by him, so that I hold but the place of a part in a universe of things.

Next, focusing in upon myself more particularly, and investigating the character of my errors (which alone provide evidence of any imperfection in me), I notice that these errors depend upon the simultaneous concurrence of two causes, namely, upon the faculty of knowing that is in me, and upon the faculty of willing, or the liberty of deciding—that is, upon the intellect together with the will. To be sure, through the intellect itself I perceive only ideas concerning which I can make a judgment, and when the intellect is precisely regarded in this way, no error can be found in it: for although perhaps innumerable things exist of which there are no ideas in me, nevertheless I am not properly called deprived of them, but rather it ought to be said, in the sense of negation only, that I am without them. This is because I can bring forward no reason by which I may prove that God ought to have given me a greater faculty of knowing than he has given me; and although I understand the craftsman is accomplished, I nevertheless do not on that account think he ought to have placed in each of his works all the perfections he can place in the others. Indeed, I also cannot question why the will, or liberty of deciding, that I received from God is not sufficiently ample and perfect; for I certainly experience that it is circumscribed within no limits. Moreover, what seems to me should very much be noted is that none of the other things in me are so perfect or great that I do not understand that there can exist the still more perfect or the greater. As an example, if I consider the faculty of understanding, I immediately recognize that in me it is very small and exceedingly finite, and at the same time I form the idea of some other much greater faculty of understanding, which by all means is the greatest and infinite; and from this very fact that I can form the idea of it, I perceive that it pertains to the nature of God. By the same reasoning, if I examine the faculty of remembering or imagining or any other, I manifestly discover none that I do not understand to be weak and circumscribed in me but immense in God. It is the will alone, or the liberty of deciding, that I experience to be so great in me that I do not apprehend an idea of any greater faculty of its kind; and so it is principally as regards will that I understand that I am an image and likeness of God. For although the will is greater beyond comparison in God than in me, both because of the knowledge and power joined to it, thus rendering it more firm and efficacious, and also because of its object, since God's will extends itself to more things; nevertheless, in itself, and formally and precisely regarded, God's will does not seem greater than mine; for the will consists only in the fact that we can either do or not do the same thing (that is, we can affirm or deny, pursue or avoid), or better still, the will consists only in that we bear ourselves in such a way toward whatever our intellect proposes ought to be affirmed or denied, or pursued or avoided, that we do not feel determined to it by any external force. Moreover, in order to be free, it is not necessary that I can bear myself to either alternative; on the contrary, the more I am inclined toward one alternative, either because I evidently understand the basis of truth and good in it, or because God so disposes the inmost aspects of my thinking toward it, so much the more freely do I choose that alternative. For assuredly divine grace and natural cognition never diminish liberty, but rather augment and strengthen it. On the contrary, that indifference I experience when no reason urges me toward one alternative more than another is the lowest grade of liberty and testifies to no perfection in the will, but merely to a defect in knowledge or some negation thereof; for were I always to see clearly what is true and good, I would never deliberate concerning what ought to be judged or chosen, and so, although I manifestly would be free, nevertheless I could never be indifferent.

Now, from these things I perceive, firstly, that the force of willing that I have from God, regarded in itself, is not the cause of my errors, for it is most ample and perfect in its kind; secondly, that the force of understanding, regarded in itself, is not the cause of my errors, for whatever I understand, my understanding of it derives from God, so that, beyond any doubt, I rightly understand it, and it is impossible that I am deceived about it. Whence then do my errors take their birth? From this one thing, that since the will extends more widely than the intellect, I do not contain the will within the limits of the intellect, but also extend it to those things I do not understand; since the will is indifferent in respect to these latter things, it easily turns aside from the true and the good, and so I make mistakes and I sin.

For example, when I examined during these days whether anything existed in the world and noticed that, from the very fact I was examining this, it evidently followed that I myself exist, I was indeed unable not to judge as true what I was so clearly understanding; not because I had been forced to judge this by any external force, but because, in conformity with the great light in the intellect, there arose a great propensity in the will; hence the less I was indifferent about this, the more spontaneously and freely I believed it. Now, however, not merely do I know that I exist insofar as I am a thinking thing, but furthermore the idea of a certain corporeal nature is presented to me, and it happens that I doubt whether the thinking nature that is in me, or better, that I myself am, is different from this very corporeal nature, or whether both are the same; and I suppose that no reason as yet presents itself to my intellect that persuades me of the one more than the other. Certainly, from this very fact I am indifferent as to which of the two ought to be affirmed or denied, or even as to whether nothing ought to be judged concerning the matter.

Also, this indifference extends not only to those things about which the intellect knows nothing manifestly, but to all those things that are not known by the intellect with sufficient perspicuity at the very time at which the will deliberates about them: for however probable the conjectures that draw me to one alternative, the mere cognition that they are only conjectures, but not certain and indubitable reasons, suffices to urge my assent toward the contrary. This I have experienced well enough during these days, when, because of the single fact that I had discerned they can in some way be doubted, I supposed false all those things I previously believed most true.

Moreover, if I do indeed abstain from casting a judgment when I do not perceive the truth sufficiently clearly and distinctly, it is clear that I act rightly, and am not deceived. But if I affirm or deny, then I do not correctly use the liberty of deciding; and if I turn myself toward that alternative which is false, I obviously will be deceived; if, however, I embrace the other alternative, I will as a matter of chance fall upon the truth, but I shall not therefore avoid blame, because it is manifest by the natural light that the perception of the intellect should always precede the determination of the will. It is in this incorrect use of the liberty of deciding that there arises that privation which constitutes the form of error: I say the privation arises from this operation insofar as the operation proceeds from me, but not that the privation inheres in the faculty that I have received from God, nor even in the operation insofar as the operation depends on him.

Moreover, I have no reason to complain that God bestowed upon me a will that extends more widely than my intellect; for since the will consists in one thing only—and is, as it were, indivisible—its nature does not seem to allow that anything can be removed from it; and to be sure, the more ample it is, so much the more ought I to give thanks to him who has bestowed it upon me.

Finally, neither ought I to complain that God concurs with me in bringing forth those acts of the will or those judgments in which I am deceived: for those acts are altogether true and good insofar as they depend upon God, and it is somehow a greater perfection in me that I can bring them forth than if I could not do so. Moreover, this privation in which the formal reason of falsity and blame alone consists does not need the concurrence of God, because it is not a thing, and it should not be said to be related to God as to its cause; rather it should be said to be only a negation. For, to be sure, it is not an imperfection in God that he has given me the liberty of assenting or of not assenting to particular things of which he has not placed in my intellect a clear and distinct perception; but undoubtedly it is an imperfection in me if I do not use this very liberty well, and cast a judgment about things I do not rightly understand. Nevertheless, I see that God could easily have arranged things so that even though I remained free and of limited knowledge I would never err; he could have arranged it so that I would never come to deliberate about any matter concerning which he had not endowed my intellect with a clear and distinct perception, or he might simply have impressed on my memory, in a way I could not forget it, that I should make no judgment about anything I do not clearly and distinctly perceive. And I easily understand that, had God made me in this way, then, considering myself as the whole, I would have come to be more perfect than I now am. But I cannot on that account deny that there is greater perfection in a universe of things when, rather than having all its parts manifestly similar, some of them are pervious to error, and others not at all. And I have no right to complain because God wished me to bear a role in the world that is neither the foremost nor most perfect.

And furthermore, although I am as yet unable to avoid errors in that first way, which requires an evident perception of all those things about which deliberation ought to take place, I can nevertheless avoid errors in the other way, which requires only that I remember that judgment is to be withheld each time the truth of a matter does not shine forth; for although I experience that I am so weak as not always to be able to remain fixed upon one and the same cognition, nevertheless I can bring it about, by an attentive and more frequently repeated meditation, that I will remember this rule each time practice demands it, and thus I will acquire a definite habit of avoiding error.

And as the greatest and foremost perfection of man consists in avoiding error, I consider today's meditation of no little worth, since I was searching for the cause of error and falsity. And certainly, that cause can be nothing else but what I have explained; for every time I so restrain my will in casting judgments that it extends itself only to those things clearly and distinctly displayed to it by the intellect, it is manifestly impossible for me to err, because every clear and distinct perception is undoubtedly something, and accordingly cannot be from nothing, but rather necessarily has God as its author—God, I say, who is most perfect and whose nature it contradicts to be a deceiver; hence every clear and distinct perception is true. Moreover, I did not learn today only what I must avoid in order never to be deceived, but at the same time I also learned what must be done in order for me to arrive at truth; for I will undoubtedly arrive at truth if only I will sufficiently attend to all those things I perfectly understand, and separate them from the remaining things that I apprehend with more confusion and obscurity. And I shall diligently devote my efforts to this tomorrow.

MEDITATION V

On the Essence of Material Things; and for a Second Time, of God, That He Exists

Many things remain for me to investigate concerning the attributes of God and concerning my own self, or the nature of my mind. Perhaps I will take these matters up at another time. But since I have already noticed what I must guard against and what I have to do in order to reach the truth, nothing seems more urgent now than to attempt to emerge from the doubts I have fallen into during the past days and to see whether anything certain can be established about material things.

And indeed before inquiring whether any material things exist outside me, I should attend to the ideas of them insofar as they are in my thinking, and I should see just which of them are distinct and which confused.

Certainly I distinctly imagine the quantity the philosophers commonly call continuous, or the extension in length, breadth, and depth of this quantity—or better still, of the thing having the quantity. I number various parts in it. I assign arbitrary magnitudes, shapes, positions, and local motions to these parts. And to these motions I assign arbitrary durations.

These things are not only manifestly known by me and perspicuous to me when they are thus generally regarded, but furthermore, in giving my attention to them, I perceive innumerable particulars regarding shapes, number, motion, and similar things, the truth of which is so obvious and so consonant with my nature that, although I am unveiling them for the first time, I do not so much seem to be learning anything new as to be remembering things I previously knew; or I seem for the first time to be taking notice of things that indeed were formerly in me, although I had not previously turned the gaze of my mind toward them.

What I think deserves the greatest consideration at this point is the following: namely, I find in myself innumerable ideas of particular things that, even if they perhaps exist nowhere outside me, nevertheless cannot be said to be nothing; and although in a certain manner they are thought of by me at my deciding, nevertheless they are not fashioned by me, but rather have their true and immutable natures. So that when, for example, I imagine a triangle, even if perhaps no such figure exists anywhere outside anyone's mind, nor ever will, there nevertheless undoubtedly exists its particular nature, or essence, or immutable and eternal form, which is not fashioned by me or dependent upon my mind. This is manifest as follows: various properties of this same triangle can be demonstrated—for example, its three angles are equal to two right angles, its largest side is subtended by its greatest angle; moreover, whether I wish it or not, I now clearly recognize these properties even though I had not in any way previously thought of them when I imagined the triangle. Therefore they have not been fashioned by me.

This conclusion is not affected if I say that, since I have occasionally seen bodies having a triangular shape, this idea of the triangle has perhaps come to me from external things through the organs of the senses; for I can also come to think of innumerable other shapes about which there can be no suspicion that they have entered into me through the senses, and nevertheless I can demonstrate various properties of them no less than of the triangle. And these indeed are all true, since they are certainly clearly known by me; accordingly, they are something, and not merely nothing: for it is manifest that everything that is true is something, and I have already demonstrated at length that everything is true that I know clearly. And even if I had not demonstrated it, nonetheless it certainly is the nature of my mind that I could not withhold assent from these things, at least as long as I perceive them clearly; and I recall that even before now, when I was attached as much as possible to the objects of the senses, I had always received truths of this kind—that is, truths that I recognized evidently concerning shapes, numbers, or other things pertaining to arithmetic, or geometry, or generally, to pure and abstract mathematics—as the most certain of all truths.

And indeed, if from the mere fact that I can draw forth the idea of anything from my thinking, it follows that all those things that I clearly and distinctly perceive to pertain to that thing truly do pertain to it, can I not also establish on that basis an argument by which God's existence may be proved? And it is certain that, no less than the idea of various figures or numbers, I also find in myself the idea of God, that is, the idea of the most perfect being; and moreover, I no less clearly perceive that it pertains to God's nature always to exist than that whatever I demonstrate concerning some figure or number also pertains to the nature of that figure or number; and accordingly, even if not everything I have thought out during these past days were true, still the existence of God should hold at least the same degree of certainty with me as had mathematical truths up until this time.

To be sure, on first appearance this is not altogether perspicuous, but it bears a certain likeness to sophisms. For since I am accustomed to distinguish essence from existence in other things, I easily persuade myself that existence can also be disjoined from the essence of God, and thus that God can be thought of as not existing. But, to one attending more diligently, it nevertheless becomes manifest that existence can no more be separated from the essence of God than the equality of its three angles to two right angles from the essence of some triangle, or the idea of a valley from the idea of a mountain: and so it becomes manifest that it is no less contradictory to think of God (that is, the most perfect being) lacking existence (that is lacking some perfection) than to think of a mountain that lacks a valley.

Nonetheless, even granting that I indeed cannot think of God except as existing, just as I cannot think of a mountain that has no valley, still it certainly does not follow that any mountain exists in the world because I think of one as having a valley, and so it likewise does not seem that God exists because of the fact that I am thinking of him as existing: for my thinking imposes no necessity on things; and in the same way as it is allowable to imagine a winged horse—although no horse has wings—so perhaps I can assign existence to God although no God exists.

On the contrary, that is where the sophism lies. For from the fact that I cannot think of a mountain that has no valley, it does not follow that a mountain or a valley exist anywhere, but merely that a mountain or a valley, whether existing or not, cannot be disjoined from one another. However, on the other hand, from the fact that I cannot think of God except as existing, it follows that existence is inseparable from God, and therefore that he truly exists: it is not that my thinking brings his existence about or imposes necessity on anything, but, on the contrary, it is because the necessity of the thing itself, namely, of the existence of God, determines me in thinking this: for I am not at liberty to think of God without existence (that is, of the most perfect being lacking the greatest perfection) as I am at liberty to imagine a horse with or without wings.

Moreover, it should not be said here that, once I have posited that God has all perfections, then, since existence is one of them, I must indeed posit an existing God, but yet that it was not necessary for me to posit what I first posited—just as it is not necessary for me to suppose that all four-sided figures can be inscribed in a circle, but yet having posited that I may suppose this, it will then be necessary for me to agree that a rhombus can be inscribed in a circle, which nevertheless is manifestly false. For although it is not necessary that I ever make my way so far as to do any thinking about God, nevertheless every time I do think of the first and greatest being, and as it were, draw the idea of him from the treasure house of my mind, it is necessary that I attribute to him every perfection, although I do not then enumerate them or attend to them singly; moreover, this necessity manifestly suffices so that afterward, when I notice that existence is a perfection, I correctly conclude that the first and greatest being exists: just as it is not necessary for me to ever imagine any triangle, but yet every time I do wish to consider a rectilinear figure having only three angles, it is necessary for me to attribute to it those things on the basis of which it may be inferred that its three angles are not greater than two right angles, even though I am not then noticing this same consequence. However, when I examine the particular figures inscribed in a circle, it is in no way necessary that all four-sided figures are included in their number; on the contrary, I can even suppose that it is not at all the case so long as I wish to admit nothing except what I clearly and distinctly understand; and accordingly there is a great difference between false postulations and true ideas that are inborn, of which the first and foremost is the idea of God. For I assuredly understand in many ways that the idea of God is not something fictitious depending upon my thinking, but that it is the image of a true and immutable nature: first, because I cannot think of any other thing, except God alone, to whose essence existence pertains; next, because I cannot understand two or more gods of this kind, and because, having posited that the one God now exists, I manifestly see that it is necessary that he has existed beforehand from eternity and will remain in existence for eternity; and last, because I perceive many other things in God that can neither be removed nor altered by me.

And so indeed, whatever reasoning I ultimately use in testing anything, I am always led back to the fact that only those things persuade me that I perceive clearly and distinctly. And although some of those things that I clearly and distinctly perceive are truly obvious to everyone, others are disclosed only by those who look more closely into them and track them down; yet once these are detected, they are considered no less certain than the former things. Thus, although in a right triangle the equality between the square of its base [*basis*] and the squares of its sides does not so easily become apparent as does the fact that this same base [*basim*] is subtended by the largest angle of the triangle, it is nevertheless no less believed—at least after it is once thoroughly seen through. Moreover, as for what pertains to God, if I were not overwhelmed by prejudices, and if the images of sensible things were not to besiege my mind at every turn, then I certainly would recognize nothing sooner or more easily than God; for what is more obvious in itself than that the greatest being or God, in whom alone existence pertains to essence, exists?

And despite the fact that attentive consideration was required for me to perceive this very thing, nevertheless I am now not only equally certain of God's existence and all other things that seem very certain, but I furthermore also notice that the certainty of the other things so depends on this very thing that without it nothing can ever be perfectly known.

For although I am of such a nature that as long as I am perceiving something very clearly and distinctly I can only believe that it is true, nevertheless since I am also of such a nature that I cannot always fasten the gaze of my mind on that same thing in order to perceive it clearly, and since the memory of judgments previously made often recurs when I am no longer attending to the reasons why I made them, if I were ignorant of God other reasons could be brought forth that would turn me away from my opinion, and so I would never have true and certain knowledge of anything but only vague and changeable opinions. Take an example: I am considering the nature of the triangle, and since I am instructed in the principles of geometry, it indeed appears very evidently to me that its three angles are equal to two right angles, and I cannot fail to believe that this is true while I am attending to its demonstration. But now, it is suddenly the time immediately thereafter! I have turned the gaze of my mind away from the demonstration, although I still remember that I had most clearly seen through it. Despite this memory, if I do not know God, it can indeed easily happen that I doubt whether the demonstration is true. For I can persuade myself that nature made me in such a way as to be occasionally deceived in those things I deem myself to perceive very evidently—since I especially remember that I had often accepted many things as true and certain that afterward, when moved by other reasons, I judged to be false.

But by now I have already perceived that God does exist, and at the same time at which I perceived his existence I also understood that everything else depends upon him, and that he is not a deceiver; moreover, I have gathered from all this that everything I clearly and distinctly perceive necessarily is true; thus, although I am no longer attending to the reasons why I judged it true that the three angles of a triangle are equal to two right angles, provided only that I remember having clearly and distinctly perceived it, I have a true and certain knowledge of it, and no contrary reasoning can be brought forth that would move me to doubt it. This does not apply merely to that one truth about the triangle, but is applicable to all the other truths I recall having demonstrated in the past, such as in geometry and in similar disciplines. For what objections may be made to me now? That I have been made in such a way as to be frequently deceived? But I now know that I cannot be deceived as regards those things I perspicuously understand. That I have accepted many other things as true and certain that I afterward discerned to be false? But even granting that, still, I had not perceived any of them clearly and distinctly; and being ignorant of this rule of truth, I had perhaps believed them for other reasons that I afterward detected to be less firm. What therefore can be said in opposition to me? Will it be said (as I not so long ago objected to myself) that perhaps I am sleeping, or that all those things I am now thinking are no more true than things that present themselves to one who is sleeping? But indeed, even that would change nothing; for certainly, even though I were dreaming, if anything is evident to my intellect, it is by all means true.

And thus I plainly see that the certainty and truth of every science depends solely upon the cognition of the true God, so that until I came to know him I could know nothing perfectly about anything else. But now, indeed, innumerable things concerning not only God himself and other intellectual things, but also concerning that entire corporeal nature that is an object of pure mathematics, can be manifestly known by me and certain for me.

MEDITATION VI

Concerning the Existence of Material Things and Concerning the Real Distinction of the Mind from the Body

It remains for me to examine whether material things exist. And I now at least know that material things, insofar as they are the object of pure mathematics, can exist, because I perceive them clearly and distinctly. For there is no doubt that God can bring about everything I am able to perceive clearly and distinctly; and I have never judged that God could not do something except for the reason that for me to distinctly perceive it would involve a contradiction. Furthermore, on the basis of the faculty of imagining, which I experience myself to use in dealing with these material things, it seems to follow that they exist; for to one more attentively considering what the imagination is, it appears to be nothing but a particular application of the faculty of knowing to a body that is intimately present to it, and that, accordingly, is existent.

But to make this manifest, I first examine the difference that exists between the imagination and pure intellection. Thus, as an example, when I imagine a triangle, I do not merely understand that it is a figure enclosed by three lines, but at the same time, with the gaze of my mind, I also intuit these three lines as if they were present; and this is what I name "to imagine." If, however, I wish to think of a chiliagon, I equally well understand that it is a figure consisting of a thousand sides just as I understand that a triangle is a figure consisting of three sides; yet I do not in the same way imagine those thousand sides or intuit them as if they were presented to me. And despite the fact that now—because of my habit of always imagining something or other whenever I think of a corporeal thing—I may perhaps be confusingly representing some figure to myself, nevertheless it is manifest that it is not a chiliagon, because it in no way differs from the figure I would represent were I thinking of a myriagon or any other figure of very many sides; moreover, the figure I am representing does not help me at all in recognizing those properties by which the chiliagon differs from other polygons. But even if it is a question of the pentagon, I can indeed understand its figure, just as I understand the figure of the chiliagon, without the activity of the imagination; however, I am also able to imagine the figure of the pentagon—that is, by applying the gaze of my mind to its five sides, and at the same time to the area contained within these five sides; and by this example of the pentagon I manifestly notice that to imagine I require some peculiar effort of the mind that I do not use for understanding; this additional effort of the mind clearly shows the difference between the imagination and the pure understanding.

In consequence of this I shall carefully speculate that the very force of imagining that is in me, according as it differs from the force of understanding, is not required for my own essence, that is, for the essence of my mind; for even if the force of imagining were to cease, undoubtedly I would nonetheless stay that same one who I now am; from which it seems to follow that the force of imagining depends upon something different from myself. And I easily understand that if some body exists with which the mind is so conjoined that the mind, at its own decision, can direct itself to, as it were, look searchingly upon that body, then it is possible that I imagine corporeal things by this means; thus this mode of thinking would differ from pure understanding only in that the mind, when it understands, in a certain way turns itself inward toward its own self and considers one of the ideas that are within it; however, when the mind imagines, it turns itself to the body, and it intuits something in the body conformable to an idea that the intellect has perceived either from itself or from the senses. I say I easily understand that imagination can be carried out this way, if indeed the body does exist; and since no other equally suitable manner of explaining imagination presents itself, from that I conclude as probable, and as probable only, that body does exist. And even though I thoroughly trace out all arguments, I nevertheless do not as yet see that any argument that proves necessarily that body exists can be derived from the distinct idea of corporeal nature I discover in my imagination.

In addition to that corporeal nature which is the object of pure mathematics, I am certainly accustomed to imagine many other things, although not so distinctly, such as colors, sounds, flavors, pain, and the like. Moreover, I perceive these things better by the sense through which, with the help of memory, they seem to have come to the imagination. Hence a more suitable treatment of them requires that at the same time I also consider sense, and see whether any certain argument for the existence of corporeal things can be derived from any of those things perceived by that mode of thinking I name sense.

Firstly, I will here recall those particular things I previously considered true in the manner perceived by sense, and I shall also recount the reasons why I thought this; next, I will set down the reasons why I afterward called them into doubt; and finally, I will consider what I should now believe about them.

Well, then, I first sensed that I had a head, hands, feet, and the other members of which this body consists—a body I regarded as if it were part of me, or even perhaps the whole of me; moreover, I sensed that this body is placed among many other bodies by which it can be variously affected, either advantageously or disadvantageously, and I measured these advantages by a certain sense of pleasure and the disadvantages by a sense of pain. And beyond pleasure and pain, I also sensed hunger, thirst, and other appetites of this kind within me; I likewise sensed certain propensities to gaiety, to sadness, to anger, as well as other similar affections. As regards the things outside me, beyond the extension, shapes, and motions of bodies, I also sensed hardness, heat, and other tactile qualities in these bodies; and furthermore I sensed light, colors, flavors, and sounds, and out of their variety I distinguished heaven, earth, the seas, and the remaining bodies from one another. Furthermore, based upon the ideas of all those qualities presented to my thinking (which ideas, properly speaking, I immediately and exclusively discerned by sense), I concluded that I also sense certain things manifestly different from my thinking, namely, the corporeal bodies from which these very ideas proceeded. Indeed, I did not draw this conclusion without reason. For I experienced that those ideas came to me without any consent of mine, in such a way that I could not sense any object, even though I wished to do so, unless it were present to the organ of sense, and could not fail to sense an object if it were present. And because the ideas perceived by sense were much more vivid and expressive, and also in their own way more distinct, than any of those ideas that I—who am practiced at and aware of my purposes in reflecting—could form, it did not seem possible that they proceeded from my own self; and accordingly, there remained the conclusion that they came to me from some other things. Since I had no notion of those things from which I concluded my ideas proceeded except the notion I had derived on the basis of the ideas themselves, the only conclusion that could enter my mind was that they are similar to the ideas. Moreover, because I recalled that I had first used the senses rather than reason, and because I saw that the ideas I myself formed were less expressive than those perceived by sense, and in very large measure composed from them, I easily persuaded myself that I manifestly have nothing in the intellect that I have not formerly had in sense. Moreover, not without reason did I decide that the particular body, that with a certain special justification I called my own, pertains more to me than does any other body; for I could never be separated from it as I could from the other bodies; I sensed in it, and in proportion to its condition, all the appetites and affections; and finally, I recognized pain and the titillation of pleasure in its parts, not, however, in the other bodies situated outside it. Yet, as to why a certain sadness of the soul follows upon that enigmatic sense of pain, or why that puzzling twitching of the stomach I call hunger puts me in mind of consuming food, or dryness in mind of drink, and so forth—indeed, I had no other explanation except that I was shown so by nature. For at least as far as I understand it, there is no manifest affinity between that twitching and the desire of consuming food, or between the sensation of the thing producing the pain and the thought of sorrow that arises from this sensation; rather I seemed to have learned from nature these and all the remaining things I judged about the objects of the senses—indeed, I had even persuaded myself of the truth of everything I judged about them before I had evaluated any reasons by which that might be proved.

Later on, numerous experiences certainly shook all the confidence I had had in the senses; for occasionally towers, which from afar had been of round appearance, appeared square from nearby, and very large statues standing at their pinnacles did not appear large to one looking up at them from the ground—in these and in innumerable other such cases I recognized that my judgments about the objects of the external senses were mistaken. I also recognized the same thing as regards my judgments concerning the internal senses; for what can be more within us than pain? Yet nevertheless, I had at one time heard from people whose leg or arm had been cut off that they still occasionally seem to themselves to feel pain in that part of the body they lack; and likewise, even as regards myself, it did not seem manifestly certain that a particular part of my body was paining me even if, on the basis of my feelings, I would be led to think the pain was in that part. To these reasons for doubting, I have also recently added two other very general grounds for doubt. The first was that while awake I never believed myself to sense anything I could not also sometimes think I sensed while sleeping; and since I do not believe that the things I seem to myself to sense in dreams come from things situated outside me, I did see why I ought to have believed this any more the case as regards the things I seem to myself to sense while awake. The other reason was that, since I still did not know the author of my origins, I saw nothing to prevent myself being so constituted by nature as to be deceived even in those things that appeared to me to be very true. And as for the reasons by which I had formerly persuaded myself concerning the truth of sensible things, I did not find it difficult to respond to them. For since I seemed to be urged on by nature to many things from which reason dissuaded me, I did not think that much confidence should be placed in the things taught by nature. And although the perceptions of the senses did not depend upon my willing, I did not therefore think it should be concluded that they proceed from things different from myself, since there perhaps could be some other faculty in me, even if as yet unknown by me, that produces them.

Now, however, after I begin to know better my own self and the author of my origin, I indeed do not think that everything I seem to be told by the senses ought to be rashly accepted, but neither do I think that everything ought to be placed into doubt.

And first, because I know that God can make all the things I clearly and distinctly understand in that manner in which I understand them, it suffices that I can clearly and distinctly understand one thing without another for me to be certain that the one thing is different from the other, since it can be set up separately from the other at least by God; moreover, to conclude that two things are different, I need not be concerned with that power by which God may separate them; and accordingly, from this very fact that I know that I exist and in the meanwhile recognize manifestly nothing else to pertain to my nature or essence except this alone, namely, that I am a thinking thing, I correctly conclude that my essence consists in this one thing, that I am a thinking thing. And although I perhaps have a body (or rather, as I shall later on say for certain, do have a body) that is very intimately conjoined with me, nevertheless because on the one hand I have a clear and a distinct idea of my own self insofar as I am only a thinking and nonextended thing, and because on the other hand I have a distinct idea of body insofar as it is only an extended and nonthinking thing, it is certain that I am truly distinct from my body and can exist without it.

Furthermore, I discover in me faculties for certain special modes of thinking, to wit, the faculties of imagining and sensing, without which I can clearly and distinctly understand myself to be a whole, but which, on the contrary, I cannot understand without me, that is, without an intelligent substance in which they inhere: for they include some intellection in their formal concept, from which I perceive that they are distinguished from me as modes from a thing. I also recognize certain other faculties, such as the faculties of changing place, of assuming various postures, and the like. These faculties, no more than the preceding ones, can be understood without some substance in which they inhere—and accordingly they cannot be understood as existing without a substance. But it is manifest that, if indeed they exist, then they must inhere in a corporeal or extended substance, and not, however, in an intelligent substance—for contained in the clear and distinct conception of them is some extension, but manifestly no intellection. Now, there is indeed in me a certain passive faculty of sensing, or of receiving and recognizing the ideas of sensible things; but I could make no use of it unless there existed either in myself or in something else a certain active faculty of producing or bringing about these ideas of sensible things. And this active faculty cannot reasonably be thought to be in my very self, since it manifestly presupposes no intellection and because these ideas of sensible things are produced without my coöperation, and often despite my wish: therefore it remains that this active faculty is in some substance different from me. As I already pointed out above, this substance must contain either formally or eminently all the reality that is objectively in the ideas produced by this faculty. Either this substance is body, or corporeal nature, containing formally everything that is objectively in the ideas produced by this faculty; or this substance is God or another creature more noble than the body, in which everything that is objectively in the ideas produced by this faculty is contained eminently. But since God is not a deceiver, it is altogether manifest that he does not directly of himself send these ideas of sensible things into me; it is also altogether manifest that he does not send them into me by means of any creature in which the objective reality of these ideas is only eminently, but not formally, contained. For since God gave me no faculty for recognizing this, but, on the contrary, has bestowed upon me a great inclination toward believing that these ideas of sensible things come from corporeal things, I do not see any argument by which He could be understood not to be a deceiver if these ideas were to come from something other than corporeal things. And consequently, corporeal things do exist. Nevertheless, perhaps they do not altogether exist in such a way as I comprehend them by sense, because this comprehension of the senses is in many respects very obscure and confused. But at least all those things exist in corporeal things that I clearly and distinctly understand in them—that is, all those things, generally regarded, that are comprehended in the object of pure mathematics.

The remaining things are all very dubious and uncertain. They are either merely particular, such as that the sun has a certain size or figure, and so on; or they are less clearly understood, such as light, sound, color, and the like. But although all these things are very dubious and uncertain, nevertheless the very fact that God is not deceiving, and that, accordingly, no falsity can be found among my thoughts unless there is also in me some faculty bestowed by God for correcting it, holds out to me an assured hope of obtaining truth even as regards these things. And indeed there is no doubt that everything I am taught by nature contains something of the truth: for through nature, generally regarded, I understand nothing other than either God himself, or the coördination of created things instituted by God; moreover, by my nature in particular I do not understand anything other than the combination of all those things that have been bestowed upon me by God.

Moreover, there is nothing this nature of mine teaches me more expressly than that I have a body that is in an improper condition when I feel pain, that lacks food or drink when I undergo hunger or thirst, and the like; and accordingly I should not doubt that there is something of the truth in this.

Nature also teaches by means of these senses of pain, hunger, thirst, and so on, that I am not merely present in my body as a sailor is present in his ship; rather I am very closely conjoined with it—and, as it were, intermingled with it—so that together with it I compose one thing. For otherwise when the body is injured, I, who am nothing other than a thinking thing, would not therefore feel pain, but would perceive this injury by the pure intellect, as a sailor perceives by sight that a part of his ship is broken. For certainly these senses of thirst, hunger, and so on, are nothing other than certain confused modes of thinking that arise from the union and, as it were, intermingling of the mind with the body.

Furthermore, I am also taught by nature that various other bodies exist round and about my own, and that I should pursue some of them and avoid others. And certainly, from the fact that I sense exceedingly differing colors, sounds, odors, flavors, degrees of warmth and hardness, and the like, I correctly conclude that these various perceptions of the senses come from correspondingly various things in bodies, even if the latter are perhaps not similar to the former; and from the fact that certain of these perceptions are agreeable to me and others disagreeable, it is manifestly certain that my body, or better said, that I as a whole, insofar as I am composed from a body and a mind, can be affected with various advantages and disadvantages by the bodies round and about me.

But there are many other things that, although I seem to be taught them by nature, I nevertheless have not really received from nature. Rather I have approved them because of my habit of judging precipitously, and consequently it may easily occur that they are false: for example, that every space is empty in which there is nothing manifestly present to make an effect on my senses; or that in a warm body there is something manifestly similar to the idea of heat in me; that in a white or a green body there is the same whiteness or greenness I sense; that in a bitter or sweet body there is the same flavor I sense, and so on; or that stars and towers and any other distant bodies have only that size and shape they display to my senses; and all other things of this kind. But in order to avoid an insufficiently distinct perception of this matter, I should define more completely for myself what I understand when I say that I am taught something by nature. And so I here use nature more strictly than for the combination of all those things bestowed upon me by God. For in this combination are contained many things that pertain to the mind alone—for example, that I perceive that what has been done cannot be undone, and all the remaining things known by the natural light, which do not concern me here. Similarly, there are also many things in this combination that regard the body alone, which also do not concern me here—for example, that the body stretches upward and downward, and so on. Hence I here use nature only in respect to those things God has bestowed upon me as a composite of mind and body. And accordingly, this nature indeed teaches us to flee from those things that bring a feeling of pain and to seek those that bring a feeling of pleasure, and the like; however, it does not appear that nature further teaches us to conclude, without a previous examination by the intellect, that any such perceptions of the senses are located in things outside us, because to know the truth about the things outside us seems to pertain to the mind alone, but not, however, to the combination of mind and body. Thus, although a star no more affects my eye than does the flame of a small torch, nevertheless that involves no real or positive inclination on my part to believe that the star is no larger than the flame; rather I have judged this without a reason from my earliest years. Again, although in approaching fire I feel warmth, and in approaching even closer feel pain, certainly no reasoning persuades me that there is something in the fire similar either to the heat or pain; rather reasoning persuades me only that there is something in the fire, whatever that thing might itself precisely be, that produces in us the aforesaid sensations of heat or pain. Again, although there is nothing in some space that moves sense, it does not therefore follow that there is no body in that space. Accordingly, I see that as regards the foregoing, and very many other things, I am accustomed to reverse abusively the order of nature. Thus the perceptions of the sense have been given by nature only to signify to the mind particular things that are advantageous or disadvantageous to the composite of which the mind is a part; and for that purpose they are sufficiently clear and distinct. However, I misuse them by considering them as if they are certain rules for immediately discerning what the particular essence is of bodies situated outside us, although they signify nothing about that except very obscurely and confusingly.

Now, I have already sufficiently examined by what reasoning, despite the goodness of God, it may happen that my judgments are false. But here a new difficulty presents itself concerning those things that nature displays to me as if they should be sought after or avoided. Moreover, the difficulty also bears on the internal senses in which I seem to have discovered faults—for example, when someone, misled by the gratifying flavor of a certain food, consumes the poison concealed within. But, to be sure, in that situation the person is urged on by nature toward seeking that in which the gratifying flavor consisted, not, however, toward seeking the poison about which he is ignorant. Thus nothing more can be concluded from this example than that this nature is not omniscient: this is not astonishing because, since a man is a limited thing, there is nothing else consonant with him but a nature of limited perfection.

But certainly we err, and not infrequently, even as regards those things toward which we are urged on by nature: as when the sick seek drink or food, which a short time afterward is harmful to them. Perhaps in this case it will be said that they err because their nature is corrupted. However, this reply does not take away the difficulty because a sick man is no less truly God's creature than a healthy man, and consequently it seems no less contradictory for God to bestow a deceiving nature upon the sick man. But let us pursue this matter. A clock, for example, is assembled from wheels and weights; moreover, it no less completely observes all the laws of nature when it is badly made and fails to indicate the correct time than when it satisfies the wishes of the craftsman in every respect. Suppose now I were to consider the body of a man insofar as it is a particular skillful contrivance made from bones, nerves, muscles, veins, blood, and skin. Suppose futhermore that I considered it so composed and adapted that, even if no mind were to exist in it, it nevertheless would have all the same motions that now occur in a man's body, not from the control of his will, and hence not on account of his mind. On these suppositions there are similarities to the clock. Thus I easily recognize that it would be natural for the man, when he has no defect in him, to be moved by dryness in the throat toward taking a drink useful to himself; but I furthermore also easily recognize that if, for example, he suffered from dropsy, it would be equally natural for him both to suffer that dryness in the throat that his mind customarily concludes is a sensation of thirst, and also to be so disposed in his nerves and remaining parts by this dryness that he takes a drink, which increases the disease. In addition, although in looking to a preconceived use of the clock I can say that, when it fails to indicate the hours correctly, it diverges from its nature; and although, in the same way, by considering the skillful contrivance of the human body, as it were, in comparison to the motions normally in it, I can also conclude that it diverges from its nature if it has a dry throat when drink is not beneficial to its conservation; nevertheless, I sufficiently recognize that this last meaning of "nature" differs much from the other meaning of "nature": for this last meaning of "nature" is nothing but a denomination by my thinking due to my comparing the sick man and the badly made clock with the idea of a healthy man and the idea of a correctly made clock, and it is extrinsic to the things spoken about; by the other meaning of "nature" I indeed understand something that truly is in things, and accordingly it contains something of the truth.

But certainly, as regards the body with dropsy, even if it is only an extrinsic denomination when it is said that its nature is corrupted because it has a dry throat but does not need drink, nevertheless it is not a pure denomination as regards the composite, that is, as regards the mind united to such a body; rather it is a true error of nature that this composite is thirsty when drink is harmful to it; and accordingly it here remains to be inquired how the goodness of God does not prevent the sick man's nature, thus understood, from being deceiving.

First of all, I call attention to the fact that there is a great difference between the mind and body in that body of its nature is always divisible, but the mind, however, is manifestly indivisible; for undoubtedly, when I consider the mind, or myself, insofar as I am only a thinking thing, I can distinguish no parts, but rather understand that I manifestly am one and an entire thing; and although the entire mind seems united to the entire body, nevertheless, when a foot or any other part of the body is cut off, nothing is therefore known to be taken away from my mind; moreover, even the faculties of willing, sensing, imagining, and so on, cannot be said to be parts of the mind, because it is one and the same mind that wills, senses, and understands. Indeed, on the contrary, I can think of no corporeal or extended thing that in my thinking I may not easily divide into parts, and from this very fact I understand that a corporeal or extended thing is divisible; and this alone would suffice to teach me that mind is altogether diverse from body if I did not as yet sufficiently well know it on other grounds.

Next, I call attention to the fact that the mind is not immediately affected by all parts of the body, but only by the brain, or perhaps even by only one very small part of it, namely, by the part in which it is said that the common sense exists. Every time this part of the brain is disposed in the same way, it displays the same thing to the mind even though the remaining parts of the body can in the meanwhile assume different conditions. This is proved by numerous experiments it is not germane to list here.

Furthermore, I call attention to the fact that it is the nature of the body that no part of it can be moved by another part that is somewhat distant from it unless it can also be moved in the same manner by whatever parts lie in between even though that more distant part does nothing. Thus, for example, in the chord *ABCD*, if its last part, *D*, is pulled, the first part, *A*, will not be moved in any way differently from how it could also be moved if one of the intermediate parts *B* or *C* were pulled and the last part, *D*, remained unmoved. By similar reasoning, when I feel the pain of my foot, physics has taught me that that sensation is brought about by means of the nerves spread out through the foot. Physics has also taught me that these nerves, which resemble strings, extend continuously from the foot to the brain and that, when they are pulled in the foot, they also pull the inmost parts of the brain to which they extend, and excite in these parts a particular motion that has been instituted by nature so that it affects the mind with a sensation of a pain existing, as it were, in the foot. But since those nerves must pass through the shinbone, legs, loins, back, and neck to come from the foot to the brain, it can occur that, although no part of the nerves in the foot is touched, but just the intermediate part, manifestly the same motion will take place in the brain as results from a foot in bad condition, and from this it will necessarily result that the mind feels the same pain.

Last, I call attention to the fact that since each of the motions that occur in that part of the brain that immediately affects the mind carries but one particular sensation to the brain, we can think of nothing better than if, from among all the sensations a particular motion can carry, it carries the one that conduces in the greatest way and most frequently to the conservation of a healthy man. Moreover, experience shows that all the senses bestowed upon us by nature are such; and accordingly, manifestly nothing is found in them that does not show the power and goodness of God. Thus, for example, when the nerves in the foot are violently and abnormally moved, that motion of the nerves through the marrow of the spine of the back reaches to the inmost part of the brain, where it provides a sign to the mind to sense something, namely, the pain existing, as it were, in the foot; and by this sign the mind is roused to rid itself as much as it can of the cause of the pain—for example, to rid itself of that which is injurious to the foot. Certainly, the nature of man could have been so constituted by God that the same motion in the brain that signifies to the mind a pain existing, as it were, in the foot would display any other thing you choose to name—for example, that motion could have displayed itself to the mind either insofar as it is a motion in the brain, or insofar as it is a motion in the foot, or insofar as it is a motion in the intermediate places; finally, that same motion could have displayed anything else whatsoever to the mind; but none of these other things would lead as well to the conservation of the body. In the same way, when we require drink there arises a dryness in the throat, moving the nerves of the throat, which in turn move the inner parts of the brain; and this motion affects the mind with the sensation of thirst, because nothing in this entire affair is more useful for us to know than that by drinking we help conserve our healthy condition; and it is the same in other cases.

From these things it is altogether manifest that, despite the immense goodness of God, the nature of man, since it is composed from mind and body, cannot fail to be occasionally deceiving. For if some cause that is not in the foot, but either is in another part of the body through which the nerves extend from the foot to the brain, or is even in the brain itself, excites what is manifestly the same motion that is customarily excited by a foot in bad condition, then pain will be felt as if it were in the foot, and sense naturally will be deceived. This is so for the following reason: since that same motion can only cause the same sensation all the time, and since that sensation customarily proceeds much more frequently from a cause that injures the foot rather than from a cause existing somewhere else, it is consonant with reason that it always display a pain in the foot rather than a pain in another part of the body. And if in certain abnormal situations dryness of the throat is caused to occur when drink is not conducive to the healthy condition of the body, as happens in the case of the victim of dropsy, it is still far better that the sense of thirst deceives us in that case than if, on the contrary, it would always deceive us even when the body is well; and the same is true of the other senses.

And this consideration helps very much, not only so that I may call attention to all the errors to which my nature is liable, but also so that I may easily correct or avoid them. For undoubtedly, since I know that all the senses have reference to the advantage of the body, and much more frequently indicate the true rather than the false; and since I can nearly always use most of them in examining the same matter; and since, moreover, I can use memory, which connects present things with preceding ones; and since I can use the intellect, which now has seen through all the causes of making errors: I should, accordingly, no longer fear that the things daily displayed by the senses are false. On the contrary, the hyperbolical doubts of the past days ought to be expelled with laughter. I ought particularly to expel that general doubt about my not distinguishing sleeping from waking; for now I notice the very large difference that separates the two of them—namely, that what occurs in sleep is never conjoined by memory with all the remaining actions of life as are the things that occur to one awake; for undoubtedly, if while I am awake someone should suddenly appear to me and immediately afterward, as happens in dreams, disappear in such a way that I would not see whence he had come or where he went, I would not unreasonably judge him to be a specter, or better, to be a phantasm depicted in my brain, rather than a real man. And since those things do indeed occur about which I distinctly notice whence and when they come to me, and since I completely connect the perception of them with the rest of my life, I am clearly certain that they occur not to one dreaming, but to one awake. Moreover, I should not doubt even in the slightest concerning the truth of these same things if, after I have employed all the senses, memory, and intellect to examine them, they do not report anything to me that clashes with the others. For from the fact that God is not deceiving, it assuredly follows that I am not deceived in such matters. But since the exigency of practice does not always permit a delay in which to make such accurate examination, it must be confessed that human life is very often liable to errors concerning particular things, and the weakness of our nature should be recognized.

SUGGESTIONS FOR FURTHER READING

Balz, Albert G. A. *Cartesian Studies.* New York: Columbia University Press, 1951.

Balz, Albert G. A. *Descartes and the Modern Mind.* New Haven: Yale University Press, 1952.

Beck, L. J. *The Metaphysics of Descartes: A Study of the Meditations.* Oxford: Clarendon Press, 1965.

Beck, L. J. *The Method of Descartes: A Study of the Regulae.* Oxford: Clarendon Press, 1952.

Cantor, Norman F., and Peter L. Klein. *Seventeenth Century Rationalism: Bacon and Descartes.* Waltham, Massachusetts: Blaisdell, 1969.

Chomsky, Noam. *Cartesian Linguistics.* New York: Harper & Row, 1966.

Doney, Willis, ed. *Descartes: A Collection of Critical Essays.* New York: Doubleday–Anchor, 1967.

Gibson, A. Boyce. *The Philosophy of Descartes.* London: Methuen, 1932.

Hooker, Michael, ed. *Descartes: Critical and Interpretive Essays.* Baltimore: Johns Hopkins University Press, 1978.

Schouls, Peter A. *The Imposition of Method: A Study of Descartes and Locke.* Oxford: Clarendon Press, 1980.

Smith, Norman Kemp. *New Studies in the Philosophy of Descartes: Descartes as Pioneer.* London: Macmillan, 1952.

Vrooman, Jack R. *René Descartes: A Biography.* New York: Putnam, 1970.

ABOUT THE AUTHOR

John J. McDermott is presently Distinguished Professor of Philosophy and Humanities and professor and head of the Department of Humanities in Medicine at Texas A&M University. The editor of scholarly editions of the writings of William James, Josiah Royce (2 vols.), John Dewey (2 vols.), he is also the author of *The Culture of Experience: Philosophical Essays in the American Grain* and some 50 papers in scholarly journals and university press collections of essays. A second volume of essays is forthcoming from The University of Massachusetts Press, as is a companion volume to the present one, *A Cultural Introduction to Philosophy: From Descartes to the Twentieth Century.*

Professor McDermott has been visiting lecturer at more than one hundred universities, symposia, and conferences, both in America and abroad. He received his Ph.D. in philosophy from Fordham University and received an honorary Doctor of Laws from The University of Hartford for distinguished service to higher education. He was a member of the Executive Committee of the American Philosophical Association, Eastern Division, and a former President of the Society for the Advancement of American Philosophy. Professor McDermott is the recipient of several teaching awards, at Queens College, C.U.N.Y., The State University of New York at Stony Brook, Texas A&M University and the National E. Harris Harbison Award for Gifted Teaching, given by the Danforth Foundation in 1969.

A NOTE ON THE TYPE

The text of this book was composed in a film version of Palatino, a type face designed by the noted German typographer Hermann Zapf. Named after Giovanbattista Palatino, a writing master of Renaissance Italy, Palatino was the first of Zapf's type faces to be introduced in America. The first designs for the face were made in 1948, and the fonts for the complete face were issued between 1950 and 1952. Like all Zapf-designed type faces, Palatino is beautifully balanced and exceedingly readable.